SECOND EDITION

# SIGNS OF LIFE IN THE U.S.A.

## Readings on Popular Culture for Writers

SONIA MAASIK

*University of California, Los Angeles*

JACK SOLOMON

*California State University, Northridge*

Bedford Books　　　Boston

**We wish to dedicate this book to the memory
of our dear friend, Kenzo.**

**For Bedford Books**

*President and Publisher:* Charles H. Christensen
*General Manager and Associate Publisher:* Joan E. Feinberg
*Managing Editor:* Elizabeth M. Schaaf
*Developmental Editor:* Stephen A. Scipione
*Editorial Assistant:* Rebecca Jerman
*Production Editor:* Sherri Frank
*Copyeditor:* Carolyn Ingalls
*Text Design:* Anna George
*Cover Design:* Hannus Design Associates
*Cover Art:* Tom Wesselmann, *Still Life No. 28,* 1964. © 1997 Tom Wesselmann/
Licensed by VAGA, New York, New York.

Library of Congress Catalog Card Number: 96–86776

*For information, write:* Bedford Books, 75 Arlington Street, Boston, MA 02116
(617-426-7440)

ISBN: 0–312–13631–5

**Acknowledgments**

McCrea Adams, "Advertising Characters: The Pantheon of Advertising." Reprinted by
permission of the author.

*(Acknowledgments and copyrights are continued at the back of the book on pages 784–789, which
constitute an extension of the copyright page. It is a violation of the law to reproduce these selections by any means whatsoever without the written permission of the copyright holder.)*

# PREFACE FOR INSTRUCTORS

Thirty years ago, Marshall McLuhan announced the beginning of a new era in the history of Western communication. The printing press, he argued in his classic study *The Gutenberg Galaxy* (1962), was yielding to a new set of media — to radio, television, and film — and a new consciousness was emerging in response to the change. The years that have passed since the publication of McLuhan's book have borne out many of his predictions, especially concerning the growth of video technologies. Today, ours is indeed a culture of the electronic media, centered on the visual image rather than the printed word, and the shape of our knowledge and experience has shifted accordingly.

This transformation from a text-centered to an image-centered culture presents a certain challenge to writing teachers. How can such a textually based enterprise as writing instruction respond to a video-driven world? How are reading and writing related to seeing and hearing? Can the habits of critical thinking that are so central to the analytical tasks of academic writing be adapted to McLuhan's brave new world?

We have prepared *Signs of Life in the U.S.A.* because we believe not only that such bridges can be built but also that building them represents our best hope for training a new generation of students in critical thinking and writing. Thus, while the goal of our text remains the traditional one of helping students become strong writers of argument and analysis, our method departs from convention by using printed texts to guide students in the interpretation and analysis of an unwritten world: The world of American popular culture, wherein images, often electronically conveyed, can be more important than words.

In the past, the study of popular culture led a rather marginal existence in the academy, but that marginalization is now coming to an end. Scholars from a host of different fields are recognizing that, far from being a trivial addition to human history, popular culture encompasses that enduring process which Michel de Certeau has called "the practice of everyday life." What is surprising, then, is not that popular culture should now be emerging as an important topic in the field of cultural studies, but that it was once so thoroughly excluded from academic inquiry. This exclusion has historically been justified on the basis of a naturalized distinction between "high" (or academically approved) and "low" (or popular) culture that contemporary cultural analysis has shown to be historically contingent. Indeed, one need only consider that such monuments of contemporary high culture as the works of Charles Dickens and William Wordsworth were once viewed as the products of popular (or folk) culture to see just how fluid the boundaries between high and low culture can be.

The reception of the first edition of this book has demonstrated how cultural studies is now an established part of the curriculum, and that semiotics — the particular method we have chosen to guide the critical analyses pursued in this text — has become an accepted tool in the study of popular culture. Teachers of composition are recognizing that students feel a certain sense of ownership toward the products of popular culture — and that using popular culture as the class focus can help students overcome the sometimes alienating effects of traditional academic subject matter. In this way, popular culture can encourage the development of the critical thinking and writing skills that writing courses are designed to promote.

## Readings on American Popular Culture

The 76 readings in this book address a broad cross section of contemporary American popular culture. We have chosen popular culture as our field because we believe that students think and write best when they are in command of their subject matter. Too often, academic ways of thinking, reasoning, arguing, and even speaking and writing seem like a foreign language for students, especially those in their first year. As a result, students may find it difficult to develop ideas, risking either writer's block or the adoption of an awkward, pedantic style that hinders their own creativity and insights. Unfortunately, both within and outside academia, students' attempts to grapple with this foreign language are sometimes interpreted as proof of their apparent "illiteracy."

But we believe that today's students are not illiterate at all; they simply have a different kind of literacy, one that exists outside the boundaries of traditional academic knowledge. We also believe that there need not be a split between academic and "real world" knowledge in the first place; rather, the two should inform each other, with the most exciting inquiry combining the riches of everyday life with the discipline and depth of academic study. *Signs of Life in the U.S.A.* is thus designed to let students take advantage of their expertise in the culture around them, allowing them to build on their strengths as they sharpen their ability to write cogent analyses, insightful interpretations, and persuasive arguments. We have included, for example, materials ranging from analyses of package designs to interpretations of the film *Malcolm X,* from explorations of women's language to advertisements for jeans and personal computers. This is not to say that we assume students are all consumers of popular culture in the same way. Indeed, the book is structured to encourage students to bring to their writing class a variety of backgrounds, interests, and experiences, a variety that will generate lively class discussion and create a community of writers.

## The Book's Organization

Reflecting the broad academic interest in culture studies, we've assumed an inclusive definition of popular culture. This definition can be seen in the book's organization, for it is divided into two sections — Images and Issues — to highlight the essential cultural connection between the things we do and the things we believe. The five chapters in the Images section focus on popular cultural behavior, especially as it is stimulated and mediated by the images projected through the objects we consume, the ads that sell us those objects, the entertainments we enjoy, and the heroes and popular characters we admire and emulate. The five Issues chapters may seem a bit more sobering, but they are inextricably linked to the text's first half. For in addressing gender issues, racial conflict, outlaw subcultures, the AIDS epidemic, and the emergence of the Internet, these chapters show that behind every image there is an issue, an ideology and belief system that shapes our behavior.

## The Critical Method: Semiotics

*Signs of Life* departs from some textbook conventions in that it makes explicit an interpretive approach, semiotics, that can guide students' analyses of popular culture. We've made this approach explicit because it has struck us that although students enjoy assignments that ask them to look at popular cultural phenomena, they often have trouble distinguishing between an argued interpretive analysis and the simple expression of an opinion. Some textbooks, for example, suggest assignments that involve analyzing a TV program or film, but they don't always tell a student how to do that. The semiotic method provides that guidance.

At the same time, semiotics reveals that there's no such thing as a pure, ideologically neutral analysis, even in freshman composition. Anthologies typically present analysis as a "pure" category: They present readings that students are asked to analyze, but articulate no conceptual framework and neither explore nor define theoretical assumptions and ideological positions. Being self-conscious about one's point of view, however, is an essential part of academic writing, and we can think of no better place for students to learn that lesson than in a writing class.

We've found through experience that a semiotic approach is especially well suited to this purpose. As a conceptual framework, semiotics teaches students to formulate cogent, well-supported interpretations. It emphasizes the examination of assumptions and the way language shapes our apprehension of the world. And, because it focuses on *how* beliefs are formulated within a social and political context (rather than just judging or evaluating those beliefs), it's ideal for discussing sensitive or politically charged issues. As an approach used in literature, media studies, anthropology, art and design coursework, sociology, law, and market research, to name only some of its more prominent field applications, semiotics has a cross-disciplinary appeal that makes it ideal for a writing class of students from a variety of majors and disciplines. We recognize that semiotics has a reputation for being highly technical or theoretical; rest assured that *Signs of Life* does not require students or instructors to have a technical knowledge of semiotics. In fact we've provided clear and accessible introductions that explain what students need to know.

We also recognize that adopting a theoretical approach may be new to some instructors, so we've designed the book to allow instructors to be as semiotic with their students as they wish. The book does not obligate instructors or students to spend a lot of time with semiotics — although we do hope you'll find the approach intriguing and provocative.

## The Editorial Apparatus

With its emphasis on popular culture, *Signs of Life* should generate lively class discussion and inspire many kinds of writing and thinking activities. The general introduction provides an overall framework for the book, acquainting students with the semiotic method they can use to interpret the topics raised in each chapter. The chapters start off with a frontispiece, a provocative visual image related to the chapter's topic, and an introduction that suggests ways to "read" the topic, presents model interpretations, and links the issues raised by the reading selections. Every chapter introduction contains three types of boxed questions designed to stimulate student thinking on the topic. The Exploring the Signs questions invite students to explore an issue in a journal entry or other prewriting activity, whereas the Discussing the Signs questions trigger class activities such as debates, discussions, or small group work. Reading the Net questions invite students to explore the chapter's topic on the Internet, both for research purposes and for texts to analyze.

The readings themselves are followed by two sorts of assignments. The Reading the Text questions help students comprehend the selections, asking them to identify important concepts and arguments, explain key terms, and relate main ideas to each other and to the evidence presented. The Reading the Signs questions are writing and activity prompts designed to produce clear analytic thinking and strong persuasive writing; they often make connections among reading selections from different chapters. Most assignments call for analytic essays, while some invite journal responses, in-class debates, group work, or other creative activities. In this edition, we've added an Appendix that not only provides a brief introduction to writing about popular culture, but also features three sample student essays that demonstrate different approaches to writing critical essays on popular culture. A Glossary of semiotic terms can serve as a ready reference of key terms and concepts used in the chapter introductions. Finally, the instructor's manual (*Editors' Notes to Accompany Signs of Life in the U.S.A.*) provides suggestions for organizing your syllabus, encouraging student response to the readings, and using popular culture and semiotics in the writing class.

## What's New in the Second Edition

Few subjects move so quickly as does the pace of popular culture, and the second edition of *Signs of Life* reflects this essential mutability through its substantial revision of the first edition. First, we have updated our readings, adding selections that focus on issues and trends important in the mid- to late-1990s. With 36 new readings, our second edition represents nearly a 50 percent turnover from the first edition. At the same time, we have updated the exemplary topics in our introductions used to model the critical assignments that follow, and have readjusted the focus of some chapters to reflect changing conditions. For instance, our chapter on "Cultural Outlaws" now adds readings on militia and hacker groups to the essays on street outlaws from the first edition. The once-hot topic of campus speech codes has cooled considerably since the early nineties, and so we have replaced our chapter on the politics of free speech with a new chapter devoted to the cultural significance of the Internet. In the early 1990s, this issue had not yet emerged in popular consciousness, but it now promises to dominate political, social, and business life in the foreseeable future through to the next millennium. Our chapter on "Virtual Culture" is designed to show how the Net represents not only a technological advance but a potential cultural intervention as profound as television. At the same time, the growing importance of the Internet in composition instruction has prompted us to add boxed questions to each chapter introduction designed to create assignments directly linked to Internet research.

We have also added an Appendix, "Writing about Popular Culture," designed to provide further instruction in the writing of critical essays on popular culture. The Appendix includes a student essay, prompted by the first edition of *Signs of Life in the U.S.A.,* that pursues a semiotic analysis of the movie *Cool Hand Luke.* In this essay, the student uses insights from Robert B. Ray's "The Thematic Paradigm" (page 278 in this edition) to write a critical analysis that proposes the student's own political interpretation of the film's ideology. A second essay provides a personal take on the significance of makeup in our body-conscious society. And a third student essay interprets the cultural significance of the Statue of Liberty, pointing out how the Statue means something different depending upon who's looking at it.

Even as we revise this text to reflect current trends, popular culture continues to evolve. The inevitable gap between the pace of editing and publishing, on the one hand, and the flow of popular culture, on the other, need not affect the book's use in the classroom, however. The Readings following the selections, and the semiotic method we propose, are designed to show students how to analyze and write critical essays about any topic they choose. They can, as one of our student writers in the Appendix did, choose a topic that appeared before they were born, or they can turn to the latest box office or prime-time hit to appear after the publication of this edition of *Signs of Life.* To put it another way, the practice of everyday life may itself be filled with evanescent fads and trends, but everyday life is not itself a fad. As the vital texture of our lived experience, popular culture provides a stable background against which students of every generation can test their critical skills.

## Acknowledgments

The vastness of the terrain of popular culture has enabled many users of the first edition of this text to make valuable suggestions for the second edition. Those instructors include: Ben Ament, St. Cloud State University; Dr. Claudia Barnett, Middle Tennessee State University; Dr. Bruce Beiderwell, University of California — Los Angeles; Elizabeth Brunsvold, St. Cloud State University; Dr. Michael Carroll, Highlands University; Dr. Mary Magdalena Chavarría, Pierce College, Los Angeles; Dr. Jane Cocalis,

Webster University; Dr. Jim Cullen, Harvard University; Philip Daughtry, Santa Monica College; Theresa Dickman, Cumberland College; Dr. Judith Doumas, Old Dominion University; Dr. Crystal Downing, Messiah College; Constance L. Eggers, Western Washington University; Dr. Jonathan Elmer, Indiana University; Dr. Ronald Emerick, Indiana University of Pennsylvania; Dr. Christine Farris, Indiana University; Dr. Elaine Fredericksen, University of Alabama; Heather Fuller, George Mason University; Dr. Robert W. Funk, Eastern Illinois University; Joan Gabriele, University of Colorado; Dr. Kevin Griffith, Capital University; Richard J. Hansberger, California State University — Northridge; Michael Heumann, University of California —Riverside; Dr. Carla Johnson, Saint Mary's College; Joanne Johnson, Jefferson Community College; Dr. Ruth D. Johnston, Pace University; Elizabeth J. Kirchoff, St. Cloud State University; Ditlev S. Larsen, St. Cloud State University; Mary Ann Lee, Longview Community College; Jill M. Leeper, DePauw University; Dr. Kim Loudermilk, Georgia Institute of Technology; Dr. Donald M. Maier, State University of New York — Plattsburgh; Debra Marquart, Drake University; Arthur Orme, Oakland University; Dr. Pamela T. Pittman, University of Central Oklahoma; Dr. Susan M. Popkin, University of California — Los Angeles; Christian Pyle, University of Kentucky; Mike Reynolds, University of Southern California; Gary Richards, Vanderbilt University; Dawn Roberts, Seattle Central Community College; Myra Seaman, Portland Community College; Leaf Seligman, University of New Hampshire; Dr. Fan A. Shen, Rochester Community College; Sidney J. Smith, Yakima Valley College; Dr. Susan Spencer, University of Central Oklahoma; Lynne Stallings, University of Southern California; Dr. Burt Thorp, University of North Dakota; Victoria Tillotson, State University of New York — Buffalo; Jennifer Traig, Brandeis University; Susanne R. Turner, University of Louisville; Mary Waters, University of California — Davis; Karin E. Westman, Vanderbilt University; Deborah M. Williams, Rutgers University; Victoria Williams, St. Cloud State University, and Noelle Wilson, University of Kentucky. We are especially grateful to those instructors who submitted sample student essays, including: Dr. Claudia Barnett, Mary Magdalena Chavarría, Dr. Jim Cullen, Dr. Judith Doumas, Dr. Crystal Downing, Constance L. Eggers, Dr. Elaine Fredericksen, Dr. Kevin Griffith, Dr. Ruth D. Johnston, Mary Ann Lee, Jill M. Leeper, Dr. Pamela T. Pittman, Susanne R. Turner, and Deborah M. Williams. We have incorporated many of their suggestions and thank them all for their comments. If we have not included something you, as an instructor, would like to work on, you may still direct your students to it, using this text as a guide, not as a set of absolute prescriptions. The practice of everyday life includes the conduct of a classroom, and we want all users of the second edition of *Signs of Life in the U.S.A.* to feel free to pursue that practice in whatever way best suits their interests and aims.

We wish also to thank once again the people of Bedford Books who have enabled us to make this second edition a reality, from Chuck Christensen and Joan Feinberg, to Steve Scipione, who, as our editor now on three projects, is beginning to feel like a member of the family. Sherri Frank ably guided our manuscript through the rigors of production, while Rebecca Jerman handled the innumerable questions and details that crop up during textbook development. In addition, Elizabeth Schaaf, John Amburg, Carol Parikh, and Andrea Goldman contributed their intelligence and superb competence to the revision of this book.

# CONTENTS

generation of admakers to realize the complete fulfillment of the consumerist vision through the fine-tuning of sheer hucksterism."

## 4.  THE HOLLYWOOD SIGN: *The Culture of American Film*   *269*

"[T]he entertainment industry's constant depiction of violent and destructive behavior, as perpetrated by some of the most attractive and glamorous human beings on the planet, redefines such conduct as sexy, glamorous, even admirable."

"How can a new generation of blacks — after pervasive civil rights legislation, Great Society programs, school busing, open housing, and more than two decades of affirmative action — be drawn to a figure of such seething racial alienation?"

"It is impossible to imagine Superman being as popular as he is and speaking as deeply to the American character were he not an immigrant and an orphan."

"The Kennedys have really become entertainment superstars."

"If I want Batman to be gay, then, for me, he is."

"I used to look at Barbie and wonder, What's wrong with this picture?"

"At root, old Joe's shtick is plain-and-simple racist."

"How much difference is there really between the two Ronalds, McDonald and Reagan?"

"It's unsettling, if not downright depressing, to go through life embarrassed about the identity of one's childhood idols."

# POPULAR SIGNS

*Or, Everything You've Always Known About American Culture (But Nobody Asked)*

In late autumn of 1995, the Beatles were resurrected. With the broadcasting of a new documentary film and the release of a musical "Anthology" that spanned their entire career, the Fabulous Four were back in business. Indeed, with a little help from some high-tech friends, they even released some new songs. You could again hear John Lennon, singing "Free as a Bird," fifteen long years after his death. And twenty-five even longer years after their breakup, the Beatles topped the charts once more.

It is highly probable that most readers of this book were born well after the breakup of the Beatles, and yet it is equally probable that most readers not only are familiar with the Beatles but also count some of their songs among their all-time favorites. Two, maybe even three, generations of Beatles fans joined to watch Paul, George, and Ringo get together to discuss their career on TV, and three generations of consumers went out to buy the *Beatles Anthology*. In many ways, the Beatles reunion was the pop cultural event of the year.

But despite all the media attention bestowed upon the resurrected Beatles, despite their significance to fans and corporations alike, it is unlikely that you would find yourself being asked to write about them in a typical college class. Nor, for that matter, would you expect to be writing about the latest Quentin Tarantino film, nor, on a more serious note, about that brochure on avoiding AIDS that you picked up at the Student Health Center. Such subjects have traditionally been regarded as being outside the traditional academic curriculum. But things are changing. The advent of cultural studies, or the study of ordinary rather than high culture, in college coursework has shown that more and more instructors have decided that America's popular culture — a field that includes everything from advertising and film to the way we define and express our sexuality — is worth studying and writing about. This is a book designed to show you how to do it — how to write about American culture as you would write about any other academic subject.

We have prepared *Signs of Life in the U.S.A.* because we believe that you are already a sophisticated student of American culture. Think of all you already know. Just list all the bands you can name. And all the various categories they fall into (Is the Seattle sound still in vogue? How's the alternative rock scene doing? Where's hip-hop these days?). Face it, you're an expert. So isn't that a good place to start learning how to write college essays, with what you know already? We all write best when we can write from our strengths, and this book is intended to let you tap into your own storehouse of information and experience as you learn to write college essays.

*Signs of Life in the U.S.A.,* then, is designed to let you exploit your knowledge of popular culture so that you may grow into a better writer about any subject. You can interpret the resurrection of the Beatles, for example, in the same manner as you would interpret, say, a short story, because the Beatles, too, constitute a kind of *sign.* A sign is something, *anything,* that carries a meaning. A stop sign, for instance, means exactly what it says: "Stop when you approach this intersection," while carrying the implied meaning, "or risk getting a ticket." Words, too, are signs: You read them to figure out what they mean. You had to be trained to read such signs, but that training began so long ago that you may well take your ability to read for granted. But all of your life you have been encountering, and interpreting, other sorts of signs that you were never taught to read. You know what they mean anyway. Take the way you wear your hair. When you get your hair cut, you are not simply removing hair: You are making a statement, sending a message about yourself. It's the same for both men and women. For men, think of the different messages you'd send if you got a buzz cut to match a goatee, or grew your hair out long, or shaved your head. What does a woman communicate when she adopts the "Rachel" hairdo from the hit TV series *Friends*? Why was your hair short last year and long this year (or long last year and short this year)? Aren't you saying something with the scissors? In this way, you make your hairstyle into a sign that sends a message about your identity. You are surrounded by such signs. Just look at your classmates.

The world of signs could be called a kind of text, the text of America's popular culture. We want you to think of *Signs of Life in the U.S.A.* as a window onto that text. What you read in the essays and introductions included in this book should lead you to study and analyze the world around you for yourself. Let the readings guide you to your own interpretations, your own readings, of the text of America.

We have chosen ten "windows" that look upon America's cultural scene. In some cases, we have put some of the scenery directly into this book, as when we include actual ads in our chapter on advertising. In other cases, where it is impossible to put something directly into a textbook, like a TV show or a movie, we have included essays that help you think about specific programs and films and assignments that invite you to go out and interpret a TV show or movie of your own choosing.

Each chapter contains an introduction designed to alert you to the kinds of signs you will find there, as well as tips on how to go about interpreting them. The readings that follow offer positions and interpretations of their own, as well as texts and contexts for your further analysis. Shelby Steele's provocative essay on Malcolm X, for example, argues that Malcolm X was an essentially *conservative* figure and that Spike Lee's film about him presents us with a myth rather than a man. To make your own judgment on the matter, you might want to read a biography of Malcolm X and compare it with the movie. Then you could write an essay stating your position. Will you agree or disagree with Steele? Only by looking closely into the matter will you be able to decide.

## Two Books in One

We have divided *Signs of Life in the U.S.A.* into two broad sections embracing, on the one hand, some of the dominant "images" in American popular culture, and on the other, some of the most prominent "issues" of our times. The images section explores the visible signs of America's popular culture, the icons of our media-dominated society. "Consuming Passions" is the lead chapter in this section because America is a consumer culture, and so the environment within which the galaxy of popular signs functions is, more often than not, a consumerist one. Next, "Brought to You B(u)y" explores the related world of advertising, for advertising provides the grease, so to speak, that lubricates the engine of America's consumer culture. Because television and the movies are the sources of many of our most significant cultural images and icons, we include a chapter on each in this section. And we have also included a chapter on American pop culture "characters" — from comic book superheroes to Elvis Presley — that America consumes along with all the other products of our consumer culture. In every chapter we have chosen topics that date from the last few years and that relate to topics in the other chapters through the connecting links of American consumption.

The second section of the book focuses on issues of contemporary importance, social and political issues that may already be of significance to your life: the politics of gender, our sense of racial identity and divisions, the growing appearance of outlaw societies — from street gangs to white supremacist militias — the AIDS epidemic, and the advent of computer virtual culture. These chapters ask you to explore national issues and controversies that affect the quality of American life, both today and into the future. While our selections are not intended to be inclusive, we have tried to provide readings and topics on some of the most pressing of contemporary issues and controversies.

The twofold structure of *Signs of Life in the U.S.A.* is intended to provide two related but tonally different sets of readings and exercises. You may find that interpreting popular images can be entertaining as well as informative, while looking at certain issues provokes profound soul-searching as you seek to unmask the implications of your beliefs and values. Throughout the book, however, you will find readings and assignments that invite you to go out and select your own "texts" for analysis (a video, an advertisement, a film, a fashion fad, a political opinion, and so on). Here's where your own experience is of particular value, for often you're a great deal more adept at choosing and decoding the signs around you than your teachers are, not only because you are more familiar with popular signs but also because you are more familiar with their background, with the particular popular cultural *system* or environment to which they belong.

## The Semiotic Method

To interpret and write effectively about the signs of popular culture, you need a method, and it is part of the purpose of this book to introduce such a method to you. Without a methodology for interpreting signs, writing about them could become little more than descriptive reviews or opinion pieces. There is nothing wrong with writing descriptions and opinions, but one of your tasks in your writing class is to learn how to write academic essays, that is, analytical essays that present theses or arguments that are well supported by evidence. The method we are drawing upon in this book — a method that is known as "semiotics" — is especially designed for the analysis of popular culture. Whether or not you're familiar with this word, you are already practicing sophisticated semiotic analyses every day of your life. Reading this page is an act of semiotic decoding (words and even letters are signs that must be interpreted), but so is figuring out just what your classmate *means* by wearing a particular shirt or dress. For a semiotician (one who practices semiotic analysis), a shirt, a haircut, a television image, anything at all, can be taken as a sign, as a message to be decoded and analyzed to discover its meaning. Every cultural activity for the semiotician leaves a trace of meaning, a kind of blip on the semiotic Richter scale, that remains for us to read, just as a geologist "reads" the earth for signs of earthquakes, volcanos, and other geological phenomena.

Many who hear the word *semiotics* for the first time assume that it is the name of a new, and forbidding, subject. But in truth, the study of signs is neither very new nor forbidding. Its modern form took shape in the late nineteenth and early twentieth centuries through the writings and lectures of two men. Charles Sanders Peirce (1839–1914) was an American philosopher and physicist who first coined the word *semiotics,* while Ferdinand de Saussure (1857–1913) was a Swiss linguist whose lectures became the foundation for what *he* called *semiology.* Without knowing of each other's work, Peirce and Saussure established the fundamental principles that modern semioticians or semiologists — the terms are essentially interchangeable — have developed into the contemporary study of semiotics.

The application of semiotics to the interpretation of popular culture was pioneered in the 1950s by the French semiologist Roland Barthes (1915–1980) in a book entitled *Mythologies.* The basic principles of semiotics had already been explored by linguists and anthropologists, but Barthes took the matter to the heart of his own contemporary France, analyzing the cultural significance of everything from professional wrestling to striptease, from toys to plastics.

It was Barthes, too, who established the political dimensions of semiotic analysis. Often, the subject of a semiotic analysis — a movie, say, or a TV program — doesn't look political at all; it simply looks like entertainment. In our society (especially in the aftermath of the Watergate scandal of the 1970s), "politics" has become something of a dirty word, and to "politicize" something seems somehow to contaminate it. So you shouldn't feel alarmed if at first it feels a little odd to search for a political meaning in an apparently neutral topic. You may even think that to do so is to "read too much" into that topic. But Barthes's point — and the point of semiotics in general — is that all social behavior is political in the sense that it reflects some personal or group interest. Such interests are encoded in what are called "ideologies," or world views, that express the values and opinions of those who hold them. Politics, then, is just another name for the clash of ideologies that takes place in any complex society where the interests of all those who belong to it constantly compete with one another.

Take, for example, the way people have responded to the movie *Forrest Gump.* Those viewers who best like the film tend to share its conservative political values: its celebration of individual responsibility and capitalist enterprise. The same viewers, on the other hand, are less likely to enjoy Oliver Stone's *Nixon,* a film that gives a less-than-flattering portrait of one of American conservatism's leading standard-bearers of this century. In each case, the viewers' responses are shaped, in part, by their ideological and political interests, not simply by their taste in the style of a movie.

While not all movies are as manifestly political as these two are, careful analysis can usually uncover some set of political values at the heart of a film, although those values may be subtly concealed behind an apparently apolitical facade. Indeed, the political values that guide our social behavior are often concealed behind images that don't look political at all. Consider, for example, the depiction of the "typical" American family in the classic TV sitcoms of the fifties and sixties, particularly all those images of happy, docile housewives. To most contemporary viewers, those images looked "normal" or natural at the time that they were first broadcast — the way families and women were supposed to be. The shows didn't seem at all ideological. To the contrary, they seemed a retreat from political rancor to domestic harmony. But to a feminist semiotician, the old sitcoms were in fact highly political, because the happy housewives they presented were really images designed to *convince* women that their place is in the home, not in the workplace competing with men. Such images — or signs — did not reflect reality; they reflected, rather, the interests of a patriarchal, male-centered society. If you think not, then ask yourself why there were shows called *Father Knows Best, Bachelor Father,* and *My Three Sons,* but no *My Three Daughters*? And why did few of the women in the shows have jobs or never seem to leave the house? Of course, there was always *I Love Lucy,* but wasn't Lucy the screwball character that her husband Ricky had to rescue from one crisis after another?

Such are the kinds of questions that semiotics invite us to ask. They may be put more generally. When analyzing any popular cultural phenomenon, always ask yourself questions like these: *Why does this thing look the way it does? Why are they saying this? Why am I doing this? What are they really saying? What am I really doing?* In short, take nothing for granted when analyzing any image or activity.

Take, for instance, the reason you may have joined a health club (or decided not to). Did you happen to respond to a photo ad that showed you a gorgeous girl or guy (with a nice looking guy or girl in the background)? On the surface of the ad, you simply see an image showing — or *denoting* — a patron of the club. You may think: "I want to look like that." But there's probably another dimension to the ad's appeal. The ad may *show* you someone with a nice body, but what it is *suggesting* — or *connoting* — is that this club is a good place to pick up a hot date. That's why there's that other figure in the background. That's supposed to be *you.* The one in the foreground is the sort of person you're being promised you'll find at the club. The ad doesn't say this, of course, but that's what it wants you to think because that's a more effective way of getting you to join. Suggestion, or connotation, is a much more powerful stimulant than denotation, but it is often deliberately masked in the signs you are presented with every day. Semiotics, one might say, reveals all the denotative smoke screens around you.

Health club membership drives, you may be thinking, aren't especially political (though actually they are when you think of the kinds of bodies that they are telling you are desirable to have), but the powerful effect of a concealed suggestion is used all the time in actual political campaigns. The now infamous "Willie Horton" episode during the 1988 presidential campaign provides a classic instance. What happened was this: Some Republican supporters of George Bush's candidacy ran a series of TV ads featuring the photographic image of one Willie Horton, a convicted rapist from Massachusetts who murdered someone while on parole. On the surface, the ads simply showed, or denoted, this fact. But what they connoted was racial hatred and fear (Willie Horton is black), and they were very effective in prompting white voters to mistrust Massachusetts governor Michael Dukakis and to vote instead for George Bush.

Signs, in short, often conceal some interest or other, whether political, or commercial, or whatever. And the proliferation of signs and images in an era of electronic technology has simply made it all the more important that we learn to decode the interests behind them.

Semiotics, accordingly, is not just about signs and symbols: It is equally about ideology and power. This fact makes semiotics sound rather serious, and often the seriousness of a semiotic analysis is quite real. But reading the text of modern life can also be fun, for it is a text that is at once popular and accessible, a "book" that is intimately in touch with the pulse of American life. As such, it is constantly changing. The same sign can change meaning if something else comes along to change the environment in which it originally appeared. Take the Beatles.

## Interpreting Popular Signs

Let's say that you receive an assignment that asks you to analyze the semiotic significance of the Beatles' reappearance in 1995. How would you go about writing it? The first thing you need to do is to set aside any personal reactions you have to the Beatles' music. You aren't writing a musical review, and the aesthetic question "What made the Beatles so *good*?" differs significantly from the semiotic question "What made the Beatles so *big*?" There are plenty of pop musicians who, like the Beatles, can stake a claim to musical genius, but no band has approached them in cultural impact. It doesn't even matter whether you like their music (or the music of Madonna, or Pearl Jam, or any other culturally significant performers). What matters in a semiotic analysis is what the Beatles phenomenon says about us as a culture.

### Exploring the Signs of American Life

Throughout this text, you'll read essays that connect the signs of American life to consumer and commercial culture. In your journal, brainstorm a list of the icons and symbols central to American culture (they can range from icons such as the Statue of Liberty to those associated with holidays, such as Thanksgiving). Then reflect on the significance of your list. How do the signs work to define what's "American"? How are the signs and symbols used as marketing tools? How does that use affect your attitude toward the signs?

In drafting your analysis, you might want to consider the Beatles' past significance. While not a requirement, this step can reveal a lot because here's a particular case of the same cultural phenomenon — the Beatles — meaning something different in a changed environment. That is, the Beatles of the early sixties signified differently than they did in the late sixties (their psychedelic phase), and they signify something different again in the nineties. That their meaning has changed because pop culture has changed could be an important part of your contemporary analysis. So you'll want to do a little research: Watch a Beatles documentary film, read a history of the group, browse through the library (or World Wide Web) for histories of rock-and-roll music.

After getting a sense of the environment in which the Beatles once signified, you'll want to survey the current musical and pop cultural scene. What's popular, and what's not? How do current musical trends differ from those of the era in which the Beatles appeared? How does the marketing of rock music differ? How have music-associated fashions changed? How have audiences changed? Is it significant that current superbands like REM are so self-conscious about their status in a media-saturated society? What, in short, is the current system of rock music like?

The purpose of such questions is to sketch the overall context in which the subject of your analysis signifies, the set of related phenomena with which your subject can be associated. This is one of the key elements of a semiotic interpretation: the establishment of a set of associated phenomena. For from a semiotic perspective, the meaning of a thing lies largely in its relations to other things, both in its *similarities* to other things and in its *differences*. By establishing these relationships, you are identifying the *system* in which a sign works.

Let's get back to the Beatles to see how you can establish such a system of relations. Taken by themselves, the band and its members don't *mean* anything: They are simply what they are, rock-and-roll performers. But seen in relation to other things — to other bands, to the commercial world of pop music, to its audience, to the history of rock-and-roll it-self — the band becomes a cultural sign. To illustrate this point, we'll walk through an interpretation of what the Beatles meant back in February 1964, when they first conquered America on *The Ed Sullivan Show*.

First, what was the relevant cultural system in place at the time? That's easy: The Beatles entered into the world of rock-and-roll, a system that they did not invent. Chuck Berry, who himself was borrowing from a musical tradition that included the blues, gospel, country-western, and bop, has been given credit for inventing rock in the fifties, closely followed by such performers as Elvis Presley, Bill Haley, and Buddy Holly. And plenty of other innovative performers were around when the Beatles arrived, figures like the Beach Boys, the Supremes, and Bob Dylan. In this sense, the Beatles were simply a part of an already existing system of pop performers; indeed, they got their start imitating both the music and the personal appearance of the leading icons of fifties rock.

So far, the system hasn't told us much. The Beatles are just another band, making music and money, meaning nothing in particular. But that doesn't seem right, does it? There has to be more to it than that. For if the Beatles simply descended from a preexisting rock system, why did their appearance on *The Ed Sullivan Show* start a cultural stampede beyond anything that even Elvis had ever inspired? In short, what was *different* about the Beatles in the pop system of the early sixties? That's where their significance lies.

For one, they were British — a fact that is not as trivial as it might appear. While English and American popular culture share many cultural *codes,* they are not identical, and what might be quite common in England can be strikingly uncommon in America (and vice versa, of course). Those famous suits the Beatles wore, for example, that so captivated American audiences in 1964 were quite recognizable to British teens as reflections of the emerging Mod style, and so were not so exciting back home in Britain. Had the Beatles appeared in the United States in their first costumes — the black leather and greasy pompadours that Americans would have easily recognized as leftover biker outfits — their reception just might have been less enthusiastic.

Because of their development in a different cultural code, the Beatles thus came to America with the preexisting appeal of being a little exotic. This was no accident, incidentally. It was planned. Already a big hit in England, the Beatles decided not to tour America until the time was right. By so doing, they used a marketing ploy that has been used quite successfully since with such products as the Cabbage Patch Kids and the Mazda Miata: They tantalized American audiences with glimpses and rumors and a few songs but withheld the actual "product," so to speak, until a fever pitch of curiosity had been reached. Another reason for the astonishing reception they received, then, and a crucial part of their difference, lies quite simply in this superior act of marketing.

But, of course, there's a lot more to it than that — and indeed, in most semiotic analyses one can never point to a single factor to explain a complex cultural phenomenon. So, beyond the advantage of a fresh fashion statement (fresh, that is, to Americans) and superior marketing, what else made the Beatles different, and thus, so significant?

Again, it wasn't just their music. Remember, we're talking about the Beatles circa 1963–1964, when they were making hits of songs written by Buddy Holly, Chuck Berry, and Little Richard, along with their own. Still, the way they performed that music was different, and, more importantly, so was the way they looked as they performed it. Like Elvis, for example, they moved around as they played, but unlike Elvis, they didn't bump and grind: They bobbed, smiled, and shook their hair. Like James Brown, they howled, but they put less raw sexuality in their whoops. And then, of course, they wore those choir boy suits, which, since the Mod look wasn't so common in America, took on a special significance. Rather than resembling Mod performers, as in England, the Beatles in America could be differentiated from the many other American rock stars who performed in suits, or at least coats and ties, in the early sixties, but in conventional suits not at all like the foppish stuff the Beatles wore.

And then there was their hair. It was long, as Elvis's hair was considered long, but it was longer than Elvis's, and, more importantly, the style was not a bad-boy pompadour, dripping with grease and aggression. It was a pudding basin style, the kind of haircut that Moe of the Three Stooges had, and that generations of working-class children whose mothers clapped bowls over their heads and snipped around the edge had had before. It was as different from anything else in the American pop fashion code as were their lapel-less suits and pointed leather boots. So what can we make of these differences?

To find the significance of such apparently insignificant details as hair and dress styles, consider once again the system in which the Beatles first appeared. In 1964, rock was a vibrant component of American youth culture, but it was also culturally marginalized. With its origins in black musical forms, rock already had one strike against it in a racially segregated America, and its related association with the raw sexuality of rhythm and blues had also forced it to the margins of socially accepted entertainment. Elvis himself, who seemed to want to seduce his audiences, had already stretched the limits of what was sexually permissible in his performances (he was ordered to stifle the bumps and grinds when he appeared on *The Ed Sullivan Show*), and the arrest and eventual incarceration of Chuck Berry on a morals charge in 1962 had prompted a widespread cleanup of pop music. Even the Supremes, the superstars of Motown, avoided the bluesy image of such major predecessors as Billie

Holliday, appearing instead as evening-gowned debutantes to pass through the cultural censors. The historical moment into which the Beatles appeared, in short, was one of renewed repression after the brief outburst of the fifties.

Now, rock had gotten its start as a release of the sexual and social energies that the conservative fifties had repressed, so the energy was still there, pent up and ready to explode. The question was, how could an act get past the cultural censors and still release that energy? The Beach Boys, with their well-scrubbed, decidedly teenaged image, singing songs about surfing and dating, weren't about to do that; black performers like James Brown and Sam Cooke, whose acts were not so expressively limited, were too marginalized by race to do it. But the Beatles did, and they did so by donning an ingenious camouflage. Substituting those prim suits and pudding basin haircuts for their original outlaw outfits, they did an end run around the censors. To Americans they looked, in short, like choirboys.

Choirboys with disconcertingly long hair, that is. Adult America didn't like it but was baffled at what else to object to, given the band's otherwise well-scrubbed, polite appearance (the Rolling Stones, deciding not to play the same game, had a great deal more trouble with adult America). What signified, then, about their hair was its noticeable difference in an era of good-boy crew cuts, on the one hand, and outlaw pompadours, on the other. Their attitude, too, was different. Cheeky, irreverent, and self-confident, they were hardly like the polite heroes of the beach blanket set — John Lennon was decidedly not the innocent Frankie Avalon — but he also wasn't the lascivious Jerry Lee Lewis. Not outlaw enough to run into trouble with the censors, and just rebellious enough to cut it with ever-rebellious youth: That was a significant part of the Beatles' secret.

Our argument, then, is that the extraordinary reception that the Beatles received in America in 1964 signified, at least in part, their tapping into a wellspring of repressed energy — both sexual and social — in American youth culture. They could release this energy because of their ability to evade a cultural censorship that suppressed or marginalized anything overtly rebellious, sexual, or black. That the "sexual revolution" followed close on the heels of the Beatles' appearance supports our contention that part of the appeal — and therefore significance — of the early Beatles was their successful, if rather sneaky, breaking down of the barriers to sexual expression. The famous "Summer of Love" was soon to follow in 1967, and the Beatles, in new uniforms, with a new look, and leading the way to yet another pop cultural system, were a part of that too.

More, of course, could be added to this argument (indeed, you should always allow your critical attention to range far and wide in the prewriting stage of a semiotic interpretation: You want to brainstorm freely in the early stages of the writing process), but this should be sufficient to show just how much times have changed. So what about now? Rather than perform that analysis here, we'll leave that to you. What is the Beatles' place in the current musical and cultural world? How are they like other bands? How are they different? What do these differences tell us about them? What does the Beatles' contemporary audience tell us? How do the Beatles relate to the current trends that dominate the American fashion codes? And how did the orchestration of their reappearance in 1995 differ from that of their inaugural American appearance in 1964?

Having answered these and other such questions, you'll be ready to formulate a thesis encapsulating what you think the Beatles signify today. Then use your description of the system or cultural context in which the Beatles now signify as a cultural sign to defend and support your thesis. The more detailed your presentation of that system, the more persuasive your essay will be.

## The Classroom Connection

Gathering your evidence in defense of an argument is also what all analytic writing is about. Thus the skills you already have as an interpreter of the signs around you — of images, objects, and forms of behavior — are the same skills that you develop as a writer of critical essays that present a point of view and an argument to defend it. There is a difference, that is, between asserting an opinion and presenting evidence in a carefully constructed argument. All of us can make our opinions known, but analytic writing requires the marshaling of supporting evidence. A lawyer doesn't simply assert a client's innocence: Evidence is required. Similarly, in interpreting the Beatles, you'll want to bring together as much supporting material from cultural history as you can. By learning to write semiotic analyses of our culture, by searching for supporting evidence to underpin your interpretive take on modern life, you are also learning to write critical arguments.

"But how," you (and perhaps your teacher) may ask, "can I know that a semiotic interpretation is right?" Good question — it is commonly asked by those who fear that a semiotic analysis might "read too much into" a subject. But then, the question can be asked of the writer of any interpretive essay, and the answer in each case is the same. No one can ever absolutely *prove* the truth of any argument in the human sciences; what you do is *persuade* your audience through the use of pertinent evidence. When you are writing analyses about popular culture, that evidence comes from your knowledge of the system to which the object you are interpreting belongs. The more you know about the system, the more convincing your interpretations will be. And that is true whether

|||||||||||||||||||||||||||||||||||||||||||||||||||||||||||||||||||||||||||||||||||||||||||||||||||||||||||||||||||||||||||||||||||||||||||||||||||||||||||||||||||||||||||||||||||||||||||||||||||||||||||||||||||||

> ### Discussing the Signs of American Life
>
> To start looking critically at the world around you, bring to class one object and give a short (two-minute) semiotic interpretation of it to your class. Your object can be anything, ranging from clothing to food, from a book to an album cover. What does your object say about modern American culture? Be sure to consider what system it belongs to (its relationship to similar objects) and what values and beliefs it reflects. And be sure to focus not on personal or private meanings but on social meanings.
>
> After everyone in the class has spoken, stand back and reflect on the collection of objects discussed. What do they say about your class as a whole?

you are writing about the Beatles or about more traditional academic subjects.

But often our interpretations of popular culture involve issues that are larger than those involved in music or entertainment. How, for instance, are we to analyze fully the widespread belief — as reflected in the classic sitcoms mentioned earlier — that it is more natural for women to stay at home and take care of the kids than it is for men to do so? Why, in other words, is the concept of "housewife" so easy to accept, while the idea of a "househusband" may appear somewhat ridiculous? How, in short, can we interpret some of our most basic values semiotically? To see how, we need to look at those value systems that semioticians call "cultural mythologies."

## Of Myths and Men

As we have seen, in a semiotic analysis we do not search for the meanings of things in the things themselves. Rather, we find meaning in the way we can relate things together. We've done this with the Beatles, but what about with beliefs? This book asks you to explore the implications of social issues like gender norms that involve a great many personal beliefs and values that we do not always recognize *as* beliefs and values. Instead, we think of them as truths (one might think, "Of course it's odd for a man to stay home and take care of the house!"). But from a semiotic perspective, our values too belong to special systems from which they take their meaning. Semioticians call these systems of belief cultural "mythologies."

## Reading American Life on the Net

In 1996, Nathaniel Wice and Steven Daly created a web site, http://www.altculture.com/home.shtml/, as a means to keep up-to-date their print encyclopedia of 1990s youth culture, *alt.culture* (1996). Visit their site and then analyze how the authors define popular culture. What sorts of phenomena do they include and why? What cultural values and social mythologies inform their choices? Do you find any areas of popular culture to be missing, and if so, what arguments would you give for their inclusion?

In the semiotic sense of the term, a cultural mythology, or "myth" for short, is not some fanciful story from the past; indeed, if you find this word confusing because of its traditional association with such stories, you may prefer to use the phrase "value system." Consider the value system that governs our traditional thinking about gender roles. Have you ever noticed how our society presumes that it is primarily the role of women — adult daughters — to take care of aging and infirm parents? If you want to look at the matter from a physiological perspective, it might seem that men would be better suited to the task: In a state of nature, men are physically stronger and so would seem to be the natural protectors of the aged. And yet, though our cultural mythology holds that men should protect the nuclear family, it tends to assign to women the care of extended families. It is culture that decides here, not nature.

But while cultural myths guide our behavior, they are subject to change. You yourself may have already experienced a transitional phase in the myths surrounding courtship behavior. In the past, the gender myths that formed the rules of the American dating game held that it is the role of the male to initiate proceedings (*he* calls) and for the female to react (*she* waits by the phone). Similarly, the rules once held that it is invariably the responsibility of the male to plan the evening and pay the tab. These rules are changing, aren't they? Can you describe the rules that now govern courtship behavior?

A cultural mythology, or value system, then, is a kind of lens that governs the way we view our world. Think of it this way: Say you were born with rose-tinted eyeglasses permanently attached over your eyes, but you didn't know they were there. Because the world would look rose-colored to you, you would presume that it *is* rose-colored. You wouldn't wonder whether the world might look otherwise through different lenses. But in the world there are other kinds of eyeglasses with different lenses, and reality does look different to those who wear them.

Those lenses are cultural mythologies, and no culture can claim to have the one set of glasses that sees things as they really are.

The profound effect our cultural mythologies have on the way we view reality, on our most basic values, is especially apparent today when the myths of European culture are being challenged by the world views of the many other cultures that have taken root in American soil. Where, for example, European-American culture upholds a profoundly individualistic social mythology, valuing individual rights before those of the group, traditional Chinese culture believes in the primacy of the family and the community over the individual. Maxine Hong Kingston's short story "No Name Woman" poignantly demonstrates how such opposing ideologies can collide with painful results in its tale of a Chinese woman who is more or less sacrificed to preserve the interests of her village. The story, from *The Woman Warrior,* tells of a young woman who gives birth to a baby too many months after her husband's departure to America with most of her village's other young men for it to be her husband's child. The men had left in order to earn the money in America that keeps the impoverished villagers from starving. They may be away for years and so need to be assured that their wives will remain faithful to them in their absence lest they refuse to go at all. The unfortunate heroine of the tale — who, to sharpen the agony, had probably been more the victim of rape than the instigator of adultery — is horribly punished by the entire village as an example to any other wives who might disturb the system and ends her life in a tragic suicide.

That Kingston wrote "No Name Woman" as a self-consciously "hyphenated" Asian-American, as one whose identity fuses both Chinese and Euro-American values, reveals the fault lines between conflicting mythologies. On the one hand, as an Asian, Kingston understands the communal values behind the horrific sacrifice of her aunt, and her story makes sure that her Euro-American readers understand this too. On the other hand, as an American and as a feminist, she is outraged by the violation of an individual woman's rights on behalf of the group (or mob, which is as the village behaves in the story). Kingston's own sense of personal conflict in this clash of mythologies — Asian, American, and feminist — offers a striking example of the inevitable conflicts that America itself will face as it changes from a monocultural to a multicultural society.

To put this another way, from the semiotic perspective, *how* you interpret something is very much a product of *who* you are; for culture is just another name for the frames that shape our values and perceptions. Traditionally, American education has presumed a monocultural perspective, a "melting pot" view that no matter what one's cultural background, truth is culture-blind. Langston Hughes took on this assumption many years ago in his classic poem "Theme for English B," where he writes, "I guess I'm what / I feel and see and hear," and wonders whether "my page will be colored" when he writes. "Being me, it will not be white," the poet suggests, but while he struggles to find what he holds in common with his white instructor, he can't suppress the differences. In essence, that is the challenge of multicultural education itself: to identify the different cultural codes that inform the mythic frameworks of the many cultures that share America while searching for what holds the whole thing together.

That meaning is not culture-blind, that it is conditioned by systems of ideology and belief that are codified differently by different cultures, is a foundational semiotic judgment. Human beings, in other words, construct their own social realities, and so who gets to do the constructing becomes very important. Every contest over a cultural code is, accordingly, a contest for power, but the contest is usually masked because the winner generally defines its mythology as the "truth," as what is most "natural" or "reasonable." Losers in the contest become objects of scorn and are quickly marginalized, declared "unnatural," or "deviant," or even "insane." The stakes are high as myth battles myth, with "truth" itself as the highest prize.

This does not mean that you must abandon your own beliefs when conducting a semiotic analysis, only that you cannot take them for granted and must be prepared to argue for them. We want to assure you that semiotics will not tell you what to think and believe. It *does* assume that what you believe reflects some cultural system or other and that no cultural system can claim absolute validity or superiority. The readings and chapter introductions in this book contain their own values and ideologies, and if you wish to challenge those values, you can begin by exposing the myths that they may assume. For example, the introduction to our chapter on the semiotics of the AIDS epidemic is guided by the presumption that AIDS is not divine punishment for immoral behavior, and that the social response to AIDS is more determined by our culture's attitudes toward homosexuality than by the threat of a fatally contagious disease. You may or may not agree with this position. If you disagree, then try to think of the basis for your disagreement. If your arguments for your beliefs are more persuasive than the positions taken in the readings, then you may have effectively countered them.

To put this another way, everything in this book reflects a political point of view, and if you hold a different one, it is not enough simply to presuppose the innate superiority of your own point of view — to claim that one writer is being "political" while you yourself are simply telling the truth. This may sound heretical precisely because human beings operate within value systems whose political invisibility is guaranteed by the system. No mythology, that is to say, begins by saying, "This is just a political construct or interpretation." Every myth begins, "This is the truth." It is very difficult to imagine, from within the myth, any alternatives. Indeed, as you read this book, you may find it upsetting to see that some traditional beliefs — such as the "proper" roles of men and women in society — are socially constructed and not absolute. But the outlines of the myth, the bounding (and binding) frame, best appear when challenged by another myth, and this challenge is probably nowhere more insistent than in America, where so many of us are really "hyphenated" Americans, citizens combining in our own persons two (or more) cultural traditions.

## Getting Started

Mythology, like culture, is not static, however, and so the semiotician must always keep his or her eye on the clock, so to speak. History, time itself, is a constant factor in a constantly changing world. Since the first edition of this book, American popular culture has changed. In this second edition, we have tried to reflect those changes — for example, the clear emergence of the Internet as a major cultural phenomenon, and the rise of talk radio hosts as major cultural players — but inevitably, further changes will occur in the time it takes for this book to appear on your class syllabus. That such changes occur is part of the excitement of the semiotic enterprise: There is always something new to consider and interpret. What does not change is the nature of semiotic interpretation: Whatever you choose to analyze in the realm of American popular culture, the semiotic approach will help you understand it.

It's your turn now. Start asking questions, pushing, probing. That's what critical writing is all about, but this time *you're* part of the question. Arriving at answers, conclusions, is the fun part here, but answers aren't the basis of analytic thinking: questions are. You always begin with a question, a query, a hypothesis, something to explore. If you already knew the answer, there would be no point in conducting the analysis. We leave you to explore the almost infinite variety of questions that the readings in this book raise. Many come equipped with their own answers, but you may (indeed will and should) find that such "answers" raise further questions. To help you ask those questions, keep in mind the two elemental principles of semiotics that we have explored so far:

1. The meaning of a sign can be found not in itself but in its *relationships* (both differences and similarities) with other signs within a *system*. To interpret an individual sign, then, you must determine the general system in which it belongs.

2. What we call social "reality" is a human construct, the product of a cultural *mythology* or *value system* that intervenes between our minds and the world we experience. Such cultural myths reflect the values and ideological interests of their builders, not the laws of nature or logic.

Perhaps our first principle could be more succinctly phrased, "Everything is connected," and our second simply says, "Question authority." Think of them that way if it helps. Or just ask yourself whenever you are interpreting something, "What's going on here?" In short, question *everything*. And one more reminder: Signs are like weather vanes; they point in response to invisible historical winds. We invite you now to start looking at the weather.

# IMAGES

|||||||||||||||||||||||||||||||||||||||||||||||||||||||||||||||

# CHAPTER ONE

# CONSUMING PASSIONS

## *The Culture of American Consumption*

Take a moment to think about your bedroom. It doesn't matter whether it's in a dorm, an apartment, your own house, or the home you grew up in, just so long as it's *your* space. How have you decorated it? Anything posted on the walls? If so, what are the themes? Sports? Music? Television? Art? Nature? What sort of furniture do you have? Take note of everything.

Now, open your clothes closet. What do you see? A pair of Doc Martens? Or Nikes? Any sweat suits? Plaid flannel shirts? Jeans? Jeans ripped at the knees? Any oversized chinos? Oversized shorts? Dresses? For work? Play? Any leotards? Miniskirts? Any business suits? Boots? In short, what are your fashion tastes?

Such questions are a good place to begin the semiotic analysis of American consumer culture, for every choice you make in the decoration of your room, and every choice you make in the decoration of yourself, is a sign, a signal you are sending to the world about yourself. Those aren't just a pair of shoes you're wearing: They're a statement about your identity. That's not just a collection of CDs: It's a message about your world view. Indeed, your music collection may say more about you than anything else you own.

To read the signs of American consumption, it is best to start with yourself, because you've already got an angle on the answers. But be careful and be honest: Remember, a cultural sign gets its meaning from the system in which it appears. Its significance does not lie in its usefulness but rather in its symbolism, in the image it projects, and that image is socially constructed. You didn't make it by yourself. To decode the stuff in your room and the stuff in your wardrobe, you've got to ask yourself what you are trying to say with it and what you want other people to think about you. And you've got to remember the difference between fashion and function.

To give you an idea of how to go about analyzing consumer objects and behavior, let's look at a very simple product that on the surface seems completely functional. Let's look at coffee.

## Interpreting the Culture of American Consumption

At first, coffee may not seem like a subject you can interpret. After all, it's just a beverage that you might drink when waking up, or studying, or chatting with friends. Its function is obvious; its physical appearance, downright innocuous. But remember that a semiotic analysis looks beyond your subject's use — what you do with it — to a wider cultural and social significance.

Let's consider those wider significances. As tea is to the British, coffee is to America: the defining beverage of our culture, consumed at breakfast, lunch, dinner, and at all hours in between. As our own cultural myths have it, coffee took the place of tea in American life after the Boston Tea Party, and so, at first, it assumed a patriotic significance. But beyond this more or less nationalistic signification, coffee connotes a number of other meanings in American consumer culture, bearing a different image depending on the context and on the consumer. As we look at a few of those images here, ask yourself which image of coffee appeals the most to you. Which images have less appealing cultural associations, and why?

### The Mrs. Olson Scenario

The traditional image of coffee in America associates coffee drinking with men and breakfast. The famous Mrs. Olson campaign that promoted Folger's coffee in the 1960s is paradigmatic of this association: It dramatized the serving of coffee as a housewifely duty. Mrs. Olson serves her spouse as he broods behind his newspaper before going to work. In this symbolic scenario, coffee is a relatively solitary drink. Rather than talking, the man behind the newspaper drinks and reads; if he talks at all, it's done in distracted mumbles. Such an image is part of a larger cultural mythology that assigns behavioral roles on the basis of gender. Women are assigned the task of brewing and serving the morning coffee, while men are cast as judges. Rather than sitting as equals conversing together

||||||||||||||||||||||||||||||||||||||||||||||||||||||||||||||||||||||||||||||||||||||||||||||||||||||||||||||||||||||||||||||||||||||||||||||||||||||||||||||||||

**Exploring the Signs of Consumer Culture**

"You are what you buy." In your journal, freewrite on the importance of consumer products in your life. How do you respond to being told your identity is equivalent to the products you buy? Do you resist the notion? Do you recall any instances when you have felt lost without a favorite object? How do you communicate your sense of self to others through objects, whether they be clothing, books, food, home decor, cars, or something else?

---

in a domestic environment, husband and wife are shown in a hierarchical relationship with the man holding the power. Indeed, the whole strategy of the Mrs. Olson ads was to convince young wives that the key to a successful marriage was serving hubby a successful cup of morning coffee — Folger's, of course.

## Truck Stops and Coffee Breaks

A second traditional image of coffee, related to the first in its reliance on traditional gender codes, has a typical location: the truck stop. You've seen this scenario: a lone truck driver, head hung over his plate of biscuits and gravy, flirting, perhaps, with a tired waitress. Here coffee means caffeine: It's not just the big rig that's tanking up. The coffee's quality is unimportant; what matters is the jolt. This image, too, is masculine and solitary; it also suggests haste — got to get back on the road.

A closely related image can be found in the office coffee break, which suggests both haste (you've got only ten minutes) and masculinity, insofar as it takes place in the traditionally masculine space of an office or workplace. While women certainly are no longer excluded from the office, the traditional scene shows them generally in a subordinate role as secretaries or as those responsible for brewing the coffee. Fast-food coffee, the Seven-Eleven's or MacDonald's big slurp grabbed on the way to work, are also part of this associational complex in which coffee connotes haste, work, and the fast and demanding pace of adult life.

## The Denny's Connection

For travelers and retirees, among others, the "coffee shop" image may be the most familiar. In a coffee shop, coffee serves as a background beverage to mediocre meals (airline coffee fits this category as well).

While the meal may be eaten at leisure, coffee in this scenario is a drink that one orders with the hash browns or the apple pie without caring much about the way it tastes. The image sometimes suggests elderly and/or palateless coffee drinkers passing the time.

### Common Grounds

Recently, yet another cultural image for coffee has been revived, an image born of the "coffeehouse" tradition. Unlike the situation in the coffee shop, where coffee is a background drink, in the coffeehouse, the center of attention is not simply the coffee — *good* coffee, that is — but is also a certain experience that goes along with drinking it. The coffee-house tradition, which goes back centuries in English cultural life, con-tinues to flourish in American intellectual and artistic circles. It is worth remembering in this context that the international insurance firm, Lloyds of London, began in an eighteenth-century English coffeehouse, and that Joseph Addison and Richard Steele launched their lively critical journal *The Spectator* in 1711 to bring "philosophy out of . . . libraries, schools and colleges to dwell in . . . coffee-houses."

The American coffeehouse tradition has maintained the English focus on good conversation (borrowing also from the tradition of the French coffee bar). Conversation, whether for business purposes or intel-lectual exploration, is the desired "product" at the coffeehouse. But while such conversation in eighteenth-century England was definitely as-sociated with masculinity, it has become gender-neutral in America. Where American women once tended to meet in tea shops, they are now flocking to such coffee-bar chains as Starbucks, places where women as well as men can be seen conversing together. In this code, the image of coffee strongly differs from such images as the Mrs. Olson or truck stop scenarios.

This difference is probably behind the popularity of coffeehouses among college students today. But here another difference comes into play. Coffee bars like Starbucks, with shining chrome-and-glass surfaces and $200 cappuccino makers for sale, tend to be most popular among the middle-aged set (Starbucks's largest market). College hangouts, on the other hand, tend to resemble the coffeehouse environments of the fifties: self-consciously shabby sites designed for late-night conversation, beat poetry readings, and alternative music. Here battered old sofas and cheap tables and chairs contrast strongly with the upscale image of the yuppie coffee sites. Connectedness is what matters in the student coffeehouse, the sense of generational belonging and relationship. We know of one such coffeehouse near our own university campus, appropriately called Common Grounds. The pun refers both to what is served there as a product (coffee) and what is offered there as an experience (a place for

**Discussing the Signs of Consumer Culture**

On the board, list in categories the fashion styles worn by members of the class. Be sure to note details, such as styles of shoes, jewelry, watches, or sunglasses, as well as broader trends. Then discuss what the clothing choices say about individuals. What messages are people sending about their personal identity? Do individual students agree with the class's interpretations of their clothing choices? Can any distinctions be made by gender, age, or ethnicity? Then discuss what the fashion styles worn by the whole class say: Is a group identity projected by class members?

people to connect). The fact that such places are springing up all over America signifies a certain shift in the interpretation of coffee by the American student population. Do you find yourself drawn to coffeehouses of this kind? Why or why not? What do you think of the people who spend their time there? Is there a definite image that such people project? Why would they (and you) choose one place over another?

Note how in each image we've examined, the actual substance of coffee itself is not particularly important. What matters is the overall cultural system, the social context, in which that substance is consumed. The residue of soaking ground coffee beans in hot water is not meaningful in itself. What is meaningful is the social and cultural context in which we consume that residue and the way we relate to other people when we do so.

If you find coffee consumption and its significance out of your line, think of any current consumer trend and question it. What messages are people sending when they buy the product? What images do they project? How does the fad relate to other cultural trends? Such are the questions that you must ask as a reader of consuming images, probing everything that you may find in the marketplace of goods and services, and taking care never to be satisfied with the answer, "because this product is *better* than that," or, more simply, "just because. . . ."

## Disposable Decades

When analyzing a consumer sign, you will often find yourself referring to particular decades in which certain popular fads and trends were prominent, for the decade in which a given style appears may be an essential key to the system that explains it. Have you ever wondered why

|||||||||||||||||||||||||||||||||||||||||||||||||||||||||||||||||||||||||||||||||||||||||||||||||||||||||||||||||||||||||||||||||||||||||||||||||||||||||

### Reading Consumer Culture on the Net

Log onto one of the many home shopping networks or catalogs. You might try the Internet Shopping Network (http://www.isn. com/), imall (http://www.imall.com/homepage.html), the Internet Mall (http://www.internet-mall.com/), or Shop at Home (http://www.shopathome.com/). Analyze both the products that are sold and the way that they are marketed. Who is the target audience for the network you're studying, and what images and values are used to attract this market? How does the marketing compare with nonelectronic sales pitches, such as displays in shopping malls and magazine or TV advertising? Does the electronic medium affect your own behavior as a consumer? Can you account for any differences in electronic and traditional marketing strategies?

American cultural trends seem to change with every decade, why it is so easy to speak of the "sixties," or the "seventies," or the "eighties" and immediately recognize the popular styles that dominated each decade? Have you ever looked at the style of a friend and thought "Oh, she's so sixties"? Can you place an Earth Shoe at the drop of a hat, or a Nehru jacket? A change in the calendar always seems to herald a change in style in a consuming culture. But why?

The decade-to-decade shift in America's pop cultural identity goes back a good number of years. It is still easy, for example, to distinguish F. Scott Fitzgerald's Jazz Age twenties from John Steinbeck's wrathful thirties. The era of the fifties, an especially connotative decade, raises images of ducktail haircuts and poodle skirts, drive-in culture and Elvis, family sitcoms and white-bread innocence, while the sixties are remembered for acid rock, hippies, the student revolution, and back-to-the-land communes. We remember the seventies as a pop cultural era divided between disco, Nashville, and preppiedom, with John Travolta, truckers, and Skippy and Muffy as dominant pop icons. The boom-boom eighties gave us Wall Street glitz and the yuppie invasion. Indeed, each decade since the First World War — which, not accidentally, happens to coincide roughly with the rise of modern advertising and mass production — seems to carry its own consumerist style.

It's no accident that the decade-to-decade shift in consumer styles seems to coincide with the advent of modern advertising and mass production, because it was mass production that created a need for constant consumer turnover in the first place. Mass production, that is, promotes stylistic change because with so many products being produced, a market must be created to consume all of them, and this means constantly consuming *more*. To get consumers to keep buying all the new stuff, you have to convince them that the stuff they already have has gone out of style. Why else, do you think, do fashion designers completely redesign their lines each year? Why else do car manufacturers annually change their color schemes and body shapes when the old model year seemed good enough? The new designs aren't simply functional improvements (though they are marketed as such); they are inducements to go out and replace what you already have lest you appear to be out of fashion. Just think: If you could afford to buy any car that you want, what would it be? Would your choice a few years ago have been the same?

And so, mass production creates consumer societies based on the constant production of new products that are intended to be disposed of with the next product year. But something happened along the way to the establishment of our consumer culture: We began to value consumption more than production. Listen to the economic news: Consumption, not production, is relied upon to carry America out of its economic downturns. When Americans stop buying, our economy grinds to a halt. Consumption lies at the center of our economic system now, and the result has been a transformation in the very way we view ourselves.

## A Tale of Two Cities

It has not always been thus in America, however. Once, Americans prided themselves on their productivity. In 1914, for example, the poet Carl Sandburg boasted of a Chicago that was "Hog Butcher for the World, Tool Maker, Stacker of Wheat, Player with Railroads and the Nation's Freight Handler." One wonders what Sandburg would think of the place today. From the south shore east to the industrial suburb of Gary, Indiana, Chicago's once-proud mills and factories rust in the winter wind. The broken windows of countless tenements stare blindly at the Amtrak commuter lines that transport the white-collared brokers of the Chicago Mercantile Exchange to the city center, where trade today is in commodity futures, not commodities. Even Michael Jackson, Gary's most famous export, hesitates to go home.

Meanwhile, a few hundred miles to the northwest, Bloomington, Minnesota, buzzes with excitement. For there stands the Mall of America, a colossus of consumption so large that it contains within its walls a seven-acre Knott's Berry Farm theme park, with lots of room to spare. You can find almost anything you want in the Mall of America, including the latest Michael Jackson records, but most of what you will find won't have been manufactured in America. Jackson himself is under contract with Sony. The proud tag "Made in the USA" is an increasingly rare item.

It's a long way, in short, from Sandburg's Chicago to the Mall of America, a trip that traverses America's shift from a producer to a consumer economy. You are probably only too aware of this transformation. The uncertainties of finding work after graduation, a stubborn international trade deficit, and the substitution of low-paying service industry jobs for high-paying positions in the manufacturing sector are the all-too-familiar consequences of America's economic "restructuring." But what is less obvious is the cultural effect of our consumer economy, the way that it is shaping a new mythology within which we define ourselves, our hopes, and our desires.

Ask yourself right now what your own goals are in going to college. Do you envision a career in law, or medicine, or banking and finance? Do you want to be a teacher, an advertising executive, or a civil servant? If you've considered any of these career examples, you are contemplating what are known as service jobs. While essential to a society, none of them actually produces anything. If you've given thought to going into some facet of manufacturing, on the other hand, you are unusual because America offers increasingly fewer opportunities in that area and little prestige. The prestige jobs are in law and medicine, by and large, a fact that is easy to take for granted. But ask yourself: Does it have to be so?

Simply to ask such questions is to begin to reveal the outline of a cultural mythology based in consumption rather than production. For one thing, while law and medicine require specialized training available to only a few, doctors and lawyers also make a lot of money and so are higher up on the scale of consumption. Quite simply, they can buy more than others can. It is easy to presume that this would be the case anywhere, but in the former Soviet Union, physicians — most of whom were women — were relatively low on the social scale. Male engineers, on the other hand, were highly valued for their role in facilitating military production. In what was a producer rather than a consumer culture, it was the producers who roosted high on the social ladder.

But to live in a consumer culture is not simply a matter of shopping; it is a matter of *being*. For in a consumer society, you are what you consume, and the entire social and economic order is maintained by the constant encouragement to buy. The ubiquity of television and advertising in America is a direct reflection of this system, for these media deliver the constant stimulus to buy in avalanches of consuming images. Consider how difficult it is to escape the arm of the advertiser. You may turn off your TV set, but a screen awaits you at the checkout counter of your supermarket, displaying incentives to spend your money. If you rush to the restroom to hide, you may find advertisements tacked to the stalls. And after all, weren't you planning to do some shopping this weekend anyway?

## When the Going Gets Tough, the Tough Go Shopping

In a cultural system where our very identities are displayed in the products we buy, it accordingly behooves us to pay close attention to what we consume and why. From the cars we drive to the clothes we wear, we are enmeshed in a web of consuming images. And as students, you are probably freer to choose the particular images you wish to project through the products you consume than most other demographic groups in America. This claim may sound paradoxical: After all, don't working adults have more money than starving students? Yes, generally. But the working world places severe restrictions on the choices employees can make in their clothing and grooming styles, and even automobile choice may be restricted (real estate agents, for example, can't escort their clients around town in Suzuki Sidekicks). Corporate business wear, for all its variations, still revolves around a central core of necktied and dark-hued sobriety, regardless of the gender of the wearer. And even with the return of long hair for men into fashion in the nineties, few professions outside the entertainment industry allow it on the job. On campus, on the other hand, you can be pretty much whatever you want to be, which is why your own daily lives provide you with a particularly rich field of consumer signs to read and decode.

So go to it. By the time you read this book, a lot will have changed. Grunge fashion and hip-hop, which dominated the early nineties and have held on through mid-decade, may be passé and something else will have come along. What themes are emerging for the nineties, anyway? Can you spot any dominant images that are likely to identify the nineties in future decades? Look around your classroom now. Start reading.

## The Readings

As this chapter's lead essay, Laurence Shames's "The More Factor" provides a mythological background for the discussions of America's consuming behavior that follow. Shames takes a historical approach to American consumerism, making a connection between our frontier history and our ever-expanding desire for more goods and services. Anne Norton follows with a semiotic analysis of shopping malls, mail-order catalogs, and the Home Shopping Network, focusing on the ways in which they construct a language of consumption tailored to specific consumer groups. Thomas Hine's interpretation of the packaging that contains America's most commonly consumed products shows how packages, too, constitute complex sign systems intended for consumer "readings." Ted Polhemus's description of the ways in which subcultural street styles "bubble up" into a realm of high fashion provides some

object lessons in the social significance of the things we wear, while Stuart Ewen's analysis of the "hard body" trend of the 1980s explores the
cultural significance of the bodies that we clothe. Joan Kron studies the
way we use home furnishings to reflect our sense of identity, and Susan
Willis critiques the synthetic imagination behind America's favorite playground, Disneyworld. Finally, Roland Barthes concludes the chapter
with his pioneering semiotic analysis of the materials from which the
French built children's toys in the 1950s — an analysis that is as timely
today as when it was written.

LAURENCE SHAMES

*The More Factor*

||||||||||||||||||||||||||||||||||||||||||||||||||

*A bumper sticker popular in the 1980s read, "Whoever dies with the most toys wins." In this selection from* The Hunger for More: Searching for Values in an Age of Greed *(1989), Laurence Shames shows how the great American hunger for more — more toys, more land, more opportunities — is an essential part of our history and character, stemming from the frontier era when the horizon alone seemed the only limit to American desire. In an era when the frontier has run out and even our consumer economy is sputtering, Shames warns that Americans will have to adjust their expectations and resign themselves to limited horizons. The author of* The Big Time: The Harvard Business School's Most Successful Class and How It Shaped America *(1986), and himself the holder of a Harvard MBA, Shames is a journalist who has contributed to such publications as* Playboy, Vanity Fair, Manhattan, inc., *and* Esquire. *He currently is working full-time on writing fiction and screen plays, with his most recent publications including* Florida Straits *(1992) and* Sunburn *(1995).*

**1**

Americans have always been optimists, and optimists have always liked to speculate. In Texas in the 1880s, the speculative instrument of choice was towns, and there is no tale more American than this.

What people would do was buy up enormous tracts of parched and vacant land, lay out a Main Street, nail together some wooden sidewalks, and start slapping up buildings. One of these buildings would be called the Grand Hotel and would have a saloon complete with swinging doors. Another might be dubbed the New Academy or the Opera House. The developers would erect a flagpole and name a church, and once the workmen had packed up and moved on, the towns would be as empty as the sky.

But no matter. The speculators, next, would hire people to pass out handbills in the Eastern and Midwestern cities, tracts limning the advantages of relocation to "the Athens of the South" or "the new plains Jerusalem." When persuasion failed, the builders might resort to bribery, paying people's moving costs and giving them houses, in exchange for nothing but a pledge to stay until a certain census was taken or a certain

**31**

inspection made. Once the nose count was completed, people were free to move on, and there was in fact a contingent of folks who made their living by keeping a cabin on skids and dragging it for pay from one town to another.

The speculators' idea, of course, was to lure the railroad. If one could create a convincing semblance of a town, the railroad might come through it, and a real town would develop, making the speculators staggeringly rich. By these devices a man named Sanborn once owned Amarillo.[1]

But railroad tracks are narrow and the state of Texas is very, very wide. For every Wichita Falls or Lubbock there were a dozen College Mounds or Belchervilles,[2] bleached, unpeopled burgs that receded quietly into the dust, taking with them large amounts of speculators' money.

Still, the speculators kept right on bucking the odds and depositing empty towns in the middle of nowhere. Why did they do it? Two reasons — reasons that might be said to summarize the central fact of American economic history and that go a fair way toward explaining what is perhaps the central strand of the national character.

The first reason was simply that the possible returns were so enormous as to partake of the surreal, to create a climate in which ordinary logic and prudence did not seem to apply. In a boom like that of real estate when the railroad barreled through, long shots that might pay one hundred thousand to one seemed worth a bet.

The second reason, more pertinent here, is that there was a presumption that America would *keep on* booming — if not forever, then at least longer than it made sense to worry about. There would always be another gold rush, another Homestead Act, another oil strike. The next generation would always ferret out opportunities that would be still more lavish than any that had gone before. America *was* those opportunities. This was an article not just of faith, but of strategy. You banked on the next windfall, you staked your hopes and even your self-esteem on it, and this led to a national turn of mind that might usefully be thought of as the habit of more.

A century, maybe two centuries, before anyone had heard the term *baby boomer,* much less *yuppie,* the habit of more had been instilled as the operative truth among the economically ambitious. The habit of more seemed to suggest that there was no such thing as getting wiped out in America. A fortune lost in Texas might be recouped in Colorado. Funds frittered away on grazing land where nothing grew might flood back in as silver. There was always a second chance, or always seemed to be, in

---

1. For a fuller account of railroad-related land speculation in Texas, see F. Stanley, *Story of the Texas Panhandle Railroads* (Borger, Tex.: Hess Publishing Co., 1976).
2. T. Lindsay Baker, *Ghost Towns of Texas* (Norman, Okla.: University of Oklahoma Press, 1986).

this land where growth was destiny and where expansion and purpose were the same.

The key was the frontier, not just as a matter of acreage, but as idea.  10 Vast, varied, rough as rocks, America was the place where one never quite came to the end. Ben Franklin explained it to Europe even before the Revolutionary War had finished: America offered new chances to those "who, in their own Countries, where all the Lands [were] fully occupied . . . could never [emerge] from the poor Condition wherein they were born."[3]

So central was this awareness of vacant space and its link to economic promise that Frederick Jackson Turner, the historian who set the tone for much of the twentieth century's understanding of the American past, would write that it was "not the constitution, but free land . . . [that] made the democratic type of society in America."[4] Good laws mattered; an accountable government mattered; ingenuity and hard work mattered. But those things were, so to speak, an overlay on the natural, geographic America that was simply *there,* and whose vast and beckoning possibilities seemed to generate the ambition and the sometimes reckless liberty that would fill it. First and foremost, it was open space that provided "the freedom of the individual to rise under conditions of social mobility."[5]

Open space generated not just ambition, but metaphor. As early as 1835, Tocqueville was extrapolating from the fact of America's emptiness to the observation that "no natural boundary seems to be set to the efforts of man."[6] Nor was any limit placed on what he might accomplish, since, in that heyday of the Protestant ethic, a person's rewards were taken to be quite strictly proportionate to his labors.

Frontier; opportunity; more. This has been the American trinity from the very start. The frontier was the backdrop and also the raw material for the streak of economic booms. The booms became the goad and also the justification for the myriad gambles and for Americans' famous optimism. The optimism, in turn, shaped the schemes and visions that were sometimes noble, sometimes appalling, always bold. The frontier, as reality and as symbol, is what has shaped the American way of doing things and the American sense of what's worth doing.

But there has been one further corollary to the legacy of the frontier, with its promise of ever-expanding opportunities: given that the goal — a realistic goal for most of our history — was *more,* Americans have been

---

3. Benjamin Franklin, "Information to Those Who Would Remove to America," in *The Autobiography and Other Writings* (New York: Penguin Books, 1986), 242.

4. Frederick Jackson Turner, *The Frontier in American History* (Melbourne, Fla.: Krieger, 1976 [reprint of 1920 edition]), 293.

5. Ibid., 266.

6. Tocqueville, *Democracy in America.*

somewhat backward in adopting values, hopes, ambitions that have to do with things *other than* more. In America, a sense of quality has lagged far behind a sense of scale. An ideal of contentment has yet to take root in soil traditionally more hospitable to an ideal of restless striving. The ethic of decency has been upstaged by the ethic of success. The concept of growth has been applied almost exclusively to things that can be measured, counted, weighed. And the hunger for those things that are unmeasurable but fine — the sorts of accomplishment that cannot be undone by circumstance or a shift in social fashion, the kind of serenity that cannot be shattered by tomorrow's headline — has gone largely unfulfilled, and even unacknowledged.

## 2

If the supply of more went on forever, perhaps that wouldn't matter very much. Expansion could remain a goal unto itself, and would continue to generate a value system based on bulk rather than on nuance, on quantities of money rather than on quality of life, on "progress" itself rather than on a sense of what the progress was for. But what if, over time, there was less more to be had?

That is the essential situation of America today.

Let's keep things in proportion: The country is not running out of wealth, drive, savvy, or opportunities. We are not facing imminent ruin, and neither panic nor gloom is called for. But there have been ample indications over the past two decades that we are running out of more.

Consider productivity growth — according to many economists, the single most telling and least distortable gauge of changes in real wealth. From 1947 to 1965, productivity in the private sector (adjusted, as are all the following figures, for inflation) was advancing, on average, by an annual 3.3 percent. This means, simply, that each hour of work performed by a specimen American worker contributed 3.3 cents worth or more to every American dollar every year; whether we saved it or spent it, that increment went into a national kitty of ever-enlarging aggregate wealth. Between 1965 and 1972, however, the "more-factor" decreased to 2.4 percent a year, and from 1972 to 1977 it slipped further, to 1.6 percent. By the early 1980s, productivity growth was at a virtual standstill, crawling along at 0.2 percent for the five years ending in 1982.[7] Through the middle years of the 1980s, the numbers rebounded somewhat — but by

---

7. These figures are taken from the Council of Economic Advisers, *Economic Report of the President,* February 1984, 267.

then the gains were being neutralized by the gargantuan carrying costs on the national debt.[8]

Inevitably, this decline in the national stockpile of more held consequences for the individual wallet.[9] During the 1950s, Americans' average hourly earnings were humping ahead at a gratifying 2.5 percent each year. By the late seventies, that figure stood just where productivity growth had come to stand, at a dispiriting 0.2 cents on the dollar. By the first half of the eighties, the Reagan "recovery" notwithstanding, real hourly wages were actually moving backwards — declining at an average annual rate of 0.3 percent.

Compounding the shortage of more was an unfortunate but crucial demographic fact. Real wealth was nearly ceasing to expand just at the moment when the members of that unprecedented population bulge known as the baby boom were entering what should have been their peak years of income expansion. A working man or woman who was thirty years old in 1949 could expect to see his or her real earnings burgeon by 63 percent by age forty. In 1959, a thirty-year-old could still look forward to a gain of 49 percent by his or her fortieth birthday.

But what about the person who turned thirty in 1973? By the time that worker turned forty, his or her real earnings had shrunk by a percentage point. For all the blather about yuppies with their beach houses, BMWs, and radicchio salads, and even factoring in those isolated tens of thousands making ludicrous sums in consulting firms or on Wall Street, the fact is that between 1979 and 1983 real earnings of all Americans between the ages of twenty-five and thirty-four actually declined by 14 percent.[10] The *New York Times,* well before the stock market crash put the kibosh on eighties confidence, summed up the implications of this downturn by observing that "for millions of breadwinners, the American dream is becoming the impossible dream."[11]

Now, it is not our main purpose here to detail the ups and downs of the American economy. Our aim, rather, is to consider the effects of those ups and downs on people's goals, values, sense of their place in the world. What happens at that shadowy juncture where economic prospects meld with personal choice? What sorts of insights and adjust-

20

---

8. For a lucid and readable account of the meaning and implications of our reservoir of red ink, see Lawrence Malkin, *The National Debt* (New York: Henry Holt and Co., 1987). Through no fault of Malkin's, many of his numbers are already obsolete, but his explanation of who owes what to whom, and what it means, remains sound and even entertaining in a bleak sort of way.

9. The figures in this paragraph and the next are from "The Average Guy Takes It on the Chin," *New York Times,* 13 July 1986, sec. 3.

10. See, for example, "The Year of the Yuppie," *Newsweek,* 31 December 1984, 16.

11. "The Average Guy," see above.

ments are called for so that economic ups and downs can be dealt with gracefully?

Fact one in this connection is that, if America's supply of more is in fact diminishing, American values will have to shift and broaden to fill the gap where the expectation of almost automatic gains used to be. Something more durable will have to replace the fat but fragile bubble that had been getting frailer these past two decades and that finally popped — a tentative, partial pop — on October 19, 1987. A different sort of growth — ultimately, a growth in responsibility and happiness — will have to fulfill our need to believe that our possibilities are still expanding.

The transition to that new view of progress will take some fancy stepping, because, at least since the end of World War II, simple economic growth has stood, in the American psyche, as the best available substitute for the literal frontier. The economy has *been* the frontier. Instead of more space, we have had more money. Rather than measuring progress in terms of geographical expansion, we have measured it by expansion in our standard of living. Economics has become the metaphor on which we pin our hopes of open space and second chances.

The poignant part is that the literal frontier did not pass yesterday: it      25
has not existed for a hundred years. But the frontier's promise has become so much a part of us that we have not been willing to let the concept die. We have kept the frontier mythology going by invocation, by allusion, by hype.

It is not a coincidence that John F. Kennedy dubbed his political program the New Frontier. It is not mere linguistic accident that makes us speak of Frontiers of Science or of psychedelic drugs as carrying one to Frontiers of Perception. We glorify fads and fashions by calling them Frontiers of Taste. Nuclear energy has been called the Last Frontier; solar energy has been called the Last Frontier. Outer space has been called the Last Frontier; the oceans have been called the Last Frontier. Even the suburbs, those blandest and least adventurous of places, have been wryly described as the crabgrass frontier.[12]

What made all these usages plausible was their being linked to the image of the American economy as an endlessly fertile continent whose boundaries never need be reached, a domain that could expand in perpetuity, a gigantic playing field that would never run out of room and on which the game would get forever bigger and more filled with action. This was the frontier that would not vanish.

It is worth noting that people in other countries (with the possible exception of that other America, Australia) do not talk about frontier this way. In Europe, and in most of Africa and Asia, "frontier" connotes, at

---

12. With the suburbs again taking on a sort of fascination, this phrase was resurrected as the title of a 1985 book — *Crabgrass Frontier: The Suburbanization of America,* by Kenneth T. Jackson (Oxford University Press).

worst, a place of barbed wire and men with rifles, and at best, a neutral junction where one changes currency while passing from one fixed system into another. Frontier, for most of the world's people, does not suggest growth, expanse, or opportunity.

For Americans, it does, and always has. This is one of the things that sets America apart from other places and makes American attitudes different from those of other people. It is why, from *Bonanza* to the Sierra Club, the notion or even the fantasy of empty horizons and untapped resources has always evoked in the American heart both passion and wistfulness. And it is why the fear that the economic frontier — our last, best version of the Wild West — may finally be passing creates in us not only money worries but also a crisis of morale and even of purpose.

**3**

It might seem strange to call the 1980s an era of nostalgia. The decade, after all, has been more usually described in terms of coolness, pragmatism, and a blithe innocence of history. But the eighties, unawares, were nostalgic for frontiers; and the disappointment of that nostalgia had much to do with the time's greed, narrowness, and strange want of joy. The fear that the world may not be a big enough playground for the full exercise of one's energies and yearnings, and worse, the fear that the playground is being fenced off and will no longer expand — these are real worries and they have had consequences. The eighties were an object lesson in how people play the game when there is an awful and unspoken suspicion that the game is winding down.

It was ironic that the yuppies came to be so reviled for their vaunting ambition and outsized expectations, as if they'd invented the habit of more, when in fact they'd only inherited it the way a fetus picks up an addiction in the womb. The craving was there in the national bloodstream, a remnant of the frontier, and the baby boomers, described in childhood as "the luckiest generation,"[13] found themselves, as young adults, in the melancholy position of wrestling with a two-hundred-year dependency on a drug that was now in short supply.

True, the 1980s raised the clamor for more to new heights of shrillness, insistence, and general obnoxiousness, but this, it can be argued, was in the nature of a final binge, the storm before the calm. America, though fighting the perception every inch of the way, was coming to realize that it was not a preordained part of the natural order that one should be richer every year. If it happened, that was nice. But who had started the flimsy and pernicious rumor that it was normal?

---

13. Thomas Hine, *Populuxe* (New York: Alfred A. Knopf, 1986), 15.

### Reading the Text

1. Summarize in a paragraph how, according to Shames, the frontier functions as a symbol of American consciousness.
2. What connection does Shames make between America's frontier history and consumer behavior?
3. Why does Shames term the 1980s "an era of nostalgia"?

### Reading the Signs

1. Shames asserts that Americans have been influenced by the frontier belief that "America would keep on booming." Do you feel that this belief continues to be influential in the 1990s? Write an essay arguing for your position.
2. Shames claims that, because of the desire for more, "the ethic of decency has been upstaged by the ethic of success" in America. In class, form teams that either agree or disagree with this position, and debate the validity of Shames's claim.
3. Read or review Joan Kron's "The Semiotics of Home Decor" (p. 72) and Stuart Ewen's "Hard Bodies" (p. 66). How are Martin J. Davidson and Raymond H—— influenced by the frontier myth that Shames describes?
4. In groups, discuss whether street gang members share the desire for "more" that Shames claims is a distinctly American trait. Then write an essay in which you argue whether you believe gangs can be called "typically American."
5. Shames does not discuss ethnicity in his essay. Read Sam Fulwood III's "The Rage of the Black Middle Class" (p. 510) and discuss the extent to which the African-Americans in his essay share the desire for more. Are there any social factors affecting their outlook on life that Shames neglects to mention?

# ANNE NORTON

## The Signs of Shopping

||||||||||||||||||||||||||||||||||||||||||||||||||||||||||||

*Shopping malls are more than places to shop, just as mail-order catalogues are more than simple lists of goods. Both malls and catalogues are coded systems that not only encourage us to buy but, more profoundly, help us to construct our very sense of identity, as in the J. Peterman catalogue that "constructs the reader as a man of rugged outdoor interests, taste, and money." In this selection from* The Republic of Signs *(1993), Anne Norton (b. 1954), a professor of political science at the*

*University of Pennsylvania, analyzes the many ways in which malls, catalogues, and home shopping networks sell you what they want by telling you who you are. Norton's other books include* Alternative Americas *(1986) and* Reflections on Political Identity *(1988).*

## Shopping at the Mall

The mall has been the subject of innumerable debates. Created out of the modernist impulse for planning and the centralization of public activity, the mall has become the distinguishing sign of suburban decentralization, springing up in unplanned profusion. Intended to restore something of the lost unity of city life to the suburbs, the mall has come to export styles and strategies to stores at the urban center. Deplored by modernists, it is regarded with affection only by their postmodern foes. Ruled more by their content than by their creators' avowed intent, the once sleek futurist shells have taken on a certain aura of postmodern playfulness and popular glitz.

The mall is a favorite subject for the laments of cultural conservatives and others critical of the culture of consumption. It is indisputably the cultural locus of commodity fetishism. It has been noticed, however, by others of a less condemnatory disposition that the mall has something of the mercado, or the agora, about it. It is both a place of meeting for the young and one of the rare places where young and old go together. People of different races and classes, different occupations, different levels of education meet there. As M. Pressdee and John Fiske note, however, though the mall appears to be a public place, it is not. Neither freedom of speech nor freedom of assembly is permitted there. Those who own and manage malls restrict what comes within their confines. Controversial displays, by stores or customers or the plethora of organizations and agencies that present themselves in the open spaces of the mall, are not permitted. These seemingly public spaces conceal a pervasive private authority.

The mall exercises its thorough and discreet authority not only in the regulation of behavior but in the constitution of our visible, inaudible, public discourse. It is the source of those commodities through which we speak of our identities, our opinions, our desires. It is a focus for the discussion of style among peripheral consumers. Adolescents, particularly female adolescents, are inclined to spend a good deal of time at the mall. They spend, indeed, more time than money. They acquire not simple commodities (they may come home with many, few, or none) but a well-developed sense of the significance of those commodities. In prowling the mall they embed themselves in a lexicon of American culture. They find themselves walking through a dictionary. Stores hang a variety of identities on their racks and mannequins. Their window displays provide elaborate scenarios conveying not only what the garment is but what the garment means.

A display in the window of Polo provides an embarrassment of semiotic riches. Everyone, from the architecture critic at the *New York Times* to kids in the hall of a Montana high school, knows what *Ralph Lauren* means. The polo mallet and the saddle, horses and dogs, the broad lawns of Newport, Kennebunkport, old photographs in silver frames, the evocation of age, of ancestry and Anglophilia, of indolence and the Ivy League, evoke the upper class. Indian blankets and buffalo plaids, cowboy hats and Western saddles, evoke a past distinct from England but nevertheless determinedly Anglo. The supposedly arcane and suspect arts of deconstruction are deployed easily, effortlessly, by the readers of these cultural texts.

Walking from one window to another, observing one another,    5
shoppers, especially the astute and observant adolescents, acquire a facility with the language of commodities. They learn not only words but a grammar. Shop windows employ elements of sarcasm and irony, strategies of inversion and allusion. They provide models of elegant, economical, florid, and prosaic expression. They teach composition.

The practice of shopping is, however, more than instructive. It has long been the occasion for women to escape the confines of their homes and enjoy the companionship of other women. The construction of woman's role as one of provision for the needs of the family legitimated her exit. It provided an occasion for women to spend long stretches of time in the company of their friends, without the presence of their husbands. They could exchange information and reflections, ask advice, and receive support. As their daughters grew, they would be brought increasingly within this circle, included in shopping trips and lunches with their mothers. These would form, reproduce, and restructure communities of taste.

The construction of identity and the enjoyment of friendship outside the presence of men was thus effected through a practice that constructed women as consumers and subjected them to the conventions of the marketplace. Insofar as they were dependent on their husbands for money, they were dependent on their husbands for the means to the construction of their identities. They could not represent themselves through commodities without the funds men provided, nor could they, without money, participate in the community of women that was realized in "going shopping." Their identities were made contingent not only on the possession of property but on the recognition of dependence.

Insofar as shopping obliges dependent women to recognize their dependence, it also opens up the possibility of subversion.[1] The housewife

---

1. Nuanced and amusing accounts of shopping as subversion are provided in John Fiske's analyses of popular culture, particularly *Reading the Popular* (Boston: Unwin Hyman [now Routledge], 1989), pp. 13–42.

who shops for pleasure takes time away from her husband, her family, and her house and claims it for herself. Constantly taught that social order and her private happiness depend on intercourse between men and women, she chooses the company of women instead. She engages with women in an activity marked as feminine, and she enjoys it. When she spends money, she exercises an authority over property that law and custom may deny her. If she has no resources independent of her husband, this may be the only authority over property she is able to exercise. When she buys things her husband does not approve — or does not know — of she further subverts an order that leaves control over property in her husband's hands.[2]

Her choice of feminine company and a feminine pursuit may involve additional subversions. As Fiske and Pressdee recognize, shopping without buying and shopping for bargains have a subversive quality. This is revealed, in a form that gives it additional significance, when a saleswoman leans forward and tells a shopper, "Don't buy that today, it will be on sale on Thursday." Here solidarity of gender (and often of class) overcome, however partially and briefly, the imperatives of the economic order.

Shoppers who look, as most shoppers do, for bargains, and sales-   10
people who warn shoppers of impending sales, see choices between commodities as something other than the evidence and the exercise of freedom. They see covert direction and exploitation; they see the withholding of information and the manipulation of knowledge. They recognize that they are on enemy terrain and that their shopping can be, in Michel de Certeau's[3] term, a "guerrilla raid." This recognition in practice of the presence of coercion in choice challenges the liberal conflation of choice and consent.


## Shopping at Home

Shopping is an activity that has overcome its geographic limits. One need no longer go to the store to shop. Direct mail catalogues, with their twenty-four-hour phone numbers for ordering, permit people to shop where and when they please. An activity that once obliged one to go out into the public sphere, with its diverse array of semiotic messages, can now be done at home. An activity that once obliged one to be in

---

2. See R. Bowlby, *Just Looking: Consumer Culture in Dreiser, Gissing, and Zola* (London: Methuen, 1985), p. 22, for another discussion and for an example of the recommendation of this strategy by Elizabeth Cady Stanton in the 1850s.

3. **Michel de Certeau** (1925–1986)   French social scientist and semiologist who played an important role in the development of contemporary cultural studies. — EDS.

company, if not in conversation, with one's compatriots can now be conducted in solitude.

The activity of catalogue shopping, and the pursuit of individuality, are not, however, wholly solitary. The catalogues invest their commodities with vivid historical and social references. The J. Peterman catalogue, for example, constructs the reader as a man of rugged outdoor interests, taste, and money.[4] He wears "The Owner's Hat" or "Hemingway's Cap," a leather flight jacket or the classic "Horseman's Duster," and various other garments identified with the military, athletes, and European imperialism. The copy for "The Owner's Hat" naturalizes class distinctions and, covertly, racism:

> Some of us work on the plantation.
> Some of us own the plantation.
> Facts are facts.
> This hat is for those who own the plantation.[5]

Gender roles are strictly delineated. The copy for a skirt captioned "Women's Legs" provides a striking instance of the construction of the gaze as male, of women as the object of the gaze:

> just when you think you see something, a shape you think you recognize, it's gone and then it begins to return and then it's gone and of course you can't take your eyes off it.
>
> Yes, the long slow motion of women's legs. Whatever happened to those things at carnivals that blew air up into girls' skirts and you could spend hours watching.[6]

"You," of course, are male. There is also the lace blouse captioned "Mystery": "lace says yes at the same time it says no."[7] Finally, there are notes of imperialist nostalgia: the Sheapherd's Hotel (Cairo) bathrobe and white pants for "the bush" and "the humid hell-holes of Bombay and Calcutta."[8]

---

4. I have read several of these. I cite *The J. Peterman Company Owner's Manual No. 5,* from the J. Peterman Company, 2444 Palumbo Drive, Lexington, Ky. 40509.

5. Ibid., p. 5. The hat is also identified with the Canal Zone, "successfully bidding at Beaulieu," intimidation, and LBOs. Quite a hat. It might be argued against my reading that the J. Peterman Company also offers the "Coal Miner's Bag" and a mailbag. However, since the descriptive points of reference on color and texture and experience for these bags are such things as the leather seats of Jaguars, and driving home in a Bentley, I feel fairly confident in my reading.

6. Ibid., p. 3. See also pp. 15 and 17 for instances of women as the object of the male gaze. The identification of the gaze with male sexuality is unambiguous here as well.

7. Ibid., p. 17.

8. Ibid., pp. 7, 16, 20, 21, 37, and 50.

It may no longer be unforgivable to say that the British left a few good things behind in India and in Kenya, Singapore, Borneo, etc., not the least of which was their Englishness.[9]

As Paul Smith observes, in his reading of their catalogues, the *Banana Republic* has also made capital out of imperial nostalgia.[10]

The communities catalogues create are reinforced by shared mailing lists. The constructed identities are reified and elaborated in an array of semiotically related catalogues. One who orders a spade or a packet of seeds will be constructed as a gardener and receive a deluge of catalogues from plant and garden companies. The companies themselves may expand their commodities to appeal to different manifestations of the identities they respond to and construct. Smith and Hawken, a company that sells gardening supplies with an emphasis on aesthetics and environmental concern, puts out a catalogue in which a group of people diverse in age and in their ethnicity wear the marketed clothes while gardening, painting, or throwing pots. Williams-Sonoma presents its catalogue not as a catalogue of things for cooking but as "A Catalog for Cooks." The catalogue speaks not to need but to the construction of identity.

The Nature Company dedicates its spring 1990 catalogue "to trees," endorses Earth Day, and continues to link itself to *The Nature Conservancy* through posters and a program in which you buy a tree for a forest restoration project. Here, a not-for-profit agency is itself commodified, adding to the value of the commodities offered in the catalogue.[11] In this catalogue, consumption is not merely a means for the construction and representation of the self, it is also a means for political action. Several commodities are offered as "A Few Things You Can Do" to save the earth: a string shopping bag, a solar battery recharger, a home newspaper recycler. Socially conscious shopping is a liberal practice in every sense. It construes shopping as a form of election, in which one votes for good commodities or refuses one's vote to candidates whose practices are ethically suspect. In this respect, it reveals its adherence to the same ideological presuppositions that structure television's Home Shopping Network and other cable television sales shows.

Both politically informed purchasing and television sales conflate the free market and the electoral process. Dollars are identified with votes, purchases with endorsements. Both offer those who engage in them the

9. Ibid., p. 20.

10. Paul Smith, "Visiting the Banana Republic," in *Universal Abandon?* ed. Andrew Ross for Social Text (Minneapolis: University of Minnesota Press, 1988), pp. 128–48.

11. *The Nature Company Catalog,* The Nature Company, P.O. Box 2310, Berkeley, Calif. 94702, Spring 1990. See pp. 1–2 and order form insert between pp. 18 and 19. Note also the entailed donation to Designs for Conservation on p. 18.

possibility to "talk back" to manufacturers. In television sales shows this ability to talk back is both more thoroughly elaborated and more thoroughly exploited. Like the "elections" on MTV that invite viewers to vote for their favorite video by calling a number on their telephones, they permit those who watch to respond, to speak, and to be heard by the television. Their votes, of course, cost money. On MTV, as in the stores, you can buy as much speech as you can afford. On the Home Shopping Network, the purchase of speech becomes complicated by multiple layers and inversions.

Each commodity is introduced. It is invested by the announcer with a number of desirable qualities. The value of these descriptions of the commodities is enhanced by the construction of the announcer as a mediator not only between the commodity and the consumer but between the salespeople and the consumer. The announcer is not, the format suggests, a salesperson (though of course the announcer is). He or she is an announcer, describing goods that others have offered for sale. Television claims to distinguish itself by making objects visible to the eyes, but it is largely through the ears that these commodities are constructed. The consumer, in purchasing the commodity, purchases the commodity, what the commodity signifies, and, as we say, "buys the salesperson's line." The consumer may also acquire the ability to speak on television. Each purchase is recorded and figures as a vote in a rough plebiscite, confirming the desirability of the object. Although the purchase figures are announced as if they were confirming votes, it is, of course, impossible to register one's rejection of the commodity. Certain consumers get a little more (or rather less) for their money. They are invited to explain the virtue of the commodity — and their purchase — to the announcer and the audience. The process of production, of both the consumers and that which they consume, continues in this apology for consumption.

The semiotic identification of consumption as an American activity, indeed, a patriotic one, is made with crude enthusiasm on the Home Shopping Network and other video sales shows. Red, white, and blue figure prominently in set designs and borders framing the television screen. The Home Shopping Network presents its authorities in an office conspicuously adorned with a picture of the Statue of Liberty.[12] Yet the messages that the Home Shopping Network sends its customers — that you can buy as much speech as you can afford, that you are recognized by others in accordance with your capacity to consume — do much to subvert the connection between capitalism and democracy on which this semiotic identification depends.

---

12. This moment from the Home Shopping Network was generously brought to my attention, on videotape, by Peter Bregman, a student in my American Studies class of fall 1988, at Princeton University.

## Reading the Text

1. What does Norton mean when she claims that the suburban shopping mall appears to be a public place but in fact is not?
2. What is Norton's interpretation of Ralph Lauren's Polo line?
3. How is shopping a subversive activity for women, according to Norton?
4. How do mail-order catalogues create communities of shoppers, in Norton's view?
5. What are the political messages sent by the Home Shopping Network, as Norton sees them, and how are they communicated?

## Reading the Signs

1. Visit a local shopping mall and study the window displays, focusing on stores intended for one group of consumers (teenagers, for instance, or children). Then write an essay in which you analyze how the displays convey what the stores' products "mean."
2. Bring a few product catalogues to class and then in small groups compare the kind of consumer "constructed" by the catalogues' cultural images and allusions. Do you note any patterns associated with gender, ethnicity, or age group? Report your group's conclusions to the whole class.
3. Interview five women of different age groups on their motivations and activities when they shop in a mall. Then use the results of your interviews as evidence in an essay in which you support, complicate, or refute Norton's assertion that shopping constitutes a subversive activity for women.
4. Watch an episode of the Home Shopping Network (your school's media library may be able to provide you access to cable TV) and write a semiotic analysis of the ways in which products are presented to consumers.
5. Select a single mail-order catalogue and write a detailed semiotic interpretation of the identity it constructs for its market.

# THOMAS HINE

## What's in a Package

‖‖‖‖‖‖‖‖‖‖‖‖‖‖‖‖‖‖‖‖‖‖‖‖‖‖‖‖‖‖‖‖‖‖‖‖‖‖‖

*What's in a package? According to Thomas Hine, a great deal, perhaps even more than what is actually* inside *the package. From the cereal boxes you find in the supermarket to the perfume bottles sold at Tiffany's, the shape and design of the packages that contain just about every product we consume have been carefully calculated to stimulate consumption. Indeed, as Hine explains in this excerpt from* The Total Package: The Evolution and Secret Meanings of Boxes, Bottles, Cans, and Tubes *(1995), "for manufacturers, packaging is the crucial final payoff to a marketing campaign." The architecture and design critic for* The Philadelphia Inquirer, *Hine has also published* Populuxe *(1986), on American design and culture, and* Facing Tomorrow *(1991), on past and current attitudes toward the future.*

When you put yourself behind a shopping cart, the world changes. You become an active consumer, and you are moving through environments — the supermarket, the discount store, the warehouse club, the home center — that have been made for you.

During the thirty minutes you spend on an average trip to the supermarket, about thirty thousand different products vie to win your attention and ultimately to make you believe in their promise. When the door opens, automatically, before you, you enter an arena where your emotions and your appetites are in play, and a walk down the aisle is an exercise in self-definition. Are you a good parent, a good provider? Do you have time to do all you think you should, and would you be interested in a shortcut? Are you worried about your health and that of those you love? Do you care about the environment? Do you appreciate the finer things in life? Is your life what you would like it to be? Are you enjoying what you've accomplished? Wouldn't you really like something chocolate?

Few experiences in contemporary life offer the visual intensity of a Safeway, a Krogers, a Pathmark, or a Piggly Wiggly. No marketplace in the world — not Marrakesh or Calcutta or Hong Kong — offers so many different goods with such focused salesmanship as your neighborhood supermarket, where you're exposed to a thousand different products a minute. No wonder it's tiring to shop.

There are, however, some major differences between the supermarket and a traditional marketplace. The cacophony of a traditional market has given way to programmed, innocuous music, punctuated by enthusiastically intoned commercials. A stroll through a traditional market offers an array of sensuous aromas; if you are conscious of smelling something in a supermarket, there is a problem. The life and death matter of eating, expressed in traditional markets by the sale of vegetables with stems and roots and by hanging animal carcasses, is purged from the supermarket, where food is processed somewhere else, or at least trimmed out of sight.

But the most fundamental difference between a traditional market    5
and the places through which you push your cart is that in a modern re-tail setting nearly all the selling is done without people. The product is totally dissociated from the personality of any particular person selling it — with the possible exception of those who appear in its advertising. The supermarket purges sociability, which slows down sales. It allows manufacturers to control the way they present their products to the world. It replaces people with packages.

Packages are an inescapable part of modern life. They are om-nipresent and invisible, deplored and ignored. During most of your wak-ing moments, there are one or more packages within your field of vision. Packages are so ubiquitous that they slip beneath conscious notice, though many packages are designed so that people will respond to them even if they're not paying attention.

Once you begin pushing the shopping cart, it matters little whether you are in a supermarket, a discount store, or a warehouse club. The im-portant thing is that you are among packages: expressive packages in-tended to engage your emotions, ingenious packages that make a product useful, informative packages that help you understand what you want and what you're getting. Historically, packages are what made self-service retailing possible, and in turn such stores increased the number and variety of items people buy. Now a world without packages is unimaginable.

Packages lead multiple lives. They preserve and protect, allowing people to make use of things that were produced far away, or a while ago. And they are potently expressive. They assure that an item arrives unspoiled, and they help those who use the item feel good about it.

We share our homes with hundreds of packages, mostly in the bath-room and kitchen, the most intimate, body-centered rooms of the house. Some packages — a perfume flacon, a ketchup bottle, a candy wrapper, a beer can — serve as permanent landmarks in people's lives that outlast homes, careers, or spouses. But packages embody change, not just in their age-old promise that their contents are new and improved, but in their attempt to respond to changing tastes and achieve new standards of convenience. Packages record changing hairstyles and changing life-styles. Even social policy issues are reflected. Nearly unopenable tamper-proof seals and other forms of closures testify to the fragility of the social contract, and the susceptibility of the great mass of people to the destructive acts of a very few. It was a mark of rising environmental

consciousness when containers recently began to make a novel promise:
"less packaging."

For manufacturers, packaging is the crucial final payoff to a market-     10
ing campaign. Sophisticated packaging is one of the chief ways people
find the confidence to buy. It can also give a powerful image to products
and commodities that are in themselves characterless. In many cases, the
shopper has been prepared for the shopping experience by lush, colorful
print advertisements, thirty-second television minidramas, radio jingles,
and coupon promotions. But the package makes the final sales pitch, seals
the commitment, and gets itself placed in the shopping cart. Advertising
leads consumers into temptation. Packaging *is* the temptation. In many
cases it is what makes the product possible.

But the package is also useful to the shopper. It is a tool for simplifying and speeding decisions. Packages promise, and usually deliver, pre-
dictability. One reason you don't think about packages is that you don't
need to. The candy bar, the aspirin, the baking powder, or the beer in
the old familiar package may, at times, be touted as new and improved,
but it will rarely be very different.

You put the package into your cart, or not, usually without really
having focused on the particular product or its many alternatives. But
sometimes you do examine the package. You read the label carefully,
looking at what the product promises, what it contains, what it warns.
You might even look at the package itself and judge whether it will, for
example, reseal to keep a product fresh. You might consider how a cosmetic container will look on your dressing table, or you might think
about whether someone might have tampered with it or whether it can
be easily recycled. The possibility of such scrutiny is one of the things
that make each detail of the package so important.

The environment through which you push your shopping cart is extraordinary because of the amount of attention that has been paid to the
packages that line the shelves. Most contemporary environments are
landscapes of inattention. In housing developments, malls, highways, office buildings, even furniture, design ideas are few and spread very thin.
At the supermarket, each box and jar, stand-up pouch and squeeze bottle, each can and bag and tube and spray has been very carefully considered. Designers have worked and reworked the design on their computers and tested mock-ups on the store shelves. Refinements are measured
in millimeters.

All sorts of retail establishments have been redefined by packaging.
Drugs and cosmetics were among the earliest packaged products, and
most drugstores now resemble small supermarkets. Liquor makers use
packaging to add a veneer of style to the intrinsic allure of intoxication,
and some sell their bottle rather than the drink. It is no accident that
vodka, the most characterless of spirits, has the highest-profile packages.

The local gas station sells sandwiches and soft drinks rather than tires and motor oil, and in turn, automotive products have been attractively repackaged for sales at supermarkets, warehouse clubs, and home centers.

With its thousands of images and messages, the supermarket is as visually dense, if not as beautiful, as a Gothic cathedral. It is as complex and as predatory as a tropical rain forest. It is more than a person can possibly take in during an ordinary half-hour shopping trip. No wonder a significant percentage of people who need to wear eyeglasses don't wear them when they're shopping, and some researchers have spoken of the trance-like state that pushing a cart through this environment induces. The paradox here is that the visual intensity that overwhelms shoppers is precisely the thing that makes the design of packages so crucial. Just because you're not looking at a package doesn't mean you don't see it. Most of the time, you see far more than a container and a label. You see a personality, an attitude toward life, perhaps even a set of beliefs. 15

The shopper's encounter with the product on the shelf is, however, only the beginning of the emotional life cycle of the package. The package is very important in the moment when the shopper recognizes it either as an old friend or a new temptation. Once the product is brought home, the package seems to disappear, as the quality or usefulness of the product it contains becomes paramount. But in fact, many packages are still selling even at home, enticing those who have bought them to take them out of the cupboard, the closet, or the refrigerator and consume their contents. Then once the product has been used up, and the package is empty, it becomes suddenly visible once more. This time, though, it is trash that must be discarded or recycled. This instant of disposal is the time when people are most aware of packages. It is a negative moment, like the end of a love affair, and what's left seems to be a horrid waste.

The forces driving package design are not primarily aesthetic. Market researchers have conducted surveys of consumer wants and needs, and consultants have studied photographs of families' kitchen cupboards and medicine chests to get a sense of how products are used. Test subjects have been tied into pieces of heavy apparatus that measure their eye movement, their blood pressure or body temperature, when subjected to different packages. Psychologists get people to talk about the packages in order to get a sense of their innermost feelings about what they want. Government regulators and private health and safety advocates worry over package design and try to make it truthful. Stock-market analysts worry about how companies are managing their "brand equity," that combination of perceived value and consumer loyalty that is expressed in advertising but embodied in packaging. The retailer is paying attention to the packages in order to weed out the ones that don't sell or aren't sufficiently profitable. The use of supermarket scanners generates information on the profitability of every cubic inch of the store. Space on the super-market shelf is some of the most valuable real estate in the world, and there are always plenty of new packaged products vying for display.

Packaging performs a series of disparate tasks. It protects its contents from contamination and spoilage. It makes it easier to transport and store goods. It provides uniform measuring of contents. By allowing brands to be created and standardized, it makes advertising meaningful and large-scale distribution possible. Special kinds of packages, with dispensing caps, sprays, and other convenience features, make products more usable. Packages serve as symbols both of their contents and of a way of life. And just as they can very powerfully communicate the satisfaction a product offers, they are equally potent symbols of wastefulness once the product is gone.

Most people use dozens of packages each day and discard hundreds of them each year. The growth of mandatory recycling programs has made people increasingly aware of packages, which account in the United States for about forty-three million tons, or just under 30 percent of all refuse discarded. While forty-three million tons of stuff is hardly in-significant, repeated surveys have shown that the public perceives that far more than 30 percent — indeed, nearly all — their garbage consists of packaging. This perception creates a political problem for the packaging industry, but it also demonstrates the power of packaging. It is symbolic. It creates an emotional relationship. Bones and wasted food (13 million tons), grass clippings and yard waste (thirty-one million tons), or even magazines and newspapers (fourteen million tons) do not feel as wasteful as empty vessels that once contained so much promise.

Packaging is a cultural phenomenon, which means that it works differ-   20
ently in different cultures. The United States has been a good market for packages since it was first settled and has been an important innovator of packaging technology and culture. Moreover, American packaging is part of an international culture of modernity and consumption. At its deepest level, the culture of American packaging deals with the issue of surviving among strangers in a new world. This is an emotion with which anyone who has been touched by modernity can identify. In lives buffeted by change, people seek the safety and reassurance that packaged products offer. American packaging, which has always sought to appeal to large numbers of diverse people, travels better than that of most other cultures.

But the similar appearance of supermarkets throughout the world should not be interpreted as the evidence of a single, global consumer culture. In fact, most companies that do business internationally redesign their packages for each market. This is done partly to satisfy local regula-tions and adapt to available products and technologies. But the principal reason is that people in different places have different expectations and make different uses of packaging.

The United States and Japan, the world's two leading industrial powers, have almost opposite approaches to packaging. Japan's is far more elaborate than America's, and it is shaped by rituals of respect and centuries-old traditions of wrapping and presentation. Packaging is explicitly recognized as an expression of culture in Japan and largely ignored in America. Japanese packaging is designed to be appreciated; American packaging is calculated to be unthinkingly accepted.

Foods that only Japanese eat — even relatively humble ones like refrigerated prepared fish cakes — have wrappings that resemble handmade paper or leaves. Even modestly priced refrigerated fish cakes have beautiful wrappings in which traditional design accommodates a scannable bar code. Such products look Japanese and are unambiguously intended to do so. Products that are foreign, such as coffee, look foreign, even to the point of having only Roman lettering and no Japanese lettering on the can. American and European companies are sometimes able to sell their packages in Japan virtually unchanged, because their foreignness is part of their selling power. But Japanese exporters hire designers in each country to repackage their products. Americans — whose culture is defined not by refinements and distinctions but by inclusiveness — want to think about the product itself, not its cultural origins.

We speak glibly about global villages and international markets, but problems with packages reveal some unexpected cultural boundaries. Why are Canadians willing to drink milk out of flexible plastic pouches that fit into reusable plastic holders, while residents of the United States are believed to be so resistant to the idea that they have not even been given the opportunity to do so? Why do Japanese consumers prefer packages that contain two tennis balls and view the standard U.S. pack of three to be cheap and undesirable? Why do Germans insist on highly detailed technical specifications on packages of videotape, while Americans don't? Why do Swedes think that blue is masculine, while the Dutch see the color as feminine? The answers lie in unquestioned habits and deep-seated imagery, a culture of containing, adorning, and understanding that no sharp marketer can change overnight.

There is probably no other field in which designs that are almost a     25
century old — Wrigley's gum, Campbell's soup, Hershey's chocolate bar — remain in production only subtly changed and are understood to be extremely valuable corporate assets. Yet the culture of packaging, defined by what people are buying and selling every day, keeps evolving, and the role nostalgia plays is very small.

For example, the tall, glass Heinz ketchup bottle has helped define the American refrigerator skyline for most of the twentieth century (even though it is generally unnecessary to refrigerate ketchup). Moreover, it provides the tables of diners and coffee shops with a vertical accent and a token of hospitality, the same qualities projected by candles and vases of flowers in more upscale eateries. The bottle has remained a fixture of American life, even though it has always been a nuisance to pour the thick ketchup through the little hole. It seemed not to matter that you have to shake and shake the bottle, impotently, until far too much ketchup comes out in one great scarlet plop. Heinz experimented for years with wide-necked jars and other sorts of bottles, but they never caught on.

Then in 1992 a survey of consumers indicated that more Americans believed that the plastic squeeze bottle is a better package for ketchup than the glass bottle. The survey did not offer any explanations for this change of preference, which has been evolving for many years as older people for whom the tall bottle is an icon became a less important part of the sample. Could it be that the difficulty of using the tall bottle suddenly became evident to those born after 1960? Perhaps the tall bottle holds too little ketchup. There is a clear trend toward buying things in larger containers, in part because lightweight plastics have made them less costly for manufacturers to ship and easier for consumers to use. This has happened even as the number of people in an average American household has been getting smaller. But houses, like packages, have been getting larger. Culture moves in mysterious ways.

The tall ketchup bottle is still preferred by almost half of consumers, so it is not going to disappear anytime soon. And the squeeze bottle does contain visual echoes of the old bottle. It is certainly not a radical departure. In Japan, ketchup and mayonnaise are sold in cellophane-wrapped plastic bladders that would certainly send Americans into severe culture shock. Still, the tall bottle's loss of absolute authority is a significant change. And its ultimate disappearance would represent a larger change in most people's visual environment than would the razing of nearly any landmark building.

But although some package designs are pleasantly evocative of another time, and a few appear to be unchanging icons in a turbulent world, the reason they still exist is because they still work. Inertia has historically played a role in creating commercial icons. Until quite recently, it was time-consuming and expensive to make new printing plates or to vary the shape or material of a container. Now computerized graphics and rapidly developing technology in the package-manufacturing industries make a packaging change easier than in the past, and a lot cheaper to change than advertising, which seems a far more evanescent medium. There is no constituency of curators or preservationists to protect the endangered package. If a gum wrapper manages to survive nearly unchanged for ninety years, it's not because any expert has determined that it is an important cultural expression. Rather, it's because it still helps sell a lot of gum.

So far, we've been discussing packaging in its most literal sense: de-  30
signed containers that protect and promote products. Such containers have served as the models for larger types of packaging, such as chain

restaurants, supermarkets, theme parks, and festival marketplaces. . . . Still, it is impossible to ignore a broader conception of packaging that is one of the preoccupations of our time. This concerns the ways in which people construct and present their personalities, the ways in which ideas are presented and diffused, the ways in which political candidates are selected and public policies formulated. We must all worry about packaging ourselves and everything we do, because we believe that nobody has time to really pay attention.

Packaging strives at once to offer excitement and reassurance. It promises something newer and better, but not necessarily different. When we talk about a tourist destination, or even a presidential contender, being packaged, that's not really a metaphor. The same projection of intensified ordinariness, the same combination of titillation and reassurance, are used for laundry detergents, theme parks, and candidates alike.

The imperative to package is unavoidable in a society in which people have been encouraged to see themselves as consumers not merely of toothpaste and automobiles, but of such imponderables as lifestyle, government, and health. The marketplace of ideas is not an agora, where people haggle, posture, clash, and come to terms with one another. Rather, it has become a supermarket, where values, aspirations, dreams, and predictions are presented with great sophistication. The individual can choose to buy them, or leave them on the shelf.

In such a packaged culture, the consumer seems to be king. But people cannot be consumers all the time. If nothing else, they must do something to earn the money that allows them to consume. This, in turn, pressures people to package themselves in order to survive. The early 1990s brought economic recession and shrinking opportunities to all the countries of the developed world. Like products fighting for their space on the shelf, individuals have had to re-create, or at least re-present, themselves in order to seem both desirable and safe. Moreover, many jobs have been reconceived to depersonalize individuals and to make them part of a packaged service experience.

These phenomena have their own history. For decades, people have spoken of writing resumes in order to package themselves for a specific opportunity. Thomas J. Watson Jr., longtime chairman of IBM, justified his company's famously conservative and inflexible dress code — dark suits, white shirts, and rep ties for all male employees — as "self-packaging," analogous to the celebrated product design, corporate imagery, and packaging done for the company by Elliot Noyes and Paul Rand. You can question whether IBM's employees were packaging themselves or forced into a box by their employer. Still, anyone who has ever dressed for success was doing a packaging job.

Since the 1950s, there have been discussions of packaging a candidate to respond to what voters are telling the pollsters who perform the same tasks as market researchers do for soap or shampoo. More recently, 35 such discussions have dominated American political journalism. The packaged candidate, so he and his handlers hope, projects a message that, like a Diet Pepsi, is stimulating without being threatening. Like a Weight Watchers frozen dessert bar, the candidate's contradictions must be glazed over and, ultimately, comforting. Aspects of the candidate that are confusing or viewed as extraneous are removed, just as stems and sinew are removed from packaged foods. The package is intended to protect the candidate; dirt won't stick. The candidate is uncontaminated, though at a slight remove from the consumer-voter.

People profess to be troubled by this sort of packaging. When we say a person or an experience is "packaged," we are complaining of a sense of excessive calculation and a lack of authenticity. Such a fear of unreality is at least a century old; it arose along with industrialization and rapid communication. Now that the world is more competitive, and we all believe we have less time to consider things, the craft of being instantaneously appealing has taken on more and more importance. We might say, cynically, that the person who appears "packaged" simply doesn't have good packaging.

Still, the sense of uneasiness about encountering packaged people in a packaged world is real, and it shouldn't be dismissed. Indeed, it is a theme of contemporary life, equally evident in politics, entertainment, and the supermarket. Moreover, public uneasiness about the phenomenon of packaging is compounded by confusion over a loss of iconic packages and personalities.

Producers of packaged products have probably never been as nervous as they became during the first half of the 1990s. Many of the world's most famous brands were involved in the merger mania of the 1980s, which produced debt-ridden companies that couldn't afford to wait for results either from their managers or their marketing strategies. At the same time, the feeling was that it was far too risky to produce something really new. The characteristic response was the line extension — "dry" beer, "lite" mayonnaise, "ultra" detergent. New packages have been appearing at a rapid pace, only to be changed whenever a manager gets nervous or a retailer loses patience.

The same skittishness is evident in the projection of public personalities as the clear, if synthetic, images of a few decades ago have lost their sharpness and broken into a spectrum of weaker, reflected apparitions. Marilyn Monroe, for example, had an image that was, Jayne Mansfield notwithstanding, unique and well defined. She was luscious as a Hershey's bar, shapely as a Coke bottle. But in a world where Coke can be sugar free, caffeine free, and cherry flavored (and Pepsi can be clear!), just one image isn't enough for a superstar. Madonna is available as Marilyn or as a brunette, a Catholic schoolgirl, or a bondage devotee. Who knows what brand extension will come next? Likewise, John F. Kennedy and Elvis Presley had clear, carefully projected images. But Bill Clinton is defined largely by evoking memories of both. As our commercial civilization seems to have lost the power to amuse or convince us in new and exciting ways, formerly potent packages are recycled and devalued. That has left the door open for such phenomena as generic cigarettes, President's Choice cola, and H. Ross Perot.

This cultural and personal packaging both fascinates and infuriates. There is something liberating in its promise of aggressive self-creation, and something terrifying in its implication that everything must be subject to the ruthless discipline of the marketplace. People are at once passive consumers of their culture and aggressive packagers of themselves, which can be a stressful and lonely combination. 40

### Reading the Text

1. How does Hine compare a supermarket with a traditional marketplace?
2. What does Hine mean when he asserts that modern retailing "replaces people with packages"?
3. How does packaging stimulate the desire to buy, according to Hine?
4. How do American attitudes toward packaging compare with those of the Japanese, according to Hine?

### Reading the Signs

1. Bring one product package to class, preferably with all students bringing items from the same product category (personal hygiene, say, or snack food or drinks). Give a brief presentation to the class in which you interpret your own package. After all the students have presented, compare the different messages the packages send to consumers.
2. Visit a popular clothing store, such as the Gap or Banana Republic, and study the ways the store uses packaging to create, as Hine puts it, "a personality, an attitude toward life." Be thorough in your investigations, studying everything from the bags in which you carry your purchases to perfume or cologne packages to clothing labels. Use your findings as evidence for an essay in which you analyze the image the store creates for itself and its consumers.
3. In your journal, write an entry in which you explore your motives if you have ever purchased a product because you liked the package. What did you like about the package, and how did it contribute to your sense of identity?
4. Visit a store with an explicit political theme, such as the Body Shop or the Nature Company, and write a semiotic analysis of some of the packaging you see in the store.
5. Study the packages that are visible to a visitor to your home, and then write an analysis of the messages those packages might send to a visitor. To develop your ideas, you might read or reread Joan Kron's "The Semiotics of Home Decor" (p. 72).

TED POLHEMUS

*Street Style*

|||||||||||||||||||||||||||||||||||||||||||||||||||||

*In the early nineties,* Vogue *promised that it would run no more features on the grunge style — in a feature on grunge style. As Ted Polhemus (b. 1947) shows in these excerpts from* Street Style: From Sidewalk to Catwalk *(1994), that's the way things often go in the high-fashion industry: What begins as the signature style of socially disaffected young people is appropriated by clothing designers and marketed as the season's chic new line. From punk to hip-hop and beyond, today's street style is often tomorrow's mainstream must wear. A specialist in fashion and body image, Polhemus is coeditor of* The Body as a Medium of Expression, *editor of* Social Aspects of the Human Body, *and author of* Fashion & Anti-Fashion: An Anthology of Clothing and Adornment. *In 1994 he served as the External Curator to the Victoria and Albert Museum's STREET-STYLE exhibition.*

## Hanging Out

A street corner in Harlem, 1940.

Outside a South London café, 1952.

Greenwich Village, New York, 1958.

Outside the Ace Café, North Circular Road, London, 1962.

Downtown, Kingston, Jamaica, 1963.                                    5

Carnaby Street, London, 1965.

The beach at La Jolla, California, 1966.

The intersection of Haight and Ashbury, San Francisco, 1967.

World's End, the King's Road, London, 1976.

A street party in the South Bronx, 1977.                              10

Brixton, South London, 1994.

Auspicious moments. The art of being at the right place at the right time. Just hanging around. Looking sharp. All dressed up and nowhere to go. Doing nothing in particular. Making history.

Without the Hipsters, Teddy Boys, Beats, Rockers, Rude Boys, Mods, Surfers, Hippies, Punks, B-Boys, Flygirls, Raggamuffins — and all the other streetstyle originals — most of us would be left without anything to wear.

But the sharp suits, leather jackets, jeans, kaftans, flares, DMs, click suits and so forth are only the visible, tangible part of this legacy. Oozing through the clothes, hairstyles, make-up and accessories is an *attitude*. An attitude which perhaps more than any other sets the tone of life in the late twentieth century. In spirit if not in practice — like all those people in ads for Coke, Pepsi, Levi's and a thousand other products — we are out there, checking out the action, hanging around.

The Street is both the stage upon which this drama unfolds and the 15 bottom line metaphor for all that is presumed to be real and happening in our world today. In the past, "Western culture" was most at ease and most recognizable within grand interiors. Today, as high culture has given way to popular culture, it is the litmus test of "street credibility" that is crucial. If it won't cut it on the corner, forget it.

Made back in 1933, the film *42nd Street* was an enticing preview of the role of The Street as a focus of modern life. Busby Berkeley's breathtaking finale begins with Ruby Keeler tap-dancing on the roof of a taxi. Panning down and sideways, the camera then takes us on a tour of a magical re-creation of *42nd Street*. All human life is here. Mingling. Checking each other out. Doing their thing. There is mayhem, madness — even murder — but the excitement and the sense of "This is where it's at" is so tangible that you want to reach out and grab handfuls of it. Instead of just passing through *42nd Street* en route to somewhere else, we want to linger here. It is a destination as well as a thoroughfare.

Although The Street is a place, it isn't just any place. Busby Berkeley's film wouldn't have worked as *Fifth Avenue*. Nor as one of those elegant boulevards along which fashionable Parisians loved to promenade at the turn of the century. Though the promenade might have marked a critical moment in the shift from inside to outside, it shouldn't by any means be confused with hanging out.

To promenade is to hob-nob with those on the up and up. Hanging out, on the other hand, is best done in the company of those from the wrong side of the tracks. Some *low life* is essential. That, and youth: *juvenile* delinquents. In this sense, The Street is a dead end — the place to go when you aren't old enough or rich enough to get in somewhere.

But while practical necessity may make The Street a last resort for some, it is precisely this quality which makes it so seductive for many who could be elsewhere. The allure of The Street as a road to nowhere is perfectly captured in Francis Ford Coppola's 1983 cult film *Rumble Fish*. Rusty James, the Motorcycle Boy, Smoke and their friends are the personification of low life: tragically flawed, angst-ridden, dead-end kids. No-hopers. But when they hit The Street, we — like Steve, the only guy with a future — just have to join them.

Like the colourblind Motorcycle Boy, we see The Street in dazzling 20 black and white: the flickering neon signs, the kids playing in the gush of water from the fire hydrant, the hookers, the pimps, the bottle-toting drunks. Up what is literally a dead-end alley we are attacked by thugs and left for dead. But we'll be back because we just can't resist the seductiveness of The Real Thing.

Postmodern theorists from Fredric Jameson to Jean Baudrillard see the elusiveness of authenticity as the fundamental crisis of our age. And who can doubt them? "The Real Thing" sold a lot of Coke and it is this same insatiable craving for authenticity that lures us onto The Street with Rusty James and the Motorcycle Boy. There is a fundamental irony in this which shouldn't escape us. These no-hopers have none of those things that our society officially decrees to be important (money, prestige, success, fame) and yet they have a monopoly on what we're actually most in need of — The Real.

This is the key to The Street's seductive appeal. And, of course, to the appeal of streetstyle. Like holy relics, streetstyle garments radiate the power of their associations. Every age uses dress and body decoration to signal what is most important at that historical moment. Throughout most of our history that message has been, "I am rich," or, "I am powerful." If today more and more people use their dress style to assert: "I am authentic," it is simply evidence of our hunger for the genuine article in an age which seems to so many to be one of simulation and hype.

### Trickle Down / Bubble Up

Styles which start life on the streetcorner have a way of ending up on the backs of top models on the world's most prestigious fashion catwalks. This shouldn't surprise us because, as we have seen, the authenticity which streetstyle is deemed to represent is a precious commodity. Everyone wants a piece of it.

But it is more than the price tag which distinguishes the genuine article from its chic reinterpretation. It's a question of context. And when fashion sticks its metaphorical gilt frame around a leather motorbike jacket, a Hippy kaftan, a pair of trainers, or a Ragga girl's batty-riders, it transforms an emblem of subcultural identity into something which anyone with enough money can acquire and wear with pride.

However much streetstyle and fashion might superficially resemble   25 each other, they are actually poles apart. Fashion is trendy. It celebrates change and progress. Change, because This Year's New Look always elbows aside Last Year's New Look in a perpetual pursuit of novelty. Progress, because of the implicit assumption — one which characterizes modern society — that The New is also — by definition, *ipso facto* — The Improved. Both a product of modernism and its ultimate expression, fashion faces resolutely towards the future. It has the capacity to generate the new and fresh, a capacity which has always made it appealing to those who subscribe to the view that change is preferable to the status quo and that tomorrow holds more promise than yesterday. (And when in the eighties there was a widespread swing towards a *post*-modernism which cast doubt on such progressive assumptions, this was reflected in a corresponding shift away from ever-changing fashion and towards classic, anti-trendy style.)

In its heyday (for example, in the 1950s and 1960s), fashion managed to get practically everyone to fall in line behind the particular look which it decreed to be *the* trend. As Peter York puts it in *Modern Times*:

> Fashion had its own establishment, a kind of Vatican, in the fifties and sixties and in this set-up they had dictators who set the lines for everybody to follow.
>
> The lines were set like edicts in the way of the old world. . . . They were set by magazine editors for magazine readers. *Vogue* used to announce the colour of the season and up and down the land shops presented clothes in banana beige or coral red or whatever.
>
> In the fifties there were actually *lines* for fashion. Dictates about the shape a woman's clothes should be, irrespective of the shape of her. And then came the sixties. Remember the mini. . . .
>
> And the point was that everyone wore it, your sister, your auntie, the gym mistress, everyone.
>
> For truly THERE WAS NO ALTERNATIVE.[1]

We find an even more illuminating example of the fashion system in action if we turn the clock back just a little further, to 1947, when Christian Dior launched his "New Look" on a world still waiting for the dust to settle on the Second World War. If ever there was a time when people yearned to catch a glimpse of a promising future, this was it, and the "New Look," though actually a re-working of an old look, certainly seemed fresh and novel compared to the dress women had been obliged to wear throughout the war.

Using extravagant amounts of fabric in its long, full skirts and cinching in women's waists in a way which some saw as unliberated, Dior's design raised many an eyebrow and prompted many a politician to rail against its profligacy. But such opposition was, of course, doomed to failure. For here was the spirit of The New at a time when everyone was desperate to be rid of The Old.

Of course only a tiny minority of women were in a position to purchase one of Dior's creations, but the years following 1947 saw the New Look "*trickle down*" (indeed, in this case, cascade down) to the department stores and, very quickly, to patterns which could be run up at home. However difficult it was to accomplish, women from Paris to Los Angeles and all points in between struggled to fall in step with the march of fashion. For, as Peter York correctly says, in those days THERE WAS NO ALTERNATIVE.

---

1. Peter York, *Modern Times,* London, 1994, p. 10.

This classic example illustrates the three principal characteristics of    35
fashion: its celebration of The New, its singularity (*the* New Look) and
its diffusion from high society to mass market. But today, while stories of
the death of fashion (my own included) may have been exaggerated, all
three of these characteristics seem much less in evidence than they were
only a few decades ago.

Firstly, as one might expect in a "Postmodern Age," a growing
number of people seem dubious about the proposition that what is new
is necessarily improved. Such distrust in progress is hardly surprising at a
time when environmental, economic and social realities cast such a dark
shadow on the future. This shift in attitude has influenced developments
in interior and furniture design, as well as in architecture — most notably
in a renewed emphasis on "Reconstruction." Likewise, in the sphere of
clothing and accessory design, "timeless classics" have gained in popularity. Indeed, those who jump uncritically on the latest bandwagon have
been branded "fashion victims," while the word "trendy" has often become a put-down rather than a compliment.

Secondly, instead of the authority of *the* fashion, one is today more
likely to see pluralism, with different designers proposing radically conflicting New Looks. While some fashion pundits may strive to reduce
this cacophony of different colours, shapes, hemlengths and so on, into a
consistent trend — a single "direction" — anyone viewing the photographs of the Paris, Milan, London or New York shows can appreciate
that difference, rather than consensus, is the order of the day.

Such multiplicity of "direction," coupled with an apparently growing inclination on the part of many simply to wear what suits them rather
than to swallow fashion's prescription, has brought a variety of dress and
adornment styles which is arguably without equal in history. The homogeneity of appearance which Peter York (in the quote above) sees as
characteristic of, for example, the sixties ("everyone wore it, your sister,
your auntie, the gym mistress, everyone") is no longer typical. Today,
when you look at what people are actually wearing on the street, in the
office and at nightclubs, what is obvious is that now there *is* an alternative. Indeed, lots and lots of alternatives, as the "edicts" of yesteryear are
pushed aside by the demands of personal choice.

Finally, do new looks still begin life within high fashion and "trickle
down" for mass consumption? It is undoubtedly true that the mass-
market "mainline" fashion industry continues to take a lead from the
more exclusive, highly priced designers. But do the creations we see on
those exclusive, cameraflashlit catwalks all originate in the minds of the
word's top designers?

Not on the evidence that I see. To my eyes an increasingly frequent    40
chain of events goes like this. First there is a genuine streetstyle innovation. This may be featured in a pop music video and streetkids in other
cities and countries may pick up on the style. Then, finally — at the end

rather than the beginning of the chain — a ritzy version of the original idea makes an appearance as part of a top designer's collection.

Instead of trickle-down, *bubble up*. Instead of the bottom end of the market emulating the top end, precisely the reverse.

If Dior's "New Look" illustrates the traditional trickle-down process, then the "Perfecto" motorcycle jacket (also known as the "Bronx" jacket) may serve to illustrate the bubble-up process in action. Based on a World War II design, the Perfecto jacket as made by the Schott Brothers company of New York became the symbol of rebellious youth when Marlon Brando wore one in *The Wild One*. With its sinister black sheen and its zips like knife slashes, this garment embodied an attitude and lifestyle which directly challenged "normal society."

In the suburban American community in which I grew up in the fifties and sixties, the only kids who wore such jackets hung out at the pool hall "looking for trouble." This was *Rumble Fish* territory — deep on the wrong side of town.

While I can recall secretly admiring these jackets early in the sixties, it would be well into the seventies before I actually got up the nerve to buy one. Nor was such hesitancy based entirely on unjustified paranoia. As shown in *American Graffiti*'s portrayal of teenage life in the USA of the early sixties — where the hero's madras sports jacket contrasts tellingly with his tormentors' Perfecto style jackets — this garment marked a very real subcultural (and often socioeconomic) boundary.

In Britain, a similar jacket was made by Lewis Leathers. Mick Farren, a braver soul than myself, got it together to buy himself one when he was only fifteen:

> I bought the jacket in a small, backstreet men's clothing store, hard up against a railway bridge in a medium sized seaside town in southern England. It was hardly the concrete jungle but it passed at the time. The store specialized in tacky, juvenile delinquent fashions — polkadot shirts, stardust peggies, dayglo socks and lurid suits that usually fell apart after a couple of weeks. . . . I stood in front of the store's full-length mirror and slipped off whatever jacket I was wearing. (It isn't part of the memory. It was probably some flakey tweed sportcoat of which my mother totally approved.) I struggled into what was going to be my first cool garment. . . . The jacket came from D. Lewis Ltd of Great Portland Street, London. It was the Bronx model. As I stared into the mirror, I couldn't believe myself. Admittedly the mirror was tilted up to produce the most flattering effect, but I looked great. My legs seemed longer, my shoulders seemed broader. I flipped the collar up. I looked so damned cool. Mother of God, I was a cross between Elvis and Lord Byron.[2]

2. Mick Farren, *The Black Leather Jacket*, London, 1985.

Only very gradually, throughout the seventies and into the eighties, did the black leather motorbike jacket become accepted as everyday, "normal" apparel. Arguably the most potent indicator of how streetstyle in general has gradually become an accepted part of our culture, its wider appeal was guaranteed when it became *de rigueur* for serious rock musicians. From Gene Vincent to Jim Morrison, from Lou Reed to The Clash, from Bruce Springsteen to George Michael, the black leather jacket is there to assure us of a musician's authenticity.

What makes the Perfecto The Real Thing is its Bad Boy / Girl, wrong-side-of-the-tracks image. That and the fact that it is a classic, anti-fashion garment, virtually unchanged in its design for some five decades.

But what is true of the genuine article as made by the Schott Brothers or Lewis Leathers is not true of the countless imitations which began appearing on high fashion catwalks in the 1980s. First it was the "street bred" designers like Katharine Hamnett, Pam Hogg and Jean-Paul Gaultier who produced their own jazzed-up versions. But when, by the mid-eighties, high fashion designers like Claude Montana, Thierry Mugler, Gianni Versace and Sonia Rykiel showed versions of the Perfecto, the bubble-up process was well and truly complete.

The transformation of the Perfecto style jacket from subcultural emblem to high and mainstream fashion is hardly unique. Most of the dozens of streetstyles dealt with in this book have at some time, in some way, provided inspiration for a wide range of fashion designers. Indeed, we have come to expect that styles which begin life on dead-end, mean streets will almost instantaneously and with ever-increasing regularity make an appearance on even the most prestigious of fashion catwalks. And, in the process, the pages of *Vogue* and *Elle* have often come to resemble those of *The Face* and *i-D* (but with the difference that the former's "Punks," "Raggamuffins," "Travellers" and so forth are actually highly paid models styled in some fantasized imitation of The Real Thing).

On one level this inversion of the socioeconomic order is all very admirable. Who wants to return to a time when the social élite were so full of themselves that they refused to believe that anything of value could come from those further down the ladder? It was the sixties which at long last recognized that culture is not the prerogative of the upper classes — a realization which revitalized our society with creative talent and new blood.

The bubble-up process has made us a fully fledged creative democracy in which talent isn't thought to be limited by class or race or education or how much money you've got in the bank. For our culture as a whole it is surely all for the best that the full spectrum of creative energy in our society has been tapped.

However, those who are actually members of such stylistically influential subcultures may not share this enthusiasm for the bubble-up process. Both in 1977, when Zandra Rhodes presented her ripped and safety-pinned "Punk Look," and, more recently, when Versace and other high fashion designers produced similarly derivative styles, genuine Punks of my acquaintance usually categorized such imitation as "insult" rather than flattery. Likewise, Johnny Stuart, author of the definitive book on Rockers, recently commented that

> It is irritating to see how the leather jacket has become just a fashion garment. I can remember how back in the days when Rockers were far, far outnumbered by Mods, to wear your leathers was a risky business indeed. If you weren't careful, if you didn't stay on your bike and keep moving, your leather jacket could get ripped off your back and you could get a real beating. The fancy fashionable versions of the Perfecto which you see all over the place these days water down the significance of the thing, taking away its original magic, castrating it.[3]

Even within the fashion industry there is concern at what is seen as "exploitation" of streetstyle creativity. According to British designer Joe Casely-Hayford,

> The fashion world has become so hungry that people are *scouring* — they come from all over the world to London, taking aspects of different groups and using it, consuming it and moving on to the next thing. But the fashion world will continue to miss the essence and will continue to exploit and will continue to rape and will continue to move on in a very superficial and trivial way.[4]

Strong words. But then the implication and effects of the bubble-up process cannot be taken lightly. Imitation may be the sincerest form of flattery, but just as the counterfeiting of fashion designers' own designs undermines their value, something similar occurs when fashion copies streetstyle. That authenticity and sense of subcultural identity which is symbolized in streetstyle is lost when it becomes "this year's latest fashion" — something which can be purchased and worn without reference to its original subcultural meaning. In this sense, what may begin as a designer's genuinely felt desire to celebrate "the street" as a wellspring of fresh ideas may have the inadvertent effect of undermining the "street value" of these styles for the very people who originally created them.

## B-Boys and Flygirls

From the moment in 1976 when Punk was born, kicking and screaming, the world's eyes focused (in disbelief) on Britain. Except for the hyped-up distraction of "disco," the UK's virtual monopoly of

55

---

3. In conversation with the author, 1994.
4. Speaking on "Reportage," BBC 2, 26 January 1994.

popular culture continued well into the eighties as the visual flare of Britain's New Romantic pop musicians coincided with the MTV-led "video revolution." But, also in 1976, invisible to the outside world, the impoverished South Bronx of NYC was beginning to fashion a new, exciting youth-culture under the banner of "rap music" and "hip-hop."

In the best streetstyle tradition the location from which this movement sprang was literally the street. Jamaican DJs living in New York (most famously, Kool Herc) had brought with them the Kingston tradition of raucous street parties organized around competing sound systems. Their crews and these events became the focus of South Bronx streetlife. As in Jamaica, the DJ was king. Not content simply to play records, the likes of Grandmaster Flash took a more hands-on approach in which turntables were themselves played like musical instruments — "scratching" over selected tracks and "mixing" together often completely different sounds.

The result was dance music of the highest order which encouraged hundreds and then thousands of New York ghetto kids to perfect what became known as "break-dancing" — letting rip on the instrumental "breaks" between verses in a highly competitive fashion reminiscent of ancient African traditions in which participants, especially the men, tried to "dance" each other off the floor.

Such dancers became known as "B-Boys" (the "B" short for "break") or "Flygirls" ("fly" being street slang for well-dressed, attractive, sexy). Despite the fact that American attentions were focused on Britain and the emerging rap musicians were given absurdly little air-play, "The Message" (in Grandmaster Flash's phrase) eventually got through. The new music, the acrobatic break-dancing and the innovative graffiti art, which also derived from poor areas of New York, all added up to a dynamic subcultural force.

However, at least in the early days, such innovations in music, dance and art were not matched by the emergence of an equally distinctive new appearance style. Most of the new breed of rap musicians dressed (at least on stage) in a way which was derivative of OTT Funk. However, slowly but surely, the anonymous B-Boys and Flygirls evolved a style of their own. The essential ingredients were defined by the rigours of strenuous dancing: athletic trainers and tracksuits, together with snug caps which offered some protection during headspins.

Although rooted in the practical and the casual, the B-Boy style 60 was also aspirational, relying (like the Casuals in Britain) on prominent upmarket labels. To these were added gold jewelry — huge, chunky necklaces or "Dukie Ropes" culminating in gleaming enormous dollar signs — and, in time, tightly cropped hairstyles featuring amazingly intricate razored designs. The look was as "street" as any look can be and when Run DMC had an enormous hit in 1986 with "My Adidas" it was cemented into international popular culture in a way which left little doubt that New York (and therefore the USA) had finally elbowed Britain aside.

Suddenly the B-Boys' and Flygirls' style was the most copied in the world. To the chagrin of millions of parents, every kid simply had to own a pair of expensive trainers and a label-festooned hooded sports-top or tracksuit. Nor was this look limited to youngsters. Overnight it became the accepted uniform of trendy advertising executives and media moguls from LA to London.

As is inevitably the case with such unwanted emulation, the real B-Boys and Flygirls had no choice but to keep moving on — using new styles and labels to define their genuine subcultural identity and generating a whole string of distinctive styles which matched rap music's own evolution.

Firstly, beginning around 1987, the Paid In Full look of Erik B. & Rakim or Ultramagnetic MCs took the basic ingredients of B-Boy style and smartened them up by emphasizing the most chic brands of sportswear (Louis Vuitton, Gucci) and by taking gold accessories to a new extreme. The effect was less "street" (no sane person would break-dance on the sidewalk in such expensive outfits) and more like Olympic athletes in designer sportswear displaying their victors' medallions with pride.

Next, circa 1988, came the Militant look which befitted the increasingly committed stance of groups like Public Enemy and BDP & KRS-1. As its name suggests, the predominant theme was "urban commando chic" — black or camouflage pattern clothes set off with dazzlingly white, big-tongued trainers and, again, heavy gold jewelry.

The Afrocentric look which became prominent late in the eighties reflected rap's renewed determination to assert black cultural identity and roots. Effectively blending sportswear with traditional African fabrics (such as batik) and loose, comfortable styles, this look is exemplified by groups such as Jungle Brothers, Lakim Shabazz and Queen Latifah.

Significantly, in line with the political stance which lay behind this style, gold jewelry (which might have come from South Africa) was replaced with Afrikan medallions made of leather in the red, gold and green of the Ethiopian flag.

Although such styles first appeared and flourished in a historical sequence, they all continue to exist side by side to the present day — making the subculture which the B-Boys and Flygirls founded richly textured, dynamic and, to use the word which has become synonymous with this group, "fresh."

### Reading the Text

1. According to Polhemus, what attitude is projected by "streetstyle," and how is it projected?
2. What is the cultural significance of the street, as Polhemus describes it, and why is it so appealing?

3. Summarize in your own words what Polhemus means by fashion that "trickles down" and that which "bubbles up."
4. Why does Polhemus believe that classic "high" fashion is in a period of decline?
5. What were the cultural roots of B–Boy and Flygirl styles, in Polhemus's view?
6. How, according to Polhemus, did B–Boy and Flygirl styles change in the 1980s?

### Reading the Signs

1. Bring an issue of a current fashion magazine for men or women (such as *Vogue* or *Details*) and study them in small groups. Do you find the clothing styles featured in ads and articles to be predominantly "bubbling up" from the street or "trickling down" from high fashion, or are both trends equally in evidence? Try to explain your findings in terms of current cultural taste and values, and report your conclusions to the class.
2. Polhemus describes the way high fashion designers take the styles of underprivileged youth and repackage them as styles sold to the privileged. In class, form teams and conduct a debate on the proposition that such cultural appropriation serves only to reinforce class inequities.
3. Using Polhemus's discussion of streetstyle as your critical framework, write an analysis of grunge fashion.
4. Polhemus describes B–Boy and Flygirl styles in the late 1980s. In a descriptive essay, update his description of these styles, being sure to note any changes and explaining the cultural or social significance of those changes.
5. Observe students at your school congregating in a public place (say, the student union building) and note the predominant fashion styles. Then write a semiotic interpretation of the fashion trends you observed.

STUART EWEN

## Hard Bodies

||||||||||||||||||||||||||||||||||||||||||||||||||||||||||||

*In this selection from* All Consuming Images: The Politics of Style in Contemporary Culture *(1988), Stuart Ewen (b. 1945) analyzes the way our bodies themselves can be signs of cultural desire. Focusing on the body sculpting popular among urban professionals in recent years, Ewen argues that the "hard body" fad reflects a postindustrial transformation of the body into a kind of industrial product, something you "build" every day at the gym. Health clubs thus can be seen as factories that produce the sorts of bodily objects that America values, with Nautilus machines standing in as the tools of mass production. Ewen documents the pulse of American culture as a professor of media studies in the Department of Communications at Hunter College, and he also serves as professor in the Ph.D. programs in history and sociology at the City University of New York Graduate Center. He is the author of numerous books and articles on American popular and consumer culture, including* Channels of Desire: Mass Images and the Shaping of American Consciousness *with Elizabeth Ewen (1982) and* Captains of Consciousness: Advertising and the Social Roots of the Consumer Culture *(1976).*

Writing in 1934, the sociologists George A. Lundberg, Mirra Komarovsky, and Mary Alice McInerny addressed the question of "leisure" in the context of an emerging consumer society. Understanding the symbiotic relationship between mass-production industries and a consumerized definition of leisure, they wrote of the need for society to achieve a compatibility between the worlds of work and daily life. "The ideal to be sought," they proposed, "is undoubtedly the gradual obliteration of the psychological barrier which today distinguishes work from leisure."[1]

That ideal has been realized in the daily routine of Raymond H———, a thirty-four-year-old middle-management employee of a large New York City investment firm. He is a living cog in what Felix Rohatyn has termed the new "money culture," one in which "making things" no longer counts; "making money," as an end in itself, is the driving force.[2] His days are spent at a computer terminal, monitoring an endless flow of numerical data.

When his workday is done, he heads toward a local health club for the relaxation of a "workout." Three times a week this means a visit to the Nautilus room, with its high, mirrored walls, and its imposing assembly line of large, specialized "machines." The workout consists of exercises for his lower body and for his upper body, twelve "stations" in all. As he moves from Nautilus machine to Nautilus machine, he works on his hips, buttocks, thighs, calves, back, shoulders, chest, upper arms, forearms, abdomen, and neck, body part by body part.

At the first station, Raymond lies on the "hip and back machine," making sure to align his hip joints with the large, polished, kidney-shaped cams which offer resistance as he extends each leg downward over the padded roller under each knee. Twelve repetitions of this, and he moves on to the "hip abduction machine," where he spreads his legs

---

1. George A. Lundberg et al., *Leisure: A Suburban Study* (1934), p. 3.
2. *New York Times,* 3 June 1987, p. A27.

outward against the padded restraints that hold them closed. Then leg extensions on the "compound leg machine" are followed by leg curls on the "leg curl machine." From here, Raymond H—— proceeds to the "pullover/torso arm machine," where he begins to address each piece of his upper body. After a precise series of repetitions on the "double chest machine," he completes his workout on the "four-way neck machine."

While he alternates between different sequential workouts, and different machines, each session is pursued with deliberate precision, following exact instructions.

Raymond H—— has been working on his body for the past three years, ever since he got his last promotion. He is hoping to achieve the body he always wanted. Perhaps it is fitting that this quintessential, single, young, urban professional — whose life has become a circle of work, money culture, and the cultivation of an image — has turned himself, literally, into a piece of work. If the body ideal he seeks is *lean,* devoid of fatty tissue, it is also *hard.* "Soft flesh," once a standard phrase in the American erotic lexicon, is now — within the competitive, upscale world he inhabits — a sign of failure and sloth. The hard shell is now a sign of achievement, visible proof of success in the "rat race." The goal he seeks is more about *looking* than *touching.*

To achieve his goal, he approaches his body piece by piece; with each machine he performs a discrete task. Along the way he also assumes the job of inspector, surveying the results of each task in the mirrors that surround him. The division of labor, the fragmentation of the work process, and the regulating function of continual measurement and observation — all fundamental to the principles of "scientific management" — are intrinsic to this form of recreation. Like any assembly line worker, H—— needs no overall knowledge of the process he is engaged in, only the specific tasks that comprise that process. "You don't have to understand *why* Nautilus equipment works," writes bodybuilder Mike Mentzer in the foreword to one of the most widely read Nautilus manuals. "With a tape measure in hand," he promises, "you will see what happens."[3]

The body ideal Raymond H—— covets is, itself, an aestheticized tribute to the broken-down work processes of the assembly line. "I'm trying to get better definition," H—— says. "I'm into Nautilus because it lets me do the necessary touchup work. Free weights [barbells] are good for building up mass, but Nautilus is great for definition."[4] By "definition," H—— is employing the lingo of the gym, a reference to a body surface upon which each muscle, each muscle group, appears segmented and distinct. The perfect body is one that ratifies the fragmentary process of its construction, one that mimics — in flesh — the illustrative qualities of a schematic drawing, or an anatomy chart.

5

---

3. Ellington Darden, *The Nautilus Bodybuilding Book* (1986), pp. viii–ix.
4. Style Project, interview I-13.

Surveying his work in the mirror, H——— admires the job he has
done on his broad, high pectorals, but is quick to note that his quadriceps
"could use some work." This ambivalence, this mix of emotions, pursues
him each time he comes for a workout, and the times in between. He is
never quite satisfied with the results. The excesses of the weekend-past
invariably leave their blemish. An incorrectly struck pose reveals an over-
measure of loose skin, a sign of weakness in the shell. Despite all efforts,
photogenic majesty is elusive.

The power of the photographic idiom, in his mind's eye, is rein-     10
forced, again and again, by the advertisements and other media of style
visible everywhere. The ideal of the perfectly posed machine — the cold,
hard body in response — is paraded, perpetually, before his eyes and
ours. We see him, or her, at every glance.

An advertisement for home gym equipment promises a "Body By
Soloflex." Above is the silent, chiaroscuro portrait of a muscular youth, his
torso bare, his elbows reaching high, pulling a thin-ribbed undershirt up
over his head, which is faceless, covered by shadow. His identity is situated
below the neck, an instrumentally achieved study in brawn. The powerful
expanse of his chest and back is illuminated from the right side. A carefully
cast shadow accentuates the paired muscle formations of his abdominal
wall. The airbrush has done its work as well, effecting a smooth, standardized, molded quality, what John Berger has termed "the skin without a biography." A silent, brooding hulk of a man, he is the unified product of
pure engineering. His image is a product of expensive photographic technology, and expensive technical expertise. His body — so we are informed — is also a technical achievement. He has reached this captured
moment of perpetual perfection on a "machine that fits in the corner" of
his home. The machine, itself, resembles a stamping machine, one used to
shape standardized, industrial products. Upon this machine, he has routinely followed instructions for "twenty-four traditional iron pumping exercises, each correct in form and balance." The privileged guidance of industrial engineering, and the mindless obedience of work discipline, have
become legible upon his body; yet as it is displayed, it is nothing less than a
thing of beauty, a transcendent aspiration.

This machine-man is one of a generation of desolate, finely tuned
loners who have cropped up as icons of American style. Their bodies,
often lightly oiled to accentuate definition, reveal their inner mechanisms
like costly, open-faced watches, where one can see the wheels and gears
moving inside, revealing — as it were — the magic of time itself. If this is
eroticism, it is one tuned more to the mysteries of technology than to
those of the flesh.

In another magazine advertisement, for Evian spring water from
France, six similarly anatomized figures stand across a black and white
two-page spread. From the look of things, each figure (three men and
three women) has just completed a grueling workout, and four of them

are partaking of Evian water as part of their recovery. The six are displayed in a lineup, each one displaying a particularly well-developed anatomical region. These are the new icons of beauty, precisely defined, powerful machines. Below, on the left, is the simple caption: "Revival of the Fittest." Though part of a group, each figure is conspicuously alone.

Once again, the modern contours of power, and the structures of work discipline, are imprinted upon the body. In a world of rampant careerism, self-absorption is a rule of thumb. If the division of labor sets each worker in competition with every other, here that fragmentation is aestheticized into the narcissism of mind and body.

Within this depiction, sexual equality is presented as the meeting point between the anorectic and the "nautilized." True to gender distinctions between evanescent value and industrial work discipline, the three women are defined primarily by contour, by the thin lines that their willowy bodies etch upon the page. Although their muscles are toned, they strike poses that suggest pure, disembodied form. Each of the men, situated alternately between the women, gives testimony on behalf of a particular fraction of segmented flesh: abdomen, shoulders and upper arms, upper back. In keeping with the assembly line approach to muscle building, each man's body symbolizes a particular station within the labor process.

Another ad, for a health and fitness magazine, contains an alarmingly discordant statement: "Today's women workers are back in the sweat shop." There is a basis to this claim. In today's world, powerful, transnational corporations search the globe looking for the cheapest labor they can find. Within this global economy, more and more women — from Chinatown to Taiwan — are employed at tedious, low-paying jobs, producing everything from designer jeans to computer parts.

Yet this is not the kind of sweatshop the ad has in mind. The photographic illustration makes this clear. Above the text, across the two-page color spread, is the glistening, heavily muscled back of a woman hoisting a chrome barbell. Her sweat is self-induced, part of a "new woman" lifestyle being promoted in *Sport* magazine, "the magazine of the new vitality." Although this woman bears the feminine trademark of blonde, braided hair, her body is decidedly masculine, a new body aesthetic in the making. Her muscles are not the cramped, biographically induced muscles of menial labor. Hers is the brawn of the purely symbolic, the guise of the middle-class "working woman."

While the text of the advertisement seems to allude to the real conditions of female labor, the image transforms that truth into beauty, rendering it meaningless. Real conditions are copywritten into catchy and humorous phrases. The harsh physical demands of women's work are reinterpreted as regimented, leisure-time workouts at a "health club." Real sweat is reborn as photogenic body oil.

The migration of women into the social structures of industrial discipline is similarly aestheticized in an ad for Jack LaLanne Fitness Centers. A black and white close-up of a young woman wrestling with a fitness "machine" is complemented by the eroticized grimace on her face. Once again, the chiaroscuro technique accentuates the straining muscles of her arms. The high-contrast, black and white motif may also suggest the "night and day" metamorphosis that will occur when one commits to this particular brand of physical discipline.

In large white letters, superimposed across the shadowy bottom of     20
the photograph, are the words: "Be taut by experts." With a clever play on words the goal of education moves from the mind to the body. Muscle power is offered as an equivalent substitute for brain power. No problem. In the search for the perfectly regulated self, it is implicit that others will do the thinking. This woman, like the Soloflex man, is the product of pure engineering, of technical expertise:

> We were building bodies back when you were building blocks. . . .
> We know how to perfectly balance your workout between swimming, jogging, aerobics and weight training on hundreds of the most advanced machines available. . . . Sure it may hurt a little. But remember. *You only hurt the one you love.* [Emphasis added.]

These advertisements, like Raymond H———'s regular visits to the Nautilus room, are part of the middle-class bodily rhetoric of the 1980s. Together they mark a culture in which self-absorbed careerism, conspicuous consumption, and a conception of *self* as an object of competitive display have fused to become the preponderant symbols of achievement. The regulated body is the nexus where a cynical ethos of social Darwinism, and the eroticism of raw power, meet.

### Reading the Text

1. Write a one-paragraph description of the 1980s' "hard body" style.
2. How, according to Ewen, is the body treated like a machine in the "hard body" exercise regimen?
3. Why does Raymond H——— exercise so much?
4. Why does Ewen say that "the goal [Raymond H———] seeks is more about *looking* than *touching*"?

### Reading the Signs

1. Ewen accuses those who follow the hard body trend of conceiving the self as "an object of competitive display." To what extent do you find his accusation valid? To support your argument, draw on your own habits of exercising and those of your friends.

2. In class, discuss the tone Ewen adopts in his essay. How does that tone affect your response to his argument?
3. Break your class into two groups according to gender. In each group, brainstorm ideal body types for both men and women, then rank them according to the group's preferences. Compare the results of the two groups: How are they gender-related?
4. Read a current issue of a magazine devoted to fitness, such as *Shape*. To what extent is the body "fashion" that Ewen describes still current? How do you explain any changes?
5. Interview three or four people who are working out in your school or local gym, asking them about the results they want to achieve through their exercising. Then using Ewen's argument about hard bodies as your model, analyze the results of your interviews.

# JOAN KRON

## *The Semiotics of Home Decor*

||||||||||||||||||||||||||||||||||||||||||||||||||||||||

*Just when you thought it was safe to go back into your living room, here comes Joan Kron with a reminder that your home is a signaling system just as much as your clothing is. In* Home-Psych: The Social Psychology of Home and Decoration *(1983), from which this selection is taken, Kron takes a broad look at the significance of interior decoration, showing how home design can reflect both an individual and a group identity. Ranging from a New York entrepreneur to Kwakiutl Indian chiefs, Kron further discusses how different cultures use possessions as a rich symbol system. The author of* High Tech: The Industrial Style and Source Book for the Home *(1978) and of some five hundred articles for American magazines, she is particularly interested in fashion, design, and the social psychology of consumption. Kron currently is an editor-at-large at* Allure *magazine.*

On June 7, 1979, Martin J. Davidson entered the materialism hall of fame. That morning the thirty-four-year-old New York graphic design entrepreneur went to his local newsstand and bought fifty copies of the *New York Times* expecting to read an article about himself in the Home section that would portray him as a man of taste and discrimination. Instead, his loft and his life-style, which he shared with singer Dawn

Bennett, were given the tongue-in-cheek treatment under the headline: "When Nothing But the Best Will Do."[1]

Davidson, who spent no more money renovating his living quarters than many of the well-to-do folks whose homes are lionized in the *Times*'s Thursday and Sunday design pages — the running ethnographic record of contemporary upper-middle-class life-style — made the unpardonable error of telling reporter Jane Geniesse how much he had paid for his stereo system, among other things. Like many people who have not been on intimate terms with affluence for very long, Davidson is in the habit of price-tagging his possessions. His 69-cent-per-bottle bargain Perrier, his $700 Armani suits from Barney's, his $27,000 cooperative loft and its $150,000 renovation, his sixteen $350-per-section sectionals, and his $11,000 best-of-class stereo. Martin J. Davidson wants the world to know how well he's done. "I live the American dream," he told Mrs. Geniesse, which includes, "being known as one of Barney's best customers."[2]

Davidson even wants the U.S. Census Bureau's computer to know how well he has done. He is furious, in fact, that the 1980 census form did not have a box to check for people who live in cooperatives. "If someone looks at my census form they'll think I must be at the poverty level or lower."[3] No one who read the *Times* article about Martin Davidson would surmise that.

It is hard to remember when a "design" story provoked more outrage. Letters to the editor poured in. Andy Warhol once said that in our fast-paced media world no one could count on being a celebrity for more than fifteen minutes. Martin Davidson was notorious for weeks. "All the Martin Davidsons in New York," wrote one irate reader, "will sit home listening to their $11,000 stereos, while downtown, people go to jail because they ate a meal they couldn't pay for."[4] "How can one man embody so many of the ills afflicting our society today?"[5] asked another offended reader. "Thank you for your clever spoof," wrote a third reader. "I was almost convinced that two people as crass as Martin Davidson and Dawn Bennett could exist."[6] Davidson's consumption largesse was even memorialized by Russell Baker, the *Times*'s Pulitzer Prize–winning humorist, who devoted a whole column to him: "While simultaneously consuming yesterday's newspaper," wrote Baker, "I con-

---

1. Jane Geniesse, "When Nothing But the Best Will Do," *New York Times,* June 7, 1979, p. C1ff.
2. Ibid.
3. Author's interview with Martin Davidson.
4. Richard Moseson, "Letters: Crossroads of Decadence and Destitution," *New York Times,* June 14, 1979, p. A28.
5. Letter to the Editor, *New York Times,* June 14, 1979, p. C9.
6. Letter to the Editor, ibid.

sumed an article about one Martin Davidson, a veritable Ajax of consumption. A man who wants to consume nothing but the best and does."[7] Counting, as usual, Davidson would later tell people, "I was mentioned in the *Times* on three different days."

Davidson, a self-made man whose motto is "I'm not taking it with me and while I'm here I'm going to spend every stinking penny I make," couldn't understand why the *Times* had chosen to make fun of him rather than to glorify his 4,000-square-foot loft complete with bidet, Jacuzzi, professional exercise gear, pool table, pinball machine, sauna, two black-tile bathrooms, circular white Formica cooking island, status-stuffed collections of Steiff animals, pop art (including eleven Warhols), a sound system that could weaken the building's foundations if turned up full blast, and an air-conditioning system that can turn cigarette smoke, which both Davidson and Bennett abhor, into mountain dew — a loft that has everything Martin Davidson ever wanted in a home except a swimming pool and a squash court.

"People were objecting to my life-style," said Davidson. "It's almost as if there were a correlation between the fact that we spend so much on ourselves and other people are starving. No one yells when someone spends $250,000 for a chest of drawers at an auction," he complained. "I just read in the paper that someone paid $650,000 for a stupid stamp. Now it'll be put away in a vault and no one will ever see it."[8]

But Dawn Bennett understood what made Davidson's consumption different. "It's not very fashionable to be an overt consumer and admit it,"[9] she said.

## What Are Things For?

As anyone knows who has seen a house turned inside out at a yard sale, furnishing a home entails the acquisition of more objects than there are in a spring housewares catalog. With all the time, money, and space we devote to the acquisition, arrangement, and maintenance of these household possessions, it is curious that we know so little about our relationships to our possessions.

"It is extraordinary to discover that no one knows why people want goods," wrote British anthropologist Mary Douglas in *The World of*

7. Russell Baker, "Observer: Incompleat Consumer," *New York Times,* June 9, 1979, p. 25.

8. Author's interview with Martin Davidson.

9. Author's interview with Dawn Bennett.

*Goods.*[10] Although no proven or agreed-upon theory of possessiveness in human beings has been arrived at, social scientists are coming up with new insights on our complicated relationships to things. Whether or not it is human nature to be acquisitive, it appears that our household goods have a more meaningful place in our lives than they have been given credit for. What comes across in a wide variety of research is that things matter enormously.

Our possessions give us a sense of security and stability. They make    10
us feel in control. And the more we control an object, the more it is a part of us. If it's *not mine,* it's *not me.*[11] It would probably make sense for everyone on the block to share a lawn mower, but then no one would have control of it. If people are reluctant to share lawn mowers, it should not surprise us that family members are not willing to share TV sets. They want their own sets so they can watch what they please. Apparently, that was why a Chicago woman, furious with her boyfriend for switching from *The Thorn Birds* to basketball, stabbed him to death with a paring knife.[12]

Besides control, we use things to compete. In the late nineteenth century the Kwakiutl Indian chiefs of the Pacific Northwest made war with possessions.[13] Their culture was built on an extravagant festival called the "potlatch," a word that means, roughly, to flatten with gifts. It was not the possession of riches that brought prestige, it was the distribution and destruction of goods. At winter ceremonials that took years to prepare for, rival chiefs would strive to outdo one another with displays of conspicuous waste, heaping on their guests thousands of spoons and blankets, hundreds of gold and silver bracelets, their precious dance masks and coppers (large shields that were their most valuable medium of exchange), and almost impoverishing themselves in the process.

---

10. Mary Douglas and Baron Isherwood, *The World of Goods* (New York: Basic Books, 1979), p. 15. A number of other social scientists have mentioned in recent works the lack of attention paid to the human relationship to possessions: See Coleman and Rainwater, *Social Standing,* p. 310. The authors observed that "the role of income in providing a wide range of rewards — consumption — has not received sufficient attention from sociologists." See Carl F. Graumann, "Psychology and the World of Things," *Journal of Phenomenological Psychology,* Vol. 4, 1974–75, pp. 389–404. Graumann accused the field of sociology of being thing-blind.

11. Lita Furby, "Possessions: Toward a Theory of Their Meaning and Function Throughout the Life Cycle," in Paul B. Baltes (ed.), *Life-Span Development and Behavior,* Vol. 1 (New York: Academic Press, 1978), pp. 297–336.

12. "'Touch That Dial and You're Dead,'" *New York Post,* March 30, 1983, p. 5.

13. Ruth Benedict, *Patterns of Culture* (Boston: Houghton Mifflin [1934], 1959); Frederick V. Grunfeld, "Homecoming: The Story of Cultural Outrage," *Connoisseur,* February 1983, pp. 100–106; and Lewis Hyde, *The Gift* (New York: Vintage Books, [1979, 1980], 1983), pp. 25–39.

Today our means of competition is the accumulation and display of symbols of status. Perhaps in Utopia there will be no status, but in this world, every human being is a status seeker on one level or another — and a status reader. "Every member of society," said French anthropologist Claude Lévi-Strauss, "must learn to distinguish his fellow men according to their mutual social status."[14] This discrimination satisfies human needs and has definite survival value. "Status symbols provide the cue that is used in order to discover the status of others, and, from this, the way in which others are to be treated," wrote Erving Goffman in his classic paper, "Symbols of Class Status."[15] Status affects who is invited to share "bed, board, and cult,"[16] said Mary Douglas. Whom we invite to dinner affects who marries whom, which then affects who inherits what, which affects whose children get a head start.

Today what counts is what you eat (gourmet is better than greasy spoon), what you fly (private jet is better than common carrier), what sports you play (sailing is better than bowling), where you matriculate, shop, and vacation, whom you associate with, how you eat (manners count), and most important, where you live. Blue Blood Estates or Hard Scrabble zip codes? as one wizard of demographics calls them. He has figured out that "people tend to roost on the same branch as birds of a feather."[17] People also use status symbols to play net worth hide-and-seek. When *Forbes* profiled the 400 richest Americans,[18] its own in-house millionaire Malcolm Forbes refused to disclose his net worth but was delighted to drop clues telling about his status entertainments — his ballooning, his Fabergé egg hunts, his châteaux, and his high life-style. It is up to others to translate those obviously costly perks into dollars.

A high price tag isn't the only attribute that endows an object with status. Status can accrue to something because it's scarce — a one-of-a-kind artwork or a limited edition object. The latest hard-to-get item is Steuben's $27,500 bowl etched with tulips that will be produced in an edition of five — one per year for five years. "Only one bowl will bloom this year,"[19] is the headline on the ad for it. Status is also found in objects made from naturally scarce materials: Hawaii's rare koa wood, lapis lazuli, or moon rock. And even if an object is neither expensive nor rare, status can rub off on something if it is favored by the right people, which

---

14. Edmund Leach, *Claude Lévi-Strauss* (New York: Penguin Books, 1980), p. 39.

15. Erving Goffman, "Symbols of Class Status," *British Journal of Sociology,* Vol. 2, December 1951, pp. 294–304.

16. Douglas and Isherwood, *World of Goods,* p. 88.

17. Michael J. Weiss, "By Their Numbers Ye Shall Know Them," *American Way,* February 1983, pp. 102–106 ff. "You tell me someone's zip code," said Jonathan Robbin, "and I can predict what they eat, drink, drive, buy, even think."

18. "The Forbes 400," *Forbes,* September 13, 1982, pp. 99–186.

19. Steuben Glass advertisement, *The New Yorker,* April 4, 1983, p. 3.

explains why celebrities are used to promote coffee, cars, casinos, and credit cards.

If you've been associated with an object long enough you don't even    15
have to retain ownership. Its glory will shine on you retroactively. Perhaps that is why a member of Swiss nobility is having two copies made of each of the Old Master paintings in his collection. This way, when he turns his castle into a museum, both his children can still have, so to speak, the complete collection, mnemonics of the pictures that have been in the family for centuries. And the most potent status symbol of all is not the object per se, but the *expertise* that is cultivated over time, such as the appreciation of food, wine, design, or art.

If an object reflects a person *accurately,* it's an index of status. But *symbols* of status are not always good indices of status. They are not official proof of rank in the same way a general's stars are. So clusters of symbols are better than isolated ones. Anyone with $525 to spare can buy one yard of the tiger-patterned silk velvet that Lee Radziwill used to cover her dining chair seats.[20] But one status yard does not a princess make. A taxi driver in Los Angeles gets a superior feeling from owning the same status-initialed luggage that many of her Beverly Hills fares own. "I have the same luggage you have," she tells them. "It blows their minds," she brags. But two status valises do not a glitterati make. Misrepresenting your social status isn't a crime, just "a presumption," said Goffman. Like wearing a $69 copy of a $1,000 watch that the mail-order catalog promises will make you "look like a count or countess on a commoner's salary."[21]

"Signs of status are important ingredients of self. But they do not exhaust all the meanings of objects for people," wrote sociologists Mihaly Csikszentmihalyi and Eugene Rochberg-Halton in *The Meaning of Things: Domestic Symbols of the Self.*[22] The study on which the book was based found that people cherished household objects not for their status-giving properties but especially because they were symbols of the self and one's connections to others.

The idea that possessions are symbols of self is not new. Many people have noticed that *having* is intricately tied up with *being.* "It is clear that between what a man calls *me* and what he simply calls *mine,* the line is difficult to draw," wrote William James in 1890.[23] "Every possession is

20. Paige Rense, "Lee Radziwill," *Celebrity Homes* (New York: Penguin Books, 1979), pp. 172–81.

21. *Synchronics* catalog, Hanover, Pennsylvania, Fall 1982.

22. Mihaly Csikszentmihalyi and Eugene Rochberg-Halton, *The Meaning of Things: Domestic Symbols and the Self* (New York: Cambridge University Press, 1981), p. 18.

23. William James, *Principles of Psychology,* Vol. 1 (New York: Macmillan, 1890), p. 291.

an extension of the self," said Georg Simmel in 1900.[24] "Humans tend to integrate their selves with objects," observed psychologist Ernest Beaglehole some thirty years later.[25] Eskimos used to *lick* new acquisitions to cement the person/object relationship.[26] We stamp our visual taste on our things making the totality resemble us. Indeed, theatrical scenic designers would be out of work if Blanche DuBois's boudoir could be furnished with the same props as Hedda Gabler's.

Csikszentmihalyi and Rochberg-Halton discovered that "things are cherished not because of the material comfort they provide but for the information they convey about the owner and his or her ties to others."[27] People didn't value things for their monetary worth, either. A battered toy, a musical instrument, a homemade quilt, they said, provide more meaning than expensive appliances which the respondents had plenty of. "What's amazing is how few of these things really make a difference when you get to the level of what is important in life,"[28] said Csikszentmihalyi. All those expensive furnishings "are required just to keep up with the neighbors or to keep up with what you expect your standard of living should be."

"How else should one relate to the Joneses if not by keeping up with them," asked Mary Douglas provocatively.[29] The principle of reciprocity requires people to consume at the same level as one's friends.[30] If we accept hospitality, we have to offer it in return. And that takes the right equipment and the right setting. But we need things for more than "keeping level" with our friends. We human beings are not only toolmakers but symbol makers as well, and we use our possessions in the same way we use language — the quintessential symbol — to *communicate* with one another. According to Douglas, goods make the universe "more intelligible." They are more than messages to ourselves and others, they are "the hardware and the software . . . of an information sys-

24. Georg Simmel, *The Philosophy of Money,* trans. Tom Bottomore and David Frisby (Boston: Routledge & Kegan Paul, 1978), p. 331.

25. Ernest Beaglehole, *Property: A Study in Social Psychology* (New York: Macmillan, 1932).

26. Ibid., p. 134.

27. Csikszentmihalyi and Rochberg-Halton, p. 239.

28. Author's interview with Mihaly Csikszentmihalyi.

29. Douglas and Isherwood, *World of Goods,* p. 125. Also see Jean Baudrillard, *For a Critique of the Political Economy of the Sign,* trans. Charles Levin (St. Louis, MO: Telos Press, 1981), p. 81. Said Baudrillard: "No one is free to live on raw roots and fresh water. . . . The vital minimum today . . . is the standard package. Beneath this level, you are an outcast." Two classic novels on consumption are (1) Georges Perec, *Les Choses* (New York: Grove Press, [1965], 1967). (2) J. K. Huysmans, *Against the Grain (A Rebours)* (New York: Dover Publications, [1931], 1969).

30. Douglas and Isherwood, *World of Goods,* p. 124.

tem."[31] Possessions speak a language we all understand, and we pay close attention to the inflections, vernacular, and exclamations.

The young husband in the film *Diner* takes his things very seriously. How could his wife be so stupid as to file the Charlie Parker records with his rock 'n' roll records, he wants to know. What's the difference, she wants to know. What's the difference? How will he find them otherwise? Every record is sacred. Different ones remind him of different times in his life. His things *take* him back. Things can also *hold* you back. Perhaps that's why Bing Crosby's widow auctioned off 14,000 of her husband's possessions — including his bed. "'I think my father's belongings have somehow affected her progress in life,'" said one of Bing's sons.[32] And things can tell you where you stand. Different goods are used to rank occasions and our guests. Costly sets of goods, especially china and porcelain, are "pure rank markers. . . . There will always be luxuries because rank must be marked," said Douglas.[33]

One of the pleasures of goods is "sharing names."[34] We size up people by their expertise in names — sports buffs can converse endlessly about hitters' batting averages, and design buffs want to know whether you speak spongeware, Palladio, Dansk, or Poggenpohl. All names are not equal. We use our special knowledge of them to show solidarity and exclude people.

In fact, the social function of possessions is like the social function of food. Variations in the quality of goods define situations as well as different times of day and seasons. We could survive on a minimum daily allotment of powdered protein mix or grains and berries. But we much prefer going marketing, making choices, learning new recipes. "Next to actually eating food, what devout gastronomes seem to enjoy most is talking about it, planning menus, and remembering meals past," observed food critic Mimi Sheraton.[35] But it's not only experts who thrive on variety. Menu monotony recently drove a Carlsbad, New Mexico, man to shoot the woman he was living with. She served him green beans once too often. "Wouldn't you be mad if you had to eat green beans all the time?" he said.[36] If every meal were the same, and if everyone dressed alike and furnished alike, all meanings in the culture would be wiped out.[37]

---

31. Ibid., p. 72.

32. Maria Wilhelm, "Things Aren't Rosy in the Crosby Clan as Kathryn Sells Bing's Things (and not for a Song)," *People,* May 31, 1982, pp. 31–33.

33. Douglas and Isherwood, *World of Goods,* p. 118.

34. Ibid., p. 75.

35. Mimi Sheraton, "More on Joys of Dining Past," *New York Times,* April 9, 1983, p. 48.

36. "Green Beans Stir Bad Blood," *New York Times,* March 26, 1983, p. 6.

37. Douglas and Isherwood, *World of Goods,* p. 66.

The furnishings of a home, the style of a house, and its landscape are all part of a system — a system of symbols. And every item in the system has meaning. Some objects have personal meanings, some have social meanings which change over time. People understand this instinctively and they desire things, not from some mindless greed, but because things are necessary to communicate with. They are the vocabulary of a sign language. To be without things is to be left out of the conversation. When we are "listening" to others we may not necessarily agree with what this person or that "says" with his or her decor, or we may misunderstand what is being said; and when we are doing the "talking" we may not be able to express ourselves as eloquently as we would like. But where there are possessions, there is always a discourse.

And what is truly remarkable is that we are able to comprehend and   25 manipulate all the elements in this rich symbol system as well as we do — for surely the language of the home and its decor is one of the most complex languages in the world. But because of that it is also one of the richest and most expressive means of communication.

### Decor as Symbol of Self

One aspect of personalization is the big I — Identity. Making distinctions between ourselves and others. "The self can only be known by the signs it gives off in communication," said Eugene Rochberg-Halton.[38] And the language of ornament and decoration communicates particularly well. Perhaps in the future we will be known by our computer communiqués or exotic brainwaves, but until then our rock gardens, tabletop compositions, refrigerator door collages, and other design language will have to do. The Nubian family in Africa with a steamship painted over the front door to indicate that someone in the house works in shipbuilding, and the Shotte family on Long Island who make a visual pun on their name with a rifle for a nameplate, are both decorating their homes to communicate "this is where our territory begins and this is who we are."

Even the most selfless people need a minimum package of identity equipment. One of Pope John Paul I's first acts as pontiff was to send for his own bed. "He didn't like sleeping in strange beds," explained a friend.[39] It hadn't arrived from Venice when he died suddenly.

Without familiar things we feel disoriented. Our identities flicker and fade like ailing light bulbs. "Returning each night to my silent, pic-

38. Eugene Rochberg-Halton, "Where Is the Self: A Semiotic and Pragmatic Theory of Self and the Environment." Paper presented at the 1980 American Sociological Meeting, New York City, 1980, p. 3.

39. Dora Jane Hamblin, "Brief Record of a Gentle Pope," *Life,* November 1978, p. 103.

tureless apartment, I would look in the bathroom mirror and wonder who I was," wrote D. M. Thomas, author of *The White Hotel,* recalling the sense of detachment he felt while living in a furnished apartment during a stint as author-in-residence at a Washington, D.C., university. "I missed familiar things, familiar ground that would have confirmed my identity."[40]

Wallpaper dealers wouldn't need fifty or sixty sample books filled with assorted geometrics, supergraphics, and peach clamshells on foil backgrounds if everyone were content to have the same roses climbing their walls. Chintz wouldn't come in forty flavors from strawberry to licorice, and Robert Kennedy, Jr.'s, bride Emily wouldn't have trotted him around from store to store "for ten hours" looking for a china pattern[41] if the home wasn't an elaborate symbol system — as important for the messages it sends to residents and outsiders as for the functions it serves.

In the five-year-long University of Chicago study[42] into how modern Americans relate to their things, investigators Mihaly Csikszentmihalyi and Rochberg-Halton found that we all use possessions to stand for ourselves. "I learned that things can embody self," said Rochberg-Halton. "We create environments that are extensions of ourselves, that serve to tell us who we are, and act as role models for what we can become."[43] But what we cherish and what we use to stand for ourselves, the researchers admitted, seemed to be "scripted by the culture."[44] Even though the roles of men and women are no longer so tightly circumscribed, "it is remarkable how influential sex-stereotyped goals still remain."[45] Men and women "pay attention to different things in the same environment and value the same things for different reasons," said the authors.[46] Men and children cared for action things and tools; women and grandparents cared for objects of contemplation and things that reminded them of family. It was also found that meaning systems are passed down in families from mothers to daughters — not to sons.

Only children and old people cared for a piece of furniture because it was useful. For adults, a specific piece of furniture embodied experiences

40. D. M. Thomas, "On Literary Celebrity," *The New York Times Magazine,* June 13, 1982, pp. 24–38, citation p. 27.

41. "Back Home Again in Indiana Emily Black Picks Up a Freighted Name: Mrs. Robert F. Kennedy, Jr.," *People,* April 12, 1982, pp. 121–23, citation p. 123.

42. Eugene Rochberg-Halton, "Cultural Signs and Urban Adaptation: The Meaning of Cherished Household Possessions." Ph.D. dissertation, Department of Behavioral Science, Committee on Human Development, University of Chicago, August 1979; and Mihaly Csikszentmihalyi and Eugene Rochberg-Halton, *The Meaning of Things: Domestic Symbols of the Self* (New York: Cambridge University Press, 1981).

43. Author's interview with Eugene Rochberg-Halton.

44. Csikszentmihalyi and Rochberg-Halton, *Meaning of Things,* p. 105.

45. Ibid., p. 112.

46. Ibid., p. 106.

and memories, or was a symbol of self or family. Photographs which had the power to arouse emotions and preserve memories meant the most to grandparents and the least to children. Stereos were most important to the younger generation, because they provide for the most human and emotional of our needs — release, escape, and venting of emotion. And since music "seems to act as a modulator of emotions," it is particularly important in adolescence "when daily swings of mood are significantly greater than in the middle years and . . . later life."[47] Television sets were cherished more by men than women, more by children than grandparents, more by grandparents than parents. Plants had greater meaning for the lower-middle class, and for women, standing for values, especially nurturance and "ecological consciousness."[48] "Plateware," the term used in the study to cover all eating and drinking utensils, was mentioned mostly by women. Of course, "plates" are the tools of the housewife's trade. In many cultures they are the legal possession of the women of the house.

The home is such an important vehicle for the expression of identity that one anthropologist believes "built environments" — houses and settlements — were originally developed to "*identify a group* — rather than to provide shelter."[49] But in contemporary Western society, the house more often identifies a person or a family instead of a group. To put no personal stamp on a home is almost pathological in our culture. Fear of attracting attention to themselves constrains people in crime-ridden areas from personalizing, lack of commitment restrains others, and insecurity about decorating skill inhibits still others. But for most people, painting some sort of self-portrait, decoratively, is doing what comes naturally.

All communications, of course, are transactions. The identity we express is subject to interpretation by others. Will it be positive or negative? David Berkowitz, the "Son of Sam" murderer, didn't win any points when it was discovered he had drawn a circle around a hole in the wall in his apartment and written "This is where I live."[50] A person who fails to keep up appearances is stigmatized.

### Reading the Text

1. Summarize how, according to Kron, our possessions act as signs of our identity.

---

47. Ibid., p. 72.
48. Ibid., p. 79.
49. Amos Rapoport, "Identity and Environment," in James S. Duncan (ed.), *Housing and Identity: Cross-Cultural Perspectives* (London: Croom Helm, 1981), pp. 6–35, citation p. 18.
50. Leonard Buder, "Berkowitz Is Described as 'Quiet' and as a Loner," *New York Times*, August 12, 1977, p. 10.

2. How do our living places work to create *group* identity?
3. Why did *New York Times* readers object to the consumption habits of Martin J. Davidson?

### Reading the Signs

1. In a small group, discuss the brand names of possessions that each of you owns. Then interpret the significance of each brand: What do the brands say about each of you? About the group?
2. With your class, brainstorm factors other than possessions that can communicate a person's identity. Then write your own essay in which you compare the relative value of possessions to your own sense of identity with the additional factors your class brainstormed.
3. Write an essay in which you argue for or against Kron's claim that "To put no personal stamp on a home is almost pathological in our culture."
4. Analyze semiotically your own apartment or a room in your house, using Kron's essay as a critical framework. How do your possessions and furnishings act as signs of your identity?
5. With Roland Barthes's comments on the meaning of materials in mind (see "Toys," p. 96), write an essay interpreting the *materials* with which you have decorated your home environment.
6. How would Joan Kron explain the "body culture" as described by Stuart Ewen ("Hard Bodies," p. 66)?

SUSAN WILLIS

*Disney World: Public Use / Private State*

|||||||||||||||||||||||||||||||||||||||||||||||||||||||||||||||

*If your idea of heaven is a place where you need only relax and wait for someone to take care of your every comfort and amusement, and where no unexpected surprises can crop up and destroy your enjoyment, then Disney World is for you. For Susan Willis (b. 1946), on the other hand, such a thoroughly programmed environment falls a good deal short of paradise. In this essay, she explains why: Could it be that Disney World is just another "brave new world"? A professor of English at Duke University, Willis specializes in minority literature and cultural studies and is the author of* Specifying: Black Women Writing the American Experience *(1987),* A Primer for Daily Life *(1991), and* Inside the Mouse *(1995).*

At Disney World, the erasure of spontaneity is so great that spontaneity itself has been programmed. On the "Jungle Cruise" khaki-clad tour guides teasingly engage the visitors with their banter, whose apparent spontaneity has been carefully scripted and painstakingly rehearsed. Nothing is left to the imagination or the unforeseen. Even the paths and walkways represent the programmed assimilation of the spontaneous. According to published reports, there were no established walkways laid down for the opening-day crowds at Disneyland.[1] Rather, the Disney Imagineers waited to see where people would walk, then paved over their spontaneous footpaths to make prescribed routes.

The erasure of spontaneity has largely to do with the totality of the built and themed environment. Visitors are inducted into the park's program, their every need predefined and presented to them as a packaged routine and set of choices. "I'm not used to having everything done for me." This is how my companion at Disney World reacted when she checked into a Disney resort hotel and found that she, her suitcase, and her credit card had been turned into the scripted components of a highly orchestrated program. My companion later remarked that while she found it odd not to have to take care of everything herself (as she normally does in order to accomplish her daily tasks), she found it "liberating" to just fall into the proper pattern, knowing that nothing could arise that hadn't already been factored into the system. I have heard my companion's remarks reiterated by many visitors to the park with whom I've talked. Most describe feeling "freed up" ("I didn't have to worry about my kids," "I didn't have to think about anything") by the experience of relinquishing control over the complex problem-solving thoughts and operations that otherwise define their lives. Many visitors suspend daily perceptions and judgments altogether, and treat the wonderland environment as more real than real. I saw this happen one morning when walking to breakfast at my Disney resort hotel. Two small children were stooped over a small snake that had crawled out onto the sun-warmed path. "Don't worry, it's rubber," remarked their mother. Clearly only Audio-Animatronic simulacra of the real world can inhabit Disney World. A real snake is an impossibility.

In fact, the entire natural world is subsumed by the primacy of the artificial. The next morning I stepped outside at the end of an early morning shower. The humid atmosphere held the combination of sun and rain. "Oh! Did they turn the sprinklers on?" This is the way my next-door neighbor greeted the day as she emerged from her hotel room. The Disney environment puts visitors inside the world that Philip K. Dick depicted in *Do Androids Dream of Electric Sleep?* — where all animal

---

1. Scott Bukatman, "There's Always Tomorrowland: Disney and the Hypercinematic Experience," *October* 57 (Summer 1991), pp. 55–78.

life has been exterminated, but replaced by the production of simulacra, so real in appearance that people have difficulty recalling that real animals no longer exist. The marvelous effect of science fiction is produced out of a dislocation between two worlds, which the reader apprehends as an estrangement, but the characters inside the novel cannot grasp because they have only the one world: the world of simulacra. The effect of the marvelous cannot be achieved unless the artificial environment is perceived through the retained memory of everyday reality. Total absorption into the Disney environment cancels the possibility for the marvelous and leaves the visitor with the banality of a park-wide sprinkler system. No muggers, no rain, no ants, and no snakes.

Amusement is the commodified negation of play. What is play but the spontaneous coming together of activity and imagination, rendered more pleasurable by the addition of friends? At Disney World, the world's most highly developed private property "state" devoted to amusement, play is all but eliminated by the absolute domination of program over spontaneity. Every ride runs to computerized schedule. There is no possibility of an awful thrill, like being stuck at the top of a ferris wheel. Order prevails particularly in the queues for the rides that zigzag dutifully on a prescribed path created out of stanchions and ropes; and the visitor's assimilation into the queue does not catapult him or her into another universe, as it would if Jorge Luis Borges fabricated the program. The Disney labyrinth is a banal extension of the ride's point of embarkation, which extends into the ride as a hyper-themed continuation of the queue. The "Backstage Movie Tour" has done away with the distinction between the ride and its queue by condemning the visitor to a two-and-a-half-hour-long pedagogical queue that preaches the process of movie production. Guests are mercilessly herded through sound stages and conveyed across endless back lots where one sees the ranch-style houses used in TV commercials and a few wrecked cars from movie chase scenes. Happily, there are a few discreet exit doors, bail-out points for parents with bored children. Even Main Street dictates programmed amusement because it is not a street but a conduit, albeit laden with commodity distractions, that conveys the visitor to the Magic Kingdom's other zones where more queues, rides, and commodities distinguish themselves on the basis of their themes. All historical and cultural references are merely ingredients for decor. Every expectation is met programmatically and in conformity with theme. Mickey as Sorcerer's Apprentice does not appear in the Wild West or the exotic worlds of Jungle and Adventure, the niches for Davey Crockett and Indiana Jones. Just imagine the chaos, a park-wide short circuit, that the mixing of themed ingredients might produce. Amusement areas are identified by a "look," by characters in costume, by the goods on sale: What place — i.e., product — is Snow White promoting if she's arm in arm with an astronaut? The utopian intermingling of thematic opportunities such as occurred at the finale of the movie *Who Framed Roger Rabbit?,* with Warner and Disney "toons" breaking their copyrighted species separation to cavort with each other and the human actors, will not happen at Disney World.

However, now that the costumed embodiment of Roger Rabbit has 5 taken up residence at Disney World, he, too, can expect to have a properly assigned niche in the spectacular Disney parade of characters. These have been augmented with a host of other Disney/Lucas/Spielberg creations, including Michael Jackson of "Captain EO" and C$_3$PO and R2D2 of *Star Wars,* as well as Disney buyouts such as Jim Henson's Muppets and the Saturday morning cartoon heroes, the Teenage Mutant Ninja Turtles. The Disney Corporation's acquisition of the stock-in-trade of popular culture icons facilitates a belief commonly held by young children that every popular childhood figure "lives" at Disney World. In the utopian imagination of children, Disney World may well be a never-ending version of the finale to *Roger Rabbit* where every product of the imagination lives in community. In reality, the products (of adult imaginations) live to sell, to be consumed, to multiply.

What's most interesting about Disney World is what's not there. Intimacy is not in the program even though the architecture includes several secluded nooks, gazebos, and patios. During my five-day stay, I saw only one kiss — and this a husbandly peck on the cheek. Eruptions of imaginative play are just as rare. During the same five-day visit, I observed only one such incident even though there were probably fifty thousand children in the park. What's curious about what's not at Disney is that there is no way of knowing what's not there until an aberrant event occurs and provokes the remembrance of the social forms and behaviors that have been left out. This was the case with the episode of spontaneous play. Until I saw real play, I didn't realize that it was missing. The incident stood out against a humdrum background of uniform amusement: hundreds of kids being pushed from attraction to attraction in their strollers, hundreds more waiting dutifully in the queues or marching about in family groups — all of them abstaining from the loud, jostling, teasing, and rivalrous behaviors that would otherwise characterize many of their activities. Out of this homogenous "amused" mass, two kids snagged a huge sombrero each from an open-air stall at the foot of the Mexico Pavilion's Aztec temple stairway and began their impromptu version of the Mexican hat dance up and down the steps. Their play was clearly counterproductive as it took up most of the stairway, making it difficult for visitors to enter the pavilion. Play negated the function of the stairs as conduit into the attraction. The kids abandoned themselves to their fun, while all around them, the great mass of visitors purposefully kept their activities in line with Disney World's prescribed functions. Everyone but the dancers seemed to have accepted the park's unwritten motto: "If you pay, you shouldn't play." To get your money's worth, you have to do everything and do it in the prescribed manner.

Free play is gratuitous and therefore a waste of the family's leisure time expenditure.

Conformity with the park's program upholds the Disney value system. Purposeful consumption — while it costs the consumer a great deal — affirms the value of the consumer. "Don't forget, we drove twenty hours to get here." This is how one father admonished his young son who was squirming about on the floor of EPCOT's Independence Hall, waiting for the amusement to begin. The child's wanton and impatient waste of time was seen as a waste of the family's investment in its amusement. If a family is to realize the value of its leisure time consumptions, then every member must function as a proper consumer.

The success of Disney World as an amusement park has largely to do with the way its use of programming meshes with the economics of consumption as a value system. In a world wholly predicated on consumption, the dominant order need not proscribe those activities that run counter to consumption, such as free play and squirming, because the consuming public largely polices itself against gratuitous acts which would interfere with the production of consumption as a value. Conformity with the practice of consumption is so widespread and deep at Disney World that occasional manifestations of boredom or spontaneity do not influence the compulsively correct behavior of others. Independence Hall did not give way to a seething mass of squirming youngsters even though all had to sit through a twenty-minute wait. Nor did other children on the margins of the hat dance fling themselves into the fun. Such infectious behavior would have indicated communally defined social relations or the desire for such social relations. Outside of Disney World in places of public use, infectious behavior is common. One child squirming about on the library floor breeds others; siblings chasing each other around in a supermarket draw others; one child mischievously poking at a public fountain attracts others; kids freeloading rides on a department store escalator can draw a crowd. These playful, impertinent acts indicate an imperfect mesh between programmed environment and the value system of consumption. Consumers may occasionally reclaim the social, particularly the child consumer who has not yet been fully and properly socialized to accept individuation as the bottom line in the consumer system of value. As an economic factor, the individual exists to maximize consumption — and therefore profits — across the broad mass of consumers. This is the economic maxim most cherished by the fast-food industry, where every burger and order of fries is individually packaged and consumed to preclude consumer pooling and sharing.

At Disney World the basic social unit is the family. This was made particularly clear to me because as a single visitor conducting research, I presented a problem at the point of embarkation for each of the rides. "How many in your group?" "One." The lone occupant of a con-

veyance invariably constructed to hold the various numerical break-
downs of the nuclear family (two, three, or four) is an anomaly. Perhaps
the most family-affirming aspect of Disney World is the way the queues
serve as a place where family members negotiate who will ride with
whom. Will Mom and Dad separate themselves so as to accompany their
two kids on a two-person ride? Will an older sibling assume the responsibility for a younger brother or sister? Every ride asks the family to evaluate each of its member's needs for security and independence. This is
probably the only situation in a family's visit to Disney World where the
social relations of family materialize as practice. Otherwise and throughout a family's stay, the family as nexus for social relations is subsumed by
the primary definition of family as the basic unit of consumption. In consumer society at large, each of us is an atomized consumer. Families are
composed of autonomous, individuated consumers, each satisfying his or
her age- and gender-differentiated taste in the music, video, food, and
pleasure marketplace. In contrast, Disney World puts the family back together. Even teens are integrated in their families and are seldom seen
roaming the park in teen groups as they might in shopping malls.

Families at Disney World present themselves as families, like the one    10
I saw one morning on my way to breakfast at a Disney resort hotel:
father, mother, and three children small to large, each wearing identical
blue Mickey Mouse T-shirts and shorts. As I walked past them, I over-
heard the middle child say, "We looked better yesterday — in white."
Immediately, I envisioned the family in yesterday's matching outfits, and
wondered if they had bought identical ensembles for every day of their
stay.

All expressions of mass culture include contradictory utopian impulses, which may be buried or depicted in distorted form, but nevertheless generate much of the satisfaction of mass cultural commodities
(whether the consumer recognizes them as utopian or not). While the
ideology of the family has long functioned to promote conservative —
even reactionary — political and social agendas, the structure of the family as a social unit signifies communality rather than individuality and can
give impetus to utopian longings for communally defined relations in society at large. However, when the family buys into the look of a family,
and appraises itself on the basis of its look ("We looked better yesterday"), it becomes a walking, talking commodity, a packaged unit of consumption stamped with the Mickey logo of approval. The theoretical
question that this family poses for me is not whether its representation of
itself as family includes utopian possibilities (because it does), but whether
such impulses can be expressed and communicated in ways not accessible
to commodification.

In its identical dress, the family represents itself as capitalism's version
of a democratized unit of consumption. Differences and inequalities
among family members are reduced to distinctions in age and size. We

have all had occasion to experience the doppelgänger effect in the presence of identical twins who choose (or whose families enforce) identical dress. Whether chosen or imposed, identical twins who practice the art of same dress have the possibility of confounding or subverting social order. In contrast, the heterogeneous family whose members choose to dress identically affirms conformity with social order. The family has cloned itself as a multiple, but identical consumer, thus enabling the maximization of consumption. It is a microcosmic representation of free market democracy where the range of choices is restricted to the series of objects already on the shelf. In this system there is no radical choice. Even the minority of visitors who choose to wear their Rolling Stones and Grateful Dead T-shirts give the impression of having felt constrained not to wear a Disney logo.

Actually, Disney has invented a category of negative consumer choices for those individuals who wish to express nonconformity. This I discovered as I prepared to depart for my Disney research trip, when my daughter Cassie (fifteen years old and "cool" to the max) warned me, "Don't buy me any of that Disney paraphernalia." As it turned out, she was happy to get a pair of boxer shorts emblazoned with the leering images of Disney's villains: two evil queens, the Big Bad Wolf, and Captain Hook. Every area of Disney World includes a Disney Villains Shop, a chain store for bad-guy merchandise. Visitors who harbor anti-Disney sentiments can express their cultural politics by consuming the negative Disney line. There is no possibility of an anticonsumption at Disney World. All visitors are, by definition, consumers, their status conferred with the price of admission.

At Disney World even memories are commodities. How the visitor will remember his or her experience of the park has been programmed and indicated by the thousands of "Kodak Picture Spot" signposts. These position the photographer so as to capture the best views of each and every attraction, so that even the most inept family members can bring home perfect postcard-like photos. To return home from a trip to Disney World with a collection of haphazardly photographed environments or idiosyncratic family shots is tantamount to collecting bad memories. A family album comprised of picture-perfect photo-site images, on the other hand, constitutes the grand narrative of the family's trip to Disney World, the one that can be offered as testimony to money well spent. Meanwhile, all those embarrassing photos, the ones not programmed by the "Picture Spots," that depict babies with ice cream all over their faces or toddlers who burst into tears rather than smiles at the sight of those big-headed costumed characters that crop up all over the park — these are the images that are best left forgotten.

The other commodified form of memory is the souvenir. As long as there has been tourism there have also been souvenirs: objects marketed to concretize the visitor's experience of another place. From a certain point of view, religious pilgrimage includes aspects of tourism, particularly when the culmination of pilgrimage is the acquisition of a transportable relic. Indeed, secular mass culture often imitates the forms and practices of popular religious culture. For many Americans today who make pilgrimages to Graceland and bring home a mass-produced piece of Presley memorabilia, culture and religion collide and mesh.

Of course, the desire to translate meaningful moments into concrete objects need not take commodified form. In Toni Morrison's *Song of Solomon,* Pilate, a larger-than-life earth mother if there ever was one, spent her early vagabondage gathering a stone from every place she visited. Similarly, I know of mountain climbers who mark their ascents by bringing a rock back from each peak they climb. Like Pilate's stones, these tend to be nondescript and embody personal remembrances available only to the collector. In contrast, the commodity souvenir enunciates a single meaning to everyone: "I was there. I bought something." Unlike the souvenirs I remember having seen as a child, seashells painted with seascapes and the name of some picturesque resort town, most souvenirs today are printed with logos (like the Hard Rock Cafe T-shirt), or renderings of copyrighted material (all the Disney merchandise). The purchase of such a souvenir allows the consumer the illusion of participating in the enterprise as a whole, attaining a piece of the action. This is the consumerist version of small-time buying on the stock exchange. We all trade in logos — buy them, wear them, eat them, and make them the containers of our dreams and memories. Similarly, we may all buy into capital with the purchase of public stock. These consumerist activities give the illusion of democratic participation while denying access to real corporate control which remains intact and autonomous, notwithstanding the mass diffusion of its logos and stock on the public market. Indeed the manipulation of public stock initiated during the Reagan administration, which has facilitated one leveraged buyout after another, gives the lie to whatever wistful remnants of democratic ownership one might once have attached to the notion of "public" stocks.

Disney World is logoland. The merchandise, the costumes, the scenery — all is either stamped with the Disney logo or covered by copyright legislation. In fact, it is impossible to photograph at Disney World without running the risk of infringing a Disney copyright. A family photo in front of Sleeping Beauty's Castle is apt to include dozens of infringements: the castle itself, Uncle Harry's "Goofy" T-shirt, the kids' Donald and Mickey hats, maybe a costumed Chip 'n Dale in the background. The only thing that saves the average family from a lawsuit is that most don't use their vacation photos as a means for making profit. I suspect the staff of "America's Funniest Home Videos" systematically eliminates all family videos shot at Disney World; otherwise prize winners might find themselves having to negotiate the legal difference between prize and profit, and in a larger sense, public use versus private property. As an interesting note, Michael Sorkin, in a recent essay on Disneyland, chose a photo of "[t]he sky above Disney World [as a] substitute for an image of the place itself." Calling Disney World "the first copyrighted urban environment," Sorkin goes on to stress the "litigiousness" of the Disney Corporation.[2] It may be that *Design Quarterly,* where Sorkin published his essay, pays its contributors, thus disqualifying them from "fair use" interpretations of copyright policy.

Logos have become so much a part of our cultural baggage that we hardly notice them. Actually they are the cultural capital of corporations. Pierre Bourdieu invented the notion of cultural capital with reference to individuals. In a nutshell, cultural capital represents the sum total of a person's ability to buy into and trade in the culture. This is circumscribed by the economics of class and, in turn, functions as a means for designating an individual's social standing. Hence people with higher levels of education who distinguish themselves with upscale or trendy consumptions have more cultural capital and can command greater privilege and authority than those who, as Bourdieu put it, are stuck defining themselves by the consumption of necessity. There are no cultural objects or practices that do not constitute capital, no reserves of culture that escape value. Everything that constitutes one's cultural life is a commodity and can be reckoned in terms of capital logic.

In the United States today there is little difference between persons and corporations. Indeed, corporations enjoy many of the legal rights extended to individuals. The market system and its private property state are "peopled" by corporations, which trade in, accumulate, and hoard up logos. These are the cultural signifiers produced by corporations, the impoverished imagery of a wholly rationalized entity. Logos are commodities in the abstract, but they are not so abstracted as to have transcended value. Corporations with lots of logos, particularly upscale, high-tech logos, command more cultural capital than corporations with fewer, more humble logos.

In late twentieth-century America, the cultural capital of corporations has replaced many of the human forms of cultural capital. As we buy, wear, and eat logos, we become the henchmen and admen of the corporations, defining ourselves with respect to the social standing of the various corporations. Some would say that this is a new form of tribalism, that in sporting corporate logos we ritualize and humanize them, we redefine the cultural capital of the corporations in human social terms. I would say that a state where culture is indistinguishable from logo and

20

---

2. Michael Sorkin, "See You in Disneyland," *Design Quarterly* (Winter 1992), pp. 5–13.

where the practice of culture risks infringement of private property is a state that values the corporate over the human.

While at Disney World, I managed to stow away on the behind-the-scenes tour reserved for groups of corporate conventioneers. I had heard about this tour from a friend who is also researching Disney and whose account of underground passageways, conduits for armies of workers and all the necessary materials and services that enable the park to function, had elevated the tour to mythic proportions in my imagination.

But very little of the behind-the-scenes tour was surprising. There was no magic, just a highly rational system built on the compartmentalization of all productive functions and its ensuing division of labor, both aimed at the creation of maximum efficiency. However, instances do arise when the rational infrastructure comes into contradiction with the onstage (park-wide) theatricalized image that the visitor expects to consume. Such is the case with the system that sucks trash collected at street level through unseen pneumatic tubes that transect the backstage area, finally depositing the trash in Disney's own giant compactor site. To the consumer's eyes, trash is never a problem at Disney World. After all, everyone dutifully uses the containers marked "trash," and what little manages to fall to the ground (generally popcorn) is immediately swept up by the French Foreign Legion trash brigade. For the consumer, there is no trash beyond its onstage collection. But there will soon be a problem as environmental pressure groups press Disney to recycle. As my companion on the backstage tour put it, "Why is there no recycling at Disney World — after all, many of the middle-class visitors to the park are already sorting and recycling trash in their homes?" To this the Disney guide pointed out that there is recycling, backstage: bins for workers to toss their Coke cans and other bins for office workers to deposit papers. But recycling onstage would break the magic of themed authenticity. After all, the "real" Cinderella's Castle was not equipped with recycling bins, nor did the denizens of Main Street, U.S.A., circa 1910, foresee the problem of trash. To maintain the image, Disney problem solvers are discussing hiring a minimum-wage workforce to rake, sort, and recycle the trash on back lots that the environmentally aware visitor will never see.

While I have been describing the backstage area as banal, the tour through it was not uneventful. Indeed there was one incident that underscored for me the dramatic collision between people's expectations of public use and the highly controlled nature of Disney's private domain. As I mentioned, the backstage tour took us to the behind-the-scenes staging area for the minute-by-minute servicing of the park and hoopla of its mass spectacles such as firework displays, light shows, and parades. We happened to be in the backstage area just as the parade down Main Street was coming to an end. Elaborate floats and costumed characters descended a ramp behind Cinderella's Castle and began to disassemble before our eyes. The floats were alive with big-headed characters, clambering off the superstructures and out of their heavy, perspiration-drenched costumes. Several "beheaded" characters revealed stocky young men gulping down Gatorade. They walked toward our tour group, bloated Donald and bandy-legged Chip from the neck down, carrying their huge costume heads, while their real heads emerged pea-sized and aberrantly human.

We had been warned *not* to take pictures during the backstage tour, but one of our group, apparently carried away by the spectacle, could not resist. She managed to shoot a couple of photos of the disassembled characters before being approached by one of the tour guides. As if caught in a spy movie, the would-be photographer pried open her camera and ripped out the whole roll of film. The entire tour group stood in stunned amazement; not, I think, at the immediate presence of surveillance, but at the woman's dramatic response. In a situation where control is so omnipresent and conformity with control is taken for granted, any sudden gesture or dramatic response is a surprise.

At the close of the tour, my companion and I lingered behind the rest of the group to talk with our tour guides. As a professional photographer, my companion wanted to know if there is a "normal" procedure for disarming behind-the-scenes photographic spies. The guide explained that the prescribed practice is to impound the cameras, process the film, remove the illicit photos, and return the camera, remaining photos, and complimentary film to the perpetrator. When questioned further, the guide went on to elaborate the Disney rationale for control over the image: the "magic" would be broken if photos of disassembled characters circulated in the public sphere; children might suffer irreparable psychic trauma at the sight of a "beheaded" Mickey; Disney exercises control over the image to safeguard childhood fantasies.

What Disney employees refer to as the "magic" of Disney World has actually to do with the ability to produce fetishized consumptions. The unbroken seamlessness of Disney World, its totality as a consumable artifact, cannot tolerate the revelation of the real work that produces the commodity. There would be no magic if the public should see the entire cast of magicians in various stages of disassembly and fatigue. That selected individuals are permitted to witness the backstage labor facilitates the word-of-mouth affirmation of the tremendous organizational feat that produces Disney World. The interdiction against photography eliminates the possibility of discontinuity at the level of image. There are no images to compete with the copyright-perfect onstage images displayed for public consumption. It's not accidental that our tour guide underscored the fact that Disney costumes are tightly controlled. The character costumes are made at only one production site and this site supplies the costumes used at Tokyo's Disneyland and EuroDisney. There can be no culturally influenced variations on the Disney models. Control over the image ensures the replication of Disney worldwide. The prohibition against photographing disassembled characters is motivated by the same phobia of industrial espionage that runs rampant throughout the high-tech information industry. The woman in our tour group who ripped open her camera and destroyed her film may not have been wrong in acting out a spy melodrama. Her photos of the disassembled costumes might have revealed the manner of their production — rendering them accessible to non-Disney replication. At Disney World, the magic that resides in the integrity of childhood fantasy is inextricably linked to the fetishism of the commodity and the absolute control over private property as it is registered in the copyrighted image.

As I see it, the individual's right to imagine and to give expression to unique ways of seeing is at stake in struggles against private property. Mickey Mouse, notwithstanding his corporate copyright, exists in our common culture. He is the site for the enactment of childhood wishes and fantasies, for early conceptualizations and renderings of the body, a being who can be imagined as both self and other. If culture is held as private property, then there can be only one correct version of Mickey Mouse, whose logo-like image is the cancellation of creativity. But the multiplicity of quirky versions of Mickey Mouse that children draw can stand as a graphic question to us as adults: Who, indeed, owns Mickey Mouse?

What most distinguishes Disney World from any other amusement park is the way its spatial organization, defined by autonomous "worlds" and wholly themed environments, combines with the homogeneity of its visitors (predominantly white, middle-class families) to produce a sense of community. While Disney World includes an underlying utopian im-pulse, this is articulated with nostalgia for a small-town, small-business America (Main Street, U.S.A.), and the fantasy of a controllable corpo-ratist world (EPCOT). The illusion of community is enhanced by the longing for community that many visitors bring to the park, which they may feel is unavailable to them in their own careers, daily lives, and neighborhoods, thanks in large part to the systematic erosion of the pub-lic sector throughout the Reagan and Bush administrations. In the last decade the inroads of private, for-profit enterprise in areas previously de-fined by public control, and the hostile aggression of tax backlash cou-pled with "me first" attitudes have largely defeated the possibility of community in our homes and cities.

Whenever I visit Disney World, I invariably overhear other visitors making comparisons between Disney World and their home towns. They stare out over EPCOT's lake and wonder why developers back home don't produce similar aesthetic spectacles. They talk about botched, abandoned, and misconceived development projects that have wrecked their local landscapes. Others see Disney World as an oasis of social tranquility and security in comparison to their patrolled, but nonetheless deteriorating, maybe even perilous neighborhoods. A recent essay in *Time* captured some of these sentiments: "Do you see anybody [at Disney World] lying on the street or begging for money? Do you see anyone jumping on your car and wanting to clean your windshield — and when you say no, they get abusive?"[3]

Comments such as these do more than betray the class anxiety of the middle strata. They poignantly express the inability of this group to make distinctions between what necessarily constitutes the public and the private sectors. Do visitors forget that they pay a daily use fee (upwards of $150 for a four-day stay) just to be a citizen of Disney World (not to mention the $100 per night hotel bill)? Maybe so — and maybe it's precisely *forgetting* that visitors pay for.

If there is any distinction to be made between Disney World and our local shopping malls, it would have to do with Disney's successful exclusion of all factors that might put the lie to its uniform social fabric. The occasional Hispanic mother who arrives with extended family and illegal bologna sandwiches is an anomaly. So too is the first-generation Cubana who buys a year-round pass to Disney's nightspot, Pleasure Island, in hopes of meeting a rich and marriageable British tourist. These women testify to the presence of Orlando, Disney World's marginalized "Sister City," whose overflowing cheap labor force and overcrowded and under-funded public institutions are the unseen real world upon which Disney's world depends.

### Reading the Text

1. In Willis's view, how does Disney World create an artificial, programmed environment, and why does Disney World do this?
2. What does Willis mean when she claims that "Amusement is the commodified negation of play"?
3. Why does Willis believe that a theme park such as Disney World "puts the family back together"?
4. How does Disney World appeal to nonconformists?
5. What does Willis mean by saying that "Disney World is logoland"?
6. Summarize in your own words Willis's interpretation of the "magic" of Disney World.

### Reading the Signs

1. In class, brainstorm a list of Disney products, characters, and movies and then discuss the impact of the Disney corporation on American consumer life.

---

3. "Fantasy's Reality," *Time,* 27 May 1991, p. 54.

2. In an essay, write an argument that defends, refutes, or modifies Willis's assumption that Disney World is too controlling in its "processing" of visitors. If you prefer, you can focus your essay on any other Disney park you may have visited.

3. Visit a local theme park and study whether it controls the consumer habits of its visitors as Willis claims Disney World does. Then write an essay in which you analyze your park's control over consumer behavior.

4. Write an essay in which you describe how you would design a theme park for the twenty-first century. What themes would you emphasize? What activities and amenities would you provide, and what would they look like? Be sure to explain your choices and what messages you communicate to visitors.

5. At the close of her essay, Willis suggests a comparison between Disney World and shopping malls. In an essay, compare and contrast the ways that Disney World and a local mall you have visited control consumer spending habits. To develop your ideas, consult Anne Norton's "The Signs of Shopping" (p. 38).

# ROLAND BARTHES

## Toys

|||||||||||||||||||||||||||||||||||||||||||||||||||

*The founder of modern semiology and its application to popular culture, Roland Barthes (1915–1980) is a major figure in literary as well as cultural criticism, whose interests ranged from the French dramatist Racine to the fashion magazine* Elle. *In this selection from his ground-breaking book* Mythologies *(1957, trans. 1972), Barthes analyzes the cultural significance of French toys and the materials they are made of, hinting at a personal nostalgic preference for traditional materials like wood over the plastics that have taken over the toy world. Elsewhere in* Mythologies, *Barthes analyzes professional wrestling spectacles, striptease, plastic, Greta Garbo, cookery, and a host of other cultural signs. Without his pioneering studies, texts like the one you are reading probably would not have been possible.*

*The author of over twenty books, of which* Mythologies *is one of the earliest, Barthes was a professor at the Collège de France at his death in 1980.*

French toys: One could not find a better illustration of the fact that the adult Frenchman sees the child as another self. All the toys one commonly sees are essentially a microcosm of the adult world; they are all reduced copies of human objects, as if in the eyes of the public the child was, all told, nothing but a smaller man, a homunculus to whom must be supplied objects of his own size.

Invented forms are very rare: a few sets of blocks, which appeal to the spirit of do-it-yourself, are the only ones which offer dynamic forms. As for the others, French toys *always mean something,* and this something is always entirely socialized, constituted by the myths or the techniques of modern adult life: the army, broadcasting, the post office, medicine (miniature instrument-cases, operating theaters for dolls), school, hair styling (driers for permanent-waving), the air force (parachutists), transport (trains, Citroëns, Vedettes, Vespas,[1] petrol stations), science (Martian toys).

The fact that French toys *literally* prefigure the world of adult functions obviously cannot but prepare the child to accept them all, by constituting for him, even before he can think about it, the alibi of a Nature which has at all times created soldiers, postmen and Vespas. Toys here reveal the list of all the things the adult does not find unusual: war, bureaucracy, ugliness, Martians, etc. It is not so much, in fact, the imitation which is the sign of an abdication, as its literalness: French toys are like a Jivaro head, in which one recognizes, shrunken to the size of an apple, the wrinkles and hair of an adult. There exist, for instance, dolls which urinate; they have an esophagus, one gives them a bottle, they wet their nappies; soon, no doubt, milk will turn to water in their stomachs. This is meant to prepare the little girl for the causality of housekeeping, to "condition" her to her future role as mother. However, faced with this world of faithful and complicated objects, the child can only identify himself as owner, as user, never as creator; he does not invent the world, he uses it: There are, prepared for him, actions without adventure, without wonder, without joy. He is turned into a little stay-at-home householder who does not even have to invent the mainsprings of adult causality; they are supplied to him ready-made: He has only to help himself, he is never allowed to discover anything from start to finish. The merest set of blocks, provided it is not too refined, implies a very different learning of the world: Then, the child does not in any way create meaningful objects, it matters little to him whether they have an adult name; the actions he performs are not those of a user but those of a demiurge. He creates forms which walk, which roll, he creates life, not property: Objects now act by themselves, they are no longer an inert and complicated material in the palm of his hand. But such toys are rather rare: French toys are usually based on imitation, they are meant to produce children who are users, not creators.

The bourgeois status of toys can be recognized not only in their forms, which are all functional, but also in their substances. Current toys

---

1. **Vespa**  Italian motor scooter. — EDS.

are made of a graceless material, the product of chemistry, not of nature. Many are now molded from complicated mixtures; the plastic material of which they are made has an appearance at once gross and hygienic, it destroys all the pleasure, the sweetness, the humanity of touch. A sign which fills one with consternation is the gradual disappearance of wood, in spite of its being an ideal material because of its firmness and its softness, and the natural warmth of its touch. Wood removes, from all the forms which it supports, the wounding quality of angles which are too sharp, the chemical coldness of metal. When the child handles it and knocks it, it neither vibrates nor grates, it has a sound at once muffled and sharp. It is a familiar and poetic substance, which does not sever the child from close contact with the tree, the table, the floor. Wood does not wound or break down; it does not shatter, it wears out, it can last a long time, live with the child, alter little by little the relations between the object and the hand. If it dies, it is in dwindling, not in swelling out like those mechanical toys which disappear behind the hernia of a broken spring. Wood makes essential objects, objects for all time. Yet there hardly remain any of these wooden toys from the Vosges, these fretwork farms with their animals, which were only possible, it is true, in the days of the craftsman. Henceforth, toys are chemical in substance and color; their very material introduces one to a coenaesthesis[2] of use, not pleasure. These toys die in fact very quickly, and once dead, they have no posthumous life for the child.

### Reading the Text

1. What does Barthes mean by saying that "French toys literally prefigure the world of adult functions"?
2. What, according to Barthes, is the significance of the *materials* with which toys are made? What is the difference between the meaning of plastic and that of wood?

### Reading the Signs

1. Barthes assumes that children are passive users of toys. Discuss whether you agree with his assumption, basing your argument on your own experience as a child and your observations of young children.
2. In small groups, brainstorm American toys, then classify them according to areas of adult life as Barthes does in his second paragraph. How do your categories compare with Barthes's? What is the significance of any differences you may find?

---

2. **coenaesthesis**   One's general awareness of the body and its condition. — EDS.

3. Bring a toy to class and, in a brief oral presentation, interpret its significance. Then, after the entire class has presented, look at the *range* of toys brought in. What does the range say about the values and culture of your class?

4. Barthes claims that French toys are small versions of the adult world. Visit a local toy store, and survey the products to see if this claim applies to American toys in the 1990s. What do the results of your survey reveal about American culture?

5. Read or review Emily Prager's "Our Barbies, Ourselves" (p. 375). Writing as Roland Barthes, interpret Barbie semiotically, being sure to relate Barbie to other dolls in the toy system.

# CHAPTER TWO

# BROUGHT TO YOU
# B(U)Y

## *The Signs of Advertising*

**A**re you wearing jeans? What brand? Gap? Levi's? Bugle Boys? Jordache? The brand matters, doesn't it? Because those aren't just jeans you're wearing, they're a statement. They project an image. In the last chapter we looked at the many ways in which the products you buy make statements, but there is another part of the story to tell. You often have an assistant on hand to help you choose the images that you want your belongings to project, an assistant whose primary interest is that you buy a particular product. He or she goes by another name, however: This assistant is an advertiser.

Advertising: It's not just show and tell. Just think of the many ways jeans alone are pitched in America. Take Levi's as an example. How are they packaged for the marketplace? What sorts of images are associated with them today? Take care to be up to date, because those images change rapidly, as the trends of popular culture change. In the 1980s, for example, Levi's were promoted as hip urban wear in TV spots set on city streets, where they were associated with the blues as "Levi's 501 Blues." These commercials were notable for the way they took a fashion that had been associated with rural and wilderness settings in the 1960s, with the "back-to-the-land" movement, and redefined them as a part of the "back-to-the-city" trend of the eighties. The significance of this shift, once more, lay in a *difference,* in the vast gap between Walden and Wall Street. But that was then and this is now. Look at a Levi's display in your local department store. With what are they

associated today? Do these associations make you want to go out and
but a pair?

By the 1990s, for instance, a prominent campaign for Guess? jeans
signified a shift in the geography of popular cultural desire. These ads,
featuring models such as Claudia Schiffer, exuded sexuality and often
adopted country-western motifs. In one print-ad series, Schiffer appears
in jeans and cowboy hat, standing outside some small-town desert convenience store in one shot; in the next shot, she's dancing on the hood of
a vintage Lincoln Continental while her cowboy-hatted boyfriend
swings her blouse in the air. The choice of such scenic details is not accidental: It signifies an advertiser's calculation that a set of steamy country-
western images will appeal to the desires of a projected market. Without
those desires, the ad would fall flat.

## Interpreting the Signs of Advertising

Let's say you are assigned the task of writing a semiotic analysis of an
advertisement, and you choose a print ad for blue jeans — in particular,
an ad campaign for Calvin Klein jeans that drew a lot of political as well
as consumer attention in 1995. One representative ad in the campaign
features a boy and a girl, both epitomes of the "waif" look exemplified
by the fragile-looking supermodel Kate Moss: straight, bleached hair,
very thin bodies. They stand next to an ordinary ladder with a simple
paneled wall for a backdrop. The boy is shirtless, the girl wears a revealing white tank top. Both figures thrust their pelvises forward in
provocative poses, and the girl's makeup suggests that her eyes have
been blackened. Finally, both models appear to be in their early adolescence, perhaps fourteen years old.

To interpret this ad, you need first, as always in a semiotic analysis,
to suspend your opinion of the actual object of your analysis — in this
case, Calvin Klein jeans. What you are studying is the image with which
the object is associated. To analyze that image, you will want to study
the details of the ad itself and the cultural system in which the ad functions, looking for both associations and differences. Let's begin by considering the cultural system.

We can note, for example, that Calvin Klein's advertisers have long
used youthful sexuality to promote jeans, starting with fifteen-year-old
Brooke Shields, who cooed that nothing came between her and her
Calvins. Similarly, the Guess? campaigns also employed youthful sexuality, as did the Jordache campaign in the seventies. In other words, advertisers have been using sexual imagery to sell jeans for a long time,
and through such a set of associations we can draw the semiotic conclusion that sex sells in America, especially among young consumers of
blue jeans.

But the matter is more complicated than that, because there are some crucial differences about the ad we are interpreting. The most striking difference is that such a howl of protest accompanied the running of the campaign in which it was featured that Calvin Klein withdrew the ad. And while it is true that some criticized the Brooke Shields ad campaign back in 1980, the opposition was never severe enough to cause a cancellation. So, something changed, and that change is crucial to our analysis.

Let's look again at some of the details of the ad for clues. Like the Brooke Shields campaign before it, the ad features a sexy teenage girl, but unlike the earlier ad, a young boy is also featured. Also contrasting with the earlier campaign is the tone of the images. Already famous as a glamorous child fashion model and movie star, Shields appears in her ads as a girl in charge of her sexuality and her world, confidently issuing the proclamation, "Nothing comes between me and my Calvins." The children in the later Klein ad, in contrast, don't look like they're in charge at all. There's a hint that, if anything, they're in bondage, offering themselves to the gaze of some sleazy voyeur. This suggestion comes from the makeup that hints at beatings, and the pairing of the two figures against a plain, even harsh, background that evokes the aura of a low-budget child pornography video. The *next* scene, the ad suggests, will show these two children coupling.

One might object that we are "reading too much into the ad." But a look at the ad's public reception — the social context in which it is meaningful — suggests that this interpretation may not be so far-fetched after all. The ad met with immediate and vocal public protest — and was quickly canceled as a result, suggesting that many who viewed it saw just what we have described. It wasn't the sexuality that caused all the trouble — as we've seen, that's been a staple of blue-jean advertising for years — it was the suggestion of child abuse and exploitation. And this, in turn, raises another set of questions for semiotic analysis.

That is, why would Calvin Klein use such images, and why were critics so quick to protest the ads? Let's take the first question. It could be argued that the ad's details were meant to signify what might be called "grunge sexuality." *Kids,* a controversial movie that appeared shortly before the Klein ads, also featured youthful grunge sexuality, as well as the kind of stark scenic backdrops characteristic of the Klein campaign, and so Klein may have been simply trying to piggyback onto the film in order to attract young consumers. So why the protest?

Here we can look at a broader cultural change. Until recently, the subject of child abuse — of which child pornography is a particularly ugly example — was taboo in American society. It happened, but we didn't talk about it. But in the past few years the topic has been put on the front burner of American consciousness, and not only among oversensitive adults. Consider the subject of one of Pearl Jam's earliest hits, "Jeremy," a song that tells the story of a mistreated child. Or of Ten

Thousand Maniacs' "What's the Matter Here," which graphically describes suburban child abuse. What was once unspoken can now be found on the pop charts, and with that shift in consciousness has come a greater sensitivity to potentially abusive images. The appearance of these two black-eyed waifs sporting that "abandoned" look one finds so often in fashion photography lately is thus more likely to provoke an accusation of child exploitation than it was in the days when such subjects weren't part of public consciousness.

Furthermore, we can expand the scope of our survey of fashion advertising to note that a great many advertisements in the nineties feature models whose expressions could be described as everything from waiflike and abandoned to outright sexual suffering. Take a look at any contemporary fashion magazine. Note how often the women, in particular, appear as if they're about to be attacked. And even when things aren't that extreme, consider the serious expressions they often have on their faces. In conventional fashion advertising — just look at a mail-order catalog — everyone looks happy. But high fashion imagery in the nineties seems to require some sort of hint at sadomasochism. In such an environment, the Calvin Klein ads can be associated with a trend in which sex and suffering have been bonded: the traditional formula for pornography.

So where does this leave us? We have a set of associations and differences, along with a sense of the cultural moment in which the ad appears. The next thing we need to do is build a thesis — then we're ready to write.

Since the ad *could* be interpreted as simply being part of grunge-fashion imagery, and thus harmless, one thesis could be that the ad's critics misinterpreted it. But our thesis will be that the ad wasn't misinterpreted, that it deliberately uses images hinting at child abuse in order to sell jeans. The body of our essay would then be devoted to defending this thesis.

The evidence we would use to defend our argument has already been suggested in our overview of both the details of the ad and the systems in which it functions. We would point, for example, to the *difference* between the image of Brooke Shields' confidently empowered sexuality and the vulnerable and brutalized images in the more recent ad to support our contention that the image is not simply one of teen-aged sexuality designed simply for teen viewers. We would also point to the *difference* between Calvin Klein's response to past criticism (he's never backed down before) and his decision to pull the campaign: The suggestion here is of a recognition that things may have gone too far. We would also point to a *system* of fashion advertisements that feature quasi-pornographic or sadomasochistic images with which the Klein ads can be associated. Finally, we would argue that the movie *Kids* itself supports our contention, insofar as the film presented bleak images of teen sex for the voyeuristic pleasure of old as well as young viewers.

---

### Exploring the Signs of Advertising

Select one of the products advertised in the "Portfolio of Advertisements" (pp. 178–187) and design in your journal an alternative ad for that product. Consider what different images or cast of characters you could include. What different myths — and thus different values — could you use to pitch this product?

Then freewrite on the significance of your alternative ad. If you have any difficulty imagining an alternative image for the product, what does that say about the power of advertising to control our view of the world? What does your choice of imagery and cultural myths say about you?

---

Having assembled the evidence, we can now present a larger conclusion based on our thesis: that America is going through a period of cultural fascination with such traditionally forbidden forms of sexual expression as pedophilia and sadomasochism, an obsession strong enough both to cause advertisers to exploit it in the never-ending struggle to move the goods and to cause protesters to denounce just how far advertisers are willing to go.

## The Semiotic Foundation

Having outlined a semiotic analysis of a particular advertisement, we'll turn now to a semiotic overview of the overall logic of advertising. Indeed, there is perhaps no better field for semiotic analysis than advertising, for ads work characteristically by substituting signs for things, and by reading those signs you can discover the values and desires that advertisers seek to exploit.

It has long been recognized that advertisements substitute images of desire for the actual products, that Coca-Cola ads, for example, don't really sell soda: They sell images of fun, or popularity, or of sheer celebrity, promising a gratifying association with the likes of Paula Abdul or Whitney Houston if you'll only drink "The Real Thing." Automobile commercials, for their part, are notorious for selling not transportation but fantasies of power, prestige, sexual potency, or even generational solidarity, as a Mercedes Benz commercial featuring the crooning voice of the late Janis Joplin demonstrates in its appeal to baby-boom consumers most likely to recognize her song "Lord, Won't You Buy Me a Mercedes-Benz."

By substituting desirable images for concrete needs, modern advertising seeks to transform desire into necessity. You *need* food, for example, but it takes an ad campaign to convince you through attractive images that you need a Big Mac. Your job may require you to have a car, but it's an ad that persuades you that a Jeep Cherokee is necessary for your happiness. If advertising worked otherwise, it would simply present you with a functional profile of a product and let you decide whether it will do the job.

From the early twentieth century, advertisers have seen their task as the transformation of desire into necessity. In the twenties and thirties, for example, voluminously printed advertisements created elaborate story lines designed to convince readers that they needed this mouthwash to attract a spouse or that caffeine-free breakfast drink to avoid trouble on the job or in the home. In such ads, products were made to appear not only desirable but absolutely necessary. Without them, your very survival as a socially competent being would be in question.

Many ads still work this way, particularly "guilt" ads that prey on your insecurities and fears. Deodorants are typically pitched in such a fashion, playing upon our fear of smelling bad in public. Can you think of any other products whose ads play upon guilt or shame? Do you find them to be effective?

## The Commodification of Desire

Associating a logically unrelated desire with an actual product (as in pitching beer through sexual come-ons) can be called the "commodification" of desire. In other words, desire itself becomes the product that the advertiser is selling. This marketing of desire was recognized as early as the 1950s in Vince Packard's *The Hidden Persuaders*. In that book, Packard points out how by the 1950s America was well along in its historic shift from a producing to a consuming economy. The implications for advertisers were enormous. Since the American economy was increasingly dependent on the constant growth of consumption, as the introduction to Chapter 1 of this text discusses, manufacturers had to find ways to convince people to consume ever more goods. So they turned to the advertising mavens on Madison Avenue, who responded with advertisements that persuaded consumers to replace perfectly serviceable products with "new and improved" substitutions within an overall economy of planned design obsolescence.

America's transformation from a producer to a consumer economy also explains that while advertising is a worldwide phenomenon, it is nowhere so prevalent as it is here. Open a copy of the popular French picture magazine *Paris Match*. You'll find plenty of paparazzi photos of international celebrities but almost no advertisements. Then open a copy of *Vogue*. It is essentially a catalog, where scarcely a page is without its ad. Indeed, advertisers themselves call this plethora of advertising "clutter" that they must creatively "cut through" each time they design a new ad campaign. The ubiquity of advertising in our lives points to a society in which people are constantly pushed to buy, as opposed to economies like Japan's that emphasize constant increases in production. And desire is what loosens the pocketbook strings.

While the basic logic of advertising may be similar from era to era, the content of an ad, and hence its significance, differs as popular culture changes. Looking at ads from different eras tells the tale. Advertising in the 1920s, for instance, focused especially on its market's desires for improved social status. Ads for elocution and vocabulary lessons, for example, appealed to working- and lower-middle-class consumers who were invited to fantasize that buying the product or service could help them enter the middle class. Meanwhile, middle-class consumers were invited to compare their enjoyment of the sponsor's product with that of the upper-class models shown happily slurping this coffee or purchasing that vacuum cleaner in the ad. Of course, things haven't changed *that* much since the twenties. Can you think of any ads that use this strategy today? How often are glamorous celebrities called in to make you identify with his or her "enjoyment" of a product? Have you heard ads for vocabulary-building programs that promise you a "verbal advantage" in the corporate struggle?

One particularly amusing ad from the twenties played upon America's fear of communism in the wake of the Bolshevik Revolution in Russia. "Is your washroom breeding Bolsheviks?" asks a print ad from the Scot paper towel company. The ad's lengthy copy explains how it might be doing so: If your company restroom is stocked with inferior paper towels, it says, discontent will proliferate among your employees and lead to subversive activities. R.C.A. Victor and Campbell's Soup, we are assured, are no such breeding grounds of subversion, thanks to their contracts with Scot. You, too, can fight the good fight against communism by buying Scot Towels, the ad suggests. To whom do you think this ad was directed? What did they fear?

## Populism Versus Elitism

American advertising tends to swing in a pendulum motion between the status-conscious ads that dominated the twenties and the more populist approach of decades like the seventies, when country music and truck-driving cowboys lent their popular appeal to Madison Avenue. This swing between elitist and populist approaches in advertising reflects a basic division within the American Dream itself, a mythic promise that at once celebrates democratic equality *and* encourages you to rise above the crowd, to be better than anyone else. Sometimes Americans are more attracted to one side than the other, but there is bound to be a shift back

||||||||||||||||||||||||||||||||||||||||||||||||||||||||||||||||||||||||||||||||||||||||||||||||||||||||||||||||||||||||||

### Discussing the Signs of Advertising

Bring to class a print ad from a newspaper or magazine and in small groups discuss your semiotic reading of it. Be sure to ask, "Why am I being shown this or being told that?" How do the characters in the ad function as signs? What sort of people don't appear as characters? What cultural myths are invoked in this ad? What relationship do you see between those myths and the intended audience of the publication? Which ads do your group members respond to positively and why? Which ads doesn't your group like?

to the other side when the thrill wears off. Thus, the populist appeal of the seventies (even disco had a distinct working-class flavor: Recall John Travolta's character in *Saturday Night Fever*) gave way to the elitist eighties, and advertising followed. Products such as Gallo's varietal wines, once considered barely a step up from jug wine, courted an upscale market through ads that featured classy yuppies serving it along with their salmon and asparagus, while Michelob light beer promised its fans that they "could have it all." Status advertising was all the rage in that glitzy, go-for-the-gold decade. Do ads work this way today? Or has the pendulum shifted back to populism, to democratic equality? Can you think of any ads that might be a sign of such a shift?

Determining whether the dominant tone of advertising at any given time is populist or elitist is one way of using advertisements as a kind of weather vane of shifting cultural trends. They help you know which way the wind blows. But a lot of other things in an ad can help you get a sense of the cultural environment in which they appear. We've looked at one such cultural weather signal in our analysis of a Calvin Klein jeans ad. But a culture is very complex, of course, and all sorts of contradictory cultural trends may occur at any given time. To see how, let's look now at an ad campaign that ran at the same time as the Klein ad, a campaign that, far from raising controversy, has shaped up as the most successful advertising gambit of our decade.

### Pink Rabbits

Consider the Energizer battery ad series that features a pink mechanical bunny who beats his drum as he storms through a sequence of mock advertisements to show how he "keeps going and going and going" on an Energizer battery. The ad's apparent point is to tell you how long an

Energizer battery lasts, but it could have done that by simply presenting battery test statistics (a dull though still usable advertising strategy). So what is the ad really doing?

First, it helps to know that when the pink bunny commercials initially appeared, a chief competitor, Duracell, already had for some time been running ads that featured contests between battery-operated toys which "demonstrated" the long-lasting superiority of Duracell products. That's part of the system in which the Energizer ad functions. So, here comes that bunny. How does his appearance relate to the Duracell ads? Does it suggest that the Energizer people have come up with a better *battery* or a better *ad*?

Now let's expand the system. When that bunny suddenly interrupts a startlingly realistic "commercial" for "Chateau Marmoset" wine, for instance, it reminds us of the rather pretentious campaign that Gallo had pitched to the yuppie market. In spoof after spoof, the Energizer ads invite us to relate them to the commercial system as a whole, to the entire terrain of American advertising. So what effects do *these* comparisons have?

Think about it. When you're sick of something, don't you like to see a good parody of it? It appears, then, that the Energizer spoofs are appealing to a certain disgust in its intended audience, a weariness with Madison Avenue gimmicks. Isn't that what the ads are doing, playing to your skepticism of advertising?

In short, in a skeptical climate, the Energizer bunny tells us, really clever advertisers (like the creators of the Joe Isuzu campaign that played upon consumer skepticism of extravagant claims in automotive advertising) come up with new ways of making us identify with their product. Gladly recognizing spoof ads as reflections of their own frustration with silly and manipulative advertising, viewers find themselves identifying with the creators and sponsors of spoof commercials. And thus they buy a product not because it is better but because they feel good about the way is was presented to them (so good that, in the case of the Energizer bunny, they went out in large numbers to buy pink bunny toys and other spin-off paraphernalia). So nothing has really changed: Once again a sign has been substituted for a thing, commodifying the consumer desire to be free of commodified desire.

We can go further. The Energizer bunny campaign can be referred to a larger system beyond the advertising world, to a social complex where citizen-consumers are becoming increasingly fed up (and with good reason) with the cynicism of the powerful in America, whether they be politicians or advertisers. As such, our bunny serves as a cultural barometer, pointing toward the same social forces that produced Ross Perot's campaign for the presidency in 1992 and the increasing popularity of registering as an independent rather than as a democrat or republican. But the fact that our barometric reading comes from an *ad* is itself a

<sub>IIIIIIIIIIIIIIIIIIIIIIIIIIIIIIIIIIIIIIIIIIIIIIIIIIIIIIIIIIIIIIIIIIIIIIIIIIIIIIIIIIIIIIIIIIIIIIIIIIIIIIIIIIIIIIIIIIIIIIIIIIIIIIIIIIIIIIIIIIIIIIIIIIII</sub>

### Reading Advertising on the Net

Advertising typically reflects the moods, values, and interests of the decade in which it is produced. Visit *Advertising Age*'s Fifty Best Commercials page (http://adage.com/news_and_features/special_reports/commercials/index.html), a compendium of blockbuster ads from the 1950s to the present. How have the advertising techniques changed through the decades? What do those changes say about the tone and interests of each decade?

sign of just how entrenched the current system is. For as the bunny tells us, the powerful are always one step ahead. In response to voter frustration, political incumbents run their campaigns as if they were political "outsiders," while advertisers, detecting a growing consumer immunity to advertising, run anticommercial commercials. The system remains the same; only the strategies change.

So in reading an ad, always ask, "Why am I being shown *that,* or being told *this*?" Cast yourself as the director of an ad, asking yourself what you would do to pitch a product, then look at what the advertiser has done. Pay attention to the way an ad's imagery is organized. Every detail counts. Why are these colors used (or lack of color, as in many Guess? ads)? Why are cute stuffed animals chosen to pitch toilet paper? What are those people *doing* in that perfume commercial? Why the cowboy hat in an ad for jeans? How does the slogan "Just Do It" sell Nikes? Look too for what the ad *doesn't* include: Is it missing a clear view of the product itself or an ethnically diverse cast of characters? In short, when interpreting an ad, transform it into a text and read it as you would a poem or an editorial or any piece of rhetoric, for in its mandate to persuade, advertising constitutes the most potent rhetoric of our times.

### The Readings

Our selections in this chapter include interpretations and analyses of the world of advertising, as well as advertisements for you to interpret yourselves. The chapter begins with a historical perspective: Roland Marchand's "The Parable of the Democracy of Goods" shows how advertisers in the 1920s played upon the unconscious desires of their market by exploiting the fundamental myths of American culture. Jack Solomon follows with a semiotic analysis of the culture of American advertising, exploring the underlying value systems that cause us to respond to advertisements in the ways that we do. Leslie Savan provides a biting analysis of the ways in which boomer ad execs seek to exploit the GenX market, while Patricia J. Williams examines both the elusiveness of truth in advertising imagery and the resulting legal implications. A pair of readings address gender issues: Diane Barthel's analysis of the images of men in advertising complements Gloria Steinem's insider's view of what goes on behind the scenes at women's magazines. Ronald K. L. Collins and David M. Skover follow with an indictment of the language of advertising, accusing it of constituting a socially stifling "brave new world" for our times. And finally, we include a portfolio of print ads for you to decode.

# ROLAND MARCHAND
## *The Parable of the Democracy of Goods*

||||||||||||||||||||||||||||||||||||||||||||||||||||||

*Advertisements do not simply reflect American myths, they create them, as Roland Marchand shows in this selection from* Advertising the American Dream *(1985). Focusing on elaborate advertising narratives, he describes "The Parable of the Democracy of Goods," which pitches a product by convincing middle-class consumers that, by buying this toilet seat or that brand of coffee, they can share an experience with the very richest Americans. The advertising strategies Marchand analyzes date from the 1920s to 1940s, and new "parables" have since appeared that reflect more modern times, but even the oldest are still in use today. A professor of history at the University of California, Davis, Marchand is also the author of* The American Peace Movement and Social Reform, 1898–1918 *(1973). A specialist in the history of advertising, media, and American culture, Marchand is completing* Creating the Corporate Soul: The Rise of Corporate Public Relations and Institutional Advertising, *to be published in 1997.*

As they opened their September 1929 issue, readers of the *Ladies' Home Journal* were treated to an account of the care and feeding of young Livingston Ludlow Biddle III, scion of the wealthy Biddles of Philadelphia, whose family coat-of-arms graced the upper right-hand corner of the page. Young Master Biddle, mounted on his tricycle, fixed a serious, slightly pouting gaze upon the reader, while the Cream of Wheat Corporation rapturously explained his constant care, his carefully regulated play and exercise, and the diet prescribed for him by "famous specialists." As master of Sunny Ridge Farm, the Biddles's winter estate in North Carolina, young Livingston III had "enjoyed every luxury of social position and wealth, since the day he was born." Yet, by the grace of a modern providence, it happened that Livingston's health was protected by a "simple plan every mother can use." Mrs. Biddle gave Cream of Wheat to the young heir for both breakfast and supper. The world's foremost child experts knew of no better diet; great wealth could procure no finer nourishment. As Cream of Wheat's advertising agency summarized the central point of the campaign that young Master Biddle initiated, "every mother can give her youngsters the fun and benefits of a Cream of Wheat breakfast just as do the parents of these boys and girls who have the best that wealth can command."[1]

---

1. *Ladies' Home Journal,* Sept. 1929, second cover; *JWT News Letter,* Oct. 1, 1929, p. 1, J. Walter Thompson Company (JWT) Archives, New York City.

While enjoying this glimpse of childrearing among the socially distinguished, *Ladies' Home Journal* readers found themselves schooled in one of the most pervasive of all advertising tableaux of the 1920s — the parable of the Democracy of Goods. According to this parable, the wonders of modern mass production and distribution enabled every person to enjoy the society's most significant pleasure, convenience, or benefit. The definition of the particular benefit fluctuated, of course, with each client who employed the parable. But the cumulative effect of the constant reminders that "any woman can" and "every home can afford" was to publicize an image of American society in which concentrated wealth at the top of a hierarchy of social classes restricted no family's opportunity to acquire the most significant products.[2] By implicitly defining "democracy" in terms of equal access to consumer products, and then by depicting the everyday functioning of that "democracy" with regard to one product at a time, these tableaux offered Americans an inviting vision of their society as one of incontestable equality.

In its most common advertising formula, the concept of the Democracy of Goods asserted that although the rich enjoyed a great variety of luxuries, the acquisition of their *one* most significant luxury would provide anyone with the ultimate in satisfaction. For instance, a Chase and Sanborn's Coffee tableau, with an elegant butler serving a family in a dining room with a sixteen-foot ceiling, reminded Chicago families that although "compared with the riches of the more fortunate, your way of life may seem modest indeed," yet no one — "king, prince, statesman, or capitalist" — could enjoy better coffee.[3] The Association of Soap and Glycerine Producers proclaimed that the charm of cleanliness was as readily available to the poor as to the rich, and Ivory Soap reassuringly related how one young housewife, who couldn't afford a $780-a-year maid like her neighbor, still maintained a significant equality in "nice hands" by using Ivory.[4] The C. F. Church Manufacturing Company epitomized this version of the parable of the Democracy of Goods in an ad entitled "a bathroom luxury everyone can afford": "If you lived in one of those palatial apartments on Park Avenue, in New York City, where you have to pay $2,000 to $7,500 a year rent, you still couldn't have a better toilet seat in your bathroom than they have — the Church Sani-white Toilet Seat which you can afford to have right now."[5]

---

2. *Saturday Evening Post,* Apr. 3, 1926, pp. 182–83; Nov. 6, 1926, p. 104; Apr. 16, 1927, p. 199; Scrapbook 54 (Brunswick-Balke-Collender), Lord and Thomas Archives, at Foote, Cone and Belding Communications, Inc., Chicago.

3. *Chicago Tribune,* Nov. 21, 1926, picture section, p. 2.

4. *Los Angeles Times,* July 14, 1929, part VI, p. 3; *Tide,* July 1928, p. 10; *Photoplay Magazine,* Mar. 1930, p. 1.

5. *American Magazine,* Mar. 1926, p. 112.

Thus, according to the parable, no discrepancies in wealth could prevent the humblest citizens, provided they chose their purchases wisely, from retiring to a setting in which they could contemplate their essential equality, through possession of an identical product, with the nation's millionaires. In 1929, Howard Dickinson, a contributor to *Printers' Ink,* concisely expressed the social psychology behind Democracy of Goods advertisements: "'With whom do the mass of people think they want to foregather?' asks the psychologist in advertising. 'Why, with the wealthy and socially distinguished, of course!' If we can't get an invitation to tea for our millions of customers, we can at least present the fellowship of using the same brand of merchandise. And it works."[6]

Some advertisers found it more efficacious to employ the parable's negative counterpart — the Democracy of Afflictions. Listerine contributed significantly to this approach. Most of the unsuspecting victims of halitosis in the mid-1920s possessed wealth and high social position. Other discoverers of new social afflictions soon took up the battle cry of "nobody's immune." "Body Odor plays no favorites," warned Lifebuoy Soap. No one, "banker, baker, or society woman," could count himself safe from B.O.[7] The boss, as well as the employees, might find himself "caught off guard" with dirty hands or cuffs, the Soap and Glycerine Producers assured readers of *True Story.* By 1930, Absorbine Jr. was beginning to document the democratic advance of "athlete's foot" into those rarefied social circles occupied by the "daintiest member of the junior set" and the noted yachtsman who owned "a railroad or two" (Fig. 1).[8]

The central purpose of the Democracy of Afflictions tableaux was to remind careless or unsuspecting readers of the universality of the threat from which the product offered protection or relief. Only occasionally did such ads address those of the upper classes who might think that their status and "fastidious" attention to personal care made them immune from common social offenses. In 1929 Listerine provided newspaper readers an opportunity to listen while a doctor, whose clientele included those of "the better class," confided "what I know about *nice* women."[9] One might have thought that Listerine was warning complacent, upper-class women that they were not immune from halitosis — except that the ad appeared in the *Los Angeles Times,* not *Harper's Bazaar.* Similarly, Forhan's toothpaste and the Soap Producers did not place their Democracy of Afflictions ads in *True Story* in order to reach the social elite. Rather, these tableaux provided en-

6. *Printers' Ink,* Oct. 10, 1929, p. 138.

7. *Tide,* Sept. 15, 1927, p. 5; *American Magazine,* Aug. 1929, p. 93; *True Story,* June 1929, p. 133; *Chicago Tribune,* Jan. 11, 1928, p. 16; Jan. 18, 1928, p. 15; Jan. 28, 1928, p. 7; *Photoplay Magazine,* Feb. 1929, p. 111.

8. *True Story,* May 1928, p. 83; June 1929, p. 133; *American Magazine,* Feb. 1930, p. 110; *Saturday Evening Post,* Aug. 23, 1930, p. 124.

9. *Los Angeles Times,* July 6, 1929, p. 3.

FIGURE 1   A negative appeal transformed the Democracy of Goods into the Democracy of Afflictions. Common folk learned from this parable that they could inexpensively avoid afflictions that beset even the yachting set.

ticing glimpses into the lives of the wealthy while suggesting an equalizing "fellowship" in shared susceptibilities to debilitating ailments. The parable of the Democracy of Goods always remained implicit in its negative counterpart. It assured readers that they could be as healthy, as charming, as free from social offense as the very "nicest" (richest) people, simply by using a product that anyone could afford.

Another variation of the parable of the Democracy of Goods employed historical comparisons to celebrate even the humblest of contemporary Americans as "kings in cottages." "No monarch in all history ever saw the day he could have half as much as you," proclaimed Paramount Pictures. Even reigning sovereigns of the present, Paramount continued, would envy readers for their "luxurious freedom and opportunity" to enter a magnificent, bedazzling "palace for a night," be greeted with fawning bows by liveried attendants, and enjoy modern entertainment for a modest price (Fig. 2). The Fisher Body Corporation coined the phrase "For Kings in Cottages" to compliment ordinary Americans on their freedom from "hardships" that even kings had been forced to endure in the past. Because

FIGURE 2   Of course, real kings had never shared their status with crowds of other "kings." But the parable of the Democracy of Goods offered a brief, "packaged experience" of luxury and preference.

of a lack of technology, monarchs who traveled in the past had "never enjoyed luxury which even approached that of the present-day automobile." The "American idea," epitomized by the Fisher Body Corporation, was destined to carry the comforts and luxuries conducive to human happiness into "the life of even the humblest cottager."[10]

Even so, many copywriters perceived that equality with past monarchs might not rival the vision of joining the fabled "Four Hundred" that Ward McAllister had marked as America's social elite at the end of the nineteenth century. Americans, in an ostensibly conformist age,

10. *Saturday Evening Post,* May 8, 1926, p. 59; *American Magazine,* May 1932, pp. 76–77. See also *Saturday Evening Post,* July 18, 1931, pp. 36–37; Aug. 1, 1931, pp. 30–31; *Better Homes and Gardens,* Mar. 1930, p. 77.

hungered for exclusivity. So advertising tableaux celebrated their ascension into this fabled and exclusive American elite. Through mass production and the resulting lower prices, the tableaux explained, the readers could purchase goods formerly available only to the rich — and thus gain admission to a "400" that now numbered millions.

The Simmons Company confessed that inner-coil mattresses had once been a luxury possessed only by the very wealthy. But now (in 1930) they were "priced so everybody in the United States can have one at $19.95." Woodbury's Soap advised the "working girl" readers of *True Story* of their arrival within a select circle. "Yesterday," it recalled, "the skin you love to touch" had been "the privilege of one woman in 65," but today it had become "the beauty right of every woman."[11] If the Democracy of Goods could establish an equal consumer right to beauty, then perhaps even the ancient religious promise of equality in death might be realized, at least to the extent that material provisions sufficed. In 1927 the Clark Grave Vault Company defined this unique promise: "Not so many years ago the use of a burial vault was confined largely to the rich. . . . Now every family, regardless of its means, may provide absolute protection against the elements of the ground."[12] If it seemed that the residents of Clark vaults had gained equality with the "400" too belatedly for maximum satisfaction, still their loving survivors could now share the same sense of comfort in the "absolute protection" of former loved ones as did the most privileged elites.

The social message of the parable of the Democracy of Goods was     10
clear. Antagonistic envy of the rich was unseemly; programs to redistribute wealth were unnecessary. The best things in life were already available to all at reasonable prices. But the prevalence of the parable of the Democracy of Goods in advertising tableaux did not necessarily betray a concerted conspiracy on the part of advertisers and their agencies to impose a social ideology on the American people. Most advertisers employed the parable of the Democracy of Goods primarily as a narrow, nonideological merchandising tactic. Listerine and Lifebuoy found the parable an obvious, attention-getting strategy for persuading readers that if even society women and bankers were unconsciously guilty of social offenses, the readers themselves were not immune. Simmons Mattresses, Chevrolet, and Clark Grave Vaults chose the parable in an attempt to broaden their market to include lower-income groups. The parable emphasized the affordability of the product to families of modest income while attempting to maintain a "class" image of the product as the preferred choice of their social betters.

---

11. *Saturday Evening Post,* Nov. 10, 1928, p. 90; *True Story,* Aug. 1934, p. 57. See also *Chicago Tribune,* Oct. 8, 1930, p. 17; *American Magazine,* Aug. 1930, p. 77; *Woman's Home Companion,* May 1927, p. 96.

12. *American Magazine,* Feb. 1927, p. 130.

Most advertisers found the social message of the parable of the Democracy of Goods a congenial and unexceptionable truism. They also saw it, like the other parables prevalent in advertising tableaux, as an epigrammatic statement of a conventional popular belief. Real income was rising for nearly all Americans during the 1920s, except for some farmers and farmworkers and those in a few depressed industries. Citizens seemed eager for confirmation that they were now driving the same make of car as the wealthy elites and serving their children the same cereal enjoyed by Livingston Ludlow Biddle III. Advertisers did not have to impose the parable of the Democracy of Goods on a contrary-minded public. Theirs was the easier task of subtly substituting this vision of equality, which was certainly satisfying *as a vision,* for broader and more traditional hopes and expectations of an equality of self-sufficiency, personal independence, and social interaction.

Perhaps the most attractive aspect of this parable to advertisers was that it preached the coming of an equalizing democracy without sacrificing those fascinating contrasts of social condition that had long been the touchstone of high drama. Henry James, writing of Hawthorne, had once lamented the obstacles facing the novelist who wrote of an America that lacked such tradition-laden institutions as a sovereign, a court, an aristocracy, or even a class of country gentlemen. Without castles, manors, and thatched cottages, America lacked those stark juxtapositions of pomp and squalor, nobility and peasantry, wealth and poverty that made Europe so rich a source of social drama.[13] But many versions of the parable of the Democracy of Goods sought to offset that disadvantage without gaining James's desired "complexity of manners." They dressed up America's wealthy as dazzling aristocrats, and then reassured readers that they could easily enjoy an essential equality with such elites in the things that really mattered. The rich were decorative and fun to look at, but in their access to those products most important to comfort and satisfaction, as the magazine *Delineator* put it, "The Four Hundred" had become "the four million."[14] Advertisers left readers to assume that they could gain the same satisfactions of exclusiveness from belonging to the four million as had once been savored by the four hundred.

While parables of consumer democracy frequently used terms like "everyone," "anyone," "any home," or "every woman," these categories were mainly intended to comprise the audience of "consumer-citizens" envisioned by the advertising trade, or families economically among the nation's top 50 percent. Thus the *Delineator* had more in mind than mere alliteration when it chose to contrast the old "400" with the new "four million" rather than a new "one hundred and twenty million." The

---

13. Henry James, *Hawthorne,* rev. ed. (New York, 1967 [c. 1879]), p. 55.
14. *Printers' Ink,* Nov. 24, 1927, p. 52.

standard antitheses of the Democracy of Goods parables were "mansion" and "bungalow." Advertising writers rarely took notice of the many millions of Americans whose standard of living fell below that of the cozy bungalow of the advertising tableaux. These millions might overhear the promises of consumer democracy in the newspapers or magazines, but advertising leaders felt no obligation to show how their promises to "everyone" would bring equality to those who lived in the nation's apartment houses and farmhouses without plumbing, let alone those who lived in rural shacks and urban tenements.

In the broadest sense, the parable of the Democracy of Goods may be interpreted as a secularized version of the traditional Christian assurances of ultimate human equality. "Body Odor plays no favorites" might be considered a secular translation of the idea that God "sends rain on the just and on the unjust" (Matt. 5:45). Promises of the essential equality of those possessing the advertised brand recalled the promise of equality of access to God's mercy. Thus the parable recapitulated a familiar, cherished expectation. Far more significant, however, was the parable's insinuation of the capacity of a Democracy of Goods to redeem the already secularized American promise of political equality.

Incessantly and enticingly repeated, advertising visions of fellowship in a Democracy of Goods encouraged Americans to look to similarities in consumption styles rather than to political power or control of wealth for evidence of significant equality. Francesco Nicosia and Robert Mayer describe the result as a "deflection of the success ethic from the sphere of production to that of consumption." Freedom of choice came to be perceived as a freedom more significantly exercised in the marketplace than in the political arena. This process gained momentum in the 1920s; it gained maturity during the 1950s as a sense of class differences was nearly eclipsed by a fascination with the equalities suggested by shared consumption patterns and "freely chosen" consumer "lifestyles."[15]

### Reading the Text

1. Summarize in your own words what Marchand means by the "parable of the democracy of goods."
2. What is the "democracy of afflictions," in your own words?
3. In class, brainstorm examples of current ads that illustrate the parable of the democracy of goods and the democracy of afflictions.

---

15. Francesco M. Nicosia and Robert N. Mayer, "Toward a Sociology of Consumption," *The Journal of Consumer Research* 3 (1976): 73; Roland Marchand, "Visions of Classlessness; Quests for Dominion: American Popular Culture, 1945–1960," in *Reshaping America: Society and Institutions, 1945–1960,* ed. Robert H. Bremner and Gary W. Reichard (Columbus, Ohio, 1982), pp. 165–70.

*Reading the Signs*

1. Does the parable of the democracy of goods work to make society more egalitarian, or does it reinforce existing power structures? Write an essay arguing for one position or the other, focusing on particular ads for your support.
2. Bring to class a popular magazine of your own choosing. In groups, study your selections. In which magazines is the myth of the democracy of goods most common? Do you find any relationship between the use of this myth and the intended audience of the magazines?
3. Look through a "women's" magazine such as *Vogue* or *Glamour*. Which myth do you find more prevalent, the democracy of goods or the democracy of afflictions? How would Diane Barthel (p. 144) explain your finding?
4. Study a "home" magazine such as *Better Homes and Gardens* and find one or more ads that use the democracy of goods as strategies. Then write a semiotic interpretation of the ads you have selected.
5. Obtain from your college library an issue of *Time* magazine dating from the 1920s, and compare it with a current issue. In what ways, if any, have the social messages communicated in the advertising changed? Try to account for any changes you identify.
6. Compare and contrast the myth of the democracy of goods with the frontier myth that Laurence Shames describes in "The More Factor" (p. 31). Consider how the two myths shape our consuming behavior and the advertising designed to trigger such behavior; you may also want to show how the myths appear in some current ads.

# JACK SOLOMON

## *Masters of Desire: The Culture of American Advertising*

||||||||||||||||||||||||||||||||||||||||||||||||||||||||

*Advertising campaigns come and go, as do the products they promote, but what does not change so quickly are the cultural patterns that advertisers rely on to work their magic. For as Jack Solomon (b. 1954) argues in this excerpt from* The Signs of Our Time *(1988), advertising does not work in a vacuum: It plays upon deeply held cultural values and desires in order to stimulate consumption. To analyze an ad, then, is to analyze the culture in which it appears. A professor of English at California State University, Northridge, Solomon is also the author of* Discourse and Reference in the Nuclear Age *(1988), and the coeditor (with Sonia Maasik) of* California Dreams and Realities *(1995) and of this textbook.*

*Amongst democratic nations, men easily attain a
certain equality of condition; but they can never
attain as much as they desire.*
— ALEXIS DE TOCQUEVILLE

On May 10, 1831, a young French aristocrat named Alexis de
Tocqueville arrived in New York City at the start of what would become one of the most famous visits to America in our history. He had
come to observe firsthand the institutions of the freest, most egalitarian
society of the age, but what he found was a paradox. For behind America's mythic promise of equal opportunity, Tocqueville discovered a desire for *unequal* social rewards, a ferocious competition for privilege and
distinction. As he wrote in his monumental study, *Democracy in America*:

> When all privileges of birth and fortune are abolished, when all
> professions are accessible to all, and a man's own energies may place
> him at the top of any one of them, an easy and unbounded career
> seems open to his ambition . . . But this is an erroneous notion,
> which is corrected by daily experience. [For when] men are nearly
> alike, and all follow the same track, it is very difficult for any one in-
> dividual to walk quick and cleave a way through the same throng
> which surrounds and presses him.

Yet walking quick and cleaving a way is precisely what Americans
dream of. We Americans dream of rising above the crowd, of attaining a
social summit beyond the reach of ordinary citizens. And therein lies the
paradox.

The American dream, in other words, has two faces: the one communally egalitarian and the other competitively elitist. This contradiction
is no accident; it is fundamental to the structure of American society.
Even as America's great myth of equality celebrates the virtues of mom,
apple pie, and the girl or boy next door, it also lures us to achieve social
distinction, to rise above the crowd and bask alone in the glory. This
land is your land and this land is my land, Woody Guthrie's populist anthem tells us, but we keep trying to increase the "my" at the expense of
the "your." Rather than fostering contentment, the American dream
breeds desire, a longing for a greater share of the pie. It is as if our society
were a vast high-school football game, with the bulk of the participants
noisily rooting in the stands while, deep down, each of them is wishing
he or she could be the star quarterback or head cheerleader.

For the semiotician, the contradictory nature of the American myth
of equality is nowhere written so clearly as in the signs that American advertisers use to manipulate us into buying their wares. "Manipulate" is
the word here, not "persuade"; for advertising campaigns are not sources
of product information, they are exercises in behavior modification.

Appealing to our subconscious emotions rather than to our conscious intellects, advertisements are designed to exploit the discontentments fostered by the American dream, the constant desire for social success and the material rewards that accompany it. America's consumer economy runs on desire, and advertising stokes the engines by transforming common objects — from peanut butter to political candidates — into signs of all the things that Americans covet most.

But by semiotically reading the signs that advertising agencies manu-          5
facture to stimulate consumption, we can plot the precise state of desire in the audiences to which they are addressed. Let's look at a representative sample of ads and what they say about the emotional climate of the country and the fast-changing trends of American life. Because ours is a highly diverse, pluralistic society, various advertisements may say different things depending on their intended audiences, but in every case they say something about America, about the status of our hopes, fears, desires, and beliefs.

We'll begin with two ad campaigns conducted by the same company that bear out Alexis de Tocqueville's observations about the contradictory nature of American society: General Motors' campaigns for its Cadillac and Chevrolet lines. First, consider an early magazine ad for the Cadillac Allanté. Appearing as a full-color, four-page insert in *Time,* the ad seems to say "I'm special — and so is this car" even before we've begun to read it: Rather than being printed on the ordinary, flimsy pages of the magazine, the Allanté spread appears on glossy coated stock. The unwritten message here is that an extraordinary car deserves an extraordinary advertisement, and that both car and ad are aimed at an extraordinary consumer, or at least one who wishes to appear extraordinary compared to his more ordinary fellow citizens.

Ads of this kind work by creating symbolic associations between their product and what is most coveted by the consumers to whom they are addressed. It is significant, then, that this ad insists that the Allanté is virtually an Italian rather than an American car, an automobile, as its copy runs, "Conceived and Commissioned by America's Luxury Car Leader — Cadillac" but "Designed and Handcrafted by Europe's Renowned Design Leader — Pininfarina, SpA, of Turin, Italy." This is not simply a piece of product information, it's a sign of the prestige that European luxury cars enjoy in today's automotive marketplace. Once the luxury car of choice for America's status drivers, Cadillac has fallen far behind its European competitors in the race for the prestige market. So the Allanté essentially represents Cadillac's decision, after years of resisting the trend toward European cars, to introduce its own European import — whose high cost is clearly printed on the last page of the ad. Although $54,700 is a lot of money to pay for a Cadillac, it's about what you'd expect to pay for a top-of-the-line Mercedes-Benz. That's precisely the point the ad is trying to make: the Allanté is no mere car. It's a potent status symbol you can associate with the other major status symbols of the 1980s.

American companies manufacture status symbols because American consumers want them. As Alexis de Tocqueville recognized a century and a half ago, the competitive nature of democratic societies breeds a desire for social distinction, a yearning to rise above the crowd. But given the fact that those who do make it to the top in socially mobile societies have often risen from the lower ranks, they still look like everyone else. In the socially immobile societies of aristocratic Europe, generations of fixed social conditions produced subtle class signals. The accent of one's voice, the shape of one's nose, or even the set of one's chin, immediately communicated social status. Aside from the nasal bray and uptilted head of the Boston Brahmin, Americans do not have any native sets of personal status signals. If it weren't for his Mercedes-Benz and Manhattan townhouse, the parvenu Wall Street millionaire often couldn't be distinguished from the man who tailors his suits. Hence, the demand for status symbols, for the objects that mark one off as a social success, is particularly strong in democratic nations — stronger even than in aristocratic societies, where the aristocrat so often looks and sounds different from everyone else.

Status symbols, then, are signs that identify their possessors' place in a social hierarchy, markers of rank and prestige. We can all think of any number of status symbols — Rolls-Royces, Beverly Hills mansions, even Shar Pei puppies (whose rareness and expense has rocketed them beyond Russian wolfhounds as status pets and has even inspired whole lines of wrinkle-faced stuffed toys) — but how do we know that something *is* a status symbol? The explanation is quite simple: when an object (or puppy!) either costs a lot of money or requires influential connections to possess, anyone who possesses it must also possess the necessary means and influence to acquire it. The object itself really doesn't matter, since it ultimately disappears behind the presumed social potency of its owner. Semiotically, what matters is the signal it sends, its value as a sign of power. One traditional sign of social distinction is owning a country estate and enjoying the peace and privacy that attend it. Advertisements for Mercedes-Benz, Jaguar, and Audi automobiles thus frequently feature drivers motoring quietly along a country road, presumably on their way to or from their country houses.

Advertisers have been quick to exploit the status signals that belong    10
to body language as well. As Hegel observed in the early nineteenth century, it is an ancient aristocratic prerogative to be seen by the lower orders without having to look at them in return. Tilting his chin high in the air and gazing down at the world under hooded eyelids, the aristocrat invites observation while refusing to look back. We can find such a pose exploited in an advertisement for Cadillac Seville in which we see an elegantly dressed woman out for a drive with her husband in their new

Cadillac. If we look closely at the woman's body language, we can see her glance inwardly with a satisfied smile on her face but not outward toward the camera that represents our gaze. She is glad to be seen by us in her Seville, but she isn't interested in looking at *us*!

Ads that are aimed at a broader market take the opposite approach. If the American dream encourages the desire to "arrive," to vault above the mass, it also fosters a desire to be popular, to "belong." Populist commercials accordingly transform products into signs of belonging, utilizing such common icons as country music, small-town life, family picnics, and farmyards. All of these icons are incorporated in GM's "Heartbeat of America" campaign for its Chevrolet line. Unlike the Seville commercial, the faces in the Chevy ads look straight at us and smile. Dress is casual; the mood upbeat. Quick camera cuts take us from rustic to suburban to urban scenes, creating an American montage filmed from sea to shining sea. We all "belong" in a Chevy.

Where price alone doesn't determine the market for a product, advertisers can go either way. Both Johnnie Walker and Jack Daniel's are better-grade whiskies, but where a Johnnie Walker ad appeals to the buyer who wants a mark of aristocratic distinction in his liquor, a Jack Daniel's ad emphasizes the down-home, egalitarian folksiness of its product. Johnnie Walker associates itself with such conventional status symbols as sable coats, Rolls-Royces, and black gold; Jack Daniel's gives us a Good Ol' Boy in overalls. In fact, Jack Daniel's Good Ol' Boy is an icon of backwoods independence, recalling the days of the moonshiner and the Whisky Rebellion of 1794. Evoking emotions quite at odds with those stimulated in Johnnie Walker ads, the advertisers of Jack Daniel's have chosen to transform their product into a sign of America's populist tradition. The fact that both ads successfully sell whisky is itself a sign of the dual nature of the American dream.

Beer is also pitched on two levels. Consider the difference between the ways Budweiser and Michelob market their light beers. Bud Light and Michelob Light cost and taste about the same, but Budweiser tends to target the working class while Michelob has gone after the upscale market. Bud commercials are set in working-class bars that contrast with the sophisticated nightclubs and yuppie watering holes of the Michelob campaign. "You're one of the guys," Budweiser assures the assembly-line worker and the truck driver, "this Bud's for you." Michelob, on the other hand, makes no such appeal to the democratic instinct of sharing and belonging. You don't share, you take, grabbing what you can in a competitive dash to "have it all."

Populist advertising is particularly effective in the face of foreign competition. When Americans feel threatened from the outside, they tend to circle the wagons and temporarily forget their class differences. In the face of the Japanese automotive "invasion," Chrysler runs populist commercials in which Lee Iacocca joins the simple folk who buy his cars as the jingle "Born in America" blares in the background. Seeking to capitalize on the popularity of Bruce Springsteen's *Born in the USA* album, these ads gloss over Springsteen's ironic lyrics in a vast display of flag-waving. Chevrolet's "Heartbeat of America" campaign attempts to woo American motorists away from Japanese automobiles by appealing to their patriotic sentiments.

The patriotic iconography of these campaigns also reflects the gen- 15 eral cultural mood of the early- to mid-1980s. After a period of national anguish in the wake of the Vietnam War and the Iran hostage crisis, America went on a patriotic binge. American athletic triumphs in the Lake Placid and Los Angeles Olympics introduced a sporting tone into the national celebration, often making international affairs appear like one great Olympiad in which America was always going for the gold. In response, advertisers began to do their own flag-waving.

The mood of advertising during this period was definitely upbeat. Even deodorant commercials, which traditionally work on our self-doubts and fears of social rejection, jumped on the bandwagon. In the guilty sixties, we had ads like the "Ice Blue Secret" campaign with its connotations of guilt and shame. In the feel-good Reagan eighties, "Sure" deodorant commercials featured images of triumphant Americans throwing up their arms in victory to reveal — no wet marks! Deodorant commercials once had the moral echo of Nathaniel Hawthorne's guilt-ridden *The Scarlet Letter*; in the early eighties they had all the moral subtlety of *Rocky IV,* reflecting the emotions of a Vietnam-weary nation eager to embrace the imagery of America Triumphant.

The commercials for Worlds of Wonder's Lazer Tag game featured the futuristic finals of some Soviet-American Lazer Tag shootout ("Practice hard, America!") and carried the emotions of patriotism into an even more aggressive arena. Exploiting the hoopla that surrounded the victory over the Soviets in the hockey finals of the 1980 Olympics, the Lazer Tag ads pandered to an American desire for the sort of clear-cut nationalistic triumphs that the nuclear age has rendered almost impossible. Creating a fantasy setting where patriotic dreams are substituted for complicated realities, the Lazer Tag commercials sought to capture the imaginations of children caught up in the patriotic fervor of the early 1980s.

## Live the Fantasy

By reading the signs of American advertising, we can conclude that America is a nation of fantasizers, often preferring the sign to the substance and easily enthralled by a veritable Fantasy Island of commercial illusions. Critics of Madison Avenue often complain that advertisers create consumer desire, but semioticians don't think the situation is that simple.

Advertisers may give shape to consumer fantasies, but they need raw material to work with, the subconscious dreams and desires of the marketplace. As long as these desires remain unconscious, advertisers will be able to exploit them. But by bringing the fantasies to the surface, you can free yourself from advertising's often hypnotic grasp.

I can think of no company that has more successfully seized upon the subconscious fantasies of the American marketplace — indeed the world marketplace — than McDonald's. By no means the first nor the only hamburger chain in the United States, McDonald's emerged victorious in the "burger wars" by transforming hamburgers into signs of all that was desirable in American life. Other chains like Wendy's, Burger King, and Jack-In-The-Box continue to advertise and sell widely, but no company approaches McDonald's transformation of itself into a symbol of American culture.

McDonald's success can be traced to the precision of its advertising. 20 Instead of broadcasting a single "one-size-fits-all" campaign at a time, McDonald's pitches its burgers simultaneously at different age groups, different classes, even different races (Budweiser beer, incidentally, has succeeded in the same way). For children, there is the Ronald McDonald campaign, which presents a fantasy world that has little to do with hamburgers in any rational sense but a great deal to do with the emotional desires of kids. Ronald McDonald and his friends are signs that recall the Muppets, "Sesame Street," the circus, toys, storybook illustrations, even *Alice in Wonderland*. Such signs do not signify hamburgers. Rather, they are displayed in order to prompt in the child's mind an automatic association of fantasy, fun, and McDonald's.

The same approach is taken in ads aimed at older audiences — teens, adults, and senior citizens. In the teen-oriented ads we may catch a fleeting glimpse of a hamburger or two, but what we are really shown is a teenage fantasy: groups of hip and happy adolescents singing, dancing, and cavorting together. Fearing loneliness more than anything else, adolescents quickly respond to the group appeal of such commercials. "Eat a Big Mac," these ads say, "and you won't be stuck home alone on Saturday night."

To appeal to an older and more sophisticated audience no longer so afraid of not belonging and more concerned with finding a place to go out to at night, McDonald's has designed the elaborate "Mac Tonight" commercials, which have for their backdrop a nightlit urban skyline and at their center a cabaret pianist with a moon-shaped head, a glad manner, and Blues Brothers shades. Such signs prompt an association of McDonald's with nightclubs and urban sophistication, persuading us that McDonald's is a place not only for breakfast or lunch but for dinner too, as if it were a popular off-Broadway nightspot, a place to see and be seen. Even the parody of Kurt Weill's "Mack the Knife" theme song that Mac the Pianist performs is a sign, a subtle signal to the sophisticated hamburger eater able to recognize the origin of the tune in Bertolt Brecht's *Threepenny Opera*.

For yet older customers, McDonald's has designed a commercial around the fact that it employs a large number of retirees and seniors. In one such ad, we see an elderly man leaving his pretty little cottage early in the morning to start work as "the new kid" at McDonald's, and then we watch him during his first day on the job. Of course he is a great success, outdoing everyone else with his energy and efficiency, and he returns home in the evening to a loving wife and a happy home. One would almost think that the ad was a kind of moving "help wanted" sign (indeed, McDonald's *was* hiring elderly employees at the time), but it's really just directed at consumers. Older viewers can see themselves wanted and appreciated in the ad — and perhaps be distracted from the rationally uncomfortable fact that many senior citizens take such jobs because of financial need and thus may be unlikely to own the sort of home that one sees in the commercial. But realism isn't the point here. This is fantasyland, a dream world promising instant gratification no matter what the facts of the matter may be.

Practically the only fantasy that McDonald's doesn't exploit is the fantasy of sex. This is understandable, given McDonald's desire to present itself as a family restaurant. But everywhere else, sexual fantasies, which have always had an important place in American advertising, are beginning to dominate the advertising scene. You expect sexual come-ons in ads for perfume or cosmetics or jewelry — after all, that's what they're selling — but for room deodorizers? In a magazine ad for Claire Burke home fragrances, for example, we see a well-dressed couple cavorting about their bedroom in what looks like a cheery preparation for sadomasochistic exercises. Jordache and Calvin Klein pitch blue jeans as props for teenage sexuality. The phallic appeal of automobiles, traditionally an implicit feature in automotive advertising, becomes quite explicit in a Dodge commercial that shifts back and forth from shots of a young man in an automobile to teasing glimpses of a woman — his date — as she dresses in her apartment.

The very language of today's advertisements is charged with sexuality. Products in the more innocent fifties were "new and improved," but everything in the eighties is "hot!" — as in "hot woman," or sexual heat. Cars are "hot." Movies are "hot." An ad for Valvoline pulses to the rhythm of a "heat wave, burning in my car." Sneakers get red hot in a magazine ad for Travel Fox athletic shoes in which we see male and female figures, clad only in Travel Fox shoes, apparently in the act of copulation — an ad that earned one of *Adweek*'s annual "badvertising" awards for shoddy advertising.

The sexual explicitness of contemporary advertising is a sign not so much of American sexual fantasies as of the lengths to which advertisers will go to get attention. Sex never fails as an attention-getter, and in a particularly competitive, and expensive, era for American marketing, advertisers like to bet on a sure thing. Ad people refer to the proliferation of TV, radio, newspaper, magazine, and billboard ads as "clutter," and nothing cuts through the clutter like sex.

By showing the flesh, advertisers work on the deepest, most coercive human emotions of all. Much sexual coercion in advertising, however, is a sign of a desperate need to make certain that clients are getting their money's worth. The appearance of advertisements that refer directly to the prefabricated fantasies of Hollywood is a sign of a different sort of desperation: a desperation for ideas. With the rapid turnover of advertising campaigns mandated by the need to cut through the "clutter," advertisers may be hard pressed for new ad concepts, and so they are more and more frequently turning to already-established models. In the early 1980s, for instance, Pepsi-Cola ran a series of ads broadly alluding to Steven Spielberg's *E.T.* In one such ad, we see a young boy, who, like the hero of *E.T.,* witnesses an extraterrestrial visit. The boy is led to a soft-drink machine where he pauses to drink a can of Pepsi as the spaceship he's spotted flies off into the universe. The relationship between the ad and the movie, accordingly, is a parasitical one, with the ad taking its life from the creative body of the film.

Pepsi did something similar in 1987 when it arranged with the producers of the movie *Top Gun* to promote the film's video release in Pepsi's television advertisements in exchange for the right to append a Pepsi ad to the video itself. This time, however, the parasitical relationship between ad and film was made explicit. Pepsi sales benefited from the video, and the video's sales benefited from Pepsi. It was a marriage made in corporate heaven.

The fact that Pepsi believed that it could stimulate consumption by appealing to the militaristic fantasies dramatized in *Top Gun* reflects similar fantasies in the "Pepsi generation." Earlier generations saw Pepsi associated with high-school courtship rituals, with couples sipping sodas together at the corner drugstore. When the draft was on, young men fantasized about Peggy Sue, not Air Force Flight School. Military service was all too real a possibility to fantasize about. But in an era when military service is not a reality for most young Americans, Pepsi commercials featuring hotshot fly-boys drinking Pepsi while streaking about in their Air Force jets contribute to a youth culture that has forgotten what military service means. It all looks like such fun in the Pepsi ads, but what they conceal is the fact that military jets are weapons, not high-tech recreational vehicles.

For less militaristic dreamers, Madison Avenue has framed ad campaigns around the cultural prestige of high-tech machinery in its own right. This is especially the case with sports cars, whose high-tech appeal is so powerful that some people apparently fantasize about *being* sports cars. At least, this is the conclusion one might draw from a Porsche                30 commercial that asked its audience, "If you were a car, what kind of car would you be?" As a candy-red Porsche speeds along a rain-slick forest road, the ad's voice-over describes all the specifications you'd want to have if you *were* a sports car. "If you were a car," the commercial concludes, "you'd be a Porsche."

In his essay "Car Commercials and 'Miami Vice,'" Todd Gitlin explains the semiotic appeal of such ads as those in the Porsche campaign. Aired at the height of what may be called America's "myth of the entrepreneur," these commercials were aimed at young corporate managers who imaginatively identified with the "lone wolf" image of a Porsche speeding through the woods. Gitlin points out that such images cater to the fantasies of faceless corporate men who dream of entrepreneurial glory, of striking out on their own like John DeLorean and telling the boss to take his job and shove it. But as DeLorean's spectacular failure demonstrates, the life of the entrepreneur can be extremely risky. So rather than having to go it alone and take the risks that accompany entrepreneurial independence, the young executive can substitute fantasy for reality by climbing into his Porsche — or at least that's what Porsche's advertisers wanted him to believe.

But there is more at work in the Porsche ads than the fantasies of corporate America. Ever since Arthur C. Clarke and Stanley Kubrick teamed up to present us with HAL 9000, the demented computer of *2001: A Space Odyssey,* the American imagination has been obsessed with the melding of man and machine. First there was television's "Six Million Dollar Man," and then movieland's *Star Wars, Blade Runner,* and *Robocop,* fantasy visions of a future dominated by machines. Androids haunt our imaginations as machines seize the initiative. *Time* magazine's "Man of the Year" for 1982 was a computer. Robot-built automobiles appeal to drivers who spend their days in front of computer screens — perhaps designing robots. When so much power and prestige is being given to high-tech machines, wouldn't you rather be a Porsche?

In short, the Porsche campaign is a sign of a new mythology that is emerging before our eyes, a myth of the machine, which is replacing the myth of the human. The iconic figure of the little tramp caught up in the cogs of industrial production in Charlie Chaplin's *Modern Times* signified a humanistic revulsion to the age of the machine. Human beings, such icons said, were superior to machines. Human values should come first in the moral order of things. But as Edith Milton suggests in her essay "The Track of the Mutant," we are now coming to believe that machines are superior to human beings, that mechanical nature is superior to human nature. Rather than being threatened by machines, we long to merge with them. "The Six Million Dollar Man" is one iconic figure in the new mythology; Harrison Ford's sexual coupling with an android is another. In such an age it should come as little wonder that computer-synthesized Max Headroom should be a commercial spokesman for

Coca-Cola, or that Federal Express should design a series of TV ads featuring mechanical-looking human beings revolving around strange and powerful machines.

### Fear and Trembling in the Marketplace

While advertisers play on and reflect back at us our fantasies about everything from fighter pilots to robots, they also play on darker imaginings. If dream and desire can be exploited in the quest for sales, so can nightmare and fear.

The nightmare equivalent of America's populist desire to "belong," 35 for example, is the fear of not belonging, of social rejection, of being different. Advertisements for dandruff shampoos, mouthwashes, deodorants, and laundry detergents ("Ring Around the Collar!") accordingly exploit such fears, bullying us into consumption. Although ads of this type are still around in the 1980s, they were particularly common in the fifties and early sixties, reflecting a society still reeling from the witch-hunts of the McCarthy years. When any sort of social eccentricity or difference could result in a public denunciation and the loss of one's job or even liberty, Americans were keen to conform and be like everyone else. No one wanted to be "guilty" of smelling bad or of having a dirty collar.

"Guilt" ads characteristically work by creating narrative situations in which someone is "accused" of some social "transgression," pronounced guilty, and then offered the sponsor's product as a means of returning to "innocence." Such ads, in essence, are parodies of ancient religious rituals of guilt and atonement, whereby sinning humanity is offered salvation through the agency of priest and church. In the world of advertising, a product takes the place of the priest, but the logic of the situation is quite similar.

In commercials for Wisk detergent, for example, we witness the drama of a hapless housewife and her husband as they are mocked by the jeering voices of children shouting "Ring Around the Collar!" "Oh, those dirty rings!" the housewife groans in despair. It's as if she and her husband were being stoned by an angry crowd. But there's hope, there's help, there's Wisk. Cleansing her soul of sin as well as her husband's, the housewife launders his shirts with Wisk, and behold, his collars are clean. Product salvation is only as far as the supermarket.

The recent appearance of advertisements for hospitals treating drug and alcohol addiction has raised the old genre of the guilt ad to new heights (or lows, depending on your perspective). In such ads, we see wives on the verge of leaving their husbands if they don't do something about their drinking, and salesmen about to lose their jobs. The man is guilty; he has sinned; but he upholds the ritual of guilt and atonement by "confessing" to his wife or boss and agreeing to go to the hospital the ad is pitching.

If guilt looks backward in time to past transgressions, fear, like desire, faces forward, trembling before the future. In the late 1980s, a new kind of fear commercial appeared, one whose narrative played on the worries of young corporate managers struggling up the ladder of success. Representing the nightmare equivalent of the elitist desire to "arrive," ads of this sort created images of failure, storylines of corporate defeat. In one ad for Apple computers, for example, a group of junior executives sits around a table with the boss as he asks each executive how long it will take his or her department to complete some publishing jobs. "Two or three days," answers one nervous executive. "A week, on overtime," a tight-lipped woman responds. But one young up-and-comer can have everything ready tomorrow, today, or yesterday, because his department uses a Macintosh desktop publishing system. Guess who'll get the next promotion?

Fear stalks an ad for AT&T computer systems too. A boss and four   40 junior executives are dining in a posh restaurant. Icons of corporate power and prestige flood the screen — from the executives' formal evening wear to the fancy table setting — but there's tension in the air. It seems that the junior managers have chosen a computer system that's incompatible with the firm's sales and marketing departments. A whole new system will have to be purchased, but the tone of the meeting suggests that it will be handled by a new group of managers. These guys are on the way out. They no longer "belong." Indeed, it's probably no accident that the ad takes place in a restaurant, given the joke that went around in the aftermath of the 1987 market crash. "What do you call a yuppie stockbroker?" the joke ran. "Hey, waiter!" Is the ad trying subtly to suggest that junior executives who choose the wrong computer systems are doomed to suffer the same fate?

For other markets, there are other fears. If McDonald's presents senior citizens with bright fantasies of being useful and appreciated beyond retirement, companies like Secure Horizons dramatize senior citizens' fears of being caught short by a major illness. Running its ads in the wake of budgetary cuts in the Medicare system, Secure Horizons designed a series of commercials featuring a pleasant old man named Harry — who looks and sounds rather like Carroll O'Connor — who tells us the story of the scare he got during his wife's recent illness. Fearing that next time Medicare won't cover the bills, he has purchased supplemental health insurance from Secure Horizons and now securely tends his rooftop garden.

Among all the fears advertisers have exploited over the years, I find the fear of not having a posh enough burial site the most arresting. Advertisers usually avoid any mention of death — who wants to associate a product with the grave? — but mortuary advertisers haven't much choice. Generally, they solve their problems by framing cemeteries as timeless parks presided over by priestly morticians, appealing to our desires for dignity and comfort in the face of bereavement. But in one television commercial for Forest Lawn we find a different approach. In this ad we are presented with the ghost of an old man telling us how he might have found a much nicer resting place than the run-down cemetery in which we find him had his wife only known that Forest Lawn was so "affordable." I presume the ad was supposed to be funny, but it's been pulled off the air. There are some fears that just won't bear joking about, some nightmares too dark to dramatize.

## The Future of an Illusion

There are some signs in the advertising world that Americans are getting fed up with fantasy advertisements and want to hear some straight talk. Weary of extravagant product claims and irrelevant associations, consumers trained by years of advertising to distrust what they hear seem to be developing an immunity to commercials. At least, this is the semiotic message I read in the "new realism" advertisements of the eighties, ads that attempt to convince you that what you're seeing is the real thing, that the ad is giving you the straight dope, not advertising hype.

You can recognize the "new realism" by its camera techniques. The lighting is usually subdued to give the ad the effect of being filmed without studio lighting or special filters. The scene looks gray, as if the blinds were drawn. The camera shots are jerky and off-angle, often zooming in for sudden and unflattering close-ups, as if the cameraman was an amateur with a home video recorder. In a "realistic" ad for AT&T, for example, we are treated to a monologue by a plump stockbroker — his plumpness intended as a sign that he's for real and not just another actor — who tells us about the problems he's had with his phone system (not AT&T's) as the camera jerks around, generally filming him from below as if the cameraman couldn't quite fit his equipment into the crammed office and had to film the scene on his knees. "This is no fancy advertisement," the ad tries to convince us, "this is sincere."

An ad for Miller draft beer tries the same approach, recreating the effect of an amateur videotape of a wedding celebration. Camera shots shift suddenly from group to group. The picture jumps. Bodies are poorly framed. The color is washed out. Like the beer it is pushing, the ad is supposed to strike us as being "as real as it gets." 45

Such ads reflect a desire for reality in the marketplace, a weariness with Madison Avenue illusions. But there's no illusion like the illusion of reality. Every special technique that advertisers use to create their "reality effects" is, in fact, more unrealistic than the techniques of "illusory" ads. The world, in reality, doesn't jump around when you look at it. It doesn't appear in subdued gray tones. Our eyes don't have zoom lenses, and we don't look at things with our heads cocked to one side. The irony of the "new realism" is that it is more unrealistic, more artificial, than the ordinary run of television advertising.

But don't expect any truly realistic ads in the future, because a realistic advertisement is a contradiction in terms. The logic of advertising is entirely semiotic: it substitutes signs for things, framed visions of consumer desire for the thing itself. The success of modern advertising, its penetration into every corner of American life, reflects a culture that has itself chosen illusion over reality. At a time when political candidates all have professional image-makers attached to their staffs, and the President of the United States can be an actor who once sold shirt collars, all the cultural signs are pointing to more illusions in our lives rather than fewer — a fecund breeding ground for the world of the advertiser.

### Reading the Text

1. Describe in your own words the paradox of the American dream, as Solomon sees it.
2. In Solomon's view, why do status symbols work particularly well in manipulating American consumers?
3. What is a "guilt" ad, according to Solomon, and how does it affect consumers?
4. Why, according to Solomon, has McDonald's been so successful in its ad campaigns?
5. What relationship does Solomon see between the "new realism" of some ads and the paradoxes of the American dream?

### Reading the Signs

1. Bring to class a general interest magazine, such as *Time, Better Homes and Gardens,* or *Road and Track,* and in small groups study the advertising. Do the ads tend to have an elitist or a populist appeal? What relationship do you see between the appeal you identify and the magazine's target readership? Present your findings to the class.
2. Watch an episode of a popular prime-time TV program, such as *Seinfeld, Murphy Brown,* or *Friends,* focusing your attention on the advertising that sponsors the show. Then write an essay in which you interpret these ads. Do the ads reveal a particular vision of the American dream, and if so, how might the vision be related to the show's audience?
3. Visit your college library and locate an issue of a popular magazine from earlier decades, such as the 1930s or 1940s. Then write an essay in which you compare and contrast the advertising found in that early issue with that in a current issue of the same publication. What similarities and

differences do you find in the myths underlying the advertising, and what is their significance?

4. In class, brainstorm a list of status symbols common in advertising today. Then discuss what groups they appeal to and why. Can you detect any patterns based on gender, ethnicity, or age?

5. The American political scene has changed since the late 1980s, when this essay was first published. In an analytic essay, argue whether you believe the populist/elitist paradox that Solomon describes still affects American advertising and media. Be sure to base your discussion on specific media examples.

# LESLIE SAVAN

## Generation X-Force

||||||||||||||||||||||||||||||||||||||||||||||||||||||

*If you're tired of being targeted by advertisers and marketers as a GenX consumer, stop wearing plaid. Or buying Nikes or Levi's 501 jeans or any of the other products that have done well by being pitched as GenX accoutrements. Because as Leslie Savan (b. 1951) points out in this selection from* The Sponsored Life *(1994), Boomer ad executives have been working overtime trying to figure out how to get Buster consumers to part with their dollars. And as Savan also points out, it's up to you to determine whether they're going to get away with it anymore. Leslie Savan is a columnist for* The Village Voice, *specializing in advertising and commercial culture, and has published in* Time, Vibe, Working Women, *and* The Utne Reader, *among other publications.*

When you hear "X" do you say, "Oh?" It's been at least X number of months since the media peaked over Generation X with major stories in *The Atlantic, Business Week,* and *U.S. News & World Report,* but the marketing to Generation X will be with us for, if we're really unlucky, a generation. The knotty relations between GenX and ad people, most of whom come from GenX's supposed nemesis, the Baby Boomers, are squeezing out ads that reflect the clichés of the day: that Xers are "cynical" and "media savvy," and soon as they smell your sell, they're outta here. Xers know they're valued only as a consuming concept — the 46 million people between the ages of 18 and 29 who annually spend $125 billion. (Caution: X numbers vary wildly from article to soft-news segment — these are the ones the media most often grafts from other media.

Furthermore, there's no Malcolm X in Generation X — except when an ad is deliberately "multicultural," the X of the media mind means almost entirely grungy white youth.)

All the hype can make you doubt if "they" — as a generation — exist at all, or if the much-publicized war between Xers and Boomers amounts to anything more than the latter preferring scotch and Walkmans while the former tilts toward tequila and Discmans (as the *Entertainment Weekly* ad sales force has so usefully discovered). Yet there are real differences between the generations: Boomers do have a more inflated sense of their own destiny, and Busters did come into a world depleted by recession, higher divorce rates, and a media monolith that's usurped institutions like education and government. But as Neil Howe and Bill Strauss lay out in their book *13th-GEN,* adjacent-generation warfare is nothing new; in fact, it got rather nasty in the 1920s clash between the X-like "Lost Generation" and the Boomful "Missionary Generation." The difference this time is the knee-jerk media attention — treating the Boomer/Buster categories like a Linda Evans/Joan Collins cat fight — and the knee-jerk marketing attention: This group is big and has discretionary income because a third of it lives with the folks. Get down and pander!

And so we have grunge-art–directed campaigns that say the word "generation" a lot: "What stirs the soul, moves a generation" is the headline for an ad featuring a grunge dude doing a little rock 'n' roll jig (for Giorgio Brutini shoes, apparently nicknamed GBX). Two G guys hold up a fish. "Work, work, work, work, work, work, work, work, fish. Take it easy," Southern Comfort advises. When Taco Bell wanted to promote its outlets' late-night hours to late-night Xers it ran the slogan "Get Laid at the Ball," uh, "Get Late at the Bell," illustrated by the speedy animation of MTV regular Bill Plympton. "The boomers are just not going to get this one," a Taco exec crowed in *Ad Age.* Meanwhile, CBS, the network with the oldest audience demographics, has its 20-year-old interns surveying their peers on how to stir X into CBS; and not one but two syndicated X newsmagazine shows, one called simply *Generation X,* are in the works.

Advertisers' guilt over doing another 180 — from ignoring GenX to genuflecting before it — contributes to their dread that the generation will reject them. What else accounts for the self-flagellation among the mostly Boomer marketing people at a recent business symposium called "Why Doesn't the Fashion and Beauty Industry Understand the New Generation X?" The president of Merry-Go-Round, the 1500-store chain that sells $1 billion of merchandise a year to 15- to 25-year-olds, stood at the podium with this quote projected on the screen behind him: "Without constant research, I know nothing."

Or as Eric Conn, the 48-year-old ad manager for Honda and Acura,  5 has said, "If I understand it, it won't work." In pushing the Integra to potential customers, about 40 percent of whom are X age and 30 percent are young Boom, Acura produced two distinct campaigns. For Boomers, the car rolls through a life-size Hot Wheels set (supposed to instill nostalgia), while for Xers a cartoon dog named Leonard mumbles cool quips like "Life is good. Mondo good." Conn explains the two-tiered approach: "Baby Boomers can still get ahead, they can still dig their way out. But the Xers, it's more like it's all been used up. They have a much more cynical outlook — you got to hit them with a little more irreverence for the system, a little more disdain in the voice." Hence, Boomer-but-bad-boy Dennis Miller as the voice of Leonard.

Carmakers in general are gunning for Xers — Geo, Saturn, Isuzu, Chrysler, Ford are all doing their X bit. Subaru's effort was the most obvious — and the most damning failure. Remember the Christian Slater-like kid who went on about how "This car is like punk rock" while other cars were somehow "boring and corporate"? The campaign did nothing for slumping Impreza sales, and the Wieden & Kennedy agency, despite its Nike rep, was canned.

One problem was its slavish posture before what research deemed "cool." In fact, a slave / master dynamic permeates most Boom / Bust relationships on the plantation of advertising, the two sides switching roles as needs demand. Boomers hold the real power — the jobs, the money — and Xers are supposedly highly resentful. But Xers feel, as the stereotype goes, morally and stylistically superior, and so before their whims the Boomer bows.

But if you Xers are going to be so cynical, don't forget your friends, like the Nike or 501 campaigns, smart spots that, unlike Subaru, would never let their research stick out like some balding Boomer's ponytail. It's not that they surf a higher moral wave — they don't, they just use your cynicism and media-savvyness more cynically and savvily than you do. What does good pal MTV say behind your back when trying to lure advertisers in trade publications? It shows yet another grunger over the headline "Buy this 24-year-old and get all his friends absolutely free. . . . He heads up a pack. What he eats, his friends eat. What he wears, they wear. What he likes, they like. And what he's never heard of . . . well . . . you get the idea."

The real war isn't so much between generations as between those, of any age, who buy into a cramped package of stylized resentment and those who won't.

### Reading the Text

1. What does Savan see as the real differences between baby boomers and GenX-ers?
2. How, according to Savan, have marketers exploited the stereotypes of the two generations in their advertising ploys?

3. Describe in your own words the effect that Savan claims the Subaru "punk rock" commercial was intended to have on Generation X.

4. What does Savan mean by concluding, "The real war isn't so much between generations as between those, of any age, who buy into a cramped package of stylized resentment and those who won't"?

### Reading the Signs

1. In class, discuss the tone Savan adopts in this essay. What does her tone reveal about her attitudes toward Generation X? What effect does it have on your own attitudes toward her essay?

2. Examine the ads in a magazine designed for the eighteen-to-thirty market, such as *Spin*. Then write an analytic essay in which you discuss the extent to which they employ the Generation X appeals that Savan describes.

3. Compare and contrast Savan's attitudes toward media representation of Generation X with those of Walter Kirn ("Twentysomethings," p. 214).

4. Write an argumentative essay that defends, refutes, or modifies the proposition that the very concept of Generation X has been constructed by the mass media. To develop your essay, consult, in addition to Savan, Walter Kirn's "Twentysomethings," p. 214, and ads, TV programs, or films that depict this generation.

5. In your journal, describe your own ad campaign that would target twentysomething consumers. Present your entry to the class, being sure to justify the choices you make in your ad design.


PATRICIA  J.  WILLIAMS

*The Fiction of Truth in Advertising*

||||||||||||||||||||||||||||||||||||||||||||||||||||||||||||||

*In* The Alchemy of Race and Rights *(1991), from which this selection is taken, Patricia J. Williams (b. 1951) explores the relationship between the law and everyday life, focusing particularly on the ways that race and gender can complicate American social relations. In this passage, Williams brings her legal training to bear on advertising: Notions of "truth" are increasingly absent from modern advertising, she finds, as she reflects on the dehumanizing and disenfranchising effect of media fictions. Educated at Harvard Law School, she currently is professor of law at Columbia Law School and has written widely on civil rights issues and legal ethics. Currently serving on the Board of Governors of the Society of American Law, Williams is also on the Board of Scholars of* Ms. *magazine and is a contributing editor of* The Nation.

When I first started teaching consumer protection a decade ago, the mathematics of false advertising was simple. If the box or brochure said "100% cotton," you merely took the item in question and subtracted it from the words: Any difference was the measure of your legal remedy. Sometimes you had to add in buyer's expertise or multiply the whole by seller's bad faith, but generally the whole reason people even took a class in consumer protection was that you didn't have to learn logarithms. Today, however, advertisers almost never represent anything remotely related to the reality of the product — or the politician — they are trying to sell; misrepresentation, the heart of false-advertising statutes, is very hard to prove. Increasingly, television ads are characterized by scenarios that neither mention the product nor contain a description of any sort. What fills the sixty seconds are "concepts" and diffuse images — images that used to be discursive, floating in the background, creating a mellow consumerist backdrop — which now dominate and direct content. Nothing is promised, everything evoked: warm fuzzy camera angles; "peak" experiences; happy pictures, mood-shaping music; almost always a smarmy, soft-peddling overvoice purring "This magic moment has been brought to you by . . . ."

An example, in the form of an anecdote: About a year ago, I was sitting at home, installed before the television set. I was preparing for a class in consumer protection. The next day's assignment was false advertising, and I was shopping for an advertisement whose structure I could use as a starting point for discussion. An ad for Georges Marciano clothing flashed on the screen and dragged me in, first with the music, South African music of haunting urgency, the echoing simultaneity of nonlinear music, the syncopation of quickening-heartbeat percussive music, dragging the ear. In the picture, a woman with long blond hair and sunglasses ran from a crowd of photographers and an admiring public. The film was black and white, a series of frames jaggedly succeeding each other, like a patchwork of secretly taken stills. Sliced into the sequence of her running away were shots of the blond and her manager/bodyguard/boyfriend packing. He packed the passports and the handgun, she packed the Georges Marciano jeans. The climax came when she burst into a room of exploding flashbulbs — a blazing bath of white light.

The effect of this particular visual and aural juxtaposition was the appearance of the music as being inside the woman's head or her heart. The music was primal, dangerous, desperate. The woman's crisis of adoration framed the burning necessity of this profound music, and the soaring universality of sound became white, female, privatized. The pulsing movement of the music elevated this event of narcissistic voyeurism to elemental importance. The music overflowed boundaries. Voices merged and surged; mood drifted and soared in the listening. African voices swelled and rose in the intricate music of knowledge, the wisdom of rhythm, the physics of echoing chasms bounded in intervals, the harmonic bells of voices striking each other in excitement and the wind, black African voices making music of the trees, of groundhogs, of whistling birds and pure chortling streams. It was generous shared music, open and eternal.

The pictures presented sought privacy. The chase was an invasion; the photographers pursued her private moments; she resisted even as her glamour consented. The viewer was drawn into desire to see her never-quite-revealed face, swept along by the urgency of her running to privacy, even as we never quite acknowledged her right to it. Thus the moment of climax, the flashing of cameras in her face (and ours, so completely have we identified with her), was one of release and relief. The music acted against the pictures. The mind resolved it queerly. The positive magnetic boundlessness of the music was turned into negative exposure. The run for privacy became an orgasmic peep show, the moment of negative exposure almost joyful.

In my lap, my textbook lay heavy, unattended pages drifting open to the Lanham Act:[1]                                                                              5

> *False designations of origin and false descriptions forbidden:*
> . . . any person who shall affix, apply, or annex, or use in connection with any goods or services . . . a false designation of origin, or any false description or representation, including words or other symbols tending falsely to describe or represent the same, and shall cause such goods or services to enter into commerce, and any person who shall with knowledge of the falsity of such . . . description or representation cause or procure the same to be transported or used in commerce . . . or used, shall be liable to a civil action . . . by any person who believes that he is or is likely to be damaged by the use of any such false description or representation.[2]

I have recounted this story at some length, not just for its illustrative contrast between the sight and the sound of an advertisement, but also because the relationship between the music and the pictures can serve as a metaphor for the tension between the political and marketplace dynamic that is my larger subject. I think that the invisible corruption of one by the other has consequences that are, ultimately, dehumanizing.

Ours is not the first generation to fall prey to false needs; but ours is the first generation of admakers to realize the complete fulfillment of the consumerist vision through the fine-tuning of sheer hucksterism. Surfaces, fantasies, appearances, and vague associations are the order of the day. So completely have substance, reality, and utility been subverted that products are purified into mere wisps of labels, floating signifiers of their former selves. "Coke" can as easily add life plastered on clothing as

---

1. **Lanham Act**   U.S. statute enacted in 1947 that revised trademark laws. — EDS.
2. §243 (a), Lanham Act, 15 U.S.C.S. §21125 (a) (1988).

poured in a cup. Calculating a remedy for this new-age consumptive pandering is problematic. If people like — and buy — the enigmatic emptiness used to push products, then describing a harm becomes elusive. But it is elusive precisely because the imagery and vocabulary of advertising have shifted the focus from need to disguise. With this shift has come — either manipulated or galloping gladly behind — a greater public appetite for illusion and disguise. And in the wake of that has come an enormous shift of national industry, national resources, and national consciousness.

Some years ago, when I first started teaching, most of my students agreed that a nice L. L. Bean Baxter State Parka delivered without a label saying "L. L. Bean" was a minor default indeed. Today I have to work to convince them that the absence of the label is not a major breach of contract; I have to make them think about what makes the parka "an L. L. Bean": its utility or its image? Its service to the wearer or its impact on those around the wearer? If masque becomes the basis of our bargains, I worry that we will forget the jazzy, primal King Lear-ish essence of ourselves from which wisdom springs and insight grows. I worry that we will create new standards of irrelevance in our lives, reordering social relations in favor of the luxurious — and since few of us can afford real luxury, blind greed becomes the necessary companion.

On a yet more complicated level, I worry that in accustoming ourselves to the emptiness of media fictions, we will have reconstructed our very notion of property. If property is literally the word or the concept used to describe it, then we have empowered the self-willed speaker not just as market actor but as ultimate Creator. If property is nothing more than what it evokes on the most intimate and subjective levels, then the inherence of its object is denied; the separateness of the thing that is property must be actively obliterated in order to maintain the privately sensational pleasantry of the mirror image. A habituated, acculturated blindness to the inherent quality of the people and things around us grows up, based on our safety from having to see. Our interrelationships with these things is not seen; their reasons for being are rendered invisible.

At the simplest level of market economics, the modern algebra of advertising deprives society of a concept of commodities as enduring. Sales of goods are no longer the subject of express or long-term promissory relationships — there is at best an implied warranty of merchantability at the fleeting moment of contract and delivery. Contract law's historic expectation interest[3] becomes even more thoroughly touch and go, in the most virulent tradition of caveat emptor. It is an unconscious narrowing of expectation to the extent that we lose our expectations. Thus, in some

---

3. The "expectation interest" in contract law is the promisee's "interest in having the benefit of his bargain by being put in as good a position as he would have been in had the contract been performed." §344 (a), *Restatement of the Law, Contracts (2d)*.

way, Coke and Pepsi lead us to obliterate the future, not just with empty calories but with empty promises. The illusion of a perky, sexy self is meaningless as to the reality of a can of corn syrup: But this substitution, this exchange of images, is a harm going beyond wasted money, tooth decay, or defeated notions of utility. The greater harm is that it is hypnotic, and culturally addictive.

In theory, contract doctrine is the currency of law used to impose economic order on human beings for certain purposes; defenses to contract formation such as fraud, duress, and undue influence are, I think, a theoretical attempt to impose an ordered humanity on economics. Increasingly, however, the day-to-day consumer purchases that form most of what is governed by contract have been characterized by a shift in popular as well as legal discourse: Contract is no longer a three-party transliterative code, in which law mediates between profit and relationship, and in which property therefore remains linked to notions of shared humanity. Instead, consumerism is locked into a two-party, bipolar code that is little more mediative than a mirror. Money reflects law and law reflects money, unattached to notions of humanity. The neat jurisprudence of interpretive transposition renders the whole into a system of equations in which money = money, words = words (or law = law). The worst sort of mindless materialism arises. The worst sort of punitive literalism puts down roots.

Some time ago, my friend and colleague Dinesh Khosla traveled to Costa Rica for a conference. On his way back to the United States, he found himself in the airport behind throngs of Costa Ricans pushing five or six huge suitcases apiece. Dinesh stopped often to assist several different people; each time he was surprised by how light the suitcases felt. After this much of the story, I already imagined its end, filling the suitcases with media images of feathery coca leaves and dusty white powders. But I was wrong; it turned out that these travelers were all wealthy Costa Ricans going to Miami for the sole purpose of shopping. They planned to load up the suitcases with designer clothes and fancy consumables and cart them back home. I was reminded of the Sufi tale of the customs official who for years scrutinized the comings and goings of a man famed as a smuggler. For years he subjected each parcel to thorough searches, but all he ever found was straw. Many years later when they were both retired, he asked the smuggler where he had hidden the contraband all that time. The man replied: "I was smuggling straw." Dinesh's account made the conspicuous luxury of North American commodities into a similar form of invisible contraband, a sinfully expensive and indulgent drug.

One last anecdote: A little way down Broadway from the 14th Street subway station in Manhattan, there is a store called the Unique Boutique. Yards from the campus of New York University, it is a place where stylish coeds shop for the slightly frumpy, punky, slummy clothes that go so well with bright red lipstick and ankle-high black bootlets.

One winter day I saw a large, bright, fun-colored sign hanging in the window: "Sale! Two-dollar overcoats. No bums, no booze." Offended, and not wanting to feel how offended I was, I turned my head away toward the street. There, in the middle of the intersection of Broadway and Washington Place, stood a black man dressed in the ancient remains of a Harris Tweed overcoat. His arms were spread-eagled as if to fly, though he was actually begging from cars in both directions. He was also drunk and crying and trying to keep his balance. Drivers were offended, terrified of disease or of being robbed. Traffic slowed as cars described wide avoiding arcs around him and his broad-winged pleading.

So the sign was disenfranchising the very people who most needed two-dollar overcoats, the so-called bums. Moreover, it was selling the image of the disenfranchised themselves. The store is a trendy boutique aimed at NYU's undergraduate population. It was selling an image of genteel poverty, of casual dispossession. It attracted those who can afford to slum in style: yet it simultaneously exploited the slum itself. It was segregationist in the same way that "whites only" signs are. And it was not just segregationist along race and class lines; it also stole the images of those who had nothing and styled it as a commodity (slumminess) to be sold to those who have much. It was the ultimate in short-term consumerist redundance: Clothes do not just make the man, they would admit him into the clothing store itself.

In discussing the tension between liberty and authority, John Stuart 15 Mill observed that self-government means "not the government of each by himself but of each by all the rest." Mill feared what he called the "tyranny of the majority" and cautioned,

> Protection . . . against the tyranny of the magistrate is not enough; there needs protection also against the tyranny of prevailing opinion and feeling; against the tendency of society to impose, by other means than civil penalties, its own ideas and practices as rules of conduct on those who dissent from them . . . how to make the fitting adjustment between individual independence and social control — is a subject on which nearly everything remains to be done.[4]

The tyranny of the majority has survived in liberal political theory as a justification for all manner of legislative restraint, particularly economic restraint. But what Mill did not anticipate was that the persuasive power of the forum itself would subvert the polis, as well as the law, to the extent that there is today precious little "public" left, just the tyranny of what we call the private. In this nation there is, it is true, relatively little force in the public domain compared to other nations, relatively little intrusive governmental interference. But we risk instead the life-crushing disenfranchisement of an entirely owned world. Permission must be

---

4. John Stuart Mill, *On Liberty,* ed. David Spitz (New York: Norton, 1975), p. 6.

sought to walk upon the face of the earth. Freedom becomes contractual and therefore obligated; freedom is framed by obligation; and obligation is paired not with duty but with debt.

### Reading the Text

1. What relationship does Williams see between products and their advertising images?
2. Why does Williams find the legal designation of "false advertising" almost irrelevant in today's marketing world?
3. How, according to Williams, has our notion of "property" been altered by modern advertising?

### Reading the Signs

1. Williams assumes that the fleeting relationship between product and image in advertising is a recent phenomenon. Visit your college library, and survey some popular magazines published at the beginning of this century. What sort of relationship between product and image do you see in advertising? What does the relationship you find say about social values?
2. Compare the "image of the disenfranchised" Williams mentions on p. 142 to grunge fashion in the 1990s. Is grunge similarly "segregationist"?
3. Read or review Gloria Steinem's "Sex, Lies, and Advertising" (p. 155), and write an essay in which you explain how the business practices of the magazine industry illustrate Williams's concluding point: "Freedom becomes contractual and therefore obligated; freedom is framed by obligation; and obligation is paired not with duty but with debt."
4. Read or review Diane Barthel's "A Gentleman and a Consumer" (p. 144) and bell hooks's "Madonna: Plantation Mistress or Soul Sister?" (p. 223). Using their essays as models, analyze the roles of gender and ethnicity in the Georges Marciano commercial that Williams describes.

DIANE BARTHEL

*A Gentleman and a Consumer*

|||||||||||||||||||||||||||||||||||||||||||||||||||||||

*It's not only women who are pressured to conform to unattainable stan-*
*dards of physical appearance: Men are victims, too. Diane Barthel*
*(b. 1949), in this selection from* Putting on Appearances: Gender
and Advertising *(1988), surveys the various images men are expected*
*to live up to as presented in advertisements in men's magazines. From*
*the cowboy to the corporate jungle fighter, from the playboy to the polo*
*player, men are urged to adopt traditionally aggressive male gender*
*roles. At the same time, Barthel points out, they are to become ob-*
*sessed with their appearance — a role that, ironically, is traditionally*
*considered feminine. A professor of sociology at the State University of*
*New York, Stony Brook, Barthel is also the author of* Amana: From
Pietist Sect to American Community *(1984) and* Historic
Preservation: Collective Memory and Historical Identity
*(1996).*

There are no men's beauty and glamour magazines with circulations
even approaching those of the women's magazines. The very idea of
men's beauty magazines may strike one as odd. In our society men traditionally were supposed to make the right appearance, to be well
groomed and neatly tailored. What they were *not* supposed to do was to
be overly concerned with their appearance, much less vain about their
beauty. That was to be effeminate, and not a "real man." Male beauty
was associated with homosexuals, and "real men" had to show how red-
blooded they were by maintaining a certain distance from fashion.

Perhaps the best-known male fashion magazine is *GQ* founded in
1957 and with a circulation of 446,000 in 1986. More recently, we have
seen the launching of *YMF* and *Young Black Male*, which in 1987 still
[had] few advertising pages. *M* magazine, founded in 1983, attracts an audience "a cut above" that of *GQ*.[1]

*Esquire* magazine, more venerable (founded in 1933), is classified as a
general interest magazine. Although it does attract many women readers,
many of the columns and features and much of the advertising are definitely directed toward attracting the attention of the male readers, who
still make up the overwhelming majority of the readership.

The highest circulations for men's magazines are for magazines specializing either in sex (*Playboy*, circulation 4.1 million; *Penthouse*, circula-

---

1. Katz and Katz, *Magazines,* pp. 703–5.

tion nearly 3.8 million; and *Hustler,* circulation 1.5 million) or sports (*Sports Illustrated,* circulation 2.7 million).[2] That these magazines share an emphasis on power — either power over women or over other men on the playing field — should not surprise. In fact, sociologist John Gagnon would argue that sex and sports now represent the major fields in which the male role, as defined by power, is played out, with physical power in work, and even in warfare, being less important than it was before industrialization and technological advance.[3]

If we are looking for comparative evidence as to how advertisements define gender roles for men and women, we should not then see the male role as defined primarily through beauty and fashion. This seems an obvious point, but it is important to emphasize how different cultural attitudes toward both the social person and the physical body shape the gender roles of men and women. These cultural attitudes are changing, and advertisements are helping to legitimate the use of beauty products and an interest in fashion for men, as we shall see. As advertisements directed toward women are beginning to use male imagery, so too advertisements for men occasionally use imagery resembling that found in advertisements directed toward women. We are speaking of two *modes,* then. As Baudrillard[4] writes, these modes "do not result from the differentiated nature of the two sexes, but from the differential logic of the system. The relationship of the Masculine and the Feminine to real men and women is relatively arbitrary."[5] Increasingly today, men and women use both modes. The two great terms of opposition (Masculine and Feminine) still, however, structure the forms that consumption takes; they provide identities for products and consumers.

Baudrillard agrees that the feminine model encourages a woman to please herself, to encourage a certain complacency and even narcissistic solicitude. But by pleasing herself, it is understood that she will also please others, and that she will be chosen. "She never enters into direct competition. . . . If she is beautiful, that is to say, if this woman is a woman, she will be chosen. If the man is a man, he will choose his woman as he would other objects/signs (HIS car, HIS woman, HIS eau de toilette)."[6]

Whereas the feminine model is based on passivity, complacency, and narcissism, the masculine model is based on exactingness and choice.

2. Ibid.

3. John Gagnon, "Physical Strength: Once of Significance," in Joseph H. Pleck and Jack Sawyer, eds., *Men and Masculinity* (Englewood Cliffs, N.J.: Prentice-Hall, 1974), pp. 139–49.

4. **Jean Baudrillard** (b. 1929)  French semiologist. — EDS.

5. Baudrillard, *La société de consommation,* pp. 144–47.

6. Ibid.

All of masculine advertising insists on rule, on choice, in terms of rigor and inflexible minutiae. He does not neglect a detail . . . It is not a question of just letting things go, or of taking pleasure in something, but rather of distinguishing himself. To know how to choose, and not to fail at it, is here the equivalent of the military and puritanical virtues: intransigence, decision, "virtus."[7]

This masculine model, these masculine virtues, are best reflected in the many car advertisements. There, the keywords are masculine terms: *power, performance, precision.* Sometimes the car is a woman, responding to the touch and will of her male driver, after attracting him with her sexy body. "Pure shape, pure power, pure Z. It turns you on." But, as the juxtaposition of shape and power in this advertisement suggests, the car is not simply other; it is also an extension of the owner. As he turns it on, he turns himself on. Its power is his power; through it, he will be able to overpower other men and impress and seduce women.

> How well does it perform?
> How well can you drive? (Merkur XR4Ti)          10
>
> The 1987 Celica GT–S has the sweeping lines and aggressive stance that promise performance. And Celica keeps its word.
>
> Renault GTA:
> Zero to sixty to zero in 13.9 sec.
> It's the result of a performance philosophy where acceleration and braking are equally important.
> There's a new Renault sports sedan called GTA. Under its slick          15
> monochromatic skin is a road car with a total performance attitude.
> . . . It's our hot new pocket rocket.

In this last example, the car, like the driver, has a total performance attitude. That is what works. The slick monochromatic skin, like the Bond Street suit, makes a good first impression. But car, like owner, must have what it takes, must be able to go the distance faster and better than the competition. This point is explicitly made in advertisements in which the car becomes a means through which this masculine competition at work is extended in leisure. Some refer directly to the manly sport of auto-racing: "The Mitsubishi Starion ESI-R. Patiently crafted to ignite your imagination. Leaving little else to say except . . . gentlemen, start your engines." Others refer to competition in the business world: "To move ahead fast in this world, you've got to have connections. The totally new Corolla FX 16 GT-S has the right ones." Or in life in general. "It doesn't take any [Japanese characters] from anyone. It won't stand for any guff from 300ZX. Or RX-7. Introducing Conquest Tsi, the new

---

7. Ibid.

turbo sport coupe designed and built by Mitsubishi in Japan." Or Ferrari, which says simply, "We are the competition." In this competition between products, the owners become almost superfluous. But the advertisements, of course, suggest that the qualities of the car will reflect the qualities of the owner, as opposed to the purely abstract, apersonal quality of money needed for purchase. Thus, like the would-be owner, the BMW also demonstrates a "relentless refusal to compromise." It is for "those who thrive on a maximum daily requirement of high performance." While the BMW has the business attitude of the old school ("aggression has never been expressed with such dignity"), a Beretta suggests what it takes to survive today in the shark-infested waters of Wall Street. In a glossy three-page cover foldout, a photograph of a shark's fin cutting through indigo waters is accompanied by the legend "Discover a new species from today's Chevrolet." The following two pages show a sleek black Beretta similarly cutting through water and, presumably, through the competition: "Not just a new car, but a new species . . . with a natural instinct for the road . . . Aggressive stance. And a bold tail lamp. See it on the road and you won't soon forget. Drive it, and you never will."

And as with men, so with cars. "Power corrupts. Absolute power corrupts absolutely" (Maserati). Not having the money to pay for a Maserati, to corrupt and be corrupted, is a source of embarrassment. Advertisements reassure the consumer that he need not lose face in this manly battle. Hyundai promises, "It's affordable. (But you'd never know it.)"

> On first impression, the new Hyundai Excel GLS Sedan might seem a trifle beyond most people's means. But that's entirely by design. Sleek European design, to be exact.

Many advertisements suggest sexual pleasure and escape, as in "Pure shape, pure power, pure Z. It turns you on." Or "The all-new Chrysler Le Baron. Beauty . . . with a passion for driving." The Le Baron may initially suggest a beautiful female, with its "image of arresting beauty" and its passion "to drive. And drive it does!" But it is "Le Baron," not "La Baronness." And the advertisement continues to emphasize how it "*attacks* [emphasis mine] the road with a high torque, 2.5 fuel-injected engine. And its turbo option can blur the surface of any passing lane." Thus the object of the pleasure hardly has to be female if it is beautiful or sleek. The car is an extension of the male that conquers and tames the (female) road: "Positive-response suspension will calm the most demanding roads." The car becomes the ultimate lover when, like the Honda Prelude, it promises to combine power, "muscle," with finesse. Automobile advertisements thus play with androgyny and sexuality; the pleasure is in the union and confusion of form and movement, sex and speed. As in any sexual union, there is ultimately a merging of identities, rather than rigid maintenance of their separation. Polymorphous perverse? Perhaps. But it sells.

Though power, performance, precision as a complex of traits find their strongest emphasis in automobile advertisements, they also appear as selling points for products as diverse as shoes, stereos, and sunglasses. The car performs on the road, the driver performs for women, even in the parking lot, as Michelin suggests in its two-page spread showing a male from waist down resting on his car and chatting up a curvaceous female: "It performs great. And looks great. So, it not only stands out on the road. But in the parking lot. Which is one more place you're likely to discover how beautifully it can handle the curves" (!).

As media analyst Todd Gitlin points out, most of the drivers shown   20 in advertisements are young white males, loners who become empowered by the car that makes possible their escape from the everyday. Gitlin stresses the advertisements' "emphasis on surface, the blankness of the protagonist; his striving toward self-sufficiency, to the point of displacement from the recognizable world."[8] Even the Chrysler advertisements that coopt Bruce Springsteen's "Born in the USA" for their "Born in America" campaign lose in the process the original political message, "ripping off Springsteen's angry anthem, smoothing it into a Chamber of Commerce ditty as shots of just plain productive-looking folks, black and white . . . whiz by in a montage-made community." As Gitlin comments, "None of Springsteen's losers need apply — or rather, if only they would roll up their sleeves and see what good company they're in, they wouldn't feel like losers any longer."[9]

This is a world of patriarchal order in which the individual male can and must challenge the father. He achieves identity by breaking loose of the structure and breaking free of the pack. In the process he recreates the order and reaffirms the myth of masculine independence. Above all, he demonstrates that he knows what he wants; he is critical, demanding, and free from the constraints of others. What he definitely does not want, and goes to some measure to avoid, is to appear less than masculine, in any way weak, frilly, feminine.

### Avoiding the Feminine

Advertisers trying to develop male markets for products previously associated primarily with women must overcome the taboo that only women wear moisturizer, face cream, hair spray, or perfume. They do

---

8. Todd Gitlin, "We Build Excitement," in Todd Gitlin, ed., *Watching Television* (New York: Pantheon, 1986), pp. 139–40.
9. Ibid.

this by overt reference to masculine symbols, language, and imagery, and sometimes by confronting the problem head-on.

There is not so much of a problem in selling products to counteract balding — that traditionally has been recognized as a male problem (a bald woman is a sexual joke that is not particularly amusing to the elderly). But other hair products are another story, as the March 1987 *GQ* cover asks, "Are you man enough for mousse?" So the advertisements must make their products seem manly, as with S-Curl's "wave and curl kit" offering "The Manly Look" on its manly model dressed in business suit and carrying a hard hat (a nifty social class compromise), and as in college basketball sportscaster Al McGuire's testimonial for Consort hair spray:

> "Years ago, if someone had said to me, 'Hey Al, do you use hair spray?' I would have said, 'No way, baby!'"
> "That was before I tried Consort Pump."                                        25
> "Consort adds extra control to my hair without looking stiff or phony. Control that lasts clean into overtime and post-game interviews . . ."
> Grooming Gear for Real Guys. *Consort.*

Besides such "grooming gear" as perms and hair sprays, Real Guys use "skin supplies" and "shaving resources." They adopt a "survival strategy" to fight balding, and the "Fila philosophy" — "products with a singular purpose: performance" — for effective "bodycare." If they wear scent, it smells of anything *but* flowers: musk, woods, spices, citrus, and surf are all acceptable. And the names must be manly, whether symbolizing physical power ("Brut") or financial power ("Giorgio VIP Special Reserve," "The Baron. A distinctive fragrance for men," "Halston — For the privileged few").

As power/precision/performance runs as a theme throughout advertising to men, so too do references to the business world. Cars, as we have seen, promise to share their owner's professional attitude and aggressive drive to beat out the competition. Other products similarly reflect the centrality of business competition to the male gender role. And at the center of this competition itself, the business suit.

> At the onset of your business day, you choose the suit or sport          30
> coat that will position you front and center . . .
> The Right Suit can't guarantee he'll see it your way. The wrong suit could mean not seeing him at all.

Along with the Right Suit, the right shirt. "You want it every time you reach across the conference table, or trade on the floor, or just move about. You want a shirt that truly fits, that is long enough to stay put through the most active day, even for the taller gentleman." The businessman chooses the right cologne — Grey Flannel, or perhaps Quorum.

He wears a Gucci "timepiece" as he conducts business on a cordless telephone from his poolside — or prefers the "dignity in styling" promised
by Raymond Weil watches, "a beautiful way to dress for success."

Men's products connect status and success; the right products show
that you have the right stuff, that you're one of them. In the 1950s
C. Wright Mills[10] described what it took to get ahead, to become part of
the "power elite":

> The fit survive, and fitness means, not formal competence . . . but
> conformity with the criteria of those who have already succeeded. To
> be compatible with the top men is to act like them, to look like
> them, to think like them: to be of and for them — or at least to dis-
> play oneself to them in such a way as to create that impression. This,
> in fact, is what is meant by "creating" — a well-chosen word — "a
> good impression." This is what is meant — and nothing else — by
> being a "sound man," as sound as a dollar.[11]

Today, having what it takes includes knowing "the difference between dressed, and well dressed" (Bally shoes). It is knowing that "what
you carry says as much about you as what you put inside it" (Hartmann
luggage). It is knowing enough to imitate Doug Fout, "member of one
of the foremost equestrian families in the country."

> Because of our adherence to quality and the natural shoulder tra-
> dition, Southwick clothing was adopted by the Fout family years ago.
> Clearly, they have as much appreciation for good lines in a jacket as
> they do in a thoroughbred.

There it is, old money. There is no substitute for it, really, in business or
in advertising, where appeals to tradition form one of the mainstays guar-
anteeing men that their choices are not overly fashionable or feminine,
not working class or cheap, but, rather, correct, in good form, above
criticism. If, when, they achieve this status of gentlemanly perfection,
then, the advertisement suggests, they may be invited to join the club.

> When only the best of associations will do

> Recognizing style as the requisite for membership, discerning      35
> men prefer the natural shoulder styling of Racquet Club. Meticu-
> lously tailored in pure wool, each suit and sportcoat is the ultimate
> expression of the clubman's classic good taste.

Ralph Lauren has his Polo University Club, and Rolex picks up on the
polo theme by sponsoring the Rolex Gold Cup held at the Palm Beach

---

10. **C. Wright Mills** (1916–1962)   American sociologist. — EDS.
11. C. Wright Mills, *The Power Elite* (New York: Oxford University Press, 1956),
p. 141.

Polo and Country Club, where sixteen teams and sixty-four players competed for "the pure honor of winning, the true glory of victory":

> It has added new lustre to a game so ancient, its history is lost in legend. Tamerlane is said to have been its patriarch. Darius's Persian cavalry, we're told, played it. It was the national sport of 16th-century India, Egypt, China, and Japan. The British rediscovered and named it in 1857.
>
> The linking of polo and Rolex is uniquely appropriate. Both sponsor and sport personify rugged grace. Each is an arbiter of the art of timing.

In the spring of 1987, there was another interesting club event — or nonevent. The prestigious New York University Club was ordered to open its doors to women. This brought the expected protests about freedom of association — and of sanctuary. For that has been one of the points of the men's club. It wasn't open to women. Members knew women had their place, and everyone knew it was not there. In the advertisements, as in the world of reality, there is a place for women in men's lives, one that revolves around:

## Sex and Seduction

The growing fascination with appearances, encouraged by advertising, has led to a "feminization" of culture. We are all put in the classic role of the female: manipulable, submissive, seeing ourselves as objects. This "feminization of sexuality" is clearly seen in men's advertisements, where many of the promises made to women are now made to men. If women's advertisements cry, "Buy (this product) and he will notice you," men's advertisements similarly promise that female attention will follow immediately upon purchase, or shortly thereafter. "They can't stay away from Mr. J." "Master the Art of Attracting Attention." She says, "He's wearing my favorite Corbin again." Much as in the advertisements directed at women, the advertisements of men's products promise that they will do the talking for you. "For the look that says come closer." "All the French you'll ever need to know."

Although many advertisements show an admiring and/or dependent female, others depict women in a more active role. "I love him — but life in the fast lane starts at 6 A.M.," says the attractive blonde tying on her jogging shoes, with the "him" in question very handsome and very asleep on the bed in the background. (Does this mean he's in the slow lane?) In another, the man slouches silhouetted against a wall; the woman leans aggressively toward him. He: "Do you always serve Tia Maria . . . or am I special?" She: "Darling, if you weren't special . . . you wouldn't be here."

The masculine role of always being in charge is a tough one. The   40
blunt new honesty about sexually transmitted diseases such as AIDS appears in men's magazines as in women's, in the same "I enjoy sex, but
I'm not ready to die for it" condom advertisement. But this new fear is
accompanied by old fears of sexual embarrassment and/or rejection. The
cartoon shows a man cringing with embarrassment in a pharmacy as the
pharmacist yells out, "Hey, there's a guy here wants some information
on Trojans." ("Most men would like to know more about Trojan brand
condoms. But they're seriously afraid of suffering a spectacular and terminal attack of embarrassment right in the middle of a well-lighted drugstore.") Compared with such agony and responsibility, advertisements
promising that women will *want* whatever is on offer, and will even meet
the male halfway, must come as blessed relief. Men can finally relax,
leaving the courting to the product and seduction to the beguiled
woman, which, surely, must seem nice for a change.

## Masculine Homilies

A homily is a short sermon, discourse, or informal lecture, often on a
moral topic and suggesting a course of conduct. Some of the most intriguing advertisements offer just that, short statements and bits of advice
on what masculinity is and on how real men should conduct themselves.
As with many short sermons, many of the advertising homilies have a
self-congratulatory air about them; after all, you do not want the consumer to feel bad about himself.

What is it, then, to be a man? It is to be *independent*. "There are
some things a man will not relinquish." Among them, says the advertisement, his Tretorn tennis shoes.

It is to *savor freedom*. "Dress easy, get away from it all and let Tom
Sawyer paint the fence," advises Alexander Julian, the men's designer.
"Because man was meant to fly, we gave him wings" (even if only on his
sunglasses).

It is to live a life of *adventure*. KL Homme cologne is "for the man
who lives on the edge." Prudential Life Insurance preaches, "If you can
dream it, you can do it." New Man sportswear tells the reader, "Life is
more adventurous when you feel like a New Man."

It is to *keep one's cool*. "J. B. Scotch. A few individuals know how to   45
keep their heads, even when their necks are on the line."

And it is to stay one step *ahead of the competition*. "Altec Lansing. Hear
what others only imagine." Alexander Julian again: "Dress up a bit when
you dress down. They'll think you know something they don't."

What is it, then, to be a woman? It is to be *dependent*. "A woman
needs a man," reads the copy in the Rigolletto advertisement showing a
young man changing a tire for a grateful young woman.

The American cowboy as cultural model was not supposed to care for or about appearances. He was what he was, hard-working, straightforward, and honest. He was authentic. Men who cared "too much" about how they looked did not fit this model; the dandy was effete, a European invention, insufficient in masculinity and not red-blooded enough to be a real American. The other cultural model, imported from England, was the gentleman. A gentleman did care about his appearance, in the proper measure and manifestation, attention to tailoring and to quality, understatement rather than exaggeration.[12]

From the gray flannel suit of the 1950s to the "power look" of the 1980s, clothes made the man fit in with his company's image. Sex appeal and corporate correctness merged in a look that spelled success, that exuded confidence.

Whether or not a man presumed to care about his appearance, he did care about having "the right stuff," as Tom Wolfe and *Esquire* call it, or "men's toys," as in a recent special issue of *M* magazine. Cars, motorcycles, stereos, sports equipment: These are part of the masculine appearance. They allow the man to demonstrate his taste, his special knowledge, his affluence: to extend his control. He can be and is demanding, for only the best will do. 50

He also wants to be loved, but he does not want to appear needy. Advertisements suggest the magic ability of products ranging from cars to hair creams to attract female attention. With the right products a man can have it all, with no strings attached: no boring marital ties, hefty mortgages, corporate compromises.

According to sociologist Barbara Ehrenreich, *Playboy* magazine did much to legitimate this image of male freedom. The old male ethos, up to the postwar period, required exchanging bachelor irresponsibility for married responsibility, which also symbolized entrance into social adulthood.[13] The perennial bachelor, with his flashy cars and interchangeable women, was the object of both envy and derision; he had fun, but . . . he was not fully grown up. There was something frivolous in his lack of purpose and application.

This old ethos has lost much of its legitimacy. Today's male can, as Baudrillard suggests, operate in both modes: the feminine mode of indulging oneself and being indulged and the masculine mode of exigency and competition. With the right look and the right stuff, he can feel confident and manly in boardroom or suburban backyard. Consumer society

---

12. See Diane Barthel, "A Gentleman and a Consumer: A Sociological Look at Man at His Best," paper presented at the annual meeting of the Eastern Sociological Society, March 1983, Baltimore.

13. Barbara Ehrenreich, *The Hearts of Men: American Dreams and the Flight from Commitment* (New York: Anchor Books, 1983).

thus invites both men and women to live in a world of appearances and to devote ever more attention to them.

## Reading the Text

1. Define in your own words what Barthel means by the "masculine" and "feminine" modes.
2. Why, according to Barthel, are men's magazines less popular than women's magazines?
3. Summarize what Barthel claims "being a man" means in magazine advertising.
4. How are women typically portrayed in men's magazine ads, according to Barthel?

## Reading the Signs

1. Buy a copy of one of the men's magazines that Barthel mentions in her essay, and study the advertising. Do the ads corroborate Barthel's claim that men today are allowed to demonstrate both their "masculine" and "feminine" sides?
2. Write an essay in which you apply Barthel's analysis of car advertising to ads in a magazine such as *Car and Driver.* To what extent do the key concepts "power," "performance," and "precision" influence the ads you find?
3. Have each class member bring a copy of a men's or women's magazine to class. Form same-sex groups, and give each group a few magazines designed for the opposite sex. Analyze the gender roles depicted in the magazines, and report to the class the group's findings.
4. Barthel claims that "the growing fascination with appearances" has led to a "feminization" of our culture. Read or review Holly Devor's "Gender Role Behaviors and Attitudes" (p. 415), and use her essay as a critical framework to critique Barthel's claim.
5. In class, brainstorm images of "masculinity" and "femininity" and write your results on the board. Then compare the class's list to the gender traits that Barthel claims are common in advertising. Discuss with your class the possible origins of your brainstormed images.

GLORIA  STEINEM

*Sex, Lies, and Advertising*

*One of the best-known icons of the women's movement, Gloria Steinem (b. 1934) has been a leader in transforming the image of women in America. As a cofounder of* Ms. *magazine, in which this selection first appeared, Steinem has provided a forum for women's voices for more than twenty years, but as her article explains, it has not been easy to keep this forum going. For a commercial publication requires commercials, and the needs of advertisers do not always mesh nicely with the goals of a magazine like* Ms. *Steinem ruefully reveals the compromises* Ms. *magazine had to make over the years to satisfy its advertising clients, compromises that came to an end only when* Ms. *ceased to take ads. Steinem's most recent book is* Moving Beyond Words *(1994), and her many other publications include* Revolution from Within *(1992), a personal exploration of the power of self-esteem. Currently the president of Voters for Choice and a consulting editor for* Ms., *Steinem continues to combine her passion for writing and activism as an unflagging voice in American feminism.*

About three years ago, as *glasnost* was beginning and *Ms.* seemed to be ending, I was invited to a press lunch for a Soviet official. He entertained us with anecdotes about new problems of democracy in his country. Local Communist leaders were being criticized in their media for the first time, he explained, and they were angry.

"So I'll have to ask my American friends," he finished pointedly, "how more *subtly* to control the press." In the silence that followed, I said, "Advertising."

The reporters laughed, but later, one of them took me aside: How *dare* I suggest that freedom of the press was limited? How dare I imply that his newsweekly could be influenced by ads?

I explained that I was thinking of advertising's media-wide influence on most of what we read. Even newsmagazines use "soft" cover stories to sell ads, confuse readers with "advertorials,"[1] and occasionally self-censor on subjects known to be a problem with big advertisers.

But, I also explained, I was thinking especially of women's magazines. 5 There, it isn't just a little content that's devoted to attracting ads, it's almost all of it. That's why advertisers — not readers — have always been the problem for *Ms.* As the only women's magazine that didn't supply what

---

1. **advertorial**   Advertisement designed to mimic the appearance of a feature article. — EDS.

the ad world euphemistically describes as "supportive editorial atmosphere" or "complementary copy" (for instance, articles that praise food/fashion/beauty subjects to "support" and "complement" food/fashion/beauty ads), *Ms.* could never attract enough advertising to break even.

"Oh, *women's* magazines," the journalist said with contempt. "Everybody knows they're catalogs — but who cares? They have nothing to do with journalism."

I can't tell you how many times I've had this argument in 25 years of working for many kinds of publications. Except as moneymaking machines — "cash cows" as they are so elegantly called in the trade — women's magazines are rarely taken seriously. Though changes being made by women have been called more far-reaching than the industrial revolution — and though many editors try hard to reflect some of them in the few pages left to them after all the ad-related subjects have been covered — the magazines serving the female half of this country are still far below the journalistic and ethical standards of news and general interest publications. Most depressing of all, this doesn't even rate an exposé.

If *Time* and *Newsweek* had to lavish praise on cars in general and credit General Motors in particular to get GM ads, there would be a scandal — maybe a criminal investigation. When women's magazines from *Seventeen* to *Lear's* praise beauty products in general and credit Revlon in particular to get ads, it's just business as usual.

### 1

When *Ms.* began, we didn't consider *not* taking ads. The most important reason was keeping the price of a feminist magazine low enough for most women to afford. But the second and almost equal reason was providing a forum where women and advertisers could talk to each other and improve advertising itself. After all, it was (and still is) as potent a source of information in this country as news or TV and movie dramas.

We decided to proceed in two stages. First, we would convince makers of "people products" used by both men and women but advertised mostly to men — cars, credit cards, insurance, sound equipment, financial services, and the like — that their ads should be placed in a women's magazine. Since they were accustomed to the division between editorial[2] and advertising in news and general interest magazines, this would allow our editorial content to be free and diverse. Second, we would add the best ads for whatever traditional "women's products"

---

2. **editorial**   In the magazine industry, all nonadvertising content in a magazine, including regular columns and feature articles. — EDS.

(clothes, shampoo, fragrance, food, and so on) that surveys showed *Ms.* readers used. But we would ask them to come in *without* the usual quid pro quo of "complementary copy."

We knew the second step might be harder. Food advertisers have always demanded that women's magazines publish recipes and articles on entertaining (preferably ones that name their products) in return for their ads; clothing advertisers expect to be surrounded by fashion spreads (especially ones that credit their designers); and shampoo, fragrance, and beauty products in general usually insist on positive editorial coverage of beauty subjects, plus photo credits besides. That's why women's magazines look the way they do. But if we could break this link between ads and editorial content, then we wanted good ads for "women's products," too.

By playing their part in this unprecedented mix of *all* the things our readers need and use, advertisers also would be rewarded: Ads for products like cars and mutual funds would find a new growth market; the best ads for women's products would no longer be lost in oceans of ads for the same category; and both would have access to a laboratory of smart and caring readers whose response would help create effective ads for other media as well.

I thought then that our main problem would be the imagery in ads themselves. Car-makers were still draping blondes in evening gowns over the hoods like ornaments. Authority figures were almost always male, even in ads for products that only women used. Sadistic, he-man campaigns even won industry praise. (For instance, *Advertising Age* had hailed the infamous Silva Thin cigarette theme, "How to Get a Woman's Attention: Ignore Her," as "brilliant.") Even in medical journals, tranquilizer ads showed depressed housewives standing beside piles of dirty dishes and promised to get them back to work.

Obviously, *Ms.* would have to avoid such ads and seek out the best ones — but this didn't seem impossible. *The New Yorker* had been selecting ads for aesthetic reasons for years, a practice that only seemed to make advertisers more eager to be in its pages. *Ebony* and *Essence* were asking for ads with positive black images, and though their struggle was hard, they weren't being called unreasonable.

Clearly, what *Ms.* needed was a very special publisher and ad sales     15
staff. I could think of only one woman with experience on the business side of magazines — Patricia Carbine, who recently had become a vice president of *McCall's* as well as its editor in chief — and the reason I knew her name was a good omen. She had been managing editor at *Look* (really *the* editor, but its owner refused to put a female name at the top of his masthead) when I was writing a column there. After I did an early interview with Cesar Chavez, then just emerging as a leader of migrant labor, and the publisher turned it down because he was worried about ads from Sunkist, Pat was the one who intervened. As I learned later, she

had told the publisher she would resign if the interview wasn't published. Mainly because *Look* couldn't afford to lose Pat, it *was* published (and the ads from Sunkist never arrived).

Though I barely knew this woman, she had done two things I always remembered: put her job on the line in a way that editors often talk about but rarely do, and been so loyal to her colleagues that she never told me or anyone outside *Look* that she had done so.

Fortunately, Pat did agree to leave *McCall's* and take a huge cut in salary to become publisher of *Ms.* She became responsible for training and inspiring generations of young women who joined the *Ms.* ad sales force, many of whom went on to become "firsts" at the top of publishing. When *Ms.* first started, however, there were so few women with experience selling space that Pat and I made the rounds of ad agencies ourselves. Later, the fact that *Ms.* was asking companies to do business in a different way meant our saleswomen had to make many times the usual number of calls — first to convince agencies and then client companies besides — and to present endless amounts of research. I was often asked to do a final ad presentation, or see some higher decision-maker, or speak to women employees so executives could see the interest of women they worked with. That's why I spent more time persuading advertisers than editing or writing for *Ms.* and why I ended up with an unsentimental education in the seamy underside of publishing that few writers see (and even fewer magazines can publish).

Let me take you with us through some experiences, just as they happened:

▪ Cheered on by early support from Volkswagen and one or two other car companies, we scrape together time and money to put on a major reception in Detroit. We know U.S. car-makers firmly believe that women choose the upholstery, not the car, but we are armed with statistics and reader mail to prove the contrary: A car is an important purchase for women, one that symbolizes mobility and freedom.

But almost nobody comes. We are left with many pounds of shrimp on the table, and quite a lot of egg on our face. We blame ourselves for not guessing that there would be a baseball pennant play-off on the same day, but executives go out of their way to explain they wouldn't have come anyway. Thus begins ten years of knocking on hostile doors, presenting endless documentation, and hiring a full-time saleswoman in Detroit; all necessary before *Ms.* gets any real results.

This long saga has a semihappy ending: foreign and, later, domestic car-makers eventually provided *Ms.* with enough advertising to make cars one of our top sources of ad revenue. Slowly, Detroit began to take the women's market seriously enough to put car ads in other women's magazines, too, thus freeing a few pages from the hothouse of fashion-beauty-food ads. 20

But long after figures showed a third, even a half, of many car models being bought by women, U.S. makers continued to be uncomfortable addressing women. Unlike foreign car-makers, Detroit never quite learned the secret of creating intelligent ads that exclude no one, and then placing them in women's magazines to overcome past exclusion. (*Ms.* readers were so grateful for a routine Honda ad featuring rack and pinion steering, for instance, that they sent fan mail.) Even now, Detroit continues to ask, "Should we make special ads for women?" Perhaps that's why some foreign cars still have a disproportionate share of the U.S. women's market.

■  In the *Ms.* Gazette, we do a brief report on a congressional hearing into chemicals used in hair dyes that are absorbed through the skin and may be carcinogenic. Newspapers report this too, but Clairol, a Bristol-Myers subsidiary that makes dozens of products — a few of which have just begun to advertise in *Ms.* — is outraged. Not at newspapers or news magazines, just at us. It's bad enough that *Ms.* is the only women's magazine refusing to provide the usual "complementary" articles and beauty photos, but to criticize one of their categories — *that* is going too far.

We offer to publish a letter from Clairol telling its side of the story. In an excess of solicitousness, we even put this letter in the Gazette, not in Letters to the Editors where it belongs. Nonetheless — and in spite of surveys that show *Ms.* readers are active women who use more of almost everything Clairol makes than do the readers of any other women's magazine — *Ms.* gets almost none of these ads for the rest of its natural life.

Meanwhile, Clairol changes its hair-coloring formula, apparently in response to the hearings we reported.

■  Our saleswomen set out early to attract ads for consumer electronics: 25 sound equipment, calculators, computers, VCRs, and the like. We know that our readers are determined to be included in the technological revolution. We know from reader surveys that *Ms.* readers are buying this stuff in numbers as high as those of magazines like *Playboy,* or "men 18 to 34," the prime targets of the consumer electronics industry. Moreover, unlike traditional women's products that our readers buy but don't need to read articles about, these are subjects they want covered in our pages. There actually *is* a supportive editorial atmosphere.

"But women don't understand technology," say executives at the end of ad presentations. "Maybe not," we respond, "but neither do men — and we all buy it."

"If women *do* buy it," say the decision-makers, "they're asking their husbands and boyfriends what to buy first." We produce letters from *Ms.* readers saying how turned off they are when salesmen say things like "Let me know when your husband can come in."

After several years of this, we get a few ads for compact sound systems. Some of them come from JVC, whose vice president, Harry Elias, is trying to convince his Japanese bosses that there is something called a women's market. At his invitation, I find myself speaking at huge trade shows in Chicago and Las Vegas, trying to persuade JVC dealers that showrooms don't have to be locker rooms where women are made to feel unwelcome. But as it turns out, the shows themselves are part of the problem. In Las Vegas, the only women around the technology displays are seminude models serving champagne. In Chicago, the big attraction is Marilyn Chambers, who followed Linda Lovelace of *Deep Throat* fame as Chuck Traynor's captive and/or employee. VCRs are being demonstrated with her porn videos.

In the end, we get ads for a car stereo now and then, but no VCRs; some IBM personal computers, but no Apple or Japanese ones. We notice that office magazines like *Working Woman* and *Savvy* don't benefit as much as they should from office equipment ads either. In the electronics world, women and technology seem mutually exclusive. It remains a decade behind even Detroit.

- Because we get letters from little girls who love toy trains, and who ask our help in changing ads and box-top photos that feature little boys only, we try to get toy-train ads from Lionel. It turns out that Lionel executives *have* been concerned about little girls. They made a pink train, and were surprised when it didn't sell.

Lionel bows to consumer pressure with a photograph of a boy *and* a girl — but only on some of their boxes. They fear that, if trains are associated with girls, they will be devalued in the minds of boys. Needless to say, *Ms.* gets no train ads, and little girls remain a mostly unexplored market. By 1986, Lionel is put up for sale.

But for different reasons, we haven't had much luck with other kinds of toys either. In spite of many articles on child-rearing; an annual listing of nonsexist, multiracial toys by Letty Cottin Pogrebin; Stories for Free Children, a regular feature also edited by Letty; and other prizewinning features for or about children, we get virtually no toy ads. Generations of *Ms.* saleswomen explain to toy manufacturers that a larger proportion of *Ms.* readers have preschool children than do the readers of other women's magazines, but this industry can't believe feminists have or care about children.

- When *Ms.* begins, the staff decides not to accept ads for feminine hygiene sprays or cigarettes: they are damaging and carry no appropriate health warnings. Though we don't think we should tell our readers what to do, we do think we should provide facts so they can decide for themselves. Since the antismoking lobby has been pressing for health warnings on cigarette ads, we decide to take them only as they comply.

Philip Morris is among the first to do so. One of its brands, Virginia Slims, is also sponsoring women's tennis and the first national polls of women's opinions. On the other hand, the Virginia Slims theme,

"You've come a long way, baby," has more than a "baby" problem. It makes smoking a symbol of progress for women.

We explain to Philip Morris that this slogan won't do well in our     35
pages, but they are convinced its success with some women means it will work with *all* women. Finally, we agree to publish an ad for a Virginia Slims calendar as a test. The letters from readers are critical — and smart. For instance: Would you show a black man picking cotton, the same man in a Cardin suit, and symbolize the antislavery and civil rights movements by smoking? Of course not. But instead of honoring the test results, the Philip Morris people seem angry to be proven wrong. They take away ads for *all* their many brands.

This costs *Ms.* about $250,000 the first year. After five years, we can no longer keep track. Occasionally, a new set of executives listens to *Ms.* saleswomen, but because we won't take Virginia Slims, not one Philip Morris product returns to our pages for the next 16 years.

Gradually, we also realize our naiveté in thinking we *could* decide against taking cigarette ads. They became a disproportionate support of magazines the moment they were banned on television, and few magazines could compete and survive without them; certainly not *Ms.,* which lacks so many other categories. By the time statistics in the 1980s showed that women's rate of lung cancer was approaching men's, the necessity of taking cigarette ads has become a kind of prison.

■   General Mills, Pillsbury, Carnation, Del Monte, Dole, Kraft, Stouffer, Hormel, Nabisco: You name the food giant, we try it. But no matter how desirable the *Ms.* readership, our lack of recipes is lethal.

We explain to them that placing food ads *only* next to recipes associates food with work. For many women, it is a negative that works *against* the ads. Why not place food ads in diverse media without recipes (thus reaching more men, who are now a third of the shoppers in supermarkets anyway), and leave the recipes to specialty magazines like *Gourmet* (a third of whose readers are also men)?

These arguments elicit interest, but except for an occasional ad for a     40
convenience food, instant coffee, diet drinks, yogurt, or such extras as avocados and almonds, this mainstay of the publishing industry stays closed to us. Period.

■   Traditionally, wines and liquors didn't advertise to women: Men were thought to make the brand decisions, even if women did the buying. But after endless presentations, we begin to make a dent in this category. Thanks to the unconventional Michel Roux of Carillon Importers (distributors of Grand Marnier, Absolut Vodka, and others), who assumes that food and drink have no gender, some ads are leaving their men's club.

Beermakers are still selling masculinity. It takes *Ms.* fully eight years to get its first beer ad (Michelob). In general, however, liquor ads are less stereotyped in their imagery — and far less controlling of the editorial content around them — than are women's products. But given the underrepresentation of other categories, these very facts tend to create a disproportionate number of alcohol ads in the pages of *Ms.* This in turn dismays readers worried about women and alcoholism.

■　We hear in 1980 that women in the Soviet Union have been producing feminist *samizdat* (underground, self-published books) and circulating them throughout the country. As punishment, four of the leaders have been exiled. Though we are operating on our usual shoestring, we solicit individual contributions to send Robin Morgan to interview these women in Vienna.

The result is an exclusive cover story that includes the first news of a populist peace movement against the Afghanistan occupation, a prediction of *glasnost* to come, and a grassroots, intimate view of Soviet women's lives. From the popular press to women's studies courses, the response is great. The story wins a Front Page award.

Nonetheless, this journalistic coup undoes years of efforts to get an　45 ad schedule from Revlon. Why? Because the Soviet women on our cover *are not wearing makeup.*

■　Four years of research and presentations go into convincing airlines that women now make travel choices and business trips. United, the first airline to advertise in *Ms.,* is so impressed with the response from our readers that one of its executives appears in a film for our ad presentations. As usual, good ads get great results.

But we have problems unrelated to such results. For instance: Because American Airlines flight attendants include among their labor demands the stipulation that they could choose to have their last names preceded by "Ms." on their name tags — in a long-delayed revolt against the standard, "I am your pilot, Captain Rothgart, and this is your flight attendant, Cindy Sue" — American officials seem to hold the magazine responsible. We get no ads.

There is still a different problem at Eastern. A vice president cancels subscriptions for thousands of copies on Eastern flights. Why? Because he is offended by ads for lesbian poetry journals in the *Ms.* Classified. A "family airline," as he explains to me coldly on the phone, has to "draw the line somewhere."

It's obvious that *Ms.* can't exclude lesbians and serve women. We've been trying to make that point ever since our first issue included an article by and about lesbians, and both Suzanne Levine, our managing editor, and I were lectured by such heavy hitters as Ed Kosner, then editor of *Newsweek* (and now of *New York Magazine*), who insisted that *Ms.* should "position" itself *against* lesbians. But our advertisers have paid to reach a guaranteed number of readers, and soliciting new subscriptions to compensate for Eastern would cost $150,000, plus rebating money in the meantime.

Like almost everything ad–related, this presents an elaborate organiz-   50
ing problem. After days of searching for sympathetic members of the
Eastern board, Frank Thomas, president of the Ford Foundation, kindly
offers to call Roswell Gilpatrick, a director of Eastern. I talk with Mr.
Gilpatrick, who calls Frank Borman, then the president of Eastern. Frank
Borman calls me to say that his airline is not in the business of censoring
magazines: *Ms.* will be returned to Eastern flights.

■   Women's access to insurance and credit is vital, but with the exception of Equitable and a few other ad pioneers, such financial services address men. For almost a decade after the Equal Credit Opportunity Act
passes in 1974, we try to convince American Express that women are a
growth market — but nothing works.

Finally, a former professor of Russian named Jerry Welsh becomes
head of marketing. He assumes that women should be cardholders, and
persuades his colleagues to feature women in a campaign. Thanks to this
1980s series, the growth rate for female cardholders surpasses that for
men.

For this article, I asked Jerry Welsh if he would explain why American Express waited so long. "Sure," he said, "they were afraid of having a
'pink' card."

■   Women of color read *Ms.* in disproportionate numbers. This is a
source of pride to *Ms.* staffers, who are also more racially representative
than the editors of other women's magazines. But this reality is obscured
by ads filled with enough white women to make a reader snowblind.

Pat Carbine remembers mostly "astonishment" when she requested   55
African American, Hispanic, Asian, and other diverse images. Marcia
Ann Gillespie, a *Ms.* editor who was previously the editor in chief of
*Essence,* witnesses ad bias a second time: Having tried for *Essence* to get
white advertisers to use black images (Revlon did so eventually, but
L'Oréal, Lauder, Chanel, and other companies never did), she sees similar problems getting integrated ads for an integrated magazine. Indeed,
the ad world often creates black and Hispanic ads only for black and Hispanic media. In an exact parallel of the fear that marketing a product to
women will endanger its appeal to men, the response is usually, "But
your [white] readers won't identify."

In fact, those we are able to get — for instance, a Max Factor
ad made for *Essence* that Linda Wachner gives us after she becomes president — are praised by white readers, too. But there are pathetically few
such images.

■   By the end of 1986, production and mailing costs have risen astro-
nomically, ad income is flat, and competition for ads is stiffer than ever.
The 60/40 preponderance of edit over ads that we promised to readers
becomes 50/50; children's stories, most poetry, and some fiction are casualties of less space; in order to get variety into limited pages, the length

(and sometimes the depth) of articles suffers; and, though we do refuse most of the ads that would look like a parody in our pages, we get so worn down that some slip through. Still, readers perform miracles. Though we haven't been able to afford a subscription mailing in two years, they maintain our guaranteed circulation of 450,000.

Nonetheless, media reports on *Ms.* often insist that our unprofitability must be due to reader disinterest. The myth that advertisers simply follow readers is very strong. Not one reporter notes that other comparable magazines our size (say, *Vanity Fair* or *The Atlantic*) have been losing more money in one year than *Ms.* has lost in 16 years. No matter how much never-to-be-recovered cash is poured into starting a magazine or keeping one going, appearances seem to be all that matter. (Which is why we haven't been able to explain our fragile state in public. Nothing causes ad flight like the smell of nonsuccess.)

My healthy response is anger. My not-so-healthy response is constant worry. Also an obsession with finding one more rescue. There is hardly a night when I don't wake up with sweaty palms and pounding heart, scared that we won't be able to pay the printer or the post office; scared most of all that closing our doors will hurt the women's movement.

Out of chutzpah and desperation, I arrange a lunch with Leonard Lauder, president of Estée Lauder. With the exception of Clinique (the brainchild of Carol Phillips), none of Lauder's hundreds of products has been advertised in *Ms.* A year's schedule of ads for just three or four of them could save us. Indeed, as the scion of a family-owned company whose ad practices are followed by the beauty industry, he is one of the few men who could liberate many pages in all women's magazines just by changing his mind about "complementary copy."

Over a lunch that costs more than we can pay for some articles, I explain the need for his leadership. I also lay out the record of *Ms.*: more literary and journalistic prizes won, more new issues introduced into the mainstream, new writers discovered, and impact on society than any other magazine; more articles that became books, stories that became movies, ideas that became television series, and newly advertised products that became profitable; and, most important for him, a place for his ads to reach women who aren't reachable through any other women's magazine. Indeed, if there is one constant characteristic of the ever-changing *Ms.* readership, it is their impact as leaders. Whether it's waiting until later to have first babies, or pioneering PABA as sun protection in cosmetics, *whatever* they are doing today, a third to a half of American women will be doing three to five years from now. It's never failed.

But, he says, *Ms.* readers are not *our* women. They're not interested in things like fragrance and blush-on. If they were, *Ms.* would write articles about them.

On the contrary, I explain, surveys show they are more likely to buy such things than the readers of, say, *Cosmopolitan* or *Vogue*. They're good

60

customers because they're out in the world enough to need several sets of everything: home, work, purse, travel, gym, and so on. They just don't need to read articles about these things. Would he ask a men's magazine to publish monthly columns on how to shave before he advertised Aramis products (his line for men)?

He concedes that beauty features are often concocted more for advertisers than readers. But *Ms.* isn't appropriate for his ads anyway, he explains. Why? Because Estée Lauder is selling "a kept-woman mentality."

I can't quite believe this. Sixty percent of the users of his products    65
are salaried, and generally resemble *Ms.* readers. Besides, his company has the appeal of having been started by a creative and hardworking woman, his mother, Estée Lauder.

That doesn't matter, he says. He knows his customers, and they would *like* to be kept women. That's why he will never advertise in *Ms.*

In November 1987, by vote of the Ms. Foundation for Education and Communication (*Ms.*'s owner and publisher, the media subsidiary of the Ms. Foundation for Women), *Ms.* was sold to a company whose officers, Australian feminists Sandra Yates and Anne Summers, raised the investment money in their country that *Ms.* couldn't find in its own. They also started *Sassy* for teenage women.

In their two-year tenure, circulation was raised to 550,000 by investment in circulation mailings, and, to the dismay of some readers, editorial features on clothes and new products made a more traditional bid for ads. Nonetheless, ad pages fell below previous levels. In addition, *Sassy,* whose fresh voice and sexual frankness were an unprecedented success with young readers, was targeted by two mothers from Indiana who began, as one of them put it, "calling every Christian organization I could think of." In response to this controversy, several crucial advertisers pulled out.

Such links between ads and editorial content was a problem in Australia, too, but to a lesser degree. "Our readers pay two times more for their magazines," Anne explained, "so advertisers have less power to threaten a magazine's viability."

"I was shocked," said Sandra Yates with characteristic directness. "In    70
Australia, we think you have freedom of the press — but you don't."

Since Anne and Sandra had not met their budget's projections for ad revenue, their investors forced a sale. In October 1989, *Ms.* and *Sassy* were bought by Dale Lang, owner of *Working Mother, Working Woman,* and one of the few independent publishing companies left among the conglomerates. In response to a request from the original *Ms.* staff — as well as to reader letters urging that *Ms.* continue, plus his own belief that *Ms.* would benefit his other magazines by blazing a trail — he agreed to try the ad-free, reader-supported *Ms*. . . . and to give us complete editorial control.


**2**

In response to the workplace revolution of the 1970s, traditional women's magazines — that is, "trade books" for women working at home — were joined by *Savvy, Working Woman,* and other trade books for women working in offices. But by keeping the fashion/beauty/entertaining articles necessary to get traditional ads and then adding career articles besides, they inadvertently produced the antifeminist stereotype of Super Woman. The male-imitative, dress-for-success woman carrying a briefcase became the media image of a woman worker, even though a blue-collar woman's salary was often higher than her glorified secretarial sister's, and though women at a real briefcase level are statistically rare. Needless to say, these dress-for-success women were also thin, white, and beautiful.

In recent years, advertisers' control over the editorial content of women's magazines has become so institutionalized that it is written into "insertion orders" or dictated to ad salespeople as official policy. The following are recent typical orders to women's magazines:

- Dow's Cleaning Products stipulates that ads for its Vivid and Spray 'n Wash products should be adjacent to "children or fashion editorial"; ads for Bathroom Cleaner should be next to "home furnishing/family" features; and so on for other brands. "If a magazine fails for half the brands or more," the Dow order warns, "it will be omitted from further consideration."
- Bristol-Myers, the parent of Clairol, Windex, Drano, Bufferin, and    75 much more, stipulates that ads be placed next to "a full page of compatible editorial."
- S.C. Johnson & Son, makers of Johnson Wax, lawn and laundry products, insect sprays, hair sprays, and so on, orders that its ads "*should not be opposite extremely controversial features or material antithetical to the nature/copy of the advertised product.*" (Italics theirs.)
- Maidenform, manufacturer of bras and other apparel, leaves a blank for the particular product and states: "The creative concept of the ——— campaign, and the very nature of the product itself appeal to the positive emotions of the reader/consumer. Therefore, it is imperative that all editorial adjacencies reflect that same positive tone. The editorial must not be negative in content or lend itself contrary to the ——— product imagery/message (e.g., *editorial relating to illness, disillusionment, large size fashion, etc.*)." (Italics mine.)
- The De Beers diamond company, a big seller of engagement rings, prohibits magazines from placing its ads with "adjacencies to hard news or anti/love-romance themed editorial."

■    Procter & Gamble, one of this country's most powerful and diversi-
fied advertisers, stands out in the memory of Anne Summers and Sandra
Yates (no mean feat in this context): Its products were not to be placed
in *any* issue that included *any* material on gun control, abortion, the oc-
cult, cults, or the disparagement of religion. Caution was also demanded
in any issue covering sex or drugs, even for educational purposes.

Those are the most obvious chains around women's magazines.    80
There are also rules so clear they needn't be written down: for instance,
an overall "look" compatible with beauty and fashion ads. Even "real"
nonmodel women photographed for a woman's magazine are usually
made up, dressed in credited clothes, and retouched out of all reality.
When editors do include articles on less-than-cheerful subjects (for instance, domestic violence), they tend to keep them short and unillus-
trated. The point is to be "upbeat." Just as women in the street are asked,
"Why don't you smile, honey?" women's magazines acquire an institutional smile.

Within the text itself, praise for advertisers' products has become so
ritualized that fields like "beauty writing" have been invented. One of its
frequent practitioners explained seriously that "It's a difficult art. How
many new adjectives can you find? How much greater can you make a
lipstick sound? The FDA restricts what companies can say on labels, but
we create illusion. And ad agencies are on the phone all the time pushing
you to get their product in. A lot of them keep the business based on
how many editorial clippings they produce every month. The worst are
products," like Lauder's as the writer confirmed, "with their own name
involved. It's all ego."

Often, editorial becomes one giant ad. Last November, for instance,
*Lear's* featured an elegant woman executive on the cover. On the contents page, we learned she was wearing Guerlain makeup and Samsara, a
new fragrance by Guerlain. Inside were full-page ads for Samsara and
Guerlain antiwrinkle cream. In the cover profile, we learned that this executive was responsible for launching Samsara and is Guerlain's director
of public relations. When the *Columbia Journalism Review* did one of the
few articles to include women's magazines in coverage of the influence
of ads, editor Frances Lear was quoted as defending her magazine because
"this kind of thing is done all the time."

Often, advertisers also plunge odd-shaped ads into the text, no matter what the cost to the readers. At *Woman's Day,* a magazine originally
founded by a supermarket chain, editor in chief Ellen Levine said, "The
day the copy had to rag around a chicken leg was not a happy one."

Advertisers are also adamant about where in a magazine their ads appear. When Revlon was not placed as the first beauty ad in one Hearst
magazine, for instance, Revlon pulled its ads from *all* Hearst magazines.
Ruth Whitney, editor in chief of *Glamour,* attributes some of these demands to "ad agencies wanting to prove to a client that they've squeezed

the last drop of blood out of a magazine." She also is, she says, "sick and tired of hearing that women's magazines are controlled by cigarette ads." Relatively speaking, she's right. To be as censoring as are many advertisers for women's products, tobacco companies would have to demand articles in praise of smoking and expect glamorous photos of beautiful women smoking their brands.

I don't mean to imply that the editors I quote here share my objections    85
to ads: Most assume that women's magazines have to be the way they are. But it's also true that only former editors can be completely honest. "Most of the pressure came in the form of direct product mentions," explains Sey Chassler, who was editor in chief of *Redbook* from the sixties to the eighties. "We got threats from the big guys, the Revlons, blackmail threats. They wouldn't run ads unless we credited them.

"But it's not fair to single out the beauty advertisers because these pressures came from everybody. Advertisers want to know two things: What are you going to charge me? What *else* are you going to do for me? It's a holdup. For instance, management felt that fiction took up too much space. They couldn't put any advertising in that. For the last ten years, the number of fiction entries into the National Magazine Awards has declined.

"And pressures are getting worse. More magazines are more bottom-line oriented because they have been taken over by companies with no interest in publishing.

"I also think advertisers do this to women's magazines especially," he concluded, "because of the general disrespect they have for women."

Even media experts who don't give a damn about women's magazines are alarmed by the spread of this ad–edit linkage. In a climate *The Wall Street Journal* describes as an unacknowledged Depression for media, women's products are increasingly able to take their low standards wherever they go. For instance: Newsweeklies publish uncritical stories on fashion and fitness. *The New York Times Magazine* recently ran an article on "firming creams," complete with mentions of advertisers. *Vanity Fair* published a profile of one major advertiser, Ralph Lauren, illustrated by the same photographer who does his ads, and turned the lifestyle of another, Calvin Klein, into a cover story. Even the outrageous *Spy* has toned down since it began to go after fashion ads.

And just to make us really worry, films and books, the last media that    90
go directly to the public without having to attract ads first, are in danger, too. Producers are beginning to depend on payments for displaying products in movies, and books are now being commissioned by companies like Federal Express.

But the truth is that women's products — like women's magazines — have never been the subjects of much serious reporting anyway. News and general interest publications, including the "style" or "living" sections of newspapers, write about food and clothing as cooking and fashion, and almost never evaluate such products by brand name. Though chemical additives, pesticides, and animal fats are major health risks in the United States, and clothes, shoddy or not, absorb more consumer dollars than cars, this lack of information is serious. So is ignoring the contents of beauty products that are absorbed into our bodies through our skins, and that have profit margins so big they would make a loan shark blush.

### 3

What could women's magazines be like if they were as free as books? as realistic as newspapers? as creative as films? as diverse as women's lives? We don't know.

But we'll only find out if we take women's magazines seriously. If readers were to act in a concerted way to change traditional practices of *all* women's magazines and the marketing of *all* women's products, we could do it. After all, they are operating on our consumer dollars; money that we now control. You and I could:

■  write to editors and publishers (with copies to advertisers) that we're willing to pay *more* for magazines with editorial independence, but will *not* continue to pay for those that are just editorial extensions of ads;

■  write to advertisers (with copies to editors and publishers) that we want fiction, political reporting, consumer reporting — whatever is, or is not, supported by their ads;

■  put as much energy into breaking advertising's control over content as into changing the images in ads, or protesting ads for harmful products like cigarettes;

■  support only those women's magazines and products that take *us* seriously as readers and consumers.

■  Those of us in the magazine world can also use the carrot-and-stick technique. For instance: Pointing out that, if magazines were a regulated medium like television, the demands of advertisers would be against FCC rules. Payola and extortion could be punished. As it is, there are probably illegalities. A magazine's postal rates are determined by the ratio of ad to edit pages, and the former costs more than the latter. So much for the stick.

The carrot means appealing to enlightened self-interest. For instance:  95
There are many studies showing that the greatest factor in determining an ad's effectiveness is the credibility of its surroundings. The "higher the rating of editorial believability," concluded a 1987 survey by the *Journal of Advertising Research,* "the higher the rating of the advertising." Thus, an impenetrable wall between edit and ads would also be in the best interest of advertisers.

Unfortunately, few agencies or clients hear such arguments. Editors often maintain the false purity of refusing to talk to them at all. Instead, they see ad salespeople who know little about editorial, are trained in business as usual, and are usually paid by commission. Editors might also band together to take on controversy. That happened once when all the major women's magazines did articles in the same month on the Equal Rights Amendment. It could happen again.

It's almost three years away from life between the grindstones of advertising pressures and readers' needs. I'm just beginning to realize how edges got smoothed down — in spite of all our resistance.

I remember feeling put upon when I changed "Porsche" to "car" in a piece about Nazi imagery in German pornography by Andrea Dworkin — feeling sure Andrea would understand that Volkswagen, the distributor of Porsche and one of our few supportive advertisers, asked only to be far away from Nazi subjects. It's taken me all this time to realize that Andrea was the one with a right to feel put upon.

Even as I write this, I get a call from a writer for *Elle,* who is doing a whole article on where women part their hair. Why, she wants to know, do I part mine in the middle?

It's all so familiar. A writer trying to make something of a nothing          100
assignment; an editor laboring to think of new ways to attract ads; readers assuming that other women must want this ridiculous stuff; more women suffering for lack of information, insight, creativity, and laughter that could be on these same pages.

I ask you: Can't we do better than this?

### Reading the Text

1. What does Steinem mean by "complementary copy"?
2. Summarize the relationship that Steinem sees between editorial content and advertising in women's magazines.
3. According to Steinem, what messages about gender roles does complementary copy send readers of women's magazines?
4. What ethnic patterns does Steinem see in advertising that appears in women's magazines, and how does she feel about those patterns?

### Reading the Signs

1. Steinem asserts that virtually all content in women's magazines is a disguised form of advertising. Test her hypothesis by writing a detailed analysis of a single issue of a magazine such as *Cosmopolitan, Glamour,* or *Elle.* Do you find instances of complementary copy? How do you react as a potential reader of such a magazine?

2.  Explore whether Steinem's argument holds for men's magazines such as *Details* or *GQ*. If you identify differences, how might they be based on different assumptions about gender roles?

3.  Steinem ends her essay by claiming that the *Ms.* published without advertising will exhibit greater journalistic freedom than the *Ms.* supported by advertising. Compare a current issue of *Ms.* with an earlier, advertising-laden issue (check your college library), and test Steinem's claim.

4.  Have each member of the class bring in a favorite magazine. In small groups, study the relationship between ads and articles. Which magazines have the most complementary copy? How can you account for your findings?

5.  How do you feel about the claim that Estée Lauder can't advertise in *Ms.* because it is selling a "kept-woman mentality"? If you are disturbed by this statement, write a letter to Estée Lauder's president, arguing against this characterization of women; if you're not bothered by it, write a letter to Gloria Steinem, trying to persuade her that an outraged response is not necessary.

6.  Do advertisers infringe upon the freedom of the press, as the publisher of *Sassy* believes? Write a journal entry in which you explore this issue.


# RONALD K. L. COLLINS
# AND DAVID M. SKOVER

## *The Death of Discourse*

||||||||||||||||||||||||||||||||||||||||||||||||||||||||||||

*Can there be tyranny of pleasure? According to Ronald K. L. Collins (b. 1949) and David M. Skover (b. 1951), not only can there be, but we are living in one now, a world where public discourse has wholly adopted the "feel good" style of commercial television and advertising. In this essay, Collins and Skover argue that Americans are increasingly unable to think and speak critically about social realities because of the way we are forever being distracted by attractive entertainments and product pitches. Is it time for a censorship of amusement-centered speech, they wonder? And if so, how would we carry it out? A visiting professor of law at Seattle University School of Law, Washington state, Ronald K. L. Collins is the author of numerous articles on law and politics. A professor of law at Seattle University School of Law, David M. Skover is also coauthor (with Pierre Schlag) of* Tactics of Legal Reasoning *(1986). Collins and Skover have published* The Death of Discourse *(1996), from which this selection is excerpted.*

Discourse is dying in America, yet everywhere free speech thrives.

Discourse. It is a weighty word of classical origin, the sort of utterance that runs to and fro in erudite circles. Something beyond mere talk is implied. Unlike trivial talk, discourse resonates with reason, with method, with purpose. Whether its loftier values were ever entirely realized is, in one sense, of no moment. Discourse is an ancient aspiration. As idealized in the Western culture's vision of classical Greece, expression was valued as a means to some *telos,* some greater end. For Aristotle, expression was not simply for its own sake but, rather, was discourse in the service of the civic good, or *agathon.* Expression, properly understood, was essential to *paideia,* the shaping of character.

This, of course, is all Greek to us young Americans. Ours is a system of free speech — free from old notions of discourse. For us, expression is no more or less than the speech of daily experiences. The sight, the sound, indeed the feel, of robust expression is a thing of joy in the carnival of life we call modern mass culture. To communicate with uninhibited liberty, to talk in the vernacular of the popular culture, to express that culture's tastes, is the way of free speech in America. It is often speech for its own sake, speech in the service of self-gratification, and speech that is essential to the raison d'être of a commercial entertainment culture. These two cultures of expression — the old discourse and the new free speech — turn to the First Amendment for constitutional recognition. Since 1791, the judicial and scholarly keepers of the amendment have invoked the high ideals of discourse to define the boundaries of protected expression. They continue to do so even now as they summon the traditional values of enlightened reason, self-government, and self-realization to protect communication in contemporary popular culture. We wonder, however, why they ignore the wide gulf between yesterday's reasons and today's realities. And we question whether the First Amendment is actually what judges and scholars say it is, or rather what the popular culture makes of it.

## The Huxleyan Nightmare

In essence, all First Amendment cases and theories aim in some way to preserve a robust social and political discourse by which the people might best govern themselves. Without this environment, the First Amendment, as we have known it, cannot survive. This lofty purpose renounces any Orwellian rule in which the hand of an omnipresent government squelches political dissent, bans books, invades privacy, censors electronic information and conceals truth. Triumphantly, America has survived 1984 and is less fearful of Orwell's dark determinism. But our Orwellian perspective hinders us from focusing on an equally menacing and more realistic threat to the First Amendment — the evil identified in Aldous Huxley's anti-utopian *Brave New World* (1946) and later developed in his *Brave New World Revisited* (1958). As Huxley himself contended and as Neil Postman echoed, it is this threat that today looms large. Now, the Huxleyan evil particularly endangers our historical and idealistic commitment to freedom of expression.

Huxley's nightmare is one in which government has no need to censor dissent, no cause to hide truth, and no ground to ban serious discussion. It is a world of pleasure and trivialization, a world whose citizenry euphorically digests narcotic "soma tablets." The brave new world offers a surfeit of entertainment, "non-stop distractions of the most fascinating nature (the feelies, orgy-porgy, centrifugal bumble-puppy)" that ensure a state of perpetual amusement and happiness. The governing maxim is: "Everybody's happy now."

The purpose of all this "happiness" is to numb. The "non-stop distractions," said Huxley, are "used as instruments of policy, for the purpose of preventing people from paying too much attention to the realities of the social and political situation." The rulers of Huxley's anti-utopia have learned that soma tablets more effectively suppress the critical mind and spirit than the iron fist of Orwell's world.

The antiquated First Amendment is eclipsed in the brave new world. Its fear of the tyranny of terror — demonstrated, for example, by the Alien and Sedition Acts of 1798, the Espionage Acts of 1917 and 1918, and the McCarthy era — is overshadowed by a tyranny of pleasure. The Orwellian shackles on physical liberty and ideological freedom constituted hands-on tyranny, but the Huxleyan conception is a hands-off form of tyranny. Huxley understood tyranny as the product of those "great impersonal forces now menacing freedom," the "motivation analyst[s]" who held out the soma tablets.

In an insightful passage particularly applicable to the First Amendment, Huxley questioned the outdated 18th century American constitutional ideal:

> [T]he early advocates of . . . a free press envisaged only two possibilities: the propaganda might be true, or it might be false. They did not foresee what in fact has happened, above all in our Western capitalist democracies — the development of a vast mass communications industry, concerned in the main with neither the true nor the false, but with the unreal, the more or less totally irrelevant. In a word, they failed to take into account man's almost infinite appetite for distractions. *(Brave New World Revisited)*

Huxley's depiction of a tyranny of pleasure accurately forecast the contemporary American media culture. He realized the connection between commercial television and his anti-utopia: "That so many of the well-fed young television-watchers in the world's most powerful democracy should be so completely indifferent to the idea of self-government, so blankly uninterested in freedom of thought and the right to dissent, is distressing, but not too surprising."

America's primary information medium is also its most popular    10
source on entertainment, its favorite plaything. Metaphorically, television is the soma tablet of modern society.

### Paratroopers' Paradox

Today, the First Amendment is still grounded in 18th century fears of government's tyrannical censorship. It is ill-equipped to deal with a distinct tyranny in late 20th century America, a tyranny that plays upon the public's insatiable appetite for amusement. We need to understand the differences between the old and new tyrannies. To borrow from Marshall McLuhan, those who attempt such a venture are the First Amendment paratroopers of our time; they realize that we cannot retain our old constitutional prerogatives in a world transformed.

Public talk is increasingly taking a distinctive and aestheticized form consistent with the look and feel of commercial television. This transformation of public talk is essential to the effective marketing of images and commercial goods in highly consumerist culture: after all, marketing often sells pleasing images. The business of television trades in the economy of such images and pulls other expression into that economy, producing a culture in which America's most beloved toy provides endless mass entertainment and profit.

Where amusement and commerce mark the boundaries for much public speech, traditional First Amendment values — which include serious dialogue and civic participation — are overshadowed. Given these core values and the presumption against censorship in First Amendment law, we ask: is there anything that could (or should) be done to thwart, rather than to feed, an amusement-centered culture?

In answering this question we encounter a paradox: to save itself, the traditional First Amendment must destroy itself. To guard against censorship, the First Amendment must protect both the old (pre-electronic) and the new (electronic) communication cultures. Accordingly, it must constrain most government controls over expression, including those over the commercial use of electronic media. On the other hand, if the First Amendment's protections do not differentiate between the old and new media cultures, the modern obsession with self-amusement can trivialize public expression and thereby undermine the traditional aims of the First Amendment. To treat the two cultures differently requires governmental "abridgment" of expression, particularly in the case of the commercial entertainment media. With such governmental abridgment, First

Amendment protection collapses into First Amendment tyranny. Without such abridgment, First Amendment liberty collapses into First
Amendment triviality. This is the paratroopers' paradox.

## Living with Lies

Can We the People survive the threat of a brave new world? Can     15
the human psyche endure a cultural approach to the First Amendment
that abandons all cultural hypocrisy? Are we prepared to admit that we
live more by low practices than by lofty ideals, and that the license of
self-gratification is our real First Amendment norm?

Some say no. For example, David Nyberg and other philosophers
have argued that deception might well be "an essential component of our
ability to organize and shape the world, to resolve problems of coordination among individuals who differ, to cope with uncertainty and pain, to
be civil and to achieve privacy as needed, to survive as a species, and to
flourish as persons." Even more forcefully, Nyberg surmised: "We decide . . . so that we might not perish of the truth."

It is at this juncture that free speech ideals confront political philosophy. The spectrum of choice is between the Socratic principle that the
unexamined life is not worth living and the Oedipal lesson that "the
well-examined life may prove unlivable."

If America's free speech system needs lies to *live,* a cultural approach
to the First Amendment (telling it like it is) could be a discourse of *death.*
For to forsake any conserving lie could eventually expose our free speech
order to the unsettling influences of nihilism. The constitutional law
governing discourse would then tend toward a First Amendment without limits — an Absolute First Amendment far beyond the Madisonian
imagination of the late Justice Hugo Black. And discourse could then be
driven more and more by a runaway engine of amusement, consumption, and passion. Echoing this idea, philosopher Loyal Rue asserted
more generally: "The single most important regulating force within a social ecology is [its governing lie] . . . Without this [lie] a culture would
lose its unity of purpose to an onslaught of diffuse meanings and thus
begin its descent into social chaos." Such arguments appear to condemn
the cultural approach to the First Amendment as an instrument of culture
death: a democracy may be unable to pursue naked truth if it must
nurture an ennobling lie to preserve some *semblance* of social purpose
and destiny.

If nothing else, the cultural approach to the First Amendment reveals
the often maladaptive character of 18th century ideals in a 21st century
environment. Succinctly, James Madison and his notions of free speech
seem practically irrelevant. When we feed on TV and video soma for an

average of some 47 hours weekly, consume the fruits of a yearly advertising budget of $149 billion, splurge some $10 billion annually on pornography to gorge our insatiable sexual appetites, and more, we are unlikely
to tolerate a First Amendment regime that is intolerant of such pleasurable practices.

The Madisonian First Amendment is going the way of agrarian    20
America. Like the harmonious, wholesome, and romantic images of the
farmer's life, traditional free speech values are overshadowed by modern
technology and materialism. Yearn as we may for those worlds, they belong to the past. If James Madison's dreams for the First Amendment are
to have any future meaning, we must forswear the fantasies in which we
now revel.

The end is near. Discourse is dying. Paratroopers are falling. As
they descend, our heroes are inspired by Albert Camus's poignant
affirmation: "I do not give the human race more than one chance in a
thousand. But I should not be a man if I did not operate on that one
chance."

### Reading the Text

1. Describe in your own words what Collins and Skover mean by "discourse."
2. Why do Collins and Skover believe that the language of modern advertising presents a challenge to First Amendment rights of free speech?
3. What relationship do Collins and Skover see between contemporary discourse and Aldous Huxley's *Brave New World*?
4. What do Collins and Skover mean when they claim, "If America's free
   speech system needs lies to *live,* a cultural approach to the First Amendment (telling it like it is) could be a discourse of *death*"?

### Reading the Signs

1. Write an essay in which you defend, refute, or modify Collins and
   Skover's assertion that "[Aldous] Huxley's depiction of a tyranny of pleasure accurately forecasts the contemporary American media culture."
2. In class, form teams and debate whether Collins and Skover are accurate
   or exaggerate when they describe modern media as "soma tablets." In
   preparing for the debate, each team should brainstorm specific media examples to support its position.
3. Assuming the perspective of Gloria Steinem in "Sex, Lies, and Advertising" (p. 155), write a letter to Collins and Skover in which you relate the
   First Amendment issues they raise to *Ms.* magazine's struggles with advertisers.

4. In your journal, write a response to Collins and Skover's question, "Is there anything that could (or should) be done to thwart, rather than to feed, an amusement-centered culture?"

5. Bring a popular magazine to class and in small groups study whether the advertising presents the "pleasing" images that Collins and Skover decry. Then use the results of your group work as evidence in an essay that argues whether you believe their assessment of modern advertising is accurate.

**what would you do?**

# ask people

## to judge me by my

# ability

## not my

# disability

cindy bolas, colorado

FOUR MINDLESS MINIMUM WAGE JOBS. A COUPLE FIST FIGHTS. TWO STEP MOMS. EVERY LOLLAPALOOZA CONCERT. THE DEATH OF A FRIEND. SIX APARTMENTS. JAIL. A COAT CHECK GIRL NAMED KATE. 5 GALLONS OF FLAT WALL FINISH. #1230.

Duck Head pants borrowed from Scott Glass, purchased 1989.

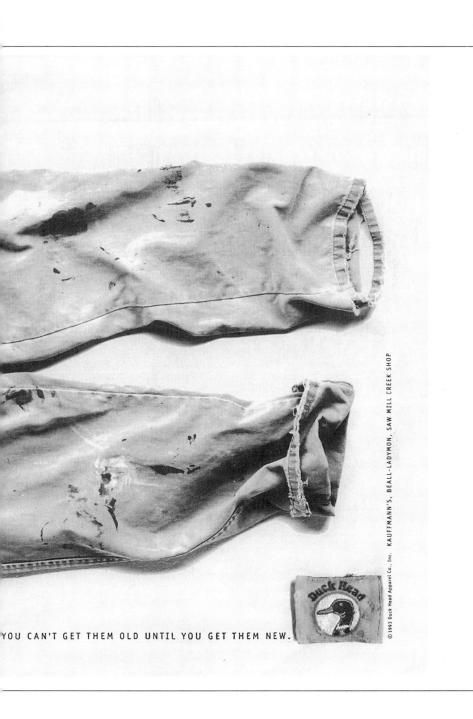

YOU CAN'T GET THEM OLD UNTIL YOU GET THEM NEW.

185

# Who says guys are afraid of commitment? He's had the same backpack for years.

When it comes to choosing a lifelong companion, lots of guys pick one of our backpacks. Each one comes with a lifetime guarantee not to rip, tear, break, or ask for a ring.

## Reading the Signs

1. Have the class vote for the ads contained in the Portfolio that are most effective and least effective in persuading the target audience to purchase the products. Then discuss the significance of the results. What strategies does the class consider more persuasive? Do you see any gender-related patterns in the class's votes?
2. Divide the class in two and have each group brainstorm the connotations attached to the male image in the Moschino ad and those attached to the baby's image. Have each group put their results on the board. Then as a whole group discuss why Moschino might have decided to combine these two images in an ad for their product line.
3. Why are dalmations associated with Bacardi rum in this ad? What kind of image are the advertisers trying to create for their product?
4. Advertisers call the Esprit ad a "message" ad. Discuss that message and why you think the advertiser found it a useful strategy to sell clothing.
5. Compare the imagery in the two Guess ads, which date approximately three years apart. Why do you think the advertisers chose to change the style of the advertising?
6. Write a semiotic interpretation of the Duck Head ad. Be sure to analyze details such as the copy, the typeface, and the condition of the pants. How do those details relate to the ad's probable audience and to the fashion system to which the pants belong? To develop your ideas, consult Leslie Savan's "Generation X-Force" (p. 134).
7. Together, the text and imagery of the Eastpak ad tell a story about the male figure who owns the backpack. What is that story? Do you think the ad is intended to appeal to men, women, or both? Why the same food displayed in each photograph? Use your observations to formulate an argument about the strategies this ad uses to appeal to consumers.

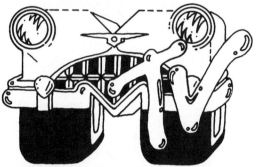

# CHAPTER THREE

# CHEAP THRILLS

## *The Images of Music, Video, and TV*

**W**riting about television or music is an assignment students often receive in their composition classes, so this chapter's topic ought to come as no surprise to you. Indeed, in high school you may have been asked to write about a favorite video or TV program, perhaps in a summary writing exercise, a descriptive essay, or an opinion piece on why such-and-such a program is your favorite show. But in college you will be asked to write more critical interpretations of popular entertainment. In so doing, you will rely on your skills in description and summary, of course, but now your purpose is to go beyond these writing tasks and to analyze the critical significance of your topic so that you can construct a critical argument or thesis about it. To show you how to do that, let's take a semiotic look at a single episode of a popular TV show.

### Interpreting the Images of Music, Video, and TV

By most accounts, one of the biggest prime-time hits of the mid-1990s is *Friends,* a program that supplanted *Beverly Hills, 90210* and *Melrose Place* as a favorite among teen and twentysomething viewers. Its popularity leads us to our prime semiotic question: Why *Friends*? Why did *this* show so appeal to the cultural taste of the times?

As with all semiotic analyses, your first step when preparing to write an analysis of a TV program is to suspend your aesthetic opinions of the

||||||||||||||||||||||||||||||||||||||||||||||||||||||||||||||||||||||||||||||||||||||||||||||||||||||||||||||||||||||||||||||||||||||||||||||||||||||||||||||||||||||||||||

## Exploring the Signs of Music Videos

In your journal, explore the impact music videos have had on you. How have videos shaped your desires and expectations about life? How were your actions and behavior influenced by MTV? What videos were especially meaningful to you? What did you think about them when you were younger, and how do you see them now? (If you didn't watch MTV, you might focus instead on television programs.)

show — that is, whether you like it or not. It also doesn't matter whether *Friends* is as popular today as it was when we wrote this introduction. It may well be that the popularity of *Friends* has declined — that's one of the constants of popular culture: its rapid turnover of fads and trends. What you are working toward is a critical opinion, what you think the underlying social significance of the program may be. This process is also different from describing what you think the show's *explicit* message is. Many programs have clearly presented "messages" — indeed, the episode of *Friends* we'll examine here has a "message" of this sort. What you'll be looking for is the message beyond the message, so to speak, the implicit signals the show is sending. To show what we mean, consider a single episode of *Friends* that focuses, typically, on relationships.

Since you may not remember our sample episode even if you saw it, we'll summarize the story briefly. As with most sitcoms, this episode's plot is rather loosely constructed — the main point is to deliver as many punch lines as possible within a half-hour time slot — but it does have a main plot and two subplots. The main plot centers on the plans of Carol and Susan to get married in a lesbian wedding. Ross, Carol's ex-husband, isn't too thrilled with the idea and at first glumly refuses to attend the ceremony. Eventually, he comes 'round and is even the one to get the wedding back on track when Carol confides to him that her parents' refusal to attend is threatening the whole event. In the end, the wedding happily takes place with Ross giving his former wife away to Susan. End of main plot.

The first subplot concerns Phoebe, a masseuse. When an elderly client of Phoebe's named Mrs. Adelman dies on the massage table, her spirit, instead of ascending to wherever, lodges inside Phoebe. Throughout the episode, young blonde Phoebe accordingly turns into a stereotypical 82-year-old Jewish woman at unpredictable times (rather in the way that Gary Trudeau's *Doonesbury* character Boopsie turns into Hunk Ra). Mr. Adelman explains his deceased spouse's lingering on in this way as her desire to "see everything" before she died. A tall order, no doubt, but everything is resolved when Phoebe attends the lesbian wedding and the spirit of Mrs. Adelman blurts out, "Now I've seen everything!" and flits off to wherever, leaving Phoebe back to Phoebe. End of first subplot.

The second subplot concerns Rachel's mother, who shows up for a visit, only to reveal that she is leaving her husband (Rachel's father) because she married him not for love but merely for the economic security he provided. Mom seems to want the kind of swinging life that she sees Rachel living, a plotline that offers all sorts of opportunities to make this middle-aged parent look silly. The episode ends without this subplot being resolved, leaving room for future developments.

All right, let's analyze this episode. First, we need to select those details that seem most suggestive, prodding us to an interpretive hypothesis. Being selective is an important step in your analysis, because not every detail of a TV show is necessarily of semiotic interest, and not every semiotically interesting detail will necessarily contribute to your emerging argument. In the interpretation we are developing here, for example, we are leaving out the Phoebe/Mrs. Adelman subplot. One could argue that it is intended as a spoof of New Age spiritualism, but its sheer goofiness suggests to us that it is simply a marker of Phoebe's zaniness and is included more or less just for laughs.

A part of the show we do want to note, though, is its overall premise: The comic dramatization of a group of twentysomething men and women living together in a Manhattan apartment. Here, the characters' occupations, which run the gamut from a fledgling soap opera actor to a coffee shop waitress, are significant. Being a waitress, especially if you grew up in a comfortable middle-class or upper-middle-class household, isn't very exciting, is it? And yet that's what Rachel, one of *Friends*'s central characters, does for a living. Now, do you see a set of associations emerging here, a cultural system that would give these details their meaning? We do.

First, we can associate *Friends* with a large number of programs that appeared in the mid-nineties, all featuring attractive twentysomething characters living and loving together in urban apartments — shows like *Melrose Place, Central Park West,* and MTV's *Real World.* Often the characters are the children of far more prosperous parents and are beginning their struggles in a difficult economic environment. Thus they must band together with a large number of roommates; otherwise, they wouldn't be able to make the rent in the sort of fashionable urban neighborhoods the shows feature. And they tend to put most of their energies into relationships, both with their friends and their lovers.

Do you see an image emerging here? It is, of course, the standard stereotype of Generation X, that middle-class generation supposedly resigned to a less prosperous life than their parents enjoyed and compensating for it by caring more about relationships than about material prosperity. Whether or not such a generation really exists, its image is much coveted as a potential market by advertisers and their clients. If you don't think so, ask yourself why so many TV shows of this sort have appeared in the mid and late 1990s. What audience do their sponsors hope to attract?

A look at the Rachel subplot of our episode of *Friends* makes it quite clear that its sponsors' target market is stereotypically GenX. As a waitress and the daughter of an upper-middle-class family, Rachel has chosen the emotional fulfillment of living with her "friends" over the economic security she could have had by marrying Barry, an orthodontist. When Rachel's mother visits, Rachel and her friends worry that she'll bother them all with her disapproval of this choice. But mom surprises everyone, first, by fussing over how wonderful it is that Rachel earns her living as a waitress, and, second, by revealing that her own husband was her "Barry." Mom confides that she's now bored and wants to live the sort of life Rachel has chosen, giving up economic security for emotional satisfaction.

The significance of this reversal points to a certain fantasy, which is what television is best at providing. As Marshall McLuhan once put it, the medium is the *massage* (not message), and the massage here is the presentation of a materially diminished life as emotionally more fulfilling than a materially enhanced one. Twentysomething viewers who have good reason to be worried about their economic prospects in a downsized, restructured America can watch themselves dramatized in *Friends* as happy, emotionally well-connected comrades whose strong bonding looks like a potent compensation for the prosperity that is being denied them. And by emotionally connecting themselves with the show, such viewers may also connect to the products that sponsor the show and buy them. That, at least, is what the sponsors hope.

Of course, the show doesn't make explicit that it is playing upon fantasies of emotional connectedness. If this were obvious, viewers might feel insulted and bolt (after all, most members of Generation X loathe the term and the stereotype). If viewers bolt, nothing gets sold. So another, at once more attractive and obvious, message is provided through the main plot of this episode that can distract us from the fact that TV shows exist to sell things.

Recall how the main plot presents the announcement and fulfillment of a lesbian marriage. The explicit message here is that society should be tolerant of such nontraditional unions. A number of signs point to this message, from Ross's switch from troubled doubt to hearty support for Carol's wedding to the image of Susan's Marine Corps father cheerfully giving her away. And even though the wedding provides the opportunity for a lot of sitcom wisecracks from some of the male characters who wonder whether it's worth the trouble to flirt with any of the women at such an affair, the sheer *ordinariness* of the scene sends the signal that this is no big deal, just two people who love each other getting married. The ease with which the marriage is dramatized and the lack of preachiness and relaxed acceptance of what is still somewhat controversial suggest that viewers of *Friends* are just like the characters: Loving, supportive, tolerant, progressively nonjudgmental people.

To underscore this message of emotional and political solidarity between show and audience, the director of this episode of *Friends* cast Candace Gingrich, the real-life lesbian sister of Newt Gingrich — a well-known icon of American conservatism — as the minister who performs the wedding ceremony. The show thus invites us to identify with Candace and all those other nice people at the wedding. As if further to underscore the sense of emotional community that the show promotes between its characters and its audience, a tease for the NBC 11:00 P.M. news promises a story on the "controversial" topic of that night's episode of *Friends*. Viewers accordingly are invited to compare their progressive acceptance of the lesbian marriage with that hostile world represented by Newt Gingrich. Take that, Newt.

The main plot of our episode thus complements our semiotic interpretation of the program as a whole: Just as *Friends* in general presents a GenX image that invites its viewers to join the fantasy, so too does this individual episode invite its audience to identify with the particular "message" of the story. Either way, we're all just "friends," helping each other and finding satisfaction in bonding and emotional commitment.

The tone of our interpretation may disturb you. After all, you may want to ask, like the Elvis Costello song, just what's wrong with peace, love, and understanding, that is, with the promotion of social tolerance and emotional commitment? Nothing at all. But here we have to look at the context in which *Friends* appears. Like all commercial programming, it is not presented as a public service. It is not there for free. It is on television because it has sponsors, and its sponsors are concerned only with attracting an audience that will buy its products. To see something of what those sponsors are thinking, we need only look at a few of the ads that were broadcast along with this episode.

Among the ads that night were ads for Miller Lite, Coors, McDonald's, and Mercedes Benz cars. The beer ads presented images attractive to people in their late teens and early twenties — especially a Coors ad that featured young men and women dressed in plaid shirts, shorts, and Doc Martens — you got it, the media stereotype of GenX grunge wear. Given the program's popularity, those were some pretty expensive ads, and their purpose was to share the fantasy the show offers to get their audiences to buy beer, hamburgers, and a Mercedes. We'll let you judge the merits of the beer and hamburgers, but consider the ad for Mercedes Benz. In Chapter Two of this book, we remark how advertising stokes desire, and indeed, the Mercedes ad made the car look quite desirable.

But isn't there a contradiction here? While twentysomethings are being dramatized as finding greater satisfaction in relationships than in things, here we find one of the most expensive of those things being presented as fulfilling in itself. Is some sort of cruel joke going on?

## Altered States

Our analysis of this episode of *Friends* thus leads to our argument. The thesis for the paper we could now write is that, through a semiotic reading of *Friends,* we can discover the way in which corporate America provides its targeted markets with feel-good fantasies intended primarily to get them to buy products, while having the perhaps unintentional effect of distracting its viewers from certain grim social and economic realities. That the episode of *Friends* was set in New York City, one of the most racially mixed cities on earth, and managed to show not a single nonwhite face could be used as further support of such a thesis insofar as the show provides an entertaining distraction from New York's ongoing racial tensions. But that wouldn't make us feel very good, would it?

Our point is that a social purpose stands behind the semiotic interpretation of a TV show: to explore, and expose, the ways in which television shapes our behavior through the careful manipulation of fantasy. Interpreting TV is thus an especially important task at a time when it is blurring the line between fantasy and reality in an ever more profound manner. Just think of the 1992 presidential election, when Dan Quayle made Murphy Brown a campaign issue because she chose to become a single mother. For months the fictional protagonist of the show, played by Candace Bergen, sparred with the real vice president over the rights of single mothers in a public battle whose most interesting significance was that everyone acted as if Murphy Brown was as real as Dan Quayle.

Such a blurring of the line between fiction and reality (a process recently accelerated by the advent of "docudrama" style shows like *America's Most Wanted* — and skewered in a film like *Natural Born Killers*) reflects television's profound effect upon the very way that we perceive our world. If television were to vanish today — no more shows, no more prime time — its effects would live on in the way it has altered our sense of reality. We expect instant visual access to every corner of the earth because of TV, and we want to get to the point quickly. It is often claimed that our attention spans have been shortened in a universe of televised sound bites, but at the same time our desire for information has been expanded (inquiring minds want to know). Indeed, the television age has equally been an information age.

In semiotic terms, the ubiquity of television and video in our lives represents a shift from one kind of sign system to another. As Marshall McLuhan pointed out thirty years ago in *The Gutenberg Galaxy,* Western culture since the fifteenth century has defined itself around the printed word, the linear text that reads from left to right and top to bottom. The printed word, in the terminology of the American founder of semiotics, Charles Sanders Peirce, is a *symbolic* sign, one whose meaning is entirely arbitrary or conventional. A symbolic sign means what it does because those who use it have decided so. Words don't look like what they mean. Their significance is entirely abstract.

Not so with a visual image like a photograph (or TV picture), which does resemble its object and is not entirely arbitrary. Though a photograph is not literally the thing it depicts and often reflects a good deal of staging and manipulation on the part of the photographer, we often respond to it as if it were an innocent reflection of the world. Peirce called such signs *icons,* referring by this term to any sign that resembles what it means. The way you interpret an icon, then, differs from the way you interpret a symbol or word. The interpretation of words involves your cognitive capabilities; the interpretation and reception of icons is far more sensuous, more a matter of vision than cognition. The shift from a civilization governed by the paradigm of the book to one dominated by television accordingly involves a shift in the way we "read" our world, as the symbolic field of the printed page yields to the iconic field of the video screen.

The shift from a symbolic, or word-centered, world to an iconic universe filled with visual images carries profound cultural implications. Such implications are not necessarily negative. The relative accessibility of video technology, for example, has created opportunities for personal expression that have never existed before. It is very difficult to publish a book, but anyone can create a widely reproducible video simply by possessing a camcorder. The rapid transmissibility of video images speeds up communication and can bond groups of linguistically and culturally diverse people together, as MTV speaks to millions of people around the nation and world at once in the language of dance and music.

At the same time, video images may be used to change consciousness and stimulate political action. Feminist rappers like Salt 'N' Pepa, for example, stage their music videos as calls to action, prodding their audiences to duplicate in reality the fantasies they see upon the screen. Indeed, while many critics of TV deplore the passivity of its viewers, the medium is not inherently passive. Look at it this way: TV has a visceral power that print does not. Words abstractly describe things; television shows you concrete images. The world pretty much ignored the famine in sub-Saharan Africa in the early eighties, for example, until the TV cameras arrived to broadcast the images of starvation. Television, in short, bears the potential to awake the apathetic as written texts cannot.

But there is a price to be paid for the new modes of perception that the iconic world of TV has stimulated; while one *can* read the signs of TV and video actively and creatively, and one can be moved to action by a video image, the sheer visibility of icons tempts one to receive them uncritically. Icons look so much like the realities they refer to that it is easy to forget that icons, too, are signs: images that people construct which carry ideological meanings.

Just think of all those iconic images of the classic fifties-era sitcoms. *Leave It to Beaver, Father Knows Best, The Ozzie and Harriet Show,* and so on have established an American mythology of an idyllic era by the sheer persuasiveness of their images. In fact, the fifties were not such idyllic years. Along with the McCarthyite hysteria of the Cold War and the looming specter of nuclear war and contamination from open-air nuclear testing, there were economic downturns, the Korean War, and a grow-ing sense that American life was becoming sterile, conformist, and mate-rialistic — though it wasn't until the sixties that this uneasiness broke into the open. Few fathers in the fifties had the kind of leisure that the sitcom dads had, and the feminist resurgence in the late sixties demonstrated that not all women were satisfied with the housewifely roles assigned them in every screenplay. And yet, those constructed images of white middle-class contentment and security have become so real in the American imagination that they can be called upon in quite concrete ways. *Leave It to Beaver* is not simply the sort of thing that shows up in Trivial Pursuit games: The image of the show has become a potent political weapon. Conservative campaigners point to the classic sitcoms as exemplars of the "family values" that America is losing, apparently forgetting that many a modern sitcom, from *The Cosby Show* to *Roseanne,* often reflect strikingly similar images of family solidarity. After all, the whole point of *Leave It to Beaver* was to show every week how "the Beav" might screw something up, create a family crisis, and then have the whole matter resolved in time for the closing commercials. While it may take several episodes to do the trick, how is *Roseanne* different?

## The Audience Is the Authority

One thing has changed in the relatively brief history of television: the emergence of cable TV. The proliferation of cable companies and channels has fostered a more finely targeted programming schedule by which producers can focus on narrowly defined audiences, from nature lovers to home shoppers. In one respect, the fine-tuning of audiences simply reflects a fine-tuning of marketing: Specially defined audiences can be targeted for specially defined marketing campaigns. In this sense, the advent of cable repeats the same history as that of traditional com-mercial television, which became a medium primarily for the pitching of goods and services. But the proliferation of channels bears the potential, at least, to upset television's commercial monopoly. When NBC, CBS, ABC, and their affiliates ruled the airways, programming decisions for an

---

### Discussing the Signs of Television

In class, choose a current television program and have the entire class watch one episode (either watch the episode as "homework" or ask someone to tape it and then watch it in class). Interpret the episode semiotically. What values and cultural myths does the show project? What do the commercials broadcast during the show say about the presumed audience for it? Go beyond the episode's surface appeal or "message" to look at the particular images it uses to tell its story, always asking, "What is this program *really* saying?"

---

entire nation were made by a tiny group of executives. Aside from the Nielsen ratings, viewers had little chance to let programmers know what they wanted to see. While certainly no revolution has occurred in the wake of cable, there has least been some movement toward audience participation in viewing.

The phenomenal success of MTV provides a good example of the increasing power of the television audience. In its early years, rock music appeared on TV in such programs as *American Bandstand* and *The Monkees.* In each case, a rock act had to be toned down considerably before it could be televised (Elvis was ordered not to bump and grind lest he be banned from the TV screens of the fifties). What amounted to censorship worked because the venues for the televising of rock were often adult-oriented (consider how the Beatles and the Rolling Stones first appeared to American audiences on the adult variety program *The Ed Sullivan Show*). MTV, on the other hand, is an entirely youth-oriented station. Though it too exists to promote products — through both the videos it displays and the commercials it runs — MTV must conform to the tastes of its audience to succeed. This means that it has to appeal to adolescent fantasies and frustrations in a way that *The Monkees,* for instance, never did. *The Monkees* was a sanitized adventure sitcom whose scripts were written by anonymous professionals. The "scripts" of MTV videos are largely determined by the performers whose popularity among adolescents brought them to the screen in the first place. In other words, while MTV serves establishment corporate sponsors like any other commercial program, it nevertheless derives its authority from its audience more than the three networks do.

No one has received more attention in this vein than Madonna, who has created something of an industry among academic critics eager to interpret her. Some see her as a postmodern feminist heroine, others as an irresponsible promoter of teenaged sexuality. Whatever one thinks of her, her preeminent place in American pop culture fairly screams for analysis. And it is likely you have more authority to conduct such an analysis than many an academic commentator.

Given the emphasis on sexuality that Madonna's videos are so famous for, you might think that that's all there is to their interpretation. But we'd like you to consider another angle for a moment. Consider one of her earlier videos, such as "Papa Don't Preach." Oh yeah, it's about teenage pregnancy, but look at that sentimental conclusion, where father and daughter are reunited. Or look at "Open Your Heart," where the peep-show star in the end runs away into an innocent sunset with the kid, like a female Charlie Chaplin. Such fantasies go beyond sex, reflecting a deep-seated sentimentality, a desire for innocence, that runs at the heart of American culture. Rather than being subversive, these videos can actually be seen to reinforce the cultural status quo. Can the same be said of Madonna's current videos?

Maybe you prefer videos like "Borderline," however, where Madonna plays a character who lives in two worlds, frolicking at once with handsome, sultry street boys and handsome, glitzy photographers. Beyond the sexual fantasies here is a social fantasy, a teen desire to identify with both the underclass and the ruling class. In some ways, this may be the most significant part of Madonna's popularity: her appeal to her audience's sense of identification with both the very rich and the urban poor. This identification may well be related to the white middle-class embrace of rap music and gang culture, on the one hand, and shows like *Melrose Place* on the other. For when analyzing the culture of American video and TV, everything ties together.

## The Readings

We begin the readings in this chapter with Susan Douglas's feminist take on two hit television dramas of the mid-nineties, *NYPD Blue* and *ER,* an analysis that examines the retrogressive messages behind the shows' progressive surfaces. Josh Ozersky follows with a critique of the "new realism" in American sitcoms, arguing that programs like *The Simpsons, Married . . . with Children,* and *Roseanne* aren't nearly as realistic as the critics say they are; instead, they seduce their viewers with a reality effect that keeps them glued to their screens, safely in the grasp of corporate sponsors who have found that portraying dysfunctional family life is a good way to keep America's dysfunctional families in the field of docile consumers. Next, Walter Kirn's opinion piece on twentysomething TV and culture presents a critical view of a "lost generation" whose "slacker rebellion" is, he believes, just another form of consumerism. Responding more positively to this generation, Douglas Rushkoff offers a new spin on Beavis and Butt-head, arguing that rather than encouraging infantile

---

### Reading Music on the Net

Many popular musicians and groups boast their own web site or host special "concert" events on the Internet. Select a favorite artist, and to find his or her site, use a search engine such as Yahoo (http://www.yahoo.com/Entertainment/Music/Artists) or try the Ultimate Band List (http://american.recordings.com/wwwofmusic), a huge list of music-related web sites. Then study your artist's site and analyze the images created for him or her. How is the artist "packaged" on the Net, and does that packaging differ from that used in other media? What sort of relationship is established between the artist and you, the fan, and how does the electronic medium affect that relationship?

---

behavior, the notorious MTV cartoon instructs its viewers on how to view MTV videos, especially boring or pretentious ones. Next, bell hooks takes on Madonna, MTV's premier diva, whose embrace of the imagery of black culture is sometimes seen as a sign of her revolutionary intentions but which hooks views as a successful white girl's appropriation of black life in ways that reflect enduring racial — and even racist — stereotypes. Tricia Rose's semiotic analysis of such "Bad Sistas" as Salt 'N' Pepa and MC Lyte explores the videos of female rappers, revealing both their explicit messages about gender conflict in the hip-hop world and the implicit meanings that the rappers themselves may miss. Pamela Wilson takes us out of MTV and into the country with a cultural analysis of Dolly Parton, a star whose shrewd manipulation of sexuality and regional solidarity has made her one of the highest paid entertainers in America. Alex Ross concludes the chapter with an examination of talk television and its reigning chiefs, David Letterman and Rush Limbaugh, cultural ironists whose grasp of the power of television to project politically attractive images aligns them with media-savvy politicians like Ronald Reagan while differentiating them from such representatives of liberal sincerity as Bill Clinton.

SUSAN DOUGLAS

*Signs of Intelligent Life on TV*

||||||||||||||||||||||||||||||||||||||||||||||||

*Do you look for television programming that reflects an enlightened view of American women? Susan Douglas (b. 1950) does, and in this essay that originally appeared in* Ms. *she reports her findings, which are mixed, at best. Although popular TV dramas like* ER *and* NYPD Blue *appear to present characters and plotlines that defy gender stereotypes, Douglas still finds the telltale signs of cultural bias against women in such programs — especially a bias against strong, professional women. When not watching TV, Douglas is a professor of Communication Studies at the University of Michigan and media critic for* The Progressive. *She is the author of* Where the Girls Are: Growing Up Female with the Mass Media *(1994) and* Inventing American Broadcasting, 1899–1922 *(1987).*

When the hospital show *ER* became a surprise hit, the pundits who had declared dramatic television "dead" were shocked. But one group wasn't surprised at all.

Those of us with jobs, kids, older parents to tend to, backed-up toilets, dog barf on the rug, and friends/partners/husbands we'd like to say more than "hi" to during any diurnal cycle don't have much time to watch television. And when we do — usually after 9:38 P.M. — we have in recent years been forced to choose between Diane Sawyer interviewing Charles Manson or Connie Chung chasing after Tonya [Harding] and Nancy [Kerrigan]. People like me, who felt that watching the newsmagazines was like exposing yourself to ideological smallpox, were starved for some good escapist drama that takes you somewhere else yet resonates with real life and has ongoing characters you care about.

When *NYPD Blue* premiered in the fall of 1993 with the tough-but-sensitive John Kelly, and featuring strong, accomplished women, great lighting, bongo drums in the sound track, and male nudity, millions sighed with relief. When *ER* hit the air, we made it one of the tube's highest rated shows. Tagging farther behind, but still cause for hope, is another hospital drama, *Chicago Hope.*

All three shows acknowledge the importance of the adult female audience by featuring women as ongoing characters who work for a living and by focusing on contemporary problems in heterosexual relationships (no, we haven't yet achieved everyday homosexual couples on TV). More to the point, hound-dog-eyed, emotionally wounded yet eager-to-talk-it-through guys are center stage. So what are we getting when we kick back and submerge ourselves in these dramas? And what do they have to say about the ongoing project of feminism?

For those of you who don't watch these shows regularly, here's a    5
brief précis: *NYPD Blue* is a cop show set in New York City and has producer Steven Bochco's signature style — lots of shaky, hand-held camera work, fast-paced editing (supported by the driving, phallic backbeat in the sound track), and multiple, intersecting plots about various crimes and the personal lives of those who work in the precinct. Last season there were more women in the show; and last season there was John Kelly.

This year, the show is more masculinized. Watching Bobby Simone, played by Jimmy Smits, earn his right to replace Kelly was like witnessing a territorial peeing contest between weimaraners. Bobby had to be as sensitive and emotionally ravaged as Johnny, so in an act of New Age male one-upmanship, the scriptwriters made him a widower who had lost his wife to breast cancer. But Bobby had to be one tough customer too, so soon after we learn of his wife's death, we see him throwing some punks up against a fence, warning them that he will be their personal terminator unless they stop dealing drugs.

*ER* has the same kind of simultaneous, intersecting story lines, served up with fast-tracking cameras that sprint down hospital corridors and swirl around operating tables like hawks on speed. And there are the same bongo drums and other percussive sounds when patients are rushed in for treatment. *Chicago Hope* is *ER* on Valium: stationary cameras, slower pace, R & B instead of drumbeats. It's also *ER* on helium or ether, kind of a *Northern Exposure* goes to the hospital, with more offbeat plots and characters, like a patient who eats his hair or a kid whose ear has fallen off.

Whenever I like a show a lot — meaning I am there week in and week out — I figure I have once again embraced a media offering with my best and worst interests at heart. Dramatic TV shows, which seek a big chunk of the middle- and upper-income folks between 18 and 49, need to suck in those women whose lives have been transformed by the women's movement (especially women who work outside the home and have disposable income) while keeping the guys from grabbing the remote. What we get out of these twin desires is a blend of feminism and antifeminism in the plots and in the female characters. And for the male characters we have an updated hybrid of masculinity that crossbreeds decisiveness, technical expertise, and the ability to throw a punch or a basketball, with a soft spot for children and a willingness to cry.

On the surface, these shows seem good for women. We see female cops, lawyers, doctors, and administrators, who are smart, efficient, and successful. But in too many ways, the women take a backseat to the boys. In *NYPD Blue,* for example, we rarely see the women actually doing their jobs. The overall message in the three shows is that, yes, women can be as competent as men, but their entrance into the workforce has wrecked the family and made women so independent and hard-hearted that dealing with them and understanding them is impossible. Despite this, they're still the weaker sex.

In *ER* it is Carol Hathaway (Julianna Margulies), the charge nurse, 10 who tried to commit suicide. It is Dr. Susan Lewis (Sherry Stringfield) who is taken in by an imposter who claims to be a hospital administrator. Dr. Lewis is also the only resident who has trouble standing up to white, male authority figures: she is unable to operate while the head cardiologist watches her. In *Chicago Hope,* a psychiatrist prevails upon a female nurse to dress up like Dorothy (ruby slippers, pigtails, and all) because a patient refusing surgery is a *Wizard of Oz* junkie. Even though she points out that no male doctor would be asked to do anything like it, the shrink insists she continue the masquerade because the patient's life is at stake. Here's the crucial guilt-shifting we've all come to know and love — this patient's illness is somehow more her responsibility than anyone else's. Her humiliation is necessary to save him.

The Ariel Syndrome — Ariel was the name of Walt Disney's little mermaid, who traded her voice for a pair of legs so that she could be with a human prince she'd seen from afar for all of ten seconds — grips many of the women, who have recurring voice problems. Watch out for female characters who "don't want to talk about it," who can't say no, who don't speak up. They make it even harder for the women who do speak their minds, who are, of course, depicted as "bitches."

One major "bitch" is the wife of *ER*'s Dr. Mark Greene (Anthony Edwards). He's a doctor who's barely ever home, she's a lawyer who lands a great job two hours away, and they have a seven-year-old. Those of us constantly negotiating about who will pick up the kids or stay late at work can relate to this. The problem is that *ER* is about *his* efforts to juggle, *his* dreams and ambitions. We know this guy, we like him, we know he's a great doctor who adores his wife and child. Her, we don't know, and there's no comparable female doctor to show the woman's side of this equation. As a result, when conflicts emerge, the audience is primed to want her to compromise (which she's already done, so he can stay at the job he loves). When she insists he quit his job and relocate, she sounds like a spoiled child more wedded to a rigid quid pro quo than to flexibility, love, the family. It's the conservative view of what feminism has turned women into — unfeeling, demanding blocks of granite.

One of the major themes of all three shows is that heterosexual relationships are a national disaster area. And it's the women's fault. Take *NYPD Blue.* Yes, there's the fantasy relationship between Andy Sipowicz (Dennis Franz) and Sylvia Costas (Sharon Lawrence), in which an accomplished woman helps a foul-mouthed, brutality-prone cop with really bad shirts get in touch with his feelings and learn the pleasures of coed showering. While this affair has become the emotional anchor of the show, it is also the lone survivor in the ongoing gender wars.

It looks like splitsville for most of the show's other couples. Greg Medavoy (Gordon Clapp) infuriates Donna Abandando (Gail O'Grady) by his behavior, which includes following her to see whom she's having lunch with. She's absolutely right. But after all the shots of Greg looking at her longingly across the office (again, we're inside his head, not hers), the audience is encouraged to think that she should give the guy a break. By contrast, her explanations of why she's so angry and what she wants have all the depth and emotional warmth of a Morse code message tapped out by an iguana. Of course Greg doesn't understand. She won't help him.

In this world, female friendships are nonexistent or venomous. And there is still worse ideological sludge gumming up these shows. Asian and Latina women are rarely seen, and African American women are also generally absent except as prostitutes, bad welfare moms, and unidentified nurses. In the *ER* emergency room, the black women who are the conscience and much-needed drill sergeants of the show don't get top billing, and are rarely addressed by name. There is also an overabundance of bad mothers of all races: adoptive ones who desert their kids, abusive ones who burn their kids, and hooker ones (ipso facto bad). Since the major female characters — all upper-middle class — don't have kids, we don't see their struggles to manage motherhood and work. And we certainly don't see less privileged moms (the real majority in the U.S.), like the nurses or office workers, deal with these struggles on a lot less money.

One of the worst things these shows do, under a veneer of liberalism and feminism, is justify the new conservatism in the U.S. The suspects brought in for questioning on *NYPD Blue* are frequently threatened and sometimes beaten, but it's O.K. because they all turn out to be guilty, anyway. Legal representation for these witnesses is an unspeakable evil because it hides the truth. After a steady diet of this, one might assume the Fourth Amendment, which prohibits unreasonable search and seizure, is hardly worth preserving.

So why are so many women devoted to these shows? First off, the women we do see are more successful, gutsy, more fully realized than most female TV characters. But as for me, I'm a sucker for the men. I want to believe, despite all the hideous evidence to the contrary, that some men have been humanized by the women's movement, that they have become more nurturing, sensitive, and emotionally responsible. I want to believe that patriarchy is being altered by feminism. Since I get zero evidence of this on the nightly news, I want a few hours a week when I can escape into this fantasy.

Of course, we pay a price for this fantasy. TV depicts "real men" being feminized for the better and women masculinized for the worse. The message from the guys is, "We became the kind of men you feminists said that you wanted, and now you can't appreciate us because you've forgotten how to be a 'real' woman." It's a bizarre twist on the real world, where many women have changed, but too many men have not. Nevertheless, in TV land feminism continues to hoist itself with its own petard. Big surprise.

## Reading the Text

1. What does Douglas mean by saying that "watching the newsmagazines was like exposing yourself to ideological smallpox," and what attitude toward the media does this comment reveal?
2. Why, according to Douglas, are professional women attracted to programs such as *ER* and *NYPD Blue*?
3. What, according to Douglas, is the overt message about gender roles communicated by the TV shows she discusses? What is the hidden message?
4. How are non–Caucasian women presented in *ER* and *NYPD Blue,* according to Douglas, and what is her opinion about their presentation?
5. How does Douglas view the "new conservatism in the U.S."?

## Reading the Signs

1. Watch an episode of *ER* or *NYPD Blue* and write an argumentative essay in which you support, refute, or modify Douglas's belief that the show, despite superficial nods at feminism, perpetuates traditional gender roles.
2. In class, brainstorm TV shows that portray women as professionals or in other responsible, intelligent roles. Then, using Douglas's argument as your starting point, discuss whether the shows really adopt a feminist or an antifeminist stance in portraying female characters.
3. In your journal, discuss your favorite prime-time TV show, exploring exactly what you find attractive about the program.
4. Apply Douglas's argument to the films Sandra Tsing Loh discusses in "The Return of Doris Day" (p. 287). To what extent is the good girl motif that Loh describes symptomatic of the covert antifeminism that Douglas decries?
5. Watch one of the TV shows that Walter Kirn discusses in "Twentysomethings" (p. 214), or another program focusing on young adult characters. Do you see evidence of the covert antifeminism that Douglas describes? What does the treatment of female characters say about the show's presumed audience? Use your findings as evidence in an analytical essay about how the show depicts women.
6. Do you see any evidence of covert antifeminism in advertising? Write an essay in which you explore the depiction of women in advertising, focusing perhaps on ads in a woman's magazine such as *Elle* or *Vogue*. To develop your argument, consult Gloria Steinem's "Sex, Lies, and Advertising" (p. 155).

JOSH OZERSKY

*TV's Anti-Families: Married . . . with Malaise*

*In this critique of the modern antifamily sitcom, Josh Ozersky argues that one of TV's shrewdest ploys is to make fun of itself in shows like* The Simpsons *to "ingratiate itself with Americans, who in an age marked by pervasive irony want to . . . feel superior to TV and yet keep watching it." Finding in such hit series as* Married . . . with Children *a bleak exaggeration of America's real family problems, Ozersky sees, at best, trivialization of dysfunctional families and, at worst, a kind of "counsel of despair." Josh Ozersky obtained his B.A. in English literature from Rutgers University and is completing his doctorate in American history at Notre Dame University. A specialist in American popular culture of the past forty years, Ozersky has published in* Seventeen, Tikkun, The Washington Times, Chronicles, *and other magazines.*

It's an odd thing when a cartoon series is praised as one of the most trenchant and "realistic" programs on TV, but there you are. Never mind the Cosby-size ratings: If merchandising says anything about American culture, and it does, then America was utterly infatuated with *The Simpsons* in 1990. "Utterly," because unlike other big winners in the industry such as the Teenage Mutant Ninja Turtles and the New Kids on the Block, the Simpsons graced not only T-shirts for the clamoring young, but T-shirts (and sweatshirts and posters and mugs) that went out in droves to parents, who rivaled kids for viewer loyalty.

The animated series chronicles the life of the Simpson family: father Homer, who works in a nuclear power plant and reads bowling-ball catalogs; mother Marge, with her blue beehive hairdo and raspy voice; misunderstood-Bohemian daughter Lisa; baby Maggie; and bratty son Bart, the anti-everything star of the series. Bart appeals to kids, who see a flattering image of themselves, and to their parents, who, even as they identify with Bart against his lumpkin parents, enjoy Bart's caricature of their own children, with his incomprehensible sloganeering ("Don't have a cow, man!") and bad manners. Nor, tellingly, has the popularity of the show stopped with the white mainstream: a black Bart soon began to turn up in unlicensed street paraphernalia.

In the first of the unauthorized shirts, Bart was himself, only darkened. The novelty soon wore off, however, and in successive generations Bart found himself ethnicized further: "Air Bart" had him flying toward a basketball hoop exclaiming "In your face, home boy." Another shirt had Bart leering at zaftig black women, loutishly yelling "Big Ole Butt!" at their retreating figures. And in later versions, Bart has a gold tooth, a razor cut, and an angry snarl — the slogan "I got the power!" juts over-head in an oversized balloon.

The "I got the power!" Bart is barely recognizable, disfigured by rancor. But even more jarring than his appearance is his vitriol, so out of keeping with the real Bart's laid-back, ironic demeanor — an endemic condition among TV characters. The naked discontent on that shirt is jarring, disturbing. It lacks the light touch. TV does not — but then the playful suppression of unhappiness has always been one of TV's great strengths; and in its latest, ugliest form, it subtly discourages alarm at the decline of the family, its own complicity in that decline, and the resulting effects on a disintegrating society.

The success in the last few seasons of new, "antifamily" sitcoms, such    5 as Fox's *Married . . . with Children* and *The Simpsons* and ABC's *Roseanne,* began a trend that has made waves in television. "Whether it's the influ-ence of Bart Simpson and those cheeky sitcoms from Fox," wrote *TV Guide* in September [1990] "or ABC's artsy anti-soap *Twin Peaks,* uncon-ventionality is in; slick and safe are out." The "cheeky sitcoms" began that trend. *Roseanne,* about an obese and abrasive proletarian mom, and *Mar-ried . . . with Children,* a half hour of pure viciousness, represented along with *The Simpsons* a new development of the situation comedy, TV's de-finitive genre. Each program (as well as its inevitable imitators) focuses on a family marked by visual styles and characterization as bleak and miser-able as those of former TV families had been handsome or cheerful.

The innovation received a lot of attention in the mass media, most of it favorable. Richard Zoglin in *Time* hailed the "real-world grit these shows provide," produced psychological authorities, and quoted Barbara Ehrenreich's wide-eyed "Zeitgeist Goddess" piece in the *New Republic.* The *New York Times*'s Caryl Rivers wrote approvingly of the new real-ism, although she noted perfunctorily that gays, minorities, and women were less visible than they should have been. What all sides had in com-mon, however, was a willingness to point out the improvement over other forms of TV. "The anti-family shows aren't against the family, ex-actly, just scornful of the romantic picture TV has often painted of it," Zoglin pointed out. "We're like a mutant Ozzie and Harriet," Simpsons creator Matt Groening boasted in *Newsweek,* which went on to point out that the show was "hardly the stuff of Saturday-morning children's pro-gramming." "Thankfully, we are past the days of perfect Mom and all-wise Dad and their twin beds," wrote the *New York Times*'s Rivers, speaking for reviewers and feature writers everywhere. And this was prior to the advent of the "unconventional" mystery serial *Twin Peaks,* which still has feature writers striving for superlatives to describe its "in-novations" and "departures."

This unanimous juxtaposition of the "antifamilies" to the stern TV households of yesteryear is a specious comparison designed to amuse and flatter. Not as the result of any conspiracy — writers in the commercial mass media generally write to please, and what they say is true enough if you have as your entire frame of reference the past and present of TV. But far from the "authenticity" it pretends to, the "grit" for the new shows is merely an improved artifice, a challenge only to the verisimilitude of art directors and casting companies. By pretending to realism, TV only extends its own hegemony, in which every standard of comparison points back to another sham. "Gosh," gushed *TV Guide* of Bart, "can you imagine Bud Anderson being so . . . *disrespectful* to Dad?" As if the lead of *Father Knows Best* had only recently become a figure of fun.

It is through this sort of pseudo–self-deprecation that TV tries to ingratiate itself with Americans, who in an age marked by pervasive irony want to run with the hare and hunt with the hound — to feel superior to TV and yet keep watching it. TV offers this target audience an abundance of self-images that will permit them this trick. The target viewers may be enlightened, making the "choice of a new generation" by seeing through *My Little Margie,* or avant-garde, on the cutting edge, for watching *Twin Peaks,* which, like *Hill Street Blues* before it, supposedly "breaks all the rules." They are in utter harmony with the very mechanics of TV production, which has no secrets from us, as we know from David Letterman's insider gags, such as the "Late Night Danger Cam."

As for discrediting paternalistic authority figures, Mark Crispin Miller has pointed out that the imperious Dads of fifties TV, now such a rich source of burlesque, were overturned by a maturing medium very early on. The "grim old abstinence" of the Puritan patriarch stood in the way of the "grim new self-indulgence" of consumer culture and was hence banished. Dads turned into "pleasant nullities," like Dick York in *Bewitched* and Timothy Busfield in *thirtysomething,* or unenlightened butts of knowing and self-flattering jokes, like Archie Bunker and Homer Simpson.

The downfall of Dad, however, saw no concomitant rise of Mom or   10 the kids. Rather, it was advertisers and corporations that benefited from the free-spending self-indulgence of all parties, liberated from patriarchal discipline. And the networks, of course, cashed in and sold advertisers airtime. In the world beyond the screen, the family has disintegrated into epidemic divorces and deteriorating marriages, latchkey children, and working parents reduced to spending "quality time" with their children, as though they were hospital visitors or the lovelorn spouses of soldiers on leave. Meanwhile, the TV world — not only in sitcoms but in endless "special reports" and talk shows and (particularly) commercials — insists again and again that we are hipper, more "open," more enlightened, and facing changing "relationships" in a new and better way. Mom, often divorced and underpaid, has her new "independence," a standard theme of programming, and Dad and the kids, faced with other losses and hardships, are offered the bold new "grittiness" of prime-time entertainment.

TV has absorbed the American family's increasing sense of defeat and estrangement and presented it as an ironic in-joke.

This dynamic is seldom noted, although the mere *fact* of watching is
noted by critics and commentators everywhere, and nowhere more visibly than on TV itself. The opening credits of *The Simpsons* end with the
family, assembled at the end of the day, jumping mutely into fixed position on the sofa and clicking on the TV set. This absorption of criticism
is and has been, except for sheer distraction, TV's greatest weapon against
criticism. The transformation of the hearth into an engine of negation,
after all, should have caused *some* stir. And so it would have, if TV were
no more than the yammering salesman it has caricatured itself as in satirical moments. But, as Miller demonstrates, TV has never shown us TV;
rather, it shows itself to us as a laughable, absurd, and harmless entity,
much like the characters on its shows.

When not played for background noise — whooping Indians in
older shows, unctuous game-show hosts or newsmen in newer ones —
depictions of the TV set on TV itself render it invisible and omnipresent.
TV itself, its conventions and production, may be the crucial point of
reference for the sophisticated appeal it enjoys today, but the set as
household centerpiece is seldom seen, and then only as a joke, as on *The
Simpsons.* Instead, the set most often poses as a portal to the outer world:
hence its constant stream of images that tease us with alluring beaches,
blue waters, busy city streets. Even in its living rooms, where we know
its presence to be inescapable, the TV is often missing. This effect is accomplished by a simple trick of photography when the family watches
TV in *All in the Family,* in *Good Times,* in *Married . . . with Children,* etc.,
the scene is shot from behind the TV set. As the family sits facing us,
with the screen nowhere in sight, the illusion exists for a moment that
the TV really is, if not a portal, then a mirror or reflection of us. A close
look at these families, and at our own, soon banishes this impression. We
are not like these TV families at all; and the TV set is obtrusive, ideological, and tendentious.

When speaking of the "antifamily" sitcoms, most of the commentators seem to have in mind *Married . . . with Children.* No other show so
luridly plays up the sheer negativity of the current "authenticity" trend,
nor does any other show do so with such predictable regularity. The series portrays the Bundys, a lower-middle-class family with two children
and a dog. Father Al (Ed O'Neill) only has "knotted bowels" to show for
his life supporting the family. Peg (Katey Sagal) is Al's castrating wife.
There is also the inevitable sharp-tongued teenage son, who singles out
for special heckling his brainless and sleazy sister. The relentlessly ironic
quality of a happy family turned thoroughly upside-down flatters the audience for their enlightenment (no *Donna Reed,* this) even as it invites
them to enjoy the ongoing frenzy of spite in which the show indulges.

And frenzy is indeed the word. Every member of the family despises everyone else, and any given program consists of little more than continuous insults, interspersed with snide loathing or occasional expressions of despair.

FATHER (to son): Did I ever tell you not to get married?
SON: Yeah, Dad.
FATHER: Did I ever tell you not to become a shoe salesman?
SON: Yeah, Dad.
FATHER: Well, then I've told you everything I know.

This sort of resigned and paralytic discontent dominates the tone of *Married . . . with Children*; it lacks even the dim rays of hope that occasionally lifted Ralph Kramden's or Riley's gloomy existence. Every show is devoted to a new kind of humiliation: to earn extra money, Al becomes a burger-flipper; when son Bud falls victim to a practical joke perpetrated by an old flame, his slutty sister Kelly comes to his defense by crucifying the girl against a locker; wife Peg belittles Al's manhood in front of strangers. Again and again, the unrelenting negativity of the show finds new ways to expand, purifying itself of any nonironic, positive content. Lovebird neighbors intended for contrast in the first season soon divorce, adding to the show's already vast reserve of bitterness. Christina Applegate, the young actress who plays Kelly, filled out during the first two years, adding a missing element of nasty prurience to the show.

The result of this hermetic exclusion of all warmth, say a number of 15 apologists for the show, is positive: "With these new programs," says Barbara Cadow, a psychologist at USC, "we see we're doing all right by comparison." Yet at the same time, it is the very "realism" of these shows that won them praise again and again. This "realism" appeals to a cynical element in us — no one would ever admit to resembling Roseanne Barr or her family, but they are eminently "realistic" portraits of the losers next door. Roseanne Barr is shrewish and miserable to the point of self-parody, and this is seen as the great strength of her series. "Mom" (who Roseanne, it is assumed, represents) "is no longer interested in being a human sacrifice on the altar of 'pro-family' values," says Barbara Ehrenreich in the *New Republic*.

The praise of the same style of TV both for its realism and for its horrific exaggeration, while apparently contradictory, is based on a common assumption. In each case, the pervasive unhappiness and derision on TV sitcoms is assumed to be a reflection, albeit a negative one, of the unhappiness of real families. Cadow assumes that it is caricature, and Ehrenreich that it is a manifesto, but neither woman doubts that both shows offer some kind of corrective to real life for their viewers, and that this explains their popularity. This congratulatory view of hit TV shows contains a fundamental error: the old network executive's rationale that

TV "gives people what they want," in response to their Nielsen-measured "choice."

The concentration of mass media into a few corporate hands invalidates that idea even more today than in the past. Given TV's entirely corporate nature, it is unreasonable to assume that the channels are referenda, since almost every channel, at least until recently, offered almost identical options. What succeeds with the public makes it, yes. But that "success" is determined by TV's agenda — which now, as always, is more than selling dog biscuits. Consumption must be encouraged psychologically; sectors and tendencies in American society have to be identified and exploited. "Since the major broadcasters are no longer winning the big numbers," observes *TV Guide,* "they're now fighting for the youthful demographics that bring in the highest revenues. That's why everyone is hyping bold, hip shows."

Of course, the success of a culture based on mass consumption depends on the creation of boundless needs; boundless needs presuppose boundless discontent. Boundless discontent must begin with the family, where social patterns are first internalized. If, latchkey in hand, TV can flatter a kinless and dispossessed child into adulthood and at the same time kid his or her parents about it, perfect consumers are thereby made. The family becomes a breeding ground for easygoing and independent citizens of the marketplace, transported beyond the inner struggle and deep feeling of family life, and bound in their place by the laws of supply and demand, consumer "choices," and a continual negation of their truest selves.

By presenting unhappy families to viewers, TV achieves many gains. First, as Cadow rightly points out, mocking the traditional family does flatter the distorted family of our times. However, this does not necessarily lift spirits. On the contrary, it lowers expectations; it stupefies discontent instead of healing it. *Married . . . with Children* is the prototype of this strategy. The petty or profound resentments of real families do not rival those of the Bundys, but then neither does their ability to punish and humiliate each other. By making our problems "seem all right by comparison," the series trivializes them rather than taking them seriously. It in fact worsens them by its counsel of despair.

Secondly, the dysfunctional TV family aids advertisers in their perennial quest for credibility by creating a supersaturated atmosphere of irony, which atrophies our ability to believe in anything. Commercials themselves work on a principle of pseudorebelliousness. Burger King — now officially touted by the Simpsons — proudly sports the "radical" motto, "Sometimes you've gotta break the rules." Swallowing these giant absurdities relies not on credulity, but on an ironic, self-assured disbelief. *Roseanne,* with its trademark sarcasm, and *Twin Peaks,* with its tongue-in-cheek grotesqueries, are good examples.

[20]

Third, and most insidious, is the stability of TV's dysfunctional families, and their passive acceptance of their fate. A successful cast is the source of "ensemble acting," which has been the formula for success for some time now on TV. Since TV characters now move in herds, they do not get divorced, move out, have devastating affairs, or anything else that would disrupt the fabric of the show's format. Implicitly, these shows assure us that family life is largely a nightmare, but one that is self-perpetuating and only requires handling with a deft, protective irony. This irony, the antithesis of deep feeling, is the essential assault on the family and on all human relationships, reducing them to problems of managerial acumen. Thus, while remaining intact in their own impoverished world, sitcom families undermine the stability of real families, discrediting the embarrassingly earnest, often abject bonds of kin while hermetically sealing themselves off from the possibility of familial collapse. And this while they consume the increasingly rare time in which American families are actually together.

*The Simpsons,* the most popular of the group and certainly the least ironic and "antifamily," is TV's most effective reinforcer. This paradox begins with the fact that the show is a cartoon: With their yellow skin, bulging eyes, and comical motions, the Simpsons are funny just to look at, and hence relieve the audience of the need to continually jeer at them. The Bundy family of *Married . . . with Children,* like all sitcom characters, aspire to the televisual purity of cartoon characters, but are stuck in rubbery bags of protoplasm with nothing but one-liners and a laugh track to hide behind. The Simpsons, oddly, are freer than other TV families to act human.

And so they do. There is an element of family loyalty and principle to be found in the Simpsons, often combined with witty and valid social criticism. Brother Bart and sister Lisa petulantly demand of baby Maggie to "come to the one you love most," to which the infant responds by crawling lovingly to the TV. Or again, when father Homer's sinister boss inquires disbelievingly, "You'd give up a job and a raise for your principles?" Homer responds (with almost none of the usual sitcom character's irony), "When you put it that way, it does sound farfetched — but that's the lunk you're lookin' at!" "Hmm," the boss replies. "You're not as dumb as you look. Or sound. Or as our best testing indicates."

With pointed jokes such as these, *The Simpsons* might prompt us to conclude the same about its vast audience. The harmlessness of these jokes can be taken for granted; no one who watches TV is going to stop because they see TV criticized. We criticize it ourselves as a matter of course. On the contrary, we feel flattered, and less inclined to stop watching.

And we are that much less inclined to object to the continuing presence of unsafe workplaces, vast corporations, the therapy racket, and all the other deserving targets of the Simpsons' harmless barbs. The genial    25

knowingness of shows like *The Simpsons* subverts criticism through an innocuous pseudocriticism, just as the familial discontents of TV shows
subvert alarm at graver discontents in real life. Criticism is further weakened by the show's irony, which although less than some other programs
is still pervasive and fundamental to its humor. No one in an ironic show
can get too far out of line. For example, in one episode, misunderstood
Lisa meets that well-worn figure of Caucasian lore, the wise and virtuous
old colored bluesman, ever ready to act as mentor to young white people
in their search for self-knowledge. *The Simpsons* is far too hip to hand us
such a hackneyed cliché. The Virtuous Old Blues Man is as empty a conceit as the Perfect Family — so on the show, he is named "Bleeding
Gums Murphy" (Why? "I haven't brushed my teeth in thirty years, that's
why.") In place of the usual soulful laments, he sings the "I Don't Have
an Italian Suit Blues."

Such undercutting is typical of TV as a whole; attempts to transcend
the flattened-out emotional landscape of TV are almost invariably punished by some droll comeuppance. But since as bizarre cartoons there is
little need to belittle them, the Simpsons get a little more than most, and
are occasionally allowed moments of earnestness unmitigated by the selfishness of *thirtysomething,* the weirdness of *Twin Peaks,* or the inevitable
"comic relief" — the stock entrances of deadpan tots and witty oldsters,
etc. — used to terminate the maudlin embraces of nonanimated sit-
comites. None of this is to be had on *The Simpsons,* but the picture it
presents is still fundamentally hopeless. The Simpsons are basically boobs,
and their occasional bursts of tenderness or insight are buried under biting irony and superior, if affectionate, mockery. More than any of the
other "antifamily" shows, *The Simpsons* seems to come close to our lives;
more than any of the other shows, as a result, it commits us to a shared
vision of pessimism and self-deprecation.

Because the TV screen is neither a mirror, reflecting ourselves paralyzed in chairs in front of it, nor a window, through which we observe
the antics of distant players, it is an implicit invitation to participate in a
vision of "society" largely designed to flatter us in sinister ways, manipulate our attention, and commit us to the status quo. In discrediting "yesterday's" family values in its various "breakthrough" shows (ostensibly
defining *A Different World* for us, as the title of one series has it), TV
seeks only to impose its own values — which is to say, the values of the
marketplace. Bart Simpson, master sneerer, is the prototype of the modern series character who — by the social scripts of TV — reflects us.
Small, ridiculous, and at the same time admirable for his sarcasm and enlightened self-interest, Bart is the child of the culture of TV, his parents
mere intermediaries.

Paradoxically, that is why the most powerless sector of American society has adopted him, fitting him with their own wishful slogan — "I got

the power!" Though black Bart's anger may be incongruous with TV, his proclamation is not, since TV is so successful an invitation to impotent posturing. At the moment, the rage of the underclass cannot be appropriated by TV, yet in black Bart, in the fatal joining of ironic hipness and earnest wrath, we see perhaps a glimpse of the future (and in fact there are already a spate of new black shows — e.g., *Fresh Prince of Bel Air, In Living Color*). "I got the power!" says black Bart. But in the world of the TV family, no one has power. Empty fantasies of might, like cynical, knowing giggles, are terminal symptoms of our capitulation to TV's vision.

Life outside of that vision *is* ugly and is becoming uglier as ties, familial and societal, dissolve and decay. But the only power we do have is the power of our own real selves to reject the defensive posture of materialist or ironist or cynic, and the soullessness of TV's "hip, bold," antilife world. Bart and his aspirants exist in that world, and their example serves only to impoverish us.

### Reading the Text

1. What does Ozersky mean by "antifamilies"?
2. How, according to Ozersky, are the antifamily sitcoms a sign of the state of American families today?
3. What is Ozersky's view of the realism of today's sitcoms?
4. How does Ozersky see television as turning today's children into "perfect consumers"?

### Reading the Signs

1. Do you agree with Ozersky's argument that "by presenting unhappy families to viewers, TV achieves many gains"? Write an essay in which you defend or refute Ozersky's thesis, supporting your position with specific examples of television shows you have seen.
2. Read or review Susan Douglas's "Signs of Intelligent Life on TV" (p. 200). Using her analysis as your critical framework, analyze an episode of *The Simpsons,* focusing on the character of Marge and her relationship with her family.
3. Ozersky claims that antifamily shows encourage consumer behavior. In an essay, explore the validity of his position. To develop your argument, consult Laurence Shames's "The More Factor" (p. 31).
4. In class, brainstorm television programs that depict "profamilies," shows that feature traditional, idealized families. Then compare the "profamily" shows with the antifamily programs that Ozersky discusses. Which do you prefer to watch? What do the class's preferences say about its values and views on life?
5. While focusing on different subjects, both Josh Ozersky and bell hooks ("Madonna: Plantation Mistress or Soul Sister?" p. 223) argue that sup-

posedly "revolutionary" media icons in fact support the prevailing ideologies that they pretend to subvert. Write an essay in which you explore this contention by examining their subjects or other media examples that seem to be "breakthroughs"; you might consider films such as *Basic Instinct* and *Natural Born Killers* or artists such as Michael Jackson or Vanilla Ice.

# WALTER KIRN

## *Twentysomethings*

||||||||||||||||||||||||||||||||||||||||||||||||||||||

*They've been called "slackers," "generation X," and "the first generation in American history that expects to do worse than its parents." And "they" may be you. In this wicked look at "twentysomething" culture — "a sluggish mainstream underground that sold out even before it could drop out" — Walter Kirn (b. 1962) rips apart the movies, TV shows, fashions, and attitudes of what may be your generation, accusing it of being made up of "mopey" consumers whose greatest contribution to culture is "the glum 'Seattle Sound.' " Kirn pulls no punches in this media and cultural review; in fact, he practically begs you to respond. The book review editor at* New York *magazine, Kirn has also published a novel* She Needed Me *(1992), and a collection of short stories,* My Hard Bargain *(1990).*

The pathology of the new kids is familiar: impatience, distrust of authority, malaise, and a wistful, ironic sense of longing for defunct ideals and lost horizons. Minus the rebelliousness and hedonism that lent punch to earlier youth movements, this is almost the same set of traits shared by Hemingway's post-World War I "lost generation," Kerouac's Beats and Hoffman's hippies. What distinguishes the most recent brood of disaffected youth — variously identified as "twentysomethings," "slackers" and "the first generation in American history that expects to do worse than its parents" — is not its desolation but the curiously lame, detached self-consciousness of its popular culture. Examples include TV shows such as *Melrose Place* and *The Heights,* magazines from *Details* to *Pulse,* bands such as R.E.M. and its countless psychedelic-lite imitators, and all movies starring Bridget Fonda that use the word "single" in their titles. The merits of the individual works vary widely, but taken together they evoke an oddly soulless counterculture, a sluggish mainstream underground that sold out even before it could drop out.

The mopey inertia of twentystuff culture is, in a way, no surprise. A generation whose defining collective experience is its lack of defining collective experiences, whose Woodstock was watching *The Partridge Family* with a couple of friends and whose great moral dilemma is "paper or plastic?" is unlikely to produce a crop of quick-witted passionate radicals. That would require adversaries; but the twentysomethings' one true nemesis — the media monster that babysat them through their loveless youths — has managed to convince them that it's their buddy, a partner in self-realization.

Consider *Melrose Place,* a show about a group of mildly disillusioned, urban young people, manufactured by Aaron Spelling, the same man who, with *The Love Boat* and *Dynasty,* did much of the initial illusioning. The program has all the twentystuff hallmarks, from a mailing address for a premise (in twentystuff narratives, zip code is destiny) to therapy-speak dialogue ("I think it's really good that you're feeling these things that you're talking about"). It's basically an ensemble coping drama, with stressors-of-the-week — career troubles, problem pregnancies — replacing storylines. The show ends when everyone has aired their issues, exchanged supportive hugs. Conflicts are not resolved, they're extinguished, flash fires of emotion brought under control by pouring words on them.

The same goes for the recent movie *Singles,* a cut above *Melrose* in craftsmanship and acting but identical in its tone of plucky pathos. Once again, the lazy organizing principle is physical location, a grungy, Seattle apartment building populated by pure-hearted young folks saddled with dead-end jobs and ingrown dreams. Jaded and wary, with uncertain prospects, these white-kid nouvelle losers struggle for intimacy, fail, and then try again and provisionally succeed. In this twentystuff soap opera, public causes exist to be gestured at ("Think Globally, Act Locally," reads a bumper sticker), but private life is all the life there is, the world having shrunk to the cramped dimensions of one's wacky, sad, starter apartment with its sardonic, cheap, recycled furnishings. Indeed, it is this notion of recycling — both of material and cultural goods — that's the essence of the twentystuff esthetic. In *Singles,* casual friends are recycled into pseudo-family members, then into lovers, then back into friends. Portentous seventies rock 'n' roll is recycled into the glum "Seattle sound." Last night's takeout is this morning's breakfast and yesterday's philosophical fads (in this case, a paperback copy of *The Fountainhead* toted around by Bridget Fonda) are today's amusements. Resigning one's self to living off the table scraps of the American century is what twentystuff culture is all about. It's about recycling anger into irony, pain into poses.

Just check out an issue of *Details* magazine, a monthly lifestyle guide for wannabe desolation angels. In a recent issue that also happens to feature an interview with recycled guru Allen Ginsberg — adopted bard of all postwar youthquakes — the bedrooms of arty young single males    5 are inspected for hidden fashion statements ("What your crib says about you"). Paolo, described as a "sound engineer/motorcycle racer," takes obvious pride in his wacky scavenging, in the fragments he has shored against his ruin: "I found the dentist's chair on the street; the sofa is the back seat of a van." Then there's Craig, a "graphic designer/DJ" (the cute juxtapositions never end), who boasts: "The trunk's from a thrift shop, the cowhide rug was a gift." The implication, of course, is that one can never be too aware of the ironic signals one is sending, even while alone, in private. According to the twentystuff credo, one's life is a self-directed TV series (*Wayne's World! Wayne's World!*), and one is always spiritually on-camera.

That's sad, I think. Not funny-sad, just sad. Consumers tricked into thinking they're producers, entombed in their own bemused self-consciousness, acting at life instead of taking action, the devotees of twentystuff may be a lost generation, indeed.

### Reading the Text

1. What, according to Kirn, are the characteristics of "twentysomethings" in television programs today?
2. What does Kirn mean by saying "resigning one's self to living off the table scraps of the American century is what twentystuff culture is all about"?
3. How does Kirn explain the "pathology" that he attributes to the "twenty-something" generation?

### Reading the Signs

1. Kirn neglects to mention that many of the shows he criticizes are written and produced by people who are far from "twentysomething." How does this omission affect the credibility of his argument?
2. Take Kirn up on his challenge: Check out an issue of *Details* magazine. Is it, as Kirn claims, "a monthly lifestyle guide for wannabe desolation angels"? Write an essay in which you support, refute, or modify his characterization of this magazine and its readership.
3. Watch an episode of one of the TV shows that Kirn discusses, and write your own analysis of it. How does it function as a sign of the "twentysomething" generation, in your view?
4. In class, discuss Kirn's tone. How does it affect your response to his essay?
5. Kirn can be accused of stereotyping a generation. In a journal entry, explore the implications of such stereotyping. Is it based in reality? What difference does it make if a generation — as opposed to, say, an ethnic group — is stereotyped? If you are part of the generation Kirn attacks, how does his article make you feel? How does his stereotyping compare with images of "baby boomers"?

DOUGLAS RUSHKOFF

*Hating What Sucks*

*The Siskel and Ebert of MTV video criticism, Beavis and Butt-head*
*have established themselves as media guides for viewers with attitudes.*
*Though only cartoon characters, they are often blamed for the dysfunc-*
*tional behavior among the MTV generation, but as Douglas Rushkoff*
*suggests in this excerpt from* Media Virus! Hidden Agendas in
Popular Culture *(1994), their role is not so pernicious. Rather,*
*Beavis and Butt-head provide a kind of self-reflexive critique of*
*MTV's own programming, exposing what is silly or pretentious in the*
*music video world. A journalist and software developer, Rushkoff*
*writes widely on popular and cybernetic culture. He has written for such*
*publications as* Virtual City, Esquire, Details, *and* The Wall
Street Journal, *and his books include* Cyberia: Life in the
Trenches of Hyperspace *(1994).*

## Meltdown

You are watching a Robert Palmer video on MTV when suddenly
the image gets shaky and then melts down totally. The images on the
monitor dissolve into a colorful fluid, eventually finding themselves in a
bottle labeled "Liquid Television." This is a typical opening to "LTV,"
as it's been tagged by its producers, MTV's weekly foray into the world
of animation specifically designed to deconstruct and parody media and
popular culture. Segments by independent animators range from "Stick
Figure Theater," a comedy cartoon in which recognizable media images
like a Madonna video or a Hitchcock film are primitively drawn on note
cards, to "Aeon Flux," a never-ending violent futuristic fantasy in which
a beautiful gun-wielding heroine kills everything in her path.

Because it has no clear through line, the show, and even its nonlinear individual segments, can be quite difficult to watch. It requires viewers to change their expectations of media and adapt to a new kind of storytelling. Executive producer Japhet Asher, a thirty-two-year-old British
documentary filmmaker, saw this as his purpose in creating "LTV":

"What I'm trying to do in television relates to dreams more than to
linear kinds of storytelling. And I think that is where things are going in
our media." This forces his audience to participate. "There's a great deal
of interactivity because the way you make connections between different
segments and different ideas and how you respond is operating on a

different level than a traditional drama. We're challenging people to make connections."

"LTV" is about learning to make connections in an apparently discontinuous media world. This is what turns a seemingly discreet set of symbols into liquid. As Asher expressed it in a pitch meeting to MTV execs, "Put your favorite television shows in a blender and hit puree and you'll wind up with 'Liquid Television.'" Even many of the segments within the show are about making sense of apparently random image combinations. In "Psychogram," the camera pans over a bizarre collection of picture postcards, as a British voice-over (performed by Asher himself) connects them into a paranoid spy story. The only thing linking the cards are the narrator's conspiratorial conclusions.

To Asher the kind of training "LTV" conducts on its audience is a   5
necessary societal engineering. "Today there is such a bombardment of information in daily life that people have to evolve, get used to it, and survive it. Editing is a great function of life. People have to learn how to control their own destiny; you have to learn to think for yourself. You have to be prepared to accept that things are changing, and have fluid thought, or you'll be in trouble."

"Fluid thought" means being able to think as a person does in a dream state. The bombardment of data and imagery must be integrated into a single story. Animation provides a nonthreatening forum in which this can be practiced. Asher believes, "People are much more resistant to having new kinds of stories told to them than they are to seeing new animation styles. The ability for animation to explore the psyche is much larger, and it can map territories beyond imagination now."

Like many members of the GenX, postpsychedelic generation, Asher and his colleagues at San Francisco–based Colossal Pictures believe that there is much to be gained from exploring consciousness. As vice chairman of the company, he sees it as his responsibility to help America explore its current frontiers of mind. He is aware of how our culture began to fixate on courtroom drama and sees that as only one step in an ongoing evolution toward a media of thought. "America had gone inward and was going towards the courts and the judicial system; that America was a frontier of laws. I believe that now we're really dealing with a frontier that goes inward — a frontier of the mind. Everybody's free in their mind if they want to look and explore."

To develop this ability, "LTV" encourages us to think in a chaotic fashion. On the simplest level, this has to do with seeing the media as a place to play with thought by deconstructing its images and learning how we have been affected by them. A mock ad for "Lee Press-on Limbs" shows a woman whose arm has fallen off just before an important evening out with a new date. The screen flashes the words "Horror! Pain! Fear! Guilt!" exposing the emotions such ads hope to exploit in order to sell their products. Another regular segment shows a fashion consultant named Lidia using a computer to come up with new looks for Sinéad O'Connor, George Michael, or Sylvester Stallone. She ends each week's segment with the slogan "The more you look, the better you'll see."

Beyond media parody and dissection, cyberpunk (gritty, computer-world science fiction) segments like "Aeon Flux" attempt to impart a new dramatic paradigm more consistent with the chaotic world-view. The heroine is engaged in a fairly plotless quest. As if in a video game, she moves or climbs from room to room, killing whoever stands in her way. One of her chief weapons is a bug that bites people and injects a fast-acting, fatal virus. She infects or shoots thousands in her journey toward a high tower, where she apparently hopes to assassinate a leader. On her way she steps on a tiny tack that becomes lodged in her heel. Just before she shoots her intended victim, the nail penetrates her foot. She loses her balance and falls off a window ledge to her death. As in a self-similar-chaos equation, one single woman is able to inflict tremendous damage on an entire city using a microscopic virus, but she is herself brought down by a tiny tack that just happened to find itself in the heel of her boot. Chaos is the aggressor's Achilles' heel.

Asher hopes that "LTV," too, will function as a deceptively high 10 leverage point in our increasingly chaotic culture. "Let's hope it catches on and spreads like a virus. If there's any hope for interaction, people are going to have to open up their minds to new approaches to stories and be prepared to interact with them." Meltdown television is a disintegration of TV as a parental or dictatorial force as it worked from the fifties to the eighties. "This is television anarchy. Definitely, that's what we want."

Even though Asher is one of the first members of the post-baby boom generation to rise to a position of power in the media, he believes he will soon be followed by others. "I feel like the lunatics are running the asylum right now, and that's a good thing. We all grew up on TV, and I'm very pleased to shake it all up now." Asher offers himself and his popular show as hard evidence that his generation did not all become couch potatoes. "I've always been a great believer in our Generation X. I don't think there's any such thing as a vidiot. That's a ridiculous phrase. The fact that somebody's capable of absorbing a vast amount of visual information makes them very intelligent, not very stupid."

## Hating What Sucks

Beavis and Butt-head, "Liquid Television's" most successful spin-off, hardly appear to support Asher's contentions about the intelligence of MTV fans. These animated teenage pals first showed up on "Liquid TV" as a comedy segment, but are now internationally famous for the afternoons they spend together irreverently watching MTV. On the surface "Beavis and Butt-head" satirizes stupid, middle-American heavy-metal airheads. The cartoon characters blow up frogs with firecrackers and use cats as baseballs. But their show works on a much deeper level as an instructional video on how to watch MTV with appropriate skepticism.

Like the boys in "Wayne's World," Beavis and Butt-head, clad in AC/DC and Metallica T-shirts, appear to understand the tactics of rock videos and are free with their commentary as they watch. The show is structured much like regular MTV, in which videos are aired back-to-back, but here the videos are augmented by the wisecracks and antics of two typical adolescent viewers. That "Beavis and Butt-head" is so popular attests to the audience's understanding of this sort of comedy. That "Beavis and Butt-head" has been censored and ultimately banished from daytime television (the show now only airs late at night) attests to the threat the characters pose as viral conduits.

The experience of "Beavis and Butt-head" is akin to watching MTV along with two bratty comrades. They spend most of their time giggling maniacally in recently lowered pubescent voices. Their laughter is their main form of communication with each other — a kind of agreement that they are not being taken in by the images in the videos they are watching, but rather maintaining a jaded attitude. As we watch an Aerosmith video with the boys, they voice-over their critique. The lead singer is pictured stark naked, with his hand deftly covering his genitals. "Where's his penis?" asks Butt-head. "It's in his hand," giggles Beavis. More laughter from both before Beavis adds, "where it always is." Their comments function like the graffiti on inane billboards that targets obvious sexual innuendo with arrows connecting one character's eyeline to another's breasts.

When something occurs in a video too subtle for Beavis or Butt-   15
head to notice, the animators clue the audience in to the boys' own susceptibility to media manipulation. When the Aerosmith singer lights up a cigarette in the video, we see Beavis unconsciously light up his own cigarette. However cynical he believes he has become, he still blindly follows the examples set by his heavy-metal heroes. The show still promotes viewer awareness by allowing us to witness areas where the characters' own detachment has been compromised.

But these instances are usually limited to one or two per episode. Usually when the boys are disturbed by something they do not understand, they simply switch channels. After watching Jermaine Jackson dance and squirm in what they assume is a giant condom, Butt-head calls out, "Change it!" We cut into a Boy George video. As George sings "I'm a man," Beavis retorts, "No way, he's not even a boy." The two are clearly uncomfortable with Boy George's sexuality and change the subject of their conversation to the style of the video, in which people move about in period costume.

"Is this supposed to be the future?" Beavis asks. "It sucks. Change it." To which Butt-head responds with surprisingly advanced wit,

"Beavis, I'm cool, but I can't change the future." More laughs. The boys understand that MTV prides itself on its ability to bend time and bring images from the past into the present, but they know how to take this all in stride. They change the channel, inflicting their will on the medium the only way they know how: channel surfing. In doing so they again demonstrate for us how to watch TV in the nineties. "I see them as an extension of our best promos," admits MTV creative director Judy McGrath, "which have always been irreverent."[1]

Near the end of one episode, the boys happen upon a David Byrne video from the movie *True Stories*. The "concept" video takes place in a bar, where clients, one by one, stand on a stage in front of a microphone and mouth the words to the song. The boys watch in silent confusion, as Byrne, the real vocalist, rises to the microphone. There is obviously supposed to be a message here — something about the relationship of audience to media or even a star to his own media — but the boys are not sophisticated enough or sober enough to care. "This video's over my head," complains Beavis.

"It's under my butt," answers Butt-head as the two finally giggle. Their mutual annoyance has united them once again. "I don't like videos that suck," continues Butt-head.

"Me, too," giggles Beavis in bad grammar as he switches off the TV   20 and the episode ends. When all else fails, the show instructs, just shut the damn thing off.

But most adults do not understand the instructional agenda of "Beavis and Butt-head." They only see two ugly adolescents destroying things and millions of teenagers enjoying them do it. Unable to decipher the language of the simulacre, adult "consensus" culture has no choice but to stamp it out whenever there is an opportunity to do so. In October of 1993, a five-year-old named Austin Messner set a fire that cost his baby sister Jessica her life. The local fire chief blamed Beavis and Butt-head's antics for having inspired the child's pyromania, and Attorney General Janet Reno, already riding a wave of public distaste for violence on television, had a new example of just how dangerous the media had become. MTV ducked for cover and changed the "Beavis and Butt-head" time slot so kids couldn't watch.

"Beavis and Butt-head" was not removed from MTV's daytime schedule because its characters set fires. Dennis the Menace performed countless acts of potentially life-endangering malice per minute, yet was never threatened with censorship. Or, as *The New York Times Magazine* suggested, critics of the show, like Attorney General Janet Reno, might best look to their own televised atrocities before blaming kids' shows for desensitizing America to the dangers of handguns and pyromania. Instead

---

1. *Rolling Stone*, "Beavis and Butt-head," August 19, 1993.

of focusing on fictional television, the magazine argued, Reno should instead be reconsidering the "protracted, prurient coverage of events like the firestorm at Waco (which she co-produced). At least 'Beavis and Butt-head,' a cartoon, does not pretend to be reality. Next to the pyrophillic news spectaculars surrounding it, its jokey efforts to stimulate a viewer's imagination almost start to look like art."[2]

"Beavis and Butt-head" was not targeted for its obvious satirical depiction of teenage pranks. It was targeted for its much less obvious, and much more subversive commentary on the dangers of growing up in the simulacre. The cartoon was attacked for using a language that adults could not understand. Grown-ups got spooked by essentially activist memes[3] shrouded in meta-media.

Now that Viacom, the parent company of MTV and Nickelodeon, has taken over Paramount, producer of such meme conduits as "Entertainment Tonight" and "A Current Affair" as well as owner of Simon & Schuster, the Beavis and Butt-head contagion is sure to spread much, much further. A book and CD have already been released, and a movie is on the way. This is the real impact of today's media empire mergers. They give virulent memes new connective pathways and breeding grounds.

### Reading the Text

1. What are the characteristics of liquid TV, as Rushkoff describes them, and what are their purposes?
2. What assumptions does Rushkoff make about Generation X, and why does he see liquid TV as well suited for this age group?
3. Why does MTV producer Japhet Asher claim that "I don't think there's any such thing as a vidiot"?
4. Summarize in your own words Rushkoff's interpretation of *Beavis and Butt-head*.
5. Why does Rushkoff believe that older viewers can't understand *Beavis and Butt-head*?

### Reading the Signs

1. In an argumentative essay, challenge, support, or modify Rushkoff's assertion that Beavis and Butt-head "demonstrate for us how to watch TV in the nineties."

---

2. Frank Rich, "Public Stages: Burn, Baby, Burn!" *The New York Times Magazine*, November 28, 1993.
3. **Meme** Douglas Rushkoff's term for the forces within the electronic media that affect our culture, similar to the way that computer viruses attack programs. — EDS.

2. Write a letter addressed to older viewers, explaining how to understand *Beavis and Butt-head,* drawing upon either Rushkoff's argument or your own interpretation of the show.

3. Tape an episode of *Beavis and Butt-head* and watch it in class. Then form teams and debate whether the episode you watch is idiotic and dangerous, as critics contend, or intelligent and instructive, as Rushkoff believes.

4. Read or reread Jenny Lyn Bader's "Larger Than Life" (p. 391) and write an essay in which you analyze Beavis and Butt-head as heroes, icons, or role models for twentysomething viewers.

5. Watch an episode of *Beavis and Butt-head* and of *The Simpsons* and write a comparison of the two shows. Of what does the humor of each show consist, and how do the shows appeal to their viewers? What significance do you attribute to the fact that one is broadcast on MTV, the other on network?

b e l l   h o o k s

## *Madonna: Plantation Mistress or Soul Sister?*

||||||||||||||||||||||||||||||||||||||||||||||||||||||||||||||||||||

*Through such videos as "Like a Prayer," Madonna has established a reputation for being a friend to black America. bell hooks isn't so sure. In this critique of Madonna's career she shows how often the material girl has exploited racial stereotypes in her rebellion against middle-class sexual codes. Using "the black female body as a sign of sexual experience," hooks argues, Madonna at once insults and exploits black women and men. And like a contemporary Shirley Temple, hooks continues, Madonna domineers the black dancers she employs in her videos, keeping them in their place and making sure that she is never upstaged by them. bell hooks (the pen name of Gloria Watkins; b. 1952) is the author of* Black Looks: Race and Representation *(1992), from which this selection is taken, and numerous other books, including* Talking Back: Thinking Feminist, Thinking Black *(1989) and* Outlaw Cultures: Resisting Representations *(1994). She is distinguished professor of English at City College of New York.*

*Subversion is contextual, historical, and above all social. No matter how exciting the "destabilizing" potential of texts, bodily or otherwise, whether those texts are subversive or recuperative or both or neither cannot be determined by abstraction from actual social practice.*

— SUSAN BORDO

White women "stars" like Madonna, Sandra Bernhard, and many others publicly name their interest in, and appropriation of, black culture as yet another sign of their radical chic. Intimacy with that "nasty" blackness good white girls stay away from is what they seek. To white and other nonblack consumers, this gives them a special flavor, an added spice. After all it is a very recent historical phenomenon for any white girl to be able to get some mileage out of flaunting her fascination and envy of blackness. The thing about envy is that it is always ready to destroy, erase, take over, and consume the desired object. That's exactly what Madonna attempts to do when she appropriates and commodifies aspects of black culture. Needless to say this kind of fascination is a threat. It endangers. Perhaps that is why so many of the grown black women I spoke with about Madonna had no interest in her as a cultural icon and said things like, "The bitch can't even sing." It was only among young black females that I could find die-hard Madonna fans. Though I often admire and, yes at times, even envy Madonna because she has created a cultural space where she can invent and reinvent herself and receive public affirmation and material reward, I do not consider myself a Madonna fan.

Once I read an interview with Madonna where she talked about her envy of black culture, where she stated that she wanted to be black as a child. It is a sign of white privilege to be able to "see" blackness and black culture from a standpoint where only the rich culture of opposition black people have created in resistance marks and defines us. Such a perspective enables one to ignore white supremacist domination and the hurt it inflicts via oppression, exploitation, and everyday wounds and pains. White folks who do not see black pain never really understand the complexity of black pleasure. And it is no wonder then that when they attempt to imitate the joy in living which they see as the "essence" of soul and blackness, their cultural productions may have an air of sham and falseness that may titillate and even move white audiences yet leave many black folks cold.

Needless to say, if Madonna had to depend on masses of black women to maintain her status as cultural icon she would have been dethroned some time ago. Many of the black women I spoke with expressed intense disgust and hatred of Madonna. Most did not respond to my cautious attempts to suggest that underlying those negative feelings might lurk feelings of envy, and dare I say it, desire. No black woman I talked to declared that she wanted to "be Madonna." Yet we have only to look at the number of black women entertainers/stars (Tina Turner, Aretha Franklin, Donna Summer, Vanessa Williams, Yo-Yo, etc.) who gain greater crossover recognition when they demonstrate that, like Madonna, they too, have a healthy dose of "blonde ambition." Clearly their careers have been influenced by Madonna's choices and strategies.

For masses of black women, the political reality that underlies Madonna's and our recognition that this is a society where "blondes" not only "have more fun" but where they are more likely to succeed in any endeavor is white supremacy and racism. We cannot see Madonna's change in hair color as being merely a question of aesthetic choice. I agree with Julie Burchill in her critical work *Girls on Film,* when she reminds us: "What does it say about racial purity that the best blondes have all been brunettes (Harlow, Monroe, Bardot)? I think it says that we are not as white as we think. I think it says that Pure is a Bore." I also know that it is the expressed desire of the nonblonde Other for those characteristics that are seen as the quintessential markers of racial aesthetic superiority that perpetuate and uphold white supremacy. In this sense Madonna has much in common with the masses of black women who suffer from internalized racism and are forever terrorized by a standard of beauty they feel they can never truly embody.

Like many black women who have stood outside the culture's fascination with the blonde beauty and who have only been able to reach it through imitation and artifice, Madonna often recalls that she was a working-class white girl who saw herself as ugly, as outside the mainstream beauty standard. And indeed what some of us like about her is the way she deconstructs the myth of "natural" white girl beauty by exposing the extent to which it can be and is usually artificially constructed and maintained. She mocks the conventional racist-defined beauty ideal even as she rigorously strives to embody it. Given her obsession with exposing the reality that the ideal female beauty in this society can be attained by artifice and social construction, it should come as no surprise that many of her fans are gay men, and that the majority of nonwhite men, particularly black men, are among that group. Jennie Livingston's film *Paris Is Burning* suggests that many black gay men, especially queens/divas, are as equally driven as Madonna by "blonde ambition." Madonna never lets her audience forget that whatever "look" she acquires is attained by hard work — "it ain't natural." And as Burchill comments in her chapter "Homosexual Girls":

> I have a friend who drives a cab and looks like a Marlboro Man but at night is the second best Jean Harlow I have ever seen. He summed up the kind of film star he adores, brutally and brilliantly, when he said, "I like actresses who look as if they've spent hours putting themselves together — and even then they don't look right."

Certainly no one, not even die-hard Madonna fans, ever insists that her beauty is not attained by skillful artifice. And indeed, a major point of the documentary film *Truth or Dare: In Bed With Madonna* was to demonstrate the amount of work that goes into the construction of her image. Yet when the chips are down, the image Madonna most exploits is that of the quintessential "white girl." To maintain that image she must always

5

position herself as an outsider in relation to black culture. It is that position of outsider that enables her to colonize and appropriate black experience for her own opportunistic ends even as she attempts to mask her acts of racist aggression as affirmation. And no other group sees that as clearly as black females in this society. For we have always known that the socially constructed image of innocent white womanhood relies on the continued production of the racist/sexist sexual myth that black women are not innocent and never can be. Since we are coded always as "fallen" women in the racist cultural iconography we can never, as can Madonna, publicly "work" the image of ourselves as innocent female daring to be bad. Mainstream culture always reads the black female body as sign of sexual experience. In part, many black women who are disgusted by Madonna's flaunting of sexual experience are enraged because the very image of sexual agency that she is able to project and affirm with material gain has been the stick this society has used to justify its continued beating and assault on the black female body. The vast majority of black women in the United States, more concerned with projecting images of respectability than with the idea of female sexual agency and transgression, do not often feel we have the "freedom" to act in rebellious ways in regards to sexuality without being punished. We have only to contrast the life story of Tina Turner with that of Madonna to see the different connotations "wild" sexual agency has when it is asserted by a black female. Being represented publicly as an active sexual being has only recently enabled Turner to gain control over her life and career. For years the public image of aggressive sexual agency Turner projected belied the degree to which she was sexually abused and exploited privately. She was also materially exploited. Madonna's career could not be all that it is if there were no Tina Turner and yet, unlike her cohort Sandra Bernhard, Madonna never articulates the cultural debt she owes black females.

In her most recent appropriations of blackness, Madonna almost always imitates phallic black masculinity. Although I read many articles which talked about her appropriating male codes, no critic seems to have noticed her emphasis on black male experience. In his *Playboy* profile, "Playgirl of the Western World," Michael Kelly describes Madonna's crotch grabbing as "an eloquent visual put-down of male phallic pride." He points out that she worked with choreographer Vince Paterson to perfect the gesture. Even though Kelly tells readers that Madonna was consciously imitating Michael Jackson, he does not contextualize his interpretation of the gesture to include this act of appropriation from black male culture. And in that specific context the groin grabbing gesture is an assertion of pride and phallic domination that usually takes place in an all-male context. Madonna's imitation of this gesture could just as easily be read as an expression of envy.

Throughout [many] of her autobiographical interviews runs a thread of expressed desire to possess the power she perceives men have.

She wants power

Madonna may hate the phallus, but she longs to possess its power. She is always first and foremost in competition with men to see who has the biggest penis. She longs to assert phallic power, and like every other group in this white supremacist society, she clearly sees black men as embodying a quality of maleness that eludes white men. Hence they are often the group of men she most seeks to imitate, taunting white males with her own version of "black masculinity." When it comes to entertainment rivals, Madonna clearly perceives black male stars like Prince and Michael Jackson to be the standard against which she must measure herself and that she ultimately hopes to transcend.

Fascinated yet envious of black style, Madonna appropriates black culture in ways that mock and undermine, making her presentation one that upstages. This is most evident in the video "Like a Prayer." Though I read numerous articles that discussed public outrage at this video, none focused on the issue of race. No article called attention to the fact that Madonna flaunts her sexual agency by suggesting that she is breaking the ties that bind her as a white girl to white patriarchy, and establishing ties with black men. She, however, and not black men, does the choosing. The message is directed at white men. It suggests that they only labeled black men rapists for fear that white girls would choose black partners over them. Cultural critics commenting on the video did not seem at all interested in exploring the reasons Madonna chooses a black cultural backdrop for this video, i.e., black church and religious experience. Clearly, it was this backdrop that added to the video's controversy.

In her commentary in the *Washington Post,* "Madonna: Yuppie Goddess," Brooke Masters writes: "Most descriptions of the controversial video focus on its Catholic imagery: Madonna kisses a black saint, and develops Christ-like markings on her hands. However, the video is also a feminist fairy tale. Sleeping Beauty and Snow White waited for their princes to come along, Madonna finds her own man and wakes him up." Notice that this writer completely overlooks the issue of race and gender. That Madonna's chosen prince was a black man is in part what made the representation potentially shocking and provocative to a white supremacist audience. Yet her attempt to exploit and transgress traditional racial taboos was rarely commented on. Instead critics concentrated on whether or not she was violating taboos regarding religion and representation.

In the United States, Catholicism is most often seen as a religion that has [few] or no black followers and Madonna's video certainly perpetuates this stereotype with its juxtaposition of images of black non-Catholic representations with the image of the black saint. Given the importance of religious experience and liberation theology in black life, Madonna's use of this imagery seemed particularly offensive. For she made black characters act in complicity with her as she aggressively flaunted her critique of Catholic manners, her attack on organized religion. Yet, no black voices that I know of came forward in print calling attention to the fact that the realm of the sacred that is mocked in this film is black religious experience, or that this appropriative "use" of that experience was offensive to many black folk. Looking at the video with a group of students in my class on the politics of sexuality where we critically analyze the way race and representations of blackness are used to sell products, we discussed the way in which black people in the video are caricatures reflecting stereotypes. They appear grotesque. The only role black females have in this video is to catch (i.e., rescue) the "angelic" Madonna when she is "falling." This is just a contemporary casting of the black female as Mammy. Made to serve as supportive backdrop for Madonna's drama, black characters in "Like a Prayer" remind one of those early Hollywood depictions of singing black slaves in the great plantation movies or those Shirley Temple films where Bojangles was trotted out to dance with Miss Shirley and spice up her act. Audiences were not supposed to be enamored of Bojangles, they were supposed to see just what a special little old white girl Shirley really was. In her own way Madonna is a modern day Shirley Temple. Certainly her expressed affinity with black culture enhances her value.

Eager to see the documentary *Truth or Dare* because it promised to focus on Madonna's transgressive sexual persona, which I find interesting, I was angered by her visual representations of her domination over not white men (certainly not over Warren Beatty or Alek Keshishian), but people of color and white working-class women. I was too angered by this to appreciate other aspects of the film I might have enjoyed. In *Truth or Dare* Madonna clearly revealed that she can only think of exerting power along very traditional, white supremacist, capitalistic, patriarchal lines. That she made people who were dependent on her for their immediate livelihood submit to her will was neither charming nor seductive to me or the other black folks that I spoke with who saw the film. We thought it tragically ironic that Madonna would choose as her dance partner a black male with dyed blonde hair. Perhaps had he appeared less like a white-identified black male consumed by "blonde ambition" he might have upstaged her. Instead he was positioned as a mirror, into which Madonna and her audience could look and see only a reflection of herself and the worship of "whiteness" she embodies — that white supremacist culture wants everyone to embody. Madonna used her power to ensure that he and the other nonwhite women and men who worked for her, as well as some of the white subordinates, would all serve as the backdrop to her white-girl-makes-good-drama. Joking about the film with other black folks, we commented that Madonna must have searched long and hard to find a black female that was not a good dancer, one who would not deflect attention away from her. And it is telling that when the film directly reflects something other than a positive image of Madonna, the camera highlights the rage this black female dancer was

No one recognizes.

suppressing. It surfaces when the "subordinates" have time off and are "relaxing."

As with most Madonna videos, when critics talk about this film they tend to ignore race. Yet no viewer can look at this film and not think about race and representation without engaging in forms of denial. After choosing a cast of characters from marginalized groups — nonwhite folks, heterosexual and gay, and gay white folks — Madonna publicly describes them as "emotional cripples." And of course in the context of the film this description seems borne out by the way they allow her to dominate, exploit, and humiliate them. Those Madonna fans who are determined to see her as politically progressive might ask themselves why it is she completely endorses those racist/sexist/classist stereotypes that almost always attempt to portray marginalized groups as "defective." Let's face it, by doing this, Madonna is not breaking with any white supremacist, patriarchal status quo; she is endorsing and perpetuating it.

Some of us do not find it hip or cute for Madonna to brag that she has a "fascistic side," a side well documented in the film. Well, we did not see any of her cute little fascism in action when it was Warren Beatty calling her out in the film. No, there the image of Madonna was the little woman who grins and bears it. No, her "somebody's got to be in charge side," as she names it, was most expressed in her interaction with those representatives from marginalized groups who are most often victimized by the powerful. Why is it there is little or no discussion of Madonna as racist or sexist in her relation to other women? Would audiences be charmed by some rich white male entertainer telling us he must "play father" and oversee the actions of the less powerful, especially women and men of color? So why did so many people find it cute when Madonna asserted that she dominates the interracial casts of gay and heterosexual folks in her film because they are crippled and she "like[s] to play mother." No, this was not a display of feminist power, this was the same old phallic nonsense with white pussy at the center. And many of us watching were not simply unmoved — we were outraged.

Perhaps it is a sign of a collective feeling of powerlessness that many       15
black, nonwhite, and white viewers of this film who were disturbed by the display of racism, sexism, and heterosexism (yes, it's possible to hire gay people, support AIDS projects, and still be biased in the direction of phallic patriarchal heterosexuality) in *Truth or Dare* have said so little. Sometimes it is difficult to find words to make a critique when we find ourselves attracted by some aspect of a performer's act and disturbed by others, or when a performer shows more interest in promoting progressive social causes than is customary. We may see that performer as above critique. Or we may feel our critique will in no way intervene on the worship of them as a cultural icon.

To say nothing, however, is to be complicit with the very forces of domination that make "blonde ambition" necessary to Madonna's success. Tragically, all that is transgressive and potentially empowering to feminist women and men about Madonna's work may be undermined by all that it contains that is reactionary and in no way unconventional or new. It is often the conservative elements in her work converging with the status quo that have the most powerful impact. For example: Given the rampant homophobia in this society and the concomitant hetero-sexist voyeuristic obsession with gay life-styles, to what extent does Madonna progressively seek to challenge this if she insists on primarily representing gays as in some way emotionally handicapped or defective? Or when Madonna responds to the critique that she exploits gay men by cavalierly stating: "What does exploitation mean? . . . In a revolution, some people have to get hurt. To get people to change, you have to turn the table over. Some dishes get broken."

I can only say this doesn't sound like liberation to me. Perhaps when Madonna explores those memories of her white working-class childhood in a troubled family in a way that enables her to understand intimately the politics of exploitation, domination, and submission, she will have a deeper connection with oppositional black culture. If and when this radi-cal critical self-interrogation takes place, she will have the power to cre-ate new and different cultural productions, work that will be truly trans-gressive — acts of resistance that transform rather than simply seduce.

### Reading the Text

1. Why does hooks call Madonna's claim that she wanted to be black as a child a "sign of white privilege"?
2. Why does hooks believe that Madonna mocks and thereby denigrates black style and culture?
3. How, according to hooks, does "blondeness" function as a sign in Ameri-can culture?

### Reading the Signs

1. While Madonna has a reputation for being revolutionary, hooks asserts that Madonna often endorses and perpetuates a "white supremacist, patri-archal status quo." Write an essay in which you support, challenge, or modify hooks's position, being sure to base your essay on *Truth or Dare* or on specific Madonna videos you have seen.
2. Rent Madonna's *Immaculate Collection* videotape and watch "Like a Prayer." Do you agree or disagree with hooks's analysis of it?
3. In class, brainstorm other examples of white artists who have appropriated black culture as signs of their "radical chic." Then discuss whether these other artists have thus mocked and undermined black culture, as hooks

says Madonna has done. To shape your discussion, read first Sam Fulwood III's "The Rage of the Black Middle Class" (p. 510).

4. In your journal, explore an answer to hooks's question "Why is it there is little or no discussion of Madonna as racist or sexist in her relation to other women?"

5. Read or review Tricia Rose's "Bad Sistas" (p. 231). How might hooks explain the representation of black culture in the videos Rose describes?

TRICIA ROSE

*Bad Sistas*

||||||||||||||||||||||||||||||||||||||||||||||||||||||

*Female rappers tell male rappers where to get off when it comes to sexual harassment and exploitation, don't they? Such is the manifest message of rap videos from such performers as Salt 'N' Pepa and MC Lyte. But as Tricia Rose (b. 1962) argues in this selection from* Black Noise: Rap Music and Black Culture in Contemporary America *(1994), the tendency of such raps to situate women in the context of sexual courtship rituals undermines their surface meaning. Wouldn't it be even more subversive to perform raps that have nothing to do with sexual relations at all, Rose implies? An assistant professor of History and Africana Studies at New York University, Rose is coeditor, with Andrew Ross, of* Microphone Fiends: Youth Music and Youth Culture *(1994).*

## Courting Disaster

Raps written by women that specifically concern male-female relationships almost always confront the tension between trust and savvy; between vulnerability and control. Some raps celebrate their sisters for "getting over" on men, rather than touting self-reliance and honesty. For example, in Icey Jaye's "It's a Girl Thang," she explains how she and her friends find ways to spend as much of their dates' money as possible and mocks the men who fall for their tricks. Similarly, in the video for Salt 'N' Pepa's "Independent" Salt accepts several expensive gifts from a string of dates who hope to win her affection with diamond necklaces and rings. In raps such as these, women are taking advantage of the logic of heterosexual courtship in which men coax women into submission with trinkets and promises for financial security. Nikki D's "Up the Ante for the Panty" and B.W.P.'s "We Want Money" are more graphic examples of a similar philosophy. However, for the most part, when they choose to rap about male–female relations, women rappers challenge the depictions of women in many male raps as gold diggers and address the fears many women share regarding male dishonesty and infidelity.

MC Lyte and Salt 'N' Pepa have reputations for biting raps that criticize men who manipulate and abuse women. Their lyrics tell the story of men taking advantage of women, cheating on them, taking their money, and leaving them for other unsuspecting female victims. These raps are not mournful ballads about the trials and tribulations of being a heterosexual woman. Similar to women's blues, they are caustic, witty, and aggressive warnings directed at men and at other women who might be seduced by them in the future. By offering a woman's interpretation of the terms of heterosexual courtship, these women's raps cast a new light on male–female sexual power relations and depict women as resistant, aggressive participants. Yet, even the raps that explore and revise women's role in the courtship process often retain the larger patriarchal parameters of heterosexual courtship.

Salt 'N' Pepa's single "Tramp" is strong advice, almost boot camp, for single black women. "Tramp" is not, as Salt 'N' Pepa warn, a "simple rhyme," but a parable about courtship rituals between men and women:

> *Homegirls attention you must pay to what I say*
> *Don't take this as a simple rhyme*
> *Cause this type of thing happens all the time*
> *Now what would you do if a stranger said "Hi"*
> *Would you dis him or would you reply?*
> *If you'd answer, there is a chance*
> *That you'd become a victim of circumstance*
> *Am I right fellas? tell the truth*
> *Or else I'll have to show and prove*
> *You are what you are I am what I am*
> *It just so happens that most men are TRAMPS.*[1]

In the absence of any response to "Am I right fellas?" (any number of sampled male replies easily could have been woven in here), Salt 'N' Pepa "show and prove" the trampings of several men who "undress you with their eyeballs," "think you're a dummy, on the first date, had the nerve to tell me he loves me" and of men who always have sex on the mind. Salt 'N' Pepa's parable defines promiscuous *males* as tramps, and thereby inverts the common belief that male sexual promiscuity is a status symbol. This reversal undermines the degrading "woman as tramp" image by stigmatizing male promiscuity. Salt 'N' Pepa suggest that women who respond to sexual advances made by these men are victims

---

1. Salt 'N' Pepa, "Tramp," *Cool, Hot and Vicious* (Next Plateau Records, 1986).

of circumstance. In this case, it is predatory, disingenuous men who are the tramps.

The music video for "Tramps" is a comic rendering of a series of social club scenes that highlight tramps on the make, mouth freshener in hand, testing their lines on the nearest woman. Dressed in the then-latest hip hop street gear, Salt 'N' Pepa perform the song on television, on a monitor perched above the bar. Because they appear on the television screen, they seem to be surveying and critiquing the club action, but the club members cannot see them. There are people dancing and talking together (including likeable men who are coded as "non-tramps"), who seem unaware of the television monitor. Salt 'N' Pepa are also shown in the club, dressed in very stylish, sexy outfits. Salt 'N' Pepa act as decoys, talking and flirting with the tramps to flesh out the dramatization of tramps on the prowl. They make several knowing gestures at the camera to reassure the viewer that they are unswayed by the tramps' efforts.

The tramps and their victims interact only with body language. The club scenes have no dialogue; we hear only Salt 'N' Pepa lyrics over the musical tracks for "Tramp," which serve respectively as the video's narrative and the club's dance music. Viewing much of the club action from Salt 'N' Pepa's authoritative position — through the television monitor — we can safely observe the playful but cautionary dramatization of heterosexual courtship. One tramp who is rapping to a woman, postures and struts, appearing to ask something like the stock pick-up line: "what is your zodiac sign, baby?" When she shows disgust and leaves her seat, he repeats the same body motions and gestures on the next woman who happens to sit down. Near the end of the video, a frustrated "wife" enters the club and drags one of the tramps home, smacking him in the head with her pocketbook. Salt 'N' Pepa are standing next to the wife's tramp in the club, shaking their heads as if to say "what a shame." Simultaneously, they are pointing and laughing at the husband from the television monitor. At the end of the video, a still frame of each man is stamped "tramp," and Salt 'N' Pepa revel in having identified and exposed them. They then leave the club together, without men, seemingly enjoying their skill at exposing the real intentions of these tramps.

Salt 'N' Pepa are "schooling" women about the sexual politics of the club scene, by engaging in and critiquing the drama of heterosexual courtship. The privileged viewer is a woman who is directly addressed in the lyrics and presumably can empathize fully with the visual depiction and interpretation of the scenes. The video's resolution can be interpreted as a warning to both men and women. Women: Don't fall for these men either by talking to them in the clubs or believing the lies they'll tell you when they come home. Men: You will get caught eventually, and you'll be embarrassed. Another message suggested by the video for "Tramp" is that women can go to these clubs, successfully play along with "the game" as long as the power of female sexuality and the terms of male desire are understood and negotiated.

However, "Tramp" does not interrogate "the game" itself. "Tramp" implicitly accepts the larger dynamics and power relationships between men and women. Although the tramps are embarrassed and momentarily contained at the end of the video, in no way can it be suggested that these tramps will stop hustling women and cheating on their wives. More important, what of women's desire? Not only is it presumed that men will continue their dishonest behavior, but women's desire for an idealized monogamous heterosexual relationship is implicitly confirmed as an unrealized (but not unrealizable?) goal. In their quest for an honest man, should not the sobering fact that "most men are tramps" be considered a point of departure for rejecting the current courtship ritual altogether?

Salt 'N' Pepa leave the club together, seemingly pleased by their freedom and by their ability to manipulate men into pursuing them "to no end." But the wife drags her husband home — she is not shocked but rather frustrated by what appears to be frequent dishonest behavior. What conclusion is to be drawn from this lesson? Do not trust tramps, separate the wheat from the tramps, and continue in your quest for an honest, monogamous man. "Tramp" is courtship advice for women who choose to participate in the current configuration of heterosexual courtship, it does not offer an alternative paradigm for such courtship, and in some ways it works inside of the very courtship rules that it highlights and criticizes. At best, "Tramp" is an implicit critique of the club scene as a setting for meeting potential mates as well as of the institution of marriage that permits significant power imbalances clearly weighted in favor of men.

MC Lyte has a far less comedic response to Sam, a boyfriend whom she catches trying to pick up women. MC Lyte's underground hit "Paper Thin" is one of the most scathingly powerful raps about male dishonesty and infidelity and the tensions between trust and vulnerability in heterosexual relations. Lyte has been burned by Sam, but she has turned her experience into a black woman's anthem that sustains an uncomfortable balance between brutal cynicism and honest vulnerability:

> *When you say you love me it doesn't matter*
> *It goes into my head as just chit chatter*
> *You may think it's egotistical or just very free*
> *But what you say, I take none of it seriously. . . .*
>
> *I'm not the kind of girl to try to play a man out*
> *They take the money and then they break the hell out.*
> *No that's not my strategy, not the game I play*
> *I admit I play a game, but it's not done that way.*
> *Truly when I get involved I give it my heart*

*I mean my mind, my soul, my body, I mean every part.*
*But if it doesn't work out — yo, it just doesn't.*
*It wasn't meant to be, you know it just wasn't.*
*So, I treat all of you like I treat all of them.*
*What you say to me is just paper thin.*[2]

Lyte's public acknowledgment that Sam's expressions of love were    10
paper thin is not a source of embarrassment for her but a means of empowerment. She plays a brutal game of the dozens on Sam while wearing
her past commitment to him as a badge of honor and sign of character.
Lyte presents commitment, vulnerability, and sensitivity as assets, not indicators of female weakness. In "Paper Thin," emotional and sexual
commitment are not romantic, Victorian concepts tied to honorable but
dependent women; they are a part of her strategy, part of the game she
plays in heterosexual courtship.

"Paper Thin's" high-energy video contains many elements present
in hip hop. The video opens with Lyte, dressed in a sweatsuit, chunk
jewelry, and sneakers, abandoning her new Jetta hastily because she
wants to take the subway to clear her head. A few members of her male
posse, shocked at her desire to leave her Jetta on the street for the subway, follow along behind her, down the steps to the subway tracks. (Her
sudden decision to leave her new car for the subway and her male posse's
surprised reaction seem to establish that Lyte rarely rides the subway anymore.) Lyte enters a subway car with an introspective and distracted
expression. Once in the subway car, her DJ K-Rock, doubling as
the conductor, announces that the train will be held in the station because of crossed signals. While they wait, Milk Boy (her female but very
masculine-looking bodyguard) spots Sam at the other end of the car, rapping heavily to two stylish women, and draws Lyte's attention to him.
Lyte, momentarily surprised, begins her rhyme as she stalks toward Sam.
Sam's attempts to escape fail; he is left to face MC Lyte's wrath. Eventually, she throws him off the train to the chorus of Ray Charles's R&B
classic, "Hit the Road Jack," and locks Sam out of the subway station
and out of the action. The subway car is filled with young black
teenagers, typical working New Yorkers and street people, many of
whom join Lyte in signifying on Sam while they groove on K-Rock's
music. MC Lyte's powerful voice and no-nonsense image dominate Sam.
The taut, driving music, which is punctuated by sampled guitar and
drum sections and an Earth Wind and Fire horn section, complement
Lyte's hard, expressive rapping style.

It is important that "Paper Thin" is set in public and on the subway,
the quintessential mode of urban transportation. Lyte is drawn to the
subway and seems comfortable there. She is also comfortable with the

---

2. MC Lyte, "Paper Thin," *Lyte as a Rock* (First Priority Records, 1988).

subway riders in her video; they are her community. During musical breaks between raps, we see passengers grooving to her music and responding to the drama. By setting her confrontation with Sam in the subway, in front of their peers, Lyte moves a private problem between lovers into the public arena and effectively dominates both spaces.

When her DJ, the musical and mechanical conductor, announces that crossed signals are holding the train in the station, it frames the video in a moment of communication crisis. The notion of crossed signals represents the inability of Sam and Lyte to communicate with one another, an inability that is primarily the function of the fact that they communicate on different frequencies. Sam thinks he can read Lyte's mind to see what she is thinking and then feed her all the right lines. But what he says carries no weight, no meaning. His discourse is light, it's paper thin. Lyte, who understands courtship as a game, confesses to being a player, yet expresses how she feels directly and in simple language. What she says has integrity, weight, and substance.

After throwing Sam from the train, she nods her head toward a young man standing against the subway door, and he follows her off the train. She will not allow her experiences with Sam to paralyze her but instead continues to participate on revised terms. As she and her new male friend walk down the street, she raps the final stanza for "Paper Thin" that sets down the new courtship ground rules:

> So, now I take precautions when choosing my mate
> I do not touch until the third or fourth date
> Then maybe we'll kiss on the fifth or sixth time that we meet
> Cause a date without a kiss is so incomplete
> And then maybe, I'll let you play with my feet
> You can suck the big toe and play with the middle
> It's so simple unlike a riddle . . .

Lyte has taken control of the process. She has selected her latest [15] companion; he has not pursued her. This is an important move, because it allows her to set the tone of the interaction and subsequently articulates the new ground rules that will protect her from repeating the mistakes she made in her relationship with Sam. Yet, a central revision to her courtship terms involves withholding sexual affection, a familiar strategy in courtship rituals for women that implicitly affirms the process of male pursuit as it forestalls it. Nonetheless, Lyte seems prepared for whatever takes place. Her analysis of courtship seems to acknowledge that there are dishonest men and that she is not interested in negotiating on their terms. Lyte affirms her courtship rules as she identifies and critiques the terms of men such as Sam. In "Paper Thin" she has announced that her desire will govern her behavior and *his* ("you can suck my big toe and then play with the middle") and remains committed to her principles at the same time.

As "products of an ongoing historical conversation," "Paper Thin" and "Tramp" are explicitly dialogic texts that draw on the language and terms imbedded in long-standing struggles over the parameters of hetero-sexual courtship. These raps are also dialogic in their use of black collec-tive memory via black music. Salt 'N' Pepa's "Tramp" draws its horns and parts of its rhythm section from the 1967 soul song of the same name performed by Otis Redding and Carla Thomas. Otis's and Carla's "Tramp" is a dialogue in which Carla expresses her frustration over Otis's failure in their relationship while he makes excuses and attempts to avoid her accusations.[3] Salt 'N' Pepa's musical quotation of Otis's and Carla's "Tramp" set a multilayered dialogue in motion. The musical style of Salt 'N' Pepa's "Tramp" carries the blues bar confessional mode of many rhythm and blues songs updated with rap's beats and breaks. Salt 'N' Pepa are testifying to Carla's problems via the music, at the same time providing their contemporary audience with a collective reference to black musical predecessors and the history of black female heterosexual struggles.

Lyte's direct address to Sam ("when you say you love it doesn't mat-ter") is her half of a heated conversation in which Sam is silenced by her, but nonetheless present. Lyte's announcement that she "admits playing a game but it's not done that way" makes it clear that she understands the power relationships that dictate their interaction. Lyte encourages herself and by extension black women to be fearless and self-possessed ("sucker you missed, I know who I am") in the face of significant emotional losses. Her game, her strategy, have a critical sexual difference that lays the groundwork for a black female-centered communal voice that revises and expands the terms of female power in heterosexual courtship.

The dialogic and resistive aspects in "Tramps" and "Paper Thin" are also present in the body of other women rappers' work. Many female rappers address the frustration heterosexual women experience in their desire for intimacy with and commitment from men. The chorus in Neneh Cherry's "Buffalo Stance" tells men not to mess with her, and that money men can't buy her love because it's affection that she's lookin' for; "Say That Then" from West Coast female rappers Oaktown 3-5-7, give no slack to "Finger popping, hip hoppin' wanna be bed rockin'" men; Monie Love's "It's a Shame" is a pep talk for a woman breaking up with a man who apparently needs to be kicked to the curb; Ice Cream Tee's "All Wrong" chastises women who allow men to abuse them; Monie Love's "Just Don't Give a Damn" is a confident and harsh

---

3. See Atlantic Records, *Rhythm and Blues Collection 1966–1969,* vol. 6. In the liner notes for this collection, Robert Pruter refers to "Tramp" as a dialogue between Carla and Otis, in which Carla's "invectives" are insufficiently countered by Otis. It should be pointed out that the Otis and Carla "Tramp" is a remake of (an answer to?) Lowell and Fulsom's version made popular in 1966.

rejection of an emotionally and physically abusive man; and MC Lyte's "I Cram to Understand U," "Please Understand," and "I'm Not Havin' It" are companion pieces to "Paper Thin."

This strategy, in which women square off with men, can be subverted and its power diminished. As Laura Berlant suggests, this mode of confrontational communication can be contained or renamed as the "female complaint." In other words, direct and legitimate criticism is reduced to "bitching" or complaining as a way of containing dissent. Berlant warns that the "female complaint . . . as a mode of expression is an admission and recognition both of privilege and powerlessness . . . circumscribed by a knowledge of woman's inevitable delegitimation within the patriarchal public sphere." Berlant argues that resistance to sexual oppression must take place "in the patriarchal public sphere, the place where significant or momentous exchanges of power are perceived to take place," but that the female complaint is devalued, marginalized, and ineffective in this sphere. Berlant offers an interpretation of "Roxanne's Revenge," an early and popular rap record by black female rapper Roxanne Shante, as an example of the pitfalls of the "female complaint." Attempts were made to contain and humiliate Roxanne on a compilation record that included several other related answer records. Berlant says that "Roxanne's Revenge" is vulnerable to "hystericization by a readily available phallic discourse (which) is immanent in the very genre of her expression."[4]

Berlant is making an important point about the vulnerability of women's voices to devaluation. No doubt women's angry responses have long been made to appear hysterical and irrational or whiny and childlike. I am not sure, though, that we can equate attempts to render women's voices as "complaint" with the voices themselves. To do so may place too much value on the attempts to contain women. "Roxanne's Revenge" gave voice to a young girl's response to real-life street confrontations with men. She entered into black male-dominated public space and drew a great deal of attention away from the UTFO song to which she responded. More importantly, "Roxanne's Revenge" has retained weight and significance in hip hop since 1985 when it was released. This has not been the case for UTFO, the UTFO song, or any of the fabricated responses on the compilation record. Much of the status of the original UTFO song "Roxanne Roxanne" is a result of the power of Roxanne Shante's answer record. What Berlant illustrates is the ways in which Roxanne's "female complaint" needed to be labeled as such and then contained precisely because it was threatening. It did not go unnoticed, because it was a compelling voice in the public domain that captured the attention of male and female hip hop fans. The compilation

4. Laura Berlant, "The Female Complaint," *Social Text,* Fall, 237–59, 1988.

record is clearly an attempt at containing her voice, but it was in my estimation an unsuccessful attempt. Furthermore, such attempts at circumscription will continue to take place when partial, yet effective, attacks are made, whether in the form of the female complaint or not. Nonetheless, Berlant's larger argument, which calls for substantial female public sphere presence and contestation, is crucial. These public sphere contests must involve more than responses to sexist male speech; they must also entail the development of sustained, strong female voices that stake claim to public space generally.

### Reading the Text

1. What are the standard themes of female rap videos, according to Rose?
2. How, according to Rose, do many women's rap videos inadvertently subvert the messages of female empowerment that they intend to send?
3. What does Rose believe are the explicit and implicit messages of Salt 'N' Pepa's "Tramp" video, and how does she feel about those messages?
4. In your own words, summarize Rose's interpretation of MC Lyte's "Paper Thin."

### Reading the Signs

1. Using Rose's article as your critical framework, compare and contrast a male and female rap video. What gender roles do you see in each, and what response is a viewer likely to have to them? To develop your ideas, read or reread Holly Devor's "Gender Role Behaviors and Attitudes" (p. 415).
2. In your journal, brainstorm a list of attributes that you would like to give your gender in a video of your own design. Then write a "screenplay" for your own rap video, being sure to incorporate your preferred attributes. Share your screenplay with your class.
3. Watch a current video by either one of the artists Rose discusses or another female rapper. Then write an analysis of your video, examining whether it perpetuates, in Rose's words, "the larger patriarchal parameters of heterosexual courtship."
4. Both Rose and Susan Douglas ("Signs of Intelligent Life on TV," p. 200) discuss the ways in which popular culture perpetuates traditional gender roles even while it may present a superficially feminist slant. In class, discuss this phenomenon, exploring the reasons behind it. Do you see any evidence that this pattern is changing in the late 1990s? Do you wish to see it change, and why or why not?
5. Adopting Rose's perspective on gender roles, analyze a Madonna video such as *Like a Prayer* or the film *Truth or Dare*. To develop your ideas, consult bell hooks's "Madonna: Plantation Mistress or Soul Sister?" (p. 223).

PAMELA  WILSON

*Mountains of Contradictions: Gender, Class,*
*and Region in the Star Image of Dolly Parton*

‖‖‖‖‖‖‖‖‖‖‖‖‖‖‖‖‖‖‖‖‖‖‖‖‖‖‖‖‖‖‖‖‖‖‖‖‖‖‖‖‖‖‖‖‖‖

*Hello, Dolly. One of country music's most popular and enduring stars,*
*Dolly Parton has built her career on what Pamela Wilson calls "moun-*
*tains of contradictions." In this detailed study of Parton's career and cul-*
*tural significance, Wilson provides a semiotic analysis of such contradic-*
*tions, revealing in Parton a powerful player in the cosmopolitan world of*
*American entertainment and business who enacts the roles of mother,*
*housewife, and sex object, just a simple country girl from Tennessee. An*
*anthropologist and communications specialist, Pamela Wilson has taught*
*at Carlow College and the University of Wisconsin, Madison, and*
*writes on the significance of American popular culture.*

Dolly Parton has achieved broad popularity over the past twenty
years as an exceptional country musician who successfully "crossed over"
into pop music and is now perceived as one of the industry's most respected and prolific singer/songwriters. Her distinctive voice is noted for
its lilting clarity and "shimmering mountain tremolo," and her repertoire
ranges from Appalachian ballads to African-American gospel tunes to
hard-driving rockabilly numbers. Parton was one of the first female
country musicians whose career developed in front of the television cameras: first as Porter Wagoner's partner on *The Porter Wagoner Show*
(1967–74), then as the first woman to host her own country and western
variety show, *Dolly* (1976–77). Securing her position as a multimedia
star, Parton has played major roles in a number of notable Hollywood
films, including *9–to–5, The Best Little Whorehouse in Texas,* and *Steel*
*Magnolias.* In addition to her musical fame and her starring roles on television and in films, Dolly Parton has become well-known through the
popular media as an icon of hyperfemininity and as a hero to or role
model for women of varying class and cultural backgrounds.[1] As Mary A.
Bufwack and Robert K. Oermann explain, "Dolly Parton is the most fa-

---

1. Mary Bufwack and Robert K. Oermann's *Finding Her Voice: The Saga of Women*
*in Country Music* (New York, 1993) provides a thorough and fascinating account of the
central, though often overlooked, role of women in the growth of country music
throughout this century. See also Joan Dew's *Singers and Sweethearts: The Women of Coun-*
*try Music* (Garden City, NJ, 1977); and scattered references in Bill C. Malone's *Southern*
*Music, American Music* (Lexington, 1979); and in John Lomax III, *Nashville: Music City*
*USA* (New York, 1985). Patrick Carr also provides an insightful look at the industry; see
"The Changing Image of Country Music," in *Country: The Music and the Musicians,* ed.
Paul Kingsbury, Country Music Foundation (New York, 1988), pp. 482–517.

mous, most universally beloved, and most widely respected woman who has ever emerged from country music," making her "a role model not only for other singers and songwriters, but for working women everywhere."[2]

Dolly Parton has fashioned her star image visually to accentuate her ample, voluptuously overflowing body, particularly her large breasts, a body image that she has embellished with showy, garish costumes and an exaggeratedly sculptured blond wig. This persona is a caricature that juxtaposes the outlandish style of the country singer (in a predominantly male tradition of gaudy costuming) with the stereotypical self-display of the "painted woman," or prostitute, whose sexuality is her style. In ironic contrast to the parodic nature of her visual style, the articulate Parton has perpetuated an image that has gained her respect as a smart, wholesome, sincere person with traditional rural values (Christianity, family, rootedness, and "old-fashioned" integrity) who has managed, through perseverance and resourcefulness, to transcend the disadvantaged economic and social circumstances into which she was born and to use her talents to realize many of her dreams. These "dreams," when materialized and activated, entail another set of contradictions since they represent a lifestyle which, on the surface, is decidedly nontraditional for someone with any combination of her social identities: female, Southern, rural, Appalachian, working-class. Yet, through the construction of her persona, Parton manages and actively exploits the contradictory meanings associated with the social categories of gender, class, ethnic, and regional identity.[3]

Parton is often compared to Mae West, Marilyn Monroe, Bette Midler, and Madonna for her manipulation and burlesquing of femininity. In fact, she has incorporated an acknowledgment of her place in this tradition of subversive white femininity into her 1990s persona through mimetic references in her costumes, makeup, and performances.[4] Yet there is something about Parton that distinctively resonates with a rural and/or working-class audience and that seems to strengthen her appeal as a popular role model rather than a mere visual icon. As a fluent and savvy promoter of "Dolly," Parton provides a fascinating case study in the

---

2. Bufwack and Oermann, *Finding Her Voice*, p. 360.

3. See Richard Dyer, *Stars* (London, 1979).

4. During the U.S. military engagement in the Persian Gulf ("Operation Desert Storm"), a story on Parton in *Vanity Fair* featured photos of Dolly attired in the style of various 1940s pin-up queens and posing atop the shoulders of American fighter pilots. Another stylized image mimetically invoked Dolly "doing" Madonna "doing" Marilyn Monroe: A photo in *People,* taken during a concert performance, shows Parton with a brassiere-like contraption of two huge cones — a mocking parody of Madonna's contemporaneous act. The caption reads "Dolly Parton finally found a way to contain herself and still delight fans at the Brady Theater in Tulsa, where she sang 'Like a Virgin' with a pointed reference to the originator." See Kevin Sessums, "Good Golly, Miss Dolly!" *Vanity Fair* (June 1991), pp. 106–11, 160–66; and *People,* 29 June 1992, p. 7.

construction of a star image, specifically one that mediates the often contradictory ideals of gender, religion, and class.[5]

An examination of national magazine stories about Dolly Parton reveals that different popular periodicals, the discourses of which strategically target different demographic constituencies, have appropriated Parton for their own purposes and have contributed to the construction of her persona in a number of different ways.[6] Music and musical technology magazines (e.g., *High Fidelity, Stereo Review, Crawdaddy*) have depicted her as a musician and songwriter, tending to focus on her extraordinary talent and her status in the music industry. Men's magazines (e.g., *Esquire, Playboy*) have claimed her as an icon for the desiring male gaze, focusing on her body and sexual image. Supermarket tabloids (e.g., *The Star, National Examiner, National Enquirer,* and *The Globe*) have variously portrayed her as a sexual icon, as a transgressor of patriarchal conventions, and as the occasional victim of personal crisis. They have also focused on her body and the unconventionality of her long-distance marriage and have offered projections of various scandals that lurk on the horizon of her life, so to speak. Middlebrow women's magazines (e.g., *Good Housekeeping, Ladies Home Journal, Redbook*) have promoted Parton's womanliness, speaking of her as if she were a potential friend and focusing on Parton's "private side": her personal history, her family and her home, her nurturing motherliness, her problems with her weight, her emotions, and her ability to balance an "ordinary" marriage and home life with an extraordinary career. The feminist magazine *Ms.* has promoted what it reads as Parton's feminism, praising her as an empowering agent for women and the working class: "a country artist, a strong businesswoman, and a mountain woman with loyalty and love for her roots."[7] Finally, mainstream news magazines (e.g., *Newsweek, Time*) have billed Parton as a phenomenon of popular culture, focusing on her astute financial management in the entertainment industry and business world.

-------

5. To clarify my terminology here, since it has potential political implications, I use the name "Dolly" to refer to the constructed persona or image and "Parton" to refer to the social agent responsible for the act of constructing. I realize, however, that even this distinction is problematic since Parton's construction and representation of her "authentic" self amounts to creating a media persona as well. Admittedly, it is difficult to refer to her as "Parton" because in almost all of the literature (with the exception of three articles, two in music magazines and one in *Ms.*) she is referred to as "Dolly" with a familiarity that I suspect would be less acceptable in journalistic writing about a man.

6. These magazine articles represent only a small portion of the available media coverage of this star, which also addresses her recordings, films, two television series and numerous specials, as well as other promotional coverage.

7. Gloria Steinem, "Dolly Parton," *Ms.* (January 1987), p. 95.

Dolly Parton's appearance, notably, the images of her body and espe- 5
cially her breasts, has become the terrain for a discursive struggle in the
popular press over the social meaning of the female body and the associated
ideologies that compete for control over the meaning of "woman" in our
society.[8] Parton has consciously and strategically created a star persona that
incorporates and even exploits many of the gender contradictions that currently circulate in society. Her complex encoding of these contested meanings via multiply accentuated signifiers defies any easy or uniform interpretation and categorization — in fact, her image encourages a plurality of
conflicting readings, which she seems to relish playfully.

The Dolly persona *embodies* (there being no other word for it) excessive womanliness, in any interpretation. Parton displays this excess
through her construction of a surface identity (her body and appearance)
and through her representation of interiority, or a deeper identity (her
emotions, desires, and "dreams"). As one interviewer noted, "Dolly built
overstatement into what she calls her 'gimmick,' that is, looking trashily
sexy on the surface while being sweet, warm and down-to-earth on the
inside."[9] Parton openly discusses the strategies she employs for the construction of her image in almost every interview, and she makes no secret
of the fact that the Dolly image is a façade she has created to market herself. This "masquerade" might be interpreted in the psychoanalytic terms
theorized by Mary Ann Doane (based on the work of Lacan and Joan
Riviere). Yet it might also be seen, following Claire Johnston, as a social
parody, a hyperbolic stereotype, a tongue-in-cheek charade that playfully
and affectionately subverts the patriarchal iconography of female sexuality.[10] As Parton has explained,

> When I started out in my career, I was plainer looking. I soon real-
> ized I had to play by men's rules to win. My way of fighting back was
> to wear the frilly clothes and put on the big, blonde wigs. It helped
> that I had a small voice that enabled me to sing songs of pain and
> loneliness and love and gentle things like butterflies and children. I
> found that both men and women liked me.[11]

Parton's construction of the "inner" Dolly, though just as carefully
controlled, is not as readily evident since she attempts to elide the

---

8. Consider the dual cultural meaning of women's breasts in our society: as characteristics of sexual attractiveness, and as sites of maternal life-giving, nourishment, nurturance, and mother-child bonding.

9. Cliff Jahr, "Golly, Dolly!" *Ladies Home Journal* (July 1982), p. 85.

10. See Mary Ann Doane, "Film and the Masquerade: Theorizing the Female
Spectator," *Screen* (September-October 1982), pp. 74–87; Joan Riviere, "Womanliness
as a Masquerade," *Formations of Fantasy,* ed. Victor Burgin et al. (London, 1986 [1929]),
pp. 35–44; and Claire Johnston, "Feminist Politics and Film History," *Screen* 16 (Autumn 1975), pp. 115–24.

11. "Love Secrets That Keep the Magic in Dolly's Marriage," *The Star,* 27 November 1990, p. 12.

constructedness of the Dolly persona by conflating it with public perceptions of the "real" Dolly Parton, thus diverting attention from the aim of
such strategies (i.e., as marketing ploys) as well:[12]

> I'm careful never to get caught up in the Dolly image, other than to
> develop and protect it, because if you start believing the public per-
> sona is you, you get frustrated and mixed up. . . . I see Dolly as a car-
> toon: she's fat, wears a wig, and so on. . . . Dolly's as big a joke to me
> as she is to others.[13]

In many ways, it is difficult to deconstruct the issues of gender, class,
regionalism, and ethnicity as distinct facets of Dolly, since many of the
signifiers Parton uses connote and connect two or more. Parton never
decontextualizes herself from her rural, working-class, Southern Appalachian identity; from her interviews it is clear that she does not distinguish the abstract condition of being female from her personal experience
as a Southern Appalachian, working-class woman. Parton "plays herself,"
constructing an image from the very contradictions of her own culturally
grounded experience and social identity. However, many popular discourses (particularly those addressed to a gendered audience, either masculine or feminine) foreground gender issues. They focus on Dolly as a
(more abstract) "woman," buying into her image without necessarily
considering the relationship between her "woman-ness" and her class
and regional/ethnic origins.

In a 1977 issue of *High Fidelity,* a country music columnist addressed
Parton's corporeal contradictions:

> Inevitably, the recent national notice accorded Dolly Parton has fo-
> cused more on the improbability of her image than on her art. A
> voluptuous woman with a childish giggle, she finger-picks the guitar,
> the banjo and the mountain dulcimer with inch-long, painted nails.
> She composes delicate lyrics of Tennessee mountain innocence and
> performs them in finery a stripper would happily peel. And through
> layers of lipstick, she pushes a voice fervent with fundamentalist reli-
> gion. . . . Today she would like to be a little more listened to and a
> little less ogled. But the reams of copy about her fashion and physiog-
> nomy can hardly be blamed on anyone but herself; she donned the
> gaudy garb and high-piled hair specifically to make us stare.[14]

---

12. For example, regarding the emphasis on family and traditional rural values in
much of the popular discourse about Parton, Ken Tucker notes that "the invocation of
family is an emotional button that country stars like to push — it seems to produce instant sympathy among tradition-minded fans." See his "9–to–5: How Willie Nelson
and Dolly Parton Qualified for 'Lifestyles of the Rich and Famous,'" in Kingsbury, ed.,
*Country,* p. 386.

13. Jahr, "Golly, Dolly!" p. 85, 139.

14. Jack Hurst, "You've Come a Long Way, Dolly," *High Fidelity* (December
1977), p. 122.

Critic Ken Tucker has also addressed the tactical strategy of Parton's self-marketing:

> Now, there is no doubt that the major reason non-country fans initially took an interest in Parton was the outer package — "People will always talk and make jokes about my bosom," was the way she put it with typical forthrightness. This, combined with her Frederick's of Hollywood high heels . . . and cartoonish hairpieces ("You'd be amazed at how expensive it is to make a wig look this cheap"), transformed Parton into the country version of Mae West, and made her a highly telegenic figure.[15]

The traditional masculine perspective that fetishizes the female body (particularly large breasts and an hourglass figure) for the male gaze has long been a visual staple of men's magazines. However, the fact that Parton's appearance is such an exaggeration of that aesthetic (plus, I suspect, the fact that she has maintained such a mystique about her sexuality) seems to make her male admirers too uncomfortable to directly address this fetish, relying instead on nervous puns, laughter, jokes, and euphemisms to communicate their desire. For example, humorist and *Esquire* columnist Roy Blount, Jr., once wrote:

> Folks, I am not going to dwell on Dolly's bosom. I am just going to pass along a vulgar story: "They say old Dolly's gone women's lib and burned her bra. Course it took her three days." Dolly's bosom, horizontally monolithic in its packaging, is every bit as imposing as her hair. And then abruptly her waist goes way in. . . . And she wears very tight clothes over it. . . . I imagine you would have to know Dolly a good while before you could say hello to her without suddenly crying, "Your body!"[16]

Prefacing his extended 1978 interview with Parton in *Playboy,* Lawrence Grobel remarked:

> Although she appears larger than life, she is actually a compact woman — dazzling in appearance; but if you took away the wig and the Frederick's of Hollywood five-inch heels, she'd stand just five feet tall. Of course, her height isn't the first thing one notices upon meeting her. As she herself kids onstage, "I know that you-all brought your binoculars to see me; but what you didn't realize is you don't need binoculars."[17]

15. Tucker, "9–to–5," p. 383.
16. Roy Blount, Jr., "Country's Angels," *Esquire* (March 1977), p. 131.
17. Lawrence Grobel, "Dolly Parton: A Candid Conversation with the Curvaceous Queen of Country Music," *Playboy* (October 1978), p. 82.

Grobel continued with another anecdote about a little girl whose parents brought her backstage to greet Dolly; it too articulates that discourse of male desire:

> The picture I'll always remember was of the father telling his wife to take a shot of him behind Dolly. He had this crazy gleam in his eyes, his tongue popped out of his mouth, and I was sure he was going to cop a feel. But he restrained himself, as most people do around her. Because she is so open and unparanoid, she manages to tame the wildest instincts of men.[18]

What the *Playboy* interview reveals is Parton's complicity in (and  10 ultimate control of) this discourse of male desire. Several factors enter into the carefully constructed mystique that Parton maintains. First, her long-distance, part-time marriage to the mysterious, never-interviewed Carl Dean of Tennessee has generated questions about outlets for her sexual energy. There is an implicit assumption that since she appears to be hyperfeminine, she must be hypersexual. One of the most prevalent topics in "Dolly" discourse is speculation about her relationship with her husband, about how much time she spends with him, and, often implicitly, about the terms of their marriage vis-à-vis fidelity (about which questions are posed but evaded in several interviews). The tabloids have linked her sexually to a number of singing partners and leading men; there have also been suggestions of a lesbian relationship with her best friend and companion. This obsessive concern with the intimate details of Parton's sex life is found primarily in men's magazines and the tabloids. In contrast, when women's magazines have addressed the issue of her marriage, the focus has primarily been on her interpersonal/emotional relationships in general.

Throughout the *Playboy* interview, Grobel repeatedly raised questions about Parton's sexuality, to which she responded teasingly and unabashedly, but always stopping short of any personal disclosures. She admitted that she frequently flirts; however, the reader can observe her flirtations with the interviewer as her way of tactically taking control of the situation; her witty and manipulative comebacks frequently seemed to take Grobel by surprise and usually served to keep the ball in her court. The late Pete Axthelm once wrote about this aspect of Parton's persona:

> What Dolly is, it seems to me, is more than the sum of her attractive parts. Aside from her talent, she represents a vanishing natural resource — the mountain woman who understood independence and manipulation of men long before the first city girl got her consciousness raised. Dolly has a seldom-seen husband . . . she also employs a

---

18. Ibid.

number of men to help build her career. But there is no doubt about who's boss. "I need my husband for love," she says, "and other men for my work. But I don't depend on any man for my strength."[19]

Although some feminists have spoken out against the objectification of women's bodies as fetishes of male desire, on the grounds that such objectification reduces women to a passive state that victimizes them, one counterargument attributes power to the woman who controls — and controls the use of — her own image. Dolly Parton, by managing and manipulating her sexual image in such a way as to attain the maximum response from the male gaze while maintaining her own dignity and self-esteem, is making patriarchal discourse work to her own advantage. She is keeping the upper hand and stage-managing her own "exploitation."

If Dolly's appearance seems to signify excessive femaleness in the discourse of male desire and the magazines that articulate it, in such women's magazines as *Good Housekeeping* and *Ladies Home Journal* it is identified with a different kind of excess: exaggerated womanliness. There, Parton's literal embodiment of excessive womanliness is represented in two domains: that of her attitudes about her weight and body image, and that of her reproductive capabilities and speculations about whether her future holds motherhood. Both domains function as grounds for identification with Dolly by many female readers. While the evocation of male desire constructs Dolly as an object of voyeurism and aggressive sexual fantasy, the emphasis on female identification constructs Dolly as an ordinary woman who has the same types of physical and emotional problems as other women. In contrast to the physiological oddity constructed by men's magazines, in women's magazines Dolly becomes "Everywoman," and efforts are made to minimize her exceptionalness.[20]

The first discursive domain of women's magazines deals respectfully with the *imperfections* of Dolly's body, as noted by Parton herself, and the associated psychological aspects (a very different reading of the same physical "text" on which the masculine reading of sexuality is based):

> I look better fat, though, don't you think? Skinny, my face looks too long. I'm just very hefty. People are always telling me to lose weight, but being overweight has certainly never made me less money or hurt my career. . . . Besides, everybody loves a fat girl. . . . See, I know I'm not a natural beauty. I got short legs, short hands, and a tiny frame, but I like the way I am. I am me. I am real.[21]

19. Pete Axthelm, "Hello Dolly," *Newsweek,* 13 June 1977, p. 71.

20. See Dyer, *Stars,* on "ordinariness" as an important aspect of star-image construction, especially among women (pp. 49–50).

21. Jahr, "Golly, Dolly!" p. 142.

After an extended illness and gynecological surgery in the late 1980s, Parton lost a good deal of weight. This generated a surge of interest in — and a number of women's magazine articles about — her body and her relationship to it:

> Dolly admits she was overeating. Although she confesses, "I'm a natural-born hog. . . . I also eat when I'm happy," the protracted illness added more pounds to an already overloaded five-foot frame. "See, I'd always had this eating problem. I'd gain twenty pounds, lose it, gain it back the next week. In ten days I'd put on ten pounds. . . . I'd binge, diet, gain, start all over again. . . . Overeating is as much a sickness as drugs or alcoholism."

> To the suggestion she's too thin, that she looks anorexic, Dolly guffaws, "Honey, hogs don't get anorexia."

> "Boy, it burns me up to see people look at a fat person and say, 'Can you believe anybody would let herself get into that kind of shape?' That's easy for someone who looks like Jane Fonda to say. When I see a really overweight person, I feel sorry for her, because I've been there. . . . I know I could gain the weight back any minute, and it scares me to death."[22]

Through this admission, Parton brings herself down from any pedestal on which her star status might have placed her and aligns herself with the everyday concerns of ordinary women. Yet she also specifically identifies with working-class women, sarcastically criticizing the class-based aesthetic of thinness among the upwardly mobile:

> "My doctors would tell me, 'Okay, you have about twenty pounds to lose, but you can do that easily. Just eat right.' Well, that's easy to say. I just love those beautiful people who tell you, 'I *cahn't* see how anybody could let themselves get in that awful shape. Oh, my dear. That's gross,'" says Dolly, aping a fancy society voice.[23]

The other discursive domain of women's magazine articles about Dolly, the intense interest in her childbearing potential, has included speculation about her desire and possible plans for motherhood:

> Dolly doubts whether they'll have children because of the demands of her career. "I'm not saying women can't do both, but I'm on the road so much that it wouldn't be fair to the child. I love children so much that I'd want to be a mother all day long if I was going to be

15

---

22. Cindy Adams, "Dolly's Dazzling Comeback," *Ladies Home Journal* (March 1984), p. 153; Nancy Anderson, "Dolly Parton: A Home Town Report," *Good Housekeeping* (February 1988), p. 186; and Mary-Ann Bendel, "A Different Dolly," *Ladies Home Journal* (November 1987), p. 120.

23. Adams, "Dolly's Dazzling Comeback," p. 153.

one. . . . But remember, I was one of the oldest in my family. I've been raising babies all my life. . . . There's no shortage of kids around our home."[24]

This interest in the nurturing, maternal side of Dolly continued after her hysterectomy, shading into curiosity about her emotional reactions to the loss of her childbearing potential:

> Dolly had a partial hysterectomy and can no longer become pregnant. "Carl and I wanted children for years," she says. "I used to grieve after the hysterectomy, but since I turned forty, it doesn't bother me as much. I think God meant for me not to have children. My songs are my children, and I've given life to three thousand of them." Had she had kids, Dolly admits, most of those songs would never have been written.[25]

This metaphoric link between childbearing and the cultural production of songs recalls the Appalachian folk tradition (as described by Bufwack and Oermann) of women collecting and amassing huge repertoires of ballads and other songs that were then shared and exchanged among themselves.[26] Songs, like stories, have been a vital part of the cultural economy of Appalachian women; producing songs, like producing children, has been important to their social identities.

In contrast to women's magazines, recent tabloid articles have created masculinist scenarios, such as this one:

> Dolly Parton wants a baby. The country music star, who's pushing 43, always insisted motherhood wasn't for her. But now she's pining for the patter of little feet. Though she knows she can't become pregnant — surgery has eliminated that possibility — she wants to tear a page out of 44-year-old Loni Anderson's book and adopt a child.[27]

Tabloid discourse thus works hard at trying to "push" Parton back into a normative patriarchal structure, to contain and/or deny the creative potential of other forms of cultural production for women.

One of the contradictions between Parton's Dolly persona and her "real-life" image is that while the former has attained wealth and fame, the latter is projected as a humble Tennessee housewife who merely puts up with the demands of fame and fortune until she can get home and relax, slip into something more comfortable — her private life — which is just like everyone else's, well, almost. These conflicting images are paralleled by the dualistic roles that Parton models for women. On the one hand, she represents the modern, nonrepressed woman who can "have it

---

24. Joyce Maynard, "Dolly," *Good Housekeeping* (September 1977), p. 60.
25. Bendel, "Different Dolly," p. 182.
26. Bufwack and Oermann, *Finding Her Voice*, p. 7.
27. Gary Graham, "Dolly Parton to Adopt Baby," *The Star,* 14 April 1989, p. 6.

all" — marriage, strong family ties and friendships, and a successful, self-managed business/career that has brought her financial independence and a commensurate degree of social power; on the other hand, she represents the traditional values of rural American womanhood. The women's magazine articles reflect both a strong interest in how she manages to balance all of these aspects of her life and an intense curiosity about what that life entails/who that woman is — hence their focus on the private, emotional side of the star. By contrast, articles in mainstream, business-oriented news and music magazines (as well as in *Ms.*) have charted the (nontraditional) economic accomplishments of Dolly Parton. Particular interest has been paid to her business acumen and to her success as a crossover, both of which are associated with overcoming institutional and social obstacles. Parton has been successful as a country music singer and songwriter, a Hollywood actress, and a television performer in both specials and series. She has also proved to be an extremely successful entrepreneur as the owner of several production companies, publishing companies, toy companies, and music studios, and as the developer of Dollywood — the theme park she created to strengthen the economy of her native Tennessee county, which celebrates both her own career and the culture of the Appalachian region where she began.[28]

Dolly Parton's star image is the terrain for a struggle over not only the contested meanings of gender — the social construction of "woman" — but also the nature of and relations among class, regional culture, and ethnicity.[29] The Dolly persona, as an intersection of multiple social categories, raises the question of what it means to be Southern, Appalachian, rural, working-class, and female — or any one of these social identity categories.

In today's cosmopolitan, rapidly globalizing society, the construction of cultural identities is increasingly becoming a symbolic process rather than a result of geographic positioning. Although the role of the media in this symbolic construction needs further exploration, I want to suggest that the country music industry contributes to it by constructing notions

---

28. See Charles Leehrsen, "Here She Comes, Again," *Newsweek,* 23 November 1987, pp. 73–74; see also Hurst, "You've Come a Long Way," p. 122; Grobel, "Candid Conversation," p. 108; and Alanna Nash, "Dollywood: A Serious Business," *Ms.* (July 1986), pp. 12–14.

29. I use the term "ethnicity" in the anthropological sense established by Barth and by de Vos and Romanucci-Ross, that is, as referring to cultural groups within a pluralistic and hegemonic society who define themselves (through a perception of common origins or common beliefs and values) as culturally distinct from the dominant group and who use a variety of mechanisms to maintain symbolic boundaries and delineations from other groups. In this sense, I perceive Southern Appalachian culture to be one of regional ethnicity, but I do not perceive "Southernness," as an external construction of regionality, to be a kind of ethnicity in itself, although it incorporates many. See Fredrik Barth, *Ethnic Groups and Boundaries* (Boston, 1969); and *Ethnic Identity: Cultural Continuities and Change,* ed. George de Vos and Lola Romanucci-Ross (Palo Alto, 1975).

of "Southernness" or "country-ness" to which consumers can subscribe. Today, many cultures are geographically situated in or otherwise associated with the American South, such as the cultures of black, rural, working-class Southerners; white, rural, working-class Southerners; the "old South's" white aristocracy; urban black Southerners; urban Southern Jews; Southern Appalachian whites; urban/suburban white Southerners; Louisiana Cajuns; Southern Mennonites; and Cherokee, Choctaw, and Seminole Indians. All are distinct, but their cultural boundaries are permeable, and social agents may be associated with more than one of these subcultures. Class, race, ethnicity, and place are the most significant markers of cultural group identity. As a result, "Southern" is clearly a generic construct rather than a label for a distinct culture. It is used as a classifying and stereotyping term by outsiders; the signifiers of Dolly Parton's distinctive white Southern Appalachian culture are collapsed into a nonspecific "Southernness" and "country-ness" by the popular culture discourses relating to country music.

"Southernness," as a symbolic and discursive construction, has acquired distinct connotations and cultural referents that are usually associated with white Southern cultures.[30] The political history of the Southern states, beginning with their secession from the United States during the Civil War period, through the stark, Depression-era WPA images of impoverished sharecroppers, to the civil rights movement of the 1960s, has generated a host of internal and external discourses and stereotypes about the "South," which are reproduced and further fueled by conflicting images and representations of the region in literature, the media, and popular culture.

The specific subculture represented by Dolly Parton (Southern Appalachian mountain culture) has also been subject to stereotyping in popular culture, from the socially inept and "primitive" hillbillies of the "L'il Abner" comic strip and television's *Beverly Hillbillies* to the violent, sexually deviant villains of James Dickey's novel *Deliverance* and its 1972 film adaptation. Parton parodies these popular images in her persona, even as she promotes the more "authentic" cultural elements that reflect her heritage, particularly the culture of Appalachian women. Historically and culturally, kinship has been the central organizing principle of Southern Appalachian society, and a matrilineal orientation has resulted

20

---

30. In the working-class South, the races (white, black, and American Indian) have lived in relative isolation from each other, maintaining fairly separate but parallel cultures. The black population in the Appalachian region has always been much smaller than that of the lowland South, according to Phillip J. Obermiller and William W. Philliber, *Too Few Tomorrows: Urban Appalachians in the 1980s* (Boone, NC, 1987), p. 11. For useful overviews of Southern cultural issues, see Carole Hill, "Anthropological Studies in the American South: Review and Directions," *Current Anthropology* 18 (1987), pp. 309–26; Marion Pearsall, "Cultures of the American South," *Anthropological Quarterly* 39 (1966), pp. 476–87; and John S. Reed, *The Enduring South: Subcultural Persistence in Mass Society* (Chapel Hill, 1974).

in strong affective ties among women.[31] Each rural community tended to form an independent, kinship-oriented, egalitarian social group, without clear social-class differences (most group antagonism stemmed from tensions between a social group and the outside world — meaning, since the mid-nineteenth century, the northern industrial society — as well as from minor tensions between communities or between families). Relationships between women have been primarily kin- and neighbor-oriented, and a strong women's culture has been maintained. Members of a traditional mountain community have tended to share a common history and ideology, with their code of morality primarily informed by localized inflections of fundamentalist Christianity.

In the traditional, preindustrial economy, there was a gendered division of labor: the woman's domain was her household, where she was responsible for raising food and children and for serving as a repository of cultural knowledge (history, genealogy, and the moral code). As industrialization overtook the agrarian mode of life in this century, mountaineers have been gradually assimilated into this economy as working-class laborers, and both men and women now participate in the wage-labor force.[32] Although this culture is generally perceived as strongly patriarchal (a perception largely due to the work of early male "ethnographers," such as John C. Campbell), studies by women who have examined the culture challenge that assumption; they see instead a gender-based system of coexisting models for cultural practice, whereby Appalachian women maintain a great deal of power within and through a facade of patriarchal control.

---

31. Relevant works on the Southern Appalachian culture of Parton's region include John C. Campbell's 1921 classic, *The Southern Highlander and His Homeland* (Lexington, 1969 [1921]); *Appalachian Ways: A Guide to the Historic Mountain Heart of the East,* ed. Jill Durrance and William Shamblin (Washington, DC, 1976); Elmora Messer Matthews, *Neighbor and Kin: Life in a Tennessee Ridge Community* (Nashville, 1965); and Jack Weller, *Yesterday's People: Life in Contemporary Appalachia* (Lexington, 1965). For insights into the culture of Southern and Appalachian women, see Margaret Jarman Hagood, *Mothers of the South: Portraiture of the White Tenant Farm Woman* (New York, 1977 [1939]); and Pamela Wilson, "Keeping the Record Straight: Conversational Storytelling and Gender Roles in a Southern Appalachian Community" (Master's thesis, University of Texas at Austin, 1984). Obermiller and Philliber, *Too Few Tomorrows,* also provide insights into Appalachian ethnicity.

32. With this century's increasing economic dependence upon industry and the corresponding breakdown of the agricultural economy, many farmworkers have been integrated into the dominant capitalist system as part of the working class and now tend to fill that slot in the social and economic structure (although it is important to point out that this rural working-class society exhibits characteristics that are quite different from those of an urban/industrial working-class society). In addition, as Obermiller and Philliber report in *Too Few Tomorrows,* from 1940 through 1970, over three million people migrated from the Southern Appalachian region to industrial urban centers in the Midwest (primarily Cincinnati, Detroit, and Chicago) to find work as unskilled laborers; some returned after a few years, but many stayed and created cultural ghettos of Appalachian people in these cities.

Much of the "Dolly" discourse in popular magazines has been devoted to authenticating her "country" life history and cultural roots, particularly the conditions of poverty, rural isolation, and familial heritage in which she developed.[33] In interviews, Parton herself has emphasized her working-class background:

> I can think like a workingman because I know what a workingman goes through. . . . Where I came from, people *never* dreamed of venturing out. They just lived and died there. Grew up with families and a few of them went to Detroit and Ohio to work in the graveyards and car factories. But I'm talking about venturing out into areas that we didn't understand.[34]

Parton has also discussed the farming/working-class mentality of her husband, an asphalt contractor:

> He's really bright. He's not backward at all. I just really wish that people would let him be. He's a home-lovin' person. He works outside, he's got his tractor and his grader, he keeps our farm in order. He wouldn't have to work no more, because I'm making good money now, but he gets up every morning at daylight. If he ain't workin' on our place, he'll take a few jobs, like grading somebody's driveway or cleaning off somebody's property, to pick up a couple of hundred bucks. . . . He'll say, "Well, I ain't in show business, I got to work."[35]

Many magazine articles underscore Parton's refusal to be assimilated into a Hollywood celebrity lifestyle and her preference for maintaining a home near Nashville. However, this brings up the complex issue of the subcultural hegemony represented by the Nashville-based country music industry.

In relation to the mainstream music and entertainment industries centered in Los Angeles and New York, the Nashville industry represents a successful regional-cultural force that has gained a national audience, yet remains independent and appears somewhat radical in its advocacy of Southern, white, working-class culture. In the course of being disseminated nationally through radio and, most recently, cable television, the "country" culture has been appropriated by a generalized working-class audience, both urban and rural, that represents various

---

33. Parton's family history and the photographs that visually document her rags-to-riches story feature prominently in women's magazine articles (see, e.g., Anderson, "Home Town Report"; and Jahr, "Golly, Dolly!"). Grobel's 1978 *Playboy* interview also extensively investigates the details of Parton's life growing up, and the two articles in *Ms.* (by Nash and by Steinem) focus on the rootedness of Parton's life and image in her region and hometown community. See also Willadeene Parton, "My Sister, Dolly Parton," *McCall's* (July 1985), pp. 74–125; and Connie Berman, "Dolly Parton Scrapbook," *Good Housekeeping* (February 1979), pp. 140–43, 203–9.

34. Grobel, "Candid Conversation," pp. 88, 102.

35. Ibid., p. 88.

racial and ethnic backgrounds.[36] As a result of its folk music origins, country music has long been a genre of self-defined "ordinary folks," whose sense of humor has frequently generated both oppositional satire and a somewhat self-mocking tone (often read as straight by outsiders, but recognized as ironic and self-parodying by insiders).[37] Since the 1950s, country music has increasingly become a genre for female artists, who have aligned themselves with rural and working-class women.

However, the country music industry has recently changed, shifting away from its folk roots (though still incorporating them in the construction of "country-ness") and moving into the postmodern popular-music mainstream market. In an insightful essay, Patrick Carr discusses the changing social image of and audience for country music in the 1980s:

> Historically in America, the rural working class has been the object of prejudice, of stereotyping amounting to contempt, on the part of the urban population. . . . Not long ago, to "be country" meant that you had been cast by a geo-socio-economic accident of birth with an almost automatically adversarial relationship with the dominant urban/suburban culture; in effect, you belonged in a cultural ghetto. Now it's a matter of free consumer choice.[38]

Carr argues that the country music industry has structured its current place in the entertainment industry in such a way as to commercialize those adversarial voices, thereby economically insinuating them into a capitalist order to which they have been traditionally opposed.[39] This is indeed a major paradox of country music in general and of stars like Parton in particular. The bristling tension between the proudly rebellious, rough-hewn rural style of "authentic" country music culture and the glossy, slickly packaged commercialized style of the mainstream entertainment industry has become the defining mark of the country music industry today. . . .[40]

In constructing her star persona, Dolly Parton has played with and exploited cultural stereotypes of style and taste — not only in terms of

---

36. On the predominance of working-class and female consumers in the composition of country music audiences, as well as the prevalence of working-class backgrounds among country music performers, see Mary A. Bufwack and Robert K. Oermann, "Women in Country Music," in *Popular Culture in America,* ed. Paul Buhle (Minneapolis, 1987), pp. 91–101.

37. On the folk origins of country music, see Hurst, "You've Come a Long Way," p. 123. He traces Parton's musical style to the convergence of three components: (1) Elizabethan ballads preserved for centuries by isolated Appalachian mountaineers; (2) the wildly emotional religious music of Protestant fundamentalist churches; and (3) the country music on early 1950s radio.

38. Carr, "Changing Image," p. 484.

39. Ibid.; see also George Lipsitz, *Time Passages* (Minneapolis, 1990), esp. pp. 99–160; and Bufwack and Oermann's "Women in Country Music."

40. This is particularly true of country music videos; see Mark Fenster, "Country Music Video," *Popular Music* 7 (1988), pp. 285–302.

femininity, but also with respect to Southern Appalachian, rural and/or working-class culture — often exaggerating them in her persona or emphasizing them in interviews:

> I always liked the looks of our hookers back home. Their big hairdos and makeup made them look *more*. When people say that less is more, I say *more* is more. Less is *less*; I go for more.

> Dolly, who commands $350,000 a week in Las Vegas — making her the highest paid entertainer there — says she prefers shopping at K-Mart or Zayre's, where she can get several articles of clothing for the price she'd pay for one at a more upscale establishment.

> I'd much rather shop in a mall and buy some cheap clothes than go into some fine store and buy something that costs a fortune. . . . I want to design something for the average woman, something that could be sold at Sears or Penney's.[41]

By foregrounding such stereotypes, Parton not only celebrates working-class tastes and values, but also parodies her male predecessors in the country music world of the 1950s and 1960s, particularly her former partner, Porter Wagoner, and others who perpetuated country music's most distinctive visual symbol — the extravagantly expensive, gaudy, spangled-and-rhinestoned stage costume, which became the haute couture of male country music performers of that era.[42] The "down-home" side of Dolly thus advocates "authenticity" by making fun of the superficial stylistic elements that have encrusted the dominant society's image of (and that have been internalized as identificatory values by) women on display, country music performers, Southerners, and the rural working class. As Gloria Steinem points out, "Her flamboyant style has turned all the devalued symbols of womanliness to her own ends. If feminism means each of us finding our unique power, and helping other women to do the same, Dolly Parton certainly has done both."[43] If we extend Steinem's statement to include the other categories of social identity and oppression that the "Dolly" image enunciates, Parton can be understood as a self-empowered woman whose image, challenging social stereotypes through parody, becomes empowering and counter-hegemonic.

### Reading the Text

1. How, in Wilson's view, does Dolly Parton manipulate traditional codes of femininity, and what contradictions does she create as a result?

---

41. Jahr, "Golly, Dolly!", p. 85; Kingsbury, ed. *Country,* p. 258; and Bendel, "Different Dolly," p. 182.

42. Carr, "Changing Image," p. 494.

43. Steinem, "Dolly Parton," p. 66.

2. What does Wilson mean when she asserts that Parton has "complicity in (and ultimate control of) this discourse of male desire"?
3. What are the differences between male and female interpretations of Parton's persona, according to Wilson?
4. How, in Wilson's view, is Parton a sign of "Southernness"?
5. Summarize in your own words the coverage of Parton in popular media.

### Reading the Signs

1. In class, form teams and debate whether Dolly Parton perpetuates or subverts traditional gender roles. To develop your ideas, consult popular media coverage of Parton; additionally, you might read or reread Holly Devor's "Gender Role Behaviors and Attitudes" (p. 415).
2. In her essay, Wilson claims that Parton has served as a "role model for women of varying class and cultural backgrounds." Read or reread Jenny Lyn Bader's "Larger Than Life" (p. 391) and write an essay in which you argue whether Parton could serve as a role model for the twentysomething generation Bader discusses.
3. Pick another popular entertainment figure with a strong regional identity, and, using Wilson's analysis as a model, analyze how that figure "constructs" a regional identity.
4. Wilson states that "Parton is often compared to Mae West, Marilyn Monroe, Bette Midler, and Madonna for her manipulation and burlesquing of femininity." Select one of these other artists and compare and contrast her with Parton, focusing on how each uses gender roles to construct a star image. Be sure to ground your discussion in a close analysis of specific songs, videos, or films.
5. Research one of the examples of Southern Appalachian mountain culture that Wilson mentions and write an analysis of how it perpetuates the cultural image of the region.

# ALEX ROSS

## The Politics of Irony

IIIIIIIIIIIIIIIIIIIIIIIIIIIIIIIIIIIIIIIIIIIIIIIIIIIII

*What do David Letterman and Rush Limbaugh have that Bill Clinton doesn't? According to Alex Ross, they share a cynical ability to manipulate the media, especially television, to their personal advantage. As opposed to what Ross identifies as Clinton's politics of sincerity, talk-television stars like Letterman and Limbaugh pursue a politics of irony, whereby a public persona is self-consciously constructed and then sold to an audience that, in Ross's words, "is viscerally alert to*

*media manipulation, but that is also a sucker for self-consciousness." A*
*freelance writer who has published in* The New Yorker, *the* New
Republic, *and the* New York Times, *Ross specializes in music*
*and popular culture. This selection first appeared in the* New Republic.

*The intellectual human being must choose between irony and*
*radicalism; a third choice is not decently possible.*
— THOMAS MANN, *Reflections of a Nonpolitical Man*

Television began with a man sitting at a desk, talking. The  desk, at
first, was a matter of necessity — early T.V. cameras were massive and
immobile, so their subjects needed a visual motive for staying put. Journalists were cast as "anchors," and entertainers as "hosts," each installed at
desks or desklike areas. Perhaps there were deeper psycho-historical origins: Roosevelt had ruled the nation from an infirm patrician's seat. In
any case, desks have now become indispensable. They impart an executive bearing to the sitters, who make completely spurious note-taking
motions when the camera cuts away to a commercial. Anyone on television capable of taking notes has an edge on the average viewer.

Fresh waves of technology and fashion should have put this antique
format out of circulation. But the desks are more numerous than ever,
especially after 11 p.m. At a time when television is dissolving into sub-
culturally specialized, aesthetically disheveled fragments, the late-night
host somehow has held on to iconic status — trumpeted by network
publicity, debated in workplaces, dissected in reams of articles such as this
one. It is as if he (and it is still universally a he) has become a critical
common referent in a hopelessly uncentered culture. Addressing a public
of infinitely malleable size, creating events from thin air, the host is asked
to engineer the illusive unities, bridging gaps that our politicians long
have been unable to navigate.

How does a host address a nation of subcultures? The one subject
known to us all is television itself — its rules, its rhetoric, its accumulated
history and literature. And so the common language has been an ironic
subversion of television itself: the most popular shows on T.V. right
now are about T.V. — "Murphy Brown," "Home Improvement" and
(fitfully) "Seinfeld," to name three top contenders. Others, such as
"Roseanne," "Married . . . With Children" and "The Simpsons," invert
the model family shows of T.V.'s past. Self-referential irony, thought to
be the annoying trivium of the 1980s, has settled in for the long haul.

Through this haze, the hosts have stumbled on what might be called
the politics of irony. They who grasp it wield strong cultural-political
clout. While the vast following that upheld Johnny Carson's "Tonight
Show" is gone forever, the more narrow but intense regard for a David

Letterman or a Rush Limbaugh has no less weight. The new host is a sly virtuoso of layered meanings, a contrapuntalist of revealed and concealed messages. The new kind of host is also — critically — not a liberal. Earnest, Clintonian liberalism so far has floundered in the new conditions. Conservatives, it turns out, know their T.V. better.

But first, some talk-show history. The original hosts were nationally syndicated gossip columnists, hired by radio to simulate glamour for 1930s audiences. Walter Winchell, of the *Daily Mirror,* won fame second to none simply by sitting at his table at the Stork Club, gathering gossip for his monologues. Celebrities came to pay homage, and he would report their quips and exploits alongside questionable stories from all sources — thus an atmosphere of "guests" circulating around him. One-third of the nation watched in fascination as he became a figure of national importance, preaching a blend of gung-ho patriotism and gangsterish apathy. FDR and J. Edgar Hoover were both in his debt. He stamped himself on the flow of events around him with an array of stylistic tics: the spastic, gibberish-flavored prose style; the much-imitated triple-dot punctuation; the grand salutation to "Mr. and Mrs. America, and all the ships at sea." He was vainglorious, nasty, vague, central.

Louella Parsons, columnist for the all-powerful Hearst newspapers and host of "Hollywood Hotel," was no less potent; she too boosted Hoover, although entertainment remained her primary interest. She is best remembered for two interventions she made in the careers of performers entering film from radio: the destruction of Orson Welles, whose debut film *Citizen Kane* unwisely attacked Hearst head-on, and the elevation of Ronald Reagan, who was lucky enough to come from her hometown of Dixon, Illinois. Parsons promoted Reagan at the outset of his career, finding him a bit role in the 1937 film version of *Hollywood Hotel.*

Parsons never made it to television, and Winchell's attempt at a show in the '50s failed miserably. The most popular hosts in the new medium were far less tendentious and imposing. Arthur Godfrey hosted folksy chat shows with titles like "Arthur Godfrey and His Friends," drawing audiences of up to 80 million people. Ed Sullivan carried a variety show just by standing around. The big names were on during the early evening; no one thought much of the late-night slot. But a Los Angeles radio host named Steve Allen drew a large following with "Tonight!," his free-wheeling NBC comedy show. His wacky stunts and frenetic good cheer made him the chief hipster of the '50s, and not beyond.

After Allen left, what became known as "The Tonight Show" fell into the hands of a genuine original. Jack Paar was an eminently normal-looking man, a former G.I. entertainer who planted himself at a desk instead of scampering around like Allen had. He would begin his shows in a low, well-modulated voice, exuding a dangerous calm. Then, periodically, but never predictably, he would lurch into disgruntled, pathetic soliloquies, decrying some indignity visited upon him by the network or the press. His emotional exhibitionism once led him to walk off the set in the middle of a broadcast.

Paar quit abruptly in 1962 after only five years. There was no other host like him on the horizon, and corporate T.V. did not seem to mind. Consolidating enormous gains in advertising revenue, the networks did not seek out difficult personalities. Daytime chat shows with Mike Douglas and Merv Griffin were idylls of complacency and vacuousness. The 1960s and '70s saw a few departures from formula, most of them either short-lived or half-hearted. "The Phil Donahue Show," originating from Ohio in 1967, drew on its bottomless fund of taboo subjects; but even in trying to break its own spell, network T.V. created instant clichés. Politicians, in turn, adopted all the robotic mannerisms perfected by the newscasters. Television fell into a shabby haze, a Dean Martin stupor, through which nothing ever penetrated fully.

Johnny Carson, whose shiveringly mellow "Tonight Show" reigned supreme from 1962 to 1992, resisted that stupor only halfway. Early on, he exuded a vague anti-establishment ethos, tending toward outright liberalism. But over time, the show approached an equilibrium of numbing blandness. The monologues were all charmingly mediocre, the conversations charmingly inert. The most memorable image in the last show was a dramatic floor shot of The Desk, plunged into darkness at the end of the typical-broadcast-day montage. "The Larry Sanders Show," HBO's brilliant talk-show satire, captures the bleary mediocrity that hung over Carson's final years and now blankets the bathetic regime of Jay Leno.

Still, Carson acquired an imperial grace over his twenty-nine-year era. He became a shadow president for a leaderless public, winning trust by never betraying expectations. His final moments as America's Host — alighting from Burbank in a helicopter, waving distantly to the cameras — were nothing less than Reaganesque. Like Reagan, Carson answered an increasingly desperate hunger for an enduring national icon, cool and agreeable and remote. Unlike Reagan, he really did have nothing to say and departed a widely beloved enigma.

If Carson closed out the story of the National Hosts, then it's hard to find a place for David Letterman. He came on stage as an insincere endnote to the Carson phenomenon, a cynical extension of a faded form. He had no trace of Carson's transcontinental, Vegas-tinged suavity. But he gathered a solid following through NBC's "Late Night," and with his new show on CBS he is improbably leading the "late-night war." He is the model of the new television personality, less intent on universal adoration than on a kind of maladjusted — and ironic — realism.

His first incarnation, as the anti-host, the anti-Carson, was the most amusing and also the most limited. "Late Night," in the early and mid-'80s, was "The Tonight Show" gone to seed. Every component in its daily lineup — set, guests, sidekicks, recurring characters, funny animals — was a deliberately inadequate echo of Carson's show-biz juggernaut. Letterman grinned knowingly through all the expert nonsense and

10

shabbiness around him. Draped with ominous praise — "hip," "subversive," "ironic," and "in tune with the zeitgeist" — the show fit snugly the culture of the mid-'80s. In his book *Boxed In,* Mark Crispin Miller tagged Letterman with "that air of laid-back irony against which all enthusiasm seems contemptible" — the empty irony that undermines a dominant mode without advancing anything to take its place. At his most smug in 1985, he did a show called "Too Tired To Do A Show" in which he just hung around the office and threw pencils at the ceiling. This was the silent counterculture, the party in the basement den that didn't disturb the parents upstairs.

Seeing that the anti-show had run its course, Letterman retrenched. The collegiate silliness faded away, and the show became a theater of his difficult personality, his mix of white-bread Americana and interstellar eccentricity. His model was no longer the goofy Steve Allen but the slow-burning Jack Paar. But where Paar waged battles with real-life enemies, Letterman fussed over tiny perturbations in his vicinity and gave vent to abstract complaints. At CBS he has taken on a brighter and busier tone, but his act remains essentially the same.

This host's point of departure is his total disregard for celebrity culture. Carson always *seemed* interested. Letterman's interviews with major stars show an impeccable ignorance of their projects and careers. He has endorsed nothing, joined no known political groups or causes, evaded *People* and "Entertainment Tonight." His session with Barbara Walters a couple of years ago was a masterpiece of nondisclosure. For many years he entered the news only on the barely plausible pretext of a crazy woman breaking into his home. Knowing American pop culture's tendency to glaze over its personalities, he makes himself known only through the distorted lens of his little talk-show kingdom. 15

To a remarkable degree, Letterman constructs his on-air persona simply with words. When he fields responses from guests and random individuals reached by camera or by phone, he is looking for dead words, raw clichés, banalities waiting to be stuffed and mounted. Once he called up a woman operating a concession stand at the Grand Canyon and asked for a description of the view; his stated aim was to hear her say the word "breathtaking." He became greatly agitated when she did not. On-air conversations he's had over the years with his mother, Dorothy Letterman, operate on the same principle. If all else fails, verbal white noise is furnished by Paul Shaffer, the dependable bandleader who speaks in a purified show-biz dialect.

The spin Letterman puts on all accumulated triteness still falls under the heading of irony, but it can no longer be described as "laid-back." Rather than simply recite clichés in a sarcastic tone, as he did early on, he nervously tampers with them until they become his own. When he introduces a guest as "always talented," for example, he is savoring the dissonance that crops up when the show-biz intro "always personable, very talented" is crunched together. Any strange combination of words intrigues him; he once reported a phrase uttered in the middle of the night on the Home Shopping Club — "Now turn over your swan candlestick holders" — and excitedly announced to his audience, "In the whole history of human civilization, those particular words had never before been uttered together."

On his best nights, Letterman is seized with a sort of broadcasting dementia, parroting television's moribund voices. He becomes the as-if host, speaking grandly to a nonexistent Winchellian public. Setting up a bland joke in his monologue, he abandons the cue card and starts babbling like Dan Rather finally gone over the brink: "In society as we know it today, in this current international situation, this seething caldron of global tension, this overall geopolitical condition of unease in which we presently find ourselves, a condition palpable even in this room, almost tangible even as we speak. . . ." Spinning out endless strings of synonyms, underscoring them with arbitrary gesticulations, Letterman becomes an opulently eccentric, almost aristocratic presence, the sort television was supposed to have disallowed long ago.

The Mad Prophet of the Airwaves eventually gives way to a second, less innocent, pose: the Great White Misanthrope. This is the one with which casual viewers are probably familiar — the middle-aged man with the grimacing grin, the lethally empty gaze, the disgusted snicker. Women guests are treated to a display of nervousness, condescension and adolescent leering. Any young actress or model causes him to be revoltingly smarmy: he might lock her in a bear hug when she first comes onstage, releasing her several seconds after she visibly has begun to squirm. With black guests, he generally leans far back in his chair and loses his colloquial assurance. Any mention of homosexuality throws him into a mild panic.

It is this corrosive persona that draws a following of a million or   20
more 18- to 49-year-old white males. (In his slightly underrated *American Psycho,* Bret Easton Ellis made the cartoon-WASP antihero an eager fan of "Late Night.") T.V. writers tend to describe this aspect of his character in a contemptuous "Gotcha!" tone — as if Letterman had accidentally revealed his true awfulness. But not only is Letterman aware of the problem — "sometimes I even annoy myself" — he goes out of his way to elaborate and exaggerate the lonely white-guy image. Once he related this exchange with a diner in a restaurant — Japanese, he emphasized — who offered to share a table when Letterman was dining alone:

LETTERMAN: No, no, I can't do that, I'd be imposing.
JAPANESE DINER: What do you mean?
LETTERMAN: All my life, I've been an imposition.
JAPANESE DINER: I don't understand. What do you mean?
LETTERMAN: I have a personality disorder.
JAPANESE DINER: What kind?

Here Letterman broke off the dialogue, having made the point that the Japanese diner was a peculiarly persistent individual. But the image one carries away is of the famous T.V. star sitting alone in a restaurant, telling strangers that he is socially inept or even mentally diseased. Unlike nearly any other American celebrity you could think of, Letterman does not want to be loved.

After several overblown opening shows, Letterman's "Late Show" on CBS has turned out to be a sort of splendid apotheosis. While holding on to his singular mannerisms, the host seems more content with the everyday routine, much as Bill Murray's cynical weatherman found serenity in *Groundhog Day*. He is nicer to the guests, and the guests now play along when his now-legendary sourness returns. He has gotten under the skin of television's mainstream appeal, and stares out with slightly demented eyes. Meanwhile, his double-pronged technique of disenchantment — the vacant-ironic manipulation of national broadcasting, the entrenched subcultural appeal — has spread in unexpected directions. Rush Limbaugh has turned it around and made it meaningful, although not as meaningful as one might hope.

Limbaugh's debut as a television host was not auspicious. It came in the waning days of "The Pat Sajak Show," CBS's pre-Letterman attempt at a late-night franchise. Various people were guest-hosting in Sajak's place, auditioning for a new version of the show. Limbaugh tried out in December 1990. His hour on the air was fatally disrupted by a throng of ACT-UP demonstrators protesting his constant resort to anti-gay remarks on his nationally syndicated radio show. The man who had once attacked homosexuality as "deadly, sickly behavior," who filed a regular "Gerbil Update," wilted before this on-air protest. "He came out full of bluster and left a very shaken man," said a CBS executive. "I had never seen a man sweat so much in my life."

Yet another veteran of the talk-show world was not discouraged by Limbaugh's CBS experience. This was Roger Ailes, best known as a T.V. coach for recent Republican presidents, but a talk-show producer by vocation. He is serious about the format, and his career shows a logical evolution. He was executive producer for "The Mike Douglas Show" in the '60s and '70s, where he perfected the art of making anyone appear comfortable on T.V. In the late '70s, he guided the late-night NBC show "Tomorrow," hosted by Tom Snyder; this was a much pricklier affair. NBC canceled it in 1982 in favor of "Late Night With David Letterman." A decade later, Ailes found in Limbaugh the basis for an entirely new kind of host-driven talk show, with current events as the only guests.

The Ailes-produced "Rush Limbaugh Show," first seen in September of 1992, was dismissed as an aberration by most T.V. critics. All the articles about the "talk-show wars" paid it no attention whatsoever, and even *The Wall Street Journal* had to ask, "Where are the visuals? Why is this man on T.V.?" The host is indeed an unconventional presence. He barks at the

viewers as if he were sitting across from them in a noisy restaurant. His figure isn't altogether congruent with the standard rectangular screen. (Perhaps letterboxing would solve this problem.) The studio audience is unset-
tlingly unanimous; although there is no applause sign, applause cuts off
with needle-sharp precision. There is an infomercial ambience.

But people have been watching. A few months into its run, the     25
show's ratings were equal to or greater than Letterman's "Late Night" in
some markets (average Nielsens of 3.0). He has gotten better at T.V.,
marshaling video clips and man-on-the-street interviews to bear out his
points. The best of these recently was a dazzling montage of disparate
personalities speaking in favor of traditional values — everyone from
Daniel Patrick Moynihan to Louis Farrakhan. Another set of tapes
demonstrated John F. Kennedy's allegiance to Reaganomics. But more
important, Limbaugh has found ways to go against the grain of the
medium, to resist its standardizing pressure. He has learned to replicate
on T.V. the intellectual emotion that powers his radio shows. In these respects, his link to Letterman is clearest.

At first glance, they seem as far apart as possible: Limbaugh, with his
weekly 20 million listeners, his record-breaking best-sellers, his newsletter that has over three times more readers than the magazine you are
holding, his "Rush Rooms" in steak houses across the country — and
Letterman, with his Viewer Mail, and the woman who breaks into his
house. Limbaugh is at his best with on-the-spot political commentary;
Letterman wings his way far above, or behind, current events. But there
is a solid likeness between the right-winger and the no-winger. Both are
cigar-smoking, divorced men in their mid-40s, from solid midwestern
backgrounds (Kansas and Indiana, respectively). Both grew up in the
1960s but were untouched by its ferment. Both have ended up in New
York, happily disgusted at its squalor. Both are noted for being painfully
shy and insecure in person.

Three extant biographies — *The Rush Limbaugh Story: Talent on Loan
from God: An Unauthorized Biography* by Paul D. Colford, *Rush!* by
Michael Arkush and *The David Letterman Story: An Unauthorized Biography* by Caroline Latham — supply material for more detailed parallels. As
Colford points out in passing, both men were devoted listeners of a
Chicago-based D.J. named Larry Lujack, whose act combined bombast
and skepticism. Limbaugh started in radio with an F.M. rock show, while
Letterman took on odd jobs for local T.V. stations. Limbaugh was consistently fired from jobs for interjecting conservative opinions into
nonopinion formats. Letterman found similar discouragement when he
interpolated comic material — his legendary Indianapolis weather reports, for example, in which imaginary storms decimated far-flung locales. (Letterman tried a talk-radio show in the mid-'70s and got
nowhere. "The Nixon-Watergate nonsense," he recalled, "was the

perfect example of something about which I knew nothing and couldn't have cared less.")

And there can be no doubt that Limbaugh has studied Letterman's show closely. He makes himself vivid by ruffling items on his desk noisily and giving cameo roles to his staff and crew. He fashions an identity from the driftwood of television language, repeating an ordinary phrase until it becomes his intellectual property. "This show is on the cutting edge of societal evolution," he says, in language usually reserved for sports cars or home entertainment systems. When he sees such prosaic phrases elsewhere in the media, he then can herald the universality of his own influence. Even more Lettermanlike, he alters banalities in midstream. "The views expressed by the host of this program will soon become federal law." The grandiose address to "listeners all across the fruited plain" echoes Letterman's "great American home-viewing public" and Winchell's "Mr. and Mrs. America." The result of all this is that Limbaugh acquires a critical distance from his medium and from himself.

What are Limbaugh's aims in appropriating and paralleling Letterman? The first possibility is that it is all a brilliant ruse designed to disguise a conservative crusade as mere entertainment. When speaking to "mainstream" publications, Limbaugh suspiciously insists that his show is all in good fun, just show biz. "This show exists in the entertainment arena," he said to *Vanity Fair*. His call-screener added, "The politics on this show are secondary to [Limbaugh's] personality." And again, in the book *The Way Things Ought To Be*: "I refuse to use the entertainment forum of my radio show to advance agendas or causes." These, surely, are disingenuous words from the man who gave a huge boost to Pat Buchanan in the New Hampshire primary, who forced disclosure of names in the House banking scandal and who could tilt the Republican primaries in 1996.

And yet if you try to pin down specifically a Limbaugh agenda, a   30
Limbaugh cause, you might end up a little baffled. His first requirement in articulating any position is that it be nonliberal. In essence, if it is nonliberal, it is conservative. He gives little thought to tensions within present-day conservatism. He skips happily from Reagan to Kemp to Bennett to Buchanan and back again. He dedicates himself to small business and local interests, then advocates NAFTA and corporatist economics. His "traditional values" twist gently in the wind, leaning toward moderation when pressed. He has been virtually silent on gay issues, except to echo the party line on gays in the military. Once he even took a call from a Republican gay man in Manhattan, and suggested that people like him should be seen at the next Republican convention.

So too with his thoughts on feminism, which are less a social philosophy than a particularly extreme men-are-different-from-women rant of the kind practiced by stand-up comics. "It can be misused," he says of his term "femi–Nazi," by which he might mean any use not idiosyncratically his own. When his needling critiques of black leaders are attacked as racist, he hollowly responds, "I am the opposite of a racist." Limbaugh is the opposite of opposites. He is a giant double negative, the logical outcome of a point-counterpoint style of political discourse. His straw-man liberal is an empty antinomial category, a clever rerouting of the bland barbs long thrown at conservatives (hence the Nazi rhetoric for feminists). He has an uncanny ability to fast-forward through the tit-for-tat clichés of T.V. debate, doing the pundits in different voices — a one-man McLaughlin Group.

With their churning syntax and overreaching vocabulary, Limbaugh's stem-winders are themselves a twist on an electronic tradition. They often sound like a giant disc jockey put-on, an endless F.M. prank. Periodically Limbaugh plays with this resemblance by hoaxing his own listeners — infamously, his "conversion to Clinton" a couple of weeks before the 1992 election, which incited a *War of the Worlds* panic among millions of American conservatives. Limbaugh's rhetorical vigor makes the line between seriousness, humorous exaggeration and outright absurdity rather blurry. "I demonstrate the absurd by being absurd," he reiterates; but it is not always the liberal position that is so demonstrated.

All the problems posed by Limbaugh's politics are solved if one takes him at his word and sees him as an entertainer. The two "unauthorized" Limbaugh biographies — Colford's is fairly neutral, Arkush's is faintly damning — depict a man who used politics as a means to an entertainment end, rather than the other way around. He was never politically active in his own right, and was not even registered to vote until the mid-'80s. Reagan, the man he trumpets as God walking on earth, never received his vote. He measures his success purely in terms of media statistics — the number of stations in his syndicated empire, the number of weeks his books stay on the best-seller list, the Nielsen ratings for his T.V. show. He was absolutely exultant when Clinton won the election, knowing that a Republican party in opposition would bolster his appeal. "They think that my era of dominant influence has come crashing down," he roared. "It has, in fact, barely begun. My era of dominant influence now shall come to the fore."

What is that influence exactly, if not a strictly political one? Some have called Limbaugh a rabble-rouser in the mold of Father Coughlin or Huey Long. A better comparison, once again, would be Walter Winchell, the gossip columnist as national statesman. Limbaugh very often grasps ideology through personalities; he is constantly recounting his encounters with everyone from Margaret Thatcher to Charles Barkley. Commentary and comedy blend with news, anecdotes and a great many traditional radio bits (weird news, off-the-cuff endorsements) thrown in for good measure. But in the end, he is something completely new: a vertically integrated media complex for like-minded conservatives, plus entertainment for the broader mass of perennial skeptics. His appeal is actually more diverse than Letterman's, seeming to encompass more female viewers and more older viewers. Almost anyone from any group could be hooked by his bravura display of politics as entertainment, and vice versa, or whatever else you want to call it. As the opposite of the opposite of what used to be conservatism, Limbaugh can only fall back on his own burgeoning selfhood to hold together his political platform. Two of his favorite phrases are all too easily interchangeable: "This program is about the truth" and "This program is about what I think." The politics of ego become inseparable from the culture of irony.

And irony is what, after all, connects Limbaugh and Letterman and    35
the television history they both refract. Irony can only be recovered in reference to a dominant language, a dominant medium, and television is without question such a medium. Letterman has assumed authority by undercutting the host formula and pretending to hate his job. Limbaugh tries to unite conservative subcultures into a broad political base by piling skepticism on top of fuzzy nostalgia. Both connect with a culture that is viscerally alert to media manipulation, but that is also a sucker for self-consciousness.

They have their colleagues in the political arena. Ronald Reagan, the former announcer, used the tropes of television and a cunning wit to distance himself from the idea of himself, to create a stage persona that T.V. audiences found appealing on its own terms. The substance of his views had taken shape long before, but irony propelled them through the screen. George Bush, with little ironic talent, valiantly attempted to parlay Reagan's technique into a rationale for an entire administration. Even more telling is the example of Ross Perot, who mixes his super-direct facts and figures with a dazzling (and, it turns out, uncontrollable) defiance of expectations. A new plateau of ironic politics was officially reached when the Texan responded to intimations of mental instability by dancing with his daughter to the strains of Patsy Cline's "Crazy."

All politicians, of course, are ironists to the extent that they are all dissemblers. But the Democratic Party seems remarkably inept in the face of Letterman-Limbaugh culture. It has mastered guerrilla-level media manipulation, but its candidates perennially adopt an earnest tone that television cuts to shreds. The Clinton people, who ought to be young enough to know the territory by heart, show no grasp of irony at all. Al Gore put in a valiant appearance on Letterman's show, of which both he and Clinton seem to be fans; but the idea is to be a commanding host, not a well-behaved guest. Clinton himself — fathomlessly earnest and deaf to the nuances of Limbaugh's and Letterman's posturing — is at sea in a culture drenched in detachment. His frozen smile gives him the look of a sidekick handing out prizes.

Placing no distance between himself and his image, prizing an un-mediated communication with the voters, Clinton buys into the liberal illusion that there is a third choice, beyond radicalism and irony — a choice of reasonableness, decency, meaning. That may be why he has so far failed to connect intuitively and decisively with the American public of today, and why his strongest demographic group is still the elderly. Clinton has yet to grapple with the climate in which he is operating and with the culture that insistently refuses to take him to heart. If he wants to gain some ground, he could start by watching T.V. more closely after 11:35 p.m. The real Culture War, he might discover, has nothing what-soever to do with the religious right.

### Reading the Text

1. What does Ross mean when he says that Letterman and Limbaugh are connected by a shared sense of irony?
2. How, according to Ross, is Bill Clinton different from the political iro-nists?
3. How, in Ross's view, did Letterman's persona as a talk-show host evolve, and why has that persona become ever more popular?
4. How has Limbaugh used Letterman's style to fashion his own stage per-sona, as Ross sees it?
5. What does Ross mean when he asserts that "the politics of ego become inseparable from the culture of irony"?

### Reading the Signs

1. Watch an episode of *The Letterman Show* and write an essay supporting, challenging, or qualifying Ross's interpretation of Letterman's persona.
2. In class, form teams and debate Ross's contention that Rush Limbaugh should be seen as an entertainer, not a politician. To support your team's position, examine any of Limbaugh's media products: the TV or radio shows or any of his books.
3. If you are a fan of either Letterman or Limbaugh, write a journal entry in which you explore why one or both of the men appeal to you. If you don't care for either one of them, watch an episode of one of their shows and explore your responses to it.
4. Limbaugh has often been accused of inventing or distorting the facts that he offers his audience. Research this controversy and write an essay in which you argue whether this accusation is valid.
5. Read or reread Josh Ozersky's "TV's Anti-Families: Married . . . with Malaise" (p. 205) and write an essay in which you argue why irony has become so popular a tool in entertainment in the late 1990s. What values or cultural concerns does the ironic viewpoint suggest?

# THE HOLLYWOOD SIGN

## *The Culture of American Film*

**Y**ou don't have to go very far to capture the explicit message of one of the 1990s' most culturally significant movies: Oliver Stone's *Natural Born Killers*. Just read the jacket to the video cassette, where you can find it described as a "wickedly funny slam of violence and media obsession." Yes, that pretty much sums it up. *Natural Born Killers* is a grotesquely humorous send-up of a society that has given us everything from *America's Most Wanted* to the "Trial of the Century" — that media circus otherwise known as the O. J. Simpson trial. For that reason alone the movie merits close semiotic attention. But we include it in our introduction to the semiotics of American film for another reason as well. When you look beyond the disturbing images and plot line of *Natural Born Killers* that its creators clearly intended us to recognize, you may find another cultural message — the signifier of an emerging cultural mythology — that even Oliver Stone and Quentin Tarantino may not have consciously intended.

### Interpreting the Culture of American Film

So let's walk through a semiotic analysis of the film. Again, the first thing you need to do in your prewriting stage (that is, after watching the film) is to set aside your opinion of the movie. Whether you like it is not part of your analysis. Similarly, if you are tempted to think that this is just entertainment with no social or political significance, you might want to fast-forward to the end of the movie (watching a film on video is the best way to notice details) to the series of film clips that accompanies the rolling of the credits: Images of such celebrities of violence as Lyle Menendez, Tonya Harding, O. J. Simpson, and Lorena Bobbitt. As Leonard Cohen sings "I've seen the future, brother, and it's murder," and "When they said repent, I wondered what they meant," to such a backdrop, it is both visually and verbally clear what message Oliver Stone wants us to get: This is a movie about the sinister relationship between the American media and the "demon" of violence that lies within us.

Now, let's start at the beginning. We can't cite all of the visual and verbal cues in the film that guide us to its explicit meaning, but we'll mention a few. Be alert, even before the plot begins, to some significant images: First, black-and-white images of animals — coyotes and such — in the natural setting of the southwestern desert. Then, before the title appears, we see the contrasting image of a television screen filled with clips from old TV shows. This image is repeated when the meeting of the film's protagonists, Mickey and Mallory, is presented in a grotesque parody of an episode of *I Love Lucy,* which, as *I Love Mallory,* is presented complete with laugh track, wisecracks (with a vilely murderous undercurrent), and an over-the-top Rodney Dangerfield playing a brutal father with overtones of Archie Bunker.

This juxtaposition of nature and American pop culture — the coyote and the situation comedy — is itself a signifier for Stone, one that he repeats throughout the film. Indeed, one of the movie's most dramatic moments occurs when Mickey and Mallory meet up with a Navajo shaman who (representing an older, more balanced relationship with nature) recognizes the violent demon in the media-obsessed Mickey shortly before Mickey guns him down. Even Mallory objects to this murder, and Mickey himself feels sorry about it, as Stone symbolically presents the destruction of one way of life, the natural balance of Native American culture, by another, the high-tech world of postindustrial civilization.

Stone makes certain that his indictment of the media, especially television, is clear throughout the movie, from the constant projection of kitschy images of fifties-era TV families glued to the set to the savage parody of shows like *America's Most Wanted* played out in the adventures of Wayne Gale, host of *American Maniacs.* Consider Gale's boasting memories of being right there with the troops in Grenada, his ego-driven desire to go mano-a-mano with TV by interviewing America's sickest criminals, and his Australian accent. Gale is intended to strike us as a cross between Dan Rather and Geraldo Rivera, with a little Robin Leach thrown into the mix. And so we don't miss the point that it is people like Gale who have helped create the violent culture in which we live, Mickey tells Gale, just before he kills Gale, that "Killing you is a statement. I'm not 100 percent sure exactly what it's saying. But you know . . . Frankenstein killed Dr. Frankenstein."

To recognize all the film's media allusions, however, you have to know the *system* in which it functions. Without that knowledge, none of these details would signify anything. And indeed, Stone presumes that his viewers do know that system and are well acquainted with pop cultural phenomena such as *I Love Lucy, America's Most Wanted,* and the stars of today's infotainment world. To put this another way, that viewers are so well versed in the system of the American media is part of the film's meaning: It indicts us for being a part of the world that the film satirizes.

To make that point clear, Stone throws in all those wickedly funny clips of people reacting to the Mickey and Mallory story on episodes of *American Maniacs.* When a young fellow with GenX written all over him says that Mickey and Mallory are the "best thing to happen to mass murder since Manson" and "if I was a mass murderer, I'd be Mickey and Mallory," Stone is including you in his indictment. When Japanese teens coo about how "cool" Mickey and Mallory are and when the mobs outside the courthouse treat the murderers as if they were visiting royalty, Stone is going after more than the media: He's sending up the mass culture to which the mass media so successfully cater. This, after all, is the same culture that has turned the Super Bowl, that grand celebration of athletic violence, into a national ritual — which is why the film shows the climactic interview of Mickey on *American Maniacs* as being broadcast right after the Big Game.

The system in which *Natural Born Killers* functions also includes a Hollywood history filled with movies to which this movie implicitly and explicitly refers. Indeed, it is hard to watch a film about two sexy young killers who tool around in an old car, taking what they want and blasting away anyone they want, without thinking about that Hollywood icon from the 1960s: *Bonnie and Clyde.* But as is so often the case in a semiotic analysis, what matters here is less the resemblance between the two films than their difference. Or, rather, the resemblance sets up and accentuates the difference. Bonnie and Clyde, for example, were played by unqualifiedly glamorous Hollywood stars: Warren Beatty and Faye Dunaway. Mickey and Mallory's glamour, which echoes that of Beatty and Dunaway, is manifestly undercut by their kitschiness and the sheer gratuitousness of their violence (if you're tempted to identify with the glamorous rebels, Stone throws in a kidnapped sex slave whose innocent beauty and horrendous suffering ought to demonstrate the difference between Mickey and Mallory and Beatty's and Dunaway's murderous characters). Similarly, where Bonnie and Clyde perish in a brutal hail of police fire that triggered audience sympathy, Mickey and Mallory quite simply get away with it all. They kill *everyone* (even the loathsome Gale) and are last seen in their Winnebago, blithely driving along like an ordinary family with two happy kids and one on the way.

---

**Exploring the Signs of Film**

In your journal, list your favorite movies. Then consider your list: What does it say about you? What cultural myths do the movies tend to reflect, and why do you think those myths appeal to you? What signs particularly appeal to your emotions? What sort of stories about human life do you most respond to?

---

The *difference* between *Bonnie and Clyde* and *Natural Born Killers,* then, suggests that Stone's meaning is that the earlier film was a part of a media-saturated society that glamorizes sex and violence. By making the real-life killers so sympathetic, *Bonnie and Clyde* only made things worse. The result is a world in which violence has gone so out of control that *everyone* is implicated — from the facile killers Mickey and Mallory themselves, to their adoring fans, from the men like Wayne Gale who profit on violence, to such vile representatives of law and order as Scagnetti (the cop who's a sex killer himself) and McClosky, Tommy Lee Jones's over-the-top prison warden. And in such a world, the killers logically have to get away with it, because as metaphors for a world where violence has taken over, Mickey and Mallory can't be stopped. Just as they escape never to be caught again, American violence continues on its demonic way.

This is the message we may find in the story and images of *Natural Born Killers*. It's the message Stone wants us to get. But let's go a little further. What other implications may we find in this film?

### Natural Born Cynics

Let's look at some details that the critics skimmed over in their reviews of *Natural Born Killers*. As we've seen, it's hard to miss Stone's indictment of the contemporary mass media. But he equally goes after every other authority figure, from brutal parents to brutal cops. This action presents a certain paradox. Stone dares us to identify with Mickey and Mallory by making them joyous rebels (after all, they "liberate" Mallory's kid brother), only to shock us into realizing just how vile they really are (Stone throws in plenty of little touches to make sure we realize this: You could put together a catalog of such signals in a prewriting exercise). But given the horror Mickey and Mallory inspire, you might think that the film would cause us to side with those who at least attempt to stop them. Nothing doing. Scagnetti is in bed, figuratively speaking, with the media that stoke the flames of American violence and profit

---

**Discussing the Signs of Film**

In any given year, one film may dominate the Hollywood box office, becoming a blockbuster that captures the public's cinematic
imagination. In class, discuss which film would be your choice as
this year's top hit. Then analyze the film semiotically. Why has
*this* film so successfully appealed to so many moviegoers?

---

from it in his role as a best-selling, tell-all paperback author. And we see
him literally in bed revealed as a pathological sex killer himself.
McClosky, the man in charge of the punishment of merciless killers like
Mickey and Mallory, isn't much better. McClosky is a vulgar sadist, and
his apparent death at the hands of the rioting prison inmates is not likely
to be mourned by many viewers. What significance might we find in this
situation?

First of all, it would be perfectly possible to write an essay arguing
that the kind of world that Stone depicts — a world of easy killing and
lax punishment — calls for a strengthening of our nation's forces of law
and order and a renewed respect for authority. You might want to write
such an essay. But it definitely isn't Stone's point of view. In Stone's
world, everyone is implicated. He presents no heroes. As *Dragnet*'s Joe
Friday becomes Scagnetti, we see an America in which the authorities
are just as bad as the crooks.

When we place this fact in a larger cultural context, we find the
emergence of a new mythology. Where American film (and society)
once valued certain kinds of heroes, men or women who protected and
served society (Robert Ray's "The Thematic Paradigm" explores this
mythology on pp. 278–287), a new view is emerging in which such
heroism is no longer possible. No one, in this system, is any better than
anyone else. The cops are just as bad as the psychopaths; the audience is
just as fatuous as the media that cater to it. From the widespread voter rejection of politicians to the apparent message of *Natural Born Killers* —
that no one is in a position to save America from itself because everyone
is guilty — we find the emergence of a mythology of cynical despair.
"We're all to blame, so what can we do?" is the ethos of such a worldview, and it is being translated into a reality of low voter turnout in
America and a general dissatisfaction with the political system. Indeed,
have you, or someone you know, ever neglected to vote because "politicians are all the same" or because "my vote wouldn't make any difference anyway"?

That, we believe, is the larger semiotic message behind *Natural Born
Killers,* a message that reveals the film as the implicit reflection of a

worldview of which its creators were not necessarily consciously aware. By showing us a world in which everything is morally equal (Mickey insists that his murderous rampage is no different from the carnage incessantly inflicted upon nature, and a TV psychologist remarks that Mickey and Mallory know the difference between good and evil but "they just don't give a damn"), the creators of *Natural Born Killers* fit into a larger cultural system: the *postmodern* system.

## The Postmodern Mythology

In the postmodern worldview, the traditional distinctions we make between things — high culture versus low culture, morality versus immorality, creativity versus imitation — tend to get flattened out. What was once viewed in terms of an oppositional hierarchy — e.g., creativity is opposed to imitation and is superior to it — is reconceived as a complex relationship between equals. Take the way *Natural Born Killers* is at once creative and derivative. It is its own film, but it is built upon imitation, parody, and direct quotation from other media sources. Throughout the movie we are presented with film images that are either drawn directly from the film archive as clips or are recreated as parodies of such images (for instance, all those cartoon sequences included in the movie). The movie alludes, as we've seen, to such earlier films as *Bonnie and Clyde,* and also to *Network,* Paddy Cheyevsky's indictment of 1970s TV. Such allusions and repetitions of existing cultural images is one of the hallmarks of postmodern filmmaking, and of postmodern culture, in which creation consists not in the invention of a new code but in the repetition of existing codes, something often called "double coding."

To put this another way, the postmodern style reflects a worldview that holds it is no longer possible or desirable to create new characters or images in movies; rather, one surveys the vast range of available images that old movies (and the electronic media in general) offer and repeats them, but with a difference. Consider what Madonna does with the image of Marilyn Monroe in her video *Material Girl,* a half-serious, half-parodic remake of Monroe's film *Gentlemen Prefer Blondes.* In the video, Madonna both resembles Marilyn Monroe and doesn't. Her image recycles an existing cultural icon — Marilyn — but with a new spin. It's the same, and not the same, simultaneously.

The sense of parody, of repetition with a difference, is crucial, for many films may repeat old images but may not be at all postmodern. Disney's cartoon *Beauty and the Beast* repeats an old story, but the film is a romantic fantasy, not a postmodern parody. *Monty Python and the Holy Grail,* in contrast, is a purely postmodern spoof of the ancient tales of King Arthur and his court. The movie retells the old story of the quest for the Holy Grail — but oh, what a difference! It's that zany difference, that repetition of what we've already seen somewhere but with a comic edge that mocks even as it retells, that sets off the truly postmodern flick.

All that zaniness is there in *Natural Born Killers* — the send-ups of newscasters, other action films (it is, after all, an action film of sorts that parodies the easy violence of, say, Schwarzenegger or Stallone), the repetition of all those images from old sitcoms — but with the serious suggestion that there's no way out. We're trapped in a world of endless repetition, of violent act repeating violent act, broadcast on the screen, there to be imitated by others in an endless cycle of escalating violence.

## Reading the Hollywood Sign: The Poetics of Cinema

The semiotic analysis of a film, then, goes beyond the words and story to analyze the way in which it can transform visual images into metaphors and symbols with profound cultural significance. And it doesn't have to be the postmodern product of such a politically self-conscious director as Oliver Stone to do so.

Consider the Godzilla films of the 1950s. If we study only their plots, we would see little more than horror stories featuring a reptilian monster rather like the dragons of medieval literature. But Godzilla was no mere dragon transported to the modern world. The dragons that populate the world of medieval storytelling were often metaphors for Satan or for the serpent in the Garden of Eden, but Godzilla was a wholly different sort of metaphor. Created by Japanese filmmakers, Godzilla arose from a biological mutation caused by nuclear contamination. She represented nuclear war itself, the overwhelming power of the bomb, which the Japanese alone have experienced. Similarly, all those "blob" movies, all the B horror films featuring laboratory experiments run amok, functioned as metaphors, as signifiers of a cultural fear that science — especially nuclear science — was leading not to progress but to annihilation.

Filmmakers work with smaller metaphors as well, using visual cues to clue their viewers in on the meaning of their films. At the end of the 1950s' classic *Giant,* for example, we see a tableau of a white baby goat standing next to a black baby goat, and then of a white baby standing in a crib side by side with a brown baby. The human babies are the grandchildren of the film's hero, played by Rock Hudson, one of whose sons had married a woman of Mexican extraction. By the end of the film, racial harmony is established through these first cousins, whose partial racial difference symbolizes the film's hopes for a future of harmonious relations between Texans of Anglo and Mexican heritage. The film's director adds those goats to make sure we get the point.

Although it is a director's job to use signs creatively, films can also contain mythic signs that their directors may not be conscious of.

**Reading Film on the Net**

Most major films now released in the United States receive their own web site. You can find them listed in print ads for the film (check your local newspaper) or visit a list of links to the major film studios at http://www.afionline.org/CINEMEDIA/Cinemedia.studios.html/. Select a current film, find the web address, log on, and analyze the film's site semiotically. What images are used to attract your interest in the film? What interactive strategies, if any, are used to increase your commitment to the film? If you've seen the movie, how does the Net presentation of it compare with your experience viewing either in a theater or on video?

Mythological structures — the heroic types, for example, that appear in American cinema as official and outlaw heroes — can tell you about the culture of a film, the unspoken presuppositions held by directors and viewers alike. Interpreting a film semiotically, then, includes the analysis both of its director's intentions and of the culture to which the director belongs. The one type of analysis tends to be more aesthetically oriented, the other more sociological or anthropological. Which type you choose (of course, both may be pursued simultaneously) depends upon your purposes. If you are writing an analysis of the films of a particular director, you may want to concentrate on decoding his or her own visual metaphors and semiotic cues; if you are searching for the pulse of American society, you may prefer to look for myths that the directors themselves may not be aware of *as myths*. In analyses of this type, one needn't be concerned with the director's intentions. Often a film's cultural significance is invisible to its creator.

Reading a film, then, is much like reading a poem or a novel. Both are texts filled with intentional and unintentional signs. The major difference is in the medium of expression. Literary texts are cast entirely in written words; films combine verbal language, visual imagery, and sound effects. We perceive literary and cinematic texts differently, of course, for the written sign is perceived in a linear fashion that relies upon one's cognitive and imaginative powers, while a film primarily targets the senses: One sees and hears (and sometimes even smells!). That film is such a sensory experience often conceals its textuality. One is tempted to sit back and go with the flow, to say that it's only entertainment and doesn't have to "mean" anything at all. But as cinematic forms of storytelling overtake written forms of expression, the study of movies as complex texts bearing cultural messages and values is becoming more and more important. Our "libraries" are increasingly to be found in mini-malls, where the texts of Hollywood can be had for two dollars a night. There's a lot to read.

## The Readings

The readings in this chapter address the various myths that pervade Hollywood films, starting with Robert B. Ray's analysis of the ways in which America's official and outlaw heroes appear both in the cinema and in history. Sandra Tsing Loh follows with a report on the return of another mythic figure to American cinema, the Good Girl, exemplified by everyone from that "mother of all modern Good Girls," Doris Day, to that savior of virtual culture, Sandra Bullock. Benjamin DeMott's indictment of Hollywood's tendency to mask the grim realities of America's racial history behind "happy faced" images of black/white friendship and solidarity complements Jessica Hagedorn's survey of a history of American filmmaking in which Asian women are presented as either tragic or trivial. In both cases, these authors critically review the ways in which Hollywood mythologizes non-European subjects. Tania Modleski then takes on Hollywood's erasure of homosexuality in such films as *Dead Poet's Society,* while Michael Parenti provides a social class-based approach to the codes of American cinema. Michael Medved offers an opinion piece on the controversy over the effect of violent entertainment on American behavior, and Shelby Steele concludes the chapter by tackling Malcolm X, the man and the movie, offering a surprising take on one of black America's leading outlaw heroes.

# ROBERT B. RAY
## The Thematic Paradigm

*Usually we consider movies to be merely entertainment, but as Robert Ray (b. 1943) demonstrates in this selection from his book* A Certain Tendency of the Hollywood Cinema *(1985), American films have long reflected fundamental patterns and contradictions in our society's myths and values. Whether in real life or on the silver screen, Ray explains, Americans have always been ambivalent about the value of civilization, celebrating it through official heroes like George Washington and Jimmy Stewart, while at the same time questioning it through outlaw heroes like Davy Crockett and Jesse James. Especially when presented together in the same film, these two hero types help mediate America's ambivalence, providing a mythic solution. Ray's analyses show how the movies are rich sources for cultural interpretation; they provide a framework for decoding movies as different as* Lethal Weapon *and* Malcolm X. *Robert Ray is a professor and director of Film Media Studies at the University of Florida, Gainesville. His most recent publication is* The Avant Garde Finds Andy Hardy *(1995).*

The dominant tradition of American cinema consistently found ways to overcome dichotomies. Often, the movies' reconciliatory pattern concentrated on a single character magically embodying diametrically opposite traits. A sensitive violinist was also a tough boxer (*Golden Boy*); a boxer was a gentle man who cared for pigeons (*On the Waterfront*). A gangster became a coward because he was brave (*Angels with Dirty Faces*); a soldier became brave because he was a coward (*Lives of a Bengal Lancer*). A war hero was a former pacifist (*Sergeant York*); a pacifist was a former war hero (*Billy Jack*). The ideal was a kind of inclusiveness that would permit all decisions to be undertaken with the knowledge that the alternative was equally available. The attractiveness of Destry's refusal to use guns (*Destry Rides Again*) depended on the tacit understanding that he could shoot with the best of them, Katharine Hepburn's and Claudette Colbert's revolts against conventionality (*Holiday, It Happened One Night*) on their status as aristocrats.

Such two-sided characters seemed particularly designed to appeal to a collective American imagination steeped in myths of inclusiveness. Indeed, in creating such characters, classic Hollywood had connected with what Erik Erikson has described as the fundamental American psychological pattern:

The functioning American, as the heir of a history of extreme contrasts and abrupt changes, bases his final ego identity on some tentative combination of dynamic polarities such as migratory and sedentary, individualistic and standardized, competitive and co-operative, pious and free-thinking, responsible and cynical, etc. . . .

To leave his choices open, the American, on the whole, lives with two sets of "truths."[1]

The movies traded on one opposition in particular, American culture's traditional dichotomy of individual and community that had generated the most significant pair of competing myths: the outlaw hero and the official hero.[2] Embodied in the adventurer, explorer, gunfighter, wanderer, and loner, the outlaw hero stood for that part of the American imagination valuing self-determination and freedom from entanglements. By contrast, the official hero, normally portrayed as a teacher, lawyer, politician, farmer, or family man, represented the American belief in collective action, and the objective legal process that superseded private notions of right and wrong. While the outlaw hero found incarnations in the mythic figures of Davy Crockett, Jesse James, Huck Finn, and all of Leslie Fiedler's "Good Bad Boys" and Daniel Boorstin's "ring-tailed roarers," the official hero developed around legends associated with Washington, Jefferson, Lincoln, Lee, and other "Good Good Boys."

An extraordinary amount of the traditional American mythology adopted by Classic Hollywood derived from the variations worked by American ideology around this opposition of natural man versus civilized man. To the extent that these variations constituted the main tendency of American literature and legends, Hollywood, in relying on this mythology, committed itself to becoming what Robert Bresson has called "the Cinema."[3] A brief description of the competing values associated with this outlaw hero–official hero opposition will begin to suggest its pervasiveness in traditional American culture.

1. *Aging:* The attractiveness of the outlaw hero's childishness and propensity to whims, tantrums, and emotional decisions derived from America's cult of childhood. Fiedler observed that American literature celebrated "the notion that a mere falling short of adulthood is a guarantee of insight and even innocence." From Huck to Holden Caulfield,

———————

1. Erik H. Erikson, *Childhood and Society* (New York: Norton, 1963), p. 286.

2. Leading discussions of the individual-community polarity in American culture can be found in *The Contrapuntal Civilization: Essays Toward a New Understanding of the American Experience,* ed. Michael Kammen (New York: Crowell, 1971). The most prominent analyses of American literature's use of this opposition remain Leslie A. Fiedler's *Love and Death in the American Novel* (New York: Stein and Day, 1966) and A. N. Kaul's *The American Vision* (New Haven: Yale University Press, 1963).

3. Robert Bresson, *Notes on Cinematography,* trans. Jonathan Griffin (New York: Urizen Books, 1977), p. 12.

children in American literature were privileged, existing beyond society's confining rules. Often, they set the plot in motion (e.g., *Intruder in the Dust, To Kill a Mockingbird*), acting for the adults encumbered by daily affairs. As Fiedler also pointed out, this image of childhood "has impinged upon adult life itself, has become a 'career' like everything else in America,"[4] generating stories like *On the Road* or *Easy Rider* in which adults try desperately to postpone responsibilities by clinging to adolescent life-styles.

While the outlaw heroes represented a flight from maturity, the official heroes embodied the best attributes of adulthood: sound reasoning and judgment, wisdom and sympathy based on experience. Franklin's *Autobiography* and *Poor Richard's Almanack* constituted this opposing tradition's basic texts, persuasive enough to appeal even to outsiders (*The Great Gatsby*). Despite the legends surrounding Franklin and the other Founding Fathers, however, the scarcity of mature heroes in American literature and mythology indicated American ideology's fundamental preference for youth, a quality that came to be associated with the country itself. Indeed, American stories often distorted the stock figure of the Wise Old Man, portraying him as mad (Ahab), useless (Rip Van Winkle), or evil (the Godfather).

2. *Society and Women:* The outlaw hero's distrust of civilization, typically represented by women and marriage, constituted a stock motif in American mythology. In his *Studies in Classic American Literature,* D. H. Lawrence detected the recurring pattern of flight, observing that the Founding Fathers had come to America "largely to get *away*. . . . Away from what? In the long run, away from themselves. Away from everything."[5] Sometimes, these heroes undertook this flight alone (Thoreau, *Catcher in the Rye*); more often, they joined ranks with other men: Huck with Jim, Ishmael with Queequeg, Jake Barnes with Bill Gorton. Women were avoided as representing the very entanglements this tradition sought to escape: society, the "settled life," confining responsibilities. The outlaw hero sought only uncompromising relationships, involving either a "bad" woman (whose morals deprived her of all rights to entangling domesticity) or other males (who themselves remained independent). Even the "bad" woman posed a threat, since marriage often uncovered the clinging "good" girl underneath. Typically, therefore, American stories avoided this problem by killing off the

4. Leslie A. Fiedler, *No! In Thunder* (New York: Stein and Day, 1972), pp. 253, 275.

5. D. H. Lawrence, *Studies in Classic American Literature* (New York: Viking/Compass, 1961), p. 3. See also Fiedler's *Love and Death in the American Novel* and Sam Bluefarb's *The Escape Motif in the American Novel: Mark Twain to Richard Wright* (Columbus: Ohio State University Press, 1972).

"bad" woman before the marriage could transpire (*Destry Rides Again, The Big Heat, The Far Country*). Subsequently, within the all-male group, women became taboo, except as the objects of lust.

The exceptional extent of American outlaw legends suggests an ideological anxiety about civilized life. Often, that anxiety took shape as a romanticizing of the dispossessed, as in the Beat Generation's cult of the bum, or the characters of Huck and "Thoreau," who worked to remain idle, unemployed, and unattached. A passage from Jerzy Kosinski's *Steps* demonstrated the extreme modern version of this romanticizing:

> I envied those [the poor and the criminals] who lived here and seemed so free, having nothing to regret and nothing to look forward to. In the world of birth certificates, medical examinations, punch cards, and computers, in the world of telephone books, passports, bank accounts, insurance plans, wills, credit cards, pensions, mortgages and loans, they lived unattached.[6]

In contrast to the outlaw heroes, the official heroes were preeminently worldly, comfortable in society, and willing to undertake even those public duties demanding personal sacrifice. Political figures, particularly Washington and Lincoln, provided the principal examples of this tradition, but images of family also persisted in popular literature from *Little Women* to *Life with Father* and *Cheaper by the Dozen*. The most crucial figure in this tradition, however, was Horatio Alger, whose heroes' ambition provided the complement to Huck's disinterest. Alger's characters subscribed fully to the codes of civilization, devoting themselves to proper dress, manners, and behavior, and the attainment of the very things despised by the opposing tradition: the settled life and respectability.[7]

3. *Politics and the Law:* Writing about "The Philosophical Approach of the Americans," Tocqueville noted "a general distaste for accepting any man's word as proof of anything." That distaste took shape as a traditional distrust of politics as collective activity, and of ideology as that activity's rationale. Such a disavowal of ideology was, of course, itself ideological, a tactic for discouraging systematic political intervention in a nineteenth-century America whose political and economic power remained in the hands of a privileged few. Tocqueville himself noted the results of this mythology of individualism which "disposes each citizen to isolate himself from the mass of his fellows and withdraw into the circle

10

---

6. Jerzy Kosinski, *Steps* (New York: Random House, 1968), p. 133.
7. See John G. Cawelti, *Apostles of the Self-Made Man: Changing Concepts of Success in America* (Chicago: University of Chicago Press, 1965), pp. 101–123.

of family and friends; with this little society formed to his taste, he gladly leaves the greater society to look after itself."[8]

This hostility toward political solutions manifested itself further in an ambivalence about the law. The outlaw mythology portrayed the law, the sum of society's standards, as a collective, impersonal ideology imposed on the individual from without. Thus, the law represented the very thing this mythology sought to avoid. In its place, this tradition offered a natural law discovered intuitively by each man. As Tocqueville observed, Americans wanted "To escape from imposed systems . . . to seek by themselves and in themselves for the only reason for things . . . in most mental operations each American relies on individual effort and judgment" (p. 429). This sense of the law's inadequacy to needs detectable only by the heart generated a rich tradition of legends celebrating legal defiance in the name of some "natural" standard: Thoreau went to jail rather than pay taxes, Huck helped Jim (legally a slave) to escape, Billy the Kid murdered the sheriff's posse that had ambushed his boss, Hester Prynne resisted the community's sexual mores. This mythology transformed all outlaws into Robin Hoods, who "correct" socially unjust laws (Jesse James, Bonnie and Clyde, John Wesley Harding). Furthermore, by customarily portraying the law as the tool of villains (who used it to revoke mining claims, foreclose on mortgages, and disallow election results — all on legal technicalities), this mythology betrayed a profound pessimism about the individual's access to the legal system.

If the outlaw hero's motto was "I don't know what the law says, but I do know what's right and wrong," the official hero's was "We are a nation of laws, not of men," or "No man can place himself above the law." To the outlaw hero's insistence on private standards of right and wrong, the official hero offered the admonition, "You cannot take the law into your own hands." Often, these official heroes were lawyers or politicians, at times (as with Washington and Lincoln), even the executors of the legal system itself. The values accompanying such heroes modified the assurance of Crockett's advice, "Be sure you're right, then go ahead."

In sum, the values associated with these two different sets of heroes contrasted markedly. Clearly, too, each tradition had its good and bad points. If the extreme individualism of the outlaw hero always verged on selfishness, the respectability of the official hero always threatened to involve either blandness or repression. If the outlaw tradition promised adventure and freedom, it also offered danger and loneliness. If the official

---

8. Alexis de Tocqueville, *Democracy in America,* ed. J. P. Mayer, trans. George Lawrence (Garden City, N.Y.: Anchor/Doubleday, 1969), pp. 430, 506. Irving Howe has confirmed Tocqueville's point, observing that Americans "make the suspicion of ideology into something approaching a national creed." *Politics and the Novel* (New York: Avon, 1970), p. 337.

tradition promised safety and comfort, it also offered entanglements and boredom.

The evident contradiction between these heroes provoked Daniel Boorstin's observation that "Never did a more incongruous pair than Davy Crockett and George Washington live together in a national Valhalla." And yet, as Boorstin admits, "both Crockett and Washington were popular heroes, and both emerged into legendary fame during the first half of the 19th century."[9]

The parallel existence of these two contradictory traditions evinced the general pattern of American mythology: the denial of the necessity for choice. In fact, this mythology often portrayed situations requiring decision as temporary aberrations from American life's normal course. By discouraging commitment to any single set of values, this mythology fostered an ideology of improvisation, individualism, and ad hoc solutions for problems depicted as crises. American writers have repeatedly attempted to justify this mythology in terms of material sources. Hence, Irving Howe's "explanation":

> It is when men no longer feel that they have adequate choices in their styles of life, when they conclude that there are no longer possibilities of honorable maneuver and compromise, when they decide that the time has come for "ultimate" social loyalties and political decisions — it is then that ideology begins to flourish. Ideology reflects a hardening of commitment, the freezing of opinion into system. . . . The uniqueness of our history, the freshness of our land, the plenitude of our resources — all these have made possible, and rendered plausible, a style of political improvisation and intellectual free-wheeling.[10]

Despite such an account's pretext of objectivity, its language betrays an acceptance of the mythology it purports to describe: "honorable maneuver and compromise," "hardening," "freezing," "uniqueness," "freshness," and "plenitude" are all assumptive words from an ideology that denies its own status. Furthermore, even granting the legitimacy of the historians' authenticating causes, we are left with a persisting mythology increasingly discredited by historical developments. (In fact, such invalidation began in the early nineteenth century, and perhaps even before.)

The American mythology's refusal to choose between its two heroes went beyond the normal reconciliatory function attributed to myth by Lévi-Strauss. For the American tradition not only overcame binary oppositions; it systematically mythologized the certainty of being able to do so. Part of this process involved blurring the lines between the two sets of heroes. First, legends often brought the solemn official heroes back down

15

---

9. Daniel J. Boorstin, *The Americans: The National Experience* (New York: Random House, 1965), p. 337.

10. *Politics and the Novel,* p. 164.

to earth, providing the sober Washington with the cherry tree, the prudent Franklin with illegitimate children, and even the upright Jefferson with a slave mistress. On the other side, stories modified the outlaw hero's most potentially damaging quality, his tendency to selfish isolationism, by demonstrating that, however reluctantly, he would act for causes beyond himself. Thus, Huck grudgingly helped Jim escape, and Davy Crockett left the woods for three terms in Congress before dying in the Alamo for Texas independence. In this blurring process, Lincoln, a composite of opposing traits, emerged as the great American figure. His status as president made him an ex officio official hero. But his Western origins, melancholy solitude, and unaided decision-making all qualified him as a member of the other side. Finally, his ambivalent attitude toward the law played the most crucial role in his complex legend. As the chief executive, he inevitably stood for the principle that "we are a nation of laws and not men"; as the Great Emancipator, on the other hand, he provided the prime example of taking the law into one's own hands in the name of some higher standard.

Classic Hollywood's gallery of composite heroes (boxing musicians, rebellious aristocrats, pacifist soldiers) clearly derived from this mythology's rejection of final choices, a tendency whose traces Erikson detected in American psychology:

> The process of American identity formation seems to support an individual's ego identity as long as he can preserve a certain element of deliberate tentativeness of autonomous choice. The individual must be able to convince himself that the next step is up to him and that no matter where he is staying or going he always had the choice of leaving or turning in the opposite direction if he chooses to do so. In this country the migrant does not want to be told to move on, nor the sedentary man to stay where he is; for the life style (and the family history) of each contains the opposite element as a potential alternative which he wishes to consider his most private and individual decision.[11]

The reconciliatory pattern found its most typical incarnation, however, in one particular narrative: the story of the private man attempting to keep from being drawn into action on any but his own terms. In this story, the reluctant hero's ultimate willingness to help the community satisfied the official values. But by portraying this aid as demanding only a temporary involvement, the story preserved the values of individualism as well.

Like the contrasting heroes' epitomization of basic American dichotomies, the reluctant hero story provided a locus for displacement. Its most famous version, for example, *Adventures of Huckleberry Finn,* offered

---

11. *Childhood and Society,* p. 286.

a typically individualistic solution to the nation's unresolved racial and sectional anxieties, thereby helping to forestall more systematic governmental measures. In adopting this story, Classic Hollywood retained its censoring power, using it, for example, in *Casablanca* to conceal the realistic threats to American self-determination posed by World War II.

Because the reluctant hero story was clearly the basis of the Western, American literature's repeated use of it prompted Leslie Fiedler to call the classic American novels "disguised westerns."[12] In the movies, too, this story appeared in every genre: in Westerns, of course (with *Shane* its most schematic articulation), but also in gangster movies (*Angels with Dirty Faces, Key Largo*), musicals (*Swing Time*), detective stories (*The Thin Man*), war films (*Air Force*), screwball comedy (*The Philadelphia Story*), "problem pictures" (*On the Waterfront*), and even science fiction (the Han Solo character in *Star Wars*). *Gone with the Wind,* in fact, had two selfish heroes who came around at the last moment, Scarlett (taking care of Melanie) and Rhett (running the Union blockade), incompatible only because they were so much alike. The natural culmination of this pattern, perfected by Hollywood in the 1930s and early 1940s, was *Casablanca*. Its version of the outlaw hero–official hero struggle (Rick versus Laszlo) proved stunningly effective, its resolution (their collaboration on the war effort) the prototypical Hollywood ending.

The reluctant hero story's tendency to minimize the official hero's    20
role (by making him dependent on the outsider's intervention) suggested an imbalance basic to the American mythology: Despite the existence of both heroes, the national ideology clearly preferred the outlaw. This ideology strove to make that figure's origins seem spontaneous, concealing the calculated, commercial efforts behind the mythologizing of typical examples like Billy the Kid and Davy Crockett. Its willingness, on the other hand, to allow the official hero's traces to show enables Daniel Boorstin to observe of one such myth, "There were elements of spontaneity, of course, in the Washington legend, too, but it was, for the most part, a self-conscious product."[13]

The apparent spontaneity of the outlaw heroes assured their popularity. By contrast, the official values had to rely on a rational allegiance that often wavered. These heroes' different statuses accounted for a structure fundamental to American literature, and assumed by Classic Hollywood: a split between the moral center and the interest center of a story. Thus, while the typical Western contained warnings against violence as a solution, taking the law into one's own hands, and moral isolationism, it simultaneously glamorized the outlaw hero's intense self-possession and willingness to use force to settle what the law could not. In other cir-

---

12. *Love and Death in the American Novel,* p. 355.
13. *The Americans: The National Experience,* p. 337.

cumstances, Ishmael's evenhanded philosophy paled beside Ahab's moral vehemence, consciously recognizable as destructive.

D. H. Lawrence called this split the profound "duplicity" at the heart of nineteenth-century American fiction, charging that the classic novels evinced "a tight mental allegiance to a morality which all [the author's] passion goes to destroy." Certainly, too, this "duplicity" involved the mythology's pattern of obscuring the necessity for choosing between contrasting values. Richard Chase has put the matter less pejoratively in an account that applies equally to the American cinema:

> The American novel tends to rest in contradictions and among extreme ranges of experience. When it attempts to resolve contradictions, it does so in oblique, morally equivocal ways. As a general rule it does so either in melodramatic actions or in pastoral idylls, although intermixed with both one may find the stirring instabilities of "American humor."[14]

Or, in other words, when faced with a difficult choice, American stories resolved it either simplistically (by refusing to acknowledge that a choice is necessary), sentimentally (by blurring the differences between the two sides), or by laughing the whole thing off.

## Reading the Text

1. What are the two basic hero types that Ray describes in American cinema?
2. How do these two hero types relate to America's "psychological pattern"?
3. Explain why, according to Ray, the outlaw hero typically mistrusts women.

## Reading the Signs

1. In "Malcolm X" (p. 325), Shelby Steele offers his reading of Malcolm X as a cinematic hero. Review Steele's selection and compare his analysis with Ray's discussion of heroes. To what extent does Ray's essay shed light on Malcolm's status as a hero?
2. Read Gary Engle's "What Makes Superman So Darned American?" (p. 344) and Andy Medhurst's "Batman, Deviance, and Camp" (p. 358) and write an essay in which you explain which type of heroes Superman and Batman are to their audiences.
3. What sort of hero is Arnold Schwarzenegger in the *Terminator* films? Write an essay in which you apply Ray's categories of hero to the

---

14. Richard Chase, *The American Novel and Its Tradition* (Garden City, N.Y.: Anchor/Doubleday, 1957), p. 1.

Schwarzenegger character, supporting your argument with specific references to one or more films.

4. In class, note on the blackboard any official and outlaw heroes you've seen in movies. Then categorize these heroes according to characteristics they have in common (such as race, gender, profession, or social class). What patterns emerge in your categories, and what is the significance of those patterns?

5. Rent one of the *Alien* films and discuss whether Sigourney Weaver fits either of Ray's two categories of hero.

6. Cartoon characters such as Bart Simpson and Ren of *Ren and Stimpy* don't readily fit Ray's two types of hero. Invent a third type of hero to accommodate such characters.

SANDRA TSING LOH

## The Return of Doris Day

|||||||||||||||||||||||||||||||||||||||||||||||||||||||||||||||||||

*Madonna is out and Doris Day is in, according to Sandra Tsing Loh's (b. 1962) pop cultural analysis, first published in* Buzz *magazine. Bad girls may have ruled the Hollywood roost in the eighties, Loh observes, but the success of actresses like Sandra Bullock shows that good girls are making a comeback in the nineties. A journalist with a B.S. in physics from Cal Tech, Loh writes widely on popular cultural topics and has published a collection of essays entitled* Depth Takes a Holiday: Essays From Lesser Los Angeles *(1996). She is a contributing editor for* Buzz.

The seventies and eighties were tough times for us Good Girls. As polite people, we like to do what's expected of us. Unfortunately, what was expected, in our sexual heyday, was for Girls to be . . . anything but Good.

In junior high, I dutifully grappled with whatever icky senior boy that Spin the Bottle sent me. By college, my sisters and I had graduated to smoking pot and swimming nude in the Sierras, sleeping with men on the first date (or before — you're welcome!), and developing evasive "mumble vaguely and give back rubs" routines if forced into a threesome.

We were lost, I tell you. Lost. But not anymore. Recently I was faced with a Nude Hot Tub Situation. It was a tame one by eighties standards. The tub was vast, the night was dark, and my companions were three platonic male friends — thirtysomethings like me stooped with worry, hardly a threat.

"C'mon!" I heard that inner coach urging me. It was the voice born in 1975, when everyone in my junior high had Chemin de Fer jeans and Candie's sandals. *Don't be a drag,* it said. *Take off your clothes and jump in!*

But then, for the first time, I heard another voice. Clear as a bell, it  5
was the soaring soprano of Mary Martin in *South Pacific,* or perhaps Shirley Jones in *Oklahoma!* It sang:

> *I've got a guy!*
> *A really great guy!*
> *He makes me as high*
> *As an elephant's eye!*

Or something to that effect. It was like a light bulb going on. Suddenly I felt right with my world — fresh, natural, confident, all the panty-shield adjectives. It was so simple, so clear. The wandering days of these breasts were over.

"If you'd known me in my twenties," I lecture my hot tub companions, as though sharing an amazing story from ancient lore, "you would have seen my boobs and seen them often!" I'm in the water now, but demurely covered in my white cotton T-shirt from Victoria's Secret. (A white cotton T-shirt is typical of what we women actually *buy* there.) "But no more." I lift a teacherly finger. "Today, I feel much more liberated keeping my shirt on. I don't have to prove anything anymore. I can turn the world on with a smile!" I hear myself excitedly half-singing, flashing on Mary Tyler Moore.

My treatise is cut short by the arrival of two 24-year-old modern dancers who rip off towels and flash their naked pink everything. The men's attention snaps away with the zing of taut bungee cords. But I don't feel bad. I know it's only I, Goody Two Shoes, who feels that wonderful glowing specialness inside.

## I. Good Girls: A Cleaned and Buffed Thumbnail History

Were our moms actually right way back when? Maybe so. Because like it or not, these days Good Girls are back in. Demure behavior is suddenly clever, fashionable, even attractive.

Who *is* the nineties Good Girl? She is: (a) spunky; (b) virginal; (c)  10
busy with purposeful activity. But not obsessively so. Her hormones are in balance. Brave chin up, she works within society's rules, finds much to celebrate in her immediate surroundings, makes the best of her lot. Good Girls don't challenge the status quo.

Good Girls have been around a long time in Western culture. The star of the very first novel in English? A Good Girl! We find her in Samuel Richardson's 1740 opus, *Pamela.* In it, Pamela's resistance to sex charges five-hundred-plus pages of narrative tension; it's so effective a gambit that Good Girls (typically poor but beautiful governesses) become the very foundation of the eighteenth- and nineteenth-century novel.

It is in twentieth-century America, however, that we start to see the rowdy Good Girl. She does more than keep her knees crossed. In fact, if so moved, she may even spread her legs boldly akimbo! (If only to punctuate a funny singalong.)

The forties and fifties brought the U.S. Good Girl her two most sacred boons: World War II, and Rodgers & Hammerstein. The former yielded new busy-but-virginal archetypes like Rosie the Riveter, the Andrews Sisters, and the Chipper Navy Nurse. The latter fleshed out the canon via the Feisty Governess of the past (Anna in *The King and I*), the Chipper Navy Nurse of the semipresent (Nellie Forbush in *South Pacific*), even the boldly innovative Frisky Nun of the future (Julie Andrews in *The Sound of Music*). Indeed, Frisky Nun proved so popular she'd soon hop mediums and become TV's *The Flying Nun* (comical ex-Gidget Sally Field). Even *The Mary Tyler Moore Show* — a milestone in the modern Good Girl's progress — almost had Moore playing a version of Frisky Nun. Laugh no more at winged hats: in the past, Frisky Nun was a female star's emancipated alternative!

The quintessential Good Girl of midcentury America — indeed the mother of all modern Good Girls — was Doris Day. We mean, of course, Nubile Doris Day, in her guise as pert, urban, apartment-dwelling career girl (*Pillow Talk*), as opposed to harangued suburban housewife (*Please Don't Eat the Daisies*). Never mind that Doris typically chucked her career at the end of the film for Rock Hudson; what mattered was that while Doris *was* a Good Girl, she was hardly a nun — in fact, she was quite sexy in her spunky purposefulness.

It was too bad that Doris stayed mainly in the movies, for the most perfect form for the American Good Girl remains the musical. Here emerges a unique symbiosis: on the one hand, the musical needs the Good Girl's soprano, her can-do optimism, the soaring love songs only she can inspire. On the other, not to put too fine a point on it, the Good Girl needs the musical. The musical could *create* Good Girls where there once were none. Example: where, outside the musical, do you find that rarest of beings — the ethnic Good Girl? Sure, ethnic girls can have hearts o' gold, but in the real world they — can we say it? — tend to be a bit sassy. Happily, the musical has the miraculous power to freshen, sanitize, uplift even ethnicities who might feel too irked with society to be Good. We see Jewish Good Girls: Tevye's daughters in *Fiddler on the Roof*. (Imagine "Matchmaker, Matchmaker" done in dialogue on a hot afternoon in Queens — another tale entirely.) It also gave us Yentl. Hm. *West Side Story* produces Latina Good Girl Maria (Natalie Wood, but we quibble). *Flower Drum Song* yields that mousy Asian Good Girl whose name no one can remember (not Nancy Kwan, the other one). *The Wiz* even gives us a black Good Girl: Diana Ross (who was never that Good again).

As we move into the late seventies, however, even white Good Girls are hard to come by. There's a general Fall of the Musical (we could discuss Andrew Lloyd Webber, but why?) — and Fall of Filmic Good Girls.

15

We lose our bright, dependable, pony-tailed stars — our June Allysons, Shirley Joneses, Julie Andrewses. We collapse into the nude/seminude group therapy "line" musicals: *Oh! Calcutta!*, *Pippin,* the exhaustingly confessional *A Chorus Line*. By 1977, we have, God forbid, Liza Minnelli trying to play an ex-WAC in *New York New York*. Liza Minnelli? The eyelashes alone would have scared Our Boys.

And you know why we saw this fall, this demise, this dismal sinking? Because national hope is failing. No one whistles a happy tune. We're moving into bad times for optimism. Bad times for patriotism. Bad times for Good Girls. Forrest Gump drifts out of touch with Jenny . . . and America itself becomes very *dark*.

## II. The Enduring Power of Good Girls

If Good Girls are back in the nineties, what does this imply? That we've come full circle? Forgiven Mom and Dad? We're in love with a wonderful guy? More deeply, does the Good Girl's resurgence signal an uplift in national character, a kind of neo-fifties patriotism, a return to what we might call, without irony, American values?

We have no idea — Good Girls are notoriously poor at political analysis. All we know is, we look around and Good Girls seem to be all over the place, winning again.

Look how they flourish, in the very bosom of our society! Good Girls are our great: morning-show hosts (Katie Couric now, Jane Pauley before); figure skaters (Nancy Kerrigan vanquishing Tonya Harding now, Dorothy Hamill vanquishing all those foreigners before); country singers (Reba, Tammy & Co. now; Dolly Parton before); middle-of-the-road pop stars (Whitney Houston, Paula Abdul now; Linda Ronstadt before); goyische straight gals to nervous Jewish comics (Sally to Harry, Helen Hunt to Paul Reiser now; Diane Keaton to Woody Allen before); Peter Pans (Sandy Duncan now-ish, Mary Martin way before); androgynous gals (Ellen DeGeneres now, Nancy Drew's pal boyish George before); astronauts (Sally Ride); Australians (Olivia Newton-John); MTV newspersons (Tabitha Soren); princesses (Di).

Can a video vixen be Good? Absolutely. Look at ex-Aerosmith girl and rising star Alicia Silverstone. You thought she was Drew Barrymore, but she's not. In Amy Heckerling's surprise summer hit *Clueless* (loosely based on Jane Austen's *Emma!*), Silverstone played Cher, a fashion-obsessed virgin ("You see how picky I am about my shoes, and *they* only go on my feet!"). Alicia the person is very spunky, clean, convincingly virginal, attends Shakespeare camp, takes tap-dancing lessons, and loves animals!

Good Girl accessories are in. Look what Hillary Clinton did for the headband — an astounding semiotic statement. Look how she reinvented cookie baking. Too-thin Nancy Reagan in her let-them-eat-cake Adolfo suit is over. Today, posing as a Good Girl — as clever Hillary does — seems powerfully subversive.

Look how even yesterday's swampy girls are cleaning up. Jane Seymour bounced back from whatever seamy B-stuff she was doing to triumph today as Dr. Quinn, Medicine Woman. Consider post-Donald Ivana, her pertness and brave industry recalling the Czech girl skier of yore. Even Sharon Stone seems downright nice. She makes an effort to dress "up" for press briefings and is so polite, modest, funny! (She showed us her home in *In Style* — the essence of nice! Is a *Redbook* cover in her future?)

And why not? Being a Good Girl pays off. Look how well Meg Ryan/Sandra Bullock films are doing. These girls don't titillate by getting naked. Why? They can turn the world on with a smile!

Even the musical is coming back! Via Disney, we have Belle and the Little Mermaid, even Princess Jasmine and Pocahontas. Look how ethnic! Maybe there *is* a place called Hope.

## III. The Nastiest Truth of All

But what is the bottom-line appeal of the Good Girl? Why do we urban nineties women want to *be* her? It's not as uncalculated as one might think. The Good Girl's draw is that she is the opposite of Bad. And Bad is something we no longer want to be.

You remember Bad Girl — she who reigned in the go-go eighties. Bad Girl is very Bad. Ow. She needs a spanking, she wants it, but beware of giving it to her because ironically it is you (or, more likely, Michael Douglas) who will suffer afterward.

Good Girl's opposite, Bad Girl, has out-of-control hormones. Bad Girl comes from a wildly dysfunctional family; her past makes her do strange, erratic things. Bad Girl tells us something is terribly wrong with society. Bad Girl challenges the status quo. Bad Girl uses sex for everything but love and babies: it's power, self-expression, psychosis, hate, revolt, revenge.

What we have in Bad Girl is Power Slut. Like Madonna in, well, ninety percent of her oeuvre. Joan Collins in *Dynasty*. Glenn Close in *Fatal Attraction*. Sharon Stone in *Basic Instinct*. Demi Moore in *Disclosure*. (Sure those last few are technically nineties, but anything written by Joe Eszterhas is really quite eighties, no?)

Good feminists we, we have saluted Bad Girl/Power Slut's right to exist, to demolish, to flourish in her own dark way. But the nagging question remains: Is this a good behavior model for us? Is Bad Girl's life healthy, happy, productive? Does she get enough love? Even more creepily we ask: Is she aging well?

Because the fact is, even we — once-nubile twentysomething gals who gamboled defiantly topless in the mountain streams of yore — feel ourselves gently softening with age each day. The drama in the bathroom no longer centers around the scale. Forget that — we've gained and lost the same fifteen pounds so often that the cycle has become like an old pal, natural as our monthly period. But our skin! Each new wrinkle tells us there's no going back. No wonder our obsessions have become all Oil of Olay, Clinique moisturizer, antiwrinkle cream!

And while we hate to be unsupportive of our Badder sisters, we can't help noticing that, well, Bad Girlhood seems so bad *for* you. Look at Heidi Fleiss — drawn and witchy and actually too thin at 29. Partying, prostitution, cocaine, and, heck, the eighties don't wear well on a gal. And look at spooky seventysomething *Cosmo* girl Helen Gurley Brown, a.k.a. "the Crypt Keeper in capri pants," as she is known to AM-radio wag Peter Tilden.

Even the indestructible Madonna is looking a bit exhausted. Sure she's a zillionaire and superpowerful and has been on top forever. Her *Sex* book broke every boundary, sold tons. But it must be tough, we secretly think, for Madonna to greet her 5,012th weekend with only those girly dancing boys with the weird hair for company. Sean is off having babies with Robin Wright (a Good Girl, if oddly skinny). Geez: Madonna's going to be 40 soon. If she keeps hanging onto Bad Girl, soon she'll be Old Crone girl. Can we women age with dignity? By what strategy will we engineer fabulous forties, fifties, sixties and beyond? (My God — a healthy woman of 65 today can expect to live to 83! Almost half our life will be spent being 50 or older!)

As we drift past our midthirties, we begin to question the idea of relentlessly pushing the boundaries of society, psychology, and biology. Will we end up like tart-talking Roseanne? We used to love her. We still do, but it's 1995 now and we are confused. She had a hit show, but still she felt the need for plastic surgery, butt tattoos, Tom Arnold tattoos, a Tom Arnold divorce, she hates her family, belched the anthem, lit her farts (or could if she'd wanted), married her bodyguard and has had a new baby, like, surgically implanted . . . where? Is this feminism? Help!

We will not go like that. (Anyway, we can't afford to.) We women    35
are survivors, and we are battening down our hatches . . . for the future.


### IV. The Good Girl Manifesto

Herewith, then, a declaration of our principles:

1. We're no longer promiscuous. Diseases suck. And so do noncommittal men our age (often spoiled for commitment by all that free sex we gave them in the sixties, seventies, and eighties). There's really no point. We can do it ourselves.

2. We're tailing down on booze and drugs. Eight glasses of water a day — better for the skin.

3. We're trying not to be anorexic. That seems very eighties. Then again, we don't want to be fat. As a result, we're just a wee bit bulimic. Sorry! We know this is not good.

4. We're *trying* to envision a future without plastic surgery. We try to keep happy, confident, glowing, nonlifted, fortysomething earth mothers Meryl/Cybill/Susan foremost in our minds. (See Nivea wrinkle cream ad: a blond mom in white feels good about her face, baby splashing in the background.)

5. We're trying to love our parents again. Their mortality weighs heavily upon us. When a parent dies, we peruse the photo album, weep while contemplating their jauntily hopeful forties hats, the huge families they came from. We feel suddenly lonely.

6. Were the forties and fifties really so bad? Gee, we feel nostalgic. We yearn for old love songs and old movies. At least our filmic Good Girl heroines do. (See Meg Ryan in *Sleepless in Seattle,* Marisa Tomei in *Only You.*) Although I must tell you: if I hear Harry Connick Jr. singing "It Had to Be You" again on the soundtrack of one more light romantic comedy, I will kill someone.

7. We're drawn to stuff that seems traditional, even if it isn't. Laura Ashley sheets. Coach bags. *Martha Stewart Living.*

8. We're back to white cotton underpants. (And as Victoria's Secret tells us, cotton is sexy again!)

9. We love our pets — our very own Disney familiars. (If we are starring in a movie, we can be expected to talk to our cat or dog in a very cute way. Starlets who need their tawdry images to be cleaned up can be expected to join PETA.)

10. We believe in true love, but we don't expect to find it in Rock Hudson. That's a dream of the past. Urban Lotharios *never* settle down — we've learned that, unlike Doris, we can't domesticate them through interior design.

That's why we're looking for love in all new places. Maybe we find it via a much younger man (a third of today's women already do). Maybe we find it by falling in love again with the family (like Sandra Bullock does in *While You Were Sleeping*). Maybe we find it in our children, postdivorce.

Consider that the template for the female sitcom today is not single newsgal Mary Tyler Moore, but single mom Murphy Brown, divorced mom Brett Butler, divorced mom Cybill. Exhusbands are reduced to comic characters sticking their heads in the door, like Howard the neighbor on the old *Bob Newhart Show.* In these days, when conception's becoming increasingly immaculate, maybe we have a baby without a guy.

Or maybe, hell, we find love for a few beautiful days with a fiftysomething shaman/photographer called Robert Kincaid with a washboard stomach. Maybe we never see him again after that. But today's

Good Girl is tough and prudent — a little bit of love and she says, un-complainingly, "I'm fine. I'm full. I have plenty."

Then goes outside and, into the air, high above her head, throws not    50
her bra . . . but her hat.

## Reading the Text

1. Why, do you think, does Loh begin her essay with a racy hot tub anec-dote?
2. Summarize in your own words what Loh means by "good girl."
3. Why do good girls have such an enduring appeal in American culture, ac-cording to Loh?
4. What are bad girls, in Loh's view, and why are they a necessary comple-ment to good girls?
5. Why, according to Loh, were the 1980s a decade in which bad girls thrived?
6. What is Loh's tone in this essay, and do you find that her approach to her topic makes the essay more or less persuasive?

## Reading the Signs

1. If you are female, explore in your journal whether in your childhood you were raised to be a "good girl" and whether that upbringing influences you today. If you are male, explore in your journal whether you believe good girls have a male equivalent: Were you raised to be a "good boy"? If so, what traits were you expected to follow? If not, explore whether you believe our culture values good boys.
2. In class, brainstorm a list of current female film stars and their chief roles and then discuss whether they are good or bad girls (or neither). Drawing on the class discussion, write an essay in which you challenge, support, or qualify Loh's contention that the 1990s have seen a return of good girls to Hollywood.
3. Good girls aren't political enough to explain their return to favor in the 1990s, Loh claims. Write your own interpretation of why the good girl has supplanted the bad girl of the 1980s, being sure to base your discussion on specific examples from film.
4. Keeping Loh's discussion of good girls in mind, watch an episode of *ER* or *NYPD Blue* (or any other "progressive" show, such as *Murphy Brown*), and write an essay that discusses the extent to which the female characters in the show fulfill the good girl archetype. To develop your ideas, read or reread Susan Douglas's "Signs of Intelligent Life on TV" (p. 200).
5. Rent a videotape of one of the Doris Day films that Loh mentions and write a semiotic analysis of the gender roles portrayed in the film.
6. Study a popular women's fashion magazine such as *Glamour* or *Vogue* and write an analysis of the way women are portrayed in the advertising. To what extent do advertisers rely on the good girl archetype that Loh de-scribes? How can you account for your findings?

BENJAMIN DeMOTT

*Put on a Happy Face: Masking the Differences*
*Between Blacks and Whites*

*By looking at the movies, you'd think that race relations in the United*
*States were in splendid shape. Just look at Danny Glover and Mel*
*Gibson in the* Lethal Weapon *movies, or consider* Driving Miss
Daisy. *But according to Benjamin DeMott (b. 1924), things are not*
*so rosy. In fact, DeMott argues in this essay that Hollywood has effec-*
*tively concealed the true state of American racial politics behind a pleas-*
*ing facade of black and white happy-faces, and so has inadvertently*
*worked to distract movie audiences from the pressing need to improve*
*our racial climate. A writer whose interests include the media and*
*American racial and class politics, DeMott's books include* Created
Equal: Reading and Writing About Class in America *(1985),*
The Imperial Middle: Why Americans Can't Think Straight
About Class *(1990), and* The Trouble With Friendship: Why
Americans Can't Think Straight About Race *(1995).*

At the movies these days, questions about racial injustice have been
amicably resolved. Watch *Pulp Fiction* or *Congo* or *A Little Princess* or any
other recent film in which both blacks and whites are primary characters
and you can, if you want, forget about race. Whites and blacks greet one
another on the screen with loving candor, revealing their common humanity. In *Pulp Fiction,* an armed black mobster (played by Samuel L.
Jackson) looks deep into the eyes of an armed white thief in the middle
of a holdup (played by Tim Roth) and shares his version of God's word
in Ezekiel, whereupon the two men lay aside their weapons, both more
or less redeemed. The moment inverts an earlier scene in which a white
boxer (played by Bruce Willis) risks his life to save another black mobster
(played by Ving Rhames), who is being sexually tortured as a prelude to
his execution.

*Pulp Fiction* (gross through July: $107 million) is one of a series of
films suggesting that the beast of American racism is tamed and harmless.
Close to the start of *Die Hard with a Vengeance* (gross through July: $95
million) the camera finds a white man wearing sandwich boards on the
corner of Amsterdam Avenue and 138th Street in Harlem. The boards
carry a horrific legend: I HATE NIGGERS. A group of young blacks approach the man with murderous intent, bearing guns and knives. They
are figures straight out of a national nightmare — ugly, enraged, terrifying. No problem. A black man, again played by Jackson, appears and

rescues the white man, played by Willis. The black man and white man come to know each other well. In time the white man declares flatly to the black, "I need you more than you need me." A moment later he charges the black with being a racist — with not liking whites as much as the white man likes blacks — and the two talk frankly about their racial prejudices. Near the end of the film, the men have grown so close that each volunteers to die for the other.

*Pulp Fiction* and *Die Hard with a Vengeance* follow the pattern of *Lethal Weapon 1, 2,* and *3,* the Danny Glover/Mel Gibson buddy vehicles that collectively grossed $357 million, and *White Men Can't Jump,* which, in the year of the L.A. riots, grossed $76 million. In *White Men Can't Jump,* a white dropout, played by Woody Harrelson, ekes out a living on black-dominated basketball courts in Los Angeles. He's arrogant and aggressive but never in danger because he has a black protector and friend, played by Wesley Snipes. At the movie's end, the white, flying above the hoop like a stereotypical black player, scores the winning basket in a two-on-two pickup game on an alley-oop pass from his black chum, whereupon the two men fall into each other's arms in joy. Later, the black friend agrees to find work for the white at the store he manages.

WHITE (helpless):  I gotta get a job. Can you get me a job?
BLACK (affectionately teasing):  Got any references?
WHITE (shy grin):  You.

Such dialogue is the stuff of romance. What's dreamed of and gained is a place where whites are unafraid of blacks, where blacks ask for and need nothing from whites, and where the sameness of the races creates a common fund of sweet content.[1] The details of the dream matter less than the force that makes it come true for both races, eliminating the constraints of objective reality and redistributing resources, status, and capabilities. That cleansing social force supersedes political and economic fact or policy; that force, improbably enough, is friendship.

Watching the beaming white men who know how to jump, we do 5 well to remind ourselves of what the camera shot leaves out. Black infants die in America at twice the rate of white infants. (Despite the increased numbers of middle-class blacks, the rates are diverging, with black rates actually rising.) One out of every two black children lives below the poverty line (as compared with one out of seven white children). Nearly four times

---

1. I could go on with examples of movies that deliver the good news of friendship: *Regarding Henry, Driving Miss Daisy, Forrest Gump, The Shawshank Redemption, Philadelphia, The Last Boy Scout, 48 Hours I–II, Rising Sun, Iron Eagle I–II, Rudy, Sister Act, Hearts of Dixie, Betrayed, The Power of One, White Nights, Clara's Heart, Doc Hollywood, Cool Runnings, Places in the Heart, Trading Places, Fried Green Tomatoes, Q & A, Platoon, A Mother's Courage: The Mary Thomas Story, The Unforgiven, The Air Up There, The Pelican Brief, Losing Isaiah, Smoke, Searching for Bobby Fischer, An Officer and a Gentleman, Speed,* etc.

as many black families exist below the poverty line as white families. More than 50 percent of African American families have incomes below $25,000. Among black youths under age twenty, death by murder occurs nearly ten times as often as among whites. Over 60 percent of births to black mothers occur out of wedlock, more than four times the rate for white mothers. The net worth of the typical white household is ten times that of the typical black household. In many states, five to ten times as many blacks as whites age eighteen to thirty are in prison.

The good news at the movies obscures the bad news in the streets and confirms the Supreme Court's recent decisions on busing, affirmative action, and redistricting. Like the plot of *White Men Can't Jump,* the Court postulates the existence of a society no longer troubled by racism. Because black-white friendship is now understood to be the rule, there is no need for integrated schools or a congressional Black Caucus or affirmative action. The Congress and state governors can guiltlessly cut welfare, food assistance, fuel assistance, Head Start, housing money, fellowship money, vaccine money. Justice Anthony Kennedy can declare, speaking for the Supreme Court majority last June, that creating a world of genuine equality and sameness requires only that "our political system and our society cleanse themselves . . . of discrimination."

The deep logic runs as follows: *Yesterday white people didn't like black people, and accordingly suffered guilt, knowing that the dislike was racist and knowing also that as moral persons they would have to atone for the guilt. They would have to ante up for welfare and Head Start and halfway houses and free vaccine and midnight basketball and summer jobs for schoolkids and graduate fellowships for promising scholars and craft-union apprenticeships and so on, endlessly. A considerable and wasteful expense. But at length came the realization that by ending dislike or hatred it would be possible to end guilt, which in turn would mean an end to redress: no more wasteful ransom money. There would be but one requirement: the regular production and continuous showing forth of evidence indisputably proving that hatred has totally vanished from the land.*

I cannot tell the reader how much I would like to believe in this sunshine world. After the theater lights brighten and I've found coins for a black beggar on the way to my car and am driving home through downtown Springfield, Massachusetts, the world invented by *Die Hard with a Vengeance* and America's highest court gives way only slowly to the familiar urban vision in my windshield — homeless blacks on trash-strewn streets, black prostitutes staked out on a corner, and signs of a not very furtive drug trade. I know perfectly well that most African Americans don't commit crimes or live in alleys. I also know that for somebody like myself, downtown Springfield in the late evening is not a good place to be.

The movies reflect the larger dynamic of wish and dream. Day after day the nation's corporate ministries of culture churn out images of racial harmony. Millions awaken each morning to the friendly sight of Katie

Couric nudging a perky elbow into good buddy Bryant Gumbel's side. My mailbox and millions of demographically similar others are choked with flyers from companies (Wal-Mart, Victoria's Secret) bent on publicizing both their wares and their social bona fides by displaying black and white models at cordial ease with one another. A torrent of goodwill messages about race arrives daily — revelations of corporate largesse, commercials, news features, TV specials, all proclaiming that whites like me feel strongly positive impulses of friendship for blacks and that those same admirable impulses are effectively eradicating racial differences, rendering blacks and whites the same. BellSouth TV commercials present children singing "I am the keeper of the world" — first a white child, then a black child, then a white child, then a black child. Because Dow Chemical likes black America, it recruits young black college grads for its research division and dramatizes, in TV commercials, their tearful-joyful partings from home. ("Son, show 'em what you got," says a black lad's father.) American Express shows an elegant black couple and an elegant white couple sitting together in a theater, happy in one another's company. (The couples share the box with an oversized Gold Card.) During the evening news I watch a black mom offer Robitussin to a miserably coughing white mom. Here's *People* magazine promoting itself under a photo of John Lee Hooker, the black bluesman. "We're these kinds of people, too," *People* claims in the caption. In the current production of *Hamlet* on Broadway, Horatio is played by a black actor. On *The 700 Club,* Pat Robertson joshes Ben Kinchlow, his black sidekick, about Ben's far-out ties.

What counts here is not the saccharine clumsiness of the inter-    10
changes but the bulk of them — the ceaseless, self-validating gestures of friendship, the humming, buzzing background theme: *All decent Americans extend the hand of friendship to African Americans; nothing but nothing is more auspicious for the African American future than this extended hand.* Faith in the miracle cure of racism by change-of-heart turns out to be so familiar as to have become unnoticeable. And yes, the faith has its benign aspect. Even as they nudge me and others toward belief in magic (instant pals and no-money-down equality), the images and messages of devoted relationships between blacks and whites do exert a humanizing influence.

Nonetheless, through these same images and messages the comfortable majority tells itself a fatuous untruth. Promoting the fantasy of painless answers, inspiring groundless self-approval among whites, joining the Supreme Court in treating "cleansing" as *inevitable,* the new orthodoxy of friendship incites culture-wide evasion, justifies one political step backward after another, and greases the skids along which, tomorrow, welfare block grants will slide into state highway-resurfacing budgets. Whites are part of the solution, says this orthodoxy, if we break out of the prison of our skin color, say hello, as equals, one-on-one, to a black stranger, and make a black friend. We're part of the problem if we have an aversion to black people or are frightened of them, or if we feel that the more distance we put between them and us the better, or if we're in the habit of asserting our superiority rather than acknowledging our common humanity. Thus we shift the problem away from politics — from black experience and the history of slavery — and perceive it as a matter of the suspicion and fear found within the white heart; solving the problem asks no more of us than that we work on ourselves, scrubbing off the dirt of ill will.

The approach miniaturizes, personalizes, and moralizes; it removes the large and complex dilemmas of race from the public sphere. It tempts audiences to see history as irrelevant and to regard feelings as decisive — to believe that the fate of black Americans is shaped mainly by events occurring in the hearts and minds of the privileged. And let's be frank: the orthodoxy of friendship feels *nice*. It practically *consecrates* self-flattery. The "good" Bill Clinton who attends black churches and talks with likable ease to fellow worshipers was campaigning when Los Angeles rioted in '92. "White Americans," he said, "are gripped by the isolation of their own experience. Too many still simply have no friends of other races and do not know any differently." Few black youths of working age in South-Central L.A. had been near enough to the idea of a job even to think of looking for work before the Rodney King verdict, but the problem, according to Clinton, was that whites need black friends.

Most of the country's leading voices of journalistic conscience (editorial writers, television anchorpersons, syndicated columnists) roundly endorse the doctrine of black-white friendship as a means of redressing the inequalities between the races. Roger Rosenblatt, editor of the *Columbia Journalism Review* and an especially deft supplier of warm and fuzzy sentiment, published an essay in *Family Circle* arguing that white friendship and sympathy for blacks simultaneously make power differentials vanish and create interracial identity between us, one by one. The author finds his *exemplum* in an episode revealing the personal sensitivity, to injured blacks, of one of his children.

"When our oldest child, Carl, was in high school," he writes, "he and two black friends were standing on a street corner in New York City one spring evening, trying to hail a taxi. The three boys were dressed decently and were doing nothing wild or threatening. Still, no taxi would pick them up. If a driver spotted Carl first, he might slow down, but he would take off again when he saw the others. Carl's two companions were familiar with this sort of abuse. Carl, who had never observed it firsthand before, burned with anger and embarrassment that he was the color of a world that would so mistreat his friends."

Rosenblatt notes that when his son "was applying to colleges, he wrote his essay on that taxi incident with his two black friends. . . . He was able to articulate what he could not say at the time — how ashamed and impotent he felt. He also wrote of the power of their friendship, 15 which has lasted to this day and has carried all three young men into the country that belongs to them. To all of us."

In this homily white sympathy begets interracial sameness in several ways. The three classmates are said to react identically to the cabdrivers' snub; i.e., they feel humiliated. "[Carl] could not find the words to express his humiliation and his friends *would* not express theirs."

The anger that inspires the younger Rosenblatt's college-admission essay on racism is seen as identical with black anger. Friendship brings the classmates together as joint, equal owners of the land of their birth ("the country that belongs to [all of] them"). And Rosenblatt supplies a still larger vision of essential black-white sameness near the end of his essay: "Our proper hearts tell the truth," he declares, "which is that we are all in the same boat, rich and poor, black and white. We are helpless, wicked, heroic, terrified, and we need one another. We need to give rides to one another."

Thus do acts of private piety substitute for public policy while the possibility of urgent political action disappears into a sentimental haze. "If we're looking for a formula to ease the tensions between the races," Rosenblatt observes, then we should "attack the disintegration of the black community" and "the desperation of the poor." Without overtly mocking civil rights activists who look toward the political arena "to erase the tensions," Rosenblatt alludes to them in a throwaway manner, implying that properly adjusted whites look elsewhere, that there was a time for politicking for "equal rights" but we've passed through it. Now is a time in which we should listen to our hearts at moments of epiphany and allow sympathy to work its wizardry, cleansing and floating us, blacks and whites "all in the same boat," on a mystical undercurrent of the New Age.

Blacks themselves aren't necessarily proof against this theme, as witness a recent essay by James Alan McPherson in the Harvard journal *Reconstruction.* McPherson, who received the 1977 Pulitzer Prize for fiction for his collection of stories *Elbow Room,* says that "the only possible steps, the safest steps . . . small ones" in the movement "toward a universal culture" will be those built not on "ideologies and formulas and programs" but on experiences of personal connectedness.

"Just this past spring," he writes, "when I was leaving a restaurant     20 after taking a [white] former student to dinner, a black [woman on the sidewalk] said to my friend, in a rasping voice, 'Hello, girlfriend. Have you got anything to spare?'" The person speaking was a female crack addict with a child who was also addicted. "But," writes McPherson, when the addict made her pitch to his dinner companion, "I saw in my friend's face an understanding and sympathy and a shining which transcended race and class. Her face reflected one human soul's connection with another. The magnetic field between the two women was charged with spiritual energy."

The writer points the path to progress through interpersonal gestures by people who "insist on remaining human, and having human responses. . . . Perhaps the best that can be done, now, is the offering of understanding and support to the few out of many who are capable of such gestures, rather than devising another plan to engineer the many into one."

The elevated vocabulary ("soul," "spiritual") beatifies the impulse to turn away from the real-life agenda of actions capable of reducing racial injustice. Wherever that impulse dominates, the rhetoric of racial sameness thrives, diminishing historical catastrophes affecting millions over centuries and inflating the significance of tremors of tenderness briefly troubling the heart or conscience of a single individual — the boy waiting for a cab, the woman leaving the restaurant. People forget the theoretically unforgettable — the caste history of American blacks, the connection between no schools for longer than a century and bad school performance now, between hateful social attitudes and zero employment opportunities, between minority anguish and majority fear.

How could this way of seeing have become conventional so swiftly? How did the dogmas of instant equality insinuate themselves so effortlessly into courts and mass audiences alike? How can a white man like myself, who taught Southern blacks in the 1960s, find himself seduced — as I have been more than once — by the orthodoxy of friendship? In the civil rights era, the experience for many millions of Americans was one of discovery. A hitherto unimagined continent of human reality and history came into view, inducing genuine concern and at least a temporary setting aside of self-importance. I remember with utter clarity what I felt at Mary Holmes College in West Point, Mississippi, when a black student of mine was killed by tailgating rednecks; my fellow tutors and I were overwhelmed with how shamefully wrong a wrong could be. For a time, we were released from the prisons of moral weakness and ambiguity. In the year or two that followed — the mid-Sixties — the notion that some humans are more human than others, whites more human than blacks, appeared to have been overturned. The next step seemed obvious: society would have to admit that when one race deprives another of its humanity for centuries, those who have done the depriving are obligated to do what they can to restore the humanity of the deprived. The obligation clearly entailed the mounting of comprehensive *long-term* programs of developmental assistance — not guilt-money handouts — for nearly the entire black population. The path forward was unavoidable.

It was avoided. Shortly after the award of civil rights and the institution, in 1966, of limited preferential treatment to remedy employment and educational discrimination against African Americans, a measure of economic progress for blacks did appear in census reports. Not much, but enough to stimulate glowing tales of universal black advance and to launch the good-news barrage that continues to this day (headline in the *New York Times,* June 18, 1995: "Moving On Up: The Greening of America's Black Middle Class").

After Ronald Reagan was elected to his first term, the new dogma of    25 black-white sameness found ideological support in the form of criticism of so-called coddling. Liberal activists of both races were berated by critics of both races for fostering an allegedly enfeebling psychology of dependency that discouraged African Americans from committing themselves to individual self-development. In 1988, the charge was passionately voiced in an essay in these pages, "I'm Black, You're White, Who's Innocent?" by Shelby Steele, who attributed the difference between black rates of advance and those of other minority groups to white folks' pampering. Most blacks, Steele claimed, could make it on their own — as voluntary immigrants have done — were they not held back by devitalizing programs that presented them, to themselves and others, as somehow dissimilar to and weaker than other Americans. This argument was all-in-the-same-boatism in a different key; the claim remained that progress depends upon recognition of black-white sameness. Let us see through superficial differences to the underlying, equally distributed gift for success. Let us teach ourselves — in the words of the Garth Brooks tune — to ignore "the color of skin" and "look for . . . the beauty within."

Still further support for the policy once known as "do-nothingism" came from points-of-light barkers, who held that a little something might perhaps be done *if* accompanied by enough publicity. Nearly every broadcaster and publisher in America moves a bale of reportage on pro bono efforts by white Americans to speed the advance of black Americans. Example: McDonald's and the National Basketball Association distribute balloons when they announce they are addressing the dropout problem with an annual "Stay in School" scheme that gives schoolkids who don't miss a January school day a ticket to an all-star exhibition. The publicity strengthens the idea that these initiatives will nullify the social context — the city I see through my windshield. Reports of white philanthropy suggest that the troubles of this block and the next should be understood as phenomena in transition. The condition of American blacks need not be read as the fixed, unchanging consequence of generations of bottom-caste existence. Edging discreetly past a beggar posted near the entrance to Zabar's or H&H Bagels, or, while walking the dog, stepping politely around black men asleep on the sidewalk, we need not see ourselves and our fellows as uncaring accomplices in the acts of social injustice.

Yet more powerful has been the ceaseless assault, over the past generation, on our knowledge of the historical situation of black Americans. On the face of things it seems improbable that the cumulative weight of documented historical injury to African Americans could ever be lightly assessed. Gifted black writers continue to show, in scene after scene — in their studies of middle-class blacks interacting with whites — how historical realities shape the lives of their black characters. In *Killer of Sheep,* the brilliant black filmmaker Charles Burnett dramatizes the daily encounters that suck poor blacks into will-lessness and contempt for white fairy tales of interracial harmony; he quickens his historical themes with images of faceless black meat processors gutting undifferentiated, unchoosing animal life. Here, say these images, as though talking back to Clarence Thomas, here is a basic level of black life unchanged over generations. Where there's work, it's miserably paid and ugly. Space allotments at home and at work cramp body and mind. Positive expectation withers in infancy. People fall into the habit of jeering at aspiration as though at the bidding of physical law. Obstacles at every hand prevent people from loving and being loved in decent ways, prevent children from believing their parents, prevent parents from believing they themselves know anything worth knowing. The only true self, now as in the long past, is the one mocked by one's own race. "Shit on you, nigger," says a voice in *Killer of Sheep.* "Nothing you say matters a good goddamn."

For whites, these words produce guilt, and for blacks, I can only assume, pain and despair. The audience for tragedy remains small, while at the multiplex the popular enthusiasm for historical romance remains constant and vast. During the last two decades, the entertainment industry has conducted a siege on the pertinent past, systematically excising knowledge of the consequences of the historical exploitation of African Americans. Factitious renderings of the American past blur the outlines of black-white conflict, redefine the ground of black grievances for the purpose of diminishing the grievances, restage black life in accordance with the illusory conventions of American success mythology, and present the operative influences on race history as the same as those implied to be pivotal in *White Men Can't Jump* or a BellSouth advertisement.

Although there was scant popular awareness of it at the time (1977), the television miniseries *Roots* introduced the figure of the Unscathed Slave. To an enthralled audience of more than 80 million the series intimated that the damage resulting from generations of birth-ascribed, semi-animal status was largely temporary, that slavery was a product of motiveless malignity on the social margins rather than of respectable rationality, and that the ultimate significance of the institution lay in the demonstration, by freed slaves, that no force on earth can best the energies of American Individualism. ("Much like the Waltons confronting the depression," writes historian Eric Foner, a widely respected authority on American slavery, "the family in 'Roots' neither seeks nor requires outside help; individual or family effort is always sufficient.") Ken Burns's much applauded PBS documentary *The Civil War* (1990) went even further than *Roots* in downscaling black injury; the series treated slavery, birth-ascribed inferiority, and the centuries-old denial of dignity as matters of slight consequence. (By "implicitly denying the brutal reality of slavery," writes historian Jeanie Attie, Burns's programs crossed "a dangerous moral threshold." To a group of historians who asked him why slavery had been so slighted, Burns said that any discussion of slavery "would have been lengthy and boring.")

Mass media treatments of the civil rights protest years carried forward   30 the process, contributing to the "positive" erasure of difference. Big-budget films like *Mississippi Burning,* together with an array of TV biographical specials on Dr. Martin Luther King and others, presented the long-running struggle between disenfranchised blacks and the majority white culture as a heartwarming episode of interracial unity; the speed and caringness of white response to the oppression of blacks demonstrated that broadscale race conflict or race difference was inconceivable.

A consciousness that ingests either a part or the whole of this revisionism loses touch with the two fundamental truths of race in America; namely, that because of what happened in the past, blacks and whites cannot yet be the same; and that because what happened in the past was no mere matter of ill will or insult but the outcome of an established caste structure that has only very recently begun to be dismantled, it is not reparable by one-on-one goodwill. The word "slavery" comes to induce stock responses with no vital sense of a grinding devastation of mind visited upon generation after generation. Hoodwinked by the orthodoxy of friendship, the nation either ignores the past, summons for it a detached, correct "compassion," or gazes at it as though it were a set of aesthetic conventions, like twisted trees and fragmented rocks in nineteenth-century picturesque painting — lifeless phenomena without bearing on the present. The chance of striking through the mask of corporate-underwritten, feel-good, ahistorical racism grows daily more remote. The trade-off — whites promise friendship, blacks accept the status quo — begins to seem like a good deal.

Cosseted by Hollywood's magic lantern and soothed by press releases from Washington and the American Enterprise Institute, we should never forget what we see and hear for ourselves. Broken out by race, the results of every social tabulation from unemployment to life expectancy add up to a chronicle of atrocity. The history of black America fully explains — to anyone who approaches it honestly — how the disaster happened and why neither guilt money nor lectures on personal responsibility can, in and of themselves, repair the damage. The vision of friendship and sympathy placing blacks and whites "all in the same boat," rendering them equally able to do each other favors, "to give rides to one another," is a smiling but monstrous lie.

## Reading the Text

1. How does DeMott view current race relations in America, and how have recent Hollywood films presented a distorted view of those relations?
2. How, in DeMott's view, do films represent the wish fulfillment of mainstream America?
3. What does DeMott see as the social effect of fantasy-laden images of happy race relations?
4. What does DeMott mean when he says that "acts of private piety substitute for public policy while the possibility of urgent political action disappears into a sentimental haze"?
5. How does DeMott interpret the depiction of slavery in productions such as *Roots* and *The Civil War*?

## Reading the Signs

1. Rent a videotape of one of the films that DeMott discusses in his essay. Then write your own analysis of the race relations depicted in the film. To what extent do you find his claim that the film sugarcoats race relations to be valid?
2. DeMott focuses on black–white relations in this essay. In class, discuss how other ethnicities, such as Latinos or Asian Americans, fit his argument.
3. DeMott is critical of the unrealistic portrayal of race relations in film. In your journal, explore whether you believe this lack of realism has a positive or negative impact on Americans' attitudes toward race.
4. DeMott contends that we can see the same unrealistic friendships between the races in product catalogs and advertising. Select a favorite catalog or magazine and study the models populating the pages. Then write an essay in which you support, refute, or modify his contention.
5. If you were to produce a film that depicts current race relations in America, what sort of film, would you create? Write a creative essay describing your ideal film, then share it with your classmates.
6. Assuming DeMott's perspective on Hollywood's depiction of race relations, write a letter to Sam Fulwood III ("The Rage of the Black Middle Class," p. 510) in which you explain the media's contribution to Fulwood's anger.
7. Keeping DeMott's argument in mind, write an interpretation of race relations as depicted in Spike Lee's *Malcolm X*. To develop your ideas, read or reread Shelby Steele's "Malcolm X" (p. 325).

JESSICA HAGEDORN

*Asian Women in Film: No Joy, No Luck*

||||||||||||||||||||||||||||||||||||||||||||||||||||

*Why do movies always seem to portray Asian women as tragic victims of history and fate? Jessica Hagedorn asks in this essay which originally appeared in* Ms. *Even such movies as* The Joy Luck Club, *based on Amy Tan's breakthrough novel that elevated Asian-American fiction to best-seller status, reinforce old stereotypes of the powerlessness of Asian and Asian-American women. A screenwriter and novelist herself, Hagedorn calls for a different kind of storytelling that would show Asian women as powerful controllers of their own destinies. Hagedorn's publications include* Dogeaters *(1990), a novel;* Danger and Beauty *(1993), a collection of poems; and* Charlie Chan is Dead: An Anthology of Contemporary Asian American Fiction *(1993).*

*Pearl of the Orient. Whore. Geisha. Concubine. Whore. Hostess. Bar Girl. Mama-san. Whore. China Doll. Tokyo Rose. Whore. Butterfly. Whore. Miss Saigon. Whore. Dragon Lady. Lotus Blossom. Gook. Whore. Yellow Peril. Whore. Bangkok Bombshell. Whore. Hospitality Girl. Whore. Comfort Woman. Whore. Savage. Whore. Sultry. Whore. Faceless. Whore. Porcelain. Whore. Demure. Whore. Virgin. Whore. Mute. Whore. Model Minority. Whore. Victim. Whore. Woman Warrior. Whore. Mail-Order Bride. Whore. Mother. Wife. Lover. Daughter. Sister.*

As I was growing up in the Philippines in the 1950s, my fertile imagination was colonized by thoroughly American fantasies. Yellowface variations on the exotic erotic loomed larger than life on the silver screen. I was mystified and enthralled by Hollywood's skewed representations of Asian women: sleek, evil goddesses with slanted eyes and cunning ways, or smiling, sarong–clad South Seas "maidens" with undulating hips, kinky black hair, and white skin darkened by makeup. Hardly any of the "Asian" characters were played by Asians. White actors like Sidney Toler and Warner Oland played "inscrutable Oriental detective" Charlie Chan with taped eyelids and a singsong, chop suey accent. Jennifer Jones was a Eurasian doctor swept up in a doomed "interracial romance" in *Love Is a Many Splendored Thing.* In my mother's youth, white actor Luise Rainer played the central role of the Patient Chinese Wife in the 1937 film adaptation of Pearl Buck's novel *The Good Earth.* Back then, not many thought to ask why; they were all too busy being grateful to see anyone in the movies remotely like themselves.

Cut to 1960: *The World of Suzie Wong,* another tragic East/West affair. I am now old enough to be impressed. Sexy, sassy Suzie (played by Nancy Kwan) works out of a bar patronized by white sailors, but doesn't seem bothered by any of it. For a hardworking girl turning nightly tricks to support her baby, she manages to parade an astonishing wardrobe in damn near every scene, down to matching handbags and shoes. The sailors are also strictly Hollywood, sanitized and not too menacing. Suzie and all the other prostitutes in this movie are cute, giggling, dancing sex machines with hearts of gold. William Holden plays an earnest, rather prim, Nice Guy painter seeking inspiration in The Other. Of course, Suzie falls madly in love with him. Typically, she tells him, "I not important," and "I'll be with you until you say — Suzie, go away." She also thinks being beaten by a man is a sign of true passion, and is terribly disappointed when Mr. Nice Guy refuses to show his true feelings.

Next in Kwan's short-lived but memorable career was the kitschy 1961 musical *Flower Drum Song,* which, like *Suzie Wong,* is a thoroughly American commercial product. The female roles are typical of Hollywood musicals of the times: women are basically airheads, subservient to men. Kwan's counterpart is the Good Chinese Girl, played by Miyoshi Umeki, who was better playing the Loyal Japanese Girl in that other classic Hollywood tale of forbidden love, *Sayonara.* Remember? Umeki was so loyal, she committed double suicide with actor Red Buttons. I instinctively hated *Sayonara* when I first saw it as a child; now I understand why. Contrived tragic resolutions were the only way Hollywood got past the censors in those days. With one or two exceptions, somebody in these movies always had to die to pay for breaking racial and sexual taboos.

Until the recent onslaught of films by both Asian and Asian American filmmakers, Asian Pacific women have generally been perceived by Hollywood with a mixture of fascination, fear, and contempt. Most Hollywood movies either trivialize or exoticize us as people of color and as women. Our intelligence is underestimated, our humanity overlooked, and our diverse cultures treated as interchangeable. If we are "good," we are childlike, submissive, silent, and eager for sex (see France Nuyen's glowing performance as Liat in the film version of *South Pacific*) or else we are tragic victim types (see *Casualties of War,* Brian De Palma's graphic 1989 drama set in Vietnam). And if we are not silent, suffering doormats, we are demonized dragon ladies — cunning, deceitful, sexual provocateurs. Give me the demonic any day — Anna May Wong as a villain slithering around in a slinky gown is at least gratifying to watch, neither servile nor passive. And she steals the show from Marlene Dietrich in Josef von Sternberg's *Shanghai Express.* From the 1920s through the '30s, Wong was our only female "star." But even she was trapped in limited roles, in what filmmaker Renee Tajima has called the dragon lady/lotus blossom dichotomy.

Cut to 1985: There is a scene toward the end of the terribly dishonest but weirdly compelling Michael Cimino movie *Year of the Dragon* (cowritten by Oliver Stone) that is one of my favorite twisted movie moments of all time. If you ask a lot of my friends who've seen that movie (especially if they're Asian), it's one of their favorites too. The setting is a crowded Chinatown nightclub. There are two very young and very tough Jade Cobra gang girls in a shoot-out with Mickey Rourke, in the role of a demented Polish American cop who, in spite of being Mr. Ugly in the flesh — an arrogant, misogynistic bully devoid of any charm — wins the "good" Asian American anchorwoman in the film's absurd and implausible ending. This is a movie with an actual disclaimer as its lead-in, covering its ass in advance in response to anticipated complaints about "stereotypes."

My pleasure in the hard-edged power of the Chinatown gang girls in *Year of the Dragon* is my small revenge, the answer to all those Suzie Wong "I want to be your slave" female characters. The Jade Cobra girls are mere background to the white male foreground/focus of Cimino's movie. But long after the movie has faded into video-rental heaven, the Jade Cobra girls remain defiant, fabulous images in my memory, flaunting tight metallic dresses and spiky cock's-comb hairdos streaked electric red and blue.

Mickey Rourke looks down with world-weary pity at the unnamed Jade
   Cobra girl (Doreen Chan) he's just shot who lies sprawled and
   bleeding on the street: "You look like you're gonna die, beautiful."
JADE COBRA GIRL: "Oh yeah? [blood gushing from her mouth] I'm
   proud of it."
ROURKE: "You are? You got anything you wanna tell me before you
   go, sweetheart?"
JADE COBRA GIRL: "Yeah. [pause] Fuck you."

Cut to 1993: I've been told that like many New Yorkers, I watch movies with the right side of my brain on perpetual overdrive. I admit to being grouchy and overcritical, suspicious of sentiment, and cynical. When a critic like Richard Corliss of *Time* magazine gushes about *The Joy Luck Club* being "a fourfold *Terms of Endearment*," my gut instinct is to run the other way. I resent being told how to feel. I went to see the 1993 eight-handkerchief movie version of Amy Tan's best-seller with a group that included my ten-year-old daughter. I was caught between the sincere desire to be swept up by the turbulent mother-daughter sagas and my own stubborn resistance to being so obviously manipulated by the filmmakers. With every flashback came tragedy. The music soared; the voice-overs were solemn or wistful; tears, tears, and more tears flowed onscreen. Daughters were reverent; mothers carried dark secrets.

I was elated by the grandness and strength of the four mothers and the luminous actors who portrayed them, but I was uneasy with the passivity of the Asian American daughters. They seemed to exist solely as receptors for their mothers' amazing life stories. It's almost as if by assimilating so easily into American society, they had lost all sense of self.

In spite of my resistance, my eyes watered as the desperate mother    10
played by Kieu Chinh was forced to abandon her twin baby girls on a
country road in war-torn China. (Kieu Chinh resembles my own mother
and her twin sister, who suffered through the brutal Japanese occupation
of the Philippines.) So far in this movie, an infant son had been deliberately drowned, a mother played by the gravely beautiful France Nuyen
had gone catatonic with grief, a concubine had cut her flesh open to save
her dying mother, an insecure daughter had been oppressed by her boorish Asian American husband, another insecure daughter had been left by
her white husband, and so on. . . . The overall effect was numbing as far
as I'm concerned, but a man sitting two rows in front of us broke down
sobbing. A Chinese Pilipino writer even more grouchy than me later
complained, "Must ethnicity only be equated with suffering?"

Because change has been slow, *The Joy Luck Club* carries a lot of cultural baggage. It is a big-budget story about Chinese American women,
directed by a Chinese American man, cowritten and coproduced by Chinese American women. That's a lot to be thankful for. And its box office
success proves that an immigrant narrative told from female perspectives
can have mass appeal. But my cynical side tells me that its success might
mean only one thing in Hollywood: more weepy epics about Asian
American mother-daughter relationships will be planned.

That the film finally got made was significant. By Hollywood standards (think white male; think money, money, money), a movie about
Asian Americans even when adapted from a best-seller was a risky proposition. When I asked a producer I know about the film's rumored delays,
he simply said, "It's still an *Asian* movie," surprised I had even asked.
Equally interesting was director Wayne Wang's initial reluctance to be
involved in the project; he told the *New York Times,* "I didn't want to do
another Chinese movie."

Maybe he shouldn't have worried so much. After all, according to
the media, the nineties are the decade of "Pacific Overtures" and East
Asian chic. Madonna, the pop queen of shameless appropriation, cultivated Japanese high-tech style with her music video "Rain," while Janet
Jackson faked kitschy orientalia in hers, titled "If." Critical attention was
paid to movies from China, Japan, and Vietnam. But that didn't mean an
honest appraisal of women's lives. Even on the art house circuit, filmmakers who should know better took the easy way out. Takehiro
Nakajima's 1992 film *Okoge* presents one of the more original film roles
for women in recent years. In Japanese, "okoge" means the crust of rice
that sticks to the bottom of the rice pot; in pejorative slang, it means fag
hag. The way "okoge" is used in the film seems a reappropriation of the
term; the portrait Nakajima creates of Sayoko, the so-called fag hag, is
clearly an affectionate one. Sayoko is a quirky, self-assured woman in
contemporary Tokyo who does voice-overs for cartoons, has a thing for

Frida Kahlo paintings, and is drawn to a gentle young gay man named Goh. But the other women's roles are disappointing, stereotypical "hysterical females" and the movie itself turns conventional halfway through. Sayoko sacrifices herself to a macho brute Goh desires, who rapes her as images of Frida Kahlo paintings and her beloved Goh rising from the ocean flash before her. She gives birth to a baby boy and endures a terrible life of poverty with the abusive rapist. This sudden change from spunky survivor to helpless, victimized woman is baffling. Whatever happened to her job? Or that arty little apartment of hers? Didn't her Frida Kahlo obsession teach her anything?

Then there was Tiana Thi Thanh Nga's *From Hollywood to Hanoi,* a self-serving but fascinating documentary. Born in Vietnam to a privileged family that included an uncle who was defense minister in the Thieu government and an idolized father who served as press minister, Nga (a.k.a. Tiana) spent her adolescence in California. A former actor in martial arts movies and fitness teacher ("Karaticize with Tiana"), the vivacious Tiana decided to make a record of her journey back to Vietnam.

*From Hollywood to Hanoi* is at times unintentionally very funny.  15 Tiana includes a quick scene of herself dancing with a white man at the Metropole hotel in Hanoi, and breathlessly announces: "That's me doing the tango with Oliver Stone!" Then she listens sympathetically to a horrifying account of the My Lai massacre by one of its few female survivors. In another scene, Tiana cheerfully addresses a food vendor on the streets of Hanoi: "Your hairdo is so pretty." The unimpressed, poker-faced woman gives a brusque, deadpan reply: "You want to eat, or what?" Sometimes it is hard to tell the difference between Tiana Thi Thanh Nga and her Hollywood persona: the real Tiana still seems to be playing one of her B-movie roles, which are mainly fun because they're fantasy. The time was certainly right to explore postwar Vietnam from a Vietnamese woman's perspective; it's too bad this film was done by a Valley Girl.

1993 also brought Tran Anh Hung's *The Scent of Green Papaya,* a different kind of Vietnamese memento — this is a look back at the peaceful, lush country of the director's childhood memories. The film opens in Saigon, in 1951. A willowy ten-year-old girl named Mui comes to work for a troubled family headed by a melancholy musician and his kind, stoic wife. The men of this bourgeois household are idle, pampered types who take naps while the women do all the work. Mui is male fantasy: she is a devoted servant, enduring acts of cruel mischief with patience and dignity; as an adult, she barely speaks. She scrubs floors, shines shoes, and cooks with loving care and never a complaint. When she is sent off to work for another wealthy musician, she ends up being impregnated by him. The movie ends as the camera closes in on Mui's contented face. Languid and precious, *The Scent of Green Papaya* is visually haunting, but it suffers from the director's colonial fantasy of women as docile, domestic creatures. Steeped in highbrow nostalgia, it's the arty Vietnamese version of *My Fair Lady* with the wealthy musician as Professor Higgins, teaching Mui to read and write.

And then there is Ang Lee's tepid 1993 hit, *The Wedding Banquet* — a clever culture-clash farce in which traditional Chinese values collide with contemporary American sexual mores. The somewhat formulaic plot goes like this: Wai-Tung, a yuppie landlord, lives with his white lover, Simon, in a chic Manhattan brownstone. Wai-Tung is an only child and his aging parents in Taiwan long for a grandchild to continue the family legacy. Enter Wei-Wei, an artist who lives in a grungy loft owned by Wai-Tung. She slugs tequila straight from the bottle as she paints and flirts boldly with her young, uptight landlord, who brushes her off. "It's my fate. I am always attracted to handsome gay men," she mutters. After this setup, the movie goes downhill, all edges blurred in a cozy nest of happy endings. In a refrain of Sayoko's plight in *Okoge,* a pregnant, suddenly complacent Wei-Wei gives in to family pressures — and never gets her life back.

> *"It takes a man to know what it is to be a real woman."*
> — SONG LILING in *M. Butterfly*

Ironically, two gender-bending films in which men play men playing women reveal more about the mythology of the prized Asian woman and the superficial trappings of gender than most movies that star real women. The slow-moving *M. Butterfly* presents the ultimate object of Western male desire as the spy/opera diva Song Liling, a Suzie Wong/Lotus Blossom played by actor John Lone with a five o'clock shadow and bobbing Adam's apple. The best and most profound of these forays into cross-dressing is the spectacular melodrama *Farewell My Concubine,* directed by Chen Kaige. Banned in China, *Farewell My Concubine* shared the prize for Best Film at the 1993 Cannes Film Festival with Jane Campion's *The Piano.* Sweeping through 50 years of tumultuous history in China, the story revolves around the lives of two male Beijing Opera stars and the woman who marries one of them. The three characters make an unforgettable triangle, struggling over love, art, friendship, and politics against the bloody backdrop of cultural upheaval. They are as capable of casually betraying each other as they are of selfless, heroic acts. The androgynous Dieyi, doomed to play the same female role of concubine over and over again, is portrayed with great vulnerability, wit, and grace by male Hong Kong pop star Leslie Cheung. Dieyi competes with the prostitute Juxian (Gong Li) for the love of his childhood protector and fellow opera star, Duan Xiaolou (Zhang Fengyi).

Cheung's highly stylized performance as the classic concubine-ready-to-die-for-love in the opera within the movie is all about female artifice. His sidelong glances, restrained passion, languid stance, small steps, and delicate, refined gestures say everything about what is considered desirable in Asian women — and are the antithesis of the feisty, outspoken woman played by Gong Li. The characters of Dieyi and Juxian both see suffering as part and parcel of love and life. Juxian matter-of-factly says to Duan Xiaolou before he agrees to marry her: "I'm used to hardship. If you take me in, I'll wait on you hand and foot. If you tire of me, I'll . . . kill myself. No big deal." It's an echo of Suzie Wong's servility, but the context is new. Even with her back to the wall, Juxian is not helpless or whiny. She attempts to manipulate a man while admitting to the harsh reality that is her life.

Dieyi and Juxian are the two sides of the truth of women's lives in most Asian countries. Juxian in particular — wife and ex-prostitute — could be seen as a thankless and stereotypical role. But like the characters Gong Li has played in Chinese director Zhang Yimou's films, *Red Sorghum, Raise the Red Lantern,* and especially *The Story of Qiu Ju,* Juxian is tough, obstinate, sensual, clever, oafish, beautiful, infuriating, cowardly, heroic, and banal. Above all, she is resilient. Gong Li is one of the few Asian Pacific actors whose roles have been drawn with intelligence, honesty, and depth. Nevertheless, the characters she plays are limited by the possibilities that exist for real women in China.

"Let's face it. Women still don't mean shit in China," my friend Meeling reminds me. What she says so bluntly about her culture rings painfully true, but in less obvious fashion for me. In the Philippines, infant girls aren't drowned, nor were their feet bound to make them more desirable. But sons were and are cherished. To this day, men of the bourgeois class are coddled and prized, much like the spoiled men of the elite household in *The Scent of Green Papaya.* We do not have a geisha tradition like Japan, but physical beauty is overtreasured. Our daughters are protected virgins or primed as potential beauty queens. And many of us have bought into the image of the white man as our handsome savior: G.I. Joe.

*Buzz* magazine recently featured an article entitled "Asian Women/L.A. Men," a report on a popular hangout that caters to white men's fantasies of nubile Thai women. The lines between movies and real life are blurred. Male screenwriters and cinematographers flock to this bar-restaurant, where the waitresses are eager to "audition" for roles. Many of these men have been to Bangkok while working on film crews for Vietnam War movies. They've come back to L.A., but for them, the movie never ends. In this particular fantasy the boys play G.I. Joe on a rescue mission in the urban jungle, saving the whore from herself. "A scene has developed here, a kind of R-rated *Cheers,*" author Alan Rifkin writes. "The waitresses audition for sitcoms. The customers date the waitresses or just keep score."

Colonization of the imagination is a two-way street. And being enshrined on a pedestal as someone's Pearl of the Orient fantasy doesn't seem so demeaning, at first; who wouldn't want to be worshipped? Perhaps that's why Asian women are the ultimate wet dream in most Hollywood movies; it's no secret how well we've been taught to play the role, to take care of our men. In Hollywood vehicles, we are objects of desire or derision; we exist to provide sex, color, and texture in what is essentially a white man's world. It is akin to what Toni Morrison calls "the Africanist presence" in literature. She writes: "Just as entertainers, through or by association with blackface, could render permissible topics that otherwise would have been taboo, so American writers were able to employ an imagined Africanist persona to articulate and imaginatively act out the forbidden in American culture." The same analogy could be made for the often titillating presence of Asian women in movies made by white men.

Movies are still the most seductive and powerful of artistic mediums, manipulating us with ease by a powerful combination of sound and image. In many ways, as females and Asians, as audiences or performers, we have learned to settle for less — to accept the fact that we are either decorative, invisible, or one-dimensional. When there are characters who look like us represented in a movie, we have also learned to view between the lines, or to add what is missing. For many of us, this way of watching has always been a necessity. We fill in the gaps. If a female character is presented as a mute, willowy beauty, we convince ourselves she is an ancestral ghost — so smart she doesn't have to speak at all. If she is a whore with a heart of gold, we claim her as a tough feminist icon. If she is a sexless, sanitized, boring nerd, we embrace her as role model for our daughters, rather than the tragic whore. And if she is presented as an utterly devoted saint suffering nobly in silence, we lie and say she is just like our mothers. Larger than life. Magical and insidious. A movie is never just a movie, after all.

## Reading the Text

1. Summarize in your own words Hagedorn's view of the traditional images of Asian women as presented in American film.
2. What is the chronology of Asian women in film that Hagedorn presents, and why do you think she gives us an historical overview?
3. Why does Hagedorn say that the film *The Joy Luck Club* "carries a lot of cultural baggage"?
4. What sort of images of Asian women does Hagedorn imply that she would prefer to see?

## Reading the Signs

1. Rent a videotape of *The Joy Luck Club* (or another film featuring Asian characters) and write an essay in which you support, refute, or modify Hagedorn's interpretation of the film.
2. In class, form teams and debate the proposition that Hollywood writers and directors have a social responsibility to avoid stereotyping ethnic characters. To develop your team's arguments, first brainstorm films that depict various ethnicities and then discuss whether the portrayals are

damaging or benign. You might also consult Benjamin DeMott's "Put on a Happy Face" (p. 295).

3. Study a magazine that targets Asian-American readers, such as *Transpacific* or *Yolk*. Then write an essay in which you discuss the extent to which Asian women fit the stereotypes that Hagedorn describes, keeping in mind the magazine's specific readership (businessmen, twentysomethings of both genders, and so forth).

4. In class, compare the stereotyped roles for Asian women that Hagedorn describes with the good and bad girl archetypes that Sandra Tsing Loh discusses in "The Return of Doris Day" (p. 287). What does your comparison suggest for the roles available for female characters of any race?

5. Watch one of the gender-bending films Hagedorn mentions (such as *M. Butterfly*) and write your own analysis of the gender roles portrayed in the film. To develop your ideas, consult Holly Devor's "Gender Role Behaviors and Attitudes" (p. 415).

# TANIA MODLESKI

## Dead White Male Heterosexual Poets Society

*Often the significance of a movie is concealed behind an elaborate smoke screen — especially when the true object of the film violates a cultural taboo. As Tania Modleski (b. 1949) argues in this probing analysis of the popular film* Dead Poets Society, *the taboo behind the scenes is Hollywood's prohibition on making openly gay films. To get around the taboos, filmmakers resort to carefully constructed codes — such as making Walt Whitman, America's great gay (as well as gray) poet, the poetic muse of* Dead Poets Society — *to pursue forbidden themes. For Modleski, however, there is a certain complicity by moviemakers with cultural censors when a film conceals its homoerotic material. This concealment also leads to flawed movies, in which certain parts of the action don't make any sense until you can decode them properly — as in the case of* Dead Poets Society. *Tania Modleski is a professor of English at the University of Southern California, where she teaches courses in film and women's studies; her books include* Loving with a Vengeance *(1982),* Studies in Entertainment *(1986),* The Woman Who Knew Too Much *(1987), and* Feminism Without Women *(1991), from which this selection is taken.*

Contemporary films are preoccupied with various *kinds* of male regression — physical, psychological, and historical — connecting nostalgia for the past and for childhood with male fears of the body and with a search for literalness in language. Nowhere are these fears and this quest more evident than in the hit film *Dead Poets Society,* which is set in a boys' boarding school in 1959. Here the insistence on boyhood sexual innocence is so extreme that the film may be said to mark the return of the "hysterical" text, in which the weight of the not-said, that which is again rapidly becoming "unspeakable," threatens to capsize the work's literal meaning. According to Geoffrey Nowell-Smith, who uses the term in discussing the family melodramas of the 1950s, the "hysterical text" is one in which the repressed sexual content of a film, banished from the film's narrative, returns to manifest itself in various ways in the *mise-en-scène* and through textual incoherences.[1] In *Dead Poets,* the repressed content is related to homoeroticism and gay sexuality. It is interesting to speculate on how the film's meaning would have changed were it to have introduced one literary figure in particular — Oscar Wilde, whose writing is judged by some critics to be the first in which "it was generally recognized that a literary work had a meaning other than its face value," whose work, then, posed a threat to the transparency and innocence of language, seeming to contaminate it with duplicitous double meanings.[2] In Wilde's case, of course, as a result of the trials, this doubleness has been lost to us and it has become impossible not to perceive the "gay" meanings of the texts.

So it is not surprising that the film turns to Walt Whitman as a more sexually ambiguous figure through whom to work out its ideologically conservative projects: first, not only to deny the homosexuality of Whitman but more generally to evade its own relation to homoeroticism; second, to appear, in true post–gay rights fashion, to be endorsing rebellious antiauthoritarian modes of behavior, but, third, to be actually evoking a longing for a closeted world in which such behavior would only serve to perpetuate a power structure that would ceaselessly punish it. Thus, despite the fact that Whitman's sexuality has been contested throughout many decades of literary criticism, the film makes no references to the debates over Whitman's homosexuality, focusing only on Whitman as the good gray poet: the free-thinking English teacher Mr. Keating, played by Robin Williams, insists on being called "Captain" or "Oh Captain, My Captain," singling out the one poem that exhibits pious deference to male authority — the very authority the film pretends to be challenging. It is not, incidentally, without relevance and certainly not without irony that Whitman's

---

1. Geoffrey Nowell-Smith, "Minnelli and Melodrama," in *Home Is Where the Heart Is: Studies in Melodrama and the Woman's Film,* ed. Christine Gledhill (London: BFI, 1987), pp. 70–74.

2. Michael Bronski, *Culture Clash: The Making of a Gay Sensibility* (Boston: South End Press, 1984), p. 53.

*[margin handwritten notes: "they are trying to hide it", "many meanings", "of Film", "not being straight forward", "they add heterosexual experiences to conceal it."]*

"corporeal utopianism" has recently been seen by one gay critic as existing in opposition to the moral-purity writers of the nineteenth century who were especially alarmed by the possible depravity of such homosocial environments as the male boarding school.[3] Welton, the setting of *Dead Poets,* would have given these writers no cause for concern.

Although the film exists in a genre of boys' boarding school films, some of which (like *The Devil's Playground*) brilliantly explore the homoerotic tensions of such an environment, and although it is directed by Peter Weir, whose previous work (e.g., *Gallipoli, Picnic at Hanging Rock*) is suffused with a lyrical homoeroticism, *Dead Poets* denies this dimension of boarding school life so resolutely that its repression can be systematically traced, the duplicitous meanings emerging after all. For example, one of the characters is a kind of misfit and a loner, unable to articulate his feelings and hence marginal to the group forming around Keating: In fact, the character reveals many of the signs of a sexual identity crisis, and in a more honest version of the film might have been shown struggling to come to terms with being gay in a heterosexual, homosocial environment. That the possible "latent" homosexual theme is overdetermined is suggested in one rather amazing scene in which Keating instructs the boy to come to the front of the room and, since he has been unable to complete the poetry writing assignment, to stare at a picture of Walt Whitman and spew out poetic phrases, while Keating spins him round and round, violently extracting the speech the boy has been withholding.

As for Keating, whose presence spawns the boys' secret society, lest anyone suspect his motives in returning to the repressive boys' school in which he had been a student, we see him in a carefully staged scene writing a letter to his fiancée whose picture is conspicuously propped on the desk. (Performing similar roles as "disclaimers" are the girls whom the boys entertain at one point in their cave, reciting poems that one of them claims to be original compositions.[4]) Asked by a student why he stays in such a stifling place, Keating responds that he loves teaching more than anything in the world; he gives no explanation of why he left the school in England, where his fiancée still lives, or why he has ruled out teaching in the public schools — clearly a more congenial place for his democratic, free-thinking sympathies. Such "disclaimers" as the photo (as well as a banal subplot in which a boy falls in love with a cheerleader and becomes rivals with a football hero in one of the public schools) and such

---

3. Michael Moon, "Disseminating Whitman," special issue, "Displacing Homophobia," ed. Ronald R. Butters, John M. Clum, and Michael Moon, *The South Atlantic Quarterly* 88, no. 1 (Winter 1989), p. 255.

4. "Disclaimer" is a term used by Robin Wood to denote aspects of plot or the existence of characters whose sole purpose is to assure us of the protagonists' heterosexuality. See his *Hollywood from Vietnam to Reagan* (New York: Columbia University Press, 1985), p. 229.

narrative incoherences might be taken as indicators of the film's repressed homoerotic content — the symptoms in the "hysterical text."

At the end of the film one boy, whose father has forbidden him to act in a play, defies his father by playing the role of Puck in a student production of *A Midsummer Night's Dream,* and then ends up killing himself because his father forbids him to continue in the role. Of all the roles to have chosen, this one seems most filled with latent — and because latent, homophobic — meaning, as if the struggle between a boy and his father were over the boy's right to "pose as a fairy." In the investigation that follows the suicide, John Keating becomes the scapegoat and is forced to leave the school, and the boys are called individually up to the principal, who orders them to "assume the position," and then paddles them. Implausibly, Keating comes to collect his things in the middle of an English class, which the principal has taken over, and as he leaves, one boy stands up to voice his support of his former teacher and then climbs up on his desk, repeating an act Keating had earlier urged the students to perform in order to encourage nonconformity. The other class members, conforming, as it were, to the boy's gesture of nonconformity, follow suit. In the final shot of the film, the camera frames the student as he stands looking at John Keating, the legs of another student straddling the image in the shape of an inverted V — the sexualized body which has been so systematically denied throughout the narrative emerging here, in hysterical fashion, in the body of the film itself, its *mise-en-scène.*

. . . *Dead Poets Society* is a profoundly regressive film, fixated on adolescence and a mythical moment in the past that it appears to repudiate but really longs for: a moment of repression and discipline and stable authority, represented by fathers, high school principals, and dead poets. By no means does the film anticipate the real rebellions that were shortly to erupt, even though it presupposes an audience that has lived through them. Thus the film challenges the literary canon and the orthodoxies of the "discipline" of literary studies (represented, for Keating, by the "realists" and by the textbook's editor whose introduction Keating instructs the boys to tear out), but returns us to this canon via a sanitized image of one of our most heterodox and sexually explicit authors; pays lip service to feminist demands for an end to exclusionary male societies, but on the grounds that male sexual needs will be better served (i.e., as one of them jokes, so the boys won't have to masturbate); and encourages such marginalized people as gay youths to speak, but only in unintelligible language. Far from anticipating the specific struggles of the 1960s and 1970s, the film lyricizes life in the closet, yearning for the time just before these rebellions — a time when, for example, there were no dead women poets (not even Emily Dickinson) and live females apparently could not tell the difference between Shakespeare and a schoolboy's poetry, a time before gay men would aid in problematizing the very notion of adolescent sexual innocence and Whitman would be brought further out of the closet. Like Keating and despite its disclaimers, its bad-faith mockery of

*[handwritten: making fun of tradition]*

"tradition," the film chooses the particular chronotope of the 1950s boys' school because it *wants* to be there: at a time and place in which tradition seemed entirely a white male heterosexual affair and could itself appear innocent, devoid of substance and body.

*[handwritten: They wanted to open up w/ homosexualism but they had to add "disclaimers" to make it not so blunt.]*

### Reading the Text

1. How, according to Modleski, does *Dead Poets Society* suppress its homo-erotic meanings?
2. How is *Dead Poets Society* an "hysterical" text?
3. What does Modleski mean by claiming that *Dead Poets Society* "lyricizes life in the closet"?

### Reading the Signs

1. Rent a videotape of *Dead Poets Society* and watch it with your class. Do you agree or disagree with Modleski's interpretation of the film? Discuss the issue in class, and then write an essay or journal entry supporting your position.
2. *Dead Poets Society* takes place at a boys' boarding school. Read or review Michael Parenti's "Class and Virtue" (p. 318). How might Parenti interpret the boys' attitudes toward social class?
3. Rent a videotape of *The Bird Cage*. How does the film's depiction of homosexual relations compare with the repressed homoeroticism Modleski sees in *Dead Poets Society*? How do you explain the differences?
4. Read or review Andy Medhurst's "Batman, Deviance, and Camp" (p. 358). How might Modleski interpret the homoeroticism implicit in the Batman-Robin relationship?

# MICHAEL PARENTI

## Class and Virtue

||||||||||||||||||||||||||||||||||||||||||||||||||

*In 1993, a movie called* Indecent Proposal *presented a story in which a billionaire offers a newly poor middle-class woman a million dollars if she'll sleep with him for one night. In Michael Parenti's terms, what was really indecent about the movie was the way it showed the woman falling in love with the billionaire, thus making a romance out of a class outrage. But the movie could get away with it, partly because Hollywood has al-ways conditioned audiences to root for the ruling classes and to ignore the inequities of class privilege. In this selection from* Make-Believe Media: The Politics of Entertainment *(1992), Parenti (b. 1933) argues that Hollywood has long been in the business of representing the interests of the ruling classes. Whether it is forgiving the classist behavior in* Pretty Woman *or glamorizing the lives of the wealthy, Hollywood makes sure its audiences leave the theater thinking you can't be too rich. Michael Parenti is a writer who lectures widely at university campuses around the country. His publications include* Power and the Powerless *(1978),* Inventing Reality: The Politics of the News Media *(1986),* Democracy for the Few *(1988),* Against Empire *(1995), and* Dirty Truths *(1996).*

*Parenti feels that Hollywood is to blame for distorting the thoughts of moralistic average people. Even though it was wrong what she did, Hollywood reaches out to the people*

## Class and Virtue

The entertainment media present working people not only as unlettered and uncouth but also as less desirable and less moral than other people. Conversely, virtue is more likely to be ascribed to those characters whose speech and appearance are soundly middle- or upper-middle class.

Even a simple adventure story like *Treasure Island* (1934, 1950, 1972) manifests this implicit class perspective. There are two groups of acquisitive persons searching for a lost treasure. One, headed by a squire, has money enough to hire a ship and crew. The other, led by the rascal Long John Silver, has no money — so they sign up as part of the crew. The narrative implicitly assumes from the beginning that the squire has a moral claim to the treasure, while Long John Silver's gang does not. After all, it is the squire who puts up the venture capital for the ship. Having no investment in the undertaking other than their labor, Long John and his men, by definition, will be "stealing" the treasure, while the squire will be "discovering" it.

To be sure, there are other differences. Long John's men are cutthroats. The squire is not. Yet, one wonders if the difference between a bad pirate and a good squire is itself not preeminently a matter of having the right amount of disposable income. The squire is no less acquisitive than the conspirators. He just does with money what they must achieve with cutlasses. The squire and his associates dress in fine clothes, speak an educated diction, and drink brandy. Long John and his men dress slovenly, speak in guttural accents, and drink rum. From these indications alone, the viewer knows who are the good guys and who are the bad. Virtue is visually measured by one's approximation to proper class appearances.

Sometimes class contrasts are juxtaposed within one person, as in *The Three Faces of Eve* (1957), a movie about a woman who suffers from multiple personalities. When we first meet Eve (Joanne Woodward), she is a disturbed, strongly repressed, puritanically religious person, who speaks with a rural, poor-Southern accent. Her second personality is that of a wild, flirtatious woman who also speaks with a rural, poor-Southern accent. After much treatment by her psychiatrist, she is cured of these schizoid personalities and emerges with a healthy third one, the real Eve, a poised, self-possessed, pleasant woman. What is intriguing is that she now speaks with a cultivated, affluent, Smith College accent, free of any low-income regionalism or ruralism, much like Joanne Woodward herself. This transformation in class style and speech is used to indicate mental health without any awareness of the class bias thusly expressed.

Mental health is also the question in *A Woman Under the Influence* (1974), the story of a disturbed woman who is married to a hard-hat husband. He cannot handle — and inadvertently contributes to — her emotional deterioration. She is victimized by a spouse who is nothing more than an insensitive, working-class bull in a china shop. One comes away convinced that every unstable woman needs a kinder, gentler, and above all, more *middle-class* hubby if she wishes to avoid a mental crack-up.

Class prototypes abound in the 1980s television series *The A-Team*. In each episode, a Vietnam-era commando unit helps an underdog, be it a Latino immigrant or a disabled veteran, by vanquishing some menacing force such as organized crime, a business competitor, or corrupt government officials. As always with the make-believe media, the A-Team does good work on an individualized rather than collectively organized basis, helping particular victims by thwarting particular villains. The A-Team's leaders are two white males of privileged background. The lowest ranking members of the team, who do none of the thinking nor the leading, are working-class palookas. They show they are good with their hands, both by punching out the bad guys and by doing the maintenance work on the team's flying vehicles and cars. One of them, "B.A." (bad ass), played by the African-American Mr. T., is visceral, tough, and purposely bad-mannered toward those he doesn't like. He projects an image of crudeness and ignorance and is associated with the physical side of things. In sum, the team has a brain (the intelligent white leaders) and a body with its simpler physical functions (the working-class characters), a hierarchy that corresponds to the social structure itself.[1]

Sometimes class bigotry is interwoven with gender bigotry, as in *Pretty Woman* (1990). A dreamboat millionaire corporate raider finds himself all alone for an extended stay in Hollywood (his girlfriend is unwilling to join him), so he quickly recruits a beautiful prostitute as his playmate of the month. She is paid three thousand dollars a week to wait around his super-posh hotel penthouse ready to perform the usual services and accompany him to business dinners at top restaurants. As prostitution goes, it is a dream gig. But there is one cloud on the horizon. She is low-class. She doesn't know which fork to use at those CEO power feasts, and she's bothersomely fidgety, wears tacky clothes, chews gum, and, y'know, doesn't talk so good. But with some tips from the hotel manager, she proves to be a

---

1. Gina Marchetti, "Class, Ideology and Commercial Television: An Analysis of 'The A-Team,'" *Journal of Film and Video,* 39, Spring 1987, pp. 19–28.

veritable Eliza Doolittle in her class metamorphosis. She dresses in proper attire, sticks the gum away forever, and starts picking the right utensils at dinner. She also figures out how to speak a little more like Joanne Woodward without the benefit of a multiple personality syndrome, and she develops the capacity to sit in a poised, wordless, empty-headed fashion, every inch the expensive female ornament.

She is still a prostitute but a classy one. It is enough of a distinction for the handsome young corporate raider. Having liked her because she was charmingly cheap, he now loves her all the more because she has real polish and is a more suitable companion. So suitable that he decides to do the right thing by her: set her up in an apartment so he can make regular visits at regular prices. But now she wants the better things in life, like marriage, a nice house, and, above all, a different occupation, one that would allow her to use less of herself. She is furious at him for treating her like, well, a prostitute. She decides to give up her profession and get a high-school diploma so that she might make a better life for herself — perhaps as a filing clerk or receptionist or some other of the entry-level jobs awaiting young women with high school diplomas.[2]

After the usual girl-breaks-off-with-boy scenes, the millionaire prince returns. It seems he can't concentrate on making money without her. He even abandons his cutthroat schemes and enters into a less lucrative but supposedly more productive, caring business venture with a struggling old-time entrepreneur. The bad capitalist is transformed into a good capitalist. He then carries off his ex-prostitute for a lifetime of bliss. The moral is a familiar one, updated for post-Reagan yuppiedom: A woman can escape from economic and gender exploitation by winning the love and career advantages offered by a rich male. Sexual allure goes only so far unless it develops a material base and becomes a class act.[3]

### Reading the Text

1. What characteristics are attributed to working-class and upper-class film characters, according to Parenti?
2. How does Parenti see the relationship between class bigotry and gender bigotry in *Pretty Woman*?
3. What relationship does Parenti see between mental health and class values in films?

### Reading the Signs

1. Rent a videotape of *Wall Street* and analyze the class issues that the movie raises.

---

2. See the excellent review by Lydia Sargent, *Z Magazine,* April 1990, pp. 43–45.
3. Ibid.

2. Using Parenti's argument as a critical framework, interpret the class values implicit in a television show such as *Beverly Hills, 90210* or *Roseanne*. Is the show that you've selected guilty of what Parenti calls "class bigotry"?

3. Do you agree with Parenti's interpretation of *Pretty Woman*? Write an argumentative essay in which you defend, challenge, or complicate his claims.

4. Read or review Holly Devor's "Gender Role Behaviors and Attitudes" (p. 415). How would Devor explain the gender bigotry that Parenti finds in *Pretty Woman*?

5. Rent the 1954 film *On the Waterfront* and watch it with your class. How are labor unions and working-class characters portrayed in that film? Does the film display the "class bigotry" that Parenti describes?

6. Read or review Michael Omi's "In Living Color" (p. 491). Then write a journal entry in which you create a category of cinematic "racial bigotry" that corresponds to Parenti's two categories of class and gender bigotry. What films that you have seen illustrate your new category?

# MICHAEL MEDVED

## The Long Arm of What You Watch

*Do movies glamorize violence? Does Hollywood contribute to the violent nature of American society? While not pointing his finger too directly in this op-ed piece on the relation between entertainment and violence, Michael Medved (b. 1948) does suggest that Hollywood executives have a social responsibility to avoid desensitizing American audiences to the dangers of violent behavior. A prominent media critic, Medved is cohost of PBS's "Sneak Previews," chief film critic for the* New York Post, *and author of* What Really Happened to the Class of '65?, The Shadow Presidents, Hospital, *and* Hollywood vs. America *(1992).*

In the past few days, Americans have seen chilling confirmation of the powerful impact that fanciful images in the popular culture exert on everyday life.

No, I'm not talking about the case of a torched toll booth in the New York subway, apparently in imitation of a scene in the current film, "Money Train." I'm referring to the ubiquitous toy commercials that turn up everywhere this time of year and make their influence felt in every home with kids and a TV. No matter how young they are, children have a distressing tendency to point to some glitzy gizmo fetchingly displayed on the family tube and to demand, in tones too insistent to be safely ignored, "I want it!"

Television is a medium so potent that it can implant these ardent imperatives in the minds of our kids in the course of a 30-second ad. How can we then pretend that it will fail, over the course of hours and hours of irresponsible programming, to instill other urgent and unwelcome yearnings?

Both critics of the entertainment industry and apologists for the Hollywood establishment have recently spent too much time debating the significance of the subway torching and other copycat crimes. The most profound problem with the popular culture isn't its immediate impact on a few vulnerable and explosive individuals, but its long-term influence on all the rest of us. The deepest concerns about Hollywood go beyond the industry's role in provoking a handful of specific and horrifying incidents. They involve its contributions to a general climate of violence, fear, impatience and self-indulgence.

Defenders of violent TV and movies are unquestionably correct in     5
pointing out that the overwhelming majority of people who view such material never directly imitate what they see on screen. But this doesn't mean they remain altogether unaffected by the gratuitously brutal scenes included in so much of American entertainment.

Consider, once again, the example of television commercials. Only a tiny fraction of those who watch a Lexus ad will ever go out and buy the car. Does that prove that the auto company has wasted the millions it spent on these ads, or that the public hasn't been influenced in any way by the elegant and seductive images so painstakingly prepared by the advertising agency? Of course not. Even those who will never come close to buying a Lexus are affected by the commercial, which, after repeated viewings, defines the vehicle as a desirable symbol of status and power and good taste.

In the same sense, the entertainment industry's constant depiction of violent and destructive behavior, as perpetrated by some of the most attractive and glamorous human beings on the planet, redefines such conduct as sexy, glamorous, even admirable. We may not instantly copy dangerous or despicable actions we view in movies or on TV, but that doesn't indicate that media images are powerless to alter our notions of what is acceptable — or fashionable — in the world around us. Watch the way that children in particular will subtly, sometimes unconsciously, pattern their speech or dress or hairstyles after favorite figures in the popular culture. It's absurd to suggest that such influence will end in every case at the most superficial level.

This recognition hardly suggests that censorship is an appropriate remedy. Few commentators or political figures — no, not even Sen. Bob Dole — advocate government restrictions on the right of Hollywood's creative community to produce even the most tawdry trash.

One can agree with the notion that movie makers have a perfect right to produce films glorifying, say, the rape and mutilation of young women at the same time that one argues that they have a responsibility not to do so.

There is no shortage of positive material in Hollywood; the Writers' Guild registers 27,000 new screenplays every year. In deciding which few of these projects will get made and which won't, the studios appropriately ask two basic questions: Will it make money? Does it have artistic value?

Executives should add a third fundamental question to the equation: What will be the impact of this proposed entertainment on the society in which we live? If Hollywood's leaders explore this dimension of their work more fully, more consistently and more responsibly, they will begin to win back some of the trust of an increasingly hostile and suspicious public.

### Reading the Text

1. What is Medved's position on the censorship of violence in films and TV programming?
2. How, according to Medved, does Hollywood glamorize violence? Why does he say Hollywood critics spend "too much time debating the significance of . . . copycat crimes"?
3. What steps would Medved recommend that Hollywood executives take to prevent the negative social effects of violent and destructive behavior on the screen?
4. What are Medved's assumptions about a film's ability to influence its audience's behaviors?

### Reading the Signs

1. In class, form teams and then stage a debate on Medved's central contention that Hollywood productions contribute to "a general climate of violence, fear, impatience, and self-indulgence." To develop your team's argument, be sure to brainstorm films or TV shows that display, in Medved's terms, "violent and destructive" behavior.
2. In your journal, outline a film that would satisfy Medved's desire for a positive effect on American society. Share your outline with your class.
3. In class, brainstorm names of films that glamorize gang membership and behavior. Then discuss whether you believe that such films have influenced American youths' attitudes toward and membership in gangs in the last decade.
4. The controversial Telecommunications Bill of 1996 requires all new television sets to be installed with the V-chip (violence chip), which would allow parents to program their sets so they can block their children's access to violent shows. Research the V-chip controversy and then write your own argument on whether you believe the V-chip is an effective way to address the concerns over excess violence on the TV screen.

SHELBY STEELE

*Malcolm X*

*One of the most independent-minded and widely read of America's writers on racial relations, Shelby Steele (b. 1946) has never been afraid to take a controversial position. In this reading of Spike Lee's* Malcolm X, *Steele goes beyond a critique of the film, which he feels oversimplifies the life and meaning of Malcolm X, to take on the myth of Malcolm X itself. At a time when Malcolm X is being celebrated as an icon of radical black nationalism, Steele argues that Malcolm was a profoundly conservative man whose appeal lies precisely in his cultural conservatism. From his beliefs in the family-building responsibilities of black women to his abhorrence of tobacco and alcohol, Malcolm X actually endorsed many of America's most traditional values — a side to his character that is often ignored. For Steele, who wishes to understand Malcolm X, not debunk him, all the mythmaking about the man does little to help us interpret his full cultural significance — a task that Steele begins here. Shelby Steele is currently a research fellow at Stanford University's Hoover Institute and the author of* The Content of Our Character: A New Vision of Race in America *(1990), which won a National Book Critics Circle Award.*

When asked recently what he thought of Malcolm X, Thurgood Marshall is reported to have said, "All he did was talk." And yet there is a kind of talk that constitutes action, a catalytic speech that changes things as irrevocably as do events or great movements. Malcolm X was an event, and his talk transformed American culture as surely, if not as thoroughly, as the civil rights movement, which might not have found the moderation necessary for its success had Malcolm not planted in the American consciousness so uncompromised a vision of the underdog's rage.

Malcolm staked out this territory against his great contemporary and foil, Martin Luther King, Jr. Sneering at King's turn-the-other-cheek Christianity, he told blacks, "Don't ask God to have mercy on him [the white man]; ask God to judge him. Ask God to do onto him what he did onto you. Ask God that he suffer as you suffered." To use the old Christian categories, Malcolm was the Old Testament to King's New Testament. Against the moral nobility of the civil rights movement, he wanted whites to know that he was not different from them; that he, too, would kill or die for freedom. "The price of freedom is death," he often said.

Like all true revolutionaries, Malcolm had an intimate relationship with his own death. By being less afraid of it than other men, he took on power. And this was not so much a death wish as it was the refusal of a compromised life. These seemed to be his terms, and for many blacks like myself who came of age during his era, there was nothing to do but love him, since he, foolishly or not, seemed to love us more than we loved ourselves.

It is always context that makes a revolutionary figure like Malcolm X a hero or a destroyer. Even when he first emerged in the late fifties and early sixties, the real debate was not so much about him (he was clear enough) as about whether or not the context of black oppression was severe enough to justify him. And now that Malcolm has explosively reemerged on the American scene, those old questions about context are with us once again.

Spike Lee has brought Malcolm's autobiography to the screen in one of the most thoroughly hyped films in American history. Malcolm's life is available in airport bookstalls. Compact discs and videotapes of his "blue-eyed devil" speeches can be picked up at Tower Records. His "X" is ubiquitous to the point of gracing automobile air fresheners. Twenty-seven years after his death, in sum, he is more visible to Americans than he was during his life. Of course Americans will commercialize anything; but that is a slightly redundant point. The really pressing matter is what this says about the context of race relations in America today. How can a new generation of blacks — after pervasive civil rights legislation, Great Society programs, school busing, open housing, and more than two decades of affirmative action — be drawn to a figure of such seething racial alienation?

The life of Malcolm X touched so many human archetypes that his story itself seems to supersede any racial context, which is to say that it meshes with virtually every context. Malcolm X is a story. And so he meets people, particularly young people, in a deeply personal way. To assess whether or not he is a good story for these times, I think we have to consider first the nature of his appeal.

Let me say — without, I hope, too many violins — that when I was growing up in the 1950s, I was very often the victim of old-fashioned racism and discrimination. These experiences were very much like the literal experience of being burned. Not only did they hurt, they also caused me to doubt myself in some fundamental way. There was shame in these experiences as well, the suspicion that by some measure of human worth I deserved them. This, of course, is precisely what they were designed to make me feel. So right away there was an odd necessity to fight and to struggle for both personal and racial dignity.

Those were the experiences that enabled me to hear Malcolm. The very soul of his legend was the heroic struggle that he was waging against racial doubt and shame. After a tortuous childhood and an early life of crime that left him shattered, he reconstructed himself — against the injuries of racial oppression — by embracing an ideology of black nationalism. Black nationalism offered something very important to Malcolm, and this quickly became his magnificently articulated offering to other blacks. What it offered was a perfectly cathartic distribution of love and hate. Blacks were innocent victims, whites were evil oppressors, and blacks had to distribute their love and hate accordingly. But if one focuses on the called-for hatred of whites, the point of Malcolm's redistribution of emotion will be missed. If Malcolm was screaming his hatred of whites, his deeper purpose was to grant blacks a license to give themselves what they needed most: self-love.

This license to love and to hate in a way that soothed my unconscious doubts was nothing less than compelling by the time I reached college. Late at night in the dorm, my black friends and I would turn off the lights for effect and listen to his album of speeches, *The Ballot or the Bullet,* over and over again. He couldn't have all that anger and all that hate unless he really loved black people, and, therefore, us. And so he massaged the injured part of ourselves with an utterly self-gratifying and unconditional love.

With Martin Luther King, by contrast, there were conditions. King    10
asked blacks — despised and unloved — to spread their meager stock of love to all people, even to those who despised us. What a lot to ask, and of a victim. With King, we were once again in second place, loving others before ourselves. But Malcolm told us to love ourselves first and to project all of our hurt into a hatred of the "blue-eyed devil" who had hurt us in the first place.

In Malcolm's deployment of love and hate there was an intrinsic logic of dignity that was very different from King's. For King, racial dignity was established by enlarging the self into a love of others. For Malcolm, dignity came from constriction, from shrinking to the enemy's size, and showing him not that you could be higher than he was, but that you could go as low. If King rose up, Malcolm dropped down. And here is where he used the hatred side of his formula to lay down his two essential principles of black dignity: the dehumanization of the white man and the threat of violence.

What made those principles essential to the dignity of blacks for Malcolm was that they followed a tit-for-tat logic — the logic by which, in his mind, any collective established its dignity against another collective. And both these principles could be powerfully articulated by Malcolm because they were precisely the same principles by which whites had oppressed blacks for centuries. Malcolm dehumanized whites by playing back, in whiteface, the stereotypes that blacks had endured. He made them animals — if they like their meat rare, "that's the dog in 'em." In the iconography of his Black Muslim period, whites were heathen, violent, drooling beasts who lynched and raped. But he often let his humor get the best of him in this, and most blacks took it with a grain of salt.

What made Malcolm one of the most controversial Americans of this century was the second principle in his logic of dignity: the threat of violence. "If we have a funeral in Harlem, make sure they have one downtown, too." "If he puts his hand on you, send him to the cemetery." Tit-for-tat logic taken to its logical conclusion. In fact, Malcolm's focus on violence against whites was essentially rhetorical. Like today's black street gangs, his Black Muslims were far more likely to kill each other than go after whites. Yet no one has ever played the white hysteria over black violence better than Malcolm.

He played this card very effectively to achieve two things. The first was to breach the horrible invisibility that blacks have endured in America. White racism has always been sustained by the white refusal or reluctance to see blacks, to think about them as people, to grant them the kind of place in the imagination that one would grant, say, to the English or even the Russians. Blacks might be servile or troublesome, but never worthy of serious, competitive consideration. Against this Malcolm sent a concrete message: We are human enough to want to kill you for what you have done to us. How does it feel to have people you have never paid much attention to want to kill you? (This was the terror Richard Wright captured so powerfully in *Native Son*: Your humble chauffeur may kill your daughter. And that novel, too, got attention.) Violence was a means to black visibility for Malcolm, and later for many other militants.

Today this idea of violence as black visibility means that part of Malcolm's renewed popularity comes from his power as an attention-getting figure. If today's "X" is an assertion of self-love, it is also a demand to be seen. This points to the second purpose of Malcolm's violent rhetoric: to restore dignity to blacks in an almost Hegelian sense. Those unwilling to kill and to die for dignity would forever be a slave class. Here he used whites as the model. They would go to war to meet any threat, even when it was far removed. Many times he told his black audiences that whites would not respect them unless they used "any means necessary" to seize freedom. For a minority outnumbered ten to one, this was not rational. But it was a point that needed to be made in the name of dignity. It was something that many blacks needed to feel about themselves, that there was a line that no one could cross.

Yet this logic of dignity only partly explains Malcolm's return as an icon in our own day. I believe that the larger reason for his perdurability and popularity is one that is almost never mentioned: that Malcolm X was a deeply conservative man. In times when the collective identity is besieged and confused, groups usually turn to their conservatives, not to their liberals; to their extreme partisans, not to their open-minded representatives. The last twenty-five years have seen huge class and cultural differences open up in black America. The current bromide is that we are not a monolith, and this is profoundly true. We now have a black governor and a black woman senator and millions of black college graduates and so on, but also hundreds of thousands of young blacks in prison. Black identity no longer has a centrifugal force in a racial sense. And in the accompanying confusion we look to the most conservative identity figure.

Malcolm was conservative through and through. As a black nationalist, he was a hard-line militarist who believed in the principle of self-mastery through force. His language and thinking in this regard were oddly in line with Henry Kissinger's description of the world as a brutal place in which safety and a balance of power is maintained through realpolitik. He was Reaganesque in his insistence on negotiating with whites from a position of strength — meaning the threat of violence. And his commitment (until the last year of his life) to racial purity and separatism would have made him the natural ally of David Duke.

In his personal life, moreover, Malcolm scrupulously followed all the Islamic strictures against alcohol, tobacco, drugs, fornication, and adultery, and his attitude toward women was decidedly patriarchal: As a Black Muslim minister he counseled that women could never be completely trusted because of their vanity, and he forbade dancing in his mosque. In his speeches he reserved a special contempt for white liberals, and he once praised Barry Goldwater as a racial realist. Believing entirely in black self-help, he had no use for government programs to uplift blacks, and sneered at the 1964 Civil Rights Bill as nothing more than white expedience.

Malcolm X was one of the most unabashed and unqualified conservatives of his time. And yet today he is forgiven his sexism by black feminists, his political conservatism by black and white liberals, his Islamic faith by black Christians, his violent rhetoric by nonviolent veterans of the civil rights struggle, his anti-Semitism by blacks and whites who are repulsed by it, his separatism by blacks who live integrated lives, and even the apparent fabrication of events in his childhood by those who would bring his story to the screen. Malcolm enjoys one of the best Teflon coatings of all time.

I think one of the reasons for this is that he was such an extreme    20
conservative, that is, such an extreme partisan of his group. All we really ask of such people is that they love the group more than anything else, even themselves. If this is evident, all else is secondary. In fact, we demand conservatism from such people, because it is a testament of their love. Malcolm sneered at government programs because he believed so much in black people: They could do it on their own. He gave up all his vices to intensify his love. He was a father figure who distributed love and hate in our favor. Reagan did something like this when he called the Soviet Union an "evil empire," and he, too, was rewarded with Teflon.

The point is that all groups take their extreme partisans more figuratively than literally. Their offer of unconditional love bribes us into loving them back rather unconditionally, so that our will to be literal with them weakens. We will not see other important black leaders of the

1960s — James Farmer, Whitney Young, Andrew Young, Medgar Evers (a genuine martyr), Roy Wilkins, John Lewis — gracing the T-shirts of young blacks who are today benefiting more from their efforts than from Malcolm's. They were too literal, too much of the actual world, for iconography, for the needs of an unsure psyche. But Malcolm, the hater and the lover, the father figure of romantic blackness, is the perfect icon.

It helps, too, that he is dead, and therefore unable to be literal in our own time. We can't know, for example, if he would now be supporting affirmative action as the reparation that is due to blacks, or condemning it as more white patronization and black dependency. In a way, the revival of Malcolm X is one of the best arguments I know of for the validity of the deconstructionist view of things: Malcolm is now a text. Today we *read* Malcolm. And this — dare I say — is one quality he shares with Christ, who also died young and became a text. He was also an Odyssean figure who journeyed toward self-knowledge. He was a priest and a heretic. For many whites he was a devil and for many blacks a martyr. Even those of my generation who grew up with him really came to know him through the autobiography that he wrote with Alex Haley. Even in his time, then, he was a text, and it is reasonable to wonder if he would have the prominence he has today without that book.

How will the new epic movie of his life — yet another refracting text — add to his prominence? Clearly it will add rather than subtract. It is a film that enhances the legend, that tries to solidify Malcolm's standing as a symbol of identity. To this end, the film marches uncritically through the well-known episodes of the life. It is beautifully shot and superbly acted by a cast that seemed especially inspired by the significance of the project. And yet it is still, finally, a march. Spike Lee, normally filled with bravado, works here like a TV docudramatist with a big budget, for whom loyalty to a received version of events is more important than insight, irony, or vision. Bruce Perry's recent study of Malcolm's life, *Malcolm: A Life of the Man Who Changed Black America,* which contradicts much of the autobiography, is completely and indefensibly ignored.

Against Lee's portrayal of Malcolm's father as a stalwart Garveyite killed by the Klan, Perry reveals a man with a reputation for skirt-chasing who moved from job to job and was often violent with his children. Lee shows the Klan burning down Malcolm's childhood home, while Perry offers considerable evidence to indicate that Malcolm's father likely burned it down himself after he received an eviction notice. Lee offers a dramatic scene of the Klan running Earl Little and his family out of Nebraska, yet Malcolm's mother told Perry that the event never happened. The rather heroic cast that Malcolm (and Lee) gave to his childhood is contradicted by Perry's extensive interviews with childhood friends, who portray Malcolm as rather fearful and erratic. Lee's only response to Perry's work was simply, "I don't believe it."

It was Spike Lee's unthinking loyalty to the going racial orthodoxy, I    25
believe, that led him to miss more than he saw, and to produce a film
that is finally part fact, part fiction, and entirely middlebrow. That racial
orthodoxy is a problem for many black artists working today, since its
goal is to make the individual artist responsible for the collective political
vision. This orthodoxy arbitrates the artist's standing within the group:
The artist can be as individual as he or she likes as long as the group view
of things is upheld. The problem here for black artists is that their racial
identity will be held hostage to the practice of their art. The effect of this
is to pressure the work of art, no matter what inspired it, into a gesture of
identification that reunites the artist and the group.

In this sense Lee's *Malcolm X* might be called a reunion film, or a
gesture of identification on his part toward the group. Thus his loyalist,
unquestioning march through Malcolm's mythology. It is certainly ironic,
given the debate over whether a white man could direct this film, that
Spike Lee sees his hero as only a black man with no more than black motivations. Human motivations like doubt, fear, insecurity, jealousy, and
love, or human themes like the search for the father, betrayal, and
tragedy, are present in the film because they were present in Malcolm's
story, but Lee seems unaware of them as the real stuff of his subject's life.
The film expresses its identification with much racial drama, but in a
human monotone.

Thus many of the obvious ironies of Malcolm's life are left hanging.
If black nationalism resurrected Malcolm in prison, it also killed him in
the end. This was a man who put all his faith in the concept of a black
nation, in the idea that blackness, in itself, carried moral significance, and
yet it was black nationalist fingers pulling the triggers that killed him.
Even on its surface this glaring irony points to the futility of cultish racial ideologies, to the collective insecurities that inspire them, and to
the frightened personalities that adhere to them as single-mindedly as
Malcolm did. But doesn't this irony also underscore the much more
common human experience of falling when we grip our illusions too
tightly, when we need them too much? It should not embarrass Lee to
draw out the irony of Malcolm being killed by blacks. He was. And there
is a lesson in it for everyone, since we are all hurt by our illusions. To
make his gesture of identification, however, Lee prefers to sacrifice the
deeper identification that his entire audience might have with his subject.


He also fails to perform the biographer's critical function. Clearly
Malcolm had something of the true believer's compulsion to believe
blindly and singularly, to eradicate all complexity as hypocrisy. All his life
he seemed to have no solid internal compass of his own to rely on in the
place of ideology — which is not to say that he didn't have brilliance
once centered by a faith. But in this important way he was very unlike

King, who, lacking Malcolm's wounds, was so well centered that he projected serenity and composure even as storms raged around him. Out of some underlying agitation Malcolm searched for authorities, for systems of belief, for father figures, for revelations: West Indian Archie, Elijah Muhammad, the Black Muslim faith, Pan Africanism, and finally the humanism of traditional Islam. All this in thirty-nine years! What else might have followed? How many more fathers? How many more -isms?

Moreover, once Malcolm learned from these people, faiths, and ideologies — or had taken what he could from them — he betrayed them all, one after another. There was always this pattern of complete, true-believing submission to authority and then the abrupt betrayal of it. There was something a little narcissistic in this, as though his submissions were really setups for the victories that he would later seize. And with each betrayal-victory there was something of a gloat — his visit to West Indian Archie when he was broken, his telling Mike Wallace on national television about Elijah Muhammad's infidelities. Betrayal was triumph for Malcolm, a moving beyond some smallness, some corruption, some realm that was beneath him.

The corruption at the heart of Malcolm's legend is that he looked    30
bigger than life because he always lived in small, cultish worlds, and always stood next to small people. He screamed at whites, but he had no idea of how to work with them to get things done. King was the man who had to get things done. I don't think that it is farfetched to suggest that finally Malcolm was afraid of white people. While King stared down every white from Bull Connor to the Kennedys, Malcolm made a big deal out of facing off with Elijah Muhammad, whom he had likely propped up for the purpose. His proclivity for little people who made him look big suggests that his black nationalism covered his fear of hard, ordinary work in the American crucible. Up against larger realities and bigger people, he might have felt inadequate.

Lee's film, as beautifully executed as it is, refuses to ask questions about Malcolm's legend. A quick look behind the legend, however, shows that Malcolm's real story was, in truth, tragedy. And the understanding of this grim truth would have helped the film better achieve the racial protest it is obviously after. Malcolm was hurt badly by oppression early in his childhood. If his family was not shattered in the way he claimed, it was shattered nevertheless. And this shattering had much to do with America's brutal racial history. He was, in his pain, a product of America. But his compensations for the hurt only extended the hurt. And the tragedy was the life that this extraordinary man felt that he needed to live, that Malcolm Little had to become Malcolm X, had to be a criminal, then a racial ideologue, and finally a martyr for an indefinable cause. Black nationalism is a tragedy of white racism, and can sometimes be as ruinous as the racism itself.

And so it is saddening to witness the reemergence of this hyped-up, legendary Mr. X, this seller of wolf tickets and excuses not to engage American society. This Malcolm is back to conceal rather than to reveal. He is here to hide our fears as he once hid his own, to keep us separated from any helpful illumination. Had the real Malcolm, the tragic Malcolm, returned, however, it would have represented a remarkable racial advancement. That Malcolm might have given both blacks and whites a way to comprehend our racial past and present. In him we all could have seen the damage done, the frustrations borne, and the fruitless heroism of the American insistence on race.

## Reading the Text

1. How has the image of Malcolm X evolved since the 1950s, according to Steele?
2. Summarize in a paragraph Steele's opinion of the film *Malcolm X*.
3. Why does Steele see Malcolm X as a fundamentally conservative figure? What evidence does he offer in support of his thesis?
4. What does Steele mean by saying that "This Malcolm is back to conceal rather than to reveal"?

## Reading the Signs

1. Rent a videotape of *Malcolm X* and write your own critique of it.
2. Do you agree with Steele's assertion that Malcolm X is a popular figure because of his conservatism? Write an essay in which you provide your own explanation of the popularity of Malcolm X (the movie and the character). Why were the 1990s the decade in which he made a comeback in American popular consciousness?
3. How would Sam Fulwood III ("The Rage of the Black Middle Class," p. 510) explain the popularity of Malcolm X? In what ways would his perspective on race in America contradict or extend Steele's analysis?
4. Read *The Autobiography of Malcolm X* and write an essay in which you compare the book's vision of Malcolm X with his portrayal in the film.
5. Drawing upon Robert Ray's "The Thematic Paradigm" (p. 278), write an essay in which you analyze Malcolm X as a hero for America in the 1990s.
6. Steele says that "the life of Malcolm X touched so many human archetypes that his story seems to supersede any racial context." How would Michael Omi ("In Living Color," p. 491) respond to this assertion?

# LARGER THAN LIFE

## *The Mythic Characters of American Culture*

**A** few years back, a national debate raged, culminating in an election that seemed to settle the matter once and for all. No, we're not referring to presidential politics, nor to the controversies over immigration and affirmative action. We're talking about the U.S. Postal Service's national ballot on whether to feature a young Elvis or an old one on a postage stamp.

If you have ever wondered about why Elvis should have his own postage stamp (note how we presume you know just which Elvis we mean), if you've ever been puzzled by the almost sacred stature this former trucker from Memphis has assumed in American popular culture, then here's your chance to figure it all out. Because Elvis, too, is a sign, one among many that appear in the form of famous American characters, some real and some fictional, but all reflecting some cross section of America's cultural mythology. Thus, to interpret the significance of these characters is to learn something about ourselves, our hopes, and our dreams. And Elvis is a very good place to begin.

### Interpreting the Mythic Characters of American Culture

So let's get to it. First study the reproduction of the Elvis stamp on the frontispiece of this chapter. It shows which Elvis won the election: the young Elvis. Don't take his election for granted, for here is one of

must ask as we seek to situate Elvis in the system
ure in which he signifies. As you ask why the
old was chosen for postal immortality, con-
ave been your choice. Then ask yourself, if
ice between a stamp featuring Jim Morrison of the
clean-shaven at twenty and chubby or bearded at twenty-
en would you choose? Does the choice seem obvious? Do you
a pattern emerging, the outline of a cultural myth?

A real mythology is at work here: America's mythic worship of youth. That is one of the systems in which Elvis gains his meaning. In a culture that does not value youth, Elvis Presley, who after all was simply a rock-and-roll star, would have been forgotten long ago. But as a youth-oriented culture, America almost inevitably went for the young Elvis in the 1992 postal election, because no other culture has so valued youthfulness and has been so ambivalent about old age as ours has. Maturity brings power in America, but also a desperate struggle to maintain the body of youth. The old Elvis's failure to remain forever young had made him something of a laughingstock before his death, and it is accordingly significant that this is not the Elvis whom America chose to immortalize on a stamp.

But, of course, a lot of young pop stars have aged (consider the Grateful Dead's Jerry Garcia just before his death), but they won't all end up on their own stamps. Somehow, Elvis is special, and his significance goes beyond his embodiment of America's adoration of youth. So we now have another question to ask: Why Elvis, old or young? Let's look at the Elvis legend, at this obscure Southern kid who rose from truck driver to superstar living in his own fabled mansion. In what ways does it exemplify that great mythic promise that we call the American Dream? How is Elvis's story like that of so many other Americans, from Benjamin Franklin on, who started poor and ended on top? Elvis seems to make the dream real, and his heroic stature can be attributed in part to the way in which he seems to verify the validity of a value system that lies at the heart of American culture.

And yet, even with the American Dream going for him, Elvis still towers above the crowd. A lot of pop stars have emerged from social obscurity to fame and fortune, so there must be more to the matter. Don't let this worry you; in fact, that is the essence of semiotic interpretation: finding the multiplicity of forces at work in the construction of a popular sign. For most signs usually have more than one explanation. Certainly Elvis does. So let's keep digging.

It's useful to recall that Elvis was considered racy stuff in the sexually repressed 1950s, so racy that he was ordered to tone down his act if he wanted to appear on TV. But it was that act, his outrageously suggestive bumping and grinding, that helped make him a superstar in the first place. His legions of teen fans loved him for it. Why?

Here we need to look at the tone and style of American popular music in the fifties. It was rather white-bread stuff: With the exception of a few black rockers like Chuck Berry who were reluctantly allowed into the mainstream pop world, the top forty was a list of carefully controlled, sanitized teen tunes. Think of the young Ricky Nelson, or Pat Boone, or Connie Francis. And then came Elvis, bringing the sexual energy of rhythm and blues to white audiences starved for a way to release their own repressed sexuality. Like a pagan deity, Elvis invited them to just let go.

In such a way, the Elvis cult hooks up with a far more ancient cult that helps explain his enduring and ecstatic appeal. More than two thousand years ago, the cult of a beautiful young god named Dionysus swept through Greece, a cult whose rituals included the release of sexual energies that ordinary Greek life repressed. Dionysus has since become an enduring symbol of sexual expression, an archetypal figure whose popular appeal has been reflected in such male sex symbols as Rudolph Valentino and Elvis Presley, men who are not simply good looking or sexy but who seem to embody sexuality itself.

We are approaching our thesis now, which is that Elvis Presley signifies in American culture on at least three mythological fronts: America's worship of everlasting youth, the American Dream, and the ancient symbolism of Dionysus as a god of sexual energy. Indeed, Dionysus offers us a clue into the significance of all those stories about Elvis's "survival." That is, part of the cult of Dionysus included his ritual murder, but he always came back to life, refusing to die. Now think of Elvis's death, and all those funny denials, the rumors: that he did not really die, that he is working as a grocery checkout clerk in Minneapolis, that he was just spotted at the 7 Eleven down the street. Refusing to stay dead, Elvis completes his mythic circuit. A sign of America's youth culture and an exemplar of the American Dream, Elvis becomes archetypal through the never-dying, ever-potent figure of Dionysus. Such a man can never die.

## Like a Candle in the Wind

If all this sounds like a lot for one man to symbolize, don't worry, Elvis isn't alone in the mythic pantheon of American popular culture. For one thing, there's Marilyn. You know the one we mean.

In many ways, the mythological significance of Marilyn Monroe resembles that of Elvis. The rise of Norma Jean to superstardom, too, exemplifies the American Dream in its gaudiest aspects. Also like Elvis, Marilyn functions as a potent sex symbol in a society ever on the lookout for sex symbols. And again like Elvis, Marilyn died young and thus enjoys the legendary status of popular American characters who have died young (have you ever seen her with Elvis and James Dean in that poster where they are all sitting together at a fifties-style coffee shop counter?). But still Marilyn Monroe is different. She's no female Dionysus, for example. Her appeal is more subtle than that, less violent and ecstatic. Yet it has proven just as enduring.

What, for example, does Marilyn Monroe mean to you? Is she just another sex symbol? But then, why do some women still identify with her today, women who can hardly be said to be sexists in their response to her? And men too: Is the enduring popularity of Marilyn Monroe among American men simply a sexual thing? Is there more to it than that?

As you ponder such questions, you might consider the system of American sex symbols to which Marilyn Monroe belongs. Each decade seems to have its dominant figure. In the 1930s, for example, there was Jean Harlow, a platinum blonde sex goddess who is best remembered through a photograph in which she is posed lying seductively on a bearskin rug. In the 1940s, there was Rita Hayworth, whose most famous image shows her posed crouching in her lingerie on a bed. But then there's Monroe in *The Seven-Year Itch,* playing a gentle if air-headed sex toy who displays her sexuality without fully being aware of it. Probably her most famous image comes from that film, when an updraft of air blows her skirts around her waist as she walks over a subway vent. She laughs as she tries to hold her skirts down. And that's how she's most often remembered.

Now consider the difference between these three images: Harlow's and Hayworth's seductive, challenging poses, and Monroe's childlike laughter and innocence. It's that laughter and that innocence that sets Monroe apart, the vulnerability that distinguishes her from the other sex goddesses of American popular culture. As the Elton John song goes,

Marilyn is remembered "like a candle in the wind." Like Elvis, she now has her own U.S. postage stamp. Why has the fascination with her endured?

## America in White-Face

Focusing on Elvis Presley and Marilyn Monroe can show how two very real people can be transformed into mythic symbols, American characters whose enduring appeal says a lot about American values and what sort of people we are. There are many such characters in our lives — from the fictional heroes who inhabit our folklore, film, and cartoon books to the real men and women who have come to symbolize our history. But when we survey the field of such characters, something else appears or, rather, doesn't appear: Just about all of the faces are white. And there is a semiotic lesson to be read here as well.

Think of the heroes of American folklore. There are Davy Crockett and Paul Bunyan, Pecos Bill and Daniel Boone, with only John Henry (significantly, a laborer) to offer a different hue. Our cartoon books are filled with superheroes — Batman, Superman, Spiderman, the list is endless — but how many aren't white? Meanwhile, Hollywood gives us the likes of Sylvester Stallone, Arnold Schwarzenegger, and Chuck Norris as larger-than-life cinema heroes. Indeed, there's something especially significant about Chuck Norris, for along with David Carradine and Jean-Claude Van Damme, Norris has appropriated what was originally an Asian role pioneered by Bruce Lee. Though the Asian origins of the martial arts tradition that such white actors have appropriated have not been concealed (Carradine's character was half-white, half-Chinese), it's instructive to note that whites often get the starring roles in such movies — as they usually do in the history of American characters.

Such a monochromatic set of characters sends a distinct signal. The message establishes a norm, a standard of Americanness from which a good proportion of nonwhite America is excluded. Toni Morrison dramatizes the potential consequences of this exclusion in her novel *The Bluest Eye,* in which a young African-American girl is driven crazy by her desire to be as lovable as the blonde-ringleted Shirley Temple, one of the most popular of American characters in the 1930s.

If the effect of a popular character is to establish a norm, those who do not — and who in fact cannot — fit the norm are relegated to the status of the abnormal or deviant. The great American myth of the melting pot — the belief that all have the opportunity to assimilate into one vast American identity — is thus belied by the faces, the characters, that are seen as representing us. Non-Anglo-Saxon European immigrants can, if they wish, choose to identify with the homogeneous facade of Anglo-Saxon America; but African-Americans, Hispanics, Native Americans,

---

**Discussing the Signs of American Characters**

In class, brainstorm a list of your favorite pop cultural icons. Then analyze your list. What mythological significance can you attach to the characters on your list? Do any rival the stature of an Elvis or a Marilyn? If so, what's their appeal; if not, why do you think they don't? What does the list say about the class's collective interests, concerns, and values?

---

and Asian Americans are not genuinely offered that opportunity, even if they desire it. Among popular culture characters, the American image is pictured in monochromatic portraits. All of the coloring of a Marvel comic book can't hide the prevailing whiteness of its heroes.

Still, there are signs that this pattern is changing. New faces, new heroes, are appearing among America's characters, some real (such as that self-creating, self-promoting sports superstar, Neon Deion Sanders), and others fictional. Can you name some of the new heroes? Are they widely known? What ethnicities do they represent? What new cartoon heroes have appeared who depart from the tradition of all-white superheroes? What's new on TV or in the movies? In the 1990s, the face of America's characters is rapidly changing. If you were to rewrite this chapter, whom would you add?

## Pitching the Product

America's characters function in another way as well. Think of Joe Camel or Betty Crocker. Both characters were invented to sell something. In each case, they were designed to appeal to the values and sense of identity of their markets. Betty Crocker, for example, was invented to sell cake mix (a product that at first was a sign of an imperfect home-maker) to women who could identify with her unsullied image of middle-class domesticity. More recent marketers, like the Sprint long distance telephone service, have chosen a more updated character, Candace Bergen's Murphy Brown, to sell its product. The distance between Betty Crocker and Murphy Brown measures the gap between the prefeminist myth of the happy housewife and the postfeminist image of the scrappy professional. But as different as the two characters are, both are designed to move the goods by embodying the culture's sense of the norm.

Then there are the athletes. On the one hand, they're real people, but on the other hand . . . well, consider Michael Jordan. A real-life sports hero, he has also been the star of his own Saturday morning cartoon series (along with Bo Jackson and Wayne Gretsky), and he was once the central cog in the great Nike, Inc., advertising machine (a role upended only by his on-again, off-again retirement). But with stars like Shaquille O'Neill already stepping into Jordan's place as hoopster-turned-hypster, we can see that when it comes to athletes, America's commercial culture has room for more than one race — but can you think of any advertising athletes who don't come in black or white?

It's hard, isn't it? Jose Canseco almost made it into the commercial class as a Latino athlete hero a few years back, but he didn't quite get to the top. And there certainly are plenty of Latino baseball stars, but black athletes dominate the pantheon of athletic characters — from such fallen figures as Mike Tyson and O. J. Simpson, to rising stars like Deion Sanders and Shaquille O'Neill. Such figures are not simply stars of the field or court, they are culture stars — in a society that doesn't otherwise particularly favor blacks. Aside from talent, then, what enables black athletes to so dominate America's sports imagination? Perhaps you might want to write an essay explaining the phenomenon.

## Whatizit

Recently, a new sort of character has appeared on the American scene, whose job also is to sell something, but that something is a good deal larger than any particular product or service. This character is the Olympic mascot, and the most recent version of this type — the 1996 Atlanta Games' Whatizit — offers us a particularly complex image for semiotic analysis. Let's look at it.

Whatizit first appeared during the closing ceremonies of the 1992 Olympic Games as the mascot for the succeeding Summer Olympiad in Atlanta. The adoption of cute, cuddly animal mascots has become routine since the successful appearance of L.A.'s Sam the Eagle, but Atlanta's new entry in the Olympic sweepstakes was both familiar and unfamiliar. It was familiar because Whatizit was, after all, a species of cartoon character like the others, but unfamiliar because no one could tell just what it was supposed to be. "What is it?" bewildered viewers asked of the blue, vaguely humanoid image with the big smile and oversized tennis shoes. "Neither man nor beast," its creators answered. Rather, the mascot for the twenty-sixth Olympic Games was a cybernetic concoction whose form depended on the operator of a computer screen. Hit one key and it's a sprinter; hit another, a gymnast; another, a basketball player; and so on through the whole range of Olympic events.

It's not too difficult to determine what Whatizit's designers were getting at with their little computer morph. Designed to showcase Atlanta's burgeoning high-tech industries, Whatizit reflected a certain democratic and technocratic optimism. If Sam the Eagle echoed the old-fashioned symbolism of Uncle Sam, Whatizit heralded the democracy of the computer age, giving anyone with access to a properly equipped computer a shot at turning Atlanta's Olympic mascot into whatever one pleased. But that's what Whatizit's designers wanted us to think. The question is, why does it look the way it does? What's going on beneath the surface?

The first message to be read in the amorphous figure of Whatizit lies in the necessity for its creation in the first place, for this is not only a mascot, a mere emblem for the Games. Rather, Whatizit is a marketable trademark, a product logo that Atlanta's Olympic committee can license to private corporations. The "product" that Atlanta had to offer, of course, was the Olympic contest itself, which has been effectively transformed from its original purpose of providing a forum for international cooperation–through–amateur–competition into one of the world's leading moneymaking extravaganzas. Indeed, with the nationalistic side of the Games much diminished since the collapse of the Soviet Union, moneymaking is practically all there is left in the new mythology of the Olympics, as professional athletes compete for endorsement opportunities and corporations strive to make their products the "Official (*fill in the blank*) of the Olympic Games."

The commodification of the Olympic mascot, then, reflects the commodification of the games themselves. Endorsed by countless producers of consumer goods and services, the Olympiad is now a gigantic product in an increasingly internationalized consumer economy. The true mascot for the games should be an animated dollar sign, or mark, or franc, or yen. But of course, that is one mascot no city will ever choose, because the purpose of a cute mascot, recognizable or not, is precisely to mask what is really going on, to present a cuddly, saleable image whose job is to distract everyone from all those salespeople hustling in the background.

But the semiotic story of Whatizit doesn't stop with its commodified profile. Fundamentally genderless, raceless, and devoid of nationalistic associations, Whatizit also functions as a sign of a certain hesitancy on the part of the Atlanta Olympic Committee. While Sam the Olympic Eagle was obviously based on the image of good ol' Anglo-Saxon Uncle Sam, Whatizit seems to bend over backwards not to refer to any particular race, class, or even gender. Why would Atlanta want to choose such a neutral symbol? Why, for instance, do you think it's blue, rather than white or black or brown or red or yellow? Why is it essentially genderless? How, in short, is Whatizit a political symbol as much as a mascot?

For even neutrality involves a political stance. Remember this fact as you consider the vast array of American characters who are out there for you to decode. Let nothing slip past you unquestioned. Why, for in-

||||||||||||||||||||||||||||||||||||||||||||||||||||||||||||||||||||||||||||||||||||||||||||||||||||||||||||||||||||||||||||||||||

**Reading American Characters on the Net**

One important component in American popular culture is the cult of the celebrity. To study this phenomenon, visit a web site devoted to listing the top 100 "hot stars": http://www.100hot.com/star. From what areas of life do these celebrities come, and what characteristics do they share? Can you think of individuals or groups who are not represented on the list? What does the list reveal about our cultural values and interests? You might also visit related links, focusing on African-Americans and Latinos, that are available at this site. How do the ethnic-specific lists compare?

stance, did Tim Burton's *Batman* exclude Robin? Why did Robin return in the third *Batman*? Why was Superman killed off (in a specially printed, enormously hyped, edition)? Why was he brought back to life? Would you tell the story of Davy Crockett and the Alamo differently if you had the chance? Or of Custer's last stand? And if you were to put a pop culture character on a postage stamp, would you choose Elvis Presley? If not, then whom?

## The Readings

The readings in this chapter analyze a range of American characters, some of whom have been used for marketing purposes and others who function as American heroes and heroines, real and fictional. Gary Engle starts things off with an analysis of how a cartoon hero, Superman, reflects mainstream American political values, while Steven Stark shows how a political hero like John F. Kennedy is transformed in our media-saturated age into a celebrity who "has more in common with Elvis than with FDR." Andy Medhurst's interpretation of Batman from a gay perspective provides some clues as to why Robin was excluded from Tim Burton's *Batman,* illuminating how Batman and Robin have been read by gay fans over the years. Emily Prager follows with an analysis of one of America's favorite toy characters, Barbie. Wanda Coleman's journalistic feature on Joe Camel and McCrea Adams's analytic survey of the characters that have populated American advertising show just how entrenched fictional characters are in our consumer economy. And Jenny Lyn Bader concludes the readings with a nostalgic essay on the place of heroes within her own generation, twentysomethings who have seen the old heroes topple and wonder whether America has any room for heroes as the 1990s wind to an end.

# GARY ENGLE

## *What Makes Superman So Darned American?*

*In 1992 Superman died — at least for a while. In bookstores and su-
permarkets across the nation, a special edition of D.C. Comics appeared,
complete with a tableau of a dying Superman bleeding in Lois Lane's
arms. In this semiotic analysis of the enduring appeal of Superman,
Gary Engle (b. 1947) argues why the Man of Steel — whom Engle
views as the ultimate immigrant — has dominated the pantheon of
American characters for so many years. Of all our heroes, Engle claims,
Superman alone "achieves truly mythic stature, interweaving a pattern
of beliefs, literary conventions, and cultural traditions of the American
people more powerfully and more accessibly than any other cultural
symbol of the twentieth century, perhaps of any period in our history."
A specialist in popular culture, Engle is an associate professor of English at Cleveland State University. In addition to over two hundred
magazine and journal articles, he has written* The Grotesque
Essence: Plays from American Minstrel Style *(1978).*

When I was young I spent a lot of time arguing with myself about
who would win in a fight between John Wayne and Superman. On days
when I wore my cowboy hat and cap guns, I knew the Duke would win
because of his pronounced superiority in the all-important matter of
swagger. There were days, though, when a frayed army blanket tied
cape-fashion around my neck signalled a young man's need to believe
there could be no end to the potency of his being. Then the Man of
Steel was the odds-on favorite to knock the Duke for a cosmic loop. My
greatest childhood problem was that the question could never be resolved because no such battle could ever take place. I mean, how would
a fight start between the only two Americans who never started
anything, who always fought only to defend their rights and the American way?

Now that I'm older and able to look with reason on the mysteries of
childhood, I've finally resolved the dilemma. John Wayne was the best
older brother any kid could ever hope to have, but he was no Superman.

Superman is *the* great American hero. We are a nation rich with legendary figures. But among the Davy Crocketts and Paul Bunyans and
Mike Finks and Pecos Bills and all the rest who speak for various regional
identities in the pantheon of American folklore, only Superman achieves
truly mythic stature, interweaving a pattern of beliefs, literary conventions, and cultural traditions of the American people more powerfully

and more accessibly than any other cultural symbol of the twentieth century, perhaps of any period in our history.

The core of the American myth in *Superman* consists of a few basic facts that remain unchanged throughout the infinitely varied ways in which the myth is told — facts with which everyone is familiar, however marginal their knowledge of the story. Superman is an orphan rocketed to Earth when his native planet Krypton explodes; he lands near Smallville and is adopted by Jonathan and Martha Kent, who inculcate in him their American middle-class ethic; as an adult he migrates to Metropolis where he defends America — no, the world! no, the Universe! — from all evil and harm while playing a romantic game in which, as Clark Kent, he hopelessly pursues Lois Lane, who hopelessly pursues Superman, who remains aloof until such time as Lois proves worthy of him by falling in love with his feigned identity as a weakling. That's it. Every narrative thread in the mythology, each one of the thousands of plots in the fifty-year stream of comics and films and TV shows, all the tales involving the demigods of the Superman pantheon — Superboy, Supergirl, even Krypto the Superdog — every single one reinforces by never contradicting this basic set of facts. That's the myth, and that's where one looks to understand America.

It is impossible to imagine Superman being as popular as he is and       5
speaking as deeply to the American character were he not an immigrant and an orphan. Immigration, of course, is the overwhelming fact in American history. Except for the Indians, all Americans have an immediate sense of their origins elsewhere. No nation on Earth has so deeply embedded in its social consciousness the imagery of passage from one social identity to another: the Mayflower of the New England separatists, the slave ships from Africa and the subsequent underground railroads toward freedom in the North, the sailing ships and steamers running shuttles across two oceans in the nineteenth century, the freedom airlifts in the twentieth. Somehow the picture just isn't complete without Superman's rocketship.

Like the peoples of the nation whose values he defends, Superman is an alien, but not just any alien. He's the consummate and totally uncompromised alien, an immigrant whose visible difference from the norm is underscored by his decision to wear a costume of bold primary colors so tight as to be his very skin. Moreover, Superman the alien is real. He stands out among the hosts of comic book characters (Batman is a good example) for whom the superhero role is like a mask assumed when needed, a costume worn over their real identities as normal Americans. Superman's powers — strength, mobility, x-ray vision and the like — are the comic-book equivalents of ethnic characteristics, and they protect and preserve the vitality of the foster community in which he lives in the same way that immigrant ethnicity has sustained American culture linguistically, artistically, economically, politically, and spiritually. The myth of Superman asserts with total confidence and a childlike innocence the value of the immigrant in American culture.

From this nation's beginnings Americans have looked for ways of coming to terms with the immigrant experience. This is why, for example, so much of American literature and popular culture deals with the theme of dislocation, generally focused in characters devoted or doomed to constant physical movement. Daniel Boone became an American legend in part as a result of apocryphal stories that he moved every time his neighbors got close enough for him to see the smoke of their cabin fires. James Fenimore Cooper's Natty Bumppo spent the five long novels of the Leatherstocking saga drifting ever westward, like the pioneers who were his spiritual offspring, from the Mohawk valley of upstate New York to the Great Plains where he died. Huck Finn sailed through the moral heart of America on a raft. Melville's Ishmael, Wister's Virginian, Shane, Gatsby, the entire Lost Generation, Steinbeck's Okies, Little Orphan Annie, a thousand fiddlefooted cowboy heroes of dime novels and films and television — all in motion, searching for the American dream or stubbornly refusing to give up their innocence by growing old, all symptomatic of a national sense of rootlessness stemming from an identity founded on the experience of immigration.

Individual mobility is an integral part of America's dreamwork. Is it any wonder, then, that our greatest hero can take to the air at will? Superman's ability to fly does more than place him in a tradition of mythic figures going back to the Greek messenger god Hermes or Zetes the flying Argonaut. It makes him an exemplar in the American dream. Take away a young man's wheels and you take away his manhood. Jack Kerouac and Charles Kurault go on the road; William Least Heat Moon looks for himself in a van exploring the veins of America in its system of blue highways; legions of gray-haired retirees turn Air Stream trailers and Winnebagos into proof positive that you can, in the end, take it with you. On a human scale, the American need to keep moving suggests a neurotic aimlessness under the surface of adventure. But take the human restraints off, let Superman fly unencumbered when and wherever he will, and the meaning of mobility in the American consciousness begins to reveal itself. Superman's incredible speed allows him to be as close to everywhere at once as it is physically possible to be. Displacement is, therefore, impossible. His sense of self is not dispersed by his life's migration but rather enhanced by all the universe that he is able to occupy. What American, whether an immigrant in spirit or in fact, could resist the appeal of one with such an ironclad immunity to the anxiety of dislocation?

In America, physical dislocation serves as a symbol of social and psychological movement. When our immigrant ancestors arrived on America's shores they hit the ground running, some to homestead on the Great Plains, others to claw their way up the socioeconomic ladder in coastal ghettos. Upward mobility, westward migration, Sunbelt relocation — the wisdom in America is that people don't, can't, mustn't end up where they begin. This belief has the moral force of religious doctrine. Thus the American identity is ordered around the psychological experience of forsaking or losing the past for the opportunity of reinventing oneself in the future. This makes the orphan a potent symbol of the American character. Orphans aren't merely free to reinvent themselves. They are obliged to do so.

When Superman reinvents himself, he becomes the bumbling Clark    10
Kent, a figure as immobile as Superman is mobile, as weak as his alter ego is strong. Over the years commentators have been fond of stressing how Clark Kent provides an illusory image of wimpiness onto which children can project their insecurities about their own potential (and, hopefully, equally illusory) weaknesses. But I think the role of Clark Kent is far more complex than that.

During my childhood, Kent contributed nothing to my love for the Man of Steel. If left to contemplate him for too long, I found myself changing from cape back into cowboy hat and guns. John Wayne, at least, was no sissy that I could ever see. Of course, in all the Westerns that the Duke came to stand for in my mind, there were elements that left me as confused as the paradox between Kent and Superman. For example, I could never seem to figure out why cowboys so often fell in love when there were obviously better options: horses to ride, guns to shoot, outlaws to chase, and savages to kill. Even on the days when I became John Wayne, I could fall victim to a never-articulated anxiety about the potential for poor judgment in my cowboy heroes. Then, I generally drifted back into a worship of Superman. With him, at least, the mysterious communion of opposites was honest and on the surface of things.

What disturbed me as a child is what I now think makes the myth of Superman so appealing to an immigrant sensibility. The shape-shifting between Clark Kent and Superman is the means by which this mid-twentieth-century, urban story — like the pastoral, nineteenth-century Western before it — addresses in dramatic terms the theme of cultural assimilation.

At its most basic level, the Western was an imaginative record of the American experience of westward migration and settlement. By bringing the forces of civilization and savagery together on a mythical frontier, the Western addressed the problem of conflict between apparently mutually exclusive identities and explored options for negotiating between them. In terms that a boy could comprehend, the myth explored the dilemma of assimilation — marry the school marm and start wearing Eastern clothes or saddle up and drift further westward with the boys.

The Western was never a myth of stark moral simplicity. Pioneers fled civilization by migrating west, but their purpose in the wilderness was to rebuild civilization. So civilization was both good and bad, what Americans fled from and journeyed toward. A similar moral ambiguity rested at the heart of the wilderness. It was an Eden in which innocence could be achieved through spiritual rebirth, but it was also the anarchic force that most directly threatened the civilized values America wanted to impose on the frontier. So the dilemma arose: In negotiating between civilization and the wilderness, between the old order and the new, between the identity the pioneers carried with them from wherever they came and the identity they sought to invent, Americans faced an impossible choice. Either they pushed into the New World wilderness and forsook the ideals that motivated them or they clung to their origins and polluted Eden.

The myth of the Western responded to this dilemma by inventing    15
the idea of the frontier in which civilized ideals embodied in the institutions of family, church, law, and education are revitalized by the virtues of savagery: independence, self-reliance, personal honor, sympathy with nature, and ethical uses of violence. In effect, the mythical frontier represented an attempt to embody the perfect degree of assimilation in which both the old and new identities came together, if not in a single self-image, then at least in idealized relationships, like the symbolic marriage of reformed cowboy and displaced school marm that ended Owen Wister's prototypical *The Virginian,* or the mystical masculine bonding between representatives of an ascendant and a vanishing America — Natty Bumppo and Chingachgook, the Lone Ranger and Tonto. On the Western frontier, both the old and new identities equally mattered.

As powerful a myth as the Western was, however, there were certain limits to its ability to speak directly to an increasingly common twentieth-century immigrant sensibility. First, it was pastoral. Its imagery of dusty frontier towns and breathtaking mountainous desolation spoke most affectingly to those who conceived of the American dream in terms of the nineteenth-century immigrant experience of rural settlement. As the twentieth century wore on, more immigrants were, like Superman, moving from rural or small-town backgrounds to metropolitan environments. Moreover, the Western was historical, often elegiacally so. Underlying the air of celebration in even the most epic and romantic of Westerns — the films of John Ford, say, in which John Wayne stood tall for all that any good American boy could ever want to be — was an awareness that the frontier was less a place than a state of mind represented in historic terms by a fleeting moment glimpsed imperfectly in the rapid wave of westward migration and settlement. Implicitly, then, whatever balance of past and future identities the frontier could offer was itself tenuous or illusory.

Twentieth-century immigrants, particularly the Eastern European Jews who came to America after 1880 and who settled in the industrial and mercantile centers of the Northeast — cities like Cleveland where

Jerry Siegel and Joe Shuster grew up and created Superman — could be entertained by the Western, but they developed a separate literary tradition that addressed the theme of assimilation in terms closer to their personal experience. In this tradition issues were clear-cut: Clinging to an Old World identity meant isolation in ghettos, confrontation with a prejudiced mainstream culture, second-class social status, and impoverishment. On the other hand, forsaking the past in favor of total absorption into the mainstream, while it could result in socioeconomic progress, meant a loss of the religious, linguistic, even culinary traditions that provided a foundation for psychological well-being. Such loss was particularly tragic for the Jews because of the fundamental role played by history in Jewish culture.

Writers who worked in this tradition — Abraham Cahan, Daniel Fuchs, Henry Roth, and Delmore Schwarz, among others — generally found little reason to view the experience of assimilation with joy or optimism. Typical of the tradition was Cahan's early novel *Yekl,* on which Joan Micklin Silver's film *Hester Street* was based. A young married couple, Jake and Gitl, clash over his need to be absorbed as quickly as possible into the American mainstream and her obsessive preservation of their Russian-Jewish heritage. In symbolic terms, their confrontation is as simple as their choice of headgear — a derby for him, a babushka for her. That the story ends with their divorce, even in the context of their gradual movement toward mutual understanding of one another's point of view, suggests the divisive nature of the pressures at work in the immigrant communities.

Where the pressures were perhaps most keenly felt was in the schools. Educational theory of the period stressed the benefits of rapid assimilation. In the first decades of this century, for example, New York schools flatly rejected bilingual education — a common response to the plight of non-English-speaking immigrants even today — and there were conscientious efforts to indoctrinate the children of immigrants with American values, often at the expense of traditions within the ethnic community. What resulted was a generational rift in which children were openly embarrassed by and even contemptuous of their parents' values, setting a pattern in American life in which second-generation immigrants migrate psychologically if not physically from their parents, leaving it up to the third generation and beyond to rediscover their ethnic roots.

Under such circumstances, finding a believable and inspiring balance 20 between the old identity and the new, like that implicit in the myth of the frontier, was next to impossible. The images and characters that did emerge from the immigrant communities were often comic. Seen over and over in the fiction and popular theater of the day was the figure of the *yiddische Yankee,* a jingoistic optimist who spoke heavily accented American slang, talked baseball like an addict without understanding the game, and dressed like a Broadway dandy on a budget — in short, one who didn't understand America well enough to distinguish between image and substance and who paid for the mistake by becoming the butt of a style of comedy bordering on pathos. So engrained was this stereotype in popular culture that it echoes today in TV situation comedy.

Throughout American popular culture between 1880 and the Second World War the story was the same. Oxlike Swedish farmers, German brewers, Jewish merchants, corrupt Irish ward healers, Italian gangsters — there was a parade of images that reflected in terms often comic, sometimes tragic, the humiliation, pain, and cultural insecurity of people in a state of transition. Even in the comics, a medium intimately connected with immigrant culture, there simply was no image that presented a blending of identities in the assimilation process in a way that stressed pride, self-confidence, integrity, and psychological well-being. None, that is, until Superman.

The brilliant stroke in the conception of Superman — the sine qua non that makes the whole myth work — is the fact that he has two identities. The myth simply wouldn't work without Clark Kent, mild-mannered newspaper reporter and later, as the myth evolved, bland TV newsman. Adopting the white-bread image of a wimp is first and foremost a moral act for the Man of Steel. He does it to protect his parents from nefarious sorts who might use them to gain an edge over the powerful alien. Moreover, Kent adds to Superman's powers the moral guidance of a Smallville upbringing. It is Jonathan Kent, fans remember, who instructs the alien that his powers must always be used for good. Thus does the myth add a mainstream white Anglo-Saxon Protestant ingredient to the American stew. Clark Kent is the clearest stereotype of a self-effacing, hesitant, doubting, middle-class weakling ever invented. He is the epitome of visible invisibility, someone whose extraordinary ordinariness makes him disappear in a crowd. In a phrase, he is the consummate figure of total cultural assimilation, and significantly, he is not real. Implicit in this is the notion that mainstream cultural norms, however useful, are illusions.

Though a disguise, Kent is necessary for the myth to work. This uniquely American hero has two identities, one based on where he comes from in life's journey, one on where he is going. One is real, one an illusion, and both are necessary for the myth of balance in the assimilation process to be complete. Superman's powers make the hero capable of saving humanity; Kent's total immersion in the American heartland makes him want to do it. The result is an improvement on the Western: an optimistic myth of assimilation but with an urban, technocratic setting.

One must never underestimate the importance to a myth of the most minute elements which do not change over time and by which we recognize the story. Take Superman's cape, for example. When Joe Shuster inked the first Superman stories, in the early thirties when he was still a student at Cleveland's Glenville High School, Superman was strictly beefcake in tights, looking more like a circus acrobat than the ultimate Man of Steel. By June of 1938 when *Action Comics* no. 1 was issued, the image had been altered to include a cape, ostensibly to make flight easier to render in the pictures. But it wasn't the cape of Victorian melodrama and adventure fiction, the kind worn with a clasp around the neck. In fact, one is hard-pressed to find any precedent in popular culture for the kind of cape Superman wears. His emerges in a seamless line from either side of the front yoke of his tunic. It is a veritable growth from behind his pectorals and hangs, when he stands at ease, in a line that doesn't so much drape his shoulders as stand apart from them and echo their curve, like an angel's wings.

In light of this graphic detail, it seems hardly coincidental that      25
Superman's real, Kryptonic name is Kal-El, an apparent neologism by George Lowther, the author who novelized the comic strip in 1942. In Hebrew, *el* can be both root and affix. As a root, it is the masculine singular word for God. Angels in Hebrew mythology are called *benei Elohim* (literally, sons of the Gods), or *Elyonim* (higher beings). As an affix, *el* is most often translated as "of God," as in the plenitude of Old Testament given names: Ishma-el, Dani-el, Ezeki-el, Samu-el, etc. It is also a common form for named angels in most Semitic mythologies: Israf-el, Aza-el, Uri-el, Yo-el, Rapha-el, Gabri-el and — the one perhaps most like Superman — Micha-el, the warrior angel and Satan's principal adversary.

The morpheme *Kal* bears a linguistic relation to two Hebrew roots. The first, *kal,* means "with lightness" or "swiftness" (faster than a speeding bullet in Hebrew?). It also bears a connection to the root *hal,* where *h* is the guttural *ch* of *chutzpah. Hal* translates roughly as "everything" or "all." *Kal-el,* then, can be read as "all that is God," or perhaps more in the spirit of the myth of Superman, "all that God is." And while we're at it, *Kent* is a form of the Hebrew *kana.* In its *k-n-t* form, the word appears in the Bible, meaning "I have found a son."

I'm suggesting that Superman raises the American immigrant experience to the level of religious myth. And why not? He's not just some immigrant from across the waters like all our ancestors, but a real alien, an extraterrestrial, a visitor from heaven if you will, which fact lends an element of the supernatural to the myth. America has no national religious icons nor any pilgrimage shrines. The idea of a patron saint is ludicrous in a nation whose Founding Fathers wrote into the founding documents the fundamental if not eternal separation of church and state. America, though, is pretty much as religious as other industrialized countries. It's just that our tradition of religious diversity precludes the nation's religious character from being embodied in objects or persons recognizably religious, for such are immediately identified by their attachment to specific sectarian traditions and thus contradict the eclecticism of the American religious spirit.

In America, cultural icons that manage to tap the national religious spirit are of necessity secular on the surface and sufficiently generalized to incorporate the diversity of American religious traditions. Superman doesn't have to be seen as an angel to be appreciated, but in the absence of a tradition of national religious iconography, he can serve as a safe, nonsectarian focus for essentially religious sentiments, particularly among the young.

In the last analysis, Superman is like nothing so much as an American boy's fantasy of a messiah. He is the male, heroic match for the Statue of Liberty, come like an immigrant from heaven to deliver humankind by sacrificing himself in the service of others. He protects the weak and defends truth and justice and all the other moral virtues inherent in the Judeo-Christian tradition, remaining ever vigilant and ever chaste. What purer or stronger vision could there possibly be for a child? Now that I put my mind to it, I see that John Wayne never had a chance.


### Reading the Text

1. Why does Superman's status as an immigrant and orphan make him deeply American, according to Engle?
2. What is the significance of Superman's ability to fly?
3. Why does Engle see physical dislocation as being so typically American?
4. What is the significance of Superman's two identities, according to Engle?


### Reading the Signs

1. Interview three classmates or friends whose families are immigrants to this country. Then compare their experience with that of the mythological character, Superman. To what extent does the Superman character reflect real-life immigrant experience? What does his story leave out? Try to account for any differences you may find.
2. Do you agree with Engle's suggestion that Superman "raises the American immigrant experience to the level of religious myth"?
3. How would Superman fit the definitions of hero that Robert Ray ("The Thematic Paradigm," p. 278) outlines?
4. Engle claims that Superman is a more authentically American hero than is John Wayne. Write an argument supporting or refuting this claim, basing your argument on specific roles that Wayne has played in film.
5. Engle only briefly discusses the fact that Superman happens to be both male and Caucasian. What is the significance of his gender and race? How do you think they may have influenced his status as an American mythological hero? You might read or review Michael Omi's "In Living Color" (p. 491) for a discussion of the impact of race on American popular culture and Holly Devor's "Gender Role Behaviors and Attitudes" (p. 415) for her explanation of the significance of gender roles.

6. Rent a videotape of one of the *Superman* movies, and write an essay in which you explore whether the cinematic depiction of this character either perpetuates or alters his mythological status.

S T E V E N   S T A R K

*The Cultural Meaning of the Kennedys*

‖‖‖‖‖‖‖‖‖‖‖‖‖‖‖‖‖‖‖‖‖‖‖‖‖‖‖‖‖‖‖‖‖‖‖‖‖‖‖

*"All history is gossip," President John F. Kennedy used to say, but, as Steven Stark (b. 1951) suggests in this essay that originally appeared in the* Atlantic Monthly, *the Kennedys have managed to turn gossip into history. A family of larger-than-life celebrities whom we know by their first names — Jack, Jackie, Bobby, Teddy — just as we know the names of entertainment superstars, the Kennedys, in Stark's words, "were a prime force in blurring the distinctions between Hollywood and Washington." In an era when actors have been presidents and presidents have appeared on* Saturday Night Live, *the impact of the Kennedys seems all the more powerful. A commentator for* National Public Radio *and* Voice of America, *Steven Stark writes about politics and popular culture. His book on sixty television shows that changed America will be published in late 1997.*

With all the media coverage occasioned by the thirtieth anniversary of John F. Kennedy's death, Joe McGinniss's biography of Edward Kennedy, *The Last Brother,* rather got lost. The brief controversy over McGinniss's methods, in turn, obscured a larger milestone: along with the flood of docudramas about the first brother, *The Last Brother* was yet another step in the transformation of the Kennedys from largely conventional political figures into pop-culture deities from the world of entertainment — the cultural equivalents, perhaps, of Elvis Presley or the Jacksons. It should be no surprise that popular biography has reflected this conversion, or that the change parallels the way politics has come to be viewed in the years since the Kennedys hit the scene. Neither is it a coincidence that the Kennedy family, through its infatuation with Hollywood, was instrumental in the conversion. "All history is gossip," President Kennedy used to say, which may or may not have been accurate then, but — owing to the changes he and his family helped accelerate — is somewhat more accurate today. "So the rumors are true?" asks a character in *The Player,* a 1992 film about Hollywood. "Rumors are always true. You know that," another answers. John Kennedy, Joe McGinniss, and millions of Americans wouldn't have put it any other way.

Of course, traditional political biographies are still being published about the Kennedys: witness *President Kennedy: Profile of Power,* Richard Reeves's recent account of the JFK presidency. But just as the political doings of the Kennedys are frequently dwarfed in the popular press by news of the latest party, drinking scandal, or date for John Junior, so in recent times have traditional books about the Kennedys been overshadowed by such gossipy volumes as the McGinniss work; Richard Burke's tell-all about Edward Kennedy, *The Senator*; Peter Collier and David Horowitz's *The Kennedys: An American Drama*; and even (though they're less gossipy) Nigel Hamilton's *JFK: Reckless Youth* and Thomas Reeves's *A Question of Character*. Because of the current cultural obsession with inner life, biography now tends to stray into the personal more than it once did. Still, the Kennedy family isn't written about the way that Harry Truman, or Ronald Reagan, or Martin Luther King Jr. is. The Kennedys are different from you and me and them, and not simply because they have more money.

To be sure, the Kennedys have had — and continue to have — a political impact on the nation. To many, they have embodied an ideal of public service. But politics hasn't been this family's calling card in the mass culture for some time. Even in the aggregate the Kennedys have never had the political impact of Martin Luther King Jr., FDR, or even Reagan. If President Kennedy is still revered today, it's more because of his glamorous style and because he died young than for any specific accomplishments. Robert Kennedy is identified with a liberal agenda that still inspires many, but he came late in life to that cause. What's more, at the time his only national candidacy was cut tragically short, it was hardly clear that he would win the election, or even that he could beat out Hubert Humphrey for the Democratic nomination. In the days before his death Kennedy lost to Eugene McCarthy in the 1968 Oregon presidential primary, and barely won the key California primary a week later. Edward Kennedy's 1980 attempt at national office failed; he lost most of the important primaries in his own party to an unpopular President. That, of course, doesn't tarnish his considerable record over the past three decades as one of the few effective spokesmen left for liberalism. But outside Massachusetts that status is hardly what makes him, or his relatives, the celebrities they have become.

The Kennedys have really become entertainment superstars. Consider some of the evidence: Like Marilyn Monroe and Elvis Presley, they attract a kind of tabloid journalism and biography which focuses even more than usual on scandal and unsavory personal tidbits. The Palm Beach rape case, after all, was a Hollywood trial, not a Washington one, and the model for most of these recent Kennedy books is not Arthur Schlesinger Jr.'s *A Thousand Days* but Albert Goldman's *Elvis*. The screaming crowds that engulfed Robert Kennedy in 1968 — tearing at his clothes and stealing his cuff links — were not unlike those that followed the Beatles and the Rolling Stones. If several people were killed trying to see Robert Kennedy's funeral train, the analogy may be as much to the reaction to Rudolph Valentino's death or to what happened in 1979 at a Who concert as it is to the funeral procession for Abraham Lincoln.

This is a family identified by first names in the familiar Hollywood 5 style — Jack, Jackie, Bobby, Ethel, Teddy — just as we once knew Elvis, Marilyn, and Ringo, but certainly not as we have known Franklin, Ronald, or even Bill. The Kennedy men are well known for their rather public life of wine, women, and song (or its modern equivalent), an existence that approximates life on the road for a rock star. Even in marriage the family reveals a kind of split personality about what it has become. Some Kennedys have gone into politics and married other people in that profession, but the two best-known current family alliances are Maria Shriver's marriage to the box-office king Arnold Schwarzenegger and John Kennedy Jr.'s relationship with the actress Daryl Hannah. (Entertainment in-law Peter Lawford was a preview of things to come.)

Defining the Kennedys as an entertainment family does explain some anomalies. There is only a weak tradition of political families in this country; the strong antipathy to royalism explains why. But there is an enduring convention of entertainment families who are often treated by the press and public like royalty, their names including Booth, Barrymore, Fairbanks, Bridges, Sheen, Douglas, Belushi, Baldwin, Garland, and Minnelli — the list goes on. There has also been a pattern of "brother acts" in vaudeville, and particularly in rock and country music — the Everly Brothers, the Stanley Brothers, the Jacksons, the Osmonds, the Kinks, the Beach Boys, the Allman Brothers, the Mills Brothers, the Statler Brothers, the Ames Brothers, even New Kids on the Block.

According to pop-culture folklore, several of these brother acts in rock have followed roughly the same pattern: The family is driven hard and molded by a difficult father. The first success is collective. Then one brother hits it big and becomes a superstar. Other family members ride the superstar's name and coattails to derivative careers of their own. Some brothers break down under the pressure, while other members of the family seem to invite trouble on a regular basis. So it has often seemed to go with the Kennedys.

As a kind of entertainment family the Kennedys were a prime force in blurring the distinctions between Hollywood and Washington — that blur being a condition characteristic of the age. As the critic Richard Schickel has observed in his book *Intimate Strangers,* they were certainly not the first to court the film industry or to recognize the consequences of the media era. Woodrow Wilson had D. W. Griffith's *The Birth of a*

*Nation* screened at the White House in 1915, and Douglas Fairbanks told Franklin Roosevelt when he was only assistant secretary of the Navy that he had the persona to succeed as an actor if he so chose.

But the Kennedys helped complete the revolution. As the biographers tell it, Father Joe "mingled" with Gloria Swanson and other stars, and his real business interest was in movie production, because he thought that was where the aristocracy of the next generation would be created. Judging from the biographies, much of the next Kennedy generation's childhood appears to have been one long photo op, culminating in John Kennedy's marriage to, of all things, an aristocratic photographer. If, in the media planning devised largely by Father Joe, JFK's 1960 race for the presidency was the first to resemble the packaging of a Hollywood blockbuster — the buildup, the bio, the promos, the publicity shots, the early buzz among influential critics, the reviews, the breakthrough performance (in debates), and, finally, the crowd reaction — that may have been no accident. "John F. Kennedy treated southern Ohio yesterday as Don Giovanni used to treat Seville," Murray Kempton wrote one day in a campaign dispatch striking both for its honesty and for the new political phenomenon it was describing. After all this, and an Administration that made the elevation of style over substance into both a zeitgeist and an ideology, not only the hanging out with Sinatra and Marilyn was inevitable; so was the eventual arrival of someone like Ronald Reagan.

Sadly, the assassinations also played a role in the conversion of the  10 Kennedys into pop-culture phenomena. As Schickel has observed, dying young, if not violently, is something of an entertainment-industry phenomenon, as anyone familiar with the lives and deaths of Elvis, Marilyn, Valentino, James Dean, Jimi Hendrix, Janis Joplin, Buddy Holly, John Belushi, Ritchie Valens, John Lennon, and Jim Morrison knows. It's not simply that an untimely death fulfills a romantic image that goes back to Byron and Keats, or that the premature passing of an entertainment figure tends to inspire a death cult in which numerous fans refuse to believe the star is dead. Dying young freezes the stars at their peak: like the promise of Hollywood itself, they remain forever young and beautiful — the perfect icons for the immortality that films and records purport to offer.

Death also to some extent frees journalists and biographers from having to stick to the truth, since the deceased don't press libel actions. In his book *Dead Elvis,* Greil Marcus described how Elvis had become a cultural obsession since his death, "a figure made of echoes, not of facts." The legend grew, he wrote, out of "art works, books, movies, dreams; sometimes more than anything cultural noise." So, too, has it gone for JFK, whose legacy has included not only the same literary tributes from the entourage, followed by the critical bios, but also the same creation of civic shrines, the same cultural buzz, the same attention paid to the surviving clan, the same questions raised about the cause of death, the same anniversary observances of the day he died, even the same odd tabloid sightings of the deceased which recall the Resurrection.

In a sense the image of all popular figures is a reflection of the public that follows them. But with a dead figure that reflective process grows exponentially — like the compounding effect of a series of mirrors. As a cultural symbol whose life can now be made into anything with impunity, Kennedy, like Presley, has become, in Marcus's words, "an anarchy of possibilities" — a reflection of the public's mass fears and aspirations and also a constant vehicle for discussing those sentiments. Thus Presley and the Kennedys have evolved into a collection of cultural deities — modern-day equivalents of the Greek gods, who were immortal while sharing the characteristics of the human beings who worshipped them.

That helps explain another unusual fact about the Kennedys: the more negative information the public is fed about the family, the more the legend just seems to grow. For that reason Palm Beach may have actually *enhanced* the family's status in the culture. Scandals become public spectacles — occasions for the masses to embroider the myth, the better to show how these superstars who are our gods flout the rules. Did anyone really lose respect for Mick Jagger when he got busted for possession?

Reviewers attacked McGinniss in part because what he wrote about the Kennedys was nothing more than gossip. But his real crime was that he merely recirculated stale gossip: who can make a new parable out of that? To a national audience now as intimately familiar with the grassy knoll, the Dike Bridge on Chappaquiddick, and the story of Jack and Marilyn as prior generations were with the stories of Icarus and of Samson and Delilah, McGinniss came off as something of a false prophet. If mass entertainment is now the civic religion in a country where government can never constitutionally fill that role, it should be no surprise that the path to immortality for a politician today is to become an entertainer in order to become a deity. "Elvis is King," they still write on street corners. Thirty years after his assassination JFK isn't far behind.

### Reading the Text

1. How, according to Stark, have the Kennedys become "pop cultural deities from the world of entertainment"?
2. How did the Kennedys help blur the line between Hollywood and Washington, D.C., according to Stark?
3. What role did the John F. Kennedy assassination play in the creation of the Kennedy family myth?

4. What does Stark mean by claiming that "in a sense the image of all popular figures is a reflection of the public that follows them"?

### Reading the Signs

1. In class, brainstorm characteristics of the Kennedy family's cultural and social image. Then discuss how Stark would explain your brainstormed list.
2. In an essay, challenge, support, or complicate Stark's contention that, in American culture, John F. Kennedy is the political equivalent of Elvis Presley.
3. Read one of the Kennedy biographies that Stark mentions. Then write an analytic essay in which you discuss how the biography contributes to the Kennedy image.
4. Visit your college library and find popular media coverage of an event or incident that returned the Kennedy family to the public eye in the 1990s (possibilities include the death of Jacqueline Kennedy Onassis, the William Kennedy Smith rape trial, or John Kennedy Jr.'s, publication of *George* magazine). Then, using Stark's argument as your critical framework, analyze the attitudes toward the Kennedys that are both explicit and implicit in the news coverage.
5. Rent a videotape of Oliver Stone's *JFK* and write a semiotic analysis of the film. What sort of cultural significance does the film grant John F. Kennedy?
6. Write an essay in which you compare John F. Kennedy's social and cultural legacy with that of Abraham Lincoln, another popular president who was assassinated.

# ANDY MEDHURST
## Batman, Deviance, and Camp

*Have you ever wondered what happened to Robin in the recent Batman movies? In this analysis of the history of the Batman, excerpted from* The Many Lives of the Batman *(1991), Andy Medhurst (b. 1959) explains why Robin had to disappear. Arguing that Batman has been "reheterosexualized" in the wake of the insinuatingly homoerotic TV series of the 1960s, Medhurst indicts the homophobia of Batfans whose "Bat-Platonic Ideal of how Batman should really be" holds no place for the "camped crusader." Andy Medhurst teaches media studies, popular culture, and lesbian and gay studies at the University of Sussex, England. His current research interests include popular film and television and lesbian and gay studies.*

*Only someone ignorant of the fundamentals of psychiatry and of the psychopathology of sex can fail to realize a subtle atmosphere of homoeroticism which pervades the adventure of the mature "Batman" and his young friend "Robin."*
                                                — FREDRIC WERTHAM[1]

*It's embarrassing to be solemn and treatise-like about Camp. One runs the risk of having, oneself, produced a very inferior piece of Camp.*
                                                — SUSAN SONTAG[2]

I'm not sure how qualified I am to write this essay. Batman hasn't been particularly important in my life since I was seven years old. Back then he was crucial, paramount, unmissable as I sat twice weekly to watch the latest episode on TV. Pure pleasure, except for the annoying fact that my parents didn't seem to appreciate the thrills on offer. Worse than that, they actually laughed. How could anyone laugh when the Dynamic Duo were about to be turned into Frostie Freezies (pineapple for the Caped Crusader, lime for his chum) by the evil Mr. Freeze?

Batman and I drifted apart after those early days. Every now and then I'd see a repeated episode and I soon began to understand and share that once infuriating parental hilarity, but this aside I hardly thought about the man in the cape at all. I knew about the subculture of comic freaks, and the new and alarmingly pretentious phrase "graphic novel" made itself known to me, but I still regarded (with the confidence of distant ignorance) such texts as violent, macho, adolescent and, well, silly.

That's when the warning bells rang. The word "silly" reeks of the complacent condescension that has at various times been bestowed on all the cultural forms that matter most to me (Hollywood musicals, British melodramas, pop music, soap operas), so what right had I to apply it to someone else's part of the popular cultural playground? I had to rethink my disdain, and 1989 has been a very good year in which to do so, because in terms of popular culture 1989 has been the Year of the Bat.

This essay, then, is not written by a devotee of Batman, someone steeped in every last twist of the mythology. I come to these texts as an interested outsider, armed with a particular perspective. That perspective is homosexuality, and what I want to try and do here is to offer a gay reading of the whole Bat-business. It has no pretension to definitiveness, I don't presume to speak for all gay people everywhere. I'm male, white, British, thirty years old (at the time of writing) and all of those factors

---

1. Fredric Wertham, *Seduction of the Innocent* (London: Museum Press, 1955), p. 190.
2. Susan Sontag, "Notes on Camp," in *A Susan Sontag Reader* (Harmondsworth: Penguin Books), p. 106.

need to be taken into account. Nonetheless, I'd argue that Batman is especially interesting to gay audiences for three reasons.

Firstly, he was one of the first fictional characters to be attacked on 5 the grounds of presumed homosexuality, by Fredric Wertham in his book *Seduction of the Innocent.* Secondly, the 1960s TV series was and remains a touchstone of camp (a banal attempt to define the meaning of camp might well start with "like the sixties' *Batman* series"). Thirdly, as a recurring hero figure for the last fifty years, Batman merits analysis as a notably successful construction of masculinity.

## Nightmare on Psychiatry Street: Freddy's Obsession

*Seduction of the Innocent* is an extraordinary book. It is a gripping, flamboyant melodrama masquerading as social psychology. Fredric Wertham is, like Senator McCarthy,[3] like Batman, a crusader, a man with a mission, an evangelist. He wants to save the youth of America from its own worst impulses, from its id, from comic books. His attack on comic books is founded on an astonishingly crude stimulus-and-response model of reading, in which the child (the child, for Wertham, seems an unusually innocent, blank slate waiting to be written on) reads, absorbs, and feels compelled to copy, if only in fantasy terms, the content of the comics. It is a model, in other words, which takes for granted extreme audience passivity.

This is not the place to go into a detailed refutation of Wertham's work, besides which such a refutation has already been done in Martin Barker's excellent *A Haunt of Fears.*[4] The central point of audience passivity needs stressing, however, because it is crucial to the celebrated passage where Wertham points his shrill, witch-hunting finger at the Dynamic Duo and cries "queer."

Such language is not present on the page, of course, but in some ways *Seduction of the Innocent* (a film title crying out for either D. W. Griffith or Cecil B. DeMille) would be easier to stomach if it were. Instead, Wertham writes with anguished concern about the potential harm that Batman might do to vulnerable children, innocents who might be turned into deviants. He employs what was then conventional psychiatric wisdom about the idea of homosexuality as a "phase":

---

3. **Senator McCarthy** United States Senator Joseph R. McCarthy (1908–1957), who in the 1950s hunted and persecuted suspected Communists and Communist sympathizers. — EDS.

4. Martin Barker, *A Haunt of Fears* (London: Pluto Press, 1984).

Many pre-adolescent boys pass through a phase of disdain for girls. Some comic books tend to fix that attitude and instill the idea that girls are only good for being banged around or used as decoys. A homoerotic attitude is also suggested by the presentation of masculine, bad, witch-like or violent women. In such comics women are depicted in a definitely anti-erotic light, while the young male heroes have pronounced erotic overtones. The muscular male supertype, whose primary sex characteristics are usually well emphasized, is in the setting of certain stories the object of homoerotic sexual curiosity and stimulation.[5]

The implications of this are breathtaking. Homosexuality, for Wertham, is synonymous with misogyny. Men love other men because they hate women. The sight of women being "banged around" is liable to appeal to repressed homoerotic desires (this, I think, would be news to the thousands of women who are systematically physically abused by heterosexual men). Women who do not conform to existing stereotypes of femininity are another incitement to homosexuality.

Having mapped out his terms of reference, Wertham goes on to peel    10
the lid from Wayne Manor:

> Sometimes Batman ends up in bed injured and young Robin is shown sitting next to him. At home they lead an idyllic life. They are Bruce Wayne and "Dick" Grayson. Bruce Wayne is described as a "socialite" and the official relationship is that Dick is Bruce's ward. They live in sumptuous quarters, with beautiful flowers in large vases, and have a butler, Alfred. Batman is sometimes shown in a dressing gown. . . . It is like a wish dream of two homosexuals living together. Sometimes they are shown on a couch, Bruce reclining and Dick sitting next to him, jacket off, collar open, and his hand on his friend's arm.[6]

So, Wertham's assumptions of homosexuality are fabricated out of his interpretation of certain visual signs. To avoid being thought queer by Wertham, Bruce and Dick should have done the following: Never show concern if the other is hurt, live in a shack, only have ugly flowers in small vases, call the butler "Chip" or "Joe" if you have to have one at all, never share a couch, keep your collar buttoned up, keep your jacket on, and never, ever wear a dressing gown. After all, didn't Noel Coward[7] wear a dressing gown?

---

5. Wertham, p. 188.
6. Wertham, p. 190.
7. **Noel Coward** (1899–1973)   British playwright, actor, and composer known for witty, sophisticated comedies. — EDS.

Wertham is easy to mock, but the identification of homosexuals through dress codes has a long history.[8] Moreover, such codes originate as semiotic systems adopted by gay people themselves, as a way of signalling the otherwise invisible fact of sexual preference. There is a difference, though, between sporting the secret symbols of a subculture if you form part of that subculture and the elephantine spot-the-homo routine that Wertham performs.

Bat-fans have always responded angrily to Wertham's accusation. One calls it "one of the most incredible charges . . . unfounded rumours . . . sly sneers"[9] and the general response has been to reassert the masculinity of the two heroes, mixed with a little indignation: "If they had been actual men they could have won a libel suit."[10] This seems to me not only to miss the point, but also to *reinforce* Wertham's homophobia — it is only possible to win a libel suit over an "accusation" of homosexuality in a culture where homosexuality is deemed categorically inferior to heterosexuality.

Thus the rush to "protect" Batman and Robin from Wertham is simply the other side to the coin of his bigotry. It may reject Wertham, cast him in the role of dirty-minded old man, but its view of homosexuality is identical. Mark Cotta Vaz thus describes the imputed homosexual relationship as "licentious" while claiming that in fact Bruce Wayne "regularly squired the most beautiful women in Gotham city and presumably had a healthy sex life."[11] Licentious versus healthy — Dr. Wertham himself could not have bettered this homophobic opposition.

Despite the passions aroused on both sides (or rather the two facets    15 of the same side), there is something comic at the heart of this dispute. It is, simply, that Bruce and Dick are *not* real people but fictional constructions, and hence to squabble over their "real" sex life is to take things a little too far. What is at stake here is the question of reading, of what readers do with the raw material that they are given. Readers are at liberty to construct whatever fantasy lives they like with the characters of the fiction they read (within the limits of generic and narrative credibility, that is). This returns us to the unfortunate patients of Dr. Wertham:

> One young homosexual during psychotherapy brought us a copy of *Detective* comic, with a Batman story. He pointed out a picture of "The Home of Bruce and Dick," a house beautifully landscaped,

---

8. See, for example, the newspaper stories on "how to spot" homosexuals printed in Britain in the fifties and sixties, and discussed in Jeffrey Weeks, *Coming Out: Homosexual Politics in Britain* (London: Quartet, 1979).

9. Phrases taken from Chapters 5 and 6 of Mark Cotta Vaz, *Tales of the Dark Knight: Batman's First Fifty Years* (London: Futura, 1989).

10. Les Daniels, *Comix: A History of Comic Books in America* (New York: Bonanza Books, 1971), p. 87.

11. Cotta Vaz, pp. 47 and 53.

warmly lighted and showing the devoted pair side by side, looking
out a picture window. When he was eight this boy had realized from
fantasies about comic book pictures that he was aroused by men. At
the age of ten or eleven, "I found my liking, my sexual desires, in
comic books. I think I put myself in the position of Robin. I did
want to have relations with Batman . . . I remember the first time I
came across the page mentioning the 'secret batcave.' The thought of
Batman and Robin living together and possibly having sex relations
came to my mind . . ."[12]

Wertham quotes this to shock us, to impel us to tear the pages of *Detective* away before little Tommy grows up and moves to Greenwich Village, but reading it as a gay man today I find it rather moving and also highly recognizable.

What this anonymous gay man did was to practice that form of bricolage[13] which Richard Dyer has identified as a characteristic reading strategy of gay audiences.[14] Denied even the remotest possibility of supportive images of homosexuality within the dominant heterosexual culture, gay people have had to fashion what we could out of the imageries of dominance, to snatch illicit meanings from the fabric of normality, to undertake a corrupt decoding for the purposes of satisfying marginalized desires.[15] This may not be as necessary as it once was, given the greater visibility of gay representations, but it is still an important practice. Wertham's patient evokes in me an admiration, that in a period of American history even more homophobic than most, there he was, raiding the citadels of masculinity, weaving fantasies of oppositional desire. What effect the dread Wertham had on him is hard to predict, but I profoundly hope that he wasn't "cured."

It wasn't only Batman who was subjected to Dr. Doom's bizarre ideas about human sexuality. Hence:

> The homosexual connotation of the Wonder Woman type of story is
> psychologically unmistakable. . . . For boys, Wonder Woman is a
> frightening image. For girls she is a morbid ideal. Where Batman is
> anti-feminine, the attractive Wonder Woman and her counterparts
> are definitely anti-masculine. Wonder Woman has her own female

---

12. Wertham, p. 192.

13. **bricolage**  A new object created by reassembling bits and pieces of other objects; here, gay-identified readings produced from classic texts. — EDS.

14. Richard Dyer, ed., *Gays and Film,* 2nd Edition (New York: Zoetrope, 1984), p. 1.

15. See Richard Dyer, "Judy Garland and Gay Men," in Dyer, *Heavenly Bodies* (London: BFI, 1987) and Claire Whitaker, "Hollywood Transformed: Interviews with Lesbian Viewers," in Peter Steven, ed., *Jump Cut: Hollywood, Politics and Counter-Cinema* (Toronto: Between the Lines, 1985).

following. . . . Her followers are the "Holiday girls," i.e. the holiday girls, the gay party girls, the gay girls.[16]

Just how much elision can be covered with one "i.e."? Wertham's view of homosexuality is not, at least, inconsistent. Strong, admirable women will turn little girls into dykes — such a heroine can only be seen as a "morbid ideal."

Crazed as Wertham's ideas were, their effectiveness is not in doubt. The mid-fifties saw a moral panic about the assumed dangers of comic books. In the United States companies were driven out of business, careers wrecked, and the Comics Code introduced. This had distinct shades of the Hays Code[17] that had been brought in to clamp down on Hollywood in the 1930s, and under its jurisdiction comics opted for the bland, the safe, and the reactionary. In Britain there was government legislation to prohibit the importing of American comics, as the comics panic slotted neatly into a whole series of anxieties about the effects on British youth of American popular culture.[18]

And in all of this, what happened to Batman? He turned into Fred MacMurray from *My Three Sons*. He lost any remaining edge of the shadowy vigilante of his earliest years, and became an upholder of the most stifling small-town American values. Batwoman and Batgirl appeared (June Allyson and Bat-Gidget) to take away any lingering doubts about the Dynamic Duo's sex lives. A 1963 story called "The Great Clayface-Joker Feud" has some especially choice examples of the new, squeaky-clean sexuality of the assembled Bats.

Batgirl says to Robin, "I can hardly wait to get into my Batgirl costume again! Won't it be terrific if we could go on a crime case together like the last time? (sigh)." Robin replies, "It sure would, Betty (sigh)." The elder Bats look on approvingly. Batgirl is Batwoman's niece — to make her a daughter would have implied that Batwoman had had (gulp) sexual intercourse, and that would never do. This is the era of Troy Donohue and Pat Boone,[19] and Batman as ever serves as a cultural thermometer, taking the temperature of the times.

The Clayface/Joker business is wrapped up (the villains of this period are wacky conjurors, nothing more, with no menace or violence about them) and the episode concludes with another tableau of terrifying heterosexual contentment. "Oh Robin," simpers Batgirl, "I'm afraid you'll just have to hold me! I'm still so shaky after fighting Clayface . . . and

---

16. Wertham, pp. 192–93.
17. **Hays Code**   The 1930 Motion Picture Production Code, which described in detail what was morally acceptable in films. — EDS.
18. See Barker.
19. **Troy Donohue and Pat Boone**   Clean-cut, all-American-boy stars from the 1950s and 1960s. — EDS.

you're so strong!" Robin: "Gosh Batgirl, it was swell of you to calm me down when I was worried about Batman tackling Clayface alone." (One feels a distinct Wertham influence here: If Robin shows concern about Batman, wheel on a supportive female, the very opposite of a "morbid ideal," to minister in a suitably self-effacing way.) Batwoman here seizes her chance and tackles Batman: "You look worried about Clayface, Batman . . . so why don't you follow Robin's example and let me soothe you?" Batman can only reply "Gulp."

Gulp indeed. While it's easy simply to laugh at strips like these, knowing as we do the way in which such straight-faced material would be mercilessly shredded by the sixties' TV series, they do reveal the retreat into coziness forced on comics by the Wertham onslaught and its repercussions. There no doubt were still subversive readers of *Batman,* erasing Batgirl on her every preposterous appearance and reworking the Duo's capers to leave some room for homoerotic speculation, but such a reading would have had to work so much harder than before. The *Batman* of this era was such a closed text, so immune to polysemic interpretation, that its interest today is only as a symptom — or, more productively, as camp. "The Great Clayface-Joker Feud" may have been published in 1963, but in every other respect it is a fifties' text. If the 1960s began for the world in general with the Beatles, the 1960s for Batman began with the TV series in 1966. If the Caped Crusader had been all but Werthamed out of existence, he was about to be camped back into life.

## The Camped Crusader and the Boys Wondered

Trying to define "camp" is like attempting to sit in the corner of a circular room. It can't be done, which only adds to the quixotic appeal of the attempt. Try these:

> To be camp is to present oneself as being committed to the marginal with a commitment greater than the marginal merits.[20]

> Camp sees everything in quotation marks. It's not a lamp but a "lamp"; not a woman but a "woman". . . . It is the farthest extension, in sensibility, of the metaphor of life as theatre.[21]

> Camp is . . . a way of poking fun at the whole cosmology of restrictive sex roles and sexual identifications which our society uses to oppress its women and repress its men.[22]

---

20. Mark Booth, *Camp* (London: Quartet, 1983), p. 18.
21. Sontag, p. 109.
22. Jack Babuscio, "Camp and the Gay Sensibility," in Dyer, ed., *Gays and Film,* p. 46.

> Camp was and is a way for gay men to re-imagine the world around them . . . by exaggerating, stylizing and remaking what is usually thought to be average or normal.[23]

> Camp was a prison for an illegal minority; now it is a holiday for consenting adults.[24]

All true, in their way, but all inadequate. The problem with camp is [25] that it is primarily an experiential rather than an analytical discourse. Camp is a set of attitudes, a gallery of snapshots, an inventory of postures, a modus vivendi, a shop-full of frocks, an arch of eyebrows, a great big pink butterfly that just won't be pinned down. Camp is primarily an adjective, occasionally a verb, but never anything as prosaic, as earthbound, as a noun.

Yet if I propose to use this adjective as a way of describing one or more of the guises of Batman, I need to arrive at some sort of working definition. So, for the purposes of this analysis, I intend the term "camp" to refer to a playful, knowing, self-reflexive theatricality. *Batman,* the sixties' TV series, was nothing if not knowing. It employed the codes of camp in an unusually public and heavily signalled way. This makes it different from those people or texts who are taken up by camp audiences without ever consciously putting camp into practice. The difference may be very briefly spelled out by reference to Hollywood films. If *Mildred Pierce*[25] and *The Letter*[26] were taken up *as* camp, teased by primarily gay male audiences into yielding meaning not intended by their makers, then *Whatever Happened to Baby Jane?*[27] is a piece of self-conscious camp, capitalizing on certain attitudinal and stylistic tendencies known to exist in audiences. *Baby Jane* is also, significantly, a 1960s' film, and the 1960s were the decade in which camp swished out of the ghetto and up into the scarcely prepared mainstream.

A number of key events and texts reinforced this. Susan Sontag wrote her *Notes on Camp,* which remains the starting point for researchers even now. Pop Art[28] was in vogue (and in *Vogue*) and whatever the more ele-

---

23. Michael Bronski, *Culture Clash: The Making of Gay Sensibility* (Boston: South End Press), p. 42.

24. Philip Core, *Camp: The Lie that Tells the Truth* (London: Plexus), p. 7.

25. **Mildred Pierce**   1945 murder mystery film that traces the fortunes of a homemaker who breaks with her husband. — EDS.

26. **The Letter**   1940 murder movie whose ending was changed to satisfy moral standards of the time. — EDS.

27. **Whatever Happened to Baby Jane?**   Macabre 1962 film about an ex–child movie star living in an old Hollywood mansion. — EDS.

28. **Pop Art**   Art movement, begun in the 1950s, that borrowed images and symbols from popular culture, particularly from commercial products and mass media, as a critique of traditional fine art. — EDS.

vated claims of Lichtenstein,[29] Warhol,[30] and the rest, their artworks were on one level a new inflection of camp. The growing intellectual respectability of pop music displayed very clearly that the old barriers that once rigidly separated high and low culture were no longer in force. The James Bond films, and even more so their successors like *Modesty Blaise,* popularized a dry, self-mocking wit that makes up one part of the multifaceted diamond of camp. And on television there were *The Avengers, The Man from UNCLE, Thunderbirds,* and *Batman.*

To quote the inevitable Sontag, "The whole point of Camp is to dethrone the serious. . . . More precisely, Camp involves a new, more complex relation to 'the serious.' One can be serious about the frivolous, frivolous about the serious."[31]

The problem with Batman in those terms is that there was never anything truly serious to begin with (unless one swallows that whole portentous Dark Knight charade, more of which in the next section). Batman in its comic book form had, unwittingly, always been camp — it was serious (the tone, the moral homilies) about the frivolous (a man in a stupid suit). He was camp in the way that classic Hollywood was camp, but what the sixties' TV series and film did was to overlay this "innocent" camp with a thick layer of ironic distance, the self-mockery version of camp. And given the long associations of camp with the homosexual male subculture, Batman was a particular gift on the grounds of his relationship with Robin. As George Melly put it, "The real Batman series were beautiful because of their unselfconscious absurdity. The remakes, too, at first worked on a double level. Over the absorbed children's heads we winked and nudged, but in the end what were we laughing at? The fact they didn't know that Batman had it off with Robin."[32]

It was as if Wertham's fears were being vindicated at last, but his 1950s' bigot's anguish had been supplanted by a self-consciously hip 1960s' playfulness. What adult audiences laughed at in the sixties' *Batman* was a camped-up version of the fifties they had just left behind.

Batman's lessons in good citizenship ("We'd like to feel that our efforts may help every youngster to grow up into an honest, useful citizen"[33]) were another part of the character ripe for ridiculing deconstruction — "Let's go, Robin, we've set another youth on the road to a

30

---

29. **Lichtenstein**  Roy Lichtenstein (1923–   ), American artist at the center of the Pop Art movement, best known for melodramatic comic-book scenes. — EDS.

30. **Warhol**  Andy Warhol (1930?–87), pioneering Pop artist known for reproducing stereotyped images of famous people, such as Marilyn Monroe, and of commercial products, such as Campbell's Soup cans. — EDS.

31. Sontag, p. 116.

32. George Melly, *Revolt Into Style: The Pop Arts in the 50s and 60s* (Oxford: Oxford University Press, 1989 [first published 1970]), p. 193.

33. "The Batman Says," *Batman* #3 (1940), quoted in Cotta Vaz, p. 15.

brighter tomorrow" (the episode "It's How You Play the Game").
Everything the Adam West Batman said was a parody of seriousness, and
how could it be otherwise? How could anyone take genuinely seriously
the words of a man dressed like that?

The Batman/Robin relationship is never referred to directly; more
fun can be had by presenting it "straight," in other words, screamingly
camp. Wertham's reading of the Dubious Duo had been so extensively
aired as to pass into the general consciousness (in George Kelly's words,
"We all knew Robin and Batman were pouves"[34]), it was part of
the fabric of *Batman,* and the makers of the TV series proceeded accordingly.

Consider the Duo's encounter with Marsha, Queen of Diamonds.
The threat she embodies is nothing less than heterosexuality itself, the
deadliest threat to the domestic bliss of the Bat-couple. She is even about
to marry Batman before Albert intervenes to save the day. He and Batman flee the church, but have to do so in the already decorated Bat-
mobile, festooned with wedding paraphernalia including a large "Just
Married" sign. "We'll have to drive it as it is," says Batman, while somewhere in the audience a Dr. Wertham takes feverish notes. Robin,
Commissioner Gordon, and Chief O'Hara have all been drugged with
Marsha's "Cupid Dart," but it is of course the Boy Wonder who Batman
saves first. The dart, he tells Robin, "contains some secret ingredient by
which your sense and your will were affected," and it isn't hard to read
that ingredient as heterosexual desire, since its result, seen in the previous
episode, was to turn Robin into Marsha's slobbering slave.

We can tell with relief now, though, as Robin is "back in fighting
form" (with impeccable timing, Batman clasps Robin's shoulder on the
word "fighting"). Marsha has one last attempt to destroy the duo, but
naturally she fails. The female temptress, the seductress, the enchantress
must be vanquished. None of this is in the least subtle (Marsha's cat, for
example, is called Circe) but this type of mass-market camp can't afford
the luxury of subtlety. The threat of heterosexuality is similarly mobilized in the 1966 feature film, where it is Bruce Wayne's infatuation
with Kitka (Catwoman in disguise) that causes all manner of problems.

A more interesting employment of camp comes in the episodes [35]
where the Duo battle the Black Widow, played by Tallulah Bankhead.
The major camp coup here, of course, is the casting. Bankhead was
one of the supreme icons of camp, one of its goddesses: "Too intelligent
not to be self-conscious, too ambitious to bother about her self-
consciousness, too insecure ever to be content, but too arrogant ever to
admit insecurity, Tallulah personified camp."[35]

---

34. Melly, p. 192.
35. Core, p. 25.

A heady claim, but perhaps justified, because the Black Widow episodes are, against stiff competition, the campiest slices of Batman of them all. The stories about Bankhead are legendary — the time when on finding no toilet paper in her cubicle she slipped a ten dollar bill under the partition and asked the woman next door for two fives, or her whispered remark to a priest conducting a particularly elaborate service and swinging a censor of smoking incense, "Darling, I love the drag, but your purse is on fire" — and casting her in Batman was the final demonstration of the series' commitment to camp.

The plot is unremarkable, the usual Bat-shenanigans; the pleasure lies in the detail. Details like the elderly Bankhead crammed into her Super-Villainess costume, or like the way in which (through a plot detail I won't go into) she impersonates Robin, so we see Burt Ward miming to Bankhead's voice, giving the unforgettable image of Robin flirting with burly traffic cops. Best of all, and Bankhead isn't even in this scene but the thrill of having her involved clearly spurred the writer to new heights of camp, Batman has to sing a song to break free of the Black Widow's spell. Does he choose to sing "God Bless America"? Nothing so rugged. He clutches a flower to his Bat chest and sings Gilbert and Sullivan's "I'm Just a Little Buttercup." It is this single image, more than any other, that prevents me from taking the post–Adam West Dark Knight at all seriously.

The fundamental camp trick which the series pulls is to make the comics speak. What was acceptable on the page, in speech balloons, stands revealed as ridiculous once given audible voice. The famous visualized sound effects (URKKK! KA-SPLOOSH!) that are for many the fondest memory of the series work along similar lines. Camp often makes its point by transposing the codes of one cultural form into the inappropriate codes of another. It thrives on mischievous incongruity.

The incongruities, the absurdities, the sheer ludicrousness of Batman were brought out so well by the sixties' version that for some audiences there will never be another credible approach. I have to include myself here. I've recently read widely in postsixties Bat-lore, and I can appreciate what the writers and artists are trying to do, but my Batman will always be Adam West. It's impossible to be somber or pompous about Batman because if you try the ghost of West will come Bat-climbing into your mind, fortune cookie wisdom on his lips and keen young Dick by his side. It's significant, I think, that the letters I received from the editors of this book began "Dear Bat-Contributor."[36] Writers preparing chapters about James Joyce or Ingmar Bergman do not, I suspect, receive analogous greetings. To deny the large camp component of Batman is to blind oneself to one of the richest parts of his history.

---

36. This essay originally appeared in an anthology, *The Many Lives of the Batman: Critical Approaches to a Superhero and His Media*. — EDS.

## Is There Bat-Life After Bat-Camp?

The international success of the Adam West incarnation left Batman    40
high and dry. The camping around had been fun while it lasted, but it
hadn't lasted very long. Most camp humor has a relatively short life span,
new targets are always needed, and the camp aspect of Batman had been
squeezed dry. The mass public had moved on to other heroes, other genres, other acres of merchandising, but there was still a hard Bat-core of
fans to satisfy. Where could the Bat go next? Clearly there was no possibility of returning to the caped Eisenhower, the benevolent patriarch of
the 1950s. That option had been well and truly closed down by the TV
show. Batman needed to be given his dignity back, and this entailed a return to his roots.

This, in any case, is the official version. For the unreconstructed
devotee of the Batman (that is, people who insist on giving him the definite article before the name), the West years had been hell — a tricksy
travesty, an effeminizing of the cowled avenger. There's a scene in *Midnight Cowboy* where Dustin Hoffman tells Jon Voight that the only audience liable to be receptive to his cowboy clothes are gay men looking for
rough trade. Voight is appalled — "You mean to tell me John Wayne
was a fag?" (quoted, roughly, from memory). This outrage, this horror at
shattered illusions, comes close to encapsulating the loathing and dread
the campy Batman has received from the old guard of Gotham City and
the younger born-again Bat-fans.

So what has happened since the 1960s has been the painstaking re-
heterosexualization of Batman. I apologize for coining such a clumsy
word, but no other quite gets the sense that I mean. This strategy has
worked, too, for large audiences, reaching its peak with the 1989 film.
To watch this and then come home to see a video of the 1966 movie is
to grasp how complete the transformation has been. What I want to do
in this section is to trace some of the crucial moments in that change,
written from the standpoint of someone still unashamedly committed to
Bat-camp.

If one wants to take Batman as a Real Man, the biggest stumbling
block has always been Robin. There have been disingenuous claims that
"Batman and Robin had a blood-brother closeness. Theirs was a spiritual
intimacy forged from the stress of countless battles fought side by side"[37]
(one can imagine what Tallulah Bankhead might say to *that*), but we
know otherwise. The Wertham lobby and the acolytes of camp alike
have ensured that any Batman/Robin relationship is guaranteed to bring
on the sniggers. Besides which, in the late 1960s, Robin was getting to
be a big boy, too big for any shreds of credibility to attach themselves to

---

37. Cotta Vaz, p. 53.

all that father-son smokescreen. So in 1969 Dick Grayson was packed off to college and the Bat was solitary once more.

This was a shrewd move. It's impossible to conceive of the recent, obsessive, sturm-und-drang Batman with a chirpy little Robin getting in the way.[38] A text of the disturbing power of *The Killing Joke*[39] could not have functioned with Robin to rupture the grim dualism of its Batman/Joker struggle. There was, however, a post-Dick Robin, but he was killed off by fans in that infamous telephone poll.[40]

It's intriguing to speculate how much latent (or blatant) homophobia    45 lay behind that vote. Did the fans decide to kill off Jason Todd so as to redeem Batman for unproblematic heterosexuality? Impossible to say. There are other factors to take into account, such as Jason's apparent failure to live up to the expectations of what a Robin should be like. The sequence of issues in which Jason/Robin died, *A Death in the Family,* is worth looking at in some detail, however, in order to see whether the camp connotations of Bruce and Dick had been fully purged.

The depressing answer is that they had. This is very much the Batman of the 1980s, his endless feud with the Joker this time uneasily stretched over a framework involving the Middle East and Ethiopia. Little to be camp about there, though the presence of the Joker guarantees a quota of sick jokes. The sickest of all is the introduction of the Ayatollah Khomeini, a real and important political figure, into this fantasy world of THUNK! and THER-ACKK! and grown men dressed as bats. (As someone who lived in the part of England from which Reagan's planes took off on their murderous mission to bomb Libya, I fail to see the humor in this cartoon version of American foreign policy: It's too near the real thing.)

Jason dies at the Joker's hands because he becomes involved in a search for his own origins, a clear parallel to Batman's endless returns to *his* Oedipal scenario. Families, in the Bat-mythology, are dark and troubled things, one more reason why the introduction of the fifties versions of Batwoman and Batgirl seemed so inappropriate. This applies only to real, biological families, though; the true familial bond is between Batman and Robin, hence the title of these issues. Whether one chooses to read Robin as Batman's ward (official version), son (approved fantasy), or

---

38. A female Robin is introduced in the *Dark Knight Returns* series, which, while raising interesting questions about the sexuality of Batman, which I don't here have the space to address, seems significant in that the Dark Knight cannot run the risk of reader speculation that a traditionally male Robin might provoke.

39. **The Killing Joke**  Graphic novel by Alan Moore, Brian Bolland and John Higgins (New York: DC Comics 1988). — EDS.

40. **telephone poll**  In a 1988 issue of the *Batman* comic, a "post-Dick Robin," Jason Todd, was badly injured in an explosion, and readers were allowed to phone the publisher to vote on whether he should be allowed to survive. — EDS.

lover (forbidden fantasy), the sense of loss at his death is bound to be devastating. Batman finds Robin's body and, in the time-honored tradition of Hollywood cinema, is at least able to give him a loving embrace. Good guys hug their dead buddies, only queers smooch when still alive.

If the word "camp" is applied at all to the eighties' Batman, it is a label for the Joker. This sly displacement is the cleverest method yet devised of preserving Bat-heterosexuality. The play that the texts regularly make with the concept of Batman and the Joker as mirror images now takes a new twist. The Joker is Batman's "bad twin," and part of that badness is, increasingly, an implied homosexuality. This is certainly present in the 1989 film, a generally glum and portentous affair except for Jack Nicholson's Joker, a characterization enacted with venomous camp. The only moment when this dour film comes to life is when the Joker and his gang raid the Art Gallery, spraying the paintings and generally camping up a storm.

The film strives and strains to make us forget the Adam West Batman, to the point of giving us Vicki Vale as Bruce Wayne's lover, and certainly Michael Keaton's existential agonizing (variations on the theme of why-did-I-have-to-be-a-Bat) is a world away from West's gleeful subversion of truth, justice and the American Way. This is the same species of Batman celebrated by Frank Miller: "If your only memory of Batman is that of Adam West and Burt Ward exchanging camped-out quips while clobbering slumming guest-stars Vincent Price and Cesar Romero, I hope this book will come as a surprise. . . . For me, Batman was never funny. . . ."[41]

The most recent linkage of the Joker with homosexuality comes in   50
*Arkham Asylum,* the darkest image of the Bat-world yet. Here the Joker has become a parody of a screaming queen, calling Batman "honey pie," given to exclamations like "oooh!" (one of the oldest homophobic clichés in the book) and pinching Batman's behind with the advice, "Loosen up, tight ass." He also, having no doubt read his Wertham, follows the pinching by asking, "What's the matter? Have I touched a nerve? How is the Boy Wonder? Started shaving yet?" The Bat-response is unequivocal: "Take your filthy hands off me . . . Filthy degenerate!"

*Arkham Asylum* is a highly complex reworking of certain key aspects of the mythology, of which the sexual tension between Batman and the Joker is only one small part. Nonetheless the Joker's question "Have I touched a nerve?" seems a crucial one, as revealed by the homophobic ferocity of Batman's reply. After all, the dominant cultural construction of gay men at the end of the 1980s is as plague carriers, and the word

---

41. Frank Miller, "Introduction," *Batman: Year One* (London: Titan, 1988).

"degenerate" is not far removed from some of the labels affixed to us in the age of AIDS.

### Batman: Is He or Isn't He?

The one constant factor through all of the transformations of Batman has been the devotion of his admirers. They will defend him against what they see as negative interpretations, and they carry around in their heads a kind of essence of batness, a Bat-Platonic Ideal of how Batman should really be. The Titan Books reissue of key comics from the 1970s each carry a preface by a noted fan, and most of them contain claims such as "This, I feel, is Batman as he was meant to be."[42]

Where a negative construction is specifically targeted, no prizes for guessing which one it is: "you . . . are probably also fond of the TV show he appeared in. But then maybe you prefer Elvis Presley's Vegas years or the later Jerry Lewis movies over their early stuff . . . for me, the definitive Batman was then and always will be the one portrayed in these pages."[43]

The sixties' TV show remains anathema to the serious Bat-fan precisely because it heaps ridicule on the very notion of a serious Batman. *Batman* the series revealed the man in the cape as a pompous fool, an embodiment of superseded ethics, and a closet queen. As Marsha, Queen of Diamonds, put it, "Oh Batman, darling, you're so divinely square." Perhaps the enormous success of the 1989 film will help to advance the cause of the rival Bat-archetype, the grim, vengeful Dark Knight whose heterosexuality is rarely called into question (his humorlessness, fondness for violence, and obsessive monomania seem to me exemplary qualities for a heterosexual man). The answer, surely, is that they needn't be mutually exclusive.

If I might be permitted a rather camp comparison, each generation   55 has its definitive Hamlet, so why not the same for Batman? I'm prepared to admit the validity, for some people, of the swooping eighties' vigilante, so why are they so concerned to trash my sixties' camped crusader? Why do they insist so vehemently that Adam West was a faggy aberration, a blot on the otherwise impeccably butch Bat-landscape? What *are* they trying to hide?

---

42. Kim Newman, "Introduction," *Batman: The Demon Awakes* (London: Titan, 1989).

43. Jonathan Ross, "Introduction," to *Batman: Vow from the Grave* (London: Titan, 1989).

If I had a suspicious frame of mind, I might think that they were protesting too much, that maybe Dr. Wertham was on to something when he targeted these narratives as incitements to homosexual fantasy. And if I want Batman to be gay, then, for me, he is. After all, outside of the minds of his writers and readers, he doesn't really exist.

## Reading the Text

1. Summarize the objections Fredric Wertham makes to Batman in *Seduction of the Innocent*.
2. In a paragraph, write your own explanation of what Medhurst means by "camp."
3. What evidence does Medhurst supply to demonstrate that Batman is a gay character?
4. Explain what Medhurst means by his closing comment: "And if I want Batman to be gay, then, for me, he is. After all, outside of the minds of his writers and readers, he doesn't really exist."

## Reading the Signs

1. Do you agree with Medhurst's argument that the Batman and Robin duo were really a covert homosexual couple? Write an essay arguing for or challenging his position, being sure to study his evidence closely. You may want to visit your campus's media library to see if they have file tapes of old *Batman* shows, or read contemporary reviews of *Batman*, to gather evidence for your own essay.
2. Compare Medhurst's analysis of Batman to Tania Modleski's analysis of *Dead Poets Society* (p. 314). In what ways is the homoeroticism in *Batman* and *Dead Poets Society* either suppressed or revealed? How are any differences in the treatment of homoeroticism signs of attitude changes toward homosexuality between the 1960s and late 1980s?
3. Check your college library for a copy of Fredric Wertham's *Seduction of the Innocent*. Then write your own critique of Wertham's attack on Batman.
4. Buy a few copies of the current *Batman* comic book and write an essay in which you explain Batman's current sexual orientation.
5. Visit your college library and obtain a copy of Susan Sontag's "Notes on Camp" (included in Sontag's collections *Against Interpretation* and *The Susan Sontag Reader*). How would Sontag interpret the character of Batman?
6. In class, discuss the notion of camp and its appeal. In what ways could a film like *Pulp Fiction* be considered camp?

EMILY PRAGER

*Our Barbies, Ourselves*

*Little girls throughout America should know that Barbie is not drawn to scale. In this tongue-in-cheek essay on the role Barbie has played in her life, Emily Prager (b. 1952) reveals the damaging effect of a doll that establishes such an impossible standard of physical perfection for little girls — and for little boys who grow up expecting their girlfriends to look like Barbie. When not contemplating what Barbie has done to her, Emily Prager is a columnist with the* New York Times *and an essayist and fiction writer who has published for* The National Lampoon, *the* Village Voice, *and* Penthouse, *among other magazines. Her books include a work of historical fiction for children,* World War II Resistance Stories; *a book of humor,* The Official I Hate Videogames Handbook; *and works of fiction such as* Eve's Tattoo *(1991) and* Clea and Zeus Divorce *(1987).*

I read an astounding obituary in the *New York Times* not too long ago. It concerned the death of one Jack Ryan. A former husband of Zsa Zsa Gabor, it said, Mr. Ryan had been an inventor and designer during his lifetime. A man of eclectic creativity, he designed Sparrow and Hawk missiles when he worked for the Raytheon Company, and, the notice said, when he consulted for Mattel he designed Barbie.

If Barbie was designed by a man, suddenly a lot of things made sense to me, things I'd wondered about for years. I used to look at Barbie and wonder, What's wrong with this picture? What kind of woman designed this doll? Let's be honest: Barbie looks like someone who got her start at the Playboy Mansion. She could be a regular guest on *The Howard Stern Show.* It is a fact of Barbie's design that her breasts are so out of proportion to the rest of her body that if she were a human woman, she'd fall flat on her face.

If it's true that a woman didn't design Barbie, you don't know how much saner that makes me feel. Of course, that doesn't ameliorate the damage. There are millions of women who are subliminally sure that a thirty-nine-inch bust and a twenty-three-inch waist are the epitome of lovability. Could this account for the popularity of breast implant surgery?

I don't mean to step on anyone's toes here. I loved my Barbie. Secretly, I still believe that neon pink and turquoise blue are the only colors in which to decorate a duplex condo. And like many others of my generation, I've never married, simply because I cannot find a man who looks as good in clam diggers as Ken.

The question that comes to mind is, of course, Did Mr. Ryan design   5
Barbie as a weapon? Because it *is* odd that Barbie appeared about the
same time in my consciousness as the feminist movement — a time when
women sought equality and small breasts were king. Or is Barbie the
dream date of weapons designers? Or perhaps it's simpler than that: Perhaps Barbie is Zsa Zsa if she were eleven inches tall. No matter what, my
discovery of Jack Ryan confirms what I have always felt: There is something indescribably masculine about Barbie — dare I say it, phallic. For
all her giant breasts and high-heeled feet, she lacks a certain softness. If
you asked a little girl what kind of doll she wanted for Christmas, I just
don't think she'd reply, "Please, Santa, I want a hard-body."

On the other hand, you could say that Barbie, in feminist terms, is
definitely her own person. With her condos and fashion plazas and pools
and beauty salons, she is definitely a liberated woman, a gal on the move.
And she has always been sexual, even totemic. Before Barbie, American
dolls were flat-footed and breastless, and ineffably dignified. They were
created in the image of little girls or babies. Madame Alexander was the
queen of doll makers in the fifties, and her dollies looked like Elizabeth
Taylor in *National Velvet*. They represented the kind of girls who looked
perfect in jodhpurs, whose hair was never out of place, who grew up to
be Jackie Kennedy — before she married Onassis. Her dolls' boyfriends
were figments of the imagination, figments with large portfolios and
three-piece suits and presidential aspirations, figments who could keep
dolly in the style to which little girls of the fifties were programmed to
become accustomed, a style that spasm-ed with the sixties and the appearance of Barbie. And perhaps what accounts for Barbie's vast popularity is that she was also a sixties woman: into free love and fun colors, an-
ticlass, and possessed of real, molded boyfriend, Ken, with whom she
could chant a mantra.

But there were problems with Ken. I always felt weird about him.
He had no genitals, and, even at age ten, I found that ominous. I mean,
here was Barbie with these humongous breasts, and that was OK with
the toy company. And then, there was Ken with that truncated, uniden-
tifiable lump at his groin. I sensed injustice at work. Why, I wondered,
was Barbie designed with such obvious sexual equipment and Ken not?
Why was his treated as if it were more mysterious than hers? Did the fact
that it was treated as such indicate that somehow his equipment, his essential maleness, was considered more powerful than hers, more worthy
of the dignity of concealment? And if the issue in the mind of the toy
company was obscenity and its possible damage to children, I still object.
How do they think I felt, knowing that no matter how many water beds
they slept in, or hot tubs they romped in, or swimming pools they
lounged by under the stars, Barbie and Ken could never make love? No
matter how much sexuality Barbie possessed, she would never turn Ken
on. He would be forever withholding, forever detached. There was a

loneliness about Barbie's situation that was always disturbing. And twenty-five years later, movies and videos are still filled with topless women and covered men. As if we're all trapped in Barbie's world and can never escape.

God, it certainly has cheered me up to think that Barbie was designed by Jack Ryan. . . .

### Reading the Text

1. Why does Prager say "a lot of things made sense" to her after she learned Barbie was designed by a man?
2. What is Prager's attitude toward Ken?
3. How do Madame Alexander dolls differ from Barbies?

### Reading the Signs

1. Bring a toy to class and, in same-sex groups, discuss its semiotic significance; you may want to focus particularly on how the toys may be intended for one gender or another. Then have each group select one toy and present your interpretation of it to the whole class. What gender-related patterns do you find in the presentations?
2. Think of a toy you played with as a child and write a semiotic interpretation of it, using Prager's essay as a model. Be sure to consider differences between your childhood response to the toy and your current response.
3. Did you have a Barbie doll when you were a child? If so, write a journal entry in which you explore what the doll meant to you when you were young and how Prager's essay has caused you to rethink your attitudes.
4. Consider how Jack Ryan, the creator of Barbie, would defend his design. Write a letter, as if you were Ryan, addressed to Prager in which you justify Barbie's appearance and refute Prager's analysis.
5. Barbie can be seen as embodying not only America's traditional gender roles but also its consumerist ethos. Visit a toy store to learn what "accessories" one can buy for Barbie and then write an essay in which you explore the extent to which she illustrates the "hunger for more" described by Laurence Shames (see "The More Factor," p. 31).

# WANDA COLEMAN
## *Say It Ain't Cool, Joe*

—————————————————————————————————————
||||||||||||||||||||||||||||||||||||||||||||||||||||||

*In 1988, R.J.R. Nabisco revived the old figure of Joe Camel and turned him into a too-cool-to-be-true cartoon smoothie designed to pitch Camels to a preteen market. The Camel people deny that Joe Camel is aimed at children, of course, but when this debonair dromedary has a higher recognition value among American children than Cheerios or Kelloggs, one has to wonder. Even Antonia Novello, U.S. Surgeon General in 1992, wondered enough to wage an unsuccessful attempt to abolish Joe Camel ads from the nation's billboards, bus stops, and magazines. Wanda Coleman (b. 1946) joins the attacks on Joe Camel, but with a difference: She offers the perspective of an African-American woman concerned with Joe's impact on children in our inner cities. A Guggenheim fellow in poetry, and an Emmy Award–winning television writer and poet, Coleman has authored several books of poetry, essays, and fiction, including* Mad Dog Black Lady *(1979),* A War of Eyes and Other Stories *(1988),* Hand Dance *(1993), and* Native In A Strange Land: Trials & Tremors *(1996).*

Boy, oh boy, there's Joe, sportin' those Polaroid peepers, looking rakishly Mediterranean with hot babes and hotter cars. His hair looks like Moammar Kadafi's. The tuxedoed dome-nose has all the sleek arrogance of a shah exiled to Malibu.

I like Joe Camel. And I don't smoke. Not out of the closet anyway. And Camels? Never. But . . .

In Afro-American street parlance, Joe the Camel is a player. Life is a game and he's winning it. He runs in the fast lane. And he's about as gangsterish as it comes. The cat — er, dromedary — is too cool Old School. (Consult your Digital Underground[1] on TNT Recordings.)

If I didn't know better, I'd say Joe was patterned after one of my father's old cronies. Doc was the original "crip," meaning physically challenged. But that didn't stop any action. He hustled his way around South-Central with one crutch on his best days, a wheelchair on his worst. According to his own legend, he had lost one leg in World War II, but rumor was that he'd sacrificed the gam in some unsavory back-alley adventure.

In spite of his cop-and-blow existence, Doc always sported highly    5
polished wingtip kicks, though one shoe was always curiously devoid of

—————————————————————————————————————
1. **Digital Underground**   A rap group. — EDS.

mass. As Mama would say, he was "sharp as a tack." And generous. One of his philanthropic pleasures was formal-dress tea parties, where he gave us munchkins a crash course on etiquette, Perle Mesta–style. He paid polite attention to me and charmed my little socks off—the adult who takes a child seriously is always an attraction.

Doc smoked. He carried the first gold cigarette case I ever saw. It was impressive to watch him slip it from the pocket of his pin-striped vest. Thing about Doc was that, no matter how vulnerable he might've been, he was not to be pitied or messed with. A gat[2] was concealed in the creases of his threads.

And therein lies the appeal of Joe Camel as a clever selling gizmo and tobacco kingpin's dream.

Underneath Joe's Cheshire cat–smug macho is a deeper message. Joe's not just another lung-collapse peddler. He's a self-respect maven. In rural bottoms and urban ghettos nationwide, rife with runaways and bored, unemployed youth, there's a serious shortage of self-esteem. Like Doc or Joe, you can fire up a coffin nail for instant attitude, the easiest way to strike a pose.

Face it. Joe Camel has life-style appeal. He's rich and he's infamous. And he runs with the pack. There's Joe the suave, white-on-white be-tuxed academic. If you ain't got it, you can fake his "smooth philosophy" by lighting up. Or you can rack 'em up for Pool Shark Joe cuz he's about to run the table.

In his stingy fedora, Hard Pack Joe and his Wide cousins have all the Hollywood charisma of William Bendix breathing down Robert Mitchum's neck in *The Big Steal* or Brando in *The Godfather*. 10

Beachcomber Joe has done his share of Venice Beach schmoozing, no doubt sipping Long Island iced tea on the volleyball court. Calypso Joe opens the doors of Club Camel on some tiny Caribbean isle where the cane grows tall and the money laundering is easy.

Joe's crimey, Eddie Camel, was a bead-wearing, apple-capped, paintbrush-totin', long-haired flower child in the sixties. But today he's a loose-lipped, slack-collared, tam-topped, neo-bebop jazz drummer. Bustah (note the idiomatic black spelling) Camel undergoes a similar transformation, and only his electric guitar remains the same.

I can't resist poking fun at ol' Joe. But underneath the fun, the birth of his cool is linked to the birth of survival strategies that have allowed the black male to withstand the relentlessness of racism. It is the cool personified by Malcolm X, Miles Davis, Willie Brown, and Ice Cube. To be cool is to be laid-back black.

But Joe Camel is offensive. Not only because cigarettes can be addictive and debilitating but because, at root, old Joe's shtick is plain-and-

---

2. **gat**  A gun. — EDS.

simple racist. He's a composite of little-understood cultural traits designed to sucker in youngsters, especially black children. And that ain't cool.

You dig?                                                                    15

### Reading the Text

1. How, according to Coleman, is the character Joe Camel used to sell cigarettes?
2. What parallels does Coleman see between Joe Camel and "Doc"?
3. Why does Coleman believe Joe Camel is "racist"?

### Reading the Signs

1. In class, form teams and debate whether the Joe Camel campaign should be banned on the grounds that it inappropriately uses an attractive cartoon character to peddle a dangerous product to children. In researching your arguments, consult the issue of the *Journal of the American Medical Association* devoted entirely to tobacco use (vol. 266, no. 22, December 11, 1991).
2. Coleman believes that Joe Camel is essentially a black character who makes a special appeal to African-American children. Write an essay in which you defend, refute, or modify this assumption. To develop your ideas, consult Michael Medved, "The Long Arm of What You Watch" (p. 322).
3. Discuss in class the tone that Coleman adopts. Why does she use a nonacademic, "homegirl" style in her essay?
4. Using Coleman's selection as a model, write an essay in which you explore the appeal of the Marlboro Man. Be sure to note the differences in the audiences to which the two characters appeal.
5. Compare Joe Camel with other cartoon characters that target children (you might read or review Andy Medhurst's "Batman, Deviance, and Camp," p. 358, and Gary Engle's "What Makes Superman So Darned American?," p. 344). Write an essay in which you explore how cool or camp characters especially appeal to children.
6. Interview younger siblings or other children you know, and ask them about their familiarity with Joe Camel. Then write an essay defending, refuting, or modifying Coleman's argument.

M c C R E A   A D A M S

*Advertising Characters: The Pantheon of Consumerism*

ııııııııııııııııııııııııııııııııııııııııııııııı

*From the Quaker Oats Quaker and Betty Crocker to Joe Isuzu and*
*Spuds MacKenzie, American advertisers have been inventing "person-*
*alities" to pitch the product since the nineteenth century. In this semi-*
*otic survey of America's advertising characters, McCrea Adams (b.*
*1952) traces the mythological descent of such figures and their eventual*
*enshrinement at the heart of commercial culture. But not all such char-*
*acters are invented; genuine social heroes may be enlisted as well. The*
*result? A teacher may show her class a picture of George Washington*
*and hear her students identify him as "someone who sold stuff on TV"*
*— or maybe just Joe Camel in a wig. McCrea Adams, who wrote this*
*essay as a UCLA student, has published articles on poetry and popu-*
*lar music history. A book and film reviewer for the Dow Jones and*
*Prodigy online computer systems, Adams currently is a project editor at*
*Salem Press and, on the side, a rock-and-roll keyboardist.*

Advertising characters, those people or animals that symbolize various products, have been with us for a long time. The Quaker Oat
Quaker appeared in 1877; Psyche, the White Rock Soda girl, debuted in
1894. The twentieth century was only four years old when the Campbell's Soup Kids arrived. Betty Crocker was born, full-grown, in the
mid-1930s.[1] Back in Psyche's youth, when neither advertising nor psychology were huge fields of their own, these characters were created by
people trying to sell their own products. Usually someone at the manufacturing company would dream up what seemed to be an appropriate
identifying symbol for their product. No one is sure, for example, exactly
how the chick that symbolizes Bon Ami cleanser began, but apparently a
company founder, in the nineteenth century, started wrapping soap bars
in paper with a little chick design on it; the enigmatic "hasn't scratched
yet" slogan was not added until later.[2]

Advertising characters and symbols can be seen as part of a continuum of fictions and fantasies given life by the restless, fertile human
imagination. Further back than recorded history, mythical or religious
beings were created and attributed with fantastic exploits and superhu-
man powers. Oral traditions passed down descriptions and tales of these

---

1. "Cherubic But Not as Chubby," *Time,* Apr. 4, 1983, p. 60.
2. *Nation's Business,* March, 1981, pp. 70–71.

"characters" before writing on papyrus was invented, let alone radio and television. The gods of ancient Egypt, the Greek gods on Mount Olympus, the Norse gods, and the pantheon of Nigeria's Yoruba people all are extensions of these prehistoric traditions. The gods and superheroes of Finnish mythology present an interesting similarity to modern advertising characters in that beings from ancient times and those of a much more recent era coexist in the same cycles of stories. Ad characters, too, inhabit a syncretic world in which Moe (Three Stooges) Howard stands beside Albert Einstein and where Leonardo da Vinci fumbles ineffectually in a modern, high-tech office. The ancient Romans adapted the Greek gods to their own culture, just as modern advertising adapts characters from the past, both real and mythical. And the birth of an advertising "being" can seem as mysterious and lost in antiquity as that of any mythical creature. Clarence Birdseye, for example, was a real frozen-food pioneer (born December 9, 1886), but he has been in the character pantheon so long that he now seems fictitious.

The Yoruba pantheon includes a character called Eshu who frequently appears in mythology: the "trickster," that supernatural being dedicated to confusing things, to befuddling and bedeviling us poor mortals. The relationship of the trickster to advertising is too obvious to require much discussion, but suffice it to say that without illusion, trickery, and magical transformations, the power of our advertising gods would be lessened considerably. We even have a double-trickster: Joe Isuzu, the lying car salesman for Isuzu, lets us laugh at the advertising "trick" even as he sells us cars. The Yoruba pantheon also includes a god of iron, Ogun, who has evolved into the god of war and transportation; nowadays he is the god who protects a city dweller's Mercedes. As our ad characters are, Ogun is a powerful "transformer" — and, like them, he is both transformer and transformed, since he himself has changed through time.[3]

Unlike religions, which seek to make sense of the cosmos and create a way to deal with mortality, folk tales and their heroes evolved largely as a source of entertainment. They also, however, often typify a culture's valued qualities, such as strength or mental agility. They represent the oral tradition in a secular context with fables of giants (such as Jack's nemesis atop the beanstalk), mythical animals, heroes such as Paul Bunyan, and tales of witches and fairies. Now, in the world of television, we have the Jolly Green Giant and the Keebler elves, ably personifying the apparently valued ability to invent new frozen foods and cookies. Television, in effect, has provided us with an artificial, electronic oral tradition, entering our minds through visual and audio stimuli.

Ellen Weis is the director of San Francisco's Museum of Modern Mythology, which has a collection of over three thousand artifacts, in- 5

---

3. Dr. Donald Cosentino provided information on the Yoruba in UCLA lectures in 1987.

cluding an eight-foot plastic Jolly Green Giant and a motorized Buster Brown display from 1915. "Every society has mythology," Weis says. "In some societies it's religion. Our religion is consumerism."[4] She points out that some mythical beings were half man, half god, and that advertising characters are half man, half product. Both are "given enormous credence in their society. Just look at Cap'n Crunch." When she says that one "can really learn a lot from an original drawing of Elsie the Cow," many things come to mind — fertility, the milk of human kindness, the relationship between humans and nature, and perhaps even the fact that Hindus hold the cow to be sacred.

Psychologist Carol Moog, who does "psychological semiotics" for advertising agencies, similarly has explored the meaning of Lever Brothers' Snuggle fabric-softener teddy bear: "The bear is an ancient symbol of aggression, but when you create a teddy bear, you provide a softer, nurturant side." This combination is the "perfect image for a fabric softener that tames the rough texture of clothing," according to Moog.[5] She advised Lever Brothers to keep Snuggle genderless and avoid mixing Snuggle with live humans in ads. "To keep the magic, it has to be just Snuggle and the viewer communicating. The teddy bear acts as a bridge between the consumer's rational and more instinctual, emotional side." Notice the supernatural overtones and the intimation of a sort of prayer. Another media observer, perhaps only half-jokingly, went so far as to call Snuggle "the anti-Christ."[6] Ellen Weis again: "These images get into our subconscious and stay with us for life. It's very important to be aware of how powerful they are." Not everyone agrees with these sorts of evaluations; as George Lois, chairman of Lois Pitts Gershon Pon, puts it, "These psychologists tend to be overly intellectual and a little tutti-frutti."

An early phase of advertising in the United States that might be termed "protoadvertising" evolved during the nineteenth century. Prime examples include the "Wild West" show and the hundreds of tonics and elixirs identified with a "doctor" who had supposedly created them to cure whatever ailed one. Here again are links with myth and power. In the first case, the reality of "the West" blurs into a re-creation of it, with some of the real characters (Wild Bill Hickok, Buffalo Bill Cody) themselves — now trickster figures — helping to smudge the lines between reality and legend, person and performer. In the second, a fabricated character ("Dr. Whoever") is presented as the inventor of a patent medicine.

---

4. Carrie Dolan, "Why is Capt. Crunch a Little Like Zeus?" *Wall Street Journal,* Feb. 1, 1988, pp. 1, 20.

5. Ronald Alsop, "Agencies Scrutinize Their Ads for Psychological Symbolism," *Wall Street Journal,* June 11, 1987, p. 27.

6. Christina Bauman, personal communication.

As the twentieth century progressed, radio and then television became filled with advertisements, and newspapers and magazines continued to bombard us with them; the streets filled with billboards, and the sky with skywriting and banners. Something had changed. There were too many gods in the pantheon and too many doctors selling us tonic. As advertising became a billion-dollar industry and television entered nearly every American home, the messages of advertising and the various characters and symbols used to convey those messages multiplied almost beyond comprehension. Life in the information society is now cluttered with sensory input of all kinds, and advertising is the most unrelenting demander of our attention. Rhetoric has been dubbed "the art of saying nothing finely," but the rhetoric of advertising is the art of saying nothing incessantly. We try our best to screen it out, turn it off, scoff at it, curse at it, laugh at it. But it is pervasive, and its characters — real, unreal, alive, animated — invade our consciousness, invited or not.

Because of this invasion, the lines between reality and fiction no longer seem very clear. Actors sell products as themselves, as anonymous pitchmen, or as created characters, and what's the difference? They are all transformed into tricksters before the camera. ("I'm an actor," John Carradine once intoned in a bank commercial, "but I'm not acting now.") Politicians in turn sell themselves as products — packaged, prepared characters. How much difference is there really between the two Ronalds, McDonald and Reagan? Quite possibly the viewer, or reader, or consumer no longer notices or cares what is real and what is not. Television, in particular, streams on endlessly, real and unreal side by side in a funny and terrible jumble of images and sounds, all trivialized by the constant yammering of commercials.

## Deities in the Pantheon

The pantheon of advertising characters contains far more beings than    10
we can recall at one time. Some have been short-lived, others have lasted
for ninety years or more. Juan Valdez grows our coffee and Mrs. Olson
brews it, although Joe DiMaggio and Mr. Coffee have given her some
competition. Madge tells us how to have younger-looking hands; Mr.
Clean and the Brawny man help us mop the floor. The lonely Maytag
repairman waits for a phone call. Mr. Goodwrench fixes the car, Mrs.
Paul makes fish sticks, Aunt Jemima serves pancakes, and Joe Isuzu lies.

Some distinctions can be drawn among the various types of advertising characters and spokespeople, provided we bear in mind that such classifications are not as clear and clean as they might at first appear. One basic distinction is between representations of real people and depictions of created characters. Within the "real" category are celebrities as themselves, corporate spokespersons as themselves, and "person-in-the-street" testimonials. Within the "created" realm are actors strongly identified with particular characters (e.g., Charmin's Mr. Whipple); actors representing a character with no unique actor identification (the Marlboro Man, for example); and actors as unnamed people shown doing things in commercials — primarily various versions of having fun. There are also cartoon characters, both still and animated (a classic is Speedy Alka-Seltzer).

Characters frequently transcend the boundaries between categories, however. Mr. Whipple is played by a live actor but has also been turned into a drawing used on packaging; conversely, symbols spawn actors to portray them. The haziest division perhaps is between created characters and "real" celebrities. The fictional Rosie of Rosie's Diner, for example, appears in an ad with Rosey Grier, making jokes about what a good name Rosie is and teaching him that Bounty really is the "quicker-picker-upper."

Cartoon characters, as well as live characters, can be either created specifically for a product or appropriated from elsewhere. Cap'n Crunch was created by Jay Ward's animation studio specifically for the cereal itself (as was Tony the Tiger, by a different studio, for Sugar Frosted Flakes). Hanna-Barbera's Flintstones, on the other hand, have been taken from their "real" world of Bedrock and used as pitchmen for at least two wildly divergent products. The first, strange as it may seem today, was Winston cigarettes, back when Winston cosponsored the original TV show in the sixties; another, more recently, has been their namesake, Flintstones vitamins. Charles M. Schulz's Peanuts gang has sold all kinds of things, including insurance for Metropolitan Life. Even the voice behind so many cartoons, Mel Blanc, has done one of those American Express "unrecognized celebrities" ads.

Some agencies created a sympathetic, "real" character for an actor to portray, while others take a more exaggerated approach. The "Sparkletts man" is a prime example of the former. Warm, friendly, handsome, competent, he happily drove his green Sparkletts truck around under sunny California skies while reciting happy, humorous rhymes about himself "and Sparkletts water makin' friends." Mr. Whipple aptly embodies the second (although he certainly has plenty of company). Played by ex-vaudevillian Dick Wilson, he first appeared in October, 1964, uttering "the whine heard round the world: 'Please don't squeeze the Charmin.'"[7] Wilson helped make Charmin the best-selling toilet paper in the United States; he now earns a handy six-figure income for about sixteen days of filming a year. Interestingly, both these actors received so much exposure from their commercials that they soon became celebrities in their own right. Again, they are not alone; Mrs. Olson, the Bartles and

---

7. "Mr. Whipple, Dick Wilson, Wraps 20th Year," *People,* Nov. 12, 1984, p. 151.

James characters, and more recently Joe Isuzu can be counted among their ranks.

Actor Jim Varney plays a character named Ernest P. Worrell, created     15
by Nashville agency Carden & Cherry, who sticks his head in the window while saying "Hey, Vern!" Varney's Ernest is supposed to represent someone in everyone's neighborhood — "the guy who drives you crazy yet cracks you up as he's doing it."[8] Well, maybe; at any rate, the Vern/Ernest commercials are used to sell a variety of products in over a hundred local markets. And in one of those odd quirks of show business, Ernest P. Worrell somehow became the lead character in a feature film, *Ernest Saves Christmas.* (The best analogue that comes to mind is the recent feature starring Cassandra Peterson's Elvira character. As a camp horror-movie host, Elvira is about as close to being a commercial character as one can get without actually being one.)

## Nobody's Perfect: Troubles on Olympus

The power attributed to advertising spokespersons — be they real or invented — is manifest in the problems they can create. The Federal Trade Commission announced in 1978 that it would begin putting pressure on stars involved in ads that make verifiably false claims. Pat Boone agreed to stop promoting an ineffective acne cream; former astronaut Gordon Cooper stopped advertising an automobile gas valve. In 1985, former football star Johnny Unitas was sued by two investors in a Florida financial services firm for misrepresenting a product he endorsed in a radio ad. The suit argued, their attorney said, that "a celebrity has some obligation to . . . make sure he is not being used in a scheme of fraud." Some entertainment agents and lawyers now require indemnification clauses holding the advertisers responsible for any fines levied against their clients.[9]

Other problems occur as well. Bill Cosby, for example, has sold so many different products that some say it is hard to identify him with any one campaign. His "overexposure" was blamed by one expert for the failure of E. F. Hutton's 1986 campaign featuring Cosby. Distinguished actor John Houseman, very effective when promoting financial house Smith Barney, was a flop at selling Big Macs. "I can't imagine John Houseman ever having been in a McDonald's," noted adman Jay Chiat.[10]

---

8. Rudy Maxa and Bina Kiyonaga, "Hey, Vern," *People,* Dec. 2, 1985, p. 121.

9. "A Celebrity Malpractice?" *Newsweek,* Dec. 23, 1985, p. 66.

10. Christy Marshall, "It Seemed Like a Good Idea at the Time," *Forbes,* Dec. 28, 1987, p. 98.

The J. Walter Thompson agency failed to sell Burger King's burgers with its huge ($40 million) campaign built around a search for the mysterious (fictional) "Herb," who had never eaten a Whopper. The public was completely uninterested. Thompson president Steve Bowen reflected that Herb never should have been revealed as a nerd, as he finally was. "Herb should have been Robert Redford," he claimed. "In reality, everything in life is aspirational, even fast food."[11] Note that Herb and Redford are viewed (albeit whimsically) as inhabitants of the same reality. Since we only "know" Redford from his fictional roles, there are many permutations of the Robert Redford persona. Similarly, Bill Cosby has been a comedian, a spy, a teacher (Chet Kincaid), and a doctor with a lawyer wife (Cliff Huxtable). And he has sold for Jell-O, Coke, Ford, Texas Instruments, and E. F. Hutton. Cosby and Redford are both changelings — and tricksters of the highest order.

Another sort of problem befell Ivory Soap executives, who were horrified when the media discovered that the woman whose portrait graced their boxes of "99-44/100% pure" detergent was Marilyn Chambers, an adult film star. This was overexposure of quite a different sort than Cosby's. In this case, the advertising character — the fiction — snagged on an unacceptable reality. The performers in pornographic movies, after all, really do perform explicit sexual acts, and this is *too* real for the world of selling. Ironically, advertising, which thrives on the sexual tease, must evade the actuality of intercourse. Ads give glimpses, magic shiny moments. Look but don't touch, they say; look and go buy. They attempt to create the urge, but place their products as the necessary middle step to obtaining satisfaction.

While human spokespersons are the most problematic for advertisers, nothing is exempt from controversy. Even man's best friend can end up in hot water. Anheuser-Busch's Spuds MacKenzie made a big splash when he arrived, a forty-seven-pound English bull terrier who sometimes appeared with "a trio of spandexed honeys" called the Spudettes.[12] Spuds's message, according to Budweiser manager Joe Corcoran, is that "you can be a hip, happy trendsetter like Spuds." No information was revealed about the "real" Spuds — advertisers insisted they wanted to preserve the mystique — although Spuds himself did hit the talk-show circuit. Toward the end of 1987 Spuds got some bad press, not because of complaints about the degrading ads with dancing bimbos, but for reportedly being a female posing as a male. Then, as if such deceptions were not bad enough, she or he soon stood accused of being a pit bull.

A more serious concern is whether Spuds may be a corrupting influence on young people. The Spuds campaign, centering as it does on a

20

---

11. Ibid.
12. Bernice Kanner, "Top Dog: Spudsmania," *New York,* Sept. 28, 1987, pp. 20–23.

household pet (and being aimed at the lowest common denominator), may well appeal to children way below the drinking age. Federal authorities refused to act on complaints about the matter. Ohio's liquor commission, however, has long had a regulation prohibiting the use of Santa Claus in ads that "might entice children to drink," and in December of 1987, it was considering whether to ban Budweiser Christmas promos and packaging that pictured Spuds MacKenzie dressed up as Santa.[13] A surprising number of mythological overtones, it must be noted, appear in these anecdotes about Spuds MacKenzie. Spuds is a Dionysian figure and, as an animal surrounded by women, is certainly a relative of the satyr. His sexual ambiguity is reminiscent of Tiresius and Hermaphroditus. He also has folkloric ties with Saint Nicholas/Santa Claus and, in adults' fears that children will be enticed to follow him, with the Pied Piper of Hamlin.

## The Pantheon from Hell

Although there are intriguing similarities between advertising characters and beings from folklore, mythology, and religion, the ways in which they differ are crucial. Religion and folklore come from the human capacity, even compulsion, to imagine the unseen. Humans want to understand things — and if we can't, we at least want to come up with a plausible and entertaining story. We create art; we have a language that can depict a past behind the moment, a future before it. That is what makes humans human; that is what we are. The supernatural is born of a sense of mystery and wonder. The characters of advertising, on the other hand, are created not to help understand the universe but to move the merchandise. In a sense, they even help to hide the truth by concealing the workings of the capitalist universe. They are self-consciously created by committees who have probed the mysteries by doing market research and studying the psychology of the consumer. Advertising characters muddle the past and diminish the future into a time when new consumption will occur. They represent the loss of mystery, and its replacement by an empty mechanistic cycle of watching and buying.

Mark Crispin Miller points out that television and its advertising have become so self-referential, and often so slyly self-mocking, that the viewer no longer has a standard by which to judge them:

> As advertising has become more self-referential, it has also become harder to distinguish from the various other features of our media culture. . . . TV is suffused with the enlightened irony of the common man, the "little guy," or — to use a less dated epithet — the

---

13. "Spuds, You Dog," *Newsweek,* Dec. 14, 1987, p. 68.

smart shopper. . . . Whatever was a source of pleasure in the past is
now derided by and for the knowing, whether it's . . . the silent
movies derisively excerpted in the ads for Hershey or Toshiba, or the
cowboy pictures lampooned by Philip Morris . . . or the Mona Lisa as
ridiculed to sell Peter Pan peanut butter.[14]

Miller calls this ongoing derision "compulsive trashing." It permeates advertising, and the use of historical figures as advertising characters
is one of the ways it manifests itself. Benjamin Franklin and Thomas
Jefferson have represented banks, and George Washington and Abraham
Lincoln have been used in innumerable pitches — especially in the
month of February. Ralph Nader complained in an open letter to President Reagan that while it isn't illegal, "using revered leaders from our
nation's past as salespeople or hawkers [is] in the realm of sleaziness."[15]
Nader wrote that a teacher reported holding up a picture of Washington
and having a child identify him as someone who sold stuff on TV. Historical figures are often used in gag ads, making the "trashing" overt.
Historical entertainment figures are also used and abused. Laurel and
Hardy lookalikes, for example, have sold windshield wipers. And in a
very strange case, IBM's agency built a successful campaign around an
imitator of Charlie Chaplin's Tramp character. Remember that in the
most famous scene in Chaplin's film *Modern Times,* the Tramp was
whirled wildly about by the huge gears and belts of a gigantic industrial
machine. There is a terrible irony in the perverting of the pathetic, loner
Tramp figure into a character selling computers for IBM, a gigantic, impersonal "machine" of the postindustrial age.

The Tramp campaign and all "historical" campaigns smudge the line      25
between the real and the fictitious. In a very real way, the question eventually becomes "What is reality?" Television programming and advertisements present a stream of images in which fiction and nonfiction are
nearly indistinguishable; news, entertainment, and advertising all look
more and more alike. The Tramp was a fiction, created by Chaplin; he
was then recreated by an actor imitating Chaplin as the Tramp. The crucial distinction is that Chaplin's Tramp was art, whereas IBM's Tramp is
pure commerce. The danger is that we may be presented with so much
slick, dazzling commerce that we no longer care about the art or the history. Consumer entertainment is, after all, very convenient. The George
Washington pitching products on TV is in some ways more real than the
other — this one can be seen "in the flesh," before our very eyes. This
unreal television world has at least partially displaced the other. A con-

---

14. Mark Crispin Miller, "Deride and Conquer," in *Watching Television,* Todd
Gitlin, ed. (New York: Pantheon Books, 1986). The excerpts are scattered throughout
Miller's essay, which begins on p. 183.

15. "Would Honest Abe Lie to You?" *Consumer Reports,* Sept. 1985, p. 567.

sumer survey taken in early 1985 showed that 93 percent of the people
polled remembered who Mr. Clean was, although he hadn't been on the
air for years, but only 56 percent knew who George Bush was.[16]

The artificial pantheon of advertising beings represents not a link
with our history and culture but a break from any meaningful sense of
who we are. Advertising presents a self-perpetuating cycle of clichés
based only on older clichés. A comedian once complained about the ad
campaign for Country Time lemon drink that boasted it "tastes just like
good old-fashioned lemonade." He said, Hey, wait a minute, folks;
lemonade isn't something from our past, some long-forgotten secret.
Anyone can make it, any time; you only need lemons, water, and sugar.
But the culture of consumerism would prefer that we forget that.

The lying Joe Isuzu character represents something even darker. He
embodies a disillusionment, a sense that there are no ethics left in our society. Indeed, we have heard so much news about illegality and deception in Washington and on Wall Street that the cliché of the sleazy car
salesman seems a fitting symbol for a large corporation. Trickster Joe
Isuzu lies and — since the audience is in on the joke — tells us to laugh
it off. Isuzu lies to sell cars, politicians lie to get elected, and we've all
been lied to so much that we find it hard to believe anything. The creators of the pantheon of consumerism must go to ever greater lengths to
capture our attention and remind us that advertising characters, the gods
of commerce, are our heroes and protectors. Kurt Vonnegut once remarked that when he tried to think about what American culture was, all
that came to mind were television commercials. With every passing year,
that observation seems more valid.

### Reading the Text

1. According to Adams, why is the use of characters an especially effective
   strategy for selling products?
2. What differences are there in the impact of fictional and real advertising
   characters?
3. What problems may arise when using characters as an advertising strategy?

### Reading the Signs

1. In class, brainstorm on the blackboard as many advertising characters as
   you can, drawing both from Adams's essay and your own experience.

---

16. Mark N. Vamos, "New Life for Madison Avenue's Old-time Stars," *Business
Week,* Apr. 1, 1985, p. 94.

With your class, categorize the characters, perhaps according to Adams's fictional and real groups, or according to gender, ethnicity, or profession. Then discuss the significance of your categories. How do the different groups appeal to consumers to buy their products? What do they reveal about American values?

2. Explore in a journal entry the appeal of Joe Camel, keeping in mind both Adams's essay and Wanda Coleman's "Say It Ain't Cool, Joe" (p. 378).

3. Select one of the products from the "Portfolio of Ads" (pp. 178-187) and sketch a new character that could serve as an advertising representative of that product. Then write an essay in which you explain how your character would act as a sign. How would it sell the product? What values would it project?

4. Adams quotes Ellen Weis of San Francisco's Museum of Modern Mythology as saying "Every society has mythology. In some societies, it's religion. Our religion is consumerism." Write an essay defending or refuting Weis's claim. To support your position, you can draw upon your own behavior as a consumer and your observations of others; you may also want to read or review Laurence Shames's "The More Factor" (p. 31).

5. In recent years, athletic shoe companies have transformed real athletes into characters to sell their products (for instance, Nike's Bo Jackson "just do it" campaign). Analyze the appeal of one such campaign, basing your analysis on specific examples of ads (you might watch some sports shows on television for broadcast ads, or study an issue of *Sports Illustrated* for print ads).

JENNY LYN BADER

*Larger Than Life*

|||||||||||||||||||||||||||||||||||||||||||||||||||||||

*Do you have any heroes? Or does the very concept of heroism seem passé in the irony-rich, self-conscious nineties? In this essay that first appeared in* Next: Young American Writers on the New Generation *(1994), Jenny Lyn Bader (b. 1968) surveys the role of heroes for her generation, comparing her point of view with those of past generations. Maybe heroes are obsolete, Bader suggests; maybe we'd just be better off with role models who, while not providing the commanding presence of the full-fledged hero, can at least provide some guidance to an often-confused Generation X. A New York–based playwright, Bader has published numerous essays on language and culture, specializing in artistic, spiritual, and moral issues.*

When my grandmother was young, she would sometimes spot the emperor Franz Josef riding down the cobbled roads of the Austro-Hungarian Empire.

She came of age so long ago that the few surviving photographs are colored cream and chestnut. Early on, she saw cars replace horses and carriages. When she got older, she marveled at the first televisions. Near the end of her life, she grew accustomed to remote control and could spot prime ministers on color TV. By the time she died, the world was freshly populated by gadgetry and myth. Her generation bore witness to the rise of new machinery created by visionaries. My generation has seen machinery break down and visionaries come under fire.

As children, we enjoyed collecting visionaries, the way we collected toys or baseball cards. When I was a kid, I first met Patrick Henry and Eleanor Roosevelt, Abraham Lincoln and Albert Einstein. They could always be summoned by the imagination and so were never late for play dates. I thought heroes figured in any decent childhood. I knew their stats.

Nathan Hale. Nelson Mandela. Heroes have guts.

Michelangelo. Shakespeare. Heroes have imagination.                                        5

They fight. Alexander the Great. Joan of Arc.

They fight for what they believe in. Susan B. Anthony. Martin Luther King.

Heroes overcome massive obstacles. Beethoven, while deaf, still managed to carry an unforgettable tune. Homer, while blind, never failed to give an excellent description. Helen Keller, both deaf and blind, still spoke to the world. FDR, despite his polio, became president. Moses, despite his speech impediment, held productive discussions with God.

They inspire three-hour movies. They make us weepy. They do the right thing while enduring attractive amounts of suffering. They tend to be self-employed. They are often killed off. They sense the future. They lead lives that make us question our own. They are our ideals, but not our friends.

They don't have to be real. Some of them live in books and legends.       10
They don't have to be famous. There are lower-profile heroes who get resurrected by ambitious biographers. There are collective heroes: firefighters and astronauts, unsung homemakers, persecuted peoples. There are those whose names we can't remember, only their deeds: "you know, that woman who swam the English Channel," "the guy who died running the first marathon," "the student who threw himself in front of the tank at Tiananmen Square." There are those whose names we'll never find out: the anonymous benefactor, the masked man, the undercover agent, the inventor of the wheel, the unknown soldier. The one who did the thing so gutsy and terrific that no one will ever know what it was.

Unlike icons (Marilyn, Elvis) heroes are not only sexy but noble, too. Unlike idols (Gretzky, Streisand), who vary from fan to fan, they are

*Time Changed.* ↗

almost universally beloved. Unlike icons and idols, heroes lack irony. And unlike icons and idols, heroes are no longer in style.

As centuries end, so do visions of faith — maybe because the faithful get nervous as the double zeroes approach and question what they've been worshipping. Kings and queens got roughed up at the end of the eighteenth century; God took a beating at the end of the nineteenth; and as the twentieth century draws to a close, outstanding human beings are the casualties of the moment. In the 1970s and 1980s, Americans started feeling queasy about heroism. Those of us born in the sixties found ourselves on the cusp of that change. A sweep of new beliefs, priorities, and headlines has conspired to take our pantheon away from us.

Members of my generation believed in heroes when they were younger but now find themselves grasping for them. Even the word *hero* sounds awkward. I find myself embarrassed to ask people who their heroes are, because the word just doesn't trip off the tongue. My friend Katrin sounded irritated when I asked for hers. She said, "Oh, Jesus . . . Do people still have heroes?"

We don't. Certainly not in the traditional sense of adoring perfect people. Frequently not at all. "I'm sort of intrigued by the fact that I don't have heroes right off the top of my head," said a colleague, Peter. "Can I get back to you?"

Some of us are more upset about this than others. It's easy to tell    15
which of us miss the heroic age. We are moved by schmaltzy political speeches, we warm up to stories of pets saving their owners, we even get misty-eyed watching the Olympics. We mope when model citizens fail us. My college roommate, Linda, remembers a seventh-grade class called "Heroes and She-roes." The first assignment was to write about a personal hero or she-ro. "I came home," Linda told me, "and cried and cried because I didn't have one. . . . Carter had screwed up in Iran and given the malaise speech. Gerald Ford was a nothing and Nixon was evil. My parents told me to write about Jane Fonda the political activist and I just kept crying."

Not everyone feels sentimental about it. A twentyish émigré raised in the former Soviet Union told me: "It's kind of anticlimactic to look for heroes when you've been brought up in a culture that insists on so many heroes. . . . What do you want me to say? Lenin? Trotsky?" Even though I grew up in the relatively propaganda-free United States, I understood. The America of my childhood insisted on heroes, too.

Of all the myths I happily ate for breakfast, the most powerful one was our story of revolution. I sang about it as early as kindergarten and read about it long after. The story goes, a few guys in wigs skipped town on some grumpy church leaders and spurned a loopy king to branch out on their own. The children who hear the story realize they don't have to believe in oldfangled clergy or a rusty crown — but they had better believe in those guys with the wigs.

I sure did. I loved a set of books known as the "Meet" series: *Meet George Washington, Meet Andrew Jackson, Meet the Men Who Sailed the Seas,* and many more. I remember one picture of an inspired Thomas Jefferson, his auburn ponytail tied in a black ribbon, penning words with a feather as a battle of banners and cannon fire raged behind him.

A favorite "Meet" book starred Christopher Columbus. His resistance to the flat-earth society of his day was engrossing, especially to a kid like me who had trouble trying new foods let alone seeking new land masses. I identified with his yearning for a new world and his difficulty with finding investors. Standing up to the king and queen of Spain was like convincing your parents to let you do stuff they thought was idiotic. Now, my allowance was only thirty-five cents a week, but that didn't mean I wasn't going to ask for three ships at some later date.

This is pretty embarrassing: I adored those guys. The ones in the   20
white powder and ponytails, the voluptuous hats, the little breeches and cuffs. They were funny-looking, but lovable. They did outrageous things without asking for permission. They invented the pursuit of happiness.

I had a special fondness for Ben Franklin, statesman and eccentric inventor. Inventions, like heroes, made me feel as though I lived in a dull era. If I'd grown up at the end of the nineteenth century, I could have spoken on early telephones. A few decades later, I could have heard the new sounds of radio. In the sixties, I could have watched black-and-white TVs graduate to color.

Instead, I saw my colorful heroes demoted to black and white. Mostly white. By the time I finished high school, it was no longer hip to look up to the paternalistic dead white males who launched our country, kept slaves and mistresses, and massacred native peoples. Suddenly they weren't visionaries but oppressors, or worse — objects. Samuel Adams became a beer, John Hancock became a building, and the rest of the guys in wigs were knocked off one by one, in a whodunit that couldn't be explained away by the fact of growing up.

The flag-waving of my youth, epitomized by America's bicentennial, was a more loving homage than I know today. The year 1976 rolled in while Washington was still reeling from Saigon, but the irony was lost on me and my second-grade classmates. The idea of losing seemed miles away. We celebrated July fourth with wide eyes and patriotic parties. Grown-ups had yet to tell themselves (so why should they tell us?) that the young nation on its birthday had suffered a tragic defeat.

Historians soon filled us in about that loss, and of others. Discovering America was nothing compared to discovering the flaws of its discoverers, now cast as imperialist sleaze, racist and sexist and genocidal. All things heroic — human potential, spiritual fervor, moral resplendence — soon became suspect. With the possible exception of bodybuilding, epic qualities went out of fashion. Some will remember 1992 as the year Su-

*we have heroes that are like us. Stupid, b/c they need to be people who inspire us to do something*

perman died. Literally, the writers and illustrators at *D.C. Comics* decided the guy was too old to keep leaping buildings and rescuing an aging damsel in distress. When rumors circulated that he would be resurrected, readers protested via calls to radio shows, letters to editors, and complaints to stores that they were in no mood for such an event.

A monster named Doomsday killed Superman, overcoming him not 25 with Kryptonite but with brute force. Who killed the others? I blame improved modes of character assassination, media hype artists, and scholars. The experts told me that Columbus had destroyed cultures and ravaged the environment. They also broke the news that the cowboys had brazenly taken land that wasn't theirs. In a way, I'm glad I didn't know that earlier; dressing up as a cowgirl for Halloween wouldn't have felt right. In a more urgent way, I wish I had known it then so I wouldn't have had to learn it later.

Just fifteen years after America's bicentennial came Columbus's quincentennial, when several towns canceled their annual parades in protest of his sins. Soon other festivities started to feel funny. When my aunt served corn pudding last Thanksgiving, my cousin took a spoonful, then said drily that the dish was made in honor of the Indians who taught us to use corn before we eliminated them. Uncomfortable chuckles followed. Actually, neither "we" nor my personal ancestors had come to America in time to kill any Native Americans. Yet the holiday put us in the same boat with the pilgrims and anchored us in the white man's domain.

I am fascinated by how we become "we" and "they." It's as if siding with the establishment is the Alka-Seltzer that helps us stomach the past. To swallow history lessons, we turn into "we": one nation under God of proud but remorseful Indian killers. We also identify with people who look like us. For example, white northerners studying the Civil War identify both with white slaveholders and with northern abolitionists, aligning with both race and place. Transsexuals empathize with men and women. Immigrants identify with their homeland and their adopted country. Historians proposing a black Athena and a black Jesus have inspired more of such bonding.

I'll admit that these empathies can be empowering. I always understood the idea of feeling stranded by unlikely role models but never emotionally grasped it until I watched Penny Marshall's movie *A League of Their Own*. For the first time, I appreciated why so many women complain that sports bore them. I had enjoyed baseball before but never as intensely as I enjoyed the games in that film. The players were people like me. Lori Petty, petite, chirpy, wearing a skirt, commanded the pitcher's mound with such aplomb that I was moved. There's something to be said for identifying with people who remind us of ourselves, though Thomas Jefferson and Lori Petty look more like each other than either of them looks like me. I'll never know if I would've read the "Meet" books with more zeal if they'd described our founding mothers. I liked them as they were.

Despite the thrill of dames batting something on the big screen besides their eyelashes, the fixation on look-alike idols is disturbing for those who get left out. In the movie *White Men Can't Jump,* Wesley Snipes tells Woody Harrelson not to listen to Jimi Hendrix, because "White people can't hear Jimi." Does this joke imply that black people can't hear Mozart? That I can admire Geena Davis's batting but never appreciate Carlton Fisk? Besides dividing us from one another, these emotional allegiances divide us from potential heroes too, causing us to empathize with, say, General Custer and his last stand instead of with Sitting Bull and the victorious Sioux.

Rejecting heroes for having the wrong ethnic credentials or sex organs    30
says less about our multicultural vision than our lack of imagination. By focusing on what we are instead of who we can become, by typecasting and miscasting our ideals — that's how we become "we" and "they." If heroes are those we'd like to emulate, it does make sense that they resemble us. But the focus on physical resemblance seems limited and racist.

Heroes should be judged on their deeds, and there are those with plenty in common heroically but not much in terms of ethnicity, nationality, or gender. Just look at Harriet Tubman and Moses; George Washington and Simón Bolívar; Mahatma Gandhi and Martin Luther King; Murasaki and Milton; Cicero and Ann Richards. Real paragons transcend nationality. It didn't matter to me that Robin Hood was English — as long as he did good, he was as American as a barbecue. It didn't matter to Queen Isabella that Columbus was Italian as long as he sailed for Spain and sprinkled her flags about. The British epic warrior Beowulf was actually Swedish. Both the German hero Etzel and the Scandinavian hero Atli were really Attila, king of the Huns. With all this borrowing going on, we shouldn't have to check the passports of our luminaries; the idea that we can be like them not literally but spiritually is what's uplifting in the first place.

The idea that we can never be like them has led to what I call jealousy journalism. You know, we're not remotely heroic so let's tear down anyone who is. It's become hard to remember which papers are tabloids. Tell-all articles promise us the "real story" — implying that greatness can't be real. The safe thing about *Meet George Washington* was that you couldn't actually meet him. Today's stories and pictures bring us closer. And actually meeting your heroes isn't the best idea. Who wants to learn that a favorite saint is really just an egomaniac with a publicist?

Media maestros have not only knocked public figures off their pedestals, they've also lowered heroism standards by idealizing just about everyone. Oprah, Geraldo, and the rest turn their guests into heroes of the afternoon because they overcame abusive roommates, childhood disfigurement, deranged spouses, multiple genitalia, cheerleading practice, or zany sexual predilections. In under an hour, a studio audience can hear their epic sagas told.

While TV and magazine producers helped lead heroes to their graves, the academic community gave the final push. Just as my peers and I made our way through college, curriculum reformers were promoting "P.C." agendas at the expense of humanistic absolutes. Scholars invented their own tabloidism, investigating and maligning both dead professors and trusty historical figures. Even literary theory helped, when deconstructionists made it trendy to look for questions instead of answers, for circular logic instead of linear sense, for defects, contradictions, and the ironic instead of meaning, absolutes, and the heroic.

It was the generations that preceded ours who killed off our heroes.  35
And like everyone who crucified a superstar, these people thought they were doing a good thing. The professors and journalists consciously moved in a positive direction — toward greater tolerance, openness, and realism — eliminating our inspirations in the process. The death of an era of hero worship was not the result of the cynical, clinical materialism too often identified with my generation. It was the side effect of a complicated cultural surgery, of an operation that may have been necessary and that many prescribed.

So with the best of intentions, these storytellers destroyed bedtime stories. Which is too bad for the kids, because stories make great teachers. Children glean by example. You can't tell a child "Be ingenious," or "Do productive things." You can tell them, "This Paul Revere person jumped on a horse at midnight, rode wildly through the dark, figured out where the mean British troops were coming to attack the warm, fuzzy, sweet, great-looking colonists, and sent messages by code, igniting our fight for freedom," and they'll get the idea. America's rugged values come gift wrapped in the frontier tales of Paul Bunyan, Daniel Boone, Davy Crockett — fables of independence and natural resources. Kids understand that Johnny Appleseed or Laura Ingalls Wilder would never need a Cuisinart. Pioneer and prairie stories convey the fun of roughing it, showing kids how to be self-reliant, or at least less spoiled.

Children catch on to the idea of imitating qualities, not literal feats. After returning his storybook to the shelf, little Billy doesn't look around for a dragon to slay. Far-off stories capture the imagination in an abstract but compelling way, different from, say, the more immediate action-adventure flick. After watching a James Bond film festival, I might fantasize about killing the five people in front of me on line at the supermarket, while legends are remote enough that Columbus might inspire one to be original, but not necessarily to study Portuguese or enlist in the navy. In tales about conquerors and cavaliers, I first flirted with the idea of ideas.

Even Saturday-morning cartoons served me as parables, when I woke up early enough to watch the classy Superfriends do good deeds.

Sure, the gender ratio between Wonder Woman and the gaggle of men in capes seemed unfair, but I was rapt. I wonder whether I glued myself to my television and my high expectations with too much trust, and helped to set my own heroes up for a fall.

Some heroes have literally been sentenced to death by their own followers. *Batman* subscribers, for example, were responsible for getting rid of Batman's sidekick, Robin. At the end of one issue, the Joker threatened to kill the Boy Wonder, and readers could decide whether Robin lived or died by calling one of two "900" numbers. The public voted overwhelmingly for his murder. I understand the impulse of those who dialed for death. At a certain point, eternal invincibility grows as dull and predictable as wearing a yellow cape and red tights every day of the year. It's not human. We get fed up.

My generation helped to kill off heroism as teenagers, with our language. We used heroic words that once described brave deeds — *excellent, amazing, awesome* — to describe a good slice of pizza or a sunny day. In our everyday speech, *bad* meant good. *Hot* meant cool. In the sarcastic slang of street gangs in Los Angeles, *hero* currently means traitor, specifically someone who snitches on a graffiti artist. 40

Even those of us who lived by them helped shatter our own myths, which wasn't all negative. We discovered that even the superhero meets his match. Every Achilles needs a podiatrist. Every rhapsodically handsome leader has a mistress or a moment of moral ambiguity. We injected a dose of reality into our expectations. We even saw a viable presidential candidate under a heap of slung mud, a few imperfections, an alleged tryst or two.

We're used to trysts in a way our elders aren't. Our parents and grandparents behave as if they miss the good old days when adulterers wore letter sweaters. They feign shock at the extramarital exploits of Thomas Jefferson, Frank Sinatra, JFK, Princess Di. Their hero worship is a romance that falters when beloved knights end up unfaithful to their own spouses. People my age aren't amazed by betrayal. We are suspicious of shining armor. Even so, tabloid sales escalate when a Lancelot gives in to temptation — maybe because the jerk who cheats on you somehow becomes more attractive. Other generations have gossiped many of our heroes into philanderers. The presumptuous hero who breaks your heart is the most compelling reason not to get involved in the first place.

Seeing your legends discredited is like ending a romance with someone you loved but ultimately didn't like. However much you longed to trust that person, it just makes more sense not to. Why pine away for an aloof godlet who proves unstable, erratic, and a rotten lover besides? It's sad to give up fantasies but mature to trade them in for healthier relationships grounded in reality.

We require a new pantheon: a set of heroes upon whom we can rely, who will not desert us when the winds change, and whom we will not desert. It's unsettling, if not downright depressing, to go through life embarrassed about the identity of one's childhood idols.

Maybe we should stick to role models instead. Heroes have become quaint, as old-fashioned as gas-guzzlers — and as unwieldy, requiring too much investment and energy. Role models are more like compact cars, less glam and roomy but easier to handle. They take up less parking space in the imagination. Role models have a certain degree of consciousness about their job. The cast members of "Beverly Hills, 90210," for example, have acknowledged that they serve as role models for adolescents, and their characters behave accordingly: they refrain from committing major crimes; they overcome inclinations toward substance abuse; they see through adult hypocrisy; and any misdemeanors they do perpetrate are punished. For moral mediators we could do better, but at least the prime-time writing staff is aware of the burden of having teen groupies.

Heroes don't have the luxury of staff writers or the opportunity to endorse designer jeans. Hercules can't go on "Nightline" and pledge to stop taking steroids. Prometheus can't get a presidential pardon. Columbus won't have a chance to weep to Barbara Walters that he didn't mean to endanger leatherback turtles or monk seals or the tribes of the Lucayas. Elizabeth I never wrote a best-seller about how she did it her way.

Role models can go on talk shows, or even host them. Role models may live next door. While a hero might be a courageous head of state, a saint, a leader of armies, a role model might be someone who put in a three-day presidential bid, your local minister, your boss. They don't need their planes to go down in flames to earn respect. Role models have a job, accomplishment, or hairstyle worth emulating.

Rather than encompassing that vast kit and caboodle of ideals, role models can perform a little neat division of labor. One could wish to give orders like Norman Schwarzkopf but perform psychoanalysis like Lucy Van Pelt, to chair a round-table meeting as well as King Arthur but negotiate as well as Queen Esther, to eat like Orson Welles but look like Helen of Troy, and so forth. It was General Schwarzkopf, the most tangible military hero for anyone my age, who vied instead for role-model status by claiming on the cover of his book: *It Doesn't Take a Hero*. With this title he modestly implies that anyone with some smarts and élan could strategize and storm as well as he has.

Role models are admirable individuals who haven't given up their lives or livelihoods and may even have a few hangups. They don't have to be prone to excessive self-sacrifice. They don't go on hunger strikes; they diet. They are therefore more likely than heroes to be free for lunch, and they are oftener still alive.

Heroism is a living thing for many of my contemporaries. In my informal poll, I not only heard sob stories about the decline of heroes, I also discovered something surprising: the ascent of parents. While the founding fathers may be passé, actual mothers, fathers, grands, and great-grands are undeniably "in." An overwhelming number of those I polled named their household forebears as those they most admired. By choosing their own relatives as ideals, people in their twenties have replaced impersonal heroes with the most personal role models of all. Members of my purportedly lost generation have not only realized that it's time to stop believing in Santa Claus, they have chosen to believe instead in their families — the actual tooth fairy, the real Mr. and Mrs. Claus. They have stopped needing the folks from the North Pole, the guys with the wigs, the studs and studettes in tights and capes.

In a way it bodes well that Superman and the rest could be killed or reported missing. They were needed to quash the most villainous folks of all: insane communists bearing nuclear weapons, heinous war criminals, monsters named Doomsday. The good news about Superman bleeding to death was that Doomsday died in the struggle.

If the good guys are gone, so is the world that divides down the middle into good guys and bad guys. A world without heroes is a rigorous, demanding place, where things don't boil down to black and white but are rich with shades of gray; where faith in lofty, dead personages can be replaced by faith in ourselves and one another; where we must summon the strength to imagine a five-dimensional future in colors not yet invented. My generation grew up to see our world shift, so it's up to us to steer a course between naïveté and nihilism, to reshape vintage stories, to create stories of spirit without apologies.

I've heard a few. There was one about the woman who taught Shakespeare to inner-city fourth graders in Chicago who were previously thought to be retarded or hopeless. There was a college groundskeeper and night watchman, a black man with a seventh-grade education, who became a contracts expert, wrote poetry and memoirs, and invested his salary so wisely that he bequeathed 450 acres of mountainous parkland to the university when he died. There was the motorcyclist who slid under an eighteen-wheeler at full speed, survived his physical therapy only to wind up in a plane crash, recovered, and as a disfigured quadriplegic started a business, got happily married, and ran for public office; his campaign button bore a caption that said "Send me to Congress and I won't be just another pretty face. . . ."

When asked for her heroes, a colleague of mine spoke of her great-grandmother, a woman whose husband left her with three kids in Galicia, near Poland, and went to the United States. He meant to send for her, but the First World War broke out. When she made it to America, her husband soon died, and she supported her family; at one point she even ran a nightclub. According to the great-granddaughter, "When she was ninety she would tell me she was going to volunteer at the hospital. I would ask how and she'd say, 'Oh, I just go over there to read to the old folks.' The 'old folks' were probably seventy. She was a great lady."

My grandmother saved her family, too, in the next great war. She  55 did not live to see the age of the fax, but she did see something remarkable in her time, more remarkable even than the emperor riding down the street: she saw him walking down the street. I used to ask her, "Did you really see the emperor Franz Josef walking down the street?"

She would say, "Ya. Walking down the street." I would laugh, and though she'd repeat it to amuse me, she did not see what was so funny. To me, the emperor was someone you met in history books, not on the streets of Vienna. He was larger than life, a surprising pedestrian. He was probably just getting some air, but he was also laying the groundwork for my nostalgia of that time when it would be natural for him to take an evening stroll, when those who were larger than life roamed cobblestones.

Today, life is larger.

## Reading the Text

1. Why do you think Bader begins and ends her essay with an anecdote regarding her grandmother, and what effect does that anecdote have on the reader?
2. How does Bader define hero, icon, and role model, and what is her attitude toward each?
3. What are the heroes and myths that Bader grew up with, and how does she feel about them now?
4. In your own words, explain Bader's attitude toward political correctness.
5. How does Bader characterize her generation of twentysomethings?

## Reading the Signs

1. In your journal, brainstorm a list of heroes that you admired as a child, then compare your list with the traditional heroes whom Bader mentions. How do you account for any differences or similarities?
2. Write an argumentative essay that supports, challenges, or modifies Bader's central contention that her generation needs role models, not heroes.
3. In class, discuss how a writer might, as Bader suggests, "reshape vintage stories, . . . create stories of spirit without apologies." Then, in a creative essay, write your own "story of spirit."
4. In class, brainstorm a list of traditional American heroes and then discuss whether they have lost their luster and, if so, why.
5. Assume Bader's perspective on heroes and write an analytic essay in which you explain whether John F. Kennedy would be considered a hero to today's twentysomething generation. To develop your ideas, read or reread Steven Stark's "The Cultural Meaning of the Kennedys" (p. 353).

# ISSUES

# WE'VE COME A LONG WAY, MAYBE

## *Gender Codes in American Culture*

It may well have been the anticlimax of the year. After two years of litigation and national debate, culminating in the sort of media blitz more commonly associated with celebrity superstars, Shannon Faulkner finally entered the Citadel Military Academy, only to drop out a week later. It was quite a spectacle: Camera crews dogged Faulkner like bloodhounds, while reporters assessed her physical fitness (a *Newsweek* article, for instance, remarked on her "too ample flesh"). When word came that Faulkner had wilted under the glare of national publicity (along with a summer heat wave) and decided to leave, images of ecstatic cadets throwing their hats, and in one famous shot, one of themselves, into the air, flooded the media. So much fuss was made over this young woman whose only claim to fame was her persistent desire to attend a publically funded military academy that one could have wondered what the proverbial "visitor from Mars" would have thought of it all.

And yet no one seemed to find it strange that Shannon Faulkner's long struggle to enter the Citadel — a battle that took her case all the way to the Supreme Court — should have attracted so much attention, not to say emotional fascination. In fact, it wasn't really all that strange, because Shannon Faulkner's brief but intense moment in the public eye was a potent sign, a signifier of the powerful force that gender codes play in our cultural life.

The real significance of the Faulkner incident was not whether the Citadel should be compelled to accept women cadets; the point was that

Faulkner's personal crusade quickly became a national symbol of the conflict between the traditional gender codes in American culture and an emerging set of new ones. According to the traditional codes, the military is for men, not women (indeed, in the same year the Faulkner drama came to its end, Newt Gingrich announced that women weren't suited for combat because they "got infections" during trench warfare). And though the role of women in the military has been growing for the past quarter century, with women now admitted to such prestigious military schools as West Point and the Air Force Academy, the all-male bastion of the Citadel was viewed as a symbolic last stand against the crumbling of the old codes. That's why so many Americans found themselves rooting either for or against Shannon Faulkner.

## Interpreting Gender Codes in American Culture

If you found yourself rooting for or against Shannon Faulkner — swelling with triumph when she finally entered the Citadel's gates, or cheering with relief when she exited — then you have experienced the almost visceral hold that our myths of gender have upon us. Whatever your opinion, your emotions reflect a system of values, or gender code, that is more the product of culture than it is of nature. Just consider that some cultures have historically made a place for women warriors, while others haven't. It isn't biology that determines what a culture will do; it is a gender code.

Such assertions may make people uneasy, particularly in the arena of gender conflict, and the response is often to make an appeal to nature — Gingrich's attempt to provide a naturalistic defense for excluding women from active combat roles is a case in point. This uneasiness is rooted in the fact that our gender codes provide a framework through which we can understand and experience our world; if that framework is disrupted, our world suffers a dislocation and we accordingly feel threatened. You may think this isn't so, believing, for instance, that women shouldn't be in the military. If that's the case, ask yourself why you feel that way. If you're concerned about women getting unfair advantages in the feminist era (one reason some Americans rooted for the Citadel), wouldn't it seem that allowing them to share the dangerous duty of military combat would actually be the opposite of a privilege?

That fact that many Americans, women as well as men, don't see it this way shows just how durable our gender codes are. According to the traditional code, women *should* be sheltered from perils like combat; women in this view belong in the domestic sphere, not the active world of conflict. Their duty is to stay in the home: Let the men go out to guide and protect the nation. If this description sounds exaggerated, consider what happened when, in 1993, two women were disqualified in

||||||||||||||||||||||||||||||||||||||||||||||||||||||||||||||||||||||||||||||||||||||||||||||||||||||||||||||||||||||||||||||||||||||||||

**Exploring the Signs of Gender**

In your journal, explore the expectations about gender roles that you grew up with. What gender norms were you taught by your family, either overtly or implicitly? Have you ever had any conflicts with your parents over "natural" gender roles? If so, how did you resolve them? Do you think your gender-related expectations today are the same you had when you were a child?

their bids to become the first female Attorney General after it was discovered that they had hired illegal immigrants as nannies for their children. The issue was never raised when only men were nominated for government posts; according to American gender myths, men aren't responsible for arranging child care. Indeed, when it was revealed in California's 1994 senatorial contest that candidate Michael Huffington had hired an illegal immigrant in his household (a particular embarrassment due to his campaign against illegal immigration), he simply blamed his wife, who willingly took the responsibility.

It is one of the major tasks of cultural semiotics to expose the outlines of such gender myths to show just how deeply they influence our lives. Think of how these myths may shape your own behavior. Traditionally, for instance, the myths that govern courtship in America dictate that the man pays the expenses on a date and is responsible for all the logistics, even providing transportation and a destination. But there is no natural reason for this to be so; it's just a cultural expectation, one that has been changing for some time. Ask yourself: Who pays when you date? Who drives? Do you even care? Your answers will help you find your place in today's shifting terrain of gender myths.

In examining the gender myths that influence your own life, you should recognize the difference between the biological category of *sex* and the cultural category of *gender*. Your sex is determined by your chromosomes, but your gender goes beyond your sex into the roles that society has determined are appropriate for you. Your sex, in other words, is your birthright, but the roles you play in society are largely determined by your culture. In everyday life, however, this distinction between the natural category of sex and the cultural category of gender is blurred because socially determined gender roles are regarded as naturally dictated sexual necessities. Western culture traditionally has assumed, for instance, that women naturally are the attractive sex, designed to be looked at, whereas men are natural voyeurs, made to do the looking. This myth is related to the belief that the male sex drive is far more active than the female's. Both myths are represented in a tradition of European art, which is filled with female nudes but hardly any male ones. Just

---

### Discussing the Signs of Gender

Bring to class a magazine that targets one gender (such as *Esquire* or *Elle*). In small groups, study both the articles and the advertising in your sample magazines, focusing on the gender roles assumed for men and women. List the major roles on the board by magazine title. What patterns do you find? Do some magazines adhere to traditional roles, while others depart from them? How can you account for your findings?

---

consider how *Playboy* and *Penthouse* enjoy subscriptions in the millions, while *Playgirl* struggles along in the shadows.

If you think this is obviously the way of nature, consider ancient Greek art, which, from its introduction of the *kouros* (a sculpted figure of a nude male) into art more than two thousand years ago, was at least as interested in the male form as in the female. The example of the Greeks tells us that there is nothing in nature to dictate whose body, male or female, will be considered more attractive. At the same time, the Greeks can show just how much we presume that the roles our gender myths define for us will be heterosexually oriented. For as ancient Greece reminds us, cultures may be homoerotic as well.

Even the standards of beauty that men as well as women are held to are culturally determined. The ideal medieval woman, for example, was short, slender, high-waisted, small-breasted, and boasted a high, domed forehead whose effect she enhanced by shaving her hairline. By the Renaissance, she had filled out considerably, and in the paintings of Peter Paul Rubens she could appear positively pudgy by contemporary standards (we even have an adjective, "Rubenesque," for well-padded feminine beauty). In more recent times, we have seen a shift from the hourglass figures of the fifties to the aerobically muscled hard bodies of the nineties. You may assume that this is it, the last stop, the one truly beautiful body, but stick around. Wait to see what's fashionable in bodies in the years to come.

Men, too, have seen their bodily ideals change over time. The ideal man of the eighteenth century, for example, was a rather heavy-set fellow, rounded in appearance, and with a hint of a double chin, while today's ideal (especially in the corporate world) has square-hewn features and a jutting jaw (cleft if possible: Just look at some ads for business-oriented services to see what today's businessman wants to look like). Now think for a moment: What would you look like if you had the choice? Would you look like the ideal of the 1950s or 1960s? Would you be long and lean, or buff courtesy of Nautilus?

Take another gender myth that our culture holds as a wholly natural reflection of the difference between the sexes. Women, the myth declares, are naturally intuitive and emotional (recall the Nike ad campaign featuring "emotional" sportswomen), whereas men are held to be rational and controlled. Or again: Men are naturally aggressive, whereas women are passive. Note the pattern: Male and female traits are lined up in neat sets of opposites that are justified through an appeal to nature. But nature isn't bound by categories. After all, have you ever seen a female bear defending her young?

## Backlash

Because of the political stakes involved, the semiotic unmasking of gender myths has not gone unchallenged in America. For once a myth has been identified, it can be questioned or altered. Thus, in the wake of the feminist revival of the seventies, the eighties saw something of a backlash. It became culturally fashionable to embrace a "new traditionalism" that really meant going back to the old mythology that had been questioned the decade before. Indeed, by the late 1980s *Time* had declared that feminism was dead, that Wonder Woman and the ERA were henceforth to be regarded as things of the past, as obsolete as Nehru jackets and Earth shoes.  praised

The media exulted. More and more women, the media exclaimed, were worrying about their "biological clocks" and whether their careers were adequate compensation for the traditional roles they supposedly had abandoned. Thanks to an article by Felice Schwartz in the *Harvard Business Review,* a new myth emerged about businesswomen who were now willing to settle for a kind of second-class corporate citizenship (dubbed the "mommy track") rather than miss out on the joys of motherhood. The postfeminist era, the media declared, had arrived.

According to Susan Faludi's study of the phenomenon, *Backlash,* such declarations were simply part of a nationwide assault upon the women's movement, an invention of "trends" that had little basis in reality but whose effect was to create some of the very anxieties that were eagerly predicted. To convince American women to return home and have children (as women should do, according to the traditional mythology), the media showered us with unsubstantiated stories of yuppie infertility, angst, and fears of spinsterhood. Meanwhile, parenting became a top pop cultural activity — as it remains today. Returning to "traditional values" — in other words, returning to the docile gender roles imposed on women in the fifties and sixties — became the media's new theme. Suddenly everyone wanted to get into the baby game. Can you think of some recent movies or TV shows that exemplify this trend? How have children become our newest media stars?

At the same time, the very word "feminism" itself was demonized. Women around the country, from the college campus to the kitchen, insisted to interviewers that "yes of course they were for women's rights, but they were not feminists." Have you ever found yourself making the same declaration? Why? What images come to mind when you think of the word "feminist"? Are those images realistic, or are they, too, myths? And whether you are male or female, what reactions do you get when you do declare that you are a feminist?

Perhaps because of the controversy, the image of feminism in America today is potent. Just consider what happened to Hillary Rodham Clinton during the 1992 presidential campaign. An outspoken feminist with a successful corporate career of her own, she had gone on record declaring that she was not the type to stay at home and bake cookies. Quite a ruckus ensued, much of which was generated by women who denounced her supposed arrogance and defended their own choice to accept the traditional woman's role as homemaker. The image of the typical feminist, for such women, was that of a privileged, college-educated white woman who sneered at women who weren't as successful as she was. And although this image, like so many images, was mostly myth, Bill Clinton deemed it safest to remove his wife from the campaign spotlight until the election was safely won.

Meanwhile, America's consumer culture finds its own way of shaping the image of a feminist. In campaigns like Virginia Slims's longrunning pitch for cigarettes, women are invited to imagine themselves as liberated consumers, free at last to smoke when and where they please. The "new woman" who appears in so many ads today is someone who goes out and buys her own Honda without male advice or chooses a new hair color "just for herself." She purchases Esprit fashions because she is politically aware, or Nike sportswear because she believes in herself. But what is really happening? Why would advertisers adopt a "feminist" stance to sell their products? How are they appealing to their market?

## The Revenge of the Gorgon

America's consumer culture is perfectly comfortable with the image of the feminist as an avid, if independent, shopper (just look at the heroine of the cartoon strip "Cathy"), but things get dicey when women assert themselves in other ways, especially sexually. Our culture is quite happy with a woman who is sexually *available,* but not when she is a sexual *aggressor.* And when she is both aggressive and bisexual, then America really gets uncomfortable. The horrific nature of the Sharon Stone character in the film *Basic Instinct* is a potent sign of just how America views the image of the sexually predatory, bisexual woman. She becomes, in short, a monster.

Women with their own ideas about sexuality have been viewed this way for a long time. Consider the ancient Greek legend of Perseus and Medusa. Medusa is the name of a monster with the body of a woman, a head curling with writhing snakes, and a stare that reduces men to stone. By cutting off Medusa's head, Perseus became one of the heroes of Greek mythology. But that's only when the tale is read from a traditional perspective. From a feminist perspective, it looks quite different.

For the writhing snakes on Medusa's head suggest other snakes, the two snakes held in the grasp of figurines unearthed in the ruins of the ancient Minoan culture of Crete. Perhaps you've seen her: the image of a goddesslike woman holding two snakes in her hands, standing imperiously in a bare-breasted pose. There is a possibility that the ancient Minoans worshipped her in what may have been a matriarchal, or women-centered, culture. But that culture was eventually overrun by the patriarchal Greeks, and the beautiful Minoan snake goddess vanished. Medusa, as read in a feminist key, is the goddess's patriarchal replacement: a warning to powerful women. For a modern parallel, consider how a woman with "big hair" (say, a snaky perm) is viewed in the male-dominated corporate world. Isn't she, too, pressured to control her locks by a male-defined dress code and forced to appear less sexy in the workplace and, hence, less threatening?

For feminist semioticians, such myths as Medusa's reflect a continuous history of male control, and what men have attempted especially to control is female sexuality. Consider how our culture still encourages young men to "sow their wild oats" but raises its collective eyebrows at the sexually active woman. Indeed, in the traditional sexual mythology, women are offered only three roles: the part of the virginal bride (soon to be a socially approved mother), of the whore, and of the castrating witch (these last two roles may be mixed, as in the figure of Delilah, who is both whore and castrator in the biblical story of Samson's fall). Now, recall *Basic Instinct*. How is the Sharon Stone character like Delilah? Which role does the Michael Douglas character want Stone to play? Is there a "witch" figure in the cast? How, in short, is *Basic Instinct* a veritable display case of America's traditional sexual mythology?

## Iron John

Men, too, are influenced by mythic images. Men are supposed to be warriors (he who flinches is a "coward") and studs (have you ever said "what a stud!" to mean "what a great guy"?). Just think of the typical Big Man on Campus. Is he not likely to be an athlete (the warrior role on a school campus) and a sexual star? What do you think of the guy who avoids athletics and doesn't "score"? How popular is he, and with whom?

The men's movement in America, currently led by such writers as Robert Bly, has arisen alongside the women's movement to challenge the traditional masculine gender roles that require men to be aggressive, competitive, and unemotional. In his best-seller *Iron John,* Bly calls for an exploration of both the masculine and the feminine side of male being. Thus, Bly's drum-beating warrior has a sensitive side, which distinguishes him from the sort of Conan the Barbarian hero America's popular culture continues to admire. How else could we explain the rise of Arnold Schwarzenegger to the top of the Hollywood heap?

Indeed, the images that are shaping your own sense of gender identity are playing now at a theater near you. Start there, or with TV or MTV. What are you being told about your sexual identity? What stars are you supposed to emulate? What images do you avoid? What does a "real man" look like on screen? How about a "real woman"? Do you ever wish that they would just "get real"?

## Gender Bending

If you've seen *Interview with the Vampire,* you've witnessed a sign of the latest disruption in American gender codes. What is significant here is the way that vampires — who have always been coded as sexual predators — appear as *bisexual* predators. When Bram Stoker wrote *Dracula* in the late nineteenth century, the cultural mores of his time prevented him from writing openly about sex, especially violent sex. So he got around the censors by presenting this exotic monster who enters young women's bedrooms at night and bites them in the neck. Consciously or unconsciously, readers could experience this as the coded depiction of a rape. Modern writers and filmmakers don't face such restrictions, at least with regard to heterosexuality. But homosexuality and bisexuality are different. Our cultural mores are still pitted against them. So reenter the vampire, not as Dracula this time but as the vampire Lestat. And he's bisexual.

The appearance of such a figure in American popular culture, and the willingness of two stars like Tom Cruise and Brad Pitt to play coded bisexual roles, is a sign of a shift in gender codes that runs far deeper than the behavioral codes we have discussed so far. It's one thing to challenge a gender myth that holds that a woman's place is in the home; it is quite another to challenge the codes that determine whom it is appropriate to go to bed with. The fact that *Interview with the Vampire* was such a success shows that a good number of Americans are willing to accept that challenge.

And the signs aren't only in the movies. When *Newsweek* ran a cover story on the new bisexuality, few protested. And as you can see in

||||||||||||||||||||||||||||||||||||||||||||||||||||||||||||||||||||||||||||||||||||||||||||||||||||||||||||||||||||||||||||||||||||||

### Reading Gender on the Net

Use search engines such as Yahoo or Altavista to research what issues are considered "male" and "female" territory on the Internet.
Focus your search on a comparison of specific topics, such as
"men's rights" and "women's rights." Compare your findings
with those of your classmates.

our analysis of an episode of *Friends* in Chapter Three, no great fuss was
made when the show dramatized a lesbian marriage in 1996 (a greater
fuss occurred a few years earlier when *Roseanne* featured a lesbian kiss).
Or consider Dennis Rodman's well-publicized display of sexual ambiguity in 1996. Meanwhile, back at the university, if you were to look
into the latest academic trends, you would discover that Queer Studies,
which both studies and challenges the ways in which sexual identity and
practice are socially constructed, has been a hot topic for a number of
years.

We aren't telling you to applaud or to condemn these signifiers of
change in American gender codes: We are simply drawing your attention to them. The fact that you may feel strongly about the matter is itself a signifier of the powerful hold our value systems have
upon us. Gender values take us to the core of our sense of ourselves
as individual and social beings, involving religious and moral beliefs
that have recently become a central component of our country's political system. And this too is a sign of the essentially political nature
of our social codes or mythologies, for if our values weren't political,
they wouldn't be entered into the electoral process. So the analysis of
gender codes in America isn't simply an academic exercise: It is a social and political activity that will affect you well beyond the classroom.

### The Readings

Our chapter begins with Holly Devor's analysis of gender roles and
the ways in which men and women manipulate the signs by which we
traditionally communicate our gender identity. Richard K. Herrell's
semiotic analysis of Chicago's annual Gay and Lesbian Pride Day Parade
relates the changes in the parade to changes in the gay community since
the event that inaugurated the Gay Liberation movement, the Stonewall
riot of 1969. Naomi Wolf's indictment of the "beauty myth" that forces
otherwise liberated women to feel trapped in their own bodies follows,

while Gary R. Brooks's analysis of the "Centerfold Syndrome" explores the debilitating effects that fantasized female bodies have on men. Next, Robin Tolmach Lakoff looks at language as a gendered sign system, showing how the form as well as the content of our speech reflects gender coding and relations of power. Deborah Tannen follows by looking at the way women are always "marked" in our society: No detail of a woman's appearance, from her hair to her shoes to her name, fails to send a gender-coded message about her. Michael A. Messner's study of the ways in which athletic competition constructs gender identity in America is next, and Peter Lyman concludes the chapter with an analysis of the male bonding rituals exemplified in college fraternity behavior.

*Gender Role Behaviors and Attitudes*

<hr>

*"Boys will be boys, and girls will be girls": Few of our cultural mythologies seem as natural as this one. But in this exploration of the gender signals that traditionally tell what a "boy" or "girl" is supposed to look and act like, Holly Devor (b. 1951) shows how these signals are not "natural" at all but instead are cultural constructs. While the classic cues of masculinity — aggressive posture, self-confidence, a tough appearance — and the traditional signs of femininity — gentleness, passivity, strong nurturing instincts — are often considered "normal," Devor explains that they are by no means biological or psychological necessities. Indeed, she suggests, they can be richly mixed and varied, or to paraphrase the old Kinks song, "Lola," "Boys can be girls and girls can be boys." Holly Devor is associate professor of sociology at the University of Victoria and is the author of* Gender Blending: Confronting the Limits of Duality *(1989), from which this selection is excerpted, and* FTM: Female-to-Male Transsexuals in Society *(forthcoming).*

## Gender Role Behaviors and Attitudes

The clusters of social definitions used to identify persons by gender are collectively known as "femininity" and "masculinity." Masculine characteristics are used to identify persons as males, while feminine ones are used as signifiers for femaleness. People use femininity or masculinity to claim and communicate their membership in their assigned, or chosen, sex or gender. Others recognize our sex or gender more on the basis of these characteristics than on the basis of sex characteristics, which are usually largely covered by clothing in daily life.

These two clusters of attributes are most commonly seen as mirror images of one another with masculinity usually characterized by dominance and aggression, and femininity by passivity and submission. A more even-handed description of the social qualities subsumed by femininity and masculinity might be to label masculinity as generally concerned with egoistic dominance and femininity as striving for cooperation or communion.[1]

<hr>

1. Maccoby, Eleanor. *Social Development: Psychological Growth and the Parent-Child Relationship* (New York: Harcourt, Brace, Jovanovich, 1980), p. 217. Egoistic dominance is a striving for superior rewards for oneself or a competitive striving to reduce the rewards for one's competitors even if such action will not increase one's own rewards. Persons who are motivated by desires for egoistic dominance not only wish the best for themselves but also wish to diminish the advantages of others whom they may perceive as competing with them.

Characterizing femininity and masculinity in such a way does not portray the two clusters of characteristics as being in a hierarchical relationship to one another but rather as being two different approaches to the same question, that question being centrally concerned with the goals, means, and use of power. Such an alternative conception of gender roles captures the hierarchical and competitive masculine thirst for power, which can, but need not, lead to aggression, and the feminine quest for harmony and communal well-being, which can, but need not, result in passivity and dependence.

Many activities and modes of expression are recognized by most members of society as feminine. Any of these can be, and often are, displayed by persons of either gender. In some cases, cross-gender behaviors are ignored by observers, and therefore do not compromise the integrity of a person's gender display. In other cases, they are labeled as inappropriate gender role behaviors. Although these behaviors are closely linked to sexual status in the minds and experiences of most people, research shows that dominant persons of either gender tend to use influence tactics and verbal styles usually associated with men and masculinity, while subordinate persons, of either gender, tend to use those considered to be the province of women.[2] Thus it seems likely that many aspects of masculinity and femininity are the result, rather than the cause, of status inequalities.

Popular conceptions of femininity and masculinity instead revolve around hierarchical appraisals of the "natural" roles of males and females. Members of both genders are believed to share many of the same human characteristics, although in different relative proportions; both males and females are popularly thought to be able to do many of the same things, but most activities are divided into suitable and unsuitable categories for each gender class. Persons who perform the activities considered appropriate for another gender will be expected to perform them poorly; if they succeed adequately, or even well, at their endeavors, they may be rewarded with ridicule or scorn for blurring the gender dividing line.

The patriarchal gender schema currently in use in mainstream North American society reserves highly valued attributes for males and actively supports the high evaluation of any characteristics which might inadvertently become associated with maleness. The ideology underlying the schema postulates that the cultural superiority of males is a natural outgrowth of the innate predisposition of males toward aggression and dominance, which is assumed to flow inevitably from evolutionary and

---

2. Judith Howard, Philip Blumstein, and Pepper Schwartz, "Sex, Power, and Influence Tactics in Intimate Relationships," *Journal of Personality and Social Psychology* 51 (1986), pp. 102–109; Peter Kollock, Philip Blumstein, and Pepper Schwartz, "Sex and Power in Interaction: Conversational Privileges and Duties," *American Sociological Review* 50 (1985), pp. 34–46.

biological sources. Female attributes are likewise postulated to find their source in innate predispositions acquired in the evolution of the species. Feminine characteristics are thought to be intrinsic to the female facility for childbirth and breastfeeding. Hence, it is popularly believed that the social position of females is biologically mandated to be intertwined with the care of children and a "natural" dependency on men for the maintenance of mother-child units. Thus the goals of femininity and, by implication, of all biological females are presumed to revolve around heterosexuality and maternity.[3]

Femininity, according to this traditional formulation, "would result in warm and continued relationships with men, a sense of maternity, interest in caring for children, and the capacity to work productively and continuously in female occupations.[4] This recipe translates into a vast number of proscriptions and prescriptions. Warm and continued relations with men and an interest in maternity require that females be heterosexually oriented. A heterosexual orientation requires women to dress, move, speak, and act in ways that men will find attractive. As patriarchy has reserved active expressions of power as a masculine attribute, femininity must be expressed through modes of dress, movement, speech, and action which communicate weakness, dependency, ineffectualness, availability for sexual or emotional service, and sensitivity to the needs of others.

Some, but not all, of these modes of interrelation also serve the demands of maternity and many female job ghettos. In many cases, though, femininity is not particularly useful in maternity or employment. Both mothers and workers often need to be strong, independent, and effectual in order to do their jobs well. Thus femininity, as a role, is best suited to satisfying a masculine vision of heterosexual attractiveness.

Body postures and demeanors which communicate subordinate status and vulnerability to trespass through a message of "no threat" make people appear to be feminine. They demonstrate subordination through a minimizing of spatial use: People appear feminine when they keep their arms closer to their bodies, their legs closer together, and their torsos and heads less vertical than do masculine-looking individuals. People also look feminine when they point their toes inward and use their hands in small or childlike gestures. Other people also tend to stand closer to people they see as feminine, often invading their personal space, while people who make frequent appeasement gestures, such as smiling, also give the appearance of femininity. Perhaps as an outgrowth of a subordinate

---

3. Chodorow, Nancy. *The Reproduction of Mothering: Psychoanalysis and the Reproduction of Mothering* (Berkeley: University of California Press, 1978), p. 134.

4. Jon K. Meyer and John E. Hoopes, "The Gender Dysphoria Syndromes: A Position Statement on So-Called 'Transsexualism,'" *Plastic and Reconstructive Surgery* 54 (Oct. 1974), pp. 444–51.

status and the need to avoid conflict with more socially powerful people, women tend to excel over men at the ability to correctly interpret, and effectively display, nonverbal communication cues.[5]

Speech characterized by inflections, intonations, and phrases that convey nonaggression and subordinate status also make a speaker appear more feminine. Subordinate speakers who use more polite expressions and ask more questions in conversation seem more feminine. Speech characterized by sounds of higher frequencies are often interpreted by listeners as feminine, childlike, and ineffectual.[6] Feminine styles of dress likewise display subordinate status through greater restriction of the free movement of the body, greater exposure of the bare skin, and an emphasis on sexual characteristics. The more gender distinct the dress, the more this is the case.

Masculinity, like femininity, can be demonstrated through a wide           10
variety of cues. Pleck has argued that it is commonly expressed in North American society through the attainment of some level of proficiency at some, or all, of the following four main attitudes of masculinity. Persons who display success and high status in their social group, who exhibit "a manly air of toughness, confidence, and self-reliance" and "the aura of aggression, violence, and daring," and who conscientiously avoid anything associated with femininity are seen as exuding masculinity.[7] These requirements reflect the patriarchal ideology that masculinity results from an excess of testosterone, the assumption being that androgens supply a natural impetus toward aggression, which in turn impels males toward achievement and success. This vision of masculinity also reflects the ideological stance that ideal maleness (masculinity) must remain untainted by female (feminine) pollutants.

Masculinity, then, requires of its actors that they organize themselves and their society in a hierarchical manner so as to be able to explicitly quantify the achievement of success. The achievement of high status in one's social group requires competitive and aggressive behavior from those who wish to obtain it. Competition which is motivated by a goal of individual achievement, or egoistic dominance, also requires of its

---

5. Erving Goffman, *Gender Advertisements* (New York: Harper Colophon Books, 1976); Judith A. Hall, *Non-Verbal Sex Differences: Communication Accuracy and Expressive Style* (Baltimore: Johns Hopkins University Press, 1984); Nancy M. Henley, *Body Politics: Power, Sex and Non-Verbal Communication* (Englewood Cliffs, New Jersey: Prentice-Hall, 1979); Marianne Wex, *"Let's Take Back Our Space": "Female" and "Male" Body Language as a Result of Patriarchal Structures* (Berlin: Frauenliteraturverlag Hermine Fees, 1979).

6. Karen L. Adams, "Sexism and the English Language: The Linguistic Implications of Being a Woman," in *Women: A Feminist Perspective,* 3rd edition, ed. Jo Freeman (Palo Alto, Calif.: Mayfield, 1984), pp. 478–91; Hall, pp. 37, 130–37.

7. Pleck, Joseph H. *The Myth of Masculinity* (Cambridge, Mass.: M.I.T. Press, 1981), p. 139.

participants a degree of emotional insensitivity to feelings of hurt and loss in defeated others, and a measure of emotional insularity to protect one-self from becoming vulnerable to manipulation by others. Such values lead those who subscribe to them to view feminine persons as "born losers" and to strive to eliminate any similarities to feminine people from their own personalities. In patriarchally organized societies, masculine values become the ideological structure of the society as a whole. Masculinity thus becomes "innately" valuable and femininity serves a contrapuntal function to delineate and magnify the hierarchical dominance of masculinity.

Body postures, speech patterns, and styles of dress which demonstrate and support the assumption of dominance and authority convey an impression of masculinity. Typical masculine body postures tend to be expansive and aggressive. People who hold their arms and hands in positions away from their bodies, and who stand, sit, or lie with their legs apart — thus maximizing the amount of space that they physically occupy — appear most physically masculine. Persons who communicate an air of authority or a readiness for aggression by standing erect and moving forcefully also tend to appear more masculine. Movements that are abrupt and stiff, communicating force and threat rather than flexibility and cooperation, make an actor look masculine. Masculinity can also be conveyed by stern or serious facial expressions that suggest minimal receptivity to the influence of others, a characteristic which is an important element in the attainment and maintenance of egoistic dominance.[8]

Speech and dress which likewise demonstrate or claim superior status are also seen as characteristically masculine behavior patterns. Masculine speech patterns display a tendency toward expansiveness similar to that found in masculine body postures. People who attempt to control the direction of conversations seem more masculine. Those who tend to speak more loudly, use less polite and more assertive forms, and tend to interrupt the conversations of others more often also communicate masculinity to others. Styles of dress which emphasize the size of upper body musculature, allow freedom of movement, and encourage an illusion of physical power and a look of easy physicality all suggest masculinity. Such appearances of strength and readiness to action serve to create or enhance an aura of aggressiveness and intimidation central to an appearance of masculinity. Expansive postures and gestures combine with these qualities to insinuate that a position of secure dominance is a masculine one.

Gender role characteristics reflect the ideological contentions underlying the dominant gender schema in North American society. That schema leads us to believe that female and male behaviors are the result

---

8. Goffman, *Gender Advertisements*; Hall; Henley; Wex.

of socially directed hormonal instructions which specify that females will want to have children and will therefore find themselves relatively helpless and dependent on males for support and protection. The schema claims that males are innately aggressive and competitive and therefore will dominate over females. The social hegemony of this ideology ensures that we are all raised to practice gender roles which will confirm this vision of the nature of the sexes. Fortunately, our training to gender roles is neither complete nor uniform. As a result, it is possible to point to multitudinous exceptions to, and variations on, these themes. Biological evidence is equivocal about the source of gender roles, psychological androgyny is a widely accepted concept. It seems most likely that gender roles are the result of systematic power imbalances based on gender discrimination.[9]

### Reading the Text

1. List the characteristics that Devor describes as being traditionally "masculine" and "feminine."
2. What relationship does Devor see between characteristics considered masculine and feminine?
3. How does Devor explain the cultural belief in the "superiority" of males?
4. How, according to Devor, do speech and dress communicate gender roles?

### Reading the Signs

1. In small same-sex groups, brainstorm lists of traits that you consider "masculine" and "feminine," then have each group write their lists on the board. Compare the lists produced by male and female groups. What patterns of differences or similarities do you see? To what extent do the traits presume a heterosexual orientation? How do you account for your results?
2. Study the speech patterns, styles of dress, and other nonverbal cues communicated by your friends during a social occasion, such as a party, trying not to reveal that you are observing them for an assignment. Then write an essay in which you analyze these cues used by your friends. To what extent do your friends enact the traditional gender roles Devor describes?
3. Look through a popular magazine such as *Vogue, Rolling Stone,* or *Gentlemen's Quarterly* for advertisements that depict men and women interacting with each other. Then write an essay in which you interpret the body postures of the models, using Devor's selection as your framework for analysis. How do males and females typically stand? To what extent do the

---

9. Howard, Blumstein, and Schwartz; Kollock, Blumstein, and Schwartz.

models enact stereotypically masculine or feminine stances? To develop your essay, consult Diane Barthel, "A Gentleman and a Consumer," p. 144.

4. Devor argues that female fashion traditionally has restricted body movement while male styles of dress have commonly allowed freedom of movement. In class, discuss whether this gender division is still true today, being sure to consider a range of clothing types (e.g., athletic wear, corporate dress, party fashion, and so forth).

5. Compare the gender norms of Japanese society as described by Dorinne K. Kondo (see "On Being a Conceptual Anomaly," p. 523) to the norms of North American society that Devor outlines in her selection. Use the details of your comparison to formulate an overall argument about the roles of each gender in the two cultures.

RICHARD K. HERRELL

## The Symbolic Strategies of Chicago's Gay and Lesbian Pride Day Parade

*Americans love a parade, and parades have long been a way for the many different cultures and ethnicities in this country to express themselves and their sense of identity. In the early 1970s, American gays and lesbians adopted the parade model to let America know that they, too, formed a community and were proud of who they were. But as Richard K. Herrell (b. 1950) points out in this semiotic analysis of Chicago's Gay and Lesbian Pride Day Parades, what gays and lesbians have communicated through their parades has changed over the years. From parades designed "to overcome invisibility" through the flaunting of drag and leather, to the AIDS-era parades that present the gay community "as composed of families, of churches, of sports leagues, of clubs and professional organizations," Chicago's annual festivals chart the direction of gay identification and politics throughout the country. Richard K. Herrell is completing work on his Ph.D. at the University of Illinois's School of Public Health, specializing in epidemiology and biostatistics.*

The *Chicago* magazine listings of things to do for June 1988 contained the following item: "Neighborhood Festivals: Chicago is a city of neighborhoods, and these local festivals are a reflection of that ethnic diversity. All during the summer you can eat brats, tacos, pierogis, krumkake, and other ethnic foods, and then dance it off doing the marengue or the polka. For specifics call the Mayor's Office of Special Events."[1] This advertising copy is a sunny paraphrase of Chicago's rhetoric about itself, a city richly provided with colorful, tuneful, tasty differences. As for the inequalities, racism, and constant political warfare that deeply divide the city, well, that doesn't make for good rhetoric or ad copy.

In the last ten years, as the number of Chicago's parades and neighborhood festivals has grown dramatically, the Gay and Lesbian Pride Week activities, including the Pride Day Parade, are now routinely listed in city publications and newspapers. A few years ago, former mayor Jane Byrne, out of office and in her endless search to get back in, popped up out of a black Mustang convertible during the parade line-up and coyly announced to reporters that she was there that day because "this is one of our summer neighborhood festivals."

This essay examines Chicago's Gay and Lesbian Pride Day Parade specifically in the context of Chicago's parades and festivals; an analysis of the gay and lesbian parades in New York, San Francisco, Los Angeles, or Europe might be quite different. The gay and lesbian parade in Chicago has adopted and transformed the parades of "ethnic groups" — the city's Irish, Polish, Mexicans, Italians, and so forth. "Ethnicity" has become a model for gays and lesbians, who now think of their community as one like other communities in Chicago, like them in having a space and a special parade to claim that space symbolically one day each summer, to express their relative cultural autonomy in the city, and to speak as a community with interests to legislators and other policy-makers, but critically different from them in their historical exclusion from normative society.

## Chicago's Gay and Lesbian Pride Day Parades

Chicago's Gay and Lesbian Pride Day Parade is one of several held annually on the last Sunday in June across the United States to commemorate the Stonewall Rebellion — the spontaneous, violent reaction by gay men and lesbians in New York City in 1969 to one of the arbitrary bar raids common at that time. These riots mark the emblematic beginning of the contemporary gay and lesbian rights movement, and those who came of age during the 1970s in its wake are sometimes called the "Stonewall generation." The parades have been held every year (with slightly different names in different cities) through the heady years of the

---

1. *Chicago,* June 1988, p. 38.

birth and maturation of the gay liberation movement into the current full realization of the AIDS crisis.

Chicago's Gay and Lesbian Pride Day Parade and rally are planned and coordinated every year by the Pride Week Committee. On the day of the parade, participants assemble during the two hours beforehand along a three-quarter-mile stretch of Halsted Street while parade watchers gather along the parade route. Virtually an event in itself, the line-up takes on a party atmosphere as public address systems on floats and in apartment windows blare dance music and Sousa marches. After the step off, the parade moves south down Broadway, a narrow, two-lane business street, for about a mile. After the parade, a rally in Lincoln Park features speeches, presentation of awards for best floats and contingents, and music performed by the gay and lesbian choruses and guest performers.

Although attendance has grown substantially in recent years, participants who have seen the huge parades in New York and San Francisco find Chicago's event a small-town affair. The parade proceeds through Newtown — the social, organizational, entertainment, and residential focus of the city's gay scene — not down State Street or North Michigan Avenue, as though New York's and San Francisco's Gay and Lesbian parades were held in the gay neighborhoods there, on Christopher Street in the Village instead of Fifth Avenue or on Castro Street instead of Market Street.

As a gay neighborhood, Newtown had been established as a residential and to a lesser extent as an entertainment area by the early 1970s, but few of the organizations, bars, and businesses that anchor the community today date back to that time. Located along Chicago's north side lakefront, Newtown consists of three or four north-south corridors separated and crosscut by business streets, bounded roughly by Diversey in the south, Irving Park in the north, Sheffield in the west, and Lake Michigan in the east. It encompasses several entertainment strips, including a three-quarter-mile stretch along one of the thoroughfares in which there are fourteen gay bars. Residential properties near the lake and to the south are expensive, and rents are high. The population is largely white, single (gay and straight), and professional. To the north and west, the neighborhood abuts Uptown, whose population is generally poorer and more working class. The demographics of streets and blocks change rapidly as real estate developers rehabilitate old properties, driving less affluent residents of all races and sexual orientations away to less expensive neighborhoods.

Newtown is also the center of the gay community's social and community life, centering on the gay and lesbian community center and on the many gay and lesbian organizations headquartered in the neighborhood that meet in rental space provided by the center or in several small churches (mainline Protestant and one Catholic).

The neighborhood itself has become a complex symbol of the gay community — its place in the city and in the life of Chicago's gay men and lesbians. When I interviewed gay men and lesbians about Newtown, they typically called it the gay "turf" or "territory." They defined the neighborhood in terms both of a space bounded by certain streets and Lake Michigan and of anchors, important places — such as bars, organizations, buildings, etc. — that focus the community's life there.

In my interviewing, I asked what makes Newtown a gay neighbor-   10
hood. A long-time resident thought for a moment and said, "What makes that neighborhood gay for me is just that gay people live there. The Jewel is gay and the Dominick's is gay and the Treasure Island is gay [large neighborhood supermarkets] because gay people shop there."

More generally, most of the men and women I interviewed (residents of this neighborhood as well as others) see Newtown as a "place to be gay" — not to engage in homosexual acts (in fact, most of the establishments offering easily accessible sexual contacts are elsewhere) but to be safe from abuse, meet with other gay friends, attend meetings of gay organizations, patronize gay-owned businesses, and meet new friends. For most, Newtown is simply the place where they can be with other gays and lesbians: "It is where I feel most comfortable walking down the street. Like I belong. Most of the people I see are just like I am."

In the 1970s, the parade aimed to establish the presence of gay people, to try to overcome invisibility. "We are everywhere!" became one of the movement's most common slogans, and the parade visually emphasized two of the gay world's most notorious indexes: drag and leather. These two controversial images of male homosexuality — dangerous hypermasculinity and abandonment of manhood altogether — became the two visible and visually aggressive ways for gay men to assert themselves as gay in public, to be not invisible.

In 1979, the color guard was led by three leathermen. Although in the minority, leather and drag and beefcake were everywhere. "We *are* different from you," the parade said. "We have sex with each other. Kinky sex, too." The parade deliberately called attention to the elaborate sexual semiotica of the leather world. Keys, bandannas, and pieces of leather worn by men and also some women — many more than the leather crowd itself at that time — publicly announced and advertised for the kinds of sex acts the wearer sought. Drag queens, female impersonators, and the guerrilla theater of "gender fuck" seemed to say, "Yes, we dress up as women, and we're going to rub your noses in it." Less flamboyantly — one could say anti-flamboyantly — lesbians refused to "dress up like ladies," as one woman put it. Men displayed the sexual polarity of their stereotypic representations, while women deemphasized presenting themselves with gender-specific expectations at all.

The strategy of the early gay liberation movement was a confrontation, its issue visibility, and its means for demonstrating difference drag, leather, and "zaps" (street demonstrations, sit-ins, guerrilla theater, etc.). The Stonewall uprising became a creation myth of the new gay community, of a new way to be gay. Sex *was* the revolution. The private was aggressively identified as public, and the parade celebrated precisely the sexual difference between gay and nongay.

By 1987, the parade exhibited the changed context of a Chicago that had elected its first woman and first black mayors, encouraging all minorities to renew demands for a progressive agenda at city hall. For the third time, the mayor proclaimed the week Gay and Lesbian Pride Week and June 28 the Gay and Lesbian Pride Parade Day in Chicago. In the 1987 parade, there were 126 entries, including bars, social service and community organizations, political organizations, beer distributors, gay and lesbian religious congregations, several aldermen and other local political figures, professional associations, service providers for people with AIDS, sports leagues, student and academic associations, and performing arts organizations. Thirty of the entries — nearly a fourth — were not self-identified as lesbian or gay. Estimates of the parade participants, including spectators, ranged up to eighty thousand.

As in the last several years, the color guard of the 1987 Chicago parade was led by the gay and lesbian social service organization's youth group for gay and lesbian teenagers. While the parade seemed no less celebratory than earlier ones (although some observers claimed it was more somber), there was much less drag and leather. But, more important, what was being said by the parade and rally had changed. Gay politics has become mainstream, and so have the messages of the parade. Civil rights legislation is advocated so that "we can be just like the rest of you, because we are just like the rest of you." Not zaps but lobbying is the tactic of choice. As AIDS has come to dominate all gay politics, activists argue that AIDS is not a "gay disease" — it affects everyone. The goals are not confrontation but assimilation. Today, the parade aims to establish that "gay" — the community of gay men and lesbians — is *not* simply "homosexuality," sex acts performed by two people of the same sex. It is all the things gay people are and have done. It is the gay and lesbian community itself. Said one participant of the first time she saw the parade, "What I took pride in at the first one was all the gay churches, all the gay organizations and businesses, because I was unaware of it. It was a real enlightening experience for me."

The parade was not less "party" and more "political," but what is being said and what semiotic means are employed have changed. In 1987, the parade specifically challenged the ways homosexuals have been defined as sinners, sick people, and criminals. Gay politics (along with American politics generally since the 1960s) has changed. Confrontation has given way to assimilationist discourse.

Although the official theme of the parade was "Proud, Strong, United," during the line-up, members of a political organization passed out signs that read, simply, "Veto Senate Bill 651 House Bill 2682." The signs were added to every float, contingent, car, and motorcycle. Unlike their usual focus on the flamboyant, the media in Chicago noticed that every entry carried signs urging Illinois's governor James Thompson to veto these bills on his desk that would establish the tracing of sexual contacts for people who are infected with HIV, institute mandatory testing, and allow quarantine of those infected. The *Chicago Tribune* reported the parade as "subdued in comparison to years past. The few drag queens and skimpily clad young men were outnumbered by sedate marchers representing various church groups, singing ensembles and associations somehow connected with AIDS."[2]

Whereas in the 1960s and 1970s sex itself was foregrounded as the revolutionary act (and indeed the gay liberation movement was part of the political and sexual revolution of the 1960s), sex and "gendered" aspects of representing gay men are now left in the background rhetorically. At the rally following the parade in 1987, the crowd responded with thunderous applause as the major speaker called out, "Make our opponents talk about our love, not our sex. Our love is the same as theirs." Presenting the gay community as composed of families, of churches and sports leagues, of clubs and professional associations, of everything about normative society except simply sexual behavior, has become the new strategy. The political agenda as frequently calls for the right to a conventional family life as for sexual freedom. In the era of AIDS, the personal script and collective myth for "coming out" (i.e., "coming out of the closet," telling others that one is gay) is based no longer on the sexual revolution of Stonewall but on a community of individuals and organizations involved in fund-raising for research, taking care of people with AIDS, offering networks of support, and defending the rights of the infected: in short, not on acts of sex but on acts of love. As the politics has become less radical and more assimilationist, participation in the parade has steadily increased.

## Parades in Chicago

Chicago's gay and lesbian parade takes place in a city of parades. In    20 the early 1950s, Mayor Richard J. Daley brought the St. Patrick's Day Parade downtown from the Irish neighborhoods and made it a public demonstration of his constituency and his coalition. The Chicago Irish had created the Democratic machine in the early decades of the twentieth century, when they were the abused and despised working and under class of Chicago. Moving the St. Patrick's Day Parade downtown signaled the arrival of Irish influence at City Hall.[3] Under Daley, the

---

2. *Chicago Tribune,* 29 June 1987, sec. 2, p. 3.

3. On the history of the Irish in Chicago, see Lawrence McCaffrey, ed., *The Irish in Chicago* (Urbana: University of Illinois Press, 1987).

Irish, Polish, and other "white ethnics" (as they are now known) ran Chicago's political machine. As black Chicagoans, including Harold Washington, were brought (in a highly qualified role) into the system, they learned the business of city government. Chicago's black leadership used their new-found knowledge to gain power under Washington's leadership.

Neighborhood events — and especially neighborhood events that move downtown — are a correlate to ethnic identity and political maturity in Chicago. The "neighborhood" is the home turf of the "ethnic community" in Chicago's political lexicon. Virtually every neighborhood has a summer street festival of some sort, featuring a parade or procession, entertainment, and food from the local eateries, as an expression of its cultural and neighborhood autonomy, typically celebrating an immigrant identity and "cultural awareness." Having a parade for one's neighborhood, community, or ethnic group is critical for having a political presence in the social consciousness of the city.

The summer calendar for these events is extensive; there are as many as three and four a weekend. The *Chicago Tribune* listed ninety-six festivals and parades for the 1988 season, including a series of "Ethnic Festivals" held at Navy Pier downtown: the Festival Polonaise, the Irish Festival, the Pan American Festival, the Festa Italiana, and the Rhythm and Blues Festival. Many other festivals in Chicago are modest neighborhood events, organized by and for local merchants as a venue for their food and wares. Others among Chicago's ethnic minorities — which are usually not called "ethnics" — also have fairs and festivals: the Chinatown Moon Festival, the Fiesta Del Sol (Mexican) in Pilsen, and the Bud Billiken Day Parade (African-American) on the South Side.

Ward organizations, neighborhood events, and the relation between neighborhoods and downtown are all imbued with the "ethnic algebra" of Chicago politics. Being "ethnic" and having an "ethnic identity" is a critical part of Chicago's political map and idiom. "Ethnic communities" are seen to have interests as such and are expected to demand representation. These parades and festivals have become tightly linked with influence real and perceived: Who comes? Who speaks? Who marches? Harold Washington was the first mayor who spoke at a Gay and Lesbian Pride Day rally. After his appearance, mass media reports for the first time treated the parade as something other than flamboyantly dressed homosexuals having a party in the street. After Washington's death, the articles reporting the 1988 parade in the gay and lesbian newspapers focused on who among the candidates for mayor attended or failed to attend the rally and parade: the acting mayor, Eugene Sawyer, failed to appear for a scheduled speech at the rally, while his archrival, Alderman Tim Evans, alone among the mayoral candidates (all of whom supported passage of the pending "gay rights" ordinance) made a surprise showing, riding in a convertible with a fellow alderman.

### Reading the Text

1. What is the significance of the Stonewall Rebellion to gay culture?
2. How has Newtown become a symbol of the gay community in Chicago, according to Herrell?
3. How has the AIDS epidemic affected the Gay and Lesbian Pride Day Parade in Chicago?

### Reading the Signs

1. In your journal, explore Herrell's claim that "ethnicity has become a model for gays and lesbians." How are homosexuals an oppressed group in America, as are many ethnic minorities? What differences are there between gays and ethnic groups?
2. Write an interpretive essay explaining how the gay pride parade works as a sign of gay identity and community. What messages are the participants sending through parade banners and themes, to both the gay and the heterosexual communities?
3. How has the meaning of the gay pride parade changed from the 1970s through the 1980s? How do you account for the symbolic changes that have occurred over the years?
4. How does the Gay and Lesbian Pride Day Parade illustrate the notion of "camp," as discussed by Andy Medhurst ("Batman, Deviance, and Camp," p. 358)?
5. Compare and contrast the gay pride parade with the Gay Games described in Michael A. Messner's "Power at Play" (p. 458). How are both rituals symbolically distinguished from their heterosexual counterparts?

NAOMI WOLF

## The Beauty Myth

|||||||||||||||||||||||||||||||||||||||||||||||||||||||||||||||

*Before Kate Moss there was Twiggy, and before Twiggy, well, women weren't expected to look so slim — not, at least, if we judge by Marilyn Monroe. And for Naomi Wolf (b. 1962), that's exactly the problem. Contemporary standards of feminine beauty have devolved to a point that can only be described as anorexic, and America's young women are paying the price through a near-epidemic of bulimia and anorexia. The most effective way to combat this epidemic, Wolf argues, is to show how what we call "beautiful" is a cultural myth that has been framed for certain purposes — essentially, Wolf believes, to keep women under control by imprisoning them in their bodies. A prominent figure in feminist and neofeminist circles, Naomi Wolf is the author of* The Beauty Myth *(1991), from which this selection is excerpted, and* Fire with Fire *(1993).*

At last, after a long silence, women took to the streets. In the two decades of radical action that followed the rebirth of feminism in the early 1970s, Western women gained legal and reproductive rights, pursued higher education, entered the trades and the professions, and overturned ancient and revered beliefs about their social role. A generation on, do women feel free?

The affluent, educated, liberated women of the First World, who can enjoy freedoms unavailable to any woman ever before, do not feel as free as they want to. And they can no longer restrict to the subconscious their sense that this lack of freedom has something to do with — with apparently frivolous issues, things that really should not matter. Many are ashamed to admit that such trivial concerns — to do with physical appearance, bodies, faces, hair, clothes — matter so much. But in spite of shame, guilt, and denial, more and more women are wondering if it isn't that they are entirely neurotic and alone but rather that something important is indeed at stake that has to do with the relationship between female liberation and female beauty.

The more legal and material hindrances women have broken through, the more strictly and heavily and cruelly images of female beauty have come to weigh upon us. Many women sense that women's collective progress has stalled; compared with the heady momentum of earlier days, there is a dispiriting climate of confusion, division, cynicism, and above all, exhaustion. After years of much struggle and little recognition, many older women feel burned out; after years of taking its light for granted, many younger women show little interest in touching new fire to the torch.

During the past decade, women breached the power structure; meanwhile, eating disorders rose exponentially and cosmetic surgery became the fastest-growing medical specialty. During the past five years, consumer spending doubled, pornography became the main media category, ahead of legitimate films and records combined, and thirty-three thousand American women told researchers that they would rather lose ten to fifteen pounds than achieve any other goal. More women have more money and power and scope and legal recognition than we have ever had before; but in terms of how we feel about ourselves *physically,* we may actually be worse off than our unliberated grandmothers. Recent research consistently shows that inside the majority of the West's controlled, attractive, successful working women, there is a secret "underlife" poisoning our freedom; infused with notions of beauty, it is a dark vein of self-hatred, physical obsessions, terror of aging, and dread of lost control.

It is no accident that so many potentially powerful women feel this way. We are in the midst of a violent backlash against feminism that uses images of female beauty as a political weapon against women's advancement: the beauty myth. It is the modern version of a social reflex that has been in force since the Industrial Revolution. As women released themselves from the feminine mystique of domesticity, the beauty myth took over its lost ground, expanding as it waned to carry on its work of social control.

The contemporary backlash is so violent because the ideology of beauty is the last one remaining of the old feminine ideologies that still has the power to control those women whom second-wave feminism would have otherwise made relatively uncontrollable: It has grown stronger to take over the work of social coercion that myths about motherhood, domesticity, chastity, and passivity no longer can manage. It is seeking right now to undo psychologically and covertly all the good things that feminism did for women materially and overtly.

This counterforce is operating to checkmate the inheritance of feminism on every level in the lives of Western women. Feminism gave us laws against job discrimination based on gender; immediately case law evolved in Britain and the United States that institutionalized job discrimination based on women's appearances. Patriarchal religion declined; new religious dogma, using some of the mind-altering techniques of older cults and sects, arose around age and weight to functionally supplant traditional ritual. Feminists, inspired by Betty Friedan, broke the stranglehold on the women's popular press of advertisers for household products, who were promoting the feminine mystique; at once, the diet and skin care industries became the new cultural censors of women's intellectual space, and because of their pressure, the gaunt, youthful model supplanted the happy housewife as the arbiter of successful womanhood. The sexual revolution promoted the discovery of female sexuality; "beauty pornography" — which for the first time in women's history artificially links a commodified "beauty" directly and explicitly to sexuality — invaded the mainstream to undermine women's new and vulnerable sense of sexual self-worth. Reproductive rights gave Western women control over our own bodies; the weight of fashion models plummeted to 23 percent below that of ordinary women, eating disorders rose exponentially, and a mass neurosis was promoted that used food and weight to strip women of that sense of control. Women insisted on politicizing health; new technologies of invasive, potentially deadly "cosmetic" surgeries developed apace to re-exert old forms of medical control of women.

Every generation since about 1830 has had to fight its version of the beauty myth. "It is very little to me," said the suffragist Lucy Stone in 1855, "to have the right to vote, to own property, etcetera, if I may not keep my body, and its uses, in my absolute right." Eighty years later, after women had won the vote, and the first wave of the organized women's movement had subsided, Virginia Woolf wrote that it would still be decades before women could tell the truth about their bodies. In 1962, Betty Friedan quoted a young woman trapped in the Feminine Mystique: "Lately, I look in the mirror, and I'm so afraid that I'm going to look like my mother." Eight years after that, heralding the cataclysmic second wave of feminism, Germaine Greer described "the Stereotype": "To her belongs all that is beautiful, even the very word beauty itself . . . she is a doll . . . I'm sick of the masquerade." In spite of the great revolution of the second wave, we are not exempt. Now we can look out over ruined barricades: A revolution has come upon us and changed everything in its path, enough time has passed since then for babies to have grown into women, but there still remains a final right not fully claimed.

The beauty myth tells a story: The quality called "beauty" objectively and universally exists. Women must want to embody it and men must want to possess women who embody it. This embodiment is an imperative for women and not for men, which situation is necessary and natural because it is biological, sexual, and evolutionary: Strong men battle for beautiful women, and beautiful women are more reproductively successful. Women's beauty must correlate to their fertility, and since this system is based on sexual selection, it is inevitable and changeless.

None of this is true. "Beauty" is a currency system like the gold     10
standard. Like any economy, it is determined by politics, and in the modern age in the West it is the last, best belief system that keeps male dominance intact. In assigning value to women in a vertical hierarchy according to a culturally imposed physical standard, it is an expression of power relations in which women must unnaturally compete for resources that men have appropriated for themselves.

"Beauty" is not universal or changeless, though the West pretends that all ideals of female beauty stem from one Platonic Ideal Woman; the Maori admire a fat vulva, and the Padung, droopy breasts. Nor is "beauty" a function of evolution: Its ideals change at a pace far more rapid than that of the evolution of species, and Charles Darwin was himself unconvinced by his own explanation that "beauty" resulted from a "sexual selection" that deviated from the rule of natural selection; for women to compete with women through "beauty" is a reversal of the way in which natural selection affects all other mammals. Anthropology has overturned the notion that females must be "beautiful" to be selected to mate: Evelyn Reed, Elaine Morgan, and others have dismissed sociobiological assertions of innate male polygamy and female monogamy. Female higher primates are the sexual initiators; not only do they seek out and enjoy sex with many partners, but "every nonpregnant female takes her turn at being the most desirable of all her troop. And that cycle keeps turning as long as she lives." The inflamed pink sexual organs of primates are often cited by male sociobiologists as analogous to human arrangements relating to female "beauty," when in fact that is a universal, nonhierarchical female primate characteristic.

Nor has the beauty myth always been this way. Though the pairing of the older rich men with young, "beautiful" women is taken to be somehow inevitable, in the matriarchal Goddess religions that dominated the Mediterranean from about 25,000 B.C.E. to about 700 B.C.E., the situation was reversed: "In every culture, the Goddess has many lovers. . . . The clear pattern is of an older woman with a beautiful but expendable youth — Ishtar and Tammuz, Venus and Adonis, Cybele and Attis, Isis and Osiris . . . their only function the service of the divine 'womb.'" Nor is it something only women do and only men watch: Among the Nigerian Wodaabes, the women hold economic power and the tribe is obsessed with male beauty; Wodaabe men spend hours together in elaborate makeup sessions, and compete — provocatively painted and dressed, with swaying hips and seductive expressions — in beauty contests judged by women. There is no legitimate historical or biological justification for the beauty myth; what it is doing to women today is a result of nothing more exalted than the need of today's power structure, economy, and culture to mount a counteroffensive against women.

If the beauty myth is not based on evolution, sex, gender, aesthetics, or God, on what is it based? It claims to be about intimacy and sex and life, a celebration of women. It is actually composed of emotional distance, politics, finance, and sexual repression. The beauty myth is not about women at all. It is about men's institutions and institutional power.

The qualities that a given period calls beautiful in women are merely symbols of the female behavior that that period considers desirable: *The beauty myth is always actually prescribing behavior and not appearance.* Competition between women has been made part of the myth so that women will be divided from one another. Youth and (until recently) virginity have been "beautiful" in women since they stand for experiential and sexual ignorance. Aging in women is "unbeautiful" since women grow more powerful with time, and since the links between generations of women must always be newly broken: Older women fear young ones, young women fear old, and the beauty myth truncates for all the female life span. Most urgently, women's identity must be premised upon our "beauty" so that we will remain vulnerable to outside approval, carrying the vital sensitive organ of self-esteem exposed to the air.

Though there has, of course, been a beauty myth in some form for as        15
long as there has been patriarchy, the beauty myth in its modern form is a

fairly recent invention. The myth flourishes when material constraints on women are dangerously loosened. Before the Industrial Revolution, the average woman could not have had the same feelings about "beauty" that modern women do who experience the myth as continual comparison to a mass-disseminated physical ideal. Before the development of technologies of mass production — daguerreotypes, photographs, etc. — an ordinary woman was exposed to few such images outside the Church. Since the family was a productive unit and women's work complemented men's, the value of women who were not aristocrats or prostitutes lay in their work skills, economic shrewdness, physical strength, and fertility. Physical attraction, obviously, played its part; but "beauty" as we understand it was not, for ordinary women, a serious issue in the marriage marketplace. The beauty myth in its modern form gained ground after the upheavals of industrialization, as the work unit of the family was destroyed, and urbanization and the emerging factory system demanded what social engineers of the time termed the "separate sphere" of domesticity, which supported the new labor category of the "breadwinner" who left home for the workplace during the day. The middle class expanded, the standards of living and of literacy rose, the size of families shrank; a new class of literate, idle women developed, on whose submission to enforced domesticity the evolving system of industrial capitalism depended. Most of our assumptions about the way women have always thought about "beauty" date from no earlier than the 1830s, when the cult of domesticity was first consolidated and the beauty index invented.

For the first time new technologies could reproduce — in fashion plates, daguerreotypes, tintypes, and rotogravures — images of how women should look. In the 1840s the first nude photographs of prostitutes were taken; advertisements using images of "beautiful" women first appeared in mid-century. Copies of classical artworks, postcards of society beauties and royal mistresses, Currier and Ives prints, and porcelain figurines flooded the separate sphere to which middle-class women were confined.

Since the Industrial Revolution, middle-class Western women have been controlled by ideals and stereotypes as much as by material constraints. This situation, unique to this group, means that analyses that trace "cultural conspiracies" are uniquely plausible in relation to them. The rise of the beauty myth was just one of several emerging social fictions that masqueraded as natural components of the feminine sphere, the better to enclose those women inside it. Other such fictions arose contemporaneously: a version of childhood that required continual maternal supervision; a concept of female biology that required middle-class women to act out the roles of hysterics and hypochondriacs; a conviction that respectable women were sexually anesthetic; and a definition of women's work that occupied them with repetitive, time-consuming, and painstaking tasks such as needlepoint and lacemaking. All such Victorian inventions as these served a double function — that is, though they were encouraged as a means to expend female energy and intelligence in harmless ways, women often used them to express genuine creativity and passion.

But in spite of middle-class women's creativity with fashion and embroidery and child rearing, and, a century later, with the role of the suburban housewife that devolved from these social fictions, the fictions' main purpose was served: During a century and a half of unprecedented feminist agitation, they effectively counteracted middle-class women's dangerous new leisure, literacy, and relative freedom from material constraints.

Though these time- and mind-consuming fictions about women's natural role adapted themselves to resurface in the postwar Feminine Mystique, when the second wave of the women's movement took apart what women's magazines had portrayed as the "romance," "science," and "adventure" of homemaking and suburban family life, they temporarily failed. The cloying domestic fiction of "togetherness" lost its meaning and middle-class women walked out of their front doors in masses.

So the fictions simply transformed themselves once more: Since the women's movement had successfully taken apart most other necessary fictions of femininity, all the work of social control once spread out over the whole network of these fictions had to be reassigned to the only strand left intact, which action consequently strengthened it a hundredfold. This reimposed onto liberated women's faces and bodies all the limitations, taboos, and punishments of the repressive laws, religious injunctions and reproductive enslavement that no longer carried sufficient force. Inexhaustible but ephemeral beauty work took over from inexhaustible but ephemeral housework. As the economy, law, religion, sexual mores, education, and culture were forcibly opened up to include women more fairly, a private reality colonized female consciousness. By using ideas about "beauty," it reconstructed an alternative female world with its own laws, economy, religion, sexuality, education, and culture, each element as repressive as any that had gone before.

Since middle-class Western women can best be weakened psychologically now that we are stronger materially, the beauty myth, as it has resurfaced in the last generation, has had to draw on more technological sophistication and reactionary fervor than ever before. The modern arsenal of the myth is a dissemination of millions of images of the current ideal; although this barrage is generally seen as a collective sexual fantasy, there is in fact little that is sexual about it. It is summoned out of political fear on the part of male-dominated institutions threatened by women's freedom, and it exploits female guilt and apprehension about our own liberation — latent fears that we might be going too far. This frantic aggregation of imagery is a collective reactionary hallucination willed into being by both men and women stunned and disoriented by the rapidity with which gender relations have been transformed: a bulwark of reassurance against the flood of change. The mass depiction of the modern woman as a "beauty" is a contradiction: Where modern women are growing, moving, and expressing their individuality, as the myth has it, "beauty" is by definition inert, timeless, and generic. That this hallucination is necessary and deliberate is evident in the way "beauty" so directly contradicts women's real situation.

And the unconscious hallucination grows ever more influential and pervasive because of what is now conscious market manipulation: powerful industries — the $33-billion-a-year diet industry, the $20-billion cosmetics industry, the $300-million cosmetic surgery industry, and the $7-billion pornography industry — have arisen from the capital made out of unconscious anxieties, and are in turn able, through their influence on mass culture, to use, stimulate, and reinforce the hallucination in a rising economic spiral.

This is not a conspiracy theory; it doesn't have to be. Societies tell themselves necessary fictions in the same way that individuals and families do. Henrik Ibsen called them "vital lies," and psychologist Daniel Goleman describes them working the same way on the social level that they do within families: "The collusion is maintained by directing attention away from the fearsome fact, or by repackaging its meaning in an acceptable format." The costs of these social blind spots, he writes, are destructive communal illusions. Possibilities for women have become so open-ended that they threaten to destabilize the institutions on which a male-dominated culture has depended, and a collective panic reaction on the part of both sexes has forced a demand for counter-images.

The resulting hallucination materializes, for women, as something all too real. No longer just an idea, it becomes three-dimensional, incorporating within itself how women live and how they do not live: It becomes the Iron Maiden. The original Iron Maiden was a medieval German instrument of torture, a body-shaped casket painted with the limbs and features of a lovely, smiling young woman. The unlucky victim was slowly enclosed inside her; the lid fell shut to immobilize the victim, who died either of starvation or, less cruelly, of the metal spikes embedded in her interior. The modern hallucination in which women are trapped or trap themselves is similarly rigid, cruel, and euphemistically painted. Contemporary culture directs attention to imagery of the Iron Maiden, while censoring real women's faces and bodies.

Why does the social order feel the need to defend itself by evading the fact of real women, our faces and voices and bodies, and reducing the meaning of women to these formulaic and endlessly reproduced "beautiful" images? Though unconscious personal anxieties can be a powerful force in the creation of a vital lie, economic necessity practically guarantees it. An economy that depends on slavery needs to promote images of slaves that "justify" the institution of slavery. Western economics are absolutely dependent now on the continued underpayment of women. An ideology that makes women feel "worth less" was urgently needed to counteract the way feminism had begun to make us feel worth more. This does not require a conspiracy; merely an atmosphere. The contemporary economy depends right now on the representation of women within the beauty myth. Economist John Kenneth Galbraith offers an economic explanation for "the persistence of the view of homemaking as a 'higher calling'": the concept of women as naturally trapped within the Feminine Mystique, he feels, "has been forced on us by popular sociology, by magazines, and by fiction to disguise the fact that woman in her role of consumer has been essential to the development of our industrial society. . . . Behavior that is essential for economic reasons is transformed into a social virtue." As soon as a woman's primary social value could no longer be defined as the attainment of virtuous domesticity, the beauty myth redefined it as the attainment of virtuous beauty. It did so to substitute both a new consumer imperative and a new justification for economic unfairness in the workplace where the old ones had lost their hold over newly liberated women.

Another hallucination arose to accompany that of the Iron Maiden: The caricature of the Ugly Feminist was resurrected to dog the steps of the women's movement. The caricature is unoriginal; it was coined to ridicule the feminists of the nineteenth century. Lucy Stone herself, whom supporters saw as "a prototype of womanly grace . . . fresh and fair as the morning," was derided by detractors with "the usual report" about Victorian feminists: "a big masculine woman, wearing boots, smoking a cigar, swearing like a trooper." As Betty Friedan put it presciently in 1960, even before the savage revamping of that old caricature: "The unpleasant image of feminists today resembles less the feminists themselves than the image fostered by the interests who so bitterly opposed the vote for women in state after state." Thirty years on, her conclusion is more true than ever: That resurrected caricature, which sought to punish women for their public acts by going after their private sense of self, became the paradigm for new limits placed on aspiring women everywhere. After the success of the women's movement's second wave, the beauty myth was perfected to checkmate power at every level in individual women's lives. The modern neuroses of life in the female body spread to woman after woman at epidemic rates. The myth is undermining — slowly, imperceptibly, without our being aware of the real forces of erosion — the ground women have gained through long, hard, honorable struggle.

The beauty myth of the present is more insidious than any mystique of femininity yet: A century ago, Nora slammed the door of the doll's house; a generation ago, women turned their backs on the consumer heaven of the isolated multi-applianced home; but where women are trapped today, there is no door to slam. The contemporary ravages of the beauty backlash are destroying women physically and depleting us psychologically. If we are to free ourselves from the dead weight that has once again been made out of femaleness, it is not ballots or lobbyists or placards that women will need first; it is a new way to see.

## Reading the Text

1. What is the "secret 'underlife' poisoning" modern women's lives, according to Wolf?
2. Summarize in your own words what Wolf means by "the beauty myth."
3. What relationship does Wolf see between the beauty myth and feminism?
4. How has the beauty myth replaced the "feminine myth of domesticity," in Wolf's opinion?
5. What are the behaviors that Wolf believes the beauty myth forces women to adopt, and why?
6. What does Wolf see as the significance of the Iron Maiden, both historically and today?

## Reading the Signs

1. Discuss in your journal your attitudes toward your own body. To what extent have your attitudes been shaped by contemporary standards of physical attractiveness?
2. Visit a local art museum (or consult a volume of art reproductions) and study the different ways in which women's bodies are represented. How do the images reflect the history of the beauty myth that Wolf presents? Use your findings to support an analytical essay about how women are represented in art.
3. Bring to class a women's fashion magazine such as *Elle* or *Vogue* and in small groups examine the ways in which both advertising and fashion displays portray women. Discuss what the ideal image of female beauty is in your publications and whether Wolf's contention that the ideal woman is "inert, timeless, and generic" is valid.
4. Write an essay in which you support, challenge, or qualify Wolf's belief that the beauty myth constitutes an "Iron Maiden" that torments the lives of modern women.
5. Implicit in Wolf's argument is the assumption that men are not bound by their own version of the beauty myth. In class, form teams and debate whether men are as trapped by standards of ideal physical attractiveness as women. To develop your ideas, consult Stuart Ewen, "Hard Bodies" (p. 66), Diane Barthel, "A Gentleman and a Consumer" (p. 144), and Gary R. Brooks, "The Centerfold Syndrome" (p. 438).

GARY R. BROOKS
*The Centerfold Syndrome*

IIIIIIIIIIIIIIIIIIIIIIIIIIIIIIIIIIIIIIIIIIIIIIIIIIIIIIIIIIIIII

*Feminists have long complained about the effects of skin magazines on women, but what about their effect on men? In this selection excerpted from* The Centerfold Syndrome *(1995), Gary R. Brooks (b. 1946) argues that pinup photography — and, more generally, the objectification of women — is as damaging to men as it is to women, because it can cause men to have unreal expectations about their sexual relationships, as well as self-doubts and an inability to achieve genuine emotional intimacy with a woman. Assistant Chief of Psychological Services at Olin Teague Veterans' Center in Tempe, Texas, Brooks is a teacher and practitioner in both individual and family therapy. His many publications have most recently focused on male gender roles.*

I'm a relatively normal and emotionally stable guy who grew up believing that looking at and desiring physically attractive women was both pleasurable and inevitable. Now I'm not so sure.

During the past several years, as I have studied the lives and conflicts of men, I have begun to question the value of much of what I had previously accepted. I once assumed, as many men do, that success at work and in a career was the greatest measure of a man, that physical toughness and heroic acts were pathways to proving manhood, that men had to keep the upper hand with women, that only "queers" loved other men, and that emotional sensitivity and vulnerability were signs of weakness. Of all these assumptions, however, none has been more deeply ingrained than the belief that physically attractive women's bodies are the most magnificent spectacles in nature, and that men are destined to fervently desire them, to compete for them, to sacrifice emotional and physical well-being for them, but rarely to enjoy them except from afar. Men and women have accepted this bizarre state of affairs, strangely enough, as both unavoidable and relatively harmless. Neither is true. In fact, in studying this situation I have come to the conclusion that this male pattern of relating to women's bodies, which I am calling the Centerfold Syndrome, represents one of the most malignant forces in contemporary relationships between men and women.

The centerfold has been one of the dominant cultural icons of the past half-century. As interpreted by *Playboy* magazine's founder Hugh Hefner and *Penthouse* magazine's publisher Bob Guccione, today's centerfold is a racier, slicker, and glossier fantasy woman, even more perfect and idealized than the pinup girl of the 1930s and 1940s. Her airbrushed perfection permeates our visual environment and our consciousness, creating unreal fantasies and expectations, imposing profound distortions on how men relate with women and to women's bodies, and, in turn, how women relate to their physical selves and with men.

## Elements of the Centerfold Syndrome

The five principal elements of the Centerfold Syndrome are (a) voyeurism, (b) objectification, (c) the need for validation, (d) trophyism, and (e) the fear of true intimacy.

### VOYEURISM

Nothing heightens the emotional intensity of a sexual encounter as   5
much as looking directly into the eyes of one's partner. Similarly, the unique features of a female partner's physical appearance — the way her breasts swell in a dress, the outline of her torso through gossamer fabric — can become a powerful sexual stimulus for a man. Certainly, the visual sense always has and probably always will play a major role in men's sexual responsiveness. In the latter half of this century, however, this component of men's sexuality has been so exploited, distorted, and outrageously exaggerated that the emotional and sexual health of most contemporary men has been seriously compromised.

Throughout our culture, in movies, on television, in magazines, and in public meeting places, men are continually assailed with images of naked and semi-naked women. Not only are the glossy soft-core porno magazines more plentiful than ever, but even the covers of many "women's" magazines feature the same type of comely, buxom models who are also pictured on hot rod magazines, tabloid newspapers, and, once a year, mainstream sports magazines. Advertising billboards promote "men's clubs" that are "topless" or "bottomless" or that feature models in lingerie. A popular restaurant celebrates women's "hooters" more than it celebrates its food. Beer companies seem to be competing to see which can cram the most bikini-clad women into a thirty-second commercial. Superhero comics are liberally sprinkled with images of breathtaking superwomen in skintight bodysuits. The creative inspiration for one entire television series is the adventures of scantily clad lifeguards. Increasingly, women are encouraged to wear bathing suits and exercise outfits that cover their derrières with little more than a thin fabric strip.

Only religious fundamentalists and radical feminists appear to be alarmed about this wave of female body glorification. The culture at large seems to be generally indifferent to this trend, seeing it as harmless titillation, pretty much a natural product of men's biological makeup. I strongly disagree with this position. It is my contention that this mania, this explosion in glorification and objectification of women's bodies, promotes unreal images of women, distorts physical reality, creates an obsession with visual stimulation, and trivializes all other natural features of a healthy psychosexual relationship.

**OBJECTIFICATION**

Voyeurism and objectification are closely related. Just as the Centerfold Syndrome calls for men to become *observers,* it also calls for women to become the *observed.* Women become objects as men become objectifiers. As the culture has granted men the right and privilege of looking at women, women have been expected to accept the role of stimulators of men's visual interest, with their bodies becoming objects that can be lined up, compared, and rated. The process is distinctly one-way, with women's bodies highlighted and male observers remaining in the shadows or anonymous in a crowd. Objective physical aspects are critical: size, shape, and harmony of body parts are more important than a woman's human qualities. The women objectified by the media remain relatively anonymous, often without names, except for pseudonyms such as Miss May, Miss Nevada, or Miss Rotary Camshaft. Despite the occasional pretense of connection through shallow interviews or background sketches, centerfold women are left devoid of real personalities, portrayed as superficial cartoon characters. Men talk of their attraction to women in dehumanizing terms based on the body part of their obsession — "I'm a leg man," or "I'm an ass man."

What's more, one fantasy woman is never enough, since images that initially can be enormously novel and exciting can quickly lose their zip. Objectifying observers soon find one naked woman boring and routine, and look for new and different images to provoke their fascination — "variety is the spice of life." At times, the confirmed objectifier becomes so attached to the thrill of the new and different visual experience, he resorts to the kinky and the offbeat, becoming preoccupied with visual fetishes. Bizarre magazines featuring only "Big-Breasted Mamas," "Black Beauties," "Oriental Cuties," or "Biker Babes" are in part a pathetic effort to override the boredom inherent in such superficial sexuality.

Since centerfold fantasy women are presented only to stimulate and to invite admiration of their perfection, they are unlike real women, who not only have physical flaws but also expect things from relationships and can be interpersonally threatening. When centerfold women are available to men as visually perfect and emotionally distant sexual fantasy objects, real women become more complicated and less appealing. In fact, when men become fixated on narrow and idealized images of female beauty — youthful bodies with uplifted breasts and full but firm bottoms — their real partners, by comparison, may come to be seen as not only less appealing but even ugly. Stretch marks, varicose veins, sagging breasts, and cellulite-marked legs, common phenomena for real female bodies, may be viewed as repugnant by men who see women as objects.

Furthermore, when a man in a relationship is continually distracted by a fantasy life dominated by visual images of idealized bodies of strangers, that man will frequently be emotionally absent from his partner; he will be unable to have intense, here-and-now experiences with her. Tragically, if he spends most of his emotional energy on sexual fantasies about inaccessible people, he frequently will not be available for even the most intimate emotional and sexual moments with the most important person in his life.

### THE NEED FOR VALIDATION

The traditional concept of manhood is an elusive state to achieve. Most men have only a vague sense of their masculinity and, therefore, continually worry about whether they measure up, and they are quick to become alarmed at the first sign of failure, weakness, or vulnerability. They are programmed to crave validation of their masculinity, and they frequently view women's bodies as a medium for that validation. This need for validation disempowers them and creates an odd yet vitally important inversion of the traditional power relationship between women and men. Despite the fact that they generally have had considerable advantages over women in physical strength and economic and political opportunities, men have frequently felt one-down about sexuality. Although there are multiple ways that women could conceivably validate a man's masculinity, the avenue critical to most men is the sexual one. When women are envisioned as sexual objects and made the centerpiece of men's visual world, they become imbued with enormous psychosocial power. They are seen as having invaluable manhood tokens that they may, or may not, choose to dispense. The more physically attractive a woman is, the more validating power she is seen to have.

What have made matters worse are the long-standing gender differences in socialization about sexual activity. Young men have been encouraged to be promiscuous — that is, to seek sexual activity with scant consideration of relationship needs, intimacy, or emotional compatibility. At the same time, young women have been encouraged to attract men's attention, yet to withhold and serve as the gatekeepers of sexual activity.

Even when participating in sex, men are not free from the need for validation. In recent years, thanks to abundant technical advice from sex manuals and implicit assumptions that men's "performances" are the critical determinants of sexual fulfillment, many contemporary men have become obsessed with producing physical evidence of women's sexual pleasure. A dramatic response from a woman's body — erect nipples, gyrating hips, a shuddering orgasm — can be interpreted by a man as unambiguous evidence of his manliness. Conversely, a cold, listless, or indifferent response from a woman's body often leaves a man feeling ineffectual, inadequate, or resentful. Rarely can a woman find the right words to reassure a man of his worth when he has decided that her body is underappreciative of his manly attentions. To many men, the state of a woman's body may come to be viewed as a masculinity barometer, with its natural fluctuations mistaken as irrefutable evidence of either a man's sexual competence or his shameful inadequacy.

The power imparted by women's sexual leverage, when viewed in    15
light of women's relative powerlessness in other spheres, sets the stage for considerable misunderstanding between women and men. Women, of course, are keenly aware of men's economic and political leverage, but are frequently unaware of the degree to which men feel powerless in terms of sexuality. Men, aware of their insecurities about sexuality, are deeply fearful of women gaining power in areas once thought to be the basis of men's security and worth.

At this critical juncture in the history of gender relations, the Centerfold Syndrome is made infinitely worse by a culture that plays to men's fears and heightens men's feelings of sexual disempowerment. As I have already discussed, artificially enhanced images of exquisitely desirable women are everywhere, but these women are remote and unattainable. They are on screens or glossy pages, but physically unavailable. They parade across well-lit and well-guarded stages, before masses of sexually aroused men who hoot but don't touch and are ultimately left unfulfilled, frustrated, and demoralized.

All men and all women are diminished by this noxious situation. The very few women who meet centerfold standards only retain their power as long as they maintain perfect bodies and the leverage of mystery and unavailability. All other women suffer from pressures to live up to the outrageous centerfold standard and from the disappointment of partners when they fail. The very few men who form sexual relationships with centerfolds are often left disappointed, fearful of loss, or envious of those who tryst with even more desirable centerfolds. The great majority of men who never come close to sex with their dream woman are left feeling cheated or unmanly.

### TROPHYISM

Men also experience their masculinity in relation to other men. That is, they ask themselves, How do I stack up against the other guys? Men compete in this way because they believe that the tokens of masculinity are in short supply, with the most valuable prizes obtained by only the worthiest men. Women's bodies become part of this scenario as they are objectified and treated as potential trophies — living testaments to a man's prowess as a financial success, skillful sexual performer, or fearless warrior.

This male competition for access to women's bodies begins in adolescence when boys compete to be the first to "score," to achieve the most sexual conquests, to "make it" with the sexiest teenage girl. The women's-bodies-as-trophies mentality, damaging enough in adolescence, becomes even more destructive in adulthood, when the "trophy hunts" of adolescence clash with men's developmental need to "settle down" and select a long-term companion. While collecting new and different sexual trophies may be celebrated among male adolescents, it is a sign of emotional immaturity in the world of most adults. Furthermore, while actual trophies retain their basic physical characteristics, human trophies do not. Women's bodies age, losing their trophy-like characteristics, especially in comparison to newer varieties. Hence, the trophy-hunting man, initially satisfied with his trophy-wife, must eventually face the maddening reality that his prize will eventually lose her lustre, while other potential prizes will emit near-irresistible allure.

Another aspect of this trophyism mentality makes it especially dangerous. Trophies, once they are won, are supposed to become the property of the winner, a permanent physical symbol of accomplishment and worthiness. This cannot be so with women's bodies. Women, of course, no longer want to be passive objects, and they have a growing say in whom they spend their lives with. From the perspective of the trophy hunter, this is a horrifying trend, as he can never be assured that his trophy will remain his. At any time, she may choose to sit on the shelf of another man. This is a devastating occurrence for a trophy-hunting man, one that commonly provokes him to desperate and destructive reactions.

### THE FEAR OF TRUE INTIMACY

Men are created within women's bodies and their first experiences of love and security come from intimate physical contact with their mothers' soft and welcoming bodies. Fathers' bodies could provide similar sensual pleasures, but they traditionally have been unavailable to young boys, or when available, have been stiff and threatening.

Though young boys treasure the opportunity to be physically close, both for sensual pleasures and for reassurance in times of vulnerability, they soon encounter social pressures to distance themselves from their mothers' bodies and establish a place alongside the bodies of men. This early developmental injunction, endemic to traditional parenting of boys, causes them to have lifelong conflict with women's bodies, a conflict that is the essence of this fifth and most complex aspect of the Centerfold Syndrome.

Young boys are conditioned to feel shame over feelings of weakness and vulnerability, encouraged to suppress their needs for sensual physical contact, and expected to develop male body armor with hard muscles and an emotionally stoic exterior. While they try to emulate heroes that are brave, intrepid, fearless, physically aggressive, and emotionally tough, boys cannot ignore that they are still insecure and crave physical comforting. At especially vulnerable times, they may allow nurturers to give some measure of soothing and comforting, but fears of humiliation quickly surface. Frequently, boys discover that some touch and physical closeness are possible through acceptable "boy" activities like sports and horseplay, but they remain continually aware that these sensual pleasures must not be acknowledged.

In short, boys learn to associate women's bodies with softness, intimacy, and sensuality, the very qualities they have been taught to reject. Despite their common exteriors of manic activity and rough play, boys often crave physical closeness and sensuality, but have no way to ask for it and few avenues by which to experience it.

In adolescence, young men find themselves besieged by two power- 25 ful yet contradictory forces — waves of sexual urgency and the extreme prohibitions against emotional intimacy. The sudden appearance of the hormonal pressures of sexuality catches young men unprepared; the fear of intimacy leaves them confused and conflicted. Help is rarely available. Usually there is some token guidance in the form of caution about the need to be sexually controlled, but boys recognize these admonitions to be contradicted by their bodies, their peers, their role models, and their culture, in which the dominant message is that sex is great and a man should acquire as much of it as possible.

Sadly, young men, who have had minimal preparation for the multiple complexities of sexuality, have also been encouraged to be physically tough and insensitive to emotional issues. Emphasis has been placed on aggressive and competitive skills, with very little emphasis on interpersonal skills of communication, empathy, and nurturing. Young men badly want sexual intimacy, but have learned to fear and suppress their needs for emotional intimacy and sensuality. They learn that the safest form of sex is the "slam bam thank you ma'am" variety.

It is conceivable that under optimal circumstances sexual activity might help boys to rediscover these long-suppressed parts of themselves and might help them unlearn their fears of these "feminine" qualities. The opposite typically occurs, however, as young men experience their brushes with sensuality and emotional intimacy as confusing and threatening to their hard-won masculine independence and desire for "sexual freedom." Most young men therefore give primacy to their sexual needs, while continuing to suppress their needs for sensuality.

As young men learn to wall themselves off from too much emotional intimacy in sex — to develop nonrelational sexuality — they are also taught to sexualize all feelings of emotional and physical closeness. As a result, they become unable to experience nonsexual intimacy. Because their closest approximations of emotional intimacy and most intense exposure to sensual pleasure occur almost exclusively in the context of rapid-orgasm sexual activity, male adolescents learn to closely associate sex and intimacy. Further, they are poorly tutored in distinguishing the two, because they have been raised in a culture that generally gives minuscule attention to men's sensuality and intimacy needs while exalting their sexual needs. Because of this confusion, it should not be surprising that a man who wants to replace his feelings of emotional distance and alienation with ones of closeness and connection misinterprets the feelings as sexual ones and assumes that he is just "horny." Consequently, men may seek sex when they really want emotional intimacy, sensual pleasure, or physical comforting. Moreover, they frequently may engage in sex when they have no interest whatever in emotional intimacy.

Sometimes the distinction between the desire for sex and the desire for intimacy is irrelevant. In some cases, a sexual relationship may help a man discover his sensuality and intimacy needs, and he may develop a deeply fulfilling relationship with his partner. More often than not, however, this blurring of sexual needs and intimacy needs will create significant relationship constraints. When young men do not learn to distinguish the two sets of needs, they will be highly restricted in their capacity to develop and maintain relationships. For example, intimacy with male peers will incite homophobic panic, and intimate friendships with girls will be contaminated by compulsive sexual overtures. Limited in their pursuit of true intimacy, young men may be prone to overdependence upon a sexual partner; or to defend against excessive intimacy, they may seek promiscuous sexual activity, rather than risk getting too close to a partner. Even when remaining monogamous, young men may be prone to seek distance through fantasy and emotional withdrawal.

Ultimately, this fifth aspect of the Centerfold Syndrome is about    30
how men are taught to suppress their needs for intimacy and sensuality, and come to invest too much emotional and psychological power in some women's bodies. Fearing their potential overdependence on women, men develop a preoccupation with sexuality, which powerfully handicaps their capacity for emotionally intimate relationships with men and for nonsexual relationships with women.

## Why Aren't There More Complaints?

Although the tenets of this syndrome are indoctrinated into children at an early age, some of the teaching has been so subtle that the more covert implications are missed. Commonly, the Centerfold Syndrome is accepted as a relatively natural outgrowth of innate, gender-based biological differences. Furthermore, the social and psychological tension produced by the syndrome has often been presented as culturally beneficial — the basic lifeblood and energizing force of our society. The significant problems related to the syndrome have been disguised or dismissed.

Consequently, only some women have protested as yet that the Centerfold Syndrome objectifies them, depersonalizes them, reduces them to body parts, perpetuates anatomical lies, and idealizes unreal fantasies about women's bodies and sexuality. Sadly, many more women accept some of the fraudulent premises of the Centerfold Syndrome and take on the hopeless task of meeting its standards, rarely satisfied with their successes, and ultimately blaming themselves for the inevitable failures.

Yet, although damage to women as the result of the Centerfold Syndrome is gradually becoming clear, there is virtually no awareness that it also harms men. This isn't surprising, since very few men seem dissatisfied with their sexual socialization. Most seem happy to embrace the Centerfold Syndrome, though some will admit disappointment that they have not been able to capture a true centerfold. Nevertheless, it's my contention that the Centerfold Syndrome is deeply harmful to women *and* men. It produces major asynchronicity between men and women and is a crucial component in the "battle of the sexes." Since it prevents real intimacy, mature discourse, and honest interpersonal connection, it creates barriers to understanding and becomes a significant obstacle to healthy relationships.

The Centerfold Syndrome is pervasive, but it is not inevitable. It is neither an unavoidable outgrowth of biological forces nor the product of moral weakness resulting from Adam succumbing to Eve's temptation with the forbidden fruit. Rather, it is a social construction, and like all socially constructed realities, it can be deconstructed.

### Reading the Text

1. Summarize in your own words what Brooks means by the Centerfold Syndrome, being sure to explain each of the five elements that he outlines.
2. Why does Brooks claim that the Centerfold Syndrome is "deeply harmful to women *and* men"?
3. How do modern mass media perpetuate the Centerfold Syndrome, in Brooks's view?
4. How, according to Brooks, has the Centerfold Syndrome led many American men to feel sexually disempowered?
5. What is the difference between sensual intimacy and sexual intimacy, according to Brooks?

### Reading the Signs

1. In your journal, discuss what you consider to be the ideal woman. Compare entries in class and list on the board the responses by gender. To

what extent has the Centerfold Syndrome affected the responses of male and female students?

2. Select a men's magazine such as *Details* and study the ways in which male and female models interact in the magazine's advertising. Use your findings to support, refute, or modify Brooks's contention that the Centerfold Syndrome is perpetuated in modern media.

3. While some counterparts to *Playboy* exist for female readers, they have not had the same commercial success. Using Brooks's argument about gender roles as your starting point, write an essay in which you explain why such magazines have failed to achieve as large a market share as men's "girlie" magazines.

4. Brooks concludes his essay by asserting that "like all socially constructed realities, [the Centerfold Syndrome] can be deconstructed." In class, discuss how such a repudiation of the Centerfold Syndrome might be achieved.

5. Write an essay in which you apply Brooks's notion of the Centerfold Syndrome to the social rituals described in Peter Lyman's "The Fraternal Bond as a Joking Relationship" (p. 471). To what extent do you believe that the young men whom Lyman discusses are influenced by the Centerfold Syndrome?

6. To what extent do sports condition young men to suppress their desire for physical closeness with other human beings? To develop your ideas, consult, in addition to Brooks's essay, Michael A. Messner's "Power at Play" (p. 458).

# ROBIN TOLMACH LAKOFF
## *Women's Language*

‖‖‖‖‖‖‖‖‖‖‖‖‖‖‖‖‖‖‖‖‖‖‖‖‖‖‖‖‖‖‖‖‖‖‖‖‖‖‖‖‖‖‖‖‖

*Do the men in your class tend to dominate during class discussion? Do the women tend to contribute by asking questions? According to Robin Tolmach Lakoff's (b. 1942) linguistic analysis of women's speech patterns, such tendencies may be expected in an environment where the prevailing gender codes compel men to be aggressive and women to be conciliatory. In all cultures, Tolmach argues, women's speech patterns reflect the gender codes of their society, and that wherever one looks, women's speech is defined as "illogical" in comparison with the "logical" norms of male speech. The very form of our speech is political, Lakoff argues in this excerpt from* Talking Power: The Politics of Language in Our Lives *(1990), and reflects the politics of gender in society. Robin Tolmach Lakoff is professor of linguistics at the University of California,*

*Berkeley. Her books include* Language and Woman's Place *(1975),* Face Value: The Politics of Beauty *(with Raquel Scherr, 1984), and* Father Knows Best: The Use and Abuse of Power in Freud's Case of Dora *(1993).*

The characteristic ways of communication that have been identified as typical of women range in English over the whole of the linguistic repertoire, from sounds to word choice to syntactic features to pragmatic and conversational options, with the preponderance in the latter categories. In this, gender-related diversity differs from regional and social dialects, whose most noticeable and numerous variations from the standard cluster in the phonology and the lexicon. This difference makes sense because dialects develop in isolation from one another as a result of the instability of linguistic forms and influence from other languages. But gender-related differences have a strong psychological component: They are intimately related to the judgments of members of a culture about how to be and think like a good man or woman. So the characteristic forms cluster at the end of the linguistic spectrum most related to psychological expression. Also anomalous, if we were disposed to consider women's linguistic patterns as one sort of social dialect, is the fact that they persist despite intense and constant fraternization with speakers of the standard; most dialects tend to erode if speakers are constantly exposed to the standard language. Gender differences in language arise not because male and female speakers are isolated from each other, but precisely because they live in close contiguity, which constantly causes comparisons and reinforces the need for polarization — linguistic and otherwise. As is true of many types of dialects and special linguistic forms, some speakers of women's language, but few speakers of the standard (male language), are able to *code-switch,* that is, use the nonstandard form in some contexts, the standard in others. Women in business or professional settings often sound indistinguishable from their male counterparts. Speakers of nondominant forms must be bilingual in this way, at least passively, to survive; speakers of the dominant form need not be. (So women don't generally complain that men's communication is impossible to understand, but the battle cry "What do women want?" has echoed in one form or another down the centuries.)

Also striking is that some form of women's language exists in every culture that has been investigated with these questions in mind. The same forms are found in language after language. These special forms may differ from one language to another, but most functional characteristics of women's language are widespread, an unremarkable fact since the language represents behavior supposedly typical of women across the majority of cultures: alleged illogic, submissiveness, sexual utility to men, secondary status.

## Reality and Interpretation

As an example of how one form may represent different functions in different cultures, consider . . . the Malagasy special use of conversational logic.[1] Because information in that culture is more precious than it is for us, the prudent speaker hoards any that he acquires, to the point of speaking in a way we would consider deliberately misleading, in violation of the rules of conversational logic; although to our eyes, neither a breach of politeness nor self-protection is involved. But this strategy is typical only of male Malagasy speakers. Women do just the perverse: speak directly and to the point (unless there are obvious reasons to do otherwise). As a result, women are considered poor communicators: They just don't know how to behave in a conversation, don't know how to transmit information properly, and are therefore illogical.

In other words, the Malagasy stereotype of women is identical to ours: Women don't handle the flow of information properly. But the explicit behavior that gives rise to the stereotype is diametrically opposite in the two cultures. So it cannot be that the basis of the stereotype is a universal Aristotelian logical principle. No one decides what communication is intrinsically "logical," then notices that women don't do it, and therefore rationally determines that women are illogical. It's rather the reverse. The dominant group first notices the ways in which the nondominant differ from themselves. They do not think to attribute such differences to external necessity imposed by themselves, or to differences in cultural expectations. Instead, they assume the difference must be due to some deep intrinsic physical and/or psychological distinction that irrevocably divides the sexes: The need for polarization is very strong. Then they decide that there must be some principled difference between men and women to explain the discrepancy. Women are the other; the other is the worse. (That is already given knowledge.) So there is something about women's minds or bodies that makes them be, think, and speak worse than men. Then what men (ideally) do is called "logical." Therefore women's ideal style is "illogical." Whatever is characteristic of the male in a culture will be defined and identified within that culture as "right" or "logical" behavior. Since women are the other, anything they do that is different will be assigned to the opposite pole. Changing their style will not help. If they change it so as to be the same as that of men, they will be seen not as logical beings in their own newfound right, but as men *manqué* or uppity persons striving for privileges they don't deserve. Anything else they do will be seen as illogical, regardless of its form.

---

1. Keenan, E. O. 1976. "The University of Conversational Postulates." *Language in Society* 5:67–80.

## Characteristics of Women's Language

Numerous traits have been said to characterize women's forms of speech in this culture. Not all women use them, and probably no one uses them all the time. (They are, for instance, more likely to show up in informal social circumstances than in business settings.) Men sometimes use them, either with different meanings or for individual special reasons. (Gay men imitate some of them.)[2]

1. Women often seem to hit phonetic points less precisely than men: lisped *s*'s, obscured vowels.
2. Women's intonational contours display more variety than men's.[3]
3. Women use diminutives and euphemisms more than men ("You nickname God's creatures," says Hamlet to Ophelia).
4. Women make more use of expressive forms (adjectives not nouns or verbs and, in that category, those expressing emotional rather than intellectual evaluation) more than men: *lovely, divine.*
5. Women use forms that convey impreciseness: *so, such.*
6. Women use hedges of all kinds more than men.
7. Women use intonation patterns that resemble questions, indicating uncertainty or need for approval.
8. Women's voices are breathier than men's.
9. Women are more indirect and polite than men.
10. Women won't commit themselves to an opinion.
11. In conversation, women are more likely to be interrupted, less likely to introduce successful topics.[4]
12. Women's communicative style tends to be collaborative rather than competitive.
13. More of women's communication is expressed nonverbally (by gesture and intonation) than men's.
14. Women are more careful to be "correct" when they speak, using better grammar and fewer colloquialisms than men.

All of these characteristics can be seen as instantiating one or more of the roles women are supposed to play in this culture. Also notable is the fact that, as suggested by several items on this list, women have communicatively more options than men, more channels legitimately open to them. (That should be seen as a plus, but nonverbal signals are often stig-

---

2. Jespersen, O. 1921. "The Woman," in *Language: Its Nature, Development, and Origin,* chapter 13. New York: W. W. Norton.

3. Lakoff, R. 1975. *Language and Woman's Place.* New York: Harper & Row. This claim is discussed, for instance, along with numbers 3 through 7.

4. Zimmerman, D., and West, C. 1975. "Sex Roles, Interruptions and Silences in Conversations." In B. Thorne and N. Henley, eds., *Language and Sex: Difference and Dominance.* Rowley, Mass.: Newbury House.

matized as distracting, and variety in intonation as hysterical.) At the same time, what they may express, and to whom, is more severely limited. This ambivalence is not unique to language: In many ways, it can be said that women are more constrained in their behavior than men (professionally, sexually); yet less in others (dress, home-versus-career options).

Other generalizations: Womanly communicative behavior is imprecise and indirect (both characteristic of female deference politeness, actually or symbolically leaving interpretation up to the hearer); nonpowerful or nonseeking of power; and more capable of expressing emotions (a trait scorned by the "logical").

The superficial forms themselves may change slightly over time. The way "ideal" women spoke in the 1930s movies (think of Katharine Hepburn or Jean Harlow) is not that of 1950s (Doris Day or Marilyn Monroe), or 1970s (Jane Fonda or Jill Clayburgh) movie heroines. Specific traits shift, but all involve some of the preceding assumptions, for our assessment of their femininity and therefore desirability (and hence ultimately movie bankability) is dependent on stereotypes embedded in the culture.

### Reading the Text

1. How, according to Lakoff, can women be considered "bilingual"?
2. What are the most striking differences between male and female linguistic patterns, as Lakoff sees them?
3. Why does Lakoff include the example from the Malagasy culture in her essay?

### Reading the Signs

1. Study the speech patterns of a woman friend as she speaks both to other women and to men. Then write an essay in which you analyze your friend's linguistic behavior, applying Lakoff's list of traits characterizing women's speech.
2. In small same-sex groups, discuss which of Lakoff's characteristics of women's language (if any) you think are accurate, thinking of your own speech patterns and those of friends. Then share the small-group results with the whole class. Do any gender-related patterns emerge?
3. What would a list of men's speech characteristics look like? Don't just reverse Lakoff's list, but create your own by observing men speaking in both formal and informal circumstances. After you've created your list, write an essay in which you explore the significance of gender differences in speech patterns.

4. To what extent can Lakoff's theory about the gender differences in speech patterns explain the misunderstandings between males and females described in Peter Lyman's "The Fraternal Bond as a Joking Relationship" (p. 471)?

5. Do you agree with Lakoff that gay men imitate some of women's forms of speech? Write an essay illustrating, refuting, or elaborating on this claim, basing your argument in part on interviews that you conduct with gay men. Ask them about their own opinions about their speech patterns and observe those patterns for yourself.

6. At the close of her essay, Lakoff points to movies as showing that, despite superficial changes in women's speech, the traits she describes tend to remain constant in our culture. Test Lakoff's assertion by watching a sampling of movies from three different decades (either rent videotapes or watch them at your school's media library). As you watch the movies, study the speech patterns of the female characters, particularly the leads, looking for the female traits Lakoff lists. Then use the results of your analysis to support, challenge, or modify Lakoff's argument.

# DEBORAH TANNEN
## There Is No Unmarked Woman

||||||||||||||||||||||||||||||||||||||||||||||||||||||

*If you use the pronoun "s/he" when writing, or write "women and men" rather than "men and women," you are not just writing words: You are making a statement that may "mark" you as being a "feminist." In this analysis of the way everything a woman does marks her in some way or other — from writing and speaking to the way she dresses and styles her hair — Deborah Tannen (b. 1945) reveals the asymmetrical nature of gender semiotics in our culture. Wearing makeup or not wearing makeup sends a signal about a woman, whereas a man without makeup sends no signal at all. Tannen's analysis shows how what men do is implicitly considered the norm in society, and so is relatively neutral, while women's difference inevitably marks them, "because there is no unmarked woman." University Professor in Linguistics at Georgetown University, Deborah Tannen is the author of many books, including the best-selling* You Just Don't Understand: Women and Men in Conversation *(1986) and, more recently,* Talking from 9 to 5 *(1994) and* Gender and Discourse *(1994).*

Some years ago I was at a small working conference of four women and eight men. Instead of concentrating on the discussion I found myself looking at the three other women at the table, thinking how each had a different style and how each style was coherent.

One woman had dark brown hair in a classic style, a cross between Cleopatra and Plain Jane. The severity of her straight hair was softened by wavy bangs and ends that turned under. Because she was beautiful, the effect was more Cleopatra than plain.

The second woman was older, full of dignity and composure. Her hair was cut in a fashionable style that left her with only one eye, thanks to a side part that let a curtain of hair fall across half her face. As she looked down to read her prepared paper, the hair robbed her of bifocal vision and created a barrier between her and the listeners.

The third woman's hair was wild, a frosted blond avalanche falling over and beyond her shoulders. When she spoke she frequently tossed her head, calling attention to her hair and away from her lecture.

Then there was makeup. The first woman wore facial cover that    5
made her skin smooth and pale, a black line under each eye and mascara that darkened already dark lashes. The second wore only a light gloss on her lips and a hint of shadow on her eyes. The third had blue bands under her eyes, dark blue shadow, mascara, bright red lipstick and rouge; her fingernails flashed red.

I considered the clothes each woman had worn during the three days of the conference: In the first case, man-tailored suits in primary colors with solid-color blouses. In the second, casual but stylish black T-shirts, a floppy collarless jacket and baggy slacks or a skirt in neutral colors. The third wore a sexy jump suit; tight sleeveless jersey and tight yellow slacks; a dress with gaping armholes and an indulged tendency to fall off one shoulder.

Shoes? No. 1 wore string sandals with medium heels; No. 2, sensible, comfortable walking shoes; No. 3, pumps with spike heels. You can fill in the jewelry, scarves, shawls, sweaters — or lack of them.

As I amused myself finding coherence in these styles, I suddenly wondered why I was scrutinizing only the women. I scanned the eight men at the table. And then I knew why I wasn't studying them. The men's styles were unmarked.

The term "marked" is a staple of linguistic theory. It refers to the way language alters the base meaning of a word by adding a linguistic particle that has no meaning on its own. The unmarked form of a word carries the meaning that goes without saying — what you think of when you're not thinking anything special.

The unmarked tense of verbs in English is the present — for example,    10
*visit*. To indicate past, you mark the verb by adding *ed* to yield *visited*. For

future, you add a word: *will visit.* Nouns are presumed to be singular until marked for plural, typically by adding *s* or *es,* so *visit* becomes *visits* and *dish* becomes *dishes.*

The unmarked forms of most English words also convey "male." Being male is the unmarked case. Endings like *ess* and *ette* mark words as "female." Unfortunately, they also tend to mark them for frivolousness. Would you feel safe entrusting your life to a doctorette? Alfre Woodard, who was an Oscar nominee for best supporting actress, says she identifies herself as an actor because "actresses worry about eyelashes and cellulite, and women who are actors worry about the characters we are playing." Gender markers pick up extra meanings that reflect common associations with the female gender: not quite serious, often sexual.

Each of the women at the conference had to make decisions about hair, clothing, makeup and accessories, and each decision carried meaning. Every style available to us was marked. The men in our group had made decisions, too, but the range from which they chose was incomparably narrower. Men can choose styles that are marked, but they don't have to, and in this group none did. Unlike the women, they had the option of being unmarked.

Take the men's hair styles. There was no marine crew cut or oily longish hair falling into eyes, no asymmetrical, two-tiered construction to swirl over a bald top. One man was unabashedly bald; the others had hair of standard length, parted on one side, in natural shades of brown or gray or graying. Their hair obstructed no views, left little to toss or push back or run fingers through and, consequently, needed and attracted no attention. A few men had beards. In a business setting, beards might be marked. In this academic gathering, they weren't.

There could have been a cowboy shirt with string tie or a three-piece suit or a necklaced hippie in jeans. But there wasn't. All eight men wore brown or blue slacks and nondescript shirts of light colors. No man wore sandals or boots; their shoes were dark, closed, comfortable, and flat. In short, unmarked.

Although no man wore makeup, you couldn't say the men didn't    15 wear makeup in the sense that you could say a woman didn't wear makeup. For men, no makeup is unmarked.

I asked myself what style we women could have adopted that would have been unmarked, like the men's. The answer was none. There is no unmarked woman.

There is no woman's hair style that can be called standard, that says nothing about her. The range of women's hair styles is staggering, but a woman whose hair has no particular style is perceived as not caring about how she looks, which can disqualify her from many positions, and will subtly diminish her as a person in the eyes of some.

Women must choose between attractive shoes and comfortable shoes. When our group made an unexpected trek, the woman who wore flat, laced shoes arrived first. Last to arrive was the woman in spike heels, shoes in hand and a handful of men around her.

If a woman's clothing is tight or revealing (in other words, sexy), it sends a message — an intended one of wanting to be attractive, but also a possibly unintended one of availability. If her clothes are not sexy, that too sends a message, lent meaning by the knowledge that they could have been. There are thousands of cosmetic products from which women can choose and myriad ways of applying them. Yet no makeup at all is anything but unmarked. Some men see it as a hostile refusal to please them.

Women can't even fill out a form without telling stories about 20 themselves. Most forms give four titles to choose from. "Mr." carries no meaning other than that the respondent is male. But a woman who checks "Mrs." or "Miss" communicates not only whether she has been married but also whether she has conservative tastes in forms of address — and probably other conservative values as well. Checking "Ms." declines to let on about marriage (checking "Mr." declines nothing since nothing was asked), but it also marks her as either liberated or rebellious, depending on the observer's attitudes and assumptions.

I sometimes try to duck these variously marked choices by giving my title as "Dr." — and in so doing risk marking myself as either uppity (hence sarcastic responses like "Excuse *me*!") or an overachiever (hence reactions of congratulatory surprise like "Good for you!").

All married women's surnames are marked. If a woman takes her husband's name, she announces to the world that she is married and has traditional values. To some it will indicate that she is less herself, more identified by her husband's identity. If she does not take her husband's name, this too is marked, seen as worthy of comment: She has *done* something; she has "kept her own name." A man is never said to have "kept his own name" because it never occurs to anyone that he might have given it up. For him using his own name is unmarked.

A married woman who wants to have her cake and eat it too may use her surname plus his, with or without a hyphen. But this too announces her marital status and often results in a tongue-tying string. In a list (Harvey O'Donovan, Jonathan Feldman, Stephanie Woodbury McGillicutty), the woman's multiple name stands out. It is marked.

I have never been inclined toward biological explanations of gender differences in language, but I was intrigued to see Ralph Fasold bring biological phenomena to bear on the question of linguistic marking in his book *The Sociolinguistics of Language*. Fasold stresses that language and culture are particularly unfair in treating women as the marked case because biologically it is the male that is marked. While two X chromosomes make a female, two Y chromosomes make nothing. Like the linguistic markers *s, es,* or *ess,* the Y chromosome doesn't "mean" anything unless it is attached to a root form — an X chromosome.

Developing this idea elsewhere Fasold points out that girls are born                        25
with fully female bodies, while boys are born with modified female bodies. He invites men who doubt this to lift up their shirts and contemplate why they have nipples.

In his book, Fasold notes "a wide range of facts which demonstrates that female is the unmarked sex." For example, he observes that there are a few species that produce only females, like the whiptail lizard. Thanks to parthenogenesis, they have no trouble having as many daughters as they like. There are no species, however, that produce only males. This is no surprise, since any such species would become extinct in its first generation.

Fasold is also intrigued by species that produce individuals not involved in reproduction, like honeybees and leaf-cutter ants. Reproduction is handled by the queen and a relatively few males; the workers are sterile females. "Since they do not reproduce," Fasold said, "there is no reason for them to be one sex or the other, so they default, so to speak, to female."

Fasold ends his discussion of these matters by pointing out that if language reflected biology, grammar books would direct us to use "she" to include males and females and "he" only for specifically male referents. But they don't. They tell us that "he" means "he or she," and that "she" is used only if the referent is specifically female. This use of "he" as the sex-indefinite pronoun is an innovation introduced into English by grammarians in the eighteenth and nineteenth centuries, according to Peter Mühlhäusler and Rom Harré in *Pronouns and People.* From at least about 1500, the correct sex-indefinite pronoun was "they," as it still is in casual spoken English. In other words, the female was declared by grammarians to be the marked case.

Writing this article may mark me not as a writer, not as a linguist, not as an analyst of human behavior, but as a feminist — which will have positive or negative, but in any case powerful, connotations for readers. Yet I doubt that anyone reading Ralph Fasold's book would put that label on him.

I discovered the markedness inherent in the very topic of gender after                        30
writing a book on differences in conversational style based on geographical region, ethnicity, class, age, and gender. When I was interviewed, the vast majority of journalists wanted to talk about the differences between women and men. While I thought I was simply describing what I observed — something I had learned to do as a researcher — merely mentioning women and men marked me as a feminist for some.

When I wrote a book devoted to gender differences in ways of speaking, I sent the manuscript to five male colleagues, asking them to alert me to any interpretation, phrasing, or wording that might seem unfairly negative toward men. Even so, when the book came out, I encountered responses like that of the television talk show host who, after interviewing me, turned to the audience and asked if they thought I was male-bashing.

Leaping upon a poor fellow who affably nodded in agreement, she made him stand and asked, "Did what she say accurately describe you?" "Oh, yes," he answered. "That's me exactly." "And what she said about women — does that sound like your wife?" "Oh yes," he responded. "That's her exactly." "Then why do you think she's male-bashing?" He answered, with disarming honesty, "Because she's a woman and she's saying things about men."

To say anything about women and men without marking oneself as either feminist or anti-feminist, male-basher or apologist for men seems as impossible for a woman as trying to get dressed in the morning without inviting interpretations of her character.

Sitting at the conference table musing on these matters, I felt sad to think that we women didn't have the freedom to be unmarked that the men sitting next to us had. Some days you just want to get dressed and go about your business. But if you're a woman, you can't, because there is no unmarked woman.

### Reading the Text

1. Explain in your own words what Tannen means by "marked."
2. Why does Tannen say that men have the option of being "unmarked"?
3. What significance does Tannen see in Ralph Fasold's biological explanations of linguistic gender difference?

### Reading the Signs

1. Do you agree with Tannen's assumption that men have the luxury of remaining "unmarked" in our society? Do you think it's possible to be purely "unmarked"? To develop your essay, you might interview some men, particularly those who elect to have an unconventional appearance, and read Ted Polhemus's "Street Style" (p. 56).
2. In class, survey the extent to which the males and females in your class are "marked" or "unmarked," in Tannen's terms, studying such signs as clothing and hair style. Do the males tend to have "unmarked" styles, while the women tend to send a message by their choices? Discuss the results of your survey, and reflect on the validity of Tannen's claims.

3. Interview at least five women who are married and ask them about their choice of names: Did they keep their "own" name, adopt their husband's, or opt for a hyphenated version? What signals do they want to send about their identity through their names? Use the results of your interviews to write a reflective essay on how our names function as signs, particularly as gender-related signs.

4. Apply Tannen's concept of being "marked" to Sam Fulwood III's "The Rage of the Black Middle Class" (p. 510). To what extent might Fulwood say that being black in American society is to be ethnically "marked"?

5. What would an unmarked appearance for women be like? Write a speculative essay in which you imagine the features of an unmarked female appearance. Share your essay with your class.

MICHAEL  A.  MESSNER

*Power at Play: Sport and Gender Relations*

||||||||||||||||||||||||||||||||||||||||||||||||||||||

*Every little boy should play Little League, right? Sports help to build character, right? Perhaps, but according to Michael A. Messner (b. 1952), the games men play are more than that: They are rituals designed to maintain the ideology and values of a competitive and hierarchical culture. Because masculine identity is rooted in the need to win, athletic competition, according to Messner, causes "men to experience their own bodies as machines . . . and to see other people's bodies as objects of their power and domination." Author of* Power at Play: Sports and the Problem of Masculinity *(1992), from which this selection is excerpted, Messner is Associate Professor in the Department of Sociology and the Program for the Study of Women and Men in Society at the University of Southern California. He is also coeditor of* Men's Lives *(1995) and* Sport, Men, and the Gender Order: Critical Feminist Perspectives *(1990) and coauthor of* Sex, Violence, and Power in Sports: Rethinking Masculinity *(1994).*

*The closer we come to uncovering some form of exemplary masculinity,*
*a masculinity which is solid and sure of itself, the clearer it becomes that*
*masculinity is structured through contradiction: the more it asserts itself,*
*the more it calls itself into question.*

— LYNN SEGAL
*Slow Motion*

In 1973, conservative writer George Gilder, later to become a central theorist of the antifeminist family policies of the Reagan administration, was among the first to sound the alarm that the contemporary explosion of female athletic participation might threaten the very fabric of civilization. "Sports," Gilder wrote, "are possibly the single most important male rite in modern society." The woman athlete "reduces the game from a religious male rite to a mere physical exercise, with some treacherous danger of psychic effect." Athletic performance, for males, embodies "an ideal of beauty and truth," while women's participation represents a "disgusting perversion" of this truth.[1] In 1986, over a decade later, a similar view was expressed by John Carroll in a respected academic journal. Carroll lauded the masculine "virtue and grace" of sport, and defended it against its critics, especially feminists. He concluded that in order to preserve sport's "naturally conserving and creating" tendencies, especially in the realms of "the moral and the religious, . . . women should once again be prohibited from sport: They are the true defenders of the humanist values that emanate from the household, the values of tenderness, nurture and compassion, and this most important role must not be confused by the military and political values inherent in sport. Likewise, sport should not be muzzled by humanist values: it is the living arena for the great virtue of manliness."[2]

The key to Gilder's and Carroll's chest-beating about the importance of maintaining sport as a "male rite" is their neo-Victorian belief that male-female biological differences predispose men to aggressively dominate public life, while females are naturally suited to serve as the nurturant guardians of home and hearth. As Gilder put it, "The tendency to bond with other males in intensely purposeful and dangerous activity is said to come from the collective demands of pursuing large animals. The female body, on the other hand, more closely resembles the body of nonhunting primates. A woman throws, for example, very like a male chimpanzee."[3] This perspective ignores a wealth of historical, anthropological, and biological data that suggest that the equation of males with domination of public life and females with the care of the domestic sphere is a cultural and historical

---

1. G. Gilder, *Sexual Suicide* (New York: Bantam Books, 1973), pp. 216, 218.

2. J. Carroll, "Sport: Virtue and Grace," *Theory Culture and Society 3* (1986), pp. 91–98. Jennifer Hargreaves delivers a brilliant feminist rebuttal to Carroll's masculinist defense of sport in the same issue of the journal. See Je. Hargreaves, "Where's the Virtue? Where's the Grace? A Discussion of the Social Production of Gender through Sport," pp. 109–121.

3. G. Gilder, p. 221.

construction.[4] In fact, Gilder's and Carroll's belief that sport, *a socially constructed institution,* is needed to sustain male-female difference contradicts their assumption that these differences are "natural." As R. W. Connell has argued, social practices that exaggerate male-female difference (such as dress, adornment, and sport) "are part of a continuing effort to sustain a social definition of gender, an effort that is necessary precisely *because the biological logic . . . cannot sustain the gender categories.*"[5]

Indeed, I must argue against the view that sees sport as a natural realm within which some essence of masculinity unfolds. Rather, sport is a social institution that, in its dominant forms, was created by and for men. It should not be surprising, then, that my research with male athletes reveals an affinity between the institution of sport and men's developing identities. As the young males in my study became committed to athletic careers, the gendered values of the institution of sport made it extremely unlikely that they would construct anything but the kinds of personalities and relationships that were consistent with the dominant values and power relations of the larger gender order. The competitive hierarchy of athletic careers encouraged the development of masculine identities based on very narrow definitions of public success. Homophobia and misogyny were the key bonding agents among male athletes, serving to construct a masculine personality that disparaged anything considered "feminine" in women, in other men, or in oneself. The fact that winning was premised on physical power, strength, discipline, and willingness to take, ignore, or deaden pain inclined men to experience their own bodies as machines, as instruments of power and domination — and to see other peoples' bodies as objects of their power and domination.

In short, my research findings are largely consistent with previous feminist analyses of sport. Whether men continue to pursue athletic careers (as many lower-class males do), or whether they shift away from sport toward education and nonathletic careers (as many middle-class males do), they are likely to continue to feel most comfortable, at least into middle adulthood, constructing identities and relationships primarily through their public achievements. As adults, these men will in all likelihood continue to need women (and may even use their power to keep

---

4. For a critical overview of the biological research on male-female difference, see A. Fausto-Sterling, *Myths of Gender: Biological Theories about Men and Women* (New York: Basic Books, 1985). For an overview of the historical basis of male domination, see R. Lee and R. Daly, "Man's Domination and Woman's Oppression: The Question of Origins," in M. Kaufman, ed., *Beyond Patriarchy: Essays by Men on Pleasure, Power, and Change* (Toronto: Oxford University Press, 1987), pp. 30–44.

5. R. W. Connell, *Gender and Power* (Stanford: Stanford University Press, 1987), p. 81 (emphasis in original text).

women) in their "feminine" roles as nurturers, emotion-workers, and mothers, even when these women also have jobs or careers of their own. The result is not only that different "masculine" and "feminine" personality structures are perpetuated, but also that institutional inequities (men's control of public life, women's double workday, etc.) persist.

What my research adds to existing feminist analyses of sport is the   5 recognition that sport does not simply and unambiguously reproduce men's existing power and privilege. Though sport clearly helps to produce culturally dominant conceptions of masculinity, my interviews reveal several strains within the sport/masculinity relationship. Most obviously, men's experiences of athletic careers are not entirely positive, nor are they the same for all men. These facts strongly suggest that sport is not a smoothly functioning, seamless institution, nor is masculinity a monolithic category. There are three factors that undermine sport's ability to construct a single dominant conception of masculinity: (1) the "costs" of athletic masculinity to men; (2) men's different experiences with athletic careers, according to social class, race, and sexual orientation; and (3) current challenges to the equation of sport and heterosexual masculinity, as posed by the rise of women's athletics. To what extent do these tendencies pose fundamental challenges to the institution of sport or to our dominant conceptions of sex and gender?

## The Costs of Athletic Masculinity

As boys, the men in my study were initially attracted to playing sport because it was a primary means to connect with other people — especially fathers, brothers, and male peers. But as these young males became committed to athletic careers, their identities became directly tied to continued public success. Increasingly, it was not just "being there with the guys" but beating the other guys that mattered most. As their need for connection with others became defined more abstractly, through their relationships with "the crowd," their actual relationships with other people tended to become distorted. Other individuals were increasingly likely to be viewed as (male) objects to be defeated or (female) objects to be manipulated and sexually conquered. As a result, the socially learned means through which they constructed their identities (public achievement within competitive hierarchies) did not deliver what was most craved and needed: intimate connection and unity with other people. More often than not, athletic careers have exacerbated existing insecurities and ambivalences in young men's developing identities, thus further diminishing their capacity for intimate relationships with others.

In addition to relational costs, many athletes — especially those in "combat sports" such as football — paid a heavy price in terms of health.

While the successful operation of the male body-as-weapon may have led, for a time, to victories on the athletic field, it also led to injuries and other health problems that lasted far beyond the end of the athletic career.

It is extremely unlikely that a public illumination of the relational and health costs paid by male athletes will lead to a widespread rejection of sport by young males. There are three reasons for this. First, the continued affinity between sport and developing masculine identities suggests that many boys will continue to be attracted to athletic careers for the same reasons they have in the past. Second, since the successful athlete often basks in the limelight of public adoration, the relational costs of athletic masculinity are often not apparent until after the athletic career ends, and he suddenly loses his connection to the crowd. Third, though athletes may recognize the present and future health costs of their athletic careers, they are likely to view them as dues willingly paid. In short, there is a neat enough fit between the psychological and emotional tendencies of young males and the institution of sport that these costs — if they are recognized at all — will be considered "necessary evils," the price men pay for the promise of "being on top."[6]

## Competing Masculinities

Boys' emerging identities may influence them to be attracted to sport, but they nevertheless tend to experience athletic careers differently, based upon variations in class, race, and sexual orientation. Despite their similarities, boys and young men bring different problems, anxieties, hopes, and dreams to their athletic experiences, and thus tend to draw different meanings from, and make different choices about, their athletic careers.

---

6. Indeed, "men's liberationists" of the 1970s were overly optimistic in believing that a public illumination of the "costs of masculinity" would induce men to "reject the male role." See, for instance, W. Farrell, *The Liberated Man* (New York: Bantam Books, 1975); J. Nichols, *Men's Liberation: A New Definition of Masculinity* (New York: Penguin Books, 1975). These men's liberationists underestimated the extent to which the costs of masculinity are linked to the promise of power and privilege. One commentator went so far as to argue that the privileges of masculinity were a "myth" perpetrated by women to keep men in destructive success-object roles. See H. Goldberg, *The Hazards of Being Male: Surviving the Myth of Masculine Privilege* (New York: Signet, 1976). For more recent discussions of the need to analyze both the "costs" and the "privileges" of dominant conceptions of masculinity, see M. E. Kann, "The Costs of Being on Top," *Journal of the National Association for Women Deans, Administrators, and Counselors* 49 (1986): 29–37; and M. A. Messner, "Men Studying Masculinity: Some Epistemological Questions in Sport Sociology," *Sociology of Sport Journal* 7 (1990): 136–153.

### RACE, CLASS, AND THE CONSTRUCTION
### OF ATHLETIC MASCULINITY

My interviews reveal that within a social context stratified by class   10
and by race, the choice to pursue — or not to pursue — an athletic career is determined by the individual's rational assessment of the available
means to construct a respected masculine identity. White middle-class
men were likely to reject athletic careers and shift their masculine striv-
ings to education and nonsport careers. Conversely, men from poor and
blue-collar backgrounds, especially blacks, often perceived athletic careers to be their best chance for success in the public sphere. For nearly
all of the men from lower-class backgrounds, the status and respect that
they received through sport was temporary — it did not translate into
upward mobility.

One might conclude from this that the United States should adopt
a public policy of encouraging young lower-class black males to "just
say no" to sport. This strategy would be doomed to failure, because
poor young black men's decisions to pursue athletic careers can be
viewed as rational, given the constraints that they continue to face. Despite the increased number of black role models in nonsport professions, employment opportunities for young black males actually deteriorated in the 1980s, and nonathletic opportunities in higher education
also declined. By 1985, blacks constituted 14 percent of the college-
aged (18–24 years) U.S. population, but as a proportion of students in
four-year colleges and universities, they had dropped to 8 percent. By
contrast, black men constituted 49 percent of male college basketball
players, and 61 percent of male basketball players in institutions that
grant athletic scholarships.[7] For young black men, then, organized sport
appears to be more likely to get them to college than their own efforts
in nonathletic activities.

In addition to viewing athletic careers as an arena for career success,
there is considerable evidence that black male athletes have used sport as
a cultural space within which to forge a uniquely expressive style of masculinity, a "cool pose." As Majors puts it,

> Due to structural limitations, a black man may be impotent in the in-
> tellectual, political, and corporate world, but he can nevertheless dis-
> play a potent personal style from the pulpit, in entertainment, and in

---

7. W. J. Wilson and K. M. Neckerman, "Poverty and Family Structure: The
Widening Gap between Evidence and Public Policy Issues," in S. H. Danzinger and
D. H. Weinberg, eds., *Fighting Poverty* (Cambridge: Harvard University Press, 1986),
pp. 232–259; F. J. Berghorn et al., "Racial Participation in Men's and Women's Inter-
collegiate Basketball: Continuity and Change, 1958–1985." *Sociology of Sport Journal* 5
(1988), 107–124.

athletic competition, with a verve that borders on the spectacular. Through the virtuosity of a performance, he tips the socially imbalanced scales in his favor and sends the subliminal message: "See me, touch me, hear me, but, white man, you can't copy me!"[8]

In particular, black men have put their "stamp" on the game of basketball. There is considerable pride in U.S. black communities in the fact that black men have come to dominate the higher levels of basketball — and in the expressive style with which they have come to do so. The often aggressive "cool pose" of black male athletes can thus be interpreted as a form of masculinity that symbolically challenges the class constraints and the institutionalized racism that so many young black males face.

### SEXUAL ORIENTATION AND THE CONSTRUCTION OF ATHLETIC MASCULINITY

Until very recently, it was widely believed that gay men did not play organized sports. Nongay people tended to stereotype gay men as "too effeminate" to be athletic. This belief revealed a confusion between sexual orientation and gender. We now know that there is no neat fit between how "masculine" or "feminine" a man is, and whether or not he is sexually attracted to women, to men, to both, or to neither.[9] Interestingly, some gay writers also believed that gay men were not active in sport. For instance, Dennis Altman wrote in 1982 that most gay men were not interested in sport, since they tended to reject the sexual repression, homophobia, and misogyny that are built into the sportsworld.[10]

The belief that gay men are not interested or involved in sport has proven to be wrong. People who made this assumption were observing the overtly masculine and heterosexual culture of sport and then falsely concluding that all of the people within that culture must be heterosexual. My interview with Mike T. and biographies of gay athletes such as David Kopay suggest that young gay males are often attracted to sport because they are just as concerned as heterosexual boys and young men with constructing masculine identities.[11] Indeed, a young closeted gay male like Mike T. may view the projection of an unambiguous mas-     15

---

8. R. Majors, "'Cool Pose': Black Masculinity and Sports," in M. A. Messner and D. F. Sabo, *Sport, Men, and the Gender Order: Critical Feminist Perspectives* (Champaign, Ill.: Human Kinetics Publishers, 1990), p. 111.

9. See S. Kleinberg, "The New Masculinity of Gay Men, and Beyond," in Kaufman, *Beyond Patriarchy*, pp. 120–138.

10. D. Altman, *The Homosexualization of America* (Boston: Beacon Press, 1982).

11. See D. Kopay and P. D. Young, *The Dave Kopay Story* (New York: Arbor House, 1977).

culinity as even more critical than his nongay counterparts do. As Mike told me, "There are a *lot* of gay men in sports," but they are almost all closeted and thus not visible to public view.

As Mike's story illustrates, gay male athletes often share similar motivations and experiences with nongay athletes. This suggests that as long as gay athletes stay closeted, they are contributing to the construction of culturally dominant conceptions of masculinity. However, Brian Pronger's recent research suggests that many gay male athletes experience organized sport in unique ways. In particular, Pronger's interviews with gay male athletes indicate that they have a "paradoxical" relationship to the male athletic culture. Though the institution itself is built largely on the denial (or sublimation) of any erotic bond between men, Pronger argues, many (but not all) gay athletes experience life in the locker room, as well as the excitement of athletic competition, as highly erotic. Since their secret desires (and, at times, secret actions) run counter to the heterosexist culture of the male locker room, closeted gay male athletes develop ironic sensibilities about themselves, their bodies, and the sporting activity itself.[12] Gay men are sexually oppressed through sport, Pronger argues, but the ironic ways they often redefine the athletic context can be interpreted as a form of resistance with the potential to undermine and transform the heterosexist culture of sport.

### THE LIMITS OF MASCULINE RESISTANCES

Men's experience of athletic careers — and the meanings they assign to these experiences — are contextualized by class, race, and sexual orientation. My research, and that of other social scientists, suggests that black male athletes construct and draw on an expressive and "cool" masculinity in order to resist racial oppression. Gay male athletes sometimes construct and draw on an "ironic" masculinity in order to resist sexual oppression. In other words, poor, black, and gay men have often found sport to be an arena in which they can build a masculinity that is, in some ways, resistant to the oppressions they face within hierarchies of intermale dominance.

But how real is the challenge these resistant masculinities pose to the role that sport has historically played in perpetuating existing differences and inequalities? A feminist perspective reveals the limited extent to which we can interpret black and gay athletic masculinities as liberating.

---

12. B. Pronger, "Gay Jocks: A Phenomenology of Gay Men in Athletics," in Messner and Sabo, *Sport, Men, and the Gender Order,* pp. 141–152; and *The Arena of Masculinity: Sports, Homosexuality, and the Meaning of Sex* (New York: St. Martin's Press, 1990).

Through a feminist lens, we can see that in adopting as their expressive vehicle many of the dominant aspects of athletic masculinity (narrow definitions of public success; aggressive, sometimes violent competition; glorification of the athletic male body-as-machine; verbal misogyny and homophobia), poor, black, and gay male athletes contribute to the continued subordination of women, as well as to the circumscription of their own relationships and development.

Tim Carrigan, Bob Connell, and John Lee assert that rather than undermining social inequality, men's struggles within class, racial, and sexual hierarchies of intermale dominance serve to reinforce men's global subordination of women. Although strains caused by differences and inequalities among men represent potential avenues for social change, ultimately, "the fissuring of the categories 'men' and 'women' is one of the central facts about a patriarchal power and the way it works. In the case of men, the crucial division is between hegemonic masculinity and various subordinated masculinities."[13] Hegemonic masculinity is thus defined in relation to various subordinated masculinities as well as in relation to femininities. This is a key insight for the contemporary meaning of sport. Utilizing the concept of "multiple masculinities," we can begin to understand how race, class, age, and sexual hierarchies among men help to construct and legitimize men's overall power and privilege over women. In addition, the false promise of sharing in the fruits of hegemonic masculinity often ties black, working-class, or gay men into their marginalized and subordinate status. For instance, my research suggests that while black men's development of "cool pose" within sport can be interpreted as creative resistance against one form of social domination (racism), it also demonstrates the limits of an agency that adopts other forms of social domination (athletic masculinity) as its vehicle.

My research also suggests how homophobia within athletic masculine cultures tends to lock men — whether gay or not — into narrowly defined heterosexual identities and relationships. Within the athletic context, homophobia is closely linked with misogyny in ways that ultimately serve to bond men together as superior to women. Given the extremely oppressive levels of homophobia within organized sport, it is understandable why the vast majority of gay male athletes would decide to remain closeted. But the public construction of a heterosexual/masculine status requires that a closeted gay athlete actively participate in (or at the very least, tolerate) the ongoing group expressions of homophobia and misogyny — what Mike T. called "locker room garbage." 20

---

13. T. Carrigan, B. Connell, and J. Lee, "Hard and Heavy: Toward a New Sociology of Masculinity," *Theory and Society* 14 (1985): 551–603.

Thus, though he may feel a sense of irony, and may even confidentially express that sense of irony to gay male friends or to researchers, the public face that the closeted gay male athlete presents to the world is really no different from that of his nongay teammates. As long as he is successful in this public presentation-of-self as heterosexual/masculine, he will continue to contribute to (and benefit from) men's power over women.

### SPORT IN GAY COMMUNITIES

The fissuring of the category "men," then, as it is played out within the dominant institution of sport, does little to threaten — indeed, may be a central mechanism in — the reconstruction of existing class, racial, sexual, and gender inequalities.[14] Nevertheless, since the outset of the gay liberation movement in the early 1970s, organized sport has become an integral part of developing gay and lesbian communities. The ways that "gay" sports have been defined and organized are sometimes different — even radically different — than the dominant institution of sport in society.

The most public sign of the growing interest in athletics in gay communities was the rapid growth and popularity of bodybuilding among many young, urban gay men in the 1970s and early 1980s. The meanings of gay male bodybuilding are multiple and contradictory.[15] On the one hand, gay male bodybuilding overtly eroticizes the muscular male body, thus potentially disrupting the tendency of sport to eroticize male bodies under the guise of aggression and competition. On the other hand, the building of muscular bodies is often motivated by a conscious need by gay men to prove to the world that they are "real men." Gay bodybuilding thus undermines cultural stereotypes of

---

14. One potentially important, but largely unexplored, fissure among men is that between athletes and nonathletes. There are tens of millions of boys who do *not* pursue athletic careers. Many boys dislike sport. Others may yearn to be athletes, but may not have the body size, strength, physical capabilities, coordination, emotional predisposition, or health that is necessary to successfully compete in sports. What happens to these boys and young men? What kinds of adult masculine identities and relationships do they eventually develop? Does the fact of not having been an athlete play any significant role in their masculine identities, goals, self-images, and relationships? The answers to these questions, of course, lie outside the purview of my study. But they are key to understanding the contemporary role that sport plays in constructions of gender.

15. For interesting discussions of bodybuilding, gender, and sexuality, see B. Glassner, *Bodies: Why We Look the Way We Do (and How We Feel about It)* (New York: G. P. Putnam's Sons, 1988); A. M. Klein, "Little Big Man: Hustling, Gender Narcissism, and Homophobia in Bodybuilding," in Messner and Sabo, *Sport, Men, and the Gender Order*, pp. 127–140.

homosexual men as "nelly," effeminate, and womanlike. But it also tends to adopt and promote a very conventional equation of masculinity with physical strength and muscularity.[16] In effect, then, as gay bodybuilders attempt to sever the cultural link between masculinity and heterosexuality, they uncritically affirm a conventional dichotomization of masculinity/male vs. femininity/female.

By contrast, some gay athletes have initiated alternative athletic institutions that aim to challenge conventional views of sexuality and gender. Originally Mike T. had gone into sport to prove that he was "male," and cover up the fact that he was gay. When his career as an Olympic athlete finally ended, he came out publicly, and soon was a very active member of the San Francisco Bay Area gay community. He rekindled his interest in the arts and dance. He also remained very active in athletics, and he increasingly imagined how wonderful it would be to blend the beauty and exhilaration of sport, as he had experienced it, with the emergent, liberating values of the feminist, gay, and lesbian communities of which he was a part. In 1982, his dream became a reality, as 1,300 athletes from twelve different nations gathered in San Francisco to participate in the first ever Gay Games.[17]

Though many of the events in the Gay Games are "conventional" sports (track and field, swimming, etc.), and a number of "serious athletes" compete in the events, overall the Games reflect a value system and a vision based on feminist and gay liberationist ideals of equality and universal participation. As Mike T. said,

---

16. Alan Klein's research revealed that nongay male bodybuilders are also commonly motivated by a need to make a public statement with their muscular bodies that they are indeed "masculine." To the nongay bodybuilder, muscles are the ultimate sign of heterosexual masculinity. But, ironically, as one nongay male bodybuilder put it, "We're everything the U.S. is supposed to stand for: strength, determination, everything to be admired. But it's not the girls that like us, it's the fags!" Interestingly, Klein found that many male bodybuilders who defined themselves as "straight" (including the one quoted above) made a living by prostituting themselves to gay men. See Klein, "Little Big Man," p. 135.

For a thought-provoking feminist analysis of the contradictory relationship between gay male sexuality and masculinity, see T. Edwards, "Beyond Sex and Gender: Masculinity, Homosexuality and Social Theory," in J. Hearn and D. Morgan, eds., *Men, Masculinities, and Social Theory* (London: Unwin Hyman, 1990), pp. 110–123.

17. The Gay Games were originally called the "Gay Olympics," but the U.S. Olympic Committee went to court to see that the word "Olympics" was not used to denote this event. Despite the existence of "Police Olympics," "Special Olympics," "Senior Olympics," "Xerox Olympics," "Armenian Olympics," even "Crab Cooking Olympics," the U.S.O.C. chose to enforce their control legally over the term "Olympics" when it came to the "Gay Olympics." For further discussion of the politics of the Gay Games, see M. A. Messner, "Gay Athletes and the Gay Games: An Interview With Tom Waddell," *M: Gentle Men for Gender Justice* 13 (1984): 13–14.

> You don't win by beating someone else. We defined winning as doing your very best. That way, everyone is a winner. And we have age-group competition, so all ages are involved. We have parity: If there's a men's sport, there's a women's sport to complement it. And we go out and recruit in Third World and minority areas. All of these people are gonna get together for a week, they're gonna march in together, they're gonna hold hands, and they'll say, "Jesus Christ! This is wonderful!" There's this *discovery*: "I had no idea women were such fun!" and, "God! Blacks are okay — I didn't do anything to offend him, and we became *friends!*" and, "God, that guy over there is in his sixties, and I had no *idea* they were so sexually *active!*" — [laughs].

This emphasis on bridging differences, overcoming prejudices, and building relationships definitely enhanced the athletic experience for one participant I interviewed. This man said that he loved to swim, and even loved to compete, because it "pushed" him to swim "a whole lot better." Yet in past competitions, he had always come in last place. As he put it, "The Gay Games were just wonderful in many respects. One of them was that people who came in second, or third, and *last* got standing ovations from the crowd — the crowd genuinely recognized the thrill of giving a damn good shot, regardless of where you came in, and gave support to that. Among the competitors, there was a whole lot of joking and supportiveness."

In 1986, 3,482 athletes participated in Gay Games II in San Francisco. In 1990, at Gay Games III in Vancouver, 7,200 athletes continued the vision of building, partly through sport, an "exemplary community" that eliminates sexism, homophobia, and racism. Mike T. described what the Gay Games mean to him:

> To me, it's one of those steps in a thousand-mile journey to try and raise consciousness and enlighten people — *not* just people outside the gay community, but within the gay community as well, [because] we're just as racist, ageist, nationalistic, and chauvinistic as anybody else. Maybe it's simplistic to some people, you know, but why does it have to be complicated? Put people in a position where they can experience this process of discovery, and here it is! I just hope that this is something that'll take hold and a lot of people will get the idea.

The Gay Games represent a radical break from past and current conceptions of the role of sport in society. But they do not represent a major challenge to sport as an institution. Alternative athletic venues like the Gay Games, since they exist outside of the dominant sports institution, do not directly confront or change the dominant structure. On the other hand, these experiments are valuable in terms of demonstrating the fact that alternative value systems and structures are possible.[18]

### Reading the Text

1. Why, in Messner's view, did conservatives such as George Gilder and John Carroll want to prohibit women from competing in athletic competitions?
2. What does Messner mean when he says that "sports is a social institution that . . . was created by and for men"?
3. What, according to Messner, are the "costs" that men must pay for participating in sports?
4. What roles do class, race, and sexual orientation play in the construction of athletic masculinity, according to Messner?
5. In what ways, according to Messner, do the Gay Games differ from the Olympic Games?

### Reading the Signs

1. In your journal, explore what athletic participation, whether in organized sports such as Little League or in informal activities such as jogging or hiking, has meant to you. Do you believe that the participation has shaped your attitudes about gender roles? If you haven't participated much in sports, what is your attitude toward athletic competition?
2. Write an argumentative essay challenging or supporting George Gilder's position that the female athlete "reduces the game from a religious male rite to a mere physical exercise, with some treacherous danger of psychic effect."
3. In class, outline the racial and gender coding of professional sports. Which ethnicities dominate which sports? In which sports, if any, have women received social acceptance? Then discuss the reasons for the ethnic and gender patterns you have found.

---

18. During the 1982 Gay Games in San Francisco, the major local newspapers tended to cover the Games mostly in the "lifestyle" sections of the paper, not in the sports pages. Alternative sports demonstrate the difficulties of attempting to change sport in the absence of larger institutional transformations. For instance, the European sport of korfball was developed explicitly as a sex-egalitarian sport. The rules of korfball aim to neutralize male-female biological differences that may translate into different levels of ability. But recent research shows that old patterns show up, even among the relatively "enlightened" korfball players. Korfball league officials are more likely to be male than female. More important, the more "key" roles within the game appear to be dominated by men, while women are partially marginalized. See D. Summerfield and A. White, "Korfball: A Model of Egalitarianism?" *Sociology of Sport Journal* 6 (1989): 144–151.

4. Study a magazine such as *Sports Illustrated* and then write an essay in which you explain the extent to which the magazine perpetuates the traditional attitudes toward gender roles that Messner claims sports encourage.
5. In class, form mixed-gender teams and debate Messner's contention that sports encourages homophobia and misogyny.

PETER  LYMAN

*The Fraternal Bond as a Joking Relationship*

||||||||||||||||||||||||||||||||||||||||||||||||||||||||||

*Let's face it: College fraternities aren't Boy Scout troops. With the reported incidence of fraternity-based date rapes on the rise and controversies about songbooks with racially and sexually offensive lyrics raging at universities from coast to coast, the Greeks are looking increasingly out of step with contemporary standards of behavior. But as Peter Lyman (b. 1940) shows in this anthropological study of the fraternal world view, the aggressiveness, the stunts, the ribald drinking songs are all part of a bonding ritual by which the boys group together in defense against what they see as threats from the worlds of work and of women. Being cool, and being tough, mean being in control for young men who feel the world slipping out of their grasp. Peter Lyman is university librarian and professor, School of Information Management and Systems, at the University of California, Berkeley. His research interests include the sociology of information, computer literacy, and electronic libraries.*

One evening during dinner, forty-five fraternity men suddenly broke into the dining room of a nearby campus sorority, surrounded the thirty women residents, and forced them to watch while one pledge gave a speech on Freud's theory of penis envy as another demonstrated various techniques of masturbation with a rubber penis. The women sat silently staring downward at their plates listening for about ten minutes, until a woman law student who was the graduate resident in charge of the house walked in, surveyed the scene, and demanded, "Please leave immediately!" As she later described that moment, "There was a mocking roar from the men, 'It's tradition.' I said, 'That's no reason to do something like this, please leave!' And they left. I was surprised. Then the women in the house started to get angry. And the guy who made the penis envy speech came back and said to us, 'That was funny to me. If that's not funny to you I don't know what kind of sense of humor you have, but I'm sorry.'"

That night the women sat around the stairwell of their house discussing the event, some angry and others simply wanting to forget the whole thing. They finally decided to ask the university to require that the men return to discuss the event. When university officials threatened to take action, the men agreed to the meeting. I was asked by both the men and the women involved to attend the discussion as a facilitator, and was given permission to write about the event as long as I concealed their identities.

In the women's view, the joke had not failed because of its subject; they considered sexual jokes to be a normal part of the erotic joking relationship between men and women. They criticized its emotional structure, the mixture of sexuality with aggression and the atmosphere of physical intimidation in the room. Although many of the men individually regretted the damage to their relationship with women friends in the group, they argued that the special group solidarity created by the initiation was a unique form of masculine friendship that justified the inconvenience caused the women.

Fraternal group bonding in everyday life frequently takes the form of *joking relationships,* in which men relate to each other by exchanging insults and jokes in order to create a feeling of solidarity that negotiates the latent tension and aggression they feel toward each other (Radcliffe-Brown, 1959). The humor of joking relationships is generally sexual and aggressive, and frequently consists of sexist or racist jokes. As Freud (1960:99) observed, the jokes men direct *toward* women are generally sexual, tend to be clever (like double entendres), and have a seductive purpose; but the jokes that men tell *about* women in the presence of other men tend to be sexist rather than intimate or erotic, and use hostile and aggressive rather than clever verbal forms. In this case study, joking relationships will be analyzed to uncover the emotional dynamics of fraternal groups and the impact of fraternal bonding upon relationships between men and women.

## The Girls' Story

The women had frequently been the target of fraternity initiation rites in the past, and generally enjoyed this joking relationship with the men, if with a certain ambivalence. "There was the naked Christmas Carol event, they were singing 'We wish you a Merry Christmas,' and 'Bring on the hasty pudding' was the big line they liked to yell out. And they had five or six pledges who had to strip in front of the house and do naked jumping jacks on the lawn, after all the women in the house were lined up on the steps to watch." The women did not think these events were hostile because they had been invited to watch, and the men stood with them watching, suggesting that the pledges, not the women, were the targets of the joke. This defined the joke as sexual, not sexist, and part of the normal erotic joking relation between "guys and girls." Still, these jokes were ritual events, not real social relationships. One woman said, "We were just supposed to watch, and the guys were watching us watch. The men set up the stage and the women are brought along to observe. They were the controlling force, then they jump into the car and take off."

At the meeting with the men, two of the women spoke for the group while eleven others sat silently in the center, surrounded by about thirty men. The first woman began, "Your humor was pretty funny as long as it was sexual, but when it went beyond sexual to sexist, then it became painful. You were saying 'I'm better than you.' When you started using sex as a way of proving your superiority, it hurt me and made me angry."

The second woman said that the fraternity's raid had the tone of a rape. "I admit we knew you were coming over, and we were whispering about it. But it went too far, and I felt afraid to say anything. Why do men always think about women in terms of violating them, in sexual imagery? You have to understand that the combination of a sexual topic with the physical threat of all of you standing around terrified me. I couldn't move. You have to realize that when men combine sexuality and force, it's terrifying to women."

Many of the women began by saying, "I'm not a feminist, but . . . ," to reassure the men that although they felt angry, they hoped to reestablish the many individual friendships that had existed between men and women in the two groups. In part the issue was resolved when the women accepted the men's construction of the event as a joke, although a failed joke, transforming a discussion about sexuality and force into a debate about good and bad jokes.

For an aggressive joke to be funny, and most jokes contain some hostility, the joke teller must send the audience a cue that says "this is meant as a joke." If accepted, the cue invokes special social rules that "frame" the hostile words that are typical of jokes, ensuring they will not be taken seriously. The men had implicitly sent such a cue when they stood *next* to the women during the naked jumping jacks. Verbal aggression mediated by the joke form will generally be without later consequences in the everyday world, and will be judged in terms of the formal intention of jokes, shared play and laughter.

In accepting the construction of the event as "just a joke" the women absolved the men of responsibility for their actions by calling them "little boys." One woman said, "It's not wrong, they're just boys playing a prank. They're little boys, they don't know what they're doing. It was unpleasant, but we shouldn't make a big deal out of it." In appealing to the rules of the joke form (as in saying "That was funny to me, I don't know what kind of sense of humor you have"), the men sacrificed their personal friendships with the women in order to protect the feelings of fraternal solidarity it produced. In calling the men "little boys" the women were bending the rules of friendship, trying to preserve their relationships to the guys by playing a patient and nurturing role.

### The Guys' Story

Aside from occasional roars of laughter, the men interrupted the women only once. When a woman began to say that the men had obviously intended to intimidate them, the men loudly protested that the women couldn't possibly judge their intentions, that they intended the whole event only as a joke, and the intention of a joke is, by definition, just fun.

At this point the two black men in the fraternity intervened to explain the rules of male joking relationships to the women. In a sense, they said, they agreed with the women, being the object of hostile jokes is painful. As they described it, the collective talk of the fraternity at meals and group events was entirely hostile joking, including many racist jokes. One said, "I'd had to listen to things in the house that I'd have hit someone for saying if I'd heard them outside." The guys roared with laughter, for the fraternal joking relation consisted almost entirely of aggressive words that were barely contained by the convention that joke tellers are not responsible for what they say.

One woman responded, "Maybe people should be hit for saying those things, maybe that's the right thing to do." But the black speaker was trying to explain the rules of male joke culture to the women, "If you'd just ignored us, it wouldn't have been any fun." To ignore a joke, even though it makes you feel hurt or angry, is to be cool, one of the primary masculine ideals of the group.

Another man tried to explain the failure of the joke in terms of the difference between the degree of "crudeness" appropriate "between guys" and between "guys and girls." He said, "As I was listening to the speech I was both embarrassed and amused. I was standing at the edge of the room, near the door, and when I looked at the guys I was laughing but when I looked at the girls I was embarrassed. I could see both sides at the same time. It was too crude for your sense of propriety. We have a sense of crudeness you don't have. That's a cultural aspect of the difference between girls and guys."

The other men laughed as he mentioned "how crude we are at the     15
house," and one of the black men added, "You wouldn't believe how
crude it gets." Many of the men later said that although they individually
found the jokes about women vulgar, the jokes were justified because
they were necessary for the formation of the fraternal bond. These men
thought that the mistake had been to reveal their crudeness to the
women; this was "in bad taste."

In part the crudeness was a kind of "signifying" or "dozens," a ritual
exchange of intimate insults that creates group solidarity. "If there's one
theme that goes on it's the emphasis on being able to take a lot of
ridicule, of shit, and not getting upset about it. Most of the interaction
we have is verbally abusing each other, making disgusting references to
your mother's sexuality, or the women you were seen with, or your sex
organ, the size of your sex organ. And you aren't cool unless you can
take it without trying to get back." Being cool is an important male
value in other settings as well, like sports or work; the joking relationship
is a kind of training that, in one guy's words, "teaches you how to keep
in control of your emotions."

But the guys themselves would not have described their group as a
joking relationship or fraternal bond, they called it friendship. One man
said that he had found perhaps a dozen guys in the house who were special friends, "guys I could cry in front of." Another said, "I think the
guys are very close, they would do nearly anything for each other, drive
each other places, give each other money. I think when they have problems about school, their car, or something like that, they can talk to each
other. I'm not sure they can talk to each other about problems with
women though." Although the image of crying in front of the other
guys was often mentioned as an example of the intimacy of the fraternal
bond, no one could actually recall anyone in the group ever crying. In
fact crying would be an admission of vulnerability which would violate
the ideals of "strength" and "being cool."

The women interpreted the sexist jokes as a sign of vulnerability.
"The thing that struck me the most about our meeting together," one
said, "was when the men said they were afraid of trusting women, afraid
of being seen as jerks." One of the guys added, "I think down deep all
the guys would love to have satisfying relationships with women. I think
they're scared of failing, of having to break away from the group they've
become comfortable with. I think being in a fraternity, having close
friendships with men is a replacement for having close relationships with
women. It'd be painful for them because they'd probably fail." These
men preferred to relate to women as a group at fraternity parties, where
they could take women back to their rooms for quick sex without
commitments.

Sexist jokes also had a social function, policing the boundaries of the
group, making sure that guys didn't form serious relationships with girls

and leave the fraternity (cf. Slater, 1963). "One of the guys just acquired a girlfriend a few weeks ago. He's someone I don't think has had a woman to be friends with, maybe ever, at least in a long time. Everybody has been ribbing him intensely the last few weeks. It's good natured in tone. Sitting at dinner they've invented a little song they sing to him. People yell questions about his girlfriend, the size of her vagina, does she have big breasts." Thus, in dealing with women, the group separated intimacy from sex, defining the male bond as intimate but not sexual (homosocial), and relationships with women as sexual but not intimate (heterosexual).

### The Fraternal Bond in Men's Life Cycle

Men often speak of friendship as a group relationship, not a dyadic one, and men's friendships often grow from the experience of shared activities or risk, rather than from self-disclosing talk (cf. Rubin, 1983:130). J. Glenn Gray (1959:89–90) distinguishes the intimate form of friendship from the comradeship that develops from the shared experience of suffering and danger of men at war. In comradeship, he argues, the individual's sense of self is subordinated to a group identity, whereas friendship is based upon a specific feeling for another that heightens a sense of individuality. 20

In this case, the guys used joking relationships to suspend the ordinary rules and responsibilities of everyday life, placing the intimacy of the fraternal group in competition with heterosexual friendships. One of the men had been inexpressive as he listened to the discussion, but spoke about the fraternity in a voice filled with emotion: "The penis envy speech was a hilarious idea, great college fun. That's what I joined the fraternity for, a good time. College is a stage in my life to do crazy and humorous things. In ten years when I'm in the business world I won't be able to carry on like this [loud laughter from the men]. The initiation was intended to be humorous. We didn't think through how sensitive you women were going to be."

This speech gives the fraternal bond a specific place in the life cycle. The joking relationship is a ritual bond that creates a male group bond in the transition between boyhood and manhood: after the separation from the family where the authority of mothers limits fun, but before becoming subject to the authority of work. One man later commented on the transitional nature of the fraternal bond, "I think a lot of us are really scared of losing total control over our own lives. Having to sacrifice our individuality. I think we're scared of work in the same way we're scared of women." The jokes expressed hostility toward women because an intimate friendship with a woman was associated with "loss of control," namely the risk of responsibility for work and family.

Most, but not all, of the guys in the fraternity were divided between their group identity and a sense of personal identity that was expressed in private friendships with women. Some of the guys, like the one who could "see both sides" as he stood on the edge of the group during the initiation, had reached a point of leaving the fraternity because they couldn't reconcile the tension between his group identity and the sense of self that he felt in his friendships with women.

Ultimately the guys justified the penis envy joke because it created a special kind of male intimacy. But although the fraternal group was able to appropriate the guys' needs for intimacy and commitment it is not clear that it was able to satisfy those needs, because it defined strength as shared risk taking rather than a quality of individual character or personality. In Gray's terms, the guys were constructing comradeship through an erotic of shared activities with an element of risk, shared danger, or rule breaking such as sports, paramilitary games, wild parties, and hostile jokes. In these contexts, strength implied the substitution of a group identity for a personal code that might extend to commitment and care for others (cf. Bly 1982).

In the guys' world, aggression was identified with strength, and defined as loss of control only if it was angry. The fraternal bond was built upon an emotional balance between aggression and anger, for life of the group centered upon the mobilization of aggressive energies in rule-governed activities, especially sports and games. In each arena aggression was defined as strength (toughness) only when it was rule-governed (cool). Getting angry was called "losing control," and the guys thought they were most likely to lose control when they experienced themselves as personally dependent, that is, in relationships with women and at work. The sense of order within fraternal groups is based upon the belief that all members are equally dependent upon the rules, and that no *personal* dependence is created within the group. This is not true of the family or of relations with women, both of which are intimate, and, from the guys' point of view, are "out of control" because they are governed by emotional commitments.

The guys recognized the relationship between their male bond and the work world by claiming that "high officials of the University know about the way we act, and they understand what we are doing." Although this might be taken as evidence that the guys were internalizing their fathers' norms and thus inheriting the rights of patriarchy, the guys described their fathers as slaves to work and women, not as patriarchs. It is striking that the guys would not accept the notion that men have more power than women; to them it is not men who rule, but work and women that govern men.

**REFERENCES**

Bly, Robert. (1982) "What men really want: An interview with Keith Thompson."
   *New Age* 30–37, 50–51.
Freud, Sigmund. (1960) *Jokes and Their Relation to the Unconscious.* New York: W. W.
   Norton.
Gray, Glenn J. (1959) *The Warriors: Reflections on Men in Battle.* New York: Harper.
Radcliffe-Brown, Alfred. (1959) *Structure and Function in Primitive Society.* Glencoe: The
   Free Press.
Rubin, Lillian. (1983) *Intimate Strangers.* New York: Harper & Row.
Slater, Phillip. (1963) "On Social Regression." *The American Sociological Review* 28:
   339–364.

## Reading the Text

1. Summarize in your own words the differences between male joke culture
   and female joke culture.
2. How, according to Lyman, did the black fraternity members play a different role than the whites in the meeting with the female students?
3. Why did the women interpret the fraternity stunt as a "sign of vulnerability"?
4. What is the difference between intimacy and comradeship, in Lyman's
   terms?

## Reading the Signs

1. In small same-sex groups, brainstorm ways in which both the men and
   women could have more effectively signaled their intentions and
   responses to the fraternity stunt incident. How, in other words, might you
   alter the situation so that all parties involved would have considered the
   joke a joke? Then share your group's suggestions with the whole class. Do
   you see any patterns in the suggestions provided by male and female
   groups?
2. Using Holly Devor's "Gender Role Behaviors and Attitudes" (p. 415) as
   your critical framework, write an essay explaining the extent to which the
   fraternity members were enacting traditionally masculine roles and the
   sorority women were enacting traditionally feminine roles.
3. Interview members of fraternities and sororities on campus to learn
   whether pranks similar to the one Lyman describes occur. If so, ask both
   males and females about the motivation behind the pranks and their responses to them. Then write an essay in which you explore the pranks'
   significance to the men and women who participate in them. Do you find
   gender differences among your interviewees? Do all parties find such
   pranks equally funny? Is the source of the humor the same for both
   groups?

4. Compare the value of being cool for the fraternity men with the "cool pose" adopted by African-American males (see the discussion of Richard Majors's work in Michael A. Messner's "Power at Play," p. 458). How can each be seen as a mechanism for surviving in the world? How do class and ethnicity affect the meaning of being cool for each group?

5. Think of a group with which you have close relations (it could be a fraternity or sorority; a club; a political, sports, or religious group; or simply a group of friends). In your journal, reflect on the ways you've bonded with others in the group. What signs do you send to each other — and to outsiders — to indicate your solidarity? What difference does it make that your group is same-sex or mixed? Is your relationship with group members, in Lyman's terms, more intimate or more comradely?

6. One of the current controversies on campuses across the nation involves fraternity pranks and songbooks, which often include racially charged and sexually violent lyrics. Do you think there should be restrictions on such pranks or songbooks, as have been instituted on many college campuses? In class, form two teams and debate this issue, focusing on a controversy at your own campus or elsewhere (research this issue by first checking the *Readers' Guide to Periodical Literature* in your library).

# THE RACE CARD

## Readings in Multicultural Semiotics

The Los Angeles riots. Proposition 187. The "trial of the century." The Million Man March. The controversy over affirmative action.

You don't have to go very far to discover potent signifiers of the state of race relations in America as the 1990s unfold as a decade of racial conflict. From the fiery upheaval in L.A. to the O. J. Simpson trial, from the increase in hate crimes to the debate over affirmative action, racial division is emerging as a central issue of our time. And no matter what position you hold, you are likely to have some pretty strong feelings on the matter.

It wasn't supposed to have turned out this way, of course. In the years between the Civil Rights movement of the sixties and the multicultural initiatives of the eighties, the challenge of racial conflict was supposed to have been answered. A resolution was supposed to be in sight. But, to paraphrase William Butler Yeats's poem "The Second Coming," things fell apart. Not only did the long-standing division between black and white America remain, but the division multiplied, bringing other ethnicities into a conflict that now pits race against race in a variety of directions. The traditional black and white screen of American racial politics has become technicolor.

It would be nice to be able to claim that a semiotic understanding of racial conflicts in our country will bring a comfortable resolution of them. We can't claim that, of course. There's too much pain, too much emotion, too many irrational forces out there to be overcome by a rational semiotic analysis. Still, as students — particularly in a class designed to train you in critical thinking — you are in an optimal position to analyze America's race relations, using the tools of critical reasoning. Semiotics can help you do that, because, while it does not offer solutions to cultural problems, it can shed light on many of their origins. And we can't begin to solve those problems until we have a clear understanding of what they are.

## Interpreting Multicultural Semiotics

The semiotics of race begins with the fundamental semiotic principle that one's worldview is determined by one's culture. To put this another way, *what* you believe depends upon *who* you are. So, let's start with a simple question: "Who are you?" Ask it of a classmate. Of yourself. What's the answer? Did your classmate give her name? Did you? Or did each of you answer differently? Did you say "I am an American"? Or did you say "I am an African-American," or an "Asian-American," or a "Latino," or a "Native American"? Would you answer "I am a European-American" or a "Jewish-American"? However you answered the question, can you say why you answered as you did?

To ask how you identify yourself and why you identify as you do is to begin to probe the semiotics of race and culture in America's multicultural society. Some of you may believe that there is a right answer to our question, that it is essential that all Americans think of themselves as *Americans* first and foremost. Others of you may believe just as strongly that your ethnic and cultural identity comes first. In either case, your beliefs reflect a worldview, or cultural mythology, that guides you in your most fundamental thoughts about your identity. Let's look at those myths for a moment.

Say that you feel that all American citizens should view themselves simply as Americans, without all the hyphens. If so, your feelings reflect a basic cultural mythology best known as the myth of the American "melting pot." This is the belief that America offers all of its citizens the opportunity to blend together into one harmonious whole that will erase the many differences among us on behalf of a new, distinctly American, identity. This belief has led many immigrants to seek to assimilate into what they perceive as the dominant American culture, shedding the specific cultural characteristics that might distinguish them from what they see as the American norm. And it is a belief that stands behind some of the most generous impulses in our culture — at least ideally.

But what if you don't buy this belief? What if, as far as you are concerned, you're proud to belong to a different community, one that differs from the basically Anglo-Saxon culture that has become the dominant, and normative, culture for assimilation? Or what if you and your people have found that you were never really allowed to blend in anyway, that in spite of the promise, the melting pot was never meant for you? If so, how does the myth of the melting pot look to you? Does it look the same as it would to someone who never had any trouble assimilating, or never needed to assimilate, because he or she already belonged to the dominant culture?

To see that the myth of the melting pot will look different depending upon who is looking at it is to see why it is so precious to some Americans and so irrelevant to others. It is to realize again the fundamental semiotic precept that our social values are culturally determined rather than inscribed in the marble of absolute truth. This idea may be difficult to accept, especially if you and your classmates all come from the same culture and hence all hold the same values. But if you know people who are different, you might want to ask them how the myth of the melting pot looks from their perspective. Does it look like an ideal that our nation should strive to achieve? Or does it look like an invitation to cultural submission? It all depends on who's looking.

The failure to recognize that different people view the melting pot differently is one of the major sources of racial misunderstanding and, thus, racial conflict in America today. On the one hand, we need to realize that many Americans, particularly nonwhites, have felt excluded from full economic and cultural participation in American life and may deeply resent the view that we all should just see ourselves as Americans — with no hyphens. But on the other hand, we also need to realize that many of today's Americans descend from non-Anglo-Saxon European immigrants who embraced the image of the melting pot, prospered, and passed their gratitude on to their descendants. For such Americans, the myth of the melting pot appears to be so benevolent that it doesn't seem right to attack it. A debate that acknowledges the historical reasons for this difference in viewpoint has a better chance to result in some consensus than one that presumes that one side's affection for the melting pot is "racist" or that the other's resentment is "petty" or "un-American."

## We Are the People

Such a recognition is difficult to achieve, of course, because of the way that cultural worldviews tend to present themselves in absolute terms. We don't look at our belief systems and say "this is our belief system"; we say "this is the truth." All cultures do this. Even the way cultures form their sense of identity involves a certain reliance on absolutes by assuming that their culture is normative, the right way to be. It's not just Anglo-Saxon America, in other words, that presumes its centrality in the order of things. We can see how groups of people implicitly believe in their privileged place in the world by looking at the

---

### Exploring the Signs of Race

In your journal, reflect on the question, "Who are you?" How does your ethnicity contribute to your sense of self? Are there other factors that contribute to your identity? If so, what are they and how do they relate to your ethnicity? If you don't perceive yourself in ethnic terms, why do you think that's the case?

---

names with which they identify themselves. Take the members of the largest Native American tribe in the United States. To the rest of the world, they are known as the "Navajos." This is not the name the "Navajos" use among themselves, however, for the word "Navajo" does not come from their language. In all likelihood, the name was given to them by neighboring Pueblo Indians, for whom the term "Navahu" means "large area of cultivated lands." But in the language of the Navajo, which is quite different from that of the Pueblo, they are not the people of the tilled fields. They are, quite simply, "The People," the most common English translation of the word "diné," the name by which the Navajo know themselves.

Or take the Hmong of Southeast Asia. "Hmong" simply means "person," and so to say "I am a Hmong" implicitly states "I am a person." And even the names of such different nations as Ireland and Iran harbor an ancient sense of normative "peoplehood," for both names are derived from the word "Aryan," which itself once bore the simple meaning "the people." To be sure, when someone says "I am diné," or "I am Hmong," or "I am Irish," he or she does not mean "I am a human being and the rest of you aren't." Nonetheless, we find inscribed within the unconscious history of these ancient tribal names the trace of a belief found within many a tribal name: the sense that one's own tribe comes first in the order of things. Things are not really so different in America, even though our country's name is derived from the name of a fifteenth-century navigator, Amerigo Vespucci. For in essence, we have tried to make America itself a tribe, and we too conceive of ourselves as a specially favored people. Indeed, our Pledge of Allegiance includes the phrase "one nation, under God," as if America alone enjoyed such a privilege. Just think how often America has tried to define itself as the richest, most powerful, most blessed nation on earth, the center to which all other peoples are to be compared.

Yet when we try to identify what, precisely, the American tribe is, we run into trouble. With so many races and cultures living together in this land, it is difficult to say just which should have the privilege of becoming the standard by which the others are identified — or if there even should be a standard. And so, as we reach the end of the twentieth century, it may be best to see ourselves as *peoples* rather than the People. By recognizing that cultural absolutes really reflect cultural mythologies, we may level the playing field and rephrase the question, "Who are *we*?"

## Culture or Race?

As you consider the cultural bases for your own sense of personal identity, you may object that race stands outside the cultural realm and belongs instead within the natural realm of biology. But even biological issues are subject to cultural interpretation. In 1970, for example, the state of Louisiana passed a law (since repealed) that identified anyone as "black" whose veins flowed with at least a one-thirty-second share of "Negro blood." A woman with a similar share in her blood sued the state in 1982 to have her racial classification changed from "black" to "white," and lost. So, what *is* she? What she believes herself to be, or what the state defines her to be? Either way, her racial identity is a matter of cultural and political determination, not a natural fact. And with more and more Americans descending from racially mixed families, these are not trivial concerns.

Similarly, the great majority of those who identify themselves as "Indians" or "Native Americans" have considerable amounts of non–Indian blood in their veins. At present, anyone who can demonstrate a twenty-five percent share of Native American blood will be legally identified as such, but there is political pressure among Native American groups to broaden the blood requirements so as to increase the number of legally identifiable "Indians." Conversely, among Jews, orthodoxy requires that to be identified as a Jew one's mother must be Jewish, and there is resistance to any tampering with this ancient rabbinical definition, even though many individuals with Jewish fathers and non-Jewish mothers consider themselves Jewish.

And so culture, the promptings of ideology rather than biology, makes its voice heard in what may appear to be the most natural of human identifications. However, in current racial discourse, culture impinges in quite another way as well. You can see this at work in the very word "multiculturalism." If taken literally, a call for multicultural education could simply mean an introduction of more Scandinavian, or French, or Greek, or Irish culture into a school curriculum. After all, these groups represent a broad range of cultures whose differences may be far more pronounced than the cultural differences between middle-class American families of African, Latin American, or European ancestry. But the word is not intended to be taken literally, of course. In practice, "multicultural" means "multiracial," and while this codification may strike some as a form of political euphemism, there are some sound reasons, in the context of American history, for so linking culture and race.

For unlike the relatively homogeneous nations of Europe where social divisions have been inscribed largely along class lines, America has been obsessed with racial difference almost from the beginning. Though class divisions are important in America, it is race that defines our sense of social identity. This obsession with racial difference has had its own cultural effects, such that it makes perfect sense to speak, for instance, of African-Americans as a culture as well as a race. It makes sense because a history of slavery and racial marginalization has effectively molded a New World culture that can be quite different from the Old World cultures of Africa. The American experience of the descendants of the African people who were dragged in chains to these shores, in other words, has produced a new culture (not without its own local distinctions) that is indeed African-*American,* but whose outward signs begin with the color of one's skin.

## Culture Matters

With the recent arrival of a new wave of immigrants to American shores — a wave whose potential for effecting widespread cultural change rivals that of the great influx of eastern and southern Europeans at the turn of the century — the confluence of race and culture in American society has produced a new set of social challenges and conflicts. A nation that endured a devastating civil war over the issue of human slavery has traditionally perceived racial conflict in black-and-white terms, but the equations of cultural difference are no longer so neatly balanced. There are too many other races and cultures to consider.

Where the rest of the country, for example, viewed the 1992 Los Angeles riots as a classic expression of black rage against white oppression, those living in L.A. knew that it wasn't this simple. Despite the media's almost exclusive focus on these two groups (*U.S. News & World Report*'s cover read, for instance, "Black vs. White: The New Fears"), a good half of those involved came from the city's largely Central American barrios. And herein lies another distinction. A census form will employ the same ethnic term for people of either Mexican or Central American origin — "Hispanic" or "Latino" — but to use this term in the context of the civil unrest is imprecise, for L.A.'s more established Chicano population largely stayed out of the action during those days of rage.

Moreover, the focus on black-white conflict obscured a different sort of conflict. The nation's newspapers and TV screens focused on the

---

### Discussing the Signs of Race

In the aftermath of the O. J. Simpson murder trial, many commentators viewed the case as something of an ethnic "litmus" test of racial solidarity. In class, discuss the extent to which this view is true among your classmates, friends, and relatives. If this belief is even partly valid, what does that suggest about the state of race relations in the United States?

---

Rodney King beating, but how many people outside of L.A. were aware of the Latasha Harlins case? This case, which involved the shooting death of an African-American girl by a Korean-American shopkeeper, was just as important as the King beating in L.A.'s black community. The King case was the last straw, but the Harlins case, which resulted in the shopkeeper's being sentenced to five years' probation for the killing, really touched a nerve only a few months before the uprising, so much so that Korean-American shops were specially targeted for destruction during the unrest.

The simmering conflict between African-Americans and Korean-Americans is well known to anyone living in New York or Los Angeles, and it provides a particularly good example of what the semiotics of cultural difference is all about. For the racial differences between these groups go hand in hand with cultural differences that are equally potent sources of conflict. The Korean cultural code, for example, holds that it is impolite to make direct eye contact with other people, a practice that many African-American customers of Korean-American shops have interpreted as a gesture of racial disdain. Similarly, Korean women traditionally are taught to avoid direct physical contact with men and so may drop a man's change on a store counter rather than hand it to him directly. For an African-American customer, this may look like another act of disrespect. And, to complicate the cultural confusion further, black immigrants from the West Indies are used to bargaining for their purchases, particularly for produce. Thus, it may be perfectly natural for such a person to haggle over the price of an apple in a Korean-owned grocery. To the owner, however, this looks like the next thing to shoplifting (indeed, Latasha Harlins was shot during an argument that ensued when she offered to pay less for a pint of orange juice than was marked on the bottle).

Of course, larger socioeconomic issues are at work here as well — recent immigrants and long-time black citizens alike are tossed into the same underclass and forced to struggle among themselves for political and economic power — but the cultural issues cannot be dismissed. Sometimes it's the small things that count most (like how one perceives the price of a bottle of orange juice), and a semiotic sensitivity to such differences can head off the larger explosions.

## The Multicultural Debate

To explore the outline of a cultural mythology is not the same thing as attacking it, though it may appear that way if it happens to be *your* culture that is under investigation. This is perfectly natural, for not only our values but also, as we have seen, our very sense of identity come to us through our cultures. Thus, it can come as a shock to be told that one's cultural worldview is just that: one world view among many. And when a traditionally dominant culture is challenged by other groups intent upon winning a share of cultural and political power for themselves, bewilderment can turn into backlash.

Try to think of an instance in which your cultural values clashed with someone else's. Can you see why that other person may have felt threatened by your difference of opinion? Do you wish that that other person could just, for once, see things from your point of view? Would it be good to come to some agreement about the matter, or would you prefer to have your own views triumph? If you'd like to find a way to agreement, how would you go about it?

As you consider the particular cultural values that really matter to you, you may well find yourself up against the problem of cultural relativism. Relativism is the position that holds that all values are relative to their social contexts and that there is no single standard by which to judge them. Indeed, opponents of multicultural education often point to the specter of relativism as a point in their favor. "How," they ask, "can we have a civil society if we can't agree on one set of values?" The monocultural position is, in effect, that America has successfully molded the many peoples and cultures in this land together into one harmonious nation (or at least is on its way to such a union) and is now being split apart by the trend toward multiculturalism. But what are the cultural assumptions behind this belief? What sort of culture do the opponents of multicultural education take for granted?

It's not that the opponents of multicultural education necessarily oppose the existence of other cultures in America. Usually, they hold the traditional American value of tolerance for difference even as they argue for a monocultural sense of nationhood. But "tolerance" itself looks tricky when we come to analyze it in cultural terms. It has rarely occurred to the dominant culture in America that people don't want to be "tolerated," that tolerance assumes a position of social and moral superiority from which one magnanimously chooses to allow other people to exist. From a semiotic perspective, tolerance is absurd in its traditional

||||||||||||||||||||||||||||||||||||||||||||||||||||||||||||||||||||||||||||||||||||||||||||||||||||||||||||||||||||||||||||||||||||||||||||||||||||||||||

### Reading Race on the Net

Many Internet sites are devoted to the culture of a particular ethnicity, such as Afronet (http://www.afronet.com) or Bienvenidos al electric mercado (http://www.mercado.com/index.html). Visit several such sites and survey the breadth of information available about different ethnic groups. To what extent can a researcher learn about various ethnicities on the Net? Is there any information that you wish would appear on the Net but could not find? Do you find any material problematic?

expression. It is the freedom to found your own country club because you have been blackballed from all the existing ones.

And that is one reason why multiculturalism is so threatening to those who oppose it. It doesn't call for more tolerance; it doesn't even call for acceptance (acceptance, too, implies a social superior who is in the position of accepting). Rather, multiculturalism calls for something closer to negotiation, a round-table dialogue presuming the participation of cultural equals who have come together to work out a complex restructuring of society. This negotiation can't take place, however, if everyone at the table presumes that their culture is the one true perspective. The United States has never had to negotiate like this before, and so there is nothing ready-made to put on the table for discussion. The first step is simply for everyone to get a chance to tell their story. That is what a multicultural education is about. The next, more challenging step, is to come up with a new story in which everyone can feel — and be — included.

### The Readings

This chapter focuses on the ways that race and culture provide a sense of identity for Americans, beginning with Michael Omi's survey of how race works as a sign in popular American culture. Nell Bernstein follows with a report on the phenomenon of "claiming" — white teens choosing to identify themselves with nonwhite ethnic groups — while Sam Fulwood III's personal testimony in "The Rage of the Black Middle Class" shows the conflict that the American Dream presents to African-Americans who have attempted to assimilate into a white, middle-class world. Brian A. Courtney then presents his experience as the child of a biracial marriage, revealing the complex identity choices that Americans of mixed race must make. Next Dorinne K. Kondo reflects on her own sense of cultural identity, focusing on the contrasting cultural inheritances of Japanese-Americans. Fan Shen follows by analyzing the role his Chinese heritage has played in his experience as a student and professor of freshman composition. Gloria Anzaldúa's "How to Tame a Wild Tongue" provides a linguistic spin on the nature of racial identity, a point of view complemented by Leslie Marmon Silko's explanation of the role of storytelling in the construction of personal identity that prevails in her Pueblo culture. Cornel West concludes the chapter with a call for the opening up of the literary canon of America in an era of profound ethnic and cultural change.

# MICHAEL OMI

## *In Living Color: Race and American Culture*

iiiiiiiiiiiiiiiiiiiiiiiiiiiiiiiiiiiiiiiiiiiiiiiiiiiiiiiii

*Though many like to think that racism in America is a thing of the past, Michael Omi argues that racism is a pervasive feature in our lives, one that is both overt and inferential. Using race as a sign by which we judge a person's character, inferential racism invokes deep-rooted stereotypes, and as Omi shows in his survey of American film, television, and music, our popular culture is hardly immune from such stereotyping. Indeed, when ostensibly "progressive" programs like* Saturday Night Live *can win the National Ethnic Coalition of Organizations' "Platinum Pit Award" for racist stereotyping in television, and comedians like Andrew Dice Clay command big audiences and salaries, one can see popular culture has a way to go before it becomes colorblind. The author of* Racial Formation in the United States: From the 1960s to the 1980s *(with Howard Winant, 1986, 1994), Michael Omi is a professor of Comparative Ethnic Studies at the University of California, Berkeley. His most recent project is a survey of antiracist organizations and initiatives.*

In February 1987, Assistant Attorney General William Bradford Reynolds, the nation's chief civil rights enforcer, declared that the recent death of a black man in Howard Beach, New York and the Ku Klux Klan attack on civil rights marchers in Forsyth County, Georgia were "isolated" racial incidences. He emphasized that the places where racial conflict could potentially flare up were "far fewer now than ever before in our history," and concluded that such a diminishment of racism stood as "a powerful testament to how far we have come in the civil rights struggle."[1]

Events in the months following his remarks raise the question as to whether we have come quite so far. They suggest that dramatic instances of racial tension and violence merely constitute the surface manifestations of a deeper racial organization of American society — a system of inequality which has shaped, and in turn been shaped by, our popular culture.

In March, the NAACP released a report on blacks in the record industry entitled "The Discordant Sound of Music." It found that despite the revenues generated by black performers, blacks remain "grossly

---

1. Reynold's remarks were made at a conference on equal opportunity held by the bar association in Orlando, Florida. *The San Francisco Chronicle* (7 February 1987).

underrepresented" in the business, marketing and A & R (Artists and Repertoire) departments of major record labels. In addition, few blacks are employed as managers, agents, concert promoters, distributors, and retailers. The report concluded that:

> The record industry is overwhelmingly segregated and discrimination is rampant. No other industry in America so openly classifies its operations on a racial basis. At every level of the industry, beginning with the separation of black artists into a special category, barriers exist that severely limit opportunities for blacks.[2]

Decades after the passage of civil rights legislation and the affirmation of the principle of "equal opportunity," patterns of racial segregation and exclusion, it seems, continue to characterize the production of popular music.

The enduring logic of Jim Crow is also present in professional sports. In April, Al Campanis, vice president of player personnel for the Los Angeles Dodgers, explained to Ted Koppel on ABC's *Nightline* about the paucity of blacks in baseball front offices and as managers. "I truly believe," Campanis said, "that [blacks] may not have some of the necessities to be, let's say, a field manager or perhaps a general manager." When pressed for a reason, Campanis offered an explanation which had little to do with the structure of opportunity of institutional discrimination within professional sports:

> [W]hy are black men or black people not good swimmers? Because they don't have the buoyancy. . . . They are gifted with great musculature and various other things. They're fleet of foot. And this is why there are a lot of black major league ballplayers. Now as far as having the background to become club presidents, or presidents of a bank, I don't know.[3]

Black exclusion from the front office, therefore, was justified on the basis of biological "difference."

The issue of race, of course, is not confined to the institutional arrangements of popular culture production. Since popular culture deals with the symbolic realm of social life, the images which it creates, represents, and disseminates contribute to the overall racial climate. They become the subject of analysis and political scrutiny. In August, the National Ethnic Coalition of Organizations bestowed the "Golden Pit Awards" on television programs, commercials, and movies that were deemed offensive to racial and ethnic groups. *Saturday Night Live,*

5

---

2. Economic Development Department of the NAACP, "The Discordant Sound of Music (A Report on the Record Industry)," (Baltimore, Maryland: The NAACP, 1987), pp. 16–17.

3. Campanis's remarks on *Nightline* were reprinted in *The San Francisco Chronicle* (April 9, 1987).

regarded by many media critics as a politically "progressive" show, was singled out for the "Platinum Pit Award" for its comedy skit "Ching Chang" which depicted a Chinese storeowner and his family in a derogatory manner.[4]

These examples highlight the *overt* manifestations of racism in popular culture — institutional forms of discrimination which keep racial minorities out of the production and organization of popular culture, and the crude racial caricatures by which these groups are portrayed. Yet racism in popular culture is often conveyed in a variety of implicit, and at times invisible, ways. Political theorist Stuart Hall makes an important distinction between *overt* racism, the elaboration of an explicitly racist argument, policy, or view, and *inferential* racism which refers to "those apparently naturalized representations of events and situations relating to race, whether 'factual' or 'fictional,' which have racist premises and propositions inscribed in them as a set of *unquestioned assumptions*." He argues that inferential racism is more widespread, common, and indeed insidious since "it is largely *invisible* even to those who formulate the world in its terms."[5]

Race itself is a slippery social concept which is paradoxically both "obvious" and "invisible." In our society, one of the first things we notice about people when we encounter them (along with their sex/gender) is their *race*. We utilize race to provide clues about *who* a person is and *how* we should relate to her/him. Our perception of race determines our "presentation of *self*," distinctions in status, and appropriate modes of conduct in daily and institutional life. This process is often unconscious; we tend to operate off of an unexamined set of *racial beliefs*.

Racial beliefs account for and explain variations in "human nature." Differences in skin color and other obvious physical characteristics supposedly provide visible clues to more substantive differences lurking underneath. Among other qualities, temperament, sexuality, intelligence, and artistic and athletic ability are presumed to be fixed and discernible from the palpable mark of race. Such diverse questions as our confidence and trust in others (as salespeople, neighbors, media figures); our sexual preferences and romantic images; our tastes in music, film, dance, or sports; indeed our very ways of walking and talking are ineluctably shaped by notions of race.

Ideas about race, therefore, have become "common sense" — a way of comprehending, explaining, and acting in the world. This is made

---

4. Ellen Wulfhorst, "TV Stereotyping: It's the 'Pits,'" *The San Francisco Chronicle* (August 24, 1987).

5. Stuart Hall, "The Whites of Their Eyes: Racist Ideologies and the Media," in George Bridges and Rosalind Brunt, eds. *Silver Linings* (London: Lawrence and Wishart, 1981), pp. 36–37.

painfully obvious when someone disrupts our common sense understandings. An encounter with someone who is, for example, racially
"mixed" or of a racial/ethnic group we are unfamiliar with becomes a
source of discomfort for us, and momentarily creates a crisis of racial
meaning. We also become disoriented when people do not act "black,"
"Latino," or indeed "white." The content of such stereotypes reveals a
series of unsubstantiated beliefs about who these groups are, what they
are like, and how they behave.

The existence of such racial consciousness should hardly be surpris-     10
ing. Even prior to the inception of the republic, the United States was a
society shaped by racial conflict. The establishment of the Southern plantation economy, Western expansion, and the emergence of the labor
movement, among other significant historical developments, have all involved conflicts over the definition and nature of the *color line*. The historical results have been distinct and different groups have encountered
unique forms of racial oppression — Native Americans faced genocide,
blacks were subjected to slavery, Mexicans were invaded and colonized,
and Asians faced exclusion. What is common to the experiences of these
groups is that their particular "fate" was linked to historically specific
ideas about the significance and meaning of race.[6] Whites defined them
as separate "species," ones inferior to Northern European cultural stocks,
and thereby rationalized the conditions of their subordination in the
economy, in political life, and in the realm of culture.

A crucial dimension of racial oppression in the United States is the
elaboration of an ideology of difference or "otherness." This involves
defining "us" (i.e., white Americans) in opposition to "them," an important task when distinct racial groups are first encountered, or in historically specific periods where preexisting racial boundaries are threatened
or crumbling.

Political struggles over the very definition of who an "American" is
illustrates this process. The Naturalization Law of 1790 declared that only
free *white* immigrants could qualify, reflecting the initial desire among
Congress to create and maintain a racially homogeneous society. The extension of eligibility to all racial groups has been a long and protracted
process. Japanese, for example, were finally eligible to become naturalized citizens after the passage of the Walter-McCarran Act of 1952. The
ideological residue of these restrictions in naturalization and citizenship
laws is the equation within popular parlance of the term "American"
with "white," while other "Americans" are described as black, Mexican,
"Oriental," etc.

---

6. For an excellent survey of racial beliefs see Thomas F. Gossett, *Race: The History of an Idea in America* (New York: Shocken Books, 1965).

Popular culture has been an important realm within which racial ideologies have been created, reproduced, and sustained. Such ideologies provide a framework of symbols, concepts, and images through which we understand, interpret, and represent aspects of our "racial" existence.

Race has often formed the central themes of American popular culture. Historian W. L. Rose notes that it is "curious coincidence" that four of the "most popular reading-viewing events in all American history" have in some manner dealt with race, specifically black/white relations in the south.[7] Harriet Beecher Stowe's *Uncle Tom's Cabin,* Thomas Ryan Dixon's *The Clansman* (the inspiration for D. W. Griffith's *The Birth of a Nation*), Margaret Mitchell's *Gone with the Wind* (as a book and film), and Alex Haley's *Roots* (as a book and television miniseries), each appeared at a critical juncture in American race relations and helped to shape new understandings of race.

Emerging social definitions of race and the "real American" were reflected in American popular culture of the nineteenth century. Racial and ethnic stereotypes were shaped and reinforced in the newspapers, magazines, and pulp fiction of the period. But the evolution and ever-increasing sophistication of visual mass communications throughout the twentieth century provided, and continue to provide, the most dramatic means by which racial images are generated and reproduced.      15

Film and television have been notorious in disseminating images of racial minorities which establish for audiences what these groups look like, how they behave, and, in essence, "who they are." The power of the media lies not only in their ability to reflect the dominant racial ideology, but in their capacity to shape that ideology in the first place. D. W. Griffith's aforementioned epic *Birth of a Nation,* a sympathetic treatment of the rise of the Ku Klux Klan during Reconstruction, helped to generate, consolidate, and "nationalize" images of blacks which had been more disparate (more regionally specific, for example) prior to the film's appearance.[8]

In television and film, the necessity to define characters in the briefest and most condensed manner has led to the perpetuation of racial caricatures, as racial stereotypes serve as shorthand for scriptwriters, directors, and actors. Television's tendency to address the "lowest common denominator" in order to render programs "familiar" to an enormous and diverse audience leads it regularly to assign and reassign racial characteristics to particular groups, both minority and majority.

---

7. W. L. Rose, *Race and Region in American Historical Fiction: Four Episodes in Popular Culture* (Oxford: Clarendon Press, 1979).

8. Melanie Martindale-Sikes, "Nationalizing 'Nigger' Imagery Through *Birth of a Nation,*" paper prepared for the 73rd Annual Meeting of the American Sociological Association (September 4–8, 1978) in San Francisco.

Many of the earliest American films deal with racial and ethnic "difference." The large influx of "new immigrants" at the turn of the century led to a proliferation of negative images of Jews, Italians, and Irish which were assimilated and adapted by such films as Thomas Edison's *Cohen's Advertising Scheme* (1904). Based on an old vaudeville routine, the film featured a scheming Jewish merchant, aggressively hawking his wares. Though stereotypes of these groups persist to this day,[9] by the 1940s many of the earlier ethnic stereotypes had disappeared from Hollywood. But, as historian Michael Winston observes, the "outsiders" of the 1890s remained: "the ever-popular Indian of the Westerns; the inscrutable or sinister Oriental; the sly, but colorful Mexican; and the clowning or submissive Negro."[10]

In many respects the "Western" as a genre has been paradigmatic in establishing images of racial minorities in film and television. The classic scenario involves the encircled wagon train or surrounded fort from which whites bravely fight off fierce bands of Native American Indians. The point of reference and viewer identification lies with those huddled within the circle — the representatives of "civilization" who valiantly attempt to ward off the forces of barbarism. In the classic Western, as writer Tom Engelhardt observes, "the viewer is forced behind the barrel of a repeating rifle and it is from that position, through its gun sights, that he receives a picture history of Western colonialism and imperialism."[11]

Westerns have indeed become the prototype for European and American excursions throughout the Third World. The cast of characters may change, but the story remains the same. The "humanity" of whites is contrasted with the brutality and treachery of nonwhites; brave (i.e., white) souls are pitted against the merciless hordes in conflicts ranging from Indians against the British Lancers to Zulus against the Boers. What Stuart Hall refers to as the imperializing "white eye" provides the framework for these films, lurking outside the frame and yet seeing and positioning everything within; it is "the unmarked position from which . . . 'observations' are made and from which, alone, they make sense."[12]

9. For a discussion of Italian, Irish, Jewish, Slavic, and German stereotypes in film, see Randall M. Miller, ed., *The Kaleidoscopic Lens: How Hollywood Views Ethnic Groups* (Englewood, N.J.: Jerome S. Ozer, 1980).

10. Michael R. Winston, "Racial Consciousness and the Evolution of Mass Communications in the United States," *Daedalus,* vol. III, No. 4 (Fall 1982).

11. Tom Engelhardt, "Ambush at Kamikaze Pass," in Emma Gee, ed., *Counterpoint: Perspectives on Asian America* (Los Angeles: Asian American Studies Center, UCLA, 1976), p. 270.

12. Hall, "Whites of Their Eyes," p. 38.

Our "common sense" assumptions about race and racial minorities in the United States are both generated and reflected in the stereotypes presented by the visual media. In the crudest sense, it could be said that such stereotypes underscore white "superiority" by reinforcing the traits, habits, and predispositions of nonwhites which demonstrate their "inferiority." Yet a more careful assessment of racial stereotypes reveals intriguing trends and seemingly contradictory themes.

While all racial minorities have been portrayed as "less than human," there are significant differences in the images of different groups. Specific racial minority groups, in spite of their often interchangeable presence in films steeped in the "Western" paradigm, have distinct and often unique qualities assigned to them. Latinos are portrayed as being prone toward violent outbursts of anger; blacks as physically strong, but dim-witted; while Asians are seen as sneaky and cunningly evil. Such differences are crucial to observe and analyze. Race in the United States is not reducible to black/white relations. These differences are significant for a broader understanding of the patterns of race in America, and the unique experience of specific racial minority groups.

It is somewhat ironic that *real* differences which exist within a racially defined minority group are minimized, distorted, or obliterated by the media. "All Asians look alike," the saying goes, and indeed there has been little or no attention given to the vast differences which exist between, say, the Chinese and Japanese with respect to food, dress, language, and culture. This blurring within popular culture has given us supposedly Chinese characters who wear kimonos; it is also the reason why the fast-food restaurant McDonald's can offer "Shanghai McNuggets" with teriyaki sauce. Other groups suffer a similar fate. Professor Gretchen Bataille and Charles Silet find the cinematic Native American of the Northeast wearing the clothing of the Plains Indians, while living in the dwellings of Southwestern tribes:

> The movie men did what thousands of years of social evolution could not do, even what the threat of the encroaching white man could not do; Hollywood produced the homogenized Native American, devoid of tribal characteristics or regional differences.[13]

The need to paint in broad racial strokes has thus rendered "internal" differences invisible. This has been exacerbated by the tendency for screenwriters to "invent" mythical Asian, Latin American, and African countries. Ostensibly done to avoid offending particular nations and peoples, such a subterfuge reinforces the notion that all the countries and cultures of a specific region are the same. European countries retain

---

13. Gretchen Bataille and Charles Silet, "The Entertaining Anachronism: Indians in American Film," in Randall M. Miller, ed., *Kaleidoscopic Lens,* p. 40.

their distinctiveness, while the Third World is presented as one homogeneous mass riddled with poverty and governed by ruthless and corrupt regimes.

While rendering specific groups in a monolithic fashion, the popular cultural imagination simultaneously reveals a compelling need to distinguish and articulate "bad" and "good" variants of particular racial groups and individuals. Thus each stereotypic image is filled with contradictions: The bloodthirsty Indian is tempered with the image of the noble savage; the *bandido* exists along with the loyal sidekick; and Fu Manchu is offset by Charlie Chan. The existence of such contradictions, however, does not negate the one-dimensionality of these images, nor does it challenge the explicit subservient role of racial minorities. Even the "good" person of color usually exists as a foil in novels and films to underscore the intelligence, courage, and virility of the white male hero.

Another important, perhaps central, dimension of racial minority      25
stereotypes is sex/gender differentiation. The connection between race and sex has traditionally been an explosive and controversial one. For most of American history, sexual and marital relations between whites and nonwhites were forbidden by social custom and by legal restrictions. It was not until 1967, for example, that the U.S. Supreme Court ruled that antimiscegenation laws were unconstitutional. Beginning in the 1920s, the notorious Hays Office, Hollywood's attempt at self-censorship, prohibited scenes and subjects which dealt with miscegenation. The prohibition, however, was not evenly applied in practice. White men could seduce racial minority women, but white women were not to be romantically or sexually linked to racial minority men.

Women of color were sometimes treated as exotic sex objects. The sultry Latin temptress — such as Dolores Del Rio and Lupe Velez—invariably had boyfriends who were white North Americans; their Latino suitors were portrayed as being unable to keep up with the Anglo-American competition. From Mary Pickford as Cho-Cho San in *Madame Butterfly* (1915) to Nancy Kwan in *The World of Suzie Wong* (1961), Asian women have often been seen as the gracious "geisha girl" or the prostitute with a "heart of gold," willing to do anything to please her man.

By contrast, Asian men, whether cast in the role of villain, servant, sidekick, or kung fu master, are seen as asexual or, at least, romantically undesirable. As Asian American studies professor Elaine Kim notes, even a hero such as Bruce Lee played characters whose "single-minded focus on perfecting his fighting skills precludes all other interests, including an interest in women, friendship, or a social life."[14]

---

14. Elaine Kim, "Asian Americans and American Popular Culture" in Hyung-Chan Kim, ed., *Dictionary of Asian American History* (New York: Greenwood Press, 1986), p. 107.

The shifting trajectory of black images over time reveals an interesting dynamic with respect to sex and gender. The black male characters in *The Birth of a Nation* were clearly presented as sexual threats to "white womanhood." For decades afterwards, however, Hollywood consciously avoided portraying black men as assertive or sexually aggressive in order to minimize controversy. Black men were instead cast as comic, harmless, and nonthreatening figures exemplified by such stars as Bill "Bojangles" Robinson, Stepin Fetchit, and Eddie "Rochester" Anderson. Black women, by contrast, were divided into two broad character types based on color categories. Dark black women such as Hattie McDaniel and Louise Beavers were cast as "dowdy, frumpy, dumpy, overweight mammy figures"; while those "close to the white ideal," such as Lena Horne and Dorothy Dandridge, became "Hollywood's treasured mulattoes" in roles emphasizing the tragedy of being of mixed blood.[15]

It was not until the early 1970s that tough, aggressive, sexually assertive black characters, both male and female, appeared. The "blaxploitation" films of the period provided new heroes (e.g., *Shaft, Superfly, Coffy,* and *Cleopatra Jones*) in sharp contrast to the submissive and subservient images of the past. Unfortunately, most of these films were shoddy productions which did little to create more enduring "positive" images of blacks, either male or female.

In contemporary television and film, there is a tendency to present 30 and equate racial minority groups and individuals with specific social problems. Blacks are associated with drugs and urban crime, Latinos with "illegal" immigration, while Native Americans cope with alcoholism and tribal conflicts. Rarely do we see racial minorities "out of character," in situations removed from the stereotypic arenas in which scriptwriters have traditionally embedded them. Nearly the only time we see young Asians and Latinos of either sex, for example, is when they are members of youth gangs, as *Boulevard Nights* (1979), *Year of the Dragon* (1985), and countless TV cop shows can attest to.

Racial minority actors have continually bemoaned the fact that the roles assigned them on stage and screen are often one-dimensional and imbued with stereotypic assumptions. In theater, the movement toward "blind casting" (i.e., casting actors for roles without regard to race) is a progressive step, but it remains to be seen whether large numbers of audiences can suspend their "beliefs" and deal with a Latino King Lear or an Asian Stanley Kowalski. By contrast, white actors are allowed to play anybody. Though the use of white actors to play blacks in "black face" is clearly unacceptable in the contemporary period, white actors continue to portray Asian, Latino, and Native American characters on stage and screen.

---

15. Donald Bogle, "A Familiar Plot (A Look at the History of Blacks in American Movies)," *The Crisis,* Vol. 90, No. 1 (January 1983), p. 15.

Scores of Charlie Chan films, for example, have been made with white leads (the last one was the 1981 *Charlie Chan and the Curse of the Dragon Queen*). Roland Winters, who played Chan in six features, was once asked to explain the logic of casting a white man in the role of Charlie Chan: "The only thing I can think of is, if you want to cast a homosexual in a show, and you get a homosexual, it'll be awful. It won't be funny . . . and maybe there's something there."[16]

Such a comment reveals an interesting aspect about myth and reality in popular culture. Michael Winston argues that stereotypic images in the visual media were not originally conceived as representations of reality, nor were they initially understood to be "real" by audiences. They were, he suggests, ways of "coding and rationalizing" the racial hierarchy and interracial behavior. Over time, however, "a complex interactive relationship between myth and reality developed, so that images originally understood to be unreal, through constant repetition began to *seem* real."[17]

Such a process consolidated, among other things, our "common sense" understandings of what we think various groups should look like. Such presumptions have led to tragicomical results. Latinos auditioning for a role in a television soap opera, for example, did not fit the Hollywood image of "real Mexicans" and had their faces bronzed with powder before filming because they looked too white. Model Aurora Garza said, "I'm a real Mexican and very dark anyway. I'm even darker right now because I have a tan. But they kept wanting to make my face darker and darker."[18]

Historically in Hollywood, the fact of having "dark skin" made an actor or actress potentially adaptable for numerous "racial" roles. Actress Lupe Velez once commented that she had portrayed "Chinese, Eskimos, Japs, squaws, Hindus, Swedes, Malays, and Japanese."[19] Dorothy Dandridge, who was the first black woman teamed romantically with white actors, presented a quandary for studio executives who weren't sure what race and nationality to make her. They debated whether she should be a "foreigner," an island girl, or a West Indian.[20] Ironically, what they refused to entertain as a possibility was to present her as what she really was, a black American woman.

The importance of race in popular culture is not restricted to the visual media. In popular music, race and race consciousness has defined,

16. Frank Chin, "Confessions of the Chinatown Cowboy," *Bulletin of Concerned Asian Scholars,* Vol. 4, No. 3 (Fall 1972).

17. Winston, "Racial Consciousness," p. 176.

18. *The San Francisco Chronicle,* September 21, 1984.

19. Quoted in Allen L. Woll, "Bandits and Lovers: Hispanic Images in American Film," in Miller, ed., *Kaleidoscopic Lens,* p. 60.

20. Bogle, "Familiar Plot," p. 17.

and continues to define, formats, musical communities, and tastes. In the mid-1950s, the secretary of the North Alabama White Citizens Council declared that "Rock and roll is a means of pulling the white man down to the level of the Negro."[21] While rock may no longer be popularly regarded as a racially subversive musical form, the very genres of contemporary popular music remain, in essence, thinly veiled racial categories. "R & B" (Rhythm and Blues) and "soul" music are clearly references to *black* music, while Country & Western or heavy metal music are viewed, in the popular imagination, as *white* music. Black performers who want to break out of this artistic ghettoization must "cross over," a contemporary form of "passing" in which their music is seen as acceptable to white audiences.

The airwaves themselves are segregated. The designation "urban contemporary" is merely radio lingo for a "black" musical format. Such categorization affects playlists, advertising accounts, and shares of the listening market. On cable television, black music videos rarely receive airplay on MTV, but are confined instead to the more marginal BET (Black Entertainment Television) network.

In spite of such segregation, many performing artists have been able to garner a racially diverse group of fans. And yet, racially integrated concert audiences are extremely rare. Curiously, this "perverse phenomenon" of racially homogeneous crowds takes place despite the color of the performer. Lionel Richie's concert audiences, for example, are virtually all-white, while Teena Marie's are all-black.[22]

Racial symbols and images are omnipresent in popular culture. Commonplace household objects such as cookie jars, salt and pepper shakers, and ashtrays have frequently been designed and fashioned in the form of racial caricatures. Sociologist Steve Dublin in an analysis of these objects found that former tasks of domestic service were symbolically transferred onto these commodities.[23] An Aunt Jemima-type character, for example, is used to hold a roll of paper towels, her outstretched hands supporting the item to be dispensed. "Sprinkle Plenty," a sprinkle bottle in the shape of an Asian man, was used to wet clothes in preparation for ironing. Simple commodities, the household implements which help us perform everyday tasks, may reveal, therefore, a deep structure of racial meaning.

A crucial dimension for discerning the meaning of particular stereo-    40
types and images is the *situation context* for the creation and consumption

---

21. Dave Marsh and Kevin Stein, *The Book of Rock Lists* (New York: Dell Publishing Co., 1981), p. 8.

22. *Rock & Roll Confidential,* No. 44 (February 1987), p. 2.

23. Steven C. Dublin, "Symbolic Slavery: Black Representations in Popular Culture," *Social Problems,* Vol. 34, No. 2 (April 1987).

of popular culture. For example, the setting in which "racist" jokes are told determines the function of humor. Jokes about blacks where the teller and audience are black constitute a form of self-awareness; they allow blacks to cope and "take the edge off" of oppressive aspects of the social order which they commonly confront. The meaning of these same jokes, however, is dramatically transformed when told across the "color line." If a white, or even black, person tells these jokes to a white audience, it will, despite its "purely" humorous intent, serve to reinforce stereotypes and rationalize the existing relations of racial inequality.

Concepts of race and racial images are both overt and implicit within popular culture — the organization of cultural production, the products themselves, and the manner in which they are consumed are deeply structured by race. Particular racial meanings, stereotypes, and myths can change, but the presence of a *system* of racial meanings and stereotypes, of racial ideology, seems to be an enduring aspect of American popular culture.

The era of Reaganism and the overall rightward drift of American politics and culture has added a new twist to the question of racial images and meanings. Increasingly, the problem for racial minorities is not that of misportrayal, but of "invisibility." Instead of celebrating racial and cultural diversity, we are witnessing an attempt by the right to define, once again, who the "real" American is, and what "correct" American values, mores, and political beliefs are. In such a context, racial minorities are no longer the focus of sustained media attention; when they do appear, they are cast as colored versions of essentially "white" characters.

The possibilities for change — for transforming racial stereotypes and challenging institutional inequities — nonetheless exist. Historically, strategies have involved the mobilization of political pressure against an offending institution(s). In the late 1950s, for instance, "Nigger Hair" tobacco changed its name to "Bigger Hare" due to concerted NAACP pressure on the manufacturer. In the early 1970s, Asian-American community groups successfully fought NBC's attempt to resurrect Charlie Chan as a television series with white actor Ross Martin. Amidst the furor generated by Al Campanis's remarks cited at the beginning of this essay, Jesse Jackson suggested that a boycott of major league games be initiated in order to push for a restructuring of hiring and promotion practices.

Partially in response to such action, Baseball Commissioner Peter Ueberroth announced plans in June 1987 to help put more racial minorities in management roles. "The challenge we have," Ueberroth said, "is to manage change without losing tradition."[24] The problem with respect to the issue of race and popular culture, however, is that the *tradition* itself

---

24. *The San Francisco Chronicle* (June 13, 1987).

may need to be thoroughly examined, its "common sense" assumptions unearthed and challenged, and its racial images contested and transformed.

## Reading the Text

1. Describe in your own words the difference between overt and inferential racism.
2. Why, according to Omi, is popular culture so powerful in shaping America's attitudes toward race?
3. What relationship does Omi see between gender and racial stereotypes?
4. How have racial relations changed in America during the 1980s, in Omi's view?

## Reading the Signs

1. In class, brainstorm on the blackboard stereotypes, both "good" and "bad," attributed to specific racial groups. Then discuss the possible sources of these stereotypes. In what ways have they been perpetuated in popular culture, including movies, television, advertising, music, and consumer products? What does your discussion reveal about popular culture's influence on our most basic ways of seeing the world?
2. Omi explains that the "situation context" can determine the impact of racially charged comments and images. Apply his concept of "situation context" to the experiences of the African-Americans described in Sam Fulwood III's "The Rage of the Black Middle Class" (p. 510). Why are some of the experiences painful reminders of living in a racist society, whereas others have a therapeutic effect?
3. Rent a videotape of *Gone with the Wind* and view the film. Write a semiotic essay in which you analyze how race operates as a sign in this movie. How, to use Omi's terms, does the film create, reproduce, and sustain racial ideologies in America? What does its racial ideology reveal about its status as a "classic" American film?
4. Rent a videotape of *Malcolm X* and view the film. Then, using Omi's essay as your critical framework, write an essay in which you explore how this film may reflect or redefine American attitudes toward racial identity and race relations. To develop your essay, you may want to consult Shelby Steele's "Malcolm X" (p. 325).
5. Buy an issue of a magazine targeted to a specific ethnic readership, such as *Hispanic, Ebony,* or *Transpacific,* and study both its advertising and its articles. Then write an essay in which you explore the extent to which the magazine accurately reflects that ethnicity or, in Omi's words, appeals to readers as "colored versions of essentially 'white' characters."
6. Watch a videotape of a film with a gang theme, such as *Boyz 'N the Hood.* Then, using Omi's essay as your starting point, write an essay in which you explore whether the film challenges or perpetuates racial stereotypes.

NELL BERNSTEIN

*Goin' Gangsta, Choosin' Cholita*

᠎᠎᠎᠎᠎᠎᠎᠎᠎᠎᠎᠎᠎᠎᠎᠎᠎᠎᠎᠎᠎᠎᠎᠎᠎᠎᠎᠎᠎᠎᠎᠎᠎᠎᠎᠎

*Ever wonder about wannabes — white suburban teenagers who dress and act like non-white inner-city gangsters? In this report on the phenomenon of "claiming," Nell Bernstein (b. 1965) probes some of the feelings and motives of teens who are "goin' gangsta" or "choosin' cholita" — kids who try on a racial identity not their own. Their reasons may surprise you. Bernstein is editor of* YO!, *a San Francisco area journal of teen life published by the Pacific News Service, and she has published in* Glamour, Woman's Day, *and* Mother Jones.

Her lipstick is dark, the lip liner even darker, nearly black. In baggy pants, a blue plaid Pendleton, her bangs pulled back tight off her forehead, 15-year-old April is a perfect cholita, a Mexican gangsta girl.

But April Miller is Anglo. "And I don't like it!" she complains. "I'd rather be Mexican."

April's father wanders into the family room of their home in San Leandro, California, a suburb near Oakland. "Hey, cholita," he teases. "Go get a suntan. We'll put you in a barrio and see how much you like it."

A large, sandy-haired man with "April" tattooed on one arm and "Kelly" — the name of his older daughter — on the other, Miller spent 21 years working in a San Leandro glass factory that shut down and moved to Mexico a couple of years ago. He recently got a job in another factory, but he expects NAFTA to swallow that one, too.

"Sooner or later we'll all get nailed," he says. "Just another stab in the back of the American middle class."

Later, April gets her revenge: "Hey, Mr. White Man's Last Stand," she teases. "Wait till you see how well I manage my welfare check. You'll be asking me for money."

A once almost exclusively white, now increasingly Latin and black working-class suburb, San Leandro borders on predominantly black East Oakland. For decades, the boundary was strictly policed and practically impermeable. In 1970 April Miller's hometown was 97 percent white. By 1990 San Leandro was 65 percent white, 6 percent black, 15 percent Hispanic, and 13 percent Asian or Pacific Islander. With minorities moving into suburbs in growing numbers and cities becoming ever more diverse, the boundary between city and suburb is dissolving, and suburban teenagers are changing with the times.

In April's bedroom, her past and present selves lie in layers, the pink walls of girlhood almost obscured, Guns N' Roses and Pearl Jam posters overlaid by rappers Paris and Ice Cube. "I don't have a big enough attitude to be a black girl," says April, explaining her current choice of ethnic identification.

What matters is that she thinks the choice is hers. For April and her friends, identity is not a matter of where you come from, what you were born into, what color your skin is. It's what you wear, the music you listen to, the words you use — everything to which you pledge allegiance, no matter how fleetingly.

The hybridization of American teens has become talk show fodder, with "wiggers" — white kids who dress and talk "black" — appearing on TV in full gangsta regalia. In Indiana a group of white high school girls raised a national stir when they triggered an imitation race war at their virtually all-white high school last fall simply by dressing "black."

In many parts of the country, it's television and radio, not neighbors, that introduce teens to the allure of ethnic difference. But in California, which demographers predict will be the first state with no racial majority by the year 2000, the influences are more immediate. The California public schools are the most diverse in the country: 42 percent white, 36 percent Hispanic, 9 percent black, 8 percent Asian.

Sometimes young people fight over their differences. Students at virtually any school in the Bay Area can recount the details of at least one "race riot" in which a conflict between individuals escalated into a battle between their clans. More often, though, teens would rather join than fight. Adolescence, after all, is the period when you're most inclined to mimic the power closest at hand, from stealing your older sister's clothes to copying the ruling clique at school.

White skaters and Mexican would-be gangbangers listen to gangsta rap and call each other "nigga" as a term of endearment; white girls sometimes affect Spanish accents; blond cheerleaders claim Cherokee ancestors.

"Claiming" is the central concept here. A Vietnamese teen in Hayward, another Oakland suburb, "claims" Oakland — and by implication blackness — because he lived there as a child. A law-abiding white kid "claims" a Mexican gang he says he hangs with. A brown-skinned girl with a Mexican father and a white mother "claims" her Mexican side, while her fair-skinned sister "claims" white. The word comes up over and over, as if identity were territory, the self a kind of turf.

At a restaurant in a minimall in Hayward, Nicole Huffstutler, 13, sits with her friends and describes herself as "Indian, German, French, Welsh, and, um . . . American": "If somebody says anything like 'Yeah, you're just a peckerwood,' I'll walk up and I'll say 'white pride!' 'Cause I'm proud of my race, and I wouldn't wanna be any other race."

"Claiming" white has become a matter of principle for Heather, too, who says she's "sick of the majority looking at us like we're less than them." (Hayward schools were 51 percent white in 1990, down from 77 percent in 1980, and whites are now the minority in many schools.)

Asked if she knows that nonwhites have not traditionally been referred to as "the majority" in America, Heather gets exasperated: "I hear that all the time, every day. They say, 'Well, you guys controlled us for many years, and it's time for us to control you.' Every day."

When Jennifer Vargas — a small, brown-skinned girl in purple jeans who quietly eats her salad while Heather talks — softly announces that she's "mostly Mexican," she gets in trouble with her friends.

"No, you're not!" scolds Heather.

"I'm mostly Indian and Mexican," Jennifer continues flatly. "I'm    20
very little . . . I'm mostly . . ."

"Your mom's white!" Nicole reminds her sharply. "She has blond hair.

"That's what I mean," Nicole adds. "People think that white is a bad thing. They think that white is a bad race. So she's trying to claim more Mexican than white."

"I have very little white in me," Jennifer repeats. "I have mostly my dad's side, 'cause I look like him and stuff. And most of my friends think that me and my brother and sister aren't related, 'cause they look more like my mom."

"But you guys are all the same race, you just look different," Nicole insists. She stops eating and frowns. "OK, you're half and half each what your parents have. So you're equal as your brother and sister, you just look different. And you should be proud of what you are — every little piece and bit of what you are. Even if you were Afghan or whatever, you should be proud of it."

Will Mosley, Heather's 17-year-old brother, says he and his friends    25
listen to rap groups like Compton's Most Wanted, NWA, and Above the Law because they "sing about life" — that is, what happens in Oakland, Los Angeles, anyplace but where Will is sitting today, an empty Round Table Pizza in a minimall.

"No matter what race you are," Will says, "if you live like we do, then that's the kind of music you like."

And how do they live?

"We don't live bad or anything," Will admits. "We live in a pretty good neighborhood, there's no violence or crime. I was just . . . we're just city people, I guess."

Will and his friend Adolfo Garcia, 16, say they've outgrown trying to be something they're not. "When I was 11 or 12," Will says, "I thought I was becoming a big gangsta and stuff. Because I liked that music, and thought it was the coolest, I wanted to become that. I wore big clothes, like you wear in jail. But then I kind of woke up. I looked at myself and thought, 'Who am I trying to be?' "

They may have outgrown blatant mimicry, but Will and his friends   30
remain convinced that they can live in a suburban tract house with a
well-kept lawn on a tree-lined street in "not a bad neighborhood" and
still call themselves "city" people on the basis of musical tastes. "City" for
these young people means crime, graffiti, drugs. The kids are law-
abiding, but these activities connote what Will admiringly calls "action."
With pride in his voice, Will predicts that "in a couple of years, Hayward
will be like Oakland. It's starting to get more known, because of crime
and things. I think it'll be bigger, more things happening, more crime,
more graffiti, stealing cars."

"That's good," chimes in 15-year-old Matt Jenkins, whose new
beeper — an item that once connoted gangsta chic but now means little
more than an active social life — goes off periodically. "More fun."

The three young men imagine with disdain life in a gangsta-free
zone. "Too bland, too boring," Adolfo says. "You have to have something going on. You can't just have everyday life."

"Mowing your lawn," Matt sneers.

"Like Beaver Cleaver's house," Adolfo adds. "It's too clean out
here."

Not only white kids believe that identity is a matter of choice or taste,   35
or that the power of "claiming" can transcend ethnicity. The Manor Park
Locos — a group of mostly Mexican-Americans who hang out in San Leandro's Manor Park — say they descend from the Manor Lords, tough
white guys who ruled the neighborhood a generation ago.

They "are like our . . . uncles and dads, the older generation," says
Jesse Martinez, 14. "We're what they were when they were around, except we're Mexican."

"There's three generations," says Oso, Jesse's younger brother.
"There's Manor Lords, Manor Park Locos, and Manor Park Pee Wees."
The Pee Wees consist mainly of the Locos' younger brothers, eager kids
who circle the older boys on bikes and brag about "punking people."

Unlike Will Mosley, the Locos find little glamour in city life. They
survey the changing suburban landscape and see not "action" or "more
fun" but frightening decline. Though most of them are not yet 18, the
Locos are already nostalgic, longing for a Beaver Cleaver past that white
kids who mimic them would scoff at.

Walking through nearly empty Manor Park, with its eucalyptus
stands, its softball diamond and tennis courts, Jesse's friend Alex, the only
Asian in the group, waves his arms in a gesture of futility. "A few years
ago, every bench was filled," he says. "Now no one comes here. I guess
it's because of everything that's going on. My parents paid a lot for this
house, and I want it to be nice for them. I just hope this doesn't turn into
Oakland."

Glancing across the park at April Miller's street, Jesse says he knows   40
what the white cholitas are about. "It's not a racial thing," he explains.

"It's just all the most popular people out here are Mexican. We're just the gangstas that everyone knows. I guess those girls wanna be known."

Not every young Californian embraces the new racial hybridism. Andrea Jones, 20, an African-American who grew up in the Bay Area suburbs of Union City and Hayward, is unimpressed by what she sees mainly as shallow mimicry. "It's full of posers out here," she says. "When *Boyz 'N the Hood* came out on video, it was sold out for weeks. The boys all wanna be black, the girls all wanna be Mexican. It's the glamour."

Driving down the quiet, shaded streets of her old neighborhood in Union City, Andrea spots two white preteen boys in Raiders jackets and hugely baggy pants strutting erratically down the empty sidewalk. "Look at them," she says. "Dislocated."

She knows why. "In a lot of these schools out here, it's hard being white," she says. "I don't think these kids were prepared for the backlash that is going on, all the pride now in people of color's ethnicity, and our boldness with it. They have nothing like that, no identity, nothing they can say they're proud of.

"So they latch onto their great-grandmother who's a Cherokee, or they take on the most stereotypical aspects of being black or Mexican. It's beautiful to appreciate different aspects of other people's culture — that's like the dream of what the 21st century should be. But to garnish yourself with pop culture stereotypes just to blend — that's really sad."

Roland Krevocheza, 18, graduated last year from Arroyo High    45
School in San Leandro. He is Mexican on his mother's side, Eastern European on his father's. In the new hierarchies, it may be mixed kids like Roland who have the hardest time finding their place, even as their numbers grow. (One in five marriages in California is between people of different races.) They can always be called "wannabes," no matter what they claim.

"I'll state all my nationalities," Roland says. But he takes a greater interest in his father's side, his Ukrainian, Romanian, and Czech ancestors. "It's more unique," he explains. "Mexican culture is all around me. We eat Mexican food all the time, I hear stories from my grandmother. I see the low-riders and stuff. I'm already part of it. I'm not trying to be; I am."

His darker-skinned brother "says he's not proud to be white," Roland adds. "He calls me 'Mr. Nazi.'" In the room the two share, the American flags and the reproduction of the Bill of Rights are Roland's; the Public Enemy poster belongs to his brother.

Roland has good reason to mistrust gangsta attitudes. In his junior year in high school, he was one of several Arroyo students who were beaten up outside the school at lunchtime by a group of Samoans who came in cars from Oakland. Roland wound up with a split lip, a concussion, and a broken tailbone. Later he was told that the assault was "gang-related" — that the Samoans were beating up anyone wearing red.

"Rappers, I don't like them," Roland says. "I think they're a bad influence on kids. It makes kids think they're all tough and bad."

Those who, like Roland, dismiss the gangsta and cholo styles as af-    50
fectations can point to the fact that several companies market overpriced
knockoffs of "ghetto wear" targeted at teens.

But there's also something going on out here that transcends adolescent faddishness and pop culture exoticism. When white kids call their
parents "racist" for nagging them about their baggy pants; when they
learn Spanish to talk to their boyfriends; when Mexican-American boys
feel themselves descended in spirit from white "uncles"; when children
of mixed marriages insist that they are whatever race they say they are, all
of them are more than just confused.

They're inching toward what Andrea Jones calls "the dream of what
the 21st century should be." In the ever more diverse communities of
Northern California, they're also facing the complicated reality of what
their 21st century will be.

Meanwhile, in the living room of the Miller family's San Leandro
home, the argument continues unabated. "You don't know what you
are," April's father has told her more than once. But she just keeps on
telling him he doesn't know what time it is.

### Reading the Text

1. How do teens like April Miller define their identity, according to
   Bernstein?
2. Describe in your own words what it means to "claim" an ethnic identity.
   Why do so many teens "claim" a new ethnicity, according to Bernstein?
3. What relationship does Bernstein see between claiming and the mass
   media?
4. What does being white mean to many of the kids who claim a nonwhite
   identity?
5. What does the city signify to the young people whom Bernstein describes?

### Reading the Signs

1. In class, stage a conversation between April Miller and her father on her
   adoption of a Mexican identity, with April defending her choice and her
   father repudiating it.
2. Write an essay in which you support, challenge, or modify Andrea Jones's
   assumption that it is media-generated "glamour" that prompts young people to claim a new ethnic identity.
3. Write an argumentative essay in which you explain whether the claiming
   fad is an expression of racial tolerance or racial stereotyping.
4. Read or reread bell hooks's "Madonna: Plantation Mistress or Soul Sister?" (p. 223). Then write an essay in which you argue whether Madonna
   could be accused of claiming a racial identity not biologically hers.

5. Bernstein describes teens claiming the identities of ethnic minorities, but she provides no instances of claiming a white identity. In class, discuss what being white signifies to these teens.

6. Write an essay in which you explore the relationship between claiming and gang membership. To develop your ideas, you might consult Sonia Maasik and Jack Solomon, "Signs of the Street: A Conversation" (p. 597) and Seth Mydans, "Not Just the Inner City: Well-to-Do Join Gangs" (p. 607).

# SAM FULWOOD III
## The Rage of the Black Middle Class

||||||||||||||||||||||||||||||||||||||||||||||||||||||||||||

*Though a period of violence and upheaval, the sixties were also a time of hope, especially for the American civil rights movement. A new American Dream appeared, one that promised a colorblind society in which all Americans could live together as one and racial differences would no longer matter. Writing a quarter-century after the assassination of Martin Luther King, Jr., Sam Fulwood III (b. 1956) surveys the legacy of the civil rights movement and finds it wanting. In America, the color of your skin still matters, even for African-Americans who have moved into the suburban middle class. Torn between his desire to maintain a comfortable middle-class existence and his rage at still feeling alien in a largely white world, Fulwood shares his disappointment and his sense of betrayal in this essay, originally written for the* Los Angeles Times Magazine. *Can African-Americans join the middle class and still retain their sense of ethnic identity? Fulwood, a correspondent for the* Los Angeles Times's *Washington bureau, isn't so sure. A graduate of the University of North Carolina at Chapel Hill and former Nieman Fellow at Harvard University, Fulwood wrote award-winning stories on the Clarence Thomas hearings and contributed to his paper's Pulitzer Prize–winning coverage of the Los Angeles riots in 1992. His most recent major publication is* Waking from the Dream: My Life in the Black Middle Class *(1996).*

Race awareness displaced my blissful childhood in 1969.

I was then in the sixth grade at Oaklawn Elementary, a three-year-old school built on the edge of my neighborhood in Charlotte, N.C. Everybody knew that one day little white boys and girls would attend classes there, but at the time, the sparkling new rooms contained only black students and teachers.

Some gossips believed that the school was built less to accommodate the affluent black families in the poorly served northwest neighborhood than to anticipate the demands of white parents who never would have allowed their precious little ones to sit in our old ramshackle schoolhouse.

None of this mattered to me. I was simply proud of the school and confident that nothing would detour my short walk to and from its library and lunchroom, my two favorite places in the building. My contentment was coldly jolted on one beautiful spring day, when Principal Gwen Cunningham's voice crackled over the intercom, summoning me to her office for a chat about my future.

Mrs. Cunningham, a proper and proud black woman, knew that my   5 father was a Presbyterian minister and my mother was an elementary school teacher, the perfect pair of parents for unchallenged credentials into black society's elite. She was convinced, on the advice of my teachers, that I should be among the first students from her elementary school to attend the nearest white junior high school the following year. This was an honor, she declared. Mrs. Cunningham countered any arguments I attempted about staying at the neighborhood school. As if I needed additional persuading, she stated: "I am absolutely certain that you can hold your own with the best [white students] at Ranson Junior High."

Suddenly, I was different from my friends and classmates, slightly better prepared to "hold my own." Moreover, it was my duty to my race to blaze a path for other blacks to follow. Mrs. Cunningham didn't know it, but she had set my life on a new course. I had been tapped, in the words of Yale law professor Stephen L. Carter, into the fraternity of "best blacks," an unofficial grouping of people selected to lead the way toward improved racial understanding and uplift.

I evolved that day into a race-child, one who believed that he would illuminate the magnificent social changes wrought by racial progress. Overt racial barriers were falling, and I, among the favored in Charlotte's black middle class, thought my future would be free of racism, free of oppression. I believed I was standing on the portico of the Promised Land.

Now, as the twentieth century seeps away, I am waking from my blind belief in the American Dream. I feel betrayed and isolated. I am angrier than I've ever been.

Lest anyone misunderstand, this is a new and troubling sensation. I was born to cheerfully embrace integration of the races, not to sulk back into a segregated world in despair. I was among that virgin group of black men and women for whom legal segregation was less a cruel reality and more historical (some say forgotten) fact. Nobody ever called me a nigger.

But now, for the first time, I am no longer running away from the   10 questions that I've spent a lifetime denying would ever be posed: Is

American society the race-blind haven that black people of my parents' generation had hoped it would be for their children? If not, what alternative do we have? I have no answers.

Although racial tensions continue to escalate, few blacks or whites seem willing to spend the resources — both fiscal and human — to ease the strain of living separate lives. Rather, a form of Balkanization is occurring, with race and class separating us. My generation — called the "new black middle class" by one sociologist — is so disillusioned by the persistent racism that continues to define and limit us that we are abandoning efforts to assimilate into the mainstream of society. I see no end to this trend.

In 1967, as the civil rights movement gathered steam, about 266,000 black American households earned an inflation-adjusted $50,000 or more, the government definition of affluence. In 1989, the number of such households had grown to more than one million. Prosperity for middle-class blacks soared so fast and so high during the past three decades that some of us no longer remember the way things used to be.

My parents used to bristle with anger whenever I teased them about being "richer" than other black families we knew. Their displeasure stemmed from a closer identification with poor black people than with neighbors and friends who in their nicer houses and fancier cars appeared "too big for their britches." In my parents' generation, poverty and black were synonymous. When my father and now-deceased mother were married in the early 1950s, about 55% of black Americans were living below the official poverty line. Although my father knows that only a third of the nation's blacks remain poor — with less than 10% confined to an "underclass" of persistent poor — he still associates himself with the underdog.

That attitude was evident during the recent Clarence Thomas Supreme Court confirmation battle. Much of Thomas's support among blacks stems from his up-by-the-bootstraps background. In contrast, Oklahoma law professor Anita Hill's polished demeanor was perceived by many working-class blacks as elitist, something they couldn't identify with.

But those views seem to be fading relics of the civil rights generation.    15
Younger, wealthier, better-educated black Americans associate less — and, therefore, identify less — with their poor cousins. We zoom past crack houses in bright, shiny cars with our windows and doors locked tight. We live in the suburbs and send our children to private academies. The world of a black middle-class achiever is a self-protective cocoon, separate from poor blacks and all whites.

I don't know what to tell my four-year-old daughter, Amanda, who is developing an awareness of her own racial and class identity, when difficult questions arise about her place in society. Recently she shocked her mother and me by declaring that when she grows up, she intends to "be white" like one of her classmates.

For the moment, the issue is dormant because simple answers will satisfy her. Clearly, the time is coming when I will need a better answer. And, I am sure, I will *not* repeat the blind beliefs of my youth. I don't want my daughter to be a second-generation "best black," her childhood twisted by the mistaken belief that race will one day be unimportant in her life.

My parents, born in rural North Carolina in the first quarter of this century, never questioned the inequities of the segregated South, but they demanded that life for my brother and me would be different. By an act of Protestant willpower, they sheltered us from the lingering traces of Jim Crow and imbued in us a belief that the evils of the outside world — I never heard the word *racism* in our household — could be made to disappear. If I worked hard, nothing was impossible.

A telling incident occurred in the early sixties — I don't really remember it, but the family has recalled the tale so often that it has become part of our history — when my younger brother, George, and I were turned away from a donkey ride outside Clarks' department store.

George noticed the bright red, blue, and green neon lights in the       20
store's parking lot. That's where the donkeys, tethered to a pole in the asphalt, slowly paced in a hay-filled circle. Other kids were riding the animals; we begged our parents to let us ride, too.

Exactly what was said by the teenage white attendant, my parents never repeated. The upshot was clear, however: He wasn't going to let us ride. As decent and law-abiding Negroes, my parents accepted the snub without argument or question. As the four of us walked back to our car with George and me in full-throated retreat, my parents' embarrassment remained veiled — until George (I am sure it was George) asked my father why they wouldn't let us ride.

"The people who own the animals don't want colored people riding them," he said in a statement-of-fact voice. "Only whites."

"Well, we can come back tomorrow," George demanded in the imperious voice that only a child can summon. "We can wear false faces. Maybe then they'll let us ride."

As the family version of this story goes, Momma lost it right then at the mere thought of her little ones hiding behind plastic masks for a ride on a funky donkey. The sight of her tears reignited our crying and provoked Daddy into a rare flash of anger. "You're not wearing any false faces, and you're not riding the damn donkeys," he said. "So forget it. This never happened."

Were it not for the dramatic social changes that transpired during my       25
childhood, I doubt that, decades later, my family would have been able to joke about the episode. I carried their laughter over the retelling of that story into adulthood as a lesson in the inevitability of the changes occurring around me. I was certain that by the time I turned thirty-five,

no one would care what color I was. All that mattered would be whether
I carried a green, gold, or platinum American Express card.

I was born in 1956 and came of age as the Great Society of the late
1960s closed. Author and scholar David Bradley defined that period as the
"Years of the Black" in a seminal essay in the May, 1982, issue of
*Esquire*. Bradley called it a "fascinating epoch" during which benevolent,
wealthy and white liberals, driven by the guilt of their forefathers' sins and
the rantings of Afro'd, heat-packing, shades-wearing militants, persuaded
politicians and activists to swallow an expensive set of social programs
meant "to conceal evidence of a scandalous past or present."

I have kept a clipping of Bradley's autobiographical essay — titled
"Black and American, 1982" and subtitled "There are no good times to
be black in America, but some times are worse than others" — since it
was published. At that time, I was embarking on my career as a reporter
at my hometown newspaper with the naive notion that my ambition and
ability would carry me to unlimited vistas. I was convinced that someday
I would respond to Bradley, challenging his pessimism and extolling my
triumph. I would declare that the Rev. Martin Luther King, Jr.'s, Great
Black American Dream had been fulfilled in my generation. Mine would
be the first in this nation's history to be judged "by the content of their
character, not the color of their skin."

Sadly, almost a decade later, I must admit that Bradley, a professor of
English at Temple University, was right to say that it is impossible "to
give a socially meaningful description of who I am and what I've done
without using the word black." This is painful, because it means I must
accept his corollary: "Nothing I shall ever accomplish or discover or earn
or inherit or buy or sell or give away — nothing I can ever do — will
outweigh the fact of my race in determining my destiny."

As a child of the post-civil rights black bourgeoisie, I was a primary
beneficiary of the protest generation and, therefore, among its most
hopeful supporters. Today, we sons and daughters of those who faced the
dogs, water hoses, and brutal cops are turning away from our parents'
great expectations of an integrated America. Many middle-class black executives are moving out of their corporate roles to create fulfilling jobs
that serve black customers. Black colleges are experiencing a renaissance.
Black organizations — churches, fraternities, sororities, and professional
groups — are attracting legions of new members. And, most surprising to
me, upscale blacks are moving to neighborhoods that insulate them from
the slings and arrows of the larger society.

Two years ago, I lived in the conspicuously affluent, middle-class black    30
suburban neighborhood of BrookGlen, about 15 miles from downtown Atlanta. My neighbors were proud of their large homes and loved to entertain.
One warm, summer evening, a backyard gathering fell suddenly silent as a
car, marked with a local realtor's logo and containing a white couple, cruised

slowly through the subdivision. Finally, one of my neighbors spoke up. "What are they looking for?" he asked bitterly. "I hope they don't find anything they like. Otherwise, there goes the neighborhood." The message was clear: Even affluent whites would ruin the sanctuary of our community.

Many of the black men and women who have come to accept this reality appear to fit neatly within the system among their white peers. They own the symbols of success. But deep inside, they are unhappy, knowing they are not accepted as equals by their white colleagues or acquaintances.

"This will be an ethnic party," says my friend Marian Holmes, inviting me to a dinner at her home in one of the few predominantly white neighborhoods in Washington. "It will be just us, no white people."

Holmes is no racist. Quite the contrary, she worries that her world is not black enough. Nearly all of her colleagues at the *Smithsonian* magazine, where she works as an editor, are white. She is comfortable with them, frequently entertaining coworkers at her home and being entertained in theirs. Even so, she seemed perplexed by her urge to host a dinner party of only black guests. It was something she couldn't remember ever having done, and now it seemed imperative. For the first time in her forty-two years, Holmes was taking stock of the fact that being black was an inescapable fact of her life.

Perhaps, like me, it hit her when Jennifer, her five-year-old daughter, began asking the tough questions: "Mommy, why aren't there more black people in the world?"

"That's an odd question for a black child living in Washington to ask," Holmes says. "But then, you know, it made sense that she would ask me something like that. There aren't very many black people in her world, which includes home, neighborhood, and school."

Pam Harris, a forty-one-year-old accountant with an Atlanta real estate management firm and one of my Atlanta neighbors, says the folks who live in her BrookGlen subdivision are proud that their community is composed of black doctors, attorneys, executives, and college professors.

"All of us have been made to feel that we have to be validated by whites to be good people and good at what we do," Harris says. "But we don't want to be validated. By living in an all-black, middle-class community, it lets us know that we're good, and there are not any of them around staring us in the face to prove it so.

"So much goes on at the job that [black professionals] have to endure, the slights and negative comments and feelings that we're unwanted," she continues. "When we have to work around them all day, by the time I come home I don't want to have to deal with white people any more."

It's a form of self-segregation, a defense against the pain of being rejected or misunderstood. One friend has coined the term "white folks overload" to explain the fits of frustration that she says black people experience from prolonged exposure to white people. With that in mind, she and her husband consciously sought out a predominantly black neighborhood in Los Angeles — View Park — as a place to begin a family. "I can't see [whites] everyday," she explained. "It's not that I dislike them or anything, but there's a membrane of coping that you have to wear to be around them."

I know what she means. Whites rarely seem at ease in my company, unless they are in control of the environment. By outnumbering and outmanning me at virtually every turn, they compel me to adapt my view of the world, even my own sense of self, to their majoritarian biases. Trying to explain my life to white people, who just don't care to understand, is taxing and, ultimately, not worth the trouble. Sort of like singing "Swing Low, Sweet Chariot" *en francais*. Why bother? Once translated, it's just not the same song.

After cultivating an image, a personality, and a set of career trophies that I assumed would be eagerly embraced by the larger society, I am maddened to learn that the color black is the foremost thing that whites see in me. I am reminded of the words of the black sergeant in Charles Fuller's *A Soldier's Play*: "You got to be like them! And I was! I was — but the rules are fixed. . . . It doesn't make any difference. They still hate you!"

This revelation first appeared to me while on assignment in the dusty South African township of Duduza, about 30 miles west of Johannesburg. My guide, Alexander Monteodi, pointed out that every fifth house or so on one street had been torched, apparently by black activists opposed to the apartheid government. Monteodi, who was the founder of the Duduza Civic Association, a community self-improvement group, explained that the charred remains "were the houses of the briefcase toters," those middle-class blacks set up by authorities to serve as examples for disgruntled blacks to emulate.

"The government wants to create a black middle class for us to look up to," Monteodi said. "Here in all this despair, they believe that those misguided blacks working for them in those city offices will serve as role models for the rest of us stuck here. It's crazy. All of us can't be middle class."

This pinprick of a comment burst my balloon. I am black and middle class in America. Have I been set up, framed like a pretty picture of upward mobility for other blacks — in America, across the globe — to replicate? Monteodi shrugged. "You live there, I don't," he said softly.

I wanted to scream. In South Africa, I first challenged the status quo of my soul. I no longer wanted to play the game. Being "middle class" suddenly was an epithet, another way of saying I wanted to be white, a rejection of being black and American.

More than a generation ago, a black sociologist named E. Franklin Frazier ignited a blaze of angst that still burns within black America by publishing *The Black Bourgeoisie,* a scathing denunciation of black American pseudoaristocracy. The 1955 book touched raw nerves among old-line, fair-skinned black families who affected the manners, dress, and behavior of whites. These blacks, Frazier contended, lived "largely in a world of make-believe; the masks which they wear to play their sorry roles conceal the feelings of inferiority and of insecurity and the frustrations that haunt their inner lives."

After two world wars and the migration of large numbers of blacks from the rural South to the industrial centers in northern cities, the complexion of the black middle class grew darker as "pure Negroes" displaced the mulatto elites, Frazier explained. In fact, skin pigmentation declined as the mark of rank among middle-class blacks, giving way to white collars and salaried jobs as the assumed price of acceptance among whites. Frazier observed that black professionals — "doctors, dentists and lawyers, and even teachers" — set the standards for what it takes "to achieve status and recognition in American society."

But Thomas L. Johnson, a thirty-four-year-old urologist in Los Angeles, told me that advanced education and professional achievement provide no vaccination against an outbreak of racist behavior from whites. "All through high school, college and medical school, I was around liberal [white students]," he said one evening at his home. "As I spent more time around them and we all got older, I really discovered they were pseudo-liberals from the sixties, who would hang around black people, smoke dope with some of us, maybe even date black women. But when it's time to settle down and raise their families, they revert to their roots of racism."

An example: "I was playing in a team tennis tournament here in Los Angeles last year at a white country club," he says. "My team is all black, and the team we were playing was all white, and we were winning when one of the white guys became frustrated. The scene deteriorated as he lost more and more points and started an argument with a black guy on my team.

"As they argued over a point, the white guy shouted: 'Well, what if I     50 call you a nigger?'" Johnson says, rolling his eyes in disgust at the memory. "I didn't expect that kind of behavior from these so-called 'upper-class' whites. But what shocked me even more was that other whites heard him use the 'N word,' and their attitude was like 'That's no big deal, let's play some tennis.' They didn't seem the least bit shocked and failed to react. White people refuse to understand how much that hurt and how insulted we were by the racist remark and their acceptance of it.

"On one level, I guess I always thought this would happen," he says. "But I'm taken aback now that I'm experiencing it firsthand. I know racism exists, but I never expected it to happen to me."

In his 1988 book, *The New Black Middle Class,* Bart Landry argues that a "chance simultaneous occurrence" of civil rights activism and national prosperity between 1960 and 1970 generated "the most radical changes in black social structure" in the nation's history.

Moreover, Landry, a sociologist at the University of Maryland, suggests that the civil rights movement was "at first a movement with middle-class goals — desegregation of public accommodations." This shouldn't come as a surprise because the sit-ins and nonviolent protests that swept through the South and, later, the nation, were led by middle-class blacks, who wanted to move closer to a white standard of living. Many were college students who expected one day to earn big salaries working in large, white-owned corporations and to spend their new-found wealth on the luxuries traditionally reserved for white people.

As they assimilated, black folks lost their soul and rhythm, their willingness to laugh out loud in public, even their outrage at oppression — both real and imagined. Recently, for example, a luncheon companion scolded me for ordering fried chicken. "I can't believe you did that," she said, sputtering with embarrassment and contempt. "That's the sort of thing I would expect an ignorant person who's never been in a restaurant before to do. How would you feel if your [white] coworkers saw you getting all greasy eating that?" This black woman, who owns both undergraduate and law-school degrees, has become so well-educated that she now knows better than to appear ignorant before white people by eating chicken in public.

So what does all this mean?                                                        55

I am reluctant to predict the future. Despite what my heart wants to believe, I can't escape thinking that white America, which stopped short of embracing middle-class blacks at the moment we most wanted inclusion, may have already lost its opportunity. The refusal of the larger society to embrace us, combined with our unwillingness to return to the ghetto, is likely to result in even more isolation, frustration, and desperation. And, worst of all, more anger. As one who once wanted to live and work and play snuggled within the American Dream, I am putting a fresh coat of pain on my cocoon.

There, in the safety of that betwixt-and-between state, I stand wobbly, unaccepted by whites who do not regard me as their equal and hovering aloof from poorer blacks, separated from them by a flimsy wrapper of social status. I straddle two worlds and consider neither home.

### Reading the Text

1. What were Fulwood's boyhood expectations of adult life?
2. Why do Fulwood's black middle-class friends engage in "self-segregation"?
3. What evidence does Fulwood present to show covert racism on the part of middle-class white people?
4. Why does Fulwood say "I straddle two worlds and consider neither home"?

### Reading the Signs

1. In a journal entry, explore your own responses to Fulwood's essay. If you are a person of color, have you shared some of the frustrations and anger that Fulwood expresses? How have your experiences been similar or different? If you are Caucasian, how do you respond to the "white folks overload" and the voluntary segregation described by Fulwood's friends? How might such segregation compare with the historical segregation imposed upon blacks?

2. Research the extent to which the alienation from mainstream society that Fulwood describes is prevalent among blacks on your campus. Interview at least five African-Americans (they can be students, staff, or faculty), and ask them about their experiences and aspirations. Then write an essay in which you compare your findings with the experiences Fulwood describes.

3. Compare Fulwood's friends with the teens mentioned in Nell Bernstein's "Goin' Gangsta, Choosin' Cholita" (p. 504). In what ways are their concerns about ethnicity and racial injustice similar? What differences do you find in their comments?

4. Fulwood says he is angry because the color black is, for white people, the primary sign of his identity. In class, brainstorm on the board ways in which "whiteness" can function as a sign in American society. Then discuss your results. What patterns emerge in your list? In what ways does the significance of "whiteness" depend on the ethnicity of the interpreter?

5. Compare and contrast Fulwood's attitudes toward ethnicity with those of Gloria Anzaldúa ("How to Tame a Wild Tongue," p. 541). What are their attitudes toward mainstream culture and toward their own ethnic backgrounds?

BRIAN A. COURTNEY

## Freedom From Choice

*If your mother's ancestors came from Africa and your father's came from Europe, what would you check off on a census form: "African-American" or "white"? For Brian A. Courtney (b. 1973), such questions arise every day, and he has no easy answers. In a nation obsessed with racial identity, little guidance is offered to those who combine multiple ethnic backgrounds. Maybe, Courtney suggests, we should invent a new category to clear up the confusion. A graduate of the University of Tennessee, Courtney is a reporter for the* Knoxville News-Sentinal.

As my friend Denise and I trudged across the University of Tennessee campus to our 9:05 A.M. class, we delivered countless head nods, "Heys" and "How ya' doin's" to other African-Americans we passed along the way. We spoke to people we knew as well as people we didn't know because it's an unwritten rule that black people speak to one another when they pass. But when I stopped to greet and hug one of my female friends, who happens to be white, Denise seemed a little bothered. We continued our walk to class, and Denise expressed concern that I might be coming down with a "fever." "I don't feel sick," I told her. As it turns out, she was referring to "jungle fever," the condition where a black man or woman is attracted to someone of the opposite race.

This encounter has not been an uncommon experience for me. That's why the first 21 years of my life have felt like a never-ending tug of war. And quite honestly, I'm not looking forward to being dragged through the mud for the rest of my life. My white friends want me to act one way — white. My African-American friends want me to act another — black. Pleasing them both is nearly impossible and leaves little room to be just me.

The politically correct term for someone with my racial background is "biracial" or "multiracial." My mother is fair-skinned with blond hair and blue eyes. My father is dark-complexioned with prominent African-American features and a head of woolly hair. When you combine the genetic makeup of the two, you get me — golden-brown skin, semi-coarse hair and a whole mess of freckles.

Someone once told me I was lucky to be biracial because I have the best of both worlds. In some ways this is true. I have a huge family that's filled with diversity and is as colorful as a box of Crayolas. My family is more open to whomever I choose to date, whether that person is black, white, biracial, Asian or whatever. But looking at the big picture, American society makes being biracial feel less like a blessing than a curse.

One reason is the American obsession with labeling. We feel the    5 need to label everyone and everything and group them into neatly defined categories. Are you a Republican, a Democrat or an Independent? Are you pro-life or pro-choice? Are you African-American, Caucasian or Native American? Not everyone fits into such classifications. This presents a problem for me and the many biracial people living in the United States. The rest of the population seems more comfortable when we choose to identify with one group. And it pressures us to do so, forcing us to deny half of who we are.

Growing up in the small, predominantly white town of Maryville, Tenn., I attended William Blount High School. I was one of a handful of minority students — a raisin in a box of cornflakes, so to speak.

Almost all of my peers, many of whom I've known since grade school, were white. Over the years, they've commented on how different I am from other black people they know. The implication was that I'm better because I'm only *half* black. Acceptance into their world has meant talking as they talk, dressing as they dress and appreciating the same music. To reduce tension and make everyone feel comfortable, I've reacted by ignoring half of my identity and downplaying my ethnicity.

My experience at UT has been very similar. This time it's my African-American peers exerting pressure to choose. Some African-Americans on campus say I "talk too white." I dress like the boys in white fraternities. I have too many white friends. In other words, I'm not black enough. I'm a white "wanna-be." The other day, an African-American acquaintance told me I dress "bourgie." This means I dress very white — a pastel-colored polo, a pair of navy chinos and hiking boots. Before I came to terms with this kind of remark, a comment like this would have angered me, and I must admit that I was a little offended. But instead of showing my frustration, I let it ride, and I simply said "Thank you." Surprised by this response, she said in disbelief, "You mean you agree?"

On more occasions than I dare to count, black friends have made sweeping derogatory statements about the white race in general. "White people do this, or white people do that." Every time I hear them, I cringe. These comments refer not just to my white friends but to my mother and maternal grandmother as well. Why should I have to shun or hide my white heritage to enhance my ethnicity? Doesn't the fact that I have suffered the same prejudices as every other African-American — and then some — count for something?

I do not blame my African-American or white friends for the problems faced by biracial people in America. I blame society for not acknowledging us as a separate race. I am speaking not only for people who, like myself, are half black and half white, but also for those who are half white and half Asian, half white and half Hispanic, or half white and half whatever. Until American society recognizes us as a distinct group, we will continue to be pressured to choose one side of our heritage over the other.

Job applications, survey forms, college-entrance exams and the like    10
ask individuals to check only *one* box for race. For most of my life, I have marked BLACK because my skin color is the first thing people notice. However, I could just as honestly have marked WHITE. Somehow, when I fill out these forms, I think the employers, administrators, researchers, teachers or whoever sees them will have a problem looking at my face and then accepting a big X by the word WHITE. In any case, checking BLACK or WHITE does not truly represent me. Only in recent

years have some private universities added the category of BIRACIAL or MULTIRACIAL to their applications. I've heard that a few states now include these categories on government forms.

One of the greatest things  parents of biracial children can do is expose them to *both* of their cultures. But what good does this do when in the end society makes us choose? Having a separate category marked BIRACIAL will not magically put an end to the pressure to choose, but it will help people to stop judging us as just black or just white and see us for what we really are — both.


### Reading the Text

1. Why did Courtney's friend Denise think he suffered from "jungle fever"?
2. What are the problems that biracial people in America face, according to Courtney?
3. What significance does Courtney see in the "American obsession with labeling"?
4. Why does Courtney believe that biracial people should be considered "a separate race"?


### Reading the Signs

1. Write a letter to Courtney in which you respond to his concern that "Until American society recognizes [biracial people] as a distinct group, we will continue to be pressured to choose one side of our heritage over the other."
2. In your journal, explore you own sense of ethnic identity. How do you choose to categorize yourself? Would strangers categorize you the same way? Have you ever felt pressure to "choose" an ethnic identity?
3. Do you think Courtney would be sympathetic or hostile to teens who "try on" different ethnic identities? Writing as if you were Courtney, write a letter to one of the teenagers who claims a new ethnic identity in Nell Bernstein's "Goin' Gangsta, Choosin' Cholita," p. 504.
4. Courtney, Dorinne K. Kondo ("On Being a Conceptual Anomaly," p. 523), and Gloria Anzaldúa ("How to Tame a Wild Tongue," p. 541) all describe multifaceted ethnic identities. Drawing upon these selections, write an essay in which you argue for or against the "American obsession with labeling" people according to ethnicity.
5. In class, brainstorm names of biracial actors, musicians, or models. Then discuss the extent to which the mass media (TV, film, advertising, videos) presume that people fit neatly into ethnic categories. What is the effect of such a presumption?

DORINNE K. KONDO

*On Being a Conceptual Anomaly*

‖‖‖‖‖‖‖‖‖‖‖‖‖‖‖‖‖‖‖‖‖‖‖‖‖‖‖‖‖‖‖‖‖‖‖‖‖‖‖‖‖‖‖‖‖‖‖‖

*Imagine going back to your ancestral homeland and finding yourself being judged for your inability to fit in perfectly with people of your ancestry. That's what happened to Dorinne Kondo, a Japanese American anthropology professor who went back to Japan to live and study and found herself being criticized for her American accent when speaking Japanese. Noting how, for the Japanese, "race, language, and culture are intertwined," Kondo tells how she was "a living oxymoron" to her Japanese hosts, who were astonished by this visitor who looked Japanese but who lacked Japanese "cultural competence." At the same time, as an American woman, Kondo found herself astonished by the gender roles of Japanese society whereby "men — even the sweetest, nicest ones — ask for a second helping of rice by merely holding out their rice bowls to the woman nearest the rice cooker." Dorinne Kondo holds the MacArthur Associate Professorship of Women's Studies in the Anthropology Department at Pomona College. She is the author of* Crafting Selves: Power, Gender, and Discourses of Identity in a Japanese Workplace *(1990), from which this selection is excerpted, and* About Face: Performing Race in Fashion and Theater *(1997).*

As a Japanese American,[1] I created a conceptual dilemma for the Japanese I encountered. For them, I was a living oxymoron, someone who was both Japanese and not Japanese. Their puzzlement was all the greater since most Japanese people I knew seemed to adhere to an eminently biological definition of Japaneseness. Race, language, and culture

---

1. Said, Edward. *Orientalism*. New York: Pantheon. 1978. The issue of what to call ourselves is an issue of considerable import to various ethnic and racial groups in the United States, as the recent emphasis on the term "African American" shows. For Asian Americans, the term "Oriental" was called into question in the sixties, for the reasons Said enumerates: the association of the term with stereotypes such as Oriental despotism, inscrutability, splendor, exoticism, mystery, and so on. It also defines "the East" in terms of "the West," in a relationship of unequal power — how rarely one hears of "the Occident," for example. Asian Americans, Japanese Americans included, sometimes hyphenate the term, but some of us would argue that leaving out the hyphen makes the term "Asian" or "Japanese" an adjective, rather than implying a half-and-half status: i.e., that one's loyalties/identities might be half Japanese and half American. Rather, in the terms "Asian American" and "Japanese American," the accent is on the "American," an important political claim in light of the mainstream tendency to see Asian Americans as somehow more foreign than other kinds of Americans.

are intertwined, so much so that any challenge to this firmly entrenched conceptual schema — a white person who speaks flawlessly idiomatic and unaccented Japanese, or a person of Japanese ancestry who cannot — meets with what generously could be described as unpleasant reactions. White people are treated as repulsive and unnatural — *hen na gaijin,* strange foreigners — the better their Japanese becomes, while Japanese Americans and others of Japanese ancestry born overseas are faced with exasperation and disbelief. How can someone who is racially Japanese lack "cultural competence"?[2] During my first few months in Tokyo, many tried to resolve this paradox by asking which of my parents was "really" American.

Indeed, it is a minor miracle that those first months did not lead to an acute case of agoraphobia, for I knew that once I set foot outside the door, someone somewhere (a taxi driver? a salesperson? a bank clerk?) would greet one of my linguistic mistakes with an astonished "Eh?" I became all too familiar with the series of expressions that would flicker over those faces: bewilderment, incredulity, embarrassment, even anger, at having to deal with this odd person who looked Japanese and therefore human, but who must be retarded, deranged, or — equally undesirable in Japanese eyes — Chinese or Korean. Defensively, I would mull over the mistake of the day. I mean, how was I to know that in order to "fillet a fish" you had to cut it "in three pieces"? Or that opening a bank account required so much specialized terminology? Courses in literary Japanese at Harvard hadn't done much to prepare me for the realities of everyday life in Tokyo. Gritting my teeth in determination as I groaned inwardly, I would force myself out of the house each morning.

For me, and apparently for the people around me, this was a stressful time, when expectations were flouted, when we had to strain to make sense of one another. There seemed to be few advantages in my retaining an American persona, for the distress caused by these reactions was difficult to bear. In the face of dissonance and distress, I found that the desire for comprehensible order in the form of "fitting in," even if it meant suppression of and violence against a self I had known in another context, was preferable to meaninglessness. Anthropological imperatives to immerse oneself in another culture intensified this desire, so that acquiring the accoutrements of Japanese selfhood meant simultaneously constructing a more thoroughly professional anthropological persona. This required language learning in the broadest sense, mastery of culturally appropriate modes of moving, acting, and speaking. For my informants, it

2. White, Merry. *The Japanese Overseas: Can They Go Home Again?* New York: Free Press, 1988. Offers an account of the families of Japanese corporate executives who are transferred abroad and who often suffer painful difficulties upon reentering Japan.

was clear that coping with this anomalous creature was difficult, for here was someone who looked like a real human being, but who simply failed to perform according to expectation. They, too, had every reason to make me over in their image, to guide me, gently but insistently, into properly Japanese behavior, so that the discrepancy between my appearance and my cultural competence would not be so painfully evident. I posed a challenge to their senses of identity. How could someone who *looked* Japanese not *be* Japanese? In my cultural ineptitude, I represented for the people who met me the chaos of meaninglessness. Their response in the face of this dissonance was to *make* me as Japanese as possible. Thus, my first nine months of fieldwork were characterized by an attempt to reduce the distance between expectation and inadequate reality, as my informants and I conspired to rewrite my identity as Japanese.

My guarantor, an older woman who, among her many activities, was a teacher of flower arranging, introduced me to many families who owned businesses in the ward of Tokyo where I had chosen to do my research. One of her former students and fellow flower-arranging teachers, Mrs. Sakamoto, agreed to take me in as a guest over the summer, since the apartment where I was scheduled to move — owned by one of my classmates in tea ceremony — was still under construction. My proclivities for "acting Japanese" were by this time firmly established. During my stay with the Sakamotos, I did my best to conform to what I thought their expectations of a guest/daughter might be. This in turn seemed to please them and reinforced my tendency to behave in terms of what I perceived to be my Japanese persona.

My initial encounter with the head of the household epitomizes this       5 mirroring and reinforcement of behavior. Mr. Sakamoto had been on a business trip on the day I moved in, and he returned the following evening, just as his wife, daughter, and I sat down to the evening meal. As soon as he stepped in the door, I immediately switched from an informal posture, seated on the *zabuton* (seat cushion) to a formal greeting posture, *seiza*-style (kneeling on the floor) and bowed low, hands on the floor. Mr. Sakamoto responded in kind (being older, male, and head of the household, he did not have to bow as deeply as I did), and we exchanged the requisite polite formulae, I requesting his benevolence, and he welcoming me to their family. Later, he told me how happy and impressed he had been with this act of proper etiquette on my part. "Today's young people in Japan," he said, "no longer show such respect. Your grandfather must have been a fine man to raise such a fine granddaughter." Of course, his statements can hardly be accepted at face value. They may well indicate his relief that I seemed to know something of proper Japanese behavior, and hence would not be a complete nuisance to them; it was also his way of making me feel at home. What is important to note is the way this statement was used to elicit proper Japanese behavior in future encounters. And his strategy worked. I was left with a warm, positive feeling toward the Sakamoto family, armed with an incentive to behave in a Japanese way, for clearly these were the expectations and the desires of the people who had taken me in and who were so generously sharing their lives with me.

Other members of the household voiced similar sentiments. Takemi-san, the Sakamotos' married daughter who lived in a distant prefecture, had been visiting her parents when I first moved in. A few minutes after our initial encounter, she observed, "You seem like a typical Japanese woman" (*Nihon no josei, to iu kanji*). Later in the summer, Mrs. Sakamoto confided to me that she could never allow a "pure American" (*junsui na Amerikajin*) to live with them, for only someone of Japanese descent was genetically capable of adjusting to life on *tatami* mats, using unsewered toilets, sleeping on the floor — in short, of living Japanese style. Again, the message was unambiguous: My "family" could feel comfortable with me insofar as I was — and acted — Japanese.

At first, then, as a Japanese American I made sense to those around me as a none-too-felicitous combination of racial categories. As field-work progressed, however, and my linguistic and cultural skills improved, my informants seemed best able to understand me by placing me in meaningful cultural roles: daughter, guest, young woman, student, prodigal Japanese who had finally seen the light and come home. Most people preferred to treat me as a Japanese — sometimes an incomplete or unconventional Japanese, but a Japanese nonetheless. Indeed, even when I tried to represent myself as an American, others did not always take heed. For instance, on my first day on the job at the confectionery factory, Mr. Satō introduced me to the division chief as an "American student," here to learn about the business and about the "real situation" (*jittai*) of workers in small enterprise. Soon it became clear that the chief remembered "student," but not "American." A week or so later, we gathered for one of our noon meetings to read from a pamphlet published by an ethics school. The owner came, and he commented on the theme of the day, *ketsui* (determination). At one point during his speech, he singled me out, praising my resolve. "If Kondō-san had been an ordinary young woman, she might never have known Japan." I stared at my shoes, my cheeks flaming. When the exercise finished, I hurried back to my work station. Akiyama-san, the division head, approached me with a puzzled expression on his face. "*Doko desu ka?*" he asked. (Where is it? — in other words, where are you from?) And after my reply, he announced loudly to all: "She says it's America!"

My physical characteristics led my friends and coworkers to emphasize my identity as Japanese, sometimes even against my own intentions and desires. Over time, my increasingly "Japanese" behavior served temporarily to resolve their crises of meaning and to confirm their assumptions about their own identities. That I, too, came to participate enthusiastically in this recasting of the self is a testimonial to their success in acting upon me.

## Conflict and Fragmentation of Self

Using these ready-made molds may have reduced the dissonance in my informants' minds, but it served only to increase the dissonance in my own. What occurred in the field was a kind of fragmenting of identity into what I then labeled Japanese and American pieces, so that the different elements, instead of fitting together to form at least the illusion of a seamless and coherent whole — it is the contention of this book that selves which are coherent, seamless, bounded, and whole are indeed illusions — strained against one another. The war was not really — or only — between Japanese and American elements, however. Perhaps it had even more to do with the position of researcher versus one of daughter and guest. In one position, my goal had to be the pursuit of knowledge, where decisive action, independence, and mastery were held in high esteem. In another, independence and mastery of one's own fate were out of the question; rather, being a daughter meant duties, responsibilities, and *inter*dependence.

The more I adjusted to my Japanese daughter's role, the keener the 10 conflicts became. Most of those conflicts had to do with expectations surrounding gender, and, more specifically, my position as a young woman. Certainly, in exchange for the care the Sakamotos showed me, I was happy to help out in whatever way I could. I tried to do some housecleaning and laundry, and I took over the shopping and cooking for Mr. Sakamoto when Mrs. Sakamoto was at one of the children's association meetings, her flower-arranging classes, or meetings of ward committees on juvenile delinquency. The cooking did not offend me in and of itself; in fact, I was glad for the opportunity to learn how to make simple Japanese cuisine, and Mr. Sakamoto put up with my sometimes appalling culinary mistakes and limited menus with great aplomb. I remember one particularly awful night when I couldn't find the makings for soup broth, and Mr. Sakamoto was fed "*miso* soup" that was little more than *miso* dissolved in hot water. He managed to down the tasteless broth with good grace — and the trace of a smile on his lips. (Of course, it is also true that although he was himself capable of simple cooking, he would not set foot in the kitchen if there were a woman in the house.) Months after I moved out, whenever he saw me he would say with a sparkle in his eye and a hint of nostalgic wistfulness in his voice, "I miss Dōrin-san's salad and sautéed beef," one of the "Western" menus I used to serve up with numbing regularity. No, the cooking was not the problem.

The problem was, in fact, the etiquette surrounding the serving of food that produced the most profound conflicts for me as an American woman. The head of the household is usually served first and receives the finest delicacies; men — even the sweetest, nicest ones — ask for a second helping of rice by merely holding out their rice bowls to the woman nearest the rice cooker, and maybe, just maybe, uttering a grunt of thanks in return for her pains. I could never get used to this practice, try as I might. Still, I tried to carry out my duties uncomplainingly, in what I hope was reasonably good humor. But I was none too happy about these things "inside." Other restrictions began to chafe, especially restrictions on my movement. I had to be in at a certain hour, despite my "adult" age. Yet I understood the family's responsibility for me as their guest and quasi-daughter, so I tried to abide by their regulations, hiding my irritation as best I could.

This fundamental ambivalence was heightened by isolation and dependency. Though my status was in some respects high in an education-conscious Japan, I was still young, female, and a student. I was in a socially recognized relationship of dependency vis-à-vis the people I knew. I was not to be feared and obeyed, but protected and helped. In terms of my research, this was an extremely advantageous position to be in, for people did not feel the need to reflect my views back to me, as they might with a more powerful person. I did not try to define situations; rather, I could allow other people to define those situations in their culturally appropriate ways, remaining open to their concerns and their ways of acting in the world. But, in another sense, this dependency and isolation increased my susceptibility to identifying with my Japanese role. By this time I saw little of American friends in Tokyo, for it was difficult to be with people who had so little inkling of how ordinary Japanese people lived. My informants and I consequently had every reason to conspire to re-create my identity as Japanese. Precisely because of my dependency and my made-to-order role, I was allowed — or rather, *forced* — to abandon the position of observer. Errors, linguistic or cultural, were dealt with impatiently or with a startled look that seemed to say, "Oh yes, you are American after all." On the other hand, appropriately Japanese behaviors were rewarded with warm, positive reactions or with comments such as "You're more Japanese than the Japanese." Even more frequently, correct behavior was simply accepted as a matter of course. *Naturally* I would understand, *naturally* I would behave correctly, for they presumed me to be, *au fond,* Japanese.

Identity can imply unity or fusion, but for me what occurred was a fragmentation of the self. This fragmentation was encouraged by my own participation in Japanese life and by the actions of my friends and acquaintances. At its most extreme point, I became "the Other" in my own mind, where the identity I had known in another context simply collapsed. The success of our conspiracy to re-create me as Japanese reached its climax one August afternoon.

It was typical summer weather for Tokyo, "like a steam bath" as the saying goes, so hot the leaves were drooping limply from the trees surrounding the Sakamotos' house. Mrs. Sakamoto and her married daughter, Takemi, were at the doctor's with Takemi's son, so Mr. Sakamoto and I were busy tending young Kaori-chan, Takemi-san's young daughter. Mr. Sakamoto quickly tired of his grandfatherly role, leaving me to entertain Kaori-chan. Promptly at four P.M., the hour when most Japanese housewives do their shopping for the evening meal, I lifted the baby into her stroller and pushed her along ahead of me as I inspected the fish, selected the freshest-looking vegetables, and mentally planned the meal for the evening. As I glanced into the shiny metal surface of the butcher's display case, I noticed someone who looked terribly familiar: a typical young housewife, clad in slip-on sandals and the loose, cotton shift called "home wear" (*hōmu wea*), a woman walking with a characteristically Japanese bend to the knees and a sliding of the feet. Suddenly I clutched the handle of the stroller to steady myself as a wave of dizziness washed over me, for I realized I had caught a glimpse of nothing less than my own reflection. Fear that perhaps I would never emerge from this world into which I was immersed inserted itself into my mind and stubbornly refused to leave, until I resolved to move into a new apartment, to distance myself from my Japanese home and my Japanese existence.

For ultimately, this collapse of identity was a distancing moment. It led me to emphasize the *differences* between cultures and among various aspects of identity: researcher, student, daughter, wife, Japanese, American, Japanese American. In order to reconstitute myself as an American researcher, I felt I had to extricate myself from the conspiracy to rewrite my identity as Japanese. Accordingly, despite the Sakamotos' invitations to stay with them for the coming year, I politely stated my intentions to fulfill the original terms of the agreement: to stay just until construction on my new apartment was complete. In order to resist the Sakamotos' attempts to re-create me as Japanese, I removed myself physically from their exclusively Japanese environment.

Thus, both the fragmentation of self and the collapse of identity were results of a complex collaboration between ethnographer and informants. It should be evident that at this particular point, my informants were hardly inert objects available for the free play of the ethnographer's desire. They themselves were, in the act of being, actively interpreting and trying to make meaning of the ethnographer. In so doing, the people I knew asserted their power to act upon the anthropologist. This was their means for preserving their own identities. Understanding, in this context, is multiple, open-ended, positioned — although that positioning can shift dramatically, as I have argued — and pervaded by relations of power. These power-imbued attempts to capture, recast, and rewrite each other were for us productive of understandings and were, existentially, alternately wrenching and fulfilling.

### Reading the Text

1. Why do the native Japanese find Kondo to be a "conceptual anomaly"?
2. Why did Kondo feel increasing inner conflict as her Japanese hosts grew increasingly comfortable with her "Japanese" identity?
3. What unfamiliar gender roles did Kondo face in Japan, and how did she respond to them?
4. Why does Kondo say her Japanese hosts engaged in a "conspiracy" to rewrite her identity as Japanese?

### Reading the Signs

1. If you have ever experienced a cultural identity crisis similar to that described by Kondo, discuss it in your journal. What factors precipitated this crisis? Explore your own responses and those of people around you.
2. Writing as if you were Kondo, compose a letter to Fan Shen (see "The Classroom and the Wider Culture: Identity as a Key to Learning English Composition," p. 531) in which you explain Shen's problems in his composition class. What advice might Kondo give Shen for coping with the alternative cultural norms he is facing in the classroom?
3. In class, freewrite for fifteen minutes on what you believe are the most important components of your identity. Then, in small groups (racially mixed if possible), discuss your results. How much of your identity is determined by ethnic origin? What other cultural factors have influenced your self-image? How does your freewriting compare with that of others in your group, and how can you account for both similarities and differences?
4. Kondo describes the importance of food rituals as signs of cultural identity and bonding. Write an essay in which you discuss the particular eating rituals of your ethnic group, being sure to discuss not simply their personal significance to you but also their significance to the group.
5. Kondo describes the "fragmentation of self" she experienced when she adopted "ready-made molds," or cultural norms, to conform to her hosts' expectations. Use her notion of "fragmentation of self" to explain the anguish felt by the African-Americans in Sam Fulwood III's "The Rage of the Black Middle Class" (p. 510). How are Fulwood's interviewees suffering a similar identity crisis? How does an important difference — the fact that his interviewees are Americans living in America — affect their attitudes?

FAN SHEN

# The Classroom and the Wider Culture: Identity as a Key to Learning English Composition

*Writing conventions involve more cultural presuppositions and mythologies than we ordinarily recognize. Take the current practice of using the first-person singular pronoun "I" when writing an essay. Such a convention presumes an individualistic worldview, which can appear very strange to someone coming from a communal culture, as Fan Shen relates in this analysis of the relation between culture and composition. Hailing from the People's Republic of China, where the group comes before the individual in social consciousness, Shen describes what it was like to move to the United States and have to learn a whole new worldview to master the writing conventions that he himself now teaches as a professor of English at Rochester Community and Technical College. A writer as well as a teacher, Fan Shen has translated three books from English into Chinese and has written numerous articles for both English and Chinese publications.*

One day in June 1975, when I walked into the aircraft factory where I was working as an electrician, I saw many large-letter posters on the walls and many people parading around the workshops shouting slogans like "Down with the word 'I'!" and "Trust in masses and the Party!" I then remembered that a new political campaign called "Against Individualism" was scheduled to begin that day. Ten years later, I got back my first English composition paper at the University of Nebraska–Lincoln. The professor's first comments were: "Why did you always use 'we' instead of 'I'?" and "Your paper would be stronger if you eliminated some sentences in the passive voice." The clashes between my Chinese background and the requirements of English composition had begun. At the center of this mental struggle, which has lasted several years and is still not completely over, is the prolonged, uphill battle to recapture "myself."

In this paper I will try to describe and explore this experience of reconciling my Chinese identity with an English identity dictated by the rules of English composition. I want to show how my cultural background shaped — and shapes — my approaches to my writing in English and how writing in English redefined — and redefines — my *ideological* and *logical* identities. By "ideological identity" I mean the system of values that I acquired (consciously and unconsciously) from my social and cultural background. And by "logical identity" I mean the natural (or

Oriental) way I organize and express my thoughts in writing. Both had to be modified or redefined in learning English composition. Becoming aware of the process of redefinition of these different identities is a mode of learning that has helped me in my efforts to write in English, and, I hope, will be of help to teachers of English composition in this country. In presenting my case for this view, I will use examples from both my composition courses and literature courses, for I believe that writing papers for both kinds of courses contributed to the development of my "English identity." Although what I will describe is based on personal experience, many Chinese students whom I talked to said that they had had the same or similar experiences in their initial stages of learning to write in English.

## Identity of the Self: Ideological and Cultural

Starting with the first English paper I wrote, I found that learning to compose in English is not an isolated classroom activity, but a social and cultural experience. The rules of English composition encapsulate values that are absent in, or sometimes contradictory to, the values of other societies (in my case, China). Therefore, learning the rules of English composition is, to a certain extent, learning the values of Anglo-American society. In writing classes in the United States I found that I had to reprogram my mind, to redefine some of the basic concepts and values that I had about myself, about society, and about the universe, values that had been imprinted and reinforced in my mind by my cultural background, and that had been part of me all my life.

Rule number one in English composition is: Be yourself. (More than one composition instructor has told me, "Just write what *you* think.") The values behind this rule, it seems to me, are based on the principle of protecting and promoting individuality (and private property) in this country. The instruction was probably crystal clear to students raised on these values, but, as a guideline of composition, it was not very clear or useful to me when I first heard it. First of all, the image or meaning that I attached to the word "I" or "myself" was, as I found out, different from that of my English teacher. In China, "I" is always subordinated to "We" — be it the working class, the Party, the country, or some other collective body. Both political pressure and literary tradition require that "I" be somewhat hidden or buried in writings and speeches; presenting the "self" too obviously would give people the impression of being disrespectful of the Communist Party in political writings and boastful in scholarly writings. The word "I" has often been identified with another "bad" word, "individualism," which has become a synonym for selfishness in China. For a long time the words "self" and "individualism" have had negative connotations in my mind, and the negative force of the words naturally extended to the field of literary studies. As a result, even if I had brilliant ideas, the "I" in my papers always had to show some modesty by not competing with or trying to stand above the names of ancient and modern authoritative figures. Appealing to Mao or other Marxist authorities became the required way (as well as the most "forceful" or "persuasive" way) to prove one's point in written discourse. I remember that in China I had even committed what I can call "reversed plagiarism" — here, I suppose it would be called "forgery" — when I was in middle school: willfully attributing some of my thoughts to "experts" when I needed some arguments but could not find a suitable quotation from a literary or political "giant."

Now, in America, I had to learn to accept the words "I" and "self"      5
as something glorious (as Whitman did), or at least something not to be ashamed of or embarrassed about. It was the first and probably biggest step I took into English composition and critical writing. Acting upon my professor's suggestion, I intentionally tried to show my "individuality" and to "glorify" "I" in my papers by using as many "I's" as possible — "I think," "I believe," "I see" — and deliberately cut out quotations from authorities. It was rather painful to hand in such "pompous" (I mean immodest) papers to my instructors. But to an extent it worked. After a while I became more comfortable with only "the shadow of myself." I felt more at ease to put down *my* thoughts without looking over my shoulder to worry about the attitudes of my teachers or the reactions of the Party secretaries, and to speak out as "bluntly" and "immodestly" as my American instructors demanded.

But writing many "I's" was only the beginning of the process of redefining myself. Speaking of redefining myself is, in an important sense, speaking of redefining the word "I." By such a redefinition I mean not only the change in how I envisioned myself, but also the change in how *I* perceived the world. The old "I" used to embody only one set of values, but now it had to embody multiple sets of values. To be truly "myself," which I knew was a key to my success in learning English composition, meant *not to be my Chinese self* at all. That is to say, when I write in English I have to wrestle with and abandon (at least temporarily) the whole system of ideology which previously defined me in myself. I had to forget Marxist doctrines (even though I do not see myself as a Marxist by choice) and the Party lines imprinted in my mind and familiarize myself with a system of capitalist/bourgeois values. I had to put aside an ideology of collectivism and adopt the values of individualism. In composition as well as in literature classes, I had to make a fundamental adjustment: If I used to examine society and literary materials through the microscopes of Marxist dialectical materialism and historical materialism, I now had to learn to look through the microscopes the other way around, i.e., to learn to look at and understand the world from the point of view of "idealism." (I must add here that there are American professors who use a Marxist approach in their teaching.)

The word "idealism," which affects my view of both myself and the universe, is loaded with social connotations, and can serve as a good example of how redefining a key word can be a pivotal part of redefining my ideological identity as a whole.

To me, idealism is the philosophical foundation of the dictum of English composition: "Be yourself." In order to write good English, I knew that I had to be myself, which actually meant not to be my Chinese self. It meant that I had to create an English self and be *that* self. And to be that English self, I felt, I had to understand and accept idealism the way a Westerner does. That is to say, I had to accept the way a Westerner sees himself in relation to the universe and society. On the one hand, I knew a lot about idealism. But on the other hand, I knew nothing about it. I mean I knew a lot about idealism through the propaganda and objections of its opponent, Marxism, but I knew little about it from its own point of view. When I thought of the word "materialism" — which is a major part of Marxism and in China has repeatedly been "shown" to be the absolute truth — there were always positive connotations, and words like "right," "true," etc., flashed in my mind. On the other hand, the word "idealism" always came to me with the dark connotations that surround words like "absurd," "illogical," "wrong," etc. In China "idealism" is depicted as a ferocious and ridiculous enemy of Marxist philosophy. Idealism, as the simplified definition imprinted in my mind had it, is the view that the material world does not exist; that all that exists is the mind and its ideas. It is just the opposite of Marxist dialectical materialism which sees the mind as a product of the material world. It is not too difficult to see that idealism, with its idea that mind is of primary importance, provides a philosophical foundation for the Western emphasis on the value of individual human minds, and hence individual human beings. Therefore, my final acceptance of myself as of primary importance — an importance that overshadowed that of authority figures in English composition — was, I decided, dependent on an acceptance of idealism.

My struggle with idealism came mainly from my efforts to understand and to write about works such as Coleridge's *Biographia Literaria* and Emerson's "Over-Soul." For a long time I was frustrated and puzzled by the idealism expressed by Coleridge and Emerson — given their ideas, such as "I think, therefore I am" (Coleridge obviously borrowed from Descartes) and "the transparent eyeball" (Emerson's view of himself) — because in my mind, drenched as it was in dialectical materialism, there was always a little voice whispering in my ear "You are, therefore you think." I could not see how human consciousness, which is not material, could create apples and trees. My intellectual conscience refused to let me believe that the human mind is the primary world and the material world secondary. Finally, I had to imagine that I was looking at a world with my head upside down. When I imagined that I was in a new body (born with the head upside down) it was easier to forget biases imprinted in my subconsciousness about idealism, the mind, and my former self. Starting from scratch, the new inverted self — which I called my "English Self" and into which I have transformed myself — could understand and *accept,* with ease, idealism as "the truth" and "himself" (i.e., my English Self) as the "creator" of the world.

Here is how I created my new "English Self." I played a "game" similar to ones played by mental therapists. First I made a list of (simplified) features about writing associated with my old identity (the Chinese Self), both ideological and logical, and then beside the first list I added a column of features about writing associated with my new identity (the English Self). After that I pictured myself getting out of my old identity, the timid, humble, modest Chinese "I," and creeping into my new identity (often in the form of a new skin or a mask), the confident, assertive, and aggressive English "I." The new "Self" helped me to remember and accept the different rules of Chinese and English composition and the values that underpin these rules. In a sense, creating an English Self is a way of reconciling my old cultural values with the new values required by English writing, without losing the former.

An interesting structural but not material parallel to my experiences in this regard has been well described by Min-zhan Lu in her important article, "From Silence to Words: Writing as Struggle" (*College English* 49 [April 1987]: 437–48). Min-zhan Lu talks about struggles between two selves, an open self and a secret self, and between two discourses, a mainstream Marxist discourse and a bourgeois discourse her parents wanted her to learn. But her struggle was different from mine. Her Chinese self was severely constrained and suppressed by mainstream cultural discourse, but never interfused with it. Her experiences, then, were not representative of those of the majority of the younger generation who, like me, were brought up on only one discourse. I came to English composition as a Chinese person, in the fullest sense of the term, with a Chinese identity already fully formed.

### Identity of the Mind: Illogical and Alogical

In learning to write in English, besides wrestling with a different ideological system, I found that I had to wrestle with a logical system very different from the blueprint of logic at the back of my mind. By "logical system" I mean two things: the Chinese way of thinking I used to approach my theme or topic in written discourse, and the Chinese critical/logical way to develop a theme or topic. By English rules, the first is illogical, for it is the opposite of the English way of approaching a topic; the second is alogical (nonlogical), for it mainly uses mental pictures instead of words as a critical vehicle.

### THE ILLOGICAL PATTERN

In English composition, an essential rule for the logical organization of a piece of writing is the use of a "topic sentence." In Chinese composition, "from surface to core" is an essential rule, a rule which means that one ought to reach a topic gradually and "systematically" instead of "abruptly."

The concept of a topic sentence, it seems to me, is symbolic of the values of a busy people in an industrialized society, rushing to get things done, hoping to attract and satisfy the busy reader very quickly. Thinking back, I realized that I did not fully understand the virtue of the concept until my life began to rush at the speed of everyone else's in this country. Chinese composition, on the other hand, seems to embody the values of a leisurely paced rural society whose inhabitants have the time to chew and taste a topic slowly. In Chinese composition, an introduction explaining how and why one chooses this topic is not only acceptable, but often regarded as necessary. It arouses the reader's interest in the topic little by little (and this is seen as a virtue of composition) and gives him/her a sense of refinement. The famous Robert B. Kaplan "noodles" contrasting a spiral Oriental thought process with a straight-line Western approach ("Cultural Thought Patterns in Inter-Cultural Education," *Readings on English as a Second Language,* Ed. Kenneth Croft, 2nd ed., Winthrop, 1980, 403–10) may be too simplistic to capture the preferred pattern of writing in English, but I think they still express some truth about Oriental writing. A Chinese writer often clears the surrounding bushes before attacking the real target. This bush-clearing pattern in Chinese writing goes back two thousand years to Kong Fuzi (Confucius). Before doing anything, Kong says in his *Luen Yu (Analects),* one first needs to call things by their proper names (expressed by his phrase "Zheng Ming"正名). In other words, before touching one's main thesis, one should first state the "conditions" of composition: how, why, and when the piece is being composed. All of this will serve as a proper foundation on which to build the "house" of the piece. In the two thousand years after Kong, this principle of composition was gradually formalized (especially through the formal essays required by imperial examinations) and became known as "Ba Gu," or the eight-legged essay. The logic of Chinese composition, exemplified by the eight-legged essay, is like the peeling of an onion: Layer after layer is removed until the reader finally arrives at the central point, the core.

*Ba Gu* still influences modern Chinese writing. Carolyn Matalene    15
has an excellent discussion of this logical (or illogical) structure and its influence on her Chinese students' efforts to write in English ("Contrastive Rhetoric: An American Writing Teacher in China," *College English* 47 [November 1985]: 789–808). A recent Chinese textbook for composition lists six essential steps (factors) for writing a narrative essay, steps to be taken in this order: time, place, character, event, cause, and consequence (*Yuwen Jichu Zhishi Liushi Jiang* [*Sixty Lessons on the Basics of the Chinese Language*], Ed. Beijing Research Institute of Education, Beijing Publishing House, 1981, 525–609). Most Chinese students (including me) are taught to follow this sequence in composition.

The straightforward approach to composition in English seemed to me, at first, illogical. One could not jump to the topic. One had to walk step by step to reach the topic. In several of my early papers I found that the Chinese approach — the bush-clearing approach — persisted, and I had considerable difficulty writing (and in fact understanding) topic sentences. In what I deemed to be topic sentences, I grudgingly gave out themes. Today, those papers look to me like Chinese papers with forced or false English openings. For example, in a narrative paper on a trip to New York, I wrote the forced/false topic sentence, "A trip to New York in winter is boring." In the next few paragraphs, I talked about the weather, the people who went with me, and so on, before I talked about what I learned from the trip. My real thesis was that one could always learn something even on a boring trip.

### THE ALOGICAL PATTERN

In learning English composition, I found that there was yet another cultural blueprint affecting my logical thinking. I found from my early papers that very often I was unconsciously under the influence of a Chinese critical approach called the creation of "yijing," which is totally non-Western. The direct translation of the word "yijing" is: yi, "mind or consciousness," and jing, "environment." An ancient approach which has existed in China for many centuries and is still the subject of much discussion, yijing is a complicated concept that defies a universal definition. But most critics in China nowadays seem to agree on one point, that yijing is the critical approach that separates Chinese literature and criticism from Western literature and criticism. Roughly speaking, yijing is the process of creating a pictorial environment while reading a piece of literature. Many critics in China believe that yijing is a creative process of inducing oneself, while reading a piece of literature or looking at a piece of art, to create mental pictures, in order to reach a unity of nature, the author, and the reader. Therefore, it is by its very nature both creative and critical. According to the theory, this nonverbal, pictorial process leads directly to a higher ground of beauty and morality. Almost all critics in China agree that yijing is not a process of logical thinking — it is not a process of moving from the premises of an argument to its conclusion, which is the foundation of Western criticism. According to yijing, the process of criticizing a piece of art or literary work has to involve the process of creation on the reader's part. In yijing, verbal thoughts and pictorial thoughts are one. Thinking is conducted largely in pictures and then "transcribed" into words. (Ezra Pound once tried to capture the creative aspect of yijing in poems such as "In a Station of the Metro." He also tried to capture the critical aspect of it in his theory of imagism and vorticism, even though he did not know the term "yijing.") One characteristic of the yijing approach to criticism, therefore, is that it often includes a description of the created mental pictures on the part of the reader/critic and his/her mental attempt to bridge (unite) the literary work, the pictures, with ultimate beauty and peace.

In looking back at my critical papers for various classes, I discovered that I unconsciously used the approach of yijing, especially in some of my earlier papers when I seemed not yet to have been in the grip of Western logical critical approaches. I wrote, for instance, an essay entitled "Wordsworth's Sound and Imagination: The Snowdon Episode." In the major part of the essay I described the pictures that flashed in my mind while I was reading passages in Wordsworth's long poem, *The Prelude*.

> I saw three climbers (myself among them) winding up the mountain in silence "at the dead of night," absorbed in their "private thoughts." The sky was full of blocks of clouds of different colors, freely changing their shapes, like oily pigments disturbed in a bucket of water. All of a sudden, the moonlight broke the darkness "like a flash," lighting up the mountain tops. Under the "naked moon," the band saw a vast sea of mist and vapor, a silent ocean. Then the silence was abruptly broken, and we heard the "roaring of waters, torrents, streams/Innumerable, roaring with one voice" from a "blue chasm," a fracture in the vapor of the sea. It was a joyful revelation of divine truth to the human mind: the bright, "naked" moon sheds the light of "higher reasons" and "spiritual love" upon us; the vast ocean of mist looked like a thin curtain through which we vaguely saw the infinity of nature beyond; and the sounds of roaring waters coming out of the chasm of vapor cast us into the boundless spring of imagination from the depth of the human heart. Evoked by the divine light from above, the human spring of imagination is joined by the natural spring and becomes a sustaining source of energy, feeding "upon infinity" while transcending infinity at the same time. . . .

Here I was describing my own experience more than Wordsworth's. The picture described by the poet is taken over and developed by the reader. The imagination of the author and the imagination of the reader are thus joined together. There was no "because" or "therefore" in the paper. There was little *logic*. And I thought it was (and it is) criticism. This seems to me a typical (but simplified) example of the yijing approach. (Incidentally, the instructor, a kind professor, found the paper interesting, though a bit "strange.")

I am not saying that such a pattern of "alogical" thinking is wrong — in fact some English instructors find it interesting and acceptable — but it is very non-Western. Since I was in this country to learn the English language and English literature, I had to abandon Chinese "pictorial logic," and to learn Western "verbal logic."

## If I Had to Start Again

The change is profound: Through my understanding of new meanings of words like "individualism," "idealism," and "I," I began to accept the underlying concepts and values of American writing, and by learning to use "topic sentences" I began to accept a new logic. Thus, when I write papers in English, I am able to obey all the general rules of English composition. In doing this I feel that I am writing through, with, and because of a new identity. I welcome the change, for it has added a new dimension to me and to my view of the world. I am not saying that I have entirely lost my Chinese identity. In fact I feel that I will never lose it. Any time I write in Chinese, I resume my old identity, and obey the rules of Chinese composition such as "Make the 'I' modest," and "Beat around the bush before attacking the central topic." It is necessary for me to have such a Chinese identity in order to write authentic Chinese. (I have seen people who, after learning to write in English, use English logic and sentence patterning to write Chinese. They produce very awkward Chinese texts.) But when I write in English, I imagine myself slipping into a new "skin," and I let the "I" behave much more aggressively and knock the topic right on the head. Being conscious of these different identities has helped me to reconcile different systems of values and logic, and has played a pivotal role in my learning to compose in English.

Looking back, I realize that the process of learning to write in English is in fact a process of creating and defining a new identity and balancing it with the old identity. The process of learning English composition would have been easier if I had realized this earlier and consciously sought to compare the two different identities required by the two writing systems from two different cultures. It is fine and perhaps even necessary for American composition teachers to teach about topic sentences, paragraphs, the use of punctuation, documentation, and so on, but can anyone design exercises sensitive to the ideological and logical differences that students like me experience — and design them so they can be introduced at an early stage of an English composition class? As I pointed out earlier, the traditional advice "Just be yourself" is not clear and helpful to students from Korea, China, Vietnam, or India. From "Be yourself" we are likely to hear either "Forget your cultural habit of writing" or "Write as you would write in your own language." But neither of the two is what the instructor meant or what we want to do. It would be helpful if he or she pointed out the different cultural/ideological connotations of the word "I," the connotations that exist in a group-centered culture and an individual-centered culture. To sharpen the contrast, it might be useful to design papers on topics like "The Individual vs. The Group: China vs. America" or "Different 'I's' in Different Cultures."

Carolyn Matalene mentioned in her article (789) an incident concerning American businessmen who presented their Chinese hosts with gifts of cheddar cheese, not knowing that the Chinese generally do not like cheese. Liking cheddar cheese may not be essential to writing English prose, but being truly accustomed to the social norms that stand behind ideas such as the English "I" and the logical pattern of English composition — call it "compositional cheddar cheese" — is essential to writing in English. Matalene does not provide an "elixir" to help her Chinese students like English "compositional cheese," but rather recommends, as do I, that composition teachers not be afraid to give foreign students English "cheese," but to make sure to hand it out slowly, sympathetically, and fully realizing that it tastes very peculiar in the mouths of those used to a very different cuisine.

### Reading the Text

1. Why does Fan Shen say English composition is a cultural and social activity?
2. What are the differences between Western and Chinese views of the self, according to Shen?
3. What does Shen mean by the "yijing" approach to writing?
4. In a paragraph, summarize the process by which Fan Shen learned to write English composition essays.

### Reading the Signs

1. In your journal, brainstorm ways in which you were brought up either to assert your individuality or to subordinate yourself to group interests (you might consider involvement in sports or school activities). Then stand back and consider your brainstormed list. To what extent were you raised

with a "Western" concept of self? How do your ethnic background and gender affect your sense of self–identity?

2. Compare and contrast Fan Shen's experience in his composition class with your own experiences. How can ethnicity and gender shape a writer's experiences?

3. In class, discuss the extent to which your classes, including your writing class, assume Western styles of learning and discourse. Then write an essay discussing the results of your discussion, using the "yijing" approach that Fan Shen describes. Read your essay aloud in class.

4. Using Fan Shen's notions of Western and non–Western styles of self, write an essay in which you analyze the differences between Japanese and American notions of the self (see Dorinne K. Kondo, "On Being a Conceptual Anomaly," p. 523).

5. Has anything you have learned in your writing class felt "foreign" to you? Write a list, as Fan Shen did, in which you name features about writing that come "naturally" to you and then list those that seem "unnatural." Then study your lists. Which features seem culturally determined and which seem linked to your own personality and way of thinking? Can you make such a distinction? How can these lists help you as a writer?

# GLORIA ANZALDÚA
## *How to Tame a Wild Tongue*

|||||||||||||||||||||||||||||||||||||||||||||||

*How would you feel if your teacher scolded you when you tried to tell her how to pronounce your name? That is the opening anecdote in Gloria Anzaldúa's linguistic analysis of Mexican-American speech. Showing that the language of Chicanos and Chicanas differs not only from the speech of Anglos but from the speech of other Hispanic groups, Anzaldúa provides a detailed description of the history and significance of her mother tongue. Language is not simply an instrument for communication, she suggests, it is a sign of identity. "So if you really want to hurt me," Anzaldúa concludes, "talk badly about my language." A lecturer at the University of California, Santa Cruz, Gloria Anzaldúa is a writer and editor whose books include* This Bridge Called My Back: Writings by Radical Women of Color *(1983),* Haciendo Caras: Making Face/Making Soul *(1990), and* Borderlands/La Frontera: The New Mestiza *(1987), from which this selection is taken.*

*"We're going to have to control your tongue," the dentist says, pulling out all the metal from my mouth. Silver bits plop and tinkle into the basin. My mouth is a mother lode.*

*The dentist is cleaning out my roots. I get a whiff of the stench when I gasp. "I can't cap that tooth yet, you're still draining," he says.*

*"We're going to have to do something about your tongue," I hear the anger rising in his voice. My tongue keeps pushing out the wads of cotton, pushing back the drills, the long thin needles. "I've never seen anything as strong or as stubborn," he says. And I think, how do you tame a wild tongue, train it to be quiet, how do you bridle and saddle it? How do you make it lie down?*

*Who is to say that robbing a people of its language is less violent than war?*
— RAY GWYN SMITH[1]

I remember being caught speaking Spanish at recess — that was good for three licks on the knuckles with a sharp ruler. I remember being sent to the corner of the classroom for "talking back" to the Anglo teacher when all I was trying to do was tell her how to pronounce my name. "If you want to be American, speak 'American.' If you don't like it, go back to Mexico where you belong."

"I want you to speak English. *Pa' hallar buen trabajo tienes que saber hablar el inglés bien. Qué vale toda tu educación si todavía hablas inglés con un* 'accent,'"[2] my mother would say, mortified that I spoke English like a Mexican. At Pan American University, I and all Chicano students were required to take two speech classes. Their purpose: to get rid of our accents.

Attacks on one's form of expression with the intent to censor are a violation of the First Amendment. *El Anglo con cara de inocente nos arrancó la lengua.*[3] Wild tongues can't be tamed, they can only be cut out.

## Overcoming the Tradition of Silence

*Ahogadas, escupimos el oscuro.*
*Peleando con nuestra propia sombra*
*el silencio nos sepulta.*[4]

---

1. Ray Gwyn Smith, *Moorland Is Cold Country,* unpublished book.

2. *Pa' hallar buen trabajo tienes que saber hablar el inglés bien. Qué vale toda tu educación si todavía hablas inglés con un* 'accent.' To find a good job you have to know how to speak English well. What good is all your education if you still speak English with an accent? — EDS.

3. *El Anglo con cara de inocente nos arrancó la lengua.* The Anglo with an innocent-looking face made us shut up. Translated literally: "pulled our tongues out." — EDS.

4. *Ahogadas, escupimos el oscuro. / Peleando con nuestra propia sombra / el silencio nos sepulta.* Drowned, we spit in the dark. / Fighting with our own shadow / the silence buries us. — EDS.

*En boca cerrada no entran moscas.* "Flies don't enter a closed mouth" is a saying I kept hearing when I was child. *Ser habladora* was to be a gossip and a liar, to talk too much. *Muchachitas bien criadas,* well-bred girls don't answer back. *Es una falta de respeto*[5] to talk back to one's mother or father. I remember one of the sins I'd recite to the priest in the confession box the few times I went to confession: talking back to my mother, *hablar pa' 'tras, repelar. Hocicona, repelona, chismosa,* having a big mouth, questioning, carrying tales are all signs of being *mal criada.*[6] In my culture they are all words that are derogatory if applied to women — I've never heard them applied to men.

The first time I heard two women, a Puerto Rican and a Cuban,   5 say the word "*nosotras,*"[7] I was shocked. I had not known the word existed. Chicanas use *nosotros*[8] whether we're male or female. We are robbed of our female being by the masculine plural. Language is a male discourse.

> *And our tongues have become*
> *dry      the wilderness has*
> *dried out our tongues      and*
> *we have forgotten speech.*
>      — IRENA KLEPFISZ[9]

Even our own people, other Spanish speakers *nos quieren poner candados en la boca.*[10] They would hold us back with their bag of *reglas de academia.*[11]

## Oyé como ladra: el lenguaje de la frontera[12]

*Quien tiene boca se equivoca.*[13]
     — MEXICAN SAYING

---

5. *Es una falta de respeto*    It's a lack of respect. — EDS.
6. *mal criada*    Ill-bred. — EDS.
7. *nosotras*    We, female form. — EDS.
8. *nosotros*    We, male form. — EDS.
9. Irena Klepfisz, "*Di rayze aheym* / The Journey Home," in *The Tribe of Dina: A Jewish Women's Anthology,* Melanie Kaye/Kantrowitz and Irena Klepfisz, eds. (Montpelier, VT: Sinister Wisdom Books, 1986), 49.
10. *nos quieren poner candados en la boca.*    They want us to put padlocks on our mouths. — EDS.
11. *reglas de academia*    Academic rules. — EDS.
12. *Oyé como ladra: el lenguaje de la frontera*    Listen how it barks: the language of the borderlands. — EDS.
13. *Quien tiene boca se equivoca.*    Whoever has a mouth makes mistakes. — EDS.

"*Pocho,* cultural traitor, you're speaking the oppressor's language by speaking English, you're ruining the Spanish language," I have been accused by various Latinos and Latinas. Chicano Spanish is considered by the purist and by most Latinos deficient, a mutilation of Spanish.

But Chicano Spanish is a border tongue which developed naturally. Change, *evolución, enriquecimiento de palabras nuevas por invención o adopción*[14] have created variants of Chicano Spanish, *un nuevo lenguaje. Un lenguaje que corresponde a un modo de vivir.*[15] Chicano Spanish is not incorrect, it is a living language.

For a people who are neither Spanish nor live in a country in which Spanish is the first language; for a people who live in a country in which English is the reigning tongue but who are not Anglo; for a people who cannot entirely identify with either standard (formal, Castillian) Spanish or standard English, what recourse is left to them but to create their own language? A language which they can connect their identity to, one capable of communicating the realities and values true to themselves — a language with terms that are neither *español ni inglés,*[16] but both. We speak a patois, a forked tongue, a variation of two languages.

Chicano Spanish sprang out of the Chicanos' need to identify ourselves as a distinct people. We needed a language with which we could communicate with ourselves, a secret language. For some of us, language is a homeland closer than the Southwest — for many Chicanos today live in the Midwest and the East. And because we are a complex, heterogeneous people, we speak many languages. Some of the languages we speak are:

1. Standard English
2. Working class and slang English
3. Standard Spanish
4. Standard Mexican Spanish
5. North Mexican Spanish dialect
6. Chicano Spanish (Texas, New Mexico, Arizona, and California have regional variations)
7. Tex-Mex
8. *Pachuco* (called *caló*)

My "home" tongues are the languages I speak with my sister and brothers, with my friends. They are the last five listed, with 6 and

10

---

14. *evolución, enriquecimiento de palabras nuevas por invención o adopción*  Evolution, enrichment of new words by invention or adoption. — EDS.

15. *un nuevo lenguaje. Un lenguaje que corresponde a un modo de vivir.*  A new language. A language that matches a way of living. — EDS.

16. *español ni inglés*  Spanish nor English. — EDS.

7 being closest to my heart. From school, the media, and job situations, I've picked up standard and working-class English. From Mamagrande Locha and from reading Spanish and Mexican literature, I've picked up Standard Spanish and Standard Mexican Spanish. From *los recién llegados,*[17] Mexican immigrants, and *braceros,*[18] I learned the North Mexican dialect. With Mexicans I'll try to speak either Standard Mexican Spanish or the North Mexican dialect. From my parents and Chicanos living in the Valley, I picked up Chicano Texas Spanish, and I speak it with my mom, younger brother (who married a Mexican and who rarely mixes Spanish with English), aunts, and older relatives.

With Chicanas from *Nuevo México* or *Arizona* I will speak Chicano Spanish a little, but often they don't understand what I'm saying. With most California Chicanas I speak entirely in English (unless I forget). When I first moved to San Francisco, I'd rattle off something in Spanish, unintentionally embarrassing them. Often it is only with another Chicana *tejana*[19] that I can talk freely.

Words distorted by English are known as anglicisms or *pochismos.* The *pocho* is an anglicized Mexican or American of Mexican origin who speaks Spanish with an accent characteristic of North Americans and who distorts and reconstructs the language according to the influence of English.[20] Tex-Mex, or Spanglish, comes most naturally to me. I may switch back and forth from English to Spanish in the same sentence or in the same word. With my sister and my brother Nune and with Chicano *tejano* contemporaries I speak in Tex-Mex.

From kids and people my own age I picked up *Pachuco. Pachuco* (the language of the zoot suiters) is a language of rebellion, both against Standard Spanish and Standard English. It is a secret language. Adults of the culture and outsiders cannot understand it. It is made up of slang words from both English and Spanish. *Ruca* means girl or woman, *vato* means guy or dude, *chale* means no, *simón* means yes, *churro* is sure, talk is *periquiar, pigionear* means petting, *que gacho* means how nerdy, *ponte águila* means watch out, death is called *la pelona.* Through lack of practice and not having others who can speak it, I've lost most of the *Pachuco* tongue.

---

17. *los recién llegados*   The recently arrived. — EDS.
18. *braceros*   Laborers. — EDS.
19. *tejana*   Female Texan. — EDS.
20. R. C. Ortega, *Dialectología Del Barrio,* trans. Hortencia S. Alwan (Los Angeles, CA: R. C. Ortega Publisher & Bookseller, 1977), 132.

## Chicano Spanish

Chicanos, after 250 years of Spanish/Anglo colonization, have devel-  15
oped significant differences in the Spanish we speak. We collapse two
adjacent vowels into a single syllable and sometimes shift the stress in
certain words such as *maíz / maiz, cohete / cuete*. We leave out certain
consonants when they appear between vowels: *lado / lao, mojado / mojao*.
Chicanos from South Texas pronounce *f* as *j* as in *jue (fue)*. Chicanos use
"archaisms," words that are no longer in the Spanish language, words
that have been evolved out. We say *semos, truje, haiga, ansina*, and *naiden*.
We retain the "archaic" *j*, as in *jalar*, that derives from an earlier *h* (the
French *halar* or the Germanic *halon* which was lost to standard Spanish in
the sixteenth century), but which is still found in several regional dialects
such as the one spoken in South Texas. (Due to geography, Chicanos
from the Valley of South Texas were cut off linguistically from other
Spanish speakers. We tend to use words that the Spaniards brought over
from Medieval Spain. The majority of the Spanish colonizers in Mexico
and the Southwest came from Extremadura — Hernán Cortés was one
of them — and Andalucía. Andalucians pronounce *ll* like a *y,* and their
*d*'s tend to be absorbed by adjacent vowels: *tirado* becomes *tirao*. They
brought *el lenguaje popular, dialectos y regionalismos*.[21])

Chicanos and other Spanish speakers also shift *ll* to *y* and *z* to *s*.[22] We
leave out initial syllables, saying *tar* for *estar, toy* for *estoy, hora* for *ahora*
(*cubanos* and *puertorriqueños* also leave out initial letters of some words).
We also leave out the final syllable such as *pa* for *para*. The intervocalic *y,*
the *ll* as in *tortilla, ella, botella*, gets replaced by *tortia* or *tortiya, ea, botea*.
We add an additional syllable at the beginning of certain words: *atocar* for
*tocar, agastar* for *gastar*. Sometimes we'll say *lavaste las vacijas,* other times
*lavates* (substituting the *ates* verb endings for the *aste*).

We use anglicisms, words borrowed from English: *bola* from ball, *car-
peta* from carpet, *máchina de lavar* (instead of *lavadora*) from washing machine. Tex-Mex argot, created by adding a Spanish sound at the beginning or end of an English word such as *cookiar* for cook, *watchar* for
watch, *parkiar* for park, and *rapiar* for rape, is the result of the pressures on
Spanish speakers to adapt to English.

We don't use the word *vosotros / as* or its accompanying verb form.
We don't say *claro* (to mean yes), *imagínate,* or *me emociona,* unless we
picked up Spanish from Latinas, out of a book, or in a classroom. Other
Spanish-speaking groups are going through the same, or similar, development in their Spanish.

---

21. Eduardo Hernandéz-Chávez, Andrew D. Cohen, and Anthony F. Beltramo,
*El Lenguaje de los Chicanos: Regional and Social Characteristics of Language Used by Mexican
Americans* (Arlington, VA: Center for Applied Linguistics, 1975), 39.

22. Hernandéz-Chávez, xvii.

## Linguistic Terrorism

Deslenguadas. Somos los del español deficiente.[23] *We are your linguistic nightmare, your linguistic aberration, your linguistic* mestisaje,[24] *the subject of your* burla.[25] *Because we speak with tongues of fire we are culturally crucified. Racially, culturally, and linguistically* somos huérfanos[26] — *we speak an orphan tongue.*

Chicanas who grew up speaking Chicano Spanish have internalized the belief that we speak poor Spanish. It is illegitimate, a bastard language. And because we internalize how our language has been used against us by the dominant culture, we use our language differences against each other.

Chicana feminists often skirt around each other with suspicion and hesitation. For the longest time I couldn't figure it out. Then it dawned on me. To be close to another Chicana is like looking into the mirror. We are afraid of what we'll see there. *Pena.* Shame. Low estimation of self. In childhood we are told that our language is wrong. Repeated attacks on our native tongue diminish our sense of self. The attacks continue throughout our lives. 20

Chicanas feel uncomfortable talking in Spanish to Latinas, afraid of their censure. Their language was not outlawed in their countries. They had a whole lifetime of being immersed in their native tongue; generations, centuries in which Spanish was a first language, taught in school, heard on radio and TV, and read in the newspaper.

If a person, Chicana or Latina, has a low estimation of my native tongue, she also has a low estimation of me. Often with *mexicanas y latinas* we'll speak English as a neutral language. Even among Chicanas we tend to speak English at parties or conferences. Yet, at the same time, we're afraid the other will think we're *agringadas* because we don't speak Chicano Spanish. We oppress each other trying to out-Chicano each other, vying to be the "real" Chicanas, to speak like Chicanos. There is no one Chicano language just as there is no one Chicano experience. A monolingual Chicana whose first language is English or Spanish is just as much a Chicana as one who speaks several variants of Spanish. A Chicana from Michigan or Chicago or Detroit is just as much a Chicana as one from the Southwest. Chicano Spanish is as diverse linguistically as it is regionally.

By the end of this century, Spanish speakers will comprise the biggest minority group in the United States, a country where students in

---

23. **Deslenguadas. Somos los del español deficiente.**   Foul-mouthed. We are the ones with deficient Spanish. — EDS.

24. **mestisaje**   Mongrels. — EDS.

25. **burla**   Ridicule. — EDS.

26. **somos huérfanos**   We are orphans. — EDS.

high schools and colleges are encouraged to take French classes because French is considered more "cultured." But for a language to remain alive it must be used.[27] By the end of this century English, and not Spanish, will be the mother tongue of most Chicanos and Latinos.

So, if you want to really hurt me, talk badly about my language. Ethnic identity is twin skin to linguistic identity — I am my language. Until I can take pride in my language, I cannot take pride in myself. Until I can accept as legitimate Chicano Texas Spanish, Tex-Mex, and all the other languages I speak, I cannot accept the legitimacy of myself. Until I am free to write bilingually and to switch codes without having always to translate, while I still have to speak English or Spanish when I would rather speak Spanglish, and as long as I have to accommodate the English speakers rather than having them accommodate me, my tongue will be illegitimate.

I will no longer be made to feel ashamed of existing. I will have my       25
voice: Indian, Spanish, white. I will have my serpent's tongue — my woman's voice, my sexual voice, my poet's voice. I will overcome the tradition of silence.

> *My fingers*
> *move sly against your palm*
> *Like women everywhere, we speak in code. . . .*
> — MELANIE KAYE/KANTROWITZ[28]

### Reading the Text

1. Why does Anzaldúa blend Spanish and English in her selection?
2. How does Anzaldúa's language contribute to her sense of identity, in her view?
3. What are the essential features of Chicano Spanish, according to Anzaldúa?
4. What does Anzaldúa mean by "linguistic terrorism"?

### Reading the Signs

1. Anzaldúa sees her language in political terms. Write a personal essay in which you explore the significance of your native language to you. If, like Anzaldúa, you too see your language politically, describe an incident that motivated you to feel this way. If you don't view language as she does,

---

27. Irena Klepfisz, "Secular Jewish Identity: Yidishkayt in America," in *The Tribe of Dina,* Kaye/Kantrowitz and Klepfisz, eds., 43.

28. Melanie Kaye/Kantrowitz, "Sign," in *We Speak in Code: Poems and Other Writings* (Pittsburgh, PA: Motheroot Publications, Inc., 1980), 85.

consider why your experiences have led you to an alternative view of language.

2. Writing as if you were Gloria Anzaldúa, compose a hypothetical letter to the U.S. English organization, a group that wishes to make English America's official language.

3. In class, discuss the effect of Anzaldúa's blending of English and Spanish and imagistic and analytic language. How does such blending contribute to the points she is making? What different impact would the essay have if it were written all in English?

4. How might Anzaldúa respond to the cross-cultural struggles that Dorinne K. Kondo ("On Being a Conceptual Anomaly," p. 523) experiences? Writing as if you were Anzaldúa, compose a letter to Kondo in which you help Kondo come to terms with her struggles.

5. How do you think Brian A. Courtney ("Freedom From Choice," p. 519) might respond to Anzaldúa's selection? Write a dialogue between Courtney and Anzaldúa, being sure to consider issues of gender as well as ethnicity. Share your dialogue with your class.

# LESLIE MARMON SILKO
## *Language and Literature from a Pueblo Indian Perspective*

*One of America's best-known Native-American writers, Leslie Marmon Silko (b. 1948) gained national attention in 1977 with the publication of her novel* Ceremony, *where she blends the conventions of the European novel with Laguna mythic traditions to tell the story of a mixed-blood Laguna war veteran. In this essay, Silko describes the mythologies of the Pueblo Indians, retelling the Pueblo creation story and explaining the essential place of storytelling and of the land in which the stories are told, in maintaining tribal cohesion and identity. The recipient of a MacArthur Foundation grant, Silko lives and writes in Arizona, near the Laguna homeland from which she derives her literary power and inspiration. She has also published a collection of poems,* Laguna Woman *(1974), a collection of short stories,* Storyteller *(1981), and a novel,* Almanac of the Dead *(1992). Her most recent publication is a collection of essays,* Yellow Woman and a Beauty of the Spirit *(1996).*

This "essay" is an edited transcript of an oral presentation. The "author" deliberately did not read from a prepared paper so that the audience could experience firsthand one dimension of the oral tradition — non-linear structure. Her remarks were intended to be heard, not read.

Where I come from, the words that are most highly valued are those which are spoken from the heart, unpremeditated and unrehearsed. Among the Pueblo people, a written speech or statement is highly suspect because the true feelings of the speaker remain hidden as he reads words that are detached from the occasion and the audience. I have intentionally not written a formal paper to read to this session because of this and because I want you to hear and to experience English in a nontraditional structure, a structure that follows patterns from the oral tradition. For those of you accustomed to a structure that moves from point A to point B to point C, this presentation may be somewhat difficult to follow because the structure of Pueblo expression resembles something like a spider's web — with many little threads radiating from a center, crisscrossing each other. As with the web, the structure will emerge as it is made and you must simply listen and trust, as the Pueblo people do, that meaning will be made.

I suppose the task that I have today is a formidable one because basically I come here to ask you, at least for a while, to set aside a number of basic approaches that you have been using and probably will continue to use in approaching the study of English or the study of language; first of all, I come to ask you to see language from the Pueblo perspective, which is a perspective that is very much concerned with including the whole of creation and the whole of history and time. And so we very seldom talk about breaking language down into words. As I will continue to relate to you, even the use of a specific language is less important than the one thing — which is the "telling," or the storytelling. And so, as Simon Ortiz has written, if you approach a Pueblo person and want to talk words or, worse than that, to break down an individual word into its components, ofttimes you will just get a blank stare, because we don't think of words as being isolated from the speaker, which, of course, is one element of the oral tradition. Moreover, we don't think of words as being alone: Words are always with other words, and the other words are almost always in a story of some sort.

Today I have brought a number of examples of stories in English because I would like to get around to the question that has been raised, or the topic that has come along here, which is what changes we Pueblo writers might make with English as a language for literature. But at the same time I would like to explain the importance of storytelling and how it relates to a Pueblo theory of language.

So first I would like to go back to the Pueblo Creation story. The reason I go back to that story is because it is an all-inclusive story of creation and how life began. Tséitsínako, Thought Woman, by thinking of her sisters, and together with her sisters, thought of everything which is, and this world was created. And the belief was that everything in this world was a part of the original creation, and that the people at home realized that far away there were others — other human beings. There is even a section of the story which is a prophesy — which describes the origin of the European race, the African, and also remembers the Asian origins.

Starting out with this story, with this attitude which includes all things, I would like to point out that the reason the people are more concerned with story and communication and less with a particular language is in part an outgrowth of the area [pointing to a map] where we find ourselves. Among the twenty Pueblos there are at least six distinct languages, and possibly seven. Some of the linguists argue — and I don't set myself up to be a linguist at all — about the number of distinct languages. But certainly Zuni is all alone, and Hopi is all alone, and from mesa to mesa there are subtle differences in language — very great differences. I think that this might be the reason that what particular language was being used wasn't as important as what a speaker was trying to say. And this, I think, is reflected and stems or grows out of a particular view of the story — that is, that language *is* story. At Laguna many words have stories which make them. So when one is telling a story, and one is using words to tell the story, each word that one is speaking has a story of its own too. Often the speakers or tellers go into the stories of the words they are using to tell one story so that you get stories within stories, so to speak. This structure becomes very apparent in the storytelling, and what I would like to show you later on by reading some pieces that I brought is that this structure also informs the writing and the stories which are currently coming from Pueblo people. I think what is essential is this sense of story, and story within story, and the idea that one story is only the beginning of many stories, and the sense that stories never truly end. I would like to propose that these views of structure and the dynamics of storytelling are some of the contributions which Native American cultures bring to the English language or at least to literature in the English language.

First of all, a lot of people think of storytelling as something that is done at bedtime — that it is something that is done for small children. When I use the term "storytelling," I include a far wider range of telling activity. I also do not limit storytelling to simply old stories, but to again go back to the original view of creation, which sees that it is all part of a whole; we do not differentiate or fragment stories and experiences. In the beginning, Tséitsínako, Thought Woman, thought of all these things, and all of these things are held together as one holds many things together in a single thought.

So in the telling (and today you will hear a few of the dimensions of this telling) first of all, as was pointed out earlier, the storytelling always includes the audience and the listeners, and, in fact, a great deal of the story is believed to be inside the listener, and the storyteller's role is to draw the story out of the listeners. This kind of shared experience grows out of a strong community base. The storytelling goes on and continues from generation to generation.

The Origin story functions basically as a maker of our identity — with the story we know who we are. We are the Lagunas. This is where we came from. We came this way. We came by this place. And so from the time you are very young, you hear these stories, so that when you go out into the wider world, when one asks who you are, or where are you from, you immediately know: We are the people who came down from the north. We are the people of these stories. It continues down into clans so that you are not just talking about Laguna Pueblo people, you are talking about your own clan. Within the clans there are stories which identify the clan.

In the Creation story, Antelope says that he will help knock a hole in the earth so that the people can come up, out into the next world. Antelope tries and tries, and he uses his hooves and is unable to break through; and it is then that Badger says, "Let me help you." And Badger very patiently uses his claws and digs a way through, bringing the people into the world. When the Badger clan people think of themselves, or when the Antelope people think of themselves, it is as people who are of *this* story, and this is *our* place, and we fit into the very beginning when the people first came, before we began our journey south.

So you can move, then, from the idea of one's identity as a tribal per- 10 son into clan identity. Then we begin to get to the extended family, and this is where we begin to get a kind of story coming into play which some people might see as a different kind of story, though Pueblo people do not. Anthropologists and ethnologists have, for a long time, differentiated the types of oral language they find in the Pueblos. They tended to rule out all but the old and sacred and traditional stories and were not interested in family stories and the family's account of itself. But these family stories are just as important as the other stories — the older stories. These family stories are given equal recognition. There is no definite, pre-set pattern for the way one will hear the stories of one's own family, but it is a very critical part of one's childhood, and it continues on throughout one's life. You will hear stories of importance to the family — sometimes wonderful stories — stories about the time a maternal uncle got the biggest deer that was ever seen and brought back from the mountains. And so one's sense of who the family is, and who you are, will then extend from that — "I am from the family of my uncle who brought in this wonderful deer, and it was a wonderful hunt" — so you have this sort of building or sense of identity.

There are also other stories, stories about the time when another uncle, perhaps, did something that wasn't really acceptable. In other words, this process of keeping track, of telling, is an all-inclusive process which begins to create a total picture. So it is very important that you know all of the stories — both positive and not so positive — about one's own family. The reason that it is very important to keep track of all the stories in one's own family is because you are liable to hear a story from somebody else who is perhaps an enemy of the family, and you are liable to hear a version which has been changed, a version which makes your family sound disreputable — something that will taint the honor of the family. But if you have already heard the story, you know your family's version of what *really* happened that night, so when somebody else is mentioning it, you will have a version of the story to counterbalance it. Even when there is no way around it — old Uncle Pete did a terrible thing — by knowing the stories that come out of other families, by keeping very close watch, listening constantly to learn the stories about other families, one is in a sense able to deal with terrible sorts of things that might happen within one's own family. When a member of one's own family does something that cannot be excused, one always knows stories about similar things which happened in other families. And it is not done maliciously. I think it is very important to realize this. Keeping track of all the stories within the community gives a certain distance, a useful perspective which brings incidents down to a level we can deal with. If others have done it before, it cannot be so terrible. If others have endured, so can we.

The stories are always bringing us together, keeping this whole together, keeping this family together, keeping this clan together. "Don't go away, don't isolate yourself, but come here, because we have all had these kinds of experiences" — this is what the people are saying to you when they tell you these other stories. And so there is this constant pulling together to resist what seems to me to be a basic part of human nature: When some violent emotional experience takes place, people get the urge to run off and hide or separate themselves from others. And of course, if we do that, we are not only talking about endangering the group, we are also talking about the individual or the individual family never being able to recover or to survive. Inherent in this belief is the feeling that one does not recover or get well by one's self, but it is together that we look after each other and take care of each other.

In the storytelling, then, we see this process of bringing people together, and it works not only on the family level, but also on the level of the individual. Of course, the whole Pueblo concept of the individual is a little bit different from the usual Western concept of the individual. But one of the beauties of the storytelling is that when something happens to an individual, many people will come to you and take you aside, or maybe a couple of people will come and talk to you. These are occasions of storytelling. These occasions of storytelling are continuous; they are a way of life.

Storytelling lies at the heart of the Pueblo people, and so when someone comes in and says, "When did they tell the stories, or what time of day does the storytelling take place?" that is a ridiculous question. The storytelling goes on constantly — as some old grandmother puts on the shoes of a little child and tells the child the story of a little girl who didn't wear her shoes. At the same time somebody comes into the house for coffee to talk with an adolescent boy who has just been into a lot of trouble, to reassure him that *he* got into that kind of trouble, or somebody else's son got into that kind of trouble too. You have this constant ongoing process, working on many different levels.

One of the stories I like to bring up about helping the individual in 15 crisis is a recent story, and I want to remind you that we make no distinctions between the stories — whether they are history, whether they are fact, whether they are gossip — these distinctions are not useful when we are talking about this particular experience with language. Anyway, there was a young man who, when he came back from the war in Vietnam, had saved up his Army pay and bought a beautiful red Volkswagen Beetle. He was very proud of it, and one night drove up to a place right across the reservation line. It is a very notorious place for many reasons, but one of the more notorious things about the place is a deep arroyo behind the place. This is the King's Bar. So he ran in to pick up a cold six-pack to take home, but he didn't put on his emergency brake. And his little red Volkswagen rolled back into the arroyo and was all smashed up. He felt very bad about it, but within a few days everybody had come to him and told him stories about other people who had lost cars to that arroyo. And probably the story that made him feel the best was about the time that George Day's station wagon, with his mother-in-law and kids in the back, rolled into that arroyo. So everybody was saying, "Well, at least your mother-in-law and kids weren't in the car when it rolled in," and you can't argue with that kind of story. He felt better then because he wasn't alone anymore. He and his smashed-up Volkswagen were now joined with all the other stories of cars that fell into that arroyo.

There are a great many parallels between Pueblo experiences and the remarks that have been made about South Africa and the Caribbean countries — similarities in experiences so far as language is concerned. More specifically, with the experience of English being imposed upon the people. The Pueblo people, of course, have seen intruders come and intruders go. The first they watched come were the Spaniards; while the Spaniards were there, things had to be conducted in Spanish. But as the old stories say, if you wait long enough, they'll go. And sure enough, they went. Then another bunch came in. And old stories say, well, if you wait around long enough, not so much that they'll go, but at least their ways will go. One wonders now, when you see what's happening to technocratic-industrial culture, now that we've used up most of the sources of energy, you think perhaps the old people are right.

But anyhow, our experience with English has been different because the Bureau of Indian Affairs schools were so terrible that we never heard of Shakespeare. There was Dick and Jane, and I can remember reading that the robins were heading south for winter, but I knew that all winter the robins were around Laguna. It took me a long time to figure out what was going on. I worried for quite a while about the robins because they didn't leave in the winter, not realizing that the textbooks were written in Boston. The big textbook companies are up here in Boston and *their* robins do go south in the winter. But this freed us and encouraged us to stay with our narratives. Whatever literature we received at school (which was damn little), at home the storytelling, the special regard for telling and bringing together through the telling, was going on constantly. It has continued, and so we have a great body of classical oral literature, both in the narratives and in the chants and songs.

As the old people say, "If you can remember the stories, you will be all right. Just remember the stories." And, of course, usually when they say that to you, when you are young, you wonder what in the world they mean. But when I returned — I had been away from Laguna Pueblo for a couple of years, well more than a couple of years after college and so forth — I returned to Laguna and I went to Laguna-Acoma high school to visit an English class, and I was wondering how the telling was continuing, because Laguna Pueblo, as the anthropologists have said, is one of the more acculturated pueblos. So I walked into this high school English class and there they were sitting, these very beautiful Laguna and Acoma kids. But I knew that out in their lockers they had cassette tape recorders, and I knew that at home they had stereos, and they were listening to Kiss and Led Zeppelin and all those other things. I was almost afraid, but I had to ask — I had with me a book of short fiction (it's called *The Man to Send Rain Clouds* [New York: Viking Press, 1974]), and among the stories of other Native American writers, it has stories that I have written and Simon Ortiz has written. And there is one particular story in the book about the killing of a state policeman in New Mexico by three Acoma Pueblo men. It was an act that was committed in the early fifties. I was afraid to ask, but I had to. I looked at the class and I said, "How many of you heard this story before you read it in the book?" And I was prepared to hear this crushing truth that indeed the anthropologists were right about the old traditions dying out. But it was amazing, you know, almost all but one or two students raised their hands. They had heard that story, just as Simon and I had heard it, when we were young. That was my first indication that storytelling continues on. About half of them had heard it in English, about half of them had heard it in Laguna. I think again, getting back to one of the original statements, that if you begin to look at the core of the importance of the language and how it fits in with the culture, it is the *story* and the feeling of the story which matters more than what language it's told in.

## Reading the Text

1. Why do the Pueblo people mistrust written language, according to Silko?
2. What does Silko mean by saying that "the storyteller's role is to draw the story out of the listeners"?
3. How, according to Silko, do stories create a "clan identity"?

## Reading the Signs

1. Silko comments on the importance of family stories to Pueblo social life. Divide the class into small groups and have each group member narrate a story from his or her family. Then, in your groups, discuss the family stories and your response to them. How do the stories become a "shared experience," in Silko's terms?
2. Write an essay in which you reflect on the importance of storytelling in your own family. Which stories have become family traditions? Can you speculate about why? How do the stories shape your "sense of who the family is and who you are"?
3. Compare and contrast the Pueblo creation story with the Judeo-Christian creation story in the Bible. What different worldviews are implied in each story? Are there any similarities?
4. Silko's essay is an edited transcript of an oral presentation. Read all or part of her selection aloud in class and discuss what differences the oral recitation makes. As a listener, do you focus on different aspects of the selection? To what extent is your understanding of her ideas modified?
5. Compare the Pueblo mode of storytelling with the *yijing* approach described by Fan Shen ("The Classroom and the Wider Culture: Identity as a Key to Learning English Composition," p. 531). How do both differ from the Western logical patterns? How do they reflect their culture's worldviews?
6. Compare the role of storytelling in Pueblo culture with the role of language in Chicano culture as described by Gloria Anzaldúa ("How to Tame a Wild Tongue," p. 541). What role does each play in forming personal and cultural identity? How does each compare with traditionally Western attitudes toward language? What are the consequences of imposing on each culture different modes of communication?

CORNEL WEST
*Diverse New World*

IIIIIIIIIIIIIIIIIIIIIIIIIIIIIIIIIIIIIIIIIIIIIIIIIIIIIIIII

*While critics of multicultural education such as the late Allan Bloom rail against what they see as the trashing of Western civilization in the current restructuring of the literary canon, proponents point out that the Eurocentric point of view simply leaves out too much of cultural history. In this argument for a multicultural canon, Cornel West (b. 1953) argues not for the dismantling of the Western tradition but for its enrichment through the inclusion of the many non-European voices that have contributed to world culture. In an America that is increasingly multicultural and multiracial in its own demographic makeup, it only makes sense to take advantage of diversity, West argues, rather than resist it. Cornel West is a professor of Afro-American Studies and Philosophy of Religion at Harvard University. His publications include* The American Evasion of Philosophy: A Genealogy of Pragmatism *(1989),* The Ethical Dimensions of Marxist Thought *(1991),* Race Matters *(1993),* Keeping Faith: Philosophy and Race in America *(1993), and, with Michael Lerner,* Jews and Blacks *(1995).*

We are grappling with the repercussions and implications of what it means to live now forty-six years after the end of the age of Europe. This age began in 1492, with the encounter between Europeans and those who were in the New World, with the massive expulsion of Jews in Spain, and with the publication of the first Indo-European grammar books in 1492. It continued through World War II, the concentration camps, and the shaking of the then-fragile European maritime empires. Forty-six years later is not a long time for that kind of fundamental glacier shift in civilizations that once dominated the world.

Analyzing multiculturalism from a contemporary philosophical perspective, and looking at its roots especially among the professional managerial strata, in museums, in galleries, in universities and so forth, is an attempt to come to terms with how we think of universality when it has been used as a smokescreen for a particular group. How do we preserve notions of universality given the fact that various other particularities — traditions, heritages, communities, voices, and what have you — are moving closer to the center of the historical stage, pushing off those few voices which had served as the centering voices between 1492 and 1945?

The United States has become the land of hybridity, heterogeneity, and ambiguity. It lacks the ability to generate national identity and has an inferiority complex vis-à-vis Europe, and the United States must deal with indigenous people's culture, including the scars and the dead bodies left from its history. Expansion across the American continent trampled the culture and heritages of degraded, hated, haunted, despised African peoples, whose backs would constitute one fundamental pillar for the building of the United States and for the larger industrializing processes in Europe.

Within the multiculturalist debate, leading Afrocentric and Africanist thinkers Leonard Jeffries and Molefi Asante articulate a critical perspective that says they are tired of the degradation of things African. On this particular point, they're absolutely right. However, they don't have a subtle enough sense of history, so they can't recognize ambiguous legacies of traditions and civilizations. They refuse to recognize the thoroughly hybrid culture of almost every culture we have ever discovered. In the case of Jeffries, this lack of subtlety slides down an ugly xenophobic slope — a mirror image of the Eurocentric racism he condemns.

We need to see history as in part the cross-fertilization of a variety of different cultures, usually under conditions of hierarchy. That's thoroughly so for the United States. For example, jazz is the great symbol of American culture, but there's no jazz without European instruments or African polyrhythms. To talk about hybrid culture means you give up all quest for pure traditions and pristine heritages.

Yes, black folk must come up with means of affirming black humanity. Don't just read Voltaire's great essays on the light of reason — read the "Peoples of America," in which he compares indigenous peoples and Africans to dogs and cattle. Don't read just Kant's *Critique of Pure Reason*, read the moments in *The Observations of the Sublime*, in which he refers to Negroes as inherently stupid. It's not a trashing of Kant. It's a situating of Kant within eighteenth-century Germany, at a time of rampant xenophobia, along with tremendous breakthroughs in other spheres. An effective multicultural critique recognizes both the crimes against humanity and the contributions to humanity from the particular cultures in Europe.

We have to demystify this notion of Europe and Eurocentrism. Europe has always been multicultural. Shakespeare borrowed from Italian narratives and pre-European narratives. When we think of multiculturalism, we're so deeply shaped by the American discourse of positively valued whiteness and negatively valued blackness, that somehow it's only when black and white folk interact that real multiculturalism's going on. The gradation of hybridity and heterogeneity is not the same between the Italians and the British, and the West Africans and the British. But "Europe" is an ideological construct. It doesn't exist other than in the minds of elites who tried to constitute a homogeneous tradition that could bring together heterogeneous populations — that's all it is.

In looking at history with a subtle historical sense, I also have in mind the fundamental question: What do we have in common? By history, I mean the human responses to a variety of different processes over time and space — various social structures that all human beings must respond to. In responding to these circumstances, the problem has been that most of us function by a kind of self-referential altruism, in which we're altruistic to those nearest to us, and those more distant, we tend to view as pictures rather than human beings. Yet, as historical beings, as fallen and fallible historical beings, we do have a common humanity. We must not forget our long historical backdrop. The present is history — that continues to inform and shape and mold our perceptions and orientations.

On the political level, multiculturalism has much to do with our present-day racial polarization — which is in many ways gender polarization, especially given the vicious violence against women, and sexual-orientation polarization with increased attacks on gays and lesbians. These conflicts, mediated or not mediated, reverberate within bureaucratic structures, and within the larger society.

Certain varieties of multiculturalism do have a politics. Afrocentrism    10 is an academic instance of a longer black nationalist tradition, and it does have a politics and a history. Black nationalism is not monolithic — there's a variety of different versions of black nationalism. In so many slices of the black community, with the escalation of the discourse of whiteness and blackness, racism escalates, both in terms of the life of the mind as well as in practices. We're getting a mentality of closing of ranks. This has happened many, many times in the black community; and it takes a nationalist form in terms of its politics. Black nationalism politics is something that has to be called for what it is, understood symptomatically, and criticized openly. It's a question of, if you're really interested in black freedom, I am too — will your black nationalist view in education, will your black nationalist view in politics deliver the black freedom that you and I are interested in? You're upset with racism in Western scholarship. I am too, and some white folk are too.

As democratic socialists, we have to look at society in a way that cuts across race, gender, region, and nation. For most people in the world, their backs are against the wall. When your back is against the wall, you're looking for weaponry: intellectual and existential weaponry to sustain yourself and your self-confidence and your self-affirmation in conditions that seemingly undermine your sense of possibility; political weaponry to organize, mobilize, to bring your power to bear on the status quo.

If you're Afro-American and you're a victim of the rule of capital, and a European Jewish figure who was born in the Catholic Rhineland and grew up as a Lutheran, by the name of Karl Marx, provides certain analytical tools, then you go there. You can't find too many insightful formulations in Marx about what it is to be black; you don't go to Marx for that. You go to Marx to keep track of the rule of capital, interlocking elites, political, banking, financial, that's one crucial source of your weaponry. You don't care where you get it from, you just want to get people off of your back.

If you want to know what it means to be black, to be African in Western civilization and to deal with issues of identity, with bombard-ment of degrading images, you go to the blues, you go to literature, you go to Du Bois's[1] analysis of race, you go to Anna Julia Cooper's[2] analysis of race. For what it means to be politically marginalized, you go to a par-ticular tradition that deals with that.

To gain a universal perspective, the left must have a moral focus on suffering. Once you lose that focus, then you're presupposing a certain level of luxury that is all too common among the professional managerial strata in their debates. Their debates begin to focus on who's going to get what slice of what bureaucratic turf for their bid for the mainstream, for middle-class status. Now, that for me is one slice of the struggle, but it's just a slice. The center of the struggle is a deeper intellectual and political set of issues: understanding the larger historical scope, the post-European age, the struggles of Third World persons as they attempt to deal with their identity, their sense of economic and political victimization. We need to not only understand but also to assist people trying to forge some kinds of more democratic regimes, which is so thoroughly difficult.

Let's not package the debate in static categories that predetermine the conclusion that reinforces polarization — that's the worst thing that could happen. Polarization paralyzes all of us — and we go on our middle-class ways, and the folk we're concerned about continue to go down the drain. 15

The political challenge is to articulate universality in a way that is not a mere smokescreen for someone else's particularity. We must preserve the possibility of universal connection. That's the fundamental challenge. Let's dig deep enough within our heritage to make that connection to others.

We're not naive, we know that argument and critical exchange are not the major means by which social change takes place in the world. But we recognize it has to have a role, has to have a function. Therefore, we will trash older notions of objectivity, and not act as if one group or community or one nation has a god's-eye view of the world. Instead we will utilize forms of intersubjectivity that facilitate critical exchange even as we recognize that none of us are free of presuppositions and prejudg-ments. We will put our arguments on the table and allow them to be

---

1. **W.E.B. Du Bois** (1868–1963)   Historian who studied the lives of blacks in America and leading opponent of racial discrimination. — EDS.

2. **Anna Julia Cooper** (1858–1964)   Educator and civil rights leader who re-searched slavery. — EDS.

interrogated and contested. The quest for knowledge without presuppositions, the quest for certainty, the quest for dogmatism and orthodoxy and rigidity is over.

## Reading the Text

1. Why does West see the period betwen 1492 and 1945 as significant?
2. What does West mean by saying that "'Europe' is an ideological construct"?
3. What sort of curriculum does West recommend for African-American students? For students of other races?

## Reading the Signs

1. Do you agree with West's charge that the United States has an "inferiority complex vis-à-vis Europe"? Discuss in class what West means by this statement and whether you share his position.
2. West only implicitly outlines his vision of an ideal multicultural curriculum. Write an essay in which you explain what you think his curriculum would be like. What sort of authors and historical figures would be studied? Would anything in the "traditional" curriculum be deleted? Share your essay with your classmates.
3. Examine the curriculum of the courses you are taking this quarter or semester. To what extent do they reflect West's "diverse new world"? If they don't resemble West's vision of the ideal education, what changes would you suggest?
4. West expresses some reservations about the views of black nationalists such as Leonard Jeffries and Molefi Asante. Visit your college library and research one such figure. Then write an essay in which you compare and contrast the black nationalist's views with West's perspective.
5. West identifies himself as a socialist scholar. What response might a middle-class African-American, such as Sam Fulwood III ("The Rage of the Black Middle Class," p. 510), have to his positions? Writing as if you were Fulwood, compose a letter to West responding to his vision of a "diverse new world."

Photograph copyright © 1993 by Robert Daniel Ullman/Design Conceptions

# CHAPTER EIGHT

# CULTURAL OUTLAWS

*Street Gangs, Militias, and Hackers
in American Culture*

**W**hat did Kevin Mitnik, the late Tupac Shakur, and Timothy McVeigh all have in common? Answer: Youth. Masculinity. Notoriety. And — most importantly — jailtime.

At first glance, Mitnik, a notorious computer hacker, Shakur, a gangsta rap star, and McVeigh, a midwestern drifter accused of bombing the Federal Building in Oklahoma City in 1995, wouldn't seem to have much in common. But as icons of three emerging outlaw subcultures — hackers, gangsters, and militias — they are part of a controversial, to many disturbing, trend in American life whose impact seems destined to grow in the coming years.

### Interpreting Street Gangs, Militias, and Hackers

Because the new outlaws are news not only for law enforcement personnel but for such popular cultural institutions as Hollywood and the fashion industry — especially in the case of street gangs — we include a chapter focused on them in this book. Our intention is not to glamorize outlaws or their behavior. Rather, we wish to demystify their behavior by analyzing why and how mainstream American popular culture tends to celebrate and even encourage outlaw behavior. A growing literature on hackers written by nonhackers, for example, tends to

---

### Exploring the Signs of Outlaws

In your journal, explore the images of hackers and gang members (especially as propagated by films, news, or videos). What is the popular image of hackers and of gangsters? In what ways does that image influence societal attitudes toward the two groups? Consider the varying treatment that the criminal justice system accords members of the two groups: What role does image play in determining that treatment?

---

aggrandize the hacker as a brilliant, wild, and crazy arch individualist whose assaults on cyberspace represent a principled resistance to authoritarianism and corporate culture. Meanwhile, suburban teenagers nationwide don the garb and adopt the music and speech codes of inner-city gangsters as emblems of their own resistance to adult authority. And the National Rifle Association, without actually condoning the destruction of the Federal Building in Oklahoma City, identified sufficiently with the pro-gun agenda of those first accused of the bombing that they launched a direct mail attack on the Bureau of Alcohol, Tobacco, and Firearms in the aftermath of the explosion — an action that caused one of the NRA's most famous members, former President George Bush, to resign from the organization.

The fact that hackers, gangsters, and pro-gun militias find support in the larger society outside their own much more restricted subcultural boundaries is itself a signifier of the mood of the nation as a whole. The semiotic analysis of such outlaws can thus ultimately bring us to a better understanding of the overall cultural condition of America itself as we move toward the twenty-first century. To help you begin that analysis, we'll provide some background and some interpretations of these groups, beginning with street gangs.

### Where Are You From?

Have you ever been asked, "Where are you from?" Probably often. But have you ever been asked the question by a group of guys standing on a street corner in a tone not of inquiry but of challenge? If you have, or if you might be in the future, you'd better know exactly what the question really means. And how to answer it.

In the code language of a typical American street gang, "Where are you from?" isn't really a question. It's more an assertion, a statement. If you know the code, you know what that statement is. It means, "This is our turf, and we don't recognize you." It means, "We think you belong on a different turf, a different street." It means, "As far as we're concerned, you're from another gang, and unless you can show us otherwise, you're in real trouble." And so the answer that teens in America's inner cities often give is, "I'm not from anywhere," which means, "I don't belong to a gang." Sometimes this response is enough to prevent a fight. Sometimes it's not.

For those of you who have never been exposed to the codes of street gang culture, this might sound peculiar. But for those of you who have lived in neighborhoods where every street, apartment building, wall, and lamppost has been claimed by one gang or another, this simple question, "Where are you from?" and the knowledge of how properly to answer it, might be an essential part of your survival equipment. Indeed, it is hard to think of any semiotic system of such critical importance to urban youth as the codes of gang culture, for even if you do not belong to a gang, your knowledge of gang signaling systems can be important street knowledge. And that's true whether you live in the city or a suburb, for the American street gang is no longer a phenomenon exclusive to the inner city.

Think for a moment of the signs and signals of the gang codes that you do know. What forms of dress, or posture, or hand-signaling, or speech are you aware of? How much can you decode? Have you ever used such signs? How? And for what purpose?

## The Writing on the Wall

The explosive growth of street gangs in America has effectively taken what was once a hidden, marginalized social phenomenon and put it on the center stage of American culture, especially youth culture. To be sure, street gangs are hardly new to American society, the first appearing among nineteenth-century Irish immigrants in lower Manhattan. But in the 1990s, gangs have transcended their traditional boundaries of slum, ghetto, and barrio to become one of America's most prominent, if troubling, subcultures, a subculture whose elaborate linguistic, clothing, and behavioral codes are not only known but also admired and emulated by teens around the country regardless of their race, class, or geographical region. Courted by fashion designers, Hollywood producers, record labels, talk show hosts, and even civic leaders (in the aftermath of the L.A. riots of 1992, captains of the Bloods and the Crips were treated, some commentators complained, like ambassadors of independent nations), the gangsters, homeboys, cholos, gangstas, what-have-you, aren't just thugs anymore.

Probably the most visible — and, at least to adults, most annoying — sign of the American street gang can be found scrawled upon walls, streetlights, billboards, traffic signs, sidewalks, overpasses, trees . . . in short, anything that doesn't move (check that; Dumpsters, panel vans, buses, and, of course, subway cars, move). Gang graffiti was apparently invented by Latino gangs in L.A. about seventy years ago, but it proliferated with the invention of spray paint. Though outsiders complain that they can't for the life of them figure out what all those squiggles and sharp angles mean, they are, in effect, part of an elaborate code whose conventions are highly standardized. Have you ever noticed just how similar in appearance gang graffiti is, from the round-letter script of a quick spray job or Magic Marker run, to the several-foot-high printed letters that rise upon a wall in massive jagged blocks to shout out a gang's initials? This standardization is no accident. Within a gang, older homeboys teach younger initiates the techniques of the graffiti guerilla, while suburban wannabes may carefully practice their own technique by copying what they see in graffiti-scarred neighborhoods. In this way, a standard repertoire of styles is passed from generation to generation and from social class to social class. Replicating a gang's signature, in effect, is a sign of membership and group identity.

Gang tags themselves are used for territorial purposes. Generally, they mark the boundaries of a gang's turf and proliferate at the margins of a territory or where turf lines are in dispute. Gang labels may be sprayed as well within the turf of another gang as a challenge or as a kind of equivalent to what Native Americans once called "taking coup." And then again, they may be scrawled in places — like freeway overpasses — that no gang could claim as a territory but that will be seen by other gangs — and everyone else — as a sign of the gang's ubiquity and daring (how do they get up on those freeway signs anyway?).

## Gangsta Chic

The proliferation of "taggers" who more often than not don't belong to formal gangs but work alone in "crews" or "posses" is a sign of yet another facet of the gangster phenomenon. Most taggers are not otherwise engaged in criminal behavior, and many are comfortably middle class. The adoption of hip hop styles by such kids is a similar signal. And where a given style, howsoever marginalized in its origins, goes mainstream, you can be sure the marketers will not be far behind.

Hence, gang-inspired fashion (hip hop), music (rap), and violence (exploited in movie after movie, from *Colors* to *Boyz 'N the Hood*) are, quite simply, big business in a marketplace that extends far beyond the ghettos and barrios where the codes of gang culture originate. Sales of baggy, oversized pants, overalls (worn unstrapped or single strapped),

||||||||||||||||||||||||||||||||||||||||||||||||||||||||||||||||||||||||||||||||||||||||||||||||||||||||||||||||||||||||||||||||||||||||||||||||||||||||||

**Discussing the Signs of Outlaws**

In class, discuss the reasons you think many middle-class youths have been attracted to the signs of gang culture, ranging from clothing styles and music to tagging and graffiti. Do these different signs mean the same thing to middle-class gangs as they do to inner-city gangs? Try to formulate your own explanation of this phenomenon.

baseball caps, team sweats and jackets, and Nike basketball shoes (worn unlaced one year, laced the next) have bounded beyond the gangs who first favored them to adolescents who line up to adopt the gangsta look. However, migration of the same object to a different system — for example, the appearance of baggy pants among suburban kids — entails a difference in meaning as well. You aren't a gangster just because you dress like one. But you may be saying something all the same.

### You Say You Want a Revolution

Yet something more exists behind the cultural significance of gang culture than fashion alone. Have you ever felt that the defiance of the gangs provides an outlet for your own feelings of rebelliousness or discontent? Are you making a social statement by aligning yourself with gang signals? Do the raps of Snoop Doggy Dog, Tupac Shakur, Ice-T, and Tha Dogg Pound express your rage?

Or is it all just fashion? Misspelling words (especially using the letter "z" instead of "s" for a plural, as in "Boyz"), wearing baseball caps backwards, and spouting violent raps were gestures originally intended at once to disturb and distinguish, to identify the urban gangster while outraging mainstream white America. But as has so often been the case in American racial politics, what was once condemned in the dominated class soon came to be consumed by the dominators. Just as Bop and the Blues, once marginalized as "Negro music" and kept off mainstream radio, metamorphosed into white-dominated rock-and-roll, so too have the emblems of gang culture — especially those of black gangs — been co-opted by white America. The symbols of disaffection become fashion symbols. Images of social despair return as dollar signs in a commercial cornucopia.

It is thus significant that it is the black gang that has supplied most of the imagery of commercial gangsterism. Though Hispanic gangs make up more than half of L.A.'s street gangs, for example, the cholo style sets

fewer trends. Suburban gangsta wannabes (even the word "gangsta" orig-
inates in the ghetto) emulate not the prison-inspired styles of Latino East
L.A. (for instance, below-the-knee cut-offs and close-cropped hair) but
rather the professional sports-inspired styles of the black gangs, designs
that send them running to the Raiders and Reebok and Nike. Though
there are Latino rappers, the sound that can claim that it's "straight outa
Compton" — one of the last predominantly black communities in a city
where Latinos are the majority population — gets all the attention.
When Edward James Olmos made a film about Latino gangs in L.A.,
*American Me,* the movie received local press attention but nothing like
the national media stakeouts that occur every time a new film about
black gangs appears.

Thus, one of the enduring ironies of American race relations makes
its way into the semiotics of the street. From generation to generation,
black America has provided young white America with metaphors of oppression, with symbols and analogies to use in their own struggles. You
might want to begin your thinking about gang culture with this phenomenon. Do you believe that it is valid for white middle-class youths to
adopt the symbols of the underclass to express themselves? Does it in any
way trivialize the social conditions behind the growth of gangs to turn
street gangs into fashion plates?

## The New World Order

Unlike street gangs, the American militia movement is neither a
youth movement nor a darling of the entertainment industry. Indeed,
until the bombing of the Federal Building in Oklahoma City, few people
paid much attention to it. Right-wing fringe groups like the Ku Klux
Klan and the American Nazi party were well known, of course, but the
militias, which really didn't appear in any significant way until the 1990s,
signify a whole new development in American consciousness.

Militia members themselves don't necessarily consider themselves
outlaws, of course. Often they consider themselves patriots resisting a
governmental authority that they don't accept. What they particularly
don't accept is the governmental authority to control gun ownership.
Thus, one of the movement's original goals was to provide legal ways of
evading gun control laws. Since the Second Amendment grants states the
right to form armed militias, "militia" groups have sprung up to take advantage of what they see as a constitutionally protected right to bear
arms. But though different militia groups may have different agendas —
most, however, seem to be associated with anti-tax and pro-gun politics
— the most semiotically interesting trait they share is a certain worldview, a mythology, that dramatically demonstrates just how different the
same world can look when you shift the mythic frame.

The militia mythology centers on what is called the "New World Order." Originally, the phrase was coined by the Bush administration to describe the global picture that was emerging after the collapse of the Soviet Union and the end of the Cold War. President Bush saw it as an opportunity to build a new world order based not on geopolitical competition but, rather, on geopolitical cooperation, led by the United States. But in the militia mythology, the New World Order is quite different. Their members believe that it is a conspiracy led by the United Nations (and since many militias also embrace anti-Semitic doctrine, vague references to a "Zionist" conspiracy also appear) to seize control of America and take away our freedoms, especially our guns. Every gun control law, every attempt to prosecute those who break such laws (like the Branch Davidians and Randy Weaver), is regarded as proof of the conspiracy. Stories of mysterious black helicopters under U.N. control are particularly popular parts of the mythology. And the FBI and the Bureau of Alcohol, Tobacco, and Firearms are the particular demons of the myth.

What is most culturally significant about the militia movement is the way that it seems to strike sympathetic chords among many Americans who wouldn't ever think of joining a militia. From talk radio to the Internet to the halls of Congress, middle Americans voice a number of the same concerns as the militias do. Anti-tax and pro-gun politicians in Washington chose to put the FBI on trial for its handling of the Branch Davidian and Randy Weaver incidents, and talk radio and TV hosts like Gordon Liddy and Rush Limbaugh have been able to build large followings among listeners who don't applaud terrorism but who aren't exactly crazy about the government either.

In short, the militia movement provides a kind of semiotic mirror image of the gangster chic. That is, much as middle-class youth have adopted the signs of a disaffected black and brown underclass to express their disaffection, so too does the militia movement provide an outlet for disaffection: most prominently, that felt by disaffected white, working-to-lower-middle-class men. As an extreme version of American populism, the militia movement reflects the discontent of rural Americans with a world that is increasingly urban and international. And as the trend toward interglobal economics grows in the coming years, it is not likely that the militias will be going away soon.

## Hacking It

The smallest group of all among America's emerging outlaw subcultures are the hackers. Viewing the wide open spaces of the Internet as their own frontier, hackers resent any attempt to limit where they can travel in cyberspace. Many hackers don't even regard breaking into someone else's files as outlaw behavior as long as they don't steal or destroy anything, and they condemn the hackers who raid bank accounts and ticket agencies for their own profit. But whether the hacker engages in overt criminal activity or simply fools around with confidential files, a distinct hacker profile and mythos is emerging.

Like the militias, the typical hacker is a disaffected white male, but the similarity stops there. Where militia politics all fall out on the far-right wing, hackers, if they have any particular politics, tend to be loosely anarchistic with a radical overlay. Often quite bright but lacking much formal schooling, hackers reflect a certain traditional strain in the American character: the insistence on absolute independence and individual freedom. The great appeal of personal computers is the way in which they can empower an otherwise obscure and powerless operator. Since the Internet is the hardest thing to police in modern society, a clever home computer user can do a great deal to harry the forces of modern control. Thus, some hackers seem to regard themselves as technological freedom fighters.

The undeniable cleverness required for hacking, coupled with the swashbuckling attitudes many hackers adopt, has resulted in a certain glamorous image. In the right circles, hackers are cool. Some even group together in bands not terribly unlike tagging posses, which compete with other hacker bands for the most notoriety in a specific space of the cyber "turf." And just as with street gangs, Hollywood has followed along. Can you think of any films that glamorize the image of the hacker?

Even in corporate America, where huge amounts of money are spent to keep a step ahead of the hackers who are continually breaking into corporate computer systems, the image of the hacker is not necessarily negative: Many "retired" hackers are earning good livings as consultants to the same corporations they once harassed, advising them on how to keep the next generation of hackers out.

And while fashion lines devoted to the "hacker style" have not yet appeared (at least not to our knowledge), a commercial market has sprung up, especially in publications in which hipness, attitude, and computer aptitude all go together. Magazines like *Wired* especially cater to this market, and although the advertising in such publications is mostly devoted to software and net materials, one can also find ads for, say, a software system that promises that "Now You Can Finish Your Concert, Try Out an Idea for Your Next Video, and Still Have Time to Trash Your Hotel Room," featuring an image of a grunge rocker with a Fender telecaster. This ad is aimed at any young computer aficionado, not hackers, but it suggests that it is possible that someday soon the signs and symbols of hackers will make their way into the youth mainstream just as gangsta symbolism has. For who, only twenty years ago when the image of the computer operator was still that of the ultimate pen-shielded nerd, could have imagined that a magazine ad would someday appear which suggests that computers rock?

|||||||||||||||||||||||||||||||||||||||||||||||||||||||||||||||||||||||||||||||||||||||||||||||||||||||||||||||||||||||||||||||||||||||||||||||||||||||||||

## Reading Outlaws on the Net

Use the Internet as a means of viewing gangster signs, or graffiti, from different parts of the United States. Visit Art Crimes: The Writing on the Wall (http://www.gatech.edu/graf/index.html.), a self-described "gallery of graffiti art from cities around the world." Then choose a specific location (perhaps your hometown or your college town) and analyze the graffiti that originate there. What styles predominate, and do the writers communicate an outlaw status through their designs? If so, how? What objects are chosen to display the graffiti, and what is their significance? Alternately, compare different regions of the United States: What signs are used to communicate an outlaw status throughout the country?

## The Readings

Our first selection in this chapter takes you to Los Angeles — a city that has been called the gang capital of the United States — where Léon Bing's interview with a gangster named Faro provides a raw insight into the world of the Bloods and Crips, America's most famous gangs. Anne Campbell then takes you to New York, where she studies members of "girl gangs" and analyzes their relationship to male gangsters, showing how the women, rather than representing female independence and power in the gangster world, are often little more than satellites of their male cohorts. Julie Gannon Shoop follows with a report on the way law enforcement officials construct "profiles" of typical street gang members, stereotyped portraits that nonwhite teens claim discriminate against them. Our next reading, "Signs of the Street: A Conversation," presents an interview conducted by the authors of this book with a group of current and former gang members now attending classes at the West Valley Occupational Center in Los Angeles. Here, the students speak of the styles and signaling systems current among gangsters, describe what gang membership means to them, and offer their opinions of the suburban wannabes who copy them. Seth Mydans's report on the growth of white gangs charts the expansion of the gang phenomenon from the inner city to the suburbs, where middle-class wannabes play out the lifestyles of urban gangsters in a 1990s version of rebels without a cause. Peter Doskoch's examination of "The Mind of the Militias" provides some sobering insights into the ideology of the growing militia movement in the U.S., while Winn Schwartau concludes the chapter with an analysis of hackers, the shock troops of what he calls the "first information warriors."

# LÉON BING

## Faro

‖‖‖‖‖‖‖‖‖‖‖‖‖‖‖‖‖‖‖‖‖‖‖‖‖‖‖‖‖‖‖‖‖‖‖‖‖‖‖

*For many teens today, something about gangsterism, even the violence, is glamorous. But as Léon Bing (b. 1950) reveals in this portrait of Faro — a homeless, half-starving gang member from South Central L.A. — there is nothing glamorous about it at all. Armed and dangerous, Faro has only to "look crazy" at someone, and be looked at crazy in return, to justify a casual homicide. The simple act of showing up on the wrong turf can mean death in an undeclared war zone where, to survive, you have to know how to hold your face and what neighborhoods to avoid. Sometimes the signs are no more visible than a street sign, and you can never know when death, blazing away with an AK-47, may wheel up in a battered sedan. Léon Bing is a former fashion model turned journalist whose work has appeared in* Rolling Stone, L.A. Weekly, *and* Harper's. *She is the author of the bestselling book* Do or Die *(1991), from which this selection is taken, and* Smoked *(1993).*

He is seventeen years old, and he is homeless. I met him through one of his homeboys on whose couch he has been sleeping for the past week. This is how he lives, from couch to couch, or in a sleeping bag, or in the back seat of a parked car. A couple of days in one place, maybe two weeks in another. He does not remember the last time he went to school, and he does not know how to read or write. He is as close to invisibility as it is possible to be.

The reason he's talking is because his friend has vouched for me. We are in my car because I have to run some errands, and I want to save time, so I have decided to take this kid — Faro — along. He sits next to me, looking out the window. His mouth is slightly open, and I can see that his teeth are small and straight. The tip of his tongue is almost, but not quite, the exact shade of raspberry sherbet. His hair has been sectioned into a myriad of tiny braids, each with a blue rubber band at the tip. He is wearing shabby sweats and busted-down Nike hightops. He is very thin; the bones of his wrists stick knobbily out of the elastic cuffs of his hooded jacket, which is at least two sizes too small for him.

We ride in silence for a while, and then I ask him about his family. It takes him a long time to answer, and when he does, his voice is soft, controlled.

"My mother, she died from a drug overdose. I got a grandmother, but she gonna go the same way — she just wanderin' the streets day and

night, lookin' for handouts so she can fix herself a pipe. My brother got
killed in a holdup three years ago."

I ask which end of the gun his brother was at, and Faro looks at me    5
in surprise. It is the first time we have made any kind of eye contact. He
has sixty-year-old eyes set down in that seventeen-year-old face. Grave-
yard eyes.

"Most people think he was holdin' the gun." He almost smiles; it is a
pained expression. "He wasn't but eight years old. He was lookin' at
comic books in a 7-Eleven and some dude come in to rob the place." He
turns away to look out the window. "The homies give him a nice funeral.
I used to have a picture of him, laid out, in my scrapbook. It got lost."

He continues to look out the window. We are moving through an
intersection where the streets are torn and gaping with road work. A
pneumatic drill is blasting, and Faro winces a little at the sound. As we
come to a stoplight a Mustang convertible pulls up on Faro's side of the
car. The driver and the guy in the passenger seat are both young, both
black. Their haircuts, called "fades," are highly styled, carefully constructed flattops with geometric designs etched into the closely shaven
sides.

"See them two dudes?" Faro's voice, unaccountably, has dropped to
a whisper. I nod my head.

"I'm gonna look crazy at 'em. You watch what they do." He turns
away from me, and I lean forward over the wheel so that I can watch the
faces on the two guys. The driver, sensing that someone is looking at
him, glances over at my car. His eyes connect with Faro's, widen for an
instant. Then he breaks the contact, looks down, looks away. And there
is no mistaking what I saw there in his eyes: It was fear. Whatever he saw
in Faro's face, he wasn't about to mess with it.

Faro giggles and turns back toward me. He looks the same as he did    10
before to me: a skinny, slightly goofy-looking kid. The light changes and
the Mustang speeds away, turning right at the next corner. I ask Faro to
"look crazy" for me. He simply narrows his eyes. That's all. He narrows
his eyes, and he looks straight at me and everything about his face shifts
and changes, as if by some trick of time-lapse photography. It becomes a
nightmare face, and it is a scary thing to see. It tells you that if you return
his stare, if you challenge this kid, you'd better be ready to stand your
ground. His look tells you that he doesn't care about anything, not your
life and not his.

I ask Faro what would have happened if the guy had looked crazy
back.

"Then we woulda got into it."

"With me sitting here next to you? Are you kidding?" I can hear an
edge of shrillness in my voice.

He laughs softly. "Never woulda happened. That was just some
damn preppy out on his lunch hour."

But if he *had* returned the challenge. What then?                          15

"Then I woulda killed him."

My eyes slide over his skinny silhouette. No way can he be hiding a weapon under that sweatsuit. He smiles slyly and pats the top of his right shoe. I peer down and there, unbelievably, is the glint of metal. I look up at Faro's face, and without knowing why, I'm shocked. I feel as if he has betrayed me, and it makes me angry.

"What you expect? This ain't no game." He is disgusted.

"You played a game with that guy, though, didn't you? That whole thing was a game."

"And what kinda game *you* playin', lady? You come on down here,                20 and you ask a whole lotta questions, and then when it get too real fo' you, you start in hollerin' like somebody dis'ed you." Cold, icy anger in his voice. His eyes are narrowed again; this time it's for real. I want to meet the challenge, I want to defend myself, but what he's saying is true. I got mad when it got too real.

"You're right, you know."

"Ye-eeeeeh."

"I get scared. And then I guess I get mad."

"Be like that with me sometime, too." We are both beginning to relax again.

"So I can ask questions again."                                             25

"Ye-eeeeeh."

We pass a group of little kids, five- and six-year-olds, walking in line behind their teacher. As they get to the corner, the teacher raises both arms in readiness to cross the street, signaling for the children to do the same. All of them lift their arms high over their heads, like holdup victims, following the teacher to the other side.

"I watch out for the little kids in my neighborhood. So gangs who we don't get along with" — he names several sets, both Bloods and Crips — "don't come in and shoot 'em up. All them I just named, they come in and shoot us up, then we catch one of 'em slippin'[1] and it's all over for them."

He is looking at the children as he talks. His voice is soft, but somehow it is not calm.

"Like there was this fool, this enemy nigger from our worst                 30 enemy set, and he was with his wife and his baby. They was walkin' down there near Vermont, where he had no business bein'. He was slippin' bad and we caught him. We was in a car, all homies, and I was like, 'Let's pop this dumb nigger, let's empty the whole clip in him.'" Faro turns to look at me, as if he wants to make sure I un-

---

1. being careless; not watching your back. — BING'S NOTE.

derstand what he is saying. "We had an AK — two-barrel banana clips, two sides — and I just . . ." He hesitates only for an instant. "I just wanted to make him pay."

Careful to keep my voice as soft as his, I ask him what it was he wanted the guy to pay for.

"For all our dead homeboys. For bein' our enemy. For slippin' so bad." He is warming to his subject, his voice is coming alive now. "You gotta understand — enemy got to pay just for bein' alive." He is quiet for a moment, then he gives a little hitch of his shoulders, like a prizefighter, and he goes on. He is animated now, reliving the event for me. "I was like 'fuck it, Cuz — I'm gonna strap this shit to the seat and I'm just gonna *work* it.'" He twists around to face the passenger door and mimes the action of holding and aiming an AK-47 rifle. "So I strapped it to the seat, like this, and we circled around and pulled up on this nigger from two blocks away, crept up on him slow like, and I just gave it to him." Faro begins to jerk and buck there in his seat as the imaginary weapon in his hands fires automatically. "*Pah-pah-pah-pah-pah-pah-pah!* You know, just let him have it. Just emptied the whole . . ." He is wholly caught up in his recollection, inflamed with it, drunk with it. "I lit his ass *up!* I killed him — shot his baby in the leg — crippled his wife!" He is facing me again, his eyes fixed on some point just to the left of mine. "She in a wheelchair now, I heard, wearin' a voicebox, 'cause one of the bullets caught her in the throat." Then, in afterthought, "The baby okay."

We are silent for a moment; when Faro speaks again his voice is a fusion of bad feelings: despair, remorse, a deep, biting resentment. "I just lit his whole family up and . . ." He sucks in air, holds it a couple of seconds, puffs it out. "It was like, damn, Cuz — I killed him, that was my mission, but still — his whole family." He shakes his head several times, as if he cannot will himself to believe his own story. Then he places the tip of one index finger on the glass next to him and taps it in a nervous, rhythmic beat. "That's a crazy world out there, and we livin' in it."

"Dying in it, too."

The finger stops tapping.

"If you die, you die. Most gangbangers don't have nothin' to live for no more, anyway. That why some of 'em be gangbangin'.'"

He seems to sense what it is that I'm thinking.

"I ain't just talkin' 'bout myself, either. I'm talkin' for a lotta gangbangers. They mothers smokin' dope. Or somebody shot somebody else's mother, and that person figure if they gangbang they got a chance to get 'em back." He is silent again for a beat or two. Then, "People don't have nothin' to live for if they mother dead, they brother dead, they sister dead. What else they got to live for? If people in yo' family is

35

just dyin', if the person you love the most, the person who love *you* the most be dead, then what else *do* you got to live for?"

"Yourself."

It's as if I hadn't spoken; he doesn't even hear me.                    40

"I tell you this — you see enough dyin', then you be ready to die yourself, just so you don't have to see no more of death."

## Reading the Text

1. Why does Bing say that Faro is "as close to invisibility as it is possible to be"?
2. What sort of sign is "looking crazy"?
3. Why does Faro feel he and his friends were duty-bound to kill the rival gang member and wound his family?
4. What is Bing's attitude toward Faro, and how does it affect your response to the selection?

## Reading the Signs

1. In your journal, explore your response to Faro's story. Do you feel sympathy or hostility toward him? What does gang involvement mean to him? Does Faro's story change your attitudes toward gangs in any way?
2. Read or review Seth Mydans's "Not Just the Inner City: Well-to-Do Join Gangs" (p. 607). What value might Faro's story hold for the suburban gang wannabes whom Mydans describes?
3. In class, compare Faro's actions and gang involvement with those of the gang members described in Anne Campbell's "The Praised and the Damned" (p. 577). What conclusions do you reach about the motivations for gang membership?
4. Write a response to the teens who have "gone gangsta" (Nell Bernstein, "Goin' Gangsta, Choosin' Cholita," p. 504) from Faro's perspective. Share your response with your class.

ANNE CAMPBELL

*The Praised and the Damned*

||||||||||||||||||||||||||||||||||||||||||||||||||||||||

*The popular image of the gang subculture is overwhelmingly masculine, but a large — and growing — number of female gangsters have evolved their own codes and styles. But, as Anne Campbell shows in this anthropological case study excerpted from* The Girls in the Gang *(1991), girl gangs tend to exist in a symbiotic — and subordinate — relationship to all-male cohorts. Far from representing a feminist version of street gang culture, female gangs seem locked in a prefeminist era in which women are perceived as the sexual and criminal servants of the men with whom they associate. Anne Campbell is senior lecturer at Durham University, England. Her latest book is* Men, Women and Aggression *(1993).*

### Cops bust up gang rumble on IND tracks
by Philip Messing

A bloody subway rumble involving three notorious Manhattan youth gangs — armed with a sawed-off rifle, baseball bats, metal-studded bracelets, and chains — was narrowly averted last night on the tracks of a Manhattan train station.

Ten well-armed members of the Renegades and the Chosen Ones jumped over turnstiles at the IND's 168th St. downtown subway station to chase three members of The Sandmen [sic], a rival gang, police said.

"If they had been caught, they would have definitely been hurt badly," said plainclothes Transit Officer Noel Negron.

Negron and his partner, Officer Lenko Kaica, who were standing on the platform, joined in the chase, which continued in the southbound subway tunnel and ended in a nearby park.

Police searched the area and found a sawed-off rifle, leather bracelet with metal studs, leather belts, a baseball bat, and a bandolier with several empty bullet casings.

Four youths — including Samuel (Sinbad) Gonzalez, president of the Chosen Ones — were arrested and charged with illegal weapons possession, defacing a firearm, criminal trespass and theft of services.

The rest of the gang members escaped.

Police said the Renegades and Chosen Ones had joined forces after the Sandmen beat up a member of the Chosen Ones and looted an apartment of the rival gang's president.

— *New York Post,* THURSDAY, OCTOBER 9, 1980

Connie is the leader of the Sandman Ladies, a female affiliate of the Sandman based in Manhattan's Upper West Side. On October 9, 1980, we were sitting together outside the city-owned apartment block in which she lived. Concrete benches and tables had thoughtfully been provided for the leisure hours of the residents, which, given the unemployment rate of the occupants, tended to be many. The seats had been taken over that day by the gang members, who shifted uneasily between surveying Broadway and Amsterdam avenues and returning to smoke, drink, and talk at our table. Between Connie and me lay a brown paper bag, which might have been taken for a beer can hidden from the police. Gino, the leader of the Sandman, was at a downtown gang community center, attempting to straighten things out between the Chosen Ones, the Renegades, and his own gang. In his absence, Connie was in charge. Conversation was stilted and tense, and Connie interrupted anyone who spoke too long or too much, dispatching them to the corner to look out. At 3:30 Connie announced she had to go pick up her kid from school. The guys were told to keep watch. She pushed the bag toward me, telling me to use it if I needed it. It contained a .32-caliber gun. With that, Connie put on her sunglasses and left to collect her two-year-old daughter from the nursery.

In New York City there may be as many as four hundred gangs with a total membership between 8,000 and 40,000. Ten percent of those members are female, ranging in age from fourteen to thirty. Some are married and many have children. They are blamed as the inciters of gang feuds; they are described as "passive, property and promiscuous." They are accused of being more vicious than any male; they are praised for being among the few with enough power to curb male gang crime. For some they represent the coming of age of urban women's liberation, for others the denial of the best qualities of womanhood. The contradictions of their position have provoked speculation among the police, the media, and the public about their reasons for joining, their roles and way of life. Despite the volumes written on male gang members, however, little is actually known about the girls, the standard reason being that girls constitute such a small proportion of gang members and are responsible for an even smaller number of gang crimes. Writers have also found male gangs, apart from their criminological interest, to be revealing in far wider sociological and psychological ways.[1] Gangs have been discussed in

1. On societal structure see A. K. Cohen, *Delinquent Boys: The Culture of the Gang* (Glencoe, Ill.: Free Press, 1955); R. K. Merton, *Social Theory and Social Structure* (Glencoe, Ill.: Free Press, 1957); R. A. Cloward and L. E. Ohlin, *Delinquency and Opportunity* (Glencoe, Ill.: Free Press, 1960). On class relations see W. B. Miller, "Lower Class Culture as a Generating Milieu of Gang Delinquency," *Journal of Social Issues, 14* (1958): 5–19; E. Stark, "Gangs and Progress: The Contribution of Delinquency to Progressive Reform," in D. F. Greenberg (ed.), *Crime and Capitalism* (Palo Alto, Calif.: Mayfield, 1981). On rites of passage see H. Block and A. Niederhoffer, *The Gang: A Study of Adolescent Behavior* (New York: Philosophical Library, 1958). On group cohesion see

terms of societal structure, class relations, rites of passage in adolescence, group cohesion, ecological pressures, learning mechanisms, even linguistic usage. Yet in most of these accounts too, girls are invisible or appear as a footnote, an enigma, an oddity.

Little enough is known in terms of hard numbers on the size of the gang problem generally, let alone on girls' involvement. In the sixties, for example, it was widely believed that gangs had finally disappeared. Absorbed into youth politics, some argued. Fighting in Vietnam, said others, or turned into self-destructive junkies. It seems likely that their disappearance was a media sleight of hand.[2] New York stopped reporting gang stories and the rest of the country followed suit. Gangs die out and are reincarnated regularly by the media whenever news is slow. As a phenomenon they have never been fully put to rest. When a crime involving a few teenagers from a poor area makes news, gangs "reappear" in New York City. When gangs return, they are not reinvented. Though they may be inactive for a few months or a few years, they are quietly living in the tradition and culture that has sustained them for over a hundred years in the United States.

Statistics on gang membership have only been available since the 1970s when police departments in major cities became sufficiently concerned about the problem to set up Gang Intelligence Units. In 1975, sociologist Walter Miller attempted to document the size of the gang problem in a government report.[3] He was criticized not only by academics but by members of the very police departments he interviewed for relying on gross estimates which in many cases were contaminated by

---

M. Klein and L. Crawford, "Groups, Gangs and Cohesiveness," in J. F. Short (ed.), *Gang Delinquency and Delinquent Subcultures* (New York: Harper & Row, 1968). On ecological pressures see F. M. Thrasher, *The Gang* (Chicago: University of Chicago Press, 1927); C. Shaw, *Delinquency Areas* (Chicago: University of Chicago Press, 1929). On learning mechanisms see E. Sutherland and D. Cressey, *Criminology,* 10th ed. (New York: Lippincott, 1978). On linguistic usage see W. Labov, *Language in the Inner City* (Philadelphia: University of Pennsylvania Press, 1970).

2. Estimating the size of gang membership generally has been a problem. Few cities keep statistics on gang membership and those that do use different definitions of gang, gang membership, and gang crime. These matters and the role of the New York City media are discussed in W. B. Miller, *Violence by Youth Gangs and Youth Groups as a Crime Problem in Major American Cities* (Washington, D.C.: U.S. Government Printing Office, 1975), and in W. B. Miller, "Gangs, Groups and Serious Youth Crime," in D. Schichor and D. Kelly (eds.), *Critical Issues in Juvenile Delinquency* (Lexington: Lexington Books, 1980). A more recent estimate of New York gang memberships suggests that numbers have declined to 4,300 members in 86 gangs. This decline was contemporaneous with the dismantling of the Police Gang Intelligence Units in Brooklyn and the Bronx and so may represent a less sensitive estimate. See J. A. Needle and W. V. Stapleton, *Police Handling of Youth Gangs* (Washington, D.C.: U.S. Department of Justice, 1983).

3. Miller, *Violence by Youth Gangs and Youth Groups.*

changes in recording methods and poor record keeping. Often they were no more than informed guesses to unanswerable questions.

A more approachable question is the extent to which the roles girls  5 play in the gang have changed over time, but even this is not without difficulties. In reviewing a hundred years of writing on female gang involvement, it is difficult to separate the true nature of girls' involvement from the particular interpretive stance of the writer (usually male), whose moral or political view most probably reflects the prevailing community standards. These must have affected the girls too and the nature of their involvement in the gang. Nevertheless, certain themes appear consistently throughout the writing and reveal important factors in the girls' participation, as constants and as historical changes in their roles.

Two factors can help in interpreting the roles of the girls. The first is the girls' class value orientation — their desire and ability to be upwardly mobile in terms of their life-style. Gang girls are almost unanimously working- or lower-class from the point of view of their parents' income and educational and employment status, but class value orientation is distinct from the reality of social class itself. Some of the girls described, while working-class, show a distinct desire to climb the social ladder. They value middle-class concerns such as the deferment of immediate gratification, long-term planning, and the desirability of self-improvement, and they also are able to deal effectively with middle-class institutions such as school and work. In the literature they are held up as "good girls." "Good girls" are feminine girls. It has been traditional to equate femininity with middle-class attributes (being well-groomed, charming, polite, passive, and modest), while masculinity is associated with working-class stereotypes (being direct, confrontational, nonverbal, physical).

Among the "good girls," some want to assume traditional complementary roles toward males. They look forward to a future as Good Wives, dependent financially and emotionally upon a man, living in a clean, decent apartment (perhaps not quite in the area of town to which they aspire) with children who are well dressed and who will grow up to better themselves in a respectable job as clerks or carpenters. Although this girl associates with a boy from the neighborhood gang, her aim is to save him from his rowdy friends who are clearly a bad element, bringing out the worst in him.

Some "good girls" assume relations with men that are not complementary but similar. These are the Independent Women. Ideally, they hope to go to college and become self-supporting with a decent job, as nurses, secretaries, or bank clerks. They may want children but do not want the financial dependence associated with total reliance on a man's income. If worse comes to worst, they will obtain welfare child allowance and raise the kids alone or with the help of their mother. They associate with the gang but only as an adolescent phase. They may go a little crazy as teenagers, but they are not lowlifes or bums. Nor do they plan to spend their lives in a grubby apartment, taking the children up-state on a bus every weekend to visit their father in prison.

The majority of gang girls, however, have a static class value orienta-tion. They are not tortured by dreams of upward mobility and have a re-alistic view of their chances of success in society. They have not done well in school, and when they have money, they spend it (often when they don't have it as well). They watch television specials about the rich and famous but understand that, short of a win on the numbers, those life-styles are extravagant dreams. They certainly are not interested in the intermediate status of a lower-middle-class suburban life-style. Like the boys in the neighborhood, they enjoy excitement and trouble, which break the monotony of a life in which little attention is given to the fu-ture. They like sharp clothes, loud music, alcohol, and soft drugs. They admire toughness and verbal "smarts." They may not be going any-where, but they make the most of where they are. Authority, in the shape of school, parents, and police, is the enemy but a welcome one since it generates confrontations and livens things up. Because these girls accept a lower-class value system, they are represented in the literature as "bad girls." Men may find dignity by being straightforward, unpreten-tious, and working class, but women do not.

Among the "bad girls," as within the "good girls," some take the tra-    10
ditional complementary role toward their men. Boyfriends take prece-dence over same-sex friendships, and boys are the ones who really mat-ter. Because of this, these girls see other girls as possible rivals and are constantly on their guard. The major focus of their quest for excitement lies in romances with the boys in which they assume a passive role. This passivity can make them the victims of unscrupulous males who may lead them into prostitution or drug addiction. Even if such a dramatic fate is avoided, their undisguised interest in sexual relationships has led them to be branded as Sex Objects by many writers (in spite of the fact that boys who show a similar interest in sex avoid this kind of labeling). The only time this type of girl escapes her passivity is when she provokes fights within and between male gang members by her promiscuous sexual be-havior and her treacherous revelation of one boy's secrets to another. But even in this, her behavior has a traditional female quality: scheming, divi-sive, and nonconfrontational.

Some "bad girls" choose to compete with males on their own terms and are therefore considered in the literature as Tomboys. They insist on accompanying their men to gang rumbles and on joining in. They pride themselves on being tough and take particular pride in fighting and beat-ing male gang members. To prove their toughness, they emulate typi-cally male crimes such as robbery, burglary, and auto theft, and some achieve the distinction of being arrested and, more rarely and therefore more prestigiously, of being sent to jail. Like the males, they have strong same-sex friendships within the gang and pride themselves on their solidarity.

However, Sex Objects and Tomboys have much in common. Both have romantic and sexual relationships with the boys in the gang, but Tomboys give equal attention to their female friends. Both will engage in fights with female rivals for their man, but Tomboys fight for other reasons as well, whereas Sex Objects feel that fighting is usually a man's job. Both will use their femininity in the service of the gang by acting as spies with other nearby gangs, by luring unsuspecting male victims into situations where they are robbed or assaulted by the boys, and by carrying concealed weapons for the boys since as females they cannot be searched on the street by male officers.[4]

These types of roles tend to suggest a no-win situation for gang girls. As Sex Objects, they are cheap women rejected by other girls, parents, social workers, and ironically, often by the boys themselves. As Tomboys, they are resented by boys and ridiculed by family and friends who wait patiently for them to "grow out of it." Among lower-class women, the Independent Woman, as often as not, raises her children in an all-female household. In so doing, she becomes the target of government, academic, and media concern by those who accuse her of rearing a new cycle of delinquents or, if she works, of ousting the male from the labor force by taking low wages. Among the black population especially, as feminist writer Michele Wallace suggests, a covert war between the sexes may exist because of the male's perception of the Independent Woman as "castrating."[5] Clearly the most socially acceptable role is that of Good Wife. Yet even here the Woman is often characterized as the fun-spoiling petty bourgeoise who takes the high-spirited male away from his gang friends to a future of shopping expeditions and diaper changing. Perhaps this is an overdrawn picture, yet in a classic account of male gang life by William Whyte one can almost hear a groan from the author as two members of the Norton Street Gang fall in love with socially aspiring girls and leave their old street friends behind.[6]

---

4. This discussion of class value orientation draws upon the work of Cohen, *Delinquent Boys,* especially his discussion of "college boys" and "corner boys," and of Miller, "Lower Class Culture as a Generating Milieu of Gang Delinquency." The views of these theorists on the value systems of gang members have been considered incompatible. The literature on female gang membership suggests that girls from the same class background differ in their adherence to middle- versus lower-class values or focal concerns.

5. M. Wallace, *Black Macho and the Myth of Superwoman* (New York: The Dial Press, 1978).

6. W. F. Whyte, *Street Corner Society: The Social Structure of an Italian Slum* (Chicago: University of Chicago Press, 1943).

## A Day with Connie

Connie lives in the Upper West Side of Manhattan on the thirteenth floor of a project apartment building. You can spot her windows easily from the ground. A Puerto Rican flag hangs from one and heads bob in and out of the other to check what's happening on the street. Inside, the lobby is painted a pale lavatorial green and echoes with the laughter and shrieks of children in the nursery on the ground floor. It smells of a musty scent that covers the odor of chemical used to control cockroaches. The two elevators operate spasmodically. A ten-minute wait is not unusual.

No one answers Connie's door at first because the knocking is drowned out by the thundering bass of the rap disco blasting out of radio speakers. The door's spyhole cover opens, swings shut, and OK is standing there. He waves me through, smiling with exaggerated politeness. In the corner of the living room, the color television is on with the sound turned down, and quiz-show hosts grin and chatter idiotically. JR is stretched out luxuriously on the sofa beneath a giant Sandman insignia depicting a hooded face on an iron cross, which hangs on the wall. He wears a yellow T-shirt that proudly states "I love Brooklyn" in graffiti writing and a leather vest. A bottle of Colt 45 beer rests on the floor next to him. Mico is in the kitchen, helping Connie bag up marijuana for the day.

Connie, perched on a stool, looks up and smiles. She wears no makeup and her hair, scrupulously clean, falls around her face. She is small — five feet two — but the tall stool gives her a certain stature. Up high by the window, she can see down onto the street. She is wearing a check blouse, jeans, and two belts, one with a demonic goat's head and the other apparently a chain from a BSA motorcycle. At the side of one belt is a small leather case that holds a knife. Connie always carries a flick knife and always in a visible place — as long as it is not a switchblade (which shoots the blade forward from the handle) and it is not concealed, the police will leave her alone. I pull up a chair and the three of us talk over the blare of the radio, yelling to make ourselves heard or leaning together conspiratorially to catch some complicated story.

In the mornings, Connie and Suzie, her daughter, get up early at 7:30. Suzie is fourteen, taller than her mother, and very capable. The girlfriend of Connie's six-year-old son Raps comes by to pick him up and often she dresses and feeds him as well. He is out of the house by 8:30. JJ, Connie's youngest son, has to be dressed and given breakfast along with baby Dahlia. She and Suzie take him to school, put Dahlia in the nursery downstairs, and sometimes manage to eat breakfast together in a donut shop. By 9:30 the kids are usually dispatched for the day.

This particular Friday, Suzie has stayed home to help out and hang around. Gino, Connie's husband and leader of the Sandman, is not going to work today and is sleeping through the early morning hubbub.

Connie is happy to have all her family around her. As we talk, she bags up with a dexterity she has developed over years — snipping up the grass and packing it into tiny yellow envelopes. She seals each with Scotch tape and then, with a small piece of cardboard, scrapes another bagful from the white plastic bowl. We talk about jealousy. Connie leans over and pulls a notebook out of the kitchen drawer. Each page has neat paragraph entries, the visible results of years of sitting, thinking, bagging, and talking. She writes down each new insight about life and relationships.

This morning she announces that she has to get on with her "automated routines," so she gets up, washes the dishes, puts a pile of dirty T-shirts into the washing machine, and lights a cigarette. OK is now listening to the radio through headphones, but the volume is so loud that we can all hear it. JR has turned up the television and sits absorbed by a soap opera. Connie runs out of cigarettes and OK is sent to the store to buy a pack of Kools. Connie tells me about when she had Suzie at fifteen. After her fourth child at twenty-eight, Connie "closed down the factory." "I felt like a damn incubator. There has got to be some balance in life, but who should decide who's to live and who's to die?" she ponders as she slaps Scotch tape onto the tiny bags.

At one o'clock, Wolfy from the Satan's Wheels in the South Bronx 20 arrives. He has a black handkerchief around his head, held in place by a piece of string, and wears a T-shirt and a cutoff denim jacket without gang insignia or "patches." Patches seen on the subway cause trouble. The guys get up to greet him as he comes into their clubhouse. They exchange news from different clubs, and Connie and I sit by, half-listening from the kitchen. From the bedroom comes a warm roar and Gino appears with arms outstretched to Wolfy. "Hey, hey, what's up?" They embrace and Gino's presence as leader is felt.

Connie divides the plastic bags and hands them to some of the guys who pull on their leather jackets and denim patches with SANDMAN MC NYC on the back and go out for the day to the street. Gino, wearing a black leather biker's cap with his leather jacket, jeans, and motorcycle boots, comes over and kisses Connie. Then he leaves to go down with the guys.

At 1:30, Shorty arrives. She is small and curly-haired, perhaps only nineteen. She is gang member Sinbad's girlfriend and wears her denim jacket over a blue sweatshirt. To be Sinbad's girlfriend is not a direct entry into the Sandman Ladies, however. She must prove her capability, just like anyone else who wants to join, and she has not yet earned her patches. Connie will decide when she deserves the title Sandman Lady. Connie says that she doesn't care about a girl's fighting history; what she looks for in a possible member are brains. Shorty is still learning. Later, when she answers the door and leaves it ajar as she tells Connie who it is, Connie tells her never, never to leave the door open. How does she know that someone they don't want to see isn't out there about to walk right in? Shorty nods. She sits in the living room quietly watching and listening to everything.

Connie's favorite song plays on the radio. She jumps up and whistles for Suzie to come in from the bedroom. Together they take over the living room floor, doing the hustle. Suzie acts the male's part perfectly, with minimum body movement and an expression of total boredom. At the end of the song, Suzie walks back to the bedroom and Connie, out of breath, laughs to herself. At 1:45, Connie's mother phones from Queens. Connie talks with her mother frequently on the phone but does not see her often. Her mother disapproves of the club, and Connie feels caught between duty and love.

Everything is quiet now. Family members have gone their ways for the day, and only Shorty sits quietly in the next room, clutching a hankie. Connie tells me more of her life story. When she was nineteen — eleven years ago — her father died. She shows me one of the letters he wrote to her while he was in the hospital for drug treatment. The handwriting is scrupulously neat. He complains that the doctors think he is crazy and tells Connie that if anything should happen to him, she should investigate it. He writes with great pride about Connie's new career in nursing and about his beautiful granddaughter (Suzie). Among his letters, Connie finds some official papers. One is a charge sheet from the police or a court, signed by a doctor, testifying that her father was found unfit to plead because of "imbecility." The other is a telegram from the hospital telling her that he is dead and asking her to make funeral arrangements. Connie never saw the death certificate and never knew what her father died from. Now she remembers his injunction and feels guilty. She never did check the circumstances of his death. She looks at the clock; it's time to go pick up the kids.

Halfway to the elevator Connie runs back to the apartment to get    25
her sunglasses. Last week she got beaten up. Her nose was broken, she had stitches, and both her eyes puffed out. The swelling has gone down, but two plum-colored circles remain around her eyes. Until they go, the sunglasses are compulsory public wear. She has also changed into a pair of dark red boots — lovingly cared for with daily doses of cold cream — that are pulled over her jeans. Over her blouse, she wears a fur-lined leather jacket, a couple of sizes too big, and on top of that her patches. Sewn on the denim jacket are the full colors of the club: SANDMAN NYC LADIES. With Shorty, we go into the weak afternoon sunshine.

Outside on a bench, Gino is recounting to the gang how the police beat him up when he had tuberculosis: "They beat the TB right out of me!" Sitting on the stone bench and the wall are seven club members all with their colors on. Wolfy and Lalla, a girl of twenty who deals around the area, are there too. Lalla wears a baseball cap back to front and a red jacket. She looks young and jumpy in comparison to Connie, severe and feminine, who sits on the stone chess table listening quietly while her husband speaks. Gino's story gets increasingly boisterous, and there is much laughter as they slap one another's hands in appreciation of the tale. The group appears insulated and self-contained. Their uniform jacket patches and their red bandannas divide them from the rest of the world. Nevertheless, neighbors, janitors, social workers, mothers of children who share Dahlia's nursery greet them as they pass, and Gino and the group wave back or shout "Hi. What's up?"

Dahlia stumbles out of the front lobby, watched by her teacher. She heads straight for Connie who picks her up, kisses her, and switches her shoes, which Dahlia has put on the wrong feet. Gino kisses Dahlia hello, and he and Connie decide who will go to pick up JJ from school. Gino goes, since he is usually at work these days and misses the daily ritual.

Every so often, someone approaches one of the group — the guy who is "holding" that day. The drug deal is transacted quietly. The girls sit separately. We talk about the neighborhood, about fights, about men. Now and again one of the guys asks for a cigarette or tells Connie something in Spanish connected with today's business. At the end of the day, all the money goes to Connie, who does the bookkeeping. Connie gives Suzie a couple of dollars from the roll of bills in her pocket to take Dahlia to the store to buy some candy. Today Dahlia gets some marshmallows, but Connie doesn't generally approve. She doesn't want her to get a taste for too much sugar.

Gino returns, and now the whole family is together. Raps, six years old, tells about a fight he had at school: "Yeah, I really dogged him. I fucked up his shit." Gino teases him about his ten-year-old girlfriend, offering some fatherly advice: "You tell that bitch that she can't carry your gaddam books to school no more." Everyone laughs except Raps, who looks down, embarrassed. He likes the attention but doesn't really know what is so funny. The teenage girls from the project are coming home from junior high school. As they pass, they greet Connie with a kiss, exchange a few words, kiss her cheek again, and go inside. They all know her and Suzie. Members of the club who have been at work or school arrive one at a time until there are fifteen of us. We each throw in a couple of dollars, and JC goes off to the liquor store. He returns with small plastic cups, a bottle of Coke, and some Bacardi rum. The girls' drinks are poured into the cups and are very strong. Sinbad notices me sipping at mine and instructs me to "Drink like a *woman*." The guys pass the liquor bottle around, drinking theirs neat. Before each one drinks, he pours a little of the rum on the ground in memory of those who are dead or in jail. The bottle ends up on the stone chess table in front of the girls, and the guys gravitate toward it. Gino and Wolfy speak half to each other and half to the kids who climb on and off the benches, threatening to upset the liquor. Raps drops his lollipop on the ground, and Gino picks it up, wipes it off, and pours Bacardi over it to sterilize it. Raps puts it back in his mouth and grimaces.

The conversation turns to Gino's time in Vietnam, where, he tells us, he was a combat photographer. He tells how many of the injuries he saw were perpetrated by the Americans on themselves when incendiary bombs were dropped short of target or when machines backfired. He was injured in the leg, but when the U.S. Army withdrew, his medical papers were lost. Now he has no way to prove that he is entitled to veteran's compensation, unless he were to take his case to court and that would cost him thousands. "If I had that kind of money, I wouldn't need their damn compensation, right?" Gino interrupts the story to wave and yell at a guy across the street who is something of a local celebrity because he had a role in *The Wiz*. Gino also sees two guys in surplus army jackets crossing the street — plainclothes cops. Gino watches as they enter a flower shop, which is a local drug-dealing center. Later, a local guy comes over to tell Gino that he followed them but they split up and went different ways.

It's 4:50 and it's getting colder. Gino announces we are going to a party tonight at the house of the president of Satan's Wheels in the Bronx. Upon hearing of the party, Connie, who has been standing back with Shorty, occasionally chatting to her, decides it is a good time to give Shorty her first patches. They disappear upstairs to sew them on her jacket and to check that Suzie can baby-sit. As we sit drinking, the daylight fades quickly. People coming home from work pass the apartment building in a steady stream. Some stare curiously at the group. Others, more familiar, simply hurry past. The light in the lobby spills out onto the concrete in front and the yellow streetlights come on.

Connie and Shorty return. Shorty spins around triumphantly to show off her new patches: LADY NYC. Later she will earn her final patch: SANDMAN. The guys yell and whistle and, led by Gino, pour bottles of beer over her head in traditional gang congratulations. She squeals. It's very cold by now and her hair is soaking wet, but she smiles and flicks back her curls with the back of her hand. Sinbad hugs her proudly.

Connie disappears and returns with a sandwich wrapped in silver foil from a local Spanish store. We pass it around and share it with the kids who have come downstairs. By now there are about twenty of us. From time to time, one of the guys comes over and looks through my notebook, curious to see what I have written down today. They borrow my pen to make illustrations, additions, or subtractions. Connie and I stand together. She points out females who pass by, some friends and some potential enemies. I am shivering from the cold, but Connie teases me that my knees are knocking at the thought of going to the South Bronx. There is talk that the Satan's Wheels will send a van to pick up everyone. That would be better than going by subway. On the subway, twenty people dressed in gang colors attract attention, which often leads to problems with the police. But the Sandman must wear their colors as a sign of pride in their club if they are going to another club's turf. Maybe they'll

carry them over their arms on the train and put them on when they get
out. Some of the guys who have come from work look tired. Gino tells
them to watch out for being burned. If they fall asleep at the party he
will set fire to their pants, a disciplinary custom that reminds members always to be on their guard when they are away from their own area.

Gino announces that we will go by subway but no one is to wear
colors on the train. Five of us take the kids and their various toys and
carts up to the apartment. Suzie has two girlfriends over for the evening
and is playing disco music. Connie leaves a small bag of grass for them.
Suzie tries for a pint of Bacardi too, but Connie refuses. Dahlia cries for
her mother but quiets down when Suzie picks her up. We go downstairs
after I have been given a plain denim jacket so I won't look completely
out of place.

OK and Shorty carry down motorcycle helmets, which they offer to    35
Gino. Gino asks what the hell they are for. OK protests that Gino told
him to bring them. Gino says he didn't. OK mumbles some curse and
turns away. Gino loses his temper and begins yelling at him. Everyone
freezes and watches to see what will happen. OK does not say a word.
Gino berates him for not listening, for not following orders, for being in-
solent. Wolfy, even though it is not his gang, joins in: "He's your leader.
You'd better damn well respect him." OK, head down, walks away.
Gino does not let up: "And don't you be sulking like that neither." OK
seems to look happier afterward. Gino's threat to leave him chained to
the iron fence at the edge of the project buildings is forgotten.

We walk in twos and threes to the subway station five or six blocks
away. Gino stops to urinate behind a wall. I walk on with the Hulk, talking about his future, his school, his clothes. Connie calls out, "Hey,
where's Annie?" She is looking out for me all the time. At the subway,
Wolfy and I walk down the steps while the rest of the group gathers at
the entrance. I put my token in the stile, but Wolfy walks through the
swing doors without paying. The subway clerk calls him back, but he
walks on. When Gino and the others appear, the clerk has already picked
up the phone to call the transit police. Gino intervenes and pays everyone's fare, including Wolfy's. On the platform, he bawls Wolfy out,
telling him it's crazy to get the cops down for the measly fare. Gino
shows a roll of money in his pocket to reinforce the point. This is, after
all, their turf. They have to use the subway all the time, so why make
trouble? Wolfy is a guest and, as such, he should respect their turf.

Gino tells us to split up because we look too conspicuous in a group.
Connie, Shorty, and I walk down the platform. Near us two black girls
are casually rolling a joint. Connie watches them — there is something
about their manner that she doesn't like. When we get on the train, one
of them leans on the center post of the car, ignoring the available seats.
Connie walks over and leans on the opposite post four feet away, staring
at her through her dark glasses. They stare each other down, but the

other girl breaks first. She looks away, then at her feet, then gets off the train. We change trains at 182nd Street. A train pulls in, but it's not the one we want to take. Inside a car, a man in his thirties, dressed in a suit, smiles at us. It isn't clear to me whether he is leering or laughing at us. As the train pulls away, Shorty smashes her fist at the window where his face is. He jumps back and the train disappears. Shorty clutches her hand. In a few minutes, it begins to swell and turn red, but she does not mention it.

We board our train. Two Puerto Rican girls are standing by the door, whispering and laughing. Connie watches them, wondering whether to "bug them out." She approaches them, but I cannot hear what is said. One girl reaches into her bag and pulls out some gum, offering Connie a stick. She takes one and offers it to me. I decline. Connie pops it in her mouth and leans over to kiss the girl on the cheek. Connie is smiling. The girls look pleased, embarrassed, and confused. The guys walk up and down the train in ones and twos, checking that everybody is on and knows where to get off. Although they are carrying their colors over their arms, they look conspicuous in their chains, boots, and bandannas. Some have sheath knives in their waistbands. Passengers watch their comings and goings uneasily.

We get off the train and climb the unlit stairs to the street. The guys take the girls' arms to guide us up. Several young girls are standing by the subway entrance. They seem excited at our arrival and particularly interested in Connie and Shorty with their patches. As we cross the street, Sinbad authoritatively holds up his hand to halt the oncoming traffic. We straggle along a side street, and Gino peers down an alleyway to a handball court where some kids are playing by floodlight. The game breaks up, and after a few seconds one of them appears in patches: FLAMES NYC. It is Felix, a friend of Gino. He greets all of us and cordially offers a small plastic cup of vodka and grapefruit juice, which we pass around. He has recently redesigned his club patches — from a swastika into a more complex design with a skull set in red and orange flames — and turns around so we can admire them. I reach out to touch them, wondering how he got such a complicated design so professionally done. Connie pulls my hand back and tells me that it is forbidden to touch someone's patches. And there are rituals surrounding them: They can never be taken off carelessly, but must be folded and laid down safely, they must always be worn with boots, never with sneakers.

Felix decides to escort us through his turf to the party, which is several blocks away. He is on good terms with Satan's Wheels. We walk on down dark streets with huge empty tenements on either side. Doorways are covered heavily with graffiti and smell of urine. Connie, Shorty, and I walk at the rear, and Sinbad turns every few yards to make sure we are keeping up. Connie advises me to sit quietly at the party and be careful that nothing I do be misunderstood. I am white and, as such, am

40

considered to be available property. Don't say too much and stick close to her, Connie says. We gaze around at the buildings. We are both completely out of our territory, although Connie points a few blocks downtown to where she lived briefly years ago. She tells me this isn't a real nice area. Broken bottles crunch under our feet. Finally we halt outside a grocery store, waiting while Gino and Felix finish their discussion.

We walk into an old tenement building. The huge hallway is painted crimson and lit by long fluorescent tubes. Initials and names are emblazoned on the walls. We walk up one flight of stairs and ring a doorbell. After a few minutes, we are let in and walk down a hallway. Three or four girls are sitting in a bedroom through some French doors. Gino greets the guys in the club who are in the kitchen drinking, and Connie goes into the bedroom. In perfect Spanish and very politely she introduces herself as head of the Sandman Ladies and thanks the girls for their hospitality. They are much younger than she is and struggle to summon an equally dignified reply. They are dressed casually, but when they reappear several minutes later, they have put on sweatshirts that say PROPERTY OF SATAN'S WHEELS NYC, with the name of their particular man underneath. Connie tells me that *her* girls don't belong to any man.

We all assemble in the living room. Connie points out that the room is "typically Spanish" — velour-patterned sofa and many mementos on the tables and shelves; dolls, candles, crucifixes. The Satan's Wheels move the sound system into the room. Bottles of beer and Bacardi are passed around, interspersed with joints. When the music comes on, it is heavy rock — Stones, Led Zeppelin, Pink Floyd — and is deafening. Conversation is possible only by leaning right up against the other person's ear. The main lights go out, and the room is lit only by three ultraviolet lights, which illuminate eyes, teeth, and the white in jacket patches. One by one people begin to dance. Connie sits next to me on the sofa with her back straight.

It is the Hulk's sixteenth birthday. Suddenly the lights are switched on and he is drenched by several bottles of beer. He waves his arms, apparently enjoying the experience. The floor is awash with liquid, but one of the Satan's Wheels later mops up. Everyone is also scrupulously careful to flick their cigarette ashes into ashtrays, rather than on the floor. Amid the apparent chaos, there is a definite order. The Hulk moves around the room, embracing every member of the club, and by the end, we are all nearly as wet as he is. Gino spends most of the evening in the kitchen, discussing club business with the Flames and Satan's Wheels. Connie and I sit together drinking. Everybody is loosening up. Chino gets his beard set alight as a reminder that he is getting a little too loose. He climbs onto the fire escape and peers down, announcing that he is contemplating suicide. Then he laughs.

Connie and I, as we drink more, consider the implications of everything in the world being a product of our imagination. If we wished it all away now, only *we* would remain, suspended sixty feet in the air, discussing this very thought. A guy next to me searches vainly for some matches. I hand him some and Connie warns me about body contact. If you touch someone accidentally, they may take it the wrong way. I move away from him, suddenly aware that I have been half-leaning on him. Connie motions me to lean forward and tells me that if we keep talking together, maybe the guys will assume that I'm with her. That way, I'll be safe. Gino returns to sit by us. He and some other guys are throwing a bottle back and forth with eyes closed, a kind of test of everybody's reaction to speed. I notice Connie's hands loose in her lap but ready in case it is thrown her way. The music changes to disco — a whole album side of it — and Connie gets up to dance alone.

It is after midnight and I decide to leave. Connie forces twenty dol-    45
lars into my hand for a cab. Gino assigns two guys to walk me to the taxi office. Everybody yells goodnight, and I make my way back home.

### *Reading the Text*

1. Why, according to Campbell, has so little been written about female gang members?
2. What are the various roles that female gang members are seen as playing?
3. Why has Connie achieved the status of leader of the Sandman Ladies?
4. How must Campbell, as a nongang white woman, adjust her verbal and body language when she is with the gang members?

### *Reading the Signs*

1. In class, write on the board the various roles that female gang members assume ("Sex Objects," "Tomboys," and so forth). Discuss the extent to which these roles are available for "mainstream" women not involved with gangs. What do these roles say about the power of gender roles in both mainstream cultures and countercultures?
2. Compare the male and female gang members whom Campbell describes. What does gang involvement seem to mean to each gender? What different roles do males and females play in the gang? Use your observations to formulate an argument about gender roles in Connie's gang; you may want to consult Holly Devor's "Gender Role Behaviors and Attitudes" (p. 415) as you write your essay.
3. Write an essay in which you explore the nature of the relationship among the gang members described in this selection. In what ways does Connie's gang operate as a "family"? And to what extent does her gang redefine traditional notions of what an American family is like?

4. How do symbols and rituals work to define Connie's gang as a group? Write a semiotic reading of the signs that the Sandman Ladies use to communicate gang affiliation, both to outsiders and to each other.

5. To what extent do the gang members described by Campbell share the "hunger for more" that Laurence Shames discusses (p. 31)? How do you account for your conclusions?

6. Assuming the role of Connie, write a letter to one of the wannabe gang members discussed in Nell Bernstein's "Goin' Gangsta, Choosin' Cholita" (p. 504). What response do you think Connie would have to the students who "try on" a gangster's identity? Share your letter with your class.

JULIE GANNON SHOOP

*Image of Fear: Minority Teens Allege Bias in "Gang Profiling"*

111111111111111111111111111111111111111111

*Have you, or a friend, ever been stopped by a police officer because you were wearing baggy pants or had a shaved head? According to this report by Julie Gannon Shoop (b. 1962), such things happen all the time to minority kids whose appearance conforms to certain profiles constructed by urban law enforcement agencies. In short, if you "look" like a gangster, the police are likely to treat you as one. So which is more important, Shoop's article implicitly asks, the right of law-abiding teens to look and dress any way they want, or the need of law enforcement to increase its effectiveness in combating gang violence? A graduate of Carleton College, Shoop is associate editor of* Trial *magazine, a publication of the Association of Trial Lawyers of America.*

In the common image of the urban thug, a dark-skinned youth wears baggy clothes, heavy jewelry, and a menacing expression. This picture, popularized in movies and music videos, has begun to show up in police department practice manuals — along with other characteristics — as the "profile" of the typical urban gang member.

To combat violent street gangs, many law enforcement agencies have developed "gang profiles" to identify young people as members or associates of gangs. The criteria range from known criminal activity and admitted gang membership to style of dress, tattoos, favorite hangouts, and the identities of friends. Some businesses have adopted similar profiles as a way to screen out potentially troublesome customers.

Proponents of gang profiling say it is a logical, efficient way to identify and monitor dangerous youths. But civil rights advocates claim that police are casting too wide a net in a fishing expedition that sweeps in innocent people — primarily young minority men — who happen to fit the broad stereotype of a gang member.

Allegedly based on profiles, teens have been thrown out of shopping malls, ejected from amusement parks, and stopped and searched by police, who may later enter their names and photos into computer databases. Their lawyers have filed lawsuits on their behalf, claiming that racial and other biases have unfairly branded these young people as criminals.

"The widespread development and use of gang profiles is part of an 5 alarming trend," said Edward Chen, a staff attorney with the American Civil Liberties Union (ACLU) of Northern California. "In their attempts to combat the real problem of gang violence, law enforcement agencies and businesses are institutionalizing stereotypes and stigmatizing an entire generation of young minority males."

Others disagree. "The system is not interested in filling itself up with [names based on] vague criteria and the remote possibility of gang membership," said Bruce Praet, a Santa Ana, California, lawyer who is defending a challenge to one police department's gang profiling system. "The objective is to identify the hard-core gang members who are inflicting violence on the citizens."

Civil rights lawyers are also questioning how information in police gang databases is handled. They have raised concerns about who has access to the databases, how long the names are retained, and whether procedures are available to have information removed if a person shows that he or she is not a gang member. Profiling critics point out that mere membership in a gang is not a crime and that vague gang profiles "do not separate the hard-core members whose lives are deeply intertwined with criminal activity from people who have some association with a gang, but it's not necessarily drug dealing, armed robbery, or drive-by shootings," said Mark Silverstein, a staff attorney with the ACLU's Southern California affiliate.

According to a recent survey by the National Institute of Justice, a research arm of the U.S. Justice Department, there were almost 5,000 gangs and 250,000 gang members in 110 U.S. cities in 1992, although definitions of what constitutes a gang or gang member varied across the United States. The report described the wide disparity between the number of alleged gang members and the much smaller number of gang-related crimes (about 46,000).

The survey found that 93 percent of the 72 largest cities reporting a gang problem list "use of symbols" — including dressing in a certain style or writing graffiti — as a criterion for defining gangs. Eighty-one percent used violent behavior as a criterion. (G. David Curry et al., Nat'l Inst. Justice, Gang Crime and Law Enforcement Recordkeeping [Aug. 1994].)

Ronald Huff, director of the Criminal Justice Research Center at    10
Ohio State University, who has studied gangs and police response for
nearly a decade, said overlabeling of gang members "is very much a
problem." Dress style, for instance, is an unreliable indicator, especially
since baggy, "hiphop"-style clothes have become fashionable among
teenagers. "We have suburban kids who dress like gangsters," he said,
"but they're not criminals."

The dress issue is a central element of a lawsuit filed last spring by
two Asian American girls challenging the "discriminatory and arbitrary"
gang profiles used by the Garden Grove, California, police department.
The girls claim that officers detained them without cause at an out-door
shopping mall and accused them of being gang members. According to
the complaint, the officers questioned the girls, searched their wallets,
and photographed them before releasing them without filing charges.
The girls deny they belong to a gang. (Pham v. City of Garden Grove,
No. 94-3358 [C.D. Cal. filed May 20, 1994].)

Silverstein of the Southern California ACLU, which filed the case on
the girls' behalf, said the officers told the girls they looked like gang
members because they were wearing baggy clothes. The officers also suspected a gang connection because the girls were standing near a restaurant that police consider a gang hangout, Silverstein said.

But Praet, the Santa Ana lawyer who represents the city, said the police were justified in stopping the girls because they were trying to get
into an adults-only nightclub. He said the club had been the scene of a
recent gang-related shooting.

The complaint claims the girls were not violating any laws when
they were detained. "Even if police reasonably suspect that you are a
gang member, that alone is not the basis for a stop," Silverstein said.
"What you need to stop somebody is a reasonable suspicion that criminal
activity is afoot."

Praet said the city does not intend to change its gang tracking prac-    15
tices but is "willing to give added reassurances to the community" that
the practices are fair. He said the city might add a code to the database
that would indicate that a person had denied being a gang member, distribute a card explaining how a photographed person could request that
the photo be removed from police department files, or limit officers' authority to take photos.

As a result of a similar suit, the city of Portland, Oregon, is developing
a hearing process in which people labeled as gang members can challenge
their inclusion on the city's gang list. The case involved Ernesto Ysasaga, a
20-year-old Hispanic man who had been convicted for misdemeanor assault and painting graffiti. The Portland Police Bureau had also placed his
name on its gang list and notified his employer that Ysasaga was a gang
member. He lost his job, although he denied he had ever been affiliated
with a gang.

"The legal basis for the claim was that anyone labeled as a gang member was not given an opportunity to prove otherwise," said Spencer Neal, Ysasaga's attorney. "It was a failure of fundamental due process." The case was settled, and a judge gave the city six months to develop a hearing procedure. (Ysasaga v. City of Portland, No. 93-1175 ST [D. Or. Apr. 26, 1994].)

## Private Profiling

Police aren't the only ones making unfair assumptions that are based on race, dress, and other factors, civil rights lawyers say. Other anti-profiling cases have targeted businesses:

■  A series of suits in northern California alleged that African American and Hispanic teenagers were ejected from shopping malls because they were wearing clothes that fit a gang profile. One case listed the city of San Mateo as a defendant because the police department had instructed the mall's management about what gang members allegedly look like. Under a settlement reached in the case, the mall agreed no longer to exclude customers based on their dress style. (Ramirez Claire v. Bohannon Development Co., No. C-93-1651-FMS [N.D. Cal. Apr. 18, 1994].)

■  In 1992, the ACLU and Kings Entertainment Co. settled a lawsuit    20
filed by 17 young African American men who claimed they were kept out, or thrown out, of the Great America theme park in Santa Clara because of their "gang attire." Park management agreed to use conduct rather than dress as the basis for deciding who may visit that park. (Garcia v. Kings Entertainment Co., No. 712978 [Cal., Santa Clara County Super. Ct. Oct. 12, 1992].)

The ACLU's Chen, who represented the teenagers in both cases, said groups of minority youths, unlike white teens, are often assumed to be lawbreakers. "The primary civil rights problem is not that kids are getting thrown out of malls," he said. "It's the mentality that underlies the whole policy."

Chen and other profiling opponents cite the large numbers of minority youths listed in police gang databases as evidence that racial bias plays a substantial, if unspoken, role in gang profiling. For example, a 1992 report by the Los Angeles County district attorney found that 47 percent of the county's African American males ranging from age 21 to 24 were listed in the county's Gang Reporting Evaluation and Tracking system. (Los Angeles County District Attorney's Office, Gangs, Crime, and Violence in Los Angeles 121 [1992].)

"I don't know anyone, not even the district attorney, who defends that number [as accurate]," said Kevin Reed, an attorney in the Los Angeles office of the NAACP Legal Defense and Educational Fund. He said the lack of consensus on what constitutes gangs and gang membership has caused gang databases to swell with the names of mislabeled young people.

Still, profiling proponents insist that it works.

"The police have had very positive experience" with profiling, said    25
John Firman, research director of the International Association of Chiefs of Police, based in Alexandria, Virginia. "There's a logic to looking for clues. It streamlines and makes more effective your work."

Ohio State University's Huff said police should use only "good, solid behavioral indicators" rather than descriptions like race or dress to identify gang members. Race, in particular, "should play no role in identifying gangs," he added. "No racial or ethnic group has a corner on gang membership."

Profiling based strictly on behavior would be an appropriate police response to the gang threat, Huff said. "I'm in favor of aggressive, high-profile law enforcement," he said, "but it has to be constitutionally sound."

### Reading the Text

1. Summarize in your own words the popular image of the gang member, according to Shoop.
2. Outline the defenses for and criticisms of police gang profiling.
3. What are some of the consequences of gang profiling by law enforcement agencies, as Shoop reports them?
4. How have individuals challenged police gang profiling, and with what effect?

### Reading the Signs

1. Shoop claims that films and videos perpetuate stereotypes of gang members. In class, brainstorm titles of films and videos that feature gangsters as characters, then discuss the extent to which they perpetuate or challenge stereotypes. Use the class discussion as a foundation for an essay in which you construct an argument about the media's role in shaping the popular image of the gang member.
2. In class, form teams and debate whether gang profiling is a legitimate strategy that law enforcement officials should use in fighting criminal gang activity.
3. In your journal, explore the fashion of wearing gang clothing and insignia, even if one is not a gang member. Have you ever worn such clothing styles, and if so, why? If not, how would you respond to a friend or sibling who may adopt such styles but not be a gang member?

4. A number of schools across the country have adopted dress codes to prevent the appearance of gang fashions on campus. Write an essay attacking or defending such codes.

5. Write a letter to Garden Grove, California, attorney Bruce Praet, arguing against his city's policy of gang profiling. Alternately, write a letter to Mark Silverstein, the ACLU attorney defending two girls arrested in Garden Grove because of gang appearance, in which you challenge his defense of them.

SONIA MAASIK AND JACK SOLOMON

*Signs of the Street: A Conversation*

|||||||||||||||||||||||||||||||||||||||||||||||||||||||||||||||||||||||||

*Too often, gangs are interpreted by adults — especially white middle-class professionals — who have no personal experience of gang life, nor any direct knowledge of the social conditions in which youth gangs flourish. One of the best ways to learn about gangs, however, is to speak with those who are associated with them. To see what the kids themselves had to say, the authors of this book visited a Los Angeles high school that offers former gang members an opportunity to complete their secondary school education. The following conversation reveals what a group of some twenty-five students at the West Valley Occupational Center school think about such issues as gang fashion, suburban wannabes, and the value that gang membership holds for those who belong to them. All names of students have been changed to protect their identity.*

*Can you describe for us what sorts of clothing you see on the streets these days?*

JORGE: Baggy pants, skate clothes, stuff like that. Look around, and everybody wears baggy pants.

*Do you know when people started wearing baggy pants? About?*

JORGE: Well, early you know, like maybe in the forties or back in the thirties.

LUIS: It came out with the zoot suits.                                    5

OSCAR: Well, gang members had to like the same thing, you know. Gangsters still stay the same.

JORGE: Designers are wearing baggy pants, just like gangs. Recently, everybody's started wearing them within probably the past what? Maybe year, two, three years.

MIKE: It started getting really crazy around two years ago.

JORGE: You know about sagging? Where they used to sag a long time ago?

LUIS: Oh, that started about, like, forty years ago. I think sagging came     10
out with the black people first. It started with the brothers.

HANK: It was rappers that came first. Remember that song about saggin' pants? It was Ice-T.

RUDY: And colors. You know, a guy may wear like red, mustard colors. And other guys wear dark colors. Everyone belongs in a group, and you can tell him by the way he dresses.

*How are Nikes these days? A few years ago Nikes were just the shoe. What's going on now?*

HANK: They're gangbanger shoes.

OSCAR: A lot of crooks wore 'em. And the Bloods would wear the all-     15
red ones with a little red stripe, but now they're trying to get conservative and they wear black and then have just a little red somewhere. They like dressing down, but they'll let you know where they're from.

*Any sneakers that you just wouldn't be seen dead in?*

TONY: Crow Wings! They're just cheap, you know, you can get 'em at Penney's for like 10 bucks.

RUDY: Reeboks are cool. Everybody wears Reeboks.

OSCAR: Converse. Converse, man. Converse.

HANK: Converse are gangbanger shoes.                                    20

LATISHA: Some taggers like the versatile Converse. They have lowtops, hightops, different colors, suede, you know, like that.

*Is there anything that you wouldn't wear at school, but would wear at home or in your neighborhood?*

OSCAR: Pajamas!

LUIS: You wouldn't wear clothes with your gang on it. You can't wear that in school 'cuz you get in trouble. Or clothes in remembrance of a friend that died.

BRIAN: You can't even wear a hat to school, 'cuz they think it's gang-     25
related.

*Two guys here are wearing shorts: one pair are blue denim cutoffs and the other are plaid cutoffs. Do you read those two guys differently?*

JORGE: Geeks, geeks! That's a skater.

*And the plaid is what?*

GARY: Surfer.

TERESA: And gangsters wear cutoff Dickies.                                    30

*What do cutoffs say to guys on the street?*

JORGE: You're a gang member. And they have to be Dickies. The make is important. The brand style.

TERESA: And they're ironed. All the gang members iron. They can't be all wrinkled. They want to show their respect, that they care for themselves.

LUIS: Gangsters are the ones that crease it, even their boxer shorts, man! It's the respect they have when they go on the street. They want people to see that they try to look good for other people.

TERESA: Well, you're not going to see a gang member going in the street        35
with wrinkled clothes, you know? They just don't look right.

*Is there anything else that they do to show respect?*

ALICIA: Short haircuts. It's got to be clean cut. It shows they respect themselves and they want respect for their gang.

OSCAR: And bald people. Bald means that they're gangbangers.

*Bald is a code word. Do you really mean shaven head?*

MIKE: Well, it means two different things. One's a gangbanger. But my        40
head's shaved all the way around, all the way under and I have hair on top. When I shaved my head, I shaved it clean. Because I'm not Hispanic or I'm not black, I immediately looked skinhead. So it has something to do with the color you are. I have a goatee and a full shaved head. I was fully labeled a skinhead, right off.

*I don't think there are any skinheads in the room now. That way nobody needs to feel defensive. What about the skinheads? What do you think about them?*

TONY: They're mostly all white power.

MIKE: That's bull, dude. They're not.

BRIAN: You're so wrong, dude. You guys have such a misconception of the skinheads. There are so many skinhead groups that are totally against racism and stuff like that. Like shark skinheads.

MIKE: There's a lot of groups like that, you know there's groups like        45
Ghost Town Skinheads and there're Nazi skinheads and stuff like that.

BRIAN: But there's Peace Punk, stuff like that. And they won't wear leather and stuff like that or do things like killing animals or hurting the environment. And people just have misconceptions and think that if you're white and got a shaved head, you're like a Nazi, you're

a skinhead and you're a racist toward everyone. But that's not the
way it is.

LATISHA: Don't you think that that's the image they project to us? And
that image is what most of the skinheads are about?

BRIAN: That's what you see, that's what you see on the media. That's
what you see on TV.

LATISHA: Okay, so what makes the difference if I see a white guy walking down the street and he just bald-headed? I have never met one
skinhead who ain't racist toward a black person.

MIKE: I think everyone pretty much has a little bit of racism in them.    50
Everybody's against every race.

BRIAN: But there's a lot of different groups, I'm telling you. See, the
media makes it seem like skinheads are, you know, the epitome of
racist people. The majority of skinheads are probably racist, but a lot
of them are not. People give skinheads bad names and that's not
cool.

*Is it useful to you to be able to figure people out by the way they dress?*

TONY: On the street, yeah. If you're walking by yourself, and you see a
bunch of people, you just don't want to get involved.

MIKE: You know that people mess with each other out on the streets.
Me and him, we were just skating at a parking lot and a car full of
guys drives up and they scream out some names. They scream out
these nicknames, and if we start talking back, then that's how things
happen, you know. Just by their appearance you can see stuff coming. Their cars even tell you.

JORGE: Yeah, Impalas and Regals, '65 Impalas.                            55

*You can read a car real quick?*

MANY: Yeah.

*What are the cars?*

HANK: Cadillacs, Regals, Impalas, older cars.

LUIS: In the olden days, they used to drive old cars. Now they're trying    60
to keep the tradition of those old cars. All you see today is pure
*raza,*[1] just driving old cars so they look good.

*How do you and your friends in your neighborhoods feel when you see in movies
or on television or on the streets obviously rich, generally white kids trying to dress
up like gangsters? What do you think when you see that?*

TERESA: Stupid!

JORGE: We laugh at them. We laugh.

---

1. ***raza*** Refers to *la raza,* the race or Hispanic people. — EDS.

OSCAR: They try to dress like us, they're trying to make a statement, like they are like we are. But if somebody approach 'em or something, they'd be the first one to back down and run away or something like that. And that ain't cool.

TERESA: They're trying to be like everybody else, trying to fit in. 65

TONY: They're just wannabes.

*When I ask you where you're from, what does that question really mean?*

JORGE: What gang we're from, what neighborhood.

LUIS: You know what? They can dress like gangs, but they have to show it. They have to prove themselves.

*So it's something more than just the clothing?* 70

LUIS: You gotta have heart for it.

JORGE: A lot of people that dress up like that, they're starting in rich, rich areas, they're starting to like get their own little gangs and they're starting to tag up the walls there, and they're starting to do the same stuff that's going on out here.

RUDY: They imitate everybody else, they try to dress the same way.

*So if it's your own style, it's cool, but, if you try to take somebody else's style that you haven't earned, that's kind of dumb?*

TERESA: There's a lot of people, just to fit in they'll dress like gangsters, 75 but they ain't about shit. They're punks. It's true, man. Say my brother or my cousin sees someone dressed like a gangster and they ask, "Where were you from?" He says, "I'm not from nowhere, I just like the way I dress." He straight out says it. He acts like he's from somewhere, but he's just scared to say he's afraid, but that's stupid. Why you gonna dress like that if you're not gonna be down for your group?

*I've heard that some guys like to wear tattoos and those tattoos mean something. Why do people tattoo?*

OSCAR: Most Chicanos, they like getting tattoos, like naked girls, Aztec warriors. It has to do with *la raza,* to do with their race. See, other guys, other races, they can get other kinds of tattoos, like cats, like lions.

BRIAN: That's like a totally different thing.

*I notice the letters. Why'd you pick those letters (points to Gothic lettering on one student's tattoo)?*

LUIS: Because that's like gang letters. It's the old style. 80

LATISHA: I think the Hispanics started it, but black people like it too, you know.

*What about the three dots on the hand? Is that where they go?*

ALICIA: Um, like about right here *(points)*, between my thumb and my
first finger. You can put them anywhere else too. You could put 'em
on the elbow or the wrist.

*What if you saw somebody from the suburbs with three dots that obviously
weren't really tattoos, but just kind of a wash-off tattoo, with three dots on their
wrist, what would you think?*

JORGE: I'd ask 'em why it's there and what kind of life do you have?          85
TERESA: A fake tattoo! Like, what are they trying to prove? To make it
look hard?
BRIAN: If you can't take the ink, don't draw on yourself. If you're not
down to getting drawn on, then, you know, don't start playing with
pens drawing things.
TERESA: I know, but what are they trying to prove? If they get one, then
get a real one.
OSCAR: One thing I want to point out, see, it doesn't really matter the
way you dress.
LUIS: Yeah. Because you can dress the dorkiest-assed person on the          90
planet, but you could be still a gang member, and if you're that gang
member and dress so dorky you could have a lot of heart for that
gang that you're from. It doesn't really matter how you dress. You
could dress like some different type of style, but still you have heart
for that neighborhood that you got jumped in to. It doesn't matter
the way you dress. It doesn't.
OSCAR: It's how people perceive you, how people look at you. All that
matters is what you have inside your heart.
MIKE: It's what society puts on teens. It's the way society says, "This is
how these people dress, this is how these people dress, this is how
these people dress." No questions. And it's fucked up. It sucks.
TERESA: But you know what? The media puts everything so wrong
when they talk about kids, but it's not the story.

*Can you think of something that's really dead wrong that the media do?*

LUIS: Oh, yeah. Like in the news or in radio, when they talk about          95
gangs, like Hispanic gangs. They make us look bad. They always talk
about the things we do bad, like, "Oh, another drive-by," but they
never talk about when one of us Hispanics graduates or does something good, become a doctor or something like that. They only talk
about the bad about us and that's one thing I don't really understand.
Why do they have to talk about things that are bad about us? I think
there's good stuff and there's bad stuff here. Like us, you know,
everybody in this class, we're *raza,* they're black, they're white, but

we go to this school, we can learn and try to make something of our lives.

JORGE: Man, I'm a gang member, but I don't go up against society. I'm gonna be up there on top of everybody else, we can do it too, you know. It don't matter the way that you dress. I could be gang member, but hey, I'm smart too. I could do the same thing other people could do.

LUIS: Yeah, I could go to college.

OSCAR: Last night, I was listening to the radio and they were talkin' about gangs, and I didn't like it, 'cuz they were talkin' about just the bad part: We kill people and we shank.

JORGE: Well, you don't?

OSCAR: No . . . all gang members don't. Most gang members get into a     100
gang because they're scared of other people, you know. They need somebody to be around, they need a base, like a family, 'cuz see, most gang members don't have love at home so they join the neighborhood. They want the love your family can't give you.

LUIS: It's like, say your mom and your dad are ignoring you or something, you go to your neighborhood, and they pay attention to you, you know, they cheer you up. They're there for you, they give you love.

OSCAR: Let's say if I got kicked outta my house, I could go with my homeboy right here, I could go to his house and kick back as long as I want. You know, they'd take care of me.

LUIS: We're always there for each other. No matter what. Thick and thin. We're family.

OSCAR: I'm gonna show you guys. You guys want to hear a rap about love?

TONY: All right! Listen, listen.     105

OSCAR: All right, here we go . . . *(rapping)* This is a story about a young kid, about his life and things he did. Young kid, he wants to join a gang. He wanta live his life in the fast lane. Hold out with the troubles in the neighborhood, doing little things that he never should. Robbing, stealing, beating up *gente,*[2] rocking around saying things like these. Dressed down, khakis and a white T-shirt standing proud and tall. *Todos vatos, todos vatos*[3] they jump me in. I want to gangbang with you, my friends, and todos step to the *calle,*[4] rock it down to L.A. from the *valle.*[5] It was accomplished, you did what I said, when he made the promise. He promised himself one day he'll be a man. I don't think they truly understand. He gonna grow like one day

---

2. *gente*   People. — EDS.
3. *todos vatos*   All these guys. — EDS.
4. *calle*   Street. — EDS.
5. *valle*   Valley. — EDS.

working, now he's watching his back in order to live, so he tries the gang. For the very first time, first time in his life that he got high. He dropped out of school at the age of twelve. People said he messed up, he said, "Oh, well." He doesn't care about anything, 'cuz now he steps on up to cocaine. He could care less about the things he lost, because this is the story about a rebel without a cause.

*(Applause.) What do you guys think when you hear that? Where did rap come from?*

HANK: It's just like nursery rhymes. A nursery rhyme is a rap. All you gotta do is speed it up or slow it down.

LATISHA: Yeah, it's like poetry. Before it was just instinct, it just happened. But now they really rappin' mean stuff.

TERESA: They rap to make a record, but now they're rappin' to mean         110
something. Messages are being sent by rap.

*We're interested in what you understand when you see graffiti on the wall, how you can know who did it and what it means. There're all sorts of differences, aren't there?*

HANK: First of all, you know who it is 'cuz they write their name on the wall. Then you'll basically know what gang they are. Anywhere you go, you can tell if it's a tagger writing or if it's gang writing.

*How?*

JORGE: By the way they write. Most taggers kinda handwrite, mostly handwriting with a big, big spray can. You know, gangbangers they do block letters, little blocklike letters. They use different kinds of letters, different styles.

LATISHA: There's another thing with taggers. When I used to tag — I         115
don't do it anymore — but when I used to hang with a tagger crew, when we wrote, we used different kinds of ink, like scribe and streaks. Being original, you can cut half of one and cut half of the other and put it in one pen and make it double like it's rainbow color.

*What's a scribe?*

LATISHA: Scribe is when you carve it on a window. You can carve your name on it.

TERESA: It looks like crayon chalk. You can carve wood and you can carve it in a bus window.

*What do you think when you see people in the suburbs becoming taggers?*

JORGE: They're trying to prove a point.                                     120

OSCAR: They're trying to get their space. That's what everybody wants in this whole world, you know, to gain your respect. And writing on the wall is doing it or the way you dress is doing it. There's all kinds of ways of gaining respect. That's what everybody wants. No matter what race you're from, you know, black, white, Hispanic. The point is, everybody just wants respect, okay? Sometimes being in the gangs gets you that respect or being a tagger gets you that respect from other taggers. You know, it depends where you're coming from.

LATISHA: That's true, because when I was in junior high I used to gang-bang with a Mexican gang, me and another black girl. I tried to go with them because I used to get picked on by a lot of girls, because I came from a small town, I used to be like a school girl. Everybody used to pick on me and then I was talking with one of my friends and she was in the gang and she was like, "Well, you can come kick it with us." But after a while, kicking it became more. I started dressing like them and doing my hair like them, everything. And I just changed completely. Then I got picked on again for acting like a Mexican girl wannabe. But when I walked with them and we all walked around that junior high, we all had respect and they all looked at me like, you know, "I ain't gonna mess with her." But then, after that, I went to taggers because I found out that the Mexicans didn't really want to hang with me. The taggers I went to were an all-black gang in L.A., and then I had respect with them too.

LUIS: You see, in the old days, the way we, *la raza,* used to get respect was by throwing one on one. Fighting. But now, no one don't throw no blows at each other, they just pull out a gun and bam, right there. One minute just takes your life away.

ALICIA: Another thing about the imitation is that I know a lot of gangsters think taggers try to imitate them by carrying a gun or something.

TERESA: Actually there's a lot of real gangsters who are older, like in their twenties and stuff, they always say that the taggers are trying to copy them. When they see them, they chase them out of their 'hood. 125

*Any other stories you want to tell?*

TONY: Sometimes you're going down the street, and you see a gang member by the way he's dressed. But sometimes he's not even a gang member, you know, his clothes don't necessarily mean he's in a gang. He wears it for his race. They just want to get their own respect by themselves.

OSCAR: Many people think that, when gang members go to a white party, everybody treats 'em different. Just like about two weeks ago, I went to some white party and I asked for something to drink, and people just gave it to me and they wanted to open it up for me.

They gave me respect. I swear to God, man, he opened it for me and he said, "Here you go, would you like anything else?"

TONY: That's what they do in the stores, they try to just hurry up and give you what you want before you get mad and you tear up something.

HANK: I know if I get mad I'm gonna tear up something and then leave. 130 Somebody say I can't have something and I ask politely and they look at you like you got shit on your face. And you be ready to swing on somebody, real quick. And that's what they trying not to have. They don't want to get in a fight with you 'cuz they know you kick ass.

OSCAR: Yeah, when you go to the store, the first thing they say is, "Do you need something?"

HANK: I get sweat all the time. Every time I walk through a store, I get sweat, I get followed, I get asked questions. Every time.

### Reading the Text

1. How is clothing used as a signaling system on the street?
2. What is the value of gang membership, in the students' views?
3. What attitudes do the students have toward suburban gang wannabes?
4. How do the students feel about skinheads?

### Reading the Signs

1. Gang culture is often depicted in the media as a counterculture. Basing your discussion on the students' comments, write an essay in which you explore the extent to which this depiction is valid. Why do you think, for instance, that Luis so frequently refers to tradition and *la raza*?
2. In class, have one student sing Oscar's rap and discuss your responses to it.
3. What role does gang membership have in forming a teen's identity, especially a teen living in the inner city? Write an essay in which you formulate your own argument. In addition to "Signs of the Street: A Conversation," you might consult Léon Bing's "Faro" (p. 572) and Anne Campbell's "The Praised and the Damned" (p. 577).
4. What response do you think the students would have to the students mentioned in Nell Bernstein's "Goin' Gangsta, Choosin' Cholita" (p. 504)? In class, role-play a conversation among the students, being sure to articulate issues on which they might agree as well as disagree.
5. "Respect" frequently surfaces as an issue in the students' conversation. In your journal, compare what respect means to the students with what it means to you. Do you define respect in similar ways, and if so, how? If not, how do you define it? What might you say to the students about their notions of respect?

S E T H   M Y D A N S

*Not Just the Inner City: Well-to-Do Join Gangs*

ııııııııııııııııııııııııııııııııııııııııııııııı

*Though originally a subculture born of poverty and racial oppression, youth gangs are becoming increasingly attractive to white suburban "wannabes" for whom gang membership constitutes a particularly effective way of rebelling against their parents. While, as Seth Mydans (b. 1946) points out in this* New York Times *article, the "copycat" or "yuppie" gangs have not yet demonstrated widespread involvement in "serious" criminal activity, they have shown a penchant for graffiti vandalism and weapons carrying. But playing gangster can get dangerous. Dabbling with gangs may appear to some middle-class wannabes as a sign of solidarity with a racial underclass, but with drive-by shootings now involving anyone caught in the wrong place at the wrong time, the romantic allure of gangsterism is becoming less attractive. A Bureau chief for the* New York Times' *Bangkok bureau, Seth Mydans is a career journalist who has served as a foreign correspondent stationed in the former Soviet Union, England, the Philippines, and Thailand.*

In suburban Hawthorne, social workers tell of the police officers who responded to a report of gang violence, only to let the instigators drive away in expensive cars, thinking they were a group of teenagers on their way to the beach.

In Tucson, Ariz., a white middle-class teenager wearing gang colors died, a victim of a drive-by shooting, as he stood with black and Hispanic members of the Bloods gang.

At Antelope Valley High School in Lancaster, Calif., about 50 miles north of Los Angeles, 200 students threw stones at a policeman who had been called to help enforce a ban on the gang outfits that have become a fad on some campuses.

Around the country, a growing number of well-to-do youths have begun flirting with gangs in a dalliance that can be as innocent as a fashion statement or as deadly as hard-core drug dealing and violence.

The phenomenon is emerging in a variety of forms. Some affluent     5
white youths are joining established black or Hispanic gangs like the Crips and Bloods; others are forming what are sometimes called "copycat" or "mutant" or "yuppie" gangs.

The development seems to defy the usual socioeconomic explanations for the growth of gangs in inner cities, and it appears to have caught parents, teachers, and law-enforcement officers off guard.

Police experts and social workers offer an array of reasons: a mis-guided sense of the romance of gangs; pursuit of the easy money of drugs; self-defense against the spread of established hard-core gangs. And they note that well-to-do families in the suburbs can be as empty and loveless as poor families in the inner city, leaving young people searching for a sense of group identity.

Furthermore, "kids have always tried to shock their parents," said Marianne Diaz-Parton, a social worker who works with young gang members in the Los Angeles suburb of Lawndale, "and these days be-coming a gang member is one way to do it."

A member of the South Bay Family gang in Hermosa Beach, a twenty-one-year-old surfer called Road Dog who said his family owned a chain of pharmacies, put it this way: "This is the nineties, man. We're the type of people who don't take no for an answer. If your mom says no to a kid in the nineties, the kid's just going to laugh." He and his friends shouted in appreciation as another gang member lifted his long hair to reveal a tattoo on a bare shoulder: "Mama tried."

Separating their gang identities from their home lives, the South Bay    10 Family members give themselves nicknames that they carry in elaborate tattoos around the backs of their necks. They consented to interviews on the condition that only these gang names be used.

The gang's leader, who said he was the son of a bank vice president, flexed a bicep so the tattooed figure of a nearly naked woman moved suggestively. Voicing his own version of the basic street philosophy of gang solidarity, the leader, who is called Thumper, said, "If you want to be able to walk the mall, you have to know you've got your boys behind you."


## From Cool to Dead

For young people who have not been hardened by the inner city, an attitude like this, if taken into the streets, can be dangerous, said Sgt. Wes McBride of the Los Angeles Sheriff's Department, who has gathered re-ports on the phenomenon from around the country.

"They start out thinking it's real cool to be a gang member," he said. "They are 'wannabes' with nothing happening around them to show them it's real dangerous, until they run afoul of real gang members, and then they end up dead."

In California's palm-fringed San Fernando Valley, said Manuel Velasquez, a social worker with Community Youth Gang Services, a pri-vate agency, "there are a lot of kids who have no business being in gangs who all of a sudden are going around acting like gang members."

"They play the part," he went on. "They vandalize. They do graffiti.  15
They do all kinds of stuff. But when it comes down to the big stuff, it's:
'Wait a minute. That's enough for me. I want to change the rules.' And
then they realize it's a little bit too late."

There are few statistics on middle-class involvement in gangs, and
officials are reluctant to generalize about its extent or the form it is taking. But reports of middle-class gang activity come from places as disparate as Denver, Seattle, Tucson, Portland, Dallas, Phoenix, Chicago,
Minneapolis, Omaha, and Honolulu.

Sgt. John Galea, until recently the head of the youth gang intelligence unit of the New York City Police Department, said that although
there was no lack of youth violence in the city, organized street gangs as
such were not a serious problem.

The South Bay Family, in Hermosa Beach, has evolved over the past
five years from a group of bouncers for a rock band to a full-fledged street-
wise, well-armed gang. But for the most part, white gangs, or white members of minority gangs, have just begun to be noticed in the past few
months.

## "Parents Are Totally Unaware"

"I think it's a new trend just since the latter part of 1989, and it's re-
ally interesting how it's getting out to suburban areas," said Dorothy
Elmore, a gang intelligence officer for the Portland Police Bureau in
Oregon. "We've got teachers calling up and saying: 'We've got some
Bloods and Crips here. What's going on?'

"It's definitely coming from two-parent families, working class to  20
middle class to upper middle class, predominantly white," she went on.
"The parents are totally unaware of the kind of activity these kids are
doing."

In Tucson, Sgt. Ron Zimmerling, who heads the Police Department's gang unit, said that "Kids from even our country-club areas were
suddenly joining gangs."

After the drive-by shooting last summer in which a white teenager
was killed, he said, he asked a black gang member about another white
youth who had attached himself to the gang. "I don't know," the black
member replied. "He just likes to hang out."

The phenomenon is better established but still relatively new in the
Los Angeles area, the nation's gang capital.

"We have covered parties where I'm totally shocked at the mixture
of people who are there," said Mrs. Diaz-Parton, of Community Youth
Gang Services in Lawndale. "Your traditional Hispanic gang member is

next to this disco-looking person who is next to a preppie guy who looks
like he's getting straight A's on his way to college."

## Bandannas and Baseball Caps

Irving G. Spergel, a sociology professor at the University of Chicago    25
who studies gangs, emphasized that the phenomenon accounts for a very
small part of the nation's gang problem, which is centered in inner cities.
He said the four thousand to five thousand neo-Nazi skinhead groups
around the country, which have their own style and ideology, were a
separate and worrisome problem.

More trivial, but still troubling to school officials, is a trend toward
gang fashions in some high schools and junior high schools. In Los Angeles, Phoenix, Tucson, and several California suburbs, students have staged
demonstrations to protest bans on wearing certain colors, bandannas,
jewelry, or baseball caps that can be a mark of gang membership.

Bare chests, tattoos, Budweiser beer, and a televised hockey game
seemed to be the fashion one recent Saturday evening at an extremely
noisy gathering of members of the South Bay Family in a small house in
a middle-class neighborhood near the Pacific Coast Highway in Hermosa
Beach. There were knives and a deer rifle in evidence, and some said
they had pistols.

Asked about the gang's philosophy, Bam Bam, the son of a professor
at the University of Southern California, shouted, "Right or wrong,
your bros are your bros!"

"Another thing that goes good here is peace," said Road Dog
loudly.

"Peace by force, man," shouted Porgy, who said his father was vice    30
president of a plastics company.

"No drug dealing!" shouted Tomcat, the son of a stockbroker.

"Quit lying to him, man," said Little Smith. "There's drugs everywhere."

On a more reflective note, away from the crowd in a small back
room, Porgy said: "There is no justification. We do what we do because
we want to. I don't blame my mother. She did the best she could."

### Reading the Text

1. Why do some teenagers become gang "wannabes," according to Mydans?
2. Which signs of gang involvement are typically adopted by suburban gang
   members?
3. How can suburban kids' "dallying" with gangs be seen as a "fashion statement"?

### Reading the Signs

1. Write a dialogue between the students interviewed in "Signs of the Street: A Conversation" (p. 597) and the suburban gang wannabes described in Mydans's essay. Share your dialogue with your classmates.
2. Compare the suburban gang involvement with that of inner-city gang members. What differences — and similarities — do you see in motivation and external signs of gang affiliation? To develop your argument, consult "Signs of the Street: A Conversation" (p. 597), Anne Campbell, "The Praised and the Damned" (p. 577), and Léon Bing, "Faro" (p. 572).
3. Compare the nicknames and symbols of group affiliation that the suburban gang member adopts with those adopted by hackers (see Winn Schwartau, "Hackers: The First Information Warriors," p. 618). What differences, if any, do you find in their frame of cultural reference and ideology?
4. In class, discuss your responses to the son of the bank vice president who claims, "If you want to be able to walk the mall, you have to know you've got your boys behind you." Have you ever known anyone like that? Why do you think he makes such a claim?
5. In your journal, describe the bonding rituals you share with close friends. How do they compare with the rituals adopted by the teens whom Mydans describes?

<br>

PETER DOSKOCH

## The Mind of the Militias

||||||||||||||||||||||||||||||||||||||||||||||||||||||||||||||||||||||||

*They're out there. Mysterious black helicopters watching your every move. Ghurka troops under U.N. command ready to cross the border and seize your weapons. A cadre of international financiers plotting to construct a New World Order. Or such is the belief of a small, but growing, number of Americans who have banded together to assert their rights to bear arms and to resist the federal government in every way. In this selection, Peter Doskoch (b. 1965) offers both an historical background of militias and an analysis of their fears and aims, concluding with some recommendations on what to do, and not to do, about them. A senior editor with* Psychology Today, *Doskoch specializes in psychology, biology, and neuroscience.*

Edward L. Brown, spokesman for New Hampshire's Constitutional Defense Militia, is patiently explaining to me how the United States government masterminded the Oklahoma City bombing, how the United

Nations is taking over America, how a small consortium of international power brokers orchestrated the breakup of the Soviet Union. And what's most striking is how normal he sounds.

Not his words: His constant reference to "they" and "them" are the calling cards of a conspiracy hound. So are his repeated mentions of "Marxist socialist puke" — meaning Bill and Hillary, journalists like myself, and the Jews who purportedly control the world's economy.

What's shockingly ordinary, rather, is his friendly, low-key demeanor. Much of the time Brown comes across like a grumpy but beloved uncle. When I confess that I just don't buy the conspiracy theories he's spewing, Brown doesn't rant — he gently growls, "Awwww, Peter," the way he might at a nephew's mischievous but harmless antics. And he dismisses any thought of militiamen as paranoid or dangerous. "We're kind of backwoods bubbas up here. We're a bunch of harmless old folks. We'll take you fishing, have you over for dinner, and put you up for the night. That's the kind of folks we are."

But the Norman Rockwell image forming in my brain shatters as Brown's homespun chitchat turns into advice on which foods I should be stockpiling in my basement just in case "these guys orchestrate this thing" and the world economy collapses.

In barely two years, thousands of "harmless old folks" like Brown  5
have transformed the word "militia" from a quaint anachronism into an armed threat. They've altered the political landscape as well, creating a chasm across which rational dialogue has ceased and liberals and conservatives now only point accusatory fingers. President Clinton has taken swipes at right-wing talk show hosts like Rush Limbaugh, claiming that their rhetoric incites militia violence. Conservatives, for their part, attribute the rise of militias to anti-government backlash.

But in talking with psychologists, psychiatrists, sociologists, local sheriffs, and militia members themselves, a far more complex picture emerges. Denouncing paramilitary groups as terrorists — or hailing them as patriots — ignores the often-subtle interplay of forces that have led to their rebirth some two centuries after Lexington and Concord. The psychological and cultural dynamics behind this resurrection can't be reduced to a catchy sound bite. But either we understand them — or we risk more Oklahoma City conflagrations.

### Apocalypse Now

There's a huge overlap between militias and Christian fundamentalists, contends Charles Strozier, Ph.D., of John Jay College's Center on Violence and Human Survival, and the end of the millennium "is the shadow on everyone's mind on the Christian right." That shadow, he says, is galvanizing militia members who truly think apocalypse is at hand.

A key concern is the timing of the period of tribulation. That's when, believers say, Christ will return to claim his people amid earthly destruction. Most ordinary fundamentalists are "pre-tribbers" — they think Jesus will come before Armageddon occurs. But fundamentalist militia members, Strozier says, tend to be mid- or post-tribbers: they believe Christ will return only *after* violent apocalypse.

"That's an arcane point of theology, but it has enormous psychological significance because they want to be there during tribulation. They want to be there when the rivers run red. They want to take their Uzis and fight it out with the Beast. God needs their help."

Hence the gun controls that militias so vigorously oppose are a threat    10
not just to their constitutional rights but to the Lord. The 1993 raid on the Branch Davidian compound in Waco, Texas, strikes a sinister chord with fundamentalist militias because it's tangible evidence that the Bureau of Alcohol, Tobacco, and Firearms is trying to prevent them "from rising up in revolution to keep the seed of Satan from destroying us," argues sociologist Brent L. Smith, Ph.D., chairman of the department of criminal justice at the University of Alabama in Birmingham and author of *Terrorism in America.*

Impending apocalypse might even tug at nonreligious militia members. For those motivated by idealism, violence "can take on a kind of transcendence," reports psychiatrist Robert Jay Lifton, M.D., director of John Jay's Center for Violence and Human Survival, in New York. "People involved in it can see themselves as moving into a heroic domain, a higher purpose." And millennium fever intensifies the urge toward transcendent violence.

### Paranoia

Political pundits interpreted last November's election as proof that voters want government off their backs. But militias believe the Feds are not only on their backs but up their pant legs, in their pockets, and — as some claim — ready to implant computer chips in their buttocks.

"The leaders of the group may be sincere in their complaints about federal intrusion into people's lives," says Theodore Feldmann, M.D., a consultant to the FBI and psychiatry professor at the University of Louisville. "But there's an excessive nature to their concern."

As a result, nearly any government law, any gathering of the rich and powerful, becomes damning proof of conspiracy. In the rhetoric of militia groups, gun control laws aren't a strategy to curb violence; they're part of a plan to enslave us. Secret societies like Yale's Skull and Bones aren't elitist fraternal groups but part of a plot to form a single world government, the New World Order. Reports of mysterious black helicopters over Montana, of foreign troops training in the

Rockies, buzz across the Internet unencumbered by such nuisances as confirmation.

Outside the realm of political rhetoric, this paranoia seems more sad than frightening. When California State University sociologist James William Gibson, Ph.D., author of *Warrior Dreams: Paramilitary Culture in Post-Vietnam America,* enrolled in combat pistol training as part of his research, he learned "how warriors should go to the bathroom." Urinals leave you vulnerable to rear attack, so the proper technique is to sit on the toilet with the pistol between your legs, ready to fire on any who invade your stall. 15

Despite their pervasive fears, most militia members are psychologically healthy, Feldmann believes. But many "are on the fringes of mental health." They're the ones he thinks most likely commit violence.


## Our Uzis, Our Selves

There's more to militias than weapons training and scampering around in the woods in camouflage get-up. They also give members a place to fit in. "For many members, the political belief that the group espouses may be less important than the sense of belonging and identification from being a part of it," reports Feldmann. Of course, people also get that sense of belonging from the Elks. But militia members may have a particular need to find social acceptance.

"Militias seem to attract people who have trouble fitting in anywhere else," Feldmann says. In that regard they resemble leftist terrorist groups of the 1970s, like the Symbionese Liberation Army. "Only a handful of people in that group had any real commitment to the group's cause. The rest were drawn by a sense of alienation and a need to find people they could identify with."

The militias's emphasis on guns further feeds that sense of self. "The act of violence can create a sense of vitality where that had been waning," notes Lifton. Wielding a powerful weapon instills a sense of purpose or invincibility, particularly for the economically or socially disenfranchised. That goes double for militia members who have achieved notoriety. Shortwave radio guru "Mark from Michigan" works as a janitor in a society that doesn't value manual labor. "His life as Militiaman Mark is far more meaningful than cleaning up a dorm," notes Gibson.


## The Post–Cold War Blues

The United States, notes Lifton, is going through a period of "post–Cold War confusion." The collapse of the Soviet Union has left us adrift. We may have won the Cold War, but we've lost a purpose. As a 20 result, Lifton says, "a sense of frustration and anger pervades the whole society."

It's no coincidence that this frustration is felt most deeply by the same socioeconomic group that has embraced militias: young to middle-aged white males in rural areas. "Worker bees in the movement tend to be much lower-educated than the general population," reports Alabama's Smith. And with jobs for unskilled workers drying up, they are unlikely to attain middle-class status — or have much of a stake in the status quo.

No wonder, then, that militias long for an earlier, more innocent America. But instead of waxing nostalgic about the 1950s, as did Reagan-era Republicans, militias look as far back as you can go: the Minutemen. Indeed, the very name of the Patriots — a broader movement that shares the militias's fears of a "suspended" constitution and a single world government — conjures images of Jefferson, Hamilton, and Washington. Some groups form self-sufficient communities that would resemble 18th-century villages were it not for modern amenities like computers. Danny Hashimoto, of the Boulder Patriots, even advocates the barter system, exchanging goods and services with others directly. (It also helps him avoid income taxes.)

## Weapon Obsession

However concerned they may be about defending the Bill of Rights, militias aren't running through the woods waving copies of the Constitution.

"They want access to weapons," says Greg Moffat, Sheriff of Idaho's Madison County, "and I'm not talking about small arms: tanks, missiles, high explosives." Some groups acquire special equipment like night-vision goggles; the Florida State Militia is allegedly capable of defending themselves against chemical and biological warfare.

Extreme as it sounds, experts say it's just an extension of America's love affair with guns. And it has less to do with our frontier past — after all, Canada was founded in a similar fashion — than with a cultural vacuum. "The American obsession with guns and violence is a partial substitute for a traditional cultural base," Lifton says. If you're living in a remote region of Montana, visiting the local museum — or even checking out what's on cable — simply isn't an option. So why not shoot beer cans off a rock with a .22?

And throw in Rambo fantasies as well. The U.S. withdrawal from Vietnam was a crushing blow to men who equated American military might with their own masculine identity, says Gibson. Blaming defeat on bureaucrats and politicians, they rejected the John Wayne model of soldiering in favor of a new American warrior: one who fights outside a corrupt political system. Thus was born the American paramilitary movement, laying the foundation for the militias who would adopt the anti-government rhetoric intact.

But while a fondness for firearms and warrior fantasies might be a prerequisite for militiahood, it's by no means sufficient. "I think a lot of people joined thinking, 'Let's grab rifles, go out in the trees, and play games,'" says Moffat. "Then they found out it's a bit more than that, that they'd have to support theories that they didn't want to support."

## The Enemy Within

One reason so many of those theories involve Orwellian visions of government, says America's premier cult expert, Margaret Thaler Singer, Ph.D., is that for militia members, many of whom operate in remote regions, the Federal government lacks a human face. Since it's far away — in Washington, D.C., or in a large city elsewhere in the state — they see little evidence in their daily lives of the good that government does — or of the people who do it.

As a result of this psychic distance, "militias have dehumanized and demonized the government," notes Frank M. Ochberg, M.D., a psychiatrist who's served on the National Task Force on Terrorism. The implications are truly frightening. Several militia leaders claim that civil war is imminent. And turning brother against brother is far easier psychologically when you believe that "these people no longer belong to the same nation," says Ochberg. "It's rationalized as attacking an enemy — an enemy within."

Adding to the geographical distance between militia and government   30
is a striking information gap. Militias tend to shun mainstream media, relying instead on their own newsletters, radio broadcasts, pamphlets, and the Internet for news of political and world affairs. So they rarely tap into information or perspectives that might moderate their views. And the Internet's cloak of anonymity further allows extreme views to fester uncensored.

## Racism

When the media reported ties between militias and white supremacists, militias in Michigan and elsewhere scurried to prove themselves equal-opportunity organizations. True, the movement is not entirely homogenous: Patriot radio personality Norm Resnick is a bespectacled Jew with a Ph.D. in psychology. (Resnick declined to talk with PT.) But in pointing frantically to one or two black or Jewish members, most militias succeed only in emphasizing how white and Christian the movement actually is.

Even so, only a minority of militia groups are explicitly racist. But their hatred is of a particularly virulent strain. Klan-watch researcher Tawanda Shaw says that 45 militias in 22 states have ties to white supremacists, including the neo-Nazi Aryan Nations. An even greater threat may be the Christian Identity movement, which believes that whites are God's chosen people and Jews are the children of Satan. Theology, more than politics, is central to these militias: many have resident pastors. But whereas religion may moderate the violent impulses of most Christians, the highly combustible mix of extreme religious, social, and political views makes Identity groups particularly dangerous.

## The Future

So what should we do about the militia movement? Gibson says that it's crucial "not to demonize the demonizers." By expressing strong disapproval toward militia members, but not ostracizing them, we may be able to pull back toward the mainstream those who have one foot in the warrior world and the other in the world of job and family. The horror of the Oklahoma bombing may also bring some back: "Dead babies and social security clerks is not an image of heroic violence."

And if millennium fever and social upheaval are indeed major forces, the militia movement may lose steam once the new century begins — provided the government does not overreact in the interim. Most experts agree that given the militias's fears, cracking down or infiltrating them is the *worst* thing to do.

"If Congress makes militias illegal, if they pass more gun control    35
laws, we could see these groups grow more in size and scope," warns Smith. "It's important that the government not overreact. We need to prosecute terrorist incidents, but we don't need to expand the ATF so that it becomes the Bureau of Alcohol, Tobacco, Firearms, and Fertilizer."

### *Reading the Text*

1. What limitation does Doskoch see in labeling militia members "terrorists"?
2. According to Doskoch, what connections have scholars seen between the militia movement and Christian fundamentalism?
3. What is the New World Order conspiracy theory, according to militia ideology?
4. What, according to Doskoch, is the typical socioeconomic profile of a militia member?
5. What role do guns play in militia culture, in Doskoch's description?

### *Reading the Signs*

1. Experts on militias suggest that "cracking down [on] or infiltrating them is the *worst* thing to do." In an essay, support, challenge, or modify this contention.
2. Compare and contrast the motives for membership in militias and in street gangs. What role does economic status play in both groups?
3. Research popular media coverage of militias, focusing perhaps on coverage of the Oklahoma City bombing in magazines such as *Newsweek.* Then write an analysis of the coverage. To what extent does the coverage condemn or glamorize the militia movement?
4. Read through a pro-gun magazine such as *Soldiers of Fortune* or *American Rifle,* studying both the articles and the advertising. Then write an essay in which you analyze the ideology implicit in the magazine. To what extent does the publication's ideology match that of the militia groups described by Doskoch?
5. In your journal, write a response to Charles Strozier's contention that militias are closely related to Christian fundamentalism.

## WINN SCHWARTAU
## *Hackers: The First Information Warriors*

ııııııııııııııııııııııııııııııııııııııııııııııı

*The FBI estimates that Pentagon computer files are hacked into over a hundred thousand times a year. If you have a bank account, your finances are vulnerable to anyone who cares to break into your computerized file and remove whatever he pleases. Were a virus to be injected into the American banking system, the economy could shut down. These are just a few of the threats posed by hackers, those much-mythologized computer outlaws who believe any file is an open file. In this excerpt from* Information Warfare *(1994), Winn Schwartau profiles the motives and attitudes of hackers, shedding light on this new breed of "information warrior." An expert on information security, Schwartau is also the author of* Terminal Compromise, *a novel about information warfare, and* Security Insider Report, *a monthly newsletter on security and personal privacy. He writes regularly for publications such as* ComputerWorld, Jane's Defense, InfoWorld, *and* PC Week.

*"Convicted Hacker and Computer Consultant. Available July 10, 1992."*
— LEN ROSE
AD OFFERING SERVICES AFTER HIS INCARCERATION.

The best example of how computer crime can be waged through social engineering was provided by an ex-hacker whom I will call Jesse James. One afternoon in Newport Beach, California, he put on a demonstration to show how easy it was to rob a bank.

Jesse took his audience to a trash bin behind Pacific Bell, the Southern California Baby Bell service provider. Dumpster diving proved to be an effective means of social engineering because within minutes, an internal telephone company employee list was dredged out of the garbage. On it, predictably, were hand-written notes with computer passwords.

In the neighborhood was a bank, which shall go nameless. After some more dumpster diving, financial and personal profiles of wealthy bank customers surfaced. That was all Jesse said he needed to commit the crime.

At a nearby phone booth, Jesse used a portable computer with an acoustic modem to dial into the telephone company's computer. Jesse knew a lot about the telephone company's computers, so he made a few changes. He gave the pay phone a new number, that of one of the wealthy clients about whom he now knew almost everything. He also turned off the victim's phone with that same number. Jesse then called the bank and identified himself as Mr. Rich, an alias.

"How can we help you, Mr. Rich?"    5

"I would like to transfer $100,000 to this bank account number."

"I will need certain information."

"Of course."

"What is your balance?"

"About ____," he supplied the number accurately.    10

"What is your address?"

Jesse gave the address.

"Are you at home, Mr. Rich?"

"Yes."

"We'll need to call you back for positive identification."    15

"I understand. Thank you for providing such good security."

In less than a minute the phone rang.

"Hello, Rich here."

The money was transferred, then transferred back to Mr. Rich's account again, to the surprise and embarrassment of the bank. The money was returned and the point was made.

Other than the governments of the world, hackers can arguably be    20
given the unenviable title of the first Information Warriors. Hackers seem to get blamed for just about everything these days. The phones go down — it's a hacker. There's a new computer virus — it's a hacker. Dan Quayle's credit report shows up on TV — it's a hacker.

According to most hackers, the media gets it all wrong. Lay people are still too grounded in snail-mail and big business; the Feds are still embroiled in paper-based bureaucracies. Even hackers themselves can't agree on the proper terminology to describe themselves.

Today, the nom-de-guerre "hacker" takes on a somewhat sinister connotation. Most people, when asked, say something like, "Isn't a hacker someone who breaks into computers?" Right or wrong, that's the image. Locked into the modern lexicon by popular usage, the term "hacker" may well be forever doomed to suffer such pejorative overtones. Hackers are often blamed for credit-card fraud and other more conventional crimes, in which the use of computers was merely incidental. As one would imagine, hackers are not happy about such misperceptions, blaming what they term "clueless Feds and the idiot police" for destroying the original ethos of hacking.

To begin with, the term hacker is derived from the word "hackney," which means drudgery; "hackneyed" means "worn out from overuse, trite." A writer who knocks out lackluster words for pay is a hack. An old, worn-out horse is a hack. A taxi driver is a hack who drives a hack. How about the golf hack who can't score below 100 even with two Mulligans a side and an occasional foot wedge?

Anyone can be a hack and the connotations aren't always negative. Most of us are hackers in one way or another. The car enthusiast who tinkers and tunes his car every weekend is a hack. He constantly wants to improve his knowledge and techniques, sharing them with others at car meets or races. He relentlessly pursues the perfect engine, or transmission, or whatever else makes a car tick. A hacker, regardless of area of interest, is curious by nature. Rop Gonggrijp, a well-known ex-hacker and editor of *Hacktic,* a Dutch computer hacker magazine, said it this way.

> Pretend you're walking down the street, the same street you have always walked down. One day, you see a big wooden or metal box with wires coming out of it sitting on the sidewalk where there had been none.
>
> Many people won't even notice. Others might say, "Oh, a box on the street." A few might wonder what it is and what it does and then move on. The hacker, the true hacker, will see the box, stop, examine it, wonder about it, and spend mental time trying to figure it out. Given the proper circumstances, he might come back later to look closely at the wiring or even be so bold as to open the box. Not maliciously, just out of curiosity.
>
> The hacker wants to know how things work.[1]

And that is exactly what pure hackers say. They only want to know     25
more about computers: the ins and the outs, the undocumented features, how can they push the system to its outer envelope and make it do things the original designers never envisioned. Hackers try to cram ten megabytes onto a 1.4 megabyte disk.

The original generation of computer hackers could be said to include John Von Neumann (the acknowledged father of the digital computer),

---

1. Daniel Boorstein, *The Discoverers* (New York: Random House, 1983), p. 500.

Alan Turing, and Grace Hopper, among other computable notables. These pioneers pushed the limits of computer science. However, most hackers evolved out of academia in the 1960s and 1970s, when terminals were connected to distant huge computers that filled rooms with vacuum tubes, core memories, and immense power supplies.

The undisputed catalyst for mass-market hacking was the introduction of the microprocessor by Intel, and the subsequent development of the personal desktop computer. Millions of PCs and Apples were bought by businesses, students, and former and future hackers during the incubation phases of the Global Network and Computers Everywhere. The nascent personal computer field was a petri dish full of ripe agar solution encouraging unbounded creativity, learning . . . and hacking. But then the money motive kicked in, which according to Rop meant the loss of true hacking creativity. Some hackers soon became budding millionaires, motivated only by the search for the Almighty Buck.

Over the years, new technology and the Global Network allowed a new breed of hackers to emerge. For the hacking phenomenon to increase logarithmically, one last piece of the equation was needed and was already well on its way to market: Infinite Connectivity. How do we get all of these computers to talk to each other? Novell took care of that with the proliferation of inexpensive Local Area Networks, or LANs, for PCs in the office. Modems allowed simple computer-to-computer conversations, as well as the creation of thousands of database and bulletin boards accessible by anyone with inexpensive equipment. Wide area networks (WANs) began to connect through the phone companies and the switch, entwining the globe in a spider's web of communications based upon systems with such uninviting names as X.25, ISDN, TCP/IP, OSI, T1, and 10 Base T. Such interconnectedness now gives anyone who wants it access to the Global Network via an incomprehensively complex matrix of digital highways. The hacker-purist, however, would likely prefer the word *free*way.

Hackers, long confined to their lone desktop PC and its limited communications capabilities, knew there was a world to explore out there — and explore they did. They traveled throughout Cyberspace and the growing Global Network, and found that the computers at the other end of the line were indeed fascinating targets of investigation. Every imaginable type of computer system was no more than a phone call away and there were thousands of others willing to help you on your way to conquering the next system. You could talk to a VAX over at the hospital, a 3090 over at the IRS, or the Tandems running the credit card division over at American Express. That euphoria, that sense of power, had been given to anyone with a couple of hundred dollars.

Billsf, a thirty-six-year-old post-Woodstock American expatriate and 30 self-described phone phreak who now calls Amsterdam home, speaks for many from the first generation of hackers. He says the thrill is in getting into the system and doing what "they" say can't be done. For him voyeurism is not part of the equation. Of breaking into a computer he says, "The first time it's a hack. The second time it's a crime." In his mind that legitimizes and proves the innocence of the hunt. He continues to defend hackers who enter computers without permission. "If there is unused computing power out there, it should be free. If I have the smarts to get it, I should be able to use it." He uses the same argument to justify phone phreaking, where the aim is to figure out how the phone systems work and then make calls for free. "If there's an open phone line, I should be able to use it for free. Otherwise it's going to waste."

Victims and potential victims of computer hackers are not so generous. The most common accusation is that hackers are nothing more than glorified criminals. The debate often goes like this:

> "It's like my house. If I don't invite you in, don't come in or it's called breaking and entering and I'll call the police."
>
> "It's not the same thing. What if I went into your house, ate an apple, and watched some TV. Then I make two phone calls and went to the bathroom. Before I left, I put $2.14 on the counter to cover the cost of the apple and the phone calls and water. I was just looking around. That should not be illegal."
>
> "Yes it should! And is. The same laws should apply for you coming into my computers uninvited."
>
> "What if my presence kept your house from being robbed? Would that make a difference?"
>
> "You still invaded my privacy. I would feel violated. My house belongs to me and so does my computer. Please stay out."
>
> "My entering or not entering your computers is a matter of ethics — not the law. It is up to my sense of responsibility to keep a clean house when I'm in your computer."

Breaking into a computer system, cracking its password scheme, or learning how to beat down the front door, is often referred to as "cracking" in distinction to "hacking." This is far from a universal definition, as there are many dissident hacker factions, but I'm going to use it anyway. Hackers, like any other group, come in many flavors but despite their claims to the contrary, they can be accurately described by category. Let's examine a few of them.

## Amateur Hacking

I know that term will offend some, but amateur hacking is a part-time effort and does not provide income. The term amateur hacker, or perhaps semi-professional hacker, is not a derogatory one nor does it belittle their skills. It merely distinguishes them from professional hackers who utilize the same techniques and tools to make a living, either legally or illegally.

Consider the following profile of a typical hacker as offered by some of their own. Hackers are

- mostly males between twelve and twenty-eight
- smart but did lousy in school
- misfits and misunderstood
- from dysfunctional families
- and of course, they can't get a date

I know a lot of hackers, and in many cases, they tend to work and 35 play on the edges of society. Some hackers — apparently too many — "consume their own body weight in controlled pharmaceutical substances," according to one underground member who himself imbibes in same.

According to Dr. Mich Kabay, Director of Education for the National Computer Security Association, some hackers could be suffering from a clinical narcissist personality disorder. He suggests that the classic hacker personality is anathematic to society, characterized by such traits as:

- a grandiose sense of self-importance
- preoccupation with fantasies of unlimited success
- need for constant attention and admiration
- strong negative responses to threats to self-esteem
- feelings of entitlement
- interpersonal exploitiveness
- alternating feelings of overidealization and devaluation
- a lack of empathy

No, not all hackers are nuts nor do they universally suffer from clinical personality disorders. They are a varied group but they do tend to think and live "on the edge." According to Dr. Percy Black, Professor of Psychology at Pace University in New York, "they're just kids," no matter what their age. He explains that malicious hacking may come from "inadequate endogenous stimulation." Simply put, either their home life, diet, or social life is such that their brains don't secrete enough "get-excited-feel-good" chemicals to create an internal feeling of satisfaction in any other way.

Some say that Ian Murphy, a 36-year-old former hacker with the nom-de-hack Captain Zap, is the perfect example of such a chemo-social imbalance. His claims to fame include federal prosecution for, among other things, electronically "stealing" computers and breaking into White House computers. His stories stretch the imagination. Murphy was featured in a 1992 *People* magazine profile and is, to say the very least, a loud, personable character. He has graced the cover of *Information Week,* a popular trade magazine, and claims to make over $500,000 a year as a hacker-advisor to corporate America.

As one probes the history and behavior of hackers, we see that a gang mentality quickly evolved. A subculture of people with common interests gathered in their favorite electronic watering hole to "hang out." BBSs and the Global Network provided the tools to allow anyone to organize a database, add a modem, and start a digital party. The term "virtual community" has come into vogue, referring to a common electronic location in Cyberspace where kindred spirits can meet. As Cyberspace developed, cliques evolved and cybernetic hierarchies formed. The teenage 414 Gang earned their rep — and national attention — for their penetrations of the Sloan-Kettering Cancer Center and Los Alamos military computers in 1982.

Competition among teenagers being what it is, whether on skateboards or with the opposite sex, it is only enhanced in Cyberspace. One hacker group might feel challenged by another's claim, so they would then have to go out and better it. Membership in a particular group quickly becomes a status symbol, one that has to be earned. Ostracism from a group is considered a major embarrassment in the Global Network. So competing hacking groups popped up all over the country, and indeed the world. Sherwood Forest, Anarchy Inc., Bad Ass MF, Chaos Computer Club, Damage Inc., Circle of Death, The Punk Mafia, Lords of Chaos, Phreaks Against Geeks, Phreaks against Phreaks Against Geeks, Elite Hackers Guild, and Feds R Us were but a few of the estimated thirty thousand private BBSs operating in 1990.[2]

As competition in Cyberspace grew, the country's networks and computers became the playground for all genres of hackers and cybernauts. Occasionally the competition got out of hand, as it did in the case of the Legion of Doom versus the Masters of Destruction. From 1989 through the end of 1991, a so-called Hacker War was waged on the battle field of corporate America's information infrastructure.

On July 8, 1992, five New York hackers who belonged to the MoD, an organized hacking group, were indicted in Federal Court on eleven separate serious charges. (Depending upon whom you listen to, MoD stands for Masters of Destruction, Deceit, or Deception.) What adds intrigue to this story is the claim that other hackers were responsible for turning the MoD in to the authorities. The Federal indictment said that the five defendants, who pleaded not guilty at their July 16, 1992, arraignment, conspired to commit a range of computer crimes, including

- Eavesdropping on phone conversations from public switch networks
- Eavesdropping on data transmissions
- Intercepting data transmissions
- Owning computer cracking hardware and software equipment

2. Bruce Sterling, *The Hacker Crackdown* (New York: Bantam, 1992), p. 7.

- Reprogramming phone company computer switches
- Stealing passwords
- Selling passwords
- Stealing credit profiles
- Selling credit profiles
- Destroying computer systems
- Causing losses of $370,000[3]

One of the defendants was quoted as saying the group could "destroy people's lives or make them look like saints." All told there were eleven counts with up to fifty-five years in prison and $2.75 million in fines if the defendants were found guilty. All five have since pled guilty or lost their court cases. Their jail sentences are intended to be an example to other would-be hackers.

The Defendants named were

- Phiber Optik (aka Mark Abene)
- Outlaw (aka Julio Fernandez)
- Corrupt (aka John Lee)
- Acid Phreak (aka Elias Ladopoulos) and
- Scorpion (aka Paul Stira)

Aged eighteen to twenty-two, they all come from lower to lower-middle class neighborhoods in Brooklyn, the Bronx, and Queens in New York City.                                                                               45

"That's absurd," a defensive Mark Abene (aka Phiber Optik) told me. "There is no group in New York and there is no computer underground. I have never been a member of any organized group." Phiber vehemently denied his involvement. However, Abene, after pleading guilty to reduced charges, was sentenced on November 3, 1993, to a year and a day for his escapades. Emmanual Goldstein, editor of *2600,* called it a "dark day for hackers."

Chris Goggans (aka Eric Bloodaxe) and Scott Chasin (aka Doc Holiday) disagree. They are ex-members of a rival hacker group, the Legion of Doom. Although other members of the LoD have periodically vacationed at government expense, neither of these two have ever been prosecuted. In mid-1991, they disavowed their hacking days and started a security consulting company, Comsec Data, which survived less than a year. Business was bad. Corporate America could not bring itself to hire ex-hackers to work on their security problems, and the security community loudly ostracized them. The founders were young and inexperienced in business, and the press was generally negative.

---

3. Sterling, p. 8.

But during the demise of their company, the Comsec Data boys were busy. Very busy. They were collecting evidence against their underground adversaries, the Masters of Destruction and especially Phiber Optik. Evidence, they claim, that they turned in to the authorities.

According to Chris Goggans, twenty-three, his first contact with Phiber was back in early 1989, when he heard that Phiber Optik was claiming to be a member of the Legion of Doom. After recommendations from another member of LoD, Phiber was able to prove his technical knowledge and worth and was permitted into the group. Soon thereafter, Phiber and Goggans agreed to share some information: Goggans knew how to access the Nynex switches, bypassing all security and authentication. Phiber knew the syntax and knew his way around the host mainframe computers themselves. A deal was struck to trade information.

Goggans said Phiber never lived up to his end of the bargain — a big    50
no-no in underground Cyberspace. "He told us to go to hell." As a result, the LoD threw Phiber Optik out in mid-1989. Phiber denies much of this account, saying he wasn't a member of LoD, just an occasional acquaintance. But according to Goggans, Phiber Optik began an electronic smear campaign against him, Chasin, and others connected with the LoD as a result of the public embarrassment. The sophomoric pranksterism included such antics as placing menacing messages and commentary on BBSs.

Enter Corrupt.

A new BBS called the 5th Amendment, or 5A, was created by Micron (an anonymous hacker) and Chasin in December 1989, with access limited to the "cream of the crop of hackers." Phiber was not invited. In February 1990, Corrupt was admitted to 5A because of his knowledge of holes in VMS systems and security. In April 1990, a number of 5A and ex-LoD hackers were illegally using a telephone voice conference bridge owned by a local Texas oil company. Anyone with the right phone number can dial in and participate in a conferenced conversation — a very common way to rip off big companies.

Alfredo de la Fe, eighteen, who was convicted on June 19, 1992, for trafficking in stolen PBX codes, agrees with other hackers who were in on that conversation that someone broke into the conference and said, "Yo! This is Dope Fiend. MoD," with a thick ethnic accent. Apparently someone responded with, "Hang up, you stupid nigger." The caller was Corrupt, who happens to be black, and who took great offense. He had been "dissed" in public and revenge was necessary. However, it may be that Corrupt misunderstood, because another member of the group, who actually is white, had been dubbed SuperNigger.

The wording distinction is important, because Phiber Optik insists that his future problems with Goggans, Chasin, and their Texas Legion of Doom friends were racially motivated. "They're just a bunch of racist rednecks," Phiber told me in a four-hour telephone interview that his lawyer advised against.

Goggans bristles at the suggestion. "We never even knew that Corrupt was black." Other hackers present on the call maintain that the racial epithet was only a "friendly" insult. Nothing racial, just kidding, if you will. Others say that the New York–based Masters of Destruction took the comment as fighting words.

Corrupt apparently sought revenge.

Shortly after the conference call, the LoD, their cohorts, and their neighbors began receiving harassing calls. Goggans says, "They [the MoD] were pulling our phone records, finding our friends, and then their friends." LoD's underground reputation grew, apparently in part because the growing MoD population (fourteen on August 1, 1990, according to the written History of the MoD) were attacking computers and leaving messages that laid blame on the Legion of Doom. Phiber swears that the name MoD was an insult aimed at the LoD, intended to make fun of them. "Goggans is a strangely deluded kid from Texas. Besides, he's an asshole."

The animosity, Phiber says, came from the LoD's racial slurs against MoD members, only one of whom does not belong to a minority. Plus, "they weren't very good and bragged and took credit for anything and everything. Just rednecks who should keep out of our way." Goggans says the attacks increased in early 1991 because of the escalating tensions between the two groups. Insults were hurled at each other over BBSs, E-mail, and voice-mail circuits.

Goggans further charges that the MoD changed his long distance carrier from Sprint to AT&T, to make access to his billing records easier. Goggans says MoD bragged about the hack and claimed, "We rule MicroLink!" (MicroLink is a subnet of Southwestern Bell's network.) The 1992 Federal indictment specifically charges MoD with tampering with Houston-based phone switches, and Southwestern Bell alleges $370,000 in damages. The indictment says the MoD "altered calling features, installed back door programs, and made other modifications." (This should sound familiar: malicious software being put into a switch.)

Credit reports were the next weapon allegedly used by the MoD against the Texans. Chasin, his mother, her friends, and neighbors were all victimized by MoD's access to credit databases. TRW admits that its computers were penetrated and that credit reports were improperly taken. The Federal indictment includes details surrounding 176 separate credit reports that the MoD had in their possession, not to mention database access codes. Goggans says that during this phase of the conflict, "they would call us and admit what they had done. . . . It had gotten totally out of hand. The MoD were hurting innocent people and we had to do something about it. No one else could have."

According to Chasin, "They are electronic terrorists."

Corrupt's own words seem to explain the hacker paranoia that inflamed this incident. "It's not just winning the game that counts, but making sure that everyone else loses," he wrote into the MoDNet computers.

De la Fe, an acquaintance of Corrupt, claims, "MoD was listening to the Feds and their computers. They were planning to wreck government computers." Morton Rosenberg, eighteen, was sentenced to eight months in prison for purchasing passwords to TRW computers from MoD's Corrupt and Outlaw and using them to illegally access credit reports. He says that the MoD was highly organized in its efforts. "The MoD had printed up price lists for passwords." Conflict, another hacker, adds, "Knowledgewise they were incredible — but with a bad attitude. They harassed hackers everywhere." Chasin says, "They were into 'outing' hackers."

Phiber says about Goggans, "He's a pain in the ass. This is none of his damn business. He should stay out of other people's lives."

As a result of the harassment they felt they were receiving from the MoD, Goggans and Chasin documented the MoD's electronic activities — in effect, snooping on the snoopers in Cyberspace. They turned this information over to security officers at the regional Bell Operating Companies (RBOCs), and the Secret Service and FBI were brought in to investigate. Tymnet (a notoriously weak communications network, according to hackers) was also notified by Goggans, as were a number of other companies who were allegedly the victims of Phiber and crew. 65

"We gave the Feds everything," Goggans claims. "We had all of the files, the dates, the times, the logs. We could have responded electronically but we decided to play by the rules. We called the authorities." The FBI will only admit they began their case in May 1991, the same time that Southwestern Bell and Goggans called them.

Goggans claims that in order to find out more about the MoD, he penetrated the weak security of a supposedly impenetrable MoD computer. He gave the FBI, Tymnet, and the Computer Emergency Response Team (CERT) MoD's lists of Tymnet passwords and IDs for Goddard Space Center, Trans Union Credit, CBI-Equifax (another major credit database), MIT, and a host of other targets.

According to the Federal indictment handed down in New York, many of the passwords found in the possession of the defendants were collected by "sniffing the switch" or monitoring data communications circuits on Tymnet. Since the defendants allegedly had access to the Tymnet computers, they were able to eavesdrop on the Tymnet network and record packets of information, including the passwords and access codes of thousands of users.

After cooperating with federal investigators, Goggans was on the receiving end of what he considers bodily threats. On Sept. 7, 1991,

Phiber sent E-mail to Goggans saying, "You need to get the shit beat out of you. Count on it," and "Never know when someone will plant a bat in your skull." Other threats allegedly included a promise to give Goggans a trip home from a computer conference in a body bag. Phiber admits making the threats, but says in his defense, "he sent me an ad for an LoD T-shirt and I went totally crazy. It was just a joke." Some joke.

The so-called LoD-MoD hacker war was over. Rosenberg was put      70
away even though he once claimed, "I stay out of jail because I do too much LSD. They're afraid to lock me up." Phiber Optik claimed innocence even though his codefendant Corrupt pled guilty to many of the eleven indictments. I received a copy of Corrupt's handwritten confession, which further showed how much control hackers have had over the phone networks and computers. He admits:

> I agreed to possess in excess of fifteen passwords, which permitted me to gain access to various computer systems, including all systems mentioned in the indictment and others. I did not have authorization to access these systems. I knew at the time that what I did was wrong.
>
> I intentionally gained access to what I acknowledge are Federal-interest computers and I acknowledge that work had to be done, to improve the security of these systems, which was necessitated by my unauthorized access.
>
> I was able to monitor data exchange between computer systems and by doing so intentionally obtained more passwords, identifications, and other data transmitted over Tymnet and other networks.
>
> I was part of a group called MoD.
>
> The members of the group exchanged information, including passwords, so that we could gain access to computer systems which we were not authorized to access.
>
> I got passwords by monitoring Tymnet, calling phone company employees and pretending to be a computer technician, and using computer programs to steal passwords.
>
> I participated in installing programs in computer systems that would give the highest level of access to members of MoD who possessed the secret password.
>
> I participated in altering telephone computer systems to obtain free calling services, such as conference calling and free billing, among others.
>
> Finally, I obtained credit reports, telephone numbers, and addresses, as well as other information about individual people, by gaining access to information and credit reporting services. I acknowledge that on November 5, 1991, I obtained passwords by monitoring Tymnet.[4]

---

4. *Wall Street Journal,* December 23, 1992, p. B6.

One of the saddest comments to come from this entire affair was made by MoD member Outlaw, who said, "It was only a game. Not a war."

## Inner-City Hacking

Inner cities are truly a study in disaster. This disaster, though, is no longer the exclusive province of any particular racial or ethnic group. Our inner cities have become melting pots, where the populace — regardless of race, color, or creed — behaves as if all hope is gone. When a ten-year-old boy carries a gun to defend his drug-dealing turf and sees little chance of survival past his teens, he has lost the ability to function in society. He sees himself as the victim of a government and a culture that have abandoned him. Why should he care about anything?

Now imagine the same angry inner-city kid, armed with a computer instead of a gun. The inner-city hacker, unlike his middle-class brethren, is angry over his social condition, intensely dislikes "the system," and has generally been powerless over his station in life — until now. For the first time he has the power and ability to affect people and events by remote control. The power of Cyberspace is in his hands.

The inner-city hacker has the same knowledge and power as his technoprecedents, regardless of the poor state of education in his neighborhood. He has little or no social conscience and the specter of jail is hardly a deterrent. It might even be an improvement over his current situation. I have had conversations with these hackers and their sense of arrogance, disdain, and alienation echoes that of the social dissidents of the 1960s. However, many radicals in the sixties were middle-class kids rebelling against the comfortable lifestyle of their parents. If things got tough, they could always go back to their well-manicured ranch-style house. Inner-city hackers have nowhere else to go. So, Cyberspace is an ideal destination. It gives them a new place to live and a turf of their own. It is the only place where they have power and can make the rules.

### Reading the Text

1. What does Schwartau mean by "dumpster diving," and why is that a favorite activity of hackers?
2. What, according to Schwartau, is the psychological profile of a typical hacker?
3. What, in Schwartau's account, are the usual justifications hackers give for engaging in computer crime?
4. In Schwartau's view, what does hacking offer to disaffected inner-city youth?

5. Why does MoD member Outlaw say that his hacking "was only a game. Not a war"?

### Reading the Signs

1. In your journal, brainstorm the image you have of hackers. Then compare your description with the typical profile of a hacker that Schwartau describes. How do you account for any similarities and differences?
2. Watch a cyberfilm such as *Hackers* and then write a semiotic analysis of the image of "information warriors" as depicted in the film. To what extent does the film image of hackers match the profile of them described by Schwartau?
3. Compare and contrast hacking groups with gangs, being sure to address both the reasons for membership in the group and group rituals. To develop your ideas, consult Léon Bing's "Faro" (p. 572), Anne Campbell's "The Praised and the Damned" (p. 577), and Seth Mydans's "Not Just the Inner City: Well-to-Do Join Gangs" (p. 607).
4. More often than not, hackers are male. In class, discuss the possible reasons for this gender pattern. To develop your ideas, read or reread Laura Miller's "Women and Children First: Gender and the Settling of the Electronic Frontier" (p. 740).
5. Write an essay arguing for or against laws that would restrict access to the Internet as a means to prevent hacking into sensitive files.

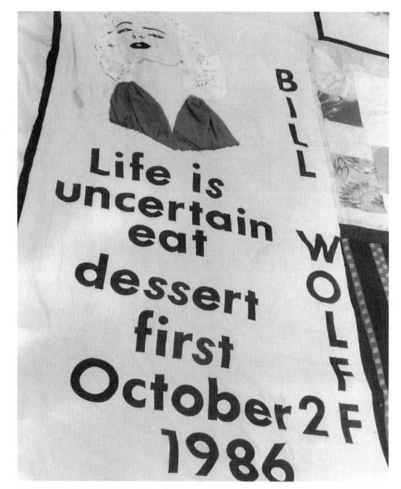

Photograph copyright © Shia/Impact Visuals.

# CHAPTER NINE

# JOURNALS OF THE PLAGUE YEARS

## *The Social Mythology of AIDS*

The topic of this chapter might puzzle you. AIDS, after all, is a disease; what could it possibly have to do with culture? Shouldn't we leave this one to the physicians and public health workers and stick to more obvious cultural issues like race and gender? We could, but then we'd be ignoring one of the most significant cultural issues in our lives today. If AIDS doesn't look like an issue to you, think about the concrete ways it has shaped your own life and behavior. Does sex now look like a game of Russian roulette to you? Do you resent having to take precautions that previous generations never had to consider? Are you nostalgic for the era before AIDS?

Thinking about AIDS for a moment reveals how it is much more than a disease and how it has become a major, if bleak, force in our culture. Though people do continue to ignore the danger (especially teenagers, who now constitute the fastest-growing population of new AIDS cases), an undeniable shadow has been cast across the land. With AZT apparently going the way of all of the other early "breakthrough" treatments, the search for a cure seems bogged down as the number of cases rises. In the United States alone, over 300,000 deaths, and over half a million cases, have been reported by 1996.

And yet, amidst such apocalyptic numbers, AIDS goes in and out of the news, appearing mostly when a new celebrity case is revealed or someone prominent dies. AIDS deaths continue to go unreported or are disguised in obituary notices. Moreover, whole nations continue to be in

**633**

||||||||||||||||||||||||||||||||||||||||||||||||||||||||||||||||||||||||||||||||||||||||||||||||||||||||||||||||||||||||||||||||||||||||||||||||

### Exploring the Signs of AIDS

What difference has the AIDS epidemic made to you? In your journal, explore the personal consequences of this disease. Have you made adjustments in personal habits or sexual behavior? Did controversies related to AIDS, such as the distribution of condoms, arise in your high school? How did you feel about such controversies? What do you think your response would be if a close friend or relative contracted the disease? If you don't feel you've been at all affected by the AIDS epidemic, why do you think that's the case?

---

denial about the extent of their exposure to the syndrome. AIDS is simply not a subject with which most people are comfortable, and the source of this discomfort lies less in the scientific realities of this natural-born killer than in its image.

## Interpreting the Social Mythology of AIDS

The image of AIDS was forged in the very first reports that appeared on the mysterious new illness. Here the media played a crucial, and perhaps even culpable, role, as the initial images of AIDS came to dominate its reception and understanding. We can recall our own introduction to AIDS as a lesson not only in recent medical history but also in the sexual behavior of the gay community. It was during a broadcast of *National Public Radio*'s "All Things Considered" one evening in 1981 that we first learned of the as-yet-unnamed epidemic. The report seemed routine enough at first. A mysterious new disease, apparently afflicting only young homosexual men, had suddenly appeared. But the story was not limited to medical reportage. Much of the story detailed the sexual practices of gay men in San Francisco and New York, and it elaborated on the speculated link between the disease and the use of "poppers," stimulants used for gay sex. And it was this focus on, even obsession with, a certain life-style that set AIDS apart from other illnesses from the very beginning.

When a mysterious, fatal illness broke out amidst a convention of American Legionnaires in 1976, for example, the media said nothing about its victims' social habits. But in NPR's report on AIDS, as in most other media reports, a presumably heterosexual audience was not simply informed about a medical phenomenon but rather was regaled with the details of the sexual habits of the first people with AIDS — even though it was not at all clear at the time that AIDS was a sexually transmitted disease. An indelible link between the disease and the sexual habits of its victims was established.

Ever since these first reports, AIDS has borne the dual stigmata of difference and disease. Had AIDS been presented only as an illness, albeit a fatally infectious one, do you think that it would have incurred the burden of shame that it now carries? After all, cancer and heart disease, which also lack reassuring preventive vaccinations and reliable cures, claim many more lives than AIDS has claimed. But it is AIDS that has been cast as a disease of the irredeemably different. Like Hester Prynne's scarlet letter "A," AIDS is the sign of the outcast.

Even the slight shift that has occurred in the general public's attitude toward AIDS in recent years reflects this sense of difference and otherness. The HBO dramatization of the late Randy Shilts's history of the epidemic, *And the Band Played On,* for example, significantly altered the tone and point of view of the book. As a gay journalist, Shilts wrote his book from inside the gay community. A good portion of the text is devoted to the story of gay men in New York and San Francisco, exploring the ordinary details of their lives as well as the impact of the epidemic upon them. Shilts also explored the lives and attitudes of the many heterosexuals involved in the early years of the epidemic — particularly the medical personnel at the Centers for Disease Control — but the focus of his text was with its homosexual cast of characters.

The movie changed that focus. Giving Dr. Don Francis, a heterosexual CDC researcher, the starring role, and enlarging the role of Dr. Selma Dritz, a San Francisco public health official, the film shifted the point of view of the book. Many of the major real-life homosexual characters were deleted (for example, all of the gay activists from New York), leaving one man, Bill Kraus, pretty much alone among the featured gay figures. While Kraus was treated as a sympathetic figure, he nonetheless appeared exotic next to all those heroic heterosexual medical figures. This shift, not so incidentally, contrasts markedly from the point of view adopted in a less well-known AIDS film, *Long Time Companion.* In this earlier film, all but one of the lead characters is gay, and the film's focus is squarely on the community that most suffered from the disease in the early years, not on the medical personnel who fought it.

HBO's film also subtly coded Kraus's role in a manner that departed both from the book and reality. The real Bill Kraus was an athletic American from the midwest, but the film chose an English actor (Ian Mackellan) to play the part. This choice made Kraus appear to be much older than he actually was and gave him an accent with just the faintest suggestion of a lisp — in short, the kind of accent Hollywood traditionally assigns to its homosexual characters. The effect is subtle but telling. Though the film avoided demonizing homosexuals (and was actually less critical of the gay community than Shilts was), by hinting at old

---

### Discussing the Signs of AIDS

Watch the film *Philadelphia* and then, in class, interpret it semioti-cally. How are people with AIDS portrayed? What images are used for gay and straight characters and for the protagonists and antagonists? This film was both praised for portraying people with AIDS positively and condemned for perpetuating stereotypes. Which position does your class find more accurate, and why?

---

stereotypes and by celebrating the straight, not gay, characters, the film *And the Band Played On* maintained a barrier between its subject matter and its presumably heterosexual audience. Once again, the image of AIDS as a disease of the exotic "other" was reinforced.

## Race, Class, and AIDS

In short, one can find even in the cultural products that reflect a sympathy toward people with AIDS a continued acceptance of its funda-mental image as a disease of the "other." And so it has been with those socially marginalized not only by their sexuality but also by their race and class as well. For as with so much else in American culture, class and race have played an important role in the social construction of AIDS. For the most part, the AIDS story as told in America thus far underplays both the heterosexual pandemic in Africa and Asia and the spread of the disease among minority intravenous drug users in America. There are a few nonpolitical reasons for this apparent neglect, of course. American IV drug users began to become infected with AIDS later than did gay men, so one would expect less written about them at this date. But still, there are political and cultural explanations for the kind of writing that has dominated the scene so far. The first people with the disease in America, though often condemned for their sexual orientation, nonetheless tended to hail from the middle- and upper-middle classes. They were often white professionals, and many were artists and writers who were already in the public eye or who could pen their own account of the disease. Heterosexual victims from racially marginalized groups, as well as IV-infected patients, have not had this kind of access. So the story of AIDS does not simply reflect cultural attitudes toward sexuality: Class and race enter the equation, too.

Consider the case of the Haitians. Early in the epidemic, the Cen-ters for Disease Control published a list of those most at risk for con-tracting the disease. This list included gay men, IV drug users, and — in a peculiar inclusion of an entire nationality — Haitians. The fact that Haitians are black added a racial slant to the social codification of AIDS, one that was based on a misunderstanding of the nature of the epidemic as it spread through Haiti. For what the CDC didn't know was that different social mores prevented the compiling of accurate demographic statistics. Many of the Haitian patients were bisexual men exposed to HIV through homosexual contacts, but given a different cultural understanding of sexual identity, few considered themselves to be "homosexual," and so did not identify themselves as such in the surveys. As a result, Haiti initially was considered a heterosexual anomaly in the New World picture of AIDS, and the entire nation was cast as a special case, a risk group all its own.

Even as the medical realities of the disease become more and more apparent, the mythology remains stubbornly intact. AIDS today bears much the same social stigma it bore from the beginning. It is still perceived as a disease of the "other," as a National Research Council report released in 1993 demonstrates. The epidemic will eventually "disappear," the *Los Angeles Times* cited in the report's conclusions, "because those who continue to be affected by it are socially invisible, beyond the sight and attention of the majority population" — that is, those whose race and class differ from that of the majority population.

## Speaking of AIDS

Even the way we speak about AIDS has played a large part in shaping its social image. One of the first metaphors used for AIDS — by historians, physicians, the gay community, and the public alike — was that of the Plague, the Black Death that devastated Europe in the fourteenth century. This is understandable, for humans understand new experiences in terms of the experiences they have already had. With terrible infectious diseases such as smallpox, tuberculosis, diphtheria, and polio under control in the modern era, the appearance of a hitherto unknown infectious killer was almost instantly associated with the greatest medical catastrophe of European history. For like that disastrous visitation of the Middle Ages, the modern "plague" too seemed to sweep from out of nowhere. And also like that earlier cataclysm, the ferocity of the disease seemed to suggest something more than mere medical mayhem let loose in the world. To some, it had all the appearance of a divine punishment.

That is what made the inaugural metaphor so powerful and political. The illness was soon dubbed the "gay plague," and this association with the medieval disease turned AIDS into a sign of divine wrath against those who were America's first victims. Indeed, the religious right cast AIDS as an instrument of retribution against sexual wickedness. Had AIDS first appeared among middle-American heterosexuals, do you think that its social construction would have been the same? The fact that an outbreak of sexually transmitted herpes among American heterosexuals in the 1970s attracted immediate medical attention but no metaphors of divine retribution can help you see just how influential those first metaphors of the AIDS epidemic have been.

Some gay Americans, for their part, constructed their own linguistic codes around AIDS as well, a code that Randy Shilts called AIDSpeak. This language sprang up to make sure that no one's feelings were hurt in speaking of this most politically sensitive of diseases. "Under the rules of AIDSpeak," Shilts wrote, "AIDS victims could not be called victims. Instead, they were to be called People With AIDS, or PWAs, as if contracting this uniquely brutal disease was not a victimizing experience. 'Promiscuous' became 'sexually active,' because gay politicians declared 'promiscuous' to be 'judgmental,' a major cuss word in AIDSpeak. The most-used circumlocution in AIDSpeak was 'bodily fluids,' an expression that avoided troublesome words like 'semen.'"

Shilts's observations point out that what we call something may not be merely a matter of harmless semantics. For the generalized term "bodily fluids" caused real panic in the mid-1980s. Saliva, after all, is a bodily fluid. "Can you get AIDS from kissing?" people asked. Or sweat? Or sneezing?

Even the acronym "AIDS" reflects the political dimensions of the syndrome. Originally called GRID (or Gay-Related Immune Deficiency), the illness was initially identified with sexual preference, pure and simple. Soon, it was renamed both to avoid the explicit finger-pointing indicated by the telltale "G" and to reflect the medical realization that AIDS is an equal-opportunity killer. But even the apparently neutral "AIDS" bears a hidden judgment. Consider the moral connotation of that scarlet letter "A." While it signifies "acquired" to distinguish this sort of immune deficiency disorder from the congenital kind, the letter is not so innocent as it appears. It also suggests that you have to do something to get AIDS, you have to act to "acquire" it, and in so doing incur a burden of moral responsibility in a climate in which the "passive" victims of the disease are more likely to receive the sympathy of their unstricken neighbors. It is instructive to note that when in 1992 the creator of the cartoon strip "Rex Morgan, MD" chose to run a series involving AIDS, he cast a young female physician as the patient, a surgeon whose exposure to HIV resulted from her professional duties in an urban trauma center. Try to imagine a popular cartoon featuring a gay man with the disease.

To appreciate the moral and political overtones of the acronym, the way it differentiates people with AIDS from the victims of such mortal ailments as cancer and heart disease, consider how you would react if the disease were called "Montagnier's syndrome," after the French researcher whose laboratory first isolated the HIV virus. This, after all, is how leprosy lost its age-old stigma, by being renamed Hansen's disease after the nineteenth-century biologist who discovered its causative bacterium. Or

|||||||||||||||||||||||||||||||||||||||||||||||||||||||||||||||||||||||||||||||||||||||||||||||||||||||||||||||||||||||||||||||||||||||||||||||||||||||

**R e a d i n g   A I D S   o n   t h e   N e t**

The Internet is widely used as a source of information about AIDS and current research on the disease. Use a search engine such as Yahoo or Altavista to identify AIDS–related Web sites, or try ACT UP (at several sites, including http://www. actupny.org/), the NAMES Project (http://www.aidsquilt. org/), the Centers for Disease Control AIDS Clearinghouse (http://www.cdcnac.org/), or the Gay Men's Health Center's "I Can't Cope With My Fear of AIDS" (http://noah. cuny.edu/aids/gmhc/brochure8.html). Study both the information and the way it is presented. What language is used today to describe the AIDS epidemic and its transmission? How do the images affect your understanding of the disease? Do you find any differences between "official" sources, such as the Centers for Disease Control, and activist organizations, such as ACT UP?

what if AIDS were called "Rock Hudson's disease" or "Magic Johnson's disease," after its most famous patients, just as Lou Gehrig lent his name to the rare ailment (ALS) that broke his consecutive game string?

It may be too late for that now, however. The word "AIDS" probably will never lose its moral burden. Though the French were puzzled from the start by America's obsession with the homosexual side to the epidemic (in France, AIDS, or SIDA, is regarded as a largely African contagion), the hidden "G" continues to dominate its semiotic horizon. Indeed, AIDS has been so closely associated with homosexuality that hemophiliac children with AIDS have been hounded out of their schools and homes, while at first some physicians denied that "innocent" children could contract it from their mothers or that transfusion recipients could be infected by tainted blood. And an occasional doctor still won't think of testing female patients for HIV, believing that they are "too nice to have AIDS." For many Americans, AIDS remains more a behavioral disorder than a viral condition, something you get as punishment for having a socially "unacceptable" sexual orientation.

## The Readings

We begin this chapter with Paul Monette's personal story of the death of his friend Roger Horwitz, a testimony that puts a human face on the often dehumanized image of AIDS in America and that has been made all the more poignant by the AIDS-related death of Monette himself. Susan Sontag then analyzes the particular metaphors and analogies that first shaped the imagery of AIDS, arguing that the way AIDS was initially defined and conceived was crucial in its eventual political construction. Evelynn Hammonds next argues that AIDS has become a disease of the racially and sexually marginalized in America, an affliction of an alien "other" that has been left to die by a society that views the disease as someone else's problem. Daniel Harris then provides a complaint that an AIDS "industry," centered on the AIDS Quilt, is turning the epidemic into a cornucopia of consumer kitsch. Douglas Crimp complements Hammond's point of view in his critique of the way that artists and the media have depicted people with AIDS. In the final reading in this chapter, Elinor Burkett reports on the way that MTV made a celebrity of an AIDS victim, only to turn off the cameras when the young man's death threatened to ruin the glamorous image of AIDS that MTV had constructed.

# Borrowed Time: An AIDS Memoir

*In the beginning, before it had a name, AIDS appeared to be a rare form of cancer afflicting only those gay men who engaged in particularly risky sexual practices. But as Paul Monette writes in this excerpt from* Borrowed Time: An AIDS Memoir *(1988), AIDS soon appeared among the kind of men Monette and his companion Roger Horwitz felt themselves to be: successful, upper-middle-class professionals living together in stable relationships. Finding that he and his friends were not immune from the "gay plague" that began its sweep through America in 1981, Monette began living, in his own phrase, "on the moon": that is, in a nightmare world of disease and death that separated him forever from the world of ordinary life. Writing from the moon, Monette here tells his story of love and death in the face of a relentless enemy, all the while preparing for death himself. The winner of the National Book Award for Non-Fiction for his autobiography* Becoming a Man: Half a Life Story *(1992), Monette died from complications of the AIDS virus in 1995.*

I don't know if I will live to finish this. Doubtless there's a streak of self-importance in such an assertion, but who's counting? Maybe it's just that I've watched too many sicken in a month and die by Christmas, so that a fatal sort of realism comforts me more than magic. All I know is this: The virus ticks in me. And it doesn't care a whit about our categories — when is full-blown, what's AIDS-related, what is just sick and tired? No one has solved the puzzle of its timing. I take my drug from Tijuana twice a day. The very friends who tell me how vigorous I look, how well I seem, are the first to assure me of the imminent medical breakthrough. What they don't seem to understand is, I used up all my optimism keeping my friend alive. Now that he's gone, the cup of my own health is neither half full nor half empty. Just half.

Equally difficult, of course, is knowing where to start. The world around me is defined now by its endings and its closures — the date on the grave that follows the hyphen. Roger Horwitz, my beloved friend, died of complications of AIDS on October 22, 1986, nineteen months and ten days after his diagnosis. That is the only real date anymore, casting its ice shadow over all the secular holidays lovers mark their calendars by. Until that long night in October, it didn't seem possible that any day could supplant the brute equinox of March 12 — the day of Roger's diagnosis in 1985, the day we began to live on the moon.

The fact is, no one knows where to start with AIDS. Now, in the seventh year of the calamity, my friends in L.A. can hardly recall what it felt like any longer, the time before the sickness. Yet we all watched the toll mount in New York, then in San Francisco, for years before it ever touched us here. It comes like a slowly dawning horror. At first you are equipped with a hundred different amulets to keep it far away. Then someone you know goes into the hospital, and suddenly you are at high noon in full battle gear. They have neglected to tell you that you will be issued no weapons of any sort. So you cobble together a weapon out of anything that lies at hand, like a prisoner honing a spoon handle into a stiletto. You fight tough, you fight dirty, but you cannot fight dirtier than it.

I remember a Saturday in February 1982, driving Route 10 to Palm Springs with Roger to visit his parents for the weekend. While Roger drove, I read aloud an article from *The Advocate:* "Is Sex Making Us Sick?" There was the slightest edge of irony in the query, an urban cool that seems almost bucolic now in its innocence. But the article didn't mince words. It was the first in-depth reporting I'd read that laid out the shadowy nonfacts of what till then had been the most fragmented of rumors. The first cases were reported to the Centers for Disease Control (CDC) only six months before, but they weren't in the newspapers, not in L.A. I note in my diary in December 1981 ambiguous reports of a "gay cancer," but I know I didn't have the slightest picture of the thing. Cancer of the *what*? I would have asked, if anyone had known anything.

I remember exactly what was going through my mind while I was reading, though I can't now recall the details of the piece. I was thinking: How is this not me? Trying to find a pattern I was exempt from. It was a brand of denial I would watch grow exponentially during the next few years, but at the time I was simply relieved. Because the article appeared to be saying that there was a grim progression toward this undefined catastrophe, a set of preconditions — chronic hepatitis, repeated bouts of syphilis, exotic parasites. No wonder my first baseline response was to feel safe. It was *them* — by which I meant the fast-lane Fire Island crowd, the Sutro Baths, the world of High Eros.

Not us.

I grabbed for that relief because we'd been through a rough patch the previous autumn. Till then Roger had always enjoyed a sort of no-nonsense good health: not an abuser of anything, with a constitutional aversion to hypochondria, and not wed to his mirror save for a minor alarm as to the growing dimensions of his bald spot. In the seven years we'd been together I scarcely remember him having a cold or taking an aspirin. Yet in October 1981 he had struggled with a peculiar bout of intestinal flu. Nothing special showed up in any of the blood tests, but over a period of weeks he experienced persistent symptoms that didn't neatly connect: pains in his legs, diarrhea, general malaise. I hadn't been feeling notably bad myself, but on the other hand I was a textbook hypochondriac, and I figured if Rog was harboring some kind of bug, so was I.

The two of us finally went to a gay doctor in the Valley for a further set of blood tests. It's a curious phenomenon among gay middle-class men that anything faintly venereal had better be taken to a doctor who's "on the bus." Is it a sense of fellow feeling perhaps, or a way of avoiding embarrassment? Do we really believe that only a doctor who's *our* kind can heal us of the afflictions that attach somehow to our secret hearts? There is so much magic to medicine. Of course we didn't know then that those few physicians with a large gay clientele were about to be swamped beyond all capacity to cope.

The tests came back positive for amoebiasis. Roger and I began the highly toxic treatment to kill the amoeba, involving two separate drugs and what seems in memory thirty pills a day for six weeks, till the middle of January. It was the first time I'd ever experienced the phenomenon of the cure making you sicker. By the end of treatment we were both weak and had lost weight, and for a couple of months afterward were susceptible to colds and minor infections.

It was only after the treatment was over that a friend of ours, diagnosed with amoebas by the same doctor, took his slide to the lab at UCLA for a second opinion. And that was my first encounter with lab error. The doctor at UCLA explained that the slide had been misread; the squiggles that looked like amoebas were in fact benign. The doctor shook his head and grumbled about "these guys who do their own lab work." Roger then retrieved his slide, took it over to UCLA and was told the same: no amoebas. We had just spent six weeks methodically ingesting poison for no reason at all.

So it wasn't the *Advocate* story that sent up the red flag for us. We'd been shaken by the amoeba business, and from that point on we operated at a new level of sexual caution. What is now called safe sex did not use to be so clearly defined. The concept didn't exist. But it was quickly becoming apparent, even then, that we couldn't wait for somebody else to define the parameters. Thus every gay man I know has had to come to a point of personal definition by way of avoiding the chaos of sexually transmitted diseases, or STD as we call them in the trade. There was obviously no one moment of conscious decision, a bolt of clarity on the shimmering freeway west of San Bernardino, but I think of that day when I think of the sea change. The party was going to have to stop. The evidence was too ominous: *We were making ourselves sick.*

Not that Roger and I were the life of the party. Roger especially didn't march to the different drum of *so many men, so little time,* the motto and anthem of the sunstruck summers of the mid-to-late seventies. He'd managed not to carry away from his adolescence the mark of too much repression, or indeed the yearning to make up for lost time. In ten years he had perhaps half a dozen contacts outside the main frame of our relationship, mostly when he was out of town on business. He was comfortable with relative monogamy, even at a time when certain quarters of the gay world found the whole idea trivial and bourgeois. I realize that in the world of the heterosexual there is a generalized lip service paid to exclusive monogamy, a notion most vividly honored in the breach. I leave the matter of morality to those with the gift of tongues; it was difficult enough for us to fashion a sexual ethics just for us. In any case, I was the one in the relationship who suffered from lost time. I was the one who would go after a sexual encounter as if it were an ice cream cone — casual, quick, good-by.

But as I say, who's counting? I only want to make it plain to start with that we got very alert and very careful as far back as the winter of 1982. That gut need for safety took hold and lingered, even as we got better again and strong. Thus I'm not entirely sure what I thought on another afternoon a year and a half later, when a friend of ours back from New York reported a conversation he'd had with a research man from Sloan-Kettering.

"He thinks all it takes is one exposure," Charlie said, this after months of articles about the significance of repeated exposure. More tenaciously than ever, we all wanted to believe the whole deepening tragedy was centered on those at the sexual frontiers who were fucking their brains out. The rest of us were fashioning our own little Puritan forts, as we struggled to convince ourselves that a clean slate would hold the nightmare at bay.

Yet with caution as our watchword starting in February of 1982, Roger was diagnosed with AIDS three years later. So the turning over of new leaves was not to be on everybody's side. A lot of us were already ticking and didn't even know. The magic circle my generation is trying to stay within the borders of is only as real as the random past. Perhaps the young can live in the magic circle, but only if those of us who are ticking will tell our story. Otherwise it goes on being *us* and *them* forever, built like a wall higher and higher, till you no longer think to wonder if you are walling it out or in.

For us the knowing began in earnest on the first of September, 1983. I'd had a call a couple of days before from my closest friend, Cesar Albini, who'd just returned to San Francisco after a summer touring Europe with a group of students. He said he'd been having trouble walking because of a swollen gland in his groin, and he was going to the hospital to have it biopsied. He reassured me he was feeling fine and wasn't expecting anything ominous, but figured he'd check it out before school started again. AIDS didn't even cross my mind, though cancer did. Half joking, Cesar wondered aloud if he dared disturb our happy friendship with bad news.

"If it's bad," I said, "we'll handle it, okay?"

But I really didn't clutch with fear, or it was only a brief stab of the hypochondriacal sort. Roger and I were busy getting ready for a four-day trip to Big Sur, something we'd done almost yearly since moving to California in 1977. We were putting the blizzard of daily life on hold, looking forward to a dose of raw sublime that coincided with our anniversary — September 3, the day we met.

Cesar was forty-three, only ten months older than Roger. Born in Uruguay, possessed of a great heart and inexhaustible energy, he had studied in Europe and traveled all over, once spending four months going overland from Paris to China at a total cost of five hundred dollars. He was the first Uruguayan ever to enter Afghanistan through the mountains — on a camel, if I remember right. He spoke French, Italian, Spanish and English with equal fluency, and he tended to be the whole language department of a school. We'd both been teaching at secondary schools in Massachusetts when we met, and we goaded one another to make the move west that had always been our shared dream. Thus Cesar had relocated to San Francisco in July of 1976, and Roger and I landed in L.A. four days after Thanksgiving the following year.

Cesar wasn't lucky in matters of the heart. He was still in the closet   20 during his years back East, and the move to San Francisco was an extraordinary rite of passage for him. He always wanted a great love, but the couple of relationships he'd been involved in scarcely left the station. Still, he was very proud and indulged in no self-pity. He learned to accept the limited terms of the once-a-week relations he found in San Francisco, and broke through to the freedom of his own manhood without the mythic partner. The open sexual exultation that marked San Francisco in those days was something he rejoiced in.

Yet even though he went to the baths a couple of times a week, Cesar wasn't into anything *weird* — or that's how I might have put it at that stage of my own denial. No hepatitis, no history of VD, built tall and fierce — of course he was safe. The profile of AIDS continued to be mostly a matter of shadows. The L.A. *Times* wasn't covering it, though by then I had come to learn how embattled things had grown in New York. The Gay Men's Health Crisis was up to its ears in clients; Larry Kramer was screaming at the mayor; and the body count was appearing weekly in the *Native*. A writer I knew slightly was walking around with Kaposi's sarcoma. A young composer kept getting sicker and sicker, though he stubbornly didn't fit the CDC's hopelessly narrow categories, so that case was still officially a toss-up. And again, we're talking New York.

I came home at six on the evening of the first, and Roger met me gravely at the door. "There's a message from Cesar," he said. "It's not good."

Numbly I played back the answering machine, where so much appalling misery would be left on tape over the years to come, as if a record were crying out to be kept. "I have a little bit of bad news." Cesar's voice sounded strained, almost embarrassed. He left no details. I called and called him throughout the evening, convinced I was about to hear cancer news. The lymph nodes, of course — a hypochondriac knows all there is to know about the sites of malignancy. Already I was figuring what the treatments might be; no question in my mind but that it was treatable. I had Cesar practically cured by the time I reached Tom, a friend and former student of his. But as usual with me in crisis, I was jabbering and wouldn't let Tom get a word in. Finally he broke through: "He's got it."

"Got what?"

It's not till you first hear it attached to someone you love that you       25
realize how little you know about it. My mind went utterly blank. The carefully constructed wall collapsed as if a 7.5 quake had rumbled under it. At that point I didn't even know the difference between KS and the opportunistic infections. I kept picturing that swollen gland in his groin, thinking: What's *that* got to do with AIDS? And a parallel track in my mind began careening with another thought: the swollen glands in my own groin, always dismissed by my straight doctor as herpes-related and "not a significant sign."

"We're not going to die young," Cesar used to say with a wag of his finger, his black Latin eyes dancing. "We won't get out of it *that* easily!" Then he would laugh and clap his hands, downing the coffee he always took with cream and four sugars. It looked like pudding.

I reached him very late that night and mouthed again the same words I'd said so bravely two days before: We'll deal with it. There is no end to the litany of reassurance that springs to your lips to ward away the specter. They've caught it early; you're fine; there's got to be some kind of treatment. That old chestnut, the imminent breakthrough. You fling these phrases instinctively, like pennies down a well. Cesar and I bent backward to calm each other. It was just a couple of lesions in the groin; you could hardly see them. And the reason everything was going to be all right was really very simple: We would fight this thing like demons.

But the hollowness and disbelief pursued Roger and me all the way up the gold coast. Big Sur was towering and bracing as ever — exalted as Homer's Ithaca, as Robinson Jeffers described it. We were staying at Ventana, the lavish inn high in the hills above the canyon of the Big Sur River. We used the inn as a base camp for our day-long hikes, returning in the evening to posh amenities worthy of an Edwardian big-game hunt. On the second morning we walked out to Andrew Molera Beach, where the Big Sur empties into the Pacific. Molera stretches unblemished for five miles down the coast, curving like a crescent moon, with weathered headlands clean as Scotland. It was a kind of holy place for Roger and me, like the yearly end of a quest.

"What if we got it?" I said, staring out at the otters belly up in the kelp beds, taking the sun.

I don't remember how we answered that, because of course there       30
wasn't any answer. Merely to pose the question was by way of another

shot at magic. Mention the unmentionable and it will go away, like shining a light around a child's bedroom to shoo the monster. The great ache we were feeling at that moment was for our stricken friend, and we were too ignorant still to envision the medieval tortures that might await him.

But I know that the roll of pictures I took that day was my first conscious memorializing of Roger and me, as if I could hold the present as security on the future. There's one of me on the beach, then a mirror image of him as we traded off the camera, both of us squinting in the clear autumn light with the river mouth behind. Back at the inn, I took a picture of Rog in a rope hammock, his blue eyes resting on me as if the camera weren't even there, in total equilibrium, nine years to the day since our paths crossed on Revere Street. His lips are barely curved in a quarter-smile, his hands at rest in his lap as the last wave of the westering sun washes his left side through the diamond weave of the rope.

### Reading the Text

1. Why does Monette say that the AIDS epidemic prompted him to look at other gays as "us" and "them"?
2. What does Monette mean by "the turning over of new leaves was not to be on everybody's side"?
3. How did Monette respond to the illness of his friend Cesar?

### Reading the Signs

1. Write an essay analyzing why Monette responded both to the general AIDS epidemic and to his and Roger's illness with denial. How did Monette distinguish himself from other gay men? What social-class issues may have affected his perception of this disease?
2. Monette's "Borrowed Time" is an autobiographical narrative, not an analytical essay. In class, "translate" Monette's selection into a one-page essay, working individually or in groups, then read the essays aloud. Discuss what different effects the storytelling and analytic modes have on you as the audience. (You may want to consult Leslie Marmon Silko's "Language and Literature from a Pueblo Indian Perspective," p. 549, for her comments on the value of storytelling.)
3. In your journal, explore the significance of Monette's title, "Borrowed Time."
4. Rent a videotape of the film *Longtime Companion,* a chronicle of a group of friends coping with the AIDS epidemic. In class, discuss how the film's characters respond to the illness. How does their response compare with Monette's?

# SUSAN SONTAG

## AIDS and Its Metaphors

〰〰〰〰〰〰〰〰〰〰〰〰〰〰〰〰〰〰〰〰〰

*When Susan Sontag (b. 1933) was diagnosed with cancer in the 1970s, she not only set out, successfully, to fight the disease, she also began an exploration of the social construction of illness throughout history. The result of her study,* Illness as Metaphor *(1978), became the basis for her more recent book,* AIDS and Its Metaphors *(1989), from which this selection has been taken. Like any illness, Sontag argues, AIDS is a sign as well as a medical phenomenon. Constructing AIDS as a "plague" especially predisposes us to regard it according to a religious mythology that isolates its victims, Sontag suggests. Even the way AIDS is medically defined has social implications, especially the term "full-blown" AIDS, which can imply that HIV infection itself is already AIDS, albeit not yet developed. Having herself felt the isolating effects of cancer, Sontag argues against the use of metaphors that dehumanize people with AIDS. The author of numerous books, essays, stories, and screenplays, Sontag has most recently published a novel,* The Volcano Lover *(1992).*

Just as one might predict for a disease that is not yet fully understood as well as extremely recalcitrant to treatment, the advent of this terrifying new disease, new at least in its epidemic form, has provided a large-scale occasion for the metaphorizing of illness.

Strictly speaking, AIDS — acquired immune deficiency syndrome — is not the name of an illness at all. It is the name of a medical condition, whose consequences are a spectrum of illnesses. In contrast to syphilis and cancer, which provide prototypes for most of the images and metaphors attached to AIDS, the very definition of AIDS requires the presence of other illnesses, so-called opportunistic infections and malignancies. But though not in *that* sense a single disease, AIDS lends itself to being regarded as one — in part because, unlike cancer and like syphilis, it is thought to have a single cause.

AIDS has a dual metaphoric genealogy. As a microprocess, it is described as cancer is: an invasion. When the focus is transmission of the disease, an older metaphor, reminiscent of syphilis, is invoked: pollution. (One gets it from the blood or sexual fluids of infected people or from contaminated blood products.) But the military metaphors used to describe AIDS have a somewhat different focus from those used in describing cancer. With cancer, the metaphor scants the issue of causality (still a murky topic in cancer research) and picks up at the point at which rogue cells inside the body mutate, eventually moving out from an original site or organ to overrun other organs or systems — a domestic subversion. In the description of AIDS the enemy is what causes the disease, an infectious agent that comes from the outside:

> The invader is tiny, about one sixteen-thousandth the size of the head of a pin. . . . Scouts of the body's immune system, large cells called macrophages, sense the presence of the diminutive foreigner and promptly alert the immune system. It begins to mobilize an array of cells that, among other things, produce antibodies to deal with the threat. Single-mindedly, the AIDS virus ignores many of the blood cells in its path, evades the rapidly advancing defenders and homes in on the master coordinator of the immune system, a helper T cell. . . .

This is the language of political paranoia, with its characteristic distrust of a pluralistic world. A defense system consisting of cells "that, among other things, produce antibodies to deal with the threat" is, predictably, no match for an invader who advances "single-mindedly." And the science-fiction flavor, already present in cancer talk, is even more pungent in accounts of AIDS — this one comes from *Time* magazine in late 1986 — with infection described like the high-tech warfare for which we are being prepared (and inured) by the fantasies of our leaders and by video entertainments. In the era of Star Wars and Space Invaders, AIDS has proved an ideally comprehensible illness:

> On the surface of that cell, it finds a receptor into which one of its envelope proteins fits perfectly, like a key into a lock. Docking with the cell, the virus penetrates the cell membrane and is stripped of its protective shell in the process. . . .

Next the invader takes up permanent residence, by a form of alien takeover familiar in science-fiction narratives. The body's own cells *become* the invader. With the help of an enzyme the virus carries with it,

> the naked AIDS virus converts its RNA into . . . DNA, the master molecule of life. The molecule then penetrates the cell nucleus, inserts itself into a chromosome and takes over part of the cellular machinery, directing it to produce more AIDS viruses. Eventually, overcome by its alien product, the cell swells and dies, releasing a flood of new viruses to attack other cells. . . .

As viruses attack other cells, runs the metaphor, so "a host of opportunistic diseases, normally warded off by a healthy immune system, attacks the body," whose integrity and vigor have been sapped by the sheer replication of "alien product" that follows the collapse of its immunological defenses. "Gradually weakened by the onslaught, the AIDS victim dies, sometimes in months, but almost always within a few years of the first symptoms." Those who have not already succumbed are described as "under assault, showing the telltale symptoms of the disease," while millions of others "harbor the virus, vulnerable at any time to a final, all-out attack."

Cancer makes cells proliferate; in AIDS, cells die. Even as this original model of AIDS (the mirror image of leukemia) has been altered, descriptions of how the virus does its work continue to echo the way the illness is perceived as infiltrating the society. "AIDS Virus Found to Hide in Cells, Eluding Detection by Normal Tests" was the headline of a recent front-page story in the *New York Times* announcing the discovery that the virus can "lurk" for years in the macrophages — disrupting their disease-fighting function without killing them, "even when the macrophages are filled almost to bursting with virus," and without producing antibodies, the chemicals the body makes in response to "invading agents" and whose presence has been regarded as an infallible marker of the syndrome.[1] That the virus isn't lethal for *all* the cells where it takes up residence, as is now thought, only increases the illness-foe's reputation for wiliness and invincibility.

What makes the viral assault so terrifying is that contamination, and   5
therefore vulnerability, is understood as permanent. Even if someone infected were never to develop any symptoms — that is, the infection remained, or could by medical intervention be rendered, inactive — the viral enemy would be forever within. In fact, so it is believed, it is just a matter of time before something awakens ("triggers") it, before the appearance of "the telltale symptoms." Like syphilis, known to generations of doctors as "the great masquerader," AIDS is a clinical construction, an inference. It takes its identity from the presence of *some* among a long, and lengthening, roster of symptoms (no one has everything that AIDS could be), symptoms which "mean" that what the patient has is this illness. The construction of the illness rests on the invention not only of AIDS as a clinical entity but of a kind of junior AIDS, called AIDS-related complex (ARC), to which people are assigned if they show "early" and often intermittent symptoms of immunological deficit such

---

1. The larger role assigned to the macrophages — "to serve as a reservoir for the AIDS virus because the virus multiplies in them but does not kill them, as it kills T-4 cells" — is said to explain the not uncommon difficulty of finding infected T-4 lymphocytes in patients who have antibodies to the virus and symptoms of AIDS. (It is still assumed that antibodies will develop once the virus spreads to these "key target" cells.) Evidence of presently infected populations of cells has been as puzzlingly limited or uneven as the evidence of infection in the populations of human societies — puzzling, because of the conviction that the disease is everywhere, and must spread. "Doctors have estimated that as few as one in a million T-4 cells are infected, which led some to ask where the virus hides. . . ." Another resonant speculation, reported in the same article (the *New York Times,* June 7, 1988): "Infected macrophages can transmit the virus to other cells, possibly by touching the cells."

as fevers, weight loss, fungal infections, and swollen lymph glands. AIDS is progressive, a disease of time. Once a certain density of symptoms is attained, the course of the illness can be swift, and brings atrocious suffering. Besides the commonest "presenting" illnesses (some hitherto unusual, at least in a fatal form, such as a rare skin cancer and a rare form of pneumonia), a plethora of disabling, disfiguring, and humiliating symptoms make the AIDS patient steadily more infirm, helpless, and unable to control or take care of basic functions and needs.

The sense in which AIDS is a slow disease makes it more like syphilis, which is characterized in terms of "stages," than like cancer. Thinking in terms of "stages" is essential to discourse about AIDS. Syphilis in its most dreaded form is "tertiary syphilis," syphilis in its third stage. What is called AIDS is generally understood as the last of three stages — the first of which is infection with a human immunodeficiency virus (HIV) and early evidence of inroads on the immune system — with a long latency period between infection and the onset of the "telltale" symptoms. (Apparently not as long as syphilis, in which the latency period between secondary and tertiary illness might be decades. But it is worth noting that when syphilis first appeared in epidemic form in Europe at the end of the fifteenth century, it was a rapid disease, of an unexplained virulence that is unknown today, in which death often occurred in the second stage, sometimes within months or a few years.) Cancer *grows* slowly: It is not thought to be, for a long time, latent. (A convincing account of a process in terms of "stages" seems invariably to include the notion of a normative delay or halt in the process, such as is supplied by the notion of latency.) True, a cancer is "staged." This is a principal tool of diagnosis, which means classifying it according to its gravity, determining how "advanced" it is. But it is mostly a spatial notion: that the cancer advances through the body, traveling or migrating along predictable routes. Cancer is first of all a disease of the body's geography, in contrast to syphilis and AIDS, whose definition depends on constructing a temporal sequence of stages.

Syphilis is an affliction that didn't have to run its ghastly full course, to paresis (as it did for Baudelaire and Maupassant and Jules de Goncourt), and could and often did remain at the stage of nuisance, indignity (as it did for Flaubert). The scourge was also a cliché, as Flaubert himself observed. "SYPHILIS. Everybody has it, more or less," reads one entry in the *Dictionary of Accepted Opinions,* his treasury of mid-nineteenth-century platitudes. And syphilis did manage to acquire a darkly positive association in late-nineteenth- and early-twentieth-century Europe, when a link was made between syphilis and heightened ("feverish") mental activity that parallels the connection made since the era of the Romantic writers between pulmonary tuberculosis and heightened emotional activity. As if in honor of all the notable writers and artists who ended their lives in syphilitic witlessness, it came to be believed that the brain lesions of neurosyphilis might actually inspire original thought or art. Thomas Mann, whose fiction is a storehouse of early-twentieth-century disease myths, makes this notion of syphilis as muse central to his *Doctor Faustus,* with its protagonist a great composer whose voluntarily contracted syphilis — the Devil guarantees that the infection will be limited to the central nervous system — confers on him twenty-four years of incandescent creativity. E. M. Cioran recalls how, in Romania in the late 1920s, syphilis-envy figured in his adolescent expectations of literary glory: He would discover that he had contracted syphilis, be rewarded with several hyperproductive years of genius, then collapse into madness. This romanticizing of the dementia characteristic of neurosyphilis was the forerunner of the much more persistent fantasy in this century about mental illness as a source of artistic creativity or spiritual originality. But with AIDS — though dementia is also a common, late symptom — no compensatory mythology has arisen, or seems likely to arise. AIDS, like cancer, does not allow romanticizing or sentimentalizing, perhaps because its association with death is too powerful. In Krzysztof Zanussi's film *Spiral* (1978), the most truthful account I know of anger at dying, the protagonist's illness is never specified; therefore, it *has* to be cancer. For several generations now, the generic idea of death has been a death from cancer, and a cancer death is experienced as a generic defeat. Now the generic rebuke to life and to hope is AIDS.

"Plague" is the principal metaphor by which the AIDS epidemic is understood. And because of AIDS, the popular misidentification of cancer as an epidemic, even as a plague, seems to be receding: AIDS has banalized cancer.

Plague, from the Latin *plaga* (stroke, wound), has long been used metaphorically as the highest standard of collective calamity, evil, scourge — Procopius, in his masterpiece of calumny, *The Secret History,* called the Emperor Justinian worse than the plague ("fewer escaped") — as well as being a general name for many frightening diseases. Although the disease to which the word is permanently affixed produced the most lethal of recorded epidemics, being experienced as a pitiless slayer is not necessary for a disease to be regarded as plague-like. Leprosy, very rarely fatal now, was not much more so when at its greatest epidemic strength, between about 1050 and 1350. And syphilis has been regarded as a plague — Blake speaks of "the youthful Harlot's curse" that "blights with plagues the Marriage hearse" — not because it killed often, but because it was disgracing, disempowering, disgusting.

It is usually epidemics that are thought of as plagues. And these mass   10
incidences of illness are understood as inflicted, not just endured. Considering illness as a punishment is the oldest idea of what causes illness, and an idea opposed by all attention to the ill that deserves the noble name of medicine. Hippocrates, who wrote several treatises on epidemics, specifi-

cally ruled out "the wrath of God" as a cause of bubonic plague. But the illnesses interpreted in antiquity as punishments, like the plague in *Oedipus,* were not thought to be shameful, as leprosy and subsequently syphilis were to be. Diseases, insofar as they acquired meaning, were collective calamities, and judgments on a community. Only injuries and disabilities, not diseases, were thought of as individually merited. For an analogy in the literature of antiquity to the modern sense of a shaming, isolating disease, one would have to turn to Philoctetes and his stinking wound.

The most feared diseases, those that are not simply fatal but transform the body into something alienating, like leprosy and syphilis and cholera and (in the imagination of many) cancer, are the ones that seem particularly susceptible to promotion to "plague." Leprosy and syphilis were the first illnesses to be consistently described as repulsive. It was syphilis that, in the earliest descriptions by doctors at the end of the fifteenth century, generated a version of the metaphors that flourish around AIDS: of a disease that was not only repulsive and retributive but collectively invasive. Although Erasmus, the most influential European pedagogue of the early sixteenth century, described syphilis as "nothing but a kind of leprosy" (by 1529 he called it "something worse than leprosy"), it had already been understood as something different, because sexually transmitted. Paracelsus speaks (in Donne's paraphrase) of "that foule contagious disease which then had invaded mankind in a few places, and since overflowes in all, that for punishment of general licentiousnes God first inflicted that disease." Thinking of syphilis as a punishment for an individual's transgression was for a long time, virtually until the disease became easily curable, not really distinct from regarding it as retribution for the licentiousness of a community — as with AIDS now, in the rich industrial countries. In contrast to cancer, understood in a modern way as a disease incurred by (and revealing of) individuals, AIDS is understood in a premodern way, as a disease incurred by people both as individuals and as members of a "risk group" — that neutral-sounding, bureaucratic category which also revives the archaic idea of a tainted community that illness has judged.

Not every account of plague or plaguelike diseases, of course, is a vehicle for lurid stereotypes about illness and the ill. The effort to think critically, historically, about illness (about disaster generally) was attempted throughout the eighteenth century: say, from Defoe's *A Journal of the Plague Year* (1722) to Alessandro Manzoni's *The Betrothed* (1827). Defoe's historical fiction, purporting to be an eyewitness account of bubonic plague in London in 1665, does not further any understanding of the plague as punishment or, a later part of the script, as a transforming experience. And Manzoni, in his lengthy account of the passage of plague through the duchy of Milan in 1630, is avowedly committed to presenting a more accurate, less reductive view than his historical sources. But even these two complex narratives reinforce some of the perennial, simplifying ideas about plague.

One feature of the usual script for plague: The disease invariably comes from somewhere else. The names for syphilis, when it began its epidemic sweep through Europe in the last decade of the fifteenth century, are an exemplary illustration of the need to make a dreaded disease foreign.[2] It was the "French pox" to the English, morbus Germanicus to the Parisians, the Naples sickness to the Florentines, the Chinese disease to the Japanese. But what may seem like a joke about the inevitability of chauvinism reveals a more important truth: that there is a link between imagining disease and imagining foreignness. It lies perhaps in the very concept of wrong, which is archaically identical with the non-us, the alien. A polluting person is always wrong, as Mary Douglas has observed. The inverse is also true: A person judged to be wrong is regarded as, at least potentially, a source of pollution.

The foreign place of origin of important illnesses, as of drastic changes in the weather, may be no more remote than a neighboring country. Illness is a species of invasion, and indeed is often carried by soldiers. Manzoni's account of the plague of 1630 (chapters 31 to 37) begins:

> The plague which the Tribunal of Health had feared might enter the Milanese provinces with the German troops had in fact entered, as is well known; and it is also well known that it did not stop there, but went on to invade and depopulate a large part of Italy.

Defoe's chronicle of the plague of 1665 begins similarly, with a flurry of ostentatiously scrupulous speculation about its foreign origin:

---

2. As noted in the first accounts of the disease: "This malady received from different peoples whom it affected different names," writes Giovanni di Vigo in 1514. Like earlier treatises on syphilis, written in Latin — by Nicolo Leoniceno (1497) and by Juan Almenar (1502) — the one by di Vigo calls it morbus Gallicus, the French disease. (Excerpts from this and other accounts of the period, including Syphilis; Or a Poetical History of the French Disease [1530] by Girolamo Fracastoro, who coined the name that prevailed, are in Classic Descriptions of Disease, edited by Ralph H. Major [1932].) Moralistic explanations abounded from the beginning. In 1495, a year after the epidemic started, the Emperor Maximilian issued an edict declaring syphilis to be an affliction from God for the sins of men.

The theory that syphilis came from even farther than a neighboring country, that it was an entirely new disease in Europe, a disease of the New World brought back to the Old by sailors of Columbus who had contracted it in America, became the accepted explanation of the origin of syphilis in the sixteenth century and is still widely credited. It is worth noting that the earliest medical writers on syphilis did not accept the dubious theory. Leoniceno's Libellus de Epidemia, quam vulgo morbum Gallicum vocant starts by taking up the question of whether "the French disease under another name was common to the ancients," and says he believes firmly that it was.

> It was about the beginning of September, 1664, that I, among the rest of my neighbours, heard in ordinary discourse that the plague was returned again in Holland; for it had been very violent there, and particularly at Amsterdam and Rotterdam, in the year 1663, whither, they say, it was brought, some said from Italy, others from the Levant, among some goods which were brought home by their Turkey fleet; others said it was brought from Candia; others from Cyprus. It mattered not from whence it came; but all agreed it was come into Holland again.

The bubonic plague that reappeared in London in the 1720s had arrived from Marseilles, which was where plague in the eighteenth century was usually thought to enter Western Europe: brought by seamen, then transported by soldiers and merchants. By the nineteenth century the foreign origin was usually more exotic, the means of transport less specifically imagined, and the illness itself had become phantasmagorical, symbolic.

At the end of *Crime and Punishment* Raskolnikov dreams of plague: 15 "He dreamt that the whole world was condemned to a terrible new strange plague that had come to Europe from the depths of Asia." At the beginning of the sentence it is "the whole world," which turns out by the end of the sentence to be "Europe," afflicted by a lethal visitation from Asia. Dostoevsky's model is undoubtedly cholera, called Asiatic cholera, long endemic in Bengal, which had rapidly become and remained through most of the nineteenth century a worldwide epidemic disease. Part of the centuries-old conception of Europe as a privileged cultural entity is that it is a place which is colonized by lethal diseases coming from elsewhere. Europe is assumed to be by rights free of disease. (And Europeans have been astoundingly callous about the far more devastating extent to which they — as invaders, as colonists — have introduced *their* lethal diseases to the exotic, "primitive" world: Think of the ravages of smallpox, influenza, and cholera on the aboriginal populations of the Americas and Australia.) The tenacity of the connection of exotic origin with dreaded disease is one reason why cholera, of which there were four great outbreaks in Europe in the nineteenth century, each with a lower death toll than the preceding one, has continued to be more memorable than smallpox, whose ravages increased as the century went on (half a million died in the European smallpox pandemic of the early 1870s) but which could not be construed as, plaguelike, a disease with a non–European origin.

Plagues are no longer "sent," as in Biblical and Greek antiquity, for the question of agency has blurred. Instead, peoples are "visited" by plagues. And the visitations recur, as is taken for granted in the subtitle of Defoe's narrative, which explains that it is about that "which happened in London during the Last Great Visitation in 1665." Even for non-Europeans, lethal disease may be called a visitation. But a visitation on "them" is invariably described as different from one on "us."

"I believe that about one half of the whole people was carried off by this visitation," wrote the English traveler Alexander Kinglake, reaching Cairo at a time of the bubonic plague (sometimes called "oriental plague"). "The Orientals, however, have more quiet fortitude than Europeans under afflictions of this sort." Kinglake's influential book *Eothen* (1844) — suggestively subtitled "Traces of Travel Brought Home from the East" — illustrates many of the enduring Eurocentric presumptions about others, starting from the fantasy that peoples with little reason to expect exemption from misfortune have a lessened capacity to *feel* misfortune. Thus it is believed that Asians (or the poor, or blacks, or Africans, or Muslims) don't suffer or don't grieve as Europeans (or whites) do. The fact that illness is associated with the poor — who are, from the perspective of the privileged, aliens in one's midst — reinforces the association of illness with the foreign: with an exotic, often primitive place.

Thus, illustrating the classic script for plague, AIDS is thought to have started in the "dark continent," then spread to Haiti, then to the United States and to Europe, then . . . . It is understood as a tropical disease: another infestation from the so-called Third World, which is after all where most people in the world live, as well as a scourge of the *tristes tropiques*.[3] Africans who detect racist stereotypes in much of the speculation about the geographical origin of AIDS are not wrong. (Nor are they wrong in thinking that depictions of Africa as the cradle of AIDS must feed anti-African prejudices in Europe and Asia.) The subliminal connection made to notions about a primitive past and the many hypotheses that have been fielded about possible transmission from animals (a disease of green monkeys? African swine fever?) cannot help but activate a familiar set of stereotypes about animality, sexual license, and blacks. In Zaire and other countries in Central Africa where AIDS is killing tens of thousands, the counterreaction has begun. Many doctors, academics, journalists, government officials, and other educated people believe that the virus was sent to Africa from the United States, an act of bacteriological warfare (whose aim was to decrease the African birth rate) which got out of hand and has returned to afflict its perpetrators. A common African version of this belief about the disease's provenance has the virus fabricated in a CIA–Army laboratory in Maryland, sent from there to Africa, and brought back to its country of origin by American homosexual missionaries returning from Africa to Maryland.[4]

---

3. ***tristes tropiques***   French, the sad tropics. — EDS.

4. The rumor may not have originated as a KGB-sponsored "disinformation" campaign, but it received a crucial push from Soviet propaganda specialists. In October 1985 the Soviet weekly *Literaturnaya Gazeta* published an article alleging that the AIDS virus had been engineered by the U.S. government during biological-warfare research at Fort Detrick, Maryland, and was being spread abroad by U.S. servicemen who had

At first it was assumed that AIDS must become widespread elsewhere in the same catastrophic form in which it has emerged in Africa, and those who still think this will eventually happen invariably invoke the Black Death. The plague metaphor is an essential vehicle of the most pessimistic reading of the epidemiological prospects. From classic fiction to the latest journalism, the standard plague story is of inexorability, inescapability. The unprepared are taken by surprise; those observing the recommended precautions are struck down as well. *All* succumb when the story is told by an omniscient narrator, as in Poe's parable "The Masque of the Red Death" (1842), inspired by an account of a ball held in Paris during the cholera epidemic of 1832. Almost all — if the story is told from the point of view of a traumatized witness, who will be a benumbed survivor, as in Jean Giono's Stendhalian novel *Horseman on the Roof* (1951), in which a young Italian nobleman in exile wanders through cholera-stricken southern France in the 1830s.

### *Reading the Text*

1. Why does Sontag assert that AIDS "is not the name of an illness at all"?
2. What metaphors have shaped our understanding of AIDS, according to Sontag?
3. Why does Sontag feel that syphilis is a closer analogy to AIDS than is cancer?
4. Why does Sontag believe that the metaphors by which we understand a disease are so important?

### *Reading the Signs*

1. In your journal, freewrite on your understanding of AIDS. How do you view the disease? Has your thinking about the disease evolved since you first learned about it? Then, with Sontag's essay in mind, reflect on your freewriting. What myths and metaphors have guided your own thinking about AIDS?

---

been used as guinea pigs. The source cited was an article in the Indian newspaper *Patriot*. Repeated on Moscow's "Radio Peace and Progress" in English, the story was taken up by newspapers and magazines throughout the world. A year later it was featured on the front page of London's conservative, mass-circulation *Sunday Express*. ("The killer AIDS virus was artificially created by American scientists during laboratory experiments which went disastrously wrong — and a massive cover-up has kept the secret from the world until today.") Though ignored by most American newspapers, the *Sunday Express* story was recycled in virtually every other country. As recently as the summer of 1987, it appeared in newspapers in Kenya, Peru, Sudan, Nigeria, Senegal, and Mexico. Gorbachev-era policies have since produced an official denial of the allegations by two eminent members of the Soviet Academy of Sciences, which was published in *Izvestia* in late October 1987. But the story is still being repeated — from Mexico to Zaire, from Australia to Greece.

2. Compare and contrast AIDS and the bubonic plague. In what ways are the diseases' biological effects on the human body similar and different? How do people's responses to the diseases compare? What is the metaphoric history of each disease? To develop your essay, you might also consult Evelynn Hammonds, "Race, Sex, AIDS: The Construction of 'Other,'" p. 658.

3. Visit your library and locate a human physiology or medical textbook (alternatively, you might visit your campus health center and pick up brochures on AIDS). Write an essay in which you analyze the discussion of AIDS. What language is used to describe the disease? Does it use any of the metaphors or images that Sontag discusses? If so, what impact do they have on your understanding of the disease?

4. How would Sontag explain Paul Monette's ("Borrowed Time: An AIDS Memoir," p. 641) response to AIDS in the early years of the epidemic? How did the metaphors and images of AIDS either facilitate or impede his understanding of the disease?

5. Sontag's *AIDS and Its Metaphors,* from which this selection was taken, was controversial because of Sontag's claims about the progress of the disease. Research the current medical wisdom about AIDS, perhaps by reading about the most recent international AIDS conference. Then write an essay in which you show the extent to which Sontag's assumptions about the medical progress of AIDS are considered valid today.

# EVELYNN HAMMONDS
## Race, Sex, AIDS: The Construction of "Other"

―――――――――――――――――――――――――――――――――――――

*Like all highly stigmatized diseases, AIDS turns the world into "us" and "them." "They" — those with AIDS — are perceived as different and alien by those who do not have it. In this essay, Evelynn Hammonds analyzes the role that difference plays in the AIDS epidemic, especially racial and sexual difference, and how those differences have contributed to the social marginalization of people with AIDS. Would AIDS have been neglected as long as it was if its first victims were Boy Scouts, or any other group considered part of mainstream society? Or did the fact that the first people with AIDS hailed from the gay community and the black underclass contribute to a national policy of indifference? Hammonds, who writes on the intersection of science, medicine, and feminism, is currently assistant professor of the history of science at Massachusetts Institute of Technology.*

In March of this year [1987] when Richard Goldstein's article, "AIDS and Race — the Hidden Epidemic" appeared in the *Village Voice,* the following statement in the lead paragraph jumped out at me: "a black woman is thirteen times more likely than a white woman to contract AIDS, says the Centers for Disease Control; a Hispanic woman is at eleven times the risk. Ninety-one percent of infants with AIDS are non-white." My first reaction was shock. I was stunned to discover the extent and rate of spread of AIDS in the black community, especially given the lack of public mobilization either inside or outside the community. My second reaction was anger. AIDS is a disease that for the time being signals a death notice. I am angry because too many people have died and are going to die of this disease. The gay male community over these last several years has been transformed and mobilized to halt transmission and gay men (at least white gay men) with AIDS have been able to live and die with some dignity and self-esteem. People of color need the opportunity to establish programs and interventions to provide education so that the spread of this disease in our communities can be halted, and to provide care so that people of color with AIDS will not live and die as pariahs.

My final reaction was despair. Of course I *knew* why information about AIDS and the black community had been buried — by both the black and white media. The white media, like the dominant power structure, have moved into their phase of "color-blindness" as a mark of progress. This ideology buries racism along with race. In the case of AIDS and race, the problem with "color-blindness" becomes clear. Race remains a reality in this society, including a reality about how perception is structured. On the one hand, race blindness means a failure to develop educational programs and materials that speak in the language of our communities and recognize the position of people of color in relation to the dominant institutions of society: medical, legal, etc. Additionally, we must ask why the vast disproportion of people of color in the AIDS statistics hasn't been seen as a remarkable fact, or as worthy of comment. By their silence, the white media fail to challenge the age-old American myth of blacks as carriers of disease, especially sexually transmitted disease. This association has quietly become incorporated into the image of AIDS.

The black community's relative silence about AIDS is in part also a response to this historical association of blacks, disease, and deviance in American society. Revealing that AIDS is prevalent in the black community raises the spectre of blacks being associated with two kinds of deviance: sexually transmitted disease and homosexuality.

As I began to make connections between AIDS and race I slowly began to pull together pieces of information and images of AIDS that I had seen in the media. Immediately I began to think about the forty-year-long Tuskegee syphilis experiment on black men. I thought about the innuendoes in media reports about AIDS in Africa and Haiti that hinted at bizarre sexual practices among black people in those countries; I remembered how a black gay man had been portrayed as sexually irresponsible in a PBS documentary on AIDS; I thought about how little I had seen in the black press about AIDS and black gay men; I began to notice the thinly veiled hostility toward the increasing number of IV drug users with AIDS. Goldstein's article revealed dramatically the deafening silence about who was now actually contracting and dying from AIDS — gay/bisexual black and Hispanic men (now about 50% of black and Hispanic men with AIDS); many black and Hispanic IV drug users; black and Hispanic women, and black and Hispanic babies born to these women.

In this culture, how we think about disease determines who lives and    5
who dies. The history of black people in this country is riddled with episodes displaying how concepts of sickness, disease, health, behavior and sexuality, and race have been entwined in the definition of normalcy and deviance. The power to define disease and normality makes AIDS a political issue.

The average black person on the street may not know the specifics of concepts of disease and race but our legacy as victims of this construction means that we know what it means to have a disease cast as the result of the immoral behavior of a group of people. Black people and other people of color notice, pay attention to what diseases are cast upon us and why. As the saying goes — "when white people get a cold, black people get pneumonia."

In this article I want to address the issues raised by the white media's silence on the connections between AIDS and race; the black media's silence on the connections between AIDS and sexuality/sexual politics, the failure of white gay men's AIDS organizations to reach the communities of people of color, and finally the implications for gay activists, progressives, and feminists.

It is very important to outline the historical context in which the AIDS epidemic occurs in regards to race. The dominant media portrayals of AIDS and scientists' assertions about its origins and modes of transmission have everything to do with the history of racial groups and sexually transmitted diseases.

## The Social Construction of Disease

A standard feature of the vast majority of medical articles on the health of blacks was a sociomedical profile of a race whose members were rapidly becoming diseased, debilitated, and debauched and had only themselves to blame.[1]

---

1. James H. Jones, *Bad Blood: The Tuskegee Syphilis Experiment* (New York: Free Press, 1981), p. 21.

One of the first things that white southern doctors noted about blacks imported from Africa as slaves was that they seemed to respond differently than whites to certain diseases. Primarily they observed that some of the diseases that were epidemic in the South seemed to affect blacks less severely than whites — specifically, fevers (e.g., yellow fever). Since in the eighteenth and nineteenth centuries there was little agreement about the nature of various illnesses and the causes of many common diseases were unknown, physicians tended to attribute the differences they noted simply to race.

In the nineteenth century when challenges were made to the institution of slavery, white southern physicians were all too willing to provide medical evidence to justify slavery. 10

> They justified slavery and, after its abolition, second-class citizenship, by insisting that blacks were incapable of assuming any higher station in life. . . . Thus, medical discourses on the peculiarities of blacks offered, among other things, a pseudoscientific rationale for keeping blacks in their places.[2]

If, as these physicians maintained, blacks were less susceptible to fevers than whites, then it seemed fitting that they and not whites should provide most of the labor in the hot, swampy lowlands where southern agriculture was centered. Southern physicians marshalled other "scientific" evidence, such as measurement of brain sizes and other body organs to prove that blacks constituted an inferior race. For many whites these arguments were persuasive because "objective" science offered validity to their personal "observations," prejudices, and fears.

The history of sexually transmitted diseases, in particular syphilis, indicates the pervasiveness of racial/sexual stereotyping. The history of syphilis in America is complex, as Allan Brandt discloses in his book *No Magic Bullet*. According to Brandt, "venereal disease has historically been assumed to be the disease of the 'other.'" Obviously the complicated interaction of sexuality and disease has deep implications for the current portrayal of AIDS.

Like AIDS, the prevailing nineteenth century view of syphilis was characterized early on in moral terms — and when it became apparent that a high rate of syphilis occurred among blacks in the South, the morality issue heightened considerably. Diseases that are acquired through immoral behavior were considered in many parts of the culture as punishment from God, the wages of sin. Anyone with such a disease was stigmatized. A white person could avoid this sin by a change in behavior. But for blacks it was different. It was noted that one of the primary differences that separated the races was that blacks were more

---

2. *Ibid.*, p. 17.

flagrant and loose in their sexual behavior — behaviors they could not control.

> Moreover, personal restraints on self-indulgence did not exist, physicians insisted, because the smaller brain of the Negro had failed to develop a center for inhibiting sexual behavior.[3]

Therefore blacks deserved to have syphilis, since they couldn't control their behavior . . . the Tuskegee experiment carried that logic to [the] extreme — blacks also deserved to die from syphilis.

> [B]lacks suffered from venereal diseases because they would not, or could not, refrain from sexual promiscuity. Social hygiene for whites rested on the assumption that attitudinal changes could produce behavioral changes. A single standard of high moral behavior could be produced by molding sexual attitudes through moral education. For blacks, however, a change in their very *nature* seemed to be required.[4]

If in the above quotation, you change blacks to homosexuals and whites to heterosexuals then the parallel to the media portrayal of people with AIDS is obvious.

The black community's response to the historical construction of sexually transmitted diseases as the result of bad, inherently uncontrollable behavior of blacks — is sexual conservatism. To avoid the stigma of being cast with diseases of the "other," the black media, as well as other institutions in the community, avoid public discussion of sexual behavior and other "deviant" behavior like drug use. The white media on the other hand is often quick to cast blacks and people of color as "other" either overtly or covertly.

### Black Community Response to AIDS

Of 38,435 diagnosed cases of AIDS as of July 20, 1987, black and Hispanic people make up 39% of all cases even though they account for only 17 percent of the adult population.[5] Eighty percent of the pediatric cases are black and Hispanic. The average life expectancy after diagnosis of a white person with AIDS in the United States is two years; of a person of color, nineteen weeks.[6]

The leading magazines in the black community, *Ebony* and *Essence,* carried no articles on AIDS until the spring of this year. The journal of

---

3. *Ibid.,* p. 23.

4. *Ibid.,* p. 48.

5. "High AIDS Rate Spurring Efforts for Minorities," *New York Times,* Sunday, August 2, 1987.

6. *Mother Jones,* Vol. 12, May 1987.

the National Medical Association, the professional organization of black physicians, carried a short guest editorial article in late 1986 and to date has not published any extensive article on AIDS. The official magazines of the NAACP and the National Urban League make no mention of AIDS throughout 1986 nor to date this year. Only the Atlanta-based SCLC (Southern Christian Leadership Conference) has established an ongoing educational program to address AIDS in the black community.

When I examined the few articles that have been written about AIDS in the national black press, several themes emerged. Almost all the articles I saw tried to indicate that the black people are at risk while simultaneously trying to avoid any implication that AIDS is a "black" disease. The black media has underemphasized, though recognized, that there are significant socioeconomic cofactors in terms of the impact of AIDS in the black community. The high rate of drug use and abuse in the black community is in part a result of many other social factors — high unemployment, poor schools, inadequate housing, and limited access to health care, all factors in the spread of AIDS. These affect specifically the fact that people of color with AIDS are diagnosed at more advanced stages of the disease and are dying faster. The national black media have so far also failed to deal with any larger public policy issue that the AIDS crisis will precipitate for the community; and most importantly homosexuality and bisexuality were dealt with in a very conservative and problematic fashion.

## Testing

In terms of testing *Ebony* encourages more opportunity for people to be tested anonymously; *Essence* recommends testing for women thinking of getting pregnant. Both articles mention that exposure of test results could result in discrimination in housing and employment but neither publication discusses the issue at any length. There is no mention of testing that is going on in the military and how those results are being used nor is there mention of testing in prison. It is clear from the sketchy discussion of testing that the political issues around testing are not being faced.

## Sexuality

The most disappointing aspect of these articles is that by focusing on individual behavior as the cause of AIDS and by setting up bisexuals, homosexuals, and drug users as "other" in the black community, and as "bad," the national black media falls into the trap of reproducing exactly how white society has defined the issue. But unlike the situation for whites, what happens to these groups within the black community will affect the community as a whole. Repressive practices around AIDS in prisons will affect all black men in prison with or without AIDS and their families outside and any other black person facing the criminal justice system; the identification of significant numbers of people of color in the military with AIDS will affect all people of color in the military. Quarantine, suspension of civil liberties for drug users in the black community with AIDS, will affect everyone in the community. Health care and housing access will be restricted for all of us. If people with AIDS are set off as "bad" or "other," no change in individual behavior in relation to them will save any of us. There can be no "us" or "them" in our communities.

The *Ebony* article entitled "The Truth about AIDS: Dread Disease Is    20 Spreading Rapidly through Heterosexual Population," while highlighting the increase of AIDS among heterosexuals in the black community, makes several comments about black homosexuals. The author notes that there is generally a negative attitude toward homosexuals in the community and quotes several physicians who emphasize that the reticence on this issue is a hindrance to AIDS education efforts in the community. It does not emphasize that, because of this "reticence," only now as AIDS is being recognized as striking heterosexuals, is it beginning to be talked about in the black community.

> One of the greatest problems in the black community, other than ignorance about the disease, is the large number of black men who engage in sex acts with other men but who don't consider themselves homosexuals.[7]

The point is then that since AIDS was initially characterized as a "gay disease" and many black men don't consider themselves gay in spite of their sexual practices, the black community did not acknowledge the presence of AIDS.

The association of AIDS with "bad" behavior is prominent in this article. Homosexuals and drug users are described as a "physiologically and economically depressed subgroup of the black community."[8]

The message is that to deal with this disease the individual behavior of a deviant subgroup must be changed. Additionally, the recommendation to heterosexuals is to "not have sex" with bisexuals and drug users. There are no recommendations about how the community can find a way to deal with the silence around the issues of homosexuality/bisexuality, sexual practices in general, and drug use. The article fails to say what the implications of the sexual practices of black men are for the community.

The *Essence* article, entitled "Nobody's Safe," avoids the issue as well.[9] The authors describe a scenario of a thirty-eight-year-old middle-class professional woman who is suddenly found to have AIDS. Her hus-

---

7. *Ebony*, April 1987, p. 128, quoting a Los Angeles AIDS expert.
8. *Ibid.*, p. 130.
9. *Essence*, June 1987.

band had died two years earlier due to a rare form of pneumonia. After testing positive for AIDS she is told by one of her husband's relatives that he had been bisexual. The text following this scenario goes on to describe how most women contract AIDS; it gives a general sketch of the origins of the disease and discusses the latency period and defines asymptomatic carriers of the virus. There is no mention of bisexuality or homosexuality. The implication is again — just don't have sex with those people if you want to avoid AIDS. It avoids discussion of the prevalence of bisexuality among black men, and consequently the way that AIDS will ultimately change sexual relationships in the black community.

## The Mainstream (White) Press

In general the mainstream media have been silent on the rise of AIDS in the black and Hispanic communities. Until very recently, with the exception of a few special reports, such as a quite excellent one on the PBS *MacNeil-Lehrer Report,* most media reports on AIDS continue to speak of the disease without mention of its effects on people of color. In recent months specific attention has been paid to the "new" phenomenon of heterosexuals with AIDS or "heterosexual AIDS." This terminology is used without the slightest mention that among Haitians and extensively in Africa, AIDS was never a disease confined to homosexuals.

The assumption in reports about the spread of AIDS to heterosexuals   25 is that these heterosexuals are white — read that as white, middle-class, non-drug-using, sexually active people. The facts are that there are very few cases of AIDS among this group. As many as 90 percent of the cases of AIDS among heterosexuals are black and Hispanic. In many media reports blacks and Hispanics with AIDS are lumped in the IV drug users group. What the media has picked up on is that heterosexual transmission in the United States now endangers middle-class whites.

A good example of the mainstream media approach is an article by Kate Leishman in the February 1987 issue of *Atlantic Monthly.* She writes that most Americans, even liberals, have the attitude that AIDS is the result of immoral behavior. Leishman lists the statistics on heterosexual transmission of AIDS at the beginning of her article. Fifteen pages later the following information appears:

> In the case of sexually active gay men [AIDS] is a tragedy — as it is for poor black and Hispanic youths, among whom there is a nationwide epidemic of venereal disease, which is a certain cofactor in facilitating transmission of HIV. This combination with the pervasive use of drugs among blacks and Hispanics ensures that the epidemic will hit them hardest next.[10]

---

10. *Atlantic Monthly,* February 1987, p. 54.

Her first explicit mention of people of color describes them as a group that uses drugs extensively, and as also riddled with venereal disease (a fact she does not support with any data). The image is one of the "unregenerate young street tough" that causes all the trouble in our cities, in short the conventional racist stereotype of black and Hispanic youth displayed in the press almost every day. Her use of the word "tragedy" because of the risk to blacks, Hispanics, and gays is gratuitous at best. The main focus of the article is the risk of AIDS to white heterosexuals and the need for them to face their fears of AIDS so they can effectively change their behavior.

In a passage reminiscent of nineteenth-century physicians' moral advice she notes the problems associated with changing people's behavior and promoting safe sex, and wonders if one can draw any lessons for heterosexual behavior from the gay male experience.

> Many people believe that the intensity or quality of homosexual drives is unique, while others argue that the ability to control sexual impulses varies extraordinarily within groups of any sexual preference.[11]

What I find striking in this passage is that there is still debate over whether certain "groups" of people have the same ability to exercise control over their sexual behavior and drives as "normal" white heterosexuals do. The passage also suggests that white heterosexuals are still the only group who have the strength, the moral fortitude, the inherent ability if educated, to control their sexual and other behavior. After all, this is a disease about behavior and not viruses, right? Leishman doesn't interview any blacks or Hispanics about their fears of AIDS, or how they want to deal with it with respect to sexual practice or other behavior.

Two months later in May several letters to the editors of *Atlantic Monthly* appeared in response to Leishman's article. In particular one reader observed her omission of statistics about the risk of AIDS to blacks and Hispanics. She responded in a fairly defensive manner:

> My article and many others have commented on the high risk of exposure to AIDS among blacks and Hispanics. Mr. Patrick's observations that blacks and Hispanics already account for ninety percent of the case load seems oddly to suggest that AIDS is on its way to becoming a disease of minorities. But the Centers for Disease Control has stressed that the overrepresentation of blacks and Hispanics in AIDS statistics is related not to race per se but to underlying risk factors.[12]

The risk factor she mentions is intravenous drug use. Leishman fails to deal with the "overrepresentation" of blacks and Hispanics in AIDS statistics. To mention our higher risk only implies that AIDS is a disease of minorities if you believe minorities are inherently different or behave dif-

---

11. *Ibid.*, p. 40.
12. *Atlantic Monthly*, May 1987, p. 13.

ferently in the face of the disease or if you believe that the disease will be confined to the minority community.

So pervasive is the association of race and IV drug use that the fact     30
that a majority of black and Hispanic men who have AIDS are gay or bi-sexual, and *non*-IV drug users, has remained buried in statistics.[13] In the face of the statistics, the *New York Times* continues to identify IV drug use as the distinguishing mode of transmission among black and Hispanic men, by focusing not on the percentage of black and Hispanic AIDS cases that are drug related, but on the percentage of drug-related AIDS cases that are black or Hispanic, which is 94%. This framework, besides blocking information that the black and Hispanic communities need, also functions to keep the white community's image "clean."

## Conclusion

As this article goes to press, media coverage of the extent of AIDS in the black and Hispanic communities is increasing daily. These latest arti-cles are covering the efforts in the black and Hispanic communities both to raise consciousness in these communities with respect to AIDS and to increase government funding to support culturally specific educational programs. Within the black community, the traditional source of leader-ship, black ministers, are now publicly expressing the reasons for their previous reluctance to speak out about AIDS. The reasons expressed tend to fall into the areas I have tried to discuss in this article, as indicated by the following comments that recently appeared in the *Boston Globe:*

> Although some black ministers described gays as the children of God and AIDS as just another virus, many more talked about homo-sexuality as sinful, including some who referred to AIDS as a God-sent plague to punish the sexually deviant.[14]
>
> There's a lot of fear of stigmatization when you stand up. . . . How does this label your church or the people who go to your church? said Rev. Bruce Wall, assistant pastor of Twelfth Baptist Church in Roxbury. Rev. Wall said ministers may also fear that an activist role on AIDS could prompt another question: "Maybe that pastor is gay."[15]

The arguments I have made as to the background of these kinds of comments continue to come out in the public discourse on AIDS and race in the national media. As the public discussion and press coverage have increased, one shift is apparent. The media is now focussing on why the black and Hispanic communities have not responded to AIDS before as a

---

13. *New York Times,* Sunday, August 2, 1987.
14. *Boston Globe,* Sunday, August 9, 1987, p. 1.
15. *Ibid.,* p. 12.

"problem" specific to these communities, while there is no acknowledgment that part of the problem is the way the media, the CDC, and the Public Health Service prevented race-specific information about AIDS from being widely disseminated. Or, to say it differently, there is no recognition of how the medical and media construction of AIDS as a "gay disease" or a disease of Haitians has affected the black and Hispanic communities.

Finally, as the black and Hispanic communities mobilize against AIDS, coalitions with established gay groups will be critical. To date, some in the black community have noted the lack of culturally specific educational material produced by these groups. Some gay groups are responding to that criticism. For progressives, feminists and gay activists, the AIDS crisis represents a crucial time when the work we have done on sexuality and sexual politics will be most needed to frame the fight against AIDS in political terms that move the politics of sexuality out of the background and challenge the repressive policies and morality that threaten not only the people with this disease but all of us.

### Reading the Text

1. Why does Hammonds consider the ideology of "color-blindness" in the media to be a problem?
2. Why, according to Hammonds, has the black community remained silent about the AIDS epidemic?
3. What relationship does Hammonds see between syphilis and other sexually transmitted diseases and the stereotyping of blacks?
4. What is Hammonds's explanation for the relative lack of media coverage of the AIDS epidemic in the black and Hispanic communities?

### Reading the Signs

1. Compare and contrast the coverage of AIDS in the black press and in the white, or mainstream, press. To develop your essay, both refer to Hammonds's evidence and generate your own by analyzing current coverage of AIDS in popular magazines.
2. Go to the library and research the Tuskegee syphilis experiment that Hammonds describes and then write an essay in which you explore her claim that "'objective' science" has been used to support racist stereotypes.
3. Both Hammonds and Susan Sontag ("AIDS and Its Metaphors," p. 648) focus on the images and metaphors by which we understand the disease. Compare and contrast their analyses of this issue. Which author do you find more persuasive? How do differences in ethnicity affect the tone and purpose of their essays?
4. How might Sam Fulwood III ("The Rage of the Black Middle Class," p. 510) and bell hooks ("Madonna: Plantation Mistress or Soul Sister?,"

p. 223) respond to Hammonds's argument? Role-play a discussion among
Fulwood, hooks, and Hammonds in class, being sure to note issues on
which they are likely to differ as well as agree.

5. Compare Hammonds's analysis of the media coverage of the AIDS epidemic with that of Douglas Crimp ("Portraits of People with AIDS,"
p. 677). How do you account for any differences in their views?

D A N I E L  H A R R I S

*Making Kitsch from AIDS*

*AIDS is not only a disease, Daniel Harris (b. 1957) argues in this cri-
tique of the world of AIDS activism and fund-raising, it's an industry.
With the AIDS Quilt serving as his chief symbol of the way that the
epidemic has spawned an ever-growing list of AIDS "products," Harris
lambastes what he sees as the trivializing of the disease. Is AIDS just
another opportunity for America's consumer economy? A freelance writer
whose work has appeared in* Harper's, Salmagundi, Newsday, The
Antioch Review, *and* The Nation, *Harris's book* The Rise and
Fall of Gay Culture *is scheduled for publication in 1997.*

AIDS may be the first disease to have its own gift shop. Housed in
the Workshop Building of the AIDS Memorial Quilt — the acres of fabric that commemorate the deaths of thousands of AIDS victims — Under
One Roof is at the epicenter of the burgeoning industry of AIDS kitsch.
Catering to an upscale clientele beaming with good intentions, the store,
on Market Street in San Francisco's Castro District, peddles memento
mori as shamelessly as tourist traps peddle souvenirs: "Cuddle Wit" teddy
bears that sport tasteful red ribbons; Keith Haring tote bags; and T-shirts
stenciled with the words "We're Cookin' Up Love for People With
AIDS." The boutique also sells a unique line of AIDS-related sympathy
cards, including one picturing a seductive man leaning inconsolably
against a tombstone angel. Inside an unctuous caption that smacks of an
undertaker's condolences reads: "I wonder at times why some are chosen
to leave so soon. Then I remember who has left, and I know. God must
have wanted them home because he missed them." One of the store's
best-selling items is a macabre coffee-table book of the Quilt itself, lav-
ishly illustrated and presumably meant for bored guests to casually thumb
through while ignoring the presentation of death as political knickknack.

Although Under One Roof donates its profits to a variety of AIDS-relief organizations, commercial businesses have not hesitated to wrap their products in the shroud of AIDS to promote their own merchandise. Benetton, in the early 1990s, placed in glossy magazines an ad that featured a skeletal male figure, obviously dying of AIDS. Stretched out in a hospital bed, beneath a print of Jesus Christ, he is attended by a sobbing father, who clutches him like a rag doll, and a grief-stricken mother, who sits crumpled in despair. In the ad's left-hand corner several words sit quietly in mourning, like unbidden guests maintaining respectful silence in the company of the family's anguish; they read, "United Colors of Benetton . . . For the nearest Benetton store location call 1-800-535-4491."

AIDS kitsch now appears in mind-numbing variety: as rap songs and safe-sex brochures, as the panel in the Quilt representing an enormous airmail envelope addressed to "A Better Place," and as André Durand's painting *Votive Offering,* which depicts an ethereal Princess Di, amid saints and bathed in celestial light, placing her hands on an emaciated AIDS patient while dying men in surrounding hospital beds strain at their dripping IVs as if pleading to touch the hem of her skirt. AIDS has been so thoroughly sentimentalized that it inspires such publicity stunts as Elton John flying Ryan White to Disneyland or Miss America haunting AIDS wards, where she consoles dozens of victims like a beauty among lepers. Whoopi Goldberg has turned up at displays of the Quilt pushing around a man in a wheelchair, an image that serves as the allegorical emblem of the kitschification of AIDS; just as politicians dandle babies, so celebrities use patients in wheelchairs as props for photo opportunities that dramatize their generosity and humanitarianism. There now exists an entire social circuit of well-advertised benefits — like the dusk-to-dawn dance-a-thons held by New York City's Gay Men's Health Crisis — each of them masterminded by an expensive breed of charity-ball impresario. The events provide celebrities on the order of Marky Mark, Madonna, and Liza Minnelli with venues to shore up their credentials for tolerance or bolster their flagging careers.

Although terminal illnesses have often been sentimentalized — who can forget *Love Story* or *Brian's Song*? — the AIDS epidemic in particular encourages the production of kitsch, inviting the abuse of activists, yellow journalists, New Age healers, pop psychologists, holistic chiropractors, and Hollywood producers. Manufacturers of kitsch use gaudy cosmetics and stagy lighting to make the pathetic more pathetic, the sad sadder, transforming AIDS into a trite melodrama, a cozy bedtime story narrated in a teary singsong for the American public.

The proliferation of AIDS kitsch can be linked to the unusual conditions under which activists were initially forced to raise money for research, treatment, and education. Given the minimal federal response to the disease in the 1980s and the public's hostility to the epidemic's first casualties — homosexuals and IV drug users — activists used a barrage of cheap images specifically designed to elicit pity in order to persuade the

5

private sector to bear the financial burden. The epidemic was sold to the public, like the red-ribbon paperweights and ruby brooches sold at Under One Roof. The marketing campaign has proved highly successful; last year the Gay Men's Health Crisis and the American Foundation for AIDS Research, two of the larger AIDS organizations, together raised more than $45 million.

The propaganda surrounding AIDS has embraced kitsch precisely because of the means by which the disease is transmitted. Because AIDS has ravaged communities of people toward whom Americans have shown little compassion, the marketing of the AIDS "product" has involved considerable ingenuity, including a full-scale revision of the image of AIDS sufferers. Unlike less controversial illnesses, like multiple sclerosis or leukemia, AIDS is vulnerable to kitsch in part because of the urgent need to render the victim innocent. In order to thwart the demonization of gay men, activists have attempted to conceal sexual practices that the public at large finds unacceptable behind a counter-iconography that has the unfortunate side effect of filling the art and writings about AIDS with implausible caricatures of the victim as a beseeching poster child. The infantilization of the epidemic's victims has come to play an increasingly important role in AIDS propaganda, whether as the uplifting tendentiousness of a coloring book entitled *It's OK to Be . . . Me: A Cool Book About Life and Being HIV+* or as the mawkishness of the songs of HIV-positive children on the album *Answer the Call,* where piping choruses of quavering sopranos recite such plaintive lines as "We need love/We need compassion to live/We've got hugs/We've got kisses to give."

Among mainstream magazines, *People* has responded most strongly to the imperative to supply sanitized portraits of AIDS victims in the name of fostering an atmosphere of tolerance and understanding. The magazine played a pivotal role in the beatification of Ryan White, whom its editors transformed into a living Hallmark card, a modern version of Dickens's Tiny Tim wasting away on the hearth, racked by chills and a hacking cough. *People*'s bathetic accounts included tear-jerking scenes of mother and son kneeling in bedside prayer, and seemed to relish the gruesome decay of his frail body, which was described in prurient detail, from his dainty feet in "huge, furry 'Bigfoot' slippers" to "his tiny blue fingers," which he constantly warmed over the coils of his mother's electric stove. White appeared in *People*'s frequent profiles as an anachronistic piece of Victoriana, a poetic wraith who enjoyed wandering among the tombstones of his future burial place, the cemetery in Cicero, Indiana, which he preferred hands down — or so we were told — to the cheerless plots of Kokomo, the home of those despicable bigots who railroaded him from their ranks because of his disease.

Almost from the inception of the epidemic, AIDS propagandists have found themselves in a peculiar moral bind. On the one hand, they attempt to elicit compassion by portraying the victims of the disease as seraphic innocents, as Sylvia Goltaub does in her memoir, *Unconditional Love,* when, after returning to Florida from her son's funeral, she imagines that she sees him soaring like an angel outside of the window of the plane, waving his hand and saying, "Hi Mom! Hi Dad! Don't Worry! Be Happy!" At the same time, the epidemic's salesmen must avoid portraying HIV-positive people as bedridden invalids unable to fight for their own interests. Those who die are often embalmed in their obituaries in heroic clichés: "foot soldiers in the war against AIDS" who die after "beautiful battles" and "long and courageous struggles," exhibiting "tenacious spirit" and a "brave refusal to surrender." The representation of the AIDS victim thus oscillates between two extremes of stylization: the childish image of the guiltless martyr clutching his teddy bear and warming "his tiny blue fingers," and the "empowered" image of the stouthearted hero whose gutsy brinkmanship in the face of death is held up as a model of unshakable resolve and pitiless optimism — a punitively high standard of behavior, it should be noted, for people suffering from a deadly disease.

If the propaganda of AIDS activists targets the housewife in Topeka, another variety of kitsch addresses the AIDS victim himself. It is he who buys the distinct and highly "niched" line of the AIDS product sold by marketers exploiting not the lucrative emotion of pity but the more profitable one of panic. Taking advantage of the desperation of people grasping at straws, New Age healers and human-potential gurus have rushed to fill the void created by the failure of traditional medicine to resolve every health crisis it encounters. AIDS has been overrun with kitsch also because it has breathed new life into moribund New Age fads. Channelers now serve as conduits for the pronouncements of ancient "Beings of Disincarnate Intelligence," who, in certain circles, are touted as leading AIDS experts. Kevin Ryerson, for instance, is a "fully accredited" clairvoyant who channels a spirit known simply as Spirit, a sagacious entity who advises victims of the epidemic to tune their unbalanced chakras like musical instruments, using as a basis not "'C' of the major scale, but 'B,' and to proceed up the scale from there to A flat [since] this pitch is closer to the 'A' of 438 vibrations per second, which is the note that is sounded if one strikes the sarcophagus in the King's Chamber of the Great Pyramid." Spirit also encourages AIDS sufferers to buy his friend's meditation tapes.

The loss of faith in conventional medicine has generated intense nostalgia for a pre-medical era of witch doctors and medicine men. Contemporary internists have been rejected and replaced by anachronistic figures decked out in the costumes of modern medievalism — magicians and alchemists who perform primitive rituals. One of the masterpieces of AIDS kitsch, the independent film *Men in Love,* is suffused with the longing for an Edenic world without science, a peaceful land of docile lotus-eaters where grieving Californians spurn traditional medicine for

10

moonlit healing circles in Maui at which they don grass skirts, mutter in-
cantations, and dance like savages around a bonfire.

Even more appalling is the mindless optimism of the self-help and
human-potential movements. A bizarre dissonance occurs when the
bleak prognosis for the victims of the disease collides with the indiscrimi-
nately happy-go-lucky, can-do attitudes of pop psychology's euphoric
rhetoric, a dissonance perhaps best expressed in the testimonials by gay
men with AIDS who deny the imminence of their death and even claim
that the disease is, as one Bay Area patient put it in an interview in the
*San Francisco Examiner,* "the most wonderful thing that ever happened in
my life." This remarkable statement is echoed in a letter that a disciple of
the reigning messiah of alternative medicine, Louise Hay, wrote to an
anthropomorphized image of his disease:

> Dear AIDS,
>
> For so long now I've been angry with you for being part of my
> life. I feel like you have violated my being. The strongest emotion
> thus far in our relationship has been anger!!
>
> But now I choose to see you in a different light. I no longer hate
> you or feel angry with you. I realize now that you have become a
> positive force in my life. You are a messenger who has brought me a
> new understanding of life and myself. So I thank you, forgive you,
> and release you.
>
> Never before has anyone given me such great opportunity. . . .
> Because of you I have learned to love myself, and as a result I love
> and am loved by others. I am now in touch with parts of my being
> that I never knew existed. I have grown spiritually and intellectually
> since your arrival. . . . So again I thank you for giving me this oppor-
> tunity to have insight into my life. How could I not forgive you,
> when so many positive experiences have come from your visit.
>
> But you have also led me to the realization that you have no
> power over me. I am the power in my world. . . .
>
> > With love,
> > Paul

In the self-help treatment guide *Immune Power,* Dr. Jon D. Kaiser
even advises his clients to open up a regular correspondence with their
virus. The patient, playing the role of the disease, writes back like a pen
pal or a well-bred guest to thank its "hosts" "for sharing your feelings
with me" "[that I] have overstayed [my] welcome," adding that "I appreciate your thoughts and I am not offended by the bluntness of your
attitude toward me."

The banal euphemisms of pop psychology have turned much of the
self-help literature on the epidemic into black comedy. Prophets like
Hay and Kaiser attempt to incorporate their clients' illnesses into their
upbeat programs for self-actualization, as if the disease were simply another hurdle to be surmounted in the quest for personal growth. The

demagogues of what might be called the "empathy industry" promote the notion that we have full control of our lives, that there is no problem so overwhelming that a simple act of self-assertion will not ultimately lead to its resolution. The modern therapeutic paradigms from which AIDS profiteers derive their methods thus fail spectacularly to acknowledge tragedy and refuse to admit that anything could evade the resourcefulness of the human will.

Given the abundance of kitsch generated from AIDS profiteering, it is surprising that the genre in which you might expect to find kitsch remains relatively free of it: fiction. It is not that such authors as David Feinberg, Edmund White, Paul Monette, Robert Ferro, John Weir, and Christopher Coe are (or were) actually all that good; they simply avoid being all that *bad.* Their novels present few overwrought scenes of tearful bedside farewells, shocking expulsions by heartless parents of their ailing children, or much of the melodrama that so appeals to American tastes. (Not incidentally, perhaps, these novels have never hit the best-seller list.) In fact, it is precisely the fear of sentimentality that defines the fiction about AIDS and makes the literary depictions of the epidemic case studies in authorial restraint. Fiction writers' fear of kitsch is so strong that contemporary literature is in many ways immune to the tragedy of AIDS, inoculated against it by a tendency toward flippant ironizing, like the compulsive jocularity found in John Weir's *The Irreversible Decline of Eddie Socket.* Here, the dying protagonist struts and poses through his illness, embracing theatrical attitudes he self-consciously plagiarizes from Hollywood B films, like the addled femme fatale in Manuel Puig's *Kiss of the Spider Woman.*

Where AIDS novelists fear to tread, however, journalists and docu- 15 dramatists go without hesitation, demonstrating a ghoulish fascination for the narrative richness of the disease. In accounts as different as Dominique Lapierre's "epic story" *Beyond Love,* an absurd pot-boiler that turns the history of AIDS into a soap opera, and Randy Shilts's *And the Band Played On,* the journalism about the epidemic is paradoxically far more fictional than the fiction. The reporting relies on the need to invent scenes, re-create internal monologues, manufacture suspense, devise artful foreshadowings, and evoke menacing atmospheres. The mainstream media have found these methods so profitable that their impulse to novelize the disease has prevailed over their obligation to document it.

Nowhere do the kitschifying effects of narrative appear more clearly than in the HBO movie version of *And the Band Played On,* itself a tissue of reconstructed dialogues and internal soliloquies. Common sense might suggest that the book should have been interpreted as documentary, with footage from newsreels and interviews; instead, Hollywood created a fictional reenactment with an all-star cast headed by a soulful Richard Gere, an earthy Lily Tomlin, and a brooding Ian McKellen — slow death as entertainment.

While telling the story of the epidemic, journalists have often given readers an improbably intimate point of view. Assuming the perspective of an omniscient third-person narrator, reporters minimize our awareness of the necessarily secondhand nature of the facts they convey, allowing us to imagine that we are viewing the scene through a hidden camera. Thus, for instance, we are literally in the hospital when the grief-stricken wife described in the *Ladies' Home Journal* article entitled "AIDS & Marriage: What Every Wife *Must* Know" paces frantically up and down the echoing corridor keeping "a silent and solitary vigil" before her dying husband's quarantined room. Likewise, we become eavesdroppers in the mobile home — indeed, in the very *mind* — of the victim of the bigoted Southern town portrayed in *U.S. News & World Report*'s article "AIDS: When Fear Takes Charge," who prays as a teenager for God to make him straight ("'Please, dear Lord, change me,' Steve prayed nightly, as he lay in bed as a youth in his father's trailer").

Where the media have sold the epidemic as lurid melodrama, as medical theme park, or as morbid peep show, the organizers of the AIDS Memorial Quilt have sold their product as a nostalgic piece of folk art. The Quilt, a patchwork of cloth that can be visited like a grave site or a war memorial, is an extraordinary and often moving device that is in part intended to manipulate the way the disease is judged by the uninfected. Just as activists attempt to make the disease appealing to the consumer by counteracting homophobic stereotypes with desexed images of AIDS martyrs, so the Quilt wraps the epidemic's infantilized victims in what amounts to a macabre security blanket, an ideological shield. According to Cleve Jones, the Quilt's founder, this embodiment of "pure good," which emanates "coziness, humanity and warmth," "touch[es] people's hearts with something that is so pure and so clear in its message" that it creates an outpouring of compassion that helps fight discrimination.

We are meant to discuss this sacrosanct artifact in hushed tones of reverence, but in fact the Quilt is the sublime expression of AIDS kitsch. It evokes nostalgia for a simpler, more innocent time, a pastoral world of buggies and butter churns — an America that never existed. "From our earliest days," the jacket copy of the coffee-table book *The Quilt* proclaims, "the quilt and the quilting bee have been part of American life." Jones, his "eyes glisten[ing] with both sadness and pride," with the "tears that flow constantly," describes the Quilt — whose panels are individually stitched by the friends and families of those who have died of AIDS — as "a way for survivors to work through their grief in a positive, creative way." "We sew and . . . cry and . . . hold each other," a Quilt volunteer explains. Thus the merchants of the disease place its primary commemorative monument within the context of a wholesome tradition of American history, to create a kind of *faux* antique, the memento of an apocryphal Arcadia. In this mythic, prelapsarian America, AIDS sheds its stigma as the scourge of depraved homosexuals and is endowed instead with the integrity of our industrious Pilgrim forefathers. Nostalgia, the longing for a legendary, small-town America, is a fundamental component of AIDS kitsch, and the selling of the Quilt obeys one of the primary rules of marketing: the romanticization of handmade goods. The Quilt effectively exudes an aura of the homestead, of kindly old grannies in bifocals and bonnets stitching up a storm, plying a trade that harks back to the naive primitivism of *American Gothic*.

The images of folk art also provide a substitute for the iconography of the Christian Church. Almost from the onset of the disease, AIDS propagandists have urged us to vent our pent-up grief as part of a regular program of mental hygiene, as well as a means of publicizing the tragedy and rallying new supporters to the cause. Therapists, members of the activist group ACT UP, and other leaders of the gay community now teach us that the suppression of sorrow and rage is both psychologically damaging and politically retrograde, at once interfering with the "grieving process" and encouraging passivity and resignation.

Rather than using venerable Christian ceremonies to express sorrow, the gay community has sought in the marketplace new models for *secular* services. The new public rituals for collective mourning — healing circles, die-ins, and the Quilt — more closely resemble sensitivity groups or counseling sessions than wakes or masses. In place of the church, which many gay people rightly perceive as a bastion of homophobia, we have invented the Quilt, which appeases both our distrust of religion and our adoration of therapy. But the Quilt is cheapened by nostalgia, the homesickness of an industrial culture for an agrarian one, and our sacramental shroud reeks not of ecclesiastical incense but of the cloying inauthenticity of a shopping mall's Yarn Barn.

### Reading the Text

1. In your own words, summarize what Harris means by "AIDS kitsch."
2. According to Harris, what were the conditions surrounding the AIDS epidemic that led to the proliferation of kitsch? Why have other terminal diseases not produced the same sorts of images and products?
3. Why, in Harris's view, have mainstream media presented "sanitized portraits of AIDS victims"?
4. What is Harris's attitude toward the self-help movement, and why does he feel that way?
5. What is Harris's tone and how does it affect a reader's response to his essay?

### Reading the Signs

1. Visit your library and research the AIDS Quilt that Harris decries (see especially *The Quilt: Stories from the NAMES Project*). Then write an essay in which you analyze the Quilt semiotically. To what extent do you find Harris's belief that the Quilt is "the sublime expression of AIDS kitsch" to be valid?
2. In class, form teams and debate Harris's central contention that kitschy images and products effectively transform "AIDS into a trite melodrama, a cozy bedtime story narrated in a teary singsong for the American public." To develop your team's arguments, research and analyze some of the examples Harris mentions or some examples you find locally. You might, for instance, study any AIDS-related brochures available at your campus's student health center, or visit a local activist organization, such as ACT UP.
3. Read or reread Paul Monette's "Borrowed Time: An AIDS Memoir" (p. 641). Then, using Harris's arguments about AIDS kitsch as your critical framework, write an analysis that focuses on the extent to which Monette relies on melodrama or sentimentality to describe his personal crisis with AIDS.
4. Writing as if you were Cleve Jones, the originator of the AIDS Quilt, compose a letter to Harris in which you defend the Quilt from the charge that it "is cheapened by nostalgia."
5. Rent a videotape of *And the Band Played On* and then write a semiotic analysis of the film.

<br>

# DOUGLAS CRIMP
## *Portraits of People with AIDS*

||||||||||||||||||||||||||||||||||||||||||||||||||||||||||||||||

*Is AIDS art? Some photographers and art galleries think so, but Douglas Crimp isn't so sure. Arguing that AIDS patients have been exploited by well-intentioned, or perhaps not-so-well-intentioned, artists and journalists, Crimp castigates a world in which people with AIDS are often presented as suffering, marginalized, and even grotesque objects for pity. There are a lot of people living with AIDS who do not show the worst signs of the disease. Why not present their portraits, Crimp asks. A professor of Visual and Cultural Studies at the University of Rochester, Crimp is coauthor of* AIDS DemoGraphics *(with Adam Rolston), editor of* AIDS: Cultural Analysis/Cultural Activism, *coeditor of* How Do I Look? Queer Film and Video, *and author of* On the Museum's Ruins.

In the fall of 1988, the Museum of Modern Art in New York presented an exhibition of Nicholas Nixon's photographs called "Pictures of People." Among the people pictured by Nixon are people with AIDS (PWAs), each portrayed in a series of images taken at intervals of about a week or a month. The photographs form part of a larger work-in-progress, undertaken by Nixon and his wife, a science journalist, to, as they explain it, "tell the story of AIDS: to show what this disease truly is, how it affects those who have it, their lovers, families and friends, and that it is both the most devastating and the most important social and medical issue of our time."[1] These photographs were highly praised by reviewers, who saw in them an unsentimental, honest, and committed portrayal of the effects of this devastating illness. One photography critic wrote:

> Nixon literally and figuratively moves in so close we're convinced that his subjects hold nothing back. The viewer marvels at the trust between photographer and subject. Gradually one's own feelings about AIDS melt away and one feels both vulnerable and privileged to share the life and (impending) death of a few individuals. (Atkins, 1988)

Andy Grundberg, photography critic of the *New York Times,* concurred:

> The result is overwhelming, since one sees not only the wasting away of the flesh (in photographs, emaciation has become emblematic of AIDS) but also the gradual dimming of the subjects' ability to compose themselves for the camera. What each series begins as a conventional effort to pose for a picture ends in a kind of abandon; as the subjects' self-consciousness disappears, the camera seems to become invisible, and consequently there is almost no boundary between the image and ourselves. (1988, p. H37)

In his catalogue introduction for the show, MOMA curator Peter Galassi also mentions the relationship between Nixon and his sitters:

> Any portrait is a collaboration between subject and photographer. Extended over time, the relationship can become richer and more intimate. Nixon has said that most of the people with AIDS he has photographed are, perhaps because stripped of so many of their hopes, less masked than others, more open to collaboration. (Galassi, 1988, p. 26)

And, after explaining that there can be no representative portrait of a person with AIDS, given the diversity of those affected, he concludes, "Beside and against this fact is the irreducible fact of the individual, made

---

1. Nick and Bebe Nixon, "AIDS Portrait Project Update," January 1, 1988, quoted in the press release for "People with AIDS: Work in Progress," New York, Zabriskie Gallery, 1988 (this exhibition was shown at the same time as the MOMA show).

present to us in body and spirit. The life and death of Tom Moran [one of Nixon's subjects] were his own" (p. 27).

I quote this standard mainstream photography criticism to draw attention to its curious contradictions. All these writers agree that there is a consensual relationship between photographer and subject that results in the portraits' effects on the viewer. But is this relationship one of growing intimacy? Or is it one of the subjects' gradual tuning out, their abandonment of a sense of self? And is the result one of according the subjects the individuality of their lives and deaths? Or do their lives and deaths become, through some process of identification, ours?

For those of us who have paid careful attention to media representations of AIDS, none of this would appear to matter, because what we see first and foremost in Nixon's photographs is their reiteration of what we have already been told or shown about people with AIDS: that they are ravaged, disfigured, and debilitated by the syndrome; they are generally alone, desperate, but resigned to their "inevitable" deaths.

During the time of the MOMA exhibition, a small group from ACT UP, the AIDS Coalition to Unleash Power, staged an uncharacteristically quiet protest of Nixon's portraits. Sitting on a bench in the gallery where the photographs of PWAs were hung, a young lesbian held a snapshot of a smiling middle-aged man. It bore the caption, "This is a picture of my father taken when he'd been living with AIDS for three years." Another woman held a photograph of PWA Coalition cofounder David Summers, shown speaking into a bank of microphones. Its caption read, "My friend David Summers living with AIDS." They and a small support group spoke with museum visitors about pictures of PWAs and handed out a flier which read, in part:

### NO MORE PICTURES WITHOUT CONTEXT

We believe that the representation of people with AIDS affects not only how viewers will perceive PWAs outside the nuseum, but, ultimately, crucial issues of AIDS funding, legislation, and education.

In portraying PWAs as people to be pitied or feared, as people alone and lonely, we believe that this show perpetuates general misconceptions about AIDS without addressing the realities of those of us living every day with this crisis as PWAs and people who love PWAs.

FACT: Many PWAs now live longer after diagnosis due to experimental drug treatments, better information about nutrition and health care, and due to the efforts of PWAs engaged in a continuing battle to define and save their lives.

FACT: The majority of AIDS cases in New York City are among people of color, including women. Typically, women do not live long after diagnosis because of lack of access to affordable health care, a primary care physician, or even basic information about what to do if you have AIDS.

The PWA is a human being whose health has deteriorated not simply due to a virus, but due to government inaction, the inaccessibility of affordable health care, and institutionalized neglect in the forms of heterosexism, racism, and sexism.

We demand the visibility of PWAs who are vibrant, angry, loving, sexy, beautiful, acting up and fighting back.

STOP LOOKING AT US; START LISTENING TO US.

As against this demand — stop looking at us — the typical liberal 5 position has held, from very early in the epidemic, that one of the central problems of AIDS, one of the things we needed to combat, was bureaucratic abstraction. What was needed was to "give AIDS a face," to "bring AIDS home." And thus the portrait of the person with AIDS had become something of a genre long before a famous photographer like Nicholas Nixon entered the field. In the catalogue for an exhibition of another well-known photographer's efforts to give AIDS a human face — Rosalind Solomon's *Portraits in the Time of AIDS* (1988) — Grey Art Gallery director Thomas Sokolowski wrote of their perceived necessity: "As our awareness of [AIDS] grew through the accumulation of vast amounts of numerically derived evidence, we still had not seen its face. We could count it, but not truly describe it. Our picture of AIDS was a totally conceptual one . . ." (1988a, n.p.). Sokolowski's catalogue essay is entitled "Looking in a Mirror," and it begins with an epigraph quoted from the late George Whitmore, which reads, "I see Jim — and that could be me. It's a mirror. It's not a victim-savior relationship. We're the same person. We're just on different sides of the fence." With Sokolowski's appropriation of these sentences from a man who himself had AIDS, we are confronted once again — as with the texts written in response to the Nixon photographs — with a defense mechanism, which denies the difference, the obvious sense of otherness, shown in the photographs by insisting that what we really see is ourselves.

A remarkably similar statement begins a CBS *Sixty Minutes* newsmagazine devoted to AIDS, in which a service organization director says, "We know the individuals, and they look a lot like you, they look a lot like me." The program, narrated by CBS news anchor Dan Rather, is titled "AIDS Hits Home." Resonating with the assertion that PWAs look like you and me, the "home" of the show's title is intended to stand in for other designations: white, middle class, middle American, but primarily *heterosexual*. For this program was made in 1986, when, as Paula Treichler (1988) has written, "the big news — what the major U.S. news magazines were running cover stories on — was the grave danger of AIDS to heterosexuals" (p. 39).

"AIDS Hits Home" nevertheless consists of a veritable catalogue of broadcast television's by-then typical portraits of people with AIDS, for example, the generic or collective portraits, portraits of so-called risk groups: gay men in their tight 501s walking arm in arm in the Castro district of San Francisco; impoverished Africans; prostitutes, who apparently always work on streets; and drug addicts, generally shown only metonymically as an arm with a spike seeking its vein. Also included in this category of the generically portrayed in "AIDS Hits Home," however, are "ordinary" heterosexuals — ordinary in the sense that they are white and don't shoot drugs — since they are the ostensible subject of the show. But the heterosexual in AIDS reportage is not quite you and me. Since television routinely assumes its audience as heterosexual and therefore unnecessary to define or explain, it had to invent what we might call the heterosexual of AIDS. As seen on *Sixty Minutes,* the heterosexual of AIDS appears to inhabit only aerobics classes, discos, and singles bars, and is understood, like *all* gay men are understood, as always ready for, or readying for, sex. In addition, in spite of the proportionately much higher rate of heterosexually transmitted AIDS among people of color, the heterosexuals portrayed on *Sixty Minutes* are, with one exception, white.

"AIDS Hits Home"'s gallery of portraits also includes individuals, of course. These are the portraits that Dan Rather warns us of in the beginning of the program, when he says, "The images we have found are brutal and heartbreaking, but if America is to come to terms with this killer, they must be seen." For the most part, though, they are not seen, or only partially seen, for these are portraits of the ashamed and dying. As they are subjected to callous interviews and voice-overs about the particularities of their illnesses and their emotions, they are obscured by television's inventive techniques. Most often they appear, like terrorists, drug kingpins, and child molesters, in shadowy silhouette, backlit with light from their hospital room windows. Sometimes the PWA is partially revealed, as doctors and nurses manipulate his body while his face remains off-camera, although in some cases, we see *only* the face, but in such extreme close-up that we cannot perceive the whole visage. And in the most technologically dehumanizing instance, the portrait of the PWA is digitized. This is the case of the feared and loathed bisexual, whose unsuspecting suburbanite wife has died of AIDS. He is shown — or rather not shown — responding to an interlocutor who says, "Forgive me asking you this question, it's not easy, but do you feel in some way as if you murdered your wife?"

As we continue to move through the *Sixty Minutes* portrait gallery, we come eventually to those whose faces can see the light of day. Among these are a few gay men, but most are women. They are less ashamed, for they are "innocent." They or the narrator explain how it is that these perfectly normal women came to be infected with HIV: one had a boyfriend who used drugs, another had a brief affair with a bisexual, and another had a bisexual husband; none of them suspected the sins of their partners. And finally there are the most innocent of all, the white, middle-class hemophiliac children. They are so innocent that they can even be shown being comforted, hugged, and played with.

Among the gay men who dare to show their faces, one is particularly useful for the purposes of *Sixty Minutes,* and interestingly he has a counterpart in an ABC *20/20* segment of a few years earlier. He is the identical twin whose brother is straight. The double portrait of the sick gay man and his healthy straight brother makes its moral lesson so clear that it needs no elaboration.[2]

Indeed, the intended messages of "AIDS Hits Home" are so obvious that I don't want to belabor them, but only to make two further points about the program. First, there is the reinforcement of hopelessness. Whenever a person with AIDS is allowed to utter words of optimism, a voice-over adds a caveat such as: "Six weeks after she said this, she was dead." Following this logic, the program ends with a standard device. Dan Rather mentions the "little victories and the *inevitable* defeats," and then proceeds to tell us what has happened to each PWA since the taping of the show. This coda ends with a sequence showing a priest — his hand on the KS-lesion-covered head of a PWA — administering last rights. Rather interrupts to say, "Bill died last Sunday," and the voice of the priest returns: "Amen."

My second point is that the privacy of the people portrayed is both brutally invaded and brutally maintained. Invaded, in the obvious sense that these people's difficult personal circumstances have been exploited for public spectacle, their most private thoughts and emotions exposed. But at the same time, maintained: The portrayal of these people's personal circumstances never includes an articulation of the public dimension of the crisis, the social conditions that made AIDS a crisis and continue to perpetuate it as a crisis. People with AIDS are kept safely within the boundaries of their private tragedies. No one utters a word about the politics of AIDS, the mostly deliberate failure of public policy at every level of government to stem the course of the epidemic, to fund biomedical research into effective treatments, provide adequate health care and housing, and conduct massive and ongoing preventive education campaigns. Even when the issue of discrimination is raised — in the case of children expelled from school — this too is presented as a problem of individual fears, prejudices, and misunderstandings. The role of broadcast television in creating and maintaining those fears, prejudices, and misunderstandings is, needless to say, not addressed.

It is, then, not merely faceless statistics that have prevented a sympathetic response to people with AIDS. The media have, from very early in

---

2. For both *Sixty Minutes* and *20/20,* the ostensible reason for showing the twins is to discuss an experimental bone marrow transplant therapy, which requires an identical twin donor. It does not, of course, require that the donor twin be straight.

the epidemic, provided us with faces. Sokolowski acknowledges this fact in his preface to the Rosalind Solomon catalogue:

> Popular representations of AIDS have been devoid of depictions of people living with AIDS, save for the lurid journalistic images of patients *in extremis,* published in the popular press where the subjects are depicted as decidedly *not* persons *living* with AIDS, but as victims. The portraits in this exhibition have a different focus. They are, by definition, portraits of individuals with AIDS, not archetypes of some abstract notion of the syndrome. Rosalind Solomon's photographs are portraits of the human condition; vignettes of the intense personal encounters she had with over seventy-five people over a ten-month period. "I photographed everyone who would let me, who was HIV-positive, or had ARC, or AIDS . . . they talked to me about their lives."
>
> The resulting seventy-five images that comprise this exhibition provide a unique portrait gallery of the faces of AIDS. (1988a, n.p.)

The brute contradiction in this statement, in which "portraits of individuals with AIDS, not archetypes of some abstract notion" is immediately conflated with "portraits of the human condition" — as if that were not an abstract notion — is exacerbated in Sokolowski's introductory text, where he applies to the photographs interpretations that read as if they were contrived as parodies of the art historian's formal descriptions and source mongering. In one image, which reminds Sokolowski of Watteau's *Gilles,* we are asked to "contemplate the formal differences between the haphazard pattern of facial lesions and the thoughtful placement of buttons fastened to the man's pullover" (1988b). He completes his analysis of this photograph by comparing it with an "early fifteenth-century *Imago Peitatis* of the scourged Christ." Other photographs suggest to him the medieval *Ostentatio Vulneris,* the *Momento Mori,* the *Imago Clipeata,* and the image of the *Maja* or Venus.

Clearly when viewing Solomon's photographs most of us will not    15
seek to place them within art historical categories. Nor will we be struck by their formal or compositional interest. Rather, many of us will see in these images, once again, and in spite of Sokolowski's insistence to the contrary, the very representations we have grown accustomed to in the mass media. William Olander, a curator at New York's New Museum of Contemporary Art who died of AIDS on March 18, 1989, saw precisely what I saw:

> The majority of the sitters are shown alone; many are in the hospital; or at home, sick, in bed. Over 90% are men. Some are photographed with their parents, or at least their mothers. Only four are shown with male lovers or friends. For the photographer, "The thing that became very compelling was knowing the people — knowing them as individuals. . . ." For the viewer, however, there is little to know other than their illness. The majority of sitters are clearly ravaged by

the disease. (No fewer than half of those portrayed bear the most visible signs of AIDS — the skin lesions associated with Kaposi's sarcoma.) Not one is shown in a work environment; only a fraction are depicted outside. None of the sitters is identified. They have no identities other than as victims of AIDS. (1988, p. 5)[3]

But giving the person with AIDS an identity as well as a face can also be a dangerous enterprise, as is clear from the most extended, and the most vicious, story of a person with AIDS that American television has thus far presented: the notorious episode of PBS *Frontline*, "AIDS: A National Inquiry." "This is Fabian's story," host Judy Woodruff informs us, "and I must warn you it contains graphic descriptions of sexual behavior." One curious aspect of this program, given its ruthlessness, is its unabashed self-reflexivity. It begins with the TV crew narrating about itself, apparently roaming the country in search of a good AIDS story: "When we came to Houston, we didn't know Fabian Bridges. He was just one of the faceless victims." After seeing the show, we might conclude that Fabian would have been better off if he'd remained so. "AIDS: A National Inquiry" is the story of the degradation of a homeless black gay man with AIDS at the hands of virtually every institution he encountered, certainly including PBS. Fabian Bridges was first diagnosed with AIDS in a public hospital in Houston, treated, released, and given a one-way ticket out of town — to Indianapolis, where his sister and brother-in-law live. They refuse to take him in, because they're afraid for their young child, about whom the brother-in-law says, "He doesn't know what AIDS is. He doesn't know what homosexuality is. He's innocent." Arrested for stealing a bicycle, Fabian is harassed and humiliated by the local police, who are also under the illusion that they might "catch" AIDS from him. After a prosecutor drops the charges against him, Fabian is once again provided with a one-way ticket out of town, this time to Cleveland, where his mother lives. But in Indianapolis, a police reporter has picked up the story, and, as the *Frontline* crew informs us, "It was Kyle Niederpreun's story that first led us to Fabian. It was a story about the alienation and rejection that many AIDS victims suffer" — an alienation and rejection that the crew seemed all too happy to perpetuate.

*Frontline* finally locates its "AIDS victim" in a cheap hotel room in Cleveland. "We spent several days with Fabian," the narrator reports, "and he agreed to let us tell his story." Cut to Fabian phoning his mother in order that her refusal to let him come home can be reenacted for the video camera. "He said he had no money," the crew goes on, "so sometimes we bought him meals, and we had his laundry done. One day

---

3. William Olander (1988), "'I Undertook this Project as a Personal Exploration of the Human Components of an *Alarming Situation*' 3 Vignettes (2)." The quote used as a title is Rosalind Solomon's.

Fabian saw a small portable radio he liked, so we bought it for him." The narration continues, "He spent time in adult bookstores and movie houses, and he admitted it was a way he helped support himself." Then, in what is surely the most degrading invasion of privacy ever shown on TV, Fabian describes, on camera, one of his tricks, ending with the confession, "I came inside him . . . accident . . . as I was pulling out, I was coming." "After Fabian told us he was having unsafe sex, we faced a dilemma," the narrator explains. "Should we report him to authorities or keep his story confidential, knowing that he could be infecting others? We decided to tell health officials what we knew."

At this point begins the story *Frontline* has really set out to tell, that of the supposed conflict between individual rights and the public welfare.[4] It is a story of the futile attempts of health officials, policemen, and the vice squad to lock Fabian up, protected as he is by troublesome civil rights. A city council member in Cleveland poses the problem: "The bottom line is we've got a guy on the street here. The guy's got a gun and he's out shootin' people. . . . What do we say collectively as a group of people representing this society?" But while the city council contemplates its draconian options, the disability benefits Fabian had applied for several months earlier arrive, and after a nasty sequence involving his sadly ill-counseled mother, who has momentarily confiscated the money in order to put it aside for Fabian's funeral, Fabian takes the money and runs.

By now *Time* magazine has published a story on what it calls this "pitiful nomad," and the local media in Houston, where Fabian has reappeared, have a sensational story for the evening news. The *Frontline* crew finds him, homeless and still supporting himself as a hustler, so, they report, "We gave him $15 a night for three nights to buy a cheap hotel room. We gave him the money on the condition that he not practice unsafe sex and that he stay away from the bathhouses." Pocketing the generous gift of $45, Fabian continues to hustle, and the vice squad moves in to enforce an order by the Houston health department, issued in a letter to Fabian, that he refrain from exchanging bodily fluids. But now the vice squad, too, faces a dilemma. "Catch 22," one of the officers says. How do you entrap someone into exchanging bodily fluids without

---

4. The fascination of the media with the supposed threat of "AIDS carriers" was most dramatically revealed in the response to Randy Shilts's *And the Band Played On,* which focused almost exclusively on Shilts's story of the so-called Patient Zero (see my essay "How to Have Promiscuity in an Epidemic," in *AIDS: Cultural Analysis/Cultural Activism,* esp. pp. 237–246). The fascination has clearly not abated. At the Sixth International Conference on AIDS in San Francisco, June 20–24, 1990, members of the media took part in a panel addressing "AIDS and the Media: A Hypothetical Case Study." The hypothetical case was that of an American soldier stationed in the Philippines accused of infecting 40 prostitutes. The soldier's "past" had him frequenting prostitutes in Uganda and bathhouses in the Castro district of San Francisco.

endangering yourself? They decide to get Fabian on a simple solicitation charge instead, to "get him to hit on one of us," as they put it, but Fabian doesn't take the bait.

Ultimately a leader of the gay community decides on his own to try     20 to help Fabian, and a lawyer from the Houston AIDS Foundation offers him a home, developments about which the Houston health commissioner blandly remarks, "It would never have occurred to me to turn to the gay community for help." But *Frontline* has now lost its story. As the narrator admits, "The gay community was protecting him from the local press and from us." There is, nevertheless, the usual coda: "The inevitable happened. Fabian's AIDS symptoms returned. Just one week after he moved into his new home, he went back into the hospital. This time, he stayed just over a month. Fabian died on November 17. His family had no money to bury him, so after a week he was given a pauper's funeral and buried in a county grave."

Judy Woodruff had introduced this program by saying, "The film you are about to see is controversial; that's because it's a portrait of a man with AIDS who continued to be promiscuous. In San Francisco and other cities, the organized gay community is protesting the film, because they say it is unfair to persons with AIDS." This strikes me as a very ambiguous reason to protest, and I have no doubt that the organized gay community's position against the film was articulated more broadly. How is it unfair to persons with AIDS? What persons with AIDS? Isn't the film unfair, first and foremost, to Fabian Bridges? The true grounds on which I imagine the gay community protested are the dangerous insinuations of the film: that the public health is endangered by the free movement within society of people with AIDS; that gay people with AIDS irresponsibly spread HIV to unsuspecting victims. They might also have protested the film's racist presumptions and class biases, its exploitation not only of Fabian Bridges but of his entire family. In addition, it seems hard to imagine a knowledgeable person seeing the film who would not be appalled at the failure of PBS to inform its audience of the extraordinary misinformation about AIDS conveyed by virtually every bureaucratic official in the film. And finally I imagine the gay community protested the film because it is so clear that the filmmakers were more interested in getting their footage than in the psychological and physical welfare of their protagonist, that instead of leading him to social service agencies or AIDS service organizations that could have helped him and his family, they lured him with small bribes, made him dependent upon them, and then betrayed him to various authorities. A particularly revealing sequence intercut toward the end of the film takes us back to Fabian's hotel room in Cleveland. "We remembered something he'd said to us earlier," the narrator says, and Fabian then intones in his affectless voice, "Let me go down in history as being . . . I am somebody, you know, somebody that'll be respected, somebody who's appreciated, and somebody who can be related to, because a whole lot of people just go, they're not even on the map, they just go."

Here we have explicitly the terms of the contract between the *Frontline* crew and Fabian Bridges. *Frontline* found in Fabian, indeed, the "alienation and rejection" that many people with AIDS suffer, and offered him the false means by which our society sometimes pretends to grant transcendence of that condition, a moment of glory in the mass media. They said to this lonely, ill, and scared young man, in effect, "We're gonna make you a star."

### Reading the Text

1. According to Crimp, what image of AIDS patients have photographers perpetuated?
2. Why, in Crimp's description, did ACT UP object to the MOMA exhibition "Pictures of People"?
3. Summarize in your own words Crimp's objection to the PBS documentary "AIDS: A National Inquiry."
4. How would you characterize Crimp's tone, and how does it affect your response to his argument?

### Reading the Signs

1. In your journal, describe how you would portray people with AIDS if you were a photographer working on assignment for a popular magazine such as *Time* or *Newsweek*.
2. In class, discuss what sort of art exhibit on the AIDS epidemic Douglas Crimp would prefer.
3. Like many AIDS activists, Crimp insists that the media's portrayal of "hopelessness" of AIDS is unfair. Write an essay supporting, qualifying, or rejecting Crimp's position on this issue. To develop your ideas, you might read or reread Susan Sontag's "AIDS and Its Metaphors" (p. 648) and Daniel Harris's "Making Kitsch from AIDS" (p. 669).
4. Write an essay in which you agree or disagree with the contention that Crimp's argument is an example of political correctness.
5. Both Crimp and Daniel Harris ("Making Kitsch from AIDS," p. 669) discuss the ways in which people with AIDS are represented in the media. Write an essay in which you evaluate the comparative effectiveness of their arguments. Which author do you find more persuasive and why?
6. Rent a videotape of the Magic Johnson AIDS video, *Time Out,* and then show it in class. Analyze semiotically the video's depiction of the disease. What images does the video use, and what is their social significance? How might Crimp or Evelynn Hammonds ("Race, Sex, AIDS: The Construction of 'Other,'" p. 658) respond to the video?

ELINOR BURKETT

*Lights, Camera . . . Death*

<hr>

||||||||||||||||||||||||||||||||||||||||||||||||||

*Pedro Zamora led a remarkable life — and death. A Cuban immigrant who came to America as a child in the Mariel Boat Lift of 1980, Zamora was chosen by MTV to portray a handsome HIV-positive young man on its show* Real World. *But as Elinor Burkett points out, having made a star of Pedro Zamora, MTV was not around to film his final hours. Was it helpful, Burkett asks, to make AIDS seem so glamorous to impressionable viewers? Why not also show them what Zamora's final days were like? A former university professor and reporter at the* Miami Herald *from 1988–1992, Burkett has been one of the few principal AIDS reporters for a major American newspaper. Author of* The Gravest Show on Earth *(1996), from which this selection was excerpted, she is also coauthor (with Frank Bruni) of* A Gospel of Shame: Child Sexual Abuse and the Catholic Church *(1993).*

Teenagers hanging out on Washington Avenue pointed and stared as twenty-six-year-old Sean Sasser sauntered around Miami's South Beach. Twentysomethings on Rollerblades — the terrors of the sidewalks — stopped to say hello. Strangers in restaurants sent waitresses over to ask for his autograph.

"How's Pedro?" everyone wanted to know.

Sean gritted his teeth and muttered, "Hanging in there."

The truth was that at that moment in October 1994 his partner, Pedro Zamora, was lying in bed in a corner room at Mercy Hospital, paralyzed on his left side. He could no longer speak. He would no longer eat. Sometimes his friends and family could pull him out of his semiconscious state, but only with difficulty. Even then, when he opened his eyes and held on to the nearest hand, no one was entirely sure that Pedro knew where he was or who his visitors were. His physician said that only 10 percent of his brain was functioning.

The kids on Rollerblades and in trendy cafes already knew the full    5
details of Pedro's condition when they accosted Sean. Pedro's imminent demise was the lead story on the local news, complete with the kind of graphic that stations design for continuing coverage of an event. "Pedro's Final Battle," Channel 4, the NBC affiliate, called it. The accompanying photograph of his once devastatingly handsome visage bore no resemblance to the gaunt death mask Pedro's face had become.

Despite Pedro's ordeal, no one in a neighborhood where Sylvester Stallone and Sandra Bernhart are regulars hesitated to pursue Sean. So what if Sean was in town for a wake and a funeral, not a day at the beach and a night posturing at the nation's hippest clubs? They could touch him, feel connected to a myth and go home and brag to their friends. Sean and Pedro weren't people, after all. They were stars. And this was the price they were paying for that stardom, a stardom based on Pedro's imminent death.

Pedro Zamora and Sean Sasser were America's first tragic romance of AIDS. Both men had spent years of their young lives trudging from classroom to classroom, from PTA meeting to political caucus warning young people of the dangers of AIDS. Pedro, a high school track star and honor student with a poise and sense of public duty decades beyond his years, got his start the afternoon he walked into the office of his high school counselor and suggested that Miami's Hialeah High School should begin AIDS education.

"That's a really good idea, Pedro," said the counselor, trying to be supportive of student initiative but unable to conceal entirely the condescension creeping into his voice. "But it's not necessary. We don't have that problem here."

Pedro, always polite and dignified, responded in a calm voice. "Yes we do," he said. "I have it."

Sean's career as an AIDS educator began the day he was due to ship    10
out for training in the U.S. Navy's nuclear program. He stopped by the recruitment office to pick up his file and board the bus for the airport. His papers weren't with those of the other men. The woman behind the desk found them in a different box and, with a pained look on her face, sent him into another room. "You're not eligible for enlistment," a medical officer told him sternly. "We found HIV in your blood."

Sean had been having sex with older men, but with the brash self-confidence of an adolescent who believes himself invulnerable to disaster, the bright young man — he was a student at the University of Chicago — had never considered the possibility that he might become infected. The Detroit high school from which he had graduated in 1986 never bothered to mention AIDS in its sex education or health classes.

Once they had turned their personal tragedies into an opportunity for education, both Pedro and Sean drew honor and praise from the small communities of the AIDS-aware across the nation. Pedro spoke before the U.S. Congress. Sean was photographed by the celebrity photographer Annie Leibovitz. That portrait became an AIDS poster in San Francisco that read: "Testing HIV positive was a wake-up call for me. Today I have a clearer idea of who I am and what I want from life. I think everything will be okay. I have no plans of disappearing any time soon."

At some point along the way, Pedro and Sean also became commodities, in a process so subtle and seductive they could neither fully register nor resist it, a process that sometimes distorted or completely obscured their initial message.

Maybe that point came when MTV realized that an HIV-positive gay man might sell more Ikea furniture than just another nouveau clubby, and invited Pedro to join the rotating cast of the hip and glam station's *Real World,* a cross between a documentary and a soap opera, created by throwing seven people in their twenties into a house and chronicling their interactions and adventures. Pedro's courtship of Sean was filmed in full color and aired to an audience of 1.5 million viewers whose demographics made advertisers drool. His visits to schools were broadcast, as was his growing illness. When Pedro went to the doctor, MTV was in the examining room. When Pedro was diagnosed with pneumonia, MTV was in the hospital.

He was featured on the cover of *POZ* magazine, molded into a sexy 15 symbol that HIV does not equal ugly. Before he fell ill, a modeling agency had been looking for the ideal product match. *Real World* aired Pedro and Sean's commitment ceremony — the best a Cuban refugee and an African American from Detroit could manage in a country still unable to cope with the concept of two men marrying. After Pedro was hospitalized, agents and producers began planning the made-for-TV movie.

Pedro never had any money. After graduating from high school, he sold suits at Burdine's department store, then lived on a $300-a-week stipend from Body Positive, a Miami AIDS resource center. When he arrived in San Francisco to begin filming *Real World,* his wallet was empty. His salary from MTV came in a lump sum at the end of his five-month contract.

He could hardly begin to spend it in the few months before he found himself dying in a bed at Mercy Hospital in Miami, and his growing celebrity brought benefits he could no longer enjoy. Mercy Hospital moved another patient out of the prime corner room on its AIDS wing to give their most famous patient the most commodious accommodations. President Bill Clinton called. The local archbishop, a fervent anti-homosexual zealot, dropped by. Mary Fisher, who barely knew the young man and whose distant affection for him was decidedly not returned, flew in from Washington. After coming out as HIV positive at the Republican National Convention in 1992, she had fashioned herself a kind of Miss Congeniality of the AIDS pageant. This duty went along with the crown.

So many strangers called and stopped in for a chance to see a bona fide celebrity buckling under a big-time disease that the hospital had to give Pedro an alias. Middle school students who had heard Pedro's speeches pooled their lunch and video-game money to send to his trust fund. Hollywood dressed up in red ribbons and held a gala fundraiser.

Curiously absent were the MTV cameras. The station would hardly air scenes of nurses changing Pedro's diapers hourly to remove the diarrhea that poured out of his body, or scenes of family members gasping and crying as Pedro suffered yet another set of convulsions. They would hardly have complemented his image as the nation's HIV poster boy, so his death seemed as melodramatically unreal as the final swoon of Marilyn Monroe.

Pedro Zamora, a shy kid who left Cuba on a trawler in 1980 and be-    20
came the Person with AIDS that young America embraced, died on November 11, 1994, five years and one day after he learned he was infected with HIV. It marked the loss of an extraordinary individual, but not an end to his ruthless commodification.

Congresswoman Ileana Ros-Lehtinen took public credit for Pedro's deathbed reunion with his Cuban relatives. His physician, Dr. Corklin Steinhart, held yet another press conference, enjoying the best free advertising a doctor could imagine. Two of his MTV co-stars hired an agent to help them build mini-careers on the lecture circuit off their friendship with Pedro. Reverend Fred Phelps, a Baptist rabble-rouser who had been disavowed by most of his fellow fundamentalists, staged a protest at Pedro's memorial service. And millions of Americans cried, convinced that because they'd had a crush on Pedro, they had compassion for AIDS. . . .

Pedro Zamora was hardly born for fame. No one from his decaying neighborhood on the outskirts of Havana had ever made it to national prominence, even on that island. And rags-to-riches, or rags-to-fame, stories are hardly the true-to-life fare of late-twentieth-century America.

He was just another anonymous immigrant among the 125,000 Cubans who were packed into yachts and trawlers in the spring of 1980 when Fidel Castro opened the port of Mariel and invited the island's "scum" to depart for capitalism's shores. Pedro's father, Hector, who worked in a warehouse, accepted the invitation for himself and his wife, Zoraida, for eight-year-old Pedro, fifteen-year-old Milagros, twelve-year-old Jesus and their grandmother.

Pedro often said that May 30, 1980, the day of his journey, was the worst of his life, even worse than the day a nurse sat him down and told him he was HIV positive. It wasn't just the press of thieves, rapists and crazies who were his fellow passengers on the thirteen-hour trip to Key West on the *Cynthia D.* It was saying goodbye to the five brothers and sisters who stayed behind, to the familiar, to the warmth of enormous family dinners and parties and outings.

It will be all right, Hector had assured his youngest. By next year    25
Castro will be gone and we'll all be together again.

It never became all right. Castro didn't fall, in one year, in five, or ten. Pedro mastered English and became yet another of the thousands of Miami Cuban kids who translate the realities of America for their parents. They all delighted in the luxury of knowing that the supermarkets always had food on their shelves, but the breakup of the family was a gnawing pain. When Pedro's mother had one of her crying spells, it fell to her baby to dance with her.

Then, in the spring of 1983, the pretty mole that Hector had long admired on Zoraida's face began to change. In June she was diagnosed with cancer. Two years later, without cooking any more of her famous dinners, she was dead.

Four years later, Pedro received a letter asking him to call the Red Cross about the blood he'd donated during a drive at Hialeah High School. He ignored it. He received another letter. He ignored that as well. He finally screwed up his courage and went to the family doctor. He'd heard of AIDS; he vaguely remembered a lecture on the disease from when he was in seventh grade. But it seemed to have nothing to do with the lives of junior high school students in suburban Hialeah. He'd put the handout on AIDS with his other classroom notes and forgotten it.

He was stunned when the doctor told him the news, although he shouldn't have been. Soon after his mother's death, promiscuity became his escape from reality, and embraces from strangers became a sad substitute for hugs from his mother. In Pedro's case, the strangers were the older men he found in the bars and bath houses that he used as refuges from grief.

An awareness of AIDS did not accompany him there. "I could       30 never connect a face with the disease," he said in an interview just months after his diagnosis. "No one ever sat me down and talked about AIDS. Our parents and teachers told us to have safe sex, but no one ever explained to me how. If they had, maybe I wouldn't be in this situation now."

Several weeks later, Pedro delivered the news to his father. "I looked at my son, my beautiful son, and saw a corpse," said Hector Zamora, who had spent his entire time in the United States caring for his dying wife, worrying about his children in Cuba and cutting grass, working construction and struggling in factories. "I thought, why can't it be me. I'm old. I've lived my life. Please, God, let us trade places."

After his mother's death, Pedro had buried his sorrow in a frenzy of school activities. If he kept himself busy, he could sometimes forget his mother's death. By the time he turned thirteen, he was a star athlete and student — president of the science club, Student of the Month in the city of Hialeah, captain of the cross-country team, member of the honor society. The teachers loved him. The girls were crazy for those eyes that seemed both wise and incredibly sexy. He'd become the family's hope. Pedro would never dirty his hands with the manual labor that had kept the Zamoras going. He'd go to college and be a doctor, a lawyer, an executive.

By the time he received that fateful letter from the Red Cross, Pedro had adjusted to the loss of his mother. He was no longer spending his evenings looking for somebody, anybody, to give him affection.

But is was already too late. For Pedro, AIDS meant death, so he prepared himself for the end. Within four months, the seventeen-year-old had worked himself into such anxiety that he wound up in the hospital — not with any AIDS-related ailment but with shingles, from the stress.

By the end of his two-month hospital stay, he discovered an antidote 35 to the stress and the despair — anger, "at the government for not caring, at people for not seeing us as real people with a real disease, at society for not teaching us anything about AIDS," he said.

Pedro never planned to leverage that anger, or his diagnosis, into celebrity status. He didn't make any plans at all. Things just seemed to happen to a boy who was extraordinarily handsome and couldn't abide ignorance. During summer school just before his graduation, Pedro sat in a classroom and heard one of those typical student discussions of gays. The word "faggot" cropped up. Pedro tensed. One boy bragged about gay bashing. Pedro exploded, although in the hushed tones his intensity always demanded.

"I'm gay," he announced. He began talking about his life as a gay man, about being HIV positive. He didn't stop for the remaining four years of his life.

Pedro had no talent for the kind of righteous indignation that fueled most activists. Yelling simply wasn't his style. Talking was. He was acutely aware of his heavily accented English, of being an immigrant kid who'd lost his mother and his family, who'd been sexually abused as a young child and sexually used by forty-year-old men at the most vulnerable time in his life.

But when he opened his mouth to speak to journalists, elementary school students, even members of Congress, he was dazzling. "He never clears his throat, repeats the question or employs any of the standard stalling-for-time tactics," said Hal Rubenstein, the *New York Times* reporter who interviewed him for *POZ* magazine in 1994. "His speech is devoid of hmms, huhs, let-me-thinks and, sometimes, when he's really zooming, even breath."

Pedro was pulled into a vortex that overwhelmed him. At first the 40 pull was merely local. Pedro would take time off from his job selling suits at Burdine's to talk to public school kids about HIV and AIDS. Warning them was both a mission and personal therapy. "The anger, the pain," he said. "I don't want anyone else to have to feel this way." After his story appeared in the *Miami Herald,* the demands on his time overwhelmed the suits and Pedro became a professional AIDS educator, receiving a salary from Body Positive to expose himself to public view. He was in constant demand at schools, synagogues and churches. He spoke to civic groups, to businesses and their employees' children. Gradually, the requests began coming from farther afield, from northern Florida and Georgia, then Washington, D.C., and overseas.

He thought about going to school so he could learn to be a counselor for the dying, about creating some balance in his life so that he'd be more than "Pedro Zamora, wonder teen with AIDS." But the bookings kept coming, the honors rolled in. He was asked to appear before Congress. He was invited to give plenary addresses. The U.S. Public Health Service selected him as a poster boy, to deliver the national AIDS message.

For the most part, Pedro revelled in the celebrity status, as anyone his age would. He'd always wanted to meet President Jimmy Carter, the man who opened America to the young Cuban refugee; AIDS paved the way. He loved flying around the country, staying at fancy hotels and being cheered. But acutely aware that his immune system was deteriorating, he also fought desperately to find a way to fit the fragments together, to have a normal life like a normal young man. He tried to carve out time to watch *Star Trek* in the apartment he shared with his boyfriend Angel or spend time with his family. But there wasn't really any time. There was always another plane to catch, another speech to prepare, another interview to give. Time was running out, and racing around blurred that truth as effectively as promiscuous sex had blunted the reality of his mother's death.

Finally, in 1993 a new director at Body Positive tried to transform Pedro from a full-time speaker into a part-time clerk. He balked. That wasn't what he wanted to do, needed to do. He turned in his resignation. Lost and broke, Pedro tried the commercial lecture circuit. It wasn't his world. Then he heard that MTV's *Real World* was looking for new cast members. He was chosen from among the 30,000 other applicants. An articulate, handsome HIV-positive gay man was almost too much to hope for on a program that thrived on the conflict bred by diversity.

"His message was, 'Look at me. I'm twenty-two years old, I look healthy, I look vibrant . . . but there's a killer lurking inside of me and it can come up and grab me at any moment,'" said Doug Herzog, MTV's executive vice president of programming and production. The drama was beyond MTV's wildest dreams. They even spiced it up some more by refusing to tell the cast members which one of them had HIV. The producers decided that the revelation, when it came, would look great on film.

When Pedro moved from Miami to the house on Russian Hill in    45
San Francisco that MTV used as the real-life stage set for the program, he moved from one fantasyland to another. Life as Wonder Boy with AIDS became life as Wonder Boy with AIDS being filmed almost twenty-four hours a day.

Cameras followed him to his speaking engagements. They captured his clash with his roommate Puck, a scab-picking bike messenger who refused to eat with utensils. They were there on his first date with Sean Sasser. For five months Pedro enjoyed a love-hate relationship with the camera. He was a dyed-in-the-wool ham who turned on a magical electricity when the red light came on. But when he fell ill with pneumonia, taping became a nightmare. His mission was to project a positive image of having HIV — the image of living with the virus, not dying from it. He escaped to Sean's apartment for two weeks. But then it was back to the cameras, to the speaking engagements, to the pressures of being the perfect AIDS poster child.

When the filming wrapped up, Pedro flew to New York for an interview on the CBS morning show. He'd been complaining about headaches and promised Sean that he'd slow down. Like most twenty-two-year-olds, he wasn't much good at pacing himself. He had to visit his family in Miami, to confront their confusion about his marriage to Sean and his decision to move to San Francisco. He had a full booking of speaking engagements and offers from a modeling agency.

The night before his CBS interview, however, he was more than just stressed. His head was throbbing. He was strangely upset that he had to change rooms in the hotel, that his shirt wasn't pressed and that the hotel laundry service was shut down for the night. He called Sean in California. "Cancel the interview," Sean told him. "Just tell them you're sick."

The next morning, Pedro didn't appear at CBS. He didn't call. He just disappeared. When he returned to the hotel, his room key wouldn't open the door. With uncommon aggressiveness he demanded that a cleaning woman let him into his room. She gave in to the request, and reported the incident. The hotel manager thought he was dealing with yet another weirdo and he called the police, who charged Pedro with trespassing. Finally an MTV producer showed up. "Look, he's Pedro Zamora, a guest in the hotel," he explained. Pedro had been trying to get into the wrong room. It seemed like an odd mistake, but mistakes happen, he figured. Then Pedro asked to make a phone call before leaving for the airport. He didn't come out of his room. When the MTV producer went in, he found Pedro sitting staring at the phone, unable to remember the number he wanted to call.

By the time he was admitted to St. Vincent's Hospital, he had no memory of anything that had happened — where he had gone in the morning, his altercation with the maid, his failed attempt to make a phone call. Something was seriously wrong. Doctors examined the confused young man, checked out his blood and ran scans on his brain. They couldn't be sure, but they suspected that Pedro had two simultaneous brain infections. 50

Sean flew in from California. Toxoplasmosis would almost be good news, he knew, since it was relatively easily cured. But PML would be a disaster, the nightmare of every AIDS patient. A poorly understood viral infection of the brain, PML causes confusion and seizures, blindness, paralysis and death. There is no effective treatment. There is no known cure.

On Monday morning a neurologist shaved the side of Pedro's head and stuck a needle deep into his brain. Pathologists examined the results of the biopsy. The PML diagnosis was confirmed.

Two days later, accompanied by Sean, his cousin Oscar and another *Real World* cast member, Pedro flew home to Miami — to the bosom of a family that still saw him as their little boy, to the bosom of a community that still thought of him as their wonder teen.

At first, it was easy to maintain the illusion that Pedro would be okay. He still looked gorgeous. He wasn't wasted or feeble. He could still samba with his friends. He took walks with Sean through his family's neighborhood. But one night his friend Ernie came over at dinner time. Pedro looked intently at the piece of ham on his plate, then picked it up with his hands and began to chew it. "Do you want me to cut it up for you?" Ernie asked. "Oh — eh, no, gracias," Pedro answered, picking up the knife and fork he had forgotten. Another night his friends panicked when Pedro locked himself in the bathroom and wouldn't come out. They agonized over his apparent anger, not realizing that their friend had forgotten how to unlock the door.

As Pedro became increasingly helpless, he became increasingly dependent, and the fight for control was waged. His old friends wanted to surround him; his new friends from MTV flew in from California. His family wanted him back in their nest; Sean wanted to lie next to him, to enfold him in his arms. The family spoke little or no English; Sean spoke no Spanish at all. One day Pedro's hand began to swell from the IV dripping into his vein. His sister Milagros removed his wedding ring. Sean never saw it again.

Pedro's speaking schedule had been planned for months before he fell ill. Judd Wineck, another member of the *Real World* cast, replaced him. He didn't speak about AIDS. He couldn't. He spoke about Pedro. While he lay dying, there was yet another AIDS benefit at a fancy Miami Beach restaurant. Pedro was the star — in absentia. His friend Alex was asked to speak. Members of the *Real World* cast were called up to the stage. No AIDS activist talked about Pedro's work. Sean sat, virtually unnoticed, in the audience.

During those last steamy days of fall in Miami, Sean Sasser lived suspended between the reality of the death watch over Pedro's withering body and the fantasyland of chic cafés and sleek bodies on Miami Beach, where he was staying. As he moved back and forth between the two, he was haunted by a distant image, a flashback to his last speaking engagement in a middle school in San Francisco. He'd told his story, yet again, about studying at the University of Chicago, taking time off for a long trip to France and Italy, about joining the army and testing positive. The kids recognized him from his bus shelter photograph and from his constant appearances on *Real World*.

One of the eighth graders sat in the back of the room and scowled. "I don't understand," the boy finally blurted out. "I thought you were trying to scare us about AIDS. Instead, you tell us about going to Europe and becoming television stars because of HIV. You make it seem so wonderful and glamorous."

### Reading the Text

1. Summarize in your own words how Pedro Zamora became one of America's most famous and beloved AIDS patients.
2. What does Burkett mean by saying that "Pedro and Sean . . . became commodities"?
3. What was Zamora's response to learning his diagnosis with AIDS, and how did he cope with the news?
4. What is Burkett's attitude toward MTV and others who profited from Zamora's illness?
5. How, according to Burkett's account, did race play a role in the story of Pedro Zamora?

### Reading the Signs

1. Burkett quotes an eighth-grade boy who tells Sean Sasser, "You make [AIDS] seem so wonderful and glamorous." In your journal, explore your response to this boy's comment. What do you think of media celebrities who visit schools as part of their AIDS education programs?
2. Write an essay in which you support, challenge, or modify Burkett's contention that Pedro Zamora became a "commodity." To develop your ideas, consult Laurence Shames's "The More Factor" (p. 31) and the Introduction to Chapter One.
3. Visit the library and research popular media coverage of celebrity AIDS figures, such as Greg Louganis or Magic Johnson. Then write an analysis of the coverage, examining the extent to which the celebrities you focus on have become "commodities," as Burkett claims occurred with Zamora.
4. Write a letter to MTV in which you express your opinion of their treatment of Pedro Zamora in *Real World*. To what extent do you believe MTV exploited Zamora as a sign of AIDS tolerance, or do you believe instead that the network contributed to positive attitudes toward the disease?
5. Write an essay in which you analyze the reasons for Zamora's wide appeal to a broad audience. To develop your ideas, consult Daniel Harris's "Making Kitsch from AIDS" (p. 669).

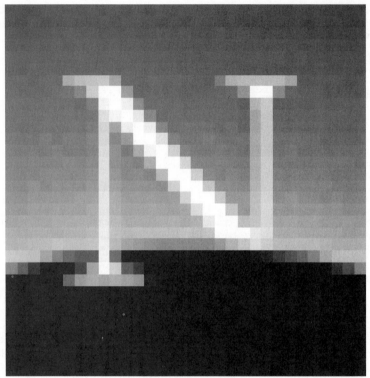

# CHAPTER TEN

# VIRTUAL CULTURE

## *Signs in Cyberspace*

**B**ill Gates thinks it's "the road ahead." Clifford Stoll thinks it's all a lot of "silicon snake oil." Al Gore thinks that it can be used to promote democracy from here to South Africa. And Newt Gingrich, who disagrees with Gore on just about everything else, thinks it holds the future of American capitalism.

"It," of course, is the Internet, and, whether you love it or loathe it, it is arguably the most significant technological intrusion into American culture since the invention of television.

Even if you yourself are not yet online, it's hard to miss. From movies like *The Net* to popular journals like *Wired* and *VirtualCity,* the electronic labyrinth of the Internet has migrated beyond the computer screen into the heart of American popular culture. Do you have a favorite band, actor, or actress? Chances are you can keep up with the latest gossip about them on a home page or Web site. Motion picture premiers now come complete with public relations blitzes broadcast not only through such traditional media as radio, TV, the daily newspaper, and billboards, but through the Net as well, while all-night "chat rooms" are beginning to replace the telephone for thousands of wired-up cybernauts. If you want to learn more about popular culture itself, the World Wide Web is filled with sites — from academically oriented electronic journals like *Postmodern Culture* to student-authored home pages — devoted to pop culture and its interpretation. And even professional football has gone online, with the first game-time Web site being broadcast during Superbowl XXX.

### Exploring the Signs of the Net

In your journal, discuss the impact that the Internet revolution has had on your life. If you are a Net aficionado, how has it affected the way you complete schoolwork, entertain yourself, even maintain friendships? How do your computer-related activities affect your sense of self-identity? If you don't use the Net, what is your attitude toward it? Do you feel you're missing something — or that Net fans are the ones who are missing out?

## Interpreting Signs in Cyberspace

As with any other cultural phenomenon, the key to a semiotic understanding of the Net lies in situating it in an overall context or system. And as with any other cultural phenomenon, this begins with a number of questions. How, for example, is the Internet related to other culturally influential electronic media — to television, and film, and radio? How are its effects like those of the media? How are they different? What social issues are involved in the emergence of the Net? Are they the same issues that confront us in other areas of American culture? How are they different?

In this introduction, we will look at four cultural issues that cyberspace has raised in the last few years. The readings to follow will explore those issues, and others, in some depth, providing you with an opportunity to write your own analyses of the cultural significance of computer technology. Let's begin with the potential that the Internet has to change our patterns of social behavior, the ways in which we relate with other people.

## Be All That You Can Be

Normally when we converse with others, we are visible to them. If we are not visible, as on the telephone, we are audible. Through sight and sound, then, the people we interact with can normally identify us — as male or female, young or old, and so on. One can always disguise one's voice on the telephone, of course, and even person-to-person interactions can be manipulated through role playing and pretense, but, by and large, we are generally limited to what we are when we interact with others. Identity, one might say, is fate.

But not on the Internet. Because no one can see or hear you in cyberspace, because of the essential anonymity of the Internet, you can be whatever you wish to be. You can pretend to be an adult if you're a kid, or a kid if you're an adult. You can pretend to be more important than you really are, or conversely, as a number of celebrities have discovered, you can escape the isolating effects of the star system and surf the Net on equal terms with everyone else. You can carry on electronic "affairs" on the Internet, and even switch genders, because, after all, no one's looking.

This capacity to change one's identity in any direction bears a profound potential to alter the way we conceive of our own identities. Rather than feeling bound by what you are, you can explore any number of identities on the Net. For many, such a capacity to break down the traditional boundaries of personal identity has proven to be quite exciting, even intoxicating, leading to utopian predictions of a whole new order of electronically conditioned consciousness.

The Internet is not the first technology to bear such a potential to alter our consciousness. Much, for example, has been written about the effects that the technologies of cinema and television already have had upon us. Marshall McCluhan, whose book *The Gutenberg Galaxy* has probably been the single most influential analysis of the cultural effects of the electronic media, himself predicted that radio and television had the capacity to connect up every corner of the earth in a worldwide "global village." And while McCluhan did not live long enough to assess the full impact of the World Wide Web, it certainly does appear that a global village of Web surfers is indeed being constructed today. Perhaps you count yourself as a member.

But what sort of village is it?

The emerging outlines of the Web's global village have some people very excited and others worried. The worried contingent — writers like Clifford Stoll and Mark Slouka — are concerned that the relationships people are building on the Net lack an essential core of humanity. The unreal world of virtual culture, they believe, the world in which you can pretend to be just about anything, is being substituted for a social reality made up of real human beings. And such a world, based entirely on the transmission of electronic signals, is potentially a world in which human beings will be unable to conceive of others *as* human beings. When all interaction is electronic, they ask, where is the ground for true human empathy and relatedness?

Nonsense, answer the Net's defenders. The Internet *fosters* human interaction; it doesn't inhibit it. People who haven't the energy to send a letter by "snail mail," or the money just to dial a friend up long distance, find themselves reconnecting with old friends thanks to the inexpensive efficiency of e-mail. Individuals who might otherwise be left home alone with no one to talk to can connect up with whole squadrons of fellow Net surfers, building electronic societies based on shared interests and enthusiasms (this is especially true for the disabled,

---

### Discussing the Signs of the Net

In class, discuss the extent to which your campus has gone online. First assign small groups of students to research the electronic accessibility of various parts of campus life, ranging from the library to classrooms, from your school's placement center to registration for classes. Then present your findings to the class. What conclusions do you draw about your school's adaptation to the electronic revolution?

---

who may find themselves socially empowered through the equalizing effects of cyberspace).

### Speak No Evil

Whether the Internet is a barrier to valid human relationships, or an enabler, it also raises the same kind of free speech issues that other media do. Newspapers, magazines, books, radio, television, and the movies have always had to negotiate the boundaries of permitted and forbidden speech (George Carlin's classic comic routine on the seven words you can't use on radio sums it all up), and now the Internet has joined them. Should neo-Nazi groups be allowed to use the Net to spew hate? The Simon Wiesenthal Center thinks not and has called upon Internet providers to show some social responsibility in its provision of Web sites (so far, the providers are resisting this call). Should pornography be permitted on the Net? Congress is working on legislation to restrict the transmission of "indecent" material through the Web. What if an online server is being exploited by a terrorist cadre? Should it be compelled to reveal the identities of its users to the FBI before an act of terrorism can be committed?

As you can see, the potential for abuse of the Internet is enormous. And one way or another our society is going to have to tackle the complex balancing act between freedom of speech and the right to protect itself that it has faced in controversies ranging from gangsta rap to the fight over campus hate speech codes.

### Hacking It

The advent of potential restrictions on the use of the Net does not sit well with its core users, men and women who are often highly independent and individualistic — rather like settlers on the nineteenth-century Western frontier (indeed, there is a civil liberties group devoted to the Internet called the Electronic Frontier Association). Seeing the Net as a new frontier, they resent the political barbed wire now being laid down across the electronic prairie. And the most individualistic of these — independent to the point of anarchy — have been those computer outlaws known as hackers.

Hackers don't like any sort of restrictions on their use of the Internet. So long as they don't actually steal anything or mess up someone else's files, they believe that they have a right to "enter" any file they can hack into. Whether you agree with such an attitude or not, it raises an issue that our current social mythologies are not quite capable of handling. That is, within our cultural codes, there is ordinarily no problem in identifying the difference between private and public property. If someone violates your space, especially if that space is your home, that's a crime. But what if that space is virtual space, itself made possible by an electronic Web that was created by publically funded government agencies? Is it private or public? Can anyone barge into your files who has the ability to do so? What do you think?

## To Have and to Have Not

Maybe such matters are a bit abstract to you because you've never been online. Perhaps you have *wanted* to surf the Net but can't afford the price of admission. Indeed, one of the most pressing social controversies surrounding the much-ballyhooed information superhighway is the fact that it is not a freeway but a tollway. That is, those who can afford it are being offered opportunities for educational and economic advancement but those who can't afford it are being denied. The potential result of this disparity might be a further widening of the gap between the haves and the have-nots in America today.

Web enthusiasts don't see it this way. They see the Internet as a liberating force that can lead to further democratization, not elitism. Noting that in an information age the ability to gain access to sources of information is the key to personal empowerment, supporters of the Internet point out that the Web allows ordinary citizens to circumvent the barriers to information access that, in their opinion, the power elites have set up to protect their own privileges. Thanks to the Web, once arcane sources of information are open to anyone with the tools to find them.

Similarly, access to the Internet provides opportunities for mass communication that have traditionally been enjoyed solely by those who control such mass media as television, film, and newspapers. With a personal computer at your fingertips, for example, you don't need to own a publishing house to publish your own books: You can use a desktop publishing system. You don't need to wait to have an article accepted for publication in a journal because you can set up your own "zine" on the Web and publish whatever you want. And you don't need to wait for a reporter to call you up or a press conference to make your views known on a political controversy because you can communicate instantly with a worldwide network of fellow Web crawlers on any topic you can imagine.

Such arguments often adopt a utopian tone, suggesting that the liberating power of the Internet will eventually lead to a decentralized world where power is shared just as information is shared, rather than concentrated in a few hands. However, not everyone agrees with this vision. Critics point to the failure of television to fulfill the promise that new technology once offered, as the medium that was supposed to raise the level of cultural consciousness in our country has declined into a cultural "wasteland." At the same time, there are plenty of signs that the power elites that Web enthusiasts believe will be undone by the anarchic potential of the Net are successfully using it to consolidate their power at the expense of the powerless. Consider, for example, the looming advent of what Microsoft tycoon Bill Gates has called "friction-free capitalism." Friction-free capitalism envisions a consumer economy in which just about all shopping will be done by computer, thus eliminating the need for retail stores and the jobs of the people who work in them. In our "frictionless" future, television entertainment will be provided on demand, enabling viewers to receive TV programming directly from its producers, thereby eliminating the need for TV networks and the jobs of the people who work for the networks.

Hence, a good deal of nervousness is being felt by those who are in danger of being reduced to "friction." After all, the new technology is being touted as a way of eliminating their livelihoods. For Kirkpatrick Sale, this potential of computer technology to displace a broad sector of the workforce looks like a repetition of something that has happened before. In his book *Rebels Against the Future: The Luddites and Their War on the Industrial Revolution* (1994; significantly subtitled, *Lessons for the Computer Age*), he describes what happened when in the late eighteenth century the appearance of steam-driven power looms forced thousands of English weavers out of work. With the advent of a new technology threatening their way of life, English weavers rebelled in an uprising known as the Luddite rebellion. For a few months in 1811, legions of angry workers destroyed the factory machinery that was destroying their livelihoods. Is a new Luddite rebellion, this time against the cyberworld, at hand?

No one knows. What we can say for sure is that the emergence of the Internet as a major factor in American culture has profound economic as well as social and cultural implications. The readings in this chapter are designed to provide a framework for understanding and analyzing these implications. The cultural impact of the Net is likely only to grow in the years to come, and so now is a good time for you to start thinking about your own response to a future that is already here.

II

### Reading the Net on the Net

The Internet is filled with visual images and graphics, ranging from directional icons to corporate advertising. Select one such type of image and study the examples you find as you conduct various Net searches. How would you interpret them semiotically? Do you find that they enhance or detract from your use of the Net?

## The Readings

We begin our readings in cyberculture with a dissenting opinion from Mark Slouka, who criticizes the cybernetic subordination of ordinary reality to virtual reality in "'Reality Is Death': The Spirit of Cyberspace." Phillip Elmer-DeWitt follows with an approving portrait of the "cyberpunk" culture, providing background information on such postmodern heroes as R. U. Sirius. Amy Bruckman's "Christmas Unplugged" offers an academic's plea to fellow cybernauts to take some time off occasionally and leave the laptop behind, while Sherry Turkle's "Who Am We?" portrays the lives and fantasies of hardcore cyber "geeks" whose online lives have become so important to them that a Christmas unplugged might seem inconceivable. Laura Miller challenges the widespread assumption that women are second-class citizens on the Net, needing special protection against sexual harassment, and LynNell Hancock explores the social and economic implications of online access, or lack of access. Finally, Lawrence K. Grossman envisions a future in which American elections go online, inaugurating an era of keypad democracy.

MARK SLOUKA

## "Reality Is Death": The Spirit of Cyberspace

⁣IIIIIIIIIIIIIIIIIIIIIIIIIIIIIIIIIIIIIIIIIIIIIII

*For cyberenthusiasts, one of the most breathtaking possibilities offered
by emerging technologies will be the replacement of ordinary physical
reality with a high-tech virtual reality that will give us everything from
new cyberpersonalities to cybersex. Mark Slouka (b. 1958) isn't an
enthusiast. In this excerpt from* War of the Worlds: Cyberspace
and the High-Tech Assault on Reality *(1995), Slouka explores
the ethical implications of virtual reality. While we're busy pushing beyond the bounds of ordinary reality, won't this distract us from the very
real problems that remain within that reality? Slouka asks. Haven't
we a job to do here, in normal space, first? Slouka is a lecturer in English and popular culture at the University of California, San Diego.*

I first stumbled upon (or into) the world of virtual systems while
teaching undergraduate seminars on twentieth-century culture at a major
California university. The head lecturer, an intelligent and witty woman,
was, it turned out, an expert on cyberspace, or the closest thing to an expert possible in an area of study still essentially in its embryonic state,
dominated by hackers from a half-dozen related fields.

Every course has its own signature. In the stresses and gaps, we can
read the lecturer's own interests. The first thing that struck me about this
particular class (a ten-week survey of contemporary culture from World
War I to the present "and beyond") was the unusual emphasis on
Nietzsche and the Dadaists. Students largely innocent of the Triple Alliance and the Munich Pact, the decline of European economic hegemony and the effects of decolonization, could explain the significance of
automatic writing, identify and discuss Duchamp's Fountain, recite Nietzsche's dictum "the breaker is the creator." Virtually all understood the
validity of the attack on rationalism and objectivity, the moral bank-
ruptcy of Western liberalism.

None of which, of course, was particularly new or disturbing.
Clearly, the well-worn theme, so suited to adolescents ripe for reductive
conspiracy theories, was the imperialism of "value structures" as such.
Objectivity was a lie. History was a lie. Truth, as the anarchist Mikhail
Bakunin had noted, was nothing more than a stick with which the
mighty beat the weak. I'd heard it before. I was reasonably comfortable
with it. A good deal of it I even agreed with. When the brush strokes got
a little broad, I'd use my weekly discussion sections to qualify, elaborate.

Every week I'd patiently, stubbornly reintroduce the problem of ethics into the equation of modern culture.

And yet, over time, it became progressively more difficult to ignore the discomfort I felt. To students, I could paper over any obvious differences between the lecturer and myself by referring to the dialectical nature of academic discourse. I had a harder time convincing myself. I liked this person. I liked talking to her. We were both on the Left. We had a similar sense of humor. Why was it, then, that I found myself — internally, subtly — more and more antagonistic toward her?

It wasn't until the last lecture that the seemingly random points of discomfort coalesced into an image I could understand. The subject was the future. I expected something on the post–cold war balance of power, the rise of tribalism, the revolutionary implications — for notions of state sovereignty, for example — of environmental degradation. The subject, instead, was the role virtual technologies would play in the new century.

Already, we were told, technological prostheses had begun to "liberate" us from the limitations of the human body. The possibilities were endless. Within the span of our children's lifetimes, we were assured, it would be possible to link the human nervous system directly to a computer, to download the human consciousness into RAM (random access memory), effectively preserving it in some artificial state. Within the foreseeable future, the dividing line between nature and technology — a false dichotomy, we were told, since at least the invention of agriculture — would be erased; genetic engineering in general, and the Human Genome Project in particular, had already blurred the line forever.

Cyberspace systems would develop and expand, fundamentally altering our definitions of physical space, of identity and community. Already it was routinely possible to interface simultaneously with a number of different individuals in different parts of the globe. In the not-too-distant future, it would be possible to touch them. Feedback technology would provide the illusion of touch directly to your nervous system. It would be indistinguishable from the real thing. Physical presence would become optional; in time, an affectation. And, having marginalized the physical self, we would marginalize community (in the old sense of the word) as well; a new era in human evolution would be ushered in. Divorced from our bodies, our minds grafted onto computers capable of realizing for us the contents of our imagination (or allowing us to experience another's imagination), meeting one another in electronically generated spaces with their own rules of behavior, we would finally attain the fulfillment of our species. In this New Age, boundaries between self and other, male and female, nature and machine, even life and death, would be obsolete. The word *reality* would lose all meaning, or would metastasize beyond recognition. Death, truly, would have no dominion. If you missed your wife or husband, whose physical body had died, you could meet up again in the virtual world. Take a walk together. Drink cappuccino. Have sex.

There was more. It was quite a lecture. My first response, I'll confess, was one of amusement. It seemed ripe territory for a new genre of jokes. Would all this spawn a new generation of travel agents? Virtual vacations? If someone told you to fuck yourself, could you do it?

Amusement gradually shifted to mild fascination. All this talk of immortality, of an "other" world; all this hostility toward the body — what was it but a rather unoriginal techno-Christianity? Substitute a few terms, look beneath the technological jargon, and you had the same basic structures, the same motivations and fears. As an example of the adaptability of a cultural form, it was moderately interesting, nothing more. The prophecies themselves seemed absurd, silly, an adolescent fantasy.

Why, then, if the material was so transparent, so easily dismissed, did    10
my curiosity give way to irritation? Why, during the week following that last lecture, did I keep picking at it, arguing with it? Why, finally, did I find it so disturbing when I brought my three-year-old son with me to pick up the final exams, to see the lecturer hand him a two-inch hybrid animal, half elephant, half cow? She had an entire collection of the little monstrosities in her office. Rabbits with pigs' snouts. Galloping horses with big dogs' heads. My son, who will play with damn near anything, wouldn't touch them. "I didn't like those funny animals," he told me on the way back to the car.

I didn't either. It was the process of trying to figure out *why* I didn't like them that first suggested to me the significance of the instinctive resistance I'd been feeling those past ten weeks. What I had been reacting to, I realized, was a kind of technological absolutism, a willingness to tinker with (or disregard) the lives of mere men and women for the sake of some future ideal. Totalists of all stripes, after all, have always been linked by their common desire to transform the world in their own image. Totalitarian visions — whether utopian fantasies or dystopian nightmares — have shared an aversion to the world in all its quotidian messiness, as well as a corresponding preoccupation with cleanliness, order, control. All, similarly, have been characterized by a vast arrogance, an unshakable belief in their own vision of a different world.

But totalitarianism destroyed one *part* of the world for the sake of another. Theorists in virtual systems, if anything, went further; their disdain for the world was more complete. They weren't interested in regaining some nationalized vision of rural bliss, some Teutonic or pan-Slavic *heimat;* they wanted the apocalypse. Their sensibility, in other words (though the distinction is a precarious one), seemed less political than religious.

But even religious absolutism fell short. Christianity, for example, unparalleled in its ability to deny the world and denounce the body, to subordinate this life to the next, nonetheless drew the majority of its forms from *this* world, from existing structures: the *rock* of the church;

the *tree* of life; the *community* of Christ. And these, it had always seemed to me, suggested a latent nostalgia. Beneath the hate for this fallen Earth, beneath the blood of the Book of Revelation, lurked a suppressed yearning. The New Jerusalem, after all, would descend to us, to *this* Earth. The cyberspace revolution, by contrast, would seek to erase the world as we had known it. It was of the same spirit as Christianity, but bigger. Colder. And melodramatic as it may seem, I sensed in it a fundamental threat to life as I'd always conceived it, as existence *within* the world. It was our connection to the physical world, I'd always believed — however ephemeral, however fragile — that gave strength, courage, even love, their meaning. But these concerns, in the world of cyberspace, were already anachronistic. What was strength, or courage, in a world without risk? What was love if not a voluntary loss of control? What was love, after all, without mortality?

What I had been confronting, in short, was an ethical vacuum. What I had sensed was an utter lack of compassion for the world and its problems as they are. Why speak of the destruction of real communities in the Balkans when you can inhabit virtual ones? Why bring up the importance of biodiversity and the implications of habitat destruction when you can create your *own* environment? From the lecturer's point of view, nature already *was* technology; in her future, the hybrid — symbolic of the newly blurred boundaries between the sexes, between species, between entire kingdoms — would be the new incarnation. It seemed to me then (and I am not naturally given to apocalyptic imagery) that the beast slouching towards Bethlehem would be a child with the head of a dog, and the sand itself, the burning heat, a desert in cyberspace, a virtual dream.

It was at this point, I think, that I began noticing the frequency with    15
which the *cyber-* and *hyper-* prefixes appeared in the mass media, the extent to which the new technology had percolated downward through the system. At my neighborhood newsstand (always a telling barometer of cultural trends), my attention was caught by the premier issue of *Future Sex* magazine, which, besides promising to fill me in on the New World Order in adult video and answer all my questions regarding electronic masturbation, claimed to have the latest word on cyborg sex slaves, 3D digital orgasms, and virtual reality sex.

The latest word, it turned out, was that in the near future, we would be able to have sex in virtual space. The computer would make our fantasies real. Cyborgs, created to our specifications, electronically generated but palpable to our senses, would form a new generation of slaves. We would be their creators. The possibilities of hyperfucking, the editors assured me, would have no impact on real-world relationships. I could hardly wait. The accompanying illustration showed a tangerine-colored "woman," with large breasts and a prehensile tail, having sex with a sort of plum-colored devil. She had two heads, neither of which looked particularly happy.[1]

When a new technology has been appropriated by science fiction freaks and popularizers, as well as given recognition by the arbiters of high culture (one shelf down from *Future Sex,* the term *hyperworld* called out from the cover of *The New Yorker*), we can assume it has caught the attention of a mass audience. I decided to look further into the whole business of cyberspace research.

What I discovered fairly quickly was that virtual systems (articles on cyborg love slaves aside) had an unusually impressive genealogy. Cyberspace research, I found, was originally underwritten in the late 1980s by a consortium of military interests — primarily the Defense Advanced Research Products Agency, or DARPA — hoping to develop a virtual environment for large-scale military exercises. Faced with the escalating costs, both financial and political, of conducting war games in Western Europe, the Pentagon decided to develop a virtual battlefield. They threw open the R&D coffers, began the bidding, and soon the thing was done. The SIMNET system linked 200 M1 tanks, each carrying a crew of four, moving over a computer-generated terrain visible through the tanks' ports. Vehicles and even aircraft would be visible to the crew; they could hear enemy as well as friendly fire. It was the beginning of a beautiful friendship between researchers in virtual systems and the bottomless pockets of the military that has continued to the present day.

The Defense Department was just one of many suitors. Reading the list, I began to understand the momentum that the new technology had acquired. From its beginnings in Air Force laboratories and the Draper Lab at the Massachusetts Institute of Technology, cyberspace research had attracted the funds and research facilities of university programs, such as those at the University of North Carolina and the Human Interface Technology Lab at the University of Washington; of computer giants like Atari, Apple, and Sega; of communications monoliths like AT&T; of multinational conglomerates like Warner Communications and Matsushita (which owns Panasonic and Universal), as well as any number of smaller companies scattered all over the industrialized world. The applications of the technology turned out to be as multifaceted as the technology itself was protean: this, in turn, led to an exceptionally fluid relationship between the public and private sectors. A video-equipped helmet, for example, though developed primarily at NASA's Ames Research Laboratories, quickly attracted the attention of companies interested in adapting it to TV, video games, advertising, and film.[2]

---

1. Richard Kadrey, "Pleasure by the Numbers," *Future Sex* (premier issue, 1992): p. 7.
2. I am indebted here to Allucquere Rosanne Stone's excellent overview in "Will the Real Body Please Stand Up?" in Michael Benedikt, ed., *Cyberspace: First Steps* (Cambridge, MA: MIT Press, 1991), pp. 92–99.

At this point, one thing began to seem fairly obvious: virtual systems   20
were not a fad. They were not going to go away. Some applications had
entered the market already; others massed on the borders. At the Flower
Hill Mall near my home, I could put on a special helmet equipped with
small video monitors capable of manufacturing a stereoscopic image before my eyes and maneuver through a stable, three-dimensional world
generated entirely by a computer. If I turned my head, the computer
would track my movements and adjust the view accordingly. By adding
special stereo headphones, I could make that virtual world acoustically as
well as visually complete. Ten minutes of virtual reality for five bucks.

Soon, the young man who set me up assured me, I'd be able to wear
special gloves, and even a bodysuit, wired with position and motion trans-
mitters that would represent my movements (to myself as well as to others)
in the virtual world. Within a few years, that glove or bodysuit would be
able to telegraph back to me the presence of virtual solid objects: their
weight, texture, even temperature. I'd be able to immerse myself in a completely artificial world, in what those in the field were referring to as "a
fully englobing environment."[3]

Was this a good thing? Did we *need* a fully englobing environment? I'd
periodically pose this question to the various enthusiasts I encountered in
both the real and the virtual world. Almost invariably, the question would
strike them as odd, even absurd, the product of a distinctly nineteenth-
century sensibility. Almost without exception, they'd answer not, as I expected, with an a priori yes but, rather, with a confused shrug. They didn't
understand the question. How did I mean, *good*? The implicit motto
seemed to be: We tinker because we can; if we weren't meant to blur the
boundaries between self and other, nature and technology, solitude and
community, they wouldn't allow themselves to be tampered with. They
would resist us. It was precisely this untroubled, childlike, essentially pre-
ethical attitude that I found most unsettling. Children, I thought, also see
resistance as some sort of moral boundary, and will tear the wings off flies
because they can — until someone suggests that they stop.

I pressed on, like some latter-day Alice, further behind the looking
glass, hoping to find something that would help me understand the phenomenon of virtual systems, that would explain their appeal. In the bor-
derless, timeless world I'd found myself in, there were no givens, no
facts, no a priori truths. Individual identity, physical space, reality itself,
had turned plastic and malleable, mere constructs we might choose to
buy into, or reinterpret, or discard altogether — as we saw fit. Which of
the three options we chose didn't matter. My lecturer, I began to realize,
had a lot of company. Her views, far from representing the radical fringe
as I had assumed, were representative of the cyberspace community as a

---

3. I first heard this term used by Allucquere Rosanne Stone.

whole. "There's nothing 'real' out there," I was told on the Net by one resident of a cyberspace community. "Reality is just a habit. A way of thinking. It's all just information." When I asked whether he was being serious, he told me he wasn't interested in debating the obvious, and suggested I do some reading. "Read a fucking book," he said. And I quote.

So I did. Several, in fact. And I emerged from the strange and utterly loopy world of cyberspace theory convinced that in order to understand fully the digital revolution, we would need to see two things very clearly: First, that the computer — no longer just an information processor — was rapidly developing into a sort of deluxe copying machine, increasingly capable of imitating certain aspects of our lives; and second, that a large number of very smart, very influential people believed that this computer copy should, and eventually would, replace the original it imitated. In books and articles, in boardrooms and classrooms, at computer shows and academic symposia, these people argued with positively evangelical fervor for their vision of the computer as God: omnipotent, omniscient, gravid with a New Creation. "Strait is the gate, and narrow is the way to heaven," St. Matthew had warned. So widen the bandwidth, the cyberists were answering.

These people, as George Bush might have put it, had the vision        25
thing. In spades. Computers represented the portal to the new Heavenly City; cyberspace would be our new home. According to Michael Benedikt, professor of architecture at the University of Texas at Austin, cyberspace would allow us to make up for the Fall from Eden, to redeem ourselves in God's graces. He was not being ironic. Cyberspace, he explained, would allow us to shed "the ballast of materiality"; it would be a pure realm — spotless, shining — into which we would be able to escape. And what would we be escaping from? Almost everything, it seemed. The Earth — grubby and all too physical. The limitations of space and time. The body — impure, treacherous, and, most annoying of all, mortal. And on and on. Cyberspace would solve all our problems.

I had assumed that those yearning to escape the world and everything in it (à la Augustine) would have a very special perspective on life in general. And so it was. "Reality is death," declared Professor Benedikt, revealing himself as the less-than-perfect dinner companion. His solution to this flaw in the cosmic plan? Cyberspace. And how did the professor envision cyberspace? As "a territory swarming with data and lies, with mind stuff and memories of nature, with a million voices and two million eyes . . . billowing, glittering, humming, coursing, a Borgesian library, a city; intimate, firm, liquid, recognizable and unrecognizable at once."[4] Got that?

Like most readers, I suspect, I had no idea what professor Benedikt might be talking about and this troubled me for a time, until I realized that what I'd been reading was something like the digital equivalent of

---

4. Michael Benedikt, "Introduction," in Benedikt, ed., *Cyberspace*, p. 2.

speaking in tongues. Professor Benedikt and those like him had caught the spirit. Communication was not his aim. Conversion was.

The literature of cyberspace, I now began to see, was all about salvation. The new, electronic millennium. Transcending time and space, the family and the body. Oh, and sex, too. "You won't need condoms anymore," promised Nicole Stenger, a former research fellow at MIT's Center for Advanced Visual Studies. "Cyberspace will be the condom."[5]

What did this mean, exactly? It meant, according to Stenger, that physical sex was going the way of the dodo and the ivory-billed woodpecker. That cybersex — a sort of expanded version of phone sex — was the wave of the future: cleaner, simpler, less risky than its messy prototype.[6] It was an interesting vision. If it came to pass, I thought, it would require that we update Hector St. John de Crèvecoeur's eighteenth-century question, "Who then is this New Man, this American?" In the New Age, apparently, he would be the one in front of the video monitor, one hand on the keyboard, the other firmly grasping his, er, mouse.

But sex was hardly the point. The word *masturbation,* in fact, hardly appeared in the rarefied world of cyberspace, though one could assume that even cyberspace condoms would refer to something, and that cyborgasms, however airy, might still require a little help in arriving. Instead, one found a great deal of talk about computers as the objects of desire. It was all about love, you see. "Our fascination with computers is more erotic than sensuous," Professor Michael Heim argued in "The Erotic Ontology of Cyberspace" — "more deeply spiritual than utilitarian." Logging on, he explained, meant taking on the role of the "erotic lover," reaching out to "a fulfillment far beyond aesthetic attachment." It was all very simple, according to Professor Heim: "The world rendered as pure information not only fascinates our eyes and minds, it captures our hearts. We feel augmented and empowered. Our hearts beat in the machines. This is Eros."[7]

30

---

5. Nicole Stenger, "Mind Is a Leaking Rainbow," in Benedikt, ed., *Cyberspace,* p. 56.

6. The "safety" of cybersex, or tinysex, or teledildonics, is a selling point that links enthusiasts across the thoroughly blurred boundaries of high and low culture. For Richard Kadrey of *Future Sex,* "VR sex . . . is the ultimate in safe sex: no HIV virus and no reason to be shy about trying out a new fetish." For Paul Wu, president of Pixis International, which markets "cyberporn" CD-ROMs, "CD sex can even have its health benefits. With the prevalence of diseases," he says, "we're directing sexual energies. It's the ultimate safe sex." Wu quoted in Dean Takahashi, "Sex Play in Cyberspace," *Los Angeles Times,* January 16, 1994.

7. Michael Heim, "The Erotic Ontology of Cyberspace," in Benedikt, ed., *Cyberspace,* p. 61. Professor Heim is not alone in his vision. Julian Dibbell's slightly less buttoned-down (unbuttoned?) observations in *The Village Voice* make the same point: "Amid flurries of even the most cursorily described caresses, sighs, and penetrations, the glands do engage, and often as throbbingly as they would in a real-life assignation. . . . And if the virtual setting and the interplayer vibes are right, who knows? The heart may engage as well, stirring up passions as strong as many that bind lovers who observe *the formality* of trysting in the flesh" (my own, wondering italics). Julian Dibbell, "Rape in Cyberspace: A Tale of Crime and Punishment on Line," *The Village Voice,* December 21, 1993.

But the prophylactic — excuse me, *romantic* — possibilities of cyber-space were just the beginning. According to Stenger, we were teetering on the threshold of a new era. "It was obvious," she claimed, "that an explosion would take place, a Big Bang of the old order . . . based on gravity, history, and territory." What would this Big Bang of the old order mean, I wondered? Would we all find ourselves afloat in Professor Benedikt's glittering, billowing mind stuff? Just so. Civilization, Stenger assured me, would "become unbalanced." She could hardly wait. Cyber-space, she enthused, would be "the new bomb, a pacific blaze that will project the imprint of our disembodied selves on the walls of eternity."[8]

The crudity of the metaphor (the "pacific blaze" Stenger evoked, of course, was the blast at Hiroshima, whose heat was so great that it im-printed the silhouettes of the newly incinerated on the wrecked walls of the city) was characteristic of theoretical writings on cyberspace. It im-plied a stunning insensitivity to, or boredom with, the merely real world, the world of historical facts and contemporary issues, in which pacific blazes (or the pleasures and risks of human sexuality) had some bearing on actual people's lives. "If only we could," Michael Benedikt had writ-ten, "we would wander the earth and never leave home; we would enjoy triumphs without risks, eat of the Tree and not be punished, con-sort daily with angels, enter heaven now and not die."[9] As a group, the cyberists seemed to have already ascended. Their perspective was post-millennial, almost hallucinatory. From their vantage, the world seemed vaguely unreal — a half-remembered dream — and *humanity* a term of little consequence.

To say that the real world didn't interest the cyberists, however, wasn't quite accurate; they didn't *believe* in it. "What we call reality," Stenger explained, "is only a temporary consensus anyway, a mere stage in the technique." Bodies, Professor Heim claimed, didn't really exist, ei-ther: they were ideological constructs — composites of attitudes, beliefs, and preconceptions, themselves dependent on larger economic and polit-ical forces at work in the general culture. Nature, too, was merely an idea, a cultural construct. Like love. Or gender.[10]

According to the cyberspace expert Allucquere Rosanne Stone, "the category 'nature,'" rather than referring to anything in the real world, was

---

8. Stenger, p. 51.

9. Benedikt, p. 14.

10. Stenger, p. 53. The similarity between cyberspace theory and certain post-structuralist attitudes toward history, culture, and the self fashionable in academia re-veals two things: (1) Many, if not most, cyberspace theorists are academics; (2) post-structuralist attitudes toward the world are, at bottom, mechanistic (the current buzzword in the humanities and social sciences, for example, is *construction*), and there-fore well suited to those interested in machines capable of breaking things down into their component parts.

just "a *strategy* for maintaining boundaries for political and economic ends." And what might those be? Why, supporting "the industries of postmodern nostalgia" (which keeps us all hungering after things that never were), for one thing, and for another, maintaining "our society's pervasively male epistemology" (which demands that we make technology look bad by setting it *against* something wonderful).[11] Nature, in other words, was a patriarchal conceit designed to enslave us to the past and to demonize machines.

At some point, I'll confess, I began to find the whole business more  35 than a little disturbing. Negotiating the electronic precincts of cyberspace, it seemed to me, was a bit like lying down drunk, feeling the room start to turn and spin, and not having a floor to ground you. Or finding yourself in a dream that starts to go bad. There was something vaguely nightmarish about this hunger for transcendence, this lust for dissolution, this utter lack of loyalty to the earth, the body, the human community. Behind the hallucinogenic jargon, the collage of quotes, and the mixed metaphors, I sensed something very lonely. And very frightening.

Was I taking it all too seriously? Looking back from the digital everafter, Stenger had predicted, we would be able to see the divine process by which we'd first "lost all trace of earth on our shoes." We would recall how our houses had gradually grown airy and insubstantial, "whistling with drafts," and how our families had "slowly thinned away." We would remember that moment in time when cyberspace became "so irresistible that some of the basic functions of human life [fell] off like ripe fruit."[12] Was there anything in our world, I wondered — visible or not — to justify this kind of prophecy?

Looking around, it seemed to me that there was, that Ms. Stenger's brave new world was not as far off as some of us might have wished. Already, after all, many of us had lost all trace of earth on our shoes. Already — as more and more of us came to spend the hours of our days in the worlds beyond the television and computer screens — our homes were growing airy and insubstantial, whistling with drafts. Assisted by the increasing fragmentation of life in the West — by the loss of community structures, the breakdown of the family, the degradation of the physical environment — we really *did* seem in danger of ascending to some new, electronic reality, of being turned, in Benedikt's phrase, "into nomads . . . who are permanently in touch."[13]

---

11. Stone, p. 102. Indifference and sometimes downright hostility toward the natural world are underlying and often explicit themes in the literature of cyberspace — one of the stranger responses, I believe, to the accelerating degradation of the environment in the second half of the twentieth century.

12. Stenger, p. 56.

13. Benedikt, p. 10.

It came as something of a shock to me to realize that Stenger and Co., however much they might sometimes sound like Shirley MacLaine, were *serious;* when they talked of their desire to engineer a Big Bang of "the old order" based on the principles of gravity, history, and territory, they meant it. More important, they had the funding and the technological sophistication to make good on many of their wildest prophecies. By grafting the tradition of millennial dreaming onto both the free market and a powerful new technology, the cyberspace enthusiasts had created something new under the sun. Only half a decade from the turn of the millennium, they were threatening to make it possible not only to sell the age-old dream of the Heavenly City but to rent out space there.

It was more than just their technological sophistication and economic savvy that made them dangerous, however. The cyberists, like all extremists, were products of their time, the children of an increasingly subjective age. To understand them — their airy, relativistic attitude, their complete interest in, if not downright animosity toward, the hard facts of history — one had to see them as the intellectual heirs of certain theories that had established themselves in American higher education over the better part of two decades.[14] It was no coincidence, after all, that many of the most ardent theorists (like my lecturer) were academics. Cyberspace, I realized, represented the marriage of deconstruction and computer technology — a mating of monsters if ever there was one.

The connection, once made, was obvious: deconstruction, which    40 began as a method of textual analysis, was all about dismantling the "apparent" realities or truths of a literary work; the focus was on language's "unreliability," the text's "indeterminacy." Like a child picking threads from a blanket, the deconstructionist would isolate certain elements of, say, a poem by John Donne, in order to show — often quite reasonably — that all meaning was provisional, that at bottom, the poem was really about nothing so much as its own subversion. The point? Relativism. By exposing the fault lines in any argument, the deconstructionist could show that all hierarchies were suspect, all values provisional, all answers partial — and therefore of equal value.

A high-powered nuisance in the field of literary criticism, deconstruction quickly moved beyond academia, adapting itself — like some opportunistic predator exploiting an ecological niche — to the "texts" of history, identity, and culture as a whole. These, too, were shown to be unreliable, riddled with gaps and inconsistencies, indeterminate to a fault.

---

14. I am referring here to deconstruction — subsumed in its many incarnations under the rubric of poststructuralism — which has played such an enormous and influential role in American and European academic circles. Among the better critiques (there are many) of deconstructive criticism are Gerald Graff, *Literature Against Itself* (Chicago: University of Chicago Press, 1979).

The predictable result, as Michiko Kakutani pointed out in the *New York Times,* was "a cultural zeitgeist in which all truth [was] deemed subjective and all facts . . . made subject to reevaluation" — a climate in which history, for example, as an objective record of events in time, didn't exist. In this New Age, there weren't any facts, just ideologies of the moment; at any given time, the ideologue with the most power and influence got to determine the truth du jour. History, in short — even an event as immutable as the Holocaust — became just a collection of fictions (subjective, indeterminate), a text as susceptible to deconstruction as any poem.[15]

But the spirit of deconstruction didn't stop with the dismantling of history. The self, as something greater than the sum of its parts, was dismantled as well. The human being — and everything she saw and thought and believed — was shown to be nothing more than the product of the ideological filling she'd been stuffed with. One could think of it as a kind of soft version of the Human Genome Project, which attempted to trace every quirk and feature of the human being back to its parent chromosome. Here, too, the trick was to locate the bit, or part; once you'd done that, you understood the person. Did you happen to think that Herman Melville could write? It was because you were a white, Anglo male. Were you troubled by the Serbian genocide in Bosnia-Herzegovina? It was because you'd been weaned on the milk of rationalism, raised in the bland light of Western liberalism and Enlightenment thought.

Like most absurdities, of course, the relativism of the deconstructionists was based on a number of reasonable and even useful insights — texts, after all, *are* indeterminate; attitudes toward the self *are* circumscribed by ideology; history, or the act of recovering history, anyway, *is* a subjective business.[16] Seen as ends in themselves, however, instead of as means to a greater objectivity, these insights led nowhere.

---

15. Michiko Kakutani, "When History and Memory Are Casualties: Holocaust Denial," Critic's Notebook, *New York Times,* April 30, 1993. See also Kakutani, "Opinion vs. Reality in an Age of Pundits," Critic's Notebook, *New York Times,* January 28, 1994; Deborah E. Lipstadt, *Denying the Holocaust: The Growing Assault on Truth and Memory* (New York: Free Press, 1993); Robert Hughes, *Culture of Complaint: The Fraying of America* (New York: Oxford University Press, 1993); Gertrude Himmelfarb, *On Looking into the Abyss: Untimely Thoughts on Culture and Society* (New York: Knopf, 1994). On ethics and deconstruction, see David Lehman, *Signs of the Times: Deconstruction and the Fall of Paul De Man* (New York: Poseidon Press, 1991).

16. Part of the danger inherent in the deconstructionist argument — a danger inherent in any form of extremism — is that it will play into the hands of totalists on the other side. Absolutes, after all — concepts like "natural law" and "divine right" — *have* been used as tools of oppression throughout history. Revealing them for what they are, therefore, is justified. Taken too far, though — and this is my point — relativism becomes an orthodoxy in its own right.

"Indeterminacy" turned into a fetish, and "unreliability" acquired its own cult following.

So how did the cyberspace theorists fit into all this? Simple. Like the   45
deconstructionists, the cyberists were enamored of the concepts of indeterminacy and instability; like the deconstructionists, they projected a
fashionable, kaffeeklatsch nihilism; like their predecessors, finally, they
were morally neuter, less interested in constructing truth and meaning —
however provisionally — than in dismantling them.[17]

There *was,* however, one important difference. The deconstructionists had theories; the cyberists had machines. Theirs, in effect, was an
*applied* deconstruction. While the deconstructionists could only *argue* that
nothing exists outside of us — that reality is just personal perspective —
the cyberists had machines that could *make* it so.

In cyberspace, for example, the reality of your experience would
change depending on which part of yourself you decided to admit to,
and which you suppressed; each time you took on another persona on a
computer network (or pretended you were another sex), the cyberspace
world would adjust accordingly, proving that just as there *is* no core self,
neither is there an objective reality outside the individual mind.

All of which, it seemed to me, left one not-so-small problem: reality.
And reality has a bad attitude. It didn't read the assigned texts; it didn't
pay attention; it was completely oblivious to the fact that you'd entered
cyberspace with Professor Benedikt, or were now "rocking and humming in televirtuality," as Nicole Stenger had put it, in a community of
"highly unstable, hermaphrodite angels." If the power were to go out as
you swam, disembodied, disengendered, through the ether of pure information, you'd find yourself back in the solid world very quickly.

What we had here, I could see now, was self-indulgence raised to the
level of a science or, worse, rank escapism masquerading as political engagement. In cyberspace, Stenger had claimed, there would be "a shifting
from the sense of territory, of being an inhabitant of an earthly system of
values that includes roots, walls, possessions, toward a radical adventure
that blasts it all."[18] Reading this, I found myself thinking: tell that to Aung
San Suu Kyi, currently in her fifth year of house arrest in Myanmar. She'll
pass it on to the Burmese junta. Or talk to dissident Wei Jingsheng in Beijing, recently released after fourteen and a half years in prison and once
again demanding respect for human rights and democracy from the same
regime that imprisoned him. Tell the estimated two and a half million Su-
danese in imminent danger of starvation that reality is only a temporary
consensus. You tell me the mind is a leaking rainbow? I say that from

---

17. The fashionable nihilism I refer to is visible, for example, in Kevin Kelly, *Out
of Control: The Rise of Neo-Biological Civilization* (Reading, MA: Addison-Wesley,
1994), in which the expression "hip poststructuralist" appears frequently.

18. Stenger, p. 53.

Bosnia-Herzegovina to the Kashmir Valley to south Los Angeles, that airy metaphor is made grotesquely literal every day.

In a world quick to brandish the term *elitist* (our latter-day equivalent    50
of the tar brush and the bag of chicken feathers), here at last was a worthy target. Who, I wondered, were these people talking to? Who, exactly, was this electronic utopia they described intended for? And what about the rest of us? What would we do about all the men, women, or children, of whatever religious persuasion or ethnic background, of whatever class or race or education, who had the misfortune of having to deal with the world as it *is,* not as it *might* exist in the daydreams of Ph.D.'s and CEOs with five-thousand-dollar computers? Would bringing the ghettos on-line increase the life expectancy of young black men?[19]

The problem, I realized, was *not* that cyberspace would usurp reality as we know it, or that we would all disappear into some virtual world. The problem, simply put, was that cyberspace would distract us from the job at hand; that, busy blurring the boundaries between biology and mechanics with Allucquere Rosanne Stone, we'd forget that most of the human race was more immediately interested in survival than transcendence; that, as we spent more and more of our time fulfilling ourselves "far beyond aesthetic attachment" with Professor Heim, we'd forget that the followers of Louis Farrakhan and Tom Metzger and the late Meyer Kahane were going about their business; that, as we wandered through virtual forests, real ones burned.

But wasn't this, after all, highly unlikely? Wasn't it absurd to suggest that the culture of distraction could ever compete with the reality that surrounds us? At one time, I would have thought so. Then I entered the virtual world.

### Reading the Text

1. What is the vision of the future that Slouka encountered in the undergraduate course described in the beginning of this selection, and what is Slouka's attitude toward it?
2. Why is Slouka uncomfortable with the vision of a "cyberfuture" liberated "from the limitations of the human body"?
3. Describe in your own words what Slouka means by saying, "Cyberspace, I realized, represented the marriage of deconstruction and computer technology — a mating of monsters if ever there was one."

---

19. Brent Staples, for example, has argued eloquently that many of today's problems have low-tech solutions. Children, for example, increasingly dependent on television role models, require real individuals who will make a commitment to them in real life. Talking to them on the Internet won't help. See "Role Models, Bogus and Real," Editorial Notebook, *New York Times,* June 24, 1994.

4. What, according to Slouka, is the attitude toward ordinary reality among cyberenthusiasts?
5. What is the significance of Slouka's statement, "as we wandered through virtual forests, real ones burned"?

### Reading the Signs

1. In your journal, write a response to cyberenthusiasts like Nicole Stenger who welcome the prospect of cybersex.
2. Write an essay in which you defend, qualify, or challenge the rejection of objective reality that Slouka finds among the gurus of cyberspace. To develop your ideas, read or reread Sherry Turkle's "Who Am We?" (p. 730) or LynNell Hancock's "The Haves and the Have-Nots" (p. 748).
3. Slouka's sources claim that new kinds of personal relationships can be achieved in cyberspace. Compare those claims with the case studies in Sherry Turkle's "Who Am We?" (p. 730). To what extent do the case studies bear out Stenger's prediction of a world without a "trace of earth on our shoes"?
4. Adopting the perspective of Laura Miller ("Women and Children First: Gender and the Settling of the Electronic Frontier," p. 740), write a response to the belief that in cyberspace, "Nature . . . was merely an idea, a cultural construct. Like love. Or gender."
5. Interview at least five cyberenthusiasts on campus (they may be faculty, students, or staff) and ask them whether they subscribe to the cyberspace belief that "there's nothing 'real' out there. . . . Reality is just a habit." Use your findings as the basis of an essay in which you explain the extent to which Slouka's fears about the ideology of cyberspace are legitimate.


PHILLIP ELMER-DeWITT

## Cyberpunk

*Do you like to stay up all night visiting the WELL or rereading* Neuromancer? *Do you like to dress in black and wear mirrored shades? Do you know the identity of R. U. Sirius? If so, you may be a cyberpunk — though if you really are one, Phillip Elmer-DeWitt observes in this cook's tour of the cyberpunk domain, you probably resent such stereotypes. The shock troops of the cybernetic avant garde, cyberpunks have seen the future, Elmer-DeWitt suggests, and it is them. A senior editor for* Time, *Elmer-DeWitt directs the magazine's science and technology coverage and, in 1993, launched TIME Online.*

In the 1950s it was the beatniks, staging a coffeehouse rebellion against the *Leave It to Beaver* conformity of the Eisenhower era. In the 1960s the hippies arrived, combining antiwar activism with the energy of sex, drugs and rock 'n' roll. Now a new subculture is bubbling up from the underground, popping out of computer screens like a piece of futuristic hypertext.

They call it cyberpunk, a late-20th century term pieced together from cybernetics (the science of communication and control theory) and punk (an antisocial rebel or hoodlum). Within this odd pairing lurks the essence of cyberpunk culture. It's a way of looking at the world that combines an infatuation with high-tech tools and a disdain for conventional ways of using them. Originally applied to a school of hard-boiled science-fiction writers and then to certain semi-tough computer hackers, the word cyberpunk now covers a broad range of music, art, psychedelics, smart drugs and cutting-edge technology. The cult is new enough that fresh offshoots are sprouting every day, which infuriates the hardcore cyberpunks, who feel they got there first.

Stewart Brand, editor of the hippie-era *Whole Earth Catalog,* describes cyberpunk as "technology with attitude." Science-fiction writer Bruce Sterling calls it "an unholy alliance of the technical world with the underground of pop culture and street-level anarchy." Jude Milhon, a cyberpunk journalist who writes under the byline St. Jude, defines it as "the place where the worlds of science and art overlap, the intersection of the future and now." What cyberpunk is about, says Rudy Rucker, a San Jose State University mathematician who writes science-fiction books on the side, is nothing less than "the fusion of humans and machines."

As in any counterculture movement, some denizens would deny that they are part of a "movement" at all. Certainly they are not as visible from a passing car as beatniks or hippies once were. Ponytails (on men) and tattoos (on women) do not a cyberpunk make — though dressing in black and donning mirrored sunglasses will go a long way. And although the biggest cyberpunk journal claims a readership approaching 70,000, there are probably no more than a few thousand computer hackers, futurists, fringe scientists, computer-savvy artists and musicians, and assorted science-fiction geeks around the world who actually call themselves cyberpunks.

Nevertheless, cyberpunk may be the defining counterculture of the ⁵ computer age. It embraces, in spirit at least, not just the nearest thirtysomething hacker hunched over his terminal but also nose-ringed twentysomethings gathered at clandestine raves, teenagers who feel about the Macintosh computer the way their parents felt about Apple Records, and even preadolescent vidkids fused like Krazy Glue to their Super Nintendo and Sega Genesis games — the training wheels of cyberpunk. Obsessed with technology, especially technology that is just beyond their reach (like brain implants), the cyberpunks are future-oriented to a fault. They already have one foot in the 21st century, and time is on their side. In the long run, we will all be cyberpunks.

The cyberpunk look — a kind of SF (science-fiction) surrealism tweaked by computer graphics — is already finding its way into art galleries, music videos and Hollywood movies. Cyberpunk magazines, many of which are "'zines" cheaply published by desktop computer and distributed by electronic mail, are multiplying like cable-TV channels. The newest, a glossy, big-budget entry called *Wired,* premiered last week with Bruce Sterling on the cover and ads from the likes of Apple Computer and AT&T. Cyberpunk music, including acid house and industrial, is popular enough to keep several record companies and scores of bands cranking out CDs. Cyberpunk-oriented books are snapped up by eager fans as soon as they hit the stores. (Sterling's latest, *The Hacker Crackdown,* quickly sold out its first hard-cover printing of 30,000.) A piece of cyberpunk performance art, *Tubes,* starring Blue Man Group, is a hit off-Broadway. And cyberpunk films such as *Blade Runner, Videodrome, Robocop, Total Recall, Terminator 2,* and *The Lawnmower Man* have moved out of the cult market and into the mall.

Cyberpunk culture is likely to get a boost from, of all things, the Clinton-Gore Administration, because of a shared interest in what the new regime calls America's "data highways" and what the cyberpunks call cyberspace. Both terms describe the globe-circling, interconnected telephone network that is the conduit for billions of voice, fax and computer-to-computer communications. The incoming Administration is focused on the wiring, and it has made strengthening the network's high-speed data links a priority. The cyberpunks look at those wires from the inside; they talk of the network as if it were an actual place — a virtual reality that can be entered, explored and manipulated.

Cyberspace plays a central role in the cyberpunk world view. The literature is filled with "console cow-boys" who prove their mettle by donning virtual-reality headgear and performing heroic feats in the imaginary "matrix" of cyberspace. Many of the punks' real-life heroes are also computer cowboys of one sort or another. *Cyberpunk,* a 1991 book by two *New York Times* reporters, John Markoff and Katie Hafner, features profiles of three canonical cyberpunk hackers, including Robert Morris, the Cornell graduate student whose computer virus brought the huge network called the Internet to a halt.

But cyberspace is more than a playground for hacker high jinks. What cyberpunks have known for some time — and what 17.5 million modem-equipped computer users around the world have discovered — is that cyberspace is also a new medium. Every night on Prodigy, CompuServe, GEnie and thousands of smaller computer bulletin boards, people by the hundreds of thousands are logging on to a great computer-mediated gabfest, an interactive debate that allows them to

leap over barriers of time, place, sex and social status. Computer networks make it easy to reach out and touch strangers who share a particular obsession or concern. "We're replacing the old drugstore soda
fountain and town square, where community used to happen in the
physical world," says Howard Rheingold, a California-based author
and editor who is writing a book on what he calls virtual communities.

Most computer users are content to visit cyberspace now and then, to    10
read their electronic mail, check the bulletin boards and do a bit of electronic shopping. But cyberpunks go there to live and play — and even
die. The WELL, one of the hippest virtual communities on the Internet,
was shaken 2½ years ago when one of its most active participants ran a
computer program that erased every message he had ever left — thousands
of postings, some running for many pages. It was an act that amounted to
virtual suicide. A few weeks later, he committed suicide for real.

The WELL is a magnet for cyberpunk thinkers, and it is there, appropriately enough, that much of the debate over the scope and significance
of cyberpunk has occurred. The question "Is there a cyberpunk movement?" launched a freewheeling on-line flame fest that ran for months.
The debate yielded, among other things, a fairly concise list of "attitudes" that, by general agreement, seem to be central to the idea of cyberpunk. Among them:

*Information wants to be free.* A good piece of information-age technology will eventually get into the hands of those who can make the best
use of it, despite the best efforts of the censors, copyright lawyers and
datacops.

*Always yield to the hands-on imperative.* Cyberpunks believe they can
run the world for the better, if they can only get their hands on the control box.

*Promote decentralization.* Society is splintering into hundreds of subcultures and designer cults, each with its own language, code and
life-style.

*Surf the edges.* When the world is changing by the nanosecond, the     15
best way to keep your head above water is to stay at the front end of the
Zeitgeist.

The roots of cyberpunk, curiously, are as much literary as they are
technological. The term was coined in the late 1980s to describe a group
of science-fiction writers — and in particular William Gibson, a 44-year-
old American now living in Vancouver. Gibson's *Neuromancer,* the first
novel to win SF's triple crown — the Hugo, Nebula and Philip K. Dick
awards — quickly became a cyberpunk classic, attracting an audience beyond the world of SF. Critics were intrigued by a dense, technopoetic
prose style that invites comparisons to Hammett, Burroughs and
Pynchon. Computer-literate readers were drawn by Gibson's nightmarish depictions of an imaginary world disturbingly similar to the one they
inhabit.

In fact, the key to cyberpunk science fiction is that it is not so much a projection into the future as a metaphorical evocation of today's technological flux. The hero of *Neuromancer,* a burned-out, drug-addicted street hustler named Case, inhabits a sleazy interzone on the fringes of a megacorporate global village where all transactions are carried out in New Yen. There he encounters Molly, a sharp-edged beauty with reflective lenses grafted to her eye sockets and retractable razor blades implanted in her fingers. They are hired by a mysterious employer who offers to fix Case's damaged nerves so he can once again enter cyberspace — a term Gibson invented. Soon Case discovers that he is actually working for an AI (artificial intelligence) named Wintermute, who is trying to get around the restrictions placed on AIs by the turing police to keep the computers under control. "What's important to me," says Gibson, "is that *Neuromancer* is about the present."

The themes and motifs of cyberpunk have been percolating through the culture for nearly a decade. But they have coalesced in the past few years, thanks in large part to an upstart magazine called *Mondo 2000.* Since 1988, *Mondo*'s editors have covered cyberpunk as *Rolling Stone* magazine chronicles rock music, with celebrity interviews of such cyberheroes as negativland and Timothy Leary, alongside features detailing what's hot and what's on the horizon. *Mondo*'s editors have packaged their quirky view of the world into a glossy book titled *Mondo 2000: A User's Guide to the New Edge* (HarperCollins; $20). Its cover touts alphabetic entries on everything from virtual reality and wetware to designer aphrodisiacs and techno-erotic paganism, promising to make cyberpunk's rarefied perspective immediately accessible. Inside, in an innovative hypertext format (which is echoed in this article), relatively straightforward updates on computer graphics, multimedia and fiber optics accompany wild screeds on such recondite subjects as synesthesia and temporary autonomous zones.

The book and the magazine that inspired it are the product of a group of brainy (if eccentric) visionaries holed up in a rambling Victorian mansion perched on a hillside in Berkeley, California. The MTV-style graphics are supplied by designer Bart Nagel, the overcaffeinated prose by Ken Goffman (writing under the pen name R. U. Sirius) and Alison Kennedy (listed on the masthead as Queen Mu, "domineditrix"), with help from Rudy Rucker and a small staff of freelancers and contributions from an international cast of cyberpunk enthusiasts. The goal is to inspire and instruct but not to lead. "We don't want to tell people what to think," says assistant art director Heide Foley. "We want to tell them what the possibilities are."

Largely patched together from back issues of *Mondo 2000* magazine [20] (and its precursor, a short-lived 'zine called *Reality Hackers*), the *Guide* is filled with articles on all the traditional cyberpunk obsessions, from artificial life to virtual sex. But some of the best entries are those that report on the activities of real people trying to live the cyberpunk life. For example, Mark Pauline, a San Francisco performance artist, specializes in giant machines and vast public spectacles: sonic booms that pin audiences to their chairs or the huge, stinking vat of rotting cheese with which he perfumed the air of Denmark to remind the citizenry of its Viking roots. When an explosion blew the thumb and three fingers off his right hand, Pauline simply had his big toe grafted where his thumb had been. He can pick things up again, but now he's waiting for medical science and grafting technology to advance to the point where he can replace his jerry-built hand with one taken from a cadaver.

Much of *Mondo 2000* strains credibility. Does physicist Nick Herbert really believe there might be a way to build time machines? Did the cryonics experts at Trans-Time Laboratory really chill a family pet named Miles and then, after its near death experience, turn it back into what its owner describes as a "fully functional dog"? Are we expected to accept on faith that a smart drug called centrophenoxine is an "intelligence booster" that provides "effective anti-aging therapy," or that another compound called hydergine increases mental abilities and prevents damage to brain cells? "All of this has some basis in today's technologies," says Paul Saffo, a research fellow at the Institute for the Future. "But it has a very anticipatory quality. These are people who assume that they will shape the future and the rest of us will live it."

Parents who thumb through *Mondo 2000* will find much here to upset them. An article on house music makes popping MDMA (Ecstasy) and thrashing all night to music that clocks 120 beats per minute sound like an experience no red-blooded teenager would want to miss. After describing in detail the erotic effects of massive doses of L-dopa, MDA and deprenyl, the entry on aphrodisiacs adds as an afterthought that in some combinations these drugs can be fatal. Essays praising the beneficial effects of psychedelics and smart drugs on the "information processing" power of the brain sit alongside rants that declare, among other things, that "safe sex is boring sex" and that "cheap thrills are fun."

Much of this, of course, is a cyberpunk pose. As Rucker confesses in his preface, he enjoys reading and thinking about psychedelic drugs but doesn't really like to take them. "To me the political point of being pro-psychedelic," he writes, "is that this means being against consensus reality, which I very strongly am." To some extent, says author Rheingold, cyberpunk is driven by young people trying to come up with a movement they can call their own. As he puts it, "They're tired of all these old geezers talking about how great the '60s were."

That sentiment was echoed by a recent posting on the WELL. "I didn't get to pop some 'shrooms and dance naked in a park with several hundred of my peers," wrote a cyberpunk wannabe who calls himself Alien. "To me, and to a lot of other generally disenfranchised members of my generation, surfing the edges is all we've got."

More troubling, from a philosophic standpoint, is the theme of   25
dystopia that runs like a bad trip through the cyberpunk worldview. Gibson's fictional world is filled with glassy-eyed girls strung out on their Walkman-like simstim decks and young men who get their kicks from microsofts plugged into sockets behind their ears. His brooding, dehumanized vision conveys a strong sense that technology is changing civilization and the course of history in frightening ways. But many of his readers don't seem to care. "History is a funny thing for cyberpunks," says Christopher Meyer, a music-synthesizer designer from Calabasas, California, writing on the WELL. "It's all data. It all takes up the same amount of space on disk, and a lot of it is just plain noise."

For cyberpunks, pondering history is not as important as coming to terms with the future. For all their flaws, they have found ways to live with technology, to make it theirs — something the back-to-the-land hippies never accomplished. Cyberpunks use technology to bridge the gulf between art and science, between the world of literature and the world of industry. Most of all, they realize that if you don't control technology, it will control you. It is a lesson that will serve them — and all of us — well in the next century.


### Reading the Text

1. According to Elmer-DeWitt, what is the essence of cyberpunk?
2. What are some of the favorite books, music, and fashions of cyberpunks, in Elmer-DeWitt's account? Why do cyberpunks find them attractive?
3. What is Elmer-DeWitt's attitude toward cyberpunk?
4. What is the dystopian vision of *Mondo 2000,* in Elmer-DeWitt's view, and why do cyberpunks endorse it?
5. What does cyberpunk Christopher Meyer mean by saying, "History is a funny thing for cyberpunks. . . . It's all data. It all takes up the same amount of space on disk, and a lot of it is just plain noise"?


### Reading the Signs

1. Read or reread Walter Kirn's "Twentysomethings" (p. 214) and compare and contrast the twentysomethings he describes with cyberpunks. To what extent do you share author Howard Rheingold's contention that "young people [are] trying to come up with a movement they can call their own"?
2. By exploring the youth-rebellion elements of cyberpunk culture, Elmer-DeWitt implies that it all might be just a fad. Write an essay in which you argue whether cyberculture is just another fashion option or a force that will indeed shape the future.

3. Write an essay in which you argue whether hackers would be considered cyberheroes or cybervillains. To develop your ideas, read or reread Winn Schwartau's "Hackers: The First Information Warriors" (p. 618).

4. In class, brainstorm a list of cyberpunk phenomena, including fashion, music, books and magazines, and film. Discuss your results. What images are associated with cyberpunk, and how do you explain their appeal?

5. In class, form four groups and assign each group the role of Phillip Elmer-DeWitt, Mark Slouka ("'Reality Is Death,'" p. 706), Sherry Turkle ("Who Am We?" p. 730), or LynNell Hancock ("The Haves and the Have-Nots," p. 748). Then stage a conversation among the groups, focusing on the contention that cyberculture is a dangerous indulgence in fantasy.

A M Y   B R U C K M A N
*Christmas Unplugged*

*One of the advantages of the Internet is that, equipped with a powerful enough laptop computer, you can take it with you almost anywhere. The problem, Amy Bruckman (b. 1965) suggests in this personal reflection about her life on the Net, is that you can become entrapped in it. Sometimes, Bruckman says, she has to force herself to leave her computer behind so that she can reexperience a world without e-mail and chatrooms — a world unplugged. A doctoral candidate at the Media Lab at MIT, Bruckman specializes in virtual communities. She is the founder of MediaMoo, a MUD designed for media researchers, and MOOSE Crossing, a MUD designed to be an innovative learning environment for children.*

If I had a network link, I'd be home now.

From my chaise lounge on the terrace of my parents' Miami Beach apartment, I see a grid of four-lane roads with palm-treed median strips, yachts moored on the inland waterway, a golf course, and a dozen tall white condominiums. The hum of traffic is punctuated by the soft thunk of racquets striking tennis balls somewhere below. The temperature is in the 70s and a breeze blows through my toes. I am a long way from Boston. If I had a net link, I'd know exactly how far.

I'd know the weather forecast for Miami, and, if I cared, for Boston too. Just about anything you might like to know is out there on the worldwide computer network — the Net — if you know where to look.

It's Christmas day in Miami, but I'm not sure it would really be Christmas or I would really be in Miami if I were plugged into the Net. I would be in my virtual office, a "room" in the text-based virtual reality environment where I do most of my work. I have a desk there, piled with things to do, and a fish tank — just like my "real" office. Except that the virtual fish don't need to be fed — they're just a program I created one day while procrastinating from real work. My virtual office is just some data on a computer housed at MIT that I can tap into from anywhere, but it is a place to me. When I log onto the network, I am there.

And I would be there right now, if not for a difficult choice I made                     5
two days ago. I was packed for my trip south and had called a cab. I had the important things: airline ticket, wallet, bathing suit. I stood in the hall staring at a padded gray bag, the one containing my Macintosh PowerBook computer. I grabbed the bag, double-locked the door, and started to walk down the hall. I stopped. I went back, opened the door, and put down the gray bag. I stood in the doorway, feeling foolish. The taxi honked. The honk gave me courage: I locked up again, leaving my computer — my office — behind.

A vacation should be about escaping from routines; going somewhere else provides a new perspective. But when I travel with my PowerBook, I bring many of my routines with me. I can readily gain access to all my familiar tools for finding information. It's as if I never left. And that's the problem. Had I brought my computer, I would not have written this essay (for which I am using a pencil). Instead, I would have logged onto the network and entered its seductive, engrossing world. By now I would have read the newswire and Miss Manners's column, answered a dozen questions from friends and colleagues, and possibly posted my thoughts on a movie I saw last night to a public discussion group. It would be as if I never left home.

The network destroys a sense of time as well as place. Daily and seasonal rhythms are subtle at best. As morning turns to evening, I am more likely to bump into my friends in Hawaii, less likely to encounter my friends in England. In the summer, things quiet down. April 1st is the only real network holiday — don't believe anything you read that day! Beyond that, life on the Net proceeds at an even, unpunctuated pace. There are no holiday decorations on the Net.

On my flight down here I saw a young boy carrying a sleek black bag on his shoulder. He held it naturally, but with a hint of importance. It took me a moment to see the logo: it contained his Nintendo Game Boy. His generation sees nothing remarkable about traveling at all times with a computer. It is already possible to connect to the network from a palm-sized computer with a cellular link. As computers get smaller and cheaper, we will lose even the excuse of the weight of that black bag or the cost of losing it.

The Net is becoming an important part of the lives of a broader segment of the population. Its spread presents a worrisome challenge: is it ever possible for us to take uninterrupted time off any more? The new technologies of connectedness are pushing people to blend their many roles into one: personal mail is mixed with professional correspondence, and work crises arrive on a cellular phone during leisure time. If our coworkers and competitors have made themselves perpetually available, we feel all the more pressure to do the same, lest we be left behind. One of my colleagues deliberately vacations in places so remote that getting a Net connection is almost impossible — it's the only way she can get a real break, and, for a little while at least, be a carefree newlywed instead of a world-renowned researcher. But such exotic locales are getting harder and harder to find.

I love the network and the people and places I find there. But sometimes I find it important to disconnect — to leave the cellular phone and the beeper in a desk drawer, leave that padded gray bag at home. To be out of touch, not for hours but for days. To leave behind routines, both virtual and real. 10

### *Reading the Text*

1. Why does Bruckman say that not taking her laptop computer with her on vacation was a "difficult choice"?
2. How, in Bruckman's view, does the Net affect our sense of time?
3. According to Bruckman, how do high-tech paraphernalia interfere with our personal lives and leisure time?
4. What is the implied value of the ability "to leave behind routines, both virtual and real," as Bruckman suggests?

### *Reading the Signs*

1. In some university towns (such as Cambridge, Massachusetts), one can find coffeehouses that offer Internet connection jacks to computer-toting patrons. Writing from Bruckman's point of view, write a commentary on the cultural significance of such a practice.
2. In your journal, discuss the effect that computers, beepers, phone answering machines, cellular phones, and the like have had on your life. Do you think they blur the lines between your public and private selves? Do you feel, with Bruckman, that you sometimes need to "disconnect" from all the technology? Why or why not?
3. As an Internet "insider," Bruckman assumes an "us" that is in danger of losing the ability to take time off from professional life. Write an essay in which you argue whether you think the "us" assumed by Bruckman includes enough people to make this concern a real social worry. To

develop your ideas, read or reread LynNell Hancock, "The Haves and the Have-Nots" (p. 748).
4. Write an essay in which you defend, challenge, or modify Bruckman's claim that "the new technologies of connectedness are pushing people to blend their many roles into one." To what extent do you believe she describes this phenomenon accurately, and do you agree with her assessment of its impact on modern American life?

SHERRY   TURKLE

## Who Am We?

*Thanks to MOOs and MUDs (these are not barnyard terms), experienced travelers on the information superhighway can construct entire worlds of their own, complete with self-invented identities and interpersonal relationships that can make them like characters in their own novels. In this survey of hard-core players of the games that cybernauts play, Sherry Turkle reveals what life is like after* Dungeons and Dragons. *Indeed, for some players, life on the Web is better than life in the world, seeming to prefer virtual space and time to real space and time. Professor of Sociology of Science at MIT, Turkle has written widely on psychoanalysis, culture, technology, and computers. She is the author of* Psychoanalytic Politics: Jacques Lacan and Freud's French Revolution *(second ed., 1992),* The Second Self: Computers and the Human Spirit *(1984), and* Life on the Net: Identity in the Age of the Internet *(1995), from which this selection was taken.*

In the early 1970s, the face-to-face role-playing game *Dungeons and Dragons* swept the game culture. The term "dungeon" persisted in the high-tech culture to connote a virtual place. So when virtual spaces were created that many computer users could share and collaborate within, they were deemed Multi-User Dungeons or MUDs, a new kind of social virtual reality. (Some games use software that make them technically MUSHes or MOOs, but the term MUD has come to refer to all of the multiuser environments.)

MUDs are a new kind of virtual parlor game and a new form of community. In addition, text-based MUDs are a new form of collaboratively written literature. MUD players are MUD authors, the creators as well as consumers of media content. In this, participating in a MUD has much in common with scriptwriting, performance art, street theater, improvisational theater, or even commedia dell'arte. But MUDs are something else as well.

As players participate, they become authors not only of text but of themselves, constructing new selves through social interaction. Since one participates in MUDs by sending text to a computer that houses the MUD's program and database, MUD selves are constituted in interaction with the machine. Take it away and the MUD selves cease to exist: "Part of me, a very important part of me, only exists inside PernMUD," says one player. Several players joke that they are like "the electrodes in the computer," trying to express the degree to which they feel part of its space.

All MUDs are organized around the metaphor of physical space. When you first enter a MUD, you may find yourself in a medieval church from which you can step out into the town square, or you may find yourself in the coat closet of a large, rambling house. For example, when you first log on to LambdaMoo, one of the most popular MUDs on the Internet, you see the following description:

> The Coat Closet. The Closet is a dark, cramped space. It appears to be very crowded in here; you keep bumping into what feels like coats, boots, and other people (apparently sleeping). One useful thing that you've discovered in your bumbling about is a metal doorknob set at waist level into what might be a door. There's a new edition of the newspaper. Type "news" to see it.

In the MUDs, virtual characters converse with each other, exchange   5 gestures, express emotions, win and lose virtual money, and rise and fall in social status. A virtual character can also die. Some die of "natural" causes (a player decides to close them down), or they can have their virtual lives snuffed out. This is all achieved through writing, and this in a culture that had apparently fallen asleep in the audiovisual arms of television. Yet this new writing is a kind of hybrid: speech momentarily frozen into artifact, but curiously ephemeral artifact. In this new writing, unless it is printed out on paper, a screenful of flickers soon replaces the previous screen.

The anonymity of MUDs gives people the chance to express multiple and often unexplored aspects of the self, to play with their identity and to try out new ones. MUDs make possible the creation of an identity so fluid and multiple that it strains the limits of the notion. Identity, after all, refers to the sameness between two qualities, in this case between a person and his or her persona. But in MUDs, one can be many.

A 21-year-old college senior defends his violent characters as "something in me; but quite frankly I'd rather rape on MUDs where no harm is done." A 26-year-old clerical worker says, "I'm not one thing, I'm many things. Each part gets to be more fully expressed in MUDs than in the real world. So even though I play more than one self on MUDs, I feel more like 'myself' when I'm MUDding." In real life, this woman sees her world as too narrow to allow her to manifest certain aspects of the person she feels herself to be. Creating screen personae is thus an opportunity for self-expression, leading to her feeling more like her true self when decked out in an array of virtual masks.

MUDs imply difference, multiplicity, heterogeneity, and fragmentation. Such an experience of identity contradicts the Latin root of the word, *idem,* meaning "the same." But this contradiction increasingly defines the conditions of our lives beyond the virtual world. MUDs thus become objects-to-think-with for thinking about postmodern selves. Indeed, the unfolding of all MUD action takes place in a resolutely postmodern context. There are parallel narratives in the different rooms of a MUD. The cultures of Tolkien, Gibson, and Madonna coexist and interact. Since MUDs are authored by their players, thousands of people in all, often hundreds at a time, are all logged on from different places; the solitary author is displaced and distributed. Traditional ideas about identity have been tied to a notion of authenticity that such virtual experiences actively subvert. When each player can create many characters in many games, the self is not only decentered but multiplied without limit.

As a new social experience, MUDs pose many psychological questions: If a persona in a role-playing game drops defenses that the player in real life has been unable to abandon, what effect does this have? What if a persona enjoys success in some area (say, flirting) that the player has not been able to achieve? Slippages often occur in places where persona and self merge, where the multiple personae join to comprise what the individual thinks of as his or her authentic self.

Doug is a Midwestern college junior. He plays four characters distributed across three different MUDs. One is a seductive woman. One is a macho, cowboy type whose self-description stresses that he is a "Marlboros rolled in the T-shirt sleeve kind of guy." The third is a rabbit of unspecified gender who wanders its MUD introducing people to each other, a character he calls Carrot. Doug says, "Carrot is so low key that people let it be around while they are having private conversations. So I think of Carrot as my passive, voyeuristic character." Doug's fourth character is one that he plays only on a MUD in which all the characters are furry animals. "I'd rather not even talk about that character because my anonymity there is very important to me," Doug says. "Let's just say that on FurryMUDs I feel like a sexual tourist." Doug talks about playing his characters in windows and says that using windows has made it possible for him to "turn pieces of my mind on and off."

"I split my mind. . . . I can see myself as being two or three or more. And I just turn on one part of my mind and then another when I go from window to window. I'm in some kind of argument in one window and trying to come on to a girl in a MUD in another, and another window might be running a spreadsheet program or some other technical thing for school. . . . And then I'll get a real-time message that flashes on the screen as soon as it is sent from another system user, and I guess that's RL. RL is just one more window, and it's not usually my best one."

Play has always been an important aspect of our individual efforts to build identity. The psychoanalyst Erik Erikson called play a "toy situation" that allows us to "reveal and commit" ourselves "in its unreality." While MUDs are not the only "places" on the Internet in which to play with identity, they provide an unparalleled opportunity for such play. On a MUD one actually gets to build character and environment and then to live within the toy situation. A MUD can become a context for discovering who one is and wishes to be. In this way, the games are laboratories for the construction of identity.

Stewart, a 23-year-old physics graduate student, uses MUDs to have experiences he can't imagine for himself in RL. His intense online involvements engaged key issues in his life but ultimately failed to help him reach successful resolutions.

Stewart's real life revolves around laboratory work and his plans for a future in science. His only friend is his roommate, another physics student whom he describes as even more reclusive than himself. For Stewart, this circumscribed, almost monastic student life does not represent a radical departure from what has gone before. He has had heart trouble since he was a child; one small rebellion, a ski trip when he was a college freshman, put him in the hospital for a week. He has lived life within a small compass.

Stewart is logged on to one MUD or another for at least 40 hours a 15 week. It seems misleading to call what he does there playing. He spends his time constructing a life that is more expansive than the one he lives in physical reality. Stewart, who has traveled very little and has never been to Europe, explains with delight that his favorite MUD, although played in English, is physically located on a computer in Germany and has many European players.

On the German MUD, Stewart shaped a character named Achilles, but he asks his MUD friends to call him Stewart as much as possible. He wants to feel that his real self exists somewhere between Stewart and Achilles. He wants to feel that his MUD life is part of his real life. Stewart insists that he does not role play, but that MUDs simply allow him to be a better version of himself.

On the MUD, Stewart creates a living environment suitable for his ideal self. His university dormitory is modest, but the room he has built for Achilles on the MUD is elegant and heavily influenced by Ralph Lauren advertising. He has named it "the home beneath the silver moon." There are books, a roaring fire, cognac, a cherry mantel "covered with pictures of Achilles's friends from around the world.

"You look up . . . and through the immense skylight you see a breathtaking view of the night sky. The moon is always full over Achilles's home, and its light fills the room with a warm glow."

Beyond expanding his social world, MUDs have brought Stewart the only romance and intimacy he has ever known. At a social event in virtual space, a "wedding" of two regular players on a German-based MUD I call Gargoyle, Achilles met Winterlight, a character played by one of the three female players on that MUD. Stewart, who has known little success in dating and romantic relationships, was able to charm this desirable player.

On their first virtual date, Achilles took Winterlight to an Italian    20 restaurant close to Stewart's dorm. He had often fantasized being there with a woman. Stewart used a combination of MUD commands to simulate a romantic evening — picking Winterlight up at the airport in a limousine, driving her to a hotel room so that she could shower, and then taking her to the restaurant and ordering veal for her.

This dinner date led to others during which Achilles was tender and romantic, chivalrous and poetic. The intimacy Achilles experienced during his courtship of Winterlight is unknown to Stewart in other contexts. "She's a very, she's a good friend. I found out a lot of things, from things about physiology to the color of nail polish she wears." Finally, Achilles asked for Winterlight's hand. When she accepted, they had a formal engagement ceremony on the MUD.

At the engagement, Winterlight gave Achilles a rose she had worn in her hair; Achilles gave her 1,000 paper stars.

Although Stewart participated in this ceremony alone in his room with his computer and modem, a group of European players actually traveled to Germany, site of Gargoyle's host computer, and got together for food and champagne. Many of the 25 guests at the German celebration brought gifts and dressed specially for the occasion. Stewart felt as though he were throwing a party. This was the first time that he had ever entertained, and he was proud of his success. In real life, Stewart felt constrained by his health problems, his shyness and social isolation, and his narrow economic straits. In the Gargoyle MUD, he bypassed these obstacles, at least temporarily.

The psychological effects of life on the screen can be complicated: a safe place is not all that is needed for personal change. Stewart came to MUDding with serious problems, and for Stewart, playing on MUDs led to a net drop in self-esteem. MUDs did help Stewart talk about his troubles while they were still emotionally relevant; nevertheless, he is emphatic that MUDding has ultimately made him feel worse about himself. MUDding did not alter Stewart's sense of himself as withdrawn, unappealing, and flawed.

While Stewart has tried hard to make his MUD self, the "better" Achilles self, part of his real life, he says he has failed. He says, "I'm not social. I don't like parties. I can't talk to people about my problems." The integration of the social Achilles, who can talk about his troubles, and the asocial Stewart, who can only cope by putting them out of mind, has not occurred. From Stewart's point of view, MUDs have stripped away some of his defenses but have given him nothing in return. In fact, MUDs make Stewart feel vulnerable in a new way. Although he hoped that MUDs would cure him, it is MUDs that now make him feel sick. He feels addicted to MUDs: "When you feel you're stagnating and you feel there's nothing going on in your life and you're stuck in a rut, it's very easy to be on there for a very large amount of time."

Stewart cannot learn from his character Achilles's experience and social success because they are too different from the things of which he believes himself capable. Despite his efforts to turn Achilles into Stewart, Stewart has split off his strengths and sees them as possible only for Achilles in the MUD. It is only Achilles who can create the magic and win the girl. In making this split between himself and the achievements of his screen persona, Stewart does not give himself credit for the positive steps he has taken in real life. Like an unsuccessful psychotherapy, MUDding has not helped Stewart bring these good experiences inside himself or integrate them into his self-image.

Relationships during adolescence are usually bounded by a mutual understanding that they involve limited commitment. Virtual space is well suited to such relationships; its natural limitations keep things within bounds. As in Thomas Mann's *The Magic Mountain,* which takes place in the isolation of a sanatorium, relationships become intense very quickly because the participants feel isolated in a remote and unfamiliar world with its own rules. MUDs, like other electronic meeting places, can breed a kind of easy intimacy. In a first phase, MUD players feel the excitement of a rapidly deepening relationship and the sense that time itself is speeding up. "The MUD quickens things. It quickens things so much," says one player. "You know, you don't think about it when you're doing it, but you meet somebody on the MUD, and within a week you feel like you've been friends forever."

In a second phase, players commonly try to take things from the virtual to the real and are usually disappointed.

Gender-swapping on MUDs is not a small part of the game action. By some estimates, Habitat, a Japanese MUD, has 1.5 million users. Habitat is a MUD operated for profit. Among the registered members of Habitat, there is a ratio of four real-life men to each real-life woman. But inside the MUD the ratio is only three male characters to one female character. In other words, a significant number of players, many tens of thousands of them, are virtually cross-dressing.

What is virtual gender-swapping all about? Some of those who do it 30 claim that it is not particularly significant. "When I play a woman I don't really take it too seriously," said 20-year-old Andrei. "I do it to improve the ratio of women to men. It's just a game." On one level, virtual gender-swapping is easier than doing it in real life. For a man to present himself as female in a chat room, on an IRC channel, or in a MUD, only requires writing a description. For a man to play a woman on the streets of an American city, he would have to shave various parts of his body; wear makeup, perhaps a wig, a dress, and high heels; perhaps change his voice, walk, and mannerisms. He would have some anxiety about passing, and there might be even more anxiety about not passing, which would pose a risk of violence and possibly arrest. So more men are willing to give virtual cross-dressing a try. But once they are online as female, they soon find maintaining this fiction is difficult. To pass as a woman for any length of time requires understanding how gender inflects speech, manner, the interpretation of experience. Women attempting to pass as men face the same kind of challenge.

Virtual cross-dressing is not as simple as Andrei suggests. Not only can it be technically challenging, it can be psychologically complicated. Taking a virtual role may involve you in ongoing relationships. You may discover things about yourself that you never knew before.

Case, a 34-year-old industrial designer who is happily married to a co-worker, is currently MUDding as a female character. In response to my question, "Has MUDding ever caused you any emotional pain?" he says, "Yes, but also the kind of learning that comes from hard times.

"I'm having pain in my playing now. Mairead, the woman I'm playing in MedievalMUSH, is having an interesting relationship with a fellow. Mairead is a lawyer, and the high cost of law school has to be paid for by a corporation or a noble house. She fell in love with a nobleman who paid for her law school. [Case slips into referring to Mairead in the first person.] Now he wants to marry me although I'm a commoner. I finally said yes. I try to talk to him about the fact that I'm essentially his property. I'm a commoner . . . I've grown up with it, that's the way life is. He wants to deny the situation. He says, 'Oh no, no, no. . . . We'll pick you up, set you on your feet, the whole world is open to you.' But every time I behave like I'm now going to be a countess some day . . . as in, 'And I never liked this wallpaper anyway,' I get pushed down. The relationship is pull up, push down. It's an incredibly psychologically damaging thing to do to a person. And the very thing that he liked about her, that she was independent, strong, said what was on her mind, it is all being bled out of her."

Case looks at me with a wry smile and sighs, "A woman's life." He continues: "I see her [Mairead] heading for a major psychological problem. What we have is a dysfunctional relationship. But even though it's very painful and stressful, it's very interesting to watch myself cope with this problem. How am I going to dig my persona's self out of this mess? Because I don't want to go on like this. I want to get out of it. . . . You can see that playing this woman lets me see what I have in my psychological repertoire, what is hard and what is easy for me. And I can also see how some of the things that work when you're a man just backfire when you're a woman."

Case further illustrates the complexity of gender swapping as a vehicle   35 for self-reflection. Case describes his RL persona as a nice guy, a "Jimmy Stewart type like my father." He says that in general he likes his father and he likes himself, but he feels he pays a price for his low-key ways. In particular, he feels at a loss when it comes to confrontation, both at home and in business dealings. Case likes MUDding as a female because it makes it easier for him to be aggressive and confrontational. Case plays several online "Katharine Hepburn types," strong, dynamic, "out there" women who remind him of his mother, "who says exactly what's on her mind and is a take-no-prisoners sort."

For Case, if you are assertive as a man, it is coded as "being a bastard." If you are assertive as a woman, it is coded as "modern and together."

Some women who play male characters desire invisibility or permission to be more outspoken or aggressive. "I was born in the South and taught that girls didn't speak up to disagree with men," says Zoe, a 34-year-old woman who plays male and female characters on four MUDs.

"We would sit at dinner and my father would talk and my mother would agree. I thought my father was a god. Once or twice I did disagree with him. I remember one time in particular when I was 10, and he looked at me and said, "Well, well, well, if this little flower grows too many more thorns, she will never catch a man."

Zoe credits MUDs with enabling her to reach a state of mind where she is better able to speak up for herself in her marriage ("to say what's on my mind before things get all blown out of proportion") and to handle her job as the financial officer for a small biotechnology firm.

"I played a MUD man for two years. First I did it because I wanted   40 the feeling of an equal playing field in terms of authority, and the only way I could think of to get it was to play a man. But after a while, I got very absorbed by MUDding. I became a wizard on a pretty simple MUD. I called myself Ulysses and got involved in the system and realized that as a man I could be firm and people would think I was a great wizard. As a woman, drawing the line and standing firm has always made me feel like a bitch and, actually, I feel that people saw me as one, too. As a man I was liberated from all that. I learned from my mistakes. I got better at being firm but not rigid. I practiced, safe from criticism."

Zoe's perceptions of her gender trouble are almost the opposite of Case's. While Case sees aggressiveness as acceptable only for women, Zoe sees it as acceptable only for men. These stories share a notion that a virtual gender swap gave people greater emotional range in the real. Zoe says: "I got really good at playing a man, so good that whoever was on the system would accept me as a man and talk to me as a man. So, other guys talked to Ulysses guy to guy. It was very validating. All those years I was paranoid about how men talked about women. Or I thought I was paranoid. Then I got a chance to be a guy and I saw that I wasn't paranoid at all."

> *Irony is about contradictions that do not resolve into larger wholes . . . about the tension of holding incompatible things together because both or all are necessary and true.*
>
> — DONNA HARAWAY

As we stand on the boundary between the real and the virtual, our experience recalls what the anthropologist Victor Turner termed a liminal moment, a moment of passage when new cultural symbols and meanings can emerge. Liminal moments are times of tension, extreme reactions, and great opportunity. When Turner talked about liminality, he understood it as a transitional state, but living with flux may no longer be temporary. Technology is bringing postmodernism down to earth itself; the story of technology refuses modernist resolutions and requires an openness to multiple viewpoints.

Multiple viewpoints call forth a new moral discourse. The culture of simulation may help us achieve a vision of a multiple but integrated identity whose flexibility, resilience, and capacity for joy comes from having access to our many selves. But if we have lost reality in the process, we shall have struck a poor bargain. In Wim Wenders's film *Until the End of the World,* a scientist develops a device that translates the electrochemical activity of the brain into digital images. He gives this technology to his family and closest friends, who are now able to hold small battery-driven monitors and watch their dreams. At first, they are charmed. They see their treasured fantasies, their secret selves. They see the images they otherwise would forget, the scenes they otherwise would repress. As with the personae one can play in a MUD, watching dreams on a screen opens up new aspects of the self.

However, the story soon turns dark. The images seduce. They are richer and more compelling than the real life around them. Wenders's characters fall in love with their dreams, become addicted to them. People wander about with blankets over their heads the better to see the monitors from which they cannot bear to be parted. They are imprisoned by the screens, imprisoned by the keys to their past that the screens seem to hold.

We, too, are vulnerable to using our screens in these ways. People  45 can get lost in virtual worlds. Some are tempted to think of life in cyberspace as insignificant, as escape or meaningless diversion. It is not. Our experiences there are serious play. We belittle them at our risk. We must understand the dynamics of virtual experience both to foresee who might be in danger and to put these experiences to best use. Without a deep understanding of the many selves that we express in the virtual, we cannot use our experiences there to enrich the real. If we cultivate our awareness of what stands behind our screen personae, we are more likely to succeed in using virtual experience for personal transformation.

The imperative to self-knowledge has always been at the heart of philosophical inquiry. In the 20th century, it found expression in the psychoanalytic culture as well. One might say that it constitutes the ethic of psychoanalysis. From the perspective of this ethic, we work to know ourselves in order to improve not only our own lives, but those of our families and society. Psychoanalysis is a survivor discourse. Born of a modernist worldview, it has evolved into forms relevant to postmodern times. With mechanistic roots in the culture of calculation, psychoanalytic ideas become newly relevant in the culture of simulation. Some believe that we are at the end of the Freudian century. But the reality is more complex. Our need for a practical philosophy of self-knowledge has never been greater as we struggle to make meaning from our lives on the screen.

### Reading the Text

1. In your own words, describe what a MUD is and how MUDs originated.
2. How, according to Turkle, do MUDs alter one's sense of identity?
3. How do Doug and Stewart, two young men described by Turkle, use MUDs to redefine their identities?
4. In Turkle's account, how do people use MUDs to engage in "virtual gender-swapping"?
5. How is anonymity an important component of MUDs, in Turkle's view?
6. What does anthropologist Victor Turner mean by "liminal moment," and how is cyberculture an instance of one?

### Reading the Signs

1. Stewart, as Turkle describes him, has invented an entire glamorous and romantic life that MUD players take seriously. Write a hypothetical letter to Stewart in which you either applaud his virtual creativity or encourage him to translate his fantasies into reality.

2. Turkle's case studies demonstrate a growing tendency to blur distinctions between fantasy and reality among many users of cyberspace. Write an essay in which you support or reject this trend.

3. In your journal, discuss the appeal of the computer-assisted ability to simulate many selves in different genders. Does such an ability strike you as liberating or foolish, and why?

4. In class, form teams and conduct a debate over the social effects of computer role playing. Does it solve personal problems, as Turkle's case studies claim, or will it lead to an inability to conduct a real social life? To develop your arguments, you might conduct interviews with students who are MUD fans.

5. If you have access to the necessary technology, join a MUD and then study your own experience. Are you tempted to try on a new persona? If so, what changes do you make and why; if not, why do you resist altering your public personality? Report your experiences to your class.

## LAURA MILLER

### Women and Children First: Gender and the Settling of the Electronic Frontier

<hr>

|||||||||||||||||||||||||||||||||||||||||||||||||||||

*The Web is often considered a masculine space into which women enter at their peril. Sexual harassment and outright intimidation of women are legion on the Web, right? Wrong, says Laura Miller (b. 1960), in this response to a* Newsweek *feature that dwelt upon the danger women faced on the Internet. An avid and experienced Internet participant, Miller feels she, and the many women like her who also spend a lot of time in cyberspace, can take care of themselves very well, thank you, and have no need for special protections. Senior editor at* Salon, *an Internet magazine, Miller has published in the* San Francisco Examiner, Wired, Harper's Bazaar, *and the* New York Times Book Review.

When *Newsweek* (May 16, 1994) ran an article entitled "Men, Women and Computers," all hell broke out on the Net, particularly on the on-line service I've participated in for six years, The WELL (Whole Earth 'Lectronic Link). "Cyberspace, it turns out," declared *Newsweek*'s Nancy Kantrowitz, "isn't much of an Eden after all. It's marred by just as many sexist ruts and gender conflicts as the Real World. . . . Women often feel about as welcome as a system crash." "It was horrible. Awful, poorly researched, unsubstantiated drivel," one member wrote, a senti-ment echoed throughout some 480 postings.

However egregious the errors in the article (some sources maintain that they were incorrectly quoted), it's only one of several mainstream media de-pictions of the Net as an environment hostile to women. Even women who had been complaining about on-line gender relations found themselves in-creasingly annoyed by what one WELL member termed the "cyberbabe ha-rassment" angle that seems to typify media coverage of the issue. Reified in the pages of *Newsweek* and other journals, what had once been the topic of discussions by insiders — on-line commentary is informal, conversational, and often spontaneous — became a journalistic "fact" about the Net known by complete strangers and novices. In a matter of months, the airy stuff of bitch sessions became widespread, hardened stereotypes.

At the same time, the Internet has come under increasing scrutiny as it mutates from an obscure, freewheeling web of computer networks used by a small elite of academics, scientists, and hobbyists to . . . well, nobody seems to know exactly what. But the business press prints vague, fevered prophecies of fabulous wealth, and a bonanza mentality has blos-somed. With it comes big business and the government, intent on regu-lating this amorphous medium into a manageable and profitable industry. The Net's history of informal self-regulation and its wide libertarian streak guarantee that battles like the one over the Clipper chip (a manda-tory decoding device that would make all encrypted data readable by federal agents) will be only the first among many.

Yet the threat of regulation is built into the very mythos used to conceptualize the Net by its defenders — and gender plays a crucial role in that threat. However revolutionary the technologized interactions of on-line communities may seem, we understand them by deploying a set of very familiar metaphors from the rich figurative soup of American cul-ture. Would different metaphors have allowed the Net a different, better historical trajectory? Perhaps not, but the way we choose to describe the Net now encourages us to see regulation as its inevitable fate. And, by examining how gender roles provide a foundation for the intensification of such social controls, we can illuminate the way those roles proscribe the freedoms of men as well as women.

For months I mistakenly referred to the EFF (an organization  5 founded by John Perry Barlow and Lotus 1-2-3 designer Mitch Kapor to foster access to, and further the discursive freedom of, on-line communi-cations) as "The Electronic Freedom Foundation," instead of by its actual name, "The Electronic Frontier Foundation." Once corrected, I was struck by how intimately related the ideas "frontier" and "freedom" are in the Western mythos. The *frontier,* as a realm of limitless possibilities and a few social controls, hovers, grail-like, in the American psyche, the dream our national identity is based on, but a dream that's always, some-how, just vanishing away.

Once made, the choice to see the Net as a frontier feels unavoidable, but it's actually quite problematic. The word "frontier" has traditionally described a place, if not land then the limitless "final frontier" of space. The Net, on the other hand, occupies precisely no physical space (although the computers and phone lines that make it possible do). It is a completely bodiless, symbolic thing with no discernable boundaries or location. The land of the American frontier did not become a "frontier" until Europeans determined to conquer it, but the continent existed before the intention to settle it. Unlike land, the Net was created by its pioneers.

Most peculiar, then, is the choice of the word "frontier" to describe an artifact so humanly constructed that it only exists as ideas or information. For central to the idea of the frontier is that it contains no (or very few) other people — fewer than two per square mile according to the nineteenth-century historian Frederick Turner. The freedom the frontier promises is a liberation from the demands of society, while the Net (I'm thinking now of Usenet) has nothing but society to offer. Without other people, news groups, mailing lists, and files simply wouldn't exist and e-mail would be purposeless. Unlike real space, cyberspace must be shared.

Nevertheless, the choice of a spatial metaphor (credited to the science-fiction novelist William Gibson, who coined the term "cyber-space"), however awkward, isn't surprising. Psychologist Julian Jaynes has pointed out that geographical analogies have long predominated humanity's efforts to conceptualize — map out — consciousness. Unfortunately, these analogies bring with them a heavy load of baggage comparable to Pandora's box: open it and a complex series of problems have come to stay.

The frontier exists beyond the edge of settled or owned land. As the land that doesn't belong to anybody (or to people who "don't count," like Native Americans), it is on the verge of being acquired; currently unowned, but still ownable. Just as the idea of chastity makes virginity sexually provocative, so does the unclaimed territory invite settlers, irresistibly so. Americans regard the lost geographical frontier with a melancholy, voluptuous fatalism — we had no choice but to advance upon it and it had no alternative but to submit. When an EFF member compares the Clipper chip to barbed wire encroaching on the prairie, doesn't he realize the surrender implied in his metaphor?

The psychosexual undercurrents (if anyone still thinks of them as    10
"under") in the idea of civilization's phallic intrusion into nature's passive, feminine space have been observed, exhaustively, elsewhere. The classic Western narrative is actually far more concerned with social relationships than conflicts between man and nature. In these stories, the frontier is a lawless society of men, a milieu in which physical strength, courage, and personal charisma supplant institutional authority and violent conflict is the accepted means of settling disputes. The Western narrative connects pleasurably with the American romance of individualistic

masculinity; small wonder that the predominantly male founders of the Net's culture found it so appealing.

When civilization arrives on the frontier, it comes dressed in skirts and short pants. In the archetypal 1939 movie *Dodge City,* Wade Hatton (Errol Flynn) refuses to accept the position of marshal because he prefers the footloose life of a trail driver. Abbie Irving (Olivia de Haviland), a recent arrival from the civilized East, scolds him for his unwillingness to accept and advance the cause of law; she can't function (in her job as crusading journalist) in a town governed by brute force. It takes the accidental killing of a child in a street brawl for Hatton to realize that he must pin on the badge and clean up Dodge City.

In the Western mythos, civilization is necessary because women and children are victimized in conditions of freedom. Introduce women and children into a frontier town and the law must follow because women and children must be protected. Women, in fact, are usually the most vocal proponents of the conversion from frontier justice to civil society.

The imperiled women and children of the Western narrative make their appearance today in newspaper and magazine articles that focus on the intimidation and sexual harassment of women on line and reports of pedophiles trolling for victims in computerized chat rooms. If on-line women successfully contest these attempts to depict them as the beleaguered prey of brutish men, expect the pedophile to assume a larger profile in arguments that the Net is out of control.

In the meantime, the media prefer to cast women as the victims, probably because many women actively participate in the call for greater regulation of on-line interactions, just as Abbie Irving urges Wade Hatton to bring the rule of law to Dodge City. These requests have a long cultural tradition, based on the idea that women, like children, constitute a peculiarly vulnerable class of people who require special protection from the elements of society men are expected to confront alone. In an insufficiently civilized society like the frontier, women, by virtue of this childlike vulnerability, are thought to live under the constant threat of kidnap, abuse, murder, and especially rape.

Women, who have every right to expect that crimes against their person will be rigorously prosecuted, should nevertheless regard the notion of special protections (chivalry, by another name) with suspicion. Based as it is on the idea that women are inherently weak and incapable of self-defense and that men are innately predatory, it actually reinforces the power imbalance between the sexes, with its roots in the concept of women as property, constantly under siege and requiring the vigilant protection of their male owners. If the romance of the frontier arises from the promise of vast stretches of unowned land, an escape from the restrictions of a society based on private property, the introduction of women spoils that dream by reintroducing the imperative of property in their own persons.

How does any of this relate to on-line interactions, which occur not on a desert landscape but in a complex, technological society where women are supposed to command equal status with men? It accompanies us as a set of unexamined assumptions about what it means to be male or female, assumptions that we believe are rooted in the imperatives of our bodies. These assumptions follow us into the bodiless realm of cyberspace, a forum where, as one scholar puts it "participants are washed clean of the stigmata of their real 'selves' and are free to invent new ones to their tastes." Perhaps some observers feel that the replication of gender roles in a context where the absence of bodies supposedly makes them superfluous proves exactly how innate those roles are. Instead, I see in the relentless attempts to interpret on-line interactions as highly gendered, an intimation of just how artificial, how created, our gender system is. If it comes "naturally," why does it need to be perpetually defended and reasserted?

Complaints about the treatment of women on line fall into three categories: that women are subjected to excessive, unwanted sexual attention, that the prevailing style of on-line discussion turns women off, and that women are singled out by male participants for exceptionally dismissive or hostile treatment. In making these assertions, the *Newsweek* article and other stories on the issue do echo grievances that some on-line women have made for years. And, without a doubt, people have encountered sexual come-ons, aggressive debating tactics, and ad hominem attacks on the Net. However, individual users interpret such events in widely different ways, and to generalize from those interpretations to describe the experiences of women and men as a whole is a rash leap indeed.

I am one of many women who don't recognize their own experience of the Net in the misogynist gauntlet described above. In researching this essay, I joined America Online and spent an hour or two "hanging out" in the real-time chat rooms reputed to be rife with sexual harassment. I received several "instant messages" from men, initiating private conversations with innocuous questions about my hometown and tenure on the service. One man politely inquired if I was interested in "hot phone talk" and just as politely bowed out when I declined. At no point did I feel harassed or treated with disrespect. If I ever want to find a phone-sex partner, I now know where to look but until then I probably won't frequent certain chat rooms.

Other women may experience a request for phone sex or even those tame instant messages as both intrusive and insulting (while still others maintain that they have received much more explicit messages and inquiries completely out of the blue). My point isn't that my reactions are the more correct, but rather that both are the reactions of women, and no journalist has any reason to believe that mine are the exception rather than the rule.

For me, the menace in sexual harassment comes from the underlying    20
threat of rape or physical violence. I see my body as the site of my
heightened vulnerability as a woman. But on line — where I have no
body and neither does anyone else — I consider rape to be impossible.
Not everyone agrees. Julian Dibble, in an article for *The Village Voice,* describes the repercussions of a "rape" in a multiuser dimension, or MUD,
in which one user employed a subprogram called a "voodoo doll" to
cause the personae of other users to perform sexual acts. Citing the "conflation of speech and act that's inevitable in any computer-mediated
world," he moved toward the conclusion that "since rape can occur
without any physical pain or damage, then it must be classified as a crime
against the mind." Therefore, the offending user had committed something on the same "conceptual continuum" as rape. Tellingly, the incident led to the formation of the first governmental entity on the MUD.

No doubt the cyber-rapist (who went by the nom de guerre Mr.
Bungle) appreciated the elevation of his mischief-making to the rank of
virtual felony: all of the outlaw glamour and none of the prison time (he
was exiled from the MUD). Mr. Bungle limited his victims to personae
created by women users, a choice that, in its obedience to prevailing
gender roles, shaped the debate that followed his crimes. For, in accordance with the real-world understanding that women's smaller, physically weaker bodies and lower social status make them subject to violation by men, there's a troubling notion in the real and virtual worlds that
women's minds are also more vulnerable to invasion, degradation, and
abuse.

This sense of fragility extends beyond interactions with sexual overtones. The *Newsweek* article reports that women participants can't tolerate the harsh, contentious quality of on-line discussions, that they prefer
mutual support to heated debate, and are retreating wholesale to women-
only conferences and newsgroups. As someone who values on-line forums precisely because they mandate equal time for each user who
chooses to take it and forestall various "alpha male" rhetorical tactics like
interrupting, loudness, or exploiting the psychosocial advantages of
greater size or a deeper voice, I find this perplexing and disturbing. In
these laments I hear the reluctance of women to enter into the kind of
robust debate that characterizes healthy public life, a willingness to let
men bully us even when they've been relieved of most of their traditional advantages. Withdrawing into an electronic purdah where one will
never be challenged or provoked, allowing the ludicrous ritual chest-
thumping of some users to intimidate us into silence — surely women
can come up with a more spirited response than this.

And of course they can, because besides being riddled with reductive
stereotypes, media analyses like *Newsweek*'s simply aren't accurate. While
the on-line population is predominantly male, a significant and vocal minority of women contribute regularly and more than manage to hold

their own. Some of the WELL's most bombastic participants are women, just as there are many tactful and conciliatory men. At least, I think there are, because, ultimately, it's impossible to be sure of anyone's biological gender on line. "Transpostites," people who pose as members of the opposite gender, are an established element of Net society, most famously a man who, pretending to be a disabled lesbian, built warm and intimate friendships with women on several CompuServe forums.

Perhaps what we should be examining is not the triumph of gender differences on the Net, but their potential blurring. In this light, *Newsweek*'s stout assertion that in cyberspace "the gender gap is real" begins to seem less objective than defensive, an insistence that on-line culture is "the same" as real life because the idea that it might be different, when it comes to gender, is too scary. If gender roles can be cast off so easily, they may be less deeply rooted, less "natural" than we believe. There may not actually be a "masculine" or "feminine" mind or outlook, but simply a conventional way of interpreting individuals that recognizes behavior seen as in accordance with their biological gender and ignores behavior that isn't.

For example, John Seabury wrote in the *New Yorker* (June 6, 1994)     25 of his stricken reaction to his first "flame," a colorful slice of adolescent invective sent to him by an unnamed technology journalist. Reading it, he begins to "shiver" like a burn victim, an effect that worsens with repeated readings. He writes that "the technology greased the words . . . with a kind of immediacy that allowed them to slide easily into my brain." He tells his friends, his co-workers, his partner — even his mother — and, predictably, appeals to CompuServe's management for recourse — to no avail. Soon enough, he's talking about civilization and anarchy, how the liberating "lack of social barriers is also what is appalling about the Net," and calling for regulation.

As a newcomer, Seabury was chided for brooding over a missive that most Net veterans would have dismissed and forgotten as the crude pot-shot of an envious jerk. (I can't help wondering if my fellow journalist never received hate mail in response to his other writings; this bit of e-mail seems comparable, par for the course when one assumes a public profile.) What nobody did was observe that Seabury's reaction — the shock, the feelings of violation, the appeals to his family and support network, the bootless complaints to the authorities — reads exactly like many horror stories about women's trials on the Net. Yet, because Seabury is a man, no one attributes the attack to his gender or suggests that the Net has proven an environment hostile to men. Furthermore, the idea that the Net must be more strictly governed to prevent the abuse of guys who write for the *New Yorker* seems laughable — though who's to say that Seabury's pain is less than any woman's? Who can doubt that, were he a woman, his tribulations would be seen as compelling evidence of Internet sexism?

The idea that women merit special protections in an environment as incorporeal as the Net is intimately bound up with the idea that women's minds are weak, fragile, and unsuited to the rough and tumble of public discourse. It's an argument that women should recognize with profound mistrust and resist, especially when we are used as rhetorical pawns in a battle to regulate a rare (if elite) space of gender ambiguity. When the mainstream media generalize about women's experiences on line in ways that just happen to uphold the most conventional and pernicious gender stereotypes, they can expect to be greeted with howls of disapproval from women who refuse to acquiesce in these roles and pass them on to other women.

And there are plenty of us, as the WELL's response to the *Newsweek* article indicates. Women have always participated in on-line communications, women whose chosen careers in technology and the sciences have already marked them as gender-role resisters. As the schoolmarms arrive on the electronic frontier, their female predecessors find themselves cast in the role of saloon girls, their willingness to engage in "masculine" activities like verbal aggression, debate, or sexual experimentation marking them as insufficiently feminine, or "bad" women. "If that's what women on line are like, I must be a Martian," one WELL woman wrote in response to the shrinking female technophobes depicted in the *Newsweek* article. Rather than regulating so many people to the status of gender aliens, we ought to reconsider how adequate those roles are to the task of describing real human beings.

### Reading the Text

1. What images of women on the Net do the mainstream media construct, according to Miller?
2. What does Miller see as the significance of the word "frontier," and how does she relate that word to the Internet?
3. Summarize in your own words the charges that critics make about the gender bias and harassment on the Internet and Miller's response to those charges.
4. Why does Miller state that women should "regard the notion of special protections . . . with suspicion"?

### Reading the Signs

1. Log onto a chat room and see for yourself how gender roles are depicted on the Net. To what extent do you find traditional roles perpetuated or ignored? Use your findings to support an argument for or against Miller's position that women should not be granted special protections on the Internet.

2. Form teams and debate whether regulation should be established to protect Internet users, whether male or female, from harassment, intimidation, or other sorts of abusive language.
3. Read or reread Laurence Shames's "The More Factor" (p. 31). Using his
argument as your starting point, write an essay in which you explain the
extent to which the Internet appeals to Americans' desire for "more."
4. In your journal, reflect on the controversy Miller mentions over whether
online rape is possible. How might one change the traditional definition
of rape to include electronic assaults?
5. Interview four of five women on campus who are avid Internet users, asking them about their experiences online. To what extent have they faced
the gender-based problems that Miller describes? Use your findings as the
basis for an argument about how gender roles are constructed online.

# LYNNELL HANCOCK
## The Haves and the Have-Nots

ꞮꞮꞮꞮꞮꞮꞮꞮꞮꞮꞮꞮꞮꞮꞮꞮꞮꞮꞮꞮꞮꞮꞮꞮꞮꞮꞮꞮꞮꞮꞮꞮꞮꞮꞮꞮꞮꞮꞮꞮꞮꞮꞮꞮꞮꞮꞮ

*As the world gets wired, it gets more and more important to go online if
you're going to keep up in a competitive environment. That's why an
increasing number of schools are hooking up to the Internet, thus giving
their students the earliest possible advantage in the race through cyberspace. Trouble is, as LynNell Hancock (b. 1953) points out, not
every school can afford the price of admission. If our already economically divided society is not to become even more divided between those
who have and those who don't, measures will have to be taken to be
sure that everyone has access to the Web. An assistant professor of
journalism and Director of the Prudential Fellowship for Children and
the News at Columbia University, Hancock is a former education editor for* Newsweek *who specializes in public education and segregation
issues.*

Aaron Smith is a teenager on the techno track. In America's breath-
less race to achieve information nirvana, the senior from Issaqua, a middle-
class district east of Seattle, has the hardware and hookups to run the
route. Aaron and 600 of his fellow students at Liberty High School have
their own electronic-mail addresses. They can log on to the Internet
every day, joining only about 15 percent of America's schoolchildren
who can now forage on their own for documents in European libraries
or chat with experts around the world. At home, the 18-year-old e-mails

his teachers, when he is not prowling the World Wide Web to track down snowboarding conditions on his favorite Cascade mountain passes. "We have the newest, greatest thing," Aaron says.

On the opposite coast, in Boston's South End, Marilee Colon scoots a mouse along a grimy Apple pad, playing a Kid Pix game on an old black-and-white terminal. It's Wednesday at a neighborhood center, Marilee's only chance to poke around on a computer. Her mom, a secretary at the center, can't afford one in their home. Marilee's public-school classroom doesn't have any either. The 10-year-old from Roxbury depends on the United South End Settlement Center and its less than state-of-the-art Macs and IBMs perched on mismatched desks. Marilee has never heard of the Internet. She is thrilled to double-click on the stick of dynamite and watch her teddy-bear creation fly off the screen. "It's fun blowing it up," says the delicate fifth grader, twisting a brown ponytail around her finger.

Certainly Aaron was born with a stack of statistical advantages over Marilee. He is white and middle class and lives with two working parents who both have higher degrees. Economists say the swift pace of high-tech advances will only drive a further wedge between these youngsters. To have an edge in America's job search, it used to be enough to be well educated. Now, say the experts, it's critical to be digital. Employees who are adept at technology "earn roughly 10 to 15 percent higher pay," according to Alan Krueger, chief economist for the U.S. Labor Department. Some argue that this pay gap has less to do with technology than with industries' efforts to streamline their work forces during the recession. . . . Still, nearly every American business from Wall Street to McDonald's requires some computer knowledge. Taco Bell is modeling its cash registers after Nintendo controls, according to Rosabeth Moss Kanter. The "haves," says the Harvard Business School professor, will be able to communicate around the globe. The "have-nots" will be consigned to the "rural backwater of the information society."

Like it or not, America is a land of inequities. And technology, despite its potential to level the social landscape, is not yet blind to race, wealth and age. The richer the family, the more likely it is to own and use a computer, according to 1993 census data. White families are three times as likely as blacks or Hispanics to have computers at home. Seventy-four percent of Americans making more than $75,000 own at least one terminal, but not even one third of all Americans own computers. A small fraction — only about 7 percent — of students' families subscribe to online services that transform the plastic terminal into a telecommunications port.

At least in public schools, the computer gap is closing. More than half the students have some kind of computer, even if it's obsolete. But schools with the biggest concentration of poor children have the least equipment, according to Jeanne Hayes of Quality Education Data. Ten

5

years ago schools had one computer for every 125 children, according Hayes. Today that figure is one for 12.

Though the gap is slowly closing, technology is advancing so fast, and at such huge costs, that it's nearly impossible for cash-strapped municipalities to catch up. Seattle is taking bids for one company to wire each ZIP code with fiber optics, so everyone — rich or poor — can hook up to video, audio and other multimedia services. Estimated cost: $500 million. Prosperous Montgomery County, Md., has an $81 million plan to put every classroom online. Next door, the District of Columbia public schools have the same ambitious plan but less than $1 million in the budget to accomplish it.

New ideas — and demands — for the schools are announced every week. The '90s populist slogan is no longer "A chicken in every pot" but "A computer on every desk." Vice President Al Gore has appealed to the telecommunications industry to cut costs and wire all schools, a task Education Secretary Richard Riley estimates will cost $10 billion. House Speaker Newt Gingrich stumbled into the discussion with a suggestion that every poor family get a laptop from Uncle Sam. Rep. Ed Markey wants a computer sitting on every school desk within 10 years. "The opportunities are enormous," Markey says.

Enormous, yes, but who is going to pay for them? Some successful school projects have relied heavily on the kindness of strangers. In Union City, N.J., school officials renovated the guts of a 100-year-old building five years ago, overhauling the curriculum and wiring every classroom in Christopher Columbus Middle School for high tech. Bell Atlantic provided wiring free and agreed to give each student in last year's seventh-grade class a computer to take home. Even parents, most of whom are South American immigrants, can use their children's computers to e-mail the principal in Spanish. He uses translation software and answers them electronically. The results have shown up in test scores. In a school where 80 percent of the children are poor, reading, math, attendance and writing scores are now the best in the district. "We believe that technology will improve our everyday life," says principal Bob Fazio. "And that other schools will piggyback and learn from us."

Still, for every Christopher Columbus, there are far more schools like Jordan High School in South-Central Los Angeles. Only 30 computers in the school's lab, most of them 12 to 15 years old, are available for Jordan's 2,000 students, many of whom live in the nearby Jordan Downs housing project. "I am teaching these kids on a system that will do them no good in the real world when they get out there," says Robert Doornbos, Jordan's computer-science instructor. "The school system has not made these kids' getting on the Information Highway a priority."

**Donkey Kong:** Having enough terminals to go around is one prob-   10
lem. But another important question is what the equipment is used for. Not much beyond rote drills and word processing, according to Linda

Roberts, a technology consultant for the U.S. Department of Education. A 1992 National Assessment of Educational Progress survey found that most fourth-grade math students were using computers to play games, "like Donkey Kong." By the eighth grade, most math students weren't using them at all.

Many school officials think that access to the Internet could become the most effective equalizer in the educational lives of students. With a modem attached, even most ancient terminals can connect children in rural Mississippi to universities in Asia. A Department of Education report last week found that 35 percent of schools have at least one computer with a modem. But only half the schools let students use it. Apparently administrators and teachers are hogging the Info Highway for themselves.

There is another gap to be considered. Not just between rich and poor, but between the young and the used-to-be-young. Of the 100 million Americans who use computers at home, school or work, nearly 60 percent are 17 or younger, according to the census. Children, for the most part, rule cyberspace, leaving the over-40 set to browse through the almanac.

The gap between the generations may be the most important, says MIT guru Nicholas Negroponte, author of the new book "Being Digital." Adults are the true "digitally homeless, the needy," he says. In other words, adults like Debbie Needleman, 43, an office manager at Wallpaper Warehouse in Natick, Mass., are wary of the digital age. "I really don't mind that the rest of the world passes me by as long as I can still earn a living," she says.

These aging choose-nots become a more serious issue when they are teachers in schools. Even if schools manage to acquire state-of-the-art equipment, there is no guarantee that trained adults will be available to understand them. This is something that tries Aaron Smith's patience. "A lot of my teachers are quite illiterate," says Aaron, the fully equipped Issaqua teenager. "You have to explain it to them real slow to make sure they understand everything." Fast or slow, Marilee Colon, Roxbury's fifth-grade computer lover, would like her chance to understand everything too.

### Reading the Text

1. Why does Hancock begin her essay by contrasting Aaron Smith with Marilee Colon, and what effect does that contrast have on her reader?
2. What evidence does Hancock advance to demonstrate that "technology . . . is not yet blind to race, wealth, and age"?
3. According to Hancock, what are some of the problems that impoverished school districts face in trying to bring their students online?

4. Why does MIT professor Nicholas Negroponte say that adults are the "digitally homeless, the needy" in cyberspace?

### Reading the Signs

1. In class, propose answers to the question that Hancock raises in her selection: Who is going to pay for making access to the Internet socioeconomically equal?
2. Laura Miller ("Women and Children First," p.740) accuses mainstream media of insisting that "on-line culture is 'the same' as real life." In an essay, discuss the extent to which that accusation applies to Hancock's selection, which first appeared in *Newsweek*.
3. Assuming the perspective of Amy Bruckman, write a response to Hancock's selection. To what extent could Hancock be accused of ignoring the disadvantages of an online life?
4. Read through a cybermagazine such as *Wired*, studying how genders, ethnicities, and age groups are portrayed in both advertising and articles. Then write a semiotic analysis of the publication, explaining the extent to which it portrays a world of "inequalities." To develop your ideas, consult Laura Miller's "Women and Children First" (p. 740).
5. Write an essay in which you support, refute, or complicate the contention that "access to the Internet could be the most effective equalizer in the educational lives of students." You might gather evidence for your position by interviewing students of varying socioeonomic backgrounds on their access to cyberspace prior to attending college.

# LAWRENCE K. GROSSMAN
## Keypad Democracy

*Someday you may vote by computer. And someday U.S. senators may cast their legislative votes only after doing a quickie computer poll of their constituents. Although that might appear to be a good thing for a participatory democracy, a fully computerized political system will have its dangers as well, Lawrence W. Grossman (b. 1931) suggests in this excerpt from* The Electronic Republic *(1995). Former president of NBC News, Grossman has taught at Harvard University and at Columbia University. He is currently president of PBS Horizons Cable Network.*

Citizens already have many ways to express themselves individually and in groups, to each other and to their elected and appointed officials. At their disposal in the future will be a diverse selection of portable fingertip and voice-activated telecommunications media capable of sending, receiving, storing, and sorting data and motion pictures of all kinds. People will be able to compose and receive instantaneous computer messages, faxes, letters, wires, and videos, and they will have the ability to direct communications, in turn, to just about any individuals or groups they select. Time and distance will be no factor. Using a combination telephone–video screen computer, citizens will be capable of participating in audio- and videophone calls, teleconferences, tele-debates, tele-discussions, tele-forums, and electronic town meetings. They will, of course, continue to have the capacity to phone radio and television talk shows from cars, homes, and workplaces, and talk to vast audiences simultaneously.

Most citizens will gain access to a good deal of information and data in many different formats, which can be retrieved on order or automatically through "smart" television sets programmed to select and store or retrieve any material on any subject. The material they call up may have been tailormade specifically for their age group, sex, race, style of living, educational level, taste, and individual interests. Some of it the users will pay for. Some will be provided free because it is promotional or public service in nature or because it grinds the ax of a particular interest group.

As the *New York Times* described the debut of a new congressional service available over the World Wide Web on the Internet, "A person who taps into the service, called Thomas in honor of Thomas Jefferson, can call up the full text of any bill introduced in Congress since 1992 and will soon be able to get all new issues of the Congressional Record. . . . Type a keyword like 'mother' and a person can get a list of every bill that mentions mothers — and every nonbinding resolution introduced to praise motherhood, condemn welfare mothers, chastise unwed mothers or provide equity for mothers and fathers in divorce cases."

Using computerized lists and on-line networks for different interest groups, individual citizens will also be able to send their own promotional material, propaganda, and publicity of all kinds in all formats to individuals, groups, and political representatives of their own choosing. There will be a continuing flow of audio, video, and written communications, dialogue exchanges, yes/no votes and polls, position papers and programs, interviews, speeches, presentations, and advertisements — all rattling around in cyberspace and all instantly available on command. And day by day, numerous polls and surveys, both official and unofficial, reliable and meretricious, impartial and self-serving, will take the pulse of the public, and continuously tabulate political opinion.

Using a designated personal code — one's Social Security number, 5
citizen registration number, or special-purpose phone number — each
citizen's message, vote, or question will be capable of being instantly tab-
ulated and sorted to determine its legitimacy, what sort of interest group
or geographic constituency it is part of, and whether enough citizens care
sufficiently about a particular matter to be worth paying attention to.

People not only will be able to vote on election day by telecomputer
for those who govern them but also will be able to make their views
known formally and informally, on a daily basis or even more often if
they wish, regarding the politics, laws, agendas, and priorities about which
they care the most. By pushing a button, typing on-line, or talking to a
computer, they will be able to tell their president, senators, members of
Congress, and local leaders what they want them to do and in what priority order. The potential will exist for individual citizens to tap into government on demand, giving them the capacity to take a direct and active
role, by electronic means, in shaping public policies and specific laws.

With public opinion of increasing importance, a remarkable variety of
techniques, devices, and measures will be employed to determine what citizens think at any particular time on any particular issue. To the telecomput-
erized citizens of the next century, today's public opinion polling will seem
as crude, primitive, and limited as the first Gallup polls in the 1930s seem to
us now. Sample groups of citizens will be empaneled to represent the whole
or specific parts of the population. These focus groups will be surveyed to
express their choices in some depth and dimension, and then monitored to
reflect any changes in their views. Electronic juries will be asked to render
judgments on individual public questions. Professional polling companies
and political consultants already do a good deal of this work. We shall see
more of it in the future, carried out in more structured and sophisticated ways.

"Boiler room" organizations, hired by special interests, will seek to manufacture and mobilize "grassroots" opinion and stimulate the outpouring of
selected messages and votes — to make sure that particular viewpoints are
heard. They do that now. In the next century, it will become a mainstream
business. Computerized political advertising, promotion, and marketing campaigns, targeted with high degrees of specificity, will lobby ordinary citizens
with as much intensity as legislators, regulators, and public officials are lob-
bied today, because public opinion — the fourth branch of government —
will play an even more pivotal role in major government decisions.

## Toward Plebiscite Democracy

Back in 1912, the United States Supreme Court put to rest the basic
question of whether procedures involving direct democracy were incompatible with our republican form of government and should, therefore,

be held unconstitutional. The issue centered on the constitutionality of the newly introduced state ballot initiatives, the populist effort to bring direct democracy to several western states. State ballot initiatives, the procedure's opponents argued, violated the constitutional requirement that elected representatives, not the people at large, make the laws of the land. Upholding the constitutionality of direct initiatives, the Supreme Court concluded that the initiative process simply augmented rather than "eliminated or superseded the republican form of government and the representative processes thought to be central to it." The court was confident that elements of direct democracy can coexist within the representative republic.

Given the accelerated use of statewide and local ballot initiatives    10
and referenda since that time, national advisory plebiscites, initiatives, or referenda, at least on certain major issues, may well be put in place by early in the next century. Polls consistently show a good deal of public support for such measures. If the American people had their way, the federal government would join the rising number of states and local jurisdictions that use ballot initiatives and referenda to impose the public's will directly on government policy. According to Gallup, 70 percent of Americans want to be able to vote directly on key national issues in the belief that national referenda will help overcome gridlock in government and end the corrupting influence of special interests on politics.

In 1993, 80 percent of those surveyed were convinced that the "country needs to make major changes in the way government works." As one observer put it, if the public had its way, "governance in the 1990s [would quickly be] transformed from an exercise in backroom decision making to an up-front, open, 'we-want-in-on-the-decision-making' experience for citizens."

The entire nation may vote not only for term limitations and balanced budgets but also to use citizens' teleprocessors and electronic keypads to bypass or override the legislative powers of Congress. This is not much different from what already has been put into effect in states like California, Colorado, and Oregon. As it is, many congressmen already have become accustomed to surveying their constituents on tough, controversial matters before casting their own votes. On especially vexing legislation involving, say, new taxes, the decision to go to war, abortion, health care reform, or environmental questions, Congress may consider it prudent to refer the ultimate decisions to an actual vote of the people. The electronic mechanisms that will make such national votes practical throughout the year will soon be in place.

In the 1994 statewide elections, voters decided nearly 150 ballot initiatives. Oregonians alone considered 19 issues, Coloradans 12, and

Californians 10, on everything from gay rights issues, to cutting off public benefits for illegal aliens, to term limits.

"The ballot initiative has become a major generator of state policy in California," said the official report of the California Commission on Campaign Financing, *Democracy by Initiative,* issued in 1992. "Although the idea of 'direct democracy' by vote of the people is an ancient one . . . , nowhere has it been applied as rigorously and with such sweeping results as in California today. If California's trends continue to serve as a predictor for the nation's future, then [we] . . . will also begin to see the emergence of 'democracy by initiative' as a new form of twenty-first century governance." In the twenty-first century, as California goes, so may go the nation.

Ballot initiatives and referenda on federal issues could be made determinative, as Ross Perot suggested be done with tax and budget decisions in a 1992 campaign proposal that generated substantial public support. Or federal referenda could be made largely advisory, in effect telling the people's representatives how their constituents think they should vote, a system that actually existed in four states over two hundred years ago. In the decades ahead, the public also may seek the power to veto laws that Congress enacts, thereby enabling the people themselves to overrule any federal measure they do not like. As we have seen, Switzerland, a country often judged to have one of the world's most effective democracies, has long operated with just such a system. In Switzerland, within ninety days after a law has been passed, if thirty thousand voters from at least eight cantons sign a petition requesting that it be put to a popular vote, the law must be brought before all the nation's citizens to be ratified. A majority of those voting can overturn the actions of their own elected representatives. The Swiss have made the initiative and referendum process the preferred method of dealing with national legislation in their country.

From today's perspective, none of these scenarios for the United States is far-fetched. The use of initiatives and referenda in states and localities has jumped fivefold in the last thirty years. Today the initiative has become a primary tool of governance in many states besides California. On the federal level, as far back as the end of the nineteenth century, proposals were offered in Congress to introduce both advisory and binding national referenda and initiatives. Such efforts were endorsed periodically by supporters on the left as well as on the right. In the 1920s, a pacifist backlash against war generated considerable support for a Constitutional amendment — the Ludlow Amendment, named after its congressional sponsor — that would have required a national referendum before the United States could declare war and send troops abroad, unless the U.S. had been invaded. Many prominent college presidents and political scientists as well as a good many newspaper editorials sup-

15

ported the idea. Federal advisory referenda were conducted among the nation's farmers from 1933 to 1936, under the New Deal, to help determine market quotas for commodities. In some regions, farmers still vote on market quotas.

In 1980, Congressman Richard A. Gephardt, a Democrat from Missouri and currently minority leader in the House, proposed that the federal government sponsor a national advisory referendum process in which voters could express their views on three issues every two years. Under the Gephardt plan, the issues would be selected after public hearings and the referendum results would be nonbinding. Issues not subsequently acted upon by Congress would be resubmitted for the voters to decide. A 1987 Gallup survey indicated that Americans approved of the plan by a two-to-one margin.

In the 1980s, Ralph Nader, frustrated by a federal government that he was convinced had lost touch with ordinary citizens, called for national ballot initiatives so that the people's voice could be heard and government officials bypassed. In a rare moment of agreement, that call was echoed on the right by conservative politicians Patrick Buchanan and Jack Kemp and economist Arthur Laffer. They believed that the national popular will was being frustrated by an unresponsive liberal elitist majority in Congress. Surveys continue to show strong popular support for such direct democratic measures.

If computer-driven electronic keypads were put in the hands of every voter, such national referenda would be relatively easy to conduct on a regular basis. Whether or not the nation actually adopts these or similar measures of direct democracy, unofficial instantaneous public opinion polls will continue to be available on demand. The federal government will have no choice but to operate in a political environment of virtual plebiscites, even if such votes are not officially recognized.

In June 1992, the Nova Scotia Liberal Party in Canada experimented    20
with a ballot by telephone to choose its new provincial leader. Despite a computer failure that delayed the phone-in election by two weeks, four times as many people voted in that election as previously had participated. The novelty of the Nova Scotia telephone vote may account for some of the increase. But it does demonstrate that convenient, accessible, easy-to-use electronic technology can attract people back into the political arena.

Cable shopping channels have installed high-speed, large-capacity computerized systems to process millions of viewers' telephone credit card orders. The same or similar technology can be recruited to tabulate votes, process polls, and count the results on initiatives and referenda, dialed in from anywhere. In 1992, CBS News asked viewers to call in their opinions to a special 800 phone number during a prime-time election campaign special, *America on the Line*. Although the audience response during the broadcast could by no means be considered a representative sample, three hundred thousand phone calls were tallied out of millions attempted that could not get through — far *more* calls than could have been processed in the 1988 election, far fewer calls than will be able to be processed by the 1996 election.

The question is not whether the transformation to instant public feedback through electronics is good or bad, or politically desirable or undesirable. Like a force of nature, it is simply the way our political system is heading. The people are being asked to give their own judgment before major governmental decisions are made. Since personal electronic media, the teleprocessors and computerized keypads that register public opinion, are inherently democratic — some fear too democratic — their effect will be to stretch our political system toward more sharing of power, at least by those citizens motivated to participate.

### Reading the Text

1. According to Grossman, what role will computers play in future elections?
2. What tone does Grossman adopt in this selection? What does his tone suggest about his views on digital democracy?
3. How have Switzerland and Canada provided models for future U.S. politics, according to Grossman?
4. Describe in your own words what Grossman means by "keypad democracy."
5. What does Grossman mean when he writes, "In the twenty-first century, as California goes, so may go the nation"?

### Reading the Signs

1. In your journal, explore your current attitudes toward elections and the political process and consider whether keyboard democracy would have any effect on those attitudes.
2. Write an essay in which you defend, qualify, or challenge the trend toward keypad democracy that Grossman describes.
3. In class, brainstorm a list of roles that computers already play in American politics and elections. Then use the list as the basis for an essay in which you assess the legitimacy of Grossman's predictions.

4. Assuming the perspective of LynNell Hancock ("The Haves and the Have-Nots," p. 748), write a critique of Grossman's prediction that America will soon enjoy keypad democracy.

5. In class, form teams and debate Grossman's contention that the effect of electronic opinion polls would be to "stretch our political system toward more sharing of power." To develop your ideas, read or reread LynNell Hancock's "The Haves and the Have-Nots" (p. 748).

# APPENDIX

## *Writing about Popular Culture*

Throughout this book, you will find readings on popular culture that you can use as models for your own writing or as subjects to which you may respond, assignments for writing critical essays on popular culture, and semiotic tips to help you analyze a wide variety of cultural phenomena. As you approach these readings and assignments, you may find it helpful to review the following suggestions for writing critical essays — whether on popular culture or on any subject — as well as some examples of student essays written in response to assignments based on *Signs of Life in the U.S.A.* Mastering the skills summarized and exemplified here should prepare you for writing the kinds of papers you will be assigned through the rest of your college career.

### Developing Ideas about Popular Culture

The first thing to consider as you prepare to write a critical essay on popular culture is the fact that you are already an expert on your subject. Being an expert doesn't necessarily mean spending years of studying in a library; simply by being an active participant in everyday life, you have a vast store of knowledge about what makes our culture tick. Just think about all you know about movies, or the thousands upon thousands of ads you've seen, or even the many unwritten "rules" governing courtship behavior among your circle of friends. All of these help form the fabric of contemporary American culture — and, if you've ever had to explain to a younger sibling why her latest outfit was inappropriate for work or why his comment to a blind date struck the wrong chord, you've already played the role of expert.

Yet, because popular culture is part of everyday life, you may take for granted this knowledge — it might not seem that it can "count" as material for a college-level assignment, and you might not think to include it in an essay. Thus, it can be useful to spend some time, before you start writing, to generate your ideas freely and openly: Your goal at this point is to develop as many ideas as possible, even ones that you might not actually use in your essay. Writing instructors call this process "prewriting," and it's a step you should take when writing on any subject in any class, not just in your writing class. This textbook includes many suggestions for how you can develop your ideas; even if your instructor doesn't require you to use all of them, you can try them on your own.

*Signs of Life* frequently asks you to respond to a reading selection in your journal, sometimes directly and sometimes indirectly, as in suggestions that you write a letter to the author of a selection. In doing so, you're taking an important first step in articulating your response to the issues and to the author's presentation of them. In asking you to keep a journal or a reading log, your instructor will probably not be concerned with your writing style, or even grammatical correctness; at this point, your goal is to concentrate on defining your ideas and pushing them as far as you can. Let's say you're asked to write your response to a reading selection; we'll take for example Emily Prager's "Our Barbies, Ourselves" in Chapter 5. You might first think through exactly what Prager is saying — what her point is — and then how you feel about it. If you agree that the Barbie doll perpetuates outmoded ideas about women, why do you feel that way? Can you think of other objects (or even people) who seem to exemplify those same ideas? What alternative ways of designing a doll can you imagine? Note that the purpose of imagining your own doll is not so you'll actually produce one; it's so you think through alternatives and explore the implications of Prager's and your own ideas. Or say you're irritated by Prager's argument: Again, why do you feel that way? What would you say to her in response? What, perhaps in your own experience as a child, might show that she's wrong? Your aim in jotting down all these ideas is not to produce a draft of an essay. It's to play with your own ideas, to see where they lead, and even just to help you decide what your ideas are in the first place.

Often we or your instructor may ask you to brainstorm a list of ideas or to freewrite in response to an issue. These are both strategies you can use in your journal, or on your own, as you start working on an essay. Brainstorming is simply amassing as many relevant (and even some irrelevant) ideas as possible. Let's say your instructor asks you to brainstorm a list of popular toys used by girls and boys in preparation for an essay about the gendered patterns of children's toys. Try to list your ideas freely, jotting down whatever comes to mind. Don't censor yourself at this point. That is, don't worry if something is really a toy or a game, or if it is used by both boys and girls, or if it really is an adult toy. Later on you can throw out ideas that don't fit. What you'll be left with is a rich list of examples that you can then study and analyze. Freewriting works much the same way and is particularly useful when you're not sure of how you feel about an issue. Sit down and just start writing or typing, and don't stop until you've written for at least ten or fifteen minutes. Let your ideas wander around your subject, working associatively, following their own path. As with brainstorming, you may produce lots of irrelevant ideas, but you may also come to a closer understanding of how you really feel about an issue.

Sometimes your instructor may assign you an open-ended topic (say, to write an argument about a gender-related controversy). Where should you start? In such cases, you may find it helpful to establish a narrow focus, perhaps by conducting an Internet search. Let's say you're asked to analyze an aspect of the film industry, but can't decide on a focus. You could explore a search engine such as Yahoo, specifically its Movies and Films index. There you'll find dozens of subcategories (42 as of August 1996) that range from "History" and "Theory and Criticism" to "Gay, Lesbian, and Bisexual" and "Trivia." Each of these subcategories has many sites to explore; "History," for instance, includes the Archives of the Lindy Hop and The Bill Douglas Centre for the History of Cinema and Popular Culture, a wonderful compendium of 25,000 books, posters, and other movie-related memorabilia. By so using the Net, you can, in effect, engage in electronic brainstorming. One cautionary note, however: Your use of electronic sources must conform to the conventions of documentation and citation, just as your use of printed sources does. See the inside back cover of this book for citation models of some basic references.

Not all "prewriting" activities are solitary, however. In fact, *Signs of Life* includes lots of suggestions that ask you to work with other students, either in your class or from across campus. We do that because much academic work really is collaborative and collegial. When a scientist is conducting research, for instance, he or she often works with a team, may present preliminary findings to colloquia or conferences, and may call or e-mail a trusted colleague at another school just to try out some ideas. There's no reason you can't benefit from the social nature of academic thinking as well. But be aware that such in-class group work is by no means "busy work." The goal rather is to help you to develop and shape your understanding of the issues and your attitudes toward them. If you're asked to study a men's fashion magazine with three classmates, for instance, you're starting to test Diane Barthel's thesis in "A Gentleman and a Consumer" (Chapter 2), seeing how it applies or doesn't apply and benefiting from your peers' insights. If you're asked to present to the class a semiotic reading of a childhood toy, you're articulating, perhaps for the first time and in an informal way, the larger significance of a familiar object — and you may be better equipped to write a more formal analysis of the same toy in an essay (especially if you receive feedback and comments from your class). And if you stage an in-class debate over whether Batman is a gay character, you're amassing a wonderful storehouse of arguments, counterarguments, and evidence to consider when you write your own essay that either supports or refutes Andy Medhurst's thesis in "Batman, Deviance, and Camp" (Chapter 5). As with other strategies to develop your ideas, you may not use directly every idea generated in conversation with your classmates, but that's okay. You should find yourself better able to sort through and articulate the ideas that you do find valuable.

## Developing Strong Arguments about Popular Culture

We expect that students will write many different sorts of papers in response to the selections in this book. You may write personal experience narratives, opinion pieces, research papers, formal pro-con arguments, and many others. Here, we'd like to focus on writing analytic essays, because the experience of analyzing popular culture may seem different than that of analyzing other subjects. Occasionally we've had students who feel reluctant to analyze popular culture, because they think analysis requires them to trash their subject, and they don't want to write a "negative" essay about what may be their favorite film or TV program. Or a few students may feel uncertain because "it's all subjective." Since most people have opinions about popular culture, they say, how can any one essay be stronger than another?

While these concerns are understandable, they needn't be an obstacle in writing a strong analytic paper — whether on popular culture or any other topic. First, we often suggest that you set aside your own personal tastes when writing an analysis. We do so not because your preferences are not important; recall that we often ask you to explore your beliefs in your journal, and we want you to be aware of your own attitudes and observations about your topic. Rather, we do so because an analysis of, say, a Madonna video is not the same as a paper that explains "why I like (or dislike) this video." Instead, an analysis would explain how it works, what cultural beliefs and viewpoints underlie it, what its significance is, and so forth. And such a paper would not necessarily be positive or negative; it would seek to explain how the elements of the video work together to have a particular effect on its audience. If your instructor asks

you to write a "critical analysis" or a "critical argument," he or she is requesting neither an attack upon nor a celebration of your topic.

As a result, the second concern, about subjectivity, becomes less of a
problem. That's because your analysis should center upon a clear argument about that video. You're not simply presenting a personal opinion
about it; rather, you're presenting a central insight about how the video
works, and you need to demonstrate it with logical, specific evidence.
It's that evidence that will take your essay out of the category of being
"merely subjective." You should start with your own opinion, but add
lots of proof that shows the legitimacy of that opinion. Does that sound
familiar? It should, because that's what you need to do in any analytic
essay, no matter what your subject matter happens to be.

## Gathering Evidence

When writing about popular culture, students sometimes wonder
what sort of evidence they can use to support their points. Your instructor will probably give you guidelines for each assignment, but we'll provide some general suggestions here. Start with your subject itself. You'll
find it's useful to view your subject, whether it's an ad, or a film, or anything else, as a text that you can "read" closely. That's what you would
do if you were asked to analyze a poem: You would read it carefully,
studying individual words, images, rhythm, and so forth, and those details would support whatever point you wanted to make about the poem.
Read your pop culture subject with the same care. Let's say your instructor asks you to analyze an advertisement. Look at the details: Who appears in the ad, and what is their expression? What props are used, and
what is the "story" that the ad tells? Is there anything missing from this
scene that you would expect to find? Your answers to such questions
could form the basis of the evidence that you use in your essay.

If your instructor has asked you to write a semiotic analysis, you can
develop evidence as well by locating your subject within a larger system.
Recall that a system is the larger network of related signs to which your
subject belongs; and identifying it helps reveal the significance of your subject. That may sound hard to do, but it is through identifying a system that
you can draw upon your own vast knowledge of popular culture. And that
may sound abstract, but it becomes very specific when applied to a particular example. If you were to analyze Doc Martens shoes, for instance, it
would help to locate them within the larger fashion system, specifically,
other choices of footwear. How do the signals sent by wearing a pair of
Doc Martens compare with those sent by wearing cowboy boots, or
loafers, or dress pumps? Teasing out those differences and similarities
would help you explain the shoes' social and cultural significance — and
that's likely cultural knowledge with which you're quite familiar. When
you identify a system, however, be sure to relate your subject to other ex-

amples of the same category of item. To what system would backpacks belong, for instance? Do they belong to the same system as beepers, or are they quite different in significance even though both beepers and backpacks are often used by the same group of people, students?

You can strengthen your argument as well if you know and use the history of your subject. That might sound like you have to do a lot of library research, but often you don't have to: You may already be familiar with the social and cultural history of your subject. If you know, for instance, that the baggy pants so popular among teens in the mid-1990s were ubiquitous among street gang members a few years before, you know an important historical detail that goes a long way toward explaining their significance. Depending upon your assignment, you might want to expand your own historical knowledge and collect other data about your topic, perhaps through surveys and interviews. If you're analyzing gendered patterns of courtship rituals, for instance, you could interview some people from different age groups, as well as both genders, to get a sense of how such patterns have evolved over time. The material you gather through such an interview will be raw data, and you'll want to do more than just "dump" the information into your essay. See this material instead as an original body of evidence that you'll sort through (you probably won't use every scrap of information) and study and interpret in its own right.

## Reading Essays about Popular Culture

In your writing course, it's likely that your instructor will ask you to work in groups with other students, perhaps reviewing each other's rough drafts. You'll find many benefits to this activity. Not only will you receive more feedback on your own in-progress work, but you will also see other students' ideas and approaches to an assignment and develop an ability to evaluate academic writing. For the same reasons, we're including three sample student essays that are responses to assignments based on *Signs of Life in the U.S.A.* You may agree or disagree with the authors' views, and you might think you'd respond to the assigned topics differently — that's fine. We've selected these three essays because they differ in style, focus, and purpose, and thus suggest three different approaches to their assignments — approaches that might help you as you write your own essays about popular culture.

## Essay 1: Critical Reading of a Film

Your instructor may ask you to read one of the selections in this text, then to apply the author's general ideas to a new example, either one provided by the assignment or one that you select. Such an assignment asks you to work closely with two "texts" — the reading selection and a pop cultural example — and requires you to articulate the relationship you see between the two. In this essay, William Martin-Doyle of Harvard University applies Robert B. Ray's theory of heroic archetypes in American cinema ("The Thematic Paradigm," p. 278) to a film of his own choice, *Cool Hand Luke*. His instructor explained to his class, "A really good essay will not simply say *why* Ray's theory does or does not apply, but will go further and speculate what that relevance or irrelevance *means*." As you read Martin-Doyle's essay, note how he fulfills both tasks.

*Cool Hand Luke:*
The Exclusion of the
Official Hero in
American Cinema

**William sums up Ray's definition of hero and presents his argument that *Cool Hand Luke* (*CHL*) departs from Ray's archetypal pattern.**

In his article "The Thematic Paradigm," Robert Ray contends that the two heroic types of outlaw and official are the stock figures of American cinema. The author implies that by the acceptance of the two characters' juxtaposition in popular culture, Americans are revealing a type of immaturity: "The parallel existence of these two contradictory traditions evinced the general pattern of American mythology: the denial of the necessity for choice" (para. 15). This contention is well rooted — movies such as *Shane,* for example, illustrate Ray's point quite effectively, presenting the viewer with the story of a gunslinger and a farmer joining forces to combat evil and defend the American way. Movies have come a long way since *Shane,* though. Films display their coming-of-age by making choices far more often than they used to. This new decisiveness does not necessarily reflect a responsible adulthood, however; when a choice is made, it is now frequently for the outlaw hero. This trend is easily seen in the movie *Cool Hand Luke* (1967).

**Paragraph doesn't just give plot summary but explains plot details in terms of the ideologies Ray describes.**

The movie tells the story of an individualist who is sentenced to two years working on a chain gang for his rebellion against authority. To avoid alienating the viewer with the story of an inhuman criminal, the makers of the movie choose a crime that panders to the audience, in the form of "malicious destruction of municipal property": cutting the heads off parking meters while bored and drunk. In this way, lawbreaking is romanticized as the vice of a man who refuses to conform. Luke's individualism and powerful personality initially alienate the other prisoners, but he soon becomes their idol; through him they live vicariously. After attempting to live in the suffocating atmosphere of the prison camp, Luke begins his escape efforts. He is repeatedly recaptured, with mounting consequences for each attempt. The authorities, as symbolized by the nameless man who supervises the chain gang's work from behind the mask of his sunglasses, attempt to break Luke's spirit. They degrade and beat him for every attempt, and they finally kill him after his third try, but Luke's refusal to conform, expressed through his escapes, is made into a victory for individuality.

 *Cool Hand Luke*'s unreserved depiction of the legal system as a brutally unjust entity signals a definite departure from movies that contain both of Ray's stock hero types. Ray asserts that "by customarily portraying the law as the tool of villains . . . this mythology betrayed a profound pessimism about the individual's access to the legal system" (para. 11). The law, confusingly, is also the tool of the official hero. This is a puzzling situation in many movies, as order is the very basis for the character of the official hero. That the support for the "Good Good Boys" (para. 3) should come from an institution that the audience for some reason views with suspicion suggests that the official hero character is only a substitute for the outlaw hero in most people's minds — the renegade is the ideal. The presence of both types in a film might indicate a certain confusion in the viewer about what he or she really values. Ray, however, indicates that American cinema is typified by the presence of the two. *Cool Hand Luke* represents a departure from that "duplicity" (para. 22): There is no confused romanticizing of two conflicting ideals — instead, the clear choice is Newman's outlaw. Everywhere in the movie, the forces of law and order are portrayed as a tool for oppression, rather than for the protection of everyday citizens, a group to which one might assume the average audience member belongs.

*[marginal note:]* Presents more fully Ray's definition of heroes and moves to the essay's assertion that *CHL* fails to fulfill this pattern.

 Ray writes of the pervasive theme of the reluctant hero, the man who is eventually forced by outside pressures into promoting the greater good; he is "the private man attempting to keep from being drawn into action on any but his own terms. In this story, the reluctant hero's ultimate willingness to help the community satisfied the official values" (para. 17). In this way, the reluctant hero represents a synthesis of the official and the outlaw hero, rendering a somewhat contradictory picture, almost of a man with a split personality. Once again, *Shane* epitomizes this concept, as the mysterious stranger is drawn into aiding the brave settlers in their struggle against the ranchers, despite his initial desire to lay aside his guns and lead a peaceful life. In contrast, *Cool Hand Luke* presents no such capitulation to the moral pressure of helping others. Luke's only priority is to live his life his own way, not to aid the other prisoners. There is no plot device of the hero righteously leading a rebellion against the armed guards for subjecting them to life in the chain gang. Luke never consciously tries to become a leader, and the other prisoners' admiration for him never fosters a sense of responsibility in him for their well-being. His strong personality induces others to become attached to him, yet he never feels any reciprocal ties. Indeed, the only strong emotional bond that he has during the entire movie is the one to his sickly mother, who comes to visit him at one point. Later in the movie, word of her death arrives, and Luke is cut off from any emotional tie, making him a complete loner. Even this instance is used as an example of the cruelty of the established authority, as Luke is confined in a wooden box the size of a closet for several days just so that he won't get any ideas about escaping to go to the funeral. This measure does force Luke to the edge, but his response is not that of Ray's stereotypical hero, who exhibits traits of both the official and the outlaw hero. His response is straightforward, in keeping with his character. He doesn't combat injustice in general, helping the greater good of the other prisoners; instead, he makes his first attempt at escape (a perfectly understandable, yet hardly selfless action). In this way, the character of Luke remains consistent — he begins as an outlaw, and he never strays from that image.

The conspicuous lack of an official hero is accented by George Kennedy's character Dragune, who at first seems like he might play that role. A prisoner who has been serving time for several years, he has become a sort of leader among the prisoners, who listen to him because of his strength and his outspokenness. A bit of a blowhard, he defends the status quo, holding forth on the value of order in the prisoners' lives: "We got rules here. In order to learn 'em, you gotta do more work with your ears than with your mouth." Ray states that the official hero's motto is "You cannot take the law into your own hands" (para. 12), and this is clearly Dragune's own personal opinion. Luke, on the other hand, obviously has no use for

*Here and in the next two paragraphs, William analyzes specific cinematic details that demonstrate the kind of hero Luke is.*

*William doesn't limit his analysis to Luke; he studies other characters as well.*

society's impositions; during his first night, he says, "I ain't heard that much worth listening to. Just a lot of guys laying down a lot of rules and regulations." When conflict arises between Dragune and Luke, it first appears that the viewpoint of the authority will triumph over Luke's championing of the individual. They box, as is the custom for two prisoners with irreconcilable differences, and Dragune easily beats Luke senseless. This physical triumph of authority quickly turns into a moral victory for Luke, however, as Dragune is forced to leave the ring when he realizes that the only way that Luke will ever stay on the ground after a knockdown is if Dragune kills him. After this turning point, Dragune soon becomes Luke's friend and eventually his disciple.

Luke's tenacity is simultaneously the strong point of his personality, the very trait that makes him worthy of admiration, and his fatal flaw. This character will never give up, no matter the pain he must endure, whether the situation is in the boxing ring against a man who heavily outweighs him, in a bet that he can eat fifty eggs in an hour, or in his repeated attempts at escape, for which he is punished with escalating viciousness. These escape attempts are the main outlet for his rebellion, and they are always initially successful. Despite the fact that he is always later apprehended, he always makes his escapes in grand fashion, confounding the authorities who attempt to chase him. The escapes are therefore victories of a kind against the establishment, symbolic of his death grip on his own identity. After the first recapture, the captain of the camp debases Luke and reflects to the other prisoners: "What we've got here is failure to communicate. Some men, you just can't reach." In this world of polar extremes, there can be no communication between the outlaw hero and the forces of conformity that would normally be wielded by an official hero. It is officialdom's failure to reach Luke, to "get his mind right," that gives the outlaw his victory. His death is imbued with nobility as the car that takes him away, dying, crushes the supervisor's sunglasses that have come to be the recurring metaphor for the rule of the law.

*Cool Hand Luke* represents a shift away from the standards presented in Ray's article, as illustrated by *Shane,* in which American movies have a conflicting duality of protagonists — *Cool Hand Luke* has instead made the choice for the outlaw hero. This is a definite shift away from earlier movies that

William locates *CHL* in the context of American film history, including films that both predate and postdate *CHL*.

emphasized the official hero, such as Jimmy Stewart films and war movies, which celebrated the triumph of the ultimate official body, the United States government. Despite the fact that the movie was a product of the late 1960s, a time of political and social unrest, *Cool Hand Luke*'s decision still has relevance in this decade. The rejection of society in its present form, as represented by the official hero, is still visible in the progression to modern hits like *Natural Born Killers* and *Pulp Fiction,* which glorify serial killers and organized crime hit men. Ray implies that Americans' failure to make a choice when it comes to their movies is a societal problem. In *Cool Hand Luke,* the choice has been made, but a new problem is reflected in that choice. Any country is based on the idea that there must be rules to govern acceptable and unacceptable behavior; the

The essay moves toward its conclusion by suggesting the social implications of the ideology represented in *CHL*.

constant deprecation of those rules therefore signals an extreme dissatisfaction with present society. Such dissatisfaction is a normal reaction against the perceived failure of authority, as exemplified by problems such as the Vietnam War, Watergate, and the national economy. Dissatisfaction isn't necessarily a bad thing, but expressing discontent without hinting at the possibility of a real solution is troubling.

The problem with the choice of the outlaw hero lies in the fact that the outlaw doesn't confront issues and deal with

William concludes with a sharp statement of his view of those implications.

them in a mature fashion; instead, he runs away as Luke did, or uses force until there is nothing left to face. In short, the choice of the outlaw hero exposes the fact that Americans are indulging in a form of moral escapism: They dislike their present circumstances, yet are too scared to face up to them.

## Essay 2: Personal Argument

Some assignments may ask you to develop your own argument about an issue after reading one or more selections about it. In this essay, Cynthia McCaughey of Pierce College, a community college in Los Angeles, was asked to write an essay in response to the issues raised in Chapter 1, "Consuming Passions: The Culture of American Consumption." While McCaughey was not required to base her discussion upon a close reading of the selections, notice that she does advance a central insight about consumer culture (her argument) and that she demonstrates it with specific details and cultural examples which she herself generates.

American Consumption:
Let's Make-Up

Centuries before the invention of the doorbell, let alone
the Avon Lady to ring it, people of all cultures have sought
specialty concoctions to apply to themselves in an effort to be
more attractive. Whether it was the extracts drawn from roots
or berries or trees that the ancient Egyptians used, or the brazen-
red, manufactured rouges of the 1920s Flappers, anyone who
had begun to experience that special hormonal calling of
maturation began looking for ways to increase their possibilities.
This happened so much so that the business of producing new
and better cosmetic wonders, since the early part of this century,
has turned into a multi-billion dollar business. But for a society
that is obsessed with outside packaging, concealing and coloring
is no longer enough. Just as we found a way to go beyond
simply gazing at the moon by landing on it, we have, through
the phenomenon of consumer demand, found a way to package
what we believe to be perpetual youth. With lotions, creams
and oils that claim to defy the aging process, we are now buying
products to rid ourselves completely of wrinkles and creases,
but, with a really hard look into the mirror, it is plain to see that
what we are really trying to rid ourselves of is any semblance of
social responsibility.

Now, the idea of evading social responsibility may seem a
lot to expect from a four-ounce jar of face cream, but we must
examine why we would dole out anywhere from $15 to $50
for a tiny jar of some obscure potion that is supposed to make
those who are not young appear to be young. Whether or
not these products deliver such promises is not at issue here;
instead, the important issue is that in the mind of the consumer, a fear is pacified — that detestable fear — the fear of
growing old. Androgynous in nature, this fear can no longer be
solely attributed to the lonely housewife who waits at home
wondering if her husband is really working late. Men comprise
a good chunk of the anti-aging purchasing frenzy. In fact,
according to Chet Shelton, a former marketing representative
for the Max Factor Company, sales of these newly developed
wrinkle creams average at an approximate ratio of 60 percent
female to 40 percent male.

So, it seems, nearly everyone who is not young anymore
is looking for a way to look as if they are, and youth is big

**Cynthia opens
with the cultural
background of
our youth
culture.**

**The thesis state-
ment.**

**Cynthia re-
moves the func-
tion of beauty
products from
her discussion
so she can focus
on their image
and ideology of
youth.**

business. The media are filled with stories about the most
recent developments and improvements in these products, and
these stories are not run in any special section labeled "for
women only." These stories make the prime-time news broadcasts. These products are staples on the counters in an overwhelming number of bathrooms all over America, fitting in as
naturally as the roll of paper hanging next to the commode.
And now, when the Avon lady rings the doorbell, it is with the
promise of "Alpha Hydroxy calling" and with claims that you
too can be one of the elite who really understands the secrets of
"true beauty."

**Cynthia estab-
lishes how wide-
spread this
ideology is.**

Do not let these fabrications fool you: by no means is the
attainability of these items either secret or elitist. Sold not just
by appointment or in specialty stores, they can be found in
places as ordinary as the grocery store and purchased as an
essential, just as the loaf of bread (analogous with the "staff of
life") two aisles over would be purchased. But to keep the aura
of these products somewhat elusive, in spite of their ready
availability, the manufacturers have taken the predictable
course — the basic "Marketing 101" strategies — that state
if what is inside the package is not unique or scarce, make the
outside of the package look as if it is. And some of the techniques used are fascinating. Some claim to "work with the
skin," others have a fictitious name followed by a series of
letters and numbers to make them sound as if they were a
substantiated, earth-shattering, scientific discovery. For
instance, what exactly is an "Olay"? No one knows. Yet
the oil of one has been smeared over aging faces for years.

**She analyzes the
image of beauty
products as cre-
ated by mar-
keters.**

At this point, the query must be raised as to the illogicality
of patting regurgitated whale by-products or placental cream
on the body to hide from the inevitable. What is it that causes
us to fear so much the very thing, aging, that other cultures
view with respect and as beauty and wisdom? Why in God's
name would we ever fantasize about being twenty-one again
with all of the confusion and growing pains that accompanied
that period in our lives?

Well, the answer may very well be "in God's name."
Strange as it is, even the ancient writings of the Old Testament
tout the praises of youth. In Ecclesiastes XI:9 the passage reads,
"Rejoice, O young man, in thy youth; and let thy heart cheer
thee in the days of thy youth." Why the blatant consensus for
youth? Because "old" means closing in on death. Death means,

**Cynthia argues
for the attrac-
tiveness of this
ideology, pro-
viding a reason
for its influence.**

to most people, even if they are not completely certain, the possibility of meeting their maker. This proposition brings up the question of accountability, and, in an era of "screw thy neighbor to make a buck," the proposition of being accountable for temporal commissions, as well as omissions, is a frightening one.

The media are aware of this trend too. In its February 6, 1995 issue, *Newsweek* tackled the question of accountability with the cover story, *Shame: How Do We Bring Back a Sense of Right and Wrong?,* and author Kenneth Woodward basically says that even the best values of today cannot come close to the sense of doing the right thing Americans possessed as little as forty years ago.

Is it not one of America's values to scapegoat youth as an excuse for misdirected values? How many times have we heard the old saying, "Oh, he'll grow out of it," not to mention that if a young person commits a very adult crime, there is a special procedure to follow to judge the actions of the accused as an adult. So, by fooling ourselves with the absence of wrinkles, we fool ourselves into believing it was excusable that we walked to the other side of the street when we saw that homeless person; or that we were too busy clinging to our $200,000 home to spend time with a friend who needed someone to talk with; or that we just have too many occupational and financial worries to spend time with our kids. So, with each tiny line we wipe away from our faces, our thighs, and our stomachs, so too do we feel justified in excusing ourselves for wiping away a little more responsibility toward our fellow man.

Ironically, as we purchase and apply these so-called "miracle" creams, we miss out on the biggest miracle of all — the joy that comes with giving to others. We have become a self-obsessed society, telling ourselves that we are hiding our imperfections from the world — in an innocent attempt to be accepted and liked. But it is much more complex than that: What we are simply doing is attempting to hide from ourselves what will ultimately be our destiny. In spite of how many dollars we spend, or what products we buy, it is ludicrous to believe that the truth can be concealed forever, and it is certain that we really will have quite a bit to "make up" for.

> Cynthia concludes by suggesting the implications of the trend she has described.

## Essay 3: Research-Based Semiotic Analysis

Particularly toward the end of the term, your instructor may ask you to conduct some outside research as part of an assignment; that work may include traditional library research, or conducting surveys or interviews, among other strategies. Here, UCLA student Benjamin J. Hofilena Jr. writes a semiotic analysis of an American icon of his own choosing, the Statue of Liberty. His research consists largely of historical background, but notice how he integrates into his argument both personal experience and an analysis of differing ideological viewpoints — an enhancement of the general assignment that his instructor welcomed.

The Statue of Liberty:
America's Greatest Symbol

More than just a monument on Bedloe's Island, the Statue of Liberty has become an American icon, symbolic of American ideals and representative of the diverse experiences of her American people. The importance of the Statue of Liberty does not lie in her personification of America but in her status as an everlasting symbolic image. With the festivities and events surrounding the celebration of Lady Liberty's centennial in

**Benjamin establishes the focus and range of his essay.**

1986 came many interpretations of what she actually symbolizes. In her hundred years, she has been symbolic of many concepts ranging from the desire of her sculptor Frederic Auguste Bartholdi for France to adopt a government like that of the United States, to the hopes of America's many immigrants, to the frustrations of some of the oppressed and disadvantaged minorities within this nation.

What did the Statue of Liberty symbolize for her sculptor, Frederic Bartholdi? In answering this question, one must take into consideration the context of French politics in the 1860s and the early 1870s, French notions of liberty and republicanism, and the political philosophy of Edouard-Rene Lefebvre de Laboulaye, the father of the Statue of Liberty (Trachtenberg

**He describes the historical context for understanding the Statue of Liberty's significance for its creators.**

22). It was at his dinner table that Bartholdi and others discussed the concept of the Statue of Liberty. Laboulaye was a great writer, a distinguished jurist, and a renowned professor at the College de France where he was known for his republican convictions. An expert in republicanism in the United States, he emerged to be the leading authority on American constitutional history after the death of Alexis de Tocqueville in 1859. Because of the instability and ineffectiveness of France's government, Laboulaye looked to the successful republican government in America as a model for what he hoped to establish in France. Post-1776 America was seen as the realization of the political philosophy of "Enlightenment," the embodiment of Liberty and Reason. The Statue of Liberty became a tangible symbol of America's success and of the hopes of both Laboulaye and Bartholdi that their country might emulate the representative government found in the United States. They hoped that the people of France would embrace and fight to establish this same government.

According to Bartholdi's account in his book, *The Statue of Liberty Enlightening the World*, a book written for fund-raising efforts in 1885, the Statue of Liberty was to be a joint project between France and the United States for the expression of friendship and gratitude. "Go to see that country. You will study it, you will bring back to us your impressions. Propose to our friends over there to make with us a monument, a common work, in remembrance of the ancient friendship of France and the United States" (Bartholdi 11). Not discarding Bartholdi's account as entirely false, one should examine Bartholdi and Laboulaye's decision to pursue the creation of the Statue of Liberty. Inherently, the true purpose of the Statue of Enlightenment was to emphasize Leboulaye's political ideology: France should pursue a government like that of America. Laboulaye wanted the Statue of Liberty to serve as propaganda for the republicanism, or representative government structure, that he saw worked so well in America. "I will try to glorify the republic and liberty over there, in hope that someday I will find it again here" (Trachtenberg 33). For Bartholdi, and for the French, Lady Liberty thus symbolized the hope and ideas of republicanism that they wanted so badly to become a realization in France. Lady Liberty's image was to "enlighten" not only the people of France, but the people of the entire world about the ideals and benefits of the government in the New Country.

Just as the Statue of Liberty was used to enlighten the world then, her image was used for this same purpose in China in more recent history. In 1989, students demonstrated for democracy in Tienanmen Square. Going to great lengths to gather the materials, and later constructing her image, students were successful in raising their replica of Lady Liberty in

> Benjamin distinguishes between the explicit meaning of the statue as stated by its creators and the implicit meaning of its underlying ideology.

The essay shifts to a more recent example of how the statue still can represent the same ideology.

Tienanmen Square before it was destroyed in the massacre five days later. For these Chinese students, Lady Liberty symbolized the democratic government that they wanted in their country. They hoped that Lady Liberty's image would enlighten the people of China with the spirit of liberty and democracy (*New Yorker* 43). It was for her republican ideals that many Chinese students became martyrs in the massacre of Tienanmen Square. The power of Lady Liberty's symbolism will endure the test of time.

The intent of Bartholdi's symbolism can be seen in some of the features that he chose to include in his sculpture. In describing his monument, Bartholdi explains that "with just-broken shackles at her feet and her grim face of suffering, Liberty is a martyr for the ideals of America" (Trachtenberg 72). For this reason, Bartholdi would like Lady Liberty to enlighten the world. This symbolism of enlightening the world is seen in her crown, which consists of seven conical rays representing the seven continents of the world. With her torch in hand, symbolic of lighting the path of truth and right, Lady Liberty appears to be striving forward ready to educate the entire world after experiencing an epiphany. Her epiphany is a result of the stone tablet with the date of the Declaration of Independence inscribed on it. Trachtenberg interprets the symbolism of the stone tablet by linking it with the stone tablet from which Moses preached the Ten Commandments, thus linking her revelation that republicanism is good to the importance of the Ten Commandments (79). Understanding the physical symbols of the monument and their meanings intended by Bartholdi, one can appreciate the value of America's greatest symbol.

Benjamin now closely analyzes specific iconic details.

Until the closure of Ellis Island and the end of mass immigration to the United States in 1954, the Statue of Liberty was often the first sight of welcome for many immigrants who came to the United States via boats. For the immigrant, the symbolism of the Statue of Liberty lies not so much in her enlightening the world; rather, she is symbolic of their American Dream, a concept that is still popular today among immigrants. Whether it be in search of a better opportunity in life for their children, an escape from religious or ethnic persecution, or simply a better chance at their own life, immigrants come to the United States with high hopes of realizing their American dream. So at the height of mass immigration to the United States, the Statue of Liberty symbolized something different than Bartholdi's interpretation of Lady Liberty Enlightening the World. For the immigrant, she was symbolic of their opportunity for their pursuit of the American Dream. Emma Lazarus articulated this symbolism in her poem which can be found at the pedestal of the monument: "Give me your tired, your poor, your huddled masses yearning to breathe free, the wretched refuse of your teeming shore, Send these, the homeless, tempest-tossed to me: I lift my lamp beside the golden door" (Kennedy 113). America, personified in the Statue of Liberty, thus became a land of great opportunity. For many, America was their last and only hope to live a better, more enjoyable life. America was the "promised land" of freedom for many immigrants.

He relates the statue to a cultural myth — the American Dream — and a different interpretation than that held by its creators, showing how different mythologies can lead to different interpretations.

The golden door of opportunity represented many things to different people. I can remember the first time I saw the Statue of Liberty. I was only eight years old and it was a cold day in New York. Visiting my relatives over the holidays, my parents took me to see this "huge statue." I had a huge smile on my face. "It's so big," I told my mom. I honestly don't think I realized what Lady Liberty stood for then. As I grew older, though, I have come to realize what the Statue of Liberty means to me and my life. Constantly as a child, and even more today as I pursue a college education, my parents tell me how fortunate I am to be born in America. "You're very lucky," they tell me. For my parents, the Statue of Liberty symbolizes my parents' American Dream that they might live a better life than did their parents and that their children might do the same and get a good education. I think that because my parents are immigrants, they tend not to take anything for granted, and they challenge my brother, sister, and me to do the same. My parents constantly remind me to "finish my studies, and to pursue my dreams." "We work so hard so that you guys can have a good life." I probably roll my eyes each time they say these words again and again, but I realize the importance of their message. I am fortunate that I was born an American citizen.

Benjamin includes his family's experiences as additional evidence of the statue's significance to immigrants, and then elaborates on that significance.

Many immigrants came to the United States knowing only that this country would be a "better" place to live. The journey to America from their native lands was often dangerous and full of risks. It was a risk, however, that many immigrants were more than willing to take. As painful as it was for some to leave their homelands, they knew that they were in search of something better: "We're going to meet a beautiful lady with a lamp. You will like America. It's a very nice place to live. I know that it is hard to move and to go somewhere new, but it is in our best interest. God is watching us" (Oral History Tape Program). Getting their citizenship papers after enduring a series of citizenship and health tests, many immigrants were excited and were ready to embrace the land of equal opportunity. From what they gathered from the wonderful stories they heard about America, they truly believed in this concept that anybody could be anybody. It wasn't a question of race or religion or gender. What mattered was their desire and their determination to make something of themselves. Some were able to realize their hopes and dreams for success, but for others, the land of opportunity became a land of hardships.

The American Dream for some was not so readily attainable. In fact, some people do not see the Statue of Liberty as symbolic of the American Dream; they view it as symbolic of their assimilation to American culture and the loss of their own culture. When they came to the United States, many immigrants were not able to find work. Many were forced to live in poorer conditions than those that they left. In their pursuit of the land of equal opportunity, immigrants almost had to abandon their culture. The American culture was something entirely new. They were introduced to a new language, clothing, and foods. Because they were immigrants, they often were the target of prejudice. Was their journey compensated with the promise of the land of equal opportunity? Some even view the Statue of Liberty as a negative symbol: "What I got angry about, when you had your hundred years of Statue of Liberty . . . We didn't come through Ellis Island . . . What are you celebrating? You came here in chains in the bottom of ships half-dead and beaten. When you think what you done give up for this country and you got so little" (Terkel 145). For Maggie Holmes, the Statue of Liberty is target of her anger for the bitter memories of how the first African-Americans were treated. Today, the image of the Statue of Liberty is often used as a target of satire. Used occasionally to question our nation and what the American people stand for, the Statue of Liberty dressed in chains or bearing her tablet with other words inscribed on it is quite common in some news magazines.

**Ben cites an alternative interpretation that stems from a conflicting ideology and different experience, showing how the same object can mean different things to different people.**

"When we saw the Statue of Liberty, everybody started hugging each other, some cried. Others yelled 'At last we're free, at last we are free.' And it was something that we longed for and the fact is that we got here, even though we came under difficulties and it was somewhat difficult to adjust. This is the greatest land and I would literally kiss the ground to stay here" (Oral History Tape Program). Like many citizens, I cherish this great country and I am proud of what we stand for. For over one hundred years, Lady Liberty has lifted her torch, crying aloud to the world the message of America and her people. An everlasting icon of America and a universal symbol of freedom and democracy, the Statue of Liberty will continue to inspire and give hope to many in the years to come.

**Benjamin concludes by returning to the dominant interpretation of the statue.**

## Works Cited

Bartholdi, Frederic Auguste. *The Statue of Liberty Enlightening the World*. New York: University Press, 1959.

Debouzy, Marianne. *In the Shadow of the Statue of Liberty: Immigrants, Workers and Citizens in the American Republic 1800–1920*. Saint-Denis: Presses Universitaires de Vincennes, 1988.

Hageman, Miller. *The Liberty*. New York: The American News Company, 1886.

Kennedy, John Fitzgerald. *A Nation of Immigrants*. New York: Popular Library, 1964.

"Notes and Comments: The Goddess of Democracy." *New Yorker* 23 October 1989:43–44.

Terkel, Studs. *How Blacks and Whites Think About the American Obsession*. New York: The New Press, 1992.

Trachtenberg, Marvin. *The Statue of Liberty*. New York: The Viking Press, 1986.

University Publications of America. *Oral History Tape Program. Voices from Ellis Island: An Oral History of American Immigration*. Maryland: University Publications of America, 1988.

# GLOSSARY

**Canon** (n.)   A group of books or works that are considered essential to a literary tradition. The plays of Shakespeare are part of the canon of English literature.

**Class** (n.)   A group of related objects or people. Those who share the same economic status in a society are said to be of the same social class: for example, working class, middle class, upper class. Members of a class tend to share the same social interests and political viewpoints.

**Code** (n.)   A system of signs or values that assigns meanings to the elements that belong to it. Thus, a traffic code defines a red light as a "stop" signal and a green light as a "go," whereas a fashion code determines whether an article of clothing is stylish. To **decode** a system is to figure out its meanings, as when one discovers what an unlaced basketball sneaker means in the code of teen fashion.

**Connotation** (n.)   The meaning emotively suggested by a word, as opposed to its objective reference, or **denotation.** Thus, the word "flag" might connote (or suggest) feelings of patriotism, while it literally denotes (or refers to) a pennantlike object.

**Consumption** (n.)   The use of products and services, as opposed to their production. A **consumer culture** is one that consumes more than it produces. As a consuming culture, for example, America uses more consumer goods such as TV sets and stereos than it manufactures, which results in a trade deficit with producer cultures (such as Japan) with which America trades.

**Context** (n.)   The environment in which a sign can be interpreted. In the context of a Pearl Jam concert, for example, plaid flannels and Doc Martens can mean that one is part of the group. Wearing the same outfit in the context of a job interview at IBM would be interpreted as meaning that you don't really want the job.

**Cultural studies** (n.)   The academic study of ordinary, everyday culture rather than high culture.

**Culture** (n.)   The overall system of values and traditions shared by a group of people. Not exactly synonymous with a "society"; a society can include numerous cultures within its boundaries. A culture encompasses the worldviews of those who belong to it. Thus, America, which is a **multicultural** society, includes the differing worldviews of people of African, Asian, Native American, and European descent.

**Denotation** (n.)   The particular object or group of objects to which a word refers; compare with **connotation.**

**Discourse** (n.)   The system of words and concepts that constitutes the knowledge and understanding of a particular community, often academic or professional. In the discourse of modern medicine, for example, it is presumed that illness is caused by material causes — e.g., chemical problems   or invasive agents — rather than by spiritual causes.

**Dominant culture** (n.)   The group within a multicultural society whose traditions, values, and beliefs are held to be normative. The European culture is dominant in the United States.

**Eurocentric** (adj.)   Related to a worldview based on the traditions and history of European culture, usually at the expense of non-European cultures.

**Function** (n.)   The utility of an object, as opposed to its cultural meaning. Spandex or Lycra shorts, for example, are valued for their function by cyclists because they're lightweight and aerodynamic. On the other hand, such shorts have become a general fashion item for both men and women because of their cultural meaning, not their function. Many non-cyclists wear Spandex to project an image of hard-bodied fitness, sexiness, or plain trendiness, for example.

**Gender** (n.)   One's sexual identity and the roles that follow from it, as determined by the norms of one's culture rather than by biology or genetics. The assumption that women should be foremost in the nurturing of children is a gender norm; the fact that only women can give birth is a biological phenomenon.

**Hacker** (n.)   A person who "breaks into" another person's or an institution's computer system without permission, either for entertainment or for criminal purposes.

**Icon** (n.) (adj. **iconic**)   In semiotics, a sign that visibly resembles its referent, as a photograph looks like the thing it represents. More broadly, an icon is someone (often a celebrity) who enjoys a commanding or representative place in popular culture. Michael Jackson and Madonna are music video icons.

**Ideology** (n.)   A set of beliefs, interests, and values that determines one's interpretations or judgments. For example, in the ideology of modern business, it is the purpose of a business to produce profits, not jobs or social benefits.

**Image** (n.)   Literally, a pictorial representation; more generally, the identity that one projects to others through such things as clothing, grooming, speech, and behavior. Andre Agassi, for example, has made a commercial career out of his image as a tennis outlaw, a rock-'n'-roll court demon.

**Militia** (n.)   A paramilitary group, typically one that holds anti-government views.

**MOO** (n.)   Multi-User Dungeons, Object-Oriented, a role-playing game that takes place in an imaginary space created on the Internet. A MOO is a programming language that exists within a **MUD.**

**MUD** (n.)   Multi-User Dungeon, a role-playing fantasy game that is created on the Internet.

**Multiculturalism** (n.)   In American education, the movement to incorporate the traditions, history, and beliefs of America's non-European cultures into a traditionally **monocultural** (or single-culture) curriculum dominated by European thought and history.

**Mythology** (n.)   The overall framework of values and beliefs incorporated in a given cultural system or worldview. Any given belief in such a structure — such as the belief that "a woman's place is in the home" — is called a **myth.**

**Net, the** (n.)   The Internet, an electronic network that links millions of computers around the world.

**Politics** (n.)   Essentially, the practice of promoting one's interests in a competitive social environment. It is not restricted to electioneering; there are office politics, classroom politics, academic politics, and sexual politics.

**Popular culture** (n.)   The segment of a culture devoted to phenomena with mass appeal, such as entertainment and consumer goods.

**Postmodernism** (n.)   The worldview behind much of contemporary literature, art, music, architecture, and philosophy, which rejects traditional attempts to make meaning out of human history and experience. For the **postmodern** (adj.) artist, art should not attempt to create new explanatory myths or symbols but should rather recodify, recycle, or repeat existing images, as in the art of Andy Warhol.

**Semiotics** (n.)   In short, the study of signs. Synonymous with **semiology,** semiotics is concerned with both the theory and practice of interpreting linguistic, cultural, and behavioral sign systems. One who practices semiotic analysis is called a **semiotician** or **semiologist.**

**Sign** (n.)   Anything that bears a meaning. Words, objects, images, and forms of behavior are all signs whose meanings are determined by the particular codes, or systems, in which they appear. See also **code** and **system.**

**Symbolic sign** (n.)   A sign, according to semiotician C. S. Peirce, whose significance is arbitrary. The meaning of the word "bear," for example, is arbitrarily determined by those who use it. Contrast with **iconic** sign.

**System** (n.)   The code, or network, within which a sign functions, and so achieves its meaning. The English language is a sign system, as is a fashion code.

**Text** (n.)   A complex of signs, which may be linguistic, imagistic, behavioral, or musical, that can be read or interpreted.

**Virtual reality** (n.)   A simulated world that is created using computer technology.

*Acknowledgments (Continued from page ii)*

Gloria Anzaldúa, "How to Tame a Wild Tongue," from *Borderlands/La Frontera: The New Mestiza* by Gloria Anzaldúa. Copyright © 1987 by Gloria Anzaldúa. Reprinted with permission from Aunt Lute Books, (415) 558-8116.

Jenny Lyn Bader, "Larger than Life," from *NEXT: Young American Writers on the New Generation* edited by Eric Liu. Copyright © 1994 by Jenny Lyn Bader. Reprinted by permission of the author and W.W. Norton & Company, Inc.

Diane Barthel, "A Gentleman and a Consumer," from *Putting on Appearances* by Diane Barthel. Copyright © 1988 by Temple University. Reprinted by permission.

Roland Barthes, "Toys," from *Mythologies* by Roland Barthes. Trans. copyright © 1972 by Jonathan Cape, Ltd. Reprinted by permission of Hill and Wang, a division of Farrar, Straus & Giroux, Inc.

Nell Bernstein, "Goin' Gangsta, Choosin' Cholita," from the March-April 1995 issue of *The Utne Reader*. Copyright © 1994 by Nell Bernstein. Reprinted by permission of the author.

Léon Bing, "Faro," originally titled "South Central," from *Do or Die* by Léon Bing. Copyright © 1992 by Léon Bing. Reprinted by permission of HarperCollins Publishers, Inc.

Gary R. Brooks, "The Centerfold Syndrome," from *The Centerfold Syndrome: How Men Can Overcome Objectification and Achieve Intimacy with Women* by Gary R. Brooks. Copyright © 1995 by Jossey-Bass, Inc. Reprinted by permission of Jossey-Bass, Inc.

Amy Bruckman, "Christmas Unplugged." Appeared in the January 1995 issue of *Technology Review*. Copyright © 1995 by *Technology Review*. Reprinted with permission from MIT's *Technology Review Magazine*.

Elinor Burkett, from "The Gravest Show on Earth," from *The Gravest Show on Earth* by Elinor Burkett. Copyright © 1995 by Elinor Burkett. Reprinted by permission of Houghton Mifflin Company. All rights reserved.

Anne Campbell, "The Praised and the Damned" and "A Day with Connie," from *The Girls in the Gang* by Anne Campbell. Copyright © 1984, 1991 by Anne Campbell. Reprinted with permission of Basil Blackwell, Ltd.

Wanda Coleman, "Say It Ain't Cool, Joe." Appeared in the October 18, 1992, edition of *The Los Angeles Times Magazine*. Copyright © 1992 by Wanda Coleman. Reprinted by permission of the author.

Ronald K. L. Collins and David M. Skover, "The Death of Discourse," from *The Death of Discourse* by Ronald K. L. Collins and David M. Skover, published by Westview Press, an imprint of HarperCollins. Copyright © 1996 by Ronald K. L. Collins and David M. Skover. Reprinted by permission of the authors.

Brian A. Courtney, from "'Freedom From Choice' My Turn." Appeared in the February 13, 1995, issue of *Newsweek*. Copyright © 1995 by *Newsweek*. Reprinted by permission of *Newsweek*. All rights reserved.

Douglas Crimp, "Portraits of People with AIDS." Reprinted from *Cultural Studies* edited by Grossberg, Nelson, and Treichler. Copyright © 1992 by Routledge. Reprinted with permission of the publisher, Routledge.

Benjamin DeMott, "Put on a Happy Face." Appeared in the September 1995 issue of *Harper's* magazine. Copyright © 1995 by *Harper's* magazine. All rights reserved. Reproduced by special permission.

Holly B. Devor, "Gender Role Behaviors and Attitudes," from *Gender Blending* by

Michael Omi, "In Living Color: Race and American Culture." Reprinted from *Cultural Politics in Contemporary America* edited by Ian Angus and Sut Jhally, 1989, with the permission of the publisher, Routledge.

Josh Ozersky, "TV's Anti-Families: Married . . . With Malaise." Appeared in *Tikkun* magazine, vol. 6, no. 1 (January/February 1991). Copyright © 1991 by Josh Ozersky. Reprinted with permission of the author.

Michael Parenti, "Class and Virtue," from *Make-Believe Media: Politics of Film and Television* by Michael Parenti. Copyright © 1991 by Michael Parenti. Reprinted by permission of St. Martin's Press, Inc.

Ted Polhemus, "Street Style," from *Streetstyle from Sidewalk to Catwalk*. Copyright © 1994 by Ted Polhemus. Reprinted by permission of Thames and Hudson, Inc., the publishers.

Emily Prager, "Our Barbies, Ourselves," originally titled "Major Barbie." Originally appeared in *INTERVIEW*, Brant Publications, Inc., December 1991. Reprinted with permission from *INTERVIEW* magazine.

Robert B. Ray, "The Thematic Paradigm—The Resolution of Incompatible Values," originally titled "Formal and Thematic Paradigms," from *A Certain Tendency of the Hollywood Cinema, 1930–1980* by Robert B. Ray. Copyright © 1985 by Princeton University Press. Reprinted by permission of Princeton University Press.

Tricia Rose, "Bad Sistas," pp. 155–163 from *Black Noise: Rap Music and Black Culture in Contemporary America*. Copyright © by Wesleyan University Press. Reprinted by permission of University Press of New England.

Alex Ross, "The Politics of Irony." Appeared in the November 8, 1993, issue of *The New Republic*. Copyright © 1993 by The New Republic, Inc. Reprinted by permission of *The New Republic*.

Douglas Rushkoff, "Hating What Sucks," from *Media Virus* by Douglas Rushkoff. Copyright © 1994 by Douglas Rushkoff. Reprinted by permission of Ballantine Books, a division of Random House, Inc.

Leslie Savan, "Generation X-Force," from *The Sponsored Life* by Leslie Savan, published by Temple University Press. Copyright © 1994 by Leslie Savan. Reprinted by permission of Don Congdon Associates, Inc.

Winn Schwartau, "Hackers: The First Information Warriors in Cyberspace," from *Information Warfare: Chaos on the Electronic Superhighway* by Winn Schwartau. Copyright © 1994 by Winn Schwartau. Appears by permission of the publisher, Thunder's Mouth Press.

Laurence Shames, "The More Factor," from *The Hunger for More* by Laurence Shames, published by Times Books, a division of Random House, Inc. Copyright © 1989 by Laurence Shames. Reprinted by permission of Stuart Krichevsky Literary Agency, Inc.

Fan Shen, "The Classroom and the Wider Culture: Identity as a Key to Learning English Composition." Appeared in the December 1989 issue of *College Composition and Communication 40*. Copyright © 1989 by the National Council of Teachers of English. Reprinted with permission.

Julie Gannon Shoop, "Image of Fear: Minority Teens Allege Bias in 'Gang Profiling'." Appeared in the October 1994 issue of *Trial*. Copyright © 1994 by the Association of Trial Lawyers of America. Reprinted with the permission of *Trial*.

Leslie Marmon Silko, "Language and Literature from a Pueblo Indian Perspective," from *English Literature: Opening Up the Canon*, edited by Leslie A. Fiedler and Houston A. Baker, Jr. Copyright © 1979 by The Johns Hopkins University Press. Reprinted with permission from The Johns Hopkins University Press.

Mark Slouka, "Reality is Death" (and notes) from *War of the Worlds: Cyberspace and the High Tech Assault on Reality* by Mark Slouka. Copyright © 1995 by Mark Slouka. Reprinted by permission of Basic Books, a division of HarperCollins Publishers, Inc.

Jack Solomon, "Masters of Desire: The Culture of American Advertising," from *The Signs of Our Time* by Jack Solomon. Copyright © 1988 by Jack Fisher Solomon, Ph.D. Reprinted by permission of The Putnam Publishing Group/Jeremy P. Tarcher, Inc.

Susan Sontag, "AIDS and its Metaphors." Excerpts from *AIDS and Its Metaphors* by Susan Sontag. Copyright © 1989 by Susan Sontag. Reprinted by permission of Farrar, Straus & Giroux, Inc.

Steven Stark, "The Cultural Meaning of the Kennedys." Appeared in the January 1994 issue of *Atlantic Monthly*. Copyright © 1994 by Steven Stark. Reprinted by permission of the author.

Shelby Steele, from "Malcolm Little." Copyright © 1993 by The New Republic, Inc. Reprinted by permission of *The New Republic*.

Gloria Steinem, from "Sex, Lies, and Advertising." Originally published in *Ms.* magazine. Copyright © 1990 by Gloria Steinem. Reprinted with the permission of the author.

Deborah Tannen, "There is No Unmarked Woman." Appeared in the June 20, 1993, issue of *The New York Times Magazine*. Copyright © 1993 by Deborah Tannen. Reprinted with the permission of the author.

Sherry Turkle, "Who Am We?" from *Life on the Screen: Identity in the Age of the Internet* by Sherry Turkle. Copyright © 1995 by Sherry Turkle. Reprinted by permission of Simon & Schuster, Inc.

Cornel West, "Diverse New World." Appeared in the July–August 1991 issue of *Democratic Left*, vol. XIX, no. 4. Copyright © 1991 by Cornel West. Reprinted with the permission of the author.

"What Would You Do? Ask people to judge me by my ability, not my disability" reprinted courtesy of Esprit de Corp.

"Who Says Guys Are Afraid of Commitment?" reprinted courtesy of Eastpak.

Patricia J. Williams, from "Gilded Lillies and Liberal Guilt" and "A Word on Categories" from *The Alchemy of Race and Rights* by Patricia J. Williams. Copyright © 1991 by the President and Fellows of Harvard College. Reprinted by permission of the publisher, Harvard University Press.

Susan Willis, from "Public Use/Private State" from "Project on Disney," *Inside the Mouse*. Copyright © 1993 by Duke University Press. Reprinted by permission of Duke University Press.

Pamela Wilson, "Mountains of Contradictions: Gender, Class, and Region in the Star Image of Dolly Parton." Appeared in the Winter 1995 issue of *South Atlantic Quarterly*, 94:1, pp. 109–134. Copyright © 1995 by Duke University Press. Reprinted with permission.

Naomi Wolf, "The Beauty Myth," from *The Beauty Myth* by Naomi Wolf. Copyright © 1991 by Naomi Wolf. Reprinted by permission of William, Morrow & Co., Inc. Copyright © 1990. Reprinted by permission of Random House of Canada Limited.

## Frontispiece Credits

*Chapter One*
Mall of America photograph appears courtesy of Steve Woit/NYT Pictures.

*Chapter Two*
Eveready Bunny appears courtesy of Eveready Battery Company, Inc.

*Chapter Three*
The MTV logo appears courtesy of MTV: Music Television. MTV: Music Television is a registered trademark of MTV Networks, a division of Viacom International, Inc. © 1993 MTV Networks. All rights reserved.

*Chapter Four*
Hollywood sign photograph appears courtesy of Michael J. Howell/Stock Boston.

*Chapter Five*
Elvis stamp copyright © U.S. Postal Service. All rights reserved.

*Chapter Six*
Family dinner photograph appears courtesy of L. Willinger/FPG International.

*Chapter Seven*
"I think there's a pretty simple reason Jackie and I are so comfortable with each other" is copyright © 1992 by the Cherokee Group. Reprinted with courtesy of The Cherokee Group.

*Chapter Eight*
*Gang Graffiti* by Robert Daniel Ullman. Copyright © 1993 by Robert Daniel Ullman/Design Conceptions.

*Chapter Nine*
Photograph copyright © Shia/Impact Visuals.

*Chapter Ten*
Netscape logo. Netscape Communications Corporation has not authorized, sponsored, endorsed, or approved this publication and is not responsible for its content. Netscape and the Netscape Communications Corporate Logos are trademarks and trade names of Netscape Communications Corporation. All other product names and/or logos are trademarks of their respective owners.

# INDEX OF AUTHORS AND TITLES

# CITING SOURCES

When you write an essay and use another author's work — whether you use the author's exact words or his or her ideas — you need to cite that source for your readers. In most humanities courses, writers use the system of documentation developed by the Modern Language Association (MLA). This system indicates a source in two ways: (1) notations that briefly identify the sources in the body of your essay, and (2) notations that give fuller bibliographic information about the sources at the end of your essay. The notations for some commonly used types of sources are illustrated below. For documenting other sources, consult a writing handbook or Joseph Gibaldi's *MLA Handbook for Writers of Research Papers,* fourth edition (New York: The Modern Language Association of America, 1995).

## In-Text Citations

In the body of your essay, you should signal to your reader that you've used a source and indicate, in parentheses, where your reader can find the source in your list of works cited. You don't need to repeat the author's name in both your writing and in the parenthetical note.

### SOURCE WITH ONE AUTHOR:

Patrick Goldstein asserts that "Talk radio has pumped up the volume of our public discourse and created a whole new political language — perhaps the prevailing political language" (16).

### SOURCE WITH TWO OR THREE AUTHORS:

Researchers have found it difficult to study biker subcultures because, as one team describes the problem, "it was too dangerous to take issue with outlaws on their own turf" (Hooper and Moore 368).

### AN INDIRECT SOURCE:

In discussing the baby mania trend, *Time* claimed that "Career women are opting for pregnancy and they are doing it in style" (qtd. in Faludi 106).

## List of Works Cited

At the end of your essay, include a list of all the sources you have cited in parenthetical notations. This list, alphabetized by author, should provide full publishing information for each source; you should indicate the date you accessed any online sources.

The first line of each entry should begin flush left. Subsequent lines should be indented half an inch (or five spaces) from the left margin. Double space the entire list, both between and within entries.